FUNDAMENTALS OF DATABASE SYSTEMS

SECOND EDITION

Ramez Elmasri

Department of Computer Science Engineering
University of Texas at Arlington

Shamkant B. Navathe

College of Computing
Georgia Institute of Technology

Addison-Wesley Publishing Company
Menlo Park, California • Reading, Massachusetts • New York
Don Mills, Ontario • Wokingham, U.K. • Amsterdam • Bonn
Sydney • Paris • Milan • Seoul • Taipei • Singapore • Tokyo
Madrid • San Juan, Puerto Rico • Mexico City

Executive Editor: Dan Joraanstad
Editorial Assistant: Laura Cheu
Production Editor: George Calmenson, The Book Company
Production Coordinator: Teri Holden
Marketing Manager: Mary Tudor
Manufacturing Coordinator: Janet Weaver
Text Design: Hal Lockwood
Cover Design: Yvo Riezebos
Copy Editor: Steven Gray
Proofreader: Martha Ghent
Composition and Illustrations: GTS Graphics, Inc.

Cover Art: "Bloom"—Original hand-pulled limited edition serigraph by Tetsuro Sawada. Exclusive Sawada publisher and distributor: Buschlen/Mowatt Fine Arts Ltd., Main Floor, 1445 West Georgia Street, Vancouver, Canada V6G 2T3 (604) 682-1234.

Library of Congress Cataloging-in-Publication Data
Elmasri, Ramez.
    Fundamentals of database systems / Ramez Elmasri, Shamkant B.
Navathe.
        p.   cm.
    Includes bibliographical references and index.
    ISBN 0-8053-1748-1
    1. Data base management.   2. Data base design.   I. Navathe, Sham.
II. Title.
QA76.9.D3E57   1994
005.74—dc20   93-36697

ISBN 0-8053-1748-1

  7 8 9 10-DO—98 97 96

Addison-Wesley Publishing Company
2725 Sand Hill Road
Menlo Park, CA 94025

In memory of my father, Dr. Aziz Elmasri,
and to my son, Thomas
R.E.

To my wife Aruna
and children Manisha and Amol,
for their support and understanding
S.B.N.

PREFACE

This book introduces the fundamental concepts necessary for designing, using, and implementing database systems. Our presentation stresses the fundamentals of database modeling and design, the languages and facilities provided by database management systems, and system implementation techniques. The book is meant to be used as a textbook for a one- or two-semester course in database systems at the junior, senior, or graduate level, and as a reference book. We assume that readers are familiar with elementary programming and data-structuring concepts, and have had some exposure to basic computer organization.

We have chosen to start in PART I with a presentation of concepts from both ends of the database spectrum—conceptual modeling principles and physical file storage techniques. We conclude the book in PART VI with a look at influential new database models, such as object-oriented and deductive models, along with an overview of emerging trends in database technology. Along the way—in PARTS II through V—we provide the reader with an in-depth treatment of the most important aspects of database fundamentals.

The key features of the second edition include:

- A self-contained, flexible organization designed for tailoring to individual needs.
- Complete coverage of the relational model and an updated coverage of SQL2 in PART II .
- Overview of legacy systems—network and hierarchical—in PART III.
- A comprehensive new chapter introducing object-oriented databases, as well as a new chapter on deductive databases.
- A running example called COMPANY allows the reader to compare different approaches that use the same application.

- Coverage of database design, including conceptual design, normalization techniques, and physical design.
- Updated presentations on DBMS system implementation concepts, including query processing, concurrency control, recovery, and security.
- State-of-the-art coverage of recent advances, including overviews of distributed, active, temporal, and multimedia databases.

Contents of *Fundamentals of Database Systems,* Second Edition

PART I describes the basic concepts necessary for a good understanding of database design and implementation. The first two chapters introduce databases, their typical users, and DBMS concepts and architecture. In Chapter 3, the concepts of the Entity-Relationship (ER) model are presented and used to illustrate conceptual database design. Chapter 4 describes the primary methods of organizing files of records on disk, including static and dynamic hashing. Chapter 5 describes indexing techniques for files, including B-tree and B+-tree data structures.

PART II describes the relational data model. Chapter 6 describes the basic relational model, its integrity constraints and update operations, and the operations of the relational algebra. It also includes an optional section that describes relational schema design starting from a conceptual ER diagram. Chapter 7 gives a detailed overview of the SQL language—updated in the second edition to include features from the SQL2 standard. Chapter 8 introduces the formal relational calculus languages, and includes overviews of the QUEL and QBE languages. Chapter 9 discusses commercial relational database systems, and includes a detailed overview of IBM's DB2 system.

PART III presents the so-called legacy database systems, namely network and hierarchical systems. These have been used as a basis for many existing commercial database applications, particularly for large databases and transaction processing systems. The network and hierarchical data models are covered in Chapters 10 and 11, respectively. Each model is first described independently of specific DBMSs. An optional section in each chapter shows how to convert the conceptual design of a database schema in the ER model into a network or hierarchical schema. Each chapter also contains an overview of a commercial system—IDMS for network and IMS for hierarchical.

PART IV covers several topics related to database design. First, in Chapters 12 and 13, we cover the formalisms, theory, and algorithms developed for relational database design by normalization. This material includes functional and other types of dependencies and normal forms for relations. Step by step intuitive normalization is presented in Chapter 12, and relational design algorithms are given in Chapter 13. Chapter 13 also defines other types of dependencies, such as multivalued and join dependencies. Chapter 14 presents an overview of the different phases of the database design process for medium-size and large applications, and it also discusses physical database design issues pertinent to relational, network, and hierarchical DBMSs.

PART V discusses techniques used in implementing database management systems (DBMSs). Chapter 15 describes implementation of the DBMS catalog, which is a vital part of any DBMS. Chapter 16 presents the techniques used for processing and optimizing queries specified in a high-level database language—such as SQL—and discusses various algorithms for implementing relational database operations. Chapters 17 through 19 discuss transaction processing, concurrency control, and recovery techniques—this material has been revised for the second edition. Chapter 20 discusses database security and authorization techniques.

PART VI covers a number of advanced topics. Chapter 21 discusses data abstraction and semantic data modeling concepts, and extends the ER model to incoporate these ideas, leading to the enhanced-ER (EER) data model. The concepts presented include subclasses, specialization, generalization, and categories. We also discuss integrity constraints and conceptual design of transactions, and give overviews of the functional, nested relational, structural, and semantic data models. Chapter 22 gives a comprehensive introduction to object-oriented databases, and gives examples from two commercial systems. In Chapter 23, we discuss distributed databases and the client–server architecture. With powerful workstations and high-speed communication networks, truly distributed databases are becoming viable. Chapter 24 introduces the concepts of deductive database systems. Finally, Chapter 25 surveys the trends in database technology and includes discussions of several emerging database technologies and applications. The next generation technologies include active, temporal, and spatial databases, scientific databases, and multimedia databases. Emerging applications include engineering design and manufacturing, office and decision support systems, and biological applications.

Appendix A gives a number of alternative diagrammatic notations for displaying a conceptual ER schema. These may be substituted for the notation we use, if the instructor so wishes. Appendix B gives some important physical parameters of disks, and Appendix C briefly compares the various data models discussed throughout the book.

Guidelines for Using *Fundamentals of Database Systems*

There are many different ways to teach a database course. The chapters in Parts I through III can be used in an introductory course on database systems in the order they are given or in the preferred order of each individual instructor. Selected chapters and sections may be left out, and the instructor can add other chapters from the rest of the book, depending on the emphasis of the course. For an emphasis on system implementation techniques, selected chapters from PART V can be used. For an emphasis on database design, chapters from PART IV can be used. The sections marked with a *star* (★) symbol are candidates for being left out, whenever a less detailed discussion of the topic in a particular chapter is desired.

Chapter 3, which covers conceptual modeling using the Entity-Relationship (ER) model, provides an important conceptual understanding of data. However, it may be left out, or covered later if the instructor so wishes. For students who have already taken a course on file organization techniques, parts of Chapters 4 and 5 could be assigned as reading material to review file organization concepts. The book has been written so that it is possible to cover topics in a variety of orders. The dependency chart below shows the major dependencies between chapters. As the chart demonstrates, it is possible to start with any of the data models (relational, ER, network, hierarchical) following the introductory chapters. It is also possible to cover file organizations and indexing early on or to postpone it. If the ER model is covered later, the sections on mapping ER in Chapters 6, 10, and 11, can be covered later after Chapter 3 is given.

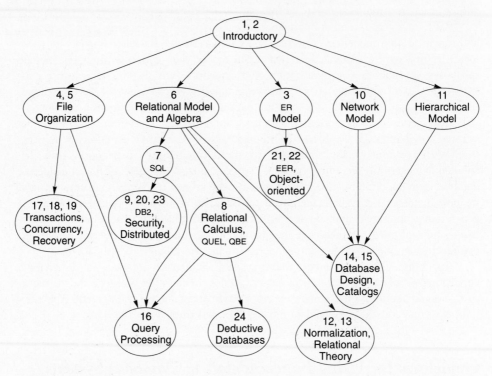

Dependency Chart

For a single-semester course based on this book, some chapters can be assigned as reading material. Chapters 4, 5, 14, 15, and 25 can be considered for such reading assignments. The book can also be used for a two-semester sequence. The first course, "Introduction to Database Systems," at the sophomore, junior, or senior level, could cover most of Chapters 1 to 12. The second course, "Database Design and Implementation Techniques," at the senior or first year graduate level, can cover the remaining chapters, and any chapters left out from the first course. PART VI can serve as introductory material for additional topics the instructor may wish to cover. Chapters from PART VI can be used selectively in either semester, and material describing the DBMS available to the students at the local institution can be covered in addition to the material in the book.

Several supplements are available for the book. These include an instructor's guide, which includes solutions to the majority of the exercises in the book, as well as a discussion on possible approaches to teaching the material in each chapter. Additional supplements are available by anonymous ftp from the site bc.aw.com under the directory bc/elmasri. Figures from every chapter are available there.

Acknowledgments

It is a great pleasure for us to acknowledge the assistance and contributions of a large number of individuals to this effort. Our editor, Dan Joraanstad, continuously encouraged and motivated us to complete the revision of the book. We would like to acknowledge the contributions of the persons who have reviewed portions of the second edition and suggested various improvements to the first edition. These include Rafi Ahmed, Antonio Albano, David Beech, Jose Blakeley, Panos Chrysanthis, Suzanne Dietrich, Vic Ghorpadey, Goetz Graefe, Eric Hanson, Junguk L. Kim, Roger King, Vram Kouramajian, Vijay Kumar, John Lowther, Sanjay Manchanda, Toshimi Minoura, Inderpal Mumick, Ed Omiecinski, Girish Pathak, Raghu Ramakrishnan, Ed Robertson, Eugene Sheng, David Stotts, Marianne Winslett, and Stan Zdonick. We would also like to acknowledge the students at the University of Texas at Arlington and Georgia Institute of Technology who used drafts of the new material in the second edition and carefully read the manuscripts.

We would like to repeat our thanks to those who reviewed and contributed to the first edition of *Fundamentals of Database Systems*. These include Alan Apt, Don Batory, Scott Downing, Dennis Heimbigner, Julia Hodges, Yannis Ioannidis, Jim Larson, Dennis McLeod, Per-Ake Larson, Rahul Patel, Nicholas Roussopoulos, David Stemple, Michael Stonebraker, Frank Tompa, and Kyu-Young Whang. Many graduate students at the University of Florida provided valuable input into the first edition.

Sham Navathe would like to acknowledge the secretarial assistance of Sharon Grant on the first edition and Gwen Baker and Jalisa Norton on the second edition.

Finally, we gratefully acknowledge the support, encouragement, and patience of our families.

R.E.
S.B.N.

ABOUT THE AUTHORS

Ramez A. Elmasri is an associate professor of computer science at the University of Texas at Arlington. His research interests include object-oriented databases and distributed systems, data modeling and query languages, and temporal databases. Well known for his research in extending the entity-relationship model, Professor Elmasri's current work focuses on incorporating time in database systems. In the 1980s as a principal research scientist at Honeywell's Computer Sciences Center in Minnesota, he worked on the design and implementation of a prototype distributed database management system: DDTS. He is a contributing author to *Temporal Databases: Theory Design and Implementation* and has published over 40 papers on database theory and design.

Shamkant B. Navathe is a professor of computing at the Georgia Institute of Technology. His research contributions include database modeling, database conversion, logical database design, distributed database design, and database integration. He has been a consultant to major computer vendors including Honeywell, Siemens, and DEC. Professor Navathe is an associate editor of the Association for Computing Machinery's *Computing Surveys*, and is the editor of Benjamin/Cummings' Series on Database Systems and Applications. Widely published, he is also the coauthor of *Conceptual Database Design: An Entity-Relationship Approach*.

BRIEF CONTENTS

★ represents that this chapter may be omitted for an introductory course

C O N T E N T S

★ represents sections that may be left out for a less detailed treatment of the chapter

PART II   RELATIONAL MODEL, LANGUAGES, AND SYSTEMS

PART III   CONVENTIONAL DATA MODELS AND SYSTEMS

PART IV   DATABASE DESIGN

PART V   SYSTEM IMPLEMENTATION TECHNIQUES

PART VI   ADVANCED DATA MODELS AND EMERGING TRENDS

CHAPTER 1

Databases and Database Users

In this chapter, we start in Section 1.1 by defining what a database is, and then we give definitions of other basic terms. In Section 1.2, we provide a simple UNIVERSITY database example to illustrate our discussion. Section 1.3 describes some of the main characteristics of database systems, and Sections 1.4 and 1.5 categorize the different types of personnel whose jobs involve using and interacting with database systems. Sections 1.6, 1.7, and 1.8 offer a more thorough discussion of the various capabilities provided by database systems and of the implications of using the database approach. Finally, Section 1.9 summarizes the chapter.

A reader who desires only a quick introduction to database systems can skip or browse through Sections 1.6 through 1.8 and then go on to Chapter 2.

1.1 Introduction

Databases and database technology are having a major impact on the growing use of computers. It is fair to say that databases will play a critical role in almost all areas where computers are used, including business, engineering, medicine, law, education, and library science, to name a few. The word *database* is in such common use that we must begin by defining what a database is. Our initial definition is quite general.

A **database** is a collection of related data.* By **data,** we mean known facts that can be recorded and that have implicit meaning. For example, consider the names, telephone numbers, and addresses of the people you know. You may have recorded this data in an indexed address book, or you may have stored it on a diskette, using a personal computer and software such as DBASE IV or V, PARADOX, or EXCEL. This is a collection of related data with an implicit meaning and hence is a database.

The preceding definition of database is quite general; for example, we may consider the collection of words that make up this page of text to be related data and hence to constitute a database. However, the common use of the term *database* is usually more restricted. A database has the following implicit properties:

- A database represents some aspect of the real world, sometimes called the **miniworld** or the **Universe of Discourse (UoD).** Changes to the miniworld are reflected in the database.

- A database is a logically coherent collection of data with some inherent meaning. A random assortment of data cannot correctly be referred to as a database.

- A database is designed, built, and populated with data for a specific purpose. It has an intended group of users and some preconceived applications in which these users are interested.

In other words, a database has some source from which data are derived, some degree of interaction with events in the real world, and an audience that is actively interested in the contents of the database.

A database can be of any size and of varying complexity. For example, the list of names and addresses referred to earlier may consist of only a few hundred records, each with a simple structure. On the other hand, the card catalog of a large library may contain half a million cards stored under different categories—by primary author's last name, by subject, by book title—with each category organized in alphabetic order. A database of even greater size and complexity is maintained by the Internal Revenue Service to keep track of the tax forms filed by taxpayers of the United States. If we assume that there are 100 million taxpayers and if each taxpayer files an average of five forms with approximately 200 characters of information per form, we would get a database of $100*(10^6)*200*5$ characters (bytes) of information. Assuming that the IRS keeps the past three returns for each taxpayer in addition to the current return, we would get a database of $4*(10^{11})$ bytes. This huge amount of information must be organized and managed so that users can search for, retrieve, and update the data as needed.

A database may be generated and maintained manually or by machine. The library card catalog is an example of a database that may be manually created and maintained. A computerized database may be created and maintained either by a group of application programs written specifically for that task or by a database management system.

A **database management system (DBMS)** is a collection of programs that enables users to create and maintain a database. The DBMS is hence a *general-purpose* software

---

*We will use the word *data* in both singular and plural, which is common in database literature. Context will determine whether it is singular or plural. In standard English, *data* is used only as the plural; datum is used as the singular.

system that facilitates the processes of defining, constructing, and manipulating databases for various applications. **Defining** a database involves specifying the data types, structures, and constraints for the data to be stored in the database. **Constructing** the database is the process of storing the data itself on some storage medium that is controlled by the DBMS. **Manipulating** a database includes such functions as querying the database to retrieve specific data, updating the database to reflect changes in the miniworld, and generating reports from the data.

It is not necessary to use general-purpose DBMS software for implementing a computerized database. We could write our own set of programs to create and maintain the database, in effect creating our own *special-purpose* DBMS software. In either case—whether we use a general-purpose DBMS or not—we usually have to employ a considerable amount of software to manipulate the database in addition to the database itself. We will call the database and software together a **database system.** Figure 1.1 illustrates these ideas.

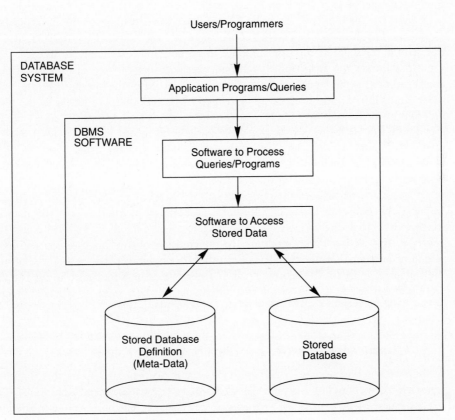

Figure 1.1 A simplified database system environment.

1.2 An Example

Let us consider an example that most readers may be familiar with: a UNIVERSITY database for maintaining information concerning students, courses, and grades in a university environment. Figure 1.2 shows the database structure and a few sample data for such a database. The database is organized as five files, each of which stores data records of the same type.* The STUDENT file stores data on each student; the COURSE file stores data on each course; the SECTION file stores data on each section of a course; the GRADE_REPORT file stores the grades that students receive in the various sections they have completed; and the PREREQUISITE file stores the prerequisites of each course.

To *define* this database, we must specify the structure of the records of each file by specifying the different types of **data elements** to be stored in each record. In Figure 1.2, each STUDENT record includes data to represent the student's Name, StudentNumber, Class (freshman or 1, sophomore or 2, . . .), and Major (MATH, computer science or COSC, . . .); each COURSE record includes data to represent the CourseName, CourseNumber, CreditHours, and Department (the department that offers the course); and so on. We must also specify a **data type** for each data element within a record. For example, we can specify that Name of STUDENT is a string of alphabetic characters, StudentNumber of STUDENT is an integer, and Grade of GRADE_REPORT is a single character from the set {A, B, C, D, F, I}. We may also use a coding scheme to represent a data item. For example, in Figure 1.2 we represent the Class of a STUDENT as 1 for freshman, 2 for sophomore, 3 for junior, 4 for senior, and 5 for graduate student.

To *construct* the UNIVERSITY database, we store data to represent each student, course, section, grade report, and prerequisite as a record in the appropriate file. Notice that records in the various files may be related to one another. For example, the record for "Smith" in the STUDENT file is related to two records in the GRADE_REPORT file that specify Smith's grades in two sections. Similarly, each record in the PREREQUISITE file relates two course records: one representing the course and the other representing the prerequisite. Most medium-size and large databases include many types of records and have many relationships among the records.

Database *manipulation* involves querying and updating. Examples of queries are "retrieve the transcript [a list of all courses and grades] of Smith"; "list the names of students who took the section of the Database course offered in Fall 1992 and their grades in that section"; and "what are the prerequisites of the Database course?" Examples of updates are "change the class of Smith to Sophomore"; "create a new section for the Database course for this semester"; and "enter a grade of A for Smith in the Database section of last semester." These informal queries and updates must be specified precisely in the database system language before they can be processed.

1.3 Characteristics of the Database Approach

A number of characteristics distinguish the database approach from the traditional approach of programming with files. In traditional **file processing,** each user defines and implements the files needed for a specific application. For example, one user, the grade

---

*We will define files and records more formally in Chapter 4.

STUDENT	Name	StudentNumber	Class	Major
	Smith	17	1	COSC
	Brown	8	2	COSC

COURSE	CourseName	CourseNumber	CreditHours	Department
	Intro to Computer Science	COSC1310	4	COSC
	Data Structures	COSC3320	4	COSC
	Discrete Mathematics	MATH2410	3	MATH
	Database	COSC3380	3	COSC

SECTION	SectionIdentifier	CourseNumber	Semester	Year	Instructor
	85	MATH2410	Fall	91	King
	92	COSC1310	Fall	91	Anderson
	102	COSC3320	Spring	92	Knuth
	112	MATH2410	Fall	92	Chang
	119	COSC1310	Fall	92	Anderson
	135	COSC3380	Fall	92	Stone

GRADE_REPORT	StudentNumber	SectionIdentifier	Grade
	17	112	B
	17	119	C
	8	85	A
	8	92	A
	8	102	B
	8	135	A

PREREQUISITE	CourseNumber	PrerequisiteNumber
	COSC3380	COSC3320
	COSC3380	MATH2410
	COSC3320	COSC1310

Figure 1.2   Example of a database.

reporting office, may keep a file on students and their grades. Programs to print a student's transcript and to enter new grades into the file are implemented. A second user, the accounting office, may keep track of students' fees and their payments. Although both users are interested in data about students, each user maintains separate files—and programs to manipulate these files—because each requires some data not available from the other user's files. This redundancy in defining and storing data results in wasted storage space and in redundant efforts to maintain common data up-to-date.

In the database approach, a single repository of data is maintained that is defined once and then is accessed by various users. The main characteristics of the database approach versus the file-processing approach are the following.

1.3.1 Self-describing Nature of a Database System

A fundamental characteristic of the database approach is that the database system contains not only the database itself but also a complete definition or description of the database. This definition is stored in the system **catalog,** which contains information such as the structure of each file, the type and storage format of each data item, and various constraints on the data. The information stored in the catalog is called **meta-data,** and it describes the structure of the primary database (Figure 1.1).

The catalog is used by the DBMS software and occasionally by database users who need information about the database structure. The DBMS software is not written for any specific database application, and hence it must refer to the catalog to know the structure of the files in a specific database, such as the type and format of data it will access. The DBMS software must work equally well with *any number of database applications*—for example, a university database, a banking database, or a company database—as long as the database definition is stored in the catalog.

In traditional file processing, data definition is typically part of the application programs themselves. Hence, these programs are constrained to work with only *one specific database*, whose structure is declared in the application programs. For example, a PASCAL program may have record structures declared in it; a C^{++} program may have "struct" or "class" declarations; and a COBOL program has Data Division statements to define its files. Whereas file-processing software can only access specific databases, DBMS software can access diverse databases by extracting the database definitions from the catalog and then using these definitions.

In our example of Figure 1.2, the DBMS stores in the catalog the definitions of all the files shown. Whenever a request is made to access, say, the Name of a STUDENT record, the DBMS software refers to the catalog to determine the structure of the STUDENT file and the position and size of the Name data item within a STUDENT record. By contrast, in a typical file-processing application, the file structure and, in some cases, the exact location of Name within a STUDENT record are already coded within each program that accesses this data item.

1.3.2 Insulation Between Programs and Data, and Data Abstraction

In traditional file processing, the structure of data files is embedded in the access programs, so any changes to the structure of a file may require *changing all programs* that access this file. By contrast, DBMS access programs are written independently of any specific files. The structure of data files is stored in the DBMS catalog separately from the access programs. We call this property **program-data independence.** For example, a file access program may be written in such a way that it can access only STUDENT records of length 42 characters (Figure 1.3). If we want to add another piece of data to each STUDENT record, say the Birthdate, such a program will no longer work and must be changed. By contrast, in a DBMS environment, we just need to change the description of STUDENT records in the catalog; no programs are changed. The next time a DBMS program refers to the catalog, the new structure of STUDENT records will be accessed and used.

Data Item Name	Starting Position in Record	Length in Characters (bytes)
Name	1	30
StudentNumber	31	4
Class	35	4
Major	39	4

Figure 1.3 Storage format for a STUDENT record.

Recent developments in object-oriented databases (see Chapter 22) and programming languages allow users to define operations on data as part of the database definitions. An **operation** (also called a *function*) is specified in two parts. The *interface* (or *signature*) of an operation includes the operation name and the data types of its arguments (or parameters). The *implementation* (or *method*) of the operation is specified separately and can be changed without affecting the interface. User application programs can operate on the data by invoking these operations through their names and arguments, regardless of how the operations are implemented. This may be termed **program-operation independence.**

The characteristic that allows program-data independence and program-operation independence is called **data abstraction.** A DBMS provides users with a **conceptual representation** of data that does not include many of the details of how the data is stored. Informally, a **data model** is a type of data abstraction that is used to provide this conceptual representation. The data model uses logical concepts, such as objects, their properties, and their interrelationships, that may be easier for most users to understand than computer storage concepts. Hence, the data model *hides* storage details that are not of interest to most database users.

For example, consider Figure 1.2. In a file-processing application, each file may be defined by its record length—the number of characters (bytes) in each record—and each data item may be specified by its starting byte within a record and its length in bytes. The STUDENT record would thus be represented as shown in Figure 1.3. But a typical database user is not concerned with where each data item is within a record or what its length is; rather, the concern is that, when a reference is made to Name of STUDENT, the correct value is returned. A conceptual representation of the STUDENT records is shown in Figure 1.2. Many other details of file-storage organization—such as the access paths specified on a file—can be hidden from database users by the DBMS; we will discuss storage details in Chapters 4 and 5.

In the database approach, the detailed structure and organization of each file are stored in the catalog. Database users refer to the conceptual representation of the files, and the DBMS extracts the details of file storage from the catalog when these are needed by the DBMS software. Many data models can be used to provide this data abstraction to database users. A major part of this book is devoted to presenting various data models and the concepts they use to abstract the representation of data.

With the recent trend toward object-oriented databases, abstraction is carried one level further to include not only the data structure but also the *operations* on the data. These operations provide an abstraction of miniworld activities commonly understood by the users. For example, an operation CALCULATE_GPA can be applied to a student object to calculate the grade point average. Such operations can be invoked by the user programs without the user's knowing the details of how they are internally implemented. In that sense, an abstraction of the miniworld activity is made available to the user as an **abstract operation.**

1.3.3 *Support of Multiple Views of the Data*

A database typically has many users, each of whom may require a different perspective or **view** of the database. A view may be a subset of the database or it may contain **virtual** data that is derived from the database files but is not explicitly stored. Some users may not need to be aware of whether the data they refer to is stored or derived. A multiuser DBMS whose users have a variety of applications must provide facilities for defining multiple views. For example, one user of the database of Figure 1.2 may be interested only in the transcript of each student; the view for this user is shown in Figure 1.4(a). A second user, who is interested only in checking that students have taken the prerequisites of each course they register for, may require the view shown in Figure 1.4(b).

1.3.4 *Sharing of Data and Multiuser Transaction Processing*

A multiuser DBMS, as its name implies, must allow multiple users to access the database at the same time. This is essential if data for multiple applications is to be integrated and maintained in a single database. The DBMS must include **concurrency control** software to ensure that several users trying to update the same data do so in a controlled manner so that the result of the updates is correct. An example is when several reservation clerks try to assign a seat on an airline flight; the DBMS should ensure that each seat can be accessed by only one clerk at a time for assignment to a passenger. These are generally called **transaction processing** applications. A fundamental role of multiuser DBMS software is to ensure that concurrent transactions operate correctly without interference.

The preceding characteristics are most important in distinguishing a DBMS from traditional file-processing software. In Section 1.6 we discuss additional functions that characterize a DBMS. First, however, we categorize the different types of persons who work in a database environment.

1.4 Actors on the Scene

For a small personal database, such as the list of addresses discussed in Section 1.1, one person typically defines, constructs, and manipulates the database. However, many persons are involved in the design, use, and maintenance of a large database with a few hundred users. In this section we identify the people whose jobs involve the day-to-day use of a large database; we call them the "actors on the scene." In Section 1.5 we consider people who may be called "workers behind the scene"—those who work to maintain the database system environment, but who are not actively interested in the database itself.

(a)

TRANSCRIPT	StudentName	StudentTranscript				
		CourseNumber	Grade	Semester	Year	SectionId
	Smith	COSC1310	C	Fall	92	119
		MATH2410	B	Fall	92	112
	Brown	MATH2410	A	Fall	91	85
		COSC1310	A	Fall	91	92
		COSC3320	B	Spring	92	102
		COSC3380	A	Fall	92	135

(b)

PREREQUISITES	CourseName	CourseNumber	Prerequisites
	Database	3380	COSC3320
			MATH2410
	Data Structures	3320	COSC1310

Figure 1.4 Two views (derived data) of the sample database in Figure 1.2. (a) The student transcript view. (b) The course prerequisites view.

1.4.1 *Database Administrators*

In any organization where many persons use the same resources, there is a need for a chief administrator to oversee and manage these resources. In a database environment, the primary resource is the database itself and the secondary resource is the DBMS and related software. Administering these resources is the responsibility of the **database administrator (DBA).** The DBA is responsible for authorizing access to the database, for coordinating and monitoring its use, and for acquiring software and hardware resources as needed. The DBA is accountable for problems such as breach of security or poor system response time. In large organizations, the DBA is assisted by a staff that helps in carrying out these functions.

1.4.2 *Database Designers*

Database designers are responsible for identifying the data to be stored in the database and for choosing appropriate structures to represent and store this data. These tasks are mostly undertaken before the database is actually implemented. It is the responsibility of database designers to communicate with all prospective database users, in order to understand their requirements, and to come up with a design that meets these requirements. In many cases, the designers are on the staff of the DBA and may be assigned other staff responsibilities after the database design is completed. Database designers typically interact with each potential group of users and develop a **view** of the database that meets the data and processing requirements of this group. These views are then analyzed and integrated with the views of other user groups. The final database design must be capable of supporting the requirements of all user groups.

1.4.3 End Users

These are the persons whose jobs require access to the database for querying, updating, and generating reports; the database primarily exists for their use. There are several categories of end users:

- **Casual end users** occasionally access the database, but they may need different information each time. They use a sophisticated database query language to specify their requests and are typically middle- or high-level managers or other occasional browsers.

- **Naive** or **parametric end users** make up a sizable portion of database end users. Their main job function revolves around constantly querying and updating the database, using standard types of queries and updates—called **canned transactions**—that have been carefully programmed and tested. We are all accustomed to dealing with several types of such users. Bank tellers check balances and post withdrawals and deposits. Reservation clerks for airlines, hotels, and car rental companies check availability for a given request and make reservations. Clerks at receiving stations for courier mail enter package identifications via bar code and descriptive information through buttons to update a central database of received and in-transit packages.

- **Sophisticated end users** include engineers, scientists, business analysts, and others who thoroughly familiarize themselves with the facilities of the DBMS so as to meet their complex requirements.

- **Stand-alone users** maintain personal databases by using ready-made program packages that provide easy-to-use menu- or graphics-based interfaces. An example is the user of a tax package that stores a variety of personal financial data for tax purposes.

A typical DBMS provides multiple facilities to access a database. Naive end users need to learn very little about the facilities provided by the DBMS; they have only to understand the types of standard transactions designed and implemented for their use. Casual users learn only a few facilities that they may use repeatedly. Sophisticated users try to learn most of the DBMS facilities in order to achieve their complex requirements. Stand-alone users typically become very proficient in using a specific software package.

1.4.4 System Analysts and Application Programmers

System analysts determine the requirements of end users, especially naive and parametric end users, and develop specifications for canned transactions that meet these requirements. **Application programmers** implement these specifications as programs; then they test, debug, document, and maintain these canned transactions. Such analysts and programmers should be familiar with the full range of capabilities provided by the DBMS to accomplish their tasks.

1.5 Workers Behind the Scene

In addition to those who design, use, and administer a database, others are associated with the design, development, and operation of the DBMS *software and system environment*. These persons are typically not interested in the database itself. We call them the workers behind the scene, and they include the following categories.

1.5.1 DBMS Designers and Implementers

These are persons who design and implement the DBMS modules and interfaces as a software package. A DBMS is a complex software system that consists of many components or **modules,** including modules for implementing the catalog, query language, interface processors, data access, and security. The DBMS must interface with other system software, such as the operating system and compilers for various programming languages.

1.5.2 Tool Developers

Tools are software packages that facilitate database system design and use, and help in improving performance. Tools are optional packages that are often purchased separately. They include packages for database design, performance monitoring, natural language or graphical interfaces, prototyping, simulation, and test data generation. Tool developers include persons who design and implement such tools. In many cases, independent software vendors develop and market these tools.

1.5.3 Operators and Maintenance Personnel

These are the system administration personnel who are responsible for the actual running and maintenance of the hardware and software environment for the database system.

Although the above categories of workers behind the scene are instrumental in making the database system available to end users, they typically do not use the database for their own purposes.

1.6 Intended Uses of a DBMS★

In this section we discuss the intended uses of a DBMS and the capabilities a good DBMS should possess. The DBA must utilize these capabilities to accomplish a variety of objectives related to the design, administration, and use of a large multiuser database.

1.6.1 Controlling Redundancy

In traditional software development utilizing file processing, every user group maintains its own files for handling its data-processing applications. For example, consider the UNI-VERSITY database example of Section 1.2; here, two groups of users could be the course registration personnel and the accounting office. In the traditional approach, each group independently keeps files on students. The accounting office also keeps data on registra-tion and related billing information, whereas the registration office keeps track of student courses and grades. Much of the data is stored twice: once in the files of each user group. Additional user groups may further duplicate some or all of the same data in their own files.

This **redundancy** in storing the same data multiple times leads to several problems. First, there is the need to perform a single logical update—such as entering data on a new student—multiple times: once for each file where student data is recorded. This leads to *duplication of effort*. Second, *storage space is wasted* when the same data is stored repeatedly, and this problem may be serious for large databases. Third, files that represent the same data may become *inconsistent*. This may happen because an update is applied to some of the files but not to others. Even if an update—such as adding a new stu-dent—is applied to all the appropriate files, the data concerning the student may still be **inconsistent** since the updates are applied independently by each user group. For example, one user group may enter a student's birthdate erroneously as JAN-19-1974, whereas the other user groups may enter the correct value of JAN-29-1974.

In the database approach, the views of different user groups are integrated during database design. For consistency, we should have a database design that stores each log-ical data item—such as a student's name or birthdate—in *only one place* in the database. This does not permit any inconsistency, and it saves storage space. In some cases, con-trolled redundancy may be useful. For example, we may store StudentName and CourseNumber redundantly in a GRADE_REPORT file (Figure 1.5(a)), because, whenever

(a)

GRADE_REPORT	StudentNumber	StudentName	SectionIdentifier	CourseNumber	Grade
	17	Smith	112	MATH2410	B
	17	Smith	119	COSC1310	C
	8	Brown	85	MATH2410	A
	8	Brown	92	COSC1310	A
	8	Brown	102	COSC3320	B
	8	Brown	135	COSC3380	A

(b)

GRADE_REPORT	StudentNumber	StudentName	SectionIdentifier	CourseNumber	Grade
	17	Brown	112	MATH2410	B

Figure 1.5 Redundant storage of data items among files. (a) Controlled redundancy: Including the StudentName and CourseNumber in the GRADE_REPORT file. (b) Uncontrolled redundancy: A GRADE_REPORT record that is inconsistent with the STUDENT records in Figure 1.2 (the Name of student number 17 is Smith, not Brown).

we retrieve a GRADE_REPORT record, we want to retrieve the student name and course number along with the grade, student number, and section identifier. By placing all the data together, we do not have to search multiple files to collect this data. In such cases, the DBMS should have the capability to **control** this redundancy so as to prohibit inconsistencies among the files. This may be done by automatically checking that the StudentName-StudentNumber values in any GRADE_REPORT record in Figure 1.5(a) match one of the Name-StudentNumber values of a STUDENT record (Figure 1.2). Similarly, the SectionIdentifier-CourseNumber values in GRADE_REPORT can be checked against SECTION records. Such checks can be specified to the DBMS during database design and automatically enforced by the DBMS whenever the GRADE_REPORT file is updated. Figure 1.5(b) shows a GRADE_REPORT record that is inconsistent with the STUDENT file of Figure 1.2, which may be entered erroneously if the redundancy is not controlled.

1.6.2   *Restricting Unauthorized Access*

When multiple users share a database, it is likely that some users will not be authorized to access all information in the database. For example, financial data is often considered confidential, and hence only authorized persons are allowed to access such data. In addition, some users may be permitted only to retrieve data, whereas others are allowed both to retrieve and to update. Hence, the type of access operation—retrieval or update— must also be controlled. Typically, users or user groups are given account numbers protected by passwords, which they can use to gain access to the database. A DBMS should provide a **security and authorization** subsystem, which the DBA uses to create accounts and to specify account restrictions. The DBMS should then enforce these restrictions automatically. Notice that we can apply similar controls to the DBMS software. For example, only the DBA's staff may be allowed to use certain **privileged** software, such as the software for creating new accounts. Similarly, parametric users may be allowed to access the database only through the canned transactions developed for their use.

1.6.3   *Persistent Storage for Program Objects and Data Structures*

A recent application of databases is to provide *persistent storage* for program objects and data structures. This is one of the main reasons for the emergence of the **object-oriented** DBMS. Programming languages typically have complex data structures, such as record types in PASCAL or class definitions in C^{++}. The values of program variables are discarded once a program terminates, unless the programmer explicitly stores them in permanent files, which often involves converting these complex structures into a format suitable for file storage. When the need arises to read this data once more, the programmer must convert from the file format to the program variable structure. Object-oriented database systems are compatible with programming languages such as C^{++} and SMALLTALK, and the DBMS software automatically performs any necessary conversions. Hence, a complex object in C^{++} can be stored permanently in an object-oriented DBMS, such as ObjectStore (see Chapter 22). Such an object is said to be **persistent,** since it survives the termination of program execution and can later be directly retrieved by another C^{++} program.

The persistent storage of program objects and data structures is an important function of database systems. Traditional database systems often suffered from the so-called *impedance mismatch problem*, since the data structures provided by the DBMS were incompatible with the programming language's data structures. Object-oriented database systems typically offer data structure *compatibility* with one or more object-oriented programming languages.

1.6.4 *Database Inferencing Using Deduction Rules*

Another recent application of database systems is to provide capabilities for defining *deduction rules* for *inferencing* new information from the stored database facts. Such systems are called **deductive** database systems. For example, there may be complex rules in the miniworld application for determining when a student is on probation. These can be specified *declaratively* as deduction rules, which when executed can determine all students on probation. In a traditional DBMS, an explicit *procedural program code* would have to be written to support such applications. But if the miniworld rules change, it is generally more convenient to change the declared deduction rules than to recode procedural programs.

1.6.5 *Providing Multiple User Interfaces*

Because many types of users, with varying levels of technical knowledge, use a database, a DBMS should provide a variety of user interfaces. These include query languages for casual users, programming language interfaces for application programmers, forms and command codes for parametric users, and menu-driven interfaces and natural language interfaces for stand-alone users.

1.6.6 *Representing Complex Relationships among Data*

A database may include numerous varieties of data that are interrelated in many ways. Consider the example shown in Figure 1.2. The record for Brown in the STUDENT file is related to four records in the GRADE_REPORT file. Similarly, each SECTION record is related to one COURSE record as well as to a number of GRADE_REPORT records—one for each student who completed that section. A DBMS must have the capability to represent a variety of complex relationships among the data as well as to retrieve and update related data easily and efficiently.

1.6.7 *Enforcing Integrity Constraints*

Most database applications have certain **integrity constraints** that must hold for the data. A DBMS should provide capabilities for defining and enforcing these constraints. The simplest type of integrity constraint involves specifying a data type for each data item. For example, in Figure 1.2, we may specify that the value of the Class data item within each STUDENT record must be an integer between 1 and 5 and that the value of Name must be a string of no more than 30 alphabetic characters. A more complex type of constraint that occurs frequently involves specifying that a record in one file must be related to records in other files. For example, in Figure 1.2, we can specify that "every SECTION record must be related to a COURSE record." Another type of constraint specifies uniqueness on data item values, such as "every COURSE record must have a unique value for CourseNumber." These constraints are derived from the meaning or **semantics** of the data and of the miniworld it represents. It is the database designers' responsibility to identify integrity constraints during database design. Some constraints can be specified to the DBMS and automatically enforced. Other constraints may have to be checked by update programs or at the time of data entry.

A data item may be entered erroneously and yet still satisfy the specified integrity constraints. For example, if a student receives a grade of A but a grade of C is entered in the database, the DBMS *cannot* discover this error automatically, because C is a valid value for the Grade data type. Such data entry errors can only be discovered manually (when the student receives the grade and complains) and corrected later by updating the database. However, a grade of X can be automatically rejected by the DBMS, because X is not a valid value for the Grade data type.

1.6.8 *Providing Backup and Recovery*

A DBMS must provide facilities for recovering from hardware or software failures. The **backup and recovery** subsystem of the DBMS is responsible for recovery. For example, if the computer system fails in the middle of a complex update program, the recovery subsystem is responsible for making sure that the database is restored to the state it was in before the program started executing. Alternatively, the recovery subsystem could ensure that the program is resumed from the point at which it was interrupted so that its full effect is recorded in the database.

1.7 **Implications of the Database Approach**★

In addition to the issues discussed in the previous section, other implications of using the database approach can benefit most organizations.

1.7.1 *Potential for Enforcing Standards*

The database approach permits the DBA to define and enforce standards among database users in a large organization. This facilitates communication and cooperation among various departments, projects, and users within the organization. Standards can be defined for names and formats of data elements, display formats, report structures, terminology, and so on. The DBA can enforce standards in a centralized database environment more easily than in an environment where each user group has control of its own files and software.

1.7.2 *Reduced Application Development Time*

A prime selling feature of the database approach is that developing a new application—such as the retrieval of certain data from the database for printing a new report—takes very little time. Designing and implementing a new database from scratch may take more time than writing a single specialized file application. However, once a database is up and running, substantially less time is generally required to create new applications using DBMS facilities. Development time using a DBMS is estimated to be one-sixth to one-fourth of that for a traditional file system.

1.7.3 Flexibility

It may be necessary to change the structure of a database as requirements change. For example, a new user group may emerge that needs additional information not currently in the database. In response, we may need to add a new file to the database or to extend the data elements in an existing file. Some DBMSs allow such changes to the structure of the database without affecting the stored data and the existing application programs.

1.7.4 Availability of Up-to-Date Information

A DBMS makes the database available to all users. As soon as one user's update is applied to the database, all other users can immediately see this update. This availability of up-to-date information is essential for many transaction processing applications, such as reservation systems or banking databases, and it is made possible by the concurrency control and recovery subsystems of a DBMS.

1.7.5 Economies of Scale

The DBMS approach permits consolidation of data and applications, thus reducing the amount of wasteful overlap between activities of data-processing personnel in different projects or departments. This enables the whole organization to invest in more powerful processors, storage devices, or communication gear, rather than having each department purchase its own (weaker) equipment separately. This reduces overall costs of operation and management.

1.8 When Not to Use a DBMS★

In spite of these advantages, there are some situations where using a DBMS may incur unnecessary overhead costs as compared to traditional file processing. The overhead costs of using a DBMS are due to the following:

- High initial investment in hardware, software, and training.
- Generality that a DBMS provides for defining and processing data.
- Overhead for providing security, concurrency control, recovery, and integrity functions.

Additional problems may arise if the database designers and DBA do not properly design the database or if the database systems applications are not implemented properly. Because of the overhead costs of using a DBMS and the potential problems of improper administration, it may be more desirable to use regular files under the following circumstances:

- The database and applications are simple, well defined, and not expected to change.
- There are stringent real-time requirements for some programs that may not be met because of DBMS overhead.
- Multiple-user access to data is not required.

1.9 Summary

In this chapter we defined a database as a collection of related data, where *data* means recorded facts. A typical database represents some aspect of the real world and is used for specific purposes by one or more groups of users. A DBMS is generalized software for implementing and maintaining a computerized database. The database and software together form a database system. We identified several characteristics that distinguish the database approach from traditional file-processing applications:

- Existence of a catalog or data dictionary.
- Data abstraction.
- Program-data independence, and program-operation independence.
- Support of multiple user views.
- Sharing of data among multiple transactions.

We then discussed the main categories of database users, or the "actors on the scene":

- Database designers and administrators.
- End users.
- Application programmers and system analysts.

We noted that, in addition to database users, there are several categories of support personnel, or "workers behind the scene," in a database environment:

- DBMS designers and implementers.
- Tool developers.
- Operators and maintenance personnel.

Then we presented a list of capabilities that should be provided by the DBMS software to the DBA, database designers, and users to help them in administering, designing, and using a database:

- Controlling redundancy.
- Restricting unauthorized access.
- Providing persistent storage for program data structures.

- Permitting inferencing by using deduction rules.
- Providing multiple interfaces.
- Representing complex relationships among data.
- Enforcing integrity constraints.
- Providing backup and recovery.

We listed some additional advantages of the database approach over traditional file-processing systems:

- Potential for enforcing standards.
- Flexibility.
- Reduced application development time.
- Availability of up-to-date information to all users.
- Economies of scale.

Finally, we discussed the overhead costs of using a DBMS and discussed some situations where it may not be advantageous to use a DBMS. A bird's-eye view of the major developments in the database field is given in the time line at the end of this chapter.

Review Questions

1.1. Define the following terms: *data, database, DBMS, database system, database catalog, program-data independence, user view, DBA, end user, canned transaction, deductive database system, persistent object, meta-data, transaction processing application.*

1.2. What three main types of actions involve databases? Briefly discuss each.

1.3. Discuss the main characteristics of the database approach and how it differs from traditional file systems.

1.4. What are the responsibilities of the DBA and the database designers?

1.5. What are the different types of database end users? Discuss the main activities of each.

1.6. Discuss the capabilities that should be provided by a DBMS.

Exercises

1.7. Identify some informal queries and update operations that you would expect to apply to the database shown in Figure 1.2.

1.8. What is the difference between controlled and uncontrolled redundancy? Illustrate with examples.

1.9. Name all the relationships among the records of the database shown in Figure 1.2.

1.10. Give some additional views that may be needed by other user groups for the database shown in Figure 1.2.

1.11. Cite some examples of integrity constraints that you think should hold on the database shown in Figure 1.2.

Selected Bibliography

The March 1976 issue of *ACM Computing Surveys* offers an early introduction to traditional data models. In this issue, Sibley (1976) and Fry and Sibley (1976) provide a good perspective on how databases evolved from traditional file processing. The October 1991 issue of *Communications of the ACM* includes several articles describing "next generation" DBMSs. Many database textbooks contain discussions of the material presented here and in Chapter 2, including Wiederhold (1986), Ullman (1988), Date (1990), and Korth and Silberschatz (1991), among others.

DATABASE SYSTEMS: A BRIEF TIME LINE

Event	Consequence
Pre-1960s	
1945 Magnetic tapes developed (the first medium to allow searching).	Replaced punch cards and paper tape.
1957 First commercial computer installed.	
1959 McGee proposed the notion of generalized access to electronically stored data.	
1959 IBM introduced the Ramac system.	Read data in a nonsequential manner, and access to files became feasible.
The '60s	
1961 The first generalized DBMS—GE's Integrated Data Store (IDS)—designed by Bachman; wide distribution by 1964. Bachman popularized data structure diagrams.	Formed the basis for Network Data Model developed by Conference on Data Systems Languages Database Task Group (CODASYL DBTG).
1965–1970 • Generalized file management systems developed by numerous vendors.	Provided two-level conceptual/user view organization of data.
• Information Management System (IMS) developed by IBM.	Formed the basis for Hierarchical Data Model.
• IMS DB/DC (database/data communication) System was the first large-scale DB/DC system.	Supported network views on top of the hierarchies.
• SABRE, developed by IBM and American Airlines.	Allowed multiple-user access to data involving a communication network.
The '70s	
Database technology experienced rapid growth.	Commercial systems followed CODASYL DBTG proposal, but none fully implemented it. IDMS system by B. F. Goodrich, Honeywell's IDS II, UNIVAC's DMS 1100, Burroughs's DMS-II, CDC's DMS-170, Phillips's PHOLAS, and Digital's DBMS-11.
	Several integrated DB/DC systems: Cincom's TOTAL plus ENVIRON/1. DBMS developed as an academic discipline and a research area.
1970 The relational model is developed by Ted Codd, an IBM research fellow.	Laid foundation for database theory.
1971 CODASYL Database Task Group Report.	
1975 ACM Special Interest Group on Management of Data organized first SIGMOD international conference.	Provided a forum for dissemination of database research.

| 1975 | Very Large Data Base Foundation organized first VLDB international conference. | Provided another forum for dissemination of database research. |

1976 Entity-relationship (ER) model introduced by Chen.

- **Research projects in the '70s:** System R (IBM), INGRES (University of California, Berkeley), System 2000 (University of Texas, Austin), Socrate Project (University of Grenoble, France), ADABAS (Technical University of Darmstadt, W. Germany).
- **Query Languages developed in the '70s:** SQUARE, SEQUEL (SQL), QBE, QUEL.

The '80s

DBMSs developed for personal computers (DBASE, PARADOX, etc).

Allowed PC users to define and manipulate data. They lacked multiview/multiaccess support and insulation between programs and data.

1983 ANSI/SPARC survey revealed >100 relational systems had been implemented by the beginning of the '80s.

Emergence of commercial relational DMBSs (DB2, ORACLE, SYBASE, INFORMIX, etc).

1985 Preliminary SQL standard published. Business world influenced by "Fourth Generation Languages." Proposal for Network Definition Language (NDL) made by ANSI.

Generated complete application programs starting from a high-level nonprogrammer language interface.

- **Trends in the '80s:** Expert Database Systems, Object-oriented DBMSs, client-server architecture for distributed databases.

Allowed new database applications, networking, and distributed data management.

The '90s

- Demand for extending DBMS capabilities to meet new applications.

DBMS features for spatial, temporal, and multimedia data, incorporating active and deductive capabilities.

- Emergence of commercial object-oriented DBMSs.
- Demand for developing applications utilizing data from a variety of sources.

Emergence of standards for data query and exchange (SQL2, PDES, STEP); extension of DBMS capabilities to heterogeneous and multi-database systems.

- Demand for exploiting massively parallel processors (MPPs).

Improved performance of commercial DBMSs.

CHAPTER 2

Database System
Concepts and
Architecture

In this chapter we discuss in more detail many of the concepts and issues that were introduced in Chapter 1. We also present the terminology that will be used throughout this book. We start, in Section 2.1, by discussing data models and defining the concepts of schemas and instances, which are fundamental to the study of database systems. We then discuss DBMS architecture and data independence, in Section 2.2; different types of interfaces and languages provided by a DBMS, in Section 2.3; the database system software environment, in Section 2.4; and classification of DBMSs, in Section 2.5.

The reader may skip or browse through the material in Sections 2.4 and 2.5.

2.1 Data Models, Schemas, and Instances

One fundamental characteristic of the database approach is that it provides some level of data abstraction by hiding details of data storage that are not needed by most database users. A data model is the main tool for providing this abstraction. A **data model** is a set of concepts that can be used to describe the structure of a database.* By *structure of*

---

*Sometimes the word *model* is used to denote a database description, or schema—for example, "the marketing data model." We will not use this interpretation.

a database, we mean the data types, relationships, and constraints that should hold for the data. Most data models also include a set of **basic operations** for specifying retrievals and updates on the database. It is gradually becoming common practice to include concepts in the data model to specify **behavior;** this refers to specifying a set of valid **user-defined operations** that are allowed on the database in addition to the basic operations provided by the data model. An example of a user-defined operation is COMPUTE_GPA, which can be applied to a STUDENT object. On the other hand, generic operations to insert, delete, modify, or retrieve an object are often included in the basic data model operations.

2.1.1 *Categories of Data Models*

Many data models have been proposed. We can categorize data models based on the types of concepts they provide to describe the database structure. **High-level** or **conceptual** data models provide concepts that are close to the way many users perceive data, whereas **low-level** or **physical** data models provide concepts that describe the details of how data is stored in the computer. Concepts provided by low-level data models are generally meant for computer specialists, not for typical end users. Between these two extremes is a class of **representational** (or **implementation**) data models, which provide concepts that may be understood by end users but that are not too far removed from the way data is organized within the computer. Representational data models hide some details of data storage but can be implemented on a computer system in a direct way.

High-level data models use concepts such as entities, attributes, and relationships. An **entity** represents a real-world object or concept, such as an employee or a project, that is stored in the database. An **attribute** represents some property of interest that further describes an entity, such as the employee's name or salary. A **relationship** among two or more entities represents an interaction among the entities; for example, a works-on relationship between an employee and a project. In Chapter 3, we will present the Entity-Relationship model—a popular high-level data model.

Representational or implementation data models are the ones used most frequently in current commercial DBMSs, and they include the three most widely used data models: relational, network, and hierarchical. Parts II and III of the book describe these models, their operations, and their languages. They represent data by using record structures and hence are sometimes called **record-based** data models. We can regard **object-oriented** data models as a new family of higher-level implementation data models that are closer to conceptual data models. We describe the general characteristics of these models, together with a description of two object-oriented DBMSs, in Chapter 22. Object-oriented models are also frequently utilized as high-level conceptual models, particularly in the software engineering domain. Additional approaches to high-level data modeling are addressed in Chapter 21.

Physical data models describe how data is stored in the computer by representing information such as record formats, record orderings, and access paths. An **access path** is a structure that makes the search for particular database records efficient. We discuss physical storage techniques and access structures in Chapters 4 and 5.

2.1.2 *Schemas and Instances*

In any data model it is important to distinguish between the *description* of the database and the *database itself*. The description of a database is called the **database schema** (or the **meta-data**). A database schema is specified during database design and is not expected to change frequently. Most data models have certain conventions for diagrammatically displaying the schemas. A displayed schema is called a **schema diagram.** Figure 2.1 shows a schema diagram for the database shown in Figure 1.2; the diagram displays the structure of each record type but not the actual instances of records. We call each object in the schema—such as STUDENT or COURSE—a **schema construct**.

A schema diagram displays only *some aspects* of a schema, such as the names of record types and data items, and some types of constraints. Other aspects are not specified in the schema diagram; for example, Figure 2.1 shows neither the data type of each data item nor the relationships among the various files. Many types of constraints are not represented in schema diagrams; for example, a constraint such as "students majoring in computer science must take COSC1310 before the end of their sophomore year" is quite difficult to represent.

The actual data in a database may change frequently; for example, the database shown in Figure 1.2 changes every time we add a new student or enter a new grade for a student. The data in the database at a particular moment in time is called a **database state** (or set of **occurrences** or **instances**). In a given database state, each schema construct has its own *current set* of instances; for example, the STUDENT construct will contain the set of individual student entities (records) as its instances. Many database states can be constructed to correspond to a particular database schema. Every time we insert or delete a record, or change the value of a data item, we change one state of the database into another state.

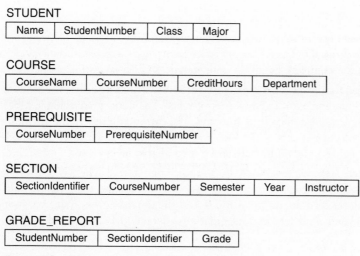

Figure 2.1 Schema diagram for the database of Figure 1.2.

The distinction between database schema and database state is very important. When we **define** a new database, we only specify its database schema to the DBMS. At this point, the corresponding database state is the "empty state" with no data. We get the "initial state" of the database when the data is first **loaded.** From then on, every time an update operation is applied to the database, we get another database state. The DBMS is partly responsible for ensuring that *every* state of the database is a **valid state**—that is, one that satisfies the structure and constraints specified in the schema. Hence, specifying a correct schema to the DBMS is extremely important, and the schema must be designed with the utmost care. The DBMS stores the schema in the DBMS catalog so that DBMS software can refer to the schema whenever it needs to. The schema is sometimes called the **intension,** and a database state is sometimes called an **extension** of the schema.

2.2 DBMS Architecture and Data Independence

Three important characteristics of the database approach, listed in Section 1.3, are (a) insulation of programs and data (program-data and program-operation independence); (b) support of multiple user views; and (c) use of a catalog to store the database description (schema). In this section we specify an architecture for database systems, called the **three-schema architecture,** * that was proposed to help achieve these characteristics. We then discuss the concept of data independence.

2.2.1 *The Three-schema Architecture*

The goal of the three-schema architecture, illustrated in Figure 2.2, is to separate the user applications and the physical database. In this architecture, schemas can be defined at the following three levels:

1. The **internal level** has an **internal schema,** which describes the physical storage structure of the database. The internal schema uses a physical data model and describes the complete details of data storage and access paths for the database.

2. The **conceptual level** has a **conceptual schema,** which describes the structure of the whole database for a community of users. The conceptual schema hides the details of physical storage structures and concentrates on describing entities, data types, relationships, user operations, and constraints. A high-level data model or an implementation data model can be used at this level.

3. The **external** or **view level** includes a number of **external schemas** or **user views.** Each external schema describes the part of the database that a particular user group is interested in and hides the rest of the database from that user group. A high-level data model or an implementation data model can be used at this level.

---

*This is also known as the ANSI/SPARC architecture, after the committee that proposed it (Tsichritzis and Klug 1978).

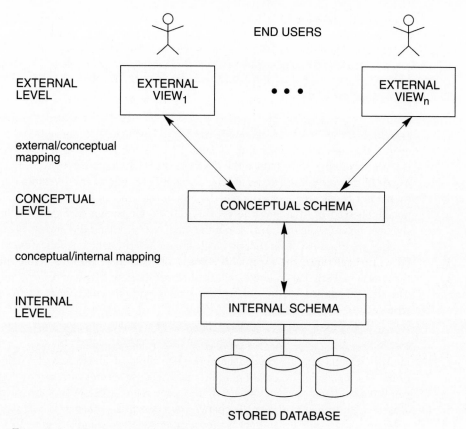

Figure 2.2   The three-schema architecture.

Most DBMSs do not separate the three levels completely, but several of them support the three-schema architecture to some extent. Some DBMSs include physical-level details in the conceptual schema. In most DBMSs that support user views, external schemas are specified in the same data model that describes the conceptual-level information. Some DBMSs allow different data models to be used at the conceptual and external levels.

Notice that the three schemas are only descriptions of data; the only data that *actually* exists is at the physical level. In a DBMS based on the three-schema architecture, each user group refers only to its own external schema. Hence, the DBMS must transform a request specified on an external schema into a request against the conceptual schema, and then into a request on the internal schema for processing over the stored database. If the request is a database retrieval, the data extracted from the stored database must be reformatted to match the user's external view. The processes of transforming requests and results between levels are called **mappings.** These mappings may be time-consuming, so some DBMSs—especially those that are meant to support small databases—do not support external views. Even in such systems, however, a certain amount of mapping is necessary to transform requests between the conceptual and internal levels.

2.2.2 *Data Independence*

The three-schema architecture can be used to explain the concept of **data independence,** which can be defined as the capacity to change the schema at one level of a database system without having to change the schema at the next higher level. We can define two types of data independence:

1. **Logical data independence** is the capacity to change the conceptual schema without having to change external schemas or application programs. We may change the conceptual schema to expand the database (by adding a new record type or data item), or to reduce the database (by removing a record type or data item). In the latter case, external schemas that refer only to the remaining data should not be affected. For example, the external schema of Figure 1.4(a) should not be affected by changing the GRADE_REPORT file shown in Figure 1.2 into the one shown in Figure 1.5(a). Only the view definition and the mappings need be changed in a DBMS that supports logical data independence. Application programs that reference the external schema constructs must work as before after the conceptual schema undergoes a logical reorganization. Changes to constraints can also be applied to the conceptual schema without affecting the external schemas.

2. **Physical data independence** is the capacity to change the internal schema without having to change the conceptual (or external) schemas. Changes to the internal schema may be needed because some physical files had to be reorganized—for example, by creating additional access structures—to improve the performance of retrieval or update. If the same data as before remains in the database, we should not have to change the conceptual schema. For example, providing an access path to improve retrieval of SECTION records (Figure 1.2) by Semester and Year should not require a query such as "list all sections offered in Fall 1991" to be changed, although the query can be executed more efficiently by the DBMS by utilizing the new access path. Because *physical data independence* refers to the insulation of an application from the physical storage structures only, it is easier to achieve than logical data independence.

Whenever we have a multiple-level DBMS, its catalog must be expanded to include information on how to map requests and data among the various levels. The DBMS uses additional software to accomplish these mappings by referring to the mapping information in the catalog. Data independence is accomplished because, when the schema is changed at some level, the schema at the next higher level remains unchanged; only the mapping between the two levels is changed. Application programs referring to the higher-level schema need not be changed. Hence, the three-schema architecture can make it easier to achieve true data independence, both physical and logical. However, the two levels of mappings create an overhead during compilation or execution of a query or program, leading to inefficiencies in the DBMS. Because of this, few DBMSs have implemented the full three-schema architecture.

2.3 Database Languages and Interfaces

In Section 1.4 we discussed the variety of users supported by a DBMS. The DBMS must provide appropriate languages and interfaces for each category of users. In this section we discuss the types of languages and interfaces provided by a DBMS and the user categories targeted by each interface.

2.3.1 DBMS Languages

Once the design of a database is completed and a DBMS is chosen to implement the database, the first order of the day is to specify conceptual and internal schemas for the database and any mappings between the two. In many DBMSs where no strict separation of levels is maintained, one language, called the **data definition language (DDL),** is used by the DBA and by database designers to define both schemas. The DBMS will have a DDL compiler whose function is to process DDL statements in order to identify descriptions of the schema constructs and to store the schema description in the DBMS catalog.

In DBMSs where a clear separation is maintained between the conceptual and internal levels, the DDL is used to specify the conceptual schema only. Another language, the **storage definition language (SDL),** is used to specify the internal schema. The mappings between the two schemas may be specified in either one of these languages. For a true three-schema architecture, we would need a third language, the **view definition language (VDL),** to specify user views and their mappings to the conceptual schema. Once the database schemas are compiled and the database is populated with data, users must have some means for manipulating the database. Typical manipulations include retrieval, insertion, deletion, and modification of the data. The DBMS provides a **data manipulation language (DML)** for these purposes.

It is common in current DBMSs not to identify the preceding types of languages as distinct; rather, a comprehensive integrated language can be used that includes constructs for conceptual schema definition, view definition, data manipulation, and storage definition. A typical example is the SQL relational database language (see Chapter 7), which represents a combination of DDL, VDL, DML, and SDL, although the SDL component is now being removed from the language.

There are two main types of DMLs. A **high-level** or **nonprocedural** DML can be used on its own to specify complex database operations in a concise manner. Many DBMSs allow high-level DML statements either to be entered interactively from a terminal or to be embedded in a general-purpose programming language. In the latter case, DML statements must be identified within the program so that they can be processed by the DBMS. A **low-level** or **procedural** DML *must* be embedded in a general-purpose programming language. This type of DML typically retrieves individual records from the database and processes each record separately. Hence, it needs to make use of programming language constructs, such as looping, to retrieve and process each individual record from a set of records. Low-level DMLs are also called **record-at-a-time** DMLs because of this property. High-level DMLs, such as SQL, can specify and retrieve many records in a single DML statement and are hence called **set-at-a-time** or **set-oriented** DMLs. A query in a high-level DML often specifies *what* data is to be retrieved rather than *how* to retrieve the data; hence, such languages are also called **declarative.**

Whenever DML commands, whether high-level or low-level, are embedded in a general-purpose programming language, that language is called the **host language** and the DML is called the **data sublanguage.** In newer DBMSs, such as object-oriented systems, the host and data sublanguages typically form one integrated language such as C^{++}. On the other hand, a high-level DML used in a stand-alone interactive manner is called a **query language.** In general, both retrieval and update commands of a high-level DML may be used interactively and are hence considered part of the query language.*

Casual end users typically use a high-level query language to specify their requests, whereas programmers use the DML in its embedded form. For naive and parametric users, there usually are **user-friendly interfaces** for interacting with the database; these can also be used by casual users or others who do not want to learn the details of a high-level query language. We discuss these types of interfaces next.

2.3.2 *DBMS Interfaces*

User-friendly interfaces provided by a DBMS may include the following.

Menu-based Interfaces. These interfaces present the user with lists of options, called **menus,** that lead the user through the formulation of a request. Menus do away with the need to memorize the specific commands and syntax of a query language; rather, the query is composed step by step by picking options from a menu list that is displayed by the system. Pull-down menus are becoming a very popular technique in window-based user interfaces. They are often used in **browsing interfaces,** which allow a user to look through the contents of a database in an unstructured manner.

Graphical Interfaces. A graphical interface typically displays a schema to the user in diagrammatic form. The user can then specify a query by manipulating the diagram. In many cases, graphical interfaces are combined with menus. Most graphical interfaces use a **pointing device,** such as a mouse, to pick certain parts of the displayed schema diagram.

Forms-based Interfaces. A forms-based interface displays a **form** to each user. Users can fill out all of the form entries to insert new data, or they fill out only certain entries, in which case the DBMS will retrieve matching data for the remaining entries. Forms are usually designed and programmed for naive users as interfaces to canned transactions. Many DBMSs have special languages, called *forms specification languages*, that help programmers specify such forms. Some systems have utilities that define a form by letting the end user interactively construct a sample form on the screen.

Natural Language Interfaces. These interfaces accept requests written in English or some other language and attempt to "understand" them. A natural language interface usually has its own "schema," which is similar to the database conceptual schema. The interface refers to the words in its schema, as well as to a set of standard words, in interpreting the request. If the interpretation is successful, the interface generates a high-level

---

*According to the meaning of the word *query* in English, it should really only be used to describe retrievals, not updates.

query corresponding to the natural language request and submits it to the DBMS for processing; otherwise, a dialogue is started with the user to clarify the request.

Interfaces for Parametric Users. Parametric users, such as bank tellers, often have a small set of operations that they must perform repeatedly. Systems analysts and programmers design and implement a special interface for a known class of naive users. Usually, a small set of abbreviated commands is included, with the goal of minimizing the number of keystrokes required for each request. For example, function keys in a terminal may be programmed to initiate the various commands. This allows the parametric user to proceed with a minimal number of keystrokes.

Interfaces for the DBA. Most database systems contain privileged commands that can be used only by the DBA's staff. These include commands for creating accounts, setting system parameters, granting account authorization, changing a schema, and reorganizing the storage structure of a database.

2.4 The Database System Environment*

A DBMS is a complex software system. In this section we discuss the types of software components that constitute a DBMS and the types of computer system software with which the DBMS interacts.

2.4.1 *DBMS Component Modules*

Figure 2.3 illustrates typical DBMS components. The database and the DBMS catalog are usually stored on disk. Access to the disk is controlled primarily by the *operating system* (OS), which schedules disk input/output. A higher-level **stored data manager** module of the DBMS controls access to DBMS information stored on disk, whether it is part of the database or of the catalog. The dotted lines and circles marked A, B, C, D, and E in Figure 2.3 illustrate accesses that are under the control of this stored data manager. The stored data manager may use basic OS services for carrying out low-level data transfer between the disk and computer main storage, but it controls other aspects of data transfer, such as handling buffers in main memory. Once the data is in main memory buffers, it can be processed by other DBMS modules.

The **DDL compiler** processes schema definitions, specified in the DDL, and stores descriptions of the schemas (meta-data) in the DBMS catalog. The catalog includes information such as the names of files, data items, storage details of each file, mapping information among schemas, and constraints. DBMS software modules that need to look up this information must access the catalog.

The **run-time database processor** handles database accesses at run time; it receives retrieval or update operations and carries them out on the database. Access to disk goes through the stored data manager. The **query compiler** handles high-level queries that are entered interactively. It parses and analyzes a query, and then generates calls to the run-time processor for executing the request.

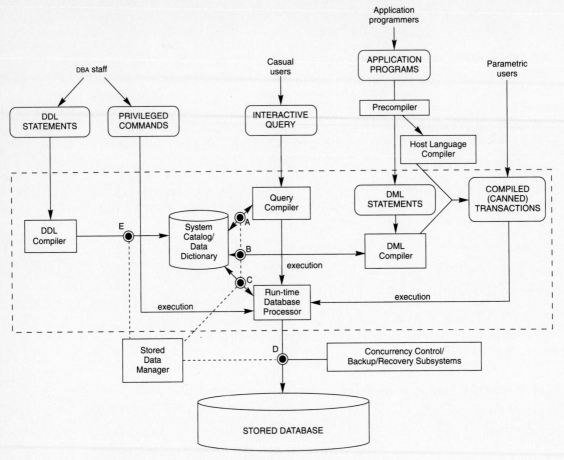

Figure 2.3 Components of a DBMS. Dotted lines show accesses that are under
the control of the stored data manager.

The **precompiler** extracts DML commands from an application program written in
a host programming language. These commands are sent to the **DML compiler** for compilation into object code for database access. The rest of the program is sent to the host
language compiler. The object codes for the DML commands and the rest of the program
are linked, forming a canned transaction whose executable code includes calls to the
run-time database processor.

Figure 2.3 is not meant to describe a specific DBMS; rather, we use it to illustrate
typical DBMS modules. The DBMS interacts with the operating system when disk
accesses—to the database or to the catalog—are needed. If the computer system is
shared by many users, the OS will schedule DBMS disk access requests and DBMS processing along with other processes. The DBMS also interfaces with compilers for general-
purpose host programming languages. User-friendly interfaces can be provided to help
any of the user types shown in Figure 2.3 in specifying their requests.

2.4.2 *Database System Utilities*

In addition to possessing the software modules just described, most DBMSs have **database utilities** that help the DBA run the database system. Common utilities have the following types of functions:

Loading: A loading utility is used to load existing data files—such as text files or sequential files—into the database. Usually, the current (source) format of the data file and the desired (target) database file structure are specified to the utility, which then automatically reformats the data and stores it in the database. With the proliferation of DBMSs, transferring data from one DBMS to another is becoming common in many organizations. Some vendors are offering products that generate the appropriate loading programs, given the existing source and target database storage descriptions (internal schemas). An example is the EXTRACT system of Evolutionary Technologies. Such tools are also called **conversion tools.**

Backup: A backup utility creates a backup copy of the database, usually by dumping the entire database onto tape. The backup copy can be used to restore the database in case of catastrophic failure.

File reorganization: This utility can be used to reorganize a database file into a different file organization to improve performance.

Performance monitoring: Such a utility monitors database usage and provides statistics to the DBA. The DBA uses the statistics in making decisions such as whether or not to reorganize files to improve performance.

Other utilities may be available for sorting files, handling data compression, monitoring access by users, and performing other functions. Another utility that can be quite useful in large organizations is an expanded **data dictionary system.** In addition to storing catalog information about schemas and constraints, the data dictionary stores other information such as design decisions, usage standards, application program descriptions, and user information. This information can be accessed *directly* by users or the DBA when needed. A data dictionary utility is similar to the DBMS catalog, but it includes a wider variety of information and is accessed mainly by users rather than by the DBMS software. A combined catalog/data dictionary, which can be accessed by both users and the DBMS software, is called a **data directory** or an **active** data dictionary. A data dictionary that can be accessed by users and the DBA but not by the DBMS software is called **passive.**

2.4.3 *Communications Facilities*

The DBMS also needs to interface with **communications software,** whose function is to allow users at locations remote from the database system site to access the database through computer terminals, workstations, or their local micro- or minicomputers. These are connected to the database site through data communications hardware such as phone lines, long-haul networks, or satellite communication devices. Many commercial database systems have communication packages that work with the DBMS. The integrated DBMS and data communications system is called a **DB/DC system.**

In addition, some distributed DBMSs are physically distributed over multiple machines. In this case, communications networks are needed to connect the machines.

These are often *local area networks* (LANs), but they can also be other types of networks. The term **client-server architecture** is used in conjunction with a DBMS if the application runs physically on one machine, called the **client,** and the data storage and access is handled by another machine, called the **server.** Various combinations of clients and servers can be offered by a vendor—for example, one server for multiple clients.

2.5 Classification of Database Management Systems*

The main criterion normally used to classify DBMSs is the **data model** on which the DBMS is based. The data models used most often in current commercial DBMSs are the relational, network, and hierarchical models. Some recent DBMSs are based on object-oriented or conceptual models. We will categorize DBMSs as **relational, network, hierarchical, object-oriented,** and **others.**

Another criterion used to classify DBMSs is the **number of users** supported by the system. **Single-user** systems support only one user at a time and are mostly used with personal computers. **Multiuser** systems, which include the majority of DBMSs, support many users concurrently.

A third criterion is the **number of sites** over which the database is distributed. Most DBMSs are **centralized,** meaning that their data is stored at a single computer site. A centralized DBMS can support multiple users, but the DBMS and the database themselves reside totally at a single computer site. A **distributed DBMS (DDBMS)** can have the actual database and DBMS software distributed over many sites, connected by a computer network. **Homogeneous DDBMSs** use the same DBMS software at multiple sites. A recent trend is to develop software to access several autonomous preexisting databases stored under **heterogeneous** DBMSs. This leads to a **federated DBMS** (or **multidatabase system),** where the participating DBMSs are loosely coupled and have a degree of local autonomy. Many DDBMSs use a client-server architecture. We discuss DDBMSs and client-server architecture in Chapter 23.

A fourth criterion is the **cost** of the DBMS. The majority of DBMS packages cost between $10,000 and $100,000. Single-user low-end systems that work with microcomputers cost between $100 and $3000. At the other end, a few elaborate packages cost more than $100,000.

We can also classify a DBMS on the basis of the **types of access path** options available for storing files. One well-known family of DBMSs is based on inverted file structures. Finally, a DBMS can be **general-purpose** or **special-purpose.** When performance is a primary consideration, a special-purpose DBMS can be designed and built for a specific application; such a system cannot be used for other applications. Many airline reservations and telephone directory systems are special-purpose DBMSs. These fall into the category of **on-line transaction processing (OLTP) systems,** which must support a large number of concurrent transactions without imposing excessive delays.

Let us briefly discuss the main criterion for classifying DBMSs: the data model. The **relational** data model represents a database as a collection of tables, where each table can be stored as a separate file. The database in Figure 1.2 is shown in a manner very

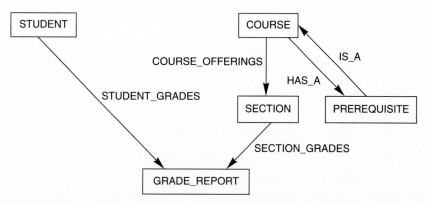

Figure 2.4   A network schema.

similar to a relational representation. Most relational databases have high-level query languages and support a limited form of user views. We discuss the relational model, its languages and operations, and a sample system in Chapters 6 to 9.

The **network** model represents data as record types and also represents a limited type of 1:N relationship, called a set type. Figure 2.4 shows a network schema diagram for the database of Figure 1.2, where record types are shown as rectangles and set types are shown as labeled directed arrows. The network model, also known as the CODASYL DBTG model,* has an associated record-at-a-time language that must be embedded in a host programming language. We present the network model and its language in Chapter 10.

The **hierarchical** model represents data as hierarchical tree structures. Each hierarchy represents a number of related records. There is no standard language for the hierarchical model, although most hierarchical DBMSs have record-at-a-time languages. We discuss the hierarchical model in Chapter 11.

The **object-oriented** model defines a database in terms of objects, their properties, and their operations. Objects with the same structure and behavior belong to a **class,** and classes are organized into hierarchies or acyclic graphs. The operations of each class are specified in terms of predefined procedures called **methods.** A number of commercial systems based on the object-oriented paradigm have become available. In addition, relational DBMSs have been extending their models to incorporate object-oriented concepts and other capabilities; these are referred to as **extended relational systems.** We discuss object-oriented models in detail in Chapter 22.

In the next chapter we present the concepts of the **Entity-Relationship** model, a popular high-level conceptual data model that is often used in database design.

---

*CODASYL DBTG stands for Computer Data Systems Language Data Base Task Group, which is the committee that specified the network model and its language.

2.6 Summary

In this chapter we introduced the main concepts used in database systems. We defined what a data model is, and we distinguished three main categories of data models:

- High-level or conceptual data models (Entity-Relationship).
- Implementation data models (record-based, object-oriented).
- Low-level or physical data models.

We distinguished the schema, or description of a database, from the database itself. The schema does not change very often, whereas the database state changes every time data is inserted, deleted, or modified. We then described the three-schema DBMS architecture, which allows three schema levels:

- External schemas describe the views of different user groups.
- A conceptual schema is a high-level description of the whole database.
- An internal schema describes the database storage structures.

A DBMS that cleanly separates the three levels must have mappings between the schemas to transform requests and results from one level to the next. Most DBMSs do not separate the three levels completely. We used the three-schema architecture to define the concepts of logical and physical data independence.

In Section 2.3 we discussed the main types of languages that DBMSs support. A data definition language (DDL) is used to define the database conceptual schema. In most DBMSs, the DDL also defines user views and storage structures; in other DBMSs, separate languages (VDL, SDL) exist for specifying views and storage structures. The DBMS compiles all schema definitions and stores them in the DBMS catalog. A data manipulation language (DML) is used for specifying database retrievals and updates. DMLs can be high-level (nonprocedural) or low-level (procedural). A high-level DML can be embedded in a host programming language, or it can be used as a stand-alone language; in the latter case it is often called a query language.

We discussed different types of interfaces provided by DBMSs, and the types of DBMS users with which each interface is associated. We then discussed the database system environment, typical DBMS software components, and DBMS utilities for helping users and the DBA perform their tasks.

Finally, we classified DBMSs according to data model, number of users, number of sites, cost, type of access paths, and generality. The main classification of DBMSs is based on the data model. We briefly discussed the main data models used in current commercial DBMSs.

Review Questions

2.1. Define the following terms: *data model, database schema, database state, internal schema, conceptual schema, external schema, data independence, DDL, DML, SDL, VDL, query language, host language, data sublanguage, database utility, active data dictionary, passive data dictionary, catalog, client-server architecture.*

2.2. Discuss the main categories of data models.

2.3. What is the difference between a database schema and a database state?

2.4. Describe the three-schema architecture. Why do we need mappings between the different schema levels? How do different schema definition languages support this architecture?

2.5. What is the difference between logical data independence and physical data independence? Which is easier to accomplish? Why?

2.6. What is the difference between procedural and nonprocedural DMLs?

2.7. Discuss the different types of user-friendly interfaces and the types of users who typically use each.

2.8. What other computer system software does a DBMS interact with?

2.9. Discuss some types of database utilities and their functions.

Exercises

2.10. Think of different users for the database of Figure 1.2. What types of applications would each user need? To which user category would each belong, and what type of interface would each need?

2.11. Choose a database application that you are familiar with. Design a schema and show a sample database for that application, using the notation of Figures 2.1 and 1.2. What types of additional information and constraints would you like to represent in the schema? Think of several users for your database, and design a view for each.

Selected Bibliography

Many database textbooks provide a discussion of the various database concepts presented here, including Wiederhold (1986), Ullman (1988), Date (1990), and Korth and Silberschatz (1991). Tsichritzis and Lochovsky (1982) is a textbook on data models. Tsichritzis and Klug (1978) and Jardine (1977) present the three-schema architecture, which was first suggested in the CODASYL DBTG report (1971) and later in an American National Standards Institute (ANSI) report (1975).

CHAPTER 3

Data Modeling Using the Entity-Relationship Model

The goal of this chapter is to present the modeling concepts of the **Entity-Relationship** (**ER**) model, which is a popular high-level conceptual data model. This model and its variations are frequently used for the conceptual design of database applications, and many database design tools employ its concepts. We describe the basic data-structuring concepts and constraints of the ER model and discuss their use in the design of conceptual schemas for database applications.

This chapter is organized as follows. In Section 3.1 we discuss the role of conceptual data models in database design. We introduce the requirements for an example database application in Section 3.2, to illustrate the use of the ER model concepts. This example database is also used in subsequent chapters. In Section 3.3 we present the concepts of the ER model, and we gradually introduce the diagrammatic technique for displaying an ER schema. Section 3.4 reviews the notation for ER diagrams; and Section 3.5 discusses the issue of how to choose the names for database schema constructs. In Section 3.6 we discuss ternary and higher-degree relationships. Finally, we conclude with a summary in Section 3.7.

The reader may skip Section 3.6 and may browse over some of the later material in Section 3.3 if desired. On the other hand, if more complete coverage of data modeling concepts and conceptual database design is desired, the reader may continue on to the material in Chapter 21 after concluding Chapter 3. In Chapter 21, we describe extensions to the ER model that lead to the Enhanced-ER (EER) model, including specialization and generalization, techniques for specifying high-level transactions, and a discussion of integrity constraints.

3.1 Using High-level Conceptual Data Models for Database Design

Figure 3.1 shows a simplified description of the database design process. The first step shown is **requirements collection and analysis.** During this step, the database designers interview prospective database users to understand and document their data requirements. The result of this step is a concisely written set of users' requirements. These requirements should be specified in as detailed and complete a form as possible. In parallel with specifying the data requirements, it is useful to specify the known *functional requirements* of the application. These consist of the user-defined operations (or **transactions)** that will be applied to the database, and they include both retrievals and updates. It is common to use techniques such as *data flow diagrams* for specifying functional requirements.

Once all the requirements have been collected and analyzed, the next step is to create a **conceptual schema** for the database, using a high-level conceptual data model. This step is called **conceptual database design**. The conceptual schema is a concise description of the data requirements of the users and includes detailed descriptions of the data types, relationships, and constraints; these are expressed using the concepts provided by the high-level data model. Because these concepts do not include any implementation details, they are usually easier to understand and can be used to communicate with nontechnical users. The high-level conceptual schema can also be used as a reference to ensure that all users' data requirements are met and that the requirements do not include any conflicts. This approach enables the database designers to concentrate on specifying the properties of the data, without being concerned with storage details. Consequently, it is easier for them to come up with a good conceptual database design.

After the conceptual schema has been designed, the basic data model operations can be used to specify high-level transactions corresponding to the user-defined operations identified during functional analysis. This also serves to confirm that the conceptual schema meets all the identified functional requirements. Modifications to the conceptual schema can be introduced if some functional requirements cannot be specified in the initial schema.

The next step in database design is the actual implementation of the database, using a commercial DBMS. Most currently available commercial DBMSs use an implementation data model, so the conceptual schema is transformed from the high-level data model into the implementation data model. This step is called **logical database design** or **data model mapping,** and its result is a database schema in the implementation data model of the DBMS.

Finally, the last step is the **physical database design** phase, during which the internal storage structures and file organizations for the database are specified. In parallel with these activities, application programs are designed and implemented as database transactions corresponding to the high-level transaction specifications. We discuss the database design process in more detail in Chapter 14.

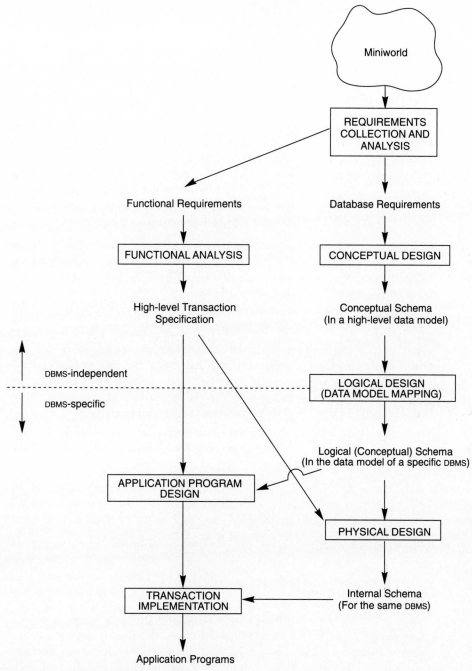

Figure 3.1   Phases of database design (simplified).

We only present the ER model concepts for conceptual schema design in this chapter. The ER model operations, which can be used to specify user-defined transactions, are discussed in Chapter 21.

3.2 An Example

In this section we describe an example database, called COMPANY, that serves to illustrate the ER model concepts and their use in schema design. We list the data requirements for the database here, and then we create its conceptual schema step-by-step as we introduce the modeling concepts of the ER model. The COMPANY database keeps track of a company's employees, departments, and projects. Suppose that, after the requirements collection and analysis phase, the database designers stated the following description of the "miniworld"—the part of the company to be represented in the database:

1. The company is organized into departments. Each department has a unique name, a unique number, and a particular employee who manages the department. We keep track of the start date when that employee began managing the department. A department may have several locations.

2. A department controls a number of projects, each of which has a unique name, a unique number, and a single location.

3. We store each employee's name, social security number, address, salary, sex, and birthdate. An employee is assigned to one department but may work on several projects, which are not necessarily controlled by the same department. We keep track of the number of hours per week that an employee works on each project. We also keep track of the direct supervisor of each employee.

4. We want to keep track of the dependents of each employee for insurance purposes. We keep each dependent's name, sex, birthdate, and relationship to the employee.

Figure 3.2 shows how the schema for this database application can be displayed by means of the graphical notation known as **ER diagrams.** We describe the process of deriving this schema from the stated requirements—and explain the ER diagrammatic notation—as we introduce the ER model concepts in the following section.

3.3 ER Model Concepts

The ER model describes data as entities, relationships, and attributes. In Section 3.3.1 we introduce the concepts of entities and their attributes. We discuss entity types and key attributes in Section 3.3.2. In Section 3.3.3 we discuss relationship types and their structural constraints. We discuss weak entity types in Section 3.3.4, and then we demonstrate the use of ER concepts in designing the COMPANY database in Section 3.3.5.

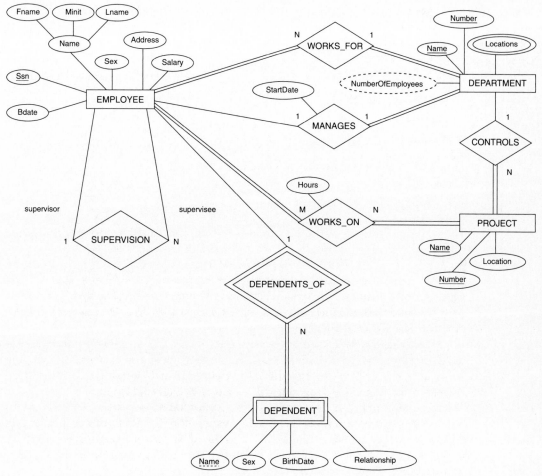

Figure 3.2 ER schema diagram for the COMPANY database.

3.3.1 Entities and Attributes

The basic object that the ER model represents is an **entity,** which is a "thing" in the real world with an independent existence. An entity may be an object with a physical existence—a particular person, car, house, or employee—or it may be an object with a conceptual existence—a company, a job, or a university course. Each entity has particular properties, called **attributes,** that describe it. For example, an employee entity may be described by the employee's name, age, address, salary, and job. A particular entity will have a **value** for each of its attributes. The attribute values that describe each entity become a major part of the data stored in the database.

Figure 3.3 shows two entities and the values of their attributes. The employee entity e_1 has four attributes: Name, Address, Age, and HomePhone; their values are "John Smith", "2311 Kirby, Houston, Texas 77001", "55", and "713-749-2630", respectively.

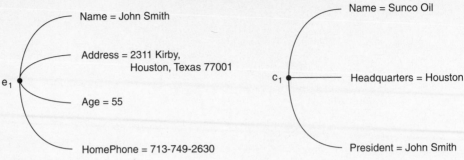

Figure 3.3   Two entities and their attribute values.

The company entity c_1 has three attributes: Name, Headquarters, and President; their values are "Sunco Oil", "Houston", and "John Smith", respectively.

Types of Attributes.   Several different types of attributes occur in the ER model: *simple* versus *composite*; *single-valued* versus *multivalued*; and *stored* versus *derived*. We first define these attribute types and illustrate their use via examples. We then introduce the concept of a *null value* for an attribute.

Composite attributes can be divided into smaller subparts, which represent more basic attributes with independent meanings of their own. For example, the Address attribute of the employee entity shown in Figure 3.3 can be subdivided into Street-Address, City, State, and Zip, with the values "2311 Kirby", "Houston", "Texas", and "77001". Attributes that are not divisible are called **simple** or **atomic** attributes. Composite attributes can form a hierarchy; for example, StreetAddress can be further sub-divided into three simple attributes, Number, Street, and ApartmentNumber, as shown in Figure 3.4. The value of a composite attribute is the concatenation of the values of its constituent simple attributes.

Composite attributes are useful to model situations in which a user sometimes refers to the composite attribute as a unit but at other times refers specifically to its compo-nents. If the composite attribute is referenced only as a whole, there is no need to sub-divide it into component attributes. For example, if there is no need to refer to the individual components of an address (Zip, Street, and so on), then the whole address is designated as a simple attribute.

Most attributes have a single value for a particular entity; such attributes are called **single-valued.** For example, Age is a single-valued attribute of person. In some cases an attribute can have a set of values for the same entity—for example, a Colors attribute for a car, or a CollegeDegrees attribute for a person. Cars with one color have a single value, whereas two-tone cars have two values for Colors. Similarly, one person may not have any college degree, another person may have one, and a third person may have two or more degrees; so different persons can have different *numbers of values* for the CollegeDegrees attribute. Such attributes are called **multivalued.** A multivalued attribute may have lower and upper bounds on the number of values for an individual entity. For

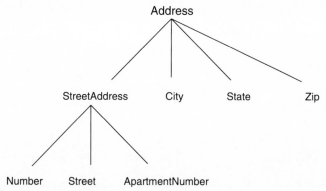

Figure 3.4 A hierarchy of composite attributes.

example, the Colors attribute of a car may have between one and five values, if we assume that a car can have at most five colors.

In some cases two (or more) attribute values are related—for example, the Age and BirthDate attributes of a person. For a particular person entity, the value of Age can be determined from the current (today's) date and the value of that person's BirthDate. The Age attribute is hence called a **derived attribute** and is said to be **derivable from** the BirthDate attribute, which is called a **stored attribute.** Some attribute values can be derived from *related entities;* for example, an attribute NumberOfEmployees of a department entity can be derived by counting the number of employees related to (working for) that department.

In some cases a particular entity may not have any applicable value for an attribute. For example, the ApartmentNumber attribute of an address applies only to addresses that are in apartment buildings and not to other types of residences such as single-family homes. Similarly, a CollegeDegrees attribute applies only to persons with college degrees. For such situations, a special value called **null** is created. An address of a single-family home would have null for its ApartmentNumber attribute, and a person with no college degree would have null for CollegeDegrees. Null can also be used if we do not know the value of an attribute for a particular entity—for example, if we do not know the home phone of "John Smith" in Figure 3.3. The meaning of the former type of null is *not applicable,* whereas the meaning of the latter is *unknown.* The unknown category of null can be further classified into two cases. The first case arises when it is known that the attribute value exists but is *missing*—for example, if the Height attribute of a person is listed as null. The second case arises when it is *not known* whether the attribute value exists—for example, if the HomePhone attribute of a person is null.

3.3.2 *Entity Types, Value Sets, and Key Attributes*

A database usually contains groups of entities that are similar. For example, a company employing hundreds of employees may want to store similar information concerning each of the employees. These employee entities share the same attributes, but each entity has

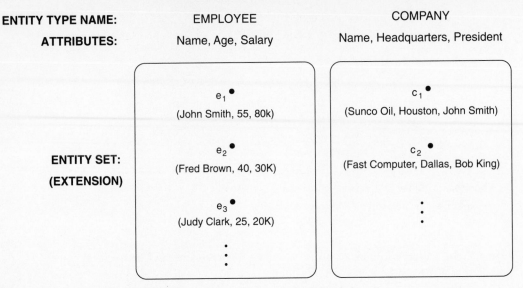

Figure 3.5   Two entity types and some of the member entities of each.

its own value(s) for each attribute. An **entity type** defines a set of entities that have the same attributes. Each entity type in the database is described by a name and a list of attributes. Figure 3.5 shows two entity types, named EMPLOYEE and COMPANY, and a list of attributes for each. A few individual entities of each type are also illustrated, along with the values of their attributes.

An entity type is represented in ER diagrams (as in Figure 3.2) as a rectangular box enclosing the entity type name. Attribute names are enclosed in ovals and are attached to their entity type by straight lines. Composite attributes are attached to their component attributes by straight lines. Multivalued attributes are displayed in double ovals.

An entity type describes the **schema** or **intension** for a *set of entities* that share the same structure. The individual entities of a particular entity type are grouped into a **collection** or **entity set,** which is also called the **extension** of the entity type.

Key Attributes of an Entity Type.   An important constraint on the entities of an entity type is the **key** or **uniqueness** constraint on attributes. An entity type usually has an attribute whose values are distinct for each individual entity. Such an attribute is called a **key attribute,** and its values can be used to identify each entity uniquely. The Name attribute is a key of the COMPANY entity type in Figure 3.5, because no two companies are allowed to have the same name. For the PERSON entity type, a typical key attribute is SocialSecurityNumber. Sometimes, several attributes together form a key, meaning that the *combination* of the attribute values must be distinct for each individual entity. A set of attributes that possess this property can be grouped into a composite attribute, which becomes a key attribute of the entity type. In ER diagrammatic notation, each key attribute has its name **underlined** inside the oval, as illustrated in Figure 3.2.

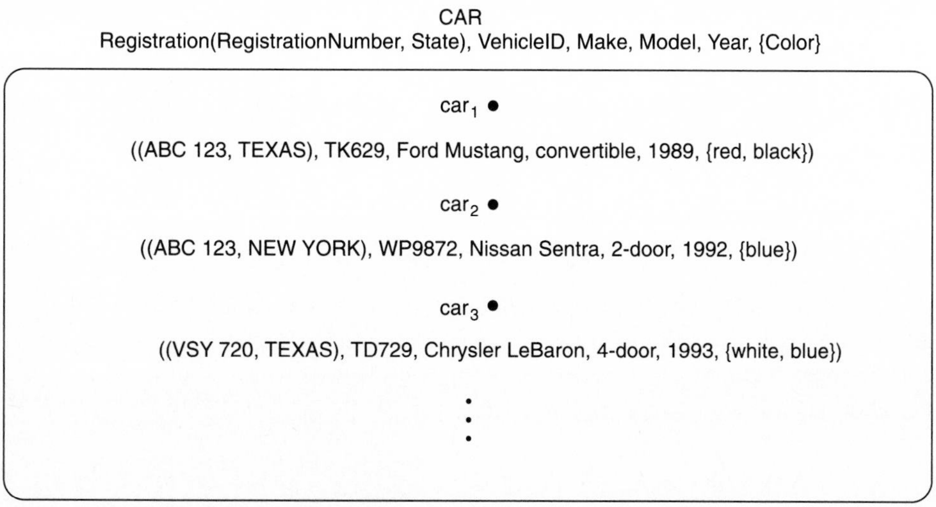

CAR
Registration(RegistrationNumber, State), VehicleID, Make, Model, Year, {Color}

car₁ ●

((ABC 123, TEXAS), TK629, Ford Mustang, convertible, 1989, {red, black})

car₂ ●

((ABC 123, NEW YORK), WP9872, Nissan Sentra, 2-door, 1992, {blue})

car₃ ●

((VSY 720, TEXAS), TD729, Chrysler LeBaron, 4-door, 1993, {white, blue})

•
•
•

Figure 3.6   The CAR entity type. Multivalued attributes are shown between set braces { }. Components of a composite attribute are shown between parentheses ( ).

Specifying that an attribute is a key of an entity type means that the preceding uniqueness property must hold for *every extension* of the entity type. Hence, it is a constraint that prohibits any two entities from having the same value for the key attribute at the same time. It is not the property of a particular extension; rather, it is a constraint on *all extensions* of the entity type. This key constraint (and other constraints we discuss later) is derived from the properties of the miniworld that the database represents.

Some entity types have *more than one* key attribute. For example, each of the VehicleID and Registration attributes of the entity type CAR (Figure 3.6) is a key in its own right. The Registration attribute is an example of a composite key formed from two simple component attributes, RegistrationNumber and State, neither of which is a key on its own.

Value Sets (Domains) of Attributes. Each simple attribute of an entity type is associated with a **value set** (or **domain**), which specifies the set of values that may be assigned to that attribute for each individual entity. In Figure 3.5, if the range of ages allowed for employees is between 16 and 70, we can specify the value set of the Age attribute of EMPLOYEE to be the set of integer numbers between 16 and 70. Similarly, we can specify the value set for the Name attribute as being the set of strings of alphabetic characters separated by blank characters; and so on. Value sets are not displayed in ER diagrams.

Mathematically, an attribute A of entity type E whose value set is V can be defined as a **function** from E to the power set* of V:

$$A : E \rightarrow P(V)$$

---

*The **power set** $P(V)$ of a set V is the set of all subsets of V.

{AddressPhone({Phone(AreaCode,PhoneNumber)},
Address(StreetAddress(Number,Street,ApartmentNumber),
City,State,Zip)) }

Figure 3.7   A multivalued composite attribute AddressPhone with multivalued and composite components.

We refer to the value of attribute A for entity e as A(e). The above definition covers both single-valued and multivalued attributes, as well as nulls. A null value is represented by the empty set. For single-valued attributes, A(e) is restricted to being a singleton* for each entity e in E whereas there is no restriction on multivalued attributes. For a composite attribute A, the value set V is the Cartesian product of $P(V_1)$, $P(V_2)$, . . ., $P(V_n)$, where V_1, V_2, . . ., V_n are the value sets of the simple component attributes that form A:

$$V = P(V_1) \times P(V_2) \times \cdots \times P(V_n)$$

Notice that composite and multivalued attributes can be nested in an arbitrary way. We can represent arbitrary nesting by grouping components of a composite attribute between parentheses ( ) and separating the components with commas, and by displaying multivalued attributes between braces { }. For example, if a person can have more than one residence and each residence can have multiple phones, an attribute AddressPhone for a PERSON entity type can be specified as shown in Figure 3.7.

Initial Conceptual Design of the COMPANY Database. We can now define the entity types for the COMPANY database described in Section 3.2. After defining several entity types and their attributes here, we *refine* our design in the next section (after introducing the concept of a relationship). According to the requirements listed in Section 3.2, we can identify four entity types—one corresponding to each of the four items in the specification (see Figure 3.8):

1. An entity type DEPARTMENT with attributes Name, Number, Locations, Manager, and ManagerStartDate. Locations is the only multivalued attribute. We can specify that each of Name and Number is a key attribute, because each was specified to be unique.

2. An entity type PROJECT with attributes Name, Number, Location, and ControllingDepartment. Each of Name and Number is a key attribute.

3. An entity type EMPLOYEE with attributes Name, SSN (for social security number), Sex, Address, Salary, BirthDate, Department, and Supervisor. Both Name and Address may be composite attributes; however, this was not specified in the requirements. We must go back to the users to see if any of them will refer to the individual components of Name—FirstName, MiddleInitial, LastName—or of Address.

4. An entity type DEPENDENT with attributes Employee, DependentName, Sex, BirthDate, and Relationship (to the employee).

---

*A singleton set is a set with only one element (value).

So far, we have not represented the fact that an employee can work on several projects, nor have we represented the number of hours per week an employee works on each project. This characteristic is listed as part of requirement 3 in Section 3.2, and it can be represented by a multivalued composite attribute of EMPLOYEE called WorksOn with simple components (Project, Hours). Alternatively, it can be represented as a multivalued composite attribute of PROJECT called Workers with simple components (Employee, Hours). We choose the first alternative in Figure 3.8, which shows each of the entity types described above. The Name attribute of EMPLOYEE is shown as a composite attribute, presumably after consultation with the users.

In Figure 3.8 there are several *implicit relationships* among the various entity types. In fact, whenever an attribute of one entity type refers to another entity type, some relationship exists. For example, the attribute Manager of DEPARTMENT refers to an employee who manages the department; the attribute ControllingDepartment of PROJECT refers to the department that controls the project; the attribute Supervisor of EMPLOYEE refers to another employee (the one who supervises this employee); the attribute Department of EMPLOYEE refers to the department for which the employee works; and so on. In the ER model, these references should not be represented as attributes but as **relationships,** which are defined in the next section. The COMPANY database schema is refined in Section 3.3.5 to represent relationships explicitly. In the initial design of entity types, relationships are typically captured in the form of attributes. As the design is refined, these attributes get converted into relationships between entity types.

3.3.3 *Relationships, Roles, and Structural Constraints*

Relationship Types and Relationship Instances. A **relationship type** R among n entity types $E_1, E_2, \ldots, E_n$ defines a set of associations among entities from these types. Mathematically, R is a set of **relationship instances** r_i, where each r_i associates n entities ($e_1, e_2, \ldots, e_n$), and each entity e_j in r_i is a member of entity type E_j, $1 \leq j \leq n$. Hence, a relationship type is a mathematical relation on $E_1, E_2, \ldots, E_n$, or alternatively it can be

DEPARTMENT
Name, Number, {Locations}, Manager, ManagerStartDate

PROJECT
Name, Number, Location, ControllingDepartment

EMPLOYEE
Name (FName, MInit, LName), SSN, Sex, Address, Salary,
BirthDate, Department, Supervisor, {WorksOn (Project, Hours)}

DEPENDENT
Employee, DependentName, Sex, BirthDate, Relationship

Figure 3.8 Preliminary design of entity types for the database described in Section 3.2. Multivalued attributes are shown between set braces { }. Components of a composite attribute are shown between parentheses ( ).

defined as a subset of the Cartesian product $E_1 \times E_2 \times \cdots \times E_n$. Each of the entity types $E_1, E_2, \ldots, E_n$ is said to **participate** in the relationship type R, and similarly each of the individual entities $e_1, e_2, \ldots, e_n$ is said to participate in the relationship instance $r_i = (e_1, e_2, \ldots, e_n)$.

Informally, each relationship instance r_i in R is an association of entities, where the association includes exactly one entity from each participating entity type. Each such relationship instance r_i represents the fact that the entities participating in r_i are related to each other in some way in the corresponding miniworld situation.

For example, consider a relationship type WORKS_FOR between the two entity types EMPLOYEE and DEPARTMENT, which associates each employee with the department the employee works for. Each relationship instance in WORKS_FOR associates one employee entity and one department entity. Figure 3.9 illustrates this example, where each relationship instance r_i is shown connected to the employee and department entities that participate in r_i. In the miniworld represented by Figure 3.9, employees e_1, e_3, and e_6 work for department d_1; e_2 and e_4 work for d_2; and e_5 and e_7 work for d_3.

In ER diagrams, relationship types are displayed as diamond-shaped boxes, which are connected by straight lines to the rectangular boxes representing the participating entity types. The relationship name is displayed in the diamond-shaped box (see Figure 3.2).

Degree of a Relationship Type. The **degree** of a relationship type is the number of participating entity types. Hence, the WORKS_FOR relationship type is of degree two. A

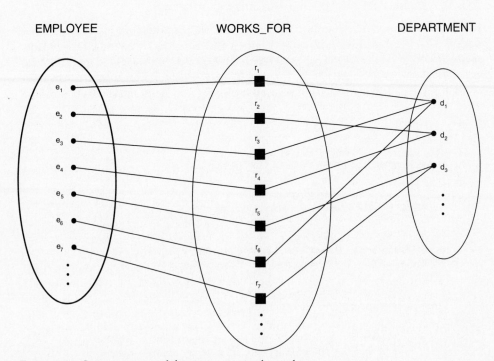

Figure 3.9   Some instances of the WORKS_FOR relationship.

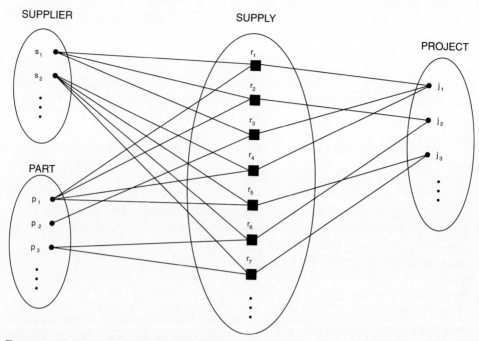

Figure 3.10   The ternary relationship SUPPLY.

relationship type of degree two is called **binary,** and one of degree three is called **ternary.** An example of a ternary relationship type is SUPPLY, shown in Figure 3.10, where each relationship instance r_i associates three entities—a supplier s, a part p, and a project j— whenever s supplies part p to project j. Relationships can be of any degree, but the ones that occur most commonly are binary relationships. We discuss higher-degree relationships further in Section 3.6.

Relationships as Attributes.   It is sometimes convenient to think of a relationship type in terms of attributes, as we discussed at the end of the previous section. Consider the WORKS_FOR relationship type of Figure 3.9. One can think of an attribute called Department of the EMPLOYEE entity type whose value for each employee entity is the *department entity* that the employee works for. Hence, the value set for this Department attribute is the *set of all DEPARTMENT entities*. This is what we did in Figure 3.8 when we specified the initial design of the entity type EMPLOYEE for the COMPANY database. However, when we think of a binary relationship as an attribute, we always have two options. In this example, the alternative is to think of a multivalued attribute Employees of the entity type DEPARTMENT whose values for each department entity is the *set of employee entities* who work for that department. The value set of this Employees attribute is the EMPLOYEE entity set. Either of these two attributes—Department of EMPLOYEE or Employees of

DEPARTMENT—can represent the WORKS_FOR relationship type. If both are represented, they are constrained to be inverses of each other.*

Role Names and Recursive Relationships. Each entity type that participates in a relationship type plays a particular **role** in the relationship. The **role name** signifies the role that a participating entity from the entity type plays in each relationship instance. For example, in the WORKS_FOR relationship type, EMPLOYEE plays the role of *employee* or *worker* and DEPARTMENT plays the role of *department* or *employer*.

Role names are not necessary in relationship types where all the participating entity types are distinct, since each entity type name can be used as the role name. However, in some cases the *same* entity type participates more than once in a relationship type in *different roles*. In such cases the role name becomes essential for distinguishing the meaning of each participation. Such relationship types are called **recursive,** and Figure 3.11 shows an example. The SUPERVISION relationship type relates an employee to a supervisor, where both employee and supervisor entities are members of the same EMPLOYEE entity type. Hence, the EMPLOYEE entity type *participates twice* in SUPERVISION: once in the *role of supervisor* (or boss), and once in the *role of supervisee* (or subordinate). Each relationship instance r_i in SUPERVISION associates two employee entities e_j and e_k, one of which plays the role of supervisor and the other the role of supervisee. In Figure 3.11, the lines marked "1" represent the supervisor role, and those marked "2" represent the supervisee role; hence, e_1 supervises e_2 and e_3; e_4 supervises e_6 and e_7; and e_5 supervises e_1 and e_4.

Constraints on Relationship Types. Relationship types usually have certain constraints that limit the possible combinations of entities that may participate in relationship instances. These constraints are determined from the miniworld situation that the relationships represent. For example, in Figure 3.9, if the company has a rule that each employee must work for exactly one department, then we would like to describe this constraint in the schema. We can distinguish two main types of relationship constraints: cardinality ratio and participation.

The **cardinality ratio** specifies the number of relationship instances that an entity can participate in. The WORKS_FOR binary relationship type DEPARTMENT:EMPLOYEE is of cardinality ratio 1:N, meaning that each department can be related to numerous employees, but an employee can be related to (work for) only one department. Common cardinality ratios for binary relationship types are 1:1, 1:N, and M:N.

An example of a 1:1 binary relationship type is MANAGES (Figure 3.12), which relates a department entity to the employee who manages that department. This represents the miniworld constraints that an employee can manage only one department and that a department has only one manager. The relationship type WORKS_ON (Figure 3.13) is of cardinality ratio M:N, if the rule is that an employee can work on several projects and that several employees can work on a project.

---

*This concept of representing relationship types as attributes is used in a class of data models called **functional data models** (see Section 21.6.1). In object-oriented (see Chapter 22) and semantic (see Section 21.6.4) data models, relationships can be represented by *reference attributes*, either in one direction or in both directions as inverses. In the relational data model (see Chapter 6), *foreign keys* are a type of reference attribute used to represent relationships.

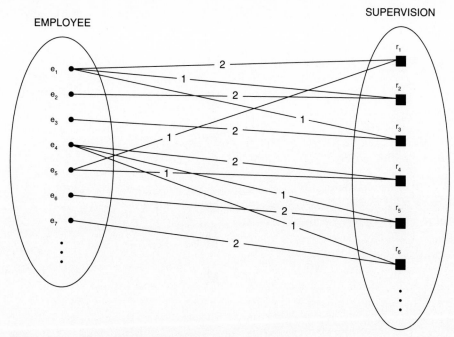

Figure 3.11   The recursive relationship SUPERVISION: EMPLOYEE plays the two roles of supervisor (1) and supervisee (2).

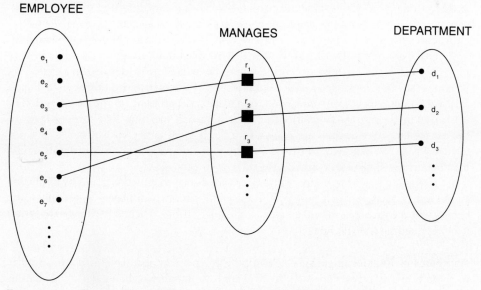

Figure 3.12   The 1:1 relationship MANAGES, with partial participation of EMPLOYEE and total participation of DEPARTMENT.

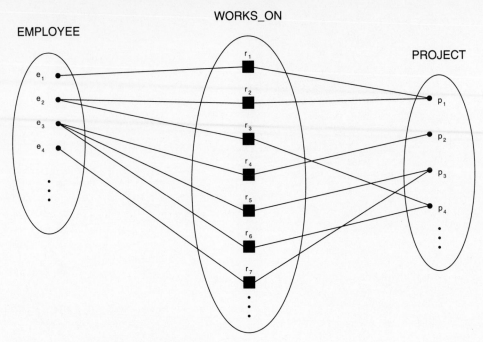

Figure 3.13   The M:N relationship WORKS_ON.

The **participation constraint** specifies whether the existence of an entity depends on its being related to another entity via the relationship type. There are two types of participation constraints—total and partial—which we illustrate by example. If a company policy states that *every* employee must work for a department, then an employee entity can exist only if it participates in a WORKS_FOR relationship instance (Figure 3.9). The participation of EMPLOYEE in WORKS_FOR is called **total,** meaning that every entity in "the total set" of employee entities must be related to a department entity via WORKS_FOR. Total participation is sometimes called **existence dependency**. In Figure 3.12 we do not expect every employee to manage a department, so the participation of EMPLOYEE in the MANAGES relationship type is **partial,** meaning that *some* or "part of the set of" employee entities are related to a department entity via MANAGES, but not necessarily all. We will refer to the cardinality ratio and participation constraints, taken together, as the **structural constraints** of a relationship type.

Cardinality ratios for binary relationships are displayed on ER diagrams by displaying 1, M, and N as shown in Figure 3.2. Total participation is displayed as a double line connecting the participating entity type to the relationship, whereas partial participation is represented by a single line.

Attributes of Relationship Types. Relationship types can also have attributes, similar to those of entity types. For example, to record the number of hours per week that an employee works on a project, we can include an attribute Hours for the WORKS_ON relationship type of Figure 3.13. Another example is to include the date on which a manager started managing a department via an attribute StartDate for the MANAGES relationship type of Figure 3.12.

Notice that attributes of 1:1 or 1:N relationship types can be migrated to one of the participating entity types. For example, the StartDate attribute for the MANAGES relationship can be an attribute of either EMPLOYEE or DEPARTMENT—although conceptually it belongs to MANAGES. This is because MANAGES is a 1:1 relationship, so every department or employee entity participates in at most one relationship instance. Hence, the value of the StartDate attribute can be determined separately, either by the participating department entity or by the participating employee (manager) entity.

For a 1:N relationship type, a relationship attribute can be migrated *only* to the entity type at the N side of the relationship. For example, in Figure 3.9, if the WORKS_FOR relationship also has an attribute StartDate that indicates when an employee started working for a department, this attribute can be included as an attribute of EMPLOYEE. This is because the relationship is 1:N, so each employee entity participates in at most one relationship instance in WORKS_FOR. In both 1:1 and 1:N relationship types, the decision as to where a relationship attribute should be placed—as a relationship type attribute or as an attribute of a participating entity type—is determined subjectively by the schema designer.

For M:N relationship types, some attributes may be determined by the *combination of participating entities* in a relationship instance, and not by any single one. Such attributes *must* be specified as relationship attributes. An example is the Hours attribute of the M:N relationship WORKS_ON (Figure 3.13); the number of hours an employee works on a project is determined by an employee-project combination and not separately by either entity.

3.3.4 *Weak Entity Types*

Some entity types may not have any key attributes of their own; these are called **weak entity types.** Entities belonging to a weak entity type are identified by being related to specific entities from another entity type in combination with some of their attribute values. We call this other entity type the **identifying owner,** and we call the relationship type that relates a weak entity type to its owner the **identifying relationship** of the weak entity type. A weak entity type always has a *total* participation constraint (existence dependency) with respect to its identifying relationship, because a weak entity cannot be identified without an owner entity. However, not every existence dependency results in a weak entity type. For example, a DRIVERS_LICENSE entity cannot exist unless it is related to a PERSON entity, even though it has its own key (DRIVERS_LICENSE_NO) and hence is not a weak entity.

Consider the entity type DEPENDENT, related to EMPLOYEE, which is used to keep track of the dependents of each employee via a 1:N relationship. The attributes of DEPENDENT are DependentName (the first name of the dependent), BirthDate, Sex, and Relationship (to the employee). Two dependents of distinct employees may have the same values for DependentName, BirthDate, Sex, and Relationship, but they are still distinct entities. They are identified as distinct entities only after determining the employee entity to which each is related. Each employee entity is said to **own** the dependent entities that are related to it.

A weak entity type normally has a **partial key,** which is the set of attributes that can uniquely identify weak entities related to *the same owner entity.* In our example, if we assume that no two dependents of the same employee ever have the same name, the attribute DependentName of DEPENDENT is the partial key.

In ER diagrams, a weak entity type and its identifying relationship are distinguished by surrounding their boxes with double lines (see Figure 3.2). The partial key attribute is underlined with a dashed or dotted line.

Weak entity types can sometimes be represented as composite, multivalued attributes. In the preceding example, we could specify a composite multivalued attribute Dependents for EMPLOYEE, composed of the attributes DependentName, BirthDate, Sex, and Relationship. The choice of which representation to use is made by the database designer. One approach is to choose the weak entity type representation if it has many attributes and participates independently in relationship types other than its identifying relationship type. In general, any number of levels of weak entity types can be defined; an owner entity type may itself be a weak entity type. In addition, a weak entity type may have more than one identifying entity type and an identifying relationship type of degree higher than two, as we illustrate in Section 3.6.

3.3.5 *Refining the* ER *Design for the* COMPANY *Database*

We can now refine the database design of Figure 3.8 by changing the attributes that represent relationships into relationship types. The cardinality ratio and participation constraint of each relationship type are determined from the requirements listed in Section 3.2. If some cardinality ratio or dependency cannot be determined from the requirements, the users must be questioned to determine these structural properties.

In our example, we specify the following relationship types:

1. MANAGES, a 1:1 relationship type between EMPLOYEE and DEPARTMENT. EMPLOYEE participation is partial. DEPARTMENT participation is not clear from the requirements. We question the users, who say that a department must have a manager at all times, which implies total participation. The attribute StartDate is assigned to this relationship type.

2. WORKS_FOR, a 1:N relationship type between DEPARTMENT and EMPLOYEE. Both participations are total.

3. CONTROLS, a 1:N relationship type between DEPARTMENT and PROJECT. The participation of PROJECT is total, whereas that of DEPARTMENT is determined to be partial, after consultation with the users.

4. SUPERVISION, a 1:N relationship type between EMPLOYEE (in the supervisor role) and EMPLOYEE (in the supervisee role). Both participations are determined to be partial, after the users indicate that not every employee is a supervisor and not every employee has a supervisor.

5. WORKS_ON, determined to be an M:N relationship type with attribute Hours, after the users indicate that a project can have several employees working on it. Both participations are determined to be total.

6. DEPENDENTS_OF, a 1:N relationship type between EMPLOYEE and DEPENDENT,

which is also the identifying relationship for the weak entity type DEPENDENT. The participation of EMPLOYEE is partial, whereas that of DEPENDENT is total.

After specifying the above six relationship types, we remove from the entity types in Figure 3.8 all attributes that have been refined into relationships. These include Manager and ManagerStartDate from DEPARTMENT; ControllingDepartment from PROJECT; Department, Supervisor, and WorksOn from EMPLOYEE; and Employee from DEPENDENT. It is important to have the least possible redundancy when we design the conceptual schema of a database. If some redundancy is desired at the storage level or at the user view level, it can be introduced later, as discussed in Section 1.6.1.

3.4 Notation for Entity-Relationship (ER) Diagrams

Figures 3.9 to 3.13 illustrate the entity types and relationship types by displaying their extensions—the individual entities and relationship instances. In ER diagrams the emphasis is on representing the schemas rather than the instances. This is more useful because a database schema changes rarely, whereas the extension changes frequently. In addition, the schema is usually easier to display than the extension of a database, because it is much smaller.

Figure 3.2 displays the COMPANY **ER database schema** as an ER diagram. We now review the full ER diagram's notation. Entity types such as EMPLOYEE, DEPARTMENT, and PROJECT are shown in rectangular boxes. Relationship types such as WORKS_FOR, MANAGES, CONTROLS, and WORKS_ON are shown in diamond-shaped boxes attached to the participating entity types with straight lines. Attributes are shown in ovals, and each attribute is attached to its entity type or relationship type by a straight line. Component attributes of a composite attribute are attached to the oval representing the composite attribute, as illustrated by the Name attribute of EMPLOYEE. Multivalued attributes are shown in double ovals, as illustrated by the Locations attribute of DEPARTMENT. Key attributes have their names underlined. Derived attributes are shown in dotted ovals, as illustrated by the NumberOfEmployees attribute of DEPARTMENT.

Weak entity types are distinguished by being placed in double rectangles and by having their identifying relationship placed in double diamonds, as illustrated by the DEPENDENT entity type and the DEPENDENTS_OF identifying relationship type. The partial key of the weak entity type is underlined with a *dotted line*.

In Figure 3.2 the cardinality ratio of each *binary* relationship type is specified by attaching a 1, M, or N on each participating edge. The cardinality ratio of DEPARTMENT:EMPLOYEE in MANAGES is 1:1, whereas it is 1:N for DEPARTMENT:EMPLOYEE in WORKS_FOR, and it is M:N for WORKS_ON. The participation constraint is specified by a single line for partial participation and by double lines for total participation (existence dependency).

In Figure 3.2 we show the role names for the SUPERVISION relationship type because the EMPLOYEE entity type plays both roles in that relationship. Notice that the cardinality is 1:N from supervisor to supervisee because, on the one hand, each employee in the role of supervisee has at most one direct supervisor, whereas an employee in the role of supervisor can supervise zero or more employees.

An alternative ER notation for specifying structural constraints involves associating a pair of integer numbers (min, max) with each *participation* of an entity type E in a relationship type R, where $0 \leq min \leq max$ and $max \geq 1$. The numbers mean that, for each entity e in E, e must participate in at least min and at most max relationship instances in R *at all times*. In this method, min = 0 implies partial participation, whereas min > 0 implies total participation. Figure 3.14 displays the COMPANY schema, using this notation. This method is more precise, and we can use it easily to specify structural constraints for relationship types *of any degree*. There are other diagrammatic notations for displaying ER diagrams. Appendix A gives some of the more popular notations.

Figure 3.14 also displays all the role names for the COMPANY database schema. Figure 3.15 summarizes the conventions for ER diagrams.

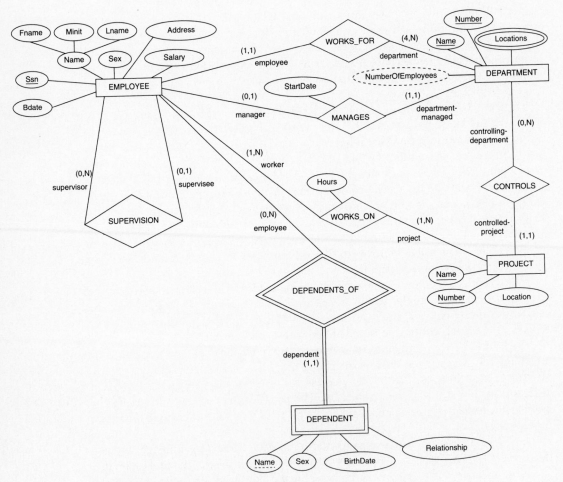

Figure 3.14   ER diagram for the COMPANY schema, with all role names included and with structural constraints on relationships specified using the alternate notation (min, max).

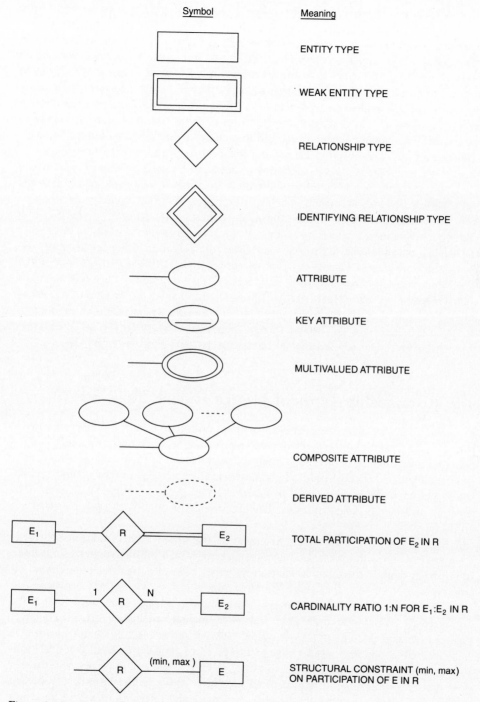

Symbol	Meaning
	ENTITY TYPE
	WEAK ENTITY TYPE
	RELATIONSHIP TYPE
	IDENTIFYING RELATIONSHIP TYPE
	ATTRIBUTE
	KEY ATTRIBUTE
	MULTIVALUED ATTRIBUTE
	COMPOSITE ATTRIBUTE
	DERIVED ATTRIBUTE
	TOTAL PARTICIPATION OF E_2 IN R
	CARDINALITY RATIO 1:N FOR $E_1:E_2$ IN R
	STRUCTURAL CONSTRAINT (min, max) ON PARTICIPATION OF E IN R

Figure 3.15   Summary of ER diagram notation.

3.5 Proper Naming of Schema Constructs

The choice of names for entity types, attributes, relationship types, and (particularly) roles is not always straightforward. One should choose names that convey, as much as possible, the meanings attached to the different constructs in the schema. We choose to use *singular names* for entity types, rather than plural ones, because the entity type name applies to each individual entity belonging to that entity type. In our ER diagrams, we will use the convention that entity type and relationship type names are in uppercase letters, attribute names are capitalized, and role names are in lowercase letters. We have already used this convention in Figures 3.2 and 3.14.

As a general practice, given a narrative description of the database requirements, the *nouns* appearing in the narrative will tend to give rise to entity type names, and the *verbs* will tend to indicate names of relationship types. Attribute names generally arise from additional nouns that describe the nouns corresponding to entity types. Another naming consideration involves choosing relationship names to make the ER diagram of the schema readable from left to right and from top to bottom. We have generally followed this guideline in Figure 3.2. One exception is the DEPENDENTS_OF relationship type, which reads from bottom to top. This is because we say that the DEPENDENT entities (bottom entity type) are DEPENDENTS_OF (relationship name) an EMPLOYEE (top entity type). To change this to read from top to bottom, we could rename the relationship type to HAS_DEPENDENTS, which would then read: an EMPLOYEE entity (top entity type) HAS_DEPENDENTS (relationship name) of type DEPENDENT (bottom entity type).

3.6 Relationship Types of Degree Higher Than Two★

In Section 3.3.3 we defined the **degree** of a relationship type as the number of participating entity types and called a relationship type of degree two **binary** and a relationship type of degree three **ternary.** The ER diagram notation for a ternary relationship type is shown in Figure 3.16(a), which displays the schema for the SUPPLY relationship type that was displayed at the instance level in Figure 3.10. In general, a relationship type R of degree n will have n edges in an ER diagram, one connecting R to each participating entity type.

Figure 3.16(b) shows an ER diagram for the three binary relationship types CAN_SUPPLY, USES, and SUPPLIES. In general, a ternary relationship type represents more information than do three binary relationship types. Consider the three binary relationship types CAN_SUPPLY, USES, and SUPPLIES. Suppose that CAN_SUPPLY, between SUPPLIER and PART, includes an instance (s, p) whenever supplier s *can supply* part p (to any project); USES, between PROJECT and PART, includes an instance (j, p) whenever project j *uses* part p; and SUPPLIES, between SUPPLIER and PROJECT, includes an instance (s, j) whenever supplier s *supplies some part* to project j. The existence of three relationship instances (s, p), (j, p), and (s, j) in CAN_SUPPLY, USES, and SUPPLIES, respectively, does not necessarily imply that an instance (s, j, p) exists in the ternary relationship SUPPLY! It is often tricky to decide whether a particular relationship should be represented as a relationship type of degree n or should be broken down into several rela-

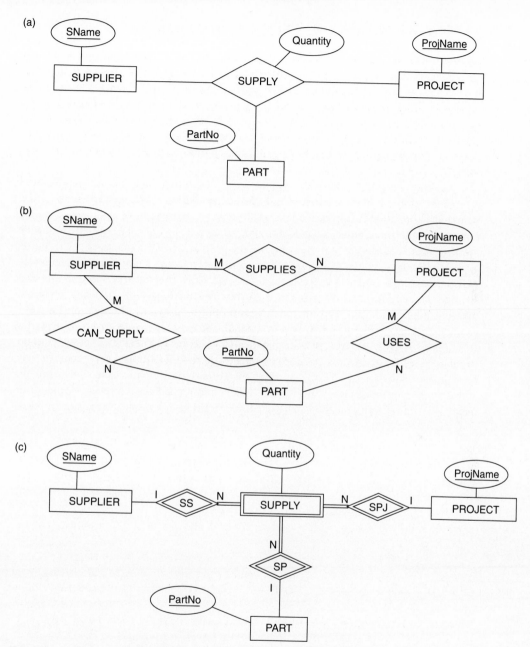

Figure 3.16   Ternary relationship types. (a) The ternary relationship type
SUPPLY. (b) Three binary relationship types that are not equivalent to the ternary relationship type SUPPLY. (c) SUPPLY represented as a weak entity type.

tionship types of smaller degrees. The designer must base this decision on the semantics or meaning of the particular situation being represented. The typical solution is to include the ternary relationship *plus* one or more of the binary relationships, as needed.

Some database design tools are based on variations of the ER model that permit binary relationships only. In this case, a ternary relationship such as SUPPLY must be represented as a weak entity type, with no partial key and with three identifying relationships. The three participating entity types SUPPLIER, PART, and PROJECT are together the owner entity types (see Figure 3.16(c)). Hence, an entity in the weak entity type SUPPLY of Figure 3.16(c) is identified by the combination of its three owner entities from SUPPLIER, PART, and PROJECT.

Another example is shown in Figure 3.17. The ternary relationship type OFFERS represents information on instructors offering courses during particular semesters; hence, it includes a relationship instance (i, s, c) whenever instructor i offers course c during semester s. The three binary relationship types shown in Figure 3.17 have the following meaning: CAN_TEACH relates a course to the instructors who *can teach* that course; TAUGHT_DURING relates a semester to the instructors who taught *some course* during that semester; and OFFERED_DURING relates a semester to the courses offered during that semester *by any instructor*. In general, these ternary and binary relationships represent different information, but certain constraints should hold among the relationships. For example, a relationship instance (i, s, c) should not exist in OFFERS *unless* an instance (i, s) exists in TAUGHT_DURING, an instance (s, c) exists in OFFERED_DURING, and an instance (i, c) exists in CAN_TEACH. However, the reverse is not always true; we may have instances (i, s), (s, c), and (i, c) in the three binary relationship types with no corresponding instance (i, s, c) in OFFERS. Under certain *additional constraints*, the latter may hold—for example, if the CAN_TEACH relationship is 1:1 (an instructor can teach

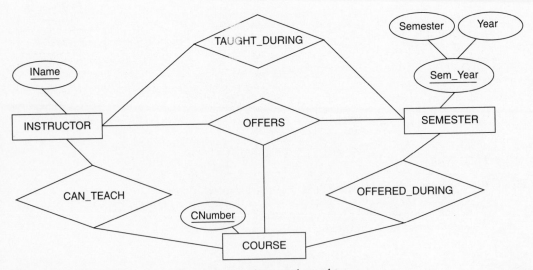

Figure 3.17   Another example of ternary versus binary relationship types.

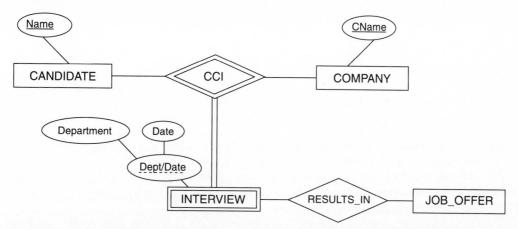

Figure 3.18 A weak entity type INTERVIEW, with a ternary identifying relationship type.

one course, and a course can be taught by only one instructor). The schema designer must analyze each specific situation to decide which of the binary and ternary relationship types are needed.

Notice that it is possible to have a weak entity type with a ternary (or n-ary) identifying relationship type. In this case, the weak entity type can have *several* owner entity types. An example is shown in Figure 3.18.

3.7 Summary

In this chapter we presented the modeling concepts of a high-level conceptual data model, the Entity-Relationship (ER) model. We started by discussing the role that a high-level data model plays in the database design process, and then we presented an example set of database requirements. We then defined the basic ER model concepts of entities and their attribute values. We discussed null values and then presented the various types of attributes, which can be nested arbitrarily:

- Simple or atomic.
- Composite.
- Multivalued.

We also briefly discussed derived attributes. We then discussed the ER model concepts at the schema or "intension" level:

- Entity types and their corresponding entity sets.
- Attributes and their value sets.
- Key attributes.

- Relationship types and their corresponding sets of instances.
- Participation roles of entity types in relationship types.

We presented two methods for specifying the structural constraints of relationship types. The first method distinguished two types of structural constraints:

- Cardinality ratios (1:1, 1:N, M:N for binary relationships).
- Participation constraints (total, partial).

We noted that, alternatively, a more general method of specifying structural constraints is to specify minimum and maximum numbers (min, max) on the participation of each entity type in a relationship type. This applies to relationship types of any degree. We then discussed weak entity types and the related concepts of owner entity types, identifying relationship types, and partial key attributes.

ER schemas can be represented diagrammatically as ER diagrams. We showed how to design an ER schema for the COMPANY database by first defining the entity types and their attributes and then refining the design to include relationship types. We displayed the ER diagram for the COMPANY database schema. Finally, we discussed ternary and higher-degree relationship types and the circumstances under which they are distinguished from a set of binary relationship types.

The ER modeling concepts we have presented thus far—entity types, relationship types, attributes, keys, and structural constraints—can model a wide variety of database applications. However, some applications—especially newer ones such as databases for engineering design or for artificial intelligence applications—require additional concepts if we want to model them with greater accuracy. We will discuss these advanced modeling concepts in Chapter 21.

Review Questions

3.1. Discuss the role of a high-level data model in the database design process.

3.2. List the various cases where use of a null value would be appropriate.

3.3. Define the following terms: *entity, attribute, attribute value, relationship instance, composite attribute, multivalued attribute, derived attribute, key attribute, value set (domain)*.

3.4. What is an entity type? What is an entity set? Explain the differences between an entity, an entity type, and an entity set.

3.5. Explain the difference between an attribute and a value set.

3.6. What is a relationship type? Explain the difference between a relationship instance and a relationship type.

3.7. What is a participation role? When is it *necessary* to use role names in the description of relationship types?

3.8. Describe the two alternatives for specifying structural constraints on relationship types. What are the advantages and disadvantages of each?

3.9. Under what conditions can an attribute of a binary relationship type be migrated to become an attribute of one of the participating entity types?

3.10. When we think of relationships as attributes, what are the value sets of these attributes? What class of data models is based on this concept?

3.11. What is meant by a recursive relationship type? Give some examples of recursive relationship types.

3.12. When is the concept of a weak entity useful in data modeling? Define the terms *owner entity type*, *weak entity type*, *identifying relationship type*, and *partial key*.

3.13. Can an identifying relationship of a weak entity type be of degree greater than two? Give examples.

3.14. Discuss the conventions for displaying an ER schema as an ER diagram.

3.15. Discuss the conditions under which a ternary relationship type can be represented by a number of binary relationship types.

Exercises

3.16. Consider the following set of requirements for a university database that is used to keep track of students' transcripts. This is similar but not identical to the database shown in Figure 1.2:

a. The university keeps track of each student's name, student number, social security number, current address and phone, permanent address and phone, birthdate, sex, class (freshman, sophomore, . . ., graduate), major department, minor department (if any), and degree program (B.A., B.S., . . ., Ph.D.). Some user applications need to refer to the city, state, and zip of the student's permanent address and to the student's last name. Both social security number and student number have unique values for each student.

b. Each department is described by a name, department code, office number, office phone, and college. Both name and code have unique values for each department.

c. Each course has a course name, description, course number, number of semester hours, level, and offering department. The value of course number is unique for each course.

d. Each section has an instructor, semester, year, course, and section number. The section number distinguishes different sections of the same course that are taught during the same semester/year; its values are 1, 2, 3, . . ., up to the number of sections taught during each semester.

e. A grade report has a student, section, letter grade, and numeric grade (0, 1, 2, 3, or 4).

Design an ER schema for this application, and draw an ER diagram for that schema. Specify key attributes of each entity type and structural constraints on each relationship type. Note any unspecified requirements, and make appropriate assumptions to make the specification complete.

3.17. Composite and multivalued attributes can be nested to any number of levels. Suppose we want to design an attribute for a STUDENT entity type to keep track of previous college education. Such an attribute will have one entry for each college previously attended, and each such entry will be composed of college name, start and end dates, degree entries (degrees awarded at that college, if any), and transcript entries (courses completed at that college, if any). Each degree entry is formed of the degree name and the month and year the degree was awarded, and each transcript entry is formed of a course name, semester, year, and grade. Design an attribute to hold this information. Use the conventions of Figure 3.8.

3.18. Show an alternative design for the attribute described in Exercise 3.17 that uses only entity types (including weak entity types, if needed) and relationship types.

3.19. Consider the ER diagram of Figure 3.19, which shows a simplified schema for an airline reservations system. Extract from the ER diagram the requirements and constraints that produced this schema. Try to be as precise as possible in your requirements and constraints specification.

3.20. In Chapters 1 and 2, we discussed the database environment and database users. We can consider many entity types to describe such an environment, such as DBMS, stored database, DBA, and catalog/data dictionary. Try to specify all the entity types that can fully describe a database system and its environment; then specify the relationship types among them, and draw an ER diagram to describe such a general database environment.

3.21. A trucking company called TRUCKERS is responsible for picking up shipments for warehouses of a retail chain called MAZE BROTHERS and delivering the shipments to individual retail store locations of MAZE BROTHERS. Currently there are 6 warehouse locations and 45 retail stores of MAZE BROTHERS. A truck may carry several shipments during a single trip, which is identified by a Trip#, and delivers those shipments to multiple stores. Each shipment is identified by a Shipment# and includes data on shipment volume, weight, destination, etc. Trucks have different capacities for both the volumes they can hold and the weights they can carry. The TRUCKERS company currently has 150 trucks, and a truck makes 3 to 4 trips each week. A database—to be used by both TRUCKERS and MAZE BROTHERS—is being designed to keep track of truck usage and deliveries and to help in scheduling trucks to provide timely deliveries to stores. Design an ER schema diagram for the above application. Make any assumptions you need, but state them clearly.

3.22. A database is being constructed to keep track of the teams and games of a sports league. A team has a number of players, not all of whom participate in each game. It is desired to keep track of the players participating in each game for each team, the positions they played in that game, and the result of the game. Try to design an ER schema diagram for this application, stating any assumptions you make. Choose your favorite sport (soccer, baseball, football, . . .).

3.23. Consider the ER diagram shown in Figure 3.20 for part of a BANK database. Each bank can have multiple branches, and each branch can have multiple accounts and loans.

a. List the (nonweak) entity types in the ER diagram.

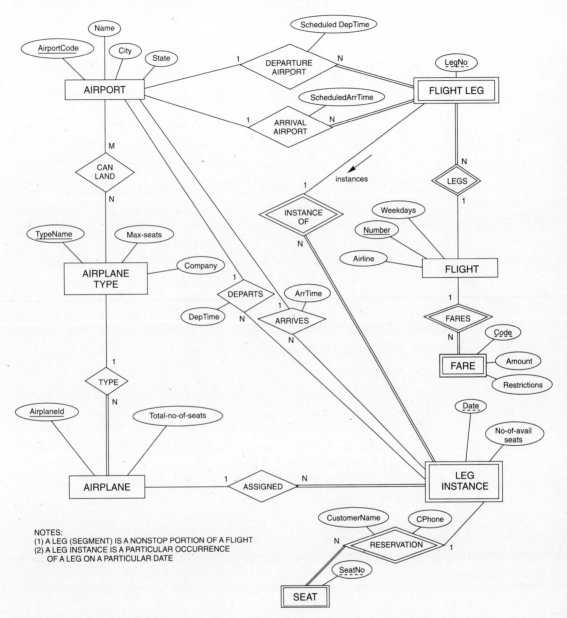

Figure 3.19   An airline schema.

b. Is there a weak entity type? If so, give its name, its partial key, and its identifying relationship.

c. What constraints do the partial key and the identifying relationship of the weak entity type specify in this diagram?

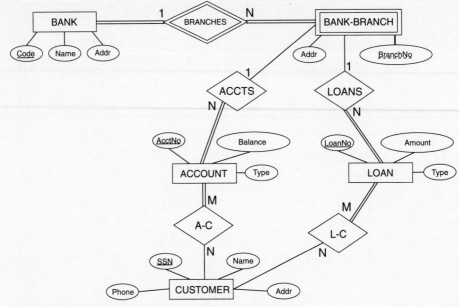

Figure 3.20 ER diagram for a BANK database.

    d. List the names of all relationship types, and specify the (min, max) constraint on each participation of an entity type in a relationship type. Justify your choices.

    e. List concisely the user requirements that led to this ER schema design.

    f. Suppose that every customer must have at least one account but is restricted to at most two loans at a time, and that a bank branch cannot have more than 1000 loans. How does this show up on the (min, max) constraints?

Selected Bibliography

The Entity-Relationship model was introduced by Chen (1976), and related work appears in Schmidt and Swenson (1975), Wiederhold and Elmasri (1979), and Senko (1975). Since then, numerous modifications to the ER model have been suggested. We have incorporated some of these in our presentation. Structural constraints on relationships are discussed in Abrial (1974), Elmasri and Wiederhold (1980), and Lenzerini and Santucci (1983). Multivalued and composite attributes are incorporated in the ER model in Elmasri et al. (1985), which also discusses ER update operations and transaction specification. A conference for the dissemination of research results related to the ER model has been held regularly since 1979. The conference has been held in Los Angeles (ER 1979, ER 1983), Washington D.C. (ER 1981), Chicago (ER 1985), Dijon, France (ER 1986), New York City (ER 1987), Rome, Italy (ER 1988), Toronto, Canada (ER 1989), Lausanne, Switzerland (ER 1990), San Mateo, California (ER 1991), and Karlsruhe, Germany (ER 1992).

CHAPTER 4

Record Storage and Primary File Organizations

In Chapters 4 and 5, we turn our attention to the techniques used for physical storage of data on the computer system. Databases are typically organized into files of records, which are stored on computer disks. We start in Section 4.1 by introducing the concepts of computer storage hierarchies. In Section 4.2 we describe disk storage devices and their characteristics, and we also briefly describe tape storage devices. Section 4.3 covers the technique of double buffering, which is used to speed up retrieval of multiple disk blocks. In Section 4.4 we discuss various ways of formatting and storing records of a file on disk. In Section 4.5 we present the various types of operations that are typically applied to records of a file. We then present three primary methods for organizing records of a file on disk: unordered records, discussed in Section 4.6; ordered records, in Section 4.7; and hashed records, in Section 4.8.

Section 4.9 very briefly discusses files of mixed records and other primary methods for organizing records, such as B-trees. In Chapter 5 we discuss techniques for creating access structures, called indexes, that speed up searching for and retrieving records. These techniques involve storage of auxiliary data besides the records themselves.

Chapters 4 and 5 may be browsed through or even skipped entirely by readers who have already studied file organizations. They can also be postponed and read later. The material covered here is necessary for understanding some of the later chapters in the book—in particular, Chapters 14 and 16 through 19.

4.1 Introduction

The collection of data that makes up a computerized database must be physically stored on some computer **storage medium.** The DBMS software can then retrieve, update, and process this data as needed. Computer storage media form a *storage hierarchy* that includes two main categories:

- Primary storage. This category includes storage media that can be operated on directly by the computer central processing unit (CPU), such as the computer main memory and smaller but faster cache memories. Primary storage usually provides fast access to data but is of limited storage capacity.

- Secondary storage. Secondary storage devices include magnetic disks, optical disks, tapes, and drums and usually are of larger capacity, cost less, and provide slower access to data than do primary storage devices. Data in secondary storage cannot be processed directly by the CPU; it must first be copied into primary storage.

Databases typically store large amounts of data that must persist over long periods of time. The data is accessed and processed repeatedly during this period. This contrasts with the notion of data structures that persist for only a limited time during program execution, which is common in programming languages. Most databases are stored permanently on **magnetic disk** secondary storage, for the following reasons:

- Generally, databases are too large to fit entirely in main memory.

- The circumstances that cause permanent loss of stored data arise less frequently for disk secondary storage than for primary storage. Hence, we refer to disk—and other secondary storage devices—as **nonvolatile storage,** whereas main memory is often called **volatile storage.**

- The cost of storage per unit of data is an order of magnitude less for disk than for primary storage.

New technologies are emerging, including optical disk storage, cheaper and larger main memories, and special-purpose database-oriented hardware. These technologies may provide viable alternatives to the use of magnetic disks in the future. For now, however, it is important to study and understand the properties and characteristics of magnetic disks and the way data files can be organized on disk in order to design effective databases with acceptable performance.

Magnetic tapes are frequently used as a storage medium for backing up the database because storage on tape costs even less than storage on disk. However, access to data on tape is quite slow. Data stored on tapes is **off-line;** that is, some intervention by an operator (or a loading device) to load a tape is needed before this data becomes available. In contrast, disks are **on-line** devices that can be directly accessed at any time.

In this and the following chapter, we describe the techniques used to store large amounts of structured data on disk. These techniques are important for database designers, the DBA, and implementers of a DBMS. Database designers and the DBA must know the advantages and disadvantages of each storage technique when they design, implement, and operate a database on a specific DBMS. Usually, the DBMS will have several options available for organizing the data, and the process of **physical database design** involves choosing the particular data organization techniques that best suit the given application requirements from among the available options. DBMS system implementers must study data organization techniques so that they can implement them efficiently and thus provide the DBA and users of the DBMS with sufficient options.

Typical database applications need only a small portion of the database at a time for processing. Whenever a certain portion of the data is needed, it must be located on disk, copied to main memory for processing, and then rewritten to the disk if the data is changed. The data stored on disk is organized as **files** of **records**. Each record is a collection of data values that can be interpreted as facts about entities, their attributes, and their relationships. Records should be stored on disk in a manner that makes it possible to locate them efficiently whenever they are needed.

There are several **primary file organizations** which determine how the records of a file are *physically placed on the disk*. A *heap file* (or *unordered file*) places the records on disk in no particular order, whereas a *sorted file* (or *sequential file*) keeps the records ordered by the value of a particular field. A *hashed file* uses a hash function to determine record placement on disk. Other primary file organizations, such as *B-trees*, use tree structures. We discuss primary file organizations in Sections 4.6 to 4.9.

4.2 Secondary Storage Devices

In this section we describe some characteristics of magnetic disk and magnetic tape storage devices. Readers who have studied these devices before may just browse through this section.

4.2.1 *Hardware Description of Disk Devices*

Magnetic disks are used for storing large amounts of data. The most basic unit of data on the disk is a single **bit** of information. By magnetizing an area on disk in certain ways, one can make it represent a bit value of either 0 (zero) or 1 (one). To code information, bits are grouped into **bytes** (or **characters**). Byte sizes are typically 4 to 8 bits, depending on the computer and the device. We assume that one character is stored in a single byte, and we use the terms *byte* and *character* interchangeably. The **capacity** of a disk is the number of bytes it can store, which is usually very large. We refer to disk capacities in kilobytes (Kbyte or 1000 bytes), megabytes (Mbyte or 1 million bytes), and gigabytes (Gbyte or 1 billion bytes). Small floppy disks used with microcomputers typically hold from 400 Kbytes to 1.2 Mbytes; hard disks for micros typically hold from 30 to 250 Mbytes; and large disk packs used with minicomputers and mainframes have capacities that range up to a few Gbytes. Disk capacities continue to grow as technology improves.

Whatever their capacity, disks are all made of magnetic material shaped as a thin circular disk (Figure 4.1(a)) and protected by a plastic or acrylic cover. A disk is **single-sided** if it stores information on only one of its surfaces and **double-sided** if both surfaces are used. To increase storage capacity, disks are assembled into a **disk pack** (Figure 4.1(b)), which may include as many as 30 surfaces. Information is stored on a disk surface in concentric circles of *small width*, each having a distinct diameter. Each circle is called a **track**. For disk packs, the tracks with the same diameter on the various surfaces are

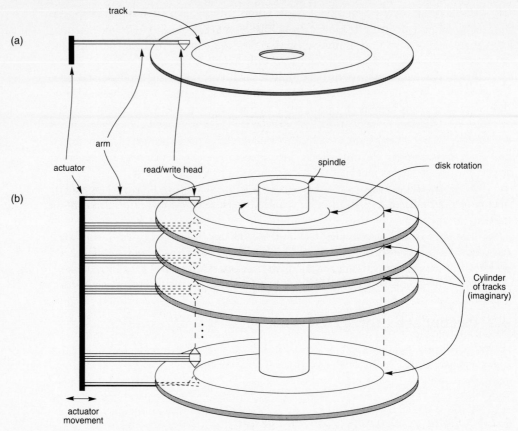

Figure 4.1   (a) A single-sided disk with read/write hardware. (b) A disk pack with read/write hardware.

called a **cylinder** because of the shape they would form if connected in space. The concept of a cylinder is important because data stored on the same cylinder can be retrieved much faster than if it were distributed among different cylinders.

Each concentric circle typically stores the same amount of information, so bits are packed more densely on the smaller-diameter tracks. The number of tracks on a disk ranges up to 800, and the capacity of each track typically ranges from 4 to 50 Kbytes. Because a track usually contains a large amount of information, it is divided into smaller blocks or sectors. The division of a track into **sectors** is hard-coded on the disk surface and cannot be changed. Sectors subtend a fixed angle at the center (Figure 4.2), and not all disks have their tracks divided into sectors. The division of a track into equal-sized **blocks** or *pages* is set by the operating system during disk **formatting** (or **initialization**). Block size is fixed during initialization and cannot be changed dynamically. Typical disk block sizes range from 512 to 4096 bytes. A disk with hard-coded sectors often has the sectors further subdivided into blocks during initialization. Blocks are separated

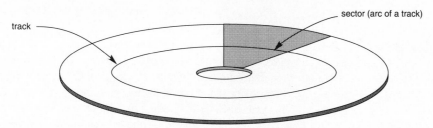

Figure 4.2   A group of sectors that subtend the same angle.

by fixed-size **interblock gaps,** which include specially coded control information written during disk initialization. This is used to determine which block on the track follows each interblock gap.

A disk is called a *random access* addressable device. Transfer of data between main memory and disk takes place in units of blocks. The **hardware address** of a block—a combination of a surface number, track number (within the surface), and block number (within the track)—is supplied to the disk input/output (I/O) hardware. The address of a **buffer**—a contiguous reserved area in main storage that holds one block—is also provided. For a **read** command, the block from disk is copied into the buffer; whereas for a **write** command, the contents of the buffer are copied into the disk block. Sometimes several contiguous blocks, called a **cluster,** may be transferred as a unit. In this case the buffer size is adjusted to match the number of bytes in the cluster.

The actual hardware mechanism that reads or writes a block is the disk **read/write head,** which is part of a system called a **disk drive.** A disk or disk pack is mounted in the disk drive, which includes a motor that rotates the disks. A read/write head includes an electronic component attached to a **mechanical arm.** Disk packs with multiple surfaces are controlled by several read/write heads—one for each surface (see Figure 4.1(b)). All arms are connected to an **actuator** attached to another electrical motor, which moves the read/write heads in unison and positions them precisely over the cylinder of tracks specified in a block address.

Disk drives for hard disks rotate the disk pack continuously at a constant speed. For a floppy disk, the disk drive begins to rotate the disk whenever a particular read or write request is initiated and ceases rotation soon after the data transfer is completed. Once the read/write head is positioned on the right track and the block specified in the block address moves under the read/write head, the electronic component of the read/write head is activated to transfer the data. Some disk units have fixed read/write heads, with as many heads as there are tracks. These are called **fixed-head** disks, whereas disk units with an actuator are called **movable-head** disks. For fixed-head disks, a track or cylinder is selected by electronically switching to the appropriate read/write head rather than by actual mechanical movement; consequently, it is much faster. However, the cost of the additional read/write heads is quite high, so fixed-head disks are not commonly used.

To transfer a disk block, given its address, the disk drive must first mechanically position the read/write head on the correct track. The time required to do this is called the **seek time.** Following that, there is another delay—called the **rotational delay** or

latency—while the beginning of the desired block rotates into position under the read/write head. Finally, some additional time is needed to transfer the data; this is called the **block transfer time**. Hence, the total time needed to locate and transfer an arbitrary block, given its address, is the sum of the seek time, rotational delay, and block transfer time. The seek time and rotational delay are usually much larger than the block transfer time. To make the transfer of multiple blocks more efficient, it is common to transfer several consecutive blocks on the same track or cylinder. This eliminates the seek time and rotational delay for all but the first block and can result in a substantial saving of time when numerous contiguous blocks are transferred. Usually, the disk manufacturer provides a **bulk transfer rate** for calculating the time required to transfer consecutive blocks. Appendix B contains a discussion of these and other disk parameters.

The time needed to locate and transfer a disk block is in the order of milliseconds, usually ranging from 15 to 60 msec. For contiguous blocks, locating the first block takes from 15 to 60 msec, but transferring subsequent blocks may only take 1 to 2 msec each. Many search techniques take advantage of consecutive retrieval of blocks when searching for data on disk. In any case, a transfer time in the order of milliseconds is considered quite high compared to the time required to process data in main memory by current CPUs. Hence, locating data on disk is a *major bottleneck* in database applications. The file structures we discuss here and in Chapter 5 attempt to *minimize the number of block transfers* needed to locate and transfer the required data from disk to main memory.

4.2.2 *Magnetic Tape Storage Devices*

Disks are **random access** secondary storage devices, because an arbitrary disk block may be accessed "at random" once we specify its address. Magnetic tapes are **sequential access** devices; to access the nth block on tape, we must first read the preceding $n - 1$ blocks. Data is stored on reels of high-capacity magnetic tape, somewhat similar to audio or video tapes. A **tape drive** is required to read the data from or to write the data to a **tape reel.** Usually, each group of bits that form a byte is stored across the tape, and the bytes themselves are stored consecutively on the tape.

A read/write head is used to read or write data on tape. Data records on tape are also stored in blocks—although the blocks may be substantially larger than those for disks, and interblock gaps are also quite large. With typical tape densities of 1600 to 6250 bytes per inch, a typical interblock gap* of 0.6 inches corresponds to 960 to 3750 bytes of wasted storage space. For better space utilization it is customary to group many records together in one block.

The main characteristic of a tape is its requirement that we access the data blocks in **sequential order.** To get to a block in the middle of a reel of tape, we must mount the tape and then read through it until the required block gets under the read/write head. For this reason, tape access can be slow and tapes are not used to store on-line data, except for some specialized applications. However, tapes serve a very important function—that of **backing up** the database. One reason for backup is to keep copies of disk files in case the data is lost because of a disk crash, which can happen if the disk read/write head touches the disk surface because of mechanical malfunction. For this reason,

---

*Called *interrecord gaps* in tape terminology.

disk files are periodically copied to tape. Tapes can also be used to store excessively large database files. Finally, database files that are seldom used or outdated but are required for historical record keeping can be **archived** on tape. Recently, smaller 8-mm magnetic tapes (similar to those used in camcorders) and CD-ROMs (compact disks–read only memory) have become popular media for backing up data files from workstations and personal computers and for storing images and system libraries.

4.3 Buffering of Blocks

When several blocks need to be transferred from disk to main memory and all the block addresses are known beforehand, several buffers can be reserved in main memory to speed up the transfer. While one buffer is being read or written, the CPU can process data in the other buffer. This is possible because an independent disk input/output (I/O) processor usually exists that, once started, can proceed to transfer a data block between memory and disk independent of and in parallel to CPU processing.

Figure 4.3 illustrates how two processes can proceed in parallel. Processes A and B are running **concurrently** in an **interleaved** fashion, whereas processes C and D are running **concurrently** in a **simultaneous** fashion. When a single CPU controls multiple processes, simultaneous execution is not possible. However, the processes can still run concurrently in an interleaved way. Buffering is most useful when processes can run concurrently in a simultaneous fashion, either because a separate disk I/O processor is available or because multiple processors exist.

Figure 4.4 illustrates how reading and processing can proceed in parallel when the time required to process a disk block in memory is less than the time required to read the next block and fill a buffer. The CPU can start processing a block once its transfer

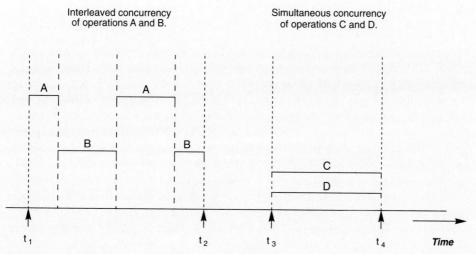

Figure 4.3   Interleaved versus simultaneous concurrency.

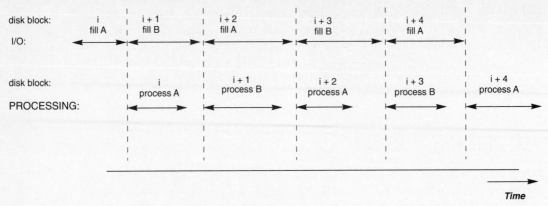

Figure 4.4 Use of two buffers, A and B, for reading from disk.

to main memory is completed; at the same time the disk I/O processor can be reading and transferring the next block into a different buffer. This technique is called **double buffering** and can also be used to write a continuous stream of blocks from memory to the disk. Double buffering permits continuous reading or writing of data on consecutive disk blocks, which eliminates the seek time and rotational delay for all but the first block transfer. Moreover, data is kept ready for processing, thus reducing the waiting time in the programs.

4.4 Placing File Records on Disk

In this section we define the concepts of records, record types, and files. Then we discuss different techniques for placing file records on disk.

4.4.1 Record Types

Data is usually stored in the form of **records.** Each record consists of a collection of related data **values** or **items,** where each value is formed of one or more bytes and corresponds to a particular **field** of the record. Records usually describe entities and their attributes. For example, an EMPLOYEE record represents an employee entity, and each field value in the record specifies some attribute of that employee, such as NAME, BIRTH-DATE, SALARY, or SUPERVISOR. A collection of field names and their corresponding data types constitutes a **record type** or **record format** definition. A **data type,** associated with each field, specifies the type of values a field can take.

The data type of a field is usually one of the standard data types used in programming. These include numeric (integer, long-integer, or real-number), string of characters (fixed-length or varying), Boolean (having 0 and 1 or TRUE and FALSE values only), and sometimes specially coded **date** and **time** data types. The number of bytes required for each data type is fixed for a given computer system. An integer may require 4 bytes, a long integer 8 bytes, a real number 4 bytes, a Boolean 1 byte, a date 4 bytes (to code the date into an integer), and a fixed-length string of k characters k bytes. Variable-length strings may require as many bytes as there are characters in each field value. For example, an EMPLOYEE record type may be defined—using PASCAL notation—as follows:

RECORD TYPE NAME	FIELD NAMES	DATA TYPES
type EMPLOYEE = record	NAME	: packed array [1..30] of character;
	SSN	: packed array [1..9] of character;
	SALARY	: integer;
	JOBCODE	: integer;
	DEPARTMENT	: packed array [1..20] of character
end;		

In recent database applications, the need may arise for storing data items that consist of large unstructured objects, which represent images, digitized video or audio streams, or free text. These are referred to as **BLOBs** (binary large objects). Normally, a BLOB data item is stored separately from its record in a pool of disk blocks, and a pointer to the BLOB is included in the record.

4.4.2 *Files, Fixed-length Records, and Variable-length Records*

A **file** is a *sequence* of records. In many cases, all records in a file are of the same record type. If every record in the file has exactly the same size (in bytes), the file is said to be made up of **fixed-length** records. If different records in the file have different sizes, the file is said to be made up of **variable-length** records. A file may have variable-length records for several reasons:

- The file records are of the same record type, but one or more of the fields are of varying size **(variable-length fields).** For example, the NAME field of EMPLOYEE can be a variable-length field.

- The file records are of the same record type, but one or more of the fields may have multiple values for individual records; such a field is called a **repeating field** and a group of values for the field is often called a **repeating group.**

- The file records are of the same record type, but one or more of the fields are **optional;** that is, they may have values for some but not all of the file records **(optional fields).**

- The file contains records of *different record types* and hence of varying size **(mixed file).** This would occur if related records of different types were placed together on disk blocks; for example, the GRADE_REPORT records of a particular student may be placed following that STUDENT's record.

The fixed-length EMPLOYEE records in Figure 4.5(a) have a record size of 71 bytes. Every record has the same fields, and field lengths are fixed, so we can identify the starting byte position of each field relative to the starting position of the record. This facilitates locating field values by programs that access such files. Notice that it is possible to represent a file that logically should have variable-length records as a fixed-length records file. For example, in the case of optional fields we could have *every field* included in *every file record* but store a special null value if no value exists for that field. For a

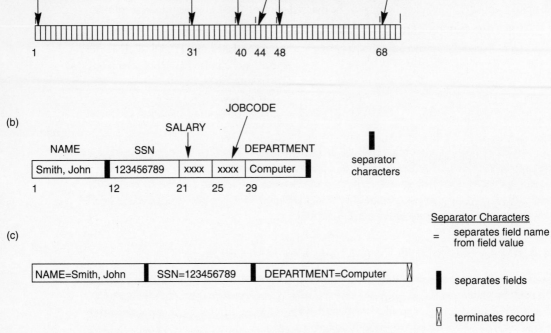

Figure 4.5   Different record storage formats. (a) A fixed-length record with six fields and size of 71 bytes. (b) A record with two variable-length fields and three fixed-length fields. (c) A variable-field record with three types of separator characters.

repeating field, we could allocate as many spaces in each record as the maximum number of values that the field can take. In either case, space is wasted when certain records do not have values for all the physical spaces provided in each record. We now consider other options for formatting records of a file of variable-length records.

For *variable-length fields*, each record has a value for each field, but we do not know the exact length of some field values. To determine the bytes within a particular record that represent each field, we can use special **separator** characters—which do not appear in any field value (such as ? or % or $)—to terminate variable-length fields (Figure 4.5(b)), or we can store the length of the field in the record.

A file of records with *optional fields* can be formatted in different ways. If the total number of fields for the record type is large but the number of fields that actually appear in a typical record is small, we can include in each record a sequence of <field-name, field-value> pairs rather than just the field values. Three types of separator characters are used in Figure 4.5(c), although we could use the same separator character for the first two purposes—separating the field name from the field value and separating one field from the next field. A more practical option is to assign a short **field type**—say, an integer number—to each field and include in each record a sequence of <field-type, field-value> pairs rather than <field-name, field-value> pairs.

A *repeating field* needs one separator character to separate the repeating values of the field and another separator character to indicate termination of the field. Finally, for a file that includes *records of different types*, each record is preceded by a **record type** indicator. Understandably, programs that process files of variable-length records need to be more complex than those for fixed-length records, where the starting position and size of each field are known and fixed.

4.4.3 Record Blocking and Spanned versus Unspanned Records

The records of a file must be allocated to disk blocks because a block is the *unit of data transfer* between disk and memory. When the block size is larger than the record size, each block will contain numerous records. Some files may have unusually large record sizes that cannot fit in one block. Suppose that the block size is B bytes. For a file of fixed-length records of size R bytes, with $B \geq R$, we can fit $bfr = \lfloor (B/R) \rfloor$ records per block, where the $\lfloor (x) \rfloor$ *(floor function)* rounds the value x down to the next integer. The value *bfr* is called the **blocking factor** for the file. In general, R may not divide B exactly, so we have some unused space in each block equal to

$$B - (bfr * R) \text{ bytes}$$

To utilize this unused space, we can store part of a record on one block and the rest on another block. A **pointer** at the end of the first block points to the block containing the remainder of the record in case it is not the next consecutive block on disk. This organization is called **spanned,** because records can span more than one block. Whenever a record is larger than a block, we *must* use a spanned organization. If records are not allowed to cross block boundaries, the organization is called **unspanned.** This is used with fixed-length records having $B \geq R$ because it makes each record start at a known location in the block, simplifying record processing. For variable-length records, either a spanned or an unspanned organization can be used. If the average record size is large, it is advantageous to use spanning to reduce the lost space in each block. Figure 4.6 illustrates spanned versus unspanned organization.

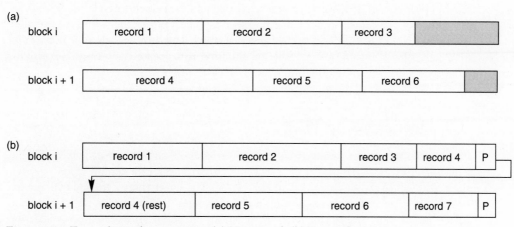

Figure 4.6 Types of record organization. (a) Unspanned. (b) Spanned.

For variable-length records using spanned organization, each block may store a different number of records. In this case, the blocking factor bfr represents the *average* number of records per block for the file. We can use bfr to calculate the number of blocks b needed for a file of r records:

$$b = \lceil (r/bfr) \rceil \text{ blocks}$$

where the $\lceil (x) \rceil$ *(ceiling function)* rounds the value x up to the next integer.

4.4.4 *Allocating File Blocks on Disk*

There are several standard techniques for allocating the blocks of a file on disk. In **contiguous allocation** the file blocks are allocated to consecutive disk blocks. This makes reading the whole file very fast using double buffering, but it makes expanding the file difficult. In **linked allocation** each file block contains a pointer to the next file block. This makes it easy to expand the file but makes it slow to read the whole file. A combination of the two allocates **clusters** of consecutive disk blocks, and the clusters are linked together. Clusters are sometimes called **segments** or **extents.** Another possibility is to use **indexed allocation,** where one or more **index blocks** contain pointers to the actual file blocks. It is also common to use combinations of these techniques.

4.4.5 *File Headers*

A **file header** or **file descriptor** contains information about a file that is needed by the programs that access the file records. The header includes information to determine the disk addresses of the file blocks as well as to record format descriptions, which may include field lengths and order of fields within a record for fixed-length unspanned records and field type codes, separator characters, and record type codes for variable-length records.

To search for a record on disk, one or more blocks are copied into main memory buffers. Programs then search for the desired record or records within the buffers, utilizing the information in the file header. If the address of the block that contains the desired record is not known, the search programs must do a **linear search** through the file blocks. Each file block is copied into a buffer and searched until either the record is located or all the file blocks have been searched unsuccessfully. This can be very time-consuming for a large file. The goal of a good file organization is to locate the block that contains a desired record with a minimal number of block transfers.

4.5 Operations on Files

Operations on files are usually grouped into **retrieval** operations and **update** operations. The former do not change any data in the file, but only locate certain records so that their field values can be examined and processed. The latter change the file by insertion or deletion of records or by modification of field values. In either case, we may have to **select** one or more records for retrieval, deletion, or modification based on a **selection condition,** which specifies criteria that the desired record or records must satisfy.

Consider an EMPLOYEE file with fields NAME, SSN, SALARY, JOBCODE, and DEPART-MENT. A **simple selection condition** may involve an equality comparison on some field value—for example, (SSN = '123456789') or (DEPARTMENT = 'Research'). More complex conditions can involve other types of comparison operators, such as $>$ or $\geq$; an example is (SALARY $\geq$ 30000). The general case is to have an arbitrary Boolean expression on the fields of the file as the selection condition.

Search operations on file systems are generally based on simple selection conditions. A complex condition must be decomposed by the DBMS (or the programmer) to extract a simple condition that can be used to locate the records on disk. Each located record is then checked to determine whether it satisfies the full selection condition. For example, we may extract the simple condition (DEPARTMENT = 'Research') from the complex condition ((SALARY $\geq$ 30000) AND (DEPARTMENT = 'Research')); each record satisfying (DEPARTMENT = 'Research') is located and then tested to see if it also satisfies (SALARY $\geq$ 30000).

When several file records satisfy a search condition, only the *first* record—with respect to the physical sequence of file records—is located. To locate other records satisfying the condition, additional operations are needed. The most recently located record of the file is designated the **current record.** Subsequent search operations commence from this record and locate the *next* record in the file satisfying the condition.

Actual operations for locating and accessing file records vary from system to system. Below, we present a set of representative operations. Typically, high-level programs, such as DBMS software programs, access the records by using these commands, so we sometimes refer to **program variables** in the following description:

- *Find* (or *Locate*): Searches for the first record satisfying a search condition. Transfers the block containing that record into a main memory buffer (if it is not already there). The record is located in the buffer and becomes the current record. Sometimes, different verbs are used to indicate whether the located record is to be retrieved (Find) or updated (Locate).

- *Read* (or *Get*): Copies the current record from the buffer to a program variable or work area in the user program. This command may also advance the current record pointer to the next record in the file, which may necessitate reading the next file block from disk.

- *FindNext*: Searches for the next record in the file that satisfies the search condition. Transfers the block containing that record into a main memory buffer (if it is not already there). The record is located in the buffer and becomes the current record.

- *Delete:* Deletes the current record and (eventually) updates the file on disk to reflect the deletion.

- *Modify:* Modifies some field values for the current record and (eventually) updates the file on disk to reflect the modification.

- *Insert:* Inserts a new record in the file by locating the block where the record is to be inserted, transferring that block into a main memory buffer (if it is not already there), writing the record into the buffer, and (eventually) writing the buffer to disk to reflect the insertion.

The preceding are called **record-at-a-time** operations, because each operation applies to a single record. In some file systems, additional **set-at-a-time** higher-level operations may be applied to a file. Examples of these are:

- *FindAll:* Locates *all* the records in the file that satisfy a search condition.
- *FindOrdered:* Retrieves all the records in the file in some specified order.
- *Reorganize:* Starts the reorganization process. As we shall see, some file organizations require periodic reorganization. An example is to reorder the file records by sorting them on a specified field.

Other operations are needed to prepare the file for access **(Open)** and to indicate that we are through using the file **(Close).** The Open operation typically retrieves the file header and prepares memory buffers for subsequent file operations.

At this point, it is worthwhile to note the difference between the terms *file organization* and *access method*. A **file organization** refers to the organization of the data of a file into records, blocks, and access structures; this includes the way records and blocks are placed on the storage medium and interlinked. An **access method,** on the other hand, consists of a group of programs that allow operations—such as those listed earlier—to be applied to a file. In general, it is possible to apply several different access methods to a file organization. Some access methods, though, can be applied only to files organized in certain ways. For example, we cannot apply an indexed access method to a file without an index (see Chapter 5).

Usually, we expect to use some search conditions more than others. Some files may be **static,** meaning that update operations are rarely performed; other, more **volatile** files may change frequently, so update operations are constantly applied to them. A successful file organization should perform as efficiently as possible the operations we expect to *apply frequently* to the file. For example, consider the EMPLOYEE file described earlier, which stores the records for current employees in a company. We expect to insert new records (when employees are hired), delete records (when employees leave the company), and modify records (say, when an employee's salary is changed). Deleting or modifying a record requires a selection condition to identify a particular record or set of records. Retrieving one or more records also requires a selection condition.

If users expect mainly to apply a search condition based on SSN, the designer must choose a file organization that facilitates locating a record given its SSN value. This may involve physically ordering the records by SSN value or defining an index on SSN (see Chapter 5). Suppose that a second application uses the file to generate employee paychecks and requires that paychecks be grouped by department. For this application it is best to store all employee records having the same department value contiguously, packing them into blocks and perhaps ordering them by name within each department. However, this arrangement conflicts with ordering the records by SSN values. If possible, the designer should choose an organization that allows both operations to be done efficiently. Unfortunately, in many cases there may not be an organization that allows all needed operations on a file to be implemented efficiently. Some file organizations make retrieval on certain search conditions very efficient, but concomitantly update becomes expensive. In such cases a compromise must be chosen that takes into account the expected mix of retrieval and update operations.

In the following sections and in Chapter 5, we discuss different methods for organizing records of a file on disk. Several general techniques, such as ordering, hashing, and indexing, are used to create access methods. In addition, various general techniques for handling insertions and deletions work with many file organizations.

4.6 Files of Unordered Records (Heap Files)

In the simplest and most basic type of organization, records are placed in the file in the order in which they are inserted, and new records are inserted at the end of the file. Such an organization is called a **heap** or **pile** file.* This organization is often used with additional access paths, such as the secondary indexes discussed in Chapter 5. It is also used to collect and store data records for future use.

Inserting a new record is *very efficient*: the last disk block of the file is copied into a buffer; the new record is added; and the block is then **rewritten** back to disk. The address of the last file block is kept in the file header. However, searching for a record using any search condition involves a **linear search** through the file block by block—an expensive procedure. If only one record satisfies the search condition, then, on the average, a program will read into memory and search half the file blocks before it finds the record. For a file of b blocks, this requires searching (b/2) blocks, on average. If no records or several records satisfy the search condition, the program must read and search all b blocks in the file.

To delete a record, a program must first find it, copy the block into a buffer, then delete the record from the buffer, and finally **rewrite the block** back to the disk. This leaves extra unused space in the disk block. Deleting a large number of records in this way results in wasted storage space. Another technique used for record deletion is to have an extra byte or bit, called a **deletion marker,** stored with each record. A record is deleted by setting the deletion marker to a certain value. A different value of the marker indicates a valid (not deleted) record. Search programs consider only valid records in a block when conducting their search. Both of these deletion techniques require periodic **reorganization** of the file to reclaim the unused space of deleted records. During reorganization, the file blocks are accessed consecutively, and records are packed by removing deleted records. After such a reorganization, the blocks are filled to capacity once more. Another possibility is to use the space of deleted records when inserting new records, although this requires extra bookkeeping to keep track of empty locations.

We can use either spanned or unspanned organization for an unordered file and either fixed-length or variable-length records. Modifying a variable-length record may require deleting the old record and inserting a modified record, because the modified record may not fit in its old space on disk.

To read all records in order of the values of some field, we create a sorted copy of the file. Sorting is an expensive operation for a large disk file, and special **external sorting** techniques are used. A common method is a variation of the merge sort technique. First,

---

*Some file systems such as Digital Equipment Corporation's VAX RMS (Record Management Services) call this organization a *sequential file*.

the records within each block are sorted. Then sorted blocks are merged to create groups of sorted records, each the size of two blocks. Each such group of sorted records is sometimes called a **run.** Runs of two blocks are then merged to form runs of four blocks, and so on, until the final run is the completely sorted file.

For a file of unordered *fixed-length records* using *unspanned blocks* and *contiguous allocation*, it is straightforward to access any record by its **position** in the file. If the file records are numbered 0, 1, 2, ..., r − 1 and the records in each block are numbered 0, 1, ..., bfr − 1, where bfr is the blocking factor, then the ith record of the file is located in block $\lfloor (i/bfr) \rfloor$ and is the (i mod bfr)th record in that block. Such a file is often called a **relative file*** because records can easily be accessed by their relative position. Accessing a record by its position does not help locate a record based on a search condition; however, it facilitates the construction of access paths on the file, such as the indexes discussed in Chapter 5.

4.7 Files of Ordered Records (Sorted Files)

We can physically order the records of a file on disk based on the values of one of their fields—called the **ordering field.** This leads to an **ordered** or **sequential** file.** If the ordering field is also a **key field** of the file—a field guaranteed to have a unique value in each record—then the field is also called the **ordering key** for the file. Figure 4.7 shows an ordered file with NAME as the ordering key field (assuming that employees have distinct names).

Ordered records have some advantages over unordered files. First, reading the records in order of the ordering field values becomes extremely efficient, since no sorting is required. Second, finding the next record from the current one in order of the ordering field usually requires no additional block accesses, because the next record is in the same block as the current one (unless the current record is the last one in the block). Third, using a search condition based on the value of an ordering key field results in faster access when the binary search technique is used, which constitutes an improvement over linear searches although it is not often used for disk files.

A **binary search** for disk files can be done on the blocks rather than on the records. Suppose that the file has b blocks numbered 1, 2, ..., b; the records are ordered by ascending value of their ordering key field; and we are searching for a record whose ordering key field value is K. Assuming that disk addresses of the file blocks are available in the file header, the binary search can be described by Algorithm 4.1. A binary search usually accesses $\log_2(b)$ blocks, whether the record is found or not—an improvement over linear searches, where, on the average, (b/2) blocks are accessed when the record is found and b blocks are accessed when the record is not found.

---

*For example, VAX RMS (Record Management Services) calls this organization a *relative file*.

**Some file systems, such as Digital Equipment Corporation's VAX RMS system, use the term *sequential file* to denote the unordered file described in Section 4.6.

	NAME	SSN	BIRTHDATE	JOB	SALARY	SEX
block 1	Aaron, Ed					
	Abbott, Diane					
	⋮					
	Acosta, Marc					
block 2	Adams, John					
	Adams, Robin					
	⋮					
	Akers, Jan					
block 3	Alexander, Ed					
	Alfred, Bob					
	⋮					
	Allen, Sam					
block 4	Allen, Troy					
	Anders, Keith					
	⋮					
	Anderson, Rob					
block 5	Anderson, Zach					
	Angeli, Joe					
	⋮					
	Archer, Sue					
block 6	Arnold, Mack					
	Arnold, Steven					
	⋮					
	Atkins, Timothy					
⋮						
block n−1	Wong, James					
	Wood, Donald					
	⋮					
	Woods, Manny					
block n	Wright, Pam					
	Wyatt, Charles					
	⋮					
	Zimmer, Byron					

Figure 4.7 Some blocks of an ordered (sequential) file of EMPLOYEE records with NAME as the ordering field.

ALGORITHM 4.1   Binary search on an ordering key of a disk file.

$l \leftarrow 1$; $u \leftarrow b$; (* b is the number of file blocks*)
while ($u \geq l$) do
   begin $i \leftarrow (l + u)$ div 2;
   read block i of the file into the buffer;
   if $K <$ ordering key field value of the first record in the block
   then $u \leftarrow i - 1$
   else if $K >$ ordering key field value of the last record in the block
      then $l \leftarrow i + 1$
      else if the record with ordering key field value = K is in the buffer
         then goto found
         else goto notfound;
  end;
  goto notfound;

A search criterion involving the conditions $>$, $<$, $\geq$, and $\leq$ on the ordering field is quite efficient, since the physical ordering of records means that all records satisfying the condition are contiguous in the file. For example, referring to Figure 4.7, if the search criterion is (NAME $<$ 'F')—where $<$ means "alphabetically before"—the records satisfying the search criterion are those from the beginning of the file up to the first record that has a NAME value starting with the letter F.

Ordering does not provide any advantages for random or ordered access of the records based on values of a *nonordering field* of the file. In these cases we do a linear search for random access. To access the records in order based on a nonordering field, it is necessary to create another sorted copy of the file.

Inserting and deleting records are expensive operations for an ordered file because the records must remain physically ordered. To insert a new record, we must find its correct position in the file, based on its ordering field value, and then make space in the file to insert the record in that position. For a large file this can be very time-consuming because, on the average, half the records of the file must be moved to make space for the new record. This means that half the file blocks must be read and rewritten after records are moved among them. For record deletion the problem is less severe, if we use deletion markers and reorganize the file periodically.

One option for making insertion more efficient is to keep some unused space in each block for new records. However, once this space is used up, the original problem resurfaces. Another frequently used method is to create a temporary *unordered* file called an **overflow** or **transaction** file. With this technique, the actual ordered file is called the **main** or **master** file. New records are inserted at the end of the overflow file rather than in their correct position in the main file. Periodically, the overflow file is merged with the master file during file reorganization. Insertion becomes very efficient, but at the cost of increased complexity in the search algorithm. The overflow file must be searched using a linear search if, after the binary search, the record is not found in the main file. For applications that do not require the most up-to-date information, overflow records can be ignored during a search.

Modifying a field value of a record depends on two factors: the search condition to locate the record, and the field to be modified. If the search condition involves the ordering key field, we can locate the record using a binary search; otherwise we must do a linear search. A nonordering field can be modified by changing the record and rewriting it in the same physical location on disk—assuming fixed-length records. Modifying the ordering field means that the record can change its position in the file, which requires deletion of the old record followed by insertion of the modified record.

Reading the file records in order of the ordering field is quite efficient if we ignore the records in overflow, since the blocks can be read consecutively using double buffering. To include the records in overflow, we must merge them in their correct positions; in this case, we can first reorganize the file, and then read its blocks sequentially. To reorganize the file, we first sort the records in the overflow file, and then merge them with the master file. The records marked deleted are removed during the reorganization.

Ordered files are rarely used in database applications unless an additional access path, called a *primary index*, is included with the file. This further improves the random access time on the ordering key field. We discuss indexes in Chapter 5.

4.8 Hashing Techniques

Another type of primary file organization is based on hashing, which provides very fast access to records on certain search conditions. This organization is usually called a **hash** or **direct** file.* The search condition must be an equality condition on a single field, called the **hash field** of the file. Often, the hash field is also a key field of the file, in which case it is called the **hash key.** The idea behind hashing is to provide a function h, called a **hash function** or **randomizing function,** that is applied to the hash field value of a record and yields the *address* of the disk block in which the record is stored. A search for the record within the block can be carried out in a main memory buffer. For most records, we need only a single block access to retrieve that record.

Hashing is also used as an internal data structure within a program whenever a small temporary file of records is accessed exclusively by using the value of one field. We describe the use of hashing for internal files in Section 4.8.1; then we show how it is modified to store external files on disk in Section 4.8.2. In Section 4.8.3 we discuss techniques for extending hashing to dynamically growing files.

4.8.1 *Internal Hashing*

For internal files, hashing is typically implemented through the use of an array of records. Suppose that the array index range is from 0 to $M - 1$ (Figure 4.8(a)); then we have M **slots** whose addresses correspond to the array indexes. We choose a hash function that transforms the hash field value into an integer between 0 and $M - 1$. One common hash function is the $h(K) = K$ **mod M** function, which returns the remainder of an integer hash field value K after division by M; this value is then used for the record address.

---

*In the VAX RMS file system of Digital Equipment Corporation, the term *direct access* refers to accessing a relative file by record position.

(a)

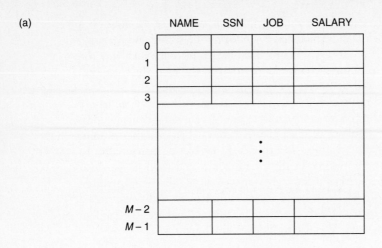

(b)

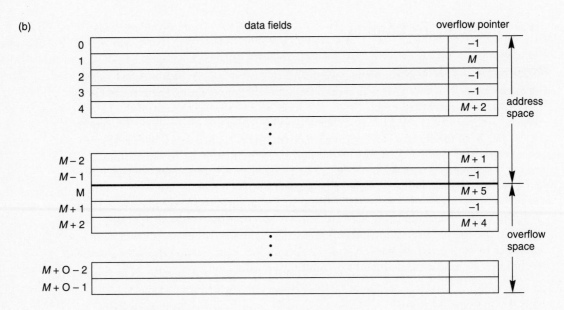

- null pointer = −1.
- overflow pointer refers to position of next record in linked list.

Figure 4.8 Internal hashing data structures. (a) Array of M positions for use in internal hashing. (b) Collision resolution by chaining records.

Noninteger hash field values can be transformed into integers before the mod function is applied. For character strings, the numeric codes associated with characters can be used in the transformation—for example, by multiplying those code values. For a hash field whose data type is a string of 20 characters, Algorithm 4.2(a) can be used to calculate the hash address. We assume that the code function returns the numeric code of a character and that we are given a hash field value K of type *array [1..20] of char.*

ALGORITHM 4.2 Two simple hashing algorithms. (a) Applying the mod hash function to a character string. (b) Collision resolution by open addressing.

(a) *temp* ← 1;
　　for *i* ← 1 to 20 do *temp* ← *temp* * code(*K*[*i*]);
　　hash_address ← *temp* mod *M*;

(b) *i* ← *hash_address*;
　　if location *i* is occupied
　　　then begin *i* ← (*i* + 1) mod *M*;
　　　　　while (*i* ≠ *hash_address*) and location *i* is occupied
　　　　　　　do *i* ← (*i* + 1) mod *M*;
　　　　　if (*i* = *hash_address*) then all positions are full
　　　　　　　　　else *new_hash_address* ← i;
　　　end;

Other hashing functions can be used. One technique, called **folding,** involves applying an arithmetic function such as addition or a logical function such as "exclusive or" to different portions of the hash field value to calculate the hash address. Another technique involves picking some digits of the hash field value—for example, the third, fifth, and eighth digits—to form the hash address. The problem with most hashing functions is that they do not guarantee that distinct values will hash to distinct addresses, because the **hash field space**—the number of possible values a hash field can take—is usually much larger than the **address space**—the number of available addresses for records. The hashing function maps the hash field space to the address space.

A **collision** occurs when the hash field value of a new record that is being inserted hashes to an address that already contains a different record. In this situation, we must insert the new record in some other position, since its hash address is occupied. The process of finding another position is called **collision resolution**. There are numerous methods for collision resolution, including the following:

- *Open addressing:* Proceeding from the occupied position specified by the hash address, the program checks the subsequent positions in order until an unused (empty) position is found. Algorithm 4.2(b) may be used for this purpose.

- *Chaining:* For this method, various overflow locations are kept, usually by extending the array with a number of overflow positions. In addition, a pointer field is added to each record location. A collision is resolved by placing the new record in an unused overflow location and setting the pointer of the occupied hash address location to the address of that overflow location. A linked list of overflow records for each hash address is maintained, as shown in Figure 4.8(b).

- *Multiple hashing:* The program applies a second hash function if the first results in a collision. If another collision results, the program uses open addressing or applies a third hash function and then uses open addressing if necessary.

Each collision resolution method requires its own algorithms for insertion, retrieval, and deletion of records. The algorithms for chaining are the simplest. Deletion algorithms for open addressing are rather tricky. Data structures textbooks discuss internal hashing algorithms in more detail.

The goal of a good hashing function is to distribute the records uniformly over the address space so as to minimize collisions while not leaving many unused locations. Simulation and analysis studies have shown that it is usually best to keep a hash table between 70% and 90% full so that the number of collisions remains low and we do not waste too much space. Hence, if we expect to have r records to store in the table, we should choose M locations for the address space such that (r/M) is between 0.7 and 0.9. It may also be useful to choose a prime number for M, since it has been demonstrated that this distributes the hash addresses better over the address space when the mod hashing function is used. Other hash functions may require M to be a power of 2.

4.8.2 *External Hashing*

Hashing for disk files is called **external hashing.** To suit the characteristics of disk storage, the target address space is made of **buckets,** each of which holds multiple records. A bucket is either one disk block or a cluster of contiguous blocks. The hashing function maps a key into a relative bucket number, rather than assigning an absolute block address to the bucket. A table maintained in the file header converts the bucket number into the corresponding disk block address, as illustrated in Figure 4.9.

The collision problem is less severe with buckets, because as many records as will fit in a bucket can hash to the same bucket without causing problems. However, we must make provisions for the case where a bucket is filled to capacity and a new record being inserted hashes to that bucket. We can use a variation of chaining in which we maintain a pointer in each bucket to a linked list of overflow records for the bucket, as shown in Figure 4.10. The pointers in the linked list should be **record pointers,** which include both a block address and a relative record position within the block.

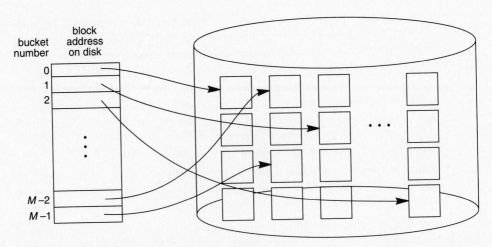

Figure 4.9 Matching bucket numbers to disk blocks.

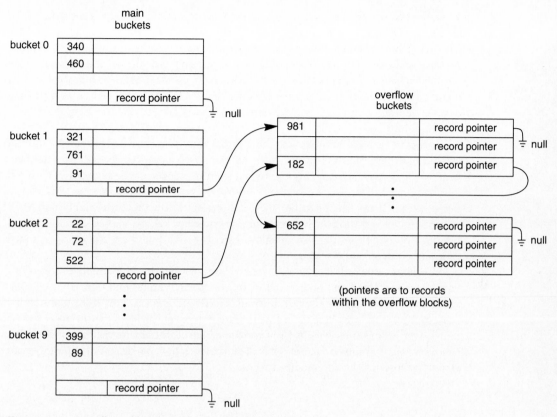

Figure 4.10   Handling overflow for buckets by chaining.

Although hashing provides the fastest possible access for retrieving an arbitrary rec-ord, given the value of its hash field, it is not very useful when other applications are required of the same file unless additional access paths are constructed. For example, if we want to retrieve records in order of their hash field values, hashing is not very suit-able, since most good hash functions do not maintain records in this order. Some hash functions, called **order preserving,** can maintain the order of records by hash field values. A simple example is to take the leftmost three digits of an invoice number field as the hash address and keep the records sorted by invoice number within each bucket. Another example is to use an integer hash key directly as an index to a relative file, if the hash key values fill up a particular interval; for example, if employee numbers in a company are assigned as 1, 2, 3, . . . up to the total number of employees, we can use the identity hash function that maintains order. Unfortunately, this only works if keys are generated in order by some application.

Another drawback of hashing is the fixed amount of space allocated to the file. Suppose that we allocate M buckets for the address space and let m be the maximum number of records that can fit in one bucket; then at most m * M records will fit in the allocated space. If the number of records turns out to be substantially less than m * M, we are left with a lot of unused space. On the other hand, if the number of records increases to substantially more than m * M, numerous collisions will result and retrieval will be slowed down because of the long lists of overflow records. In either case, we may have to change the number of blocks allocated and then use a different hashing function to redistribute the records among the buckets. Newer file organizations based on hashing allow the number of buckets to vary dynamically; we discuss some of these techniques in Section 4.8.3.

In regular external hashing, searching for a record given a value of some field other than the hash field is as expensive as in the case of an unordered file. Record deletion can be implemented by removing the record from its bucket. If the bucket has an overflow chain, we can move one of the overflow records into the bucket to replace the deleted record. If the record to be deleted is already in overflow, we simply remove it from the linked list. Notice that removing an overflow record implies that we should keep track of empty positions in overflow. This is easily done by maintaining a linked list of unused overflow locations.

Modifying a record's field value depends on two factors: the search condition to locate the record, and the field to be modified. If the search condition is an equality comparison on the hash field, we can locate the record efficiently by using the hashing function; otherwise, we must do a linear search. A nonhash field can be modified by changing the record and rewriting it in the same bucket. Modifying the hash field means that the record can move to another bucket, which requires deletion of the old record followed by insertion of the modified record.

4.8.3 *Hashing Techniques That Allow Dynamic File Expansion*★

A major drawback of the *static* hashing scheme just discussed is that the hash address space is fixed. Hence, it is difficult to expand or shrink the file dynamically. The schemes described in this section attempt to remedy this situation. The first two schemes— dynamic hashing and extendible hashing—store an access structure in addition to the file, and hence are somewhat similar to indexing (Chapter 5). The main difference is that the access structure is based on the values that result after application of the hash function to the search field. In indexing, the access structure is based on the value of the search field itself. The third technique—linear hashing—does not require use of any additional access structures.

These hashing schemes take advantage of the fact that the result of most hashing functions is a nonnegative integer and hence can be represented as a binary number. The access structure is built on the **binary representation** of the hashing function result, which is a string of **bits.** We call this the **hash value** of a record. Records are distributed among buckets based on the values of the *leading bits* in their hash values.

Dynamic Hashing. In dynamic hashing, the number of buckets is not fixed (as in regular hashing) but grows or diminishes as needed. The file can start with a single bucket; once that bucket is full, and a new record is inserted, the bucket **overflows** and is split into

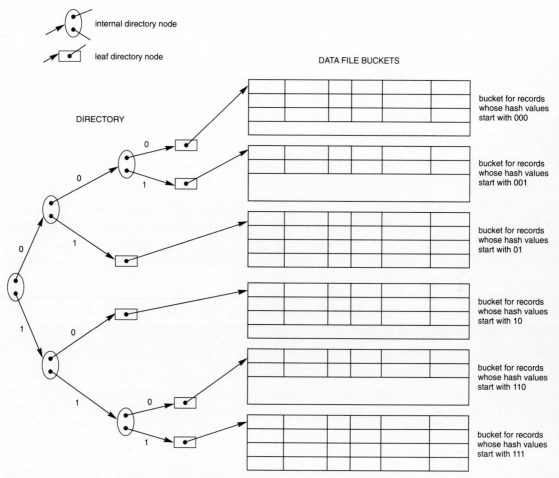

Figure 4.11   Structure of the dynamic hashing scheme.

two buckets. The records are distributed among the two buckets based on the value of the first (leftmost) bit of their hash values. Records whose hash values start with a 0 bit are stored in one bucket, and those whose hash values start with a 1 bit are stored in the other bucket. At this point, a binary tree structure called a **directory** (or **index**) is built. The directory has two types of nodes:

- **Internal nodes** guide the search; each has a left pointer corresponding to a 0 bit and a right pointer corresponding to a 1 bit.
- **Leaf nodes** hold a pointer to a bucket—a bucket address. Figure 4.11 illustrates a directory and the buckets of the data file.

ALGORITHM 4.3   The search procedure for dynamic hashing.

```
h ← hash value of record;
t ← root node of directory;
i ← 1;
while t is an internal node of the directory do
   begin
   if the i^th bit of h is a 0
        then t ← left son of t
        else t ← right son of t;
   i ← i + 1
   end;
search the bucket whose address is in node t;
```

The search for a record proceeds as shown in Algorithm 4.3. The directory can be stored in main memory unless it becomes too large. If the directory does not fit in one block, it is distributed over two or more levels. Note that directory entries are quite compact. Each internal node holds a tag bit to specify the type of node, plus the left and right pointers. A parent pointer may also be needed. Each leaf node holds a bucket address. Special representations of binary trees can be used to reduce the space needed by left, right, and parent pointers of internal nodes. In general, if a directory of x levels is stored on disk, we need x + 1 block accesses to retrieve a bucket.

If a bucket overflows, it is split into two, and the records are distributed based on the next significant bit in their hash value. For example, if a new record is inserted into the bucket for records whose hash values start with 10—the fourth bucket in Figure 4.11—and causes overflow, then all records whose hash value starts with 100 are placed in the first split bucket, and the second bucket contains those whose hash value starts with 101. The directory is expanded with a new internal node to reflect the split; this node points to two leaf nodes that point to the two buckets. The levels of the binary tree can then expand dynamically. However, the number of levels cannot exceed the number of bits in the hash value.

If the hash function distributes the records uniformly, the directory tree will be balanced. Buckets can be combined if one becomes empty or if the total number of records in two neighboring buckets can fit in a single bucket. In this case, the directory loses an internal node and the two leaf nodes are combined to form a single leaf node that points to the new bucket. Thus the levels of the binary tree can shrink dynamically.

Extendible Hashing. In extendible hashing, a different type of **directory**—an array of 2^d bucket addresses—is maintained, where d is called the **global depth** of the directory. The integer value corresponding to the first (high-order) d bits of a hash value is used as an index to the array to determine a directory entry, and the address in that entry determines the bucket in which the corresponding records are stored. However, there does not have to be a distinct bucket for each of the 2^d directory locations. Several directory locations with the same first d' bits for their hash values may contain the same bucket address if all the records that hash to these locations fit in a single bucket. A

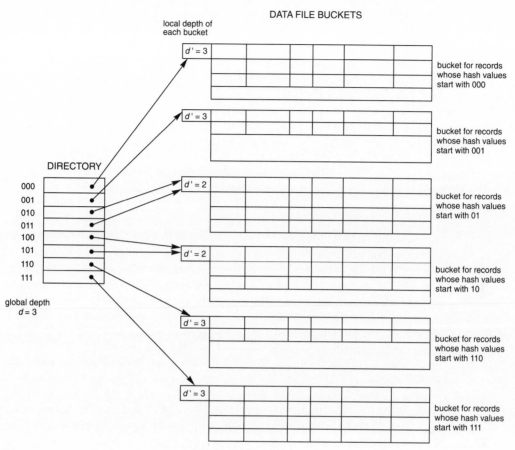

DATA FILE BUCKETS

local depth of
each bucket

$d' = 3$ — bucket for records whose hash values start with 000

$d' = 3$ — bucket for records whose hash values start with 001

DIRECTORY

000
001
010
011
100
101
110
111

global depth
$d = 3$

$d' = 2$ — bucket for records whose hash values start with 01

$d' = 2$ — bucket for records whose hash values start with 10

$d' = 3$ — bucket for records whose hash values start with 110

$d' = 3$ — bucket for records whose hash values start with 111

Figure 4.12   Structure of the extendible hashing scheme.

local depth d'—stored with each bucket—specifies the number of bits on which the
bucket contents are based. Figure 4.12 shows a directory with global depth d = 3.

The value of d can be increased or decreased by one at a time, thus doubling or
halving the number of entries in the directory array. Doubling is needed if a bucket
whose local depth d' is equal to the global depth d overflows. Halving occurs if d > d'
for all the buckets after some deletions occur. Most record retrievals require two block
accesses—one to the directory, and the other to the bucket.

To illustrate bucket splitting, suppose that a new inserted record causes overflow in
the bucket whose hash values start with 01—the third bucket in Figure 4.12. The
records will be distributed among two buckets: the first contains all records whose hash
values start with 010, and the second all those whose hash values start with 011. Now
the two directory locations for 010 and 011 point to the two new distinct buckets. Before
the split, they pointed to the same bucket. The local depth d' of the two new buckets
is 3, which is one more than the local depth of the old bucket.

If a bucket that overflows and is split used to have a local depth d' equal to the global depth d of the directory, then the size of the directory must now be doubled so that we can use an extra bit to distinguish the two new buckets. For example, if the bucket for records whose hash values start with 111 in Figure 4.12 overflows, the two new buckets need a directory with global depth $d = 4$, because the two buckets are now labeled 1110 and 1111, and hence their local depths are both 4. The directory size is hence doubled, and each of the other original locations in the directory is also split into two locations, both of which have the same pointer as did the original location. The maximum directory size is 2^k, where k is the number of bits in a hash value.

Linear Hashing. The idea behind linear hashing is to allow a hash file to expand and shrink its number of buckets dynamically *without* needing a directory. Suppose that the file starts with M buckets numbered 0, 1, . . ., M − 1 and uses the mod hash function $h(K) = K \bmod M$; this hash function is called the initial hash function h_0. Overflow because of collisions is still handled by maintaining individual overflow chains for each bucket. However, when a collision leads to an overflow record in *any* file bucket, the *first* bucket in the file—bucket 0—is split into two buckets: the original bucket 0 and a new bucket M at the end of the file. The records originally in bucket 0 are distributed among the two buckets based on a different hashing function $h_1(K) = K \bmod 2M$. A key property of the two hash functions h_0 and h_1 is that any records that hashed to bucket 0 based on h_0 will hash to either bucket 0 or bucket M based on h_1; this is necessary for linear hashing to work.

As further collisions leading to overflow records occur, additional buckets are split in the *linear* order 1, 2, 3, ... If enough overflows occur, all file buckets are split, so the records in overflow are redistributed into regular buckets, using the function h_1 via a *delayed split* of their buckets. There is no directory; only a value n is needed to determine which buckets have been split. To retrieve a record with hash key value K, first apply the function h_0 to K; if $h_0(K) < n$, then apply the function h_1 on K because the bucket is already split. Initially, $n = 0$, indicating that the function h_0 applies to all buckets; n grows linearly as buckets are split.

When $n = M$, all the original buckets have been split and the hash function h_1 applies to all records in the file. At this point, n is reset to 0 (zero), and any new collisions causing overflow lead to the use of a new hashing function $h_2(K) = K \bmod 4M$. In general, a sequence of hashing functions $h_j(K) = K \bmod (2^j M)$ is used, where $j = 0$, 1, 2, . . . ; a new hashing function h_{j+1} is needed whenever all the buckets 0, 1, . . ., $(2^j M) - 1$ have been split and n is reset to 0. The search for a record with hash key value K is given by Algorithm 4.4.

Buckets that have been split can also be recombined if the load of the file falls below a certain threshold. In general, the **file load factor** l can be defined as $l = r/(\text{bfr} * N)$, where r is the current number of file records, bfr is the maximum number of records that can fit in a bucket, and N is the current number of file buckets. Blocks are combined linearly, and N is decremented appropriately. The file load can be used to trigger both splits and combinations; in this manner the file load can be kept within a desired range. Splits can be triggered when the load exceeds a certain threshold—say, 0.9—and combinations can be triggered when the load falls below another threshold—say, 0.7.

ALGORITHM 4.4   The search procedure for linear hashing.

```
if n = 0
   then m ← hⱼ(K) (* m is the hash value of record with hash key K *)
   else begin
        m ← hⱼ(K);
        if m<n then m ← h_{j+1} (K)
        end;
search the bucket whose hash value is m (and its overflow, if any);
```

4.9   Other Primary File Organizations⋆

4.9.1   *Files of Mixed Records*

The file organizations we have studied so far assume that all records of a particular file are of the same record type. The records could be of EMPLOYEEs, PROJECTs, STUDENTs, or DEPARTMENTs, but each file contains records of only one type. In most database applications, we encounter situations in which numerous types of entities are interrelated in various ways, as we saw in Chapter 3. Relationships among records in various files can be represented by **connecting fields.** For example, a STUDENT record can have a connecting field MAJORDEPT whose value gives the name of the DEPARTMENT in which the student is majoring. This MAJORDEPT field *refers* to a DEPARTMENT entity, which should be represented by a record of its own in the DEPARTMENT file. If we want to retrieve field values from two related records, we must retrieve one of the records first. Then we can use its connecting field value to retrieve the related record in the other file. Hence, relationships are implemented by **logical field references** among the records in distinct files.

File organizations in hierarchical and network DBMSs implement relationships among records as **physical relationships** realized by physical contiguity of related records or by physical pointers. These file organizations typically assign an **area** of the disk to hold records of more than one type so that records of different record types can be physically related. If a particular relationship is expected to be used very frequently, implementing the relationship physically can increase the system's efficiency at retrieving related records. For example, if the query to retrieve a DEPARTMENT record and all records for STUDENTs majoring in that department is very frequent, it would be desirable to place each DEPARTMENT record and its cluster of STUDENT records contiguously on disk in a mixed file.

To distinguish the records in a mixed file, each record has—in addition to its field values—a **record type** field, which specifies the type of record. This is typically the first field in each record and is used by the system software to determine the type of record it is about to process. Using the catalog information, the DBMS can determine the fields of that record type and their sizes, in order to interpret the record data.

4.9.2 B-Trees and Other Data Structures

Other data structures can be used for primary file organizations. For example, if both the record size and the number of records in a file are small, some DBMSs offer the option of using a B-tree data structure as the primary file organization. We will describe B-trees in Section 5.3.1, when we discuss the use of the B-tree data structure for indexing. In general, any data structure that can be adapted to the characteristics of disk devices can be used as a primary file organization for record placement on disk.

4.10 Summary

In this chapter we started by discussing the characteristics of secondary storage devices. We concentrated on magnetic disks because they are used most often to store on-line database files. Data on disk is stored in blocks; accessing a disk block is expensive because of the seek time, rotational delay, and block transfer time. Double buffering can be used when accessing consecutive disk blocks, to reduce the average block access time. Other disk parameters are discussed in Appendix B.

We discussed different ways of storing records of a file on disk. Records of a file are grouped into disk blocks and can be of fixed length or variable length, spanned or unspanned, and same record type or mixed. We discussed the file header, which describes the record formats and keeps track of the disk addresses of the file blocks. Information in the file header is used by system software accessing the file records.

We then presented a set of typical commands for accessing individual file records and discussed the concept of the current record of a file. We discussed how complex record search conditions are transformed into simple search conditions that are used to locate records in the file.

Three primary file organizations were then discussed: unordered, ordered, and hashed. Unordered files require a linear search to locate records, but record insertion is very simple. We discussed the deletion problem and the use of deletion markers.

Ordered files shorten the time required to read records in order of the ordering field. The time required to search for an arbitrary record, given the value of its ordering key field, is also reduced if a binary search is used. However, maintaining the records in order makes insertion very expensive; thus the technique of using an unordered overflow file to reduce the cost of record insertion was discussed. Overflow records are merged with the master file periodically during file reorganization.

Hashing provides very fast access to an arbitrary record of a file, given the value of its hash field. The most suitable method for external hashing is the bucket technique, with one or more contiguous blocks corresponding to each bucket. Collisions causing bucket overflow are handled by chaining. Access on any nonhash field is slow, and so is sequential access of the records on any field. We then discussed hashing techniques that allow the file to expand and shrink dynamically, including dynamic, extendible, and linear hashing.

Finally, we briefly discussed other possibilities for primary file organizations, such as B-trees, and files of mixed records, which implement relationships among records of different types physically as part of the storage structure.

Review Questions

4.1. What is the difference between primary and secondary storage?

4.2. Why are disks and not tapes used to store on-line database files?

4.3. Define the following terms: *disk, disk pack, track, block, cylinder, sector, interblock gap, read/write head.*

4.4. Discuss the process of disk initialization.

4.5. Discuss the mechanism used to read data from or write data to the disk.

4.6. What are the components of a disk block address?

4.7. Why is accessing a disk block expensive? Discuss the time components involved in accessing a disk block.

4.8. How does double buffering improve block access time?

4.9. What are the different reasons for having variable-length records? What type of separator characters is needed for each?

4.10. Discuss the different techniques for allocating file blocks on disk.

4.11. What is the difference between a file organization and an access method?

4.12. What is the difference between a selection condition and a search condition?

4.13. What are the typical record-at-a-time operations for accessing a file? Which of these depend on the current record of a file?

4.14. Discuss the different techniques for record deletion.

4.15. Discuss the advantages and disadvantages of using (a) an unordered file, (b) an ordered file, and (c) a regular (static) hash file with buckets and chaining. Which operations can be efficiently performed on each of these organizations, and which operations are expensive?

4.16. Discuss the different techniques for allowing a hash file to expand and shrink dynamically. What are the advantages and disadvantages of each?

4.17. What are mixed files used for? What are other types of primary file organizations?

Exercises

4.18. Consider a disk with the following characteristics (these are not parameters of any particular disk unit): block size B = 512 bytes; interblock gap size G = 128 bytes; number of blocks per track = 20; number of tracks per surface = 400. A disk pack consists of 15 double-sided disks.

   a. What is the total capacity of a track, and what is its useful capacity (excluding interblock gaps)?

   b. How many cylinders are there?

   c. What are the total capacity and the useful capacity of a cylinder?

   d. What are the total capacity and the useful capacity of a disk pack?

e. Suppose that the disk drive rotates the disk pack at a speed of 2400 rpm (revolutions per minute); what are the transfer rate in bytes/msec and the block transfer time (btt) in msec? What is the average rotational delay (rd) in msec? What is the bulk transfer rate (see Appendix B)?

f. Suppose that the average seek time is 30 msec. How much time does it take (on the average) in msec to locate and transfer a single block, given its block address?

g. Calculate the average time it would take to transfer 20 random blocks, and compare this with the time it would take to transfer 20 consecutive blocks using double buffering to save seek time and rotational delay.

4.19. A file has r = 20,000 STUDENT records of *fixed length*. Each record has the following fields: NAME (30 bytes), SSN (9 bytes), ADDRESS (40 bytes), PHONE (9 bytes), BIRTHDATE (8 bytes), SEX (1 byte), MAJORDEPTCODE (4 bytes), MINORDEPTCODE (4 bytes), CLASSCODE (4 bytes, integer), and DEGREEPROGRAM (3 bytes). An additional byte is used as a deletion marker. The file is stored on the disk whose parameters are given in Exercise 4.18.

a. Calculate the record size R in bytes.

b. Calculate the blocking factor bfr and the number of file blocks b, assuming an unspanned organization.

c. Calculate the average time it takes to find a record by doing a linear search on the file if (i) the file blocks are stored contiguously, and double buffering is used; (ii) the file blocks are not stored contiguously.

d. Assume that the file is ordered by SSN; calculate the time it takes to search for a record given its SSN value, by doing a binary search.

4.20. Suppose that only 80% of the STUDENT records from Exercise 4.19 have a value for PHONE, 85% for MAJORDEPTCODE, 15% for MINORDEPTCODE, and 90% for DEGREEPROGRAM; and suppose that we use a variable-length record file. Each record has a 1-byte *field type* for each field occurring in the record, plus the 1-byte deletion marker and a 1-byte end-of-record marker. Suppose that we use a *spanned* record organization, where each block has a 5-byte pointer to the next block (this space is not used for record storage).

a. Calculate the average record length R in bytes.

b. Calculate the number of blocks needed for the file.

4.21. Suppose that a disk unit has the following parameters: seek time s = 20 msec; rotational delay rd = 10 msec; block transfer time btt = 1 msec; block size B = 2400 bytes; interblock gap size G = 600 bytes. An EMPLOYEE file has the following fields: SSN, 9 bytes; LASTNAME, 20 bytes; FIRSTNAME, 20 bytes; MIDDLE INIT, 1 byte; BIRTHDATE, 10 bytes; ADDRESS, 35 bytes; PHONE, 12 bytes; SUPERVISORSSN, 9 bytes; DEPARTMENT, 4 bytes; JOBCODE, 4 bytes; *deletion marker*, 1 byte. The EMPLOYEE file has r = 30000 records, fixed-length format, and unspanned blocking. Write down appropriate formulas *and* calculate the following values for the above EMPLOYEE file:

a. The record size R (including the deletion marker), the blocking factor Bfr, and the number of disk blocks b.

b. Calculate the wasted space in each disk block because of the unspanned organization.

c. Calculate the transfer rate tr and the bulk transfer rate btr for this disk unit (see Appendix B for definitions of tr and btr).

d. Calculate the average *number of block accesses* needed to search for an arbitrary record in the file, using linear search.

e. Calculate the average *time* needed in msec to search for an arbitrary record in the file, using linear search, if the file blocks are stored on consecutive disk blocks and double buffering is used.

f. Calculate the average *time* needed in msec to search for an arbitrary record in the file, using linear search, if the file blocks are *not* stored on consecutive disk blocks.

g. Assume that the records are ordered via some key field. Calculate the average *number of block accesses* and the *average time* needed to search for an arbitrary record in the file, using binary search.

4.22. A PARTS file with Part# as hash key includes records with the following Part# values: 2369, 3760, 4692, 4871, 5659, 1821, 1074, 7115, 1620, 2428, 3943, 4750, 6975, 4981, 9208. The file uses eight buckets, numbered 0 to 7. Each bucket is one disk block and holds two records. Load these records into the file in the given order, using the hash function h(K) = K mod 8. Calculate the average number of block accesses for a random retrieval on Part#.

4.23. Load the records of Exercise 4.22 into expandable hash files based on (i) dynamic hashing and (ii) extendible hashing. Show the structure of the directory at each step. For extendible hashing, show the global and local depths at each stage. Use the hash function h(K) = K mod 32.

4.24. Load the records of Exercise 4.22 into an expandable hash file, using linear hashing. Start with a single disk block, using the hash function $h_0 = K \bmod 2^0$, and show how the file grows and how the hash functions change as the records are inserted. Assume that blocks are split whenever an overflow occurs, and show the value of n at each stage.

4.25. Compare the file commands listed in Section 4.5 to those available on a file access method you are familiar with.

4.26. Suppose that we have an unordered file of fixed-length records that uses an unspanned record organization. Outline algorithms for insertion, deletion, and modification of a file record. State any assumptions you make.

4.27. Suppose that we have an ordered file of fixed-length records and an unordered overflow file to handle insertion. Both files use unspanned records. Outline algorithms for insertion, deletion, and modification of a file record and for reorganizing the file. State any assumptions you make.

4.28. Can you think of techniques other than an unordered overflow file that can be used to make insertion in an ordered file more efficient?

4.29. Suppose that we have a hash file of fixed-length records, and suppose that overflow is handled by chaining. Outline algorithms for insertion, deletion, and modification of a file record. State any assumptions you make.

4.30. Can you think of techniques other than chaining to handle bucket overflow in external hashing?

4.31. Write program code that can be used to access individual fields of records under each of the following circumstances. For each case, state the assumptions you make concerning pointers, separator characters, etc. Determine the type of information needed in the file header in order for your code to be general in each case.

   a. Fixed-length records with unspanned blocking.

   b. Fixed-length records with spanned blocking.

   c. Variable-length records with variable-length fields and spanned blocking.

   d. Variable-length records with repeating groups and spanned blocking.

   e. Variable-length records with optional fields and spanned blocking.

   f. Variable-length records that allow all three cases in parts c, d, and e.

Selected Bibliography

Wiederhold (1983) has a detailed discussion and analysis of secondary storage devices and file organizations. Optical disks are described in Berg and Roth (1989) and analyzed in Ford and Christodoulakis (1991). Other textbooks, listed in the bibliography at the end of Chapters 1 and 2, include discussions of the material presented here. Most data structures textbooks, including Knuth (1973), discuss static hashing in more detail; Knuth has a complete discussion of hash functions and collision resolution techniques, as well as of their performance comparison. Knuth also offers a detailed discussion of techniques for sorting external files. Salzberg et al. (1991) describes a distributed external sorting algorithm.

Morris (1968) is an early paper on hashing. Dynamic hashing is due to Larson (1978), and extendible hashing is described in Fagin et al. (1979). Linear hashing is described by Litwin (1980). There are many proposed variations for dynamic, extendible, and linear hashing; for examples, see Cesarini and Soda (1991), Du and Tong (1991), and Hachem and Berra (1992).

Several textbooks have appeared whose main topic is file organizations and access methods: Smith and Barnes (1987), Salzberg (1988), Miller (1987), and Livadas (1989).

CHAPTER 5

Index Structures for Files

In this chapter, we describe **access structures** called **indexes,** which are used to speed up the retrieval of records in response to certain search conditions. Some types of indexes, termed **secondary access paths,** do not affect the physical placement of records on disk; rather, they provide alternative search paths for locating the records efficiently based on the **indexing fields.** Other types of indexes can only be constructed on a file with a particular primary organization. In general, any of the data structures discussed in Chapter 4 can be used to construct a secondary access path. However, the most prevalent types of indexes are based on ordered files (single-level indexes) and tree data structures (multilevel indexes, B^+-trees). Indexes can also be constructed based on hashing or other data structures.

We describe different types of single-level indexes—primary, secondary, and clustering—in Section 5.1. In Section 5.2 we show how single-level indexes can themselves be viewed as ordered files, and we develop the concept of multilevel indexes. We describe B-trees and B^+-trees, which are commonly used to implement dynamically changing multilevel indexes, in Section 5.3. In Section 5.4, we discuss how other data structures—such as hashing—can be used to construct indexes. We also distinguish between logical indexes and physical indexes.

5.1 Types of Single-level Ordered Indexes

The idea behind an ordered index access structure is similar to that behind the indexes used commonly in textbooks. A textbook index lists important terms at the end of the book in alphabetic order. Along with each term, a list of page numbers where the term appears is given. We can search the index to find a list of *addresses*—page numbers in this case—and use these addresses to locate the term in the textbook by *searching* the specified pages. The alternative, if no other guidance is given, is to sift slowly through the whole textbook word by word to find the term we are interested in; this corresponds to doing a linear search on a file. Of course, most books do have additional information, such as chapter and section titles, that can help us find a term without having to search through the whole book. However, the index is the only exact indication of where each term occurs in the book.

An index access structure is usually defined on a single field of a file, called an **indexing field.** The index typically stores each value of the index field along with a list of pointers to all disk blocks that contain records with that field value. The values in the index are *ordered* so that we can do a binary search on the index. The index file is much smaller than the data file, so searching the index using a binary search is reasonably efficient. Multilevel indexing does away with the need for a binary search at the expense of creating indexes to the index itself! Multilevel indexing is discussed in Section 5.2.

There are several types of ordered indexes. A **primary index** is an index specified on the *ordering key field* of an ordered file of records. Recall from Section 4.7 that an ordering key field is used to *physically order* the file records on disk, and every record has a *unique value* for that field. If the ordering field is not a key field—that is, if several records in the file can have the same value for the ordering field—another type of index, called a **clustering index,** can be used. Notice that a file can have *at most one* physical ordering field, so it can have at most one primary index or one clustering index, *but not both.* A third type of index, called a **secondary index,** can be specified on any *nonordering* field of a file. A file can have several secondary indexes in addition to its primary access method. In the next three subsections we discuss these three types of indexes.

5.1.1 *Primary Indexes*

A **primary index** is an ordered file whose records are of fixed length with two fields. The first field is of the same data type as the ordering key field of the data file, and the second field is a pointer to a disk block—a block address. The ordering key field is called the **primary key** of the data file. There is one **index entry** (or **index record**) in the index file for each *block* in the data file. Each index entry has the value of the primary key field for the *first* record in a block and a pointer to that block as its two field values. We will refer to the two field values of index entry i as $<K(i), P(i)>$.

To create a primary index on the ordered file shown in Figure 4.7, we use the NAME field as primary key, because that is the ordering key field of the file (assuming that each value of NAME is unique). Each entry in the index has a NAME value and a pointer. The first three index entries are as follows:

$<K(1) = (Aaron,Ed), P(1) = $ address of block 1$>$
$<K(2) = (Adams,John), P(2) = $ address of block 2$>$
$<K(3) = (Alexander,Ed), P(3) = $ address of block 3$>$

Figure 5.1 illustrates this primary index. The total number of entries in the index is the same as the *number of disk blocks* in the ordered data file. The first record in each block of the data file is called the **anchor record** of the block, or simply the **block**

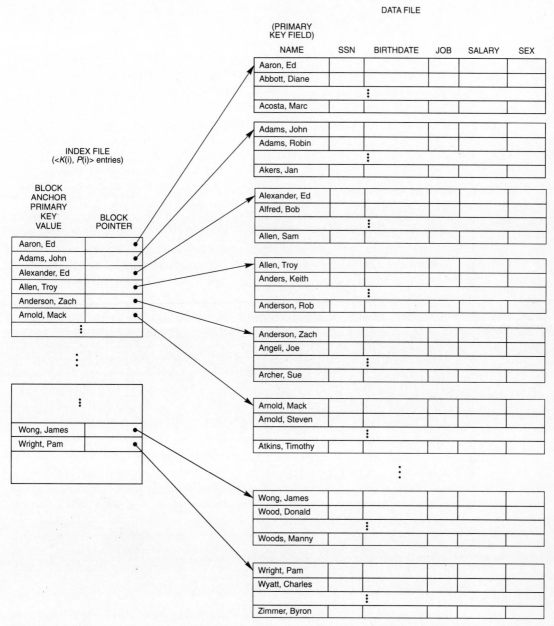

Figure 5.1 Primary index on the ordering key field of the file shown in Figure 4.7.

anchor.* A primary index is an example of a **nondense index:** it includes an entry for each disk block of the data file rather than for *every record* in the data file. A **dense index,** on the other hand, contains an entry for every record in the file.

The index file for a primary index needs substantially fewer blocks than does the data file, for two reasons. First, there are *fewer index entries* than there are records in the data file, because an entry exists for each whole block of the data file rather than for each record. Second, each index entry is typically *smaller in size* than a data record because it has only two fields; consequently, more index entries than data records can fit in one block. A binary search on the index file hence requires fewer block accesses than a binary search on the data file.

A record whose primary key value is K lies in the block whose address is P(i), where $K(i) \le K < K(i + 1)$. The ith block in the data file contains all such records because of the physical ordering of the file records on the primary key field. To retrieve a record, given the value K of its primary key field, we do a binary search on the index file to find the appropriate index entry i, and then retrieve the data file block whose address is P(i). Notice that the above formula would not be correct if the data file were ordered on a *nonkey field* that allowed multiple records to have the same ordering field value. In that case the same index value as that in the block anchor could be repeated in the last records of the previous block. Example 1 illustrates the saving in block accesses that is attainable when an index is used to search for a record.

EXAMPLE 1:   Suppose that we have an ordered file with $r = 30,000$ records stored on a disk with block size $B = 1024$ bytes. File records are of fixed size and are unspanned, with record length $R = 100$ bytes. The blocking factor for the file would be bfr = $\lfloor (B/R) \rfloor = \lfloor (1024/100) \rfloor = 10$ records per block. The number of blocks needed for the file is $b = \lceil (r/bfr) \rceil = \lceil (30,000/10) \rceil = 3000$ blocks. A binary search on the data file would need approximately $\lceil (\log_2 b) \rceil = \lceil (\log_2 3000) \rceil = 12$ block accesses.

Now suppose that the ordering key field of the file is $V = 9$ bytes long, a block pointer is $P = 6$ bytes long, and we have constructed a primary index for the file. The size of each index entry is $R_i = (9 + 6) = 15$ bytes, so the blocking factor for the index is $bfr_i = \lfloor (B/R_i) \rfloor = \lfloor (1024/15) \rfloor = 68$ entries per block. The total number of index entries r_i is equal to the number of blocks in the data file, which is 3000. The number of blocks needed for the index is hence $b_i = \lceil (r_i/bfr_i) \rceil = \lceil (3000/68) \rceil = 45$ blocks. To perform a binary search on the index file would need $\lceil (\log_2 b_i) \rceil = \lceil (\log_2 45) \rceil = 6$ block accesses. To search for a record using the index, we need one additional block access to the data file for a total of $6 + 1 = 7$ block accesses—an improvement over binary search on the data file, which required 12 block accesses. ■

A major problem with a primary index—as with any ordered file—is insertion and deletion of records. With a primary index, the problem is compounded because, if we attempt to insert a record in its correct position in the data file, we not only have to move records to make space for the new record but also have to change some index

---

*We can use a scheme similar to the one described here, with the last record in each block (rather than the first) as the block anchor. This slightly improves the efficiency of the search algorithm.

entries, since moving records will change the anchor records of some blocks. We can use an unordered overflow file, as discussed in Section 4.7, to reduce this problem. Another possibility is to use a linked list of overflow records for each block in the data file. This is similar to the method of dealing with overflow records described with hashing in Section 4.8.2. Records within each block and its overflow linked list can be sorted to improve retrieval time. Record deletion is handled using deletion markers.

5.1.2 Clustering Indexes

If records of a file are physically ordered on a nonkey field that *does not have a distinct value* for each record, that field is called the **clustering field.** We can create a different type of index, called a **clustering index,** to speed up retrieval of records that have the same value for the clustering field. This differs from a primary index, which requires that the ordering field of the data file have a *distinct value* for each record.

A clustering index is also an ordered file with two fields; the first field is of the same type as the clustering field of the data file, and the second field is a block pointer. There is one entry in the clustering index for each *distinct value* of the clustering field, containing the value and a pointer to the *first block* in the data file that has a record with that value for its clustering field. Figure 5.2 shows an example of a data file with a clustering index. Notice that record insertion and record deletion still cause problems, because the data records are physically ordered. To alleviate the problem of insertion, it is common to reserve a whole block for *each value* of the clustering field; all records with that value are placed in the block. If more than one block is needed to store the records for a particular value, additional blocks are allocated and linked together. This makes insertion and deletion relatively straightforward. Figure 5.3 shows this scheme.

A clustering index is another example of a *nondense* index, because it has an entry for every *distinct value* of the indexing field rather than for every record in the file. There is some similarity between Figures 5.1 to 5.3, on the one hand, and Figures 4.11 and 4.12, on the other. An index is somewhat similar to the directory structures used for dynamic and extendible hashing, described in Section 4.8.3. Both are searched to find a pointer to the data block containing the desired record. A main difference is that an index search uses the values of the search field itself, whereas a hash directory search uses the hash value that is calculated by applying the hash function to the search field.

5.1.3 Secondary Indexes

A **secondary index** also is an ordered file with two fields. The first field is of the same data type as some *nonordering field* of the data file and is called an **indexing field** of the file. The second field is either a *block* pointer or a *record* pointer. There can be *many* secondary indexes (and hence, indexing fields) for the same file.

We first consider a secondary index access structure on a key field—a field having a *distinct value* for every record in the data file. Such a field is sometimes called a **secondary key.** In this case there is one index entry for *each record* in the data file, which contains the value of the secondary key for the record and a pointer either to the block in which the record is stored or to the record itself. A secondary index on a key field is a **dense** index: it contains one entry for each record in the data file.

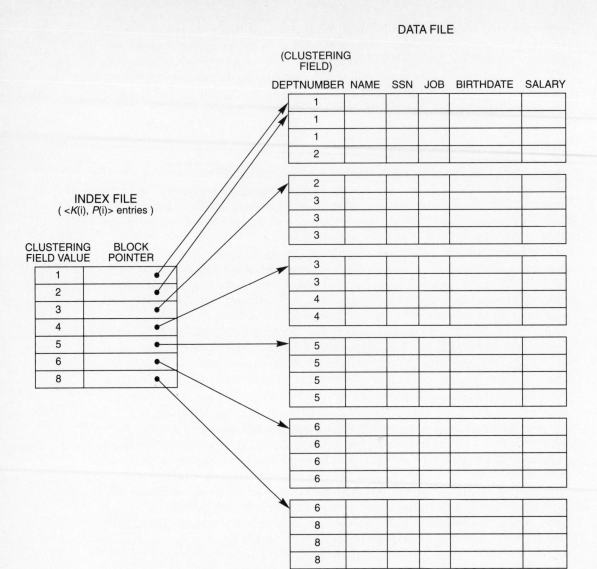

Figure 5.2   A clustering index on the DEPTNUMBER ordering field of an
EMPLOYEE file.

We again refer to the two field values of index entry i as $<K(i), P(i)>$. The entries are **ordered** by value of $K(i)$, so we can perform a binary search on the index. Because the records of the data file are *not* physically ordered by values of the secondary key field, we cannot use block anchors. That is why an index entry is created for each record in the data file, rather than for each block as in the case of a primary index. Figure 5.4 illustrates a secondary index in which the pointers $P(i)$ in the index entries are *block pointers*, not record pointers. Once the appropriate block is transferred to main memory, a search for the desired record within the block can be carried out.

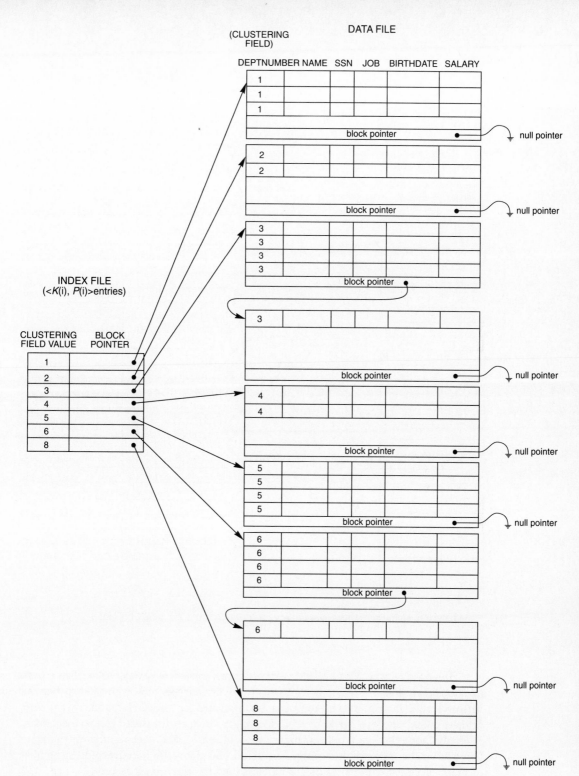

Figure 5.3 Clustering index with separate blocks for each group of records that share the same value for the clustering field.

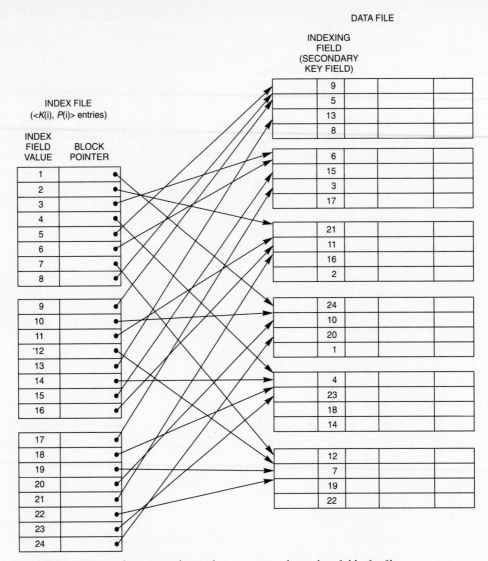

Figure 5.4   A dense secondary index on a nonordering key field of a file.

A secondary index usually needs more storage space and longer search time than does a primary index, because of its larger number of entries. However, the *improvement* in search time for an arbitrary record is much greater for a secondary index than for a primary index, since we would have to do a *linear search* on the data file if the secondary index did not exist. For a primary index, we could still use a binary search on the main file, even if the index did not exist. Example 2 illustrates the improvement in number of blocks accessed when a secondary index is used to search for a record.

EXAMPLE 2: Consider the file of Example 1 with $r = 30,000$ fixed-length records of size $R = 100$ bytes stored on a disk with block size $B = 1024$ bytes. The file has $b = 3000$ blocks, as calculated in Example 1. To do a linear search on the file, we would require $b/2 = 3000/2 = 1500$ block accesses on the average. Suppose that we construct a secondary index on a nonordering key field of the file that is $V = 9$ bytes long. As in Example 1, a block pointer is $P = 6$ bytes long, so each index entry is $R_i = (9 + 6) = 15$ bytes, and the blocking factor for the index is $bfr_i = \lfloor (B/R_i) \rfloor = \lfloor (1024/15) \rfloor = 68$ entries per block. In a dense secondary index such as this, the total number of index entries r_i is equal to the *number of records* in the data file, which is 30,000. The number of blocks needed for the index is hence $b_i = \lceil (r_i/bfr_i) \rceil = \lceil (30,000/68) \rceil = 442$ blocks. Compare this to the 45 blocks needed by the nondense primary index in Example 1.

A binary search on this secondary index needs $\lceil (\log_2 b_i) \rceil = \lceil (\log_2 442) \rceil = 9$ block accesses. To search for a record using the index, we need an additional block access to the data file for a total of $9 + 1 = 10$ block accesses—a vast improvement over the 1500 block accesses needed on the average for a linear search, but slightly worse than the 7 block accesses required for the primary index. ■

We can also create a secondary index on a *nonkey field* of a file. In this case, numerous records in the data file can have the same value for the indexing field. There are several options for implementing such an index:

- Option 1 is to include several index entries with the same $K(i)$ value—one for each record. This would be a dense index.

- Option 2 is to have variable-length records for the index entries, with a repeating field for the pointer. We keep a list of pointers $<P(i,1), \ldots, P(i,k)>$ in the index entry for $K(i)$—one pointer to each block that contains a record whose indexing field value equals $K(i)$. In either option 1 or option 2, the binary search algorithm on the index must be modified appropriately.

- Option 3, which is more commonly used, is to keep the index entries themselves at a fixed length and have a single entry for each *index field value*, but create an extra level of indirection to handle the multiple pointers. In this nondense scheme, the pointer $P(i)$ in index entry $<K(i), P(i)>$ points to a *block of record pointers*; each record pointer in that block points to one of the data file records with value $K(i)$ for the indexing field. If some value $K(i)$ occurs in too many records, so that their record pointers cannot fit in a single disk block, a linked list of blocks is used. This technique is illustrated in Figure 5.5. Retrieval via the index requires an additional block access because of the extra level, but the algorithms for searching the index and (more important) for inserting of new records in the data file are straightforward. In addition, retrievals on complex selection conditions may be handled by referring to the pointers, without having to retrieve many unnecessary file records (see Exercise 5.16).

Notice that a secondary index provides a **logical ordering** on the records by the indexing field. If we access the records in order of the entries in the secondary index, we get them in order of the indexing field.

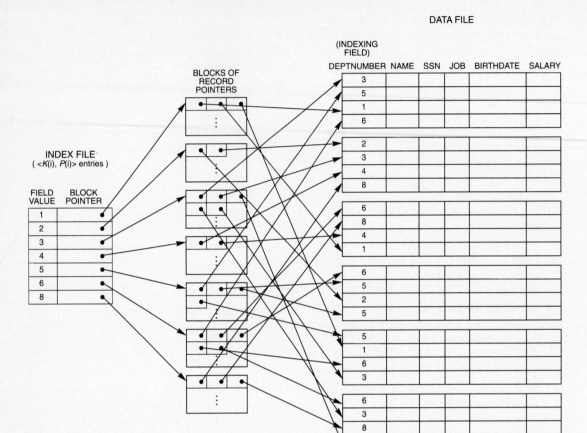

Figure 5.5   A secondary index on a nonkey field implemented using one level
of indirection so that index entries are of fixed length and have
unique field values.

5.1.4 *Summary*

To conclude this section, we summarize the discussion on index types in two tables. Table
5.1 shows the index field characteristics of each type of ordered single-level index discussed—primary, clustering, and secondary. Table 5.2 summarizes the properties of each
type of index by comparing the number of index entries and specifying which indexes
are dense and which use block anchors of the data file.

Table 5.1   Types of Indexes

	Ordering Field	**Nonordering Field**
Key field	Primary index	Secondary index (key)
Nonkey field	Clustering index	Secondary index (nonkey)

Table 5.2 Properties of Index Types

		Properties of Index Type		
		Number of (First-level) Index Entries	Dense or Nondense	Block Anchoring on the Data File
	Primary	Number of blocks in data file	Nondense	Yes
Type	Clustering	Number of distinct index field values	Nondense	Yes/no[a]
of	Secondary	Number of records in data file	Dense	No
Index	(key)			
	Secondary	Number of records[b] or	Dense or	No
	(nonkey)	Number of distinct index field values[c]	Nondense	

[a]Yes if every distinct value of the ordering field starts a new block; no otherwise.
[b]For option 1.
[c]For options 2 and 3.

5.2 Multilevel Indexes

The indexing schemes we have described thus far involve an ordered index file. A binary search is applied to the index to locate pointers to a record (or records) in the file having a specific index field value. A binary search requires approximately $(\log_2 b_i)$ block accesses for an index with b_i blocks, because each step of the algorithm reduces the part of the index file that we continue to search by a factor of 2. This is why we take the log function to the base 2. The idea behind a **multilevel index** is to reduce the part of the index that we continue to search by bfr_i, the blocking factor for the index, which is larger than 2. Hence, the search space is reduced much faster. The value bfr_i is called the **fan-out** of the multilevel index, and we will refer to it by the symbol **fo**. Searching a multilevel index requires approximately $(\log_{fo} b_i)$ block accesses, which is a smaller number than for binary search if the fan-out is larger than 2.

A multilevel index considers the index file, which we will now refer to as the **first** (or **base**) **level** of a multilevel index, as an *ordered file* with a *distinct value* for each K(i). Hence we can create a primary index for the first level; this index to the first level is called the **second level** of the multilevel index. Because the second level is a primary index, we can use block anchors so that the second level has one entry for *each block* of the first level. The blocking factor bfr_i for the second level—and for all subsequent levels—is the same as that for the first-level index, because all index entries are the same size; each has one field value and one block address. If the first level has r_1 entries, and the blocking factor—which is also the fan-out—for the index is $bfr_i = fo$, then the first level needs $\lceil (r_1/fo) \rceil$ blocks, which is therefore the number of entries r_2 needed at the second level of the index.

We can repeat this process for the second level. The **third level**, which is a primary index for the second level, has an entry for each second-level block, so the number of third-level entries is $r_3 = \lceil (r_2/fo) \rceil$. Notice that we require a second level only if the first level needs more than one block of disk storage, and, similarly, we require a third level only if the second level needs more than one block. We can repeat the preceding process until all the entries of some index level t fit in a single block. This block at the tth level is called the **top** index level.* Each level reduces the number of entries at the previous level by a factor of fo—the index fan-out—so we can use the formula $1 \leq (r_1/((fo)^t))$ to calculate t. Hence, a multilevel index with r_1 first-level entries will have approximately t levels, where $t = \lceil (\log_{fo}(r_1)) \rceil$.

The multilevel scheme described here can be used on any type of index, whether it is a primary, a clustering, or a secondary index, as long as the first-level index has *distinct values for K(i) and fixed-length entries*. Figure 5.6 shows a multilevel index built over a primary index. Example 3 illustrates the improvement in number of blocks accessed when a multilevel index is used to search for a record.

EXAMPLE 3: Suppose that the dense secondary index of Example 2 is converted into a multilevel index. We calculated the index blocking factor $bfr_i = 68$ index entries per block, which is also the fan-out fo for the multilevel index; the number of first-level blocks $b_1 = 442$ blocks was also calculated. The number of second-level blocks will be $b_2 = \lceil (b_1/fo) \rceil = \lceil (442/68) \rceil = 7$ blocks, and the number of third-level blocks will be $b_3 = \lceil (b_2/fo) \rceil = \lceil (7/68) \rceil = 1$ block. Hence, the third level is the top level of the index, and $t = 3$. To access a record by searching the multilevel index, we must access one block at each level plus one block from the data file, so we need $t + 1 = 3 + 1 = 4$ block accesses. Compare this to Example 2, where 10 block accesses were needed when a single-level index and binary search were used. ∎

Notice that we could also have a multilevel primary index, which would be non-dense. Exercise 5.10c illustrates this case, where we *must* access the data block from the file before we can determine whether the record being searched for is in the file. For a dense index, this can be determined by accessing the first index level (without having to access a data block), since there is an index entry for *every* record in the file.

Algorithm 5.1 outlines the search procedure for a record in a data file that uses a nondense multilevel primary index with t levels. We refer to entry i at level j of the index as $<K_j(i), P_j(i)>$, and we search for a record whose primary key value is K. We assume that any overflow records are ignored. If the record is in the file, there must be some entry at level 1 with $K_1(i) \leq K < K_1(i + 1)$ and the record will be in the block of the data file whose address is $P_1(i)$. Exercise 5.15 discusses modifying the search algorithm for other types of indexes.

ALGORITHM 5.1 Searching a nondense multilevel primary index with t levels.

$p \leftarrow$ address of top level block of index;
for $j \leftarrow t$ step $- 1$ to 1 do
    begin
    read the index block (at j^{th} index level) whose address is p;
    search block p for entry i such that $K_j(i) \leq K < K_j(i + 1)$ (if $K_j(i)$ is the
        last entry in the block, it is sufficient to satisfy $K_j(i) \leq K$);

---

*The numbering scheme for index levels used here is the *reverse* of the way levels are commonly defined for tree data structures. In tree data structures, t is referred to as level 0 (zero), $t - 1$ is level 1, etc.

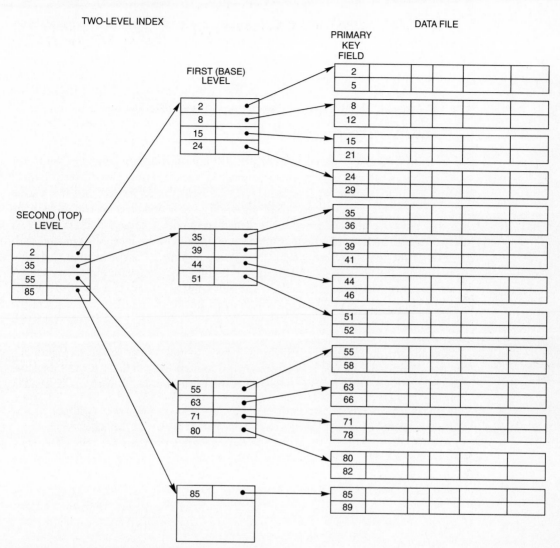

Figure 5.6 A two-level primary index.

         $p \leftarrow P_j(i)$ (* picks appropriate pointer at j^{th} index level *)
         end;
    read the data file block whose address is p;
    search block p for record with key = K;

As we have seen, a multilevel index reduces the number of blocks accessed when searching for a record, given its indexing field value. We are still faced with the problems of dealing with index insertions and deletions, because all index levels are *physically ordered files*. To retain the benefits of using multilevel indexing while reducing index insertion and deletion problems, designers often adopt a multilevel index that leaves some space in each of its blocks for inserting new entries. This is called a **dynamic multilevel index** and is often implemented by using data structures called B-trees and B^+-trees.

5.3 Dynamic Multilevel Indexes Using B-Trees and B^+-Trees

B-trees and B^+-trees are special cases of the well-known tree data structure. We introduce very briefly the terminology used in discussing tree data structures. A **tree** is formed of **nodes**. Each node in the tree, except for a special node called the **root,** has one **parent** node and several—zero or more—**child** nodes. The root node has no parent. A node that does not have any child nodes is called a **leaf** node; a nonleaf node is called an **internal** node. The **level** of a node is always one more than the level of its parent, with the level of the root node being zero.* A **subtree** of a node consists of that node and all its **descendent** nodes—its child nodes, the child nodes of its child nodes, etc. A precise recursive definition of a subtree is that it consists of a node n and the subtrees of all the child nodes of n. Figure 5.7 illustrates a tree data structure. In this figure the root node is A; and its child nodes are B, C, and D. Nodes E, J, C, G, H, and K are leaf nodes.

Usually, we display a tree with the root node at the top, as shown in Figure 5.7. One way to implement a tree is to have as many pointers in each node as there are child nodes of that node. In some cases, a parent pointer is also stored in each node. In addi-

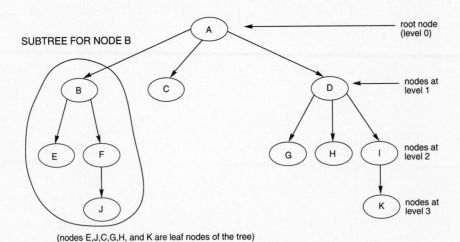

(nodes E,J,C,G,H, and K are leaf nodes of the tree)

Figure 5.7   A tree data structure.

*This standard definition of the level of a tree node, which we use throughout Section 5.3, is different from the one we gave for multilevel indexes in Section 5.2.

tion to pointers, a node usually contains some kind of stored information. When a multi-level index is implemented as a tree structure, this information includes the values of the file's indexing field that are used to guide the search for a particular record.

In Section 5.3.1, we introduce search trees and then discuss B-trees, which can be used as dynamic multilevel indexes to guide the search for records in a data file. B-tree nodes are kept between 50% and 100% full, and pointers to the data blocks are stored in both internal nodes and leaf nodes of the B-tree structure. In Section 5.3.2 we discuss B$^+$-trees, a variation of B-trees in which pointers to the data blocks of a file are stored only in leaf nodes; this can lead to fewer levels and higher-capacity indexes.

5.3.1 Search Trees and B-Trees

A search tree is a special type of tree that is used to guide the search for a record, given the value of one of its fields. The multilevel indexes discussed in Section 5.2 can be thought of as a variation of a search tree. Each node in the multilevel index can have as many as *fo* pointers and *fo* key values, where *fo* is the index fan-out. The index field values in each node guide us to the next node, until we reach the data file block that contains the required records. By following a pointer, we restrict our search at each level to a subtree of the search tree and ignore all nodes not in this subtree.

Search Trees. A search tree is slightly different from a multilevel index. A **search tree** of order p is a tree such that each node contains *at most* p − 1 search values and p pointers in the order $<P_1, K_1, P_2, K_2, \ldots, P_{q-1}, K_{q-1}, P_q>$, where q ≤ p, each P_i is a pointer to a child node (or a null pointer), and each K_i is a search value from some ordered set of values. All search values are assumed to be unique.* Figure 5.8 illustrates a node of a search tree. Two constraints must hold at all times on the search tree:

1. Within each node, $K_1 < K_2 < \cdots < K_{q-1}$.
2. For all values X in the subtree pointed at by P_i, we have $K_{i-1} < X < K_i$ for 1 < i < q, $X < K_i$ for i = 1, and $K_{i-1} < X$ for i = q (see Figure 5.8).

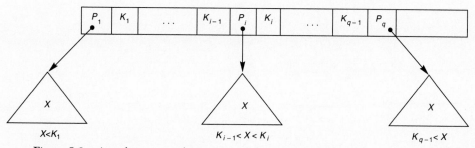

Figure 5.8 A node in a search tree.

---

*This restriction can be relaxed, but then the following formulas must be modified.

Whenever we search for a value X, we follow the appropriate pointer P_i according to the formulas in condition 2 above. Figure 5.9 illustrates a search tree of order p = 3 and integer search values. Notice that some of the pointers P_i in a node may be **null** pointers.

We can use a search tree as a mechanism to search for records stored in a disk file. The values in the tree can be the values of one of the fields of the file, called the **search field** (same as the index field if a multilevel index guides the search). Each value in the tree is associated with a pointer to the record in the data file having that value. Alternatively, the pointer could be to the disk block containing that record. The search tree itself can be stored on disk by assigning each tree node to a disk block. When a new record is inserted, we must update the search tree by including the search field value of the new record and a pointer to the new record in the search tree.

Algorithms are necessary for inserting and deleting search values into and from the search tree while maintaining the preceding two constraints. In general, these algorithms do not guarantee that a search tree is **balanced,** meaning that all of its leaf nodes are at the same level.* Keeping a search tree balanced is important because it guarantees that no nodes will be at very high levels and hence require many block accesses during a tree search. Another problem with search trees is that record deletion may leave some nodes in the tree nearly empty, thus wasting storage space and increasing the number of levels.

B-Trees. The B-tree—a search tree with some additional constraints on it—solves both of the above problems to some extent. The additional constraints ensure that the tree is always balanced and that the space wasted by deletion, if any, never becomes excessive. The algorithms for insertion and deletion, though, become more complex in order to maintain these constraints. Nonetheless, most insertions and deletions are simple processes; they become complicated only under special circumstances—namely, whenever we attempt an insertion into a node that is already full or a deletion from a node that

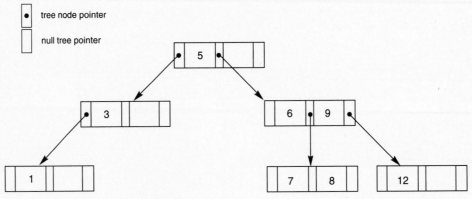

Figure 5.9   A search tree of order p = 3.

---

*The definition of *balanced* is different for binary trees. Balanced binary trees are known as AVL trees.

makes it less than half full. More formally, a **B-tree** of **order** p, when used as an access structure on a *key field* to search for records in a data file, can be defined as follows:

1. Each internal node in the B-tree (Figure 5.10(a)) is of the form

   $$<P_1, <K_1, Pr_1>, P_2, <K_2, Pr_2>, \ldots, <K_{q-1}, Pr_{q-1}>, P_q>$$

   where $q \leq p$. Each P_i is a **tree pointer**—a pointer to another node in the B-tree. Each Pr_i is a **data pointer***—a pointer to the record whose search key field value is equal to K_i (or to the data file block containing that record).

2. Within each node, $K_1 < K_2 < \cdots < K_{q-1}$.

3. For all search key field values X in the subtree pointed at by P_i, we have

   $K_{i-1} < X < K_i$ for $1 < i < q$, $X < K_i$ for $i = 1$, and $K_{i-1} < X$ for $i = q$
   (see Figure 5.10(a)).

4. Each node has at most p tree pointers.

5. Each node, except the root and leaf nodes, has at least $\lceil (p/2) \rceil$ tree pointers. The root node has at least two tree pointers unless it is the only node in the tree.

6. A node with q tree pointers, $q \leq p$, has $q - 1$ search key field values (and hence has $q - 1$ data pointers).

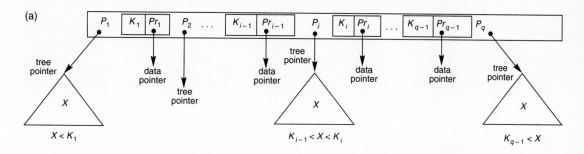

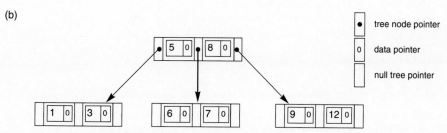

Figure 5.10 B-tree structures. (a) A node in a B-tree with $q - 1$ search values. (b) A B-tree of order $p = 3$. The values were inserted in the order 8,5,1,7,3,12,9,6.

---

*A data pointer is either a block address, or a record address; the latter is essentially a block address *and* an offset.

7. All leaf nodes are at the same level. Leaf nodes have the same structure as internal nodes except that all of their *tree pointers* P_i are **null**.

Figure 5.10(b) illustrates a B-tree of order p = 3. Notice that all search values K in the B-tree are unique because we assumed that the tree is used as an access structure on a key field. If we use a B-tree on a nonkey field, we must change the definition of the file pointers Pr_i to point to a block—or linked list of blocks—that contain pointers to the file records themselves. This extra level of indirection is similar to Option 3, discussed in Section 5.1.3, for secondary indexes.

A B-tree starts with a single root node (which is also a leaf node) at level 0 (zero). Once the root node is full with p − 1 search key values and we attempt to insert another entry in the tree, the root node splits into two nodes at level 1. Only the middle value is kept in the root node, and the rest of the values are split evenly between the other two nodes. When a nonroot node is full and a new entry is inserted into it, that node is split into two nodes at the same level, and the middle entry is moved to the parent node along with two pointers to the split nodes. If the parent node is full, it is also split. Splitting can propagate all the way to the root node, creating a new level every time the root is split. We do not discuss algorithms for B-trees in detail here; rather, we outline search and insertion procedures for B^+-trees in the next section.

If deletion of a value causes a node to be less than half full, it is combined with its neighboring nodes, and this can also propagate all the way to the root. Hence, deletion can reduce the number of tree levels. It has been shown by analysis and simulation that, after numerous random insertions and deletions on a B-tree, the nodes are approximately 69% full when the number of values in the tree stabilizes. This is also true of B^+-trees. If this happens, node splitting and combining will occur only rarely, so insertion and deletion become quite efficient. If the number of values grows, the tree will expand without a problem—although splitting of nodes may occur, so some insertions will take more time. Example 4 illustrates how we calculate the order p of a B-tree stored on disk.

EXAMPLE 4: Suppose the search field is V = 9 bytes long, the disk block size is B = 512 bytes, a record (data) pointer is P_r = 7 bytes, and a block pointer is P = 6 bytes. Each B-tree node can have *at most* p tree pointers, p − 1 data pointers, and p − 1 search key field values (see Figure 5.10(a)). These must fit into a single disk block if each B-tree node is to correspond to a disk block. Hence, we must have

$$(p * P) + ((p - 1) * (P_r + V)) \leq B$$
$$(p * 6) + ((p - 1) * (7 + 9)) \leq 512$$
$$(22 * p) \leq 528$$

We can choose p to be a large value that satisfies the above inequality, which gives p = 23 (p = 24 is not chosen because of the reasons given next). ∎

In general, a B-tree node may contain additional information needed by the algorithms that manipulate the tree, such as the number of entries q in the node and a pointer to the parent node. Hence, before we do the preceding calculation for p, we should reduce the block size by the amount of space needed for all such information. Next, we illustrate how to calculate the number of blocks and levels for a B-tree.

EXAMPLE 5: Suppose that the search field of Example 4 is a nonordering key field, and we construct a B-tree on this field. Assume that each node of the B-tree is 69% full. Each node, on the average, will have $p * 0.69 = 23 * 0.69$ or approximately 16 pointers and, hence, 15 search key field values. The **average fan-out** $fo = 16$. We can start at the root and see how many values and pointers exist, on the average, at each subsequent level:

Root:	1 node	15 entries	16 pointers
Level 1:	16 nodes	240 entries	256 pointers
Level 2:	256 nodes	3840 entries	4096 pointers
Level 3:	4096 nodes	61,440 entries	

At each level, we calculated the number of entries by multiplying the total number of pointers at the previous level by 15, the average number of entries in each node. Hence, for the given block size, pointer size, and search key field size, a two-level B-tree holds up to $3840 + 240 + 15 = 4095$ entries on the average; a three-level B-tree holds up to 65,535 entries on the average. ∎

B-trees are sometimes used as primary file organizations. In this case, whole records are stored within the B-tree nodes rather than just the <search key, record pointer> entries. This works well for files with a relatively *small number of records*, and a *small record size*. Otherwise, the fan-out and the number of levels become too great to permit efficient access.

5.3.2 B⁺-Trees

Most implementations of a dynamic multilevel index use a variation of the B-tree data structure called a **B⁺-tree.** In a B-tree, every value of the search field appears once at some level in the tree, along with a data pointer. In a B⁺-tree, data pointers are stored *only at the leaf nodes* of the tree; hence, the structure of leaf nodes differs from the structure of internal nodes. The leaf nodes have an entry for *every* value of the search field, along with a data pointer to the record (or to the block that contains this record) if the search field is a key field. For a nonkey search field, the pointer points to a block containing pointers to the data file records, creating an extra level of indirection.

The leaf nodes of the B⁺-tree are usually linked together to provide ordered access on the search field to the records. These leaf nodes are similar to the first (base) level of an index. Internal nodes of the B⁺-tree correspond to the other levels of a multilevel index. Some search field values from the leaf nodes are repeated in the internal nodes of the B⁺-tree to guide the search. The structure of the *internal nodes* of a B⁺-tree of order p (Figure 5.11(a)) is as follows:

1. Each internal node is of the form

   $$<P_1, K_1, P_2, K_2, \ldots, P_{q-1}, K_{q-1}, P_q>$$

   where $q \leq p$ and each P_i is a **tree pointer.**

2. Within each internal node, $K_1 < K_2 < \cdots < K_{q-1}$.

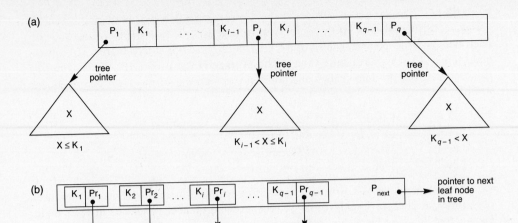

Figure 5.11   The nodes of a B^+-tree. (a) Internal node of a B^+-tree with $q - 1$ search values. (b) Leaf node of a B^+-tree.

3. For all search field values X in the subtree pointed at by P_i, we have $K_{i-1} < X \le K_i$ for $1 < i < q$, $X \le K_i$ for $i = 1$, and $K_{i-1} < X$ for $i = q$ (see Figure 5.11(a)).*

4. Each internal node has at most p tree pointers.

5. Each internal node, except the root, has at least $\lceil (p/2) \rceil$ tree pointers. The root node has at least two tree pointers if it is an internal node.

6. An internal node with q pointers, $q \le p$, has $q - 1$ search field values.

The structure of the *leaf nodes* of a B^+-tree of order p (Figure 5.11(b)), is as follows:

1. Each leaf node is of the form

$$< <K_1, Pr_1>, <K_2, Pr_2>, \ldots, <K_{q-1}, Pr_{q-1}>, P_{next}>$$

where $q \le p$, each Pr_i is a data pointer, and P_{next} points to the next *leaf node* of the B^+-tree.

2. Within each leaf node, $K_1 < K_2 < \cdots < K_{q-1}$, $q \le p$.

3. Each Pr_i is a **data pointer** that points to the record whose search field value is K_i or to a file block containing the record (or to a block of record pointers that point to records whose search field value is K_i if the search field is not a key).

4. Each leaf node has at least $\lfloor (p/2) \rfloor$ values.

5. All leaf nodes are at the same level.

---

*Our definition follows Knuth (1973). One can define a B^+-tree differently by exchanging the $<$ and $\le$ symbols ($K_{i-1} \le X < K_i$; $X < K_1$; $K_{q-1} \le X$), but the principles remain the same.

For a B$^+$-tree constructed on a key field, the pointers in internal nodes are *tree pointers* to blocks that are tree nodes, whereas the pointers in leaf nodes are *data pointers* to the data file records or blocks—except for the P$_{next}$ pointer, which is a tree pointer to the next leaf node. By starting at the leftmost leaf node, it is possible to traverse leaf nodes as a linked list, using the P$_{next}$ pointers. This provides ordered access to the data records on the indexing field. A P$_{previous}$ pointer can also be included. For a B$^+$-tree on a nonkey field, an extra level of indirection is needed similar to the one shown in Figure 5.5, so the Pr pointers are block pointers to blocks that contain a set of record pointers to the actual records in the data file, as discussed in Option 3 of Section 5.1.3.

Because entries in the *internal nodes* of a B$^+$-tree include search values and tree pointers without any data pointers, more entries can be packed into an internal node of a B$^+$-tree than for a similar B-tree. Thus, for the same block (node) size, the order p will be larger for the B$^+$-tree than for the B-tree, as we illustrate in Example 6. This can lead to fewer B$^+$-tree levels, improving search time. Because the structures for internal and for leaf nodes of a B$^+$-tree are different, the order p can be different. We will use p to denote the order for *internal nodes* and p$_{leaf}$ to denote the order for *leaf nodes*, which we define as being the maximum number of data pointers in a leaf node.

EXAMPLE 6:   To calculate the order p of a B$^+$-tree, suppose that the search key field is V = 9 bytes long, the block size is B = 512 bytes, a record pointer is P$_r$ = 7 bytes, and a block pointer is P = 6 bytes, as in Example 4. An internal node of the B$^+$-tree can have up to p tree pointers and p − 1 search field values; these must fit into a single block. Hence, we have:

$$(p * P) + ((p - 1) * V) \leq B$$
$$(p * 6) + ((p - 1) * 9) \leq 512$$
$$(15 * p) \leq 521$$

We can choose p to be the largest value satisfying the above inequality, which gives p = 34. This is larger than the value of 23 for the B-tree, resulting in a larger fan-out and more entries in each internal node of a B$^+$-tree than in the corresponding B-tree. The leaf nodes of the B$^+$-tree will have the same number of values and pointers, except that the pointers are data pointers and a next pointer. Hence, the order p$_{leaf}$ for the leaf nodes can be calculated as follows:

$$(p_{leaf} * (P_r + V)) + P \leq B$$
$$(p_{leaf} * (7 + 9)) + 6 \leq 512$$
$$(16 * p_{leaf}) \leq 506$$

It follows that each leaf node can hold up to p$_{leaf}$ = 31 key value/data pointer combinations, assuming that the data pointers are record pointers. ∎

As with the B-tree, we may need additional information—to implement the insertion and deletion algorithms—in each node. This information can include the type of node (internal or leaf), the number of current entries q in the node, and pointers to the parent and sibling nodes. Hence, before we do the above calculations for p and p$_{leaf}$, we should reduce the block size by the amount of space needed for all such information. The next example illustrates how we can calculate the number of entries in a B$^+$-tree.

EXAMPLE 7:   Suppose that we construct a B^+-tree on the field of Example 6. To calculate the approximate number of entries of the B^+-tree, we assume that each node is 69% full. On the average, each internal node will have 34 * 0.69 or approximately 23 pointers, and hence 22 values. Each leaf node, on the average, will hold $0.69 * p_{leaf} = 0.69 * 31$ or approximately 21 data record pointers. A B^+-tree tree will have the following average number of entries at each level:

Root:	1 node	22 entries	23 pointers
Level 1:	23 nodes	506 entries	529 pointers
Level 2:	529 nodes	11,638 entries	12,167 pointers
Leaf level:	12,167 nodes	255,507 record pointers	

For the block size, pointer size, and search field size given above, a three-level B^+-tree holds up to 255,507 record pointers, on the average. Compare this to the 65,535 entries for the corresponding B-tree in Example 5. ∎

Search, Insertion, and Deletion with B^+-Trees.   Algorithm 5.2 outlines the procedure using the B^+-tree as access structure to search for a record. Algorithm 5.3 illustrates the procedure for inserting a record in a file with a B^+-tree access structure. These algorithms assume the existence of a key search field, and they must be modified appropriately for the case of a B^+-tree on a nonkey field. We now illustrate insertion and deletion with an example.

ALGORITHM 5.2   Searching for a record with search key field value K, using a B^+-tree.

```
n ← block containing root node of B⁺-tree;
read block n;
while (n is not a leaf node of the B⁺-tree) do
   begin
   q ← number of tree pointers in node n;
   if K ≤ n.K₁ (*n.kᵢ refers to the iᵗʰ search field value in node n*)
      then n ← n.P₁ (*n.Pᵢ refers to the iᵗʰ tree pointer in node n*)
      else if K > n.K_{q−1}
            then n ← n.P_q
            else begin
                 search node n for an entry i such that n.K_{i−1} < K ≤ n.Kᵢ;
                 n ← n.Pᵢ
                 end;
      read block n
   end;
search block n for entry (Kᵢ,Prᵢ) with K = Kᵢ; (* search leaf node *)
if found
   then read data file block with address Prᵢ and retrieve record
   else record with search field value K is not in the data file;
```

ALGORITHM 5.3 Inserting a record with search key field value K in a B$^+$-tree of order p.

n ← block containing root node of B$^+$-tree;
read block n; set stack S to empty;
while (n is not a leaf node of the B$^+$-tree) do
   begin
   push address of n on stack S;
      (*stack S holds parent nodes that are needed in case of split*)
   q ← number of tree pointers in node n;
   if K ≤ n.K$_1$ (*n.K$_i$ refers to the ith search field value in node n*)
      then n ← n.P$_1$ (*n.P$_i$ refers to the ith tree pointer in node n*)
      else if K > n.K$_{q-1}$
         then n ← n.P$_q$
         else begin
            search node n for an entry i such that n.K$_{i-1}$ < K ≤ n.K$_i$;
            n ← n.P$_i$
         end;
   read block n
   end;
search block n for entry (K$_i$,Pr$_i$) with K = K$_i$; (*search leaf node n*)
if found
   then record already in file—cannot insert
   else (*insert entry in B$^+$-tree to point to record*)
   begin
   create entry (K,Pr) where Pr points to new record;
   if leaf node n is not full
   then insert entry (K, Pr) in correct position in leaf node n
   else
   begin (*leaf node n is full with p$_{leaf}$ record pointers—is split*)
   copy n to temp (*temp is an oversize leaf node to hold extra entry*);
   insert entry (K, Pr) in temp in correct position;
      (*temp now holds p$_{leaf}$ + 1 entries of the form (K$_i$, Pr$_i$)*)
   new ← a new empty leaf node for the tree; new.P$_{next}$ ← n.P$_{next}$;
   j ← ⌈(p$_{leaf}$ + 1)/2⌉;
   n ← first j entries in temp (up to entry (K$_j$,Pr$_j$)); n.P$_{next}$ ← new;
   new ← remaining entries in temp; K ← K$_j$;
(*now we must move (K,new) and insert in parent internal node
   —however, if parent is full, split may propagate*)
   finished ← false;
   repeat
   if stack S is empty
      then (*no parent node—new root node is created for the tree*)
      begin
      root ← a new empty internal node for the tree;
      root ← <n, K, new>; finished ← true;
      end

```
        else
            begin
            n ← pop stack S;
            if internal node n is not full
                then
                begin (*parent node not full—no split*)
                insert (K, new) in correct position in internal node n;
                finished ← true
                end
            else
                begin (*internal node n is full with p tree pointers—is split*)
                copy n to temp (*temp is an oversize internal node*);
                insert (K,new) in temp in correct position;
                    (*temp now has p+1 tree pointers*)
                new ← a new empty internal node for the tree;
                j ← ⌊((p + 1)/2⌋;
                n ← entries up to tree pointer Pⱼ in temp;
                    (*n contains <P₁, K₁, P₂, K₂, . . ., Pⱼ₋₁, Kⱼ₋₁, Pⱼ >*)
                new ← entries from tree pointer Pⱼ₊₁ in temp;
                    (*n contains < Pⱼ₊₁, Kⱼ₊₁, . . ., Kₚ₋₁, Pₚ, Kₚ, Pₚ₊₁ >*)
                K ← Kⱼ
            (*now we must move (K,new) and insert in parent internal node*)
                end
            end
        until finished
        end;
    end;
```

Figure 5.12 illustrates insertion of records in a B^+-tree of order $p = 3$ and $p_{leaf} = 2$. First, we observe that the root is the only node in the tree, so it is also a leaf node. As soon as more than one level is created, the tree is divided into internal nodes and leaf nodes. Notice that *every value must exist at the leaf level*, because all data pointers are at the leaf level. However, only some values exist in internal nodes to guide the search. Notice also that every value appearing in an internal node also appears as *the rightmost value* in the subtree pointed at by the tree pointer to the left of the value.

When a *leaf node* is full and a new entry is inserted there, the node **overflows** and must be split. The first $j = \lceil ((p_{leaf} + 1)/2) \rceil$ entries in the original node are kept there, and the remaining entries are moved to a new leaf node. The jth search value is replicated in the parent internal node, and an extra pointer to the new node is created in the parent. These must be inserted in the parent node in their correct sequence. If the parent internal node is full, the new value will cause it to overflow also, so it must be split. The entries in the internal node up to P_j—the jth tree pointer after inserting the new value and pointer, where $j = \lfloor ((p + 1)/2) \rfloor$—are kept, while the jth search value is *moved* to the parent, not replicated. A new internal node will hold the entries from P_{j+1} to the end of the entries in the node (see Algorithm 5.3). This splitting can propagate all the way up to create a new root node and hence a new level for the B^+-tree.

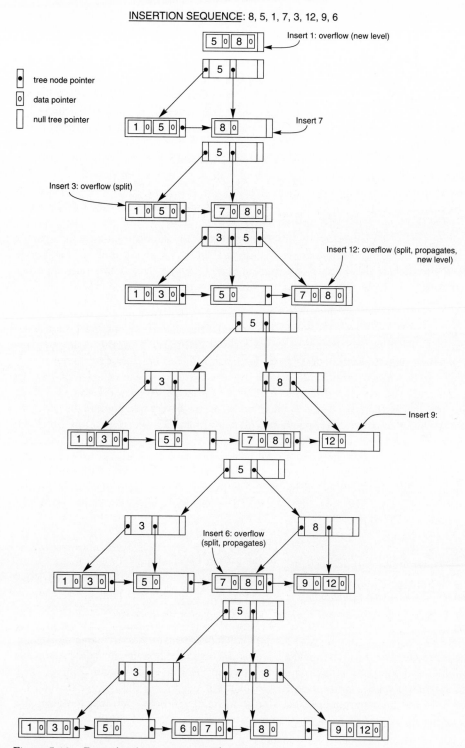

Figure 5.12 Example of insertion in a B+-tree.

Figure 5.13 illustrates deletion from a B^+-tree. When an entry is deleted, it is always removed from the leaf level. If it happens to occur in an internal node, it must also be removed from there. In the latter case, the value to its left in the leaf node must replace it in the internal node, because that node is now the rightmost entry in the subtree. Deletion may cause **underflow** by reducing the number of entries in the leaf node to below the minimum required. In this case we try to find a **sibling** leaf node—a leaf node directly to the left or to the right of the node with underflow—and **redistribute** the entries among the node and its sibling so that both are at least half full; otherwise, the node is merged with its siblings and the number of leaf nodes is reduced. A common method is to try redistributing entries with the left sibling; if this is not possible, an attempt to redistribute with the right sibling is made. If this is not possible either, the three nodes are merged into two leaf nodes. In such a case, underflow may propagate to **internal** nodes because one fewer tree pointer and search value are needed. This can propagate and reduce the tree levels.

Notice that implementing the insertion and deletion algorithms may require parent and sibling pointers for each node, or the use of a stack as in Algorithm 5.3. Each node should also include the number of entries in it and its type (leaf or internal). Another alternative is to implement insertion and deletion as recursive procedures.

Variations of B-Trees and B^+-Trees. To conclude this section, we briefly mention some variations of B-trees and B^+-trees. In some cases, constraint 5 on the B-tree (or B^+-tree), which requires each node to be at least half full, can be changed to require each node to be at least two-thirds full. In this case the B-tree has been called a **B*-tree**. In general, some systems allow the user to choose a **fill factor** between 0.5 and 1.0, where the latter means that the B-tree (index) nodes are to be completely full. In addition, some systems allow the user to specify two fill factors for a B^+-tree: one for the leaf level, and one for the internal nodes of the tree. When the index is first constructed, each node is filled up to approximately the fill factors specified. Recently, investigators have suggested relaxing the requirement that a node be half full, and instead allow a node to become completely empty before merging, to simplify the deletion algorithm. Studies show that this does not waste too much additional space under randomly distributed insertions and deletions.

5.4 Other Types of Indexes★

5.4.1 *Using Hashing and Other Data Structures as Indexes*

It is also possible to create access structures similar to indexes that are based on *hashing*. The index entries <K, Pr> (or <K, P>) can be organized as a dynamically expandable hash file, using one of the techniques described in Section 4.8.3; searching for an entry uses the hash search algorithm on K. Once an entry is found, the pointer Pr (or P) is used to locate the corresponding record in the data file. Other search structures can also be used as indexes.

DELETION SEQUENCE: 5, 12, 9

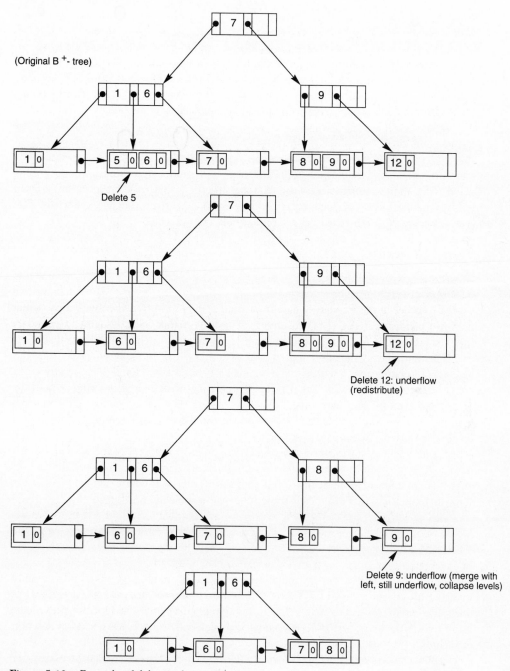

Figure 5.13   Example of deletion from a B^+-tree.

5.4.2 *Logical Versus Physical Indexes*

So far, we have assumed that the index entries <K, Pr> (or <K, P>) always include a physical pointer Pr (or P) that specifies the physical record address on disk as a block number and offset. This is sometimes called a **physical index,** and it has the disadvantage that the pointer must be changed if the record is moved to another disk location. For example, suppose that a primary file organization is based on linear hashing or extendible hashing; then, each time a bucket is split, some records are allocated to new buckets and hence have new physical addresses. If there was a secondary index on the file, the pointers to those records would have to be found and updated—a difficult task.

To remedy this situation, we can use a structure called a **logical index,** whose index entries are of the form <K, K$_p$>. Each entry has one value K for the secondary indexing field matched with the value K$_p$ of the field used for the primary file organization. By searching the secondary index on the value of K, a program can locate the corresponding value of K$_p$ and use this to access the record, using the primary file organization. Logical indexes are used when physical record addresses are expected to change frequently. The cost is the extra search based on the primary file organization.

5.4.3 *Discussion*

In many systems, an index is not an integral part of the data file but can be created and discarded dynamically. That is why it is often called an access structure. Whenever we expect to access a file frequently based on some search condition involving a particular field, we can request the DBMS to create an index on that field. Usually, a secondary index is created, to avoid physical ordering of the records in the data file on disk.

The main advantage of secondary indexes is that—theoretically, at least—they can be created in conjunction with *virtually any record organization*. Hence, a secondary index could be used to complement other primary access methods such as ordering or hashing, or it could even be used with mixed files. To create a B$^+$-tree secondary index on some field of a file, we must go through all records in the file to create the entries at the leaf level of the tree. These entries are then sorted and filled according to the specified fill factor; simultaneously, the other index levels are created. It is more expensive and much harder to create primary indexes and clustering indexes dynamically, because the records of the data file must be physically sorted on disk in order of the indexing field. However, some systems allow users to create these indexes dynamically on their files.

It is common to use an index to enforce a *key constraint* on the index field of a file. While searching the index to insert a new record, it is straightforward to check at the same time whether another record in the file—and hence in the tree—has the same value for the index field. If so, the insertion can be rejected.

A file that has a secondary index on every one of its fields is often called a **fully inverted file**. Because all indexes are secondary, new records are inserted at the end of the file; therefore, the data file itself is an unordered (heap) file. The indexes are usually implemented as B$^+$-trees, so they are updated dynamically to reflect insertion or deletion of records.

Another common file organization is an ordered file with a multilevel primary index on its ordering key field. Such an organization is often called an **indexed sequential file** and is commonly used in business data processing. Insertion is handled by some form of overflow file that is merged periodically with the data file. The index is re-created during file reorganization. IBM's **indexed sequential access method (ISAM)** incorporates a two-level index that is closely related to the disk. The first level is a cylinder index, which has the key value of an anchor record for each cylinder of a disk pack and a pointer to the track index for the cylinder. The track index has the key value of an anchor record for each track in the cylinder and a pointer to the track. The track can then be searched sequentially for the desired record or block. Another IBM method, the **virtual storage access method (VSAM),** is somewhat similar to the B^+-tree access structure.

5.5 Summary

In this chapter we presented file organizations that involve additional access structures, called indexes, to improve the efficiency of retrieval of records from a data file. These access structures may be used *in conjunction with* the primary file organizations discussed in Chapter 4, which are used to organize the file records themselves on disk.

We first discussed three types of ordered single-level indexes: primary, secondary, and clustering. Each index is specified on a field of the file. Primary and clustering indexes are constructed on the physical ordering field of a file, whereas secondary indexes are specified on nonordering fields. The field for a primary index must also be a key of the file, whereas it is a nonkey field for a clustering index. A single-level index is an ordered file and is searched using a binary search. We showed how multilevel indexes can be constructed to improve the efficiency of searching an index.

We then showed how multilevel indexes can be implemented as B-trees and B^+-trees, which are dynamic structures that allow an index to expand and shrink dynamically. The nodes (blocks) of these index structures are kept between half full and completely full by the insertion and deletion algorithms. Nodes eventually stabilize at an average occupancy of 69% full, allowing space for insertions without requiring reorganization of the index for the majority of insertions. B^+-trees generally can hold more entries in their internal nodes than can B-trees, so they may have fewer levels or hold more entries than does a corresponding B-tree.

In Section 5.4, we showed how an index can be constructed based on hash data structures; then we introduced the concept of a logical index as compared to the physical indexes we described before. Finally, we discussed how combinations of the above organizations can be used. For example, secondary indexes are often used with mixed files, as well as with unordered and ordered files. Secondary indexes can also be created for hash files and dynamic hash files.

Review Questions

5.1. Define the following terms: *indexing field, primary key field, clustering field, secondary key field, block anchor, dense index, nondense index.*

5.2. What are the differences among primary, secondary, and clustering indexes? How do these differences affect the ways in which these indexes are implemented? Which of the indexes are dense, and which are not?

5.3. Why can we have at most one primary or clustering index on a file, but several secondary indexes?

5.4. How does multilevel indexing improve the efficiency of searching an index file?

5.5. What is the order p of a B-tree? Describe the structure of B-tree nodes.

5.6. What is the order p of a B$^+$-tree? Describe the structure of both internal and leaf nodes of a B$^+$-tree.

5.7. How does a B-tree differ from a B$^+$-tree? Why is a B$^+$-tree usually preferred as an access structure to a data file?

5.8. What is a fully inverted file? What is an indexed sequential file?

5.9. How can hashing be used to construct an index? What is the difference between a logical index and a physical index?

Exercises

5.10. Consider a disk with block size B = 512 bytes. A block pointer is P = 6 bytes long, and a record pointer is P_R = 7 bytes long. A file has r = 30,000 EMPLOYEE records of *fixed length*. Each record has the following fields: NAME (30 bytes), SSN (9 bytes), DEPARTMENTCODE (9 bytes), ADDRESS (40 bytes), PHONE (9 bytes), BIRTHDATE (8 bytes), SEX (1 byte), JOBCODE (4 bytes), SALARY (4 bytes, real number). An additional byte is used as a deletion marker.

a. Calculate the record size R in bytes.

b. Calculate the blocking factor bfr and the number of file blocks b, assuming an unspanned organization.

c. Suppose that the file is *ordered* by the key field SSN and we want to construct a *primary index* on SSN. Calculate (i) the index blocking factor bfr_i (which is also the index fan-out fo); (ii) the number of first-level index entries and the number of first-level index blocks; (iii) the number of levels needed if we make it into a multilevel index; (iv) the total number of blocks required by the multilevel index; and (v) the number of block accesses needed to search for and retrieve a record from the file—given its SSN value—using the primary index.

d. Suppose that the file is *not ordered* by the key field SSN and we want to construct a *secondary index* on SSN. Repeat the previous exercise (part c) for the secondary index and compare with the primary index.

e. Suppose that the file is *not ordered* by the nonkey field DEPARTMENTCODE and we want to construct a *secondary index* on DEPARTMENTCODE, using option 3 of Section 5.1.3, with an extra level of indirection that stores record pointers. Assume there are 1000 distinct values of DEPARTMENTCODE and that the EMPLOYEE records are evenly distributed among these values. Calculate (i) the index blocking factor bfr_i (which is also the index fan-out fo); (ii) the number of blocks needed by the level of indirection that stores record pointers; (iii) the number of first-level index entries and the number of first-level index blocks; (iv) the number of levels needed if we make it into a multilevel index;

(v) the total number of blocks required by the multilevel index and the blocks used in the extra level of indirection; and (vi) the approximate number of block accesses needed to search for and retrieve *all* records in the file that have a specific DEPARTMENTCODE value, using the index.

f. Suppose that the file is *ordered* by the nonkey field DEPARTMENTCODE and we want to construct a *clustering index* on DEPARTMENTCODE that uses block anchors (every new value of DEPARTMENTCODE starts at the beginning of a new block). Assume there are 1000 distinct values of DEPARTMENTCODE and that the EMPLOYEE records are evenly distributed among these values. Calculate (i) the index blocking factor bfr_i (which is also the index fan-out fo); (ii) the number of first-level index entries and the number of first-level index blocks; (iii) the number of levels needed if we make it into a multilevel index; (iv) the total number of blocks required by the multilevel index; and (v) the number of block accesses needed to search for and retrieve all records in the file that have a specific DEPARTMENTCODE value, using the clustering index (assume that multiple blocks in a cluster are either contiguous or linked by pointers).

g. Suppose that the file is *not* ordered by the key field SSN and we want to construct a B^+-tree access structure (index) on SSN. Calculate (i) the orders p and p_{leaf} of the B^+-tree; (ii) the number of leaf-level blocks needed if blocks are approximately 69% full (rounded up for convenience); (iii) the number of levels needed if internal nodes are also 69% full (rounded up for convenience); (iv) the total number of blocks required by the B^+-tree; and (v) the number of block accesses needed to search for and retrieve a record from the file—given its SSN value—using the B^+-tree.

h. Repeat part g, but for a B-tree rather than for a B^+-tree. Compare your results for the B-tree and for the B^+-tree.

5.11. A PARTS file with Part# as key field includes records with the following Part# values: 23, 65, 37, 60, 46, 92, 48, 71, 56, 59, 18, 21, 10, 74, 78, 15, 16, 20, 24, 28, 39, 43, 47, 50, 69, 75, 8, 49, 33, 38. Suppose that the search field values are inserted in the given order in a B^+-tree of order p = 4 and p_{leaf} = 3; show how the tree will expand and what the final tree will look like.

5.12. Repeat Exercise 5.11, but use a B-tree of order p = 4 instead of a B^+-tree.

5.13. Suppose that the following search field values are deleted, in the given order, from the B^+-tree of Exercise 5.11; show how the tree will shrink and show the final tree. The deleted values are 65, 75, 43, 18, 20, 92, 59, 37.

5.14. Repeat Exercise 5.13, but for the B-tree of Exercise 5.12.

5.15. Algorithm 5.1 outlines the procedure for searching a nondense multilevel primary index to retrieve a file record. Adapt the algorithm for each of the following cases:

a. A multilevel secondary index on a nonkey nonordering field of a file. Assume that option 3 of Section 5.1.3 is used, where an extra level of indirection stores pointers to the individual records with the corresponding index field value.

b. A multilevel secondary index on a nonordering key field of a file.

c. A multilevel clustering index on a nonkey ordering field of a file.

5.16. Suppose that several secondary indexes exist on nonkey fields of a file, implemented using option 3 of Section 5.1.3; for example, we could have secondary indexes on the fields DEPARTMENTCODE, JOBCODE, and SALARY of the EMPLOYEE file of Exercise 5.10. Describe an efficient way to search for and retrieve records satisfying a complex selection condition on these fields, such as (DEPARTMENT-CODE = 5 AND JOBCODE = 12 AND SALARY > 50,000), using the record pointers in the indirection level.

5.17. Adapt Algorithms 5.2 and 5.3, which outline search and insertion procedures for a B$^+$-tree, to a B-tree.

5.18. It is possible to modify the B$^+$-tree insertion algorithm to delay the case where a new level is produced by checking for a possible *redistribution* of values among the leaf nodes. Figure 5.14 illustrates how this could be done for our example of Figure

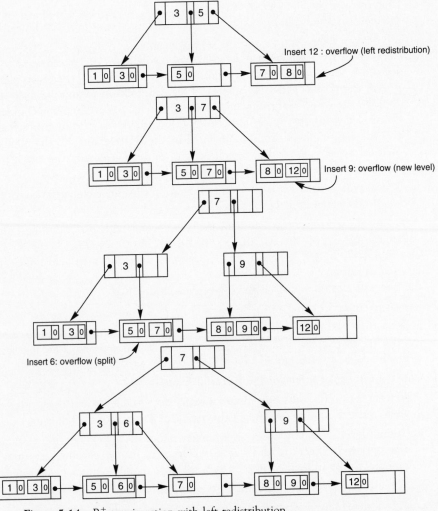

Figure 5.14   B$^+$-tree insertion with left redistribution.

5.12; rather than splitting the leftmost leaf node when 12 is inserted, we do a *left redistribution* by moving 7 to the leaf node to its left (if there is space in this node). Figure 5.14 shows how the tree would look when redistribution is considered. It is also possible to consider *right redistribution*. Try to modify the B^+-tree insertion algorithm to take redistribution into account.

5.19. Outline an algorithm for deletion from a B^+-tree.

5.20. Repeat Exercise 5.19 for a B-tree.

Selected Bibliography

Nievergelt (1974) discusses the use of binary search trees for file organization. Bayer and McCreight (1972) defines B-trees; and Comer (1979) provides a survey of B-trees and their variations and history. Knuth (1973) provides detailed analysis of many search techniques, including B-trees and some of their variations. Wirth (1972), Salzberg (1988), and Smith and Barnes (1987) provide search, insertion, and deletion algorithms for B-trees and B^+-trees. Larson (1981) analyzes index-sequential files; and Held and Stonebraker (1978) compares static multilevel indexes with B-tree dynamic indexes. Lehman and Yao (1981) and Srinivasan and Carey (1991) discuss concurrent access to B-trees. The books by Wiederhold (1983), Smith and Barnes (1987), and Salzberg (1988) among others, discuss many of the techniques described in this chapter.

New techniques and applications of indexes and B^+-trees are discussed in Lanka and Mays (1991), Mohan and Narang (1992), Zobel et al. (1992), and Faloutsos and Jagadish (1992). The performance of various B-tree and B^+-tree algorithms is assessed in Baeza-Yates and Larson (1989) and Johnson and Shasha (1993). Buffer management for indexes is discussed in Mackert and Lohman (1989) and Chan et al. (1992).

CHAPTER 6

The Relational Data Model and Relational Algebra

The relational model of data was introduced by Codd (1970). It is based on a simple and uniform data structure—the relation—and has a solid theoretical foundation. We will discuss various aspects of the relational model in several chapters, since there is more conceptual material to cover on the relational model than on other data models. The relational model is also becoming firmly established in the database application world, and there are many commercial relational DBMS packages.

In this chapter, we will concentrate on describing the basic principles of the relational model of data. Commercial relational languages and systems are discussed in subsequent chapters. We begin this chapter by defining the modeling concepts and notation of the relational model in Section 6.1. In Section 6.2 we identify the integrity constraints that are now considered an important part of the relational model. Section 6.3 defines the update operations of the relational model and discusses their effect on integrity constraints. Section 6.4 shows how relations can be declared in a database system. In Section 6.5 we present a detailed discussion of the relational algebra, which is a collection of operations for manipulating relations and specifying queries. We consider the relational algebra to be an integral part of the relational data model. Section 6.6 defines additional relational operations that are useful in many database applications. We give examples of specifying queries that use relational operations in Section 6.7. Section 6.8 presents algorithms for designing a relational database schema by mapping a conceptual design from the ER model (see Chapter 3) to the relational model. Finally, Section 6.9 is a summary.

For the reader who is interested in a less detailed introduction to relational concepts, Sections 6.1.2, 6.5.7, and 6.6 may be skipped. Section 6.8 on relational database design assumes that the reader is familiar with the material in Chapter 3, and it may also be skipped.

The whole of Part II of this textbook is devoted to the relational model. In Chapter 7, we describe the SQL query language, which is becoming the standard in commercial relational DBMSs. We present another formal language for the relational model—the relational calculus—in Chapter 8; this language provides a theoretical foundation for commercial relational query languages and is used as the basis for advanced relational systems such as deductive databases (see Chapter 24). We also discuss the QUEL and QBE languages in Chapter 8. Finally, Chapter 9 presents an overview of one commercial relational DBMS. Chapters 12 and 13 in Part IV of the book present the formal constraints of functional and multivalued dependencies and explain how they are used to develop a relational database design theory based on normalization.

6.1 Relational Model Concepts

The relational model represents the database as a collection of relations. Informally, each relation resembles a table or, to some extent, a simple file. For example, the database of files shown in Figure 1.2 is considered to be in the relational model. However, there are important differences between relations and files, as we shall soon see.

When a relation is thought of as a **table** of values, each row in the table represents a collection of related data values. These values can be interpreted as facts describing a real-world entity or relationship. The table name and column names are used to help in interpreting the meaning of the values in each row of the table. For example, the first table of Figure 1.2 is called STUDENT because each row represents facts about a particular student entity. The column names—Name, StudentNumber, Class, Major—specify how to interpret the data values in each row, based on the column each value is in. All values in a column are of the same data type.

In relational model terminology, a row is called a *tuple*, a column header is called an *attribute*, and the table is called a *relation*. The data type describing the types of values that can appear in each column is called a *domain*. We now define these terms—*domain*, *tuple*, *attribute*, and *relation*—more precisely.

6.1.1 *Domains, Tuples, Attributes, and Relations*

A **domain** D is a set of atomic values. By **atomic** we mean that each value in the domain is indivisible as far as the relational model is concerned. A common method of specifying a domain is to specify a data type from which the data values forming the domain are drawn. It is also useful to specify a name for the domain, to help in interpreting its values. Some examples of domains follow:

- USA_phone_numbers: The set of 10-digit phone numbers valid in the United States.
- Local_phone_numbers: The set of 7-digit phone numbers valid within a particular area code.
- Social_security_numbers: The set of valid 9-digit social security numbers.
- Names: The set of names of persons.

- Grade_point_averages: Possible values of computed grade point averages; each must be a value between 0 and 4.

- Employee_ages: Possible ages of employees of a company; each must be a value between 16 and 80 years old.

- Academic_departments: The set of academic departments, such as Computer Science, Economics, and Physics, in a university.

The preceding are logical definitions of domains. A **data type** or **format** is also specified for each domain. For example, the data type for the domain USA_phone_numbers can be declared as a character string of the form (ddd)ddd-dddd, where each d is a numeric (decimal) digit and the first three digits form a valid telephone area code. The data type for Employee_ages is an integer number between 16 and 80. For Academic_departments, the data type is the set of all character strings that represent valid department names or codes.

A domain is thus given a name, data type, and format. Additional information for interpreting the values of a domain can also be given; for example, a numeric domain such as Person_weights should have the units of measurement—pounds or kilograms—specified. Next we define the concept of a relation schema, which describes the structure of a relation.

A **relation schema** R, denoted by $R(A_1, A_2, \ldots, A_n)$, is made up of a relation name R and a list of attributes $A_1, A_2, \ldots, A_n$. Each **attribute** A_i is the name of a role played by some domain D in the relation schema R. D is called the **domain** of A_i and is denoted by $dom(A_i)$. A relation schema is used to *describe* a relation; R is called the **name** of this relation. The **degree of a relation** is the number of attributes n of its relation schema.

An example of a relation schema for a relation of degree 7, which describes university students, is the following:

STUDENT(Name, SSN, HomePhone, Address, OfficePhone, Age, GPA)

For this relation schema, STUDENT is the name of the relation, which has seven attributes. We can specify the following domains for some of the attributes of the STUDENT relation: dom(Name) = Names; dom(SSN) = Social_security_numbers; dom(HomePhone) = Local_phone_numbers; dom(OfficePhone) = Local_phone_numbers; dom(GPA) = Grade_point_averages.

A **relation** (or **relation instance**) r of the relation schema $R(A_1, A_2, \ldots, A_n)$, also denoted by r(R), is a set of n-tuples $r = \{t_1, t_2, \ldots, t_m\}$. Each **n-tuple** t is an ordered list of n values $t = <v_1, v_2, \ldots, v_n>$, where each value v_i, $1 \leq i \leq n$, is an element of $dom(A_i)$ or is a special **null** value. The terms relation **intension** for the schema R and relation **extension** (or **state**) for a relation instance r(R) are also commonly used.

Figure 6.1 shows an example of a STUDENT relation, which corresponds to the STUDENT schema specified above. Each tuple in the relation represents a particular student entity. We display the relation as a table, where each tuple is shown as a row and each attribute corresponds to a column header indicating a role or interpretation of the values in that column. *Null values* represent attributes whose values are unknown or do not exist for some individual STUDENT tuples.

The above definition of a relation can be *restated* as follows. A relation r(R) is a **subset of the Cartesian product** of the domains that define R:

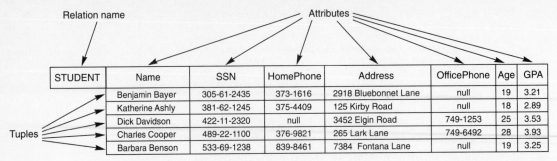

Figure 6.1   The attributes and tuples of a relation STUDENT.

$$r(R) \subseteq (dom(A_1) \textbf{ X } dom(A_2) \textbf{ X } \cdots \textbf{ X } dom(A_n))$$

The Cartesian product specifies all possible combinations of values from the underlying domains. Hence, if we denote the number of values or **cardinality** of a domain D by |D|, and assume that all domains are finite, the total number of tuples in the Cartesian product is

$$|dom(A_1)| * |dom(A_2)| * \cdots * |dom(A_n)|$$

Out of all these possible combinations, a relation instance at a given time—the **current relation state**—reflects only the valid tuples that represent a particular state of the real world. In general, as the state of the real world changes, so does the relation, by being transformed into another relation state. However, the schema R is relatively static and does *not* change except very infrequently—for example, as a result of adding an attribute to represent new information that was not originally stored in the relation.

It is possible for several attributes to *have the same domain*. The attributes indicate different **roles,** or interpretations, for the domain. For example, in the STUDENT relation, the same domain Local_phone_numbers plays the role of HomePhone, referring to the "home phone of a student," and the role of OfficePhone, referring to the "office phone of the student."

6.1.2 *Characteristics of Relations*⋆

The earlier definition of relations implies certain characteristics that make a relation different from a file or a table. We now discuss some of these characteristics.

Ordering of Tuples in a Relation. A relation is defined as a set of tuples. Mathematically, elements of a set have *no order* among them; hence, tuples in a relation do not have any particular order. However, in a file, records are physically stored on disk so there always is an order among the records. This ordering indicates first, second, i^{th}, and last records in the file. Similarly, when we display a relation as a table, the rows are displayed in a certain order.

Tuple ordering is not part of a relation definition, because a relation attempts to represent facts at a logical or abstract level. Many logical orders can be specified on a

STUDENT	Name	SSN	HomePhone	Address	OfficePhone	Age	GPA
	Dick Davidson	422-11-2320	null	3452 Elgin Road	749-1253	25	3.53
	Barbara Benson	533-69-1238	839-8461	7384 Fontana Lane	null	19	3.25
	Charles Cooper	489-22-1100	376-9821	265 Lark Lane	749-6492	28	3.93
	Katherine Ashly	381-62-1245	375-4409	125 Kirby Road	null	18	2.89
	Benjamin Bayer	305-61-2435	373-1616	2918 Bluebonnet Lane	null	19	3.21

Figure 6.2 The same relation STUDENT of Figure 6.1 with a different order of rows.

relation; for example, tuples in the STUDENT relation of Figure 6.1 could be logically ordered by values of Name, SSN, Age, or some other attribute. The definition of a relation does not specify any order: there is *no preference* for one logical ordering over another. Hence, the relation displayed in Figure 6.2 is considered *identical* to the one shown in Figure 6.1. When a relation is implemented as a file, a physical ordering may be specified on the records of the file.

Ordering of Values Within a Tuple, and Alternative Definition of Relation. According to the preceding definition of a relation, an n-tuple is an *ordered list* of n values, so the ordering of values in a tuple—and hence of attributes in a relation schema definition— is important. However, at a logical level, the order of attributes and their values are *not* really important as long as the correspondence between attributes and values is maintained.

An **alternative definition of a relation** can be given, making the ordering of values in a tuple *unnecessary*. In this definition, a relation schema $R = \{A_1, A_2, \ldots, A_n\}$ is a *set* of attributes, and a relation r(R) is a finite set of **mappings** $r = \{t_1, t_2, \ldots, t_m\}$, where each tuple t_i is a mapping from R to D, and D is the union of the attribute domains; that is, $D = dom(A_1) \cup dom(A_2) \cup \cdots \cup dom(A_n)$. In this definition, $t(A_i)$ must be in $dom(A_i)$ for $1 \leq i \leq n$ for each mapping t in r. Each mapping t_i is called a tuple.

According to this definition, a **tuple** can be considered as a **set** of (<attribute>, <value>) pairs, where each pair gives the value of the mapping from an attribute A_i to a value v_i from $dom(A_i)$. The ordering of attributes is *not* important, because the attribute name appears with its value. By this definition, the two tuples shown in Figure 6.3 are identical. This makes sense at an abstract or logical level, since there really is no reason to prefer having one attribute value appear before another in a tuple.

When a relation is implemented as a file, the attributes can be physically ordered as fields within a record. We will use the **first definition** of relation, where the attributes

t = < (Name ,Dick Davidson),(SSN, 422-11-2320),(HomePhone,null),(Address, 3452 Elgin Road),
(OfficePhone ,749-1253),(Age ,25),(GPA ,3.53)>

t = < (Address,3452 Elgin Road),(Name,Dick Davidson),(SSN, 422-11-2320),(Age ,25),
(OfficePhone ,749-1253),(GPA,3.53),(HomePhone,null)>

Figure 6.3 Two identical tuples when order of attributes and values is not part of the definition of a relation.

and the values within tuples *are ordered*, because it simplifies much of the notation. However, the alternative definition given here is more general.

Values in the Tuples. Each value in a tuple is an **atomic** value; that is, it is not divisible into components within the framework of the relational model. Hence, composite and multivalued attributes (see Chapter 3) are not allowed. Much of the theory behind the relational model was developed with this assumption in mind, which is called the **first normal form** assumption. Multivalued attributes must be represented by separate relations, and composite attributes are represented only by their simple component attributes. Recent research in the relational model attempts to remove these restrictions by using the concept of **nonfirst normal form** or **nested** relations (see Chapter 21).

The values of some attributes within a particular tuple may be unknown or may not apply to that tuple. A special value, called **null,** is used for these cases. For example, in Figure 6.1, some student tuples have null for their office phones because they do not have an office. Another student has a null for home phone, presumably because either he does not have a home phone or he has one but we do not know it. In general, we can have *several types* of null values, such as "value unknown," "attribute does not apply to this tuple," or "this tuple has no value for this attribute." Some implementations actually devise different codes for different types of null values. Incorporating different types of null values into relational model operations has proved difficult, and a full discussion lies outside the scope of this book.

Interpretation of a Relation. The relation schema can be interpreted as a declaration or a type of **assertion**. For example, the schema of the STUDENT relation of Figure 6.1 asserts that, in general, a student entity has a Name, SSN, HomePhone, Address, OfficePhone, Age, and GPA. Each tuple in the relation can then be interpreted as a **fact** or a particular instance of the assertion. For example, the first tuple in Figure 6.1 asserts the fact that there is a STUDENT whose name is Benjamin Bayer, SSN is 305-61-2435, Age is 19, and so on.

Notice that some relations may represent facts about *entities*, whereas other relations may represent facts about *relationships*. For example, a relation schema MAJORS (StudentSSN, DepartmentCode) asserts that students major in academic departments; a tuple in this relation relates a student to his or her major department. Hence, the relational model represents facts about both entities and relationships *uniformly* as relations.

An alternative interpretation of a relation schema is as a **predicate;** in this case, the values in each tuple are interpreted as values that *satisfy* the predicate. This interpretation is quite useful in the context of logic programming languages, such as PROLOG, because it allows the relational model to be used within these languages. This is further discussed in Chapter 24 on deductive databases.

6.1.3 *Relational Model Notation*

We will use the following notation in our presentation:

- A relation schema R of degree n is denoted by $R(A_1, A_2, \ldots, A_n)$.

- An n-tuple t in a relation r(R) is denoted by $t = <v_1, v_2, \ldots, v_n>$, where v_i is the value corresponding to attribute A_i. The following notation refers to **component values** of tuples:

  – $t[A_i]$ refers to the value v_i in t for attribute A_i.

  – $t[A_u, A_w, \ldots, A_z]$, where $A_u, A_w, \ldots, A_z$ is a list of attributes from R, refers to the subtuple of values $<v_u, v_w, \ldots, v_z>$ from t corresponding to the attributes specified in the list.

- The letters Q, R, S denote relation names.

- The letters q, r, s denote relation states.

- The letters t, u, v denote tuples.

- In general, the name of a relation such as STUDENT indicates the current set of tuples in that relation—the *current relation state*, or *instance*—whereas STUDENT(Name, SSN, . . .) refers to the relation schema.

- Attribute names are sometimes qualified with the relation name to which they belong—for example, STUDENT.Name or STUDENT.Age.

Consider the tuple t = <'Barbara Benson', '533-69-1238', '839-8461', '7384 Fontana Lane', null, 19, 3.25> from the STUDENT relation in Figure 6.1; we have t[Name] = <'Barbara Benson'>, and t[SSN, GPA, Age] = <'533-69-1238', 3.25, 19>.

6.2 Relational Model Constraints

In this section, we discuss the various types of constraints that can be specified on a relational database schema. These include domain constraints, key constraints, entity integrity, and referential integrity constraints. Other types of constraints, called *data dependencies* (which include *functional dependencies* and *multivalued dependencies*), are used mainly for database design by normalization and will be discussed in Chapters 12 and 13.

6.2.1 *Domain Constraints*

Domain constraints specify that the value of each attribute A must be an atomic value from the domain dom(A) for that attribute. We have already discussed the ways in which domains can be specified in Section 6.1.1. The data types associated with domains typically include standard numeric data types for integers (such as short-integer, integer, long-integer) and real numbers (float and double-precision float). Characters, fixed-length strings, and variable-length strings are also available, as are date, time, timestamp, and money data types. Other possible domains may be described by a subrange of values from a data type or as an enumerated data type where all possible values are explicitly listed. Rather than describe these in detail here, we discuss the data types offered by the SQL2 relational standard in Section 7.1.2.

6.2.2 *Key Constraints*

A relation is defined as a *set of tuples*. By definition, all elements of a set are distinct; hence, all tuples in a relation must also be distinct. This means that no two tuples can have the same combination of values for *all* their attributes. Usually, there are other **subsets of attributes** of a relation schema R with the property that no two tuples in any relation instance r of R should have the same combination of values for these attributes. Suppose that we denote one such subset of attributes by SK; then for any two distinct tuples t_1 and t_2 in a relation instance r of R, we haves the constraint that:

$$t_1[SK] \neq t_2[SK]$$

Any such set of attributes SK is called a **superkey** of the relation schema R. Every relation has at least one superkey—the set of all its attributes. A superkey can have redundant attributes, however, so a more useful concept is that of a *key*, which has no redundancy. A **key** K of a relation schema R is a superkey of R with the additional property that removing any attribute A from K leaves a set of attributes K' that is not a superkey of R. Hence, a key is a *minimal superkey*; a superkey from which we cannot remove any attributes and still have the uniqueness constraint hold.

For example, consider the STUDENT relation of Figure 6.1. The attribute set {SSN} is a key of STUDENT because no two student tuples can have the same value for SSN. Any set of attributes that includes SSN—for example, {SSN, Name, Age}—is a superkey. However, the superkey {SSN, Name, Age} is not a key of STUDENT, because removing Name or Age or both from the set still leaves us with a superkey.

The value of a key attribute can be used to identify uniquely a tuple in the relation. For example, the SSN value 305-61-2435 identifies uniquely the tuple corresponding to Benjamin Bayer in the STUDENT relation. Notice that a set of attributes constituting a key is a property of the relation schema; it is a constraint that should hold on *every* relation instance of the schema. A key is determined from the meaning of the attributes in the relation schema. Hence, the property is *time-invariant*; it must continue to hold when we insert new tuples in the relation. For example, we cannot and should not designate the Name attribute of the STUDENT relation in Figure 6.1 as a key, because there is no guarantee that two students with identical names will never exist.*

In general, a relation schema may have more than one key. In this case, each of the keys is called a **candidate key**. For example, the CAR relation in Figure 6.4 has two candidate keys: LicenseNumber and EngineSerialNumber. It is common to designate one of the candidate keys as the **primary key** of the relation. This is the candidate key whose values are used to *identify* tuples in the relation. We use the convention that the attributes that form the primary key of a relation schema are underlined, as shown in Figure 6.4. Notice that, when a relation schema has several candidate keys, the choice of one to become primary key is arbitrary; however, it is usually better to choose a primary key with a single attribute or a small number of attributes.

6.2.3 *Relational Database Schemas and Integrity Constraints*

So far, we have discussed single relations and relation schemas. A relational database usually contains many relations, with tuples in relations that are related in various ways. In this section we define a relational database and a relational database schema. A **rela-**

---

*Names are sometimes used as keys, but then some artifact—such as appending an ordinal number—must be used to distinguish between identical names.

CAR	LicenseNumber	EngineSerialNumber	Make	Model	Year
	Texas ABC-739	A69352	Ford	Mustang	90
	Florida TVP-347	B43696	Oldsmobile	Cutlass	93
	New York MPO-22	X83554	Oldsmobile	Delta	89
	California 432-TFY	C43742	Mercedes	190-D	87
	California RSK-629	Y82935	Toyota	Camry	92
	Texas RSK-629	U028365	Jaguar	XJS	92

Figure 6.4 The CAR relation with two candidate keys: LicenseNumber and EngineSerialNumber.

tional database schema S is a set of relation schemas S = {R_1, R_2, ..., R_m} and a set of **integrity constraints** IC. A **relational database instance** DB of S is a set of relation instances DB = {r_1, r_2, ..., r_m} such that each r_i is an instance of R_i and such that the r_i relations satisfy the integrity constraints specified in IC. Figure 6.5 shows a relational database schema that we call COMPANY, and Figure 6.6 shows a relational database instance corresponding to the COMPANY schema. We use this schema and database in this chapter and in Chapters 7 through 9 for developing example queries in different relational languages. When we refer to a relational database, we implicitly include both its schema and its current instance.

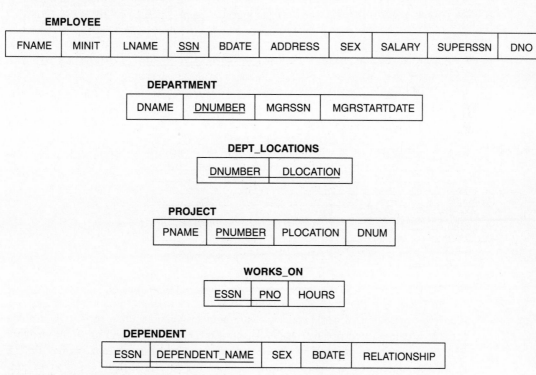

Figure 6.5 The COMPANY relational database schema; primary keys are underlined.

EMPLOYEE	FNAME	MINIT	LNAME	SSN	BDATE	ADDRESS	SEX	SALARY	SUPERSSN	DNO
	John	B	Smith	123456789	09-JAN-55	731 Fondren, Houston, TX	M	30000	333445555	5
	Franklin	T	Wong	333445555	08-DEC-45	638 Voss, Houston, TX	M	40000	888665555	5
	Alicia	J	Zelaya	999887777	19-JUL-58	3321 Castle, Spring, TX	F	25000	987654321	4
	Jennifer	S	Wallace	987654321	20-JUN-31	291 Berry, Bellaire, TX	F	43000	888665555	4
	Ramesh	K	Narayan	666884444	15-SEP-52	975 Fire Oak, Humble, TX	M	38000	333445555	5
	Joyce	A	English	453453453	31-JUL-62	5631 Rice, Houston, TX	F	25000	333445555	5
	Ahmad	V	Jabbar	987987987	29-MAR-59	980 Dallas, Houston, TX	M	25000	987654321	4
	James	E	Borg	888665555	10-NOV-27	450 Stone, Houston, TX	M	55000	null	1

DEPT_LOCATIONS		DNUMBER	DLOCATION
		1	Houston
		4	Stafford
		5	Bellaire
		5	Sugarland
		5	Houston

DEPARTMENT	DNAME	DNUMBER	MGRSSN	MGRSTARTDATE
	Research	5	333445555	22-MAY-78
	Administration	4	987654321	01-JAN-85
	Headquarters	1	888665555	19-JUN-71

WORKS_ON	ESSN	PNO	HOURS
	123456789	1	32.5
	123456789	2	7.5
	666884444	3	40.0
	453453453	1	20.0
	453453453	2	20.0
	333445555	2	10.0
	333445555	3	10.0
	333445555	10	10.0
	333445555	20	10.0
	999887777	30	30.0
	999887777	10	10.0
	987987987	10	35.0
	987987987	30	5.0
	987654321	30	20.0
	987654321	20	15.0
	888665555	20	null

PROJECT	PNAME	PNUMBER	PLOCATION	DNUM
	ProductX	1	Bellaire	5
	ProductY	2	Sugarland	5
	ProductZ	3	Houston	5
	Computerization	10	Stafford	4
	Reorganization	20	Houston	1
	Newbenefits	30	Stafford	4

DEPENDENT	ESSN	DEPENDENT_NAME	SEX	BDATE	RELATIONSHIP
	333445555	Alice	F	05-APR-76	DAUGHTER
	333445555	Theodore	M	25-OCT-73	SON
	333445555	Joy	F	03-MAY-48	SPOUSE
	987654321	Abner	M	29-FEB-32	SPOUSE
	123456789	Michael	M	01-JAN-78	SON
	123456789	Alice	F	31-DEC-78	DAUGHTER
	123456789	Elizabeth	F	05-MAY-57	SPOUSE

Figure 6.6   A relational database instance (state) of the COMPANY schema.

In Figure 6.5, the DNUMBER attribute in both DEPARTMENT and DEPT_LOCATIONS stands for the same real-world concept—the number given to a department. That same concept is called DNO in EMPLOYEE and DNUM in PROJECT. We will allow an attribute that represents the same real world concept to have names that may or may not be identical in different relations. Similarly, we allow attributes that represent different concepts to have the same name in different relations. For example, we could have used the attribute name NAME for both PNAME of PROJECT and DNAME of DEPARTMENT; in this case, we would have two attributes that share the same name but represent different real-world concepts—project names and department names.

In some *early versions of the relational model*, an assumption was made that the same real-world concept, when represented by an attribute, would have *identical* attribute names in all relations. This creates problems when the same real-world concept is used in different roles (meanings) in the same relation. For example, the concept of social security number appears twice in the EMPLOYEE relation of Figure 6.5: once in the role of employee social security number, and once in the role of supervisor social security number. To avoid problems, we gave them distinct attribute names—SSN and SUPERSSN, respectively.

Integrity constraints are specified on a database schema and are expected to hold on every database instance of that schema. In addition to domain and key constraints, two other types of constraints are considered part of the relational model: entity integrity and referential integrity.

6.2.4 *Entity Integrity, Referential Integrity, and Foreign Keys*

The **entity integrity constraint** states that no primary key value can be null. This is because the primary key value is used to identify individual tuples in a relation; having null values for the primary key implies that we cannot identify some tuples. For example, if two or more tuples had null for their primary keys, we might not be able to distinguish them.

Key constraints and entity integrity constraints are specified on individual relations. The **referential integrity constraint** is specified between two relations and is used to maintain the consistency among tuples of the two relations. Informally, the referential integrity constraint states that a tuple in one relation that refers to another relation must refer to an *existing tuple* in that relation. For example, in Figure 6.6, the attribute DNO of EMPLOYEE gives the department number for which each employee works; hence, its value in every EMPLOYEE tuple must match the DNUMBER value of some tuple in the DEPARTMENT relation.

To define referential integrity more formally, we must first define the concept of a foreign key. The conditions for a foreign key, given below, specify a referential integrity constraint between the two relation schemas R_1 and R_2. A set of attributes FK in relation schema R_1 is a **foreign key** of R_1 if it satisfies the following two rules:

1. The attributes in FK have the same domain as the primary key attributes PK of another relation schema R_2; the attributes FK are said to **reference** or **refer to** the relation R_2.

2. A value of FK in a tuple t_1 of R_1 either occurs as a value of PK for some tuple t_2 in R_2 or is null. In the former case, we have $t_1[FK] = t_2[PK]$, and we say that the tuple t_1 **references** or **refers to** the tuple t_2.

In a database of many relations, there are usually many referential integrity constraints. To specify these constraints, we must first have a clear understanding of the meaning or role that each set of attributes plays in the various relation schemas of the database. Referential integrity constraints typically arise from the *relationships among the entities* represented by the relation schemas. For example, consider the database shown in Figure 6.6. In the EMPLOYEE relation, the attribute DNO refers to the department for which an employee works; hence, we designate DNO to be a foreign key of EMPLOYEE, referring to the DEPARTMENT relation. This means that a value of DNO in any tuple t_1 of the EMPLOYEE relation must match a value of the primary key of DEPARTMENT—the DNUMBER attribute—in some tuple t_2 of the DEPARTMENT relation, or the value of DNO *can be null* if the employee does not belong to a department. In Figure 6.6 the tuple for employee "John Smith" references the tuple for the "Research" department, indicating that "John Smith" works for this department.

Notice that a foreign key can *refer to its own relation*. For example, the attribute SUPERSSN in EMPLOYEE refers to the supervisor of an employee; this is another employee, represented by a tuple in the EMPLOYEE relation. Hence, SUPERSSN is a foreign key that references the EMPLOYEE relation itself. In Figure 6.6 the tuple for employee "John Smith" references the tuple for employee "Franklin Wong," indicating that "Franklin Wong" is the supervisor of "John Smith."

We can *diagrammatically display referential integrity constraints* by drawing a directed arc from each foreign key to the relation it references. For clarity, the arrowhead may

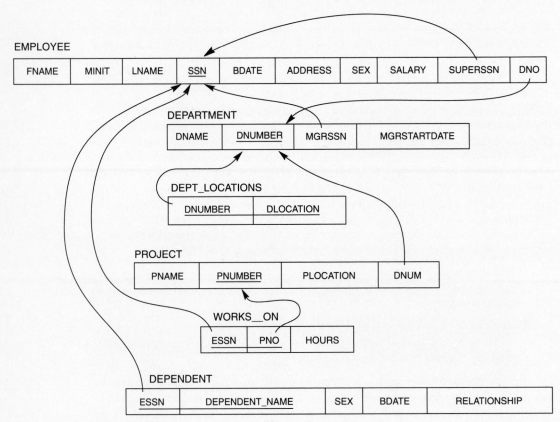

Figure 6.7   Referential integrity constraints displayed on the COMPANY relational database schema.

point to the primary key of the referenced relation. Figure 6.7 shows the schema in Figure 6.5 with the referential integrity constraints displayed in this manner.

All integrity constraints should be specified on the relational database schema if we are interested in maintaining these constraints on all database instances. Hence, in a relational system, the data definition language (DDL) should include provisions for specifying the various types of constraints so that the DBMS can automatically enforce them. Most relational database management systems support key and entity integrity constraints, and many systems are now making provisions to support referential integrity.

The preceding types of constraints do not include a large class of general constraints, sometimes called *semantic integrity constraints*, that may have to be specified and enforced on a relational database. Examples of such constraints are "the salary of an employee should not exceed the salary of the employee's supervisor" and "the maximum number of hours an employee can work on all projects per week is 56." Such constraints are not enforced by most commercial relational DBMSs, but mechanisms for specifying and enforcing these constraints are being developed.

6.3 Update Operations on Relations

The operations of the relational model can be categorized into retrievals and updates. Relational algebra operations, which can be used to specify retrievals, are discussed in detail in Section 6.5. In this section, we concentrate on the update operations. There are three basic update operations on relations: insert, delete, and modify. **Insert** is used to insert a new tuple or tuples in a relation; **delete** is used to delete tuples; and **modify** is used to change the values of some attributes. Whenever update operations are applied, the integrity constraints specified on the relational database schema should not be violated. In this section we discuss the types of constraints that may be violated by each update operation and the types of actions that may be taken if an update does cause a violation. We use the database shown in Figure 6.6 for examples and discuss only key constraints, entity integrity constraints, and the referential integrity constraints shown in Figure 6.7. For each type of update, we give some example operations and discuss any constraints that each operation may violate.

6.3.1 *The Insert Operation*

The **Insert** operation provides a list of attribute values for a new tuple t that is to be inserted into a relation R. Insert can violate any of the four types of constraints discussed in the previous section. Domain constraints can be violated if an attribute value is given that does not appear in the corresponding domain. Key constraints can be violated if a key value in the new tuple t already exists in another tuple in the relation r(R). Entity integrity can be violated if the primary key of the new tuple t is null. Referential integrity can be violated if the value of any foreign key in t refers to a tuple that does not exist in the referenced relation. Here are some examples to illustrate this discussion.

1. Insert < 'Cecilia', 'F', 'Kolonsky', '677678989', '05-APR-50', '6357 Windy Lane, Katy, TX', F, 28000, null, 4 > into EMPLOYEE.

   —This insertion satisfies all constraints, so it is acceptable.

2. Insert < 'Alicia', 'J', 'Zelaya', '999887777', '05-APR-50', '6357 Windy Lane, Katy, TX', F, 28000, '987654321', 4 > into EMPLOYEE.

    —This insertion violates the key constraint because another tuple with the same SSN value already exists in the EMPLOYEE relation.

3. Insert < 'Cecilia', 'F', 'Kolonsky', null, '05-APR-50', '6357 Windy Lane, Katy, TX', F, 28000, null, 4 > into EMPLOYEE.

    —This insertion violates the entity integrity constraint (null for the primary key SSN), so it is unacceptable.

4. Insert < 'Cecilia', 'F', 'Kolonsky', '677678989', '05-APR-50', '6357 Windswept, Katy, TX', F, 28000, '987654321', 7 > into EMPLOYEE.

    —This insertion violates the referential integrity constraint specified on DNO because no DEPARTMENT tuple exists with DNUMBER = 7.

If an insertion violates one or more constraints, two options are available. The first option is to *reject the insertion*. In this case, it would be useful if the DBMS could explain to the user why the insertion was rejected. The second option is to attempt to *correct the reason for rejecting the insertion*. For example, in operation 3 above, the DBMS could ask the user to provide a value for SSN and could accept the insertion if a valid SSN value were provided. In operation 4, the DBMS could either ask the user to change the value of DNO to some valid value (or set it to null), or it could ask the user to insert a DEPARTMENT tuple with DNUMBER = 7 and could accept the insertion only after such an operation was accepted. Notice that, in the latter case, the insertion can **cascade** back to the EMPLOYEE relation if the user attempts to insert a tuple for department 7 with a value for MGRSSN that does not exist in the EMPLOYEE relation.

6.3.2 *The Delete Operation.*

The **Delete** operation can violate only referential integrity, if the tuple being deleted is referenced by the foreign keys from other tuples in the database. To specify deletion, a condition on the attributes of the relation selects the tuple (or tuples) to be deleted. Here are some examples.

1. Delete the WORKS_ON tuple with ESSN = '999887777' and PNO = 10.
    —This deletion is acceptable.

2. Delete the EMPLOYEE tuple with SSN = '999887777'.
    —This deletion is not acceptable, because two tuples in WORKS_ON refer to this tuple. Hence, if the tuple is deleted, referential integrity violations will result.

3. Delete the EMPLOYEE tuple with SSN = '333445555'.
    —This deletion will result in even worse referential integrity violations, because the tuple involved is referenced by tuples from the EMPLOYEE, DEPARTMENT, WORKS_ON, and DEPENDENT relations.

Three options are available if a deletion operation causes a violation. The first option is to *reject the deletion*. The second option is to *attempt to cascade (or propagate) the deletion* by deleting tuples that reference the tuple that is being deleted. For example, in operation 2, the DBMS could automatically delete the two offending tuples from

WORKS_ON with ESSN = '999887777'. A third option is to *modify the referencing attribute values* that cause the violation; each such value is either set to null or changed to reference another valid tuple. Notice that, if a referencing attribute that causes a violation is *part of the primary key,* it cannot be set to null; otherwise, it would violate entity integrity.

Combinations of these three options are also possible. For example, to avoid having operation 3 cause a violation, the DBMS may automatically delete all tuples from WORKS_ON and DEPENDENT with ESSN = '333445555'. Tuples in EMPLOYEE with SUPERSSN = '333445555' and the tuple in DEPARTMENT with MGRSSN = '333445555' can either be deleted or have their SUPERSSN and MGRSSN values changed to other valid values or to null. Although it may make sense to delete automatically the WORKS_ON and DEPENDENT tuples that refer to an EMPLOYEE tuple, it may not make sense to delete other EMPLOYEE tuples or a DEPARTMENT tuple. In general, when a referential integrity constraint is specified, the DBMS should allow the user to *specify which of the three options* applies in case of a violation of the constraint.

6.3.3   *The Modify Operation*

The **Modify** operation is used to change the values of one or more attributes in a tuple (or tuples) of some relation R. It is necessary to specify a condition on the attributes of the relation R to select the tuple (or tuples) to be modified. Here are some examples.

1. Modify the SALARY of the EMPLOYEE tuple with SSN = '999887777' to 28000.
   —Acceptable.

2. Modify the DNO of the EMPLOYEE tuple with SSN = '999887777' to 1.
   —Acceptable.

3. Modify the DNO of the EMPLOYEE tuple with SSN = '999887777' to 7.
   —Unacceptable, because it violates referential integrity.

4. Modify the SSN of the EMPLOYEE tuple with SSN = '999887777' to '987654321'.
   —Unacceptable, because it violates primary key and referential integrity constraints.

Modifying an attribute that is neither a primary key nor a foreign key usually causes no problems; the DBMS need only check to confirm that the new value is of the correct data type and domain. Modifying a primary key value is similar to deleting one tuple and inserting another in its place, because we use the primary key to identify tuples. Hence, the issues discussed earlier under both Insert and Delete come into play. If a foreign key attribute is modified, the DBMS must make sure that the new value refers to an existing tuple in the referenced relation.

6.4   Defining Relations

When a relational database is to be implemented for a complex application, designers commonly begin by carefully *designing* the database schema. This involves deciding which attributes belong together in each relation, choosing appropriate names for the relations and their attributes, specifying the domains and data types of the various attributes, identifying the candidate keys and choosing a primary key for each relation, and specifying all foreign keys. We will discuss two techniques for relational database design. Section 6.8 demonstrates how a relational database scheme can be designed by mapping a conceptual database design developed using the ER model (see Chapter 3). Chapters 12 and 13 describe normalization theory and relational design algorithms based on functional and multivalued dependencies. In this section, we assume that the design of a relational database schema has already been accomplished, and we discuss how a database user may declare the individual relations.

Each relational DBMS must have a Data Definition Language (DDL) for defining the relation schemas. Most DDLs are based on the SQL language, and we present the SQL DDL in Section 7.1. Here, we discuss the (idealized) language components needed to declare a relation schema. The first step is to give a name to the whole relational database schema so that individual relations can be assigned to it, using a statement such as the following:

DECLARE SCHEMA COMPANY;

The next step is to declare the domains needed for the attributes, giving each domain a name and data type. We declare possible domains for the attributes of the EMPLOYEE and DEPARTMENT relations of Figure 6.7 as follows.

DECLARE DOMAIN PERSON_SSNS **TYPE** FIXED_CHAR (9) ;
DECLARE DOMAIN PERSON_NAMES **TYPE** VARIABLE_CHAR (15) ;
DECLARE DOMAIN PERSON_INITIALS **TYPE** ALPHABETIC_CHAR (1) ;
DECLARE DOMAIN DATES **TYPE** DATE ;
DECLARE DOMAIN ADDRESSES **TYPE** VARIABLE_CHAR (35) ;
DECLARE DOMAIN PERSON_SEX **TYPE** ENUMERATED {M, F} ;
DECLARE DOMAIN PERSON_SALARIES **TYPE** MONEY ;
DECLARE DOMAIN DEPT_NUMBERS **TYPE** INTEGER_RANGE [1,10] ;
DECLARE DOMAIN DEPT_NAMES **TYPE** VARIABLE_CHAR (20) ;

The individual relations can now be defined. Constructs are needed for specifying the relation name, attribute names and domains, primary and other keys, and foreign keys. To declare the EMPLOYEE and DEPARTMENT relations of Figure 6.7, we can use the following:

DECLARE RELATION EMPLOYEE
FOR SCHEMA COMPANY
ATTRIBUTES   FNAME   **DOMAIN** PERSON_NAMES,
                 MINIT   **DOMAIN** PERSON_INITIALS,
                 LNAME   **DOMAIN** PERSON_NAMES,
                 SSN   **DOMAIN** PERSON_SSNS,
                 BDATE   **DOMAIN** DATES,
                 ADDRESS   **DOMAIN** ADDRESSES,
                 SEX   **DOMAIN** PERSON_SEX,
                 SALARY   **DOMAIN** PERSON_SALARIES,
                 SUPERSSN   **DOMAIN** PERSON_SSNS,
                 DNO   **DOMAIN** DEPT_NUMBERS

```
CONSTRAINTS PRIMARY_KEY (SSN),
            FOREIGN_KEY (SUPERSSN) REFERENCES EMPLOYEE,
            FOREIGN_KEY (DNO) REFERENCES DEPARTMENT;

DECLARE RELATION DEPARTMENT
FOR SCHEMA COMPANY
ATTRIBUTES   DNAME         DOMAIN DEPT_NAMES,
             DNUMBER       DOMAIN DEPT_NUMBERS,
             MGRSSN        DOMAIN PERSON_SSNS,
             MGRSTARTDATE  DOMAIN DATES
CONSTRAINTS PRIMARY_KEY (DNUMBER),
            KEY (DNAME),
            FOREIGN_KEY (MGRSSN) REFERENCES EMPLOYEE;
```

The preceding examples offer a brief introduction to the constructs needed in a relational DDL. We discuss the main constructs of SQL DDL, which is used as the basis for most commercial relational DBMSs, in Chapter 7.

6.5 The Relational Algebra

So far, we have discussed the concepts that the relational model provides for defining the structure and constraints of a database, and for performing the relational update operations. Now we turn our attention to the relational algebra, which is a collection of operations that are used to manipulate entire relations. These operations are used, for example, to select tuples from individual relations and to combine related tuples from several relations for the purpose of specifying a query—a retrieval request—on the database. The result of each operation is a new relation, which can be further manipulated.

The relational algebra operations are usually divided into two groups. One group includes set operations from mathematical set theory; these are applicable because each relation is defined to be a set of tuples. Set operations include UNION, INTERSECTION, DIFFERENCE, and CARTESIAN PRODUCT. The other group consists of operations developed specifically for relational databases; these include SELECT, PROJECT, and JOIN, among others. The SELECT and PROJECT operations are discussed first, because they are the simplest. Then we discuss set operations. Finally, we discuss JOIN and other complex operations. The relational database shown in Figure 6.6 is used for our examples.

6.5.1 *The* SELECT *Operation*

The SELECT operation is used to select a *subset* of the tuples in a relation that satisfy a **selection condition.** For example, to select the subset of EMPLOYEE tuples who work in department 4 or whose salary is greater than $30,000, we can individually specify each of these two conditions with the SELECT operation, as follows:

$$\sigma_{DNO=4}(EMPLOYEE)$$
$$\sigma_{SALARY>30000}(EMPLOYEE)$$

In general, the SELECT operation is denoted by

$$\sigma_{<\text{selection condition}>}(<\text{relation name}>)$$

where the symbol σ (sigma) is used to denote the SELECT operator, and the selection condition is a Boolean expression specified on the relation attributes.

The relation resulting from the SELECT operation has the *same attributes* as the relation specified in <relation name>. The Boolean expression specified in <selection condition> is made up of a number of **clauses** of the form:

<attribute name> <comparison op> <constant value>,   or
<attribute name> <comparison op> <attribute name>

where <attribute name> is the name of an attribute of <relation name>, <comparison op> is normally one of the operators $\{=, <, \le, >, \ge, \ne\}$, and <constant value> is a constant value from the attribute domain. Clauses can be arbitrarily connected by the Boolean operators AND, OR, and NOT to form a general selection condition. For example, to select the tuples for all employees who either work in department 4 and make over $25,000 per year, or work in department 5 and make over $30,000, we can specify the following SELECT operation:

$$\sigma_{(\text{DNO}=4 \text{ AND SALARY}>25000) \text{ OR } (\text{DNO}=5 \text{ AND SALARY}>30000)}(\text{EMPLOYEE})$$

The result is shown in Figure 6.8(a).

Notice that the comparison operators in the set $\{=, <, \le, >, \ge, \ne\}$ apply to attributes whose domains are *ordered values*, such as numeric or date domains. Domains of strings of characters are considered ordered based on the collating sequence of the characters. If the domain of an attribute is a set of *unordered values*, then only the comparison operators in the set $\{=, \ne\}$ can be applied to that attribute. An example of an unordered

(a)

FNAME	MINIT	LNAME	SSN	BDATE	ADDRESS	SEX	SALARY	SUPERSSN	DNO
Franklin	T	Wong	333445555	08-DEC-45	638 Voss,Houston,TX	M	40000	888665555	5
Jennifer	S	Wallace	987654321	20-JUN-31	291 Berry,Bellaire,TX	F	43000	888665555	4
Ramesh	K	Narayan	666884444	15-SEP-52	975 FireOak,Humble,TX	M	38000	333445555	5

(b)

LNAME	FNAME	SALARY
Smith	John	30000
Wong	Franklin	40000
Zelaya	Alicia	25000
Wallace	Jennifer	43000
Narayan	Ramesh	38000
English	Joyce	25000
Jabbar	Ahmad	25000
Borg	James	55000

(c)

SEX	SALARY
M	30000
M	40000
F	25000
F	43000
M	38000
M	25000
M	55000

Figure 6.8   Results of SELECT and PROJECT operations.
(a) $\sigma_{(\text{DNO}=4 \text{ AND SALARY}>25000) \text{ OR } (\text{DNO}=5 \text{ AND SALARY}>30000)}$ (EMPLOYEE)
(b) $\pi_{\text{LNAME, FNAME, SALARY}}$(EMPLOYEE).
(c) $\pi_{\text{SEX, SALARY}}$ (EMPLOYEE).

domain is the domain Color = {red, blue, green, white, yellow, . . .} where no order is specified among the various colors. Some domains allow additional types of comparison operators; for example, a domain of character strings may allow the comparison operator SUBSTRING_OF.

In general, the result of a SELECT operation can be determined as follows. The <selection condition> is applied independently to each tuple t in the relation R specified by <relation name>. This is done by substituting for each occurrence of an attribute A_i in the selection condition with its value in the tuple $t[A_i]$. If the condition evaluates to true, then tuple t is **selected**. All the selected tuples appear in the result of the SELECT operation. The Boolean conditions AND, OR, and NOT have their normal interpretation as follows:

- (cond1 AND cond2) is true if both (cond1) and (cond2) are true; otherwise, it is false.

- (cond1 OR cond2) is true if either (cond1) or (cond2) or both are true; otherwise, it is false.

- (NOT cond) is true if cond is false; otherwise, it is false.

The SELECT operator is unary; that is, it is applied on a single relation. Hence, SELECT cannot be used to select tuples from more than one relation. Moreover, the selection operation is applied to *each tuple individually*; hence, selection conditions cannot apply over more than one tuple. The **degree** of the relation resulting from a SELECT operation is the same as that of the original relation R on which the operation is applied, because it has the same attributes as R. The number of tuples in the resulting relation is always *less than or equal to* the number of tuples in the original relation R. The fraction of tuples selected by a selection condition is referred to as the **selectivity** of the condition.

Notice that the SELECT operation is **commutative;** that is,

$$\sigma_{<cond1>}(\sigma_{<cond2>}(R)) = \sigma_{<cond2>}(\sigma_{<cond1>}(R))$$

Hence, a sequence of SELECTs can be applied in any order. In addition, we can always combine a **cascade** of SELECT operations into a single SELECT operation with a conjunctive (AND) condition; that is,

$$\sigma_{<cond1>}(\sigma_{<cond2>}(\cdots(\sigma_{<condn>}(R))\cdots)) = \sigma_{<cond1> \text{ AND } <cond2> \text{ AND } \cdots \text{ AND } <condn>}(R)$$

6.5.2 *The PROJECT Operation*

If we think of a relation as a table, the SELECT operation selects some of the *rows* from the table while discarding other rows. The **PROJECT** operation, on the other hand, selects certain *columns* from the table and discards the other columns. If we are interested in only certain attributes of a relation, we use the PROJECT operation to "project" the relation over these attributes. For example, to list each employee's first and last names and salary, we can use the PROJECT operation as follows:

$\pi_{\text{LNAME, FNAME, SALARY}}(\text{EMPLOYEE})$

The resulting relation is shown in Figure 6.8(b). The general form of the PROJECT operation is

$$\pi_{<\text{attribute list}>}(<\text{relation name}>)$$

where π (pi) is the symbol used to represent the PROJECT operation and <attribute list> is a list of attributes of the relation specified by <relation name>. The resulting relation has only the attributes specified in <attribute list> and *in the same order as they appear in the list*. Hence, its **degree** is equal to the number of attributes in <attribute list>.

If the attribute list includes only nonkey attributes of a relation, duplicate tuples are likely to appear in the result. The PROJECT operation implicitly *removes any duplicate tuples*, so the result of the PROJECT operation is a set of tuples and hence a valid relation. For example, consider the following PROJECT operation:

$$\pi_{\text{SEX, SALARY}}(\text{EMPLOYEE})$$

The result is shown in Figure 6.8(c). The tuple <F, 25000> appears only once in Figure 6.8(c), even though this combination of values appears twice in the EMPLOYEE relation. Whenever two or more identical tuples appear when applying a PROJECT operation, only one is kept in the result; this is known as **duplicate elimination** and is necessary to ensure that the result of the PROJECT operation is also a relation—a *set* of tuples.

The number of tuples in a relation resulting from a PROJECT operation is always less than or equal to the number of tuples in the original relation. If the projection list includes a key of the relation, the resulting relation has the *same number* of tuples as the original one. Moreover,

$$\pi_{<\text{list1}>}(\pi_{<\text{list2}>}(R)) = \pi_{<\text{list1}>}(R)$$

as long as <list2> contains the attributes in <list1>; otherwise, the left-hand side is incorrect. It is also noteworthy that commutativity *does not* hold on PROJECT.

6.5.3 *Sequences of Operations and Renaming of Attributes*

The relations shown in Figure 6.8 do not have any names. In general, we may want to apply several relational algebra operations one after the other. Either we can write the operations as a single **relational algebra expression** by nesting the operations, or we can apply one operation at a time and create intermediate result relations. In the latter case, we must name the relations that hold the intermediate results. For example, to retrieve the first name, last name, and salary of all employees who work in department number 5, we must apply a SELECT and a PROJECT operation. We can write a single relational algebra expression as follows:

$$\pi_{\text{FNAME, LNAME, SALARY}}(\sigma_{\text{DNO}=5}(\text{EMPLOYEE}))$$

Figure 6.9(a) shows the result of this relational algebra expression. Alternatively, we can explicitly show the sequence of operations, giving a name to each intermediate relation, as follows:

(a)

FNAME	LNAME	SALARY
John	Smith	30000
Franklin	Wong	40000
Ramesh	Narayan	38000
Joyce	English	25000

(b)

TEMP	FNAME	MINIT	LNAME	SSN	BDATE	ADDRESS	SEX	SALARY	SUPERSSN	DNO
	John	B	Smith	123456789	09-JAN-55	731 Fondren,Houston,TX	M	30000	333445555	5
	Franklin	T	Wong	333445555	08-DEC-45	638 Voss,Houston,TX	M	40000	888665555	5
	Ramesh	K	Narayan	666884444	15-SEP-52	975 Fire Oak,Humble,TX	M	38000	333445555	5
	Joyce	A	English	453453453	31-JUL-62	5631 Rice,Houston,TX	F	25000	333445555	5

R	FIRSTNAME	LASTNAME	SALARY
	John	Smith	30000
	Franklin	Wong	40000
	Ramesh	Narayan	38000
	Joyce	English	25000

Figure 6.9 Results of relational algebra expressions. (a) $\pi_{\text{LNAME, FNAME,}}$ $_{\text{SALARY}} (\sigma_{\text{DNO}=5} (\text{EMPLOYEE}))$. (b) The same expression using intermediate relations and renaming of attributes.

DEP5_EMPS ← $\sigma_{\text{DNO}=5}$(EMPLOYEE)
RESULT ← $\pi_{\text{FNAME, LNAME, SALARY}}$(DEP5_EMPS)

It is often simpler to break down a complex sequence of operations by specifying intermediate result relations than to write a single relational algebra expression. We can also use this technique to **rename the attributes** in the intermediate and result relations. This can be useful in connection with more complex operations such as UNION and JOIN, as we shall see. We will introduce the notation for renaming here. To rename the attributes in a relation that results from applying a relational algebra operation, we simply list the new attribute names in parentheses, as in the following example:

TEMP ← $\sigma_{\text{DNO}=5}$(EMPLOYEE)
R(FIRSTNAME,LASTNAME,SALARY) ← $\pi_{\text{FNAME, LNAME, SALARY}}$(TEMP)

The above two operations are illustrated in Figure 6.9(b). If no renaming is applied, the names of the attributes in the resulting relation of a SELECT operation are the same as those in the original relation and in the same order. For a PROJECT operation with no renaming, the resulting relation has the same attribute names as those in the projection list and in the same order.

6.5.4 Set Theoretic Operations

The next group of relational algebra operations are the standard mathematical operations on sets. They apply to the relational model because a relation is defined to be a set of tuples and can be used to process the tuples in two relations as sets. For example, to retrieve the social security numbers of all employees who either work in department 5 or directly supervise an employee who works in department 5, we can use the UNION operation as follows:

DEP5_EMPS ← $\sigma_{DNO=5}$(EMPLOYEE)
RESULT1 ← π_{SSN}(DEP5_EMPS)
RESULT2(SSN) ← $\pi_{SUPERSSN}$(DEP5_EMPS)
RESULT ← RESULT1 ∪ RESULT2

The relation RESULT1 has the social security numbers of all employees who work in department 5, whereas RESULT2 has the social security numbers of all employees who directly supervise an employee who works in department 5. The UNION operation produces the tuples that are in either RESULT1 or RESULT2 or both (see Figure 6.10).

Several set theoretic operations are used to merge the elements of two sets in various ways, including UNION, INTERSECTION, and DIFFERENCE. These operations are binary; that is, they are applied to two sets. When these operations are adapted to relational databases, we must make sure that the operations can be applied to two relations so that the result is also a valid relation. To achieve this, the two relations on which any of the above three operations are applied must have the same **type of tuples;** this condition is called *union compatibility.* Two relations $R(A_1, A_2, \ldots, A_n)$ and $S(B_1, B_2, \ldots, B_n)$ are said to be **union compatible** if they have the same degree n, and if $dom(A_i) = dom(B_i)$ for $1 \leq i \leq n$. This means that the two relations have the same number of attributes and that each pair of corresponding attributes have the same domain.

We can define the three operations UNION, INTERSECTION, and DIFFERENCE on two union-compatible relations R and S as follows:

- *UNION:* The result of this operation, denoted by R ∪ S, is a relation that includes all tuples that are either in R or in S or in both R and S. Duplicate tuples are eliminated.

- *INTERSECTION:* The result of this operation, denoted by R ∩ S, is a relation that includes all tuples that are in both R and S.

- *DIFFERENCE:* The result of this operation, denoted by R − S, is a relation that includes all tuples that are in R but not in S.

We will adopt the convention that the resulting relation has the same attribute names as the *first* relation R. Figure 6.11 illustrates the three operations. The relations STUDENT and INSTRUCTOR in Figure 6.11(a) are union compatible, and their tuples represent the names of students and instructors, respectively. The result of the UNION oper-

RESULT1	SSN
	123456789
	333445555
	666884444
	453453453

RESULT2	SSN
	333445555
	888665555

RESULT	SSN
	123456789
	333445555
	666884444
	453453453
	888665555

Figure 6.10   RESULT ← RESULT1 ∪ RESULT2.

ation (Figure 6.11(b)) shows the names of all students and instructors. Note that duplicate tuples appear only once in the result. The result of the INTERSECTION operation (Figure 6.11(c)) includes only those who are both students and instructors. Notice that both UNION and INTERSECTION are *commutative operations*; that is,

$$R \cup S = S \cup R, \quad \text{and} \quad R \cap S = S \cap R$$

Either operation can be applied to *any number of relations*, and both are *associative operations*; that is,

$$R \cup (S \cup T) = (R \cup S) \cup T, \quad \text{and}$$
$$(R \cap S) \cap T = R \cap (S \cap T)$$

(a)

STUDENT	FN	LN
	Susan	Yao
	Ramesh	Shah
	Johnny	Kohler
	Barbara	Jones
	Amy	Ford
	Jimmy	Wang
	Ernest	Gilbert

INSTRUCTOR	FNAME	LNAME
	John	Smith
	Ricardo	Browne
	Susan	Yao
	Francis	Johnson
	Ramesh	Shah

(b)

FN	LN
Susan	Yao
Ramesh	Shah
Johnny	Kohler
Barbara	Jones
Amy	Ford
Jimmy	Wang
Ernest	Gilbert
John	Smith
Ricardo	Browne
Francis	Johnson

(c)

FN	LN
Susan	Yao
Ramesh	Shah

(d)

FN	LN
Johnny	Kohler
Barbara	Jones
Amy	Ford
Jimmy	Wang
Ernest	Gilbert

(e)

FNAME	LNAME
John	Smith
Ricardo	Browne
Francis	Johnson

Figure 6.11 The set operations UNION, INTERSECTION. and DIFFERENCE. (a) Two union compatible relations. (b) STUDENT ∪ INSTRUCTOR. (c) STUDENT ∩ INSTRUCTOR. (d) STUDENT − INSTRUCTOR. (e) INSTRUCTOR − STUDENT.

The DIFFERENCE operation is *not commutative*; that is, in general,

$$R - S \neq S - R$$

Figure 6.11(d) shows the names of students who are not instructors, and Figure 6.11(e) shows the names of instructors who are not students.

Next we discuss the CARTESIAN PRODUCT, denoted by **X**. This is also a binary set operation, but the relations on which it is applied do *not* have to be union compatible. This operation, also known as CROSS PRODUCT or CROSS JOIN, is used to combine tuples from two relations so that related tuples can be identified. In general, the result of $R(A_1, A_2, \ldots, A_n)$ **X** $S(B_1, B_2, \ldots, B_m)$ is a relation Q with n + m attributes $Q(A_1, A_2, \ldots, A_n, B_1, B_2, \ldots, B_m)$, in that order. The resulting relation Q has one tuple for each combination of tuples—one from R and one from S. Hence, if R has n_R tuples and S has n_S tuples, then R **X** S will have $n_R * n_S$ tuples. To illustrate the use of CARTESIAN PRODUCT, suppose that we want to retrieve for each female employee a list of the names of her dependents; we can do this as follows:

FEMALE_EMPS ← $\sigma_{SEX='F'}$(EMPLOYEE)
EMPNAMES ← $\pi_{FNAME, LNAME, SSN}$(FEMALE_EMPS)
EMP_DEPENDENTS ← EMPNAMES X DEPENDENT
ACTUAL_DEPENDENTS ← $\sigma_{SSN=ESSN}$(EMP_DEPENDENTS)
RESULT ← $\pi_{FNAME, LNAME, DEPENDENT\_NAME}$(ACTUAL_DEPENDENTS)

The resulting relations from the above sequence of operations are shown in Figure 6.12. The EMP_DEPENDENTS relation is the result of applying the CARTESIAN PRODUCT operation to EMPNAMES from Figure 6.12 with DEPENDENT from Figure 6.6. In EMP_DEPENDENTS, every tuple from EMPNAMES is combined with every tuple from DEPENDENT, giving a result that is not very meaningful. We only want to combine a female employee tuple with her dependents—namely, the DEPENDENT tuples whose ESSN values match the SSN value of the EMPLOYEE tuple. The ACTUAL_DEPENDENTS relation accomplishes this.

The CARTESIAN PRODUCT creates tuples with the combined attributes of two relations. We can then SELECT only related tuples from the two relations by specifying an appropriate selection condition, as we did in the preceding example. Because this sequence of CARTESIAN PRODUCT followed by SELECT is used quite commonly to identify and select related tuples from two relations, a special operation, called JOIN, was created to specify this sequence as a single operation. We discuss the JOIN operation next. The CARTESIAN PRODUCT is rarely used as a meaningful operation by itself.

6.5.5 *The JOIN Operation*

The JOIN operation, denoted by ⋈, is used to combine *related tuples* from two relations into single tuples. This operation is very important for any relational database with more than a single relation, because it allows us to process relationships among relations. To illustrate JOIN, suppose that we want to *retrieve the name of the manager of each department*. To get the manager's name, we need to combine each department tuple with the employee tuple whose SSN value matches the MGRSSN value in the department tuple.

FEMALE_ EMPS	FNAME	MINIT	LNAME	SSN	BDATE	ADDRESS	SEX	SALARY	SUPERSSN	DNO
	Alicia	J	Zelaya	999887777	19-JUL-58	3321 Castle,Spring,TX	F	25000	987654321	4
	Jennifer	S	Wallace	987654321	20-JUN-31	291 Berry,Bellaire,TX	F	43000	888665555	4
	Joyce	A	English	453453453	31-JUL-62	5631 Rice,Houston,TX	F	25000	333445555	5

EMPNAMES	FNAME	LNAME	SSN
	Alicia	Zelaya	999887777
	Jennifer	Wallace	987654321
	Joyce	English	453453453

EMP_DEPENDENTS	FNAME	LNAME	SSN	ESSN	DEPENDENT_NAME	SEX	BDATE	• • •
	Alicia	Zelaya	999887777	333445555	Alice	F	05-APR-76	• • •
	Alicia	Zelaya	999887777	333445555	Theodore	M	25-OCT-73	• • •
	Alicia	Zelaya	999887777	333445555	Joy	F	03-MAY-48	• • •
	Alicia	Zelaya	999887777	987654321	Abner	M	29-FEB-32	• • •
	Alicia	Zelaya	999887777	123456789	Michael	M	01-JAN-78	• • •
	Alicia	Zelaya	999887777	123456789	Alice	F	31-DEC-78	• • •
	Alicia	Zelaya	999887777	123456789	Elizabeth	F	05-MAY-57	• • •
	Jennifer	Wallace	987654321	333445555	Alice	F	05-APR-76	• • •
	Jennifer	Wallace	987654321	333445555	Theodore	M	25-OCT-73	• • •
	Jennifer	Wallace	987654321	333445555	Joy	F	03-MAY-48	• • •
	Jennifer	Wallace	987654321	987654321	Abner	M	29-FEB-32	• • •
	Jennifer	Wallace	987654321	123456789	Michael	M	01-JAN-78	• • •
	Jennifer	Wallace	987654321	123456789	Alice	F	31-DEC-78	• • •
	Jennifer	Wallace	987654321	123456789	Elizabeth	F	05-MAY-57	• • •
	Joyce	English	453453453	333445555	Alice	F	05-APR-76	• • •
	Joyce	English	453453453	333445555	Theodore	M	25-OCT-73	• • •
	Joyce	English	453453453	333445555	Joy	F	03-MAY-48	• • •
	Joyce	English	453453453	987654321	Abner	M	29-FEB-32	• • •
	Joyce	English	453453453	123456789	Michael	M	01-JAN-78	• • •
	Joyce	English	453453453	123456789	Alice	F	31-DEC-78	• • •
	Joyce	English	453453453	123456789	Elizabeth	F	05-MAY-57	• • •

ACTUAL_DEPENDENTS	FNAME	LNAME	SSN	ESSN	DEPENDENT_NAME	SEX	BDATE
	Jennifer	Wallace	987654321	987654321	Abner	M	29-FEB-32

RESULT	FNAME	LNAME	DEPENDENT_NAME
	Jennifer	Wallace	Abner

Figure 6.12 The CARTESIAN PRODUCT operation.

We do this by using the JOIN operation, and then projecting the result over the necessary attributes:

$$\text{DEPT\_MGR} \leftarrow \text{DEPARTMENT} \bowtie_{\text{MGRSSN=SSN}} \text{EMPLOYEE}$$
$$\text{RESULT} \leftarrow \pi_{\text{DNAME, LNAME, FNAME}}(\text{DEPT\_MGR})$$

DEPT_MGR	DNAME	DNUMBER	MGRSSN	• • •	FNAME	MINIT	LNAME	SSN	• • •
	Research	5	333445555	• • •	Franklin	T	Wong	333445555	• • •
	Administration	4	987654321	• • •	Jennifer	S	Wallace	987654321	• • •
	Headquarters	1	888665555	• • •	James	E	Borg	888665555	• • •

Figure 6.13   The JOIN operation.

The first operation is illustrated in Figure 6.13. The example we gave earlier to illustrate the CARTESIAN PRODUCT operation can be specified, using the JOIN operation, by replacing the two operations

EMP_DEPENDENTS ← EMPNAMES X DEPENDENT
ACTUAL_DEPENDENTS ← $\sigma_{SSN=ESSN}$(EMP_DEPENDENTS)

with

ACTUAL_DEPENDENTS ← EMPNAMES ⋈ $_{SSN=ESSN}$DEPENDENT

The general form of a JOIN operation on two relations $R(A_1, A_2, \ldots, A_n)$ and $S(B_1, B_2, \ldots, B_m)$ is

R ⋈ $_{<join\ condition>}$ S

The result of the JOIN is a relation Q with n + m attributes $Q(A_1, A_2, \ldots, A_n, B_1, B_2, \ldots, B_m)$ in that order; Q has one tuple for each combination of tuples—one from R and one from S—*whenever the combination satisfies the join condition*. This is the main difference between CARTESIAN PRODUCT and JOIN: in JOIN, only combinations of tuples satisfying the join condition appear in the result; whereas in the CARTESIAN PRODUCT *all* combinations of tuples are included in the result. The join condition is specified on attributes from the two relations R and S and is evaluated for each combination of tuples. Each tuple combination for which the join condition evaluates to true for its attribute values is included in the resulting relation Q as a single tuple.

A join condition is of the form:

<condition> AND <condition> AND ⋯ AND <condition>

where each condition is of the form $A_i \theta B_j$, A_i is an attribute of R, B_j is an attribute of S, A_i and B_j have the same domain, and θ is one of the comparison operators $\{=, <, \leq, >, \geq, \neq\}$. A JOIN operation with such a general join condition is called a **THETA JOIN.** Tuples whose join attributes are null *do not* appear in the result.

The most common JOIN involves join conditions with equality comparisons only. Such a JOIN, where the only comparison operator used is =, is called an **EQUIJOIN.** Both examples we have considered were EQUIJOINs. Notice that in the result of an EQUIJOIN we always have one or more pairs of attributes that have *identical values* in every tuple. For example, in Figure 6.13, the values of the attributes MGRSSN and SSN are identical in every tuple of DEPT_MGR because the equality join condition is specified on these two attributes. Because one of each pair of attributes with identical values is superfluous, a new operation, called **NATURAL JOIN,** was created to get rid of the second attribute in an equijoin condition. We denote natural join by *. It is basically an equijoin followed by removal of the superfluous attributes. The standard definition of NATURAL JOIN requires that the two join attributes (or each pair of join attributes) have the same name. If this is not the case, a renaming operation is applied first. An example is

DEPT (DNAME,DNUM,MGRSSN,MGRSTARTDATE) ← DEPARTMENT
PROJ_DEPT ← PROJECT * DEPT

The attribute DNUM is called the **join attribute.** The resulting relation is illustrated in Figure 6.14(a). In the PROJ_DEPT relation, each tuple combines a PROJECT tuple with the DEPARTMENT tuple for the department that controls the project. In the resulting relation we keep only one *join attribute*.

If the attributes on which the natural join is specified *have the same names in both relations*, renaming is unnecessary. To apply a natural join on the DNUMBER attribute of DEPARTMENT and DEPT_LOCATIONS, it is sufficient to write

DEPT_LOCS ← DEPARTMENT * DEPT_LOCATIONS

The resulting relation is shown in Figure 6.14(b), which combines each department with its locations and has one tuple for each location. In general, NATURAL JOIN is performed by equating *all* attribute pairs that have the same name in the two relations. There can be a list of join attributes from each relation, and each corresponding pair must have the same name.

A more general definition for NATURAL JOIN is

$$Q \leftarrow R *_{(<list1>),(<list2>)} S$$

In this case, $<list1>$ specifies a list of i attributes from R, and $<list2>$ specifies a list of i attributes from S. The lists are used to form equality comparison conditions between pairs of corresponding attributes; the conditions are then ANDed together. Only the list corresponding to attributes of the first relation R—$<list 1>$—is kept in the result Q.

Notice that, if no combination of tuples satisfies the join condition, the result of a JOIN is an empty relation with zero tuples. In general, if R has n_R tuples and S has n_S tuples, the result of a JOIN operation $R \bowtie_{<join condition>} S$ will have between zero and

(a)

PROJ_DEPT	PNAME	PNUMBER	PLOCATION	DNUM	DNAME	MGRSSN	MGRSTARTDATE
	ProductX	1	Bellaire	5	Research	333445555	22-MAY-78
	ProductY	2	Sugarland	5	Research	333445555	22-MAY-78
	ProductZ	3	Houston	5	Research	333445555	22-MAY-78
	Computerization	10	Stafford	4	Administration	987654321	01-JAN-85
	Reorganization	20	Houston	1	Headquarters	888665555	19-JUN-71
	Newbenefits	30	Stafford	4	Administration	987654321	01-JAN-85

(b)

DEPT_LOCS	DNAME	DNUMBER	MGRSSN	MGRSTARTDATE	LOCATION
	Headquarters	1	888665555	19-JUN-71	Houston
	Administration	4	987654321	01-JAN-85	Stafford
	Research	5	333445555	22-MAY-78	Bellaire
	Research	5	333445555	22-MAY-78	Sugarland
	Research	5	333445555	22-MAY-78	Houston

Figure 6.14 The NATURAL JOIN operation. (a) PROJ_DEPT ← PROJECT * DEPT. (b) DEPT_LOCS ← DEPARTMENT * DEPT_LOCATIONS.

$n_R * n_S$ tuples. The expected size of the join result divided by the maximum size $n_R * n_S$ leads to a ratio called **join selectivity,** which is a property of each join condition. If there is no <join condition> to satisfy, all combinations of tuples qualify and the JOIN becomes a CARTESIAN PRODUCT, also called a CROSS JOIN.

6.5.6 *Complete Set of Relational Algebra Operations*

It has been shown that the set of relational algebra operations $\{\sigma, \pi, \cup, -, \times\}$ is a **complete** set; that is, any of the other relational algebra operations can be expressed as a *sequence of operations from this set*. For example, the INTERSECTION operation can be expressed by using UNION and DIFFERENCE as follows:

$$R \cap S \equiv (R \cup S) - ((R - S) \cup (S - R))$$

Although, strictly speaking, INTERSECTION is not required, it is inconvenient to specify this complex expression every time we wish to specify an intersection. As another example, a JOIN operation can be specified as a CARTESIAN PRODUCT followed by a SELECT operation, as we discussed:

$$R \bowtie_{<condition>} S \equiv \sigma_{<condition>} (R \times S)$$

Similarly, a NATURAL JOIN can be specified as a CARTESIAN PRODUCT followed by SELECT and PROJECT operations. Hence, the various JOIN operations are also *not strictly necessary* for the expressive power of the relational algebra; however, they are very important—as is the INTERSECTION operation—because they are convenient to use and are very commonly applied in database applications. Other operations have been included in the relational algebra for convenience rather than necessity. We discuss one of these—the DIVISION operation—in the next section.

6.5.7 *The DIVISION Operation*★

The DIVISION operation is useful for a special kind of query that sometimes occurs in database applications. An example is: "Retrieve the names of employees who work on *all* the projects that 'John Smith' works on." To express this query using the DIVISION operation, proceed as follows. First, retrieve the list of project numbers that 'John Smith' works on in the intermediate relation SMITH_PNOS:

SMITH $\leftarrow \sigma_{FNAME='John' \text{ AND } LNAME='Smith'}(EMPLOYEE)$
SMITH_PNOS $\leftarrow \pi_{PNO}(WORKS\_ON *_{ESSN=SSN} SMITH)$

Next, create a relation that includes a tuple <PNO, ESSN> whenever the employee whose social security number is ESSN works on the project whose number is PNO in the intermediate relation SSN_PNOS:

SSN_PNOS $\leftarrow \pi_{PNO, ESSN}(WORKS\_ON)$

Finally, apply the DIVISION operation to the two relations, which gives the desired employees' social security numbers:

SSNS(SSN) $\leftarrow$ SSN_PNOS $\div$ SMITH_PNOS
RESULT $\leftarrow \pi_{FNAME, LNAME}(SSNS * EMPLOYEE)$

The previous operations are shown in Figure 6.15(a). In general, the DIVISION operation is applied to two relations $R(Z) \div S(X)$, where $X \subseteq Z$. Let $Y = Z - X$; that is, let Y be the set of attributes of R that are not attributes of S. The result of DIVISION is a relation $T(Y)$ that includes a tuple t if a tuple t_R whose $t_R[Y] = t$ appears in R, with $t_R[X] = t_S$ *for every tuple* t_S in S. This means that, for a tuple t to appear in the result T of the DIVISION, the values in t must appear in R in combination with *every* tuple in S.

Figure 6.15(b) illustrates a DIVISION operator where $X = \{A\}$ and $Y = \{B\}$ are both single attributes. Notice that b_1 and b_4 appear in R in combination with all three tuples in S; that is why they appear in the resulting relation T. All other values of B in R do not appear with all the tuples in S and are not selected: b_2 does not appear with a_2 and b_3 does not appear with a_1.

The DIVISION operator can be expressed as a sequence of π, X, and $-$ operations as follows:

$$T_1 \leftarrow \pi_Y(R)$$
$$T_2 \leftarrow \pi_Y((S \; X \; T_1) - R)$$
$$T \leftarrow T_1 - T_2$$

6.6 Additional Relational Operations⋆

Some common database requests cannot be performed with the standard relational algebra operations described in Section 6.5. Most commercial query languages for relational DBMSs include capabilities to perform these requests. In this section we define additional operations to express these requests. These operations enhance the expressive power of the relational algebra.

6.6.1 *Aggregate Functions*

The first type of request that cannot be expressed in relational algebra is to specify mathematical **aggregate functions** on collections of values from the database. An example involves retrieving the average or total salary of all employees or the number of employee tuples. Common functions applied to collections of numeric values include SUM, AVERAGE, MAXIMUM, and MINIMUM. The COUNT function is used for counting tuples. Each of these functions can be applied to a collection of tuples.

Another common type of request involves grouping the tuples in a relation by the value of some of their attributes and then applying an aggregate function independently to each group. An example would be to group employee tuples by DNO, so that each group includes the tuples for employees working in the same department. We can then list each DNO value along with, say, the average salary of employees within the department.

We can define a FUNCTION operation,⋆ using the symbol $\mathfrak{F}$ (pronounced "script F"), to specify these types of requests as follows:

<grouping attributes> $\mathfrak{F}$ <function list> (<relation name>)

⋆There is no single agreed-upon notation for specifying aggregate functions.

(a)

SSN_PNOS	ESSN	PNO
	123456789	1
	123456789	2
	666884444	3
	453453453	1
	453453453	2
	333445555	2
	333445555	3
	333445555	10
	333445555	20
	999887777	30
	999887777	10
	987987987	10
	987987987	30
	987654321	30
	987654321	20
	888665555	20

SMITH_PNOS	PNO
	1
	2

SSNS	SSN
	123456789
	453453453

(b)

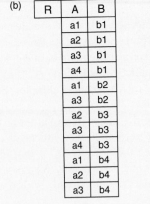

Figure 6.15   The DIVISION operation. (a) Dividing SSN_PNOS by SMITH_PNOS. (b) T ← R ÷ S.

where <grouping attributes> is a list of attributes of the relation specified in <relation name>, and <function list> is a list of (<function> <attribute>) pairs. In each such pair, <function> is one of the allowed functions—such as SUM, AVERAGE, MAXIMUM, MINIMUM, COUNT—and <attribute> is an attribute of the relation specified by <relation name>. The resulting relation has the grouping attributes plus one attribute for each element in the function list. For example, to retrieve each department number, the number of employees in the department, and their average salary, we write

$$R(\text{DNO, NUMBER\_OF\_EMPLOYEES, AVERAGE\_SAL}) \leftarrow$$
$$_{\text{DNO}} \Im_{\text{ COUNT SSN, AVERAGE SALARY}}(\text{EMPLOYEE})$$

The result of this operation is shown in Figure 6.16(a).

In the above example, we specified a list of attribute names—between parentheses—for the resulting relation R. If no such list is specified, then the attributes of the resulting relation that correspond to the function list will each be the concatenation of the function name with the attribute name on which the function is applied in the form <function>_<attribute>. For example, the result of the following operation is shown in Figure 6.16(b).

$$_{\text{DNO}} \Im_{\text{ COUNT SSN, AVERAGE SALARY}}(\text{EMPLOYEE})$$

If no grouping attributes are specified, the functions are applied to the attribute values of *all the tuples* in the relation, so the resulting relation has a *single tuple only*. For example, the result of the following operation is shown in Figure 6.16(c).

$$\Im_{\text{ COUNT SSN, AVERAGE SALARY}}(\text{EMPLOYEE})$$

(a)

R	DNO	NO_OF_EMPLOYEES	AVERAGE_SAL
	5	4	33250
	4	3	31000
	1	1	55000

(b)

DNO	COUNT_SSN	AVERAGE_SALARY
5	4	33250
4	3	31000
1	1	55000

(c)

COUNT_SSN	AVERAGE_SALARY
8	35125

Figure 6.16 The FUNCTION operation.
(a) R (DNO,NO_OF_EMPLOYEES,AVERAGE_SAL)$\leftarrow$ $_{\text{DNO}} \Im$ COUNT SSN,AVERAGE SALARY (EMPLOYEE). (b) $_{\text{DNO}}\Im$COUNT SSN,AVERAGE SALARY (EMPLOYEE). (c) $\Im$COUNT SSN,AVERAGE SALARY (EMPLOYEE).

It is worth emphasizing that the result of applying an aggregate function is a relation, not a scalar number—even if it has a single value.

6.6.2 *Recursive Closure Operations*

Another type of operation that, in general, cannot be specified in the relational algebra is **recursive closure.** This operation is applied to a **recursive relationship** between tuples of the same type, such as the relationship between an employee and a supervisor. This relationship is described by the foreign key SUPERSSN of the EMPLOYEE relation in Figures 6.6 and 6.7, which relates each employee tuple (in the role of supervisee) to another employee tuple (in the role of supervisor). An example of a recursive operation is to retrieve all supervisees of an employee e at all levels—that is, all employees e' directly supervised by e, all employees e'' directly supervised by each employee e', all employees e''' directly supervised by each employee e'', and so on. Although it is straightforward in the relational algebra to specify all employees supervised by e *at a specific level*, it is difficult to specify all supervisees at *all* levels. For example, to specify the SSNs of all employees e' directly supervised—*at level one*—by the employee e whose name is 'James Borg' (see Figure 6.6), we can apply the following operations:

$$\text{BORG\_SSN} \leftarrow \pi_{\text{SSN}}(\sigma_{\text{FNAME}='\text{James}' \text{ AND LNAME}='\text{Borg}'}(\text{EMPLOYEE}))$$
$$\text{SUPERVISION(SSN1, SSN2)} \leftarrow \pi_{\text{SSN, SUPERSSN}}(\text{EMPLOYEE})$$
$$\text{RESULT1(SSN)} \leftarrow \pi_{\text{SSN1}}(\text{SUPERVISION} \bowtie_{\text{SSN2=SSN}} \text{BORG\_SSN})$$

To retrieve all employees supervised by Borg at level two—that is, all employees e'' supervised by some employee e' who is directly supervised by Borg—we can apply another JOIN to the result of the first query, as follows:

$$\text{RESULT2(SSN)} \leftarrow \pi_{\text{SSN1}}(\text{SUPERVISION} \bowtie_{\text{SSN2=SSN}} \text{RESULT1})$$

To get both sets of employees supervised at levels one and two by 'James Borg,' we can apply the UNION operation to the two results, as follows:

$$\text{RESULT3} \leftarrow (\text{RESULT1} \cup \text{RESULT2})$$

The results of these queries are illustrated in Figure 6.17. Although it is possible to retrieve employees at each level and then take their UNION, we cannot, in general, specify a query such as "retrieve the supervisees of 'James Borg' at all levels" if we do not know the *maximum number of levels*, because we would need a looping mechanism.

6.6.3 *OUTER JOIN and OUTER UNION Operations*

Finally, we discuss some extensions of the JOIN and UNION operations. The JOIN operations described earlier match tuples that satisfy the join condition. For example, for a NATURAL JOIN operation R * S, only tuples from R that have matching tuples in S—and vice versa—appear in the result. Hence, tuples without a "related tuple" are eliminated from the result. Tuples with null in the join attributes are also eliminated. A set of operations, called OUTER JOINs, can be used when we want to keep all tuples in R or S or both in the result—whether or not they have matching tuples in the other relation.

(Borg's SSN is 888665555)

	(SSN)	(SUPERSSN)
SUPERVISION	SSN1	SSN2
	123456789	333445555
	333445555	888665555
	999887777	987654321
	987654321	888665555
	666884444	333445555
	453453453	333445555
	987987987	987654321
	888665555	null

RESULT 1	SSN
	333445555
	987654321

(Supervised by Borg)

RESULT 2	SSN
	123456789
	999887777
	666884444
	453453453
	987987987

(Supervised by Borg's subordinates)

RESULT	SSN
	123456789
	999887777
	666884444
	453453453
	987987987
	333445555
	987654321

(RESULT1 ∪ RESULT2)

Figure 6.17 Two-level recursion.

For example, suppose that we want a list of all employee names and also the name of the departments they manage, *if they happen to manage a department*; we can apply an operation **LEFT OUTER JOIN,** denoted by ⟕, to retrieve the result as follows:

TEMP ← (EMPLOYEE ⟕ $_{SSN=MGRSSN}$ DEPARTMENT)
RESULT ← $\pi_{FNAME, MINIT, LNAME, DNAME}$(TEMP)

The LEFT OUTER JOIN operation keeps every tuple in the *first* or left relation R in R ⟕ S; if no matching tuple is found in S, then the attributes of S in the result are filled or "padded" with null values. The result of these operations is shown in Figure 6.18.

A similar operation, RIGHT OUTER JOIN, denoted by ⟖, keeps every tuple in the *second* or right relation S in the result of R ⟖ S. A third operation, FULL OUTER JOIN, denoted by ⟗, keeps all tuples in both the left and the right relations when no matching tuples are found, padding them with null values as needed.

The **OUTER UNION** operation was developed to take the union of tuples from two relations that are *not union compatible*. This operation will take the UNION of tuples in two relations that are **partially compatible,** meaning that only some of their attributes are union compatible. The attributes that are not union compatible from either relation are kept in the result, and tuples that have no values for these attributes are padded with

RESULT	FNAME	MINIT	LNAME	DNAME
	John	B	Smith	null
	Franklin	T	Wong	Research
	Alicia	J	Zelaya	null
	Jennifer	S	Wallace	Administration
	Ramesh	K	Narayan	null
	Joyce	A	English	null
	Ahmad	V	Jabbar	null
	James	E	Borg	Headquarters

Figure 6.18 The LEFT OUTER JOIN operation.

null values. For example, an OUTER UNION can be applied to two relations whose schemas are STUDENT(Name, SSN, Department, Advisor) and FACULTY(Name, SSN, Department, Rank). The resulting relation schema is R(Name, SSN, Department, Advisor, Rank), and all the tuples from both relations are included in the result. Student tuples will have a null for the Rank attribute, whereas faculty tuples will have a null for the Advisor attribute. A tuple that exists in both will have values for all its attributes.

Another capability that exists in most commercial languages (but not in the relational algebra) is that of specifying operations on values after they are extracted from the database. For example, arithmetic operations such as $+$, $-$, and $*$ can be applied to numeric values.

6.7 Examples of Queries in the Relational Algebra

We now give additional examples to illustrate the use of the relational algebra operations. All examples refer to the database of Figure 6.6. In general, the same query can be stated in numerous ways using the various operations. We will state each query in one way and leave it to the reader to come up with equivalent formulations.

QUERY 1
Retrieve the name and address of all employees who work for the 'Research' department.

RESEARCH_DEPT ← $\sigma_{DNAME='Research'}$(DEPARTMENT)
RESEARCH_DEPT_EMPS ← (RESEARCH_DEPT $\bowtie$ $_{DNUMBER=DNO}$ EMPLOYEE)
RESULT ← $\pi_{FNAME, LNAME, ADDRESS}$(RESEARCH_DEPT_EMPS)

This query could be specified in other ways; for example, the order of the JOIN and SELECT operations could be reversed, or the JOIN could be replaced by a NATURAL JOIN.

QUERY 2
For every project located in 'Stafford', list the project number, the controlling department number, and the department manager's last name, address, and birthdate.

STAFFORD_PROJS ← $\sigma_{PLOCATION='Stafford'}$(PROJECT)
CONTR_DEPT ← (STAFFORD_PROJS ⋈ $_{DNUM=DNUMBER}$ DEPARTMENT)
PROJ_DEPT_MGR ← (CONTR_DEPT ⋈ $_{MGRSSN=SSN}$ EMPLOYEE)
RESULT ← $\pi_{PNUMBER, DNUM, LNAME, ADDRESS, BDATE}$ (PROJ_DEPT_MGR)

QUERY 3

Find the names of employees who work on *all* the projects controlled by department number 5.

DEPT5_PROJS(PNO) ← $\pi_{PNUMBER}(\sigma_{DNUM=5}$(PROJECT))
EMP_PROJ(SSN, PNO) ← $\pi_{ESSN, PNO}$(WORKS_ON)
RESULT_EMP_SSNS ← EMP_PROJ ÷ DEPT5_PROJS
RESULT ← $\pi_{LNAME, FNAME}$(RESULT_EMP_SSNS * EMPLOYEE)

QUERY 4

Make a list of project numbers for projects that involve an employee whose last name is 'Smith', either as a worker or as a manager of the department that controls the project.

SMITHS(ESSN) ← $\pi_{SSN}(\sigma_{LNAME='Smith'}$(EMPLOYEE))
SMITH_WORKER_PROJS ← π_{PNO}(WORKS_ON * SMITHS)
MGRS ← $\pi_{LNAME, DNUMBER}$(EMPLOYEE ⋈ $_{SSN=MGRSSN}$ DEPARTMENT)
SMITH_MGRS ← $\sigma_{LNAME='Smith'}$(MGRS)
SMITH_MANAGED_DEPTS(DNUM) ← $\pi_{DNUMBER}$(SMITH_MGRS)
SMITH_MGR_PROJS(PNO) ← $\pi_{PNUMBER}$(SMITH_MANAGED_DEPTS * PROJECT)
RESULT ← (SMITH_WORKER_PROJS ∪ SMITH_MGR_PROJS)

QUERY 5

List the names of all employees with two or more dependents.

Strictly speaking, this query *cannot be done in the relational algebra*. We have to use the FUNCTION operation with the COUNT aggregate function. We assume that dependents of the *same* employee have *distinct* DEPENDENT_NAME values.

T_1(SSN, NO_OF_DEPS) ← $_{ESSN}$ ℑ $_{COUNT\ DEPENDENT\_NAME}$(DEPENDENT)
T_2 ← $\sigma_{NO\_OF\_DEPS\geq2}(T_1)$
RESULT ← $\pi_{LNAME, FNAME}(T_2$ * EMPLOYEE)

QUERY 6

Retrieve the names of employees who have no dependents.

ALL_EMPS ← π_{SSN}(EMPLOYEE)
EMPS_WITH_DEPS(SSN) ← π_{ESSN}(DEPENDENT)
EMPS_WITHOUT_DEPS ← (ALL_EMPS − EMPS_WITH_DEPS)
RESULT ← $\pi_{LNAME, FNAME}$(EMPS_WITHOUT_DEPS * EMPLOYEE)

QUERY 7

List the names of managers who have at least one dependent.

MGRS(SSN) ← π_{MGRSSN}(DEPARTMENT)
EMPS_WITH_DEPS(SSN) ← π_{ESSN}(DEPENDENT)
MGRS_WITH_DEPS ← (MGRS ∩ EMPS_WITH_DEPS)
RESULT ← $\pi_{LNAME, FNAME}$(MGRS_WITH_DEPS * EMPLOYEE)

As we mentioned earlier, the same query can, in general, be specified in many different ways. For example, the operations can often be applied in various sequences. In addition, some operations can be used to replace others; for example, the INTERSECTION operation in Query 7 can be replaced by a natural join. As an exercise, try to do each of the above example queries using different operations. In Chapters 7 and 8 we will show how these queries are stated in other relational languages.

6.8 Relational Database Design Using ER-to-Relational Mapping★

In this section, we show how a relational database schema can be derived from a conceptual schema developed using the Entity-Relationship (ER) model (see Chapter 3). Many CASE (computer-aided software engineering) tools are based on the ER model and its variations. These computerized tools are used interactively by database designers to develop an ER schema for their database application. Many tools use ER diagrams or variations to develop the schema graphically, and then automatically convert it into a relational database schema in the DDL of a specific relational DBMS.

In Section 6.8.1, we give the outline of an algorithm that can map an ER schema into the corresponding relational database schema. Then, in Section 6.8.2, we provide a summary of the correspondences between ER model constructs and relational model constructs.

6.8.1 *ER-to-Relational Mapping Algorithm*

We now informally describe the steps of an algorithm for ER-to-relational mapping.

The COMPANY relational schema shown in Figure 6.5 can be derived from the ER schema of Figure 3.2 by following these steps. We illustrate each step by using examples from the COMPANY schema.

STEP 1: For each regular entity type E in the ER schema, create a relation R that includes all the simple attributes of E. Include only the simple component attributes of a composite attribute. Choose one of the key attributes of E as primary key for R. If the chosen key of E is composite, the set of simple attributes that form it will together form the primary key of R.

In our example, we create the relations EMPLOYEE, DEPARTMENT, and PROJECT in Figure 6.5 to correspond to the regular entity types EMPLOYEE, DEPARTMENT, and PROJECT from Figure 3.2. These are sometimes called "entity" relations. The foreign key and relationship attributes are not included yet; they will be added during subsequent steps. These include the attributes SUPERSSN and DNO of EMPLOYEE; MGRSSN and MGRSTART-

DATE of DEPARTMENT; and DNUM of PROJECT. We choose SSN, DNUMBER, and PNUMBER as primary keys for the relations EMPLOYEE, DEPARTMENT, and PROJECT, respectively.

STEP 2:   For each weak entity type W in the ER schema with owner entity type E, create a relation R, and include all simple attributes (or simple components of composite attributes) of W as attributes of R. In addition, include as foreign key attributes of R the primary key attribute(s) of the relation(s) that correspond to the owner entity type(s); this takes care of the identifying relationship type of W. The primary key of R is the combination of the primary key(s) of the owner(s) and the partial key of the weak entity type W, if any.

In our example, we create the relation DEPENDENT in this step to correspond to the weak entity type DEPENDENT. We include the primary key of the EMPLOYEE relation—which corresponds to the owner entity type—as a foreign key attribute of DEPENDENT; we renamed it ESSN, although this was not necessary. The primary key of the DEPENDENT relation is the combination {ESSN, DEPENDENT_NAME} because DEPENDENT_NAME is the partial key of DEPENDENT.

STEP 3:   For each binary 1:1 relationship type R in the ER schema, identify the relations S and T that correspond to the entity types participating in R. Choose one of the relations—S, say—and include as foreign key in S the primary key of T. It is better to choose an entity type with total participation in R in the role of S. Include all the simple attributes (or simple components of composite attributes) of the 1:1 relationship type R as attributes of S.

In our example, we map the 1:1 relationship type MANAGES from Figure 3.2 by choosing the participating entity type DEPARTMENT to serve in the role of S, because its participation in the MANAGES relationship type is total (every department has a manager). We include the primary key of the EMPLOYEE relation as foreign key in the DEPARTMENT relation and rename it MGRSSN. We also include the simple attribute StartDate of the MANAGES relationship type in the DEPARTMENT relation and rename it MGRSTARTDATE.

Notice that an alternative mapping of a 1:1 relationship type is possible by merging the two entity types and the relationship into a single relation. This is particularly appropriate when both participations are total and when the entity types do not participate in any other relationship types.

STEP 4:   For each regular (nonweak) binary 1:N relationship type R, identify the relation S that represents the participating entity type at the *N-side* of the relationship type. Include as foreign key in S the primary key of the relation T that represents the other entity type participating in R; this is because each entity instance on the N-side is related to at most one entity instance on the 1-side of the relationship type. Include any simple attributes (or simple components of composite attributes) of the 1:N relationship type as attributes of S.

In our example, we now map the 1:N relationship types WORKS_FOR, CONTROLS, and SUPERVISION from Figure 3.2. For WORKS_FOR we include the primary key of the DEPARTMENT relation as foreign key in the EMPLOYEE relation and call it DNO. For SUPERVISION we include the primary key of the EMPLOYEE relation as foreign key in the

EMPLOYEE relation itself(!) and call it SUPERSSN. The CONTROLS relationship is mapped to the foreign key attribute DNUM of PROJECT.

STEP 5: For each binary M:N relationship type R, create a new relation S to represent R. Include as foreign key attributes in S the primary keys of the relations that represent the participating entity types; their combination will form the primary key of S. Also include any simple attributes of the M:N relationship type (or simple components of composite attributes) as attributes of S. Notice that we cannot represent an M:N relationship type by a single foreign key attribute in one of the participating relations—as we did for 1:1 or 1:N relationship types—because of the M:N cardinality ratio.

In our example, we map the M:N relationship type WORKS_ON from Figure 3.2 by creating the relation WORKS_ON in Figure 6.5. The relation WORKS_ON is sometimes called a "relationship" relation, since it corresponds to a relationship type. We include the primary keys of the PROJECT and EMPLOYEE relations as foreign keys in WORKS_ON and rename them PNO and ESSN, respectively. We also include an attribute HOURS in WORKS_ON to represent the Hours attribute of the relationship type. The primary key of the WORKS_ON relation is the combination of the foreign key attributes {ESSN, PNO}.

Notice that we can always map 1:1 or 1:N relationships in a manner similar to M:N relationships. This alternative is particularly useful when few relationship instances exist, in order to avoid null values in foreign keys. In this case, the primary key of the "relationship" relation will be the foreign key of *only one* of the participating "entity" relations. For a 1:N relationship, this will be the entity relation on the N-side. For a 1:1 relationship, the entity relation with total participation (if any) is chosen.

STEP 6: For each multivalued attribute A, create a new relation R that includes an attribute corresponding to A plus the primary key attribute K (as a foreign key in R) of the relation that represents the entity type or relationship type that has A as an attribute. The primary key of R is the combination of A and K. If the multivalued attribute is composite, we include its simple components.

In our example, we create a relation DEPT_LOCATIONS. The attribute DLOCATION represents the multivalued attribute Locations of DEPARTMENT, while DNUMBER—as foreign key—represents the primary key of the DEPARTMENT relation. The primary key of DEPT_LOCATIONS is the combination of {DNUMBER, DLOCATION}. A separate tuple will exist in DEPT_LOCATIONS for each location that a department has.

Figure 6.5 shows the relational database schema obtained through the preceding steps, and Figure 6.6 shows a sample database instance. Notice that we did not discuss the mapping of n-ary relationship types (n > 2), because none exist in Figure 3.2; these can be mapped in a similar way to M:N relationship types by including the following additional step in the mapping procedure.

STEP 7: For each n-ary relationship type R, n > 2, create a new relation S to represent R. Include as foreign key attributes in S the primary keys of the relations that represent the participating entity types. Also include any simple attributes of the n-ary relationship type (or simple components of composite attributes) as attributes of S. The primary key of S is usually a combination of all the foreign keys that reference the relations representing the participating entity types. However, if the participation constraint (min, max) of one of the entity types E participating in R has max $= 1$, then the primary key of S can be the single foreign key attribute that references the relation E' corresponding to E; this is because, in this case, each entity e in E will participate in at most one relationship instance of R and hence can uniquely identify that relationship instance. This concludes the mapping procedure. ∎

For example, consider the relationship type SUPPLY of Figure 3.16(a). This can be mapped to the relation SUPPLY shown in Figure 6.19, whose primary key is the combination of foreign keys {SNAME, PARTNO, PROJNAME}.

The main point to note in a relational schema, as compared to an ER schema, is that relationship types are not represented explicitly; instead, they are represented by having two attributes A and B, one a primary key and the other a foreign key—over the same domain—included in two relations S and T. Two tuples in S and T are related when they have the same value for A and B. By using the EQUIJOIN (or NATURALJOIN) operation over S.A and T.B, we can combine all pairs of related tuples from S and T and materialize the relationship. When a binary 1:1 or 1:N relationship type is involved, a single join operation is usually needed. For a binary M:N relationship type, two join operations are needed, whereas for n-ary relationship types, n joins are needed.

For example, to form a relation that includes the employee name, project name, and hours that the employee works on each project, we need to connect each EMPLOYEE tuple to the related PROJECT tuples via the WORKS_ON relation of Figure 6.5. Hence, we must apply the EQUIJOIN operation to the EMPLOYEE and WORKS_ON relations with the join condition SSN = ESSN, and then apply another EQUIJOIN operation to the resulting relation and the PROJECT relation with join condition PNO = PNUMBER. In general, when multiple relationships need to be traversed, numerous join operations must be specified. A relational database user must always be aware of the foreign key attributes in order to use them correctly in combining related tuples from two or more relations.

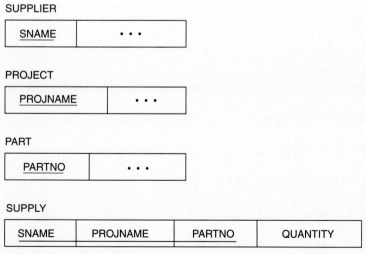

Figure 6.19 Mapping the n-ary relationship type SUPPLY from Figure 3.16(a).

Table 6.1 Join Conditions for Materializing the Relationship Types of the COMPANY ER Schema

ER Relationship	Participating Relations	Join Condition
WORKS_FOR	EMPLOYEE, DEPARTMENT	EMPLOYEE.DNO = DEPARTMENT.DNUMBER
MANAGES	EMPLOYEE, DEPARTMENT	EMPLOYEE.SSN = DEPARTMENT.MGRSSN
SUPERVISION	EMPLOYEE(E) EMPLOYEE(S)	EMPLOYEE(E).SUPERSSN = EMPLOYEE(S).SSN
WORKS_ON	EMPLOYEE, WORKS_ON, PROJECT	EMPLOYEE.SSN = WORKS_ON.ESSN AND PROJECT.PNUMBER = WORKS_ON.PNO
CONTROLS	DEPARTMENT, PROJECT	DEPARTMENT.DNUMBER = PROJECT.DNUM
DEPENDENTS_OF	EMPLOYEE, DEPENDENT	EMPLOYEE.SSN = DEPENDENT.ESSN

Table 6.1 shows the pairs of attributes that are used in EQUIJOIN operations to materialize each relationship type in the COMPANY schema of Figure 3.2. To materialize the 1:N relationship type WORKS_ON, we apply EQUIJOIN to the relations EMPLOYEE and DEPARTMENT on the attributes DNO of EMPLOYEE and DNUMBER of DEPARTMENT. According to the database in Figure 6.6, the employees Smith, Wong, Narayan, and English work for department 5 (Research); Zelaya, Wallace, and Jabbar work for department 4 (Administration); and Borg works for department 1 (Headquarters).

Another point to note in the relational schema is that we create a separate relation for *each* multivalued attribute. For a particular entity with a set of values for the multivalued attribute, the key attribute value of the entity is repeated once for each value of the multivalued attribute in a separate tuple. This is because the basic relational model does *not* allow multiple values (or a set of values) for an attribute in a single tuple. For example, because department 5 has three locations, three tuples exist in the DEPT_LOCATIONS relation of Figure 6.6; each tuple specifies one of the locations. An equijoin is needed to relate the values of the multivalued attribute to the values of other attributes of an entity or a relationship instance, but we still get multiple tuples. The relational algebra does not have a NEST or COMPRESS operation that would produce from the DEPT_LOCATIONS relation of Figure 6.6 a set of tuples of the form {<1, Houston>, <4, Stafford>, <5, {Bellaire, Sugarland, Houston}>}. This is a serious drawback of the current normalized or "flat" version of the relational model. The relational languages SQL, QUEL, and QBE also have no features for handling such sets of values within tuples. On this score, the object-oriented, hierarchical, and network models have better facilities than does the relational model. The nested relational model (see Chapter 21) attempts to remedy this.

Table 6.2   Correspondence Between ER and Relational Models

ER Model	Relational Model
entity type	"entity" relation
1:1 or 1:N relationship type	foreign key (or "relationship" relation)
M:N relationship type	"relationship" relation and two foreign keys
n-ary relationship type	"relationship" relation and n foreign keys
simple attribute	attribute
composite attribute	set of simple component attributes
multivalued attribute	relation and foreign key
value set	domain
key attribute	primary (or secondary) key

In our example, we apply EQUIJOIN to DEPT_LOCATIONS and DEPARTMENT on the DNUMBER attribute to get the values of all locations along with other DEPARTMENT attributes. In the resulting relation, the values of the other department attributes are repeated in separate tuples for every location that a department has.

6.8.2 *Summary of Mapping for Model Construct and Constraints*

We now summarize the correspondences between ER and relational model constructs and constraints in Table 6.2.

6.9 Summary

In this chapter we presented the modeling concepts provided by the relational model of data. We also discussed the relational algebra and additional operations that can be used to manipulate relations. We started by introducing the concepts of domains, tuples, and attributes. We then defined a relation schema as a list of attributes that describe the structure of a relation. A relation, or relation instance, is a set of tuples.

Several characteristics differentiate relations from ordinary tables or files. The first is that tuples in a relation are not ordered. The second involves the ordering of attributes in a relation schema and the corresponding ordering of values within a tuple. We gave an alternative definition of relation that does not require these two orderings, but we continued to use the first definition, which requires attributes and tuple values to be ordered, for convenience. We then discussed values in tuples and introduced null values to represent missing or unknown information.

We then defined a relational database schema and a relational database. Several types of constraints can be considered part of the relational model. The concepts of superkey, candidate key, and primary key specify key constraints. The entity integrity constraint prohibits primary key attributes from being null. The interrelation constraint of referential integrity is used to maintain consistency of references among tuples from different relations.

The update operations on the relational model are Insert, Delete, and Modify. Each operation may violate certain types of constraints. Whenever an update is applied, the database consistency after the update must be checked to ensure that no constraints are violated. Relational schemas are declared via a relational DDL.

The relational algebra is a set of operations for manipulating relations. We presented the various operations and illustrated the types of manipulations each is used for. Table 6.3 lists the various relational algebra operations we discussed. The unary relational oper-

Table 6.3   Operations of the Relational Algebra

Operation	Purpose	Notation
SELECT	Selects all tuples that satisfy the selection condition from a relation R.	$\sigma_{\text{<selection condition>}}(R)$
PROJECT	Produces a new relation with only some of the attributes of R, and removes duplicate tuples.	$\pi_{\text{<attribute list>}}(R)$
THETA JOIN	Produces all combinations of tuples from R_1 and R_2 that satisfy the join condition.	$R_1 \bowtie_{\text{<join condition>}} R_2$
EQUIJOIN	Produces all the combinations of tuples from R_1 and R_2 that satisfy a join condition with only equality comparisons.	$R_1 \bowtie_{\text{<join condition>}} R_2$, or $R_1 \bowtie_{(\text{<join attributes 1>})},$ $(\text{<join attributes 2>})$ R_2
NATURAL JOIN	Same as EQUIJOIN except that the join attributes of R_2 are not included in the resulting relation; if the join attributes have the same names, they do not have to be specified at all.	$R_1 *_{\text{<join condition>}} R_2$, or $R_1 *_{(\text{<join attributes 1>})},$ $(\text{<join attributes 2>})$ R_2 or $R_1 * R_2$
UNION	Produces a relation that includes all the tuples in R_1 or R_2 or both R_1 and R_2; R_1 and R_2 must be union compatible.	$R_1 \cup R_2$
INTERSECTION	Produces a relation that includes all the tuples in both R_1 and R_2; R_1 and R_2 must be union compatible.	$R_1 \cap R_2$
DIFFERENCE	Produces a relation that includes all the tuples in R_1 that are not in R_2; R_1 and R_2 must be union compatible.	$R_1 - R_2$
CARTESIAN PRODUCT	Produces a relation that has the attributes of R_1 and R_2 and includes as tuples all possible combinations of tuples from R_1 and R_2.	$R_1 \times R_2$
DIVISION	Produces a relation R(X) that includes all tuples $t[X]$ in $R_1(Z)$ that appear in R_1 in combination with every tuple from $R_2(Y)$, where $Z = X \cup Y$.	$R_1(Z) \div R_2(Y)$

ators SELECT and PROJECT were discussed first. Then we discussed binary set operations that require that relations on which they are applied be union compatible; these include UNION, INTERSECTION, and DIFFERENCE. The CARTESIAN PRODUCT operation is used to combine tuples from two relations into single larger tuples. We showed how CARTESIAN PRODUCT followed by SELECT can identify related tuples from two relations. The JOIN operations can directly identify and combine related tuples. Join operations include THETA JOIN, EQUIJOIN, and NATURAL JOIN.

We then discussed some types of queries that cannot be stated with the relational algebra operations. We introduced the FUNCTION operation to deal with aggregate types of requests. We discussed recursive queries and showed how some types of recursive queries can be specified. We then presented the OUTER JOIN and OUTER UNION operations, which extend JOIN and UNION.

We also gave examples in Section 6.7 to illustrate the use of relational operations to specify queries on a relational database. We use these queries in subsequent chapters in discussing various query languages.

In Section 6.8, we showed how a conceptual schema design in the ER model can be mapped to a relational database schema. An algorithm for ER-to-relational mapping was given and illustrated by examples from the COMPANY database. Table 6.2 summarizes the correspondences between the ER and relational model constructs and constraints.

Review Questions

6.1. Define the following terms: *domain, attribute, n-tuple, relation schema, relation instance, degree of a relation, relational database schema, relational database instance*.

6.2. Why are tuples in a relation not ordered?

6.3. Why are duplicate tuples not allowed in a relation?

6.4. What is the difference between a key and a superkey?

6.5. Why do we designate one of the candidate keys of a relation to be primary key?

6.6. Discuss the characteristics of relations that make them different from ordinary tables and files.

6.7. Discuss the various reasons that lead to the occurrence of null values in relations.

6.8. Discuss the entity integrity and referential integrity constraints. Why is each considered important?

6.9. Define *foreign key*. What is this concept used for?

6.10. Discuss the various update operations on relations and the types of integrity constraints that must be checked for each update operation.

6.11. List the operations of the relational algebra and the purpose of each.

6.12. What is union compatibility? Why do the UNION, INTERSECTION, and DIFFERENCE operations require that the relations on which they are applied be union compatible?

6.13. Discuss some types of queries for which renaming of attributes is necessary in order to specify the query unambiguously.

6.14. Discuss the various types of JOIN operations.

6.15. What is the FUNCTION operation? What is it used for?

6.16. How are the OUTER JOIN operations different from the JOIN operations? How is the OUTER UNION operation different from UNION?

6.17. Discuss the correspondences between the ER model constructs and the relational model constructs. Show how each ER model construct can be mapped to the relational model, and discuss any alternative mappings.

Exercises

6.18. Show the result of each of the example queries in Section 6.7 as they would apply to the database of Figure 6.6.

6.19. Specify the following queries on the database schema shown in Figure 6.5, using the relational operators discussed in this chapter. Also show the result of each query as it would apply to the database of Figure 6.6.

   a. Retrieve the names of all employees in department 5 who work more than 10 hours per week on the 'ProductX' project.

   b. List the names of all employees who have a dependent with the same first name as themselves.

   c. Find the names of all employees who are directly supervised by 'Franklin Wong'.

   d. For each project, list the project name and the total hours per week (by all employees) spent on that project.

   e. Retrieve the names of all employees who work on every project.

   f. Retrieve the names of all employees who do not work on any project.

   g. For each department, retrieve the department name and the average salary of all employees working in that department.

   h. Retrieve the average salary of all female employees.

   i. Find the names and addresses of all employees who work on at least one project located in Houston but whose department has no location in Houston.

   j. List the last names of all department managers who have no dependents.

6.20. Suppose that each of the following update operations is applied directly to the database of Figure 6.6. Discuss *all* integrity constraints violated by each operation, if any, and the different ways of enforcing these constraints.

   a. Insert < 'Robert', 'F', 'Scott', '943775543', '21-JUN-42', '2365 Newcastle Rd, Bellaire, TX', M, 58000, '888665555', 1 > into EMPLOYEE.

   b. Insert < 'ProductA', 4, 'Bellaire', 2 > into PROJECT.

   c. Insert < 'Production', 4, '943775543', '01-OCT-88' > into DEPARTMENT.

   d. Insert < '677678989', null, '40.0' > into WORKS_ON.

   e. Insert < '453453453', 'John', M, '12-DEC-60', 'SPOUSE' > into DEPENDENT.

   f. Delete the WORKS_ON tuples with ESSN = '333445555'.

   g. Delete the EMPLOYEE tuple with SSN = '987654321'.

h. Delete the PROJECT tuple with PNAME = 'ProductX'.

i. Modify the MGRSSN and MGRSTARTDATE of the DEPARTMENT tuple with DNUMBER = 5 to '123456789' and '01-OCT-93', respectively.

j. Modify the SUPERSSN attribute of the EMPLOYEE tuple with SSN = '999887777' to '943775543'.

k. Modify the HOURS attribute of the WORKS_ON tuple with ESSN = '999887777' and PNO = 10 to '5.0'.

6.21. Consider the AIRLINE relational database schema shown in Figure 6.20, which describes a database for airline flight information. Each FLIGHT is identified by a

AIRPORT

AIRPORT_CODE	NAME	CITY	STATE

FLIGHT

NUMBER	AIRLINE	WEEKDAYS

FLIGHT_LEG

FLIGHT_NUMBER	LEG_NUMBER	DEPARTURE_AIRPORT_CODE	SCHEDULED_DEPARTURE_TIME
		ARRIVAL_AIRPORT_CODE	SCHEDULED_ARRIVAL_TIME

LEG_INSTANCE

FLIGHT_NUMBER	LEG_NUMBER	DATE	NUMBER_OF_AVAILABLE_SEATS	AIRPLANE_ID
DEPARTURE_AIRPORT_CODE	DEPARTURE_TIME	ARRIVAL_AIRPORT_CODE	ARRIVAL_TIME	

FARES

FLIGHT_NUMBER	FARE_CODE	AMOUNT	RESTRICTIONS

AIRPLANE_TYPE

TYPE_NAME	MAX_SEATS	COMPANY

CAN_LAND

AIRPLANE_TYPE_NAME	AIRPORT_CODE

AIRPLANE

AIRPLANE_ID	TOTAL_NUMBER_OF_SEATS	AIRPLANE_TYPE

SEAT_RESERVATION

FLIGHT_NUMBER	LEG_NUMBER	DATE	SEAT_NUMBER	CUSTOMER_NAME	CUSTOMER_PHONE

Figure 6.20 The AIRLINE relational database schema.

flight NUMBER, and consists of one or more FLIGHT_LEGS with LEG_NUMBERs 1, 2, 3, etc. Each leg has scheduled arrival and departure times and airports and has many LEG_INSTANCES—one for each DATE on which the flight travels. FARES are kept for each flight. For each leg instance, SEAT_RESERVATIONS are kept, as are the AIRPLANE used on the leg and the actual arrival and departure times and airports. An AIRPLANE is identified by an AIRPLANE_ID and is of a particular AIRPLANE_TYPE. CAN_LAND relates AIRPLANE_TYPEs to the AIRPORTs in which they can land. An AIRPORT is identified by an AIRPORT_CODE. Specify the following queries in relational algebra:

a. For each flight, list the flight number, the departure airport for the first leg of the flight, and the arrival airport for the last leg of the flight.

b. List the flight numbers and weekdays of all flights or flight legs that depart from Houston Intercontinental Airport (airport code 'IAH') and arrive in Los Angeles International Airport (airport code 'LAX').

c. List the flight number, departure airport code, scheduled departure time, arrival airport code, scheduled arrival time, and weekdays of all flights or flight legs that depart from some airport in the city of Houston and arrive at some airport in the city of Los Angeles.

d. List all fare information for flight number 'CO197'.

e. Retrieve the number of available seats for flight number 'CO197' on '09-OCT-93'.

6.22. Consider an update for the AIRLINE database to enter a reservation on a particular flight or flight leg on a given date.

a. Give the operations for this update.

b. What types of constraints would you expect to check?

c. Which of these constraints are key, entity integrity, and referential integrity constraints, and which are not?

d. Specify all the referential integrity constraints on Figure 6.20.

6.23. Consider the relation

CLASS(Course#, Univ_Section#, InstructorName, Semester, BuildingCode, Room#, TimePeriod, Weekdays, CreditHours).

This represents classes taught in a university, with unique Univ_Section#. Identify what you think should be various candidate keys, and write in your own words the constraints under which each candidate key would be valid.

6.24. Figure 6.21 shows an ER schema for a database that may be used to keep track of transport ships and their locations for maritime authorities. Map this schema into a relational schema, and specify all primary keys and foreign keys.

6.25. Map the BANK ER schema of Exercise 3.23 (shown in Figure 3.20) into a relational schema. Specify all primary keys and foreign keys.

6.26. Consider the LIBRARY relational schema shown in Figure 6.22, which is used to keep track of books, borrowers, and book loans. Referential integrity constraints

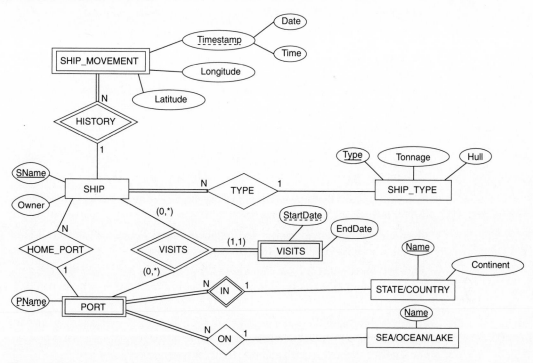

Figure 6.21   An ER schema for a SHIP_TRACKING database.

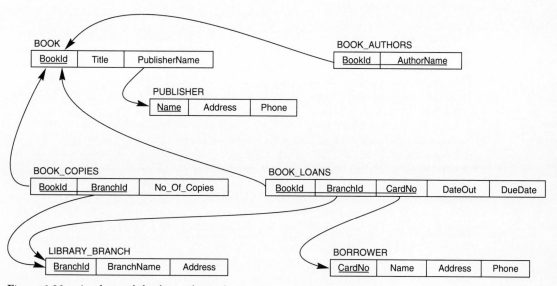

Figure 6.22   A relational database schema for a LIBRARY database.

are shown as directed arcs in Figure 6.22, as in the notation of Figure 6.7. Write down relational expressions for the following queries on the LIBRARY database:

a. How many copies of the book titled *The Lost Tribe* are owned by the library branch whose name is "Sharpstown"?

b. How many copies of the book titled *The Lost Tribe* are owned by each library branch?

c. Retrieve the names of all borrowers who do not have any books checked out.

d. For each book that is loaned out from the "Sharpstown" branch and whose DueDate is today, retrieve the book title, the borrower's name, and the borrower's address.

e. For each library branch, retrieve the branch name and the total number of books loaned out from that branch.

f. Retrieve the names, addresses, and number of books checked out for all borrowers who have more than five books checked out.

g. For each book authored (or co-authored) by "Stephen King," retrieve the title and the number of copies owned by the library branch whose name is "Central."

6.27. Try to map the relational schema of Figure 6.22 into an ER schema. This is part of a process known as *reverse engineering*, where a conceptual schema is created for an existing implemented database. State any assumption you make.

Selected Bibliography

The relational model was introduced by Codd (1970) in a classic paper. Codd also introduced the relational algebra and laid the theoretical foundations for the relational model in a series of papers (Codd 1971, 1972, 1972a, 1974); he was later given the Turing award, the highest honor of the ACM, for his work on the relational model. In a later paper, Codd (1979) discussed extending the relational model and incorporating NULLs in the relational algebra. The resulting model is known as RM/T. Earlier work by Childs (1968) used set theory to model databases.

Much research has been conducted on various aspects of the relational model. Todd (1976) describes an experimental DBMS that directly implements the relational algebra operations. Date (1983a) discusses outer joins. Schmidt and Swenson (1975) introduces additional semantics into the relational model by classifying different types of relations. Wiederhold and Elmasri (1979) introduces various types of connections between relations to enhance its constraints. Work on extending relational operations is discussed by Carlis (1986) and Ozsoyoglu et al. (1985). Cammarata et al. (1989) extends the relational model integrity constraints and joins. Additional bibliographic notes for other aspects of the relational model and its languages, systems, extensions, and theory are given in Chapters 7, 8, 9, 12, 13, 16, 20, 21, and 23.

CHAPTER 7

SQL—A Relational Database Language

In Chapter 6 we discussed the relational algebra operations; these operations are very important for understanding the types of requests that may be specified on a relational database. They are also important for query processing and optimization in a relational DBMS, as we shall see in Chapter 16. The relational algebra is generally classified as a high-level query language because its operations are applied to entire relations. However, there are few commercial DBMS languages based directly on the relational algebra.* This is because a query in the relational algebra is written as a sequence of operations that, when executed, produce the required result. When specifying a relational algebra query, the user must specify *how*—in what order—to execute the query operations. Most commercial relational DBMSs provide a high-level *declarative* language interface, so the user only specifies *what* the result is, leaving the actual optimization and decisions on how to execute the query to the DBMS.

In this chapter and in Chapter 8, we discuss several languages that have been partially or fully implemented and are available on commercial DBMSs. The best known of these is SQL, whose name is derived from Structured Query Language. We present two other languages, QUEL and QBE, in Chapter 8 after we have discussed the relational calculus, which is the formal language on which QUEL and QBE (and to some extent, SQL) are based.

Originally, SQL was called SEQUEL (for Structured English QUEry Language) and was designed and implemented at IBM Research as the interface for an experimental relational database system called SYSTEM R. SQL is now the language for IBM's DB2 and

---

*An early experimental DBMS, called ISBL, implemented the relational algebra operations as its query language (Todd 1976).

SQL/DS commercial relational DBMSs and was the earliest of the high-level database languages, along with QUEL. Variations of SQL have been implemented by most commercial DBMS vendors. A joint effort under way by ANSI (the American National Standards Institute) and ISO (the International Standards Organization) has led to a standard version of SQL (ANSI 1986), called SQL1. A revised and much expanded standard called SQL2 (also referred to as SQL-92) has also been developed. Plans are already underway for SQL3, which will further extend SQL with object-oriented and other recent database concepts.

SQL is a comprehensive database language; it has statements for data definition, query, and update. Hence, it is both a DDL *and* a DML. In addition, it has facilities for defining views on the database, for creating and dropping indexes on the files that represent relations (although these have been dropped from SQL2), and for embedding SQL statements into a general-purpose programming language such as C or PASCAL. We will discuss these topics in the following subsections. In our discussion, we will mostly follow SQL2. However, we will describe some features, such as CREATE INDEX, that were dropped from SQL2 based on earlier SQL versions, since they are still supported by many relational DBMSs. We briefly discuss catalog and dictionary facilities of SQL in Chapter 15, and we give an overview of SQL commands for authorization of privileges in Chapter 20.

For the reader who desires a less comprehensive introduction to SQL, parts or all of the following sections may be skipped: 7.2.5 to 7.2.9, 7.5, 7.6, and 7.7.

7.1 Data Definition in SQL

SQL uses the terms **table, row,** and **column** for relation, tuple, and attribute, respectively. We will use the corresponding terms interchangeably. The SQL commands for data definition are CREATE, ALTER, and DROP; these are discussed in Sections 7.1.2 to 7.1.4. First, however, we discuss schema and catalog concepts. We only give an overview of the most important features. Details can be found in the SQL2 document.

7.1.1 *Schema and Catalog Concepts in SQL2*

Early versions of SQL included no concept of a relational database schema; all tables (relations) were considered part of the same schema. The concept of an SQL schema was incorporated into SQL2 in order to group together tables and other constructs that belong to the same database application. An SQL **schema** is identified by a **schema name,** and includes an authorization identifier to indicate the user or account who owns the schema, as well as **descriptors** for *each element* in the schema. Schema elements include the tables, views, domains, and other constructs (such as authorization grants and assertions) that describe the schema. A schema is created via the CREATE SCHEMA statement, which can include all the schema elements' definitions. Alternatively, the schema can be assigned a name and authorization identifier, and the elements can be defined later. For example, the following statement creates a schema called COMPANY, owned by the user with authorization identifier JSMITH:

CREATE SCHEMA COMPANY **AUTHORIZATION** JSMITH;

In addition to using the concept of schema, SQL2 uses the concept of **catalog**—a named collection of schemas in an SQL environment. A catalog always contains a special schema called INFORMATION_SCHEMA, which provides information on all the element descriptors of all the schemas in the catalog to authorized users. Integrity constraints such as referential integrity can be defined between relations only if they exist in schemas within the same catalog. Schemas within the same catalog can also share certain elements, such as domain definitions.

7.1.2 *The CREATE TABLE Command and SQL Data Types and Constraints*

The CREATE TABLE command is used to specify a new relation by giving it a name and specifying its attributes and constraints. The attributes are specified first; and each attribute is given a name, a data type to specify its domain of values, and possibly some constraints. The key, entity integrity, and referential integrity constraints are then specified. Figure 7.1(a) shows sample data definition statements in SQL for the relational database schema shown in Figure 6.7. Typically, the SQL schema in which the relations are declared is implicitly specified in the environment in which the CREATE TABLE statements are executed. Alternatively, one can explicitly attach the schema name to the relation name, separated by a period. For example, by writing the command

CREATE TABLE COMPANY.EMPLOYEE...

rather than

CREATE TABLE EMPLOYEE ...

as in Figure 7.1(a), one can explicitly make the EMPLOYEE table part of the COMPANY SQL schema.

The **data types** available for attributes include numeric, character-string, bit-string, date, and time. **Numeric** data types include integer numbers of various sizes (INTEGER or INT, and SMALLINT), and real numbers of various precisions (FLOAT, REAL, DOUBLE PRECISION). Formatted numbers can be declared by using DECIMAL(i,j) (or DEC(i,j) or NUMERIC(i,j)), where i, the *precision*, is the total number of decimal digits and j, the *scale*, is the number of digits after the decimal point. The default for scale is zero, and the default for precision is implementation-defined.

Character-string data types are either fixed-length (CHAR(n) or CHARACTER(n), where n is the number of characters) or varying-length (VARCHAR(n) or CHAR VARYING(n) or CHARACTER VARYING(n), where n is the maximum number of characters). **Bit-string** data types are either of fixed length n (BIT(n)) or varying length (BIT VARYING(n), where n is the maximum number of bits). The default for n, the length of a character string or bit string, is one.

There are new data types for **date** and **time** in SQL2. The DATE data type has ten positions, and its components are YEAR, MONTH, and DAY typically in the form YYYY-MM-DD. The TIME data type has at least eight positions, with the components HOUR, MINUTE, and SECOND, typically in the form HH:MM:SS. Only valid dates and times should be allowed by the SQL implementation. In addition, a data type TIME(i), where i is called *time fractional seconds precision*, specifies $i + 1$ additional positions for TIME—one position for an additional separator character, and i positions for specifying decimal fractions of a second. A TIME WITH TIME ZONE data type includes an additional six positions for

(a)

```
CREATE TABLE EMPLOYEE
        ( FNAME           VARCHAR(15)       NOT NULL ,
          MINIT           CHAR ,
          LNAME           VARCHAR(15)       NOT NULL ,
          SSN             CHAR(9)           NOT NULL ,
          BDATE           DATE
          ADDRESS         VARCHAR(30) ,
          SEX             CHAR ,
          SALARY          DECIMAL(10,2) ,
          SUPERSSN        CHAR(9) ,
          DNO             INT               NOT NULL ,
      PRIMARY KEY (SSN) ,
      FOREIGN KEY (SUPERSSN) REFERENCES EMPLOYEE(SSN) ,
      FOREIGN KEY (DNO) REFERENCES DEPARTMENT(DNUMBER) ) ;
CREATE TABLE DEPARTMENT
        ( DNAME           VARCHAR(15)       NOT NULL ,
          DNUMBER         INT               NOT NULL ,
          MGRSSN          CHAR(9)           NOT NULL ,
          MGRSTARTDATE    DATE ,
      PRIMARY KEY (DNUMBER) ,
      UNIQUE (DNAME) ,
      FOREIGN KEY (MGRSSN) REFERENCES EMPLOYEE(SSN) ) ;
CREATE TABLE DEPT_LOCATIONS
        ( DNUMBER         INT               NOT NULL ,
          DLOCATION       VARCHAR(15)       NOT NULL ,
      PRIMARY KEY (DNUMBER, DLOCATION) ,
      FOREIGN KEY (DNUMBER) REFERENCES DEPARTMENT(DNUMBER) ) ;
CREATE TABLE PROJECT
        ( PNAME           VARCHAR(15)       NOT NULL ,
          PNUMBER         INT               NOT NULL ,
          PLOCATION       VARCHAR(15) ,
          DNUM            INT               NOT NULL ,
      PRIMARY KEY (PNUMBER) ,
      UNIQUE (PNAME) ,
      FOREIGN KEY (DNUM) REFERENCES DEPARTMENT(DNUMBER) ) ;
CREATE TABLE WORKS_ON
        ( ESSN            CHAR(9)           NOT NULL ,
          PNO             INT               NOT NULL ,
          HOURS           DECIMAL(3,1)      NOT NULL ,
      PRIMARY KEY (ESSN, PNO) ,
      FOREIGN KEY (ESSN) REFERENCES EMPLOYEE(SSN) ,
      FOREIGN KEY (PNO) REFERENCES PROJECT(PNUMBER) ) ;
CREATE TABLE DEPENDENT
        ( ESSN                 CHAR(9)           NOT NULL ,
          DEPENDENT_NAME  VARCHAR(15)       NOT NULL ,
          SEX             CHAR ,
          BDATE           DATE ,
          RELATIONSHIP    VARCHAR(8) ,
      PRIMARY KEY (ESSN, DEPENDENT_NAME) ,
      FOREIGN KEY (ESSN) REFERENCES EMPLOYEE(SSN) ) ;
```

Figure 7.1 SQL2 data definitions. (a) SQL2 statements defining the COMPANY
        schema of Figure 6.7. (b) Specifying referential triggered actions.

(b)
CREATE TABLE EMPLOYEE
      (. . . ,
        DNO   INT   **NOT NULL**   **DEFAULT** 1,
     CONSTRAINT EMPPK
      PRIMARY KEY (SSN) ,
     CONSTRAINT EMPSUPERFK
      FOREIGN KEY (SUPERSSN) **REFERENCES** EMPLOYEE(SSN)
            ON DELETE SET NULL   **ON UPDATE** CASCADE ,
     CONSTRAINT EMPDEPTFK
      FOREIGN KEY (DNO) **REFERENCES** DEPARTMENT(DNUMBER)
            ON DELETE SET DEFAULT   **ON UPDATE** CASCADE);

CREATE TABLE DEPARTMENT
      (. . . ,
      MGRSSN   CHAR(9) **NOT NULL DEFAULT** "888665555" ,
      . . . ,
     CONSTRAINT DEPTPK
      PRIMARY KEY (DNUMBER) ,
     CONSTRAINT DEPTSK
      UNIQUE (DNAME),
     CONSTRAINT DEPTMGRFK
      FOREIGN KEY (MGRSSN) **REFERENCES** EMPLOYEE(SSN)
         ON DELETE SET DEFAULT   **ON UPDATE** CASCADE);

CREATE TABLE DEPT_LOCATIONS
      (. . . ,
     PRIMARY KEY (DNUMBER, DLOCATION),
     FOREIGN KEY (DNUMBER) **REFERENCES** DEPARTMENT(DNUMBER)
      ON DELETE CASCADE   **ON UPDATE** CASCADE) ;

Figure 7.1   *(continued)*

specifying the *displacement* from the standard universal time zone, which is in the range +13:00 to −12:59 in units of HOURS:MINUTES. If WITH TIME ZONE is not included, the default is the local time zone for the SQL session. Finally, a **timestamp** data type (TIMESTAMP) includes both the DATE and TIME fields, plus a minimum of six positions for fractions of seconds and an optional WITH TIME ZONE qualifier.

Another data type related to DATE, TIME, and TIMESTAMP is the INTERVAL data type. This specifies an **interval**—a *relative value* that can be used to increment or decrement an absolute value of a date, time, or timestamp. Intervals are qualified to be either YEAR/MONTH intervals or DAY/TIME intervals.

In SQL2, it is possible to specify the data type of each attribute directly, as in Figure 7.1(a); alternatively, a domain can be declared, and the domain name used. This makes it easier to change the data type for a domain that is used by numerous attributes in a schema, and improves schema readability. For example, we can create a domain SSN_TYPE by the following statement:

CREATE DOMAIN SSN_TYPE **AS** CHAR(9) ;

We can use SSN_TYPE in place of CHAR(9) in Figure 7.1(a) for the attributes SSN and SUPERSSN of EMPLOYEE, MGRSSN of DEPARTMENT, ESSN of WORKS_ON, and ESSN of DEPARTMENT. A domain can also have an optional default specification via a DEFAULT clause, as we will discuss for attributes.

Because SQL allows NULLs as attribute values, a *constraint* NOT NULL may be specified if NULL is not permitted for that attribute. This should always be specified for the primary key attributes of each relation, as well as for any other attributes whose values are required not to be NULL, as shown in Figure 7.1(a). It is also possible to define a *default value* for an attribute by appending the clause DEFAULT <value> to an attribute definition. The default value is included in any new tuple if an explicit value is not provided for that attribute. Figure 7.1(b) illustrates an example of specifying a default manager for a new department and a default department for a new employee. If no default clause is specified, the default default value (!) is NULL.

Following the attribute (or column) specifications, additional *table constraints* can be specified on a table, including keys and referential integrity, as illustrated in Figure 7.1(a).* The **PRIMARY KEY** clause specifies one or more attributes that make up the primary key of a relation. The **UNIQUE** clause specifies alternate keys. Referential integrity is specified via the **FOREIGN KEY** clause.

As we discussed in Section 6.2.4, a referential integrity constraint can be violated when tuples are inserted or deleted or when a foreign key attribute value is modified. The schema designer can specify the action to be taken if a referential integrity constraint is violated upon deletion of a referenced tuple or upon modification of a referenced primary key value, by attaching a *referential triggered action* clause to any foreign key constraint. The options include SET NULL, CASCADE, and SET DEFAULT. An option must be qualified with either ON DELETE or ON UPDATE. We illustrate this with the example shown in Figure 7.1(b). Here, the database designer chose SET NULL ON DELETE and CASCADE ON UPDATE for the foreign key SUPERSSN of EMPLOYEE. This means that if the tuple for a supervising employee is *deleted*, the value of SUPERSSN is *set to* NULL for all employee tuples referencing the deleted employee tuple. If the SSN value for a supervising employee is *updated* (say, because it was entered incorrectly), the new value is *cascaded* to SUPERSSN for all employee tuples referencing the updated employee tuple.

In general, the action taken by the DBMS for SET NULL or SET DEFAULT is the same for both ON DELETE or ON UPDATE; the value of the affected referencing attributes is changed to NULL for SET NULL, and to the specified default value for SET DEFAULT. The action for CASCADE ON DELETE is to delete all the referencing tuples, whereas the action for CASCADE ON UPDATE is to change the value of the foreign key to the updated (new) primary key value for all referencing tuples. It is the responsibility of the database designer to choose the appropriate action and to specify it in the DDL. As a general rule, the CASCADE option is suitable for "relationship" relations such as WORKS_ON, for relations that represent multivalued attributes such as DEPT_LOCATIONS, and for relations that represent weak entity types such as DEPENDENT.

Figure 7.1(b) also illustrates how a constraint may be given a name, following the keyword **CONSTRAINT.** The names of all constraints within a particular schema must be

---

*Key and referential integrity constraints were not included in earlier versions of SQL. In some implementations, keys were specified implicitly at the internal level via the CREATE INDEX command (see Section 7.5).

unique. A constraint name is used to identify a particular constraint in case the constraint must be dropped later and replaced with another constraint, as we shall discuss in Section 7.1.4. Giving names to constraints is optional.

The relations declared through CREATE TABLE statements are called **base tables** (or base relations) in SQL terminology; this means that the relation and its tuples are actually created and stored as a file by the DBMS. Base relations are distinguished from **virtual relations,** created through the CREATE VIEW statement (see Section 7.4), which may or may not correspond to an actual physical file. In SQL the attributes in a base table are considered to be *ordered in the sequence in which they are specified* in the CREATE TABLE statement. However, rows (tuples) are not considered to be ordered.

7.1.3 The DROP SCHEMA and DROP TABLE Commands

If a whole schema is not needed any more, the DROP SCHEMA command can be used. There are two *drop behavior* options: CASCADE and RESTRICT. For example, to remove the COMPANY database schema and all its tables, domains, and other elements, the CASCADE option is used as follows:

DROP SCHEMA COMPANY **CASCADE**;

If the RESTRICT option is chosen in place of CASCADE, the schema is dropped only if it has *no elements* in it; otherwise, the DROP command will not be executed.

If a base relation within a schema is not needed any longer, the relation and its definition can be deleted by using the DROP TABLE command. For example, if we no longer wish to keep track of dependents of employees in the COMPANY database of Figure 6.6, we can get rid of the DEPENDENT relation by issuing the command

DROP TABLE DEPENDENT **CASCADE**;

If the RESTRICT option is chosen instead of CASCADE, a table is dropped only if it is *not referenced* in any constraints (such as by foreign key definitions in another relation) or views (see Section 7.4). With the CASCADE option, all such constraints and views that reference the table are dropped automatically from the schema, along with the table itself.

7.1.4 The ALTER TABLE Command

The definition of a base table can be changed by using the ALTER TABLE command. The possible *alter table actions* include adding or dropping a column (attribute), changing a column definition, and adding or dropping table constraints. For example, to add an attribute for keeping track of jobs of employees to the EMPLOYEE base relations in the COMPANY schema, we can use the command

ALTER TABLE COMPANY.EMPLOYEE **ADD** JOB VARCHAR(12);

We must still enter a value for the new attribute JOB for each EMPLOYEE tuple. This can be done either by specifying a default clause or by using the UPDATE command (see Section 7.3). If no default clause is specified, the new attribute will have NULLs in all the tuples of the relation immediately after the command is executed; hence, the NOT NULL constraint is *not allowed* in this case.

To drop a column, one must choose either CASCADE or RESTRICT for drop behavior. If CASCADE is chosen, all constraints and views that reference the column are dropped automatically from the schema, along with the column. If RESTRICT is chosen, the command is successful only if no views or constraints reference the column. For example, the following command removes the attribute ADDRESS from the EMPLOYEE base table:

ALTER TABLE COMPANY.EMPLOYEE **DROP** ADDRESS **CASCADE**;

It is also possible to alter a column definition by dropping an existing default clause or by defining a new default clause. The following examples illustrate this clause:

ALTER TABLE COMPANY.DEPARTMENT **ALTER** MGRSSN **DROP DEFAULT**;
ALTER TABLE COMPANY.DEPARTMENT **ALTER** MGRSSN **SET DEFAULT** "333445555";

Finally, one can change the constraints specified on a table by adding or dropping a constraint. To be dropped, a constraint must have been given a name when it was specified. For example, to drop the constraint named EMPSUPERFK in Figure 7.1(b) from the EMPLOYEE relation, we write

ALTER TABLE COMPANY.EMPLOYEE **DROP CONSTRAINT** EMPSUPERFK **CASCADE**;

Once this is done, we can redefine a replacement constraint by adding a new constraint to the relation, if needed. This is specified by using the **ADD** keyword followed by the new constraint, which can be named or unnamed and can be of any of the table constraint types discussed in Section 7.1.2.

The preceding subsections gave an overview of the data definition commands of SQL. There are many other details and options, and we refer the interested reader to the SQL and SQL2 documents listed in the bibliographical notes. The next section discusses the querying capabilities of SQL.

7.2 Queries in SQL

SQL has one basic statement for retrieving information from a database: the **SELECT statement**. The SELECT statement *has no relationship* to the SELECT operation of the relational algebra, which was discussed in Chapter 6. There are many options and flavors to the SELECT statement in SQL, so we will introduce its features gradually. We will use example queries specified on the schema of Figure 6.5 and will refer to the sample database state shown in Figure 6.6 to show the results of some of the example queries.

Before proceeding, we must point out an important distinction between SQL and the formal relational model discussed in Chapter 6: SQL allows a table (relation) to have two or more tuples that are identical in all their attribute values. Hence, in general, an SQL table is not a *set of tuples*, because a set does not allow two identical members; rather it is a **multiset** (sometimes called a *bag*) of tuples. Some SQL relations are constrained to be sets because a key constraint has been declared or because the DISTINCT option has been used with the SELECT statement (described later in this section). We should be aware of this distinction as we discuss the examples.

7.2.1 *Basic SQL Queries*

The basic form of the SELECT statement, sometimes called a **mapping** or a **SELECT FROM WHERE block,** is formed of the three clauses SELECT, FROM, and WHERE and has the following form:

SELECT \<attribute list>
FROM \<table list>
WHERE \<condition>

where

- \<attribute list> is a list of attribute names whose values are to be retrieved by the query.
- \<table list> is a list of the relation names required to process the query.
- \<condition> is a conditional (Boolean) search expression that identifies the tuples to be retrieved by the query.

We now illustrate the basic SELECT statement with some example queries. We will label the queries here with the same query numbers that appear in Chapter 6 and in Chapter 8, for easy cross reference.

QUERY 0

Retrieve the birthdate and address of the employee whose name is 'John B. Smith'. (This is a new query that did not appear in Chapter 6.)

Q0: **SELECT** BDATE, ADDRESS
    FROM EMPLOYEE
    WHERE FNAME='John' **AND** MINIT='B' **AND** LNAME='Smith'

This query involves only the EMPLOYEE relation listed in the FROM clause. The query selects the EMPLOYEE tuples that satisfy the condition of the WHERE clause, then projects the result on the BDATE and ADDRESS attributes listed in the SELECT clause. Q0 is similar to the relational algebra expression

$$\pi_{<\textbf{BDATE,ADDRESS}>}(\sigma_{\text{FNAME}='\text{John' AND MINIT}='\text{B' AND LNAME}='\text{Smith'}} (\textbf{EMPLOYEE}))$$

Hence, a simple SQL query with a single relation name in the FROM clause is similar to a SELECT–PROJECT pair of relational algebra operations. The SELECT clause of SQL specifies the *projection attributes,* and the WHERE clause specifies the *selection condition.* The only difference is that in the SQL query we may get duplicate tuples in the result of the query, because the constraint that a relation is a set is not enforced. Figure 7.2(a) shows the result of query Q0 on the database of Figure 6.6.

QUERY 1

Retrieve the name and address of all employees who work for the 'Research' department.

Q1: **SELECT** FNAME, LNAME, ADDRESS
    FROM EMPLOYEE, DEPARTMENT
    WHERE DNAME='Research' **AND** DNUMBER=DNO

(a)

BDATE	ADDRESS
09-JAN-55	731 Fondren, Houston, TX

(b)

FNAME	LNAME	ADDRESS
John	Smith	731 Fondren, Houston, TX
Franklin	Wong	638 Voss, Houston, TX
Ramesh	Narayan	975 Fire Oak, Humble, TX
Joyce	English	5631 Rice, Houston, TX

(c)

PNUMBER	DNUM	LNAME	ADDRESS	BDATE
10	4	Wallace	291 Berry, Bellaire, TX	20-JUN-31
30	4	Wallace	291 Berry, Bellaire, TX	20-JUN-31

(d)

E.FNAME	E.LNAME	S.FNAME	S.LNAME
John	Smith	Franklin	Wong
Franklin	Wong	James	Borg
Alicia	Zelaya	Jennifer	Wallace
Jennifer	Wallace	James	Borg
Ramesh	Narayan	Franklin	Wong
Joyce	English	Franklin	Wong
Ahmad	Jabbar	Jennifer	Wallace

(e)

SSN
123456789
333445555
999887777
987654321
666884444
453453453
987987987
888665555

(f)

SSN	DNAME
123456789	Research
333445555	Research
999887777	Research
987654321	Research
666884444	Research
453453453	Research
987987987	Research
888665555	Research
123456789	Administration
333445555	Administration
999887777	Administration
987654321	Administration
666884444	Administration
453453453	Administration
987987987	Administration
888665555	Administration
123456789	Headquarters
333445555	Headquarters
999887777	Headquarters
987654321	Headquarters
666884444	Headquarters
453453453	Headquarters
987987987	Headquarters
888665555	Headquarters

(g)

FNAME	MINIT	LNAME	SSN	BDATE	ADDRESS	SEX	SALARY	SUPERSSN	DNO
John	B	Smith	123456789	09-JAN-RR	731 Fondren, Houston, TX	M	30000	333445555	5
Franklin	T	Wong	333445555	08-DEC-45	638 Voss, Houston, TX	M	40000	888665555	5
Ramesh	K	Narayan	666884444	15-SEP-52	975 Fire Oak, Humble, TX	M	38000	333445555	5
Joyce	A	English	453453453	31-JUL-62	5631 Rice, Houston, TX	F	25000	333445555	5

Figure 7.2   Results of queries specified on the database of Figure 6.6. (a) Result of Q0. (b) Result of Q1. (c) Result of Q2. (d) Result of Q8. (e) Result of Q9. (f) Result of Q10. (g) Result of Q1C.

Query Q1 is similar to a SELECT–PROJECT–JOIN sequence of relational algebra operations. Such queries are often called **select–project–join queries.** In the WHERE clause of Q1, the condition DNAME = 'Research' is a **selection condition** and corresponds to a SELECT operation in the relational algebra. The condition DNUMBER = DNO is a **join condition,** which corresponds to the condition under which a JOIN is performed in the relational algebra. The result of query Q1 may be displayed as shown in Figure 7.2(b). In general, any number of select and join conditions may be specified in a single SQL query. The next example is a select–project–join query with *two* join conditions.

QUERY 2

For every project located in 'Stafford', list the project number, the controlling department number, and the department manager's last name, address, and birthdate.

Q2:	**SELECT**	PNUMBER, DNUM, LNAME, ADDRESS, BDATE
	FROM	PROJECT, DEPARTMENT, EMPLOYEE
	WHERE	DNUM=DNUMBER **AND** MGRSSN=SSN **AND**
		PLOCATION='Stafford'

The join condition DNUM = DNUMBER relates a project to its controlling department, whereas the join condition MGRSSN = SSN relates the controlling department to the employee who manages that department. The result of query Q2 is shown in Figure 7.2(c).

7.2.2 *Dealing with Ambiguous Attribute Names and Aliasing*

In SQL the same name can be used for two (or more) attributes as long as the attributes are in *different relations*. If this is the case, and a query refers to two or more attributes with the same name, we must **qualify** the attribute name with the relation name, to prevent ambiguity. This is done by *prefixing* the relation name to the attribute name and separating the two by a period. To illustrate this, suppose that in Figures 6.5 and 6.6 the DNO and LNAME attributes of the EMPLOYEE relation were called DNUMBER and NAME and the DNAME attribute of DEPARTMENT was also called NAME; then, to prevent ambiguity, query Q1 would be rephrased as shown in Q1A. We must prefix the attributes NAME and DNUMBER in Q1A to specify which ones we are referring to, because the attribute names are used in both relations:

Q1A:	**SELECT**	FNAME, EMPLOYEE.NAME, ADDRESS
	FROM	EMPLOYEE, DEPARTMENT
	WHERE	DEPARTMENT.NAME='Research' **AND**
		DEPARTMENT.DNUMBER=EMPLOYEE.DNUMBER

Ambiguity also arises in the case of queries that refer to the same relation twice, as in the following example. This query did not appear in Chapter 6; hence it is given the number 8 to distinguish it from queries 1 through 7 of Section 6.7.

QUERY 8

For each employee, retrieve the employee's first and last name and the first and last name of his or her immediate supervisor.

Q8:	**SELECT**	E.FNAME, E.LNAME, S.FNAME, S.LNAME
	FROM	EMPLOYEE E, EMPLOYEE S
	WHERE	E.SUPERSSN=S.SSN

In this case, we are allowed to declare alternative relation names E and S, called **aliases,** for the EMPLOYEE relation. An alias can directly follow the relation name, as in Q8, or it can follow the keyword **AS**—for example, EMPLOYEE **AS** E. It is also possible to rename the relation attributes within the query by giving them aliases; for example, if we write

EMPLOYEE **AS** E(FN, MI, LN, SSN, BD, ADDR, SEX, SAL, SSSN, DNO)

in the FROM clause, FN becomes an alias for FNAME, MI for MINIT, LN for LNAME, and so on. In Q8, we can think of E and S as two *different copies* of the EMPLOYEE relation; the first, E, represents employees in the role of supervisees; and the second, S, represents employees in the role of supervisors. We can now join the two copies. Of course, in reality there is *only one* EMPLOYEE relation, and the join condition is meant to join the relation with itself by matching the tuples that satisfy the join condition E.SUPERSSN = S.SSN. Notice that this is an example of a one-level recursive query, as we discussed in Section 6.6.2. As in the relational algebra, we *cannot* specify a general recursive query, with an unknown number of levels, in a single SQL statement.

The result of query Q8 is shown in Figure 7.2(d). Whenever one or more aliases are given to a relation, we can use these names to represent different references to that relation. This permits multiple references to the same relation. Notice that, if we want to, we can use this alias-naming mechanism in any SQL query, whether or not the same relation needs to be referenced more than once. For example, we could specify query Q1A as in Q1B just to shorten the relation names that prefix the attributes:

Q1B:	**SELECT**	E.FNAME, E.NAME, E.ADDRESS
	FROM	EMPLOYEE E, DEPARTMENT D
	WHERE	D.NAME='Research' **AND** D.DNUMBER=E.DNUMBER

7.2.3 *Unspecified WHERE Clauses and Use of '*'*

We discuss two more features of SQL here. A *missing WHERE clause* indicates no condition on tuple selection; hence, *all tuples* of the relation specified in the FROM clause qualify and are selected for the query result. This is equivalent to the condition WHERE TRUE, which means *every row in the table*. If more than one relation is specified in the FROM clause and there is no WHERE clause, then the CROSS PRODUCT—*all possible tuple combinations*—of these relations is selected. For example, Query 9 selects all EMPLOYEE SSNs (Figure 7.2(e)), and Query 10 selects all combinations of an EMPLOYEE SSN and a DEPARTMENT DNAME (Figure 7.2(f)).

QUERIES 9 AND 10
Select all EMPLOYEE SSNs (Q9), and all combinations of EMPLOYEE SSN and DEPARTMENT DNAME (Q10) in the database.

Q9:	**SELECT**	SSN
	FROM	EMPLOYEE
Q10:	**SELECT**	SSN, DNAME
	FROM	EMPLOYEE, DEPARTMENT

It is extremely important to specify every selection and join condition in the WHERE clause; if any such condition is overlooked, incorrect and very large relations may result.

Notice that Q10 is similar to a CROSS PRODUCT operation followed by a PROJECT operation in the relational algebra. If we specify all the attributes of EMPLOYEE and DEPARTMENT in Q10, we get the CROSS PRODUCT.

To retrieve all the attribute values of the selected tuples, we do not have to list the attribute names explicitly in SQL; we just specify an *asterisk* (*), which stands for *all the attributes*. For example, query Q1C retrieves all the attribute values of EMPLOYEE tuples who work in DEPARTMENT number 5 (Figure 7.2(g)); query Q1D retrieves all the attributes of an EMPLOYEE and the attributes of the DEPARTMENT he or she works in for every employee of the 'Research' department; and Q10A specifies the CROSS PRODUCT of the EMPLOYEE and DEPARTMENT relations.

    Q1C: SELECT   *
            FROM   EMPLOYEE
            WHERE   DNO=5

    Q1D: SELECT   *
            FROM   EMPLOYEE, DEPARTMENT
            WHERE   DNAME='Research' AND DNO=DNUMBER

    Q10A: SELECT   *
            FROM   EMPLOYEE, DEPARTMENT

7.2.4 Tables as Sets in SQL

As we mentioned earlier, in general, SQL does not treat a relation as a set; *duplicate tuples can appear more than once* in a relation or in the result of a query. SQL does not automatically eliminate duplicate tuples in the results of queries, for the following reasons:

- Duplicate elimination is an expensive operation. One way to implement it is to sort the tuples first and then eliminate duplicates.
- The user may want to see duplicate tuples in the result of a query.
- When an aggregate function (see Section 7.2.9) is applied to tuples, in most cases we do not want to eliminate duplicates.

If we *do want* to eliminate duplicate tuples from the result of an SQL query, we use the key word **DISTINCT** in the SELECT clause, meaning that only distinct tuples should remain in the result. This causes the result of an SQL query to be a relation—a set of tuples—according to the definition of relation given in Chapter 6. For example, Query 11 retrieves the salary of every employee; if several employees have the same salary, that salary value will appear as many times in the result of the query, as shown in Figure 7.3(a).

QUERY 11
Retrieve the salary of every employee.

    Q11:   SELECT   SALARY
            FROM   EMPLOYEE

(a)	SALARY		(b)	SALARY
	30000			30000
	40000			40000
	25000			25000
	43000			43000
	38000			38000
	25000			55000
	25000			
	55000			

(c)	FNAME	LNAME		(d)	FNAME	LNAME
					James	Borg

Figure 7.3   Results of some other queries specified on the database shown in Figure 6.6. (a) Result of Q11. (b) Result of Q11A. (c) Result of Q12. (d) Result of Q14.

If we are interested only in distinct salary values, we want each value to appear only once, regardless of how many employees earn that salary. By using the keyword **DISTINCT** as in Q11A we accomplish this, as shown in Figure 7.3(b):

Q11A: **SELECT**   **DISTINCT** SALARY
FROM   EMPLOYEE

SQL has directly incorporated some of the set operations of the relational algebra. There is a set union operation (**UNION**), and in SQL2 there are also set difference (**EXCEPT**) and set intersection (**INTERSECT**) operations. The relations resulting from these set operations are sets of tuples; that is, *duplicate tuples are eliminated from the result* (unless the operation is followed by the keyword ALL). Because the set operations apply only to *union-compatible relations*, we must make sure that the two relations on which we apply the operation have the same attributes and that the attributes appear in the same order in both relations. The next example illustrates the use of UNION.

QUERY 4
Make a list of all project numbers for projects that involve an employee whose last name is 'Smith', either as a worker or as a manager of the department that controls the project.

Q4:   **(SELECT**   PNUMBER
FROM   PROJECT, DEPARTMENT, EMPLOYEE
WHERE   DNUM=DNUMBER **AND** MGRSSN=SSN **AND** LNAME='Smith')
UNION
(SELECT   PNUMBER
FROM   PROJECT, WORKS_ON, EMPLOYEE
WHERE   PNUMBER=PNO **AND** ESSN=SSN **AND** LNAME='Smith')

The first SELECT query retrieves the projects that involve a 'Smith' as manager of the department that controls the project, and the second retrieves the projects that involve a 'Smith' as a worker on the project. Notice that, if several employees have the last name 'Smith', the project names involving any of them will be retrieved. Applying the UNION operation to the two SELECT queries gives the desired result.

7.2.5 *Nested Queries and Set Comparisons*★

Some queries require that existing values in the database be fetched and then used in a comparison condition. Such queries can be conveniently formulated by using **nested queries,** which are complete SELECT queries within the WHERE clause of another query. That other query is called the **outer query**. Query 4 is formulated in Q4 without a nested query, but it can be rephrased to use nested queries as shown in Q4A:

```
Q4A:   SELECT    DISTINCT PNUMBER
       FROM      PROJECT
       WHERE     PNUMBER IN    (SELECT   PNUMBER
                               FROM      PROJECT, DEPARTMENT,
                                         EMPLOYEE
                               WHERE     DNUM=DNUMBER AND
                                         MGRSSN=SSN
                                         AND LNAME='Smith')
                 OR
                 PNUMBER IN    (SELECT   PNO
                               FROM      WORKS_ON, EMPLOYEE
                               WHERE     ESSN=SSN AND LNAME='Smith')
```

The first nested query selects the project numbers of projects that have a 'Smith' involved as manager, while the second selects the project numbers of projects that have a 'Smith' involved as worker. In the outer query, we select a PROJECT tuple if the PNUMBER value of that tuple is in the result of either nested query. The comparison operator IN compares a value v with a set (or multiset) of values V and evaluates to TRUE if v is one of the elements in V.

The IN operator can also compare a tuple of values in parentheses with a set of union-compatible tuples. For example, the query

```
SELECT DISTINCT ESSN
FROM WORKS_ON
WHERE (PNO, HOURS) IN (SELECT PNO, HOURS FROM WORKS_ON
                       WHERE SSN='123456789');
```

will select the social security numbers of all employees who work the same (hours, project) combination on some project that employee 'John Smith' (whose SSN = '123456789') works on.

In addition to the IN operator, a number of other comparison operators can be used to compare a single value v (typically an attribute name) to a set V (typically a nested query). The = ANY (or = SOME) operator returns TRUE if the value v is equal to *some value* in the set V and is hence equivalent to IN. The keywords ANY and SOME have the same meaning. Other operators that can be combined with ANY (or SOME) include >, >=, <, <=, and <>. The keyword ALL can also be combined with one of these operators. For example, the comparison condition (v > ALL V) returns TRUE if the value v is greater than *all* the values in the set V. An example is the following query, which returns the names of employees whose salary is greater than the salary of all the employees in department 5:

SELECT	LNAME, FNAME
FROM	EMPLOYEE
WHERE	SALARY > **ALL** (**SELECT** SALARY **FROM** EMPLOYEE
	WHERE DNO=5) ;

In general, we can have several levels of nested queries. We are once again faced with possible ambiguity among attribute names if attributes of the same name exist— one in a relation in the FROM clause of the *outer query*, and the other in a relation in the FROM clause of the *nested query*. The rule is that a reference to an *unqualified attribute* refers to the relation declared in the **innermost nested query**. For example, in the SELECT clause and WHERE clause of the first nested query of Q4A, a reference to any unqualified attribute of the PROJECT relation refers to the PROJECT relation specified in the FROM clause of the nested query. To refer to an attribute of the PROJECT relation specified in the outer query, we can specify and refer to an *alias* for that relation. These rules are similar to scope rules for program variables in a programming language such as PASCAL, which allows nested procedures and functions. To illustrate the potential ambiguity of attribute names in nested queries, consider Query 12, whose result is shown in Figure 7.3(c).

QUERY 12
Retrieve the name of each employee who has a dependent with the same first name and same sex as the employee.

Q12:	**SELECT**	E.FNAME, E.LNAME	
	FROM	EMPLOYEE E	
	WHERE	E.SSN **IN**	(**SELECT** ESSN
			FROM DEPENDENT
			WHERE ESSN=E.SSN **AND**
			E.FNAME=DEPENDENT_NAME **AND**
			SEX=E.SEX)

In the nested query of Q12, we must qualify E.SEX because it refers to the SEX attribute of EMPLOYEE from the outer query, and DEPENDENT also has an attribute called SEX. All unqualified references to SEX in the nested query refer to SEX of DEPENDENT. However, we do not *have to* qualify FNAME and SSN because the DEPENDENT relation does not have attributes called FNAME and SSN, so there is no ambiguity. Notice that we need the SSN = ESSN condition in the WHERE clause of the nested query; without this condition, we would select employees whose first name and sex match those of *any* dependent, whether or not the dependent is of that particular employee.

Whenever a condition in the WHERE clause of a nested query references some attribute of a relation declared in the outer query, the two queries are said to be **correlated**. We can understand a correlated query better by considering that the *nested query is eval-*

uated once for each tuple (or combination of tuples) in the outer query. For example, we can think of Q12 as follows: for *each* EMPLOYEE tuple, evaluate the nested query, which retrieves the ESSN values for all DEPENDENT tuples with the same social security number, sex, and name as the EMPLOYEE tuple; if the SSN value of the EMPLOYEE tuple is *in* the result of the nested query, then select that EMPLOYEE tuple.

In general, a query written with nested SELECT... FROM... WHERE... blocks and using the = or IN comparison operators can *always* be expressed as a single block query. For example, Q12 may be written as in Q12A:

Q12A: **SELECT** E.FNAME, E.LNAME
FROM EMPLOYEE E, DEPENDENT D
WHERE E.SSN=D.ESSN **AND** E.SEX=D.SEX **AND**
E.FNAME=D.DEPENDENT_NAME

The original SQL implementation on SYSTEM R also had a **CONTAINS** comparison operator, which is used to compare two sets. This operator was subsequently dropped from the language, possibly because of the difficulty in implementing it efficiently. Most commercial implementations of SQL do *not* have this operator. The CONTAINS operator compares two sets of values and returns TRUE if one set contains all values in the other set. Query 3 illustrates the use of the CONTAINS operator.

QUERY 3
Retrieve the name of each employee who works on *all* the projects controlled by department number 5.

Q3: **SELECT** FNAME, LNAME
FROM EMPLOYEE
WHERE ((**SELECT** PNO
FROM WORKS_ON
WHERE SSN=ESSN)
CONTAINS
(**SELECT** PNUMBER
FROM PROJECT
WHERE DNUM=5))

In Q3, the second nested query (which is not correlated with the outer query) retrieves the project numbers of all projects controlled by department 5. For *each* employee tuple, the first nested query (which is correlated) retrieves the project numbers on which the employee works; if these contain all projects controlled by department 5, the employee tuple is selected and the name of that employee is retrieved. Notice that the CONTAINS comparison operator is similar in function to the DIVISION operation of the relational algebra, described in Section 6.5.7.

7.2.6 *The EXISTS and UNIQUE Functions in SQL*★

Next, we discuss a function, called EXISTS, in SQL that is used to check whether the result of a correlated nested query is empty (contains no tuples). We illustrate the use of EXISTS—and also NOT EXISTS—with some examples. First, we formulate Query 12 in an alternative form that uses EXISTS. This is shown as Q12B:

Q12B: **SELECT**   E.FNAME, E.LNAME
              FROM   EMPLOYEE E
              WHERE   **EXISTS**   **(SELECT**   *
                                FROM   DEPENDENT
                                WHERE   E.SSN=ESSN **AND** SEX=E.SEX
                                            AND E.FNAME=DEPENDENT_NAME)

EXISTS and NOT EXISTS are usually used in conjunction with a correlated nested query. In Q12B, the nested query references the SSN, FNAME, and SEX attributes of the EMPLOYEE relation from the outer query. We can think of Q12B as follows: for each EMPLOYEE tuple, evaluate the nested query, which retrieves all DEPENDENT tuples with the same social security number, sex, and name as the EMPLOYEE tuple; if at least one tuple EXISTS in the result of the nested query, then select that EMPLOYEE tuple. In general, EXISTS(Q) returns **TRUE** if there is *at least one tuple* in the result of query Q, and it returns **FALSE** otherwise; NOT EXISTS(Q) returns **TRUE** if there are *no tuples* in the result of query Q, and it returns **FALSE** otherwise. Next, we illustrate the use of NOT EXISTS.

QUERY 6
Retrieve the names of employees who have no dependents.

Q6:   **SELECT**   FNAME, LNAME
        FROM   EMPLOYEE
        WHERE   **NOT EXISTS**   **(SELECT**   *
                                     FROM   DEPENDENT
                                     WHERE   SSN=ESSN)

In Q6, the correlated nested query retrieves all DEPENDENT tuples related to an EMPLOYEE tuple. If *none exist*, the EMPLOYEE tuple is selected. We may understand the query better if we think about it in the following way: for *each* EMPLOYEE tuple, the nested query selects all DEPENDENT tuples whose ESSN value matches the EMPLOYEE SSN; if the result of the nested query is empty, then no dependents are related to the employee, so we select that EMPLOYEE tuple and retrieve its FNAME and LNAME. There is another SQL function UNIQUE(Q) that returns TRUE if there are no duplicate tuples in the result of query Q; otherwise, it returns FALSE.

QUERY 7
List the names of managers who have at least one dependent.

Q7:   **SELECT**   FNAME, LNAME
        FROM   EMPLOYEE
        WHERE   **EXISTS**   **(SELECT**   *
                                  FROM   DEPENDENT
                                  WHERE   SSN=ESSN)
              AND
              EXISTS   **(SELECT**   *
                                  FROM   DEPARTMENT
                                  WHERE   SSN=MGRSSN)

One way to write this query is shown in Q7, where we specify two nested correlated queries; the first selects all DEPENDENT tuples related to an EMPLOYEE, and the second selects all DEPARTMENT tuples managed by the EMPLOYEE. If at least one of the first and at least one of the second exist, we select the EMPLOYEE tuple and retrieve its FNAME and LNAME values. Can you rewrite this query using only a single nested query or no nested queries?

Query 3, which we used to illustrate the CONTAINS comparison operator, can be stated using EXISTS and NOT EXISTS in SQL systems that *do not have the CONTAINS operator*. We show this rephrasing of Query 3 as Q3A below. Notice that we need two-level nesting in Q3A and that this formulation is quite a bit more complex than Q3, which used the CONTAINS comparison operator:

```
Q3A:  SELECT    LNAME, FNAME
      FROM      EMPLOYEE
      WHERE     NOT EXISTS
                (SELECT *
                FROM WORKS_ON B
                WHERE (B.PNO IN    (SELECT   PNUMBER
                                    FROM      PROJECT
                                    WHERE     DNUM=5) )
                AND
                NOT EXISTS  (SELECT  *
                             FROM    WORKS_ON C
                             WHERE   C.ESSN=SSN
                                     AND C.PNO=B.PNO) )
```

In Q3A, the outer nested query selects any WORKS_ON (B) tuples whose PNO is of a project controlled by department 5, *if* there is not a WORKS_ON (C) tuple with the same PNO and the same SSN as that of the EMPLOYEE tuple under consideration in the outer query. If no such tuple exists, we select the EMPLOYEE tuple. The form of Q3A matches the following rephrasing of Query 3: select each employee such that there does not exist a project controlled by department 5 that the employee does not work on.

Notice that Query 3 is typically stated in the relational algebra by using the DIVISION operation. Moreover, Query 3 requires a type of quantifier called a **universal quantifier** in the relational calculus (see Section 8.1.5). The negated existential quantifier NOT EXISTS can be used to express a universally quantified query, as we shall discuss in Chapter 8.

7.2.7 *Explicit Sets and NULLs in SQL*★

We have seen several queries with a nested query in the WHERE clause. It is also possible to use an **explicit set of values** in the WHERE clause, rather than a nested query. Such a set is enclosed in parentheses in SQL.

QUERY 13
Retrieve the social security numbers of all employees who work on project number 1, 2, or 3.

Q13:	SELECT	DISTINCT ESSN
	FROM	WORKS_ON
	WHERE	PNO IN (1, 2, 3)

SQL allows queries that check whether a value is NULL—missing or undefined or not applicable. However, rather than using = or ≠ to compare an attribute to NULL, SQL uses IS or IS NOT. This is because SQL considers each null value distinct from other null values, so equality comparison is not appropriate. It follows that, when a join search (comparison) condition is specified, tuples with null values for the join attributes are not included in the result (unless it is an OUTER JOIN; see Section 7.2.8). Query 14 illustrates this; its result is shown in Figure 7.3(d).

QUERY 14
Retrieve the names of all employees who do not have supervisors.

Q14:	SELECT	FNAME, LNAME
	FROM	EMPLOYEE
	WHERE	SUPERSSN IS NULL

7.2.8 Renaming Attributes and Joined Tables★

It is possible to rename any attribute that appears in the result of a query by adding the qualifier AS followed by the desired new name. Hence, the AS construct can be used to alias both attribute and relation names. For example, Q8A below shows how query Q8 can be slightly changed to retrieve the last name of each employee and his or her supervisor, while renaming the resulting attribute names as EMPLOYEE_NAME and SUPERVISOR_NAME. The new names will appear as column headers in the query result:

Q8A:	SELECT	E.LNAME AS EMPLOYEE_NAME, S.LNAME AS
		SUPERVISOR_NAME
	FROM	EMPLOYEE AS E, EMPLOYEE AS S
	WHERE	E.SUPERSSN=S.SSN

The concept of a **joined table** (or **joined relation**) was incorporated into SQL2 to permit users to specify a table resulting from a join operation *in the FROM clause of a* query. This construct may be easier to comprehend than mixing together all the select and join conditions in the WHERE clause. For example, consider query Q1, which retrieves the name and address of every employee who works for the 'Research' department. For some users, it may be easier first to specify the join of the EMPLOYEE and DEPARTMENT relations, and then to select the desired tuples and attributes. This can be written in SQL2 as in Q1A:

Q1A:	SELECT	FNAME, LNAME, ADDRESS
	FROM	(EMPLOYEE JOIN DEPARTMENT ON DNO=DNUMBER)
	WHERE	DNAME='Research'

The FROM clause in Q1A contains a single *joined table*. The attributes of such a table are all the attributes of the first table, EMPLOYEE, followed by all the attributes of the second table, DEPARTMENT. The concept of a joined table also allows the user to specify different types of join, such as NATURAL JOIN and various types of OUTER JOIN. In a NATURAL JOIN on two relations R and S, no join condition is specified; an implicit (equi-)join condition for *each pair of attributes with the same name* from R and S is created. Each such pair of attributes is included only once in the resulting relation (see Section 6.5.5.)

If the names of the join attributes are not the same in the base relations, it is possible to rename the attributes so that they match, and then to apply NATURAL JOIN. In this case, the AS construct can be used to rename a relation and all its attributes. This is illustrated in Q1B, where the DEPARTMENT relation is renamed as DEPT and its attributes are renamed as DNAME, DNO (to match the name of the desired join attribute DNO in EMPLOYEE), MSSN, and MSDATE. The implied join condition for this NATURAL JOIN is EMPLOYEE.DNO = DEPT.DNO, because this is the only pair of attributes with the same name:

Q1B: **SELECT** FNAME, LNAME, ADDRESS
      FROM (EMPLOYEE **NATURAL JOIN** (DEPARTMENT **AS** DEPT
           (DNAME, DNO, MSSN, MSDATE)))
      WHERE DNAME='Research

The default type of join in a joined table is an **inner** join, where a tuple is included in the result only if a matching tuple exists in the other relation. For example, in query Q8A, only employees that *have a supervisor* are included in the result; an EMPLOYEE tuple whose value for SUPERSSN is NULL is excluded. If the user requires that all employees be included, an outer join must be used explicitly (see Section 6.6.3). In SQL2, this is handled by explicitly specifying the OUTER JOIN in a joined table, as illustrated in Q8B:

Q8B: **SELECT** E.LNAME **AS** EMPLOYEE_NAME, S.LNAME **AS**
           SUPERVISOR_NAME
      FROM (EMPLOYEE E **LEFT OUTER JOIN** EMPLOYEE S **ON**
           E.SUPERSSN=S.SSN)

The options available for specifying joined tables in SQL2 include INNER JOIN (same as JOIN), LEFT OUTER JOIN, RIGHT OUTER JOIN, and FULL OUTER JOIN. In the latter three, the keyword OUTER may be omitted. It is also possible to *nest* join specifications; that is, one of the tables in a join may itself be a joined table. This is illustrated by Q2A, which is a different way of specifying query Q2, using the concept of a joined table:

Q2A: **SELECT** PNUMBER, DNUM, LNAME, ADDRESS, BDATE
      FROM ((PROJECT **JOIN** DEPARTMENT **ON** DNUM=DNUMBER) **JOIN**
           EMPLOYEE **ON** MGRSSN=SSN)
      WHERE PLOCATION='Stafford'

7.2.9 *Aggregate Functions and Grouping*★

In Section 6.6.1, we introduced the concept of an aggregate function as a relational operation. Because grouping and aggregation are required in many database applications, SQL has features that incorporate these concepts. The first of these features is a number of built-in functions: **COUNT, SUM, MAX, MIN,** and **AVG.** The COUNT function returns the number of tuples or values specified in a query. The functions SUM, MAX, MIN, and AVG are applied to a set or multiset of numeric values and return, respectively, the sum, maximum value, minimum value, and average (mean) of those values. These functions can be used in the SELECT clause or in a HAVING clause (which we will introduce later). We illustrate the use of these functions with example queries.

QUERY 15
Find the sum of the salaries of all employees, the maximum salary, the minimum salary, and the average salary.

Q15:   **SELECT**   **SUM** (SALARY), **MAX** (SALARY), **MIN** (SALARY),
                      AVG (SALARY)
          FROM   EMPLOYEE

If we want to get the preceding function values for employees of a specific department—say the 'Research' department—we can write Query 16, where the EMPLOYEE tuples are restricted by the WHERE clause to employees who work for the 'Research' department.

QUERY 16
Find the sum of the salaries of all employees of the 'Research' department, as well as the maximum salary, the minimum salary, and the average salary in this department.

Q16:   **SELECT**   **SUM** (SALARY), **MAX** (SALARY), **MIN** (SALARY),
                      AVG (SALARY)
          FROM   EMPLOYEE, DEPARTMENT
          WHERE   DNO=DNUMBER **AND** DNAME='Research'

QUERIES 17 AND 18
Retrieve the total number of employees in the company (Q17) and the number of employees in the 'Research' department (Q18).

Q17:   **SELECT**   **COUNT** (*)
          FROM   EMPLOYEE

Q18:   **SELECT**   **COUNT** (*)
          FROM   EMPLOYEE, DEPARTMENT
          WHERE   DNO=DNUMBER **AND** DNAME='Research'

Here the asterisk (*) refers to the *rows* (tuples), so COUNT (*) returns the number of rows in the result of the query. We may also use the COUNT function to count values in a column rather than tuples, as in the next example.

QUERY 19
Count the number of distinct salary values in the database.

Q19:   **SELECT**   **COUNT (DISTINCT** SALARY)
          FROM   EMPLOYEE

Notice that, if we write COUNT(SALARY) instead of COUNT(DISTINCT SALARY) in Q19, we get the same result as COUNT(*) because duplicates will not be eliminated. The preceding examples show how functions are applied to retrieve a summary value from the database. In some cases we may need to use functions to select particular tuples. In such cases we specify a correlated nested query with the desired function, and we use that nested query in the WHERE clause of an outer query. For example, to retrieve the names of all employees who have two or more dependents (Query 5), we can write

Q5:	SELECT	LNAME, FNAME
	FROM	EMPLOYEE
	WHERE	(SELECT COUNT (*)
	FROM	DEPENDENT
	WHERE	SSN=ESSN) $\geq$ 2

The correlated nested query counts the number of dependents that each employee has; if this is greater than or equal to 2, the employee tuple is selected.

In many cases we want to apply the aggregate functions *to subgroups of tuples in a relation*, based on some attribute values. For example, we may want to find the average salary of employees in each department or the number of employees who work on each project. In these cases we need to group the tuples that have the same value of some attribute(s), called the **grouping attribute**(s), and we need to apply the function to each such group independently. SQL has a **GROUP BY** clause for this purpose. The GROUP BY clause specifies the grouping attributes, which should *also appear in the SELECT clause*, so that the value resulting from applying each function to a group of tuples appears along with the value of the grouping attribute(s).

QUERY 20
For each department, retrieve the department number, the number of employees in the department, and their average salary.

Q20:	SELECT	DNO, **COUNT** (*), **AVG** (SALARY)
	FROM	EMPLOYEE
	GROUP BY	DNO

In Q20, the EMPLOYEE tuples are divided into groups—each group having the same value for the grouping attribute DNO. The COUNT and AVG functions are applied to each such group of tuples. Notice that the SELECT clause includes only the grouping attribute and the functions to be applied on each group of tuples. Figure 7.4(a) illustrates how grouping works on Q20, and it also shows the result of Q20.

QUERY 21
For each project, retrieve the project number, the project name, and the number of employees who work on that project.

Q21:	SELECT	PNUMBER, PNAME, **COUNT** (*)
	FROM	PROJECT, WORKS_ON
	WHERE	PNUMBER=PNO
	GROUP BY	PNUMBER, PNAME

(a)

FNAME	MINIT	LNAME	SSN	• • •	SALARY	SUPERSSN	DNO
John	B	Smith	123456789		30000	333445555	5
Franklin	T	Wong	333445555		40000	888665555	5
Ramesh	K	Narayan	666884444		38000	333445555	5
Joyce	A	English	453453453	• • •	25000	333445555	5
Alicia	J	Zelaya	999887777		25000	987654321	4
Jennifer	S	Wallace	987654321		43000	888665555	4
Ahmad	V	Jabbar	987987987		25000	987654321	4
James	E	Bong	888665555		55000	null	1

DNO	COUNT (*)	AVG (SALARY)
5	4	33250
4	3	31000
1	1	55000

Result of Q20.

Grouping EMPLOYEE tuples by the value of DNO.

(b)

PNAME	PNUMBER		ESSN	PNO	HOURS
ProductX	1		123456789	1	32.5
ProductX	1		453453453	1	20.0
ProductY	2		123456789	2	7.5
ProductY	2		453453453	2	20.0
ProductY	2		333445555	2	10.0
ProductZ	3		666884444	3	40.0
ProductZ	3		333445555	3	10.0
Computerization	10	• • •	333445555	10	10.0
Computerization	10		999887777	10	10.0
Computerization	10		987987987	10	35.0
Reorganization	20		333445555	20	10.0
Reorganization	20		987654321	20	15.0
Reorganization	20		888665555	20	null
Newbenefits	30		987987987	30	5.0
Newbenefits	30		987654321	30	20.0
Newbenefits	30		999887777	30	30.0

These groups are not selected by the HAVING condition of Q22.

After applying the WHERE clause but before applying HAVING.

PNAME	PNUMBER		ESSN	PNO	HOURS
ProductY	2		123456789	2	7.5
ProductY	2		453453453	2	20.0
ProductY	2		333445555	2	10.0
Computerization	10	• • •	333445555	10	10.0
Computerization	10		999887777	10	10.0
Computerization	10		987987987	10	35.0
Reorganization	20		333445555	20	10.0
Reorganization	20		987654321	20	15.0
Reorganization	20		888665555	20	null
Newbenefits	30		987987987	30	5.0
Newbenefits	30		987654321	30	20.0
Newbenefits	30		999887777	30	30.0

PNAME	COUNT (*)
ProductY	3
Computerization	3
Reorganization	3
Newbenefits	3

Result of Q22
(PNUMBER not shown).

After applying the HAVING clause condition.

Figure 7.4 Results of GROUP BY and HAVING. (a) Results for Query 20. (b) Results for Query 22.

Q21 shows how we can use a join condition in conjunction with GROUP BY. In this case, the grouping and functions are applied *after* the joining of the two relations. Sometimes we want to retrieve the values of these functions only for *groups that satisfy certain conditions*. For example, suppose that we want to modify Query 21 so that only projects with more than two employees appear in the result. SQL provides a **HAVING clause,** which can appear in conjunction with a GROUP BY clause, for this purpose. HAVING provides a condition on the group of tuples associated with each value of the grouping attributes; and only the groups that satisfy the condition are retrieved in the result of the query. This is illustrated by Query 22.

QUERY 22
For each project *on which more than two employees work*, retrieve the project number, the project name, and the number of employees who work on the project.

```
Q22:   SELECT      PNUMBER, PNAME, COUNT (*)
       FROM        PROJECT, WORKS_ON
       WHERE       PNUMBER=PNO
       GROUP BY    PNUMBER, PNAME
       HAVING      COUNT (*) > 2
```

Notice that, while selection conditions in the WHERE clause limit the *tuples* to which functions are applied, the HAVING clause limits *whole groups*. Figure 7.4(b) illustrates the use of HAVING and displays the result of Q22.

QUERY 23
For each project, retrieve the project number, the project name, and the number of employees from department 5 who work on the project.

```
Q23:   SELECT      PNUMBER, PNAME, COUNT (*)
       FROM        PROJECT, WORKS_ON, EMPLOYEE
       WHERE       PNUMBER=PNO AND SSN=ESSN AND DNO=5
       GROUP BY    PNUMBER, PNAME
```

Here we restrict the tuples in each group to those that satisfy the condition specified in the WHERE clause—namely, that they work in department number 5. Notice that we must be extra careful when two different conditions apply (one to the function in the SELECT clause, and another to the function in the HAVING clause). For example, suppose that we want to count the *total* number of employees whose salaries exceed $40,000 in each department, but only for departments where more than five employees work. Here, the condition (SALARY > 40000) applies only to the COUNT function in the SELECT clause. Suppose that we write the following *incorrect* query:

```
SELECT      DNAME, COUNT (*)
FROM        DEPARTMENT, EMPLOYEE
WHERE       DNUMBER=DNO AND SALARY>40000
GROUP BY    DNAME
HAVING      COUNT (*) > 5
```

This is incorrect because it will select only departments that have more than five employees *who each earn more than $40,000*. The rule is that the WHERE clause is executed first, to select individual tuples; the HAVING clause is applied later, to select individual groups of tuples. Hence, the tuples are already restricted to employees who earn more than $40,000, *before* the function in the HAVING clause is applied. One way to write the query correctly is to use a nested query, as shown in Query 24.

QUERY 24
For each department having more than five employees, retrieve the department number and the number of employees making more than $40,000.

Q24:	**SELECT**	DNAME, **COUNT** (*)
	FROM	DEPARTMENT, EMPLOYEE
	WHERE	DNUMBER=DNO **AND** SALARY>40000 **AND**
		DNO **IN** (**SELECT** DNO
		FROM EMPLOYEE
		GROUP BY DNO
		HAVING **COUNT** (*) > 5)
	GROUP BY	DNAME

7.2.10 *Substring Comparisons, Arithmetic Operators, and Ordering*

In this section we discuss three more features of SQL. The first feature allows comparison conditions on only parts of a character string, using the LIKE comparison operator. Partial strings are specified by using two reserved characters: '%' replaces an arbitrary number of characters, and '_' replaces a single arbitrary character. For example, consider the following query.

QUERY 25
Retrieve all employees whose address is in Houston, Texas.

Q25:	**SELECT**	FNAME, LNAME
	FROM	EMPLOYEE
	WHERE	ADDRESS **LIKE** '%Houston,TX%'

To retrieve all employees who were born during the 1950s, we can use Query 26. Here, '5' must be the third character of the string (according to our format for date), so we use the value '__5_____', with each underscore serving as a placeholder for an arbitrary character.

QUERY 26
Find all employees who were born during the 1950s.

Q26:	**SELECT**	FNAME, LNAME
	FROM	EMPLOYEE
	WHERE	BDATE **LIKE** '__5_____'

Another feature allows the use of arithmetic in queries. The standard arithmetic operators '+', '−', '*', and '/' (for addition, subtraction, multiplication, and division, respectively) can be applied to numeric values in a query. For example, suppose that we want to see the effect of giving all employees who work on the 'ProductX' project a 10% raise; we can issue Query 27 to see what their salaries would become.

QUERY 27
Show the resulting salaries if every employee working on the 'ProductX' project is given a 10% raise.

Q27:   **SELECT**   FNAME, LNAME, 1.1*SALARY
        FROM   EMPLOYEE, WORKS_ON, PROJECT
        WHERE   SSN=ESSN **AND** PNO=PNUMBER **AND** PNAME='ProductX'

For string data types, the concatenate operator '‖' can be used in a query to append two string values. For date, time, timestamp, and interval data types, operators include incrementing ('+') or decrementing ('−') a date, time, or timestamp by a type-compatible interval. In addition, an interval value can be specified as the difference between two date, time, or timestamp values.

Finally, SQL allows the user to order the tuples in the result of a query by the values of one or more attributes, using the **ORDER BY** clause. For example, suppose that we want to retrieve a list of employees and the projects each works in, but we want the list ordered by the employees' departments and we want the names within each department ordered alphabetically.

QUERY 28
Retrieve a list of employees and the projects they are working on, ordered by department and, within each department, alphabetically by last name, first name.

Q28:   **SELECT**   DNAME, LNAME, FNAME, PNAME
       FROM   DEPARTMENT, EMPLOYEE, WORKS_ON, PROJECT
       WHERE   DNUMBER=DNO **AND** SSN=ESSN **AND** PNO=PNUMBER
       ORDER BY DNAME, LNAME, FNAME

The default order is in ascending order of values. We can specify the keyword **DESC** if we want a descending order of values. The keyword **ASC** can be used to specify ascending order explicitly. If we want descending order on DNAME and ascending order on LNAME, FNAME, the ORDER BY clause of Q28 becomes

ORDER BY   DNAME **DESC**, LNAME **ASC**, FNAME **ASC**

7.2.11 *Discussion*

A query in SQL can consist of up to six clauses, but only the first two—SELECT and FROM—are mandatory. The clauses are specified in the following order, with the clauses between [. . .] being optional:

SELECT <attribute list>
FROM <table list>
[WHERE <condition>]
[GROUP BY <grouping attribute(s)>]
[HAVING <group condition>]
[ORDER BY <attribute list>]

The SELECT clause lists the attributes or functions to be retrieved. The FROM clause specifies all relations needed in the query, including joined relations, but not those needed in nested queries. The WHERE clause specifies the conditions for selection of tuples from these relations. GROUP BY specifies grouping attributes, whereas HAVING specifies a condition on the groups being selected rather than on the individual tuples. The built-in aggregate functions COUNT, SUM, MIN, MAX, and AVG are used in conjunction with grouping. Finally, ORDER BY specifies an order for displaying the result of a query.

A query is evaluated by applying first the FROM clause, followed by the WHERE clause, and then GROUP BY and HAVING. If none of the last three clauses (GROUP BY, HAVING, ORDER BY) are specified, we can *think* of a query as being executed as follows: for *each combination of tuples*—one from each of the relations specified in the FROM clause—evaluate the WHERE clause; if it evaluates to TRUE, place the values of attributes specified in the SELECT clause from this tuple combination in the result of the query. Of course, this is not an efficient way to implement the query, and each DBMS has special query optimization routines to decide on an execution plan. We discuss query processing and optimization in Chapter 16.

In general, there are numerous ways to specify the same query in SQL. This flexibility in specifying queries has advantages and disadvantages. The main advantage is that a user can choose the technique he or she is most comfortable with when specifying a query. For example, many queries may be specified with join conditions in the WHERE clause, or by using joined relations in the FROM clause, or with some form of nested queries and the IN comparison operator. Some users may be more comfortable with one approach, whereas others may be more comfortable with another. From the programmer's and the system's query optimization point of view, it is generally preferable to write a query with as little nesting and implied ordering as possible.

The disadvantage of having numerous ways of specifying the same query is that this may confuse the user. The user may not know which technique to use to specify particular types of queries.

Another problem is that it may be more efficient to execute a query specified in one way than the same query specified in an alternative way. Ideally, this should not be the case: the DBMS should process the same query in the same way, regardless of how the query is specified. But this is quite difficult in practice, as each DBMS has different methods for processing queries specified in different ways. An additional burden on the user is to figure out which of the alternative specifications is the most efficient. Ideally, the user should worry only about specifying the query correctly. It is the responsibility of the DBMS to execute the query efficiently. In practice, however, it helps if the user is somewhat aware of which types of constructs in a query are more expensive to process than others. For example, a join condition specified on fields on which no indexes exist (see Section 7.5) can be quite expensive when specified on two large relations; hence, the user should create the appropriate indexes *before* specifying such a query.

7.3 Update Statements in SQL

In SQL three commands can be used to modify the database: INSERT, DELETE, and UPDATE. We discuss each of these in turn.

7.3.1   *The* INSERT *Command*

In its simplest form, INSERT is used to add a single tuple to a relation. We must specify the relation name and a list of values for the tuple. The values should be listed *in the same order* in which the corresponding attributes were specified in the CREATE TABLE command. For example, to add a new tuple to the EMPLOYEE relation shown in Figure 6.5 and specified in the CREATE TABLE EMPLOYEE command in Figure 7.1, we can use U1:

U1:	**INSERT INTO**	EMPLOYEE
	VALUES	('Richard','K', 'Marini', '653298653', '30-DEC-52','98 Oak Forest,Katy,TX', 'M', 37000, '987654321', 4)

A second form of the INSERT statement allows the user to specify explicit attribute names that correspond to the values in the INSERT command. In this case, attributes with NULL or DEFAULT values can be *left out*. For example, to enter a tuple for a new EMPLOYEE for whom we only know the FNAME, LNAME, and SSN attributes, we can use U1A:

U1A:	**INSERT INTO**	EMPLOYEE (FNAME, LNAME, SSN)
	VALUES	('Richard', 'Marini', '653298653')

Attributes not specified in U1A are set to their DEFAULT or to NULL, and the values are listed in the same order *as the attributes are listed in the* INSERT *command itself*. It is also possible to insert into a relation *multiple tuples* separated by commas in a single INSERT command. The attribute values forming each tuple are enclosed in parentheses.

A DBMS that fully implements SQL2 should support and enforce all the integrity constraints that can be specified in the DDL. However, some DBMSs do not incorporate all the constraints, in order to maintain the efficiency of the DBMS and because of the complexity of enforcing all constraints. In a system that does not support some constraint—say, referential integrity—the users or programmers must enforce the constraint. For example, if we issue the command in U2 on the database shown in Figure 6.6, a DBMS not supporting referential integrity will do the insertion even though no DEPARTMENT tuple exists in the database with DNUMBER = 2. It is the responsibility of the user to check that any such unchecked constraints are not violated. However, the DBMS must implement checks to enforce all the SQL integrity constraints *it supports*. A DBMS enforcing NOT NULL will reject an INSERT command in which an attribute declared to be NOT NULL does not have a value; for example, U2A would be *rejected* because no SSN value is provided:

U2:	**INSERT INTO**	EMPLOYEE (FNAME, LNAME, SSN, DNO)
	VALUES	('Robert', 'Hatcher', '980760540', 2)
U2A:	**INSERT INTO**	EMPLOYEE (FNAME, LNAME, DNO) (∗ rejected update ∗)
	VALUES	('Robert', 'Hatcher', 2)

A variation of the INSERT command inserts multiple tuples into a relation in conjunction with creating the relation and loading it with the *result of a query*. For example, to create a temporary table that has the name, number of employees, and total salaries for each department, we write the statements in U3A and U3B:

U3A:	**CREATE TABLE**	**DEPTS_INFO**	(DEPT_NAME VARCHAR(15),
			NO_OF_EMPS INTEGER,
			TOTAL_SAL INTEGER) ;

U3B:	**INSERT INTO**	DEPTS_INFO (DEPT_NAME, NO OF EMPS,
		TOTAL SAL)
	SELECT	DNAME, COUNT (*), SUM (SALARY)
	FROM	DEPARTMENT, EMPLOYEE
	WHERE	DNUMBER=DNO
	GROUP BY	DNAME ;

A table DEPTS_INFO is created by U3A and is loaded with the summary information retrieved from the database by the query in U3B. We can now query DEPTS_INFO as we could any other relation; and when we do not need it any more, we can remove it by using the DROP TABLE command. Notice that the DEPTS_INFO table may not be up to date; that is, if we update either the DEPARTMENT or the EMPLOYEE relations after issuing U3B, the information in DEPTS_INFO *becomes outdated*. We have to create a view (see Section 7.4) to keep such a table up to date.

7.3.2 *The DELETE Command*

The DELETE command removes tuples from a relation. It includes a WHERE clause, similar to that used in an SQL query, to select the tuples to be deleted. Tuples are explicitly deleted from only one table at a time. However, the deletion may propagate to tuples in other relations if such a result is specified in the referential integrity constraints of the DDL (see Section 7.1.2). Depending on the number of tuples selected by the condition in the WHERE clause, zero, one, or several tuples can be deleted by a single DELETE command. A missing WHERE clause specifies that all tuples in the relation are to be deleted; however, the table remains in the database as an empty table. We must use the DROP TABLE command to remove the table completely. The DELETE commands in U4A to U4D, if applied independently to the database of Figure 6.6, will delete zero, one, four, and all tuples, respectively, from the employee relation:

U4A:	**DELETE FROM**	EMPLOYEE		
	WHERE	LNAME='Brown'		

U4B:	**DELETE FROM**	EMPLOYEE		
	WHERE	SSN='123456789'		

U4C:	**DELETE FROM**	EMPLOYEE		
	WHERE	DNO **IN**	(**SELECT**	DNUMBER
			FROM	DEPARTMENT
			WHERE	DNAME='Research')

U4D:	**DELETE FROM**	EMPLOYEE

7.3.3 *The* UPDATE *Command*

The **UPDATE** command is used to modify attribute values of one or more selected tuples. As in the DELETE command, a WHERE clause in the UPDATE command selects the tuples to be modified from a single relation. However, updating a primary key value may propagate to the foreign key values of tuples in other relations if such a result is specified in the referential integrity constraints of the DDL (see Section 7.1.2). An additional SET **clause** specifies the attributes to be modified and their new values. For example, to change the location and controlling department number of project number 10 to 'Bellaire' and 5, respectively, we use U5:

```
U5:   UPDATE   PROJECT
      SET      PLOCATION = 'Bellaire', DNUM = 5
      WHERE    PNUMBER=10
```

Several tuples can be modified with a single UPDATE command. An example is to give all employees in the 'Research' department a 10% raise in salary, as shown in U6. In this request, the modified SALARY value depends on the original SALARY value in each tuple, so two references to the SALARY attribute are needed. In U6, the reference to the SALARY attribute on the right refers to the old SALARY value *before modification*, and the one on the left refers to the new SALARY value *after modification*:

```
U6:   UPDATE   EMPLOYEE
      SET      SALARY = SALARY *1.1
      WHERE    DNO IN   (SELECT   DNUMBER
                         FROM     DEPARTMENT
                         WHERE    DNAME='Research')
```

It is also possible to specify NULL or DEFAULT as the new attribute value. Notice that each UPDATE command explicitly specifies a single relation only. To modify multiple relations, we must issue several UPDATE commands. These (and other SQL commands) could be embedded in a general-purpose program, as we discuss in Section 7.7.

7.4 Views in SQL

In this section we introduce the concept of a view in SQL. We then show how views are specified, and we discuss the problem of updating a view.

7.4.1 *Concept of a View in SQL*

A **view** in SQL terminology is a single table that is derived from other tables.* These other tables could be base tables or previously defined views. A view does not necessarily exist in physical form; it is considered a **virtual table,** in contrast to base tables whose tuples are actually stored in the database. This limits the possible update operations that can be applied to views, but it does not provide any limitations on querying a view.

---

*As used here, the term *view* is more limited than the term *user views* discussed in Chapters 1 and 2.

We can think of a view as a way of specifying a table that we need to reference frequently, even though it may not exist physically. For example, in Figure 6.5 we may frequently issue queries that retrieve the employee name and the project names that the employee works on. Rather than having to specify the join of the EMPLOYEE, WORKS_ON, and PROJECT tables every time we issue that query, we can define a view that is a result of these joins and hence already includes the attributes we wish to retrieve frequently. We can then issue queries on the view, which are specified as single-table retrievals rather than as retrievals involving two joins on three tables. We call the tables EMPLOYEE, WORKS_ON, and PROJECT the **defining tables** of the view.

7.4.2 *Specification of Views in* SQL

The command to specify a view is **CREATE VIEW.** The view is given a (virtual) table name, a list of attribute names, and a query to specify the contents of the view. If none of the view attributes result from applying functions or arithmetic operations, we do not have to specify attribute names for the view, as they will be the same as the names of the attributes of the defining tables. The views in V1 and V2 create virtual tables whose schemas are illustrated in Figure 7.5 when applied to the database schema of Figure 6.5.

```
V1:  CREATE VIEW   WORKS_ON1
     AS  SELECT    FNAME, LNAME, PNAME, HOURS
         FROM      EMPLOYEE, PROJECT, WORKS_ON
         WHERE     SSN=ESSN AND PNO=PNUMBER ;

V2:  CREATE VIEW   DEPT_INFO   (DEPT_NAME, NO_OF_EMPS, TOTAL_ SAL)
     AS  SELECT    DNAME, COUNT (*), SUM (SALARY)
         FROM      DEPARTMENT, EMPLOYEE
         WHERE     DNUMBER=DNO
         GROUP BY  DNAME ;
```

In V1, we did not specify any new attribute names for the view WORKS_ON1 (although we could have); in this case, WORKS_ON1 inherits the names of the view attributes from the defining tables EMPLOYEE, PROJECT, and WORKS_ON. View V2 explicitly specifies new attribute names for the view DEPT_INFO, using a one-to-one correspondence between the attributes specified in the CREATE VIEW clause and those specified in the SELECT clause of the query that defines the view. We can now specify SQL queries on a view—or virtual table—in the same way we specify queries involving

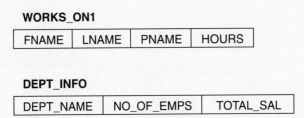

WORKS_ON1

FNAME	LNAME	PNAME	HOURS

DEPT_INFO

DEPT_NAME	NO_OF_EMPS	TOTAL_SAL

Figure 7.5   Two views specified on the database schema of Figure 6.5.

base tables. For example, to retrieve the last name and first name of all employees who work on 'ProjectX', we can utilize the WORKS_ON1 view and specify the query as in QV1:

QV1:   **SELECT**   PNAME, FNAME, LNAME
           FROM   WORKS_ON1
           WHERE   PNAME='ProjectX' ;

The same query would require the specification of two joins if specified on the base relations; the main advantage of a view is to simplify the specification of certain queries. Views can also be used as a security mechanism (see Chapter 20).

A view is *always up to date*; if we modify the tuples in the base tables on which the view is defined, the view automatically reflects these changes. Hence, the view is not realized at the time of view definition but rather at the time we specify a query on the view. It is the responsibility of the DBMS and not the user to make sure that the view is up to date.

If we do not need a view any more, we can use the **DROP VIEW** command to dispose of it. For example, to get rid of the two views defined in V1 and V2, we can use the SQL statements in V1A and V2A:

V1A: **DROP VIEW**   WORKS_ON1 ;

V2A: **DROP VIEW**   DEPT_INFO ;

7.4.3 *Updating of Views and View Implementation*

Updating of views is complicated and can be ambiguous. In general, an update on a view defined on a *single table* without any *aggregate functions* can be mapped to an update on the underlying base table. For a view involving joins, an update operation may be mapped to update operations on the underlying base relations *in multiple ways*. The topic of updating views is still an active research area. To illustrate potential problems with updating a view defined on multiple tables, consider the WORKS_ON1 view, and suppose that we issue the command to update the PNAME attribute of 'John Smith' from 'ProductX' to 'ProductY'. This view update is shown in UV1:

UV1:   **UPDATE**   WORKS_ON1
           SET   PNAME = 'ProductY'
           WHERE   LNAME='Smith' **AND** FNAME='John' **AND** PNAME='ProductX'

This query can be mapped into several updates on the base relations to give the desired update on the view. Two possible updates (a) and (b) on the base relations corresponding to UV1 are shown here:

(a):   **UPDATE**   WORKS_ON
           SET   PNO = (**SELECT** PNUMBER **FROM** PROJECT
                             WHERE PNAME='ProductY')
           WHERE   ESSN = (**SELECT** SSN **FROM** EMPLOYEE
                             WHERE LNAME='Smith' **AND** FNAME='John') **AND**
                     PNO = (**SELECT** PNUMBER **FROM** PROJECT
                             WHERE PNAME='ProductX')

(b):   **UPDATE**   PROJECT
           SET   PNAME = 'ProductY'
           WHERE   PNAME = 'ProductX'

Update (a) relates 'John Smith' to the 'ProductY' PROJECT tuple in place of the 'ProductX' PROJECT tuple and is the most likely desired update. However, (b) would also give the desired update effect on the view, but it accomplishes this by changing the name of the 'ProductX' tuple in the PROJECT relation to 'ProductY'. It is quite unlikely that the user who specified the view update UV1 wants the update to be interpreted as in (b), since it also has the effect of changing all the view tuples with PNAME = 'ProductX'.

Some view updates may not make much sense; for example, modifying the TOTAL_SAL attribute of DEPT_INFO does not make sense because TOTAL_SAL is defined to be the sum of the individual employee salaries. This request is shown as UV2:

UV2:   **UPDATE**   DEPT_INFO
           SET   TOTAL_SAL=100000
           WHERE   DNAME='Research' ;

Many possible updates on the underlying base relations can satisfy this view update.

In general, we cannot guarantee that any view can be updated. A view update is feasible when only *one possible update* on the base relations can accomplish the desired update effect on the view. Whenever an update on the view can be mapped to *more than one update* on the underlying base relations, we must have a certain procedure to choose the desired update. Some researchers have developed methods for choosing the most likely update, while other researchers prefer to have the user choose the desired update mapping during view definition.

In summary, we can make the following observations:

• A view with a single defining table is updatable if the view attributes contain the primary key or some other candidate key of the base relation, because this maps each (virtual) view tuple to a single base tuple.

• Views defined on multiple tables using joins are generally not updatable.

• Views defined using grouping and aggregate functions are not updatable.

In SQL2, the clause WITH CHECK OPTION must be added at the end of the view definition if a view is to be updated. This allows the system to check for view updatability and to plan an execution strategy for view updates.

The problem of efficiently implementing a view for querying is also complex. Two approaches have been suggested. One strategy, called **query modification,** involves modifying the view query into a query on the underlying base tables. The disadvantage of this approach is that it is inefficient for views defined via complex queries that are time-consuming to execute, especially if multiple queries are applied to the view within a short period of time. The other strategy, called **view materialization,** involves physically creating a temporary view table when the view is first queried and keeping that table on the assumption that other queries on the view will follow. In this case, a strategy for incrementally updating the view table when the base tables are updated must be developed in order to keep the view up to date. If the view is not referenced for a certain period of time, the system may then remove the physical view table and recompute it when future queries reference the view.

7.5 Specifying Additional Constraints as Assertions★

In SQL2, users can specify constraints that do not fall into any of the categories described in Section 7.1.2 (such as keys, entity integrity, and referential integrity) via **declarative assertions,** using the **CREATE ASSERTION statement** of the DDL. Each assertion is given a constraint name and is specified via a condition similar to the WHERE clause of an SQL query. For example, to specify the constraint "The salary of an employee must not be greater than the salary of the manager of the department that the employee works for" in SQL2, we can write the following assertion:

CREATE ASSERTION SALARY_CONSTRAINT
CHECK (**NOT EXISTS** (**SELECT** ∗ **FROM** EMPLOYEE E, EMPLOYEE M,
          DEPARTMENT D
       WHERE E.SALARY>M.SALARY **AND**
          E.DNO=D.DNUMBER **AND** D.MGRSSN=M.SSN));

The constraint name SALARY_CONSTRAINT is followed by the keyword **CHECK,** which is followed by a **condition** in parentheses that must hold true on the database state for the assertion to be satisfied. The constraint name can be used later to refer to the constraint, to modify or drop it. The DBMS is responsible for ensuring that the condition is not violated. Any WHERE clause condition can be used, but many constraints can be specified using the EXISTS and NOT EXISTS style of conditions. Whenever some tuples in the database cause the condition of an ASSERTION statement to evaluate to FALSE, the constraint is **violated.** The constraint is **satisfied** by a database state if *no combination of tuples* in that database state violates the constraint. Note that the CHECK clause and constraint condition can also be used in conjunction with the CREATE DOMAIN statement (see Section 7.1.2) to specify constraints on a particular domain, such as restricting the values of a domain to a *subrange* of the data type for the domain.

Earlier versions of SQL had two types of statements to declare constraints: ASSERT and TRIGGER. The **ASSERT statement** is somewhat similar to CREATE ASSERTION of SQL2 with a different syntax. We can specify the constraint "The salary of an employee must not be greater than the salary of the manager of the department that the employee works for," using ASSERT, as follows:

ASSERT SALARY_CONSTRAINT **ON** EMPLOYEE E, EMPLOYEE M, DEPARTMENT D:
NOT (E.SALARY>M.SALARY **AND** E.DNO=D.DNUMBER **AND** D.MGRSSN=M.SSN);

The keyword **ASSERT** indicates that a constraint is being defined; it is followed by the name of the constraint, SALARY_CONSTRAINT. Following the ON keyword are the relations affected by the constraint. Finally, the assertion condition is specified, which is again similar to the condition of a WHERE clause.

In many cases it is convenient to specify the type of action to be taken in case of a constraint violation. Rather than offering users only the option of aborting the transaction that causes a violation, the DBMS should make other options available. For example, it may be useful to specify a constraint that, if violated, causes some user to be informed. A manager may want to be informed if an employee's travel expenses exceed a certain limit by receiving a message whenever this occurs. The action that the DBMS must take in this case is to send an appropriate message to that user, and the constraint is thus used to **monitor** the database. Other actions may be specified, such as executing a specific procedure or triggering other updates. A mechanism called a *trigger* has been proposed to implement such actions in earlier versions of SQL.*

A **trigger** specifies a **condition** and an **action** to be taken in case that condition is satisfied. The condition is usually specified as an assertion that invokes or "triggers" the action when it becomes TRUE. A DEFINE TRIGGER statement was proposed to specify triggers. For example, we can specify a trigger that notifies the department manager if any employee in the manager's department has a higher salary than the manager, as follows:

> **DEFINE TRIGGER** SALARY_TRIGGER **ON** EMPLOYEE E, EMPLOYEE
> M, DEPARTMENT D:
> E.SALARY>M.SALARY **AND** E.DNO=D.DNUMBER **AND**
> D.MGRSSN=M.SSN
>   **ACTION_PROCEDURE** INFORM_MANAGER (D.MGRSSN) ;

The above trigger specifies that the procedure INFORM_MANAGER should be executed whenever the trigger condition occurs. Notice the difference between ASSERT and TRIGGER: an ASSERT statement prohibits an update that violates the assertion condition (makes it FALSE), whereas a trigger allows the update to take place but executes the action procedure when the trigger condition occurs (becomes TRUE). Hence, the condition specified earlier in the SALARY_CONSTRAINT using ASSERT and the TRIGGER condition given above are *inverses* of each other.

Notice that triggers combine the declarative and procedural approaches used in implementing integrity constraints. The trigger condition is declarative, while its action is procedural.

7.6 Specifying Indexes★

Earlier versions of SQL had statements for creating and dropping indexes on attributes of base relations. However, because an index is a physical access path rather than a logical concept, these statements were dropped from SQL2. We include this section because some DBMSs still include the CREATE INDEX statements. In early versions, the SQL DDL did not have clauses for specifying key and referential integrity constraints in the CREATE TABLE statement. Rather, specifying a *key constraint* was combined with index specification.

Recall from Chapter 5 that an index is a physical access structure that is specified on one or more attributes of a file. In SQL a file corresponds, more or less, to a base relation, so indexes are specified on base relations. The attribute(s) on which an index

---

*Recently, concepts have been developed for so-called **active database systems** (see Section 25.3.2), which define general mechanisms for incorporating automatic database actions into the database design.

is created are termed **indexing attributes.** An index makes accessing tuples based on conditions that involve its indexing attributes more efficient. This means that, in general, executing a query takes less time if some attributes involved in the query conditions have been indexed than if they have not. This improvement can be dramatic for queries where large relations are involved. In general, if attributes used in selection and join conditions of a query are indexed, the execution time of the query is greatly reduced.

In relational DBMSs, indexes can be created and dropped dynamically. The CREATE INDEX command is used to specify an index. Each index is given a name, which is used to drop the index when it is not needed any more. For example, to create an index on the LNAME attribute of the EMPLOYEE base relation from Figure 6.5, we can issue the command shown in I1:

```
I1:   CREATE   INDEX   LNAME_INDEX
              ON      EMPLOYEE ( LNAME );
```

In general, the index is arranged in ascending order of the indexing attribute values. If we want the values in descending order, we can add the keyword DESC after the attribute name. The default is ASC, for ascending. We can also create an index on a combination of attributes. For example, to create an index on the combination of FNAME, MINIT, and LNAME, we use I2. In I2 we assume that we want LNAME in ascending order and that we want FNAME in descending order within the same LNAME value:

```
I2:   CREATE   INDEX   NAMES_INDEX
              ON      EMPLOYEE ( LNAME ASC, FNAME DESC, MINIT );
```

There are two additional options on indexes in SQL. The first permits specifying the **key constraint** on the indexing attribute or combination of attributes.* The key word UNIQUE following the CREATE command is used to specify a key. For example, to specify an index on the SSN attribute of EMPLOYEE *and at the same time* to specify that SSN is a key attribute of the EMPLOYEE base relation, we use I3:

```
I3:   CREATE UNIQUE   INDEX   SSN_INDEX
                      ON      EMPLOYEE ( SSN );
```

Notice that specifying a key is best done before any tuples are inserted in the relation, so that the system will enforce the constraint. An attempt to create a unique index on an existing base table will fail if the current tuples in the table do not obey the uniqueness constraint on the indexing attribute.

The reason behind linking the definition of a key constraint with specification of an index in earlier versions of SQL is that it is much more efficient to enforce uniqueness of key values on a file if an index is defined on the key attribute. We can check whether a duplicate value exists in the index while searching the index. If no index exists, it is necessary in most cases to search the entire file to discover whether a duplicate value exists for an attribute.

The second option on index creation permits specifying whether an index is a clustering index (see Chapter 5). Join and selection conditions are even more efficient when specified on an attribute with a clustering index. The key word CLUSTER is used in this

---

*This was the only way to specify key constraints in early versions of SQL.

case at the end of the CREATE INDEX command. For example, if we want the EMPLOYEE records indexed and clustered by department number, we create a clustering index on DNO, as in I4:

I4:   **CREATE   INDEX**   DNO_INDEX
       ON   EMPLOYEE (DNO)
       CLUSTER;

A base relation can have *at most one* clustering index but any number of nonclustering indexes.

A *clustering and unique* index is similar to the *primary index* of Chapter 5. A *clustering but nonunique* index is similar to the *clustering index* of Chapter 5. Finally, a *nonclustering* index is similar to the *secondary index* of Chapter 5. Each DBMS may have its own type of index implementation technique; for example, multilevel indexes may use B-trees or B^+-trees or some other variations similar to the ones discussed in Chapter 5. Many relational DBMSs now also provide hash-based storage structures.

The **DROP INDEX** command is used to drop an index. The reason for dropping indexes is that they are expensive to maintain whenever the base relation is updated and they require additional storage. Hence, if we no longer expect to issue queries involving an indexed attribute, we should drop that index. An example of dropping the DNO index is given next:

I5:   **DROP INDEX**   DNO_INDEX;

7.7 Embedded SQL★

SQL can also be used in conjunction with a general-purpose programming language such as C, ADA, PASCAL, COBOL, or PL/I. The programming language is called the **host language**. Any SQL statement—data definition, query, update, or view definition—can be embedded in a host language program. The embedded SQL statement is distinguished from programming language statements by prefixing it with a special character or command so that a **preprocessor** can separate the embedded SQL statements from the host language code. In SQL2, the keywords EXEC SQL or the sequence &SQL(precedes any embedded SQL statement, and the statements can be terminated by a matching END-EXEC., ")", or ";". In some earlier implementations SQL statements were passed as parameters in procedure calls.

In general, different systems follow different conventions for embedding SQL statements. To illustrate the concepts of embedded SQL, we will use PASCAL as the host programming language and define our own syntax. We will use a "$" sign to identify SQL statements in the program, and ";" as the terminator character. Within an embedded SQL command, we may refer to program variables, which are prefixed by a ":" sign.* This allows program variables and database schema objects, such as attributes and relations, to have the same names without any ambiguity.

---

*The "%" sign was used in some earlier versions of SQL.

Suppose that we want to write PASCAL programs to process the database of Figure 6.5. We need to declare program variables to match the types of the database attributes that the program will process. These program variables may or may not have names that are identical to their corresponding attributes. We will use the PASCAL program variables declared in Figure 7.6 for all our examples, and we will show PASCAL program segments without variable declarations.

As a first example, we write a repeating program segment (loop) that reads a social security number and prints out some information from the corresponding EMPLOYEE tuple. The PASCAL program code is shown in E1, where we assume that appropriate program variables SOC_SEC_NUM and LOOP have been declared elsewhere. The program reads (inputs) a social security number value and then retrieves the EMPLOYEE tuple with that social security number via the embedded SQL command. Embedded SQL retrieval commands need an **INTO** clause, which specifies the program variables into which attribute values from the database are retrieved. PASCAL program variables in the INTO clause are prefixed with the ":" sign. Here is the E1 program segment:

```
E1:    LOOP:= 'Y';
       while LOOP = 'Y' do
           begin
           writeln('input social security number:');
           readln(SOC_SEC_NUM);
           $SELECT FNAME, MINIT, LNAME, ADDRESS, SALARY
           INTO :E.FNAME, :E.MINIT, :E.LNAME, :E.ADDRESS, :E.SALARY
           FROM EMPLOYEE
           WHERE SSN=:SOC_SEC_NUM ;
           writeln( E.FNAME, E.MINIT, E.LNAME, E.ADDRESS, E.SALARY);
           writeln('more social security numbers (Y or N)? ');
           readln(LOOP)
           end;
```

In E1 a single tuple is selected by the embedded SQL query; that is why we are able to assign its attribute values directly to program variables. In general, an SQL query can retrieve many tuples. In the latter case, the PASCAL program will typically go through the retrieved tuples and process them one at a time. The concept of a cursor is used to allow tuple-at-a-time processing by the PASCAL host language program.

We can think of a **cursor** as a pointer that points to a *single tuple (row)* from the result of a query. The cursor is declared when the SQL query command is declared in the

```
var DNAME: packed array [1..15] of char;
    DNUMBER, RAISE: integer;
    E: record FNAME,  LNAME: packed array [1..15] of char;
            MINIT, SEX: char;
            SSN, BDATE, SUPERSSN: packed array [1..9] of  char;
            ADDRESS: packed array [1..30] of char;
            SALARY, DNO: integer
       end;
```

Figure 7.6   PASCAL program variables used in E1 and E2.

program. Later in the program, an **OPEN** cursor command fetches the query result from the database and sets the cursor to a position *before the first row* in the result of the query. This becomes the **current row** for the cursor. Subsequently, FETCH commands are issued in the program; each FETCH moves the cursor to the *next row* in the result of the query, making it the current row and copying its attribute values into PASCAL program variables specified in the FETCH command. This is similar to traditional record-at-a-time file processing.

To determine when all the tuples in the result of the query have been processed, an implicit variable, called **SQLCODE,**[*] is used to communicate to the program the status of SQL embedded commands. When an SQL command is executed successfully, a code of 0 (zero) is returned in SQLCODE. Different codes are returned to indicate exceptions and errors. If a FETCH command is issued that results in moving the cursor past the last tuple in the result of the query, a special END_OF_CURSOR code is returned. The programmer uses this to terminate a loop over the tuples in a query result. In general, numerous cursors can be opened at the same time. A **CLOSE** cursor command is issued to indicate that we are done with the result of the query.

An example of using cursors is shown in E2, where the EMP cursor is explicitly declared. We assume that appropriate PASCAL program variables have been declared as in Figure 7.6. The program segment in E2 reads (inputs) a department name and then lists the names of employees who work in that department, one at a time. The program reads a raise amount for each employee's salary and updates the employee's salary by that amount:

```
E2:    writeln('enter the department name:'); readln(DNAME);
       $SELECT DNUMBER INTO :DNUMBER
       FROM DEPARTMENT
       WHERE DNAME=:DNAME;
       $DECLARE    EMP CURSOR FOR
                      SELECT SSN, FNAME, MINIT, LNAME, SALARY
                      FROM EMPLOYEE
                      WHERE DNO=:DNUMBER
       FOR UPDATE OF SALARY;
       $OPEN EMP;
       $FETCH EMP INTO :E.SSN, :E.FNAME, :E.MINIT, :E.LNAME, :E.SALARY;
       while SQLCODE = 0 do
           begin
           writeln('employee name: ', E.FNAME, E.MINIT, E.LNAME);
           writeln('enter raise amount: '); readln(RAISE);
           $UPDATE EMPLOYEE SET SALARY = SALARY + :RAISE
                            WHERE CURRENT OF EMP;
           $FETCH EMP INTO :E.SSN, :E.FNAME, :E.MINIT, :E.LNAME,
           :E.SALARY;
           end;
       $CLOSE CURSOR EMP;
```

---

[*] This is now called SQLSTATE in SQL2.

In SQL2, it is possible to position the cursor in other ways than for purely sequential access. A **fetch orientation** can be added whose values can be one of NEXT, PRIOR, FIRST, LAST, ABSOLUTE i, and RELATIVE i. In the latter two commands, i must evaluate to an integer value that specifies an absolute tuple position or a tuple position relative to the current cursor position. The default fetch orientation is NEXT. This allows the programmer to move the cursor around the tuples in the query result with greater flexibility, providing random access by position. The general form of a FETCH command is as follows, with the parts in square brackets being optional:

FETCH [[<fetch orientation>] **FROM**]
<cursor name> **INTO** <fetch target list> ;

When a cursor is defined for rows that are to be updated, we must add the clause **FOR UPDATE OF** in the cursor declaration and list the names of any attributes that will be updated by the program. This is illustrated in E2. If rows are to be deleted, the keywords FOR UPDATE must be added. In the embedded UPDATE (or DELETE) command, the condition **WHERE CURRENT OF** cursor specifies that the current tuple is the one to be updated (or deleted).

7.8 Summary

In this chapter we presented the SQL database language. This language or variations of it have been implemented as interfaces to several commercial relational DBMSs, including IBM's DB2 and SQL/DS, ORACLE, INGRES, and UNIFY. The original version of SQL was implemented in the experimental DBMS called SYSTEM R, which was developed at IBM Research. SQL is designed to be a comprehensive language that includes statements for data definition, queries, updates, and view definition. We discussed each of these in separate sections of this chapter. Our emphasis was on the SQL2 standard, but we did discuss a few features from older SQL versions, such as CREATE INDEX, in order to provide the appropriate historical perspective.

In the final section we discussed embedding SQL in a general-purpose programming language. We presented the concept of a CURSOR, which allows a programmer to process the result of a high-level query one tuple at a time.

Table 7.1 shows a summary of the syntax or structure of various SQL statements. This summary is not meant to be comprehensive and to describe every possible SQL construct; rather, it is meant to serve as a quick reference to the major types of constructs available in SQL. We use BNF notation, where nonterminal symbols are shown in angled brackets <...>, optional parts are shown in square brackets [...], repetitions are shown in braces {...}, and alternatives are shown in parentheses (...|...|...).*

---

*The full syntax of SQL2 is described in a document of over 500 pages.

Table 7.1   Summary of SQL Syntax

CREATE TABLE <table name> (<column name> <column type> [<attribute constraint>]
{, <column name> <column type> [<attribute constraint>] }
[<table constraint> {,<table constraint>}])

DROP TABLE <table name>

ALTER TABLE <table name> ADD <column name> <column type>

SELECT [DISTINCT] <attribute list>
FROM (<table name> { <alias>} | <joined table>) {, (<table name> { <alias>} | <joined table>) }
[WHERE <condition>]
[GROUP BY <grouping attributes> [HAVING <group selection condition>]]
[ORDER BY <column name> [<order>] {, <column name> [<order>] }]

<attribute list>::= (* | (<column name> | <function>(([DISTINCT]<column name> | *)))
{,(<column name> | <function>(([DISTINCT] <column name> | *)) }))
<grouping attributes>::= <column name> { , <column name>}
<order>::= (ASC | DESC)

INSERT INTO <table name> [(<column name>{, <column name>})]
(VALUES (<constant value> , { <constant value>}){,(<constant value>{,<constant value>})}
| <select statement>)

DELETE FROM <table name>
[WHERE <selection condition>]

UPDATE <table name>
SET <column name>=<value expression> { , <column name>=<value expression> }
[WHERE <selection condition>]

CREATE [UNIQUE] INDEX <index name>
ON <table name> (<column name> [<order>] { , <column name> [<order>] })
[CLUSTER]

DROP INDEX <index name>

CREATE VIEW <view name> [(<column name> { , <column name> })]
AS <select statement>

DROP VIEW <view name>

Review Questions

7.1. How do the relations (tables) in SQL differ from the relations defined formally in Chapter 6? Discuss the other differences in terminology.

7.2. Why does SQL allow duplicate tuples in a table or in a query result?

7.3. Why did earlier SQL implementations permit a key to be defined only in conjunction with an index?

7.4. How does SQL allow implementation of the entity integrity and referential integrity constraints described in Chapter 6? What about general integrity constraints?

7.5. What is a view in SQL, and how is it defined? Discuss the problems that may arise when one attempts to update a view. How are views typically implemented?

7.6. What is a cursor? How is it used in embedded SQL? How are cursors positioned for accessing rows non-sequentially?

Exercises

7.7. Consider the database shown in Figure 1.2, whose schema is shown in Figure 2.1. What are the referential integrity constraints that should hold on the schema? Write appropriate SQL DDL statements to define the database.

7.8. Repeat Exercise 7.7, but use the AIRLINE database schema of Figure 6.20.

7.9. Consider the LIBRARY relational database schema of Figure 6.22. Choose the appropriate action (reject, cascade, set to null, set to default) for each referential integrity constraint, both for *delete* of a referenced tuple, and for *update* of a primary key attribute value in a referenced tuple. Justify your choices.

7.10. Write appropriate SQL DDL statements for declaring the LIBRARY relational database schema of Figure 6.22. Use the referential action chosen in Exercise 7.9.

7.11. Write SQL queries for the LIBRARY database queries given in Exercise 6.26.

7.12. How can the key and foreign key constraints be enforced by the DBMS? Is the enforcement technique you suggest difficult to implement? Can the constraint checks be executed efficiently when updates are applied to the database?

7.13. Specify the queries of Exercise 6.19 in SQL. Show the result of each query if it is applied to the COMPANY database of Figure 6.6.

7.14. Specify the following additional queries on the database of Figure 6.5 in SQL. Show the query results if each query is applied to the database of Figure 6.6.

   a. For each department whose average employee salary is more than $30,000, retrieve the department name and the number of employees working for that department.

   b. Suppose that we want the number of *male* employees in each department rather than all employees (as in Exercise 7.14a). Can we specify this query in SQL? Why or why not?

7.15. Specify the updates of Exercise 6.20, using the SQL update commands.

7.16. Specify the following queries in SQL on the database schema of Figure 2.1.

    a. Retrieve the names of all senior students majoring in 'COSC' (computer science).

    b. Retrieve the names of all courses taught by Professor King in 1985 and 1986.

    c. For each section taught by Professor King, retrieve the course number, semester, year, and number of students who took the section.

    d. Retrieve the name and transcript of each senior student (Class = 5) majoring in COSC. A transcript includes course name, course number, credit hours, semester, year, and grade for each course completed by the student.

    e. Retrieve the names and major departments of all straight-A students (students who have a grade of A in all their courses).

    f. Retrieve the names and major departments of all students who do not have a grade of A in any of their courses.

7.17. Write SQL update statements to do the following on the database schema shown in Figure 2.1.

    a. Insert a new student <'Johnson', 25, 1, 'MATH'> in the database.

    b. Change the class of student 'Smith' to 2.

    c. Insert a new course <'Knowledge Engineering','COSC4390', 3,'COSC'>.

    d. Delete the record for the student whose name is 'Smith' and whose student number is 17.

7.18. Write PASCAL programs with embedded SQL statements in the style shown in Section 7.7 to do the following tasks on the database schema of Figure 2.1. Define appropriate program variables for each program code.

    a. Enter the grades of students in a section. The program should input the section ID and then have a loop that inputs each student's number and grade and inserts this information in the database.

    b. Print the transcript of a student. The program should input the student's ID, and it should print the student's name and a list of <course number, course name, section ID, semester, year, grade> for each section that the student has completed.

7.19. Write statements to create indexes on the database schema shown in Figure 2.1 on the following attributes:

    a. A unique clustering index on the StudentNumber attribute of STUDENT.

    b. A clustering index on the StudentNumber attribute of GRADE_REPORT.

    c. An index on the Major attribute of STUDENT.

7.20. What types of queries would become more efficient for each of the indexes specified in Exercise 7.19?

7.21. Specify the following views in SQL on the COMPANY database schema shown in Figure 6.5.

    a. A view that has the department name, manager name, and manager salary for every department.

b. A view that has the employee name, supervisor name, and employee salary for each employee who works in the 'Research' department.

c. A view that has project name, controlling department name, number of employees, and total hours worked per week on the project for each project.

d. A view that has project name, controlling department name, number of employees, and total hours worked per week on the project for each project *with more than one employee working on it.*

7.22. Consider the following view DEPT_SUMMARY, defined on the COMPANY database of Figure 6.6:

CREATE VIEW   DEPT_SUMMARY (D, C, TOTAL_S, AVERAGE_S)
AS   SELECT   DNO, COUNT (*), SUM (SALARY), AVG (SALARY)
     FROM   EMPLOYEE
     GROUP BY   DNO;

State which of the following queries and updates would be allowed on the view. If a query or update would be allowed, show what the corresponding query or update on the base relations would look like, and give its result when applied to the database of Figure 6.6.

a. **SELECT**   *
    FROM   DEPT_SUMMARY

b. **SELECT**   D, C
    FROM   DEPT_SUMMARY
    WHERE   TOTAL_S > 100000

c. **SELECT**   D, AVERAGE_S
    FROM   DEPT_SUMMARY
    WHERE   C > (**SELECT** C **FROM** DEPT_SUMMARY **WHERE** D=4)

d. **UPDATE**   DEPT_SUMMARY
    SET   D=3
    WHERE   D=4

e. **DELETE FROM**   DEPT_SUMMARY
    WHERE   C > 4

7.23. Consider the relation schema CONTAINS(Parent_part #, Sub_part #); a tuple $<P_i, P_j>$ in CONTAINS means that part P_i contains part P_j as a direct component. Suppose that we choose a part P_k that contains no other parts, and we want to find the part numbers of all parts that contain P_k, directly or indirectly at any level; this is a *recursive query* that requires computing the **transitive closure** of CONTAINS. Show that this query cannot be directly specified as a single SQL query. Can you suggest extensions to SQL to allow the specification of such queries?

7.24. Specify the queries and updates of Exercises 6.21 and 6.22, which refer to the AIRLINE database, in SQL.

7.25. Choose some database application that you are familiar with.

a. Design a relational database schema for your database application.

b. Declare your relations, using the SQL DDL.

c. Specify a number of queries in SQL that are needed by your database application.

d. Based on your expected use of the database, choose some attributes that should have indexes specified on them.

e. Implement your database, if you have an SQL system available.

Selected Bibliography

The SQL language, originally named SEQUEL, was a sequel to the language SQUARE (Specifying Queries *as* Relational Expressions), described by Boyce et al. (1975). The syntax of SQUARE was modified into SEQUEL (Chamberlin and Boyce 1974) and then into SEQUEL 2 (Chamberlin et al. 1976), on which SQL is based. The original implementation of SEQUEL was done at IBM Research, San Jose, California.

Reisner (1977) describes a human factors evaluation of SEQUEL in which she found that users have some difficulty with specifying join conditions and grouping correctly. Date (1984b) contains a critique of the SQL language that points out its strengths and shortcomings. Date and Darwen (1993) describes SQL2. ANSI (1986) outlines the original SQL standard, and ANSI (1992) describes the new SQL2 standard. Various vendor manuals describe the characteristics of SQL as implemented on DB2, SQL/DS, ORACLE, INGRES, UNIFY, and other commercial DBMS products. Horowitz (1992) discusses some of the problems related to referential integrity and propagation of updates in SQL2.

The question of view updates is addressed by Dayal and Bernstein (1978), Keller (1982), and Langerak (1990), among others. View implementation is discussed in Blakeley et al. (1989) and Roussopoulos (1990). Negri et al. (1991) describes formal semantics of SQL queries.

The Relational Calculus, QUEL, and QBE

In Chapter 6 we presented the relational data model and discussed the operations of the relational algebra, which are fundamental for manipulating a relational database. Although we described the relational algebra as an integral part of the relational model, it is actually only one type of formal query language for specifying retrievals and forming new relations from a relational database. In this chapter we discuss another formal language for relational databases, the **relational calculus**. Many commercial relational database languages are based on some aspects of relational calculus, including the SQL language discussed in Chapter 7. However, some languages are more similar to the relational calculus than others; for example, the QUEL and QBE languages presented in Sections 8.2 and 8.4 are closer to relational calculus than SQL is.

How does relational calculus differ from relational algebra? The main difference is that in relational calculus we write one **declarative** expression to specify a retrieval request, whereas in relational algebra we must write a *sequence of operations*. It is true that these operations can be nested to form a single expression; however, a certain order among the operations is always explicitly specified in a relational algebra expression. This order also specifies a partial strategy for evaluating the query. In relational calculus, there is no description of how to evaluate a query; a calculus expression specifies *what* is to be retrieved rather than *how* to retrieve it. Therefore, the relational calculus is considered to be a declarative or **nonprocedural** language.

In one important way, relational algebra and relational calculus are identical. It has been shown that any retrieval that can be specified in the relational algebra can also be specified in the relational calculus, and vice versa; in other words, the **expressive power** of the two languages is *identical*. This has led to definition of the concept of a relationally complete language. A relational query language L is called **relationally complete** if we can express in L any query that can be expressed in the relational calculus. Relational completeness has become an important benchmark for comparing the expressive power of high-level query languages. However, as we saw in Section 6.6, certain frequently required queries in database applications cannot be expressed in relational algebra or calculus. Most relational query languages are relationally complete but have *more expressive power* than relational algebra or relational calculus because of additional operations such as aggregate functions, grouping, and ordering.

The relational calculus is a formal language, based on the branch of mathematical logic called predicate calculus. There are two well-known ways in which the predicate calculus can be adapted into a language for relational databases. The first is called the **tuple relational calculus,** and the second is called the **domain relational calculus.** Both are adaptations of first-order predicate calculus.* In tuple relational calculus, variables range over tuples; whereas in domain relational calculus, variables range over domain values of attributes. We discuss these in Sections 8.1 and 8.3, respectively. All our examples will again refer to the database shown in Figures 6.5 and 6.6.

We will also present in this chapter two early relational query languages that are important for historical reasons. The QUEL query language was originally developed at the same time as SQL; but it has lost ground, in spite of its popularity among researchers, because of the need for standardization. The QBE language is important because it is one of the first graphical query languages developed for database systems. We present a summary of the concepts of QUEL in Section 8.2 and an overview of QBE in Section 8.4.

The reader may skip Sections 8.2, 8.3, and 8.4 if only a brief introduction to relational calculus is desired.

8.1 Tuple Relational Calculus

8.1.1 *Tuple Variables and Range Relations*

The tuple relational calculus is based on specifying a number of **tuple variables**. Each tuple variable usually **ranges over** a particular database relation, meaning that the variable may take as its value any individual tuple from that relation. A simple tuple relational calculus query is of the form

$\{t \mid \text{COND}(t)\}$

where t is a tuple variable and COND(t) is a conditional expression involving t. The result of such a query is the set of all tuples t that satisfy COND(t). For example, to find all employees whose salary is above $50,000, we can write the following tuple calculus expression:

$\{t \mid \text{EMPLOYEE}(t) \textbf{ and } t.\text{SALARY}>50000\}$

---

*In our presentation, we *do not* assume that the reader is familiar with first-order predicate calculus, which deals with quantified variables and values. To deal with quantified relations or sets of sets, we have to use a higher-order predicate calculus.

The condition EMPLOYEE(t) specifies that the *range relation* of tuple variable t is EMPLOYEE. Each EMPLOYEE tuple t that satisfies the condition t.SALARY>50000 will be retrieved. Notice that t.SALARY references attribute SALARY of tuple variable t; this notation resembles how attribute names are qualified with relation names or aliases in SQL. In the notation of Chapter 6, t.SALARY is the same as writing t[SALARY].

The above query retrieves all attribute values for each selected EMPLOYEE tuple t. To retrieve only *some* of the attributes—say, the first and last names—we write

{t.FNAME, t.LNAME | EMPLOYEE(t) **and** t.SALARY>50000}

This is equivalent to the following SQL query:

```
SELECT    T.FNAME, T.LNAME
FROM      EMPLOYEE T
WHERE     T.SALARY>50000
```

Informally, we need to specify the following information in a tuple calculus expression:

1. For each tuple variable t, the **range relation** R of t. This value is specified by a condition of the form R(t).

2. A condition to select particular combinations of tuples. As tuple variables range over their respective range relations, the condition is evaluated for every possible combination of tuples to identify the **selected combinations** for which the condition evaluates to **TRUE.**

3. A set of attributes to be retrieved, the **requested attributes.** The values of these attributes are retrieved for each selected combination of tuples.

Observe the correspondence of the preceding items to a simple SQL query: item 1 corresponds to the FROM clause relation names; item 2 corresponds to the WHERE clause condition; and item 3 corresponds to the SELECT clause attribute list. Before we discuss the formal syntax of tuple relational calculus, consider another query we have seen before.

QUERY 0
Retrieve the birthdate and address of the employee (or employees) whose name is 'John B. Smith'.

Q0 : {t.BDATE, t.ADDRESS | EMPLOYEE(t) **and** t.FNAME='John' **and** t.MINIT='B' **and** t.LNAME='Smith'}

In tuple relational calculus, we first specify the requested attributes t.BDATE and t.ADDRESS for each selected tuple t. Then we specify the condition for selecting a tuple following the bar (|)—namely, that t be a tuple of the EMPLOYEE relation whose FNAME, MINIT, and LNAME attribute values are 'John', 'B', and 'Smith', respectively.

8.1.2 *Formal Specification of Tuple Relational Calculus*

A general **expression** of the tuple relational calculus is of the form

$$\{t_1.A_1, t_2.A_2, \ldots, t_n.A_n \mid \text{COND}(t_1, t_2, \ldots, t_n, t_{n+1}, t_{n+2}, \ldots, t_{n+m})\}$$

where t_1, t_2, ..., t_n, t_{n+1}, ..., t_{n+m} are tuple variables, each A_i is an attribute of the relation on which t_i ranges, and COND is a **condition** or **formula*** of the tuple relational calculus. A formula is made up of predicate calculus **atoms**, which can be one of the following:

1. An atom of the form $R(t_i)$, where R is a relation name and t_i is a tuple variable. This atom identifies the range of the tuple variable t_i as the relation whose name is R.

2. An atom of the form $t_i.A$ **op** $t_j.B$, where **op** is one of the comparison operators in the set $\{ =, \neq, <, \leq, >, \geq \}$, t_i and t_j are tuple variables, A is an attribute of the relation on which t_i ranges, and B is an attribute of the relation on which t_j ranges.

3. An atom of the form $t_i.A$ **op** c or c **op** $t_j.B$, where **op** is one of the comparison operators in the set $\{ =, \neq, <, \leq, >, \geq \}$, t_i and t_j are tuple variables, A is an attribute of the relation on which t_i ranges, B is an attribute of the relation on which t_j ranges, and c is a constant value.

Each of the preceding atoms evaluates to either **TRUE** or **FALSE** for a specific combination of tuples; this is called the **truth value** of an atom. In general, a tuple variable ranges over all possible tuples "in the universe." For atoms of type 1, if the tuple variable is assigned a tuple that is a *member of the specified relation* R, the atom is **TRUE**; otherwise it is **FALSE**. In atoms of types 2 and 3, if the tuple variables are assigned to tuples such that the values of the specified attributes of the tuples satisfy the condition, then the atom is **TRUE**.

A **formula** (condition) is made up of one or more atoms connected via the logical operators **and, or,** and **not** and is defined recursively as follows:

1. Every atom is a formula.

2. If F_1 and F_2 are formulas, then so are $(F_1$ **and** $F_2)$, $(F_1$ **or** $F_2)$, **not**(F_1), and **not** (F_2). The truth values of these four formulas are derived from their component formulas F_1 and F_2 as follows:

   a. $(F_1$ **and** $F_2)$ is **TRUE** if both F_1 and F_2 are **TRUE**; otherwise, it is **FALSE**.

   b. $(F_1$ **or** $F_2)$ is **FALSE** if both F_1 and F_2 are **FALSE;** otherwise it is **TRUE**.

   c. **not**(F_1) is **TRUE** if F_1 is **FALSE**; it is **FALSE** if F_1 is **TRUE**.

   d. **not**(F_2) is **TRUE** if F_2 is **FALSE**; it is **FALSE** if F_2 is **TRUE**.

In addition, two special symbols called **quantifiers** can appear in formulas; these are the **universal quantifier** ($\forall$) and the **existential quantifier** ($\exists$). Truth values for formulas with quantifiers are described in 3 and 4 below; first, however, we need to define the concepts of free and bound tuple variables in a formula. Informally, a tuple variable t is bound if it is quantified, meaning that it appears in an ($\exists$ t) or ($\forall$ t) clause; otherwise, it is free. Formally, we define a tuple variable in a formula as **free** or **bound** according to the following rules:

---

*Also called a **well-formed formula** or **wff** in mathematical logic.

- An occurrence of a tuple variable in a formula F that *is an atom* is free in F.
- An occurrence of a tuple variable t is free or bound in a formula made up of logical connectives—$(F_1$ **and** $F_2)$, $(F_1$ **or** $F_2)$, **not**(F_1), and **not**(F_2)—depending on whether it is free or bound in F_1 or F_2 (if it occurs in either). Notice that in a formula of the form $F = (F_1$ **and** $F_2)$ or $F = (F_1$ **or** $F_2)$, a tuple variable may be free in F_1 and bound in F_2, or vice versa. In this case, one occurrence of the tuple variable is bound and the other is free in F.
- All *free* occurrences of a tuple variable t in F are **bound** in a formula F' of the form $F' = (\exists\ t)(F)$ or $F' = (\forall\ t)(F)$. The tuple variable is bound to the quantifier specified in F'. For example, consider the two formulas:

F_1 : d.DNAME='Research'
F_2 : (∃t) (d.DNUMBER=t.DNO)

The tuple variable d is free in both F_1 and F_2, whereas t is bound to the ∃ quantifier in F_2.

We can now give the rules 3 and 4, to continue the definition of a formula we started earlier:

3. If F is a formula, then so is $(\exists\ t)(F)$, where t is a tuple variable. The formula $(\exists\ t)(F)$ is TRUE if the formula F evaluates to TRUE for *some* (at least one) tuple assigned to free occurrences of t in F; otherwise $(\exists\ t)(F)$ is FALSE.

4. If F is a formula, then so is $(\forall\ t)(F)$, where t is a tuple variable. The formula $(\forall\ t)(F)$ is TRUE if the formula F evaluates to TRUE for *every tuple* (in the universe) assigned to free occurrences of t in F; otherwise $(\forall\ t)(F)$ is FALSE.

The (∃) quantifier is called an existential quantifier because a formula $(\exists\ t)(F)$ is TRUE if "there exists" some tuple t that makes F TRUE. For the universal quantifier, $(\forall\ t)(F)$ is TRUE if every possible tuple that can be assigned to free occurrences of t in F is substituted for t, and F is TRUE for *every such substitution*. It is called the universal quantifier because every tuple in "the universe of" tuples must make F TRUE.

8.1.3 *Example Queries Using the Existential Quantifier*

We will use many of the same queries shown in Chapter 6 so as to give a flavor of how the same queries are specified in relational algebra and in relational calculus. Notice that some queries are easier to specify in the relational algebra than in the relational calculus, and vice versa.

QUERY 1
Retrieve the name and address of all employees who work for the 'Research' department.

Q1 : {t.FNAME, t.LNAME, t.ADDRESS | EMPLOYEE(t) **and** ((∃d) (DEPARTMENT(d) **and** d.DNAME='Research' **and** d.DNUMBER=t.DNO)) }

The *only free tuple variables* in a relational calculus expression should be those that appear to the left of the bar (|). In Q1, t is the only free variable; it is then *bound successively* to each tuple that *satisfies the conditions* specified in Q1, and the attributes FNAME, LNAME, and ADDRESS are retrieved for each such tuple. The conditions EMPLOYEE(t) and DEPARTMENT(d) specify the range relations for t and d. The condition d.DNAME = 'Research' is a **selection condition** and corresponds to a SELECT operation in the relational algebra, whereas the condition d.DNUMBER = t.DNO is a **join condition** and serves a similar purpose to the JOIN operation (see Chapter 6).

QUERY 2
For every project located in 'Stafford', list the project number, the controlling department number, and the department manager's last name, birthdate, and address.

Q2 : {p.PNUMBER, p.DNUM, m.LNAME, m.BDATE, m.ADDRESS | PROJECT(p)
     and EMPLOYEE(m) **and** p.PLOCATION='Stafford' **and**
     (($\exists$d)(DEPARTMENT(d) **and** p.DNUM=d.DNUMBER **and** d.MGRSSN=m.SSN)) }

In Q2 there are two free tuple variables, p and m. Tuple variable d is bound to the existential quantifier. The query condition is evaluated for every combination of tuples assigned to p and m; and out of all possible combinations of tuples to which p and m are bound, only the combinations that satisfy the condition are selected.

Several tuple variables in a query can range over the same relation. For example, to specify the query Q8—for each employee, retrieve the employee's first and last name and the first and last name of his or her immediate supervisor—we specify two tuple variables e and s that both range over the EMPLOYEE relation:

Q8 : {e.FNAME,e.LNAME,s.FNAME,s.LNAME | EMPLOYEE(e) **and** EMPLOYEE(s)
     and e.SUPERSSN=s.SSN}

QUERY 3'
Find the name of each employee who works on *some* project controlled by department number 5. This is a variation of query 3 in which "all" is changed to "some." In this case we need two join conditions and two existential quantifiers.

Q3' : {e.LNAME, e.FNAME | EMPLOYEE(e) **and** (($\exists$ x)($\exists$ w)
     (PROJECT(x) **and** WORKS_ON(w) **and** x.DNUM=5 **and** w.ESSN=e.SSN **and**
     x.PNUMBER=w.PNO)) }

QUERY 4
Make a list of project numbers for projects that involve an employee whose last name is 'Smith', either as a worker or as manager of the controlling department for the project.

Q4 : {p.PNUMBER | PROJECT(p) **and**
     ((($\exists$ e)($\exists$ w)(EMPLOYEE(e) **and** WORKS_ON(w) **and**
     w.PNO=p.PNUMBER **and** e.LNAME='Smith' **and** e.SSN=w.ESSN))
     or
     (($\exists$ m)($\exists$ d)(EMPLOYEE(m) **and** DEPARTMENT(d) **and**
     p.DNUM=d.DNUMBER **and** d.MGRSSN=m.SSN **and** m.LNAME='Smith'))) }

Compare this with the relational algebra version of this query in Chapter 6. The UNION operation in relational algebra can usually be substituted with an **or** connective in relational calculus. In the next section we discuss the relationship between the universal and existential quantifiers and show how one can be transformed into the other.

8.1.4 *Transforming the Universal and Existential Quantifiers*

We now introduce some well-known transformations from mathematical logic that relate the universal and existential quantifiers. It is possible to transform a universal quantifier into an existential quantifier, and vice versa, and get an equivalent expression. One general transformation can be described informally as follows: transform one type of quantifier into the other with negation (preceded by **not**); **and** and **or** replace one another; a negated formula becomes unnegated; and an unnegated formula becomes negated. Some special cases of this transformation can be stated as follows, where $\not\exists$ denotes **not**($\exists$):

$(\forall\ x)\ (P(x)) \equiv (\not\exists\ x)\ (\textbf{not}\ (P(x)))$

$(\exists\ x)\ (P(x)) \equiv \textbf{not}\ (\forall\ x)\ (\textbf{not}\ (P(x)))$

$(\forall\ x)\ (P(x)\ \textbf{and}\ Q(x)) \equiv (\not\exists\ x)\ (\textbf{not}\ (P(x))\ \textbf{or not}\ (Q(x)))$

$(\forall\ x)\ (P(x)\ \textbf{or}\ Q(x)) \equiv (\not\exists\ x)\ (\textbf{not}\ (P(x))\ \textbf{and not}\ (Q(x)))$

$(\exists\ x)\ (P(x)\ \textbf{or}\ Q(x)) \equiv \textbf{not}\ (\forall\ x)\ (\textbf{not}\ (P(x))\ \textbf{and not}\ (Q(x)))$

$(\exists\ x)\ (P(x)\ \textbf{and}\ Q(x)) \equiv \textbf{not}\ (\forall\ x)\ (\textbf{not}\ (P(x))\ \textbf{or not}\ (Q(x)))$

Notice also that the following is true, where the $\Rightarrow$ symbol stands for **implies:**

$(\forall\ x)\ (P(x)) \Rightarrow (\exists\ x)\ (P(x))$

$(\not\exists\ x)\ (P(x)) \Rightarrow \textbf{not}\ (\forall\ x)\ (P(x))$

However, the following is *not true:*

$\textbf{not}\ (\forall\ x)\ (P(x)) \Rightarrow (\not\exists\ x)\ (P(x))$

8.1.5 *Using the Universal Quantifier*

Whenever we use a universal quantifier, it is quite judicious to follow a few rules to ensure that our expression makes sense. We discuss these rules with respect to Query 3.

QUERY 3
Find the names of employees who work on *all* the projects controlled by department number 5. One way of specifying this query is by using the universal quantifier as shown.

Q3 : {e.LNAME, e.FNAME | EMPLOYEE(e) **and** (($\forall$ x)**(not** (PROJECT(x)) **or**
(**not** (x.DNUM=5) **or**
(($\exists$ w)(WORKS_ON(w) **and** w.ESSN=e.SSN **and** x.PNUMBER=w.PNO))))}

We can break up Q3 into its basic components as follows:

Q3 : {e.LNAME, e.FNAME | EMPLOYEE(e) **and** F'}
F' = ($\forall$ x) **(not** (PROJECT(x)) **or** F$_1$)

$F_1 =$ (**not** (x.DNUM=5) **or** F_2)
$F_2 = (\exists$ w)(WORKS_ON(w) **and** w.ESSN= e.SSN **and** x.PNUMBER=w.PNO)

The trick is to exclude from the universal quantification all tuples that we are not interested in. We can do this by making the condition TRUE *for all such tuples*. This is necessary because a universally quantified tuple variable, such as x in Q3, must evaluate to TRUE *for every possible tuple* assigned to it. The first tuples to exclude are those that are not in the relation R of interest. Then we exclude the tuples we are not interested in from R itself. Finally, we specify a condition F_2 that must hold on all the remaining tuples in R. In Q3, R is the PROJECT relation. Each tuple e that makes F_2 TRUE *for all remaining PROJECT tuples that have not been excluded* is selected for the query result. Hence, we can explain Q3 as follows:

1. For the formula $F' = (\forall x)(F)$ to be TRUE, we must have the formula F be TRUE *for all tuples in the universe that can be assigned to x*. However, in Q3 we are only interested in F being TRUE for all tuples of the PROJECT relation that are controlled by department 5. Hence, the formula F is of the form (**not**(PROJECT(x)) **or** F_1). The '**not**(PROJECT(x)) **or** ... ' condition is TRUE for all tuples *not in the PROJECT relation* and has the effect of eliminating these tuples from consideration in the truth value of F_1. For *every tuple* in the PROJECT relation, F_1 must be TRUE if F is to be TRUE.

2. Using the same line of reasoning, we do not want to consider tuples in the PROJECT relation that are not of interest. Because we want a selected EMPLOYEE tuple to work on all projects controlled by department number 5, we are only interested in PROJECT tuples whose DNUM = 5. We can therefore say

   if (x.DNUM=5) **then** F_2

   which is equivalent to

   (**not** (x.DNUM=5) **or** F_2)

   Formula F_1, hence, is of the form (PROJECT(x) **and** (**not**(x.DNUM=5) **or** F_2)). In the context of Q3, this means that, for a tuple x in the PROJECT relation, either its DNUM $\neq$ 5 or it must satisfy F_2.

3. Finally, F_2 gives the condition that we want to hold for a selected EMPLOYEE tuple: that the employee works on *every PROJECT tuple that has not been excluded yet*. Such EMPLOYEE tuples are selected by the query.

In English, Q3 gives the following condition for selecting an EMPLOYEE tuple e: for every tuple x in the PROJECT relation with x.DNUM = 5, there must exist a tuple w in WORKS_ON such that w.ESSN = e.SSN and w.PNO = x.PNUMBER. This is equivalent to saying that EMPLOYEE e works on every PROJECT x in DEPARTMENT number 5. (Whew!)

Using the general transformation from universal to existential quantifiers given in Section 8.1.4, we can rephrase the query in Q3 as shown in Q3A:

Q3A : {e.LNAME, e.FNAME | EMPLOYEE(e) **and** (**not** ($\exists$ x) (PROJECT(x)
    and (x.DNUM=5) **and**
(**not** ($\exists$ w)(WORKS_ON(w) **and** w.ESSN=e.SSN **and** x.PNUMBER=w.PNO))))}

We now give some additional examples of queries that use quantifiers.

QUERY 6
Find the names of employees who have no dependents.

Q6 : {e.FNAME, e.LNAME | EMPLOYEE(e) **and (not** (∃d)(DEPENDENT(d) **and**
e.SSN=d.ESSN))}

Using the general transformation rule, we can rephrase Q6 as follows:

Q6A : {e.FNAME, e.LNAME | EMPLOYEE(e) **and** ((∀ d) **(not** (DEPENDENT(d)) **or**
not (e.SSN=d.ESSN)))}

QUERY 7
List the names of managers who have at least one dependent.

Q7 : {e.FNAME, e.LNAME | EMPLOYEE(e) **and** ((∃ d) (∃ p)
(DEPARTMENT(d) **and** DEPENDENT(p) **and** e.SSN=d.MGRSSN **and**
p.ESSN=e.SSN))}

8.1.6 *Safe Expressions*

Whenever we use universal quantifiers, existential quantifiers, or negation of predicates
in a calculus expression, we must make sure that the resulting expression makes sense.
A **safe expression** in relational calculus is one that is guaranteed to yield a *finite number
of tuples* as its result; otherwise, the expression is called **unsafe**. For example, the
expression

{t | **not** (EMPLOYEE(t))}

is *unsafe* because it yields all tuples in the universe that are *not* EMPLOYEE tuples, which
are infinitely numerous. If we follow the rules for Q3 discussed earlier, we will get a safe
expression when using universal quantifiers. We can define "safe expressions" more precisely by introducing the concept of the *domain of a tuple relational calculus expression*:
This is the set of all values that either appear as constant values in the expression or
exist in any tuple of the relations referenced in the expression. The domain of
{t | **not**(EMPLOYEE(t)) } is the set of all attribute values appearing in some tuple of the
EMPLOYEE relation (for any attribute). The domain of the expression Q3A would
include all values appearing in EMPLOYEE, PROJECT, and WORKS_ON (UNIONed with the
value 5 appearing in the query itself).

An expression is said to be **safe** if all values in its result are from the domain of the
expression. Notice that the result of {t | **not**(EMPLOYEE(t)) } is unsafe, since it will, in
general, include tuples (and hence values) from outside the EMPLOYEE relation; such values are not in the domain of the expression. All of our other examples are safe
expressions.

8.1.7 *Quantifiers in* SQL

The EXISTS function in SQL is similar to the existential quantifier of the relational calculus. When we write

```
SELECT    ...
FROM      ...
WHERE     EXISTS    (SELECT    *
                     FROM      R X
                     WHERE     P(X) )
```

in SQL, it is equivalent to saying that a tuple variable X ranging over the relation R is existentially quantified. The nested query on which the EXISTS function is applied is normally correlated with the outer query; that is, the condition P(X) includes some attribute from the outer query relations. The WHERE condition of the outer query evaluates to TRUE if the nested query returns a nonempty result that contains one or more tuples.

SQL does not include a universal quantifier. Use of a negated existential quantifier ($\not\exists$ x) by writing NOT EXISTS is how SQL supports universal quantification, as illustrated by Q3 in Chapter 7.

8.2 The QUEL Language*

QUEL is a data definition and manipulation language originally developed for the popular INGRES relational DBMS. The first version of INGRES, which stands for *I*nteractive *Gr*aph*ics and R*etrieval *S*ystem, was developed as a research project at the University of California at Berkeley in the mid-1970s; this is often called university INGRES. A commercial INGRES DBMS has been available since 1980. QUEL can be used as an interactive query language or it can be embedded within a host programming language. It includes a range of functionality similar to that provided by early SQL versions. Our presentation here will follow a pattern similar to that used in the presentation of SQL in Chapter 7, but in a brief summary form. The query aspects of QUEL are closely related to the tuple relational calculus discussed in the previous section, but enhanced with aggregate functions and grouping.

8.2.1 *Data and Storage Definition in QUEL*

The CREATE Command and QUEL Data Types. The CREATE command is used to specify a **base relation**—a relation whose tuples are physically stored in the database—and its attributes. Several data types are available for attributes. Numeric data types include I1, I2, and I4 for integers of 1, 2, and 4 bytes length, and F4 and F8 for real floating-point numbers of 4 and 8 bytes length. Character string data types include Cn and CHAR(n) for a fixed-length string of n characters and TEXT(n) and VARCHAR(n) for a varying-length string with a maximum length of n characters.* In addition, a DATE data type is available; this provides flexible formats, such as absolute date/time values like '19-OCT-1920 12:00 pm' or relative values like '2 years 4 months' or '1 day 4 hours 30 minutes'. A MONEY data type, which is a 16-digit number with the two rightmost digits representing cents, is also available. Figure 8.1 shows how the EMPLOYEE and DEPARTMENT relations of Figure 6.5 may be declared in QUEL.

---

*Cn was used in university INGRES and has some peculiar behavior when string comparisons are applied. TEXT(n) was introduced in commercial INGRES and gives more predictable results.

```
L1: CREATE EMPLOYEE      (   FNAME            =   TEXT(15),
                             MINIT            =   C1,
                             LNAME            =   TEXT(15),
                             SSN              =   C9,
                             BDATE            =   DATE,
                             ADDRESS          =   TEXT(30),
                             SEX              =   C1,
                             SALARY           =   MONEY,
                             SUPERSSN         =   C9,
                             DNO              =   I4 );

     CREATE DEPARTMENT    (   DNAME            =   TEXT(15),
                             DNUMBER          =   I4,
                             MGRSSN           =   C9,
                             MGRSTARTDATE     =   DATE );
```

Figure 8.1   Declaring the EMPLOYEE and DEPARTMENT relations of Figure 6.5 in QUEL.

The INDEX Command.   The INDEX command is used to specify a (first-level only) index on a relation; in fact, an index is treated as an ordered base relation where the only attributes are the indexing attributes, and the DBMS maintains pointers to the corresponding records. In our terminology of Chapter 5, it is a *single-level secondary index*. A multilevel index can be created by specifying a B-TREE over an existing INDEX.

The MODIFY Command and Use of UNIQUE.   To specify or change the storage structure on a base relation or an index, the MODIFY command is used. The available storage structures are ISAM (indexed sequential), HASH, BTREE, HEAP (unordered file), and HEAP-SORT (sort the records now, but do not maintain the order when new tuples are inserted). The letter C appended before any storage structure name—for example, CHASH or CBTREE—indicates that the files and their access paths will be stored in a compressed form, thus saving space but increasing retrieval and update time. Each base relation (or index) can have at most one storage structure defined over it. The usual default storage structure for a base relation is HEAP.

Key attributes are specified by including the key word UNIQUE in a MODIFY command; hence, as in early SQL, we cannot specify key attributes independently of a specific storage structure on the relation. To illustrate the use of MODIFY, suppose that we want to specify the following: a key and a B-tree on the SSN attribute of EMPLOYEE, an index on the combination of LNAME and FNAME attributes of EMPLOYEE, a key and hash access on the DNAME attribute of DEPARTMENT, and a key and compressed B-tree index on the DNO attribute of DEPARTMENT. The statements in L1 perform all of these tasks:

```
L1:   MODIFY EMPLOYEE TO BTREE UNIQUE ON SSN;
      INDEX ON EMPLOYEE IS NAME_INDEX (LNAME, FNAME);
      MODIFY DEPARTMENT TO HASH UNIQUE ON DNAME;
      INDEX ON DEPARTMENT IS DNO_INDEX (DNO);
      MODIFY DNO_INDEX TO CBTREE UNIQUE ON DNO;
```

If a base relation or index is not needed any longer, we can delete it by using the DESTROY command. An example is given in L2:

L2:   **DESTROY** DNO_INDEX, NAME_INDEX ;

The original QUEL does not have commands to add attributes to tables (ALTER in SQL), nor does it have explicit NULL values as in SQL. A missing value is represented by a blank for string data types and by 0 (zero) for numeric data types.

8.2.2 *Overview of QUEL Query Constructs*

Basic QUEL retrieval queries of the **select–project–join** type are very similar to tuple relational calculus. Two clauses, RETRIEVE and WHERE, are used; RETRIEVE specifies the attributes to be retrieved—the projection attributes—and WHERE specifies the select and join conditions. QUEL does not have a FROM clause as SQL does; rather, all attributes in a QUEL query *must be explicitly qualified*, either by their relation name or by a tuple variable declared to range over their relation. Tuple variables are declared explicitly in the RANGE statement of QUEL.

QUERY 0
Retrieve the birthdate and address of the employee whose name is 'John B. Smith'.

Q0:   **RETRIEVE**   (EMPLOYEE.BDATE, EMPLOYEE.ADDRESS)
    WHERE   EMPLOYEE.FNAME='John' **AND** EMPLOYEE.MINIT='B'
       AND EMPLOYEE.LNAME='Smith'

Alternatively, we can specify tuple variables in RANGE statements and use the tuple variables in the query. For the remaining examples, we assume that the RANGE variables in L3 have been declared:

L3:   **RANGE OF**   E, S **IS** EMPLOYEE,
       D **IS** DEPARTMENT,
       P **IS** PROJECT,
       W **IS** WORKS_ON,
       DEP **IS** DEPENDENT,
       DL **IS** DEPT_LOCATIONS

QUERY 1
Retrieve the name and address of all employees who work for the 'Research' department.

Q1:   **RETRIEVE**   (E.FNAME, E.LNAME, E.ADDRESS)
    WHERE   D.DNAME='Research' AND D.DNUMBER=E.DNO

QUERY 2
For every project located in 'Stafford', list the project number, the controlling department number, and the department manager's last name, birthdate, and address.

Q2:   **RETRIEVE**   (P.PNUMBER, P.DNUM, E.LNAME, E.BDATE, E.ADDRESS)
    WHERE   P.DNUM=D.DNUMBER **AND** D.MGRSSN=E.SSN **AND**
       P.PLOCATION='Stafford'

QUERY 8

For each employee, retrieve the employee's first and last name and the first and last name of his or her immediate supervisor.

Q8:	RETRIEVE	(E.FNAME, E.LNAME, S.FNAME, S.LNAME)
	WHERE	E.SUPERSSN=S.SSN

To retrieve *all the attributes* of the selected tuples, we use the key word ALL. Query Q1D retrieves all attributes of an EMPLOYEE and the DEPARTMENT he or she works in for every employee in the 'Research' department:

Q1D:	RETRIEVE	(E.ALL, D.ALL)
	WHERE	D.DNAME='Research' **AND** E.DNO=D.DNUMBER

As in SQL, the result of a query in QUEL may have duplicate tuples. To eliminate duplicate tuples, the key word UNIQUE is specified in the RETRIEVE clause (similar to DISTINCT in SQL). Query 11 retrieves all salaries of employees, keeping duplicates, whereas Q11A removes duplicate salaries from the result of the query:

Q11:	RETRIEVE	(E.SALARY)

Q11A:	RETRIEVE	UNIQUE (E.SALARY)

QUERY 3'

Retrieve the names of employees who work on *some* project that is controlled by department 5.

Q3':	RETRIEVE	UNIQUE (E.FNAME, E.LNAME)
	WHERE	P.DNUM=5 **AND** P.PNUMBER=W.PNO **AND**
		W.ESSN=E.SSN

In QUEL, any range variable appearing in the WHERE clause of a QUEL query that does not appear in the RETRIEVE clause *is implicitly quantified by an existential quantifier.* The P and W tuple variables are implicitly quantified by the existential quantifier in Q3'. For queries that involve universal quantifiers or negated existential quantifiers, we must use either the COUNT function or the ANY function. QUEL has the built-in functions **COUNT, SUM, MIN, MAX,** and **AVG.** Additional functions **COUNTU, SUMU,** and **AVGU** *eliminate duplicate tuples before applying the functions* COUNT, SUM, and AVG.

All QUEL functions can be used either in the RETRIEVE clause or in the WHERE clause. Whenever a function is used in the RETRIEVE clause, we must give it an *independent attribute name*, which appears as a column header for the query result. In Q15, the resulting relation would have column names SUMSAL, MAXSAL, MINSAL, and AVGSAL.

QUERY 15

Find the sum of the salaries of all employees, the maximum salary, the minimum salary, and the average salary.

Q15:	RETRIEVE	(SUMSAL = **SUM** (E.SALARY), MAXSAL = **MAX** (E.SALARY),
		MINSAL = **MIN** (E.SALARY), AVGSAL = **AVG** (E.SALARY))

QUERIES 17 AND 18

Retrieve the total number of employees in the company (Q17) and the number of employees in the 'Research' department (Q18).

Q17:   RETRIEVE   (TOTAL_EMPS = **COUNT** (E.SSN))

Q18:   RETRIEVE   (RESEARCH_EMPS = **COUNT** (E.SSN **WHERE** E.DNO= D.DNUMBER **AND** D.DNAME='Research'))

The BY qualifier in QUEL can be used within each function specification to specify a particular grouping of tuples; hence, different groupings can be used in the same query. Each function can have its own grouping attributes, as well as its own WHERE conditions, and grouping can be used in the RETRIEVE clause *or* in the WHERE clause.

QUERY 20

For each department, retrieve the department number, the number of employees in the department, and their average salary.

Q20:   RETRIEVE   (E.DNO, NO_OF_EMPS = **COUNT** (E.SSN **BY** E.DNO), AVG_SAL = **AVG** (E.SALARY **BY** E.DNO))

Q20 groups EMPLOYEE tuples by department number, using the BY qualifier, by writing "BY E.DNO." Counting the employees by department is written as COUNT(E.SSN BY E.DNO). The grouping attribute E.DNO must also appear independently in the RETRIEVE list for the query to make sense.

QUERY 21

For each project, retrieve the project number, the project name, and the number of employees who work on that project.

Q21:   RETRIEVE   (W.PNO, P.PNAME, NO_OF_EMPS = **COUNT** (W.ESSN **BY** W.PNO, P.PNAME **WHERE** W.PNO=P.PNUMBER))

Q21 illustrates a grouping example where two relations are joined based on the condition W.PNO = P.PNUMBER, and then tuples are grouped by (W.PNO, P.PNAME) and the query result is calculated. Q21 illustrates the use of both grouping and a WHERE condition *within the specification of an aggregate function.* This allows several functions to be applied to different sets of tuples within the same query.

QUERY 22

For each project on which more than two employees work, retrieve the project number and the number of employees who work on that project.

Q22:   RETRIEVE   (W.PNO, NO_OF_EMPS = **COUNT** (W.ESSN BY W.PNO))
    WHERE   **COUNT** (W.ESSN BY W.PNO) >2

Another function in QUEL, ANY, is used to specify explicit existential quantification. ANY is applied to a subquery; if the result includes at least one tuple, ANY returns 1; otherwise, it returns 0. Hence, ANY is somewhat similar to the EXISTS function in SQL, except that EXISTS returns TRUE or FALSE rather than 1 or 0. ANY is usually applied to a nested subquery that uses grouping or a WHERE condition.

QUERY 12
Retrieve the name of each employee who has a dependent with the same first name and same sex as the employee.

Q12:   RETRIEVE   (E.FNAME, E.LNAME)
                        WHERE ANY (DEP.DEPENDENT_NAME **BY** E.SSN **WHERE**
                        E.SSN=DEP.ESSN
                        AND E.FNAME=DEP.DEPENDENT_NAME **AND**
                        E.SEX=DEP.SEX) = 1

QUERY 6
Retrieve the names of employees who have no dependents.

Q6:   RETRIEVE   (E.FNAME, E.LNAME)
        WHERE   **ANY**   (DEP.DEPENDENT_NAME **BY** E.SSN
                            WHERE E.SSN=DEP.SSN) = 0

QUERY 3
Find the social security numbers of employees who work on *all* projects controlled by department number 5.

Q3:   RETRIEVE   (E.SSN)
        WHERE   **ANY** (P.PNUMBER
                            WHERE   (P.DNUM=5)
                            AND
                            ANY (W.PNO **BY** E.SSN
                                WHERE   E.SSN=W.ESSN **AND**
                                P.PNUMBER=W.PNO) =0) =0

QUEL provides partial string comparisons by using two reserved characters: "*" replaces an arbitrary number of characters; and "?" replaces a single arbitrary character. For example, to retrieve all employees whose address is in Houston, Texas, we can use Q25.

Q25:   RETRIEVE   (E.LNAME, E.FNAME)
        WHERE   E.ADDRESS = '*Houston,TX*'

QUEL permits the use of standard arithmetic operators "+", "−," "*", and "/." QUEL also permits retrieval of the result of a query *into a relation*; the **INTO** keyword is used for this purpose. For example, to keep the result of Q27 in a relation called PROD-UCTX_RAISES that also includes the current salary in each tuple, plus a column called PROJ whose value is 'ProductX' for all tuples, we can use Q27A:

Q27A: RETRIEVE INTO PRODUCTX_RAISES (PROJ = 'ProductX', E.FNAME,
                        E.LNAME, CURRENT_SALARY = E.SALARY,
                        PROPOSED_ SALARY = E.SALARY * 1.1)
        WHERE   E.SSN=W.ESSN **AND** W.PNO=P.PNUMBER **AND** P.PNAME=
                        'ProductX'

QUEL also has a SORT BY clause similar to the ORDER BY clause of SQL. In QUEL three statements can be used to modify the database: APPEND, DELETE, and REPLACE.

QUEL also has facilities for defining views and a mechanism for embedding QUEL in a programming language (called EQUEL). We briefly discuss QUEL updates. To insert a new tuple in a relation, QUEL provides the **APPEND** command. For example, to add a new tuple to the EMPLOYEE relation of Figure 6.6, we can use U1:

U1:   APPEND TO EMPLOYEE (FNAME = 'Richard', MINIT = 'K', LNAME = 'Marini',
              SSN ='653298653', BDATE = '30-DEC-52',
              ADDRESS = '98 Oak Forest,Katy,TX',
              SEX = 'M',
              SALARY = 37000, SUPERSSN = '987654321', DNO = 4)

The APPEND command also permits insertion of multiple tuples into a relation by selecting the result of another query. The DELETE command is used to remove tuples from a relation. It includes a WHERE clause to select the tuples to be deleted:

U4A: DELETE   EMPLOYEE
         WHERE   E.LNAME='Brown'

U4B: DELETE   EMPLOYEE
         WHERE   E.SSN='123456789'

U4C: DELETE   EMPLOYEE
         WHERE   E.DNO=D.DNUMBER **AND** D.DNAME='Research'

The REPLACE command is used to modify attribute values. A WHERE clause selects the tuples to be modified from a single relation. For example, to change the location and controlling department of project 10 to 'Bellaire' and department 5, respectively, we use U5:

U5:   REPLACE   PROJECT (PLOCATION = 'Bellaire', DNUM = 5)
        WHERE   P.PNUMBER=10

8.2.3 Comparison of QUEL with SQL

In this section we briefly compare QUEL and SQL. The following points are noteworthy:

- Both QUEL and SQL are based on variations of the tuple relational calculus; however, QUEL is much closer to the tuple relational calculus than is SQL.
- In SQL, nesting of SELECT ... FROM ... WHERE ... blocks can be repeated arbitrarily to any number of levels; in QUEL, nesting is restricted to one level.
- Both SQL and QUEL use implicit existential quantifiers. Both handle universal quantification in terms of equivalent existential quantification.
- The grouping facility of QUEL—the BY...WHERE... clause—can occur any number of times in the RETRIEVE or WHERE clauses, allowing different groupings in the same query. In SQL only a single grouping per query is permitted via the GROUP BY ... HAVING ... clause, so nesting of queries is needed to allow different groupings.
- SQL allows some explicit set operations from the relational algebra, such as UNION; these are not available in QUEL but are handled by specifying more complex selection and join conditions.

- QUEL allows the specification of a temporary file to receive the output of a query in a single statement; in SQL, we must use a separate CREATE statement to create a table before we can do this.

- The ANY operator returns an integer value of 0 or 1 in QUEL; the EXISTS operator, which is used for similar purposes in SQL, returns a Boolean value of TRUE or FALSE.

- SQL has evolved dramatically and become a de facto standard for relational databases.

8.3 Domain Relational Calculus★

Domain relational calculus, or simply **domain calculus**, is the other type of formal predicate calculus–based language for relational databases. There is one commercial query language, QBE (see Section 8.4), that is somewhat related to the domain calculus, although QBE was developed prior to the formal specification of domain calculus.

The domain calculus differs from the tuple calculus in the *type of variables* used in formulas: rather than having variables range over tuples, the variables range over single values from domains of attributes. To form a relation of degree n for a query result, we must have n of these **domain variables**—one for each attribute. An expression of the domain calculus is of the form

$$\{x_1, x_2, \ldots, x_n \mid COND(\ x_1, x_2, \ldots, x_n, x_{n+1}, x_{n+2}, \ldots, x_{n+m})\}$$

where $x_1, x_2, \ldots, x_n, x_{n+1}, x_{n+2}, \ldots, x_{n+m}$ are domain variables that range over domains (of attributes) and COND is a **condition** or **formula** of the domain relational calculus. A formula is made up of **atoms**. The atoms of a formula are slightly different from those for the tuple calculus and can be one of the following:

1. An atom of the form $R(x_1, x_2, \ldots, x_j)$, where R is the name of a relation of degree j and each x_i, $1 \le i \le j$, is a domain variable. This atom states that a list of values of $<x_1, x_2, \ldots, x_j>$ must be a tuple in the relation whose name is R, where x_i is the value of the ith attribute value of the tuple. To make a domain calculus expression more concise, we *drop the commas* in a list of variables; thus, we write

   $$\{x_1\ x_2 \ldots x_n \mid R(x_1\ x_2\ x_3)\ \textbf{and} \ldots\}$$

   instead of:

   $$\{x_1, x_2, \ldots, x_n \mid R(x_1, x_2, x_3)\ \textbf{and} \ldots\}$$

2. An atom of the form x_i **op** x_j, where **op** is one of the comparison operators in the set $\{ =, \neq, <, \le, >, \ge \}$ and x_i and x_j are domain variables.

3. An atom of the form x_i **op** c or c **op** x_j, where **op** is one of the comparison operators in the set $\{ =, \neq, <, \le, >, \ge \}$, x_i and x_j are domain variables, and c is a constant value.

As in tuple calculus, atoms evaluate to either **TRUE** or **FALSE** for a specific set of values, called the **truth values** of the atoms. In case 1, if the domain variables are assigned values corresponding to a tuple of the specified relation R, then the atom is TRUE. In cases 2 and 3, if the domain variables are assigned values that satisfy the condition, then the atom is TRUE.

In a similar way to the tuple relational calculus, formulas are made up of atoms, variables, and quantifiers, so we will not repeat the specifications for formulas here. Some examples of queries specified in the domain calculus follow. We will use lowercase letters l, m, n, ..., x, y, z for domain variables.

QUERY 0
Retrieve the birthdate and address of the employee whose name is 'John B. Smith'.

Q0: {uv | (∃ q) (∃ r) (∃ s)
       (EMPLOYEE(qrstuvwxyz) **and** q='John' **and** r='B' **and** s='Smith')}

We need ten variables for the EMPLOYEE relation, one to range over the domain of each attribute in order. Of the ten variables q, r, s, ..., z, only q, r, and s are bound to an existential quantifier; the rest are free. We first specify the requested attributes, BDATE and ADDRESS, by the domain variables u for BDATE and v for ADDRESS. Then we specify the condition for selecting a tuple following the bar (|)—namely, that the sequence of values assigned to the variables qrstuvwxyz be a tuple of the EMPLOYEE relation and that the values for q (FNAME), r (MINIT), and s (LNAME) be 'John', 'B', and 'Smith', respectively. Notice that we existentially quantify only the variables participating in a condition.

An alternative notation for writing this query is to assign the constants 'John', 'B', and 'Smith' directly as shown in Q0A, where all variables are free:

Q0A: {uv | EMPLOYEE('John','B','Smith',t,u,v,w,x,y,z)}

QUERY 1
Retrieve the name and address of all employees who work for the 'Research' department.

Q1: {qsv | (∃ z) (EMPLOYEE(qrstuvwxyz) **and** (∃ l) (∃ m)
       (DEPARTMENT(lmno) **and** l='Research' **and** m=z))}

A condition relating two domain variables that range over attributes from two relations, such as m = z in Q1, is a **join condition;** whereas a condition that relates a domain variable to a constant, such as l = 'Research', is a **selection condition**.

QUERY 2
For every project located in 'Stafford', list the project number, the controlling department number, and the department manager's last name, birthdate, and address.

Q2: {iksuv | (∃ j) (PROJECT(hijk) **and** (∃ t) (EMPLOYEE(qrstuvwxyz) **and**
       (∃ m)(∃ n) (DEPARTMENT(lmno) **and** k=m **and** n=t **and** j='Stafford'))}

QUERY 6
Find the names of employees who have no dependents.

Q6:{qs | (∃ t) (EMPLOYEE(qrstuvwxyz) **and** (**not**(∃ l) (DEPENDENT(lmnop) **and** t=l))))}

Query 6 can be restated using universal quantifiers instead of the existential quantifiers, as shown in Q6A:

Q6A:{qs | (∃ t) (EMPLOYEE(qrstuvwxyz) **and** ((∀ l) (**not**(DEPENDENT(lmnop)) **or** **not**(t=l)))))}

QUERY 7

List the names of managers who have at least one dependent.

Q7:{sq | (∃ t) (EMPLOYEE(qrstuvwxyz) **and** ((∃ j) (DEPARTMENT(hijk) **and** ((∃ l) (DEPENDENT(lmnop) **and** t=j **and** l=t)))))}

As we mentioned earlier, it can be shown that any query that can be expressed in the relational algebra can also be expressed in the domain or tuple relational calculus. In addition, any safe expression in the domain or tuple relational calculus can be expressed in the relational algebra.

8.4 Overview of the QBE Language★

QBE (Query By Example) is a user-friendly relational query language that was developed at IBM Research. QBE is available as an IBM commercial product as part of the QMF (Query Management Facility) interface option to DB2. It differs from SQL and QUEL in that the user does not have to specify a structured query explicitly; rather, the query is formulated by filling in **templates** of relations that are displayed on a terminal screen. Figure 8.2 shows how these templates may look for the database of Figure 6.6. The user does not

EMPLOYEE	FNAME	MINIT	LNAME	SSN	BDATE	ADDRESS	SEX	SALARY	SUPERSSN	DNO

DEPARTMENT	DNAME	DNUMBER	MGRSSN	MGRSTARTDATE

DEPT_LOCATIONS	DNUMBER	DLOCATION

WORKS_ON	ESSN	PNO	HOURS

PROJECT	PNAME	PNUMBER	PLOCATION	DNUM

DEPENDENT	ESSN	DEPENDENT_NAME	SEX	BDATE	RELATIONSHIP

Figure 8.2 The relational schema of Figure 6.6 as it may be displayed by QBE.

have to remember the names of attributes or relations, because they are displayed as part of these templates. In addition, the user does not have to follow any rigid syntax rules for query specification; rather, constants and variables are entered in the columns of the templates to construct an **example** related to the retrieval or update request. QBE is related to the domain relational calculus, as we shall see, and its original specification has been shown to be relationally complete.

Retrieval queries are specified by filling in certain columns of the relation templates. When entering constant values into a template, we type them as they are; however, **example values,** which are preceded by the "_" (underscore) character, can also be entered. The prefix "P." is used to indicate that the values of a particular column are to be retrieved, where P stands for Print. For example, consider the query Q0: Retrieve the birthdate and address of 'John B. Smith'; this may be specified in QBE as shown in Figure 8.3(a).

In Figure 8.3(a), we specified an example of the *type of row* in which we are interested. The example values preceded by "_" represent *free domain variables* (see Section 8.3). Actual constant values, such as John, B., and Smith, are used to select tuples from the database with matching values. All columns in which the prefix P. appears have their values retrieved in the query result.

Q0 can be abbreviated as shown in Figure 8.3(b). There is no need to specify example values for columns in which we are not interested. Moreover, because example values are completely arbitrary, we can just specify variable names for them, as shown in Figure 8.3(c). We can also leave out the example values entirely, as shown in Figure 8.3(d), and just specify a P. under the columns to be retrieved.

To see how retrieval queries in QBE are similar to the domain relational calculus, compare Figure 8.3(d) with Q0 (simplified) in domain calculus, which is as follows:

Q0 : { uv | EMPLOYEE(qrstuvwxyz) **and** q='John' **and** r='B' **and** s='Smith'}

We can think of each column in a QBE template as an *implicit domain variable*; hence, FNAME corresponds to the domain variable q, MINIT corresponds to r, . . ., and DNO corresponds to z. In the QBE query, the columns with P. correspond to variables specified to

(a)

EMPLOYEE	FNAME	MINIT	LNAME	SSN	BDATE	ADDRESS	SEX	SALARY	SUPERSSN	DNO
	John	B	Smith	_123456789	P._9/1/60	P._100 Main, Houston, TX	_M	_25000	_123456789	_3

(b)

EMPLOYEE	FNAME	MINIT	LNAME	SSN	BDATE	ADDRESS	SEX	SALARY	SUPERSSN	DNO
	John	B	Smith		P._9/1/60	P._100 Main, Houston, TX				

(c)

EMPLOYEE	FNAME	MINIT	LNAME	SSN	BDATE	ADDRESS	SEX	SALARY	SUPERSSN	DNO
	John	B	Smith		P._X	P._Y				

(d)

EMPLOYEE	FNAME	MINIT	LNAME	SSN	BDATE	ADDRESS	SEX	SALARY	SUPERSSN	DNO
	John	B	Smith		P.	P.				

Figure 8.3 Four ways of specifying the query Q0 in QBE.

the left of the bar (|) in domain calculus, whereas the columns with constant values correspond to tuple variables with equality selection conditions on them. The condition EMPLOYEE(qrstuvwxyz), and the existential quantifiers are implicit in the QBE query because the template corresponding to the EMPLOYEE relation is used.

In QBE, the user interface first allows the user to choose the tables (relations) needed to formulate a query by displaying a list of all relation names. The templates for the chosen relations are then displayed. The user moves to the appropriate columns in the templates and specifies the query. Special function keys are used to move to the next or previous column in the current template, to move to the next or previous relation template, and to perform other common functions.

We now give examples to illustrate basic facilities of QBE. We must explicitly enter comparison operators other than = (such as > or ≥) before typing a constant value. For example, the query Q0A, "List the social security numbers of employees who work more than 20 hours per week on project number 1," can be specified as shown in Figure 8.4(a). For more complex conditions, the user can ask for a **condition box**, which is created by pressing a particular function key. The user can then type the complex condition.* For example, the query Q0B, "List the social security numbers of employees who work more than 20 hours per week on either project 1 or project 2", can be specified as shown in Figure 8.4(b).

Some complex conditions can be specified without a condition box. The rule is that all conditions specified on the same row of a relation template are connected by the **and** logical connective (*all* must be satisfied by a selected tuple), whereas conditions specified on distinct rows are connected by **or** (*at least one* must be satisfied). Hence, Q0B can also be specified, as shown in Figure 8.4(c), by entering two distinct rows in the template.

(a)

WORKS_ON	ESSN	PNO	HOURS
	P.	1	>20

(b)

WORKS_ON	ESSN	PNO	HOURS
	P.	_PX	_HX

CONDITIONS

_HX>20 AND (_PX = 1 OR _PX = 2)

(c)

WORKS_ON	ESSN	PNO	HOURS
	P.	1	>20
	P.	2	>20

Figure 8.4 Specifying complex conditions in QBE. (a) The query Q0A. (b) The query Q0B with a condition box. (c) The query Q0B without a condition box.

*Negation with the ¬ symbol is *not* allowed in a condition box.

Now consider the query Q0C "List the social security numbers of employees who work on *both* project 1 and project 2"; this cannot be specified as in Figure 8.5(a), which lists those who work on *either* project 1 or project 2. The example variable _ES will bind itself to ESSN values in <-, 1, -> tuples *as well as* to those in <-, 2, -> tuples. Figure 8.5(b) shows how to specify Q0C correctly, where the condition (_EX = _EY) in the box makes the _EX and _EY variables bind only to identical ESSN values.

In general, once a query is specified, the resulting values are displayed in the template under the appropriate columns. If the result contains more rows than can be displayed on the screen, most QBE implementations have function keys to allow scrolling up and down the rows. Similarly, if a template or several templates are too wide to appear on the screen, it is possible to scroll sideways to examine all the templates.

A join operation is specified in QBE by using the *same variable** in the columns to be joined. For example, the query Q1, "List the name and address of all employees who work for the 'Research' department," can be specified as shown in Figure 8.6(a). Any number of joins can be specified in a single query. We can also specify a **result table** to display the result of the join query, as shown in Figure 8.6(a); this is needed if the result includes attributes from two or more relations. If no result table is specified, the system provides the query result in the columns of the various relations, which may make it difficult to interpret. Figure 8.6(a) also illustrates the feature of QBE for specifying that all attributes of a relation should be retrieved, by placing the P. operator under the relation name in the relation template.

To join a table with itself, we specify different variables to represent the different references to the table. For example, the query Q8, "for each employee retrieve the employee's first and last name as well as the first and last name of his or her immediate supervisor," can be specified as shown in Figure 8.6(b), where the variables starting with E refer to an employee and those starting with S refer to a supervisor.

(a)

WORKS_ON	ESSN	PNO	HOURS
	P._ES	1	
	P._ES	2	

(b)

WORKS_ON	ESSN	PNO	HOURS
	P._EX	1	
	P._EY	2	

CONDITIONS

_EX = _EY

Figure 8.5   Specifying EMPLOYEES who work on both projects. (a) Incorrect specification of an AND condition. (b) Correct specification.

---

*A variable is called an **example element** in QBE manuals.

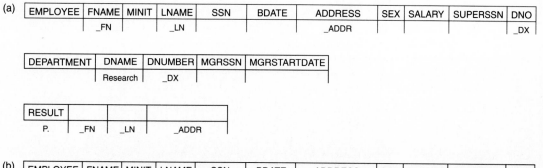

Figure 8.6 Illustrating JOIN and result relations in QBE. (a) The query Q1.
(b) The query Q8.

Next, consider the types of queries that require grouping or aggregate functions. A grouping operator G. can be specified in a column to indicate that tuples should be grouped by the value of that column. Common functions can be specified, such as AVG., SUM., CNT. (count), MAX., and MIN. In QBE the functions AVG., SUM., and CNT. are applied to *distinct values* within a group in the default case. If we want these functions to apply to all values, we must use the prefix ALL.* This convention is *different* in SQL and QUEL, where the default is to apply a function to all values.

Figure 8.7(a) shows query Q19, which counts the number of *distinct* salary values in the EMPLOYEE relation. Query Q19A (Figure 8.7(b)) counts all salary values, which is the same as counting the number of employees. Figure 8.7(c) shows Q20, which retrieves each department number and the number of employees and average salary within each department; hence, the DNO column is used for grouping as indicated by the G. function. Several of the operators G., P., and ALL can be specified in a single column. Figure 8.7(d) shows query Q22A, which displays each project name and the number of employees working on the project for projects on which more than two employees work.

QBE has a negation symbol, ¬, which is used in a manner similar to the NOT EXISTS function of SQL. Figure 8.8 shows query Q6, which lists the names of employees who have no dependents. The negation symbol ¬ says that we will select values of the _SX variable from the EMPLOYEE relation only if they do not occur in the DEPENDENT relation. The same effect can be produced by placing a ≠ _SX in the ESSN column.

Although the QBE language as originally proposed was shown to support the equivalent of the EXISTS and NOT EXISTS functions of SQL, the QBE implementation in QMF

---

*ALL in QBE is unrelated to the universal quantifier. Also, the use of ALL in QUEL is for a different purpose.

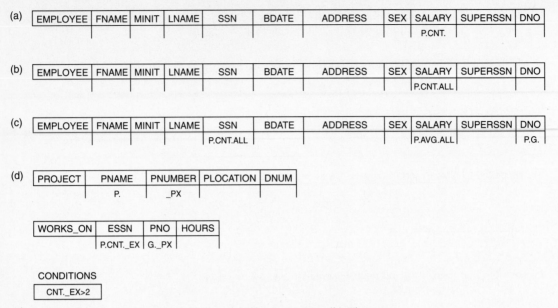

Figure 8.7   Functions and grouping in QBE. (a) The query Q19. (b) The query Q19A. (c) The query Q20. (d) The query Q22A.

(under the DB2 system) does *not* provide this support. Hence, the QMF version of QBE, which we discuss here, is *not relationally complete*. Queries such as Q3, "Find employees who work on *all* projects controlled by department 5," *cannot* be specified.

There are three QBE operators for modifying the database: I. for insert, D. for delete, and U. for update. The insert and delete operators are specified in the template column under the relation name, whereas the update operator is specified under the columns to be updated. Figure 8.9(a) shows how to insert a new EMPLOYEE tuple. For deletion, we first enter the D. operator and then specify the tuples to be deleted by a condition (Figure 8.9(b)). To update a tuple, we specify the U. operator under the attribute name, followed by the new value of the attribute. We should also select the tuple or tuples to be updated in the usual way. Figure 8.9(c) shows an update request to increase the salary of 'John Smith' by 10% and also to reassign him to department number 4.

QBE also has data definition capabilities. The tables of a database can be specified interactively, and a table definition can also be updated by adding, renaming, or removing a column. We can also specify various characteristics for each column, such as

EMPLOYEE	FNAME	MINIT	LNAME	SSN	BDATE	ADDRESS	SEX	SALARY	SUPERSSN	DNO
	P.		P.	_SX						

DEPENDENT	ESSN	DEPENDENT_NAME	SEX	BDATE	RELATIONSHIP
¬	_SX				

Figure 8.8   Illustrating negation by the query Q6.

(a)

EMPLOYEE	FNAME	MINIT	LNAME	SSN	BDATE	ADDRESS	SEX	SALARY	SUPERSSN	DNO
I.	Richard	K	Marini	653298653	30-DEC-52	98 Oak Forest, Katy, TX	M	37000	987654321	4

(b)

EMPLOYEE	FNAME	MINIT	LNAME	SSN	BDATE	ADDRESS	SEX	SALARY	SUPERSSN	DNO
D.				653298653						

(c)

EMPLOYEE	FNAME	MINIT	LNAME	SSN	BDATE	ADDRESS	SEX	SALARY	SUPERSSN	DNO
	John		Smith					U._S•1.1		U.4

Figure 8.9   Modifying the database in QBE. (a) Insertion. (b) Deletion.
(c) Update in QBE.

whether it is a key of the relation, what its data type is, and whether an index should be created on that field. QBE also has facilities for view definition, authorization, storing query definitions for later use, and so on.

QBE does not use the "linear" style of QUEL and SQL; rather, it is a "two-dimensional" language, because users specify a query moving around the full area of the screen. Tests on users have shown that QBE is easier to learn than SQL, especially for nonspecialists. In this sense, QBE was the first user-friendly relational database language.

More recently, numerous other user-friendly interfaces have been developed for commercial database systems. The use of menus, graphics, and forms is now quite common.

8.5 Summary

The relational calculus is a declarative formal query language for the relational model, which is based on the branch of mathematical logic called predicate calculus. There are two types of relational calculi: the tuple relational calculus uses tuple variables that range over relations; the domain relational calculus uses domain variables.

A query is specified in a single declarative statement, without specifying any order or method for retrieving the query result. Hence, the relational calculus is often considered to be a higher-level language than the relational algebra. A relational algebra expression implicitly specifies an ordering of operations to retrieve the result of a query, whereas a relational calculus expression specifies only what we want to retrieve regardless of how the query may be executed.

We discussed the syntax of relational calculus queries. We also discussed the existential quantifier ($\exists$) and the universal quantifier ($\forall$). We saw that relational calculus variables are bound by these quantifiers. We saw in detail how queries with universal quantification are written, and we discussed the problem of specifying safe queries whose results are finite. We also discussed rules for transforming universal into existential quantifiers, and vice versa. It is the quantifiers that give expressive power to the relational calculus, making it equivalent to relational algebra.

The SQL language, described in Chapter 7, has its roots in the tuple relational calculus. A SELECT–PROJECT–JOIN query in SQL is similar to a tuple relational calculus expression, if we consider each relation name in the FROM clause of the SQL query to be a tuple variable with an implicit existential quantifier. The EXISTS function in SQL is equivalent to the existential quantifier and can be used in its negated form (NOT EXISTS) to specify universal quantification. There is no explicit equivalent of a universal quantifier in SQL. There is no analog to grouping and aggregation functions in the relational calculus.

We also discussed two database languages that are related to relational calculus. The language QUEL is very similar to the tuple relational calculus, without the universal quantifier. The QBE language has similarities to the domain relational calculus.

Review Questions

8.1. In what sense does relational calculus differ from relational algebra, and in what sense are they similar?

8.2. How does tuple relational calculus differ from domain relational calculus?

8.3. Discuss the meanings of the existential quantifier ($\exists$) and the universal quantifier ($\forall$).

8.4. Define the following terms with respect to the tuple calculus: *tuple variable, range relation, atom, formula, expression.*

8.5. Define the following terms with respect to the domain calculus: *domain variable, range relation, atom, formula, expression.*

8.6. What is meant by a *safe expression* in relational calculus?

8.7. When is a query language called relationally complete?

8.8. Discuss the rules for specifying grouping attributes and functions in QUEL.

8.9. Discuss the rules for nesting of functions in QUEL.

8.10. Compare the various features of SQL and QUEL, and discuss why you may prefer one over the other for each feature.

8.11. Discuss the rules for nesting operators in QBE.

8.12. Why must the insert I. and delete D. operators of QBE appear under the relation name in a relation template and not under a column name?

8.13. Why must the update U. operators of QBE appear under a column name in a relation template and not under the relation name?

Exercises

8.14. Specify queries a, b, c, e, f, i, and j of Exercise 6.19 in both the tuple relational calculus and the domain relational calculus.

8.15. Specify queries a, b, c, and d of Exercise 6.21 in both the tuple relational calculus and the domain relational calculus.

8.16. Specify queries of Exercise 7.16 in both the tuple relational calculus and the domain relational calculus. Also specify these queries in the relational algebra.

8.17. In a tuple relational calculus query with n tuple variables, what would be the typical minimum number of join conditions? Why? What is the effect of having a smaller number of join conditions?

8.18. Rewrite the domain relational calculus queries that followed Q0 in Section 8.3 in the style of the abbreviated notation of Q0A, where the objective is to minimize the number of domain variables by writing constants in place of variables wherever possible.

8.19. Consider this query: Retrieve the SSNs of employees who work on at least those projects on which the employee with SSN = 123456789 works. This may be stated as (FORALL x) (IF P THEN Q), where:

• x is a tuple variable that ranges over the PROJECT relation.

• P ≡ employee with SSN = 123456789 works on project x.

• Q ≡ employee e works on project x.

Express the query in tuple relational calculus, using the rules:

• $(\forall x)(P(x)) \equiv (\nexists x)(not(P(x)))$.

• (IF P THEN Q) ≡ (not(P) or Q).

8.20. Show how you may specify the following relational algebra operations in both tuple and domain relational calculus.

  a. $\sigma_{A=C}(R(A, B, C))$.

  b. $\pi_{<A,\ B>}(R(A, B, C))$.

  c. R(A, B, C) * S(C, D, E).

  d. R(A, B, C) ∪ S(A, B, C).

  e. R(A, B, C) ∩ S(A, B, C).

  f. R(A, B, C) − S(A, B, C).

  g. R(A, B, C) × S(D, E, F).

  h. R(A, B) ÷ S(A).

8.21. Suggest extensions to the relational calculus so that it may express the following types of operations discussed in Section 6.6: (a) aggregate functions and grouping; (b) OUTER JOIN operations; (c) recursive closure queries.

8.22. Write appropriate QUEL data definition statements for some of the database schemas shown in Figure 6.5, Figure 2.1, Figure 6.19, and Figure 6.22.

8.23. Specify the queries of Exercises 6.19 and 7.14 in QUEL.

8.24. Consider the following query, which is a variation on Q24: List the SSN of the youngest person in department 5 among employees earning more than $50,000. Can this be done as a single QUEL query? What about in SQL? If it can-not be done as a single query, show how it can be done in steps by storing temporary results.

8.25. Specify the updates of Exercise 6.20, using the QUEL update commands.

8.26. Specify the queries of Exercise 7.16 in QUEL.

8.27. Specify the updates of Exercise 7.17, using the QUEL update commands.

8.28. Specify the queries of Exercise 6.26 in QUEL.

8.29. Write QUEL statements to create the indexes specified in Exercise 7.19.

8.30. Specify the queries and updates of Exercises 6.21 and 6.22 in QUEL.

8.31. Repeat Exercise 7.25, but use QUEL instead of SQL.

8.32. Specify some of the queries of Exercises 6.19 and 7.14 in QBE.

8.33. Can you specify the query of Exercise 8.24 as a single QBE query?

8.34. Specify the updates of Exercise 6.20 in QBE.

8.35. Specify the queries of Exercise 7.16 in QBE.

8.36. Specify the updates of Exercise 7.17 in QBE.

8.37. Specify the queries and updates of Exercises 6.21 and 6.22 in QBE.

Selected Bibliography

Codd (1971) introduced the language ALPHA, which is based on concepts of tuple relational calculus. ALPHA also includes the notion of aggregate functions, which goes beyond relational calculus. The original formal definition of relational calculus was given by Codd (1972), which also provided an algorithm that transforms any tuple relational calculus expression to relational algebra. Codd defined a language as relationally complete if it is at least as powerful as relational calculus. Ullman (1988) describes a formal proof of the equivalence of relational algebra with the safe expressions of tuple and domain relational calculus.

Ideas of domain relational calculus appeared initially in the QBE language (Zloof 1975). The concept is formally defined by Lacroix and Pirotte (1977). The ILL language (Lacroix and Pirotte 1977a) is based on domain relational calculus. The QUEL language (Stonebraker et al. 1976) is based on tuple relational calculus, with implicit existential quantifiers but no universal quantifiers, and was implemented in the INGRES system. Zook et al. (1977) describes the language for "university INGRES," and the commercial version of QUEL is described in RTI (1983). A book (Stonebraker 1986) contains a compilation of research and survey papers related to the INGRES system.

Thomas and Gould (1975) reports the results of experiments comparing the ease of use of QBE to SQL. The commercial QBE functions are described in an IBM manual (1978), and a quick reference card is available (IBM 1978a). Appropriate DB2 reference manuals discuss the QBE implementation for that system. Whang et al. (1990) extends QBE with universal quantifiers.

CHAPTER 9

A Relational Database System—DB2

In this chapter we discuss a representative relational database management system (RDBMS) called DB2. The basic architecture of DB2 is overviewed in Section 9.2. Section 9.3 discusses data definition in DB2, and Section 9.4 discusses data manipulation. Section 9.5 gives an overview of DB2 storage structures, and Section 9.6 discusses some additional features. First, we give a historical perspective on the development of relational database systems in Section 9.1.

For the reader who desires to get a general introduction to the DB2 system, Sections 9.5 and 9.6, which discuss physical aspects of DB2, may be skipped.

9.1 Introduction to Relational Database Management Systems

After Codd introduced the relational model in 1970, there was a flurry of experimentation with relational ideas. A major research and development effort was initiated at IBM's San Jose (now called Almaden) Research Center. It led to the announcement of two commercial relational DBMS products by IBM in the 1980s: SQL/DS for DOS/VSE (disk operating system/virtual storage extended) and for VM/CMS (virtual machine/conversational monitoring system) environments, introduced in 1981; and DB2 for the MVS operating system, introduced in 1983. Another major relational DBMS is INGRES, developed at the University of California, Berkeley, in the early 1970s and commercialized by Relational Technology, Inc., in the late 1970s. Now INGRES is a commercial RDBMS marketed by Ingres, Inc., a subsidiary of ASK Inc. Other popular commercial RDBMSs include ORACLE of Oracle, Inc.; Sybase of Sybase, Inc.; RDB of Digital Equipment Corp.; INFORMIX of Informix, Inc.; and UNIFY of Unify, Inc. It is not possible to describe the features of each of these RDBMSs in detail. In this chapter we will discuss the features of IBM's DB2 product to give the reader a feel for what is typically offered in a commercial RDBMS product. The other systems have similar architectures, language support, and tools for application development.

Besides the RDBMSs mentioned above, many implementations of the relational data model appeared on the personal computer (PC) platform in the 1980s. These include RIM, RBASE 5000, PARADOX, OS/2 Database Manager, DBase IV, XDB, WATCOM SQL, SQL Server (of Sybase, Inc.), and most recently ACCESS (of Microsoft, Inc.). They were initially single-user systems, but more recently, they have started offering the client/server database architecture (see Chapter 23 for definition) and are becoming compliant with the Microsoft *Open Database Connectivity* (ODBC) standard. This standard permits the use of many front-end tools with these systems. We will not survey the PC RDBMSs here.

The word *relational* is also used somewhat inappropriately by several vendors to refer to their products as a marketing gimmick. To qualify as a genuine relational DBMS, a system must have at least the following properties:*

1. It must store data as relations such that each column is independently identified by its column name and the ordering of rows is immaterial.

2. The operations available to the user, as well as those used internally by the system, should be true relational operations; that is, they should be able to generate new relations from old relations.

3. The system must support at least one variant of the JOIN operation.

Although we could add to this list, we propose these criteria as a very minimal set for testing whether a system is relational. It is easy to see that many so-called relational DBMSs do not satisfy these criteria.

We now describe DB2, which is currently one of the more widely used mainframe relational systems.

9.2 Basic Architecture of DB2

The name DB2 is an abbreviation for Database 2. It is a relational DBMS product of IBM for the MVS operating system. Our discussion in this chapter refers to DB2 Version 2 Release 3 and, to some extent, to DB2 Version 3. Emphasis is placed on conveying the complexity of an RDBMS product like DB2 and its variety of features, rather than on an exact enumeration of features and facilities in a specific version of DB2.

DB2 cooperates with ("attaches to," in the product terminology) any of the three MVS subsystem environments: CICS, TSO, and IMS. These systems cooperate with DB2 facilities to provide data communications and transaction management. Figure 9.1 shows the relationships among various components of DB2. DB2 allows concurrent access to databases by IMS/VS-DC (Information Management System/Virtual Storage-Data Communications), CICS (Customer Information Control System), and TSO (Time Sharing

---

*Codd (1985) specified 12 rules for determining whether a DBMS is relational. We have listed the rules in the appendix to this chapter. Codd (1990) presents a treatise on extended relational models and systems, identifying over 330 features of relational systems, divided into 18 categories.

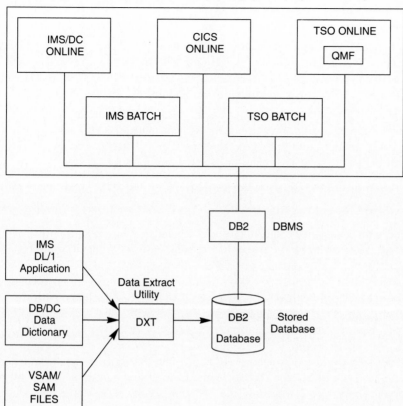

Figure 9.1   Overview of the organization of DB2 system, with a partial view of supporting features.

Option) users, both interactive and batch. CICS is a teleprocessing monitoring system— a popular IBM product used by many industries for processing of business transactions. (We discuss transaction processing in Chapter 17.) IMS/DC is a data communication environment that supports hierarchical IMS databases (we discuss IMS in Section 11.7). TSO is a longstanding time-sharing environment product of IBM. The "call attach" facility CAF (not shown in Figure 9.1) allows an application to interact with a DB2 database without the help of these monitors. The DB2 databases can be accessed by application programs written in COBOL, PL/1, FORTRAN, C, PROLOG, or IBM assembly language.

The following points further describe the use of various subsystems shown in Figure 9.1:

1. A DB2 application consisting of programs written in the aforementioned languages runs under the control of *exactly one* of the three subsystems—IMS, CICS, or TSO. The IMS, CICS, and TSO DB2 applications run distinctly. In fact, they are described in separate sets of manuals.

2. The same DB2 databases may be shared by IMS, CICS, and TSO applications. CSP (Cross Systems Product) allows an application developed under TSO to run under CICS and vice versa.

3. There are two main online facilities with DB2: QMF (Query Management Facility) under CICS or CAF, and DB2 Interactive (DB2I) under TSO. DB2I comes with DB2; it allows professional users to enter SQL interactively through an interface called SPUFI and helps them prepare programs and utilities for execution.

4. Besides DB2 databases, IMS databases are also accessible from a DB2 application under the IMS or CICS environment, but not under the TSO environment. The same TSO application may be executed either as batch or on line, by directing the I/O in the program to files or by using terminals for I/O.

As shown in Figure 9.1, two other facilities—QMF and DXT—play important roles in the use of DB2.

QMF (Query Management Facility). QMF is a separate product from DB2 that acts as a query language and report writer. It simply runs as an on-line TSO application. It supports ad hoc querying by nontechnical end users in either SQL or QBE and displays the results of SQL or QBE queries as formatted reports. It can access both DB2 and SQL/DS databases. The output of QMF can be directed to other utilities to draw bar charts (with the Interactive Chart Utility) and other graphical data displays (with the Graphical Data Display Manager). Users interactively build forms to control the display of query results.

DXT (Data Extract). Data Extract is a utility program that extracts data from IMS databases or VSAM (Virtual Storage Access Method) or SAM (Sequential Access Method) files and converts it into a sequential file. DXT can specify extraction requests interactively or as batch jobs. This sequential file is in a format suitable for direct loading into a DB2 database. DXT is an independent IBM product.

9.2.1 *The DB2 Family and DB2/2*

SQL/DS is IBM's first relational DBMS that belongs to the "DB2 family." The data definition and manipulation facilities of the two systems are essentially the same, with only minor syntactic differences. Both systems use SQL as an interactive query language, as well as a database programming language, by embedding it in a host language (see Section 7.7). The DB2 system initially used the SQL/DS code for the upper parts of the system (for example, the query optimization and query processing features). The "lower" parts of DB2 were built from scratch. The QMF and DXT facilities may be used for both DB2 and SQL/DS. However, the physical storage of data in SQL/DS and DB2 differs. For example, concepts such as DB2 tablespaces have no analog in SQL/DS. DB2 also supports specialized techniques for handling large databases and heavy workloads that are unique to the MVS operating system. Whereas DB2 provides an interactive SQL facility for end users via DB2I, SQL/DS is able to provide some end-user facilities via its ISQL (interactive SQL) component. The IBM Database 2 OS/2 (called DB2/2 for short) is the latest of the IBM RDBMSs. It runs on OS/2 and was introduced in 1988 as OS/2 Extended Edition Database Manager. Note that AS/400 DBMS is different from the RDBMSs in the DB2 family. Most of its functionality resides in proprietary hardware.

9.2.2   *Organization of Data and Processes in DB2*

Let us first see how DB2 databases are perceived by users and application programs. All data is viewed as relations or "tables," a legitimate DB2 term. Tables are of two types: *base tables*, which physically exist as stored data; and *views*, which are virtual tables without a separate physical identity in storage. A base table consists of one or more VSAM files.

Application Processing. Figure 9.2 shows the preparation of a DB2 application in embedded SQL, in a simplified manner. It indicates the sequence of processes through which a user application must pass in order to access a DB2 database. The major components of the SQL application flow are the precompiler, the bind, the run-time supervisor,* and the stored data manager. Briefly, they perform the following functions:

- **Precompiler:** As discussed in Chapters 1 and 7, the job of the precompiler is to process embedded SQL statements in a host language program. The precompiler generates two kinds of output: the original source program, with the embedded SQL replaced by CALLs; and database request modules (DBRMs), which are collections of SQL statements in a parse tree form input to the bind process.

- **Bind:** This component accommodates both types of SQL requests: those arising in application programs to be executed over and over again, and ad hoc queries that execute only once. For the first category, following a detailed analysis and query optimization, as discussed in Chapter 16, one or more related DBRMs are compiled *only once* into an application plan. The cost of this binding is thus amortized across the repeated executions of the program and is found to be well justified. The bind process also permits an application to construct and submit a (dynamic) SQL statement for immediate execution. Bind parses all SQL statements. Whereas manipulative statements of SQL are bound to produce executable code, the definition and control statements in SQL are parsed by bind and left in a form that is interpreted at run time. The output of bind is called a plan or a package.

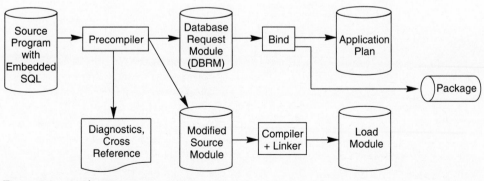

Figure 9.2   Application preparation.

---

*The terms *run-time supervisor* and *stored data manager* are not in DB2 manuals. They are adapted from Date and White (1988). The term in IBM manuals called *Relational Data System* (RDS) came from the original System R implementation. It encompasses the precompiler, the bind, and the run-time supervisor.

- **Run-time supervisor:** This refers to the services of DB2 that control the application execution at run time. The execution of an SQL call within an actual application program goes through the processing steps shown in Figure 9.3. When the load module of the application program is executing and comes to a CALL inserted by the precompiler, control goes to the run-time supervisor via the appropriate language interface module of DB2. The run-time supervisor retrieves the application plan, uses the control information in it, and requests that the stored data manager actually access the database.

- **Stored data manager:** This is the system component that manages the physical database. It includes what DB2 calls the Data Manager, as well as the Buffer Manager, Log Manager, and so on. Together they perform all the necessary functions involved in dealing with the stored database—search, retrieve, update—as required by the application plan. This component appropriately updates the indexes. To get the best performance out of buffer pools, it employs sophisticated buffering techniques such as read-ahead buffering and look-aside buffering. The stored data manager is able to provide hashed and linked access to the system tables in the system catalog. The data manager accesses data or indexes by supplying page identifiers to the buffer manager. The page size is 4096 bytes and corresponds to the page size of the operating system.

Interactive Processing. DB2 also allows on-line users to access the database by using the DB2I (DB2 interactive) facility, which is an on-line application running under DB2. For

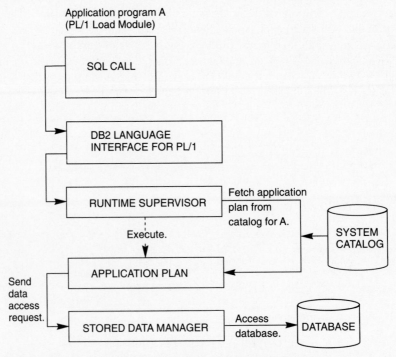

Figure 9.3 A PL/1 application execution example in DB2.

an on-line user to establish communication with this on-line application, the services of a data communication (DC) manager must be used. In the case of a DB2 user wishing to gain such access, the (DC) manager function is performed by the TSO component of MVS, by the data communication facility DC of IMS, or by the CICS (see Figure 9.1). DB2I accepts SQL statements from a terminal and passes them to DB2 for execution. Even during interactive execution, SQL is compiled and an application plan is generated for it; the results are passed back from the execution to the terminal. This plan is discarded after execution.

Utilities. The database services include a set of utilities. These are described later (see Section 9.5.3).

9.2.3 *Other Related Functions for Compilation and Execution of SQL*

Several functions are required during the compilation and execution of SQL queries or applications. We quickly review the more important ones here:

- *Optimization:* This function deals with the choice of an optimum access plan to implement an SQL retrieval or update request.
- *Recompilation of application plans:* Whenever an index is created or dropped by using CREATE INDEX or DROP INDEX, the corresponding application plan is marked "invalid" in the catalog by the run-time supervisor. At a subsequent invocation of an invalid plan, the bind is invoked to recompile it on the basis of the then-current set of indexes. This whole process of *automatic binding* is transparent to the user.
- *Authorization checking:* Bind also checks whether the user who invoked bind is allowed to perform the operations involved in the DBRM(s) to be bound. DB2 uses an authorization identifier of the requester to determine whether access privileges are allowed. IMS and CICS supply authorization identifiers and control their use. TSO defaults to the user identifier. Each connecting environment tells DB2 its connection type through the IDENTIFY facility. To prevent unauthorized IDENTIFY requests, an installation can control who may connect to DB2 and what connection type they may use.

9.3 Data Definition in DB2

We discussed the data definition facilities of SQL in Section 7.1. The definition facilities allow the creation, deletion, and alteration (when appropriate) of base tables, views, and indexes. The statements include the following:

For Tables	For Views	For Indexes
CREATE TABLE	CREATE VIEW	CREATE INDEX
ALTER TABLE		ALTER INDEX
DROP TABLE	DROP VIEW	DROP INDEX

There is no ALTER VIEW statement. ALTER INDEX does exist, but it deals with the physical parameters of an index. In Chapter 7 (Figure 7.1) we showed a complete definition of a relational database in terms of CREATE TABLE statements. No ordering of tuples is explicitly imposed on base tables during creation. The ordering of columns is implicit by virtue of the order of the column names in the CREATE TABLE statement.

DB2 supports the concept of null values. Any column can contain a null value unless the definition of that column in CREATE TABLE explicitly specifies **NOT NULL**. A column in which null values are allowed is physically represented in the stored database by two columns: the data column itself, and a hidden, 1-byte-wide indicator column where a value of X'FF' means that the corresponding data value is to be ignored (that is, is a null) and a value of X'00' indicates that the corresponding value is a true (nonnull) value.

9.3.1 *The System Catalog*

In DB2 the tables called *catalog* are accessible via SQL for the database administrator or other authorized users. The DB2 system catalog contains a variety of information including the definitions of base tables, views, indexes, applications, users, access privileges, and application plans. These descriptions are referred to by the system in order to perform certain tasks; for example, during query optimization the bind component accesses the catalog to obtain index information.

DB2 takes a uniform approach to storing the data and the catalog: both are stored as tables. Instead of giving an exhaustive description of the catalog, we will highlight its contents by referring only to a few important tables:

1. SYSTABLES: This has one entry for every base table in the system. The information for each table contains, among other things, its name, the name of its creator, and the total number of columns it contains.

2. SYSCOLUMNS: This contains one entry for every column (attribute) defined in the system. For every column name, the name of the table to which it belongs, its type, and other information are stored. The same column name may appear in multiple tables.

3. SYSINDEXES: This contains for each index the name of the index, the name of the indexed table, the name of the user who created the index, and so on.

Querying Catalog Information. Because the catalog is organized in terms of the tables, it can be queried by using SQL, just as any other table can. For example, consider the query

```
SELECT    NAME
FROM      SYSTABLES
WHERE     COLCOUNT>5
```

This SQL query accesses the catalog to list the names of tables containing more than five columns.

The name of the creator for the catalog tables is SYSIBM. Hence, the complete name of a table like SYSTABLES is referenced as SYSIBM.SYSTABLES. The system automatically creates catalog entries for the catalog tables. Authorized users have access to the catalog for querying. Thus, those having SELECT privilege on system catalogs, if they are not familiar with the structure of the database, can query the catalog to find out more about it.

For example, the query

SELECT TBNAME
FROM   SYSIBM.SYSCOLUMNS
WHERE   NAME='DNUMBER'

lists the names of tables DEPARTMENT and DEPT_LOCATIONS (see Figure 6.5) that contain the column DNUMBER. The availability to the user of the same SQL interface to access meta-data, and not just data, is an important facility of DB2.

Updating Catalog Information. Whereas querying the catalog is informative for users, updating the catalog can be really devastating. For example, a routine SQL update request such as

DELETE
FROM   SYSIBM.SYSTABLES
WHERE   CREATOR=NAVATHE

removes all the tables created by NAVATHE in the catalog. As a result, the definitions of these tables no longer exist, even though the tables themselves do still exist. The tables have essentially become inaccessible! To guard against such situations, UPDATE, DELETE, and INSERT operations are *not* permitted against the tables in the catalog. The corresponding functionality is offered by ALTER TABLE, DROP TABLE, and CREATE TABLE, respectively, which are the data definition statements in SQL. The SQL COMMENT statement serves the useful purpose of storing textual information about a table or a column in the catalog.

For example, referring to the database definition in Figure 7.1, the statement "COMMENT ON COLUMN DEPENDENT.ESSN IS 'If dependent has both parents as employees, the dependent is represented twice.' " is stored in the appropriate REMARKS columns of the entry in the SYSCOLUMNS table.

9.4 Data Manipulation in DB2

SQL is the primary data manipulation language of DB2. In Chapter 7, we discussed a version of SQL that closely corresponds to its implementation in DB2. For quick reference, we offer the following list of some types of retrievals and updates that are supported by DB2 SQL (the numbers refer to example queries in Chapter 7). Newer versions of DB2 may support some of the currently unavailable features:

1. Simple retrievals from tables (Q0).
2. Listing the entire width of the table on rows meeting a prespecified condition (Q1C).
3. Retrievals with elimination of duplicate rows (Q11A).

4. Retrievals with computed values from columns (Q15).

5. Ordering of the result of a query (Q28).

6. Retrievals with conditions involving sets and ranges. These are effected with various types of constructors:

   a. Using IN (Q13).

   b. Using BETWEEN (this is not discussed in Chapter 7): DB2 allows a construction with BETWEEN or NOT BETWEEN; e.g., "WHERE SALARY BETWEEN 50,000 AND 100,000" is permitted.

   c. Using LIKE (Q25, Q26).

   d. Using NULL in comparisons (Q14).

7. Multitable retrievals involving JOINS (Q1, Q2, Q8, and so on).

8. Nested queries: The nesting can be achieved by passing the results of the inner subquery to the outer query, using IN (see Q12, Q4A). In general, queries can be nested to any level. As demonstrated in Q4A, the inner and outer subqueries may refer to the same table.

9. Using EXISTS: Existential quantification (Chapter 8) is supported by connecting two subqueries with EXISTS (Q12B, Q7). Since there is no direct support for universal quantification, it is achieved by means of NOT EXISTS (Q6, Q3A).

10. Using built-in functions: The functions in DB2 SQL include COUNT, SUM, AVG, MAX, and MIN. EXISTS is also considered a built-in function, although, instead of returning a numeric or string value, it returns a truth value.

11. Grouping (Q20, Q21) and conditions on groups (Q22).

12. UNION: It is possible to take a union of the results of subqueries. The results must be union-compatible (see Chapter 6 for definition). The facility to include strings in the SELECT statement comes in handy in conjunction with UNION in DB2. For example, to obtain a list of people who worked more than 40 hours and a list of those who worked on project P5, we could input

```
SELECT    ESSN, 'worked more than 40 hours'
FROM      WORKS_ON
WHERE     HOURS>40
UNION     SELECT    ESSN, 'worked on project P5'
          FROM      WORKS_ON
          WHERE     PNO = P5
```

The results may look like this:

    1000 worked more than 40 hours.
    1002 worked more than 40 hours.
    1003 worked more than 40 hours.
    1002 worked on project P5.
    1007 worked on project P5.

Notice that, if there had been no string constraints in the SELECT clause, the duplicate entity (1002) would have been eliminated.

13. CONTAINS, INTERSECTION, and MINUS: DB2 SQL does *not* support these operators. They must be handled by using EXISTS and NOT EXISTS. Also, OUTER UNION is *not* supported in DB2.

14. Insertion (U1, U1A, U3B).

15. Deletion: Accomplished by using DELETE (U4A–U4D). To delete the definition of the table completely, a DROP TABLE must be used.

16. Modification: Accomplished by using UPDATE (U5, U6).

Updating facilities in DB2 SQL have the shortcoming that, when an INSERT, DELETE, or UPDATE involves a subquery, the nested subquery cannot refer to the table that is the target of the operation. For example, to update the value of hours in all rows to the average of hours, the following type of construction would be desirable, but it is *not* permissible in DB2:

```
UPDATE    WORKS_ON
SET       HOURS=X
WHERE     X =  ( SELECT  AVG(HOURS)
                 FROM    WORKS_ON )
```

(A construction that eliminates X by eliminating the WHERE clause and nests SELECT within UPDATE would work even better.) In actuality, the result is accomplished by first obtaining the average and then using that average to set up another query.

DB2 Version 2 Release 3 (and Version 3) conforms to ISO/ANSI SQL89 specifications. As such, some of the following features of SQL 2 discussed in Chapter 7 may not be available in DB2:

1. The CREATE DOMAIN command (as a means of defining new types to use in referring to value sets).

2. Use of joined tables within the FROM clause (Section 7.2.8).

3. The CREATE ASSERTION statement (Section 7.5), and TRIGGERs with action procedures.

9.4.1 *View Processing*

As discussed in Section 7.4, a view may be defined in DB2 by using CREATE VIEW AS followed by an SQL query. The following points apply to view definition in DB2:

- A view definition may involve one or more tables; it may use joins as well as built-in functions.

- If column names are not specified in the view definition, they may be assigned automatically except when built-in functions, arithmetic expressions, or constraints are used.

- The SQL query used in view definition may not use UNION or ORDER BY.

- Views may be defined on top of existing views.

- When a view is defined by using the clause WITH CHECK OPTION, an INSERT or UPDATE against such a view undergoes a check to confirm that the view-defining predicate is indeed satisfied. For example, in the following instruction, the view-defining predicate is Balance > 500:

CREATE VIEW CREDIT_WORTHY
AS **SELECT** CUST#, Name, Phone#
FROM CUST
WHERE BALANCE>500
WITH CHECK OPTION

Retrievals from Views. Views are treated like any base tables for specifying retrieval queries. Problems can occur when an attribute of the view is a result of a built-in function applied to an underlying base table. For example, consider the following view definition:

CREATE VIEW DEPT_SUMMARY (D#, TOTSALARY)
AS **SELECT** DNO, SUM(SALARY)
FROM EMPLOYEE
GROUP BY DNO

Now let us consider two queries. First, the query

SELECT D#
FROM DEPT_SUMMARY
WHERE TOTSALARY > 100000

is *not* valid, because after conversion of the WHERE clause it looks like WHERE SUM(SALARY) > 100,000, and a built-in function is *not* allowed in a WHERE clause. The correct conversion (can you write what it should be?) contains a HAVING clause, but DB2 cannot come up with such a converted query. Second, the query

SELECT SUM(TOTSALARY)
FROM DEPT_SUMMARY

is *also invalid*, because SUM(TOTSALARY) is equivalent to SUM(SUM(SALARY)), and DB2 does not allow a nested built-in function.

Updating of Views. We discussed view update problems in Section 7.4.3. DB2 has no facility for investigating what a user wants to do when he or she specifies a view update. In addition, there is no facility for analyzing and determining whether a certain update provides a unique set of updates on the base relations. Therefore, DB2 takes a rather restricted approach by allowing updates only on single-relation views. Furthermore, *even for single-relation views*, the following restrictions apply:

• A view is not updatable if (a) its definition involves a built-in function, (b) its definition involves DISTINCT in the SELECT clause, (c) its definition includes a subquery and the FROM clause in that subquery refers to the base table on which the view is defined, or (d) there is a GROUP BY in the view definition.

• If a field of the view is derived from an arithmetic expression or a constant, INSERT or UPDATE is *not* allowed; however, DELETE is allowed (since a corresponding row may be deleted from the base table).

9.4.2 *Use of Embedded SQL*

Embedded SQL has been covered in detail in Section 7.7. Here we give a few details regarding the use of embedded SQL in DB2. As we discussed, SQL can be embedded in PL/1, COBOL, FORTRAN, C, PROLOG, and assembly language programs. The embedding guidelines are as follows:

- Any base tables or views used by the program should be declared by means of a DECLARE statement. This makes the program easy to follow, and it also helps the precompiler perform syntax checks.

- Embedded SQL statements must be preceded by EXEC SQL and are entered at a place where any host language *executable* statement can go.

- Embedded SQL may involve data definition facilities, such as CREATE TABLE and DECLARE CURSOR, that are purely declarative.

- SQL statements may reference host language variables preceded by colons.

- Host variables that receive values from SQL must have data types compatible with the SQL field definitions. Compatibility is defined very loosely; for instance, character strings of varying length or numeric data of binary or decimal nature are considered compatible. DB2 performs appropriate conversions.

- SQL Communication Area (SQLCA) serves as the common feedback area between the application program and DB2. A status indicator SQLCODE contains a numeric value showing the result of a query (for instance, zero indicates successful completion, whereas +100 indicates that the query executed but the result is null).

- No cursor is required for an SQL retrieval query that returns a single tuple or for UPDATE, DELETE, or INSERT statements (except when the CURRENT OF a record is required—see Section 7.7).

- A special utility program called DCLGEN (declarations generator) may be used to construct DECLARE TABLE statements automatically in PL/1 from the CREATE TABLE definitions in SQL. PL/1 or COBOL structures corresponding to the table definitions are also automatically generated.

- The WHENEVER statement, placed out of line, allows the SQLCODE to be checked for a specific condition. Examples are

```
WHENEVER    NOTFOUND PERFORM X;
WHENEVER    SQLERROR GO TO Y;
```

In these examples, NOTFOUND and SQLERROR are system key words corresponding to SQLCODE = 100 and SQLCODE = other than 0 or 100, respectively.

9.4.3 *Referential Integrity*

We defined the notion of referential integrity in Section 6.2.4. It is based on the notion of foreign keys in one relation that depend on the primary keys in some other relations. Simply put, the integrity constraint states that the foreign key may either be null or have a value that refers to a valid value *already present* as a primary key value in some other table. If this constraint is violated during an update operation, the RDBMS is supposed either to reject the update or to take a *corrective action*. These actions were discussed in Section 6.3.

The CREATE TABLE command we introduced in Section 7.1.2, together with the PRIMARY KEY and FOREIGN KEY specification, applies in DB2. DB2 permits the designation of primary and foreign keys in the CREATE TABLE and ALTER TABLE commands. We also discussed the options called SET NULL and CASCADE, which may be used in case of a referential integrity violation (see the schema in Figure 7.1). They are applicable in DB2. There is also a RESTRICT option in DB2. For example, to prevent deletion of a department in which employees are currently employed, the CREATE TABLE EMPLOYEE statement of Figure 7.1(a) can be modified to contain the following specification:

FOREIGN KEY (DNO) **REFERENCES** DEPARTMENT (DNUMBER) **ON DELETE RESTRICT;**

DB2 allows primary keys to be declared NOT NULL or NOT NULL WITH DEFAULT. The latter allows a blank or a zero to be used as a primary key value. With a unique index on the primary key column, if NOT NULL WITH DEFAULT is specified, only one key with a zero or blank value is allowed.

In DB2, certain rules apply to the insertion, deletion, or modification of foreign key values, as well as to deletion or modification of primary key values. Notice that deletion of a foreign key (setting it to a null value) or insertion of a primary key value does *not* cause an integrity constraint violation. The rules can be summarized as follows:

1. A primary key value may be modified if it has no matching foreign key value(s).
2. If a user attempts to delete a primary key value, and a matching foreign key value exists, then:
   a. Deletion is barred if the foreign key constraint is RESTRICT.
   b. Corresponding tuples (in other tables) with matching foreign key values are deleted if the constraint specification is CASCADE.
   c. Corresponding foreign key values are set to null if the constraint specification is SET NULL.
3. Insertion or modification of a foreign key value is allowed only if a matching primary key value exists.

Enforcement of referential integrity constraints according to the preceding rules implies that the system performs internal processing involving the necessary I/O operations, concurrency control locks, and so on. In general, the system uses indexes, if available, for checking. The system does the checking at the Data Manager level without passing the data to the "upper layers" of the system called the Relational Data System. Thus, the process tends to be more efficient than it would be if it were done by an application. For batch operations involving deletion or insertion of a large number of rows, it may be more efficient for an application to enforce referential integrity constraints by taking an appropriate large-scale corrective action, rather than letting the system check the constraint for the deletion or insertion on each row.

Utilities such as LOAD (see Section 9.5.3) provide a means of shutting off the checking of constraints. To shut off constraint checking during batch updates, the ALTER

TABLE facility can be used to drop the foreign key specifications temporarily. Then, after the update, the CHECK DATA utility can be used to make sure that the data is consistent.

The catalog maintains referential integrity information in a variety of places, including the following:

- SYSFOREIGNKEYS contains the foreign key constraint name called RELNAME and the columns that contain the key.
- SYSCOLUMNS.KEYSEQ, FOREIGNKEY indicates whether the column is part of a primary key or part of a foreign key.
- SYSTABLESPACE.STATUS indicates whether the tablespace is in check pending status with respect to integrity constraint checking.

Different RDBMSs provide referential integrity specification and enforcement at different levels of detail. In some systems, these functions are left for the application to provide.

9.5 Storage of Data in DB2★

A database in DB2 is a collection of logically related objects. These objects are the various physically stored tables and indexes. DB2 uses a special terminology to describe the partitioned areas of storage. **Tablespace** refers to the part of secondary storage where tables are stored, and **indexspace** refers to the part where indexes are stored. Figure 9.4 shows a schematic of the DB2 storage structure. The total collection of data in a system consisting of user databases DBX and DBY and the system catalog database are shown.

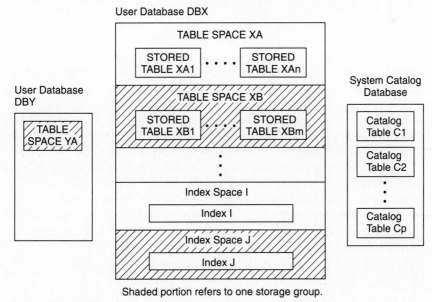

Figure 9.4   Schematic of DB2 storage structure.

A **page** is the basic unit of data transfer between secondary and primary storage. A dynamically extendible collection of pages is called a **space**. Each space belongs to a **storage group,** which is a collection of direct-access storage areas from the same device type. There is no 1:1 correspondence between a database and a storage group. In Figure 9.4, the same storage group contains an indexspace and a tablespace from database DBX and a tablespace from database DBY. A **database** is a unit of **start/stop** that the console operator enables or disables via a START or STOP command. Tables can be moved from one database to another without producing any effect on the users or the user programs.

Storage groups are managed by using VSAM files (entry-sequenced data sets). Within a page, DB2 manages the reorganization without using VSAM at all. DB2 allows the DBA and the system administrator to specify the details of the storage structure, using different statements. For each object described (such as table, tablespace, index, indexspace, database, or storage group), the three statements used uniformly are CREATE, ALTER, and DROP. Users are *not* required to know about the internal storage organization in order to use the system. Although a tablespace is required to store a table, the system assigns a *default* tablespace when the creator of a table fails to specify one. A database is a logical entity whose physical components can be freely moved and manipulated without affecting the integrity of the database. CREATE TABLESPACE identifies the database to which the tablespace belongs.

9.5.1 *Tablespaces and Stored Tables*

A tablespace for a given table is specified in the CREATE TABLE statement for that table. The page size in a tablespace is either 4096 or 32,768 bytes. A tablespace can grow in size if more storage is added from a storage group, to an upper limit of 64 gigabytes. A tablespace is the unit of storage subjected to reorganization or recovery by a console command. Since it would be very inefficient to manage a large tablespace in this way, DB2 allows tablespaces to be partitioned.

A nonpartitioned tablespace is called a **simple tablespace**. In most cases a simple tablespace holds one table. Multiple tables—say, EMPLOYEE and DEPARTMENT—may be stored in the same tablespace to improve performance if they have a high probability of being accessed together. The index, if any, for a table goes into an indexspace. A table with a clustering index (see Chapter 5) is initially loaded into the tablespace in order by the key, using a load utility. Intermittent gaps are included to hold subsequently inserted records. Without a clustering index, records may be loaded in any order. Insertions go to the end of the file.

A **partitioned tablespace** contains one table that is partitioned into (grouped by) value ranges of some partitioning field(s). A clustering index is *required* on those fields and cannot be changed. Thus, the EMPLOYEE table may be partitioned by using a clustering index on DNO. The advantage of partitioned tablespaces is that each partition is treated as a separate storage object for recovery and reorganization and so may be associated with a different storage group.

Partitioning a tablespace provides several advantages for large tables:

- *Improved data availability*: A user can perform normal maintenance on one partition of the table while the rest of the table remains available for utility or SQL processing.

- *Improved utility performance:* A utility job can work on all partitions simultaneously, instead of working on one partition at a time. This can significantly reduce the amount of time needed to complete a utility job.

- *Improved query response time:* When DB2 scans data to answer a query, it can sometimes scan through partitions simultaneously, instead of scanning through the entire tablespace from beginning to end. This improvement is most significant for queries that are complex or that require DB2 to scan large amounts of data.

A **segmented tablespace** is designed to hold more than one table. The available space is divided into groups of pages called *segments*, each having the same size. Each segment contains rows from only one table. To search all the rows for one table, it is unnecessary to scan the entire table space, but only the segments that contain that table. If a table is dropped, its segments immediately become reusable. All the segments must reside in the same user-defined data set or in the same storage group.

Each row in a table constitutes a **stored record**—a string of bytes comprising a prefix containing system control information and up to n stored fields, where n is the number of columns in the base table. Null fields at the end of a varying-length record are *not* stored. Internally, each record has a unique **record id (RID)** within a database; it consists of the page number and the byte offset from the start of the page of a slot that, in turn, contains the record's starting position within the page.

Each **stored field** includes three elements:

- A prefix field that contains the length of data, if it is varying.

- A null indicator prefix that indicates whether the field contains a null value.

- An encoded data value.

DB2 has adopted a strategy of storing all data types in such a way that they are regarded as byte strings and the "compare logical" instruction always yields a correct result (even for data type INTEGER). The interpretation of byte strings is not the concern of the stored data manager. Varying fields occupy only the actual space required. Data compression or encryption is left open to a user-provided procedure, which may be interposed each time a stored record is read or stored. Records *within a page* can be reorganized without changing their RIDs.

9.5.2 *Indexspaces and Indexes*

An indexspace corresponds to the storage occupied by an index. Unlike tablespace, it is automatically created. Index pages are 4096 bytes long, but they can be locked a quarter page at a time. An indexspace that contains a clustering index for a partitioned tablespace is itself considered partitioned.

Indexes are B^+-trees (see Chapter 5) in which each node is a page. The leaf pages are chained together to provide sequential access to the rows (in the tablespace). A table may have one clustered and any number of nonclustered indexes. The leaf pages of a nonclustered index access the rows of the tablespace in an order different from their physical order. Hence, for efficient sequential processing of a table, it is essential to have a clustering index.

9.5.3 *DB2 Utilities*

DB2 provides various utilities that can be used by application developers to manipulate stored data and to avoid writing individual programs. Following is a list of some of the utilities used to manage DB2 "data objects" (as in DB2 terminology):

- **LOAD:** The LOAD utility loads data from basic sequential access method (BSAM) data sets, unloaded SQL/DS tables, and unloaded DB2 tables into DB2 tables. The partition of a tablespace can be replaced by using LOAD REPLACE. The load utility ensures that the data loaded in the table and index is consistent and usable.

- **REORG:** The REORG utility reorganizes tablespaces and tableindexes. It can reestablish free space and the physical sequence described by a clustering index. It reclaims space lost by fragmentation and dropped tables.

- **CHECK:** The CHECK INDEX utility tests whether indexes are consistent with the data they index and issues warning messages when it finds an inconsistency. The CHECK DATA utility searches for referential constraint violations and indicates where they exist. CHECK DATA can be used to delete referential constraint violations.

- **STOSPACE:** The STOSPACE utility reports information about the current use of space by tablespaces and indexspaces in a given DB2 storage group. The STOSPACE utility can update the DB2 catalog with this information.

- **RUNSTATS:** The RUNSTATS utility reports statistical information about tables, tablespaces, and tableindexes. The RUNSTATS utility can update the DB2 catalog with this information. DB2 uses these statistics to optimize the performance of SQL statements (we discuss this as part of query optimization in Chapter 16). Database administrators can use them to assess the status of a particular tablespace or indexspaces.

- **REPAIR:** The REPAIR utility repairs data. The data involved can be a user's own data or data the user would not normally access explicitly, such as index entries.

- **Utilities for Diagnosis:** DB2 also provides a series of utilities to help database application development teams diagnose problems. Among other things, these utilities can create dumps based on DB2 events, verify the integrity of catalog table spaces, and display the contents of recovery logs.

9.6 Internal Features of DB2★

In this section we summarize features of DB2 related to security, authorization, and transaction processing.

9.6.1 *Security and Authorization*

Generally speaking, security of data is addressed at two levels in DB2:

1. The view mechanism can be used to hide sensitive data from unauthorized users.

2. The authorization subsystem, which gives specific privileges to certain users, allows them to grant those privileges to other users selectively and dynamically and to revoke them at will.

The DB2 GRANT and REVOKE commands and the GRANT OPTION feature are discussed in Section 20.2. Specific considerations with respect to these commands that apply in DB2 are given here. The DBA or an appropriate administrator is entrusted with the decisions related to granting specific privileges to users and to revoking those privileges. This policy decision may be conveyed to DB2 in the form of CREATE VIEW or GRANT and REVOKE statements. This information resides in the system catalog. The system's responsibility is to enforce these decisions at run time when retrieval or update operations are attempted; this function is performed by the bind component (see Figure 9.2).

User Identification. Legitimate users are known to DB2 in terms of an authorization ID (identifier) called AUTHID, which is assigned by system administrators. It is the user's responsibility to use that ID when signing onto the system. Users of DB2 sign first on either CICS, IMS, or TSO; that subsystem passes the ID on to DB2. Hence, the responsibility for checking the user ID falls to one of these subsystems. The keyword USER refers to a system variable whose value is an authorization ID. If a certain user is using a view (for retrieval or update), the variable USER contains the ID of the user who is *using* the view and *not* the ID of the one who created it. Thus,

```
CREATE    VIEW    OWN_TABLES
AS                SELECT    *
                  FROM      SYSIBM.SYSTABLES
                  WHERE     CREATOR=USER
```

is a view definition that selects the tables created by the currently logged-in user. SYSIBM.SYSTABLES and CREATOR are keywords in DB2. If a user with ID sbn134 is logged on and executes the query

```
SELECT    *
FROM      OWN_TABLES
```

the USER in the view is bound to sbn134, and the result of the query is a retrieval from SYSTABLES of the entries that were created by sbn134.

Views as a Security Mechanism. It is possible to use views for security purposes by blocking out unwanted data from unauthorized users. By choosing appropriate conditions in the WHERE clause, as well as including only the columns in the SELECT clause that a user is permitted to see, the system designer can keep certain data hidden from a user. Views defined over system catalog information, such as the view illustrated above, permit a user to see only selected parts of the catalog. By applying aggregation functions such as AVG and SUM, the designer may permit a user to see a statistical summary of the base table and not individual values.

In DB2, when a record is INSERTed or UPDATEd through a view, the requirement that the new or updated row in the table must obey the view-defining condition(s) or predicates is *not* enforced. This can sometimes lead to a situation where the new or updated record disappears immediately from the user's view but appears in the underlying base table. To prevent such insertions or deletions, the CHECK OPTION should be used in the view definition.

Grant and Revoke Mechanisms. GRANT and REVOKE statements in SQL determine specific operations granted to or revoked from a user. (The general discussion of Section 20.2 holds here.) Privileges GRANTed to users may be classified into the following broad categories:

- Table and view privileges: Apply to base tables and views.
- Database privileges: Apply to operations with a database (such as creating a table).
- Application plan privileges: Refer to execution of application plans.
- Storage privileges: Deal with the use of certain storage objects, namely tablespaces, storage groups, and buffer pools.
- System privileges: Apply to system operations (such as creating a new database).

There are also certain "bundled" privileges, a term that refers to a tailor-made assortment of privileges:

- SYSADM (system administrator) privilege is the highest-order privilege and includes all possible privileges in the system.
- DBADM (database administrator) privilege on a specific database allows the holder to execute any operation on that database.
- DBACTRL (database control) privilege on a specific database is similar to DBADM except that only control operations, and no data manipulation operations (for example, in SQL), are allowed.
- DBMAINT (database maintenance) privilege on a specific database allows the holder to execute read-only maintenance operations (such as backup) on the database. It is a subset of the DBACTRL privilege.
- SYSOPR (system operator) privilege allows the holder to perform only console operator functions, with no access to the database.

One authorization ID has the SYSADM privilege, and it represents the system administration function. Other IDs may hold the SYSADM privilege, but that privilege may be revoked. PUBLIC is a system keyword and includes all authorization IDs.

A few final notes on the way in which these features are implemented in DB2:

- A major performance benefit results from the fact that many authorization checks can be applied at the time of bind (compile time) instead of being delayed until execution time.
- DB2 works with various accompanying systems; together with them, it provides system security. The individual control mechanisms of MVS, VSAM, IMS, and CICS offer additional protection.
- The entire array of authorization and security mechanisms is optional. Thus, they may be disabled, permitting any user to have full access privileges.

9.6.2 *Transaction Processing*

We discuss the concept of transactions and the problems of recovery and concurrency control related to transaction processing in Chapters 17 through 19. Here we describe only the features specific to DB2 and SQL. Interested readers may want to read the concepts presented in Chapters 17 through 19 prior to reading the rest of this section.

First, let us use the embedded SQL example E2 from Section 7.7 and modify it to demonstrate how an actual transaction is written in DB2. We use PL/1 here, since DB2 does not accept PASCAL. The transaction consists of giving a raise R to an employee with social security number S:

```
TRANS1: PROC OPTIONS (MAIN);
EXEC SQL WHENEVER SQLERROR GO TO ERROR_PROC;
DCL S FIXED DECIMAL (9.0);
DCL R FIXED DECIMAL (7.2);
GET LIST (S, R);
EXEC SQL UPDATE EMPLOYEE
SET SALARY = SALARY + :R
WHERE SSN = :S;
EXEC SQL WHENEVER NOTFOUND GO TO PRINT_MSG;
COMMIT;
GO TO EXIT;
PRINT_MSG: PUT LIST ('EMPLOYEE', S, 'NOT IN DATABASE'); GO TO EXIT;
ERROR_PROC: ROLLBACK;
EXIT: RETURN;
END TRANS1;
```

In this example, the transaction may fail if no employee has social security number S (NOTFOUND) or if SQLCODE returns a negative value (SQLERROR).

We may also insert checks into the program, such as to make sure that the salary is not null, failure of which may cause the transaction to fail. The COMMIT operation signals a successful end of transaction; it instructs the transaction manager to commit the change to the database—that is, to make it permanent, leaving the database in a consistent state. The ROLLBACK operation, on the other hand, signals an unsuccessful end of transaction. It instructs the transaction manager *not* to make any permanent change to the database, but to leave it in the state it was in before this transaction execution began.

A typical transaction may involve a number of retrievals and updates; however, there is *only one* COMMIT operation in the program, so either *all* changes are applied or *none* is applied. The ROLLBACK operation uses the log entries and appropriately restores an updated item to its previous value.

Every DB2 operation is executed in the context of some transaction. This *includes* those entered interactively through DB2I. An application consists of a series of transactions. Transactions *cannot* be nested inside one another.

Commit and Rollback in DB2. The DB2 DBMS is *subordinate* to the transaction manager (IMS, CICS, or TSO) under which it is running. It acts as one of the resource managers providing a service to the transaction manager. Hence, the following points must be noted:

- COMMIT and ROLLBACK are not database operations. They are instructions to the transaction manager, which is not part of the DBMS.

- If a transaction updates an IMS database and a DB2 database, either all of the updates (both to IMS and to DB2) should be committed or all should be rolled back.

- A "synchronization point" (abbreviated *syncpoint*) defines a point at which the database is in a consistent state. The beginning of a transaction, COMMIT, and ROLLBACK each establishes a syncpoint. Nothing else establishes a syncpoint.

- The COMMIT operation signals a successful end of transaction, establishes a syncpoint, commits all updates to the database made since the previous syncpoint, closes all open cursors, and releases all locks (with some exceptions).

- The ROLLBACK operation signals an unsuccessful end of transaction, establishes a syncpoint, closes all open cursors, and releases all locks (with some exceptions).

Explicit Locking Facilities. DB2 supports a number of different lock types. The DB2 user is mainly concerned with the exclusive (X) and shared (S) locks. We discuss different kinds of locks and their uses in Chapter 18. Besides the internal locking mechanism, DB2 provides some explicit locking facilities. A transaction can issue the following statement:

LOCK TABLE <table-name> IN <mode-type> MODE;

The mode-type can be EXCLUSIVE or SHARE. The table-name must be a base table. An exclusive lock allows the transaction to lock the table entirely; the lock is released when the program (not the transaction) terminates. However, a shared lock allows other transactions to acquire a shared lock concurrently on the same table or on part of the table. Until all shared locks are released, no exclusive lock may be acquired on the table or on part of it.

This facility is provided to improve the efficiency of transactions that need to process a single large table (for example, produce a listing of 10,000 employees from the employee table) by dispensing with the locking overhead of issuing and releasing individual record-level locks.

A negative SQLCODE value returned after an SQL operation that requests a lock signifies a deadlock. To break a deadlock, the transaction manager chooses one of the deadlocked transactions as a *victim* and rolls it back automatically, or requests that it roll itself back. This transaction releases all locks and enables some other transaction to proceed.

9.6.3 *Dynamic* SQL

The dynamic SQL facility is designed exclusively for supporting on-line applications. In some applications characterized by a great deal of variability, instead of writing a specific SQL query for every possible condition, a designer may find it much more convenient to construct parts of the SQL query dynamically (at run time) and then to bind and execute them dynamically. This process occurs when SQL statements are interactively entered through DB2I or QMF. However, we will consider how *embedded* SQL statements are constructed dynamically. Without getting into the details of the syntax, we will outline this facility.

A character string is defined in the host language with some initial content:

```
DCL QSTRING CHAR (256) VARYING INITIAL
'DELETE FROM EMPLOYEE WHERE CONDITION'.
```

An SQL variable (SQLVARBL, in this case) is declared, to hold the SQL query at run time:

```
EXEC SQL DECLARE SQLVARBL STATEMENT;
```

The QSTRING is appropriately modified by changing, say, the CONDITION in the WHERE part of the query from the terminal. The following PREPARE statement would cause the QSTRING to be precompiled, bound, converted into object code, and stored in SQLVARBL:

```
EXEC SQL PREPARE SQLVARBL FROM :QSTRING;
```

Finally, the EXECUTE statement actually executes this compiled code:

```
EXEC SQL EXECUTE SQLVARBL;
```

Notice that PREPARE accepts all the different SQL statements except an EXEC SQL. Statements to be prepared may not contain references to host variables. However, they may contain parameters that are denoted by question marks. The parameter values are supplied at run time via program variables. For example, suppose that the WHERE condition in QSTRING in our example were replaced by "SALARY >? AND SALARY <?"; then

```
EXEC SQL EXECUTE SQLVARBL USING :LOW_LIMIT, :UPPER_LIMIT
```

would substitute the values of *program variables* LOW_LIMIT and HIGH_LIMIT in place of the two question marks.

This discussion pertains to SQL statements that do not return any data to the program. When data values have to be retrieved via a SELECT statement that is generated dynamically, the program typically does not know about such variables in advance. Hence, that information is supplied dynamically by using another dynamic SQL statement, called DESCRIBE. The description of expected results is returned in an area called SQL Descriptor Area (SQLDA). Storage is allocated for such variables by using the host programming language. Finally, the result is retrieved a row at a time, using cursor operations. Updating of the results by using the CURRENT option is also supported.

9.6.4 *Features for Performance Improvement*

In this section we mention a few of the facilities present in Version 2.3 of DB2 that help enhance the performance of applications. The following list is not exhaustive:

- Packages: A source program P1, after precompiling, may be converted into a corresponding database request module—say, DBRM P1 (see Figure 9.2). It is possible for two different application plans to use the same DBRM P1. In that case, it is possible to define a package for P1 and include it in both plans. If the access paths to be used for DBRM P1 change, the package can be subjected to the bind process again, which will run *only once* on P1. Eventually, what is executed is an application plan and not the package. But the intermediate package notion prevents duplication of the bind activities for DBRMs that are used in many application plans.

- The OPTIMIZE for n ROWS clause: This can be added to any SQL statement. Its purpose is to override the calculated estimate of rows in the result of a query. By setting n low, users can avoid intermediate buffering of the result (called "list prefetch").

- The Index Lookaside feature: This is useful when the data affected by a query— particularly an update or a join—involves keys located close together. Instead of causing a repetitive scan of the index, this feature forces a scan of the adjacent leaf pages of the index or the range of pages under an intermediate index node, before returning to the root for a top–down scan.

- "SLOW CLOSE" feature: This allows all data sets (including table and/or index) to remain open even after a user has issued the VSAM CLOSE command, until the count of currently open data sets exceeds a certain parameter.

- A CICS-related feature for cursors: We showed in example E2 of Section 7.7 how a cursor must be opened when a corresponding embedded SQL query has to be executed in an application program. If the same cursor is utilized repeatedly, instead of doing multiple OPENS, we can perform multiple FETCHES.

- Hybrid joins: New join algorithms that combine the features of a nested loop join and a sort merge join (discussed in Section 16.3) have been implemented. They also allow a reduction in temporary tables by using a list of matching key values, which corresponds to a join technique called "semijoin."

Features introduced in Versions 2.3 and 3 of DB2 include the following:

- Buffer pools: DB2 permits a user to store data temporarily in buffer pools. This makes data available without I/O processing. Only when this data is changed is it written to the physical disk. Up to 1.6 gigabytes of data can be stored in these buffer pools, known as **virtual buffer pools.** Version 3 of DB2 allows backing of virtual buffer pools with an additional 8 gigabytes of fast-access, expanded storage. The expanded storage comes in units known as *hiperspaces* (for high-performance spaces), 2-gigabyte blocks that are built dynamically when needed for data stored in hiperpools. *Hiperpools* (high-performance pools) are extensions to virtual buffer pools; infrequently accessed data in a virtual buffer pool is moved to its hiperpool with no I/O processing.

- Partition independence: DB2 Version 3 lets an application work on one partition of a tablespace or indexspace without locking the other partitions; partitions are thus independent of each other. It is possible to increase data availability by taking advantage of partition independence in the following ways:

  – Perform maintenance on partitions instead of on whole tablespaces and index-spaces. For example, recover, reorganize, or load one partition, and leave the other available for utility or SQL processing.

– Use the START DATABASE and STOP DATABASE commands on partitions instead of on whole tablespaces. This frees up the other partitions for utility or SQL processing.

9.7 Summary

In this chapter we introduced the various commercial products known as relational database management systems or RDBMSs and surveyed the features of one major product: IBM's DB2. The DB2 system owes its origin to a research prototype called System R of IBM; other RDBMSs similar to it exist in the DB2 family.

We presented the basic modular organization of DB2. Our purpose was not to give an exhaustive description of these modules or DB2 features, but to introduce the reader to a typical set of internal features and to the organizational detail of a commercial RDBMS. We pointed out how DB2 basically supports the SQL language described in Chapter 7, with additional details on its referential integrity specification and enforcement. For the sake of completeness, we also commented on the transaction-processing and security features of DB2, for which detailed concepts are described in Chapters 17 through 20. Finally, we noted a few of the features introduced in the current versions of DB2—Version 2.3 and Version 3.

Appendix to Chapter 9

E. F. Codd, the originator of the relational data model, published a two-part article in *Computerworld* (Codd 1985) that lists 12 rules* for how to determine whether a DBMS is relational and to what extent it is relational [see also Codd (1986)]. We list these here because they provide a very useful yardstick for evaluating a relational system. Codd also mentions that, according to these rules, no fully relational system is available as yet. In particular, rules 6, 9, 10, 11, and 12 are difficult to satisfy.

Rule 1: The Information Rule

All information in a relational database is represented explicitly at the logical level in exactly one way—by values in tables.

Rule 2: Guaranteed Access Rule

Each and every datum (atomic value) in a relational database is guaranteed to be logically accessible by resorting to a combination of table name, primary key value, and column name.

Rule 3: Systematic Treatment of Null Values

Null values (distinct from the empty character string or a string of blank characters and distinct from zero or any other number) are supported in the fully relational DBMS for representing missing information in a systematic way, independent of data type.

---

*The rules in the appendix are derived from two papers by Ted Codd that appeared in *Computerworld*: "Is your DBMS really relational?" (October 14, 1985) and "Does your DBMS run by the rules?" (October 21, 1985), copyright © 1988 by CW Publishing, Inc.

Rule 4: Dynamic On-line Catalog Based on the Relational Model

The database description is represented at the logical level in the same way as ordinary data, so authorized users can apply the same relational language to its interrogation as they apply to regular data.

Rule 5: Comprehensive Data Sublanguage Rule

A relational system may support several languages and various modes of terminal use (for example, the fill-in-the-blanks mode). However, there must be at least one language whose statements are expressible, per some well-defined syntax, as character strings and whose ability to support all of the following items is comprehensive: data definition, view definition, data manipulation (interactive and by program), integrity constraints, and transaction boundaries (begin, commit, and rollback).

Rule 6: View Updating Rule

All views that are theoretically updatable are also updatable by the system.

Rule 7: High-level Insert, Update, and Delete

The capability of handling a base relation or a derived relation as a single operand applies not only to the retrieval of data but also to the insertion, update, and deletion of data.

Rule 8: Physical Data Independence

Application programs and terminal activities remain logically unimpaired whenever any changes are made in either storage representation or access methods.

Rule 9: Logical Data Independence

Application programs and terminal activities remain logically unimpaired when information-preserving changes of any kind that theoretically permit unimpairment are made to the base tables.

Rule 10: Integrity Independence

Integrity constraints specific to a particular relational database must be definable in the relational data sublanguage and storable in the catalog, not in the application programs.

A minimum of the following two integrity constraints must be supported:

1. Entity integrity: No component of a primary key is allowed to have a null value.
2. Referential integrity: For each distinct nonnull foreign key value in a relational database, there must exist a matching primary key value from the same domain.

Rule 11: Distribution Independence

A relational DBMS has distribution independence. Distribution independence implies that users should not have to be aware of whether a database is distributed.

Rule 12: Nonsubversion Rule

If a relational system has a low-level (single-record-at-a-time) language, that low-level language cannot be used to subvert or bypass the integrity rules or constraints expressed in the higher-level (multiple-records-at-a-time) relational language.

There is a rider to these 12 rules known as **Rule Zero:** "For any system that is claimed to be a relational database management system, that system must be able to manage data entirely through its relational capabilities."

On the basis of the above rules, there is no fully relational DBMS available today.

Selected Bibliography

Several books are dedicated to describing the DB2 system. These include Date & White (1988), Martin, Chapman & Leben (1989), and Wiorkowski & Kull (1992). Chamberlin et al. (1981) provides a history of System R, the precursor to DB2 system, and the SQL/Data System. Blasgen et al. (1981) gives an architectural overview of System R. Codd (1990) describes the relational model, Version 2, where he points out 18 categories of features of the relational model and their implementation in RDBMSs. The DB2 system is described in various manuals, including the following:

GC26-4886	General Information
SC26-4888	Administration Guide
SC26-4889	Application Programming and SQL Guide
SC26-4891	Command and Utility Reference
LY27-9603	Diagnosis Guide and Reference
GC26-4886	General Information
GC26-4887	Licensed Program Specifications
GC26-4894	Master Index
SC26-4892	Messages and Codes
SX26-3801	Reference Summary
SC26-4890	SQL Reference
SC26-3077	Usage of Distributed Data Management Commands

Other manuals of interest in the DBL library include the following:

GC26-4341	SAA: An Overview
SC26-4650	Planning for Distributed Relational Database
GH24-5065	SQL/DS Concepts and Facilities
SO4G-1022	ES OS/2 Database Manager Programming Guide and Reference

Advanced facilities in DB2 are discussed by Lucyk (1993). Chang et al. (1988) provides an overview of the OS/2 Data Manager. The SAA architecture is described in IBM (1992). Mohan (1993) gives an overview of the IBM RDBMS products. Several periodicals are dedicated to the DB2 system. One of the more technical ones is a monthly called the *DB2 Journal*.

CHAPTER 10

The Network
Data Model and
the IDMS System

In Chapters 6 through 9 we discussed the relational data model, its languages, and a relational DBMS. We now discuss the network model, which, together with the hierarchical data model, was a major data model for implementing numerous commercial DBMSs. We will discuss the hierarchical model in the next chapter. Historically, the network model structures and language constructs were defined by the CODASYL (Conference on Data Systems Languages) committee, so it is often referred to as the CODASYL network model. More recently, ANSI (American National Standards Institute) made a recommendation for a network definition language (NDL) standard [ANSI 1984].

The original network model and language were presented in the CODASYL Data Base Task Group's 1971 report [DBTG 1971]; this is sometimes called the DBTG model. Revised reports in 1978 and 1981 incorporated more recent concepts. In this chapter, rather than concentrating on the details of a particular CODASYL report, we present the general concepts behind network-type databases and use the term **network model** rather than CODASYL model or DBTG model. We present the network model concepts independently of the entity-relationship, relational, or hierarchical data models. We show in Section 10.4 how a network model schema may be designed, starting from the ER model.

We will use PASCAL as the host language when we present the commands for a network database language, to be consistent with the rest of the book. The original CODASYL/DBTG report used COBOL as the host language. Regardless of the host programming language, the basic database manipulation commands of the network model remain the same.

In Section 10.1 we discuss record types and set types, which are the two main data-structuring constructs in the network model. Section 10.2 discusses network model constraints, and Section 10.3 presents a data definition language (DDL) for the network model. Section 10.4 shows how a network schema can be designed by mapping a conceptual ER schema into the network model. In Section 10.5 we present a data manipulation language for network databases which is a record-at-a-time language. Such languages contrast with the high-level relational languages discussed in Chapters 6 through 9, which specify a set of records for retrieval in a single command. Traditionally, the network and hierarchical models are associated with low-level record-at-a-time languages. Section 10.6 gives an overview of the IDMS commercial network DBMS.

It is possible to skip some or all of Sections 10.4 through 10.6 if a less detailed presentation of the network model is desired.

10.1 Network Database Structures

There are two basic data structures in the network model: records and sets. We discuss records and record types in Section 10.1.1. In Section 10.1.2 we introduce sets and their basic properties. Section 10.1.3 presents special types of sets. We show how sets are represented and implemented in Section 10.1.4. Finally, we show how 1:1 and M:N relationships are represented in the network model in Section 10.1.5.

10.1.1 Records, Record Types, and Data Items

Data is stored in **records**; each record consists of a group of related data values. Records are classified into **record types,** where each record type describes the structure of a group of records that store the same type of information. We give each record type a name, and we also give a name and format (data type) for each **data item** (or attribute) in the record type. Figure 10.1 shows a record type STUDENT with data items NAME, SSN, ADDRESS, MAJORDEPT, and BIRTHDATE. The **format** (or **data type**) of each data item is also shown in Figure 10.1.

The network model allows complex data items to be defined. A **vector** is a data item that may have multiple values in a single record.* A **repeating group** allows inclusion of a set of composite values for a data item in a single record.** For example, if we want to include the transcript of each student within each student record, we can define a TRANSCRIPT repeating group for the student record; TRANSCRIPT consists of the four data items YEAR, COURSE, SEMESTER, and GRADE, as shown in Figure 10.2. The repeating group is not essential to the modeling capability of the network model, since we can represent the same situation with two record types and a set type (see Section 10.1.2). Repeating groups can be nested several levels deep.

All the above types of data items are called **actual data items,** because their values are actually stored in the records. **Virtual** (or **derived**) **data items** can also be defined. The value of a virtual data item is not actually stored in a record; instead, it is derived from the actual data items by using some procedure that is defined specifically for this purpose. For example, we can declare a virtual data item AGE for the record type shown

---

*This corresponds to a *simple* multivalued attribute in the terminology of Chapter 3.
**This corresponds to a *composite* multivalued attribute in the terminology of Chapter 3.

STUDENT				
NAME	SSN	ADDRESS	MAJORDEPT	BIRTHDATE

data item name	format
NAME	CHARACTER 30
SSN	CHARACTER 9
ADDRESS	CHARACTER 40
MAJORDEPT	CHARACTER 10
BIRTHDATE	CHARACTER 9

Figure 10.1 A record type STUDENT.

in Figure 10.1 and write a procedure to calculate the value of AGE from the value of the actual data item BIRTHDATE in each record.

A typical database application has numerous record types—from a few to a few hundred. To represent relationships between records, the network model provides the modeling construct called *set type*, which we discuss next.

10.1.2 Set Types and Their Basic Properties

A **set type** is a description of a 1:N relationship between two record types. Figure 10.3 shows how we represent a set type diagrammatically as an arrow. This type of diagrammatic representation is called a **Bachman diagram**. Each set type definition consists of three basic elements:

• A name for the set type.
• An owner record type.
• A member record type.

The set type in Figure 10.3 is called MAJOR_DEPT; DEPARTMENT is the **owner** record type, and STUDENT is the **member** record type. This represents the 1:N relationship

STUDENT					
NAME	· · ·	TRANSCRIPT			
		YEAR	COURSE	SEMESTER	GRADE

Smith	· · ·	1984	COSC3320	Fall	A
		1984	COSC3340	Fall	A
		1984	MATH312	Fall	B
		1985	COSC4310	Spring	C
		1985	COSC4330	Spring	B

Figure 10.2 A repeating group TRANSCRIPT.

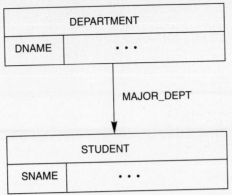

Figure 10.3   The set type MAJOR_DEPT (which is MANUAL OPTIONAL).

between academic departments and students majoring in those departments. In the database itself, there will be many **set occurrences** (or **set instances**) corresponding to a set type. Each instance relates one record from the owner record type—a DEPARTMENT record in our example—to the set of records from the member record type related to it—the set of STUDENT records for students who major in that department. Hence, each set occurrence is composed of:

- One owner record from the owner record type.
- A number of related member records (zero or more) from the member record type.

A record from the member record type *cannot exist in more than one set occurrence* of a particular set type. This maintains the constraint that a set type represents a 1:N relationship. In our example a STUDENT record can be related to at most one major DEPARTMENT and hence is a member of at most one set occurrence of the MAJOR_DEPT set type.

A set occurrence can be identified either by the *owner record* or by *any of the member records*. Figure 10.4 shows four set occurrences (instances) of the MAJOR_DEPT set type. Notice that each set instance *must* have one owner record but can have any number of member records (**zero** or more). Hence, we usually refer to a set instance by its owner record. The four set instances in Figure 10.4 can be referred to as the 'Computer Science', 'Mathematics', 'Physics', and 'Geology' sets. It is customary to use a different representation of a set instance (Figure 10.5) where the records of the set instance are shown linked together by pointers, which corresponds to a commonly used technique for implementing sets.

In the network model, a set instance is *not identical* to the concept of a set in mathematics. There are two principal differences:

- The set instance has one *distinguished element*—the owner record—whereas in a mathematical set there is no such distinction among the elements of a set.
- In the network model, the member records of a set instance are *ordered*, whereas order of elements is immaterial in a mathematical set. Hence, we can refer to the

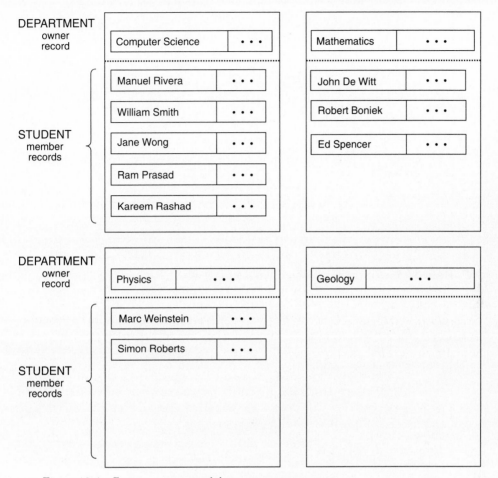

Figure 10.4 Four set instances of the set type MAJOR_DEPT.

first, second, i^{th}, and last member records in a set instance. Figure 10.5 shows an alternate "linked" representation of an instance of the set MAJOR_DEPT. In Figure 10.5 the record of 'Manuel Rivera' is the first STUDENT (member) record in the 'Computer Science' set, and that of 'Kareem Rashad' is the last member record. The set of the network model is sometimes referred to as an **owner-coupled set** or **co-set,** to distinguish it from a mathematical set.

10.1.3 *Special Types of Sets*

Two special types of sets are allowed in the CODASYL network model: SYSTEM-owned sets and multimember sets. A third type, called a recursive set, was not allowed in the original CODASYL report. We discuss these three special types of sets next.

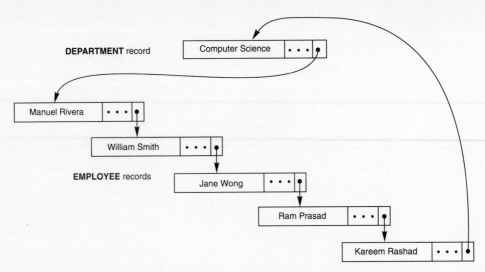

Figure 10.5   Alternate representation of a set instance.

System-owned (Singular) Sets.   A **system-owned** set is a set with no owner record type; instead, the system* is the owner. We can think of the system as a special "virtual" owner record type with only a single record occurrence. System-owned sets serve two main purposes in the network model:

- They provide *entry points* into the database via the records of the specified member record type. Processing can commence by accessing members of that record type, and then retrieving related records via other sets.

- They can be used to *order* the records of a given record type by using the set ordering specifications. By specifying several system-owned sets on the same record type, a user can access its records in different orders.

A system-owned set allows the processing of records of a record type by using the regular set operations that we will discuss in Section 10.5.3. This type of set is called a **singular** set because there is only one set occurrence of it. The diagrammatic representation of the system-owned set ALL_DEPTS is shown in Figure 10.6(a), which allows DEPARTMENT records to be accessed in order of some field—say, NAME—with an appropriate set-ordering specification.

Multimember Sets.   **Multimember** sets are used in instances where member records of a set may be of *more than one* record type. They are not supported in most commercial network DBMSs. The member records of a set occurrence of a multimember set type may include records from any combination of member record types. A multimember set using three member record types is shown in Figure 10.6(b). The constraint that each member record may appear in at most one set occurrence is still valid, to enforce the 1:N nature of the relationship.

---

*By *system*, we mean the DBMS software.

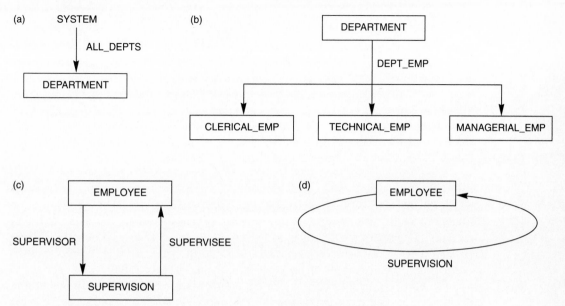

Figure 10.6   Special types of sets. (a) A singular (SYSTEM-owned) set. (b) A
multimember set. (c) The recursive set SUPERVISION represented
by using a linking record type. (d) Prohibited recursive set
representation.

Recursive Sets. A set type in which the same record type plays the role of both owner
and member is called a **recursive** set. An example of a recursive 1:N relationship that
can be represented by a recursive set is the SUPERVISION relationship, which relates a
supervisor employee to the list of employees directly under his or her supervision. In this
relationship the EMPLOYEE record type plays both the roles: that of the owner record type
(the supervisor employee), and that of the member record type (the supervisee
employees).

　　　Recursive sets were prohibited in the original CODASYL model because it is difficult
to process them using the CODASYL data manipulation language (DML). The DML (see
Section 10.5.2) assumes that a record belongs to a single set occurrence of each set type.
With recursive sets, the same record can be an owner of one set occurrence and a member of another, both set occurrences being of the same set type. Because of this problem,
it has become customary to represent a recursive set in the network model by creating
an additional **linking** (or **dummy**) record type. The same technique is used to represent
M:N relationships, as we shall see in Section 10.1.5. Figure 10.6(c) shows the representation of the SUPERVISION relationship, using two set types and a linking record type.
In Figure 10.6(c) the SUPERVISOR set type is really a 1:1 relationship; that is, at most
one SUPERVISION member record will exist in each SUPERVISOR set occurrence. We can
think of each SUPERVISION linking record as representing an employee *in the role of super-*
visor. The direct recursive set representation—usually prohibited in the network
model—is shown in Figure 10.6(d). Most network DBMS implementations do not allow
the same record type to participate as both owner and member in the same set type.

10.1.4 *Stored Representations of Set Instances*

A set instance is commonly represented as a **ring (circular linked list)** linking the owner record and all member records of the set, as shown in Figure 10.5. This is also sometimes called a **circular chain**. The ring representation is symmetric with respect to all records; hence, to distinguish between the owner record and the member records, the DBMS includes a special field, called the **type field**, that has a distinct value (assigned by the DBMS) for each record type. By examining the type field, the system can tell whether the record is the owner of the set instance or is one of the member records. This type field is hidden from the user and is used only by the DBMS.

In addition to the type field, a record type is automatically assigned a **pointer field** by the DBMS for *each set type in which it participates as owner or member*. This pointer can be considered to be *labeled* with the set type name to which it corresponds; hence, the system internally maintains the correspondence between these pointer fields and their set types. A pointer is usually called the **NEXT** pointer in a member record and the **FIRST** pointer in an owner record because these point to the next and first member records, respectively. In our example of Figure 10.5, each student record has a NEXT pointer to the next STUDENT record within the set occurrence. The NEXT pointer of the *last member record* in a set occurrence points back to the owner record. If a record of the member record type does not participate in any set instance, its NEXT pointer has a special **nil** pointer. If a set occurrence has an owner but no member records, the FIRST pointer points right back to the owner record itself or it can be **nil**.

The preceding representation of sets is one method for implementing set instances. In general, a DBMS can implement sets in various ways. However, the chosen representation must allow the DBMS to do all the following operations:

- Given an owner record, find all member records of the set occurrence.
- Given an owner record, find the first, i^{th}, or last member record of the set occurrence. If no such record exists, give an indication of that fact.
- Given a member record, find the next (or previous) member record of the set occurrence. If no such record exists, give an indication of that fact.
- Given a member record, find the owner record of the set occurrence.

The circular linked list representation allows the system to do all of the preceding operations with varying degrees of efficiency. In general, a network database schema has many record types and set types, so a record type may participate as owner and member in numerous set types. For example, in the network schema that appears later as Figure 10.9, the EMPLOYEE record type participates as owner in four set types—MANAGES, IS_A_SUPERVISOR, E_WORKSON, and DEPENDENTS_OF—and participates as member in two set types—WORKS_FOR and SUPERVISEES. In the circular linked list representation, six additional pointer fields are added to the EMPLOYEE record type. However, no confusion arises, because each pointer is labeled by the system and plays the role of FIRST or NEXT pointer for a specific set type.

Other representations of sets allow more efficient implementation of some of the operations on sets noted previously. We briefly mention five of them here:

- Doubly linked circular list representation: Besides the NEXT pointer in a member record type, a **PRIOR** pointer points back to the prior member record of the set occurrence. The PRIOR pointer of the first member record can point back to the owner record.

- Owner pointer representation: This can be used in combination with either the linked list or the doubly linked list representation. For each set type an additional **OWNER** pointer is included in the member record type. The OWNER pointer points directly to the owner record of the set.

- Contiguous member records: Rather than being linked by pointers, the member records are actually placed in contiguous physical locations, typically following the owner record.

- Pointer arrays: An array of pointers is stored with the owner record. The ith element in the array points to the ith member record of the set instance. This is usually implemented in conjunction with the owner pointer.

- Indexed representation: A small index is kept with the owner record *for each set occurrence.* An index entry contains the value of a key indexing field and a pointer to the actual member record that has this field value. The index may be implemented as a linked list chained by next and prior pointers (the IDMS system allows this option; see Section 10.6).

These representations support the network DML operations with varying degrees of efficiency. Ideally, the programmer should not be concerned with how sets are implemented, but only with confirming that they are implemented correctly by the DBMS. However, in practice, the programmer can benefit from the particular implementation of sets, to write more efficient programs. Most systems allow the database designer to choose from among several options for implementing each set type, using a MODE statement to specify the chosen representation.

10.1.5 *Using Sets to Represent 1:1 and M:N Relationships*

A set type represents a 1:N relationship between two record types. This means that *a record of the member record type can appear in only one set occurrence.* This constraint is automatically enforced by the DBMS in the network model.

To represent a 1:1 relationship between two record types by using a set type, we must restrict each set occurrence to having *a single member record.* The network model does not provide for automatically enforcing this constraint, so the *programmer* must check that the constraint is not violated every time a member record is inserted into a set occurrence.

An M:N relationship between two record types cannot be represented by a single set type. For example, consider the WORKS_ON relationship between EMPLOYEEs and PROJECTs. Assume that an employee can be working on several projects simultaneously and that a project typically has several employees working on it. If we try to represent this by a set type, neither the set type in Figure 10.7(a) nor that in Figure 10.7(b) will represent the relationship correctly. Figure 10.7(a) enforces the incorrect constraint that a PROJECT record is related to only one EMPLOYEE record, whereas Figure 10.7(b) enforces the incorrect constraint that an EMPLOYEE record is related to only one PROJECT record. Using both set types E_P and P_E simultaneously, as in Figure 10.7(c), leads to the problem of enforcing the constraint that P_E and E_P are mutually consistent inverses, plus the problem of dealing with relationship attributes.

The correct method for representing an M:N relationship in the network model is to use two set types and an additional record type, as shown in Figure 10.7(d). This additional record type—WORKS_ON, in our example—is called a **linking** (or **dummy**) record type. Each record of the WORKS_ON record type must be owned by one EMPLOYEE record through the E_W set and by one PROJECT record through the P_W set and serves to relate these two owner records. This is illustrated conceptually in Figure 10.7(e).

Figure 10.7(f) shows an example of individual record and set occurrences in the linked list representation corresponding to the schema in Figure 10.7(d). Each record of the WORKS_ON record type has two NEXT pointers: the one marked NEXT(E_W) points to the next record in an instance of the E_W set, and the one marked NEXT(P_W) points

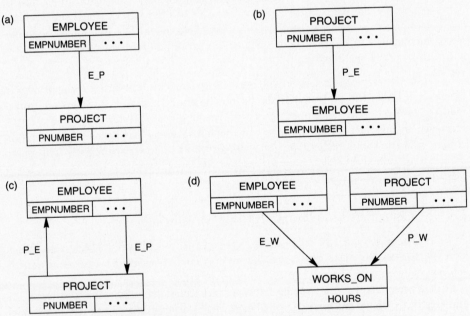

Figure 10.7   Representing M:N relationships using sets. (a)–(c) Incorrect representations of M:N relationship. (d) Correct representation of an M:N relationship using a linking (dummy) record type.
(*continued on next page*)

(e)

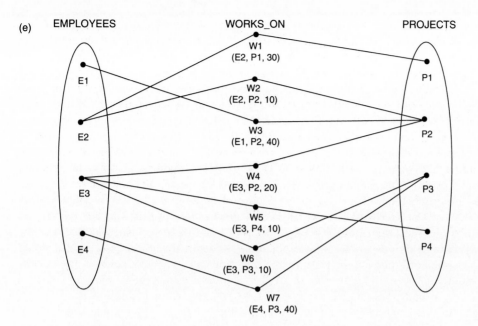

(f)

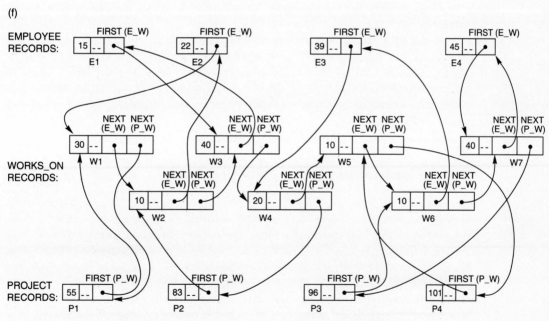

Figure 10.7 *(continued)* (e) Representing some occurrences of an M:N relationship with "linking occurrences." (f) Some occurrences of the set types E_W and P_W and the linking record type WORKS_ON corresponding to the M:N relationship instances shown in Figure 10.7(e).

to the next record in an instance of the P_W set. Each WORKS_ON record relates its two owner records. Each WORKS_ON record also contains the number of hours per week that an employee works on a project. The same occurrences in Figure 10.7(f) are shown in Figure 10.7(e) by displaying the W records individually, without showing the pointers.

To find all projects that a particular employee works on, we start at the EMPLOYEE record and then trace through all WORKS_ON records owned by that EMPLOYEE, using the FIRST(E_W) and NEXT(E_W) pointers. At each WORKS_ON record in the set occurrence, we find its owner PROJECT record by following the NEXT(P_W) pointers until we find a record of type PROJECT. For example, for the E2 EMPLOYEE record, we follow the FIRST(E_W) pointer in E2 leading to W1, the NEXT(E_W) pointer in W1 leading to W2, and the NEXT(E_W) pointer in W2 leading back to E2. Hence, W1 and W2 are identified as the member records in the set occurrence of E_W owned by E2. By following the NEXT(P_W) pointer in W1, we reach P1 as its owner; and by following the NEXT(P_W) pointer in W2 (and through W3 and W4), we reach P2 as its owner. Notice that the existence of direct OWNER pointers for the P_W set in the WORKS_ON records would have simplified the process of identifying the owner PROJECT record of each WORKS_ON record.

In a similar fashion, we can find all EMPLOYEE records related to a particular PROJECT. In this case the existence of owner pointers for the E_W set would simplify processing. All this pointer tracing is done *automatically by the DBMS*; the programmer has DML commands for directly finding the owner or the next member, as we shall discuss in Section 10.5.3.

Notice that we could represent the M:N relationship as in Figure 10.7(a) (or 10.7(b)) if we were allowed to duplicate PROJECT (or EMPLOYEE) records. In Figure 10.7(a) a PROJECT record would be duplicated as many times as there were employees working on the project. However, duplicating records creates problems in maintaining consistency among the duplicates whenever the database is updated, and it is not recommended in general.

10.2 Constraints in the Network Model

In explaining the network model so far, we have already discussed "structural" constraints that govern how record types and set types are structured. In the present section we discuss "behavioral" constraints that apply to (the behavior of) the members of sets when insertion, deletion, and update operations are performed on sets. Several constraints may be specified on set membership. These are usually divided into two main categories, called **insertion options** and **retention options** in CODASYL terminology. These constraints are determined during database design by knowing how a set is required to *behave* when member records are inserted or when owner or member records are deleted. The constraints are specified to the DBMS when we declare the database structure, using the data definition language (see Section 10.3). Not all combinations of the constraints are possible. We first discuss each type of constraint and then give the allowable combinations.

10.2.1 *Insertion Options (Constraints) on Sets*

The insertion constraints—or options, in CODASYL terminology—on set membership specify what is to happen when we insert a new record in the database that is of a member record type. A record is inserted by using the STORE command (see Section 10.5.4). There are two options:

- AUTOMATIC: The new member record is *automatically connected* to an appropriate* set occurrence when the record is inserted.

- MANUAL: The new record is not connected to any set occurrence. If desired, the programmer can explicitly *(manually)* connect the record to a set occurrence subsequently, by using the CONNECT command.

For example, consider the MAJOR_DEPT set type of Figure 10.3. In this situation we can have a STUDENT record that is not related to any department through the MAJOR_DEPT set (if the corresponding student has not declared a major). We should therefore declare the MANUAL insertion option, meaning that when a member STUDENT record is inserted in the database it is not automatically related to a DEPARTMENT record through the MAJOR_DEPT set. The database user may later insert the record "manually" into a set instance when the corresponding student declares a major department. This manual insertion is accomplished by using an update operation called CONNECT, submitted to the database system, as we shall see in Section 10.5.4.

The AUTOMATIC option for set insertion is used in situations where we want to insert a member record into a set instance automatically upon storage of that record in the database. We must specify a criterion for *designating the set instance* of which each new record becomes a member. As an example, consider the set type shown in Figure 10.8(a), which relates each employee to the set of dependents of that employee. We can declare the EMP_DEPENDENTS set type to be AUTOMATIC, with the condition that a new DEPENDENT record with a particular EMPSSN value is inserted into the set instance owned by the EMPLOYEE record with the same SSN value. The DBMS locates the EMPLOYEE record such that EMPLOYEE.SSN = DEPENDENT.EMPSSN and connects the new DEPENDENT record automatically to that set instance. Notice that the SSN field should be declared so that no two EMPLOYEE records have the same SSN; otherwise, more than one set instance is identified by the above condition. In Section 10.3.2 we discuss other criteria for automatically identifying and selecting a set occurrence.

10.2.2 *Retention Options (Constraints) on Sets*

The retention constraints—or options, in CODASYL terminology—specify whether a record of a member record type can exist in the database on its own or whether it must always be related to an owner as a member of some set instance. There are three retention options:

- OPTIONAL: A member record can exist on its own *without being* a member in any occurrence of the set. It can be connected and disconnected to set occurrences at

---

*The appropriate set occurrence is determined by a specification that is part of the definition of the set type, the SET OCCURRENCE SELECTION, which we discuss in Section 10.3.2 as a part of the network DDL.

(a)
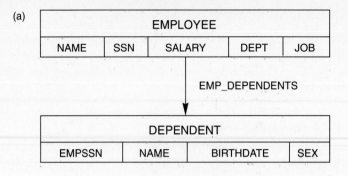

(b)
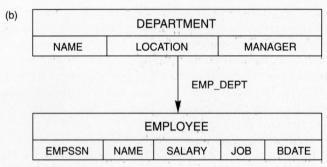

Figure 10.8   Different set options. (a) An AUTOMATIC FIXED set type
EMP_DEPENDENTS. (b) An AUTOMATIC MANDATORY set type
EMP_DEPT.

will by means of the CONNECT and DISCONNECT commands of the network DML
(see Section 10.5.4).

- MANDATORY: A member record *cannot* exist on its own; it must *always* be a member in some set occurrence of the set type. It can be reconnected in a single operation from one set occurrence to another by means of the RECONNECT command of the network DML (see Section 10.5.4).

- FIXED: As in MANDATORY, a member record *cannot* exist on its own. Moreover, once it is inserted in a set occurrence, it is *fixed*; it *cannot* be reconnected to another set occurrence.

We now illustrate the differences among these options by examples showing when each option should be used. First, consider the MAJOR_DEPT set type of Figure 10.3. To provide for the situation where we may have a STUDENT record that is not related to any department through the MAJOR_DEPT set, we declare the set to be OPTIONAL. In Figure 10.8(a) EMP_DEPENDENTS is an example of a FIXED set type, because we do not expect a dependent to be moved from one employee to another. In addition, every DEPENDENT record must be related to some EMPLOYEE record at all times. In Figure 10.8(b) a MANDATORY set EMP_DEPT relates an employee to the department the

Table 10.1 Set Insertion and Retention Options

| | | Retention Option | | |
		OPTIONAL	MANDATORY	FIXED
Insertion Option	MANUAL	Application program is in charge of inserting member record into set occurence. Can CONNECT, DISCONNECT, RECONNECT	Not very useful.	Not very useful.
	AUTOMATIC	DBMS inserts a new member record into a set occurrence automatically. Can CONNECT, DISCONNECT, RECONNECT.	DBMS inserts a new member record into a set occurrence automatically. Can RECONNECT member to a different owner.	DBMS inserts a new member record into a set occurrence automatically. *Cannot* RECONNECT member to a different owner.

employee works for. Here, every employee must be assigned to exactly one department at all times; however, an employee can be reassigned from one department to another.

In general, the MANDATORY and FIXED options are used in situations where a member record should not exist in the database without being related to an owner through some set occurrence. For FIXED, the additional requirement of never moving a member record from one set instance to another is enforced. By using an appropriate insertion/ retention option, the DBA is able to specify the behavior of a set type as a constraint, which is then *automatically* held good by the system.

10.2.3 Combinations of Insertion and Retention Options

Not all combinations of insertion and retention options are useful. For example, FIXED and MANDATORY retention options imply that a member record should always be related to an owner, so they should be used with the AUTOMATIC insertion option. While any combination of these options is technically valid, only three combinations normally make sense, and most implementations of the network model allow only these "reasonable" combinations: AUTOMATIC-FIXED, AUTOMATIC-MANDATORY, and MANUAL-OPTIONAL.* We can also think of applications where an AUTOMATIC-OPTIONAL set might be useful—namely, when the member record is automatically connected to an owner if a particular owner is specified, but otherwise the new member record is not connected to any set instance. These combinations are summarized in Table 10.1.

---

*The original CODASYL DBTG report did not place these restrictions on possible combinations of options.

10.2.4 *Set Ordering Options*

The member records in a set instance can be ordered in various ways. Order can be based on an ordering field or controlled by the time sequence of insertion of new member records. The available options for ordering can be summarized as follows:

- Sorted by an ordering field: The values of one or more fields from the member record type are used to order the member records within *each set occurrence* in ascending or descending order. The system maintains the order when a new member record is connected to the set instance by automatically inserting the record in its correct position in the order.

- System default: A new member record is inserted in an arbitrary position determined by the system.

- First or last: A new member record becomes the first or last record in the set occurrence *at the time it is inserted.* Hence, this corresponds to having the member records in a set instance stored in chronological (or reverse chronological) order.

- Next or prior: The new member record is inserted after or before the current record of the set occurrence. This will become clearer when we discuss currency indicators in Section 10.5.1.

The desired options for insertion, retention, and ordering are specified when the set type is declared in the data definition language. Details of declaring record types and set types are discussed in Section 10.3 in connection with the network model data definition language (DDL).

10.3 Data Definition in the Network Model

After designing a network database schema, we must declare all the record types, set types, data item definitions, and schema constraints to the network DBMS. The network DDL is used for this purpose. Each network DBMS has a slightly different syntax and options included in its DDL, so rather than presenting the exact syntax of the CODASYL DBTG DDL, we will concentrate on understanding the different concepts and options available in most network DBMSs.

10.3.1 *Record Type and Data Item Declarations*

Network DDL declarations for the record types of the COMPANY schema shown in Figure 10.9 are shown in Figure 10.10(a). Each record type is given a name by using the **RECORD NAME IS** clause. A format (data type) is specified for each of its data items (fields), along with any constraints on the data items. (The f.k. and * markings in Figure 10.9 are explained in Section 10.4, when we discuss ER-to-network mapping.) The usual data types available depend on the types definable in the host programming language. We

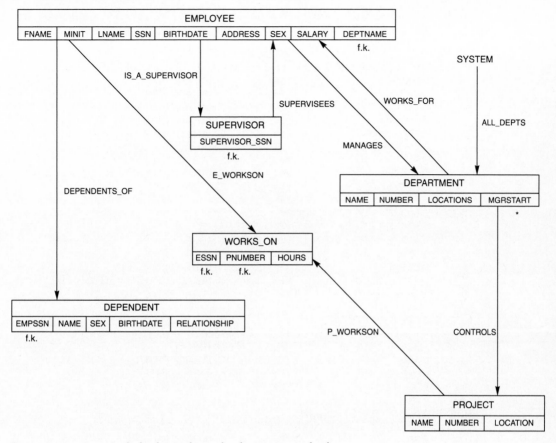

Figure 10.9 A network database schema for the COMPANY database.

will assume that character strings, integer numbers, and formatted numbers are available.*

To specify key constraints on fields, or on combinations of fields that cannot have the same value in more than one record of a record type, the **DUPLICATES ARE NOT ALLOWED** clause is used. For example, in Figure 10.10(a), SSN is a key of the EMPLOYEE record type, and the combination (ESSN, PNUMBER) is a key of the WORKS_ON record type. Additional constraints available on fields include a constraint on the values a numeric field can take, using the **CHECK** clause. For example, we may specify that a numeric field cannot have a value greater than some number.

---

*Formatted numbers are usually specified by two numbers (i,j), where i is the total number of digits in the number and j is the number of digits after the decimal point; they are of the same size as a character string of size i+1 (one character is needed for the decimal point). A format of (7,2) permits numbers of the form ddddd.dd, where each d stands for a decimal digit.

```
SCHEMA NAME IS COMPANY

RECORD NAME IS EMPLOYEE
    DUPLICATES ARE NOT ALLOWED FOR SSN
    DUPLICATES ARE NOT ALLOWED FOR FNAME, MINIT, LNAME
        FNAME            TYPE IS      CHARACTER 15
        MINIT            TYPE IS      CHARACTER 1
        LNAME            TYPE IS      CHARACTER 15
        SSN              TYPE IS      CHARACTER 9
        BIRTHDATE        TYPE IS      CHARACTER 9
        ADDRESS          TYPE IS      CHARACTER 30
        SEX              TYPE IS      CHARACTER 1
        SALARY           TYPE IS      CHARACTER 10
        DEPTNAME         TYPE IS      CHARACTER 15

RECORD NAME IS DEPARTMENT
    DUPLICATES ARE NOT ALLOWED FOR NAME
    DUPLICATES ARE NOT ALLOWED FOR NUMBER
        NAME             TYPE IS      CHARACTER 15
        NUMBER           TYPE IS      NUMERIC INTEGER
          LOCATIONS      TYPE IS      CHARACTER 15    VECTOR
        MGRSTART         TYPE IS      CHARACTER 9

RECORD NAME IS PROJECT
    DUPLICATES ARE NOT ALLOWED FOR NAME
    DUPLICATES ARE NOT ALLOWED FOR NUMBER
        NAME             TYPE IS      CHARACTER 15
        NUMBER           TYPE IS      NUMERIC INTEGER
        LOCATION         TYPE IS      CHARACTER 15

RECORD NAME IS WORKS_ON
    DUPLICATES ARE NOT ALLOWED FOR ESSN, PNUMBER
        ESSN             TYPE IS      CHARACTER 9
        PNUMBER          TYPE IS      NUMERIC INTEGER
        HOURS            TYPE IS      NUMERIC (4,1)

RECORD NAME IS SUPERVISOR
    DUPLICATES ARE NOT ALLOWED FOR SUPERVISOR_SSN
        SUPERVISOR_SSN   TYPE IS      CHARACTER 9

RECORD NAME IS DEPENDENT
    DUPLICATES ARE NOT ALLOWED FOR EMPSSN, NAME
        EMPSSN           TYPE IS      CHARACTER 9
        NAME             TYPE IS      CHARACTER 15
        SEX              TYPE IS      CHARACTER 1
        BIRTHDATE        TYPE IS      CHARACTER 9
        RELATIONSHIP     TYPE IS      CHARACTER 10
```

Figure 10.10   (a) Record type declarations for the schema in Figure 10.9.
                     (*continued on next page*)

```
SET NAME IS ALL_DEPTS
    OWNER IS SYSTEM
        ORDER IS SORTED BY DEFINED KEYS
    MEMBER IS DEPARTMENT
        KEY IS ASCENDING NAME

SET NAME IS WORKS_FOR
    OWNER IS DEPARTMENT
        ORDER IS SORTED BY DEFINED KEYS
    MEMBER IS EMPLOYEE
        INSERTION IS MANUAL
        RETENTION IS OPTIONAL
        KEY IS ASCENDING LNAME, FNAME, MINIT
        CHECK IS DEPTNAME IN EMPLOYEE = NAME IN DEPARTMENT

SET NAME IS CONTROLS
    OWNER IS DEPARTMENT
        ORDER IS SORTED BY DEFINED KEYS
    MEMBER IS PROJECT
        INSERTION IS AUTOMATIC
        RETENTION IS MANDATORY
        KEY IS ASCENDING NAME
        SET SELECTION IS BY APPLICATION

SET NAME IS MANAGES
    OWNER IS EMPLOYEE
        ORDER IS SYSTEM DEFAULT
    MEMBER IS DEPARTMENT
        INSERTION IS AUTOMATIC
        RETENTION IS MANDATORY
        SET SELECTION IS BY APPLICATION

SET NAME IS P_WORKSON
    OWNER IS PROJECT
        ORDER IS SYSTEM DEFAULT
        DUPLICATES ARE NOT ALLOWED
    MEMBER IS WORKS_ON
        INSERTION IS AUTOMATIC
        RETENTION IS FIXED
        KEY IS ESSN
        SET SELECTION IS STRUCTURAL NUMBER IN PROJECT = PNUMBER IN
        WORKS_ON

SET NAME IS E_WORKSON
    OWNER IS EMPLOYEE
        ORDER IS SYSTEM DEFAULT
        DUPLICATES ARE NOT ALLOWED
    MEMBER IS WORKS_ON
        INSERTION IS AUTOMATIC
        RETENTION IS FIXED
        KEY IS PNUMBER
        SET SELECTION IS STRUCTURAL SSN IN EMPLOYEE = ESSN IN WORKS_ON
```

Figure 10.10   (b) Set type declarations for the schema in Figure 10.9. *(contin-ued on next page)*

```
SET NAME IS SUPERVISEES
    OWNER IS SUPERVISOR
        ORDER IS BY DEFINED KEY
        DUPLICATES ARE NOT ALLOWED
    MEMBER IS EMPLOYEE
        INSERTION IS MANUAL
        RETENTION IS OPTIONAL
        KEY IS LNAME, MINIT, FNAME

SET NAME IS IS_A_SUPERVISOR
    OWNER IS EMPLOYEE
        ORDER IS SYSTEM DEFAULT
        DUPLICATES ARE NOT ALLOWED
    MEMBER IS SUPERVISOR
        INSERTION IS AUTOMATIC
        RETENTION IS MANDATORY
        KEY IS SUPERVISOR_SSN
        SET SELECTION IS BY VALUE OF SSN IN EMPLOYEE
        CHECK IS SUPERVISOR_SSN IN SUPERVISION = SSN IN EMPLOYEE

SET NAME IS DEPENDENTS_OF
    OWNER IS EMPLOYEE
        ORDER IS BY DEFINED KEY
        DUPLICATES ARE NOT ALLOWED
    MEMBER IS DEPENDENT
        INSERTION IS AUTOMATIC
        RETENTION IS FIXED
        KEY IS ASCENDING NAME
        SET SELECTION IS STRUCTURAL SSN IN EMPLOYEE = EMPSSN IN
        DEPENDENT
```

Figure 10.10   (*continued*) (b) Set type declarations for the schema in Figure
10.9.

10.3.2 *Set Type Declarations and Set Selection Options*

Figure 10.10(b) shows network DDL declarations for the set types of the COMPANY
schema shown in Figure 10.9. These are more complex than record type declarations,
because more options are available. Each set type is given a name by using the SET NAME
IS clause. The insertion and retention options (constraints), discussed in Section 10.2,
are specified for each set type by using the INSERTION IS and RETENTION IS clauses. If
the insertion option is AUTOMATIC, we must also specify how the system will *select a set
occurrence automatically* to connect a new member record to that occurrence when the
record is first inserted into the database. The SET SELECTION clause is used for this purpose. Three common methods of specifying SET SELECTION are as follows:

- SET SELECTION IS STRUCTURAL: We can specify set selection by values of two
  fields that must match—one field from the owner record type, and one from the
  member record type. This is called a structural constraint in network terminology.
  Examples are the P_WORKSON and E_WORKSON set type declarations in Figure
  10.10(b). The specified field of the owner record type must have the constraint

DUPLICATES ARE NOT ALLOWED so that it specifies a single owner record and hence a single set occurrence.

- SET SELECTION BY APPLICATION: The set occurrence is determined via the application program, which should make the desired set occurrence the current of set (see Section 10.5.1) before the new member record is stored. The new member record is then automatically connected to the current set occurrence. An example is the MANAGES set in Figure 10.10(b); to connect an EMPLOYEE record to a DEPARTMENT as manager of that department, we must first make that EMPLOYEE record the current of set for the MANAGES set type. Storing a new DEPARTMENT record then *automatically* connects it to its manager EMPLOYEE record as owner.

- SET SELECTION IS BY VALUE OF <field name> IN <record type name>: A third option is to specify a field of the owner record type whose value is used to specify a set occurrence by identifying the owner record of the set. An example is the IS_A_SUPERVISOR set type declared in Figure 10.10(b), where we must set the SSN field of the UWA program variable (see Section 10.5.1) corresponding to EMPLOYEE to the value in the desired owner record before storing a new SUPERVISOR record. The field specified in the owner record type should have the constraint DUPLICATES ARE NOT ALLOWED so that it identifies a unique owner record and hence a unique set occurrence.

Another option for sets is to specify how individual member records in a set instance will be ordered, as we discussed in Section 10.2.4. This is important because of the record-at-a-time nature of the network DML. The **ORDER IS** clause is used for this purpose, sometimes in conjunction with the **KEY IS** clause. Options for the ORDER IS clause include the following:

- ORDER IS SORTED BY DEFINED KEYS: We use the KEY IS clause to specify one or more fields from the member record type; the system uses the values of these fields to order the member records within each set instance. The KEY IS clause also specifies whether the records should be ordered in ASCENDING or DESCENDING order. An example is the WORKS_FOR set type, where EMPLOYEE records owned by a DEPARTMENT are ordered in ascending values of LNAME, FNAME, and MINIT values.

- ORDER IS FIRST (or LAST): A new member record is inserted as the first (or last) record in the set occurrence.

- ORDER IS BY SYSTEM DEFAULT: No particular order is specified on the member records in a set instance.

- ORDER IS NEXT (or PRIOR): A new member record is inserted immediately after (before) the current record of the set. The program must make the current of set (see Section 10.5.1) point to the particular record after (before) which we want the new record to be inserted in the set.

Another clause that works in conjunction with the KEY IS clause is the **DUPLICATES ARE NOT ALLOWED** clause. Both clauses apply to member record types within sets. This combination specifies that no two member records *within a set occurrence* are allowed to have the same values for their fields declared as keys. An example is the ESSN field that is declared to be KEY for the P_WORKSON set type, meaning that no two WORKS_ON records *within the same set occurrence* of P_WORKSON have the same value for ESSN. This is specified because we do not want to connect the same employee twice as a worker on the same project.

Finally, let us consider the CHECK clause, which is used to specify a structural constraint between the owner and the member records within a set occurrence. This is used with MANUAL sets to specify a condition that some fields of a member record must have the same values as some fields of the owner record. If an attempt is made to connect a member record that does not satisfy the condition of the CHECK clause, the system generates an exception condition and does not connect the member record. An example is given in the declaration of the WORKS_FOR set type in Figure 10.10(b). This constraint is similar to the SET SELECTION IS STRUCTURAL, which is used for AUTOMATIC sets.

10.4 Network Database Design Using ER-to-Network Mapping★

We now show how a conceptual database design specified as an ER schema (see Chapter 3) can be mapped to a network schema. We use the COMPANY ER schema shown in Figure 3.2 to illustrate our discussion. In a network schema we can explicitly represent a relationship type as a set type if it is 1:N; however, no explicit representation exists if it is 1:1 or M:N. One simple method of representing a 1:1 relationship type is to use a set type but to make each set instance have at most one member record. This constraint must be enforced by the programs that update the database, since the DBMS itself does not enforce it. For M:N relationship types, the standard representation is to use two set types and a linking record type. The network model allows vector fields and repeating groups, which can be used directly to represent composite and multivalued attributes or even weak entity types, as we shall see.

The COMPANY network schema shown in Figure 10.9 can be derived from the ER schema of Figure 3.2 by the following general mapping procedure. We illustrate each step by using examples from the COMPANY schema.

STEP 1: Regular Entities: For each regular entity type E in the ER schema, create a record type R in the network schema. All simple (or composite) attributes of E are included as simple (or composite) fields of R. All multivalued attributes of E are included as vector fields or repeating groups of R.

In our example we create the record types EMPLOYEE, DEPARTMENT, and PROJECT and include all their fields shown in Figure 10.9 except the fields marked by an f.k. (foreign key) or a * (relationship attribute). Notice that the LOCATIONS field of the DEPARTMENT record type is a vector field because it represents a multivalued attribute.

STEP 2: Weak Entities: For each weak entity type WE with the owner identifying entity type IE, either (a) create a record type W to represent WE, making W the member record type in a set type that relates W to the record type representing IE as owner, or (b) make a repeating group in the record type representing IE to represent the attributes of WE. If the first alternative is chosen, the key field of the record type representing IE in W can be repeated.

In Figure 10.9 we choose the first alternative; a record type DEPENDENT is created and made the member record type of the DEPENDENTS_OF set type, which is owned by EMPLOYEE. We duplicated the SSN key of EMPLOYEE in DEPENDENT and called it EMPSSN.

STEP 3: One-to-One and One-to-Many Relationships: For each nonrecursive binary 1:1 or 1:N relationship type R between entity types E1 and E2, create a set type relating the record types S1 and S2 that represent E1 and E2, respectively. For a 1:1 relationship type, arbitrarily choose one of S1 and S2 as owner and the other as member; however, it is preferable to choose as member a record type that represents a total participation in the relationship type. Another option for mapping a 1:1 binary relationship type R between E1 and E2 is to create a single record type S that merges E1, E2, and R and includes all their attributes; this is useful if both participations of E1 and E2 in R are total and E1 and E2 do not participate in numerous other relationship types.

For a 1:N relationship type, the record type S1 that represents the entity type E1 at the 1-side of the relationship type is chosen as owner, and the record type S2 that represents the entity type E2 at the N-side of the relationship type is chosen as member. Any attributes of the relationship type R are included as fields in the *member* record type S2.

In general, we can arbitrarily duplicate one (or more) attributes of an owner record type of a set type—whether it represents a 1:1 or a 1:N relationship—in the member record type. If the duplicated attribute is a unique key attribute of the owner, it can be used to declare a structural constraint on the set type or to specify automatic owner selection on set membership, as discussed in Section 10.2.1.

In our example we represent the 1:1 relationship type MANAGES from Figure 3.2 by the set type MANAGES, and we choose DEPARTMENT as member record type because of its total participation. The StartDate attribute of MANAGES becomes a field MGRSTART of the member record type DEPARTMENT. The two nonrecursive 1:N relationship types from Figure 3.2, WORKS_FOR and CONTROLS, are represented by the two set types WORKS_FOR and CONTROLS in Figure 10.9. For the WORKS_ON set type, we choose to repeat a unique key field NAME of the owner record type DEPARTMENT in the member record type EMPLOYEE, and we call it DEPTNAME. We decline to repeat any key field for the CONTROLS set type. In general, a unique field from an owner record type could be repeated in the member record type.

STEP 4: Binary Many-to-Many Relationships: For each binary M:N relationship type R between entity types E1 and E2, create a linking record type X and make it the member record type in two set types. The set type owners are the record types S1 and S2 that represent E1 and E2. Any attributes of R are made fields of X. The designer may arbitrarily duplicate the unique (key) fields of the owner record types as fields of X.

In Figure 10.9 we create the linking record type WORKS_ON to represent the M:N relationship type WORKS_ON, and we include HOURS as its field. Two set types E_WORKSON and P_WORKSON are created with WORKS_ON as member record type. We choose to duplicate the unique key fields SSN and NUMBER of the owner record types EMPLOYEE and PROJECT in WORKS_ON, calling them ESSN and PNUMBER, respectively.

STEP 5: Recursive Relationships: For each recursive 1:1 or 1:N binary relationship type in which entity type E participates in both roles, create a "dummy" linking record type D and two set types to relate D to the record type X representing E. One or both of the set types will be constrained to have set instances with a single member record— one in the case of a 1:N relationship type, and both in the case of a 1:1 relationship type.

In Figure 3.2 we have one recursive 1:N relationship type SUPERVISION. We create the dummy linking record type SUPERVISOR and the two set types IS_A_SUPERVISOR and SUPERVISEES. The IS_A_SUPERVISOR set type is constrained to have single member records by the database update programs in its set instances. We can think of each dummy SUPERVISOR member record of the IS_A_SUPERVISOR set type as representing its owner EMPLOYEE record *in a supervisory role*. The SUPERVISEES set type is used to relate the "dummy" SUPERVISOR record to all EMPLOYEE records that represent the employees that are his or her direct supervisees.

The preceding steps consider only binary relationship types. Step 6 shows how n-ary relationship types with n > 2 are mapped by creating a linking record type, similar to the case of an M:N relationship type.

STEP 6: n-ary Relationships: For each n-ary relationship type R, n > 2, create a linking record type X and make it the member record type in n set types. The owner of each set type is the record type that represents one of the entity types participating in the relationship type R. Any attributes of R are made fields of X. The designer may arbitrarily duplicate the unique (key) fields of the owner record types as fields of X.

For example, consider the relationship type SUPPLY in the ER model, as shown in Figure 10.11(a). This can be mapped to the record type SUPPLY and the three set types shown in Figure 10.11(b), where we choose not to duplicate any fields of the owners.

Notice that composite and multivalued attributes can be directly represented in the network model. In addition, we can represent weak entity types either as separate record types or as repeating groups within the owner; the latter is useful if the weak entity type does not participate in any additional relationship types. By duplicating a unique (key) field from the owner record type in the member record type, we can specify a structural constraint on set membership or automatic set selection; the DBMS will connect a member record to a set instance only if the same key field value is stored in both owner and member records. This amounts to getting the DBMS to enforce the constraint automatically. Although it is not required to duplicate a matching key field from the owner record type in the member record type, it is a recommended practice. The cost is the extra storage space required for the duplicate field in each member record. The benefits are the automatic constraint enforcement and the availability of the duplicated field in the member record without the need first to retrieve its owner.

By duplicating the key fields of owner records in member records for all set types in a network schema, we create record types that are practically identical to the relations of a relational database schema! The only differences are for recursive relationship types, multivalued attributes, and weak entity types. For recursive 1:1 or 1:N relationship types, we need not create a dummy relation in the relational schema, as we must in the network model. For weak entity types and multivalued attributes, we need not create additional record types in the network schema, as we must in the relational model. ■

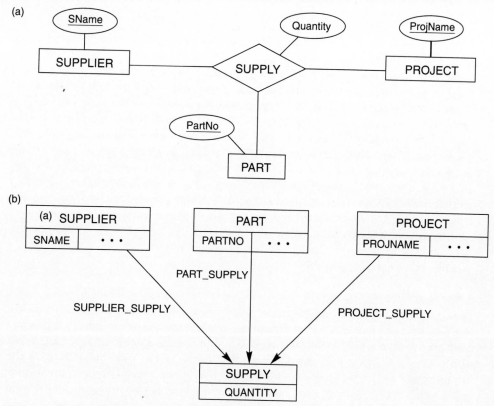

Figure 10.11 Mapping the n-ary (n = 3) relationship type SUPPLY of the ER model in the network model: (a) The ER model. (b) The network model.

— Not on final

10.5 Programming a Network Database★

In this section we discuss how to write programs that manipulate a network database—including such tasks as searching for and retrieving records from the database; inserting, deleting, and modifying records; and connecting and disconnecting records from set occurrences. A **data manipulation language** is used for these purposes. The DML associated with the network model consists of record-at-a-time commands that are embedded in a general-purpose programming language called the **host language**.★ In practice, the most commonly used host languages are COBOL★★ and PL/I. In our examples, however, we will write program segments in PASCAL notation augmented with network DML commands.

★Embedded commands of the DML are also called the **data sublanguage.**
★★The CODASYL DML in the DBTG report was originally proposed as a data sublanguage for COBOL.

10.5.1 Basic Concepts for Network Database Manipulation

To write programs for manipulating a network database, we first need to discuss some basic concepts related to how data manipulation programs are written. The database system and the host programming language are two separate software systems that are linked together by a common interface and communicate only through this interface. Because DML commands are record-at-a-time, it is necessary to identify specific records of the database as **current records**. The DBMS itself keeps track of a number of current records and set occurrences by means of a mechanism known as **currency indicators**. In addition, the host programming language needs local program variables to hold the records of different record types so that their contents can be manipulated by the host program. The set of these local variables in the program is usually referred to as the **user work area (UWA)**. Communication between the DBMS and the host programming language is mainly accomplished through currency indicators and the user work area.

In this section we discuss these two concepts. Our examples refer to the network database schema shown in Figure 10.9, which is the network version of the COMPANY schema used in previous chapters.

The User Work Area (UWA). The UWA is a set of program variables, declared in the host program, to communicate the contents of individual records between the DBMS and the host program. For each record type in the database schema, a corresponding program variable with the same format must be declared in the program. It is customary to use the same record type names and the same field names in the UWA variables as in the database schema. In fact, the UWA variables can be automatically declared in the program by a software package that creates program variables that are equivalent to the record types declared in the DDL for a database schema.

For the COMPANY schema of Figure 10.9, if an interface between PASCAL and the network DBMS were available, it could create the PASCAL program variables shown in Figure 10.12. A single record of each record type can be copied from or written into the database by using the corresponding program variable of the UWA. The GET command (see Section 10.5.3) physically reads a record and copies it into the corresponding program variable. Then we can refer to the field values to print or to use for calculations. To write a record into the database, we first assign its field values to the fields of the program variable and then use the STORE command (see Section 10.5.3) to physically store the record in the database.

Currency Indicators. In the network DML, retrievals and updates are handled by moving or **navigating** through the database records; hence, keeping a trace of the search is critical. Currency indicators are a means of keeping track of the most recently accessed records and set occurrences by the DBMS. They play the role of position holders so that we may process new records starting from the ones most recently accessed until we retrieve all the records that contain the information we need. Each currency indicator can be thought of as a record pointer (or record address) that points to a single database record. In a network DBMS, several currency indicators are used:

- **Current of record type:** For each record type, the DBMS keeps track of the most recently accessed record of that record type. If no record has been accessed yet from that record type, the current record is undefined.

```
type LOCATIONRECORD    = ( * this is for the vector field LOCATIONS of DEPARTMENT *)
                         record
                         LOCATION : packed array [1..15] of char ;
                         NEXT : ^LOCATIONRECORD
                         end ;

     var  EMPLOYEE    :  record
                         FNAME : packed array  [1..15] of char ;
                         MINIT : char ;
                         LNAME : packed array [1..15] of char ;
                         SSN : packed array [1..9] of char ;
                         BIRTHDATE : packed array [1..9] of char ;
                         ADDRESS : packed array [1..30] of char ;
                         SEX : char ;
                         SALARY : packed array [1..10] of char ;
                         DEPTNAME : packed array [1..15] of char
                         end ;
          DEPARTMENT  :  record
                         NAME : packed array [1..15] of char ;
                         NUMBER : integer ;
                         LOCATIONS : ^LOCATIONRECORD ;
                         MGRSTART : packed array [1..9] of char
                         end ;
          PROJECT     :  record
                         NAME : packed array [1..15] of char ;
                         NUMBER : integer ;
                         LOCATION : packed array [1..15] of char
                         end ;
          WORKS_ON    :  record
                         ESSN ; packed array [1..9] of char ;
                         PNUMBER : integer ;
                         HOURS : packed array [1..4] of char
                         end ;
          SUPERVISOR  :  record
                         SUPERVISOR_SSN : packed array [1..9] of char
                         end ;
          DEPENDENT   :  record
                         EMPSSN : packed array [1..9] of char ;
                         NAME : packed array [1..15] of char ;
                         SEX : char ;
                         BIRTHDATE : packed array [1..9] of char ;
                         RELATIONSHIP : packed array [1..10] of char
                         end;
```

Figure 10.12   PASCAL program variables for the UWA corresponding to the network schema in Figure 10.9.

- **Current of set type:** For each set type in the schema, the DBMS keeps track of the most recently accessed set occurrence from the set type. The set occurrence is specified by a single record from that set, which is *either the owner or one of the member* records. Hence, the current of set (or current set) points to a record, even though it is used to keep track of a set occurrence. If the program has not accessed any record from that set type, the current of set is undefined.

- **Current of run unit (CRU):** A run unit is a database access program that is executing (running) on the computer system. For each run unit, the CRU keeps track of the record most recently accessed by the program; this record can be from *any* record type in the database.

Each time a program executes a DML command, the currency indicators for the record types and set types affected by that command are updated by the DBMS. A clear understanding of how each DML command affects the currency indicators is necessary. Many DML commands both affect and depend on the currency indicators. In Section 10.5.3 we illustrate how the different DML commands affect currency indicators.

Status Indicators. Several **status indicators** return an indication of success or failure after each DML command is executed. The program can check the values of these status indicators and take appropriate action—either to continue execution or to transfer to an error-handling routine.

We call the main status variable DB_STATUS and assume that it is implicitly declared in the host program. After each DML command, the value of DB_STATUS indicates whether the command was successful or whether an error or an exception occurred. The most common exception that occurs is the END_OF_SET (**EOS**) exception. This is not an error; it only indicates that no more member records exist in a set occurrence. Thus it is frequently used to terminate a program loop that processes every member element of a set instance. A DML command to find the next (or prior) member of a set returns an EOS exception when no next (or prior) member record exists. The program checks for DB_STATUS = EOS to terminate the loop. We will assume that a DB_STATUS value of 0 (zero) indicates a successfully executed command with no exceptions occurring.

Illustration of Currency Indicators and the UWA. Suppose that a program executes database commands that result in the following events on the database instances shown in Figure 10.7(f):

- The EMPLOYEE record E3 is accessed.
- By following the FIRST(E_W) pointer in E3, the WORKS_ON record W4 is accessed; by continuing with the NEXT(E_W) pointers in WORKS_ON records, W5 and W6 are accessed.
- The record W6 is retrieved into the corresponding UWA variable.

Figure 10.13 illustrates the effects of these events on the UWA variables and the DBMS currency indicators when applied to the instances of Figure 10.7(f). Figure 10.14 shows how the currency indicators change as the events take place, with an additional event that locates the owner record P3 of W6 in the P_W set. In Figure 10.14 a pointer to a record x is shown as $^{\wedge}$x. Notice that, after the first command, the current of set for *all* set types in which EMPLOYEE participates in Figure 10.9 are set to point to E3; these are E_WORKSON and DEPENDENTS_OF, which are shown in Figure 10.14, as well as SUPERVISEES, IS_A_SUPERVISOR, MANAGES, and WORKS_FOR, which are not shown. The current of EMPLOYEE record type continues to hold during the later commands, whereas that of DEPENDENT is never set (remains undefined). Notice how the currency changes for the set type E_W as we move from owner to member and for P_W as we move from member to owner.

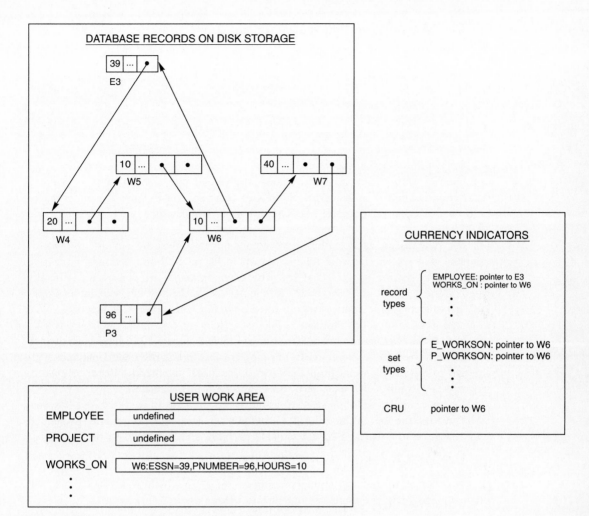

Figure 10.13 UWA variables and currency indicators.

Step	Record Currencies					Set Currencies					CRU
	EMPLOYEE	WORKS_ON	PROJECT	DEPENDENT	...	E_WORKSON (E_W)	P_WORKSON (P_W)	DEPENDENTS_OF	CONTROLS	...	
FIND E3	^E3					^E3		^E3			^E3
FIND W6 (member of E_W)	^E3	^W6				^W6	^W6	^E3			^W6
FIND P3 (owner of P_W)	^E3	^W6	^P3			^W6	^P3	^E3	^P3		^P3

Figure 10.14 How currency indicators change.

10.5.2 *Network Data Manipulation Language (DML)*

The commands for manipulating a network database are called the network DML. These commands are typically embedded in a general-purpose programming language, called the host programming language. The DML commands can be grouped into navigation commands, retrieval commands, and update commands. **Navigation** commands are used to set the currency indicators to specific records and set occurrences in the database. **Retrieval** commands retrieve the current record of the run unit (CRU). **Update** commands can be divided into two subgroups—one for updating records, and the other for updating set occurrences. Record update commands are used to store new records, delete unwanted records, and modify field values, whereas set update commands are used to connect or disconnect a member record in a set occurrence or to move a member record from one set occurrence to another. The full set of commands is summarized in Table 10.2.

We now discuss each of these DML commands and illustrate our discussion with examples that use the network schema shown in Figure 10.9 and defined by the DDL statements in Figures 10.10(a) and (b). The DML commands we present are generally based on the CODASYL DBTG proposal. We use PASCAL as the host language in our examples, but students may practice writing these programs with other host languages. The examples consist of short program segments without any variable declarations. We assume that the UWA (user work area) variables shown in Figure 10.12 have been defined elsewhere in the PASCAL program. In our programs, we prefix the DML commands with a $-sign to distinguish them from the PASCAL language statements. We write PASCAL language key words—such as *if, then, while,* and *for*—in lowercase.

In our examples we often need to assign values to fields of the PASCAL UWA variables. We use the PASCAL notation for assignment. For example, to set the FNAME and LNAME fields of the EMPLOYEE UWA variable to 'John' and 'Smith', we write:

```
EMPLOYEE.FNAME := 'John'; EMPLOYEE.LNAME := 'Smith';
```

Notice that, in the COBOL programming langauge (for which the CODASYL DML was originally designed), the same assignments are written as:

```
MOVE 'John' TO FNAME IN EMPLOYEE
MOVE 'Smith' TO LNAME IN EMPLOYEE
```

10.5.3 *DML Commands for Retrieval and Navigation*

The DML command for retrieving a record is the **GET** command. Before the GET command is issued, the program should specify the record it wants to retrieve as the CRU, by using the appropriate navigational **FIND** commands. There are many variations of FIND; we will first discuss the use of FIND in locating record instances of a record type and then discuss the variations for processing set occurrences.

DML Commands for Locating Records of a Record Type. There are two main variations of the FIND command for locating a record of a certain record type and making that record the CRU and current of record type. Other currency indicators may also be

Table 10.2   Summary of Network DML Commands

(RETRIEVAL)	
GET	RETRIEVE THE CURRENT OF RUN UNIT (CRU) INTO THE CORRESPONDING USER WORK AREA (UWA) VARIABLE
(NAVIGATION)	
FIND	RESET THE CURRENCY INDICATORS; ALWAYS SETS THE CRU; ALSO SETS CURRENCY INDICATORS OF INVOLVED RECORD TYPES AND SET TYPES. THERE ARE MANY VARIATIONS OF FIND.
(RECORD UPDATE)	
STORE	STORE THE NEW RECORD IN THE DATABASE AND MAKE IT THE CRU
ERASE	DELETE FROM THE DATABASE THE RECORD THAT IS THE CRU
MODIFY	MODIFY SOME FIELDS OF THE RECORD THAT IS THE CRU
(SET UPDATE)	
CONNECT	CONNECT A MEMBER RECORD (THE CRU) TO A SET INSTANCE
DISCONNECT	REMOVE A MEMBER RECORD (THE CRU) FROM A SET INSTANCE
RECONNECT	MOVE A MEMBER RECORD (THE CRU) FROM ONE SET INSTANCE TO ANOTHER

affected, as we shall see. The format of these two commands is as follows, where optional parts of the command are shown in brackets, [. . .]:

- **FIND ANY** <record type name> [**USING** <field list>]
- **FIND DUPLICATE** <record type name> [**USING** <field list>]

We now illustrate the use of these commands with examples. To retrieve the EMPLOYEE record for the employee whose name is John Smith and to print out his salary, we can write EX1:

```
EX1:  1   EMPLOYEE.FNAME := 'John'; EMPLOYEE.LNAME := 'Smith';
      2   $FIND ANY EMPLOYEE USING FNAME, LNAME;
      3   if DB_STATUS = 0
      4      then begin
      5         $GET EMPLOYEE;
      6         writeln (EMPLOYEE.SALARY)
      7      end
      8      else writeln ('no record found');
```

The **FIND ANY** command finds the *first* record in the database of the specified <record type name> such that the field values of the record match the values initialized earlier in the corresponding UWA fields specified in the USING clause of the command.

In EX1, lines 1 and 2 are equivalent to saying: "Search for the first EMPLOYEE record that satisfies the condition FNAME = 'John' and LNAME = 'Smith' and make it the current record of the run unit (CRU)." The GET statement is equivalent to saying: "Retrieve the CRU record into the corresponding UWA program variable." In general, whenever a FIND command is used, the program should check whether it successfully located a record, by testing the value of DB_STATUS. A value of 0 means that a record was successfully located, so we write the if ... then statement starting in line 3 before issuing the GET command in line 5 of EX1.

The FIND statement not only sets the CRU but also sets additional currency indicators—namely, those for the record type whose name is specified in the command and for any set types in which that record type participates as owner or member. Hence, the preceding FIND command also sets the currency indicators for the EMPLOYEE record type and for every set type in which the located record participates as owner or member of a set occurrence. However, the GET command always retrieves the CRU, *which may not be the same as the current of record type*.* The IDMS system combines FIND and GET into a single command, called OBTAIN.

Two variations of EX1 are worth considering. First, if we replace line 5 by just $GET, we retrieve exactly the same result as before. The difference is that including the record type name in the GET command—as in EX1—makes the system check that the CRU is of the specified record type; if not, an error is generated and the CRU is not retrieved into the UWA variable. As a second variation, if we replace line 5 by, say, $GET DEPARTMENT, an error is generated because the record type specified in the GET command, DEPARTMENT, does not match the record type of the CRU, EMPLOYEE.

If more than one record satisfies our search and we want to retrieve all of them, we must write a looping construct in the host programming language. For example, to retrieve all EMPLOYEE records for employees who work in the Research department and to print their names, we can write EX2.

```
EX2:    EMPLOYEE.DEPTNAME := 'Research';
        $FIND ANY EMPLOYEE USING DEPTNAME;
        while DB_STATUS = 0 do
            begin
            $GET EMPLOYEE;
            writeln ( EMPLOYEE.FNAME, ", EMPLOYEE.LNAME );
            $FIND DUPLICATE EMPLOYEE USING DEPTNAME
            end;
```

The **FIND DUPLICATE** command finds the *next* (or duplicate) record, starting from the current record, that satisfies the search. We cannot use FIND ANY, because it always locates the first record satisfying the search. Notice that "first" and "next" records have no special meaning here, because we did not specify any order on EMPLOYEE records in the DDL of Figure 10.10(b). The system searches for EMPLOYEE records physically in the order in which they are stored. However, once all EMPLOYEE records have been checked

---

*A variation of the network DML has been suggested which uses the GET command to retrieve the *current record of the specified record type*. This makes some programs easier to write. However, most network DBMSs use the GET command to retrieve the CRU, as we discuss here.

in the while-loop, the system sets DB_STATUS to a "no more records found" exception condition and the loop terminates.

DML Commands for Set Processing. For set processing, we have the following variations of FIND:

- FIND (FIRST | NEXT | PRIOR | LAST | ...) <record type name>
  WITHIN <set type name> [USING <field names>]
- FIND OWNER WITHIN <set type name>

Once we have established a current set occurrence of a set type, we can use the FIND command to locate various records that participate in the set occurrence. We can locate either the owner record or one of the member records and make that record the CRU. We use **FIND OWNER** to locate the owner record and one of **FIND FIRST, FIND NEXT, FIND LAST**, or **FIND PRIOR** to locate the first, next, last, or prior member record of the set instance, respectively.

Recall that the current of set indicator may be pointing to either the owner or to any member record of a set occurrence. The FIND OWNER, FIND FIRST, and FIND LAST commands have the same effect regardless of the particular record in the set occurrence that the current of set points to. However, FIND NEXT and FIND PRIOR *do depend* on the current of set. For FIND NEXT, if the current of set is the owner, it locates the first member; if the current of set is any member record except the last member, it locates the next member record; finally, if the current of the set is the last member record in the set, it sets DB_STATUS to the EOS (end-of-set) exception. For FIND PRIOR, corresponding similar actions are taken.

The next example illustrates the use of FIND FIRST and FIND NEXT. The query is to print the names of employees who work in the Research department alphabetically by last name, which is shown in EX3. This is similar to EX2 except for the alphabetic ordering requirement. EX3 retrieves first the 'Research' DEPARTMENT record and then the member EMPLOYEE records owned by that record via the WORKS_FOR set. Recall that, in the declaration of the WORKS_FOR set type in Figure 10.10(b), we specified that the member records in each set instance of WORKS_FOR are stored by ascending value of LNAME, FNAME, and MINIT. By retrieving the EMPLOYEE member records in order, we can print the employee names alphabetically in EX3. Notice how we terminate the loop by checking DB_STATUS. Once the last member record of the set occurrence is located, the subsequent FIND NEXT command sets DB_STATUS to the EOS (end-of-set) exception.

```
EX3:    DEPARTMENT.NAME := 'Research';
        $FIND ANY DEPARTMENT USING NAME;
        if DB_STATUS = 0 then
            begin
            $FIND FIRST EMPLOYEE WITHIN WORKS_FOR;
            while DB_STATUS = 0 do
                begin
                $GET EMPLOYEE;
                writeln ( EMPLOYEE.LNAME, ", EMPLOYEE.FNAME );
                FIND NEXT EMPLOYEE WITHIN WORKS_FOR
                end
            end;
```

The next example illustrates the use of FIND OWNER. The query is to print the project name, project number, and hours per week for each project that employee John Smith works on (assuming there is only one such employee). This is shown in EX4. The FIND ANY command sets the CRU as well as the current record of the EMPLOYEE record type and the current of set of the E_WORKSON set type. We then loop through each WORKS_ON member record in the current E_WORKSON set, and within each loop we find the PROJECT record that owns the WORKS_ON record via the P_WORKSON set type, using the FIND OWNER command. Note that we do not have to check DB_STATUS after the FIND OWNER command, because the retention option for the set P_WORKSON is FIXED, so every WORKS_ON record must belong to a P_WORKSON set instance:

```
EX4:    EMPLOYEE.FNAME := 'John'; EMPLOYEE.LNAME := 'Smith';
        $FIND ANY EMPLOYEE USING FNAME, LNAME;
        if DB_STATUS = 0 then
            begin
            $FIND FIRST WORKS_ON WITHIN E_WORKSON;
            while DB_STATUS = 0 do
                begin
                $GET WORKS_ON;
                $FIND OWNER WITHIN P_WORKSON;
                $GET PROJECT;
                writeln ( PROJECT.NAME, PROJECT.NUMBER,
                        WORKS_ON.HOURS );
                $FIND NEXT WORKS_ON WITHIN E_WORKSON
                end
            end;
```

In EX3 and EX4, we processed all member records of a set instance. Alternatively, we can selectively process only the member records that satisfy some condition. If the condition is an equality comparison on one (or more) fields, we can append a USING clause to the FIND command. To illustrate this, consider the request to print the names of all employees who work full-time—40 hours per week—on the 'ProductX' project; this example is shown as EX5:

```
EX5:    PROJECT.NAME := 'ProductX';
        $FIND ANY PROJECT USING NAME;
        if DB_STATUS = 0 then
            begin
            WORKS_ON.HOURS:= '40.0';
            $FIND FIRST WORKS_ON WITHIN P_WORKSON USING HOURS;
            while DB_STATUS = 0 do
                begin
                $GET WORKS_ON;
                $FIND OWNER WITHIN E_WORKSON; $GET EMPLOYEE;
                writeln (EMPLOYEE.FNAME, EMPLOYEE.LNAME);
                $FIND NEXT WORKS_ON WITHIN P_WORKSON USING HOURS
                end
            end;
```

In EX5, the qualification USING HOURS in FIND FIRST and FIND NEXT specifies that only the WORKS_ON records in the current set instance of P_WORKSON whose HOURS field value matches the value in WORKS_ON.HOURS of the UWA, which is set to '40.0' in the program, are found. Notice that the USING clause with FIND NEXT is used to find the *next member record within the same set occurrence*; when we process records of a record type *regardless of the sets they belong to*, we use FIND DUPLICATE rather than FIND NEXT.

If the condition that selects specific member records of a set instance involves comparison operators *other than equality*, such as less than or greater than, we must retrieve each member record and check whether it satisfies the condition in the host program itself. The reader should attempt to modify EX4 so that only the projects for which the WORKS_ON.HOURS value exceeds 5 are retrieved. This condition must be placed immediately after the WORKS_ON record is physically retrieved.

We use numerous embedded loops in the same program segment to process several sets. For example, consider the following query: For each department, print the department's name and its manager's name; and for each employee who works in that department, print the employee's name and the list of project names that the employee works on.

This query requires us to process the system-owned set ALL_DEPTS to retrieve DEPARTMENT records. Using the WORKS_FOR set, the program retrieves the EMPLOYEE records for each DEPARTMENT. Then, for each employee found, the E_WORKSON set is accessed to locate the WORKS_ON records. For each WORKS_ON record located, a "FIND OWNER WITHIN P_WORKSON" locates the appropriate PROJECT.

Using the Host Programming Language Facilities. Because the network DML is a record-at-a-time language, we need to use the facilities of the host programming language any time a query requires a set of records. We also need to use the host programming language to calculate functions on sets of records, such as COUNTs or AVERAGEs, which must be explicitly implemented by the programmer. This compares with the easy specification of such functions in high-level languages such as SQL (Chapter 7) and QUEL (Chapter 8).

A final example illustrates how we can calculate functions such as COUNT and AVERAGE. Suppose that we want to calculate the number of employees who are supervisors in each department and their average salary; this is shown in EX6. We assume that a PASCAL function convert_to_real, which converts the string value of the SALARY field into a real number, has been declared elsewhere. We must also have program variables total_sal:real and no_of_supervisors:integer declared elsewhere to accumulate the total salary and number of supervisors in each department. In EX6, notice how we test whether an employee is a supervisor by determining whether an EMPLOYEE record participates as owner in some instance of the IS_A_SUPERVISOR set:

```
EX6:    $FIND FIRST DEPARTMENT WITHIN ALL_DEPTS;
        while DB_STATUS = 0 do
            begin
            $GET DEPARTMENT;
            write (DEPARTMENT.NAME); (* department name *)
            total_sal:= 0; no_of_supervisors:= 0;
            $FIND FIRST EMPLOYEE WITHIN WORKS_FOR;
            while DB_STATUS = 0 do
                begin
                $GET EMPLOYEE;
                $FIND FIRST SUPERVISOR WITHIN IS_A_SUPERVISOR;
                (* employee is a supervisor if it owns a SUPERVISOR record via
                IS_A_SUPERVISOR *)
                if DB_STATUS = 0 then (* test if employee is a supervisor *)
                    begin
                    total_sal:= total_sal + convert_to_real (EMPLOYEE.SALARY);
                    no_of_supervisors:= no_of_supervisors+1
                    end;
                $FIND NEXT EMPLOYEE WITHIN WORKS_FOR;
                end;
            writeln('number of supervisors =', no_of_supervisors);
            writeln('average salary of supervisors =', total_sal/no_of_supervisors);
            writeln( );
            $FIND NEXT DEPARTMENT WITHIN ALL_DEPTS
            end;
```

10.5.4 *DML Commands for Updating the Database*

The DML commands for updating a network database are summarized in Table 10.2. Here, we first discuss the commands for updating records—namely the STORE, ERASE, and MODIFY commands. These are used to insert a new record, delete a record, and modify some fields of a record, respectively. Following this, we illustrate the commands that modify set instances, which are the CONNECT, DISCONNECT, and RECONNECT commands.

The STORE Command. The STORE command is used to insert a new record. Before issuing a STORE, we must first set up the UWA variable of the corresponding record type so that its field values contain the field values of the new record. For example, to insert a new EMPLOYEE record for John F. Smith, we can use EX7:

```
EX7:    EMPLOYEE.FNAME := 'John';
        EMPLOYEE.LNAME := 'Smith';
        EMPLOYEE.MINIT := 'F';
        EMPLOYEE.SSN := '567342739';
        EMPLOYEE.ADDRESS := '40 Walcott Road, Minneapolis, Minnesota 55433';
        EMPLOYEE.BIRTHDATE := '10-JAN-55';
```

```
EMPLOYEE.SEX := 'M';
EMPLOYEE.SALARY := '25000.00';
EMPLOYEE.DEPTNAME := '';
$STORE EMPLOYEE;
```

The result of the STORE command is insertion of the current contents of the UWA record of the specified record type into the database. In addition, if the record type is an AUTOMATIC member of a set type, the record is automatically inserted into a set instance, which is determined by the SET SELECTION declaration. The newly inserted record also becomes the CRU and the current record for its record type, as well as the current of set for any set type that has the record type as owner or member.

Effects of SET SELECTION Options on the STORE Command. AUTOMATIC SET SELECTION options have different effects on the execution of the STORE command. Recall that, in a set type with AUTOMATIC insertion option, a new record of the member record type must be connected to a set instance at the same time it is inserted into the database by a STORE command. We briefly discuss three of the SET SELECTION options—BY STRUCTURAL, BY APPLICATION, and BY VALUE—next.

First, we illustrate the **BY STRUCTURAL** option. Recall from Section 10.3 (Figure 10.10) that, in the network DDL, this option has the following format:

SET SELECTION IS STRUCTURAL
<data item> **IN** <member record type> = <data item> **IN** <owner record type>

This allows the DBMS to determine *by itself* the set occurrence in which a newly inserted member record is to be connected; it is illustrated by the declarations for the P_WORKSON and E_WORKSON set types in Figure 10.10(b). For example, to relate the EMPLOYEE record with SSN = '567342739', just inserted in EX7, as a 40-hour-per-week worker on the project whose project number is 55, we must create and store a new linking WORKS_ON record with the appropriate ESSN and PNUMBER values, as shown in EX8. The STORE WORKS_ON command in EX8 automatically connects the newly inserted WORKS_ON record into the E_WORKSON set instance owned by the EMPLOYEE record with SSN = '567342739' and into the P_WORKSON set instance owned by the PROJECT record with NUMBER = 55 by automatically locating these owner records and their set instances. The newly inserted record also becomes the current of set for both these set types. If either of the owner records did not exist in the database, the STORE command would generate an error and the new WORKS_ON record would not be inserted into the database.

```
EX8:   WORKS_ON.ESSN := '567342739';
       WORKS_ON.PNUMBER := 55;
       WORKS_ON.HOURS := '40.0';
       $STORE WORKS_ON;
```

In the network DDL, the **BY APPLICATION** option has the following format:

SET SELECTION IS BY APPLICATION

The application program is responsible for selecting the proper set occurrence *before* storing the new member record. For example, to insert a new PROJECT record for a project that is controlled by the Research department, we must explicitly make the Research DEPARTMENT record the current of set for CONTROLS *before* issuing the STORE PROJECT command.

In the network DDL, the **BY VALUE** option has the following format:

SET SELECTION IS BY VALUE OF <data item> **IN** <owner record type>

It is illustrated by the declaration of the IS_A_SUPERVISOR set type in Figure 10.10(b). In this case we just set the value of the field specified in the SET SELECTION IS BY VALUE declaration—SSN of EMPLOYEE for the IS_A_SUPERVISOR set—before issuing the STORE command. This should be a key field of the owner record type, and the DBMS uses that value to find the (unique) owner of the new record. For example, to insert a new SUPERVISOR record to correspond to the employee with SSN = '567342739', we use EX9. This provides the value of EMPLOYEE.SSN in the program, which the DBMS uses to select the appropriate owner EMPLOYEE record and to automatically connect the new SUPERVISOR record to its set instance.

Notice that we could have declared SET SELECTION BY STRUCTURAL for the IS_A_SUPERVISOR set type; in fact, this would have been more appropriate in Figure 10.10(b). However, if the SUPERVISOR_SSN field was not included in the SUPERVISOR record type, the BY STRUCTURAL option cannot be used and BY VALUE would be the most appropriate choice. In general, when a UNIQUE field value from the owner record type is duplicated in the member record type, it is most appropriate to specify SET SELECTION BY STRUCTURAL for automatic sets; otherwise, SET SELECTION must be either BY VALUE or BY APPLICATION:

```
EX9:    SUPERVISOR.SUPERVISOR_SSN := '567342739';
        (* create new SUPERVISION record in UWA *)
        EMPLOYEE.SSN := '567342739';
        (* set VALUE of SSN for automatic set selection *)
        $STORE SUPERVISOR;
```

The ERASE and ERASE ALL Commands. Next, we discuss deletion of records. To delete a record from the database, we first make that record the CRU and then issue the **ERASE** command. For example, to delete the EMPLOYEE record inserted in EX7, we can use EX10:

```
EX10:   EMPLOYEE.SSN := '567342793';
        $FIND ANY EMPLOYEE USING SSN;
        if DB_STATUS = 0 then $ERASE EMPLOYEE;
```

The effect of an ERASE command on any member records that are *owned by the record being deleted* is determined by the set retention option. For example, the effect of the ERASE command in EX10 depends on the set retention for each set type that has EMPLOYEE as an owner. If retention is OPTIONAL, member records are kept in the database but are disconnected from the owner record before it is deleted. If retention is FIXED, all member records are deleted along with their owner. Finally, if retention is MANDATORY and some member records are owned by the record to be deleted, the ERASE command is rejected and an error message is generated. We cannot delete the owner, because the member records would then have no owner, which is not permitted for a MANDA-TORY set. These rules are recursively applied to any additional records owned by other records whose deletion is automatically triggered by an ERASE command. Deletion can thus propagate through the database and can be very damaging if it is not used carefully.

In EX10, when we ERASE the EMPLOYEE record, all WORKS_ON and DEPENDENT records owned by it are automatically deleted, because the E_WORKSON and DEPEND-ENTS_OF sets have a FIXED retention. However, if that EMPLOYEE record owns a SUPER-VISOR record via the IS_A_SUPERVISOR set or a DEPARTMENT record via the MANAGES set, the deletion is rejected by the system because the IS_A_SUPERVISOR and MANAGES sets have MANDATORY retention. We must first explicitly remove those member records from such MANDATORY sets before issuing the ERASE command on their owner record. If the EMPLOYEE record does not own any SUPERVISOR or DEPARTMENT records via IS_A_SUPERVISOR or MANAGES, the EMPLOYEE record is deleted.

A variation of the ERASE command, **ERASE ALL,** allows the programmer to remove a record and all records owned by it directly or indirectly. This means that *all* member records owned by the record are deleted. In addition, member records owned by any of the deleted records are also deleted, down to any number of repetitions. For example, EX11 deletes the Research DEPARTMENT record, as well as all EMPLOYEE records that are owned by that DEPARTMENT via WORKS_FOR and any PROJECT records that are owned by that DEPARTMENT via CONTROLS. In addition, any DEPENDENT, SUPERVISOR, DEPART-MENT, or WORKS_ON records owned by the deleted EMPLOYEE or PROJECT records are also deleted *automatically*:

```
EX11:   DEPARTMENT.NAME := 'Research';
        $FIND ANY DEPARTMENT USING NAME;
        if DB_STATUS = 0 then $ERASE ALL DEPARTMENT;
```

We can also use a looping program to delete a number of records. For example, suppose that we want to delete all employees who work for the Research department, but not the DEPARTMENT record itself; to do this we can use EX12. Notice that the CRU and the current of record type for the record just deleted point to an *"empty" position* where the record that was deleted used to be. That is why the FIND NEXT statement in EX12 works correctly:

```
EX12:   DEPARTMENT.NAME := 'Research';
        $FIND ANY DEPARTMENT USING NAME;
        if DB_STATUS = 0 then
            begin
            $FIND FIRST EMPLOYEE WITHIN WORKS_FOR;
            while DB_STATUS = 0 do
                begin
                $ERASE EMPLOYEE;
                $FIND NEXT EMPLOYEE WITHIN WORKS_FOR
                end
            end;
```

The MODIFY Command. The final command for updating records is the MODIFY command, which changes some field values of a record. We should take the following sequence of steps to modify field values of a record:

- Make the record to be modified the CRU.
- Retrieve the record into the corresponding UWA variable.
- Modify the desired fields in the UWA variable.
- Issue the MODIFY command.

For example, to give all employees in the Research department a 10% raise, we can use EX13. We assume the existence of two PASCAL functions—convert_to_real and convert_to_string—that have been declared elsewhere; the first converts a string value of the SALARY field to a real number, and the second formats a real value to the SALARY field format.

```
EX13:    DEPARTMENT.NAME := 'Research';
         $FIND ANY DEPARTMENT USING NAME;
         if DB_STATUS = 0 then
             begin
             $FIND FIRST EMPLOYEE WITHIN WORKS_FOR;
             while DB_STATUS = 0 do
                 begin
                 $GET EMPLOYEE;
                 EMPLOYEE.SALARY := convert_to_string (convert_to_real
                                          (EMPLOYEE.SALARY)*1.1);
                 $MODIFY EMPLOYEE;
                 $FIND NEXT EMPLOYEE WITHIN WORKS_FOR
                 end
         end;
```

Commands for Updating Set Instances. We now consider the three set update operations—CONNECT, DISCONNECT, and RECONNECT—which are used to insert and remove member records in set instances. The CONNECT command inserts a member record into a set instance. The member record should be the current of run unit and is connected to the set instance that is the current of set for the set type. For example, to connect the EMPLOYEE record with SSN = '567342793' to the WORKS_FOR set owned by the Research DEPARTMENT record, we can use EX14:

```
EX14:    DEPARTMENT.NAME := 'Research';
         $FIND ANY DEPARTMENT USING NAME;
         if DB_STATUS = 0 then
             begin
             EMPLOYEE.SSN := '567342793';
             $FIND ANY EMPLOYEE USING SSN;
```

```
        if DB_STATUS = 0 then
             $CONNECT EMPLOYEE TO WORKS_FOR;
        end;
```

In EX14, we first locate the Research DEPARTMENT record so that the current of set of the WORKS_FOR set type becomes the set instance owned by the Research DEPARTMENT record. Then we locate the required EMPLOYEE record so that it becomes the CRU. Finally, we issue a CONNECT command. Notice that the EMPLOYEE record to be connected should *not be a member* of any set instance of WORKS_FOR before the CONNECT command is issued. We must use the RECONNECT command for the latter case. The CONNECT command can be used only with MANUAL sets or with AUTOMATIC OPTIONAL sets. With other AUTOMATIC sets, the system automatically connects a member record to a set instance, governed by the SET SELECTION option specified, as soon as the record is stored.

The DISCONNECT command is used to remove a member record from a set instance without connecting it to another set instance. Hence, it can be used only with OPTIONAL sets. We make the record to be disconnected the CRU before issuing the DISCONNECT command. For example, to remove the EMPLOYEE record with SSN = '836483873' from the SUPERVISEES set instance of which it is a member, we use EX15:

```
EX15:    EMPLOYEE.SSN := '836483873';
         $FIND ANY EMPLOYEE USING SSN;
         if DB_STATUS = 0
             then $DISCONNECT EMPLOYEE FROM SUPERVISEES;
```

Finally, the **RECONNECT** command can be used with both OPTIONAL and MAN-DATORY sets, but not with FIXED sets. The RECONNECT command moves a member record from one set instance to another set instance of the *same* set type. It cannot be used with FIXED sets because a member record cannot be moved from one set instance to another under the FIXED constraint. Before we issue the RECONNECT command, the set instance to which the member record is to be connected should be the current of set for the set type, and the member record to be connected should be the CRU. To do this, we need to use an additional phrase with the FIND command—called the RETAINING CURRENCY phrase—which we now discuss.

The RETAINING CURRENCY Phrase. The RECONNECT command and the **RETAINING CURRENCY** phrase are illustrated in the context of EX16, which removes the current manager of the Research department and assigns the employee with SSN = '836483873' to become its new manager. Notice that the MANAGES set is declared to be AUTOMATIC MANDATORY, so another EMPLOYEE record currently owns the Research DEPARTMENT record in the MANAGES set type. Before issuing the RECONNECT command, we should make the EMPLOYEE record with SSN = '836483873' the current of set for the MANAGES set type. We should also make the Research DEPARTMENT record into the CRU, as this is the record to be RECONNECTED to its new manager within the set MANAGES. However, the Research DEPARTMENT record is already a member of a different MANAGES set instance, so when it is made the CRU it will also become the current of set for the MANAGES set type:

EX16:   EMPLOYEE.SSN := '836483873';
         $FIND ANY EMPLOYEE **USING** SSN; (* set current of set for MANAGES *)
         if DB_STATUS = 0 then
             begin
             DEPARTMENT.NAME = 'Research';
             $FIND ANY DEPARTMENT **USING** NAME **RETAINING** MANAGES
             CURRENCY;
             (* set CRU *without changing* the current of set for MANAGES *)
             if DB_STATUS = 0 then **$RECONNECT** DEPARTMENT **WITHIN**
             MANAGES
             end;

To make the record become the CRU *without changing the current of set*, we use the RETAINING CURRENCY phrase appended to the FIND command. In EX16, we use the RETAINING MANAGES CURRENCY phrase appended to the FIND command. This changes the CRU to the Research DEPARTMENT record but leaves the current of set of MANAGES unchanged; it remains the set instance owned by the EMPLOYEE record whose SSN is 836483873.

Notice that the record to be moved should be a member of a set instance of the same set type before the RECONNECT command is issued; otherwise, we should use the CONNECT command. A RECONNECT can be replaced by a DISCONNECT and a CONNECT for OPTIONAL sets. However, for MANDATORY sets we must use the RECONNECT command if we want to move a member record from one set instance to another, because it must remain connected to an owner at all times.

10.6 A Network Database System—IDMS*

10.6.1 *Introduction*

In this section we survey a popular DBMS based on the network model called the Integrated Database Management System (IDMS). It is currently marketed by Computer Associates under the name CA-IDMS. The network model has had a number of major commercial DBMS implementations: IDS II of Honeywell, DMS II of Burroughs (now UNISYS), DMS 1100 of UNIVAC (now UNISYS), VAX-DBMS of Digital Equipment, IMAGE of Hewlett-Packard, and IDMS. Most of these systems (with the exception of the original IDS) were developed following the 1971 CODASYL DBTG report (DBTG 1971) and implemented the concepts specified in that report. The DBTG report was revised in 1978 and 1981, adding some concepts and deleting others. For example, data structure descriptions or views over multiple record types (which we did not discuss) were added in the 1978 report. LOCATION MODE for record type definition and the AREA concept from the original report (which we did not discuss either) were dropped. When we analyze any particular CODASYL system (sometimes called a DBTG system), we should typically explore most of the features of the network model. Otherwise, the CODASYL DBTG classification of the system becomes questionable. Minor variations exist, some of which can be attributed to the DBTG report updates of 1978 and 1981.

DMS II of UNISYS is not a true CODASYL DBTG implementation, since it does not follow the network data model strictly. It supports embedded record types and hence can be considered as hierarchical as well as network. The TOTAL system of CINCOM also does *not* follow the DBTG concepts. It represents data in terms of two types of record types, called *master* and *variable*. Relationships can be defined from any master record type to any variable record type, but no relationships are possible among variable record types. TOTAL has since been enhanced into SUPRA.

The DBTG proposed three languages:

- Schema DDL—to describe a network-structured database. This is equivalent to the ANSI/SPARC conceptual schema (Section 2.2).

- Subschema DDL—to describe the part of the database relevant to one application. This corresponds to the ANSI/SPARC external schema.

- DML—data manipulation language for processing the data defined by the preceding two languages. The DML in DBTG (1971) was proposed to be used in conjunction with COBOL and hence was called COBOL DML.

All network model implementations have their own syntax for these three languages. Our DML syntax in this chapter is quite close to that in IDMS. All systems use the concept of user work areas (UWAs) and currency indicators, as shown in Figure 10.13. Some DBMSs (including IDMS) also use a device media control language (DMCL), which defines the physical characteristics of the storage media, such as buffer and page sizes to which the schema definition is mapped.

IDMS is an implementation of the CODASYL DBTG concepts originally by Cullinet Software. It is designed to run on IBM mainframes under all standard operating systems. The name of the product was officially changed to IDMS/R (IDMS/Relational) in 1983, when relational facilities were added on top of the base product. Currently, it is known as CA-IDMS and has two versions: DB and DC. In this section we concentrate on the basic network-oriented facilities that correspond to the original IDMS. IDMS is closely integrated with a dictionary product called **Integrated Data Dictionary** (IDD).

10.6.2 *Basic Architecture of* IDMS

The IDMS family of products provides various facilities based on the central DBMS and the IDD. The IDD stores a variety of entities (an IDD term). Basic entities include users, systems, files, data items, reports, transactions, programs, and program entry points. Teleprocessing entities include messages, screens, display formats, queues, destinations, lines, terminals, and encoding tables. A number of relationships and cross-references among these entities are also stored.

Data definition facilities include three compilers that compile the schema DDL, the subschema DDL, and the DMCL. IDMS is invoked by a CALL interface for data manipulation. Users do not code the calls in their programs (unlike with IMS). Instead, they use a set of DML statements similar to those in Table 10.2. A **DML preprocessor** translates the DML statements into calling sequences appropriate to the host language. IDMS provides DML facilities within the following host languages: COBOL, PL/1, and IBM assembler language. The relational extensions in IDMS/R include the Automatic System Facility

(ASF)—a menu-driven front end to the system that permits a set of form-based functions to define and manipulate relational views in the form of logical records. The Logical Record Facility (LRF) creates a view of the underlying database as virtual tables for relational processing.

Computer Associates provide a set of supporting products for use with IDMS. Besides IDD, they include the following:

- *Application generator* (Application Development System/On-Line Application Generator—ADS): With this tool, an application developer defines the application functions and responses to the dictionary. It acts as a prototype tool and enables the user to have an on-line preview of the application.

- *On-line query (OLQ):* This interface allows users to ask ad hoc queries against the database or to obtain formatted reports by using predefined queries.

- *Report writer (CULPRIT):* This is a parameter-driven report writer. It actively uses the definition stored in the dictionary to generate reports. Report definitions can be stored in the dictionary and invoked by supplying the report name and parameters.

Other products are mentioned under various boxes in the CA-IDMS Environment (see Figure 10.15).

Starting from the preceding repertoire of facilities, development of an IDMS application proceeds as follows:

1. Database schema, subschema, and so on are defined by means of interactive tools called IDD utilities.

2. The schemas are compiled by using the schema compiler.

3. A DMCL description to define the physical characteristics of the database is compiled by the DMCL compiler.

4. Subschemas for various applications are compiled by the subschema compiler. The logical records or views are a part of the subschema in IDMS/R.

5. Application source programs are written in a host language with embedded DML statements and precompiled. The precompilers record in the dictionary the operations that each program performs on specific data. This information is automatically monitored by the IDD. Hence it is called an *active* dictionary.

10.6.3 *Data Definition in* IDMS

The schema is defined by using the schema DDL. The online schema compiler allows a free-form syntax, incremental schema modification, and schema validation. A schema has five different parts: schema description, file description, area description, record description, and set description. We will concentrate on the last two. The record and set type definitions for defining the schema of Figure 10.9 that are shown in Figure 10.10 can be used with minor syntax variations in IDMS record definitions. We will not discuss the full syntax; instead, we just highlight the differences between IDMS's DDL and the DDL in Section 10.3. The main differences are as follows:

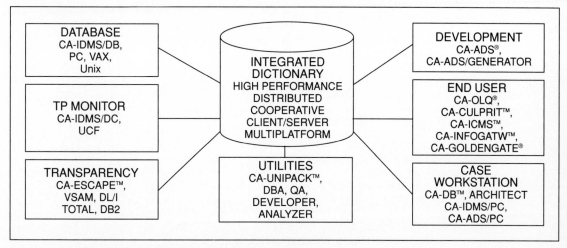

Figure 10.15   The IDMS product family. (Courtesy: Computer Associates, *CA-IDMS/DB: Product Concepts and Facilities Manual*)

- A record type must be assigned to an AREA when it is defined, using the phrase "WITHIN AREA."
- A record type must have a LOCATION MODE specification.

An **area** is a DBTG concept that refers to a group of record types. An area is typically mapped to a physically contiguous storage space. This concept has physical overtones and compromises data independence. Hence it was removed from the 1981 DBTG report. The **location mode** for record type is a specification of how a new occurrence of that record should be stored and how existing occurrences should be retrieved. IDMS allows the following location modes:

- CALC—The record is stored by using a CALC key from within the record; this key is used for hashing to calculate a page address, and the record is stored in or near that page. The CALC key may be declared to be unique (DUPLICATES NOT ALLOWED).
- VIA—The VIA followed by a set type name means that a member record is stored physically as close as possible to the owner record (if they belong to the same area). If they are assigned to different areas, the member record is stored at the *same relative position* in the area as the owner in its area. This feature was valid up to release 10.0 of IDMS.
- VIA INDEX—In this option, available after release 10.0, a record is stored via a "system-owned index" that provides a system owner record and a B^+-tree index. The system owner record contains the name of the index, and it points to the B^+-tree, which, in turn, points to the member records.
- DIRECT—A record is placed on or near a user-specified page.

```
SCHEMA NAME IS COMPANY

RECORD NAME IS EMPLOYEE
LOCATION MODE IS CALC USING SSN
DUPLICATES NOT ALLOWED
WITHIN EMP_AREA
02 FNAME    PIC X(15)
02 MINIT    PIC X
02 LNAME    PIC X(15)
02 SSN      PIC 9(9)
02 BIRTHDATE PIC X(9)
02 ADDRESS  PIC X(30)
02 SEX      PIC X
02 SALARY   PIC 9(10)
02 DEPTNAME PIC X(15)

RECORD NAME IS WORKS_ON
LOCATION MODE IS VIA E_WORKSON SET
WITHIN EMP_AREA
02 ESSN     PIC 9(9)
02 PNUMBER  PIC 999 USAGE COMP-3
02 HOURS    PIC 99  USAGE COMP-3

SET NAME IS WORKS_FOR
OWNER IS DEPARTMENT
MEMBER IS EMPLOYEE MANUAL OPTIONAL
ORDER IS SORTED
MODE IS CHAINED
ASCENDING KEY IS LNAME, FNAME
DUPLICATES ALLOWED
```

Figure 10.16   Sample record and set type definitions in IDMS schema DDL.

Another option, called physical sequential, is also available. In Figure 10.16 we give sample definitions of record types EMPLOYEE and WORKS_ON from the database shown in Figure 10.9. Data items are defined in the style of COBOL. See the similarity of this definition to that in Figure 10.10. EMPLOYEE is accessed by the unique CALC key of SSN, whereas WORKS_ON is accessed by using VIA E_WORKSON set type. To allow a user to start searching a database directly at a record type, that record must have been declared with location mode CALC or DIRECT. Another option is to use a system-owned set (Section 10.1.3) with that record type as a member.

IDMS also uses the concept of **database keys,** which we omitted in the earlier discussion. IDMS assigns a unique identifier called a database key to each record occurrence when it is entered into the database. Its value is a 4-byte identifier containing a page number and a line number.

Set Definitions. IDMS set definitions differ from the set features described earlier in the following ways:

1. The SET SELECTION clause is missing. Thus, to insert a record automatically into the set, the program must select an appropriate set occurrence, making it current.

2. The FIXED set retention is not provided; only MANDATORY and OPTIONAL are allowed.

3. There is no CHECK facility to check that a member in a set satisfies a certain constraint before it is added into the set (see the example of CHECK on the WORKS_FOR set in Figure 10.10(b)).

4. Set definition includes the choice of implementation by means of "MODE IS CHAINED or INDEXED." The former links up the members in every set occurrence by means of a circular linked list; the latter sets up an index for each set occurrence (see Section 10.1.4).

5. It is possible to designate the order in which pointers such as next or prior pointers or owner pointers (see Section 10.1.4) should be allocated within the record. This is another example of how a low-level physical specification is done as part of the DDL in IDMS.

In Figure 10.16 we show how the set type WORKS_FOR in Figure 10.9 would be defined in the DDL.

Subschema Definition. A subschema in IDMS is a subset of the original schema obtained by omitting data items, record types, and set types. Whenever a record type is omitted, all set types in which it participates as an owner or member must be eliminated. Subschema definition has two data divisions: identification division and subschema data division. The latter specifies the areas, the record types or parts thereof, and the sets to be included. An on-line subschema compiler is available. Figure 10.17 shows a hypothetical subschema definition that includes a subset of the schema in Figure 10.9 related to employees, departments, and supervisors. Subschema definition can also include logical record and path-group statements.

There are some problems with the ERASE command when applied to a record in the subschema. The deletion may propagate via set membership to a number of other records that may not be part of the subschema. The subschema designer must include all such record types to which a delete may propagate when defining the subschema.

Device Media Control Language (DMCL) Description. The DMCL allows a specification of the physical storage parameters that govern the mapping of the instances of data into storage for a given schema description. It specifies buffer size in terms of number of pages, and page size in bytes; it associates area names with names of buffer pools and states the names of journal files, specifying the types of device on which journal files will reside. We do not give any details of the syntax of DMCL here.

10.6.4 *Data Manipulation in IDMS*

The data manipulation language concepts introduced in Section 10.5 are applicable with minor changes to IDMS. All DML commands in Table 10.2 are available in some form. The variations are discussed next.

```
ADD
          SUBSCHEMA NAME IS EMP_DEPT OF SCHEMA  NAME COMPANY
          DMCL NAME IS ED_DMCL
          PUBLIC ACCESS IS ALLOWED FOR DISPLAY
ADD
          AREA NAME IS EMP_AREA
          DEFAULT USAGE IS SHARED UPDATE
ADD
          AREA NAME IS DEP_AREA
ADD
          RECORD NAME IS EMPLOYEE
                    ELEMENTS ARE ALL
ADD
          RECORD NAME IS SUPERVISOR
                    ELEMENTS ARE ALL
ADD
          RECORD NAME IS DEPARTMENT
                    ELEMENTS ARE NUMBER, NAME
ADD
          SET NAME IS IS_A_SUPERVISOR
ADD
          SET NAME IS SUPERVISEES
ADD
          SET NAME IS MANAGES
ADD
          SET NAME IS WORKS_FOR
```

Figure 10.17   Subschema definition for the schema in Figure 10.9 (details omitted).

Retrieval Commands

- The FIND CALC <record-type-name> is applicable when a key value is already supplied in the Calc-Key field of the UWA.

- FIND <record-type-name> DBKEY is <dbkey-value> is a way of finding a record, given the database key value. This form can be used whether or not the location mode of that record is DIRECT, but it requires that the program supply the database key value (absolute location id) of the record. This is normally done if a record that has been retrieved previously is to be retrieved again in the program. The DBKEY is saved and reused.

- For retrieving a record within a set type, or within an area, the following FIND is available:

    FIND (FIRST | NEXT | PRIOR | LAST) <record-type-name> [WITHIN <set-type-name> | WITHIN <area-name>]

The available types of FINDs are summarized in Figure 10.18. IDMS also allows the verb OBTAIN in place of the FIND-GET combination.

- The fourth type of FIND in Figure 10.18 can be used not only within a set type but also within an area.

1 FIND ANY (or CALC) <record-type-name>
   FIND DUPLICATE   <record-type-name>
2 FIND <record-type-name> DBKEY IS <dbkey-value>
3 FIND CURRENT [<record-type-name> | WITHIN <set-type-name> |
       WITHIN <area-name >]
4 FIND [NEXT| PRIOR| FIRST| LAST| NTH] <record-type-name> WITHIN
       [<set-type-name> | WITHIN <area-name>]
5 FIND <record-type-name> WITHIN <set-type-name> USING
       <ordering-field-name>

Figure 10.18   Available types of FIND in IDMS.

Update Commands. The STORE, ERASE, and MODIFY commands of Section 10.5.4 apply to IDMS. The IDMS ERASE has four options:

- ERASE—Deletes the CRU (current of run unit) record if it is not the owner of any nonempty set occurrence. The system takes into account all sets for which the record type is an owner.

- ERASE PERMANENT—Deletes the CRU record, together with MANDATORY member occurrences of that record in any set type. OPTIONAL member occurrences are not deleted but are disconnected.

- ERASE SELECTIVE—Deletes the CRU record, the MANDATORY members, *and* the OPTIONAL members that do not participate in any other set occurrence.

- ERASE ALL—Deletes the CRU record and all members, whether they are MANDATORY or OPTIONAL.

In all of these options, deletion propagates recursively—that is, as if the member record that was deleted were itself an object of the ERASE command. IDMS CONNECT and DISCONNECT work as discussed in Section 10.5.4. There is no RECONNECT in IDMS.

10.6.5 *Storage of Data in IDMS*

In IDMS a database is logically composed of one or more areas. Areas are made up of database pages. Each page corresponds to a physical block in a file, which makes a page the basic unit of input/output. The relationship among areas and files is many-to-many; that is, an area may be mapped to a number of files and vice versa. Notice the similarity of this relationship to spaces in DB2 (and storage groups in IMS). This correspondence is stored as a part of schema description. Files are divided into fixed-length blocks called pages. Each record in a page has a prefix containing a line# (assigned from bottom of page), a record-id, and a record length. The record also includes pointers—a minimum of one per set type in which it is an owner or a member. The database key of a record on page 1051, line 3 is considered to be (1051,3).

Sets are implemented in two ways: as linked sets (MODE IS CHAIN) or as indexed sets (MODE IS INDEXED). A forward pointer is included for a set type in its owner and member record types. The designer may also request reverse pointers (LINKED TO PRIOR),

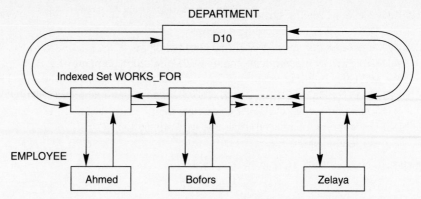

Figure 10.19   One occurrence of an ordered indexed set type WORKS_FOR.

which are assigned in both the owner and the member, and pointer to owner (LINKED TO OWNER), which is assigned to the member record.

In the indexed set representation, every set occurrence is represented by the owner and a small (local) index represented by a set of index records. Figure 10.19 shows the indexed set WORKS_FOR for the schema defined in Figure 10.16. The owner and the index records are linked along a linked list using next, prior, and owner pointers. Each member record points back to its index entry. It is *not* necessary that an indexed set be ordered.

The system-owned sets are maintained as indexed sets. There the set-ordering specification is used to order the values of the ordering field. Each index record contains this value and the database key value. There is one occurrence of each set, and the one index so created is equivalent to a clustering index. However, many system-owned sets can be defined with different set orderings for the same record type. The CALC option provides hashed access on a CALC key to a record type (in IMS it is available *only for root records*). With the VIA SET option, if that set is defined by using MODE IS INDEX and ORDER IS SORTED, not only are the member records stored close to the owner (same page or a nearby page), but also the physical order of the member records closely approximates their logical order.

The product that deals with centralized database processing (without telecommunications) is called CA-IDMS/DB. IDMS is also available, providing an integrated communications facility in the form of the product CA-IDMS/DC. Details are outside our scope here, since we have not yet discussed distributed databases and "client-server" architectures.

For compatibility with the relational model, IDMS has been enhanced to support the coexistence of both navigational and relational processing—even within the same application. It naturally involves allowing records to be treated as rows of a table, where the record type is equivalent to a table or relation definition. The querying and programming facilities allow three ways of accessing data: by using the navigational DML; by using the SQL language; and by using dynamic SQL, where the SQL query is formulated within a program at run-time. These multiple-access mechanisms are supported on top of the "logical level." The "physical level" deals with stored data in the form of files stored in BDAM (Basic Direct Access Method) and VSAM (Virtual Sequential Access Method).

CA-IDMS/DB SQL is based on ANSI SQL standard, level 2. The language includes GRANT and REVOKE options (see Chapter 20), besides standard SQL (discussed in Chapter 7). The product called CA Extended SQL includes more advanced facilities including dynamic SQL and data/time/substring features in SQL. We will not get into the details of processing the network model's stored databases by using the relational model, but the trend is likely to be in that direction with existing network DBMS products.

10.7 Summary

In this chapter we discussed the network model, which represents data by using the building blocks of record types and set types. Each set type defines a 1:N relationship between an owner record type and a member record type. A record type can participate as owner or member in any number of set types. This is the main distinction between set types of the network model and the parent-child relationships of the hierarchical model discussed in Chapter 11. In the hierarchical model, relationships must obey a strictly hierarchical pattern. Because of the restrictions on the different types of parent-child relationships in most hierarchical DBMSs, the network model has a better modeling capability than does the hierarchical model. The modeling capability of the network model is also superior to that of the original relational model in that it *explicitly* models relationships, although the incorporation of foreign keys in the relational model alleviates this weakness. The JOIN operations in the relational model actually become visible and substantial as set types in the network model.

We discussed three special types of sets. SYSTEM-owned or singular sets are used to define entry points to the database. Multimember sets are used for the case when member records can be from more than one record type. Recursive sets are sets that have the same record type participating both as owner and as member. Because of implementation difficulties, recursive sets were prohibited in the original CODASYL network model, and it is now customary to represent them by using an additional linking record type and two set types.

We then discussed the types of integrity constraints on set membership that can be specified on a network schema. These are classified into insertion options (MANUAL or AUTOMATIC), retention options (OPTIONAL, MANDATORY, or FIXED), and ordering options.

The circular linked list (or ring) representation of implementing set instances was discussed; and we also discussed other implementation options for set instances that can be used to improve the performance of the circular linked list, such as double-linking and owner pointers. Other techniques that can be used to implement sets instead of linked lists, such as contiguous storage or pointer arrays, were also briefly discussed.

M:N relationships, or relationships in which more than two record types participate, can also be represented by using a linking record type. In the case of an M:N relationship with two participating record types, two set types and a linking record type are used. In the case of an n-ary relationship in which n record types participate, one linking record type and n set types are needed. One-to-one relationships are not represented explicitly;

they can be represented as a set type, but the application programs must make sure that each set instance has at most one member record at all times.

A data definition language (DDL) was presented for the network model. We saw how record types and set types are defined, and we discussed the various SET SELECTION options that are used with AUTOMATIC sets. These options specify how the DBMS identifies the appropriate set instance of an AUTOMATIC set type where a new member record is to be connected when the record is stored in the database.

We presented the commands of a record-at-a-time data manipulation language (DML) for the network model. We saw how to write programs with embedded DML commands to retrieve information from a network database and to update the database. The FIND command is used to "navigate" through the database, setting various currency indicators, whereas the GET command is used to retrieve the CRU into the corresponding UWA program variable. Commands for inserting, deleting, and modifying records and for modifying set instances were covered, as well.

Finally, we gave an overview of the IDMS commercial network DBMS.

Review Questions

10.1. Discuss the various types of fields (data items) that can be defined for record types in the network model.

10.2. Define the following terms: *set type, owner record type, member record type, set instance (set occurrence), AUTOMATIC set type, MANUAL set type, MANDATORY set type, OPTIONAL set type, FIXED set type*.

10.3. How are the set instances of a set type identified?

10.4. Discuss the various constraints on set membership and the cases in which each constraint should be used.

10.5. In the circular linked list (ring) representation of set instances, how does the DBMS distinguish between member records and the owner record of a set instance?

10.6. Discuss the various methods of implementing set instances. For each method, discuss which types of set-processing FIND commands can be implemented efficiently and which cannot.

10.7. What are SYSTEM-owned (singular) set types used for?

10.8. What are multimember set types used for?

10.9. What are recursive set types? Why are they not allowed in the original CODASYL network model? How can they be implemented via a linking record type?

10.10. Show how each of the following types of relationships is represented in the network model: (a) M:N relationships; (b) n-ary relationships with n > 2; (c) 1:1 relationships. Discuss how an ER schema can be mapped into a network schema.

10.11. Discuss the following concepts, and explain what each is used for when writing a network DML database program: (a) the user work area (UWA); (b) currency indicators; (c) the database status indicator.

10.12. Discuss the different types of currency indicators, and tell how each type of navigational FIND command affects each currency indicator.

10.13. Describe the various SET SELECTION options for AUTOMATIC set types, and specify the circumstances under which each SET SELECTION option should be chosen.

10.14. State what each of the following clauses in the network DDL specifies: (a) DUPLICATES ARE NOT ALLOWED; (b) ORDER IS; (c) KEY IS; (d) CHECK.

10.15. For what purpose is the RETAINING CURRENCY clause used with the FIND command in the network DDL?

10.16. How does the ERASE ALL command differ from the ERASE command?

10.17. Discuss the CONNECT, DISCONNECT, and RECONNECT commands, and specify the types of set constraints under which each can be used.

Exercises

10.18. Specify the queries of Exercise 6.19, using network DML commands embedded in PASCAL on the network database schema of Figure 10.9. Use the PASCAL program variables declared in Figure 10.12, and declare any additional variables you may need.

10.19. How would you modify the program segment in EX3 so that it retrieves for *each* department the department name and the names of all employees who work in that department, ordered alphabetically?

10.20. Consider the following query: "For each department, print the department name and its manager's name; for each employee who works in that department, print the employee's name and the list of project names the employee works on." First write a program segment for this query. Then modify it so that the following conditions are met, one at a time:

   a. Only departments with greater than 10 employees are listed.

   b. Only employees who work more than 20 total hours are listed.

   c. Only employees with dependents are listed.

10.21. Consider the network database schema shown in Figure 10.20, which corresponds to the relational schema of Figure 2.1. Write appropriate network DDL statements to define the record types and set types of the schema. Choose appropriate set constraints for each set type, and justify your choices.

10.22. Write PASCAL program segments with embedded network DML commands to specify the queries of Exercise 7.16 on the schema of Figure 10.20.

10.23. Write PASCAL program segments with embedded network DML commands to do the updates and tasks of Exercises 7.17 and 7.18 on the network database schema of Figure 10.20. Specify any program variables you need.

10.24. During processing of the query "Find all courses offered by the COSC department; and for each course, list its name, its sections, and its prerequisites" on the schema of Figure 10.20, the following steps are performed by the DBMS: (a) find

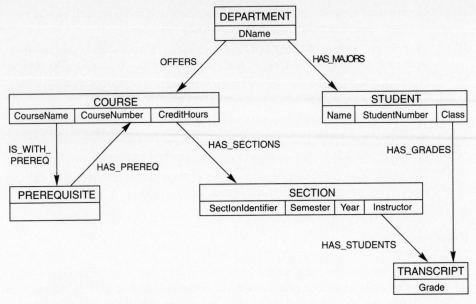

Figure 10.20   Network schema for a university database.

the DEPARTMENT record for COSC; (b) find a COURSE record for COSC541 as a member of OFFERS; (c) find a SECTION record for section S32491 as a member of HAS_SECTIONS; (d) find a PREREQUISITE record occurrence—say, P1—as a member of IS_WITH_PREREQ; (e) find a member course record of HAS_PREREQ—say, the course MATH143. Show the currency indicators of set types, record types, and the CRU after each of these events, using the notation in Figure 10.14. Assume that all currency indicators were nil originally. What happens to the currency of the COURSE record type after step (e)? Suppose that we did FIND NEXT COURSE WITHIN OFFERS after step (e); what problem would arise, and how could we solve it? (*Hint:* Consider using the RETAINING CURRENCY phrase in some of the commands.)

10.25. Write procedures in pseudocode (PASCAL style) that may be part of the DBMS software, and outline the action taken by the following DML commands:

   a. Process the STORE <record type> command. This should check for set type definitions in the DBMS catalog to determine which sets the record type participates in as owner or member, and take appropriate action.

   b. Process the ERASE <record type> and ERASE ALL <record type> commands.

10.26. Choose some database application that you are familiar with or interested in.

   a. Design a network database schema for your database application.

   b. Declare your record types and set types using the network DDL.

   c. Specify a number of queries and updates that are needed by your database application, and write a PASCAL program segment with embedded network DML commands for each of your queries.

   d. Implement your database if you have a network DBMS system available.

10.27. Map the following ER schemas into network schemas. Specify for each set type the insertion and retention options and any ordering options, and justify your choices.

   a. The AIRLINES ER schema of Figure 3.19.

   b. The BANK ER schema of Figure 3.20.

   c. The SHIP_TRACKING ER schema of Figure 6.21.

10.28. Consider the network schema diagram for a LIBRARY database shown in Figure 10.21, which corresponds to the relational schema of Figure 6.22.

   a. Specify appropriate PASCAL UWA variables for the LIBRARY schema.

   b. Write PASCAL program segments with embedded network DML commands for each of the queries in Exercise 6.26.

   c. Compare the relational (Figure 6.22) and network (Figure 10.21) schemas for the LIBRARY database. Identify their similarities and differences. How can you make the network schema more similar to the relational schema?

10.29. Try to map the network schema of Figure 10.21 into an ER schema. This is part of a process known as *reverse engineering*, where a conceptual schema is created for an existing implemented database. State any assumptions you make.

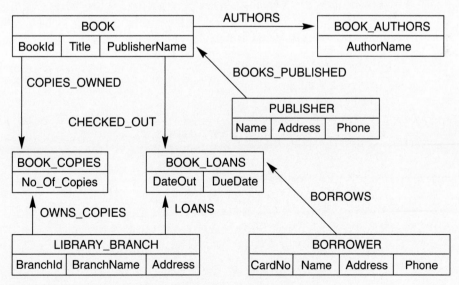

Figure 10.21   Network schema diagram for a LIBRARY database.

Selected Bibliography

Early work on the network data model was done by Charles Bachman during the development of the first commercial DBMS, IDS (Bachman and Williams 1964) at General Electric and later at Honeywell. Bachman also introduced the earliest diagrammatic technique for representing relationships in database schemas, called data structure diagrams (Bachman 1969) or Bachman diagrams. Bachman won the 1973 Turing Award, ACM's highest honor, for his work, and his Turing Award lecture (Bachman 1973) presents the view of the database as a primary resource and the programmer as a "navigator" through the database. In a 1974 debate between proponents and opponents of the relational approach, he represented the latter (Bachman 1974). Other work on the network model was performed by George Dodd (Dodd 1966) at General Motors Research. Dodd (1969) gives an early survey of database management techniques.

The DBTG (Data Base Task Group) of CODASYL (Conference on Data Systems Languages) was set up to propose DBMS standards. The DBTG 1971 report (DBTG 1971) contains schema and subschema DDLs and a DML for use with COBOL. A revised report (CODASYL 1978) was made in 1978, and another draft revision was made in 1981. The X3H2 committee of ANSI (the American National Standards Institute) proposed a standard network language called NDL.

The design of network databases is discussed by Dahl and Bubenko (1982), Whang et al. (1982), Schenk (1974), Gerritsen (1975), and Bubenko et al. (1976). Irani et al. (1979) discusses optimization techniques for designing network schemas from user requirements. Bradley (1978) proposes a high-level query language for the network model. Navathe (1980) discusses structural mapping of network schemas to relational schemas. Mark et al. (1992) discusses an approach to maintaining a network and relational database in a consistent state.

Network database management is surveyed by Taylor and Frank (1976). Extensive treatments of the network model are offered in the books by Cardenas (1985), Kroenke and Dolan (1988), and Olle (1978). The IDMS system is described in several CA-IDMS/DB manuals published by Computer Associates.

The Hierarchical Data Model and the IMS System

The hierarchical model of data was developed to model the many types of hierarchical organizations that exist in the real world. Humans have long used hierarchical organization of information to help them better understand the world. There are many examples, such as classification schemes for species in the plant and animal worlds and classification schemes for human languages. Humans also adopted hierarchical structures and naming schemes to deal with the structures they created, such as corporate organization charts, library classification schemes, and governmental hierarchies. The hierarchical data model represents hierarchical organizations in a direct and natural way and may be the best choice in some situations, but it has problems when representing situations with nonhierarchical relationships.

There is no original document that describes the hierarchical model, as there are for the relational and network models. Rather, several early computer information management systems were developed using hierarchical storage structures. Recent examples of these systems include Control Data Corporation's Multi-Access Retrieval System (MARS VI), IBM's Information Management System (IMS), and MRI's System-2000 (now sold by SAS Institute).

In this chapter we present the principles behind the hierarchical model independent of any specific system and relate them to IMS, which is the dominant hierarchical system in use today. Section 11.1 discusses hierarchical schemas and instances. In Section 11.2 the concept of a virtual parent-child relationship, which is used to overcome the limitations of pure hierarchies, is discussed. Section 11.3 discusses constraints on the hierarchical model. Section 11.5 addresses the mapping of schemas from the ER model into the hierarchical model. Sections 11.4 and 11.6 discuss data definition and data manipulation languages for the hierarchical data model as defined here. A representative hierarchical system (namely, IMS) is discussed in Section 11.7. Some features of another hierarchical system called System 2000 are also mentioned. Section 11.8 summarizes this chapter.

For readers seeking only a brief overview of the hierarchical model, some or all of Sections 11.4 through 11.7 may be skipped.

11.1 Hierarchical Database Structures

In this section, the data structuring concepts of the hierarchical model are discussed. We first discuss parent-child relationships and how they can be used to form a hierarchical schema (in Section 11.1.1). Then we discuss the properties of a hierarchical schema (in Section 11.1.2). Hierarchical occurrence trees are discussed in Section 11.1.3 and a common method for storing these trees—called the hierarchical sequence—is discussed (in Section 11.1.4).

11.1.1 Parent-Child Relationships and Hierarchical Schemas

The hierarchical model employs two main data structuring concepts: records and parent-child relationships. A **record** is a collection of **field values** that provide information on an entity or a relationship instance. Records of the same type are grouped into **record types**. A record type is given a name, and its structure is defined by a collection of named **fields** or **data items**. Each field has a certain data type, such as integer, real, or string.

A **parent-child relationship type (PCR type)** is a 1:N relationship between two record types. The record type on the 1-side is called the **parent record type,** and the one on the N-side is called the **child record type** of the PCR type. An **occurrence** (or **instance) of the PCR type** consists of *one record* of the parent record type and *a number of records* (zero or more) of the child record type.

A **hierarchical database schema** consists of a number of hierarchical schemas. Each **hierarchical schema** (or **hierarchy**) consists of a number of record types and PCR types.

A hierarchical schema is displayed as a **hierarchical diagram,** in which record type names are displayed in rectangular boxes and PCR types are displayed as lines connecting the parent record type to the child record type. Figure 11.1 shows a simple hierarchical diagram for a hierarchical schema with three record types and two PCR types. The record

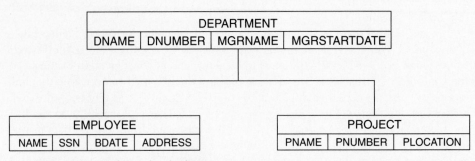

Figure 11.1 A hierarchical schema.

types are DEPARTMENT, EMPLOYEE, and PROJECT. Field names can be displayed under each record type name, as shown in Figure 11.1. In some diagrams, for brevity, we display only the record type names.

We refer to a PCR type in a hierarchical schema by listing the pair (parent record type, child record type) between parentheses. The two PCR types in Figure 11.1 are (DEPARTMENT, EMPLOYEE) and (DEPARTMENT, PROJECT). Notice that PCR types *do not* have a name in the hierarchical model. However, a certain meaning is associated with each PCR type by the database designer. In Figure 11.1 each *occurrence* of the (DEPARTMENT, EMPLOYEE) PCR type relates one department record to the records of the *many* (zero or more) employees who work in that department. An *occurrence* of the (DEPARTMENT, PROJECT) PCR type relates a department record to the records of projects controlled by that department. Figure 11.2 shows two PCR occurrences (or instances) for each of these two PCR types.

11.1.2 *Properties of a Hierarchical Schema*

A hierarchical schema of record types and PCR types must have the following properties:

1. One record type, called the **root** of the hierarchical schema, does not participate as a child record type in any PCR type.

2. Every record type except the root participates as a child record type in *exactly one* PCR type.

3. A record type can participate as parent record type in any number (zero or more) of PCR types.

4. A record type that does not participate as parent record type in any PCR type is called a **leaf** of the hierarchical schema.

5. If a record type participates as parent in more than one PCR type, then *its child*

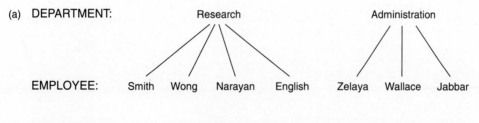

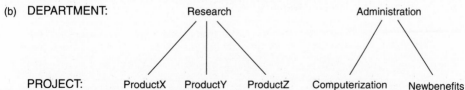

Figure 11.2   Occurrences of PCR types. (a) Two occurrences of the PCR type (DEPARTMENT, EMPLOYEE). (b) Two occurrences of the PCR type (DEPARTMENT, PROJECT).

record types are ordered. The order is displayed, by convention, from left to right in a hierarchical diagram.

The definition of a hierarchical schema defines a **tree data structure**. In the terminology of tree data structures, a record type corresponds to a **node** of the tree, and a PCR type corresponds to an **edge** (or **arc**) of the tree. We will use the terms *node* and *record type*, and *edge* and *PCR type*, interchangeably. The usual convention of displaying a tree is slightly different from that used in hierarchical diagrams, in that each tree edge is shown separately from other edges (Figure 11.3). In hierarchical diagrams the convention is that all edges emanating from the same parent node are joined together (Figure 11.1). We will use this latter hierarchical diagram convention.

The preceding properties of a hierarchical schema mean that every node except the root has exactly one parent node. However, a node can have several child nodes, and in this case they are ordered from left to right. In Figure 11.1 EMPLOYEE is the first child of DEPARTMENT, and PROJECT is the second child. The previously identified properties also limit the types of relationships that can be represented in a hierarchical schema. In particular, M:N relationships between record types *cannot* be directly represented, because parent-child relationships are 1:N relationships, and a record type *cannot participate as child* in two or more distinct parent-child relationships.

An M:N relationship may be handled in the hierarchical model by allowing *duplication of child record instances.* For example, consider an M:N relationship between EMPLOYEE and PROJECT, where a project can have several employees working on it, and an employee can work on several projects. We can represent the relationship as a (PROJECT, EMPLOYEE) PCR type as shown in Figure 11.4(a). In this case a record describing the same employee can be duplicated by appearing once under *each* project that the employee works for. Alternatively, we can represent the relationship as an (EMPLOYEE, PROJECT) PCR type as shown in Figure 11.4(b), in which case project records may be duplicated.

EXAMPLE 1:   Consider the following instances of the EMPLOYEE:PROJECT relationship:

Project	Employees Working on the Project
A	E1, E3, E5
B	E2, E4, E6
C	E1, E4
D	E2, E3, E4, E5

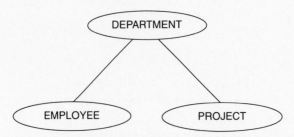

Figure 11.3   Tree representation of the hierarchical schema in Figure 11.1.

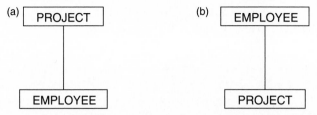

Figure 11.4 Representing an M:N relationship. (a) One representation of the M:N relationship. (b) Alternative representation of the M:N relationship.

If these instances are stored using the hierarchical schema of Figure 11.4(a), there will be four occurrences of the (PROJECT, EMPLOYEE) PCR type—one for each project. The employee records for E1, E2, E3, and E5 will appear *twice each* as child records, however, because each of these employees works on two projects. The employee record for E4 will appear three times—once under each of projects B, C, and D. Some data field values in the employee records may be context-dependent; that is, these field values depend on both EMPLOYEE and PROJECT. Such data may differ in each occurrence of a duplicated employee record because it also depends on the parent project record. An example is a field that gives the number of hours per week that an employee works on the project. However, the majority of the field values in the employee records, such as employee name, social security number, and salary, would certainly be duplicated under each project that the employee works for. ■

To avoid such duplication, a technique is used whereby several hierarchical schemas can be specified in the same hierarchical database schema. Relationships like the preceding PCR type can now be defined *across* hierarchical schemas, allowing us to circumvent the problem of duplication discussed earlier. This technique, called "virtual" relationships, causes a departure from the "strict" hierarchical model. We discuss this technique in Section 11.2.

11.1.3 *Hierarchical Occurrence Trees*

Corresponding to a hierarchical schema, many hierarchical occurrences exist in the database. Each **hierarchical occurrence,** also called an **occurrence tree,** is a **tree** structure whose root is a single record from the root record type. The occurrence tree also contains all the children record occurrences of the root record, all children record occurrences within the PCRs of each of the child records of the root record, and so on, all the way to records of the leaf record types.

For example, consider the hierarchical diagram shown in Figure 11.5, which represents part of the COMPANY database introduced in Chapter 3 and also used in Chapters 6 to 10. Figure 11.6 shows one hierarchical occurrence tree of this hierarchical schema. In the occurrence tree, each node is a record occurrence, and each arc represents a parent-child relationship between two records. In both Figures 11.5 and 11.6, we use the characters **D, E, P, T, S,** and **W** to represent **type indicators** for the record types DEPART-

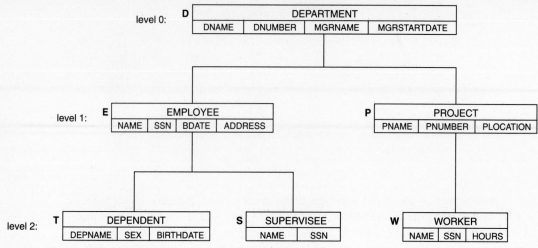

Figure 11.5   Hierarchical schema for part of the COMPANY database.

MENT, EMPLOYEE, PROJECT, DEPENDENT, SUPERVISEE, and WORKER, respectively. We shall see the significance of these type indicators when we discuss hierarchical sequences in the next section.

We can define occurrence trees more formally by using the terminology for tree structures, which we need in our subsequent discussion. In a tree structure, the root is said to have **level** zero. The level of a nonroot node is one more than the level of its parent node, as shown in Figures 11.5 and 11.6. A **descendent** D of a node N is a node connected to N via one or more arcs such that the level of D is greater than the level of N. A node N and all its descendent nodes form a **subtree** of node N. An **occurrence tree** can now be defined as the subtree of a record whose type is of the root record type.

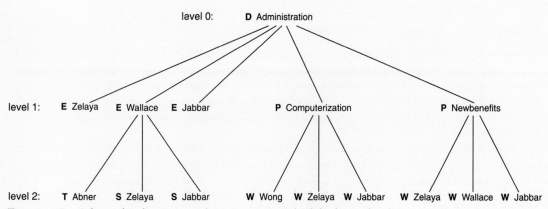

Figure 11.6   A hierarchical occurrence (or occurrence tree) of the hierarchical schema in Figure 11.5.

The root of an occurrence tree is a single record occurrence of the root record type. There may be a varying number of occurrences of each nonroot record type, and each such occurrence must have a parent record in the occurrence tree; that is, each such occurrence must participate in a PCR occurrence. Notice that each nonroot node, together with all its descendent nodes, forms a **subtree**, which, taken alone, satisfies the structure of an occurrence tree for a portion of the hierarchical diagram. Notice, too, that the level of a record in an occurrence tree is the same as the level of its record type in the hierarchical diagram.

11.1.4 *Linearized Form of a Hierarchical Occurrence*

A hierarchical occurrence tree can be represented in storage by using any of a variety of data structures. However, a particularly simple storage structure that can be used is the **hierarchical record,** which is a linear ordering of the records in an occurrence tree in the *preorder traversal* of the tree. This order produces a sequence of record occurrences known as the **hierarchical sequence** (or **hierarchical record sequence**) of the occurrence tree; it can be obtained by applying the following recursive procedure to the root of an occurrence tree:

```
procedure Pre_order_traverse ( root record );
    begin
    output ( root record );
    for each child record of root record in left to right order do
            Pre_order_traverse ( child record )
    end;
```

The above procedure, when applied to the occurrence tree in Figure 11.6, gives the hierarchical sequence shown in Figure 11.7. If we use the hierarchical sequence to implement occurrence trees, we need to store a record type indicator with each record because of the different record types and the variable number of child records in each parent-child relationship. The system needs to examine the type of each record as it goes

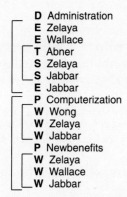

```
      D  Administration
      E  Zelaya
      E  Wallace
      T  Abner
      S  Zelaya
      S  Jabbar
      E  Jabbar
      P  Computerization
      W  Wong
      W  Zelaya
      W  Jabbar
      P  Newbenefits
      W  Zelaya
      W  Wallace
      W  Jabbar
```

Figure 11.7   Hierarchical sequence for the occurrence tree in Figure 11.6.

sequentially through the records. Notice that these record type indicators are implementation structures and are not seen by the hierarchical DBMS user.

The hierarchical sequence is often desirable because the child nodes follow their parent node in storage. Hence, given a parent record, all descendent records in its subtree follow it in the hierarchical sequence and can be retrieved efficiently. However, child records are collectively placed after their parent record only if the child records are leaf nodes in the occurrence tree. Otherwise, whole subtrees of each child node are placed after their parent record in left-to-right order.

The hierarchical sequence is also important because some hierarchical data-manipulation languages, such as that used in IMS, use it as a basis for defining hierarchical database operations. The HDML language we discuss in Section 11.4 is based on the hierarchical sequence.

Next, we define two additional terms that are used by some hierarchical languages. A **hierarchical path** is a sequence of nodes $N_1, N_2, \ldots, N_i$, where N_1 is the root of a tree and N_j is a child of N_{j-1} for $j = 2, 3, \ldots, i$. A hierarchical path can be defined either on a hierarchical schema or on an occurrence tree. A hierarchical path is **complete** if N_i is a leaf of the tree. A **broom** is a set of hierarchical paths resulting from the hierarchical path $N_1, N_2, \ldots, N_i$ along with all the hierarchical paths in the subtree of N_i. For example, (DEPARTMENT, EMPLOYEE, SUPERVISEE) is a complete path in the hierarchical schema of Figure 11.5. In the occurrence tree of Figure 11.6, (Administration, Wallace) is a path, and (Administration, Wallace, {Abner, Zelaya, Jabbar}) is a broom.

We can now define a **hierarchical database occurrence** as a sequence of all the occurrence trees that are occurrences of a hierarchical schema. This is similar to the definition of a **forest** of trees in data structures. For example, a hierarchical database occurrence of the hierarchical schema shown in Figure 11.5 would consist of a number of occurrence trees similar to the one shown in Figure 11.6. There would be one occurrence tree for each DEPARTMENT record, and they would be ordered as the first, second, . . ., last occurrence tree.

11.2 Virtual Parent-Child Relationships

The hierarchical model has problems when modeling certain types of relationships. These include the following relationships and situations:

1. M:N relationships.

2. The case where a record type participates as child in more than one PCR type.

3. N-ary relationships with more than two participating record types.

As we saw in Section 11.1.2, case 1 can be represented as a PCR type at the expense of duplicating record occurrences of the child record type. Case 2 can be represented in a similar fashion, with more duplication of records. Case 3 presents a problem because the PCR is a binary relationship.

Record duplication, in addition to wasting storage space, causes problems with maintaining consistent duplicate copies of the same record. The concept of a virtual (or pointer) record type is used in the IMS system to deal with all three problem cases identified earlier. The idea is to include more than one hierarchical schema in the hierarchical database schema and to use pointers from nodes of one hierarchical schema to the other to represent the relationships. We do *not* follow IMS terminology, but instead develop the concepts more generally.

A **virtual** (or **pointer**) **record type** VC is a record type with the property that each of its records contains a pointer to a record of another record type VP. VC plays the role of "virtual child" and VP of "virtual parent" in a "virtual parent-child relationship." Each record occurrence c of VC points to exactly one record occurrence p of VP. Rather than duplicating the record p itself in an occurrence tree, we include the virtual record c that contains a pointer to p. Several virtual records may point to p, but only a single copy of p itself is stored in the database.

Figure 11.8 shows the M:N relationship between EMPLOYEE and PROJECT represented with virtual records EPOINTER and PPOINTER. Compare this with Figure 11.4, where the same relationship was represented without virtual records. Figure 11.9 shows the occurrence trees and pointers for the data instances given in Example 1 when the hierarchical schema shown in Figure 11.8(a) is used. In Figure 11.9 there is only a single copy of each EMPLOYEE record; however, several virtual records may point to the same EMPLOYEE record. Hence, the information stored in an EMPLOYEE record is not duplicated. Information that depends on both parent and child records—such as hours per week that an employee works on a project—is included in the virtual pointer record; such data is popularly known among hierarchical database users as **intersection data**.

Notice that the relationship between EMPLOYEE and EPOINTER in Figure 11.8(a) is a 1:N relationship and hence qualifies as a PCR type. Such a relationship is called a **virtual parent-child relationship (VPCR) type**. EMPLOYEE is called the **virtual parent** of EPOINTER; and conversely, EPOINTER is called a **virtual child** of EMPLOYEE. Conceptually, PCR types and VPCR types are similar. The main difference between the two lies in the way they are implemented. A PCR type is usually implemented by using the hierarchical sequence, whereas a VPCR type is usually implemented by establishing a pointer (a phys-

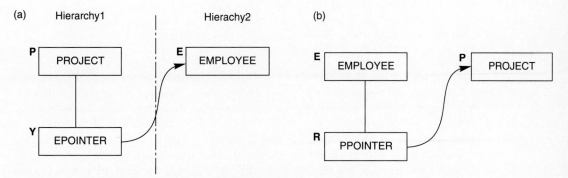

Figure 11.8 Representing an M:N relationship by using VPCR types. (a) One representation of the M:N relationship, with virtual parent EMPLOYEE. (b) Alternative representation of the M:N relationship, with virtual parent PROJECT.

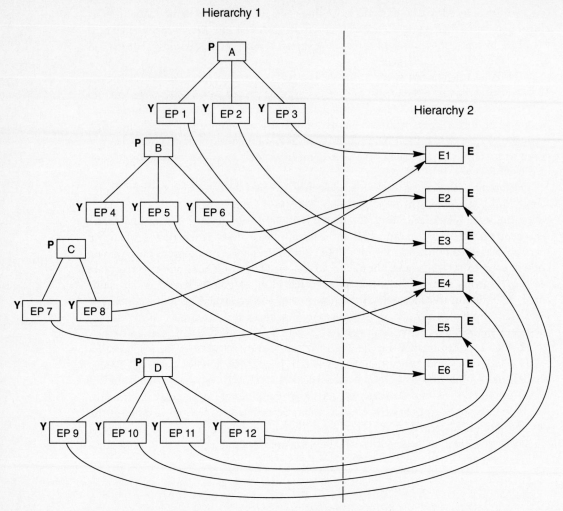

Figure 11.9 The occurrences of Example 1 corresponding to the hierarchical schema in Figure 11.8(a).

ical one containing an address, or a logical one containing a key) from a virtual child record to its virtual parent record. This mainly affects the efficiency of certain queries.

Figure 11.10 shows a hierarchical database schema of the COMPANY database that uses some VPCRs and has no redundancy in its record occurrences. The hierarchical database schema is made up of two hierarchical schemas—one with root DEPARTMENT, and the other with root EMPLOYEE. Four VPCRs, all with virtual parent EMPLOYEE, are included to represent the relationships without redundancy. Notice that IMS *may not allow this* because an implementation constraint in IMS limits a record to being virtual parent of at most one VPCR; to get around this constraint, one can create dummy children record types of EMPLOYEE in Hierarchy 2 so that each VPCR points to a distinct virtual parent record type.

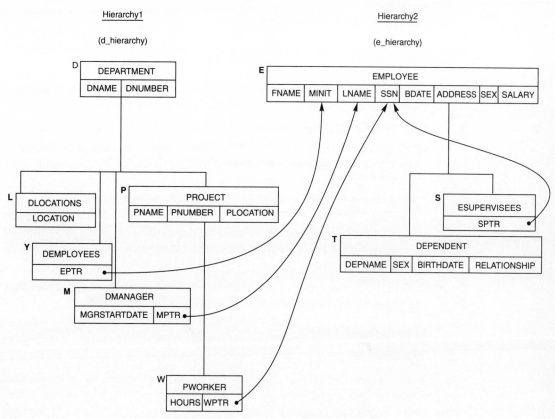

Figure 11.10 A hierarchical schema for the COMPANY database, using VPCR types among two hierarchies to eliminate redundant record instances.

In general, there are many feasible methods of designing a database using the hierarchical model. In many cases, performance considerations are the most important factor in choosing one hierarchical database schema over another. Performance depends on the implementation options available on each specific system, as well as on specific limits set by the DBA at a particular installation—for example, whether certain types of pointers are provided by the system and whether certain limits on number of levels are imposed by the DBA.

One thing to consider about VPCRs is that they can be implemented in different ways. One option is just to have a pointer in the virtual child to the virtual parent, as we discussed earlier. A second option is to have, in addition to the child-to-parent pointer, a backward link from the virtual parent to a linked list of virtual child records. The pointer from the virtual parent to the first virtual child record is called a **virtual child pointer,** whereas a pointer from one virtual child to the next is called a **virtual twin pointer**. In this case, the hierarchical model becomes *very similar* to the network model, which was discussed in Chapter 10. This backward link makes it easy to retrieve all the virtual child records of a particular virtual parent record.

11.3 Integrity Constraints in the Hierarchical Model

A number of built-in **inherent constraints** exist in the hierarchical model whenever we specify a hierarchical schema. These include the following constraints:

1. No record occurrences except root records can exist without being related to a parent record occurrence. This has the following implications:

   a. A child record cannot be inserted unless it is linked to a parent record.

   b. A child record may be deleted independently of its parent; however, deletion of a parent record automatically results in deletion of all its child and descendent records.

   c. The above rules do not apply to virtual child records and virtual parent records. The rule here is that a pointer in a virtual child record must point to an actual occurrence of a virtual parent record. Deletion of a record should not be allowed while pointers exist to it from virtual child records, making it a virtual parent.

2. If a child record has two or more parent records from the *same* record type, the child record must be duplicated once under each parent record.

3. A child record having two or more parent records of *different* record types can do so only by having at most one real parent, with all the others represented as virtual parents.

In addition, each hierarchical DBMS may have its own additional integrity rules that are unique to its own implementation. For example, in IMS a record type can be the virtual parent in *only one* VPCR type. This implies that the schema of Figure 11.10 is *not* allowed by IMS, because the EMPLOYEE record is virtual parent in four distinct VPCRs. Another rule in IMS is that a root record type *cannot* be a virtual child record type in a VPCR type.

Any other constraints that are not implicit in a hierarchical schema must be enforced explicitly by the programmers in the database update programs. For example, if a duplicated record is updated, it is the responsibility of the update program to ensure that all copies are updated in the same way.

11.4 Data Definition in the Hierarchical Model*

In this section we give an example of a hierarchical data definition language (HDDL), which is *not* the language of any specific hierarchical DBMS but is used to illustrate the language concepts for a hierarchical database. The HDDL demonstrates how a hierarchical database schema can be defined. Some of the terminology used here is different from that of IMS and other hierarchical DBMSs. To define a hierarchical database schema, we must define the fields of each record type, the data type of each field, and any key constraints on fields. In addition, we must specify a root record type as such; and for every nonroot record type, we must specify its (real) parent in a PCR type. Any VPCR types must also be specified.

Figure 11.11 shows the HDDL specification of the database schema shown in Figure 11.10. Most of the statements are self-explanatory. In actual hierarchical DBMSs, the syntax is usually more complicated, and (as we mentioned earlier) the terminology may be different. Notice also that some of the structures, such as the representation of EMPLOYEE as a virtual parent of more than one VPCR type, may not be allowed in some hierarchical DBMSs such as IMS.

In Figure 11.11, either each record type is declared to be of type root or a single (real) parent record type is declared for the record type. The data items of the record are then listed along with their data types. We must specify a virtual parent for data items that are of type *pointer*. Data items declared under the KEY clause are constrained to have unique values for each record. Each KEY clause specifies a separate key; and if a single KEY clause lists more than one field, the combination of these field values must be unique in each record.

The CHILD NUMBER clause specifies the left-to-right order of a child record type under its (real) parent record type. In Figure 11.11 these correspond to the left-to-right order shown in Figure 11.10 and are needed to specify the order of the child subtrees of different child record types under a parent record in the hierarchical sequence. For example, under an EMPLOYEE record we first have all subtrees of its DEPENDENT child records (CHILD NUMBER = 1), followed by all subtrees of its ESUPERVISEES child records (CHILD NUMBER = 2) in the hierarchical sequence.

The ORDER BY clause specifies the order of individual records of the same record type in the hierarchical sequence. For a root record type, this specifies the order of the occurrence trees. For example, EMPLOYEE records are ordered alphabetically by LNAME, FNAME, so the occurrence trees of these records are ordered alphabetically by these fields. For nonroot record types, the ORDER BY clause specifies how the records should be ordered *within each parent record*, by specifying a field called a **sequence key**. For example, PROJECT records controlled by a particular DEPARTMENT have their subtrees ordered alphabetically within the same parent DEPARTMENT record by PNAME, according to Figure 11.11.

11.5 Hierarchical Database Design Using ER-to-Hierarchical Mapping★

In the hierarchical model, only 1:N relationship types can be represented in a particular hierarchy as parent-child relationship (PCR) types. In addition, a record type can have at most one (real) parent record type; hence, M:N relationship types are difficult to represent. Possible ways to represent M:N relationship types in a hierarchical database include the following:

- Represent the M:N relationship type as though it were a 1:N relationship type. In this case, record instances at the N-side are duplicated because each record may be related to several parents. This representation keeps all record types in a single hierarchy *at the cost of duplicating record instances*. The application programs that update the database must maintain the consistency of duplicate copies.

```
SCHEMA NAME = COMPANY

HIERARCHIES = HIERARCHY1, HIERARCHY2

RECORD
    NAME = EMPLOYEE
    TYPE = ROOT OF HIERARCHY2
    DATA ITEMS =
        FNAME       CHARACTER 15
        MINIT       CHARACTER 1
        LNAME       CHARACTER 15
        SSN         CHARACTER 9
        BDATE       CHARACTER 9
        ADDRESS     CHARACTER 30
        SEX         CHARACTER 1
        SALARY      CHARACTER 10
    KEY = SSN
    ORDER BY LNAME, FNAME

RECORD
    NAME = DEPARTMENT
    TYPE = ROOT OF HIERARCHY1
    DATA ITEMS =
        DNAME       CHARACTER 15
        DNUMBER     INTEGER
    KEY = DNAME
    KEY = DNUMBER
    ORDER BY DNAME

RECORD
    NAME = DLOCATIONS
    PARENT = DEPARTMENT
    CHILD NUMBER = 1
    DATA ITEMS =
        LOCATION    CHARACTER 15

RECORD
    NAME = DMANAGER
    PARENT = DEPARTMENT
    CHILD NUMBER = 3
    DATA ITEMS =
        MGRSTARTDATE    CHARACTER 9
        MPTR            POINTER WITH VIRTUAL PARENT = EMPLOYEE

RECORD
    NAME = PROJECT
    PARENT = DEPARTMENT
    CHILD NUMBER = 4
    DATA ITEMS =
        PNAME       CHARACTER 15
        PNUMBER     INTEGER
        PLOCATION   CHARACTER 15
    KEY = PNAME
    KEY = PNUMBER
    ORDER BY PNAME
```

Figure 11.11   Declarations for the hierarchical schema in Figure 11.10. *(continued on next page)*

```
RECORD
    NAME = PWORKER
    PARENT = PROJECT
    CHILD NUMBER = 1
    DATA ITEMS =
        HOURS          CHARACTER 4
        WPTR           POINTER WITH VIRTUAL PARENT = EMPLOYEE

RECORD
    NAME = DEMPLOYEES
    PARENT = DEPARTMENT
    CHILD NUMBER = 2
    DATA ITEMS =
        EPTR           POINTER WITH VIRTUAL PARENT = EMPLOYEE

RECORD
    NAME IS ESUPERVISEES
    PARENT = EMPLOYEE
    CHILD NUMBER = 2
    DATA ITEMS =
        SPTR           POINTER WITH VIRTUAL PARENT = EMPLOYEE

RECORD
    NAME = DEPENDENT
    PARENT = EMPLOYEE
    CHILD NUMBER = 1
    DATA ITEMS =
        DEPNAME        CHARACTER 15
        SEX            CHARACTER 1
        BIRTHDATE      CHARACTER 9
        RELATIONSHIP   CHARACTER 10
    ORDER BY DESC BIRTHDATE
```

Figure 11.11   *(continued)* Declarations for the hierarchical schema in Figure 11.10.

• Create more than one hierarchy and have virtual parent-child relationship (VPCR) types (logical pointers) from a record type that appears in one hierarchy to the root record type of another hierarchy. These pointers can be used to represent the M:N relationship type in a manner similar to the one used in the network model. Even then, a constraint, adopted from the IMS DBMS model, restricts each record type to having at most one virtual child.

Because multiple options may be considered, there is no standard method for mapping an ER schema into a hierarchical schema. We will illustrate the two possibilities discussed above with two hierarchical schemas, in Figures 11.12(a) and (b), that can be used to represent the ER schema shown in Figure 3.2. A third alternative is shown in Figure 11.10.

Figure 11.12(a) shows a single hierarchy that can be used to represent the ER schema of Figure 3.2. We choose DEPARTMENT as the root record type of the hierarchy. The 1:N relationship types WORKS_FOR and CONTROLS and the 1:1 relationship type MANAGES are represented at the first level of the hierarchy by the record types EMPLOYEE, PROJECT, and DEPT_MANAGER, respectively. However, to limit redundancy, we keep only some of the attributes of an employee who is a manager in the DEPTMANAGER record type. The EMPLOYEE records in a hierarchical tree owned by a particular DEPARTMENT record will

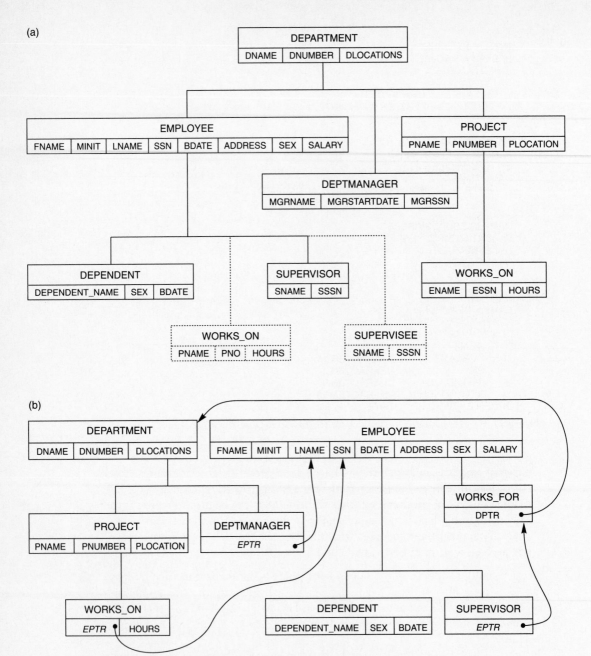

Figure 11.12   Mapping the ER schema of Figure 3.2 to the hierarchical model. (a) A hierarchical database schema for the COMPANY database with a single hierarchy. (b) Another hierarchical database schema for the same database with two hierarchies and four VPCRs.

represent the employees who work for that department. Similarly, the PROJECT records will represent the projects controlled by that department, and the DEPTMANAGER record will represent the employee who manages the department. An employee who is a manager is thus represented twice—once as an instance of EMPLOYEE, and the second time as an instance of DEPTMANAGER. The application programs are responsible for maintaining these copies in consistent form.

The 1:N relationship type DEPENDENTS_OF is represented by the record type DEPENDENT as a subordinate of EMPLOYEE (we did not include the RELATIONSHIP attribute of DEPENDENT here). The M:N relationship type WORKS_ON is represented as a subordinate of PROJECT, but only an employee's ENAME and ESSN are included in WORKS_ON, along with the relationship attribute HOURS. An employee who works on several different projects will be stored in as many copies of WORKS_ON record instances with identical ENAME, ESSN values. The rest of the information on employees is not replicated in WORKS_ON, in order to limit redundancy. Notice that each WORKS_ON record represents one of the employees working on a particular project. Alternatively, we could represent WORKS_ON as a subordinate record type of EMPLOYEE; in this case, each WORKS_ON record would represent one of the projects that an EMPLOYEE works on, and its fields would be PNAME, PNUMBER, and HOURS, as shown by the dotted WORKS_ON box in Figure 11.12(a). In the latter case, PROJECT information would be duplicated in multiple copies of WORKS_ON records.

Finally, the SUPERVISION relationship type is represented as a subordinate of EMPLOYEE. We could choose to represent it in either the role of a supervisor or that of a supervisee. In Figure 11.12(a) each SUPERVISOR record represents the supervisor of the owner EMPLOYEE record in the hierarchy, so the hierarchical relationship represents the supervisor role; each employee has a single child record SUPERVISOR representing his or her direct supervisor. Alternatively, we could represent the role of a supervisee in the hierarchical relationship; then every EMPLOYEE record that represents a supervisory employee would be related to (potentially) many direct supervisees as child records. This is shown in dotted lines in the box SUPERVISEE in Figure 11.12(a). In either case, EMPLOYEE information is replicated in the SUPERVISOR or SUPERVISEE records, so we include only a few of the attributes of EMPLOYEE.

There is excessive replication in Figure 11.12(a) of employee information in the record types EMPLOYEE, DEPTMANAGER, WORKS_ON, and SUPERVISOR, because they all represent employees in various roles. We can somewhat limit the replication by representing the ER schema of Figure 3.2 with two or more hierarchies. In Figure 11.12(b) two hierarchies are used. The first hierarchy has DEPARTMENT as root record type and represents the relationship types CONTROLS, MANAGES, and WORKS_ON. The second hierarchy has EMPLOYEE as root record type and represents the relationship types DEPENDENTS_OF and SUPERVISION. By using virtual parent-child relationships and virtual pointers in the WORKS_ON, DEPTMANAGER, and SUPERVISOR record types, we do not replicate any employee information. Each pointer will point to an EMPLOYEE record, but EMPLOYEE information is stored only once as a root record of the second hierarchy. The WORKS_FOR relationship type is represented by a child of the EMPLOYEE record called WORKS_FOR with virtual parent DEPARTMENT.*

---

*This is done because the root record EMPLOYEE is *not* allowed to have a virtual parent in IMS.

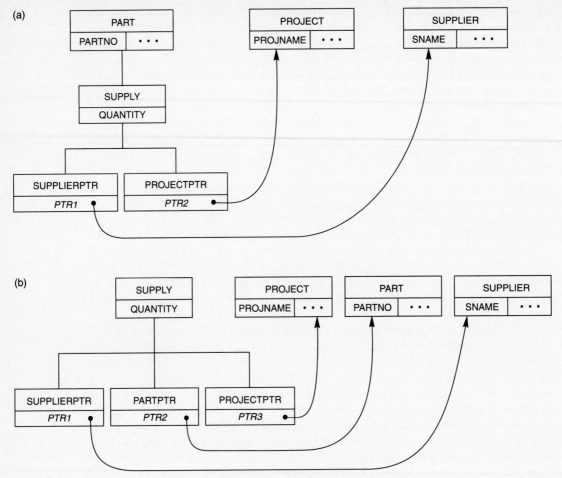

Figure 11.13   Mapping an n-ary (n = 3) relationship type SUPPLY from ER to hierarchical. (a) One option for representing a ternary relationship. (b) Representing a ternary relationship using three VPCR types.

Finally, consider the mapping of n-ary relationship types, n > 2. Figure 11.13 shows two options for mapping the SUPPLY ternary relationship type of Figure 3.16(a). Because of the constraint, derived from IMS, that a record type can have at most one virtual parent, we cannot place SUPPLY under PART, say, and include two pointers to two virtual parents PROJECT and SUPPLIER. The option in Figure 11.13(a) creates *two pointer record types* under SUPPLY with virtual parents PROJECT and SUPPLIER. Another option, shown in Figure 11.13(b), is to have SUPPLY as root of a hierarchy and create three pointer record types under it to point to the participating record types as virtual parents. This option is the most flexible one.

Clearly, the hierarchical model offers many options for representing the same ER schema. Many other representations, besides those discussed above, could have been used. The issues of efficient data access and of limiting redundancy versus facilitating retrieval are important in choosing a particular representation. The hierarchical model is generally considered inferior in its modeling capability to both the relational model and the network model, for the following reasons:

- M:N relationship types can be represented only by adding redundant records or by using virtual parent-child relationships and pointer records.

- All 1:N relationship types in a hierarchy must be maintained in the same direction.

- A record type in a hierarchy can have at most one (real) owner record type.

- A record type can have at most two parents—one real and one virtual. (This limitation is specific to IMS.)

11.6 Data Manipulation Language for the Hierarchical Model★

We now discuss HDML (Hierarchical Data Manipulation Language), which is a record-at-a-time language for manipulating hierarchical databases. The commands of the language must be embedded in a general-purpose programming language, called the **host** language. Although it is more common to have COBOL or PL/I as the host language, we use PASCAL in our examples to maintain consistency with the rest of this book. Notice that HDML is *not* a language for a particular hierarchical DBMS; rather, it is introduced to illustrate the concepts of a hierarchical database manipulation language. We begin by introducing the general concept of a user work area for communication with the system, together with some currency concepts.

11.6.1 *User Work Area (UWA) and Currency Concepts for Using HDML Commands*

In a record-at-a-time language, a database retrieval operation retrieves database records into **program variables**. In our examples, database records are retrieved into PASCAL program variables. The program can then refer to the program variables to access the field values of the database records. We assume that a PASCAL record type has been declared for each record type in the schema of Figure 11.10. The PASCAL program variables, shown in Figure 11.14, use the *same field names* as those in the database schema of Figure 11.10, whereas *record names* are prefixed with a P_. These program variables exist in what is often called the **user work area**. Notice that it is possible to have these variables declared automatically by referring to the database schema declared in Figure 11.11. Initially, the values of these record variables are undefined. Whenever a data retrieval operation retrieves a database record of a particular type, it is placed in the corresponding UWA program variable.

```
var P_EMPLOYEE        :    record
                           FNAME: packed array [1..15] of char;
                           MINIT: char;
                           LNAME: packed array [1..15] of char;
                           SSN: packed array [1..9] of char;
                           BDATE: packed array [1..9] of char;
                           ADDRESS: packed array [1..30] of char;
                           SEX: char;
                           SALARY : packed array [1..10] of char
                           end;
    P_DEPARTMENT      :    record
                           DNAME: packed array [1..15] of char;
                           DNUMBER: integer
                           end;
    P_DLOCATIONS      :    record
                           LOCATION: packed array [1..15] of char
                           end;
    P_DMANAGER        :    record
                           MGRSTARTDATE: packed array [1..9] of char;
                           MPTR: database pointer to EMPLOYEE
                           end;
    P_PROJECT         :    record
                           PNAME: packed array [1..15] of char;
                           PNUMBER: integer;
                           PLOCATION: packed array [1..15] of char
                           end;
    P_PWORKER         :    record
                           HOURS: packed array [1..4] of char;
                           WPTR: database pointer to EMPLOYEE
                           end;
    P_DEMPLOYEES      :    record
                           EPTR: database pointer to EMPLOYEE
                            end;
    P_ESUPERVISEE     :    record
                           SPTR: database pointer to EMPLOYEE
                           end;
    P_DEPENDENT       :    record
                           DEPNAME: packed array [1..15] of char;
                           SEX: char;
                           BIRTHDATE: packed array [1..9] of char;
                           RELATIONSHIP: packed array [1..10] of char
                           end;
```

Figure 11.14   PASCAL program variables in the UWA corresponding to part of the hierarchical schema in Figure 11.10.

The HDML is based on the concept of **hierarchical sequence** defined in Section 11.1. Following each database command, the last record accessed by the command is called the **current database record**. The DBMS maintains a pointer to the current record. Subsequent database commands proceed *from the current record* and may define a new current record, depending on the type of command. Hence, HDML commands traverse through a hierarchical database retrieving the records required by the query. Originally, the current database record is an "imaginary record" located just before the root record of the first occurrence tree in the database.

If a database has more than one hierarchical schema in it, and these hierarchies are processed together, the IMS system allows the definition of a user view to create a tailor-made hierarchical schema that includes the desired record types connected by VPCR types.* Such a view is treated as a single **hierarchical schema** and has its own **current database record**. Since we do not intend to go into the details of defining and processing these views, we will assume for convenience that *each hierarchical schema* has its own **current of hierarchy record**. IMS also has provisions for remembering the last record accessed of *each record type,* so we assume that the system keeps track of the **current of record type** for *each record type*—this is a pointer to the last record accessed from the record type. The HDML commands implicitly refer to these three types of **currency indicators:**

- Current of database.
- Current of hierarchy for each hierarchical schema.
- Current of record type for each record type.

Record-at-a-time programming requires continuous interaction between the user program and the DBMS. **Status information** at the end of each database command must be communicated back to the program. This is accomplished by a variable called **DB_STATUS,** whose value is set by the DBMS software after each database command is executed. We will assume that a value of DB_STATUS = 0 specifies that the last database command was successfully executed.

HDML commands can be categorized as retrieval commands, update commands, and currency retention commands. **Retrieval commands** retrieve one or more database records into the corresponding program variables and may change some currency indicators. **Update commands** are used to insert, delete, and modify database records. **Currency retention commands** are used to mark the current record so that it can be updated or deleted by a subsequent command. The HDML commands are summarized in Table 11.1.

We now discuss each of these commands and illustrate our discussion with examples based on the schema shown in Figure 11.10. In the program segments, *HDML commands are prefixed with a $-sign* to distinguish them from the PASCAL language statements. PASCAL language key words—such as if, then, while, and for—are written in lowercase.

11.6.2 *The GET Command*

The HDML command for retrieving a record is the **GET** command. There are many variations of GET; the structure of two of these variations is as follows, with optional parts shown between brackets [...]:

- GET FIRST** <record type name> [WHERE <condition>]
- GET NEXT <record type name> [WHERE <condition>]

The simplest variation is the **GET FIRST** command, which always starts searching the database from the *beginning of the hierarchical sequence* until it finds the first record occurrence of <record type name> that satisfies <condition>. This record also becomes

---

*These "view" schemas are called **logical databases** in IMS and will be discussed briefly in Section 11.7.3.
This is similar to the **GET UNIQUE (GU) command of IMS.

Table 11.1   Summary of HDML Commands

RETRIEVAL

GET — RETRIEVE A RECORD INTO THE CORRESPONDING PROGRAM VARIABLE AND MAKE IT THE CURRENT RECORD. VARIATIONS INCLUDE GET FIRST, GET NEXT, GET NEXT WITHIN PARENT, AND GET PATH.

RECORD UPDATE

INSERT — STORE A NEW RECORD IN THE DATABASE AND MAKE IT THE CURRENT RECORD

DELETE — DELETE THE CURRENT RECORD (AND ITS SUBTREE) FROM THE DATABASE

REPLACE — MODIFY SOME FIELDS OF THE CURRENT RECORD

CURRENCY RETENTION

GET HOLD — RETRIEVE A RECORD AND HOLD IT AS THE CURRENT RECORD SO IT CAN SUBSEQUENTLY BE DELETED OR REPLACED

---

the current of database, current of hierarchy, and current of record type and is retrieved into the corresponding UWA program variable. For example, to retrieve the "first" EMPLOYEE record in the hierarchical sequence whose name is John Smith, we write EX1:

> EX1:   **$GET FIRST** EMPLOYEE **WHERE** FNAME='John' AND LNAME='Smith';

The DBMS uses the condition following WHERE to search for the first record in order of the hierarchical sequence that satisfies the condition and is of the specified record type. The value of DB_STATUS is set to 0 (zero) if the record is *found successfully;* otherwise, DB_STATUS is set to some other value—1, say—that indicates *not found.* Other errors or exceptions are indicated by different values for DB_STATUS.

If more than one record in the database satisfies the WHERE condition and we want to retrieve all of them, we must write a looping construct in the host program and use the GET NEXT command. We assume that the GET NEXT starts its search from the *current record of the record type specified in GET NEXT** and searches forward in the hierarchical sequence to find another record of the specified type satisfying the WHERE condition. For example, to retrieve records of all EMPLOYEEs whose salary is less than $20,000 and obtain a printout of their names, we can write the program segment shown in EX2:

> EX2:   **$GET FIRST** EMPLOYEE **WHERE** SALARY < '20000.00';
> while **DB_STATUS** = 0 do
>   begin
>   writeln (P_EMPLOYEE.FNAME, P_EMPLOYEE.LNAME);
>   **$GET NEXT** EMPLOYEE **WHERE** SALARY < '20000.00'
>   end;

---

* IMS commands generally proceed forward from the *current of database,* rather than from the current of specified record type as HDML commands do.

In EX2, the while loop continues until no more EMPLOYEE records in the database satisfy the WHERE condition; hence, the search goes through to the last record in the database (hierarchical sequence). When no more records are found, DB_STATUS becomes nonzero, with a code indicating "end of database reached," and the while loop terminates. Notice that the WHERE condition in the GET commands is optional. If there is no condition, the very next record in the hierarchical sequence of the specified record type is retrieved. For example, to retrieve all EMPLOYEE records in the database, we can use EX3:

```
EX3:    $GET FIRST EMPLOYEE;
        while DB_STATUS = 0 do
            begin
            writeln ( P_EMPLOYEE.FNAME, P_EMPLOYEE.LNAME );
            $GET NEXT EMPLOYEE
            end;
```

11.6.3 The GET PATH and GET NEXT WITHIN PARENT Commands

So far we have considered retrieving single records by using the GET command. But when we have to locate a record deep in the hierarchy, the retrieval may be based on a series of conditions on records along the entire hierarchical path. To accommodate this, we introduce the GET PATH command:

```
GET ( FIRST | NEXT ) PATH <hierarchical path> [ WHERE <condition> ]
```

Here, <hierarchical path> is a list of record types that starts from the root along a path in the hierarchical schema, and <condition> is a Boolean expression specifying conditions on the individual record types along the path. Because several record types may be specified, the field names are prefixed by the record type names in <condition>. For example, consider the following query: "List the lastname and birthdates of all employee-dependent pairs, where both have the first name John." This is shown in EX4:

```
EX4:    $GET FIRST PATH EMPLOYEE, DEPENDENT
        WHERE EMPLOYEE.FNAME='John' AND DEPENDENT.DEPNAME='John';
        while DB_STATUS = 0 do
            begin
            writeln (P_EMPLOYEE.LNAME, P_EMPLOYEE.BDATE,
                    P_DEPENDENT.BIRTHDATE);
            $GET NEXT PATH EMPLOYEE, DEPENDENT
                WHERE EMPLOYEE.FNAME='John' AND
                DEPENDENT.DEPNAME='John'
            end;
```

We assume that a GET PATH command retrieves *all records along the specified path* into the UWA variables,* and the last record along the path becomes the current database record. In addition, all records along the path become the *current records of their respective record types*.

---

*IMS provides the capability of specifying that only *some* of the records along the path are to be retrieved.

Another common type of query is to find all records of a given type that have *the same parent record*. In this case we need the GET NEXT WITHIN PARENT command, which can be used to loop through the child records of a parent record and has the following format:

```
GET NEXT <child record type name>
    WITHIN [ VIRTUAL ] PARENT [ <parent record type name> ]*
    [ WHERE <condition> ]
```

This command retrieves the next record of the child record type by searching forward from the *current of the child record type* for the next child record *owned by the current parent record.* If no more child records are found, DB_STATUS is set to a nonzero value to indicate that "there are no more records of the specified child record type that have the same parent as the current parent record." The <parent record type name> is *optional,* and the default is the immediate (real) parent record type of <child record type name>. For example, to retrieve the names of all projects controlled by the 'Research' department, we can write the program segment shown in EX5:

```
EX5:    $GET FIRST PATH DEPARTMENT, PROJECT
            WHERE DNAME='Research';
            (* the above establishes the 'Research' DEPARTMENT record as
                current parent of type DEPARTMENT, and retrieves the first child
                PROJECT record under that DEPARTMENT record *)
        while DB_STATUS = 0 do
            begin
            writeln ( P_PROJECT.PNAME );
            $GET NEXT PROJECT WITHIN PARENT
            end;
```

In EX5, we can write "WITHIN PARENT DEPARTMENT" rather than just "WITHIN PARENT" in the GET NEXT command with the same effect, because DEPARTMENT is the immediate parent record type of PROJECT. However, if we want to retrieve all records owned by a parent that is *not the immediate parent*—for example, all the PWORKER records owned by the same DEPARTMENT record—then we must specify DEPARTMENT as the parent record type in the "WITHIN PARENT" clause.

Notice that there are two main methods for explicitly establishing a parent record as the current record:

- If we use GET FIRST or GET NEXT, the record retrieved becomes the current parent record.

- If we use a GET PATH command, a hierarchical path of current parent records of the respective record types is established. This can also retrieve the *first child record,* as demonstrated in EX5, so that subsequent GET NEXT WITHIN PARENT commands can be issued.

---

*There is no provision for retrieving all children of a virtual parent in IMS in this way without defining a view of the database.

We can rewrite EX4 without the GET PATH command by using one loop to find EMPLOYEEs with FNAME = 'John' and a nested loop using GET NEXT WITHIN PARENT to find any DEPENDENTs of each such EMPLOYEE with DEPNAME = 'John'. However, the GET PATH command allows us to do this more directly and with a *smaller number of calls* to the DBMS.

Another variation of the GET command can be used to locate the real or virtual parent record of the *current record of a specified child record type:**

```
GET [ VIRTUAL ] PARENT <parent record type name>
OF <child record type name>
```

For example, to retrieve the names and hours per week for each employee who works on 'ProjectX', we can use the GET PARENT command, as in EX6.

EX6:   **$GET FIRST PATH** DEPARTMENT PROJECT, PWORKER
               WHERE PNAME='ProjectX'; (* establish parent record and retrieve first
                                                      child *)
       while **DB_STATUS** = 0 do
           begin
           $GET VIRTUAL PARENT EMPLOYEE OF PWORKER;
           if DB_STATUS=0 then
                   writeln (P_EMPLOYEE.LNAME, P_EMPLOYEE.FNAME,
                   P_PWORKER.HOURS)
                   else writeln ('error--has no EMPLOYEE
                   virtual parent');
           $GET NEXT PWORKER **WITHIN** PARENT PROJECT
           end;

Notice that we can use a WHERE condition with the GET NEXT WITHIN PARENT command. For example, to retrieve the names of employees who work more than 5 hours per week on 'ProjectX', we can modify the GET NEXT PWORKER WITHIN PARENT command in EX6 to:

$GET NEXT PWORKER **WITHIN** PARENT PROJECT **WHERE** HOURS > '5.0';

We must also modify the GET FIRST PATH command appropriately. Just as we permitted traversing a VPCR from child to parent, as illustrated in EX6, we can also traverse from parent to child, using the following command modification:

```
GET NEXT <virtual child record type name>
    WITHIN PARENT <virtual parent record type name>
```

11.6.4 *Calculating Aggregate Functions*

Aggregate functions such as COUNT and AVERAGE must be explicitly implemented by the programmer, using the facilities of the host programming language. For example, to

---

*IMS does not have a counterpart for this command without using what IMS calls a **logical database,** which "hides" this operation by thinking of a virtual parent and a virtual child as a single record.

calculate the number of employees who work in each department and their average salary, we can write EX7:

```
EX7:    $GET FIRST PATH DEPARTMENT, DEMPLOYEES;
        while DB_STATUS = 0 do
            begin
            total_sal:= 0; no_of_emps:= 0; writeln (P_DEPARTMENT.DNAME);
            (* department name *)
            while DB_STATUS = 0 do
                begin
                $GET VIRTUAL PARENT EMPLOYEE;
                total_sal:= total_sal + conv_sal (P_EMPLOYEE.SALARY);
                no_of_emps:= no_of_emps + 1;
                $GET NEXT DEMPLOYEES WITHIN PARENT DEPARTMENT
                end;
                    writeln( 'no of emps =', no_of_emps,'avg sal of emps =',
                    total_sal/no_of_emps);
                    $GET NEXT PATH DEPARTMENT, DEMPLOYEES
                    end;
```

To accumulate the total salary and number of employees, we must have program variables declared, so we assume that the program variables total_sal:real and no_of_ emps:integer are declared in the program header and that a PASCAL function conv_ sal:real is also declared that converts a salary value from string to real number.

11.6.5 HDML Commands for Update

The HDML commands for updating a hierarchical database are shown in Table 11.1. The INSERT command is used to insert a new record. Before inserting a record of a particular record type, we must first place the field values of the new record in the appropriate user work area program variable. For example, suppose that we want to insert a new EMPLOYEE record for John F. Smith; we can use the program segment in EX8:

```
EX8:    P_EMPLOYEE.FNAME := 'John';
        P_EMPLOYEE.LNAME := 'Smith';
        P_EMPLOYEE.MINIT := 'F';
        P_EMPLOYEE.SSN := '567342739';
        P_EMPLOYEE.ADDRESS := '40 N.W. 80th Blvd., Gainesville, Florida, 32607'
        P_EMPLOYEE.BDATE := '10-JAN-55';
        P_EMPLOYEE.SEX := 'M';
        P_EMPLOYEE.SALARY:='30000.00'
        $INSERT EMPLOYEE FROM P_EMPLOYEE;
```

The INSERT command inserts a record into the database. The newly inserted record also becomes the current record for the database, its hierarchical schema, and its record type. If it is a root record, as in EX8, it creates a new hierarchical occurrence tree with the new record as root. The record is inserted in the hierarchical sequence in the order specified by any ORDER BY fields in the schema definition. For example, the new

EMPLOYEE record in EX8 is inserted in alphabetical order of its LNAME, FNAME combined value, according to the schema definition in Figure 11.11. If no ordering fields are specified in the definition of the root record of a hierarchical schema, a new root record is inserted following the occurrence tree that contained the current database record before the insertion.

To insert a child record, we should make its parent, or one of its sibling records, the *current record* of the hierarchical schema before issuing the INSERT command. We should also set any virtual parent pointers before inserting the record. To do that, we need a command SET VIRTUAL PARENT, which sets the pointer field in the program variable to the current record of the virtual parent record type.* The record is inserted after finding an appropriate place for it in the hierarchical sequence past the current record. For example, suppose that we want to relate the EMPLOYEE record inserted in EX8 as a 40-hour-per-week worker on the project whose project number is 55; we can use EX9:

EX9: **$GET FIRST** EMPLOYEE **WHERE** SSN='567342739'; (* find virtual parent *)
　　if **DB_STATUS**=0 then
　　　　begin
　　　　P_PWORKER.WPTR := **SET VIRTUAL PARENT;** (* virtual
　　　　parent pointer to current record *)
　　　　P_PWORKER.HOURS := '40.0';
　　　　$GET FIRST PROJECT **WHERE** PNUMBER=55; (* make (real) parent the
　　　　current record *)
　　　　if **DB_STATUS**=0 then **$INSERT** PWORKER **FROM** P_PWORKER;
　　　　end;

To delete a record from the database, we first make it the current record and then issue the **DELETE** command. The **GET HOLD** is used to make the record the current record, where the HOLD key word indicates to the DBMS that the program will delete or update the record just retrieved. For example, to delete all male EMPLOYEEs, we can use EX10, which also lists the deleted employee names *before* deleting their records:

EX10:　**$GET HOLD FIRST** EMPLOYEE **WHERE** SEX='M';
　　　while **DB_STATUS**=0 do
　　　　begin
　　　　writeln (P_EMPLOYEE.LNAME, P_EMPLOYEE.FNAME);
　　　　$DELETE EMPLOYEE;
　　　　$GET HOLD NEXT EMPLOYEE **WHERE** SEX='M';
　　　　end;

Notice that deleting a record means automatically deleting all its descendent records—all records in its subtree. However, virtual child records in other hierarchies are not deleted. In fact, before deleting a record, the DBMS should make sure that no virtual child records point to it. Following a successful DELETE command, the current record becomes an "empty position" in the hierarchical sequence corresponding to the record just deleted. Subsequent operations continue from that position.

---

*The SET VIRTUAL PARENT action is done implicitly in IMS when a logical record that includes the virtual parent in its definition is inserted.

To modify field values of a record, we take the following steps:

1. Make the record to be modified the current record, and retrieve it into the corresponding UWA program variable by using the GET HOLD command.

2. Modify the desired fields in the UWA program variable.

3. Issue the REPLACE command.

For example, to give all employees in the 'Research' department a 10% raise, we can use the program shown in EX11:

```
EX11:   $GET FIRST PATH DEPARTMENT, DEMPLOYEES
                WHERE DNAME='Research';
        while DB_STATUS = 0 do
           begin
           $GET HOLD VIRTUAL PARENT EMPLOYEE OF DEMPLOYEES;
           P_EMPLOYEE.SALARY := P_EMPLOYEE.SALARY * 1.1;
           $REPLACE EMPLOYEE FROM P_EMPLOYEE;
           $GET NEXT DEMPLOYEES WITHIN PARENT DEPARTMENT
           end;
```

11.7 Overview of the IMS Hierarchical Database System*

11.7.1 Introduction

In this section we survey a major hierarchical system—Information Management System, or IMS. Although IMS essentially implements the hypothetical hierarchical data model described earlier in this chapter, many features are peculiar to this complex system. We highlight the architecture and special types of view processing and storage structures in IMS, and we compare DL/1, IMS's data language, with the HDDL and HDML discussed earlier.

IMS is one of the earliest DBMSs, and it ranks as the dominant system in the commercial market for support of large-scale accounting and inventory systems. IBM manuals refer to the full product as IMS/VS (Virtual Storage); and typically, the full product is installed under the MVS operating system. IMS DB/DC is the term used for installations that utilize the product's own subsystems to support the physical database (DB) and to provide data communications (DC).

However, other important versions exist that support only the IMS data language (DL/1). Such DL/1-only configurations can be implemented under MVS, but they may also use the DOS/VSE operating system. These systems issue their calls to VSAM files and use IBM's Customer Information Control System (CICS) for data communications. The trade-off is a sacrifice of support features for the sake of simplicity and improved throughput.

The original IMS/360 Version 1 product was introduced by IBM in 1968 following a joint development project with North American Rockwell. A number of major revisions to IMS have followed. These have incorporated or accommodated major technological advances: modern communications networking, direct record access (augmented "fast path"), and secondary indexes, among others. IMS development now embodies several thousand man-years of effort, much of that driven by the needs of an articulate user community.

IMS has no built-in query language, which can be seen as a major shortcoming. Partial responses to this situation appeared early on, with IBM's IQF (interactive query facility) and other add-on products sold by vendors or developed by users. One common and high-flexibility solution today is to download information from the typically enormous IMS database to a separate relational system. Then, with relevant summary data moved to a microcomputer or to the mainframe's SQL/DS or DB2 system, individual corporate entities can carry out their own information system functions.

A number of versions of IMS have been marketed to work with various IBM operating systems, including (among the recent systems) OS/VS1, OS/VS2, MVS, MVS/XA, and ESA. The system comes with various options. IMS runs under different versions on the IBM 370 and 30XX family of computers. The data definition and manipulation language of IMS is Data Language One, or DL/1. Application programs written in COBOL, PL/1, FORTRAN, and BAL (Basic Assembly Language) interface with DL/1.

System 2000 (S2K) is another popular hierarchical system that follows a different version of the hierarchical data model. It operates on a wide range of systems, including IBM 360/370, 43XX, and 30XX models, as well as UNIVAC, CDC, and CYBER hardware. System S2K can be configured with options such as a nonprocedural query language for nonprogrammers, a procedural language interface to COBOL, PL/1, and FORTRAN, a sequential file processing capability, and a teleprocessing monitor. In the rest of this section, we describe various aspects of IMS.

11.7.2 *Basic Architecture of IMS*

The internal organization of IMS can be described in terms of various layers of definitions and mappings. IMS uses its own terminology, which is sometimes confusing or misleading. A stored hierarchy in IMS is called a **physical database (PDB)**. For a given installation, the data in the database comprises several physical databases. Each physical database has a data definition or a schema written in DL/1. IMS calls this definition a DBD, for *database description*. The compiled form of a DBD is stored internally; it includes information on how the database definition is mapped into storage and what access methods are applicable.

IMS provides a view facility that is fairly complex. A view can be defined by choosing part of a physical database or by choosing parts of a number of physical databases and interlinking them into a new hierarchy. We shall refer to these as type 1 and type 2 views, respectively. (The type nomenclature is our own.)

A type 1 view is a subhierarchy and is defined by means of a **Program Communication Block** or PCB. A type 2 view must be defined in DL/1 in terms of a *logical DBD*. The resulting structure is called a **logical database (LDB)**. Physical and logical databases are discussed in Section 11.7.3.

A user application program needs to access data from several isolated physical databases or from type 1 or type 2 views. In high-volume on-line transaction systems, reentrant data access modules are used. All the data descriptions needed by an application are packaged in a **Program Specification Block** or PSB. A PSB contains different chunks of description, corresponding to type 1 or type 2 view definitions. These chunks are stored as Program Communication Blocks. *Each application must have a distinct PSB, even though it may be identical to another PSB.* The application program in COBOL, PL/1, FOR-TRAN, or BAL invokes DL/1 via a call to get IMS to service a retrieval or update operation. The IMS system in turn communicates with the user via the PCB, which is (defined in the application program as) an area addressable via a pointer passed to the program. Current status information is posted to the PCB. IMS mainly supports five access methods, HSAM, HISAM, HDAM, HIDAM, and MSDB, which in turn use the built-in access methods of the operating system to manage various files.

Figure 11.15 shows how two applications called SALES and GENERAL LEDGER may actually share underlying physical databases in IMS via DBDs, PCBs, and PSBs.

11.7.3 *Logical Organization of Data in* IMS

In IMS, records are called segments, and relationships are distinguished into physical and logical (instead of real and virtual). Our terminology is cross-referenced with that of IMS and System 2000 in Table 11.2.

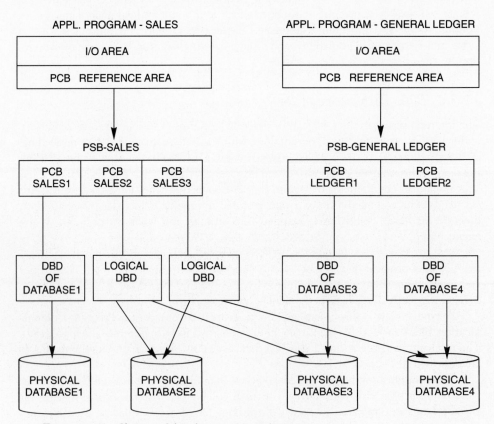

Figure 11.15   Sharing of data by two IMS applications.

Table 11.2   Hierarchical Data Model Terminology

Hierarchical Data Model	IMS Term	System 2000 Term
1. Record type	Segment type	Repeating group record
2. Record occurrence	Segment occurrence	Record occurrence
3. Field or data item	Field	Data item
4. Sequence field as key	Sequence field	Key
5. Parent-child relationship type	Physical parent-child relationship type	Hierarchical schema relationship
6. Virtual parent-child relationship type	Logical parent-child relationship type	Not provided except at run time
7. Hierarchical database schema	Physical or logical database definition (done in DBD)	Schema tree
8. Root of hierarchy	Root segment	Root record
9. Occurrence tree of a hierarchy	Physical database record	Data tree
10. Hierarchical record sequence	Hierarchical sequence	No special term
11. Pointer record type	Pointer segment type	No similar concept

Physical Databases.   An IMS physical database (PDB) refers to the hierarchy that is actually stored. It is defined in the form of a physical DBD using the DL/1 language. Figure 11.16 shows the definition of a physical database that corresponds to the hierarchy shown in Figure 11.5. It contains six segment types, each of which can have an arbitrary number of occurrences in the database. For the schema of Figure 11.10, we would need to use two physical database definitions. Later, appropriate logical databases would be defined based on these physical databases. The definition of the virtual parent-child relationships shown in Figure 11.10 is included in both of these physical DBDs and is quite complicated.

We make the following important points about the database definition:

- The database description is written in terms of the macros DBD, SEGM, FIELD, DBDGEN, FINISH, and END. The SEGM macro defines a segment, and the FIELD macro defines a field. Other macro names are self-explanatory.

- Each macro uses certain keywords. The hierarchical logical structure of the database is defined by virtue of the "PARENT =" specifications of the segments.

- The order of occurrence of the SEGM statements is the means of ordering segments within the logical schema. This top-to-bottom left-to-right ordering is significant. Changing this ordering yields a *different* physical database.

- A *sequence field* (optionally) designates a field within a segment type by which its occurrences may be ordered. The specific value of a sequence field is called the key of that segment occurrence.

```
1 DBD   NAME = COMPANY
2 SEGM NAME = DEPARTMENT, BYTES = 28
3 FIELD NAME = DNAME, BYTES = 10, START = 1
4 FIELD NAME = (DNUMBER, SEQ), BYTES = 6, START = 11
5 FIELD NAME = MGRNAME, BYTES = 3, START = 17
6 FIELD NAME = MGRSTARTDATE, BYTES = 9, START = 20

7 SEGM  NAME = EMPLOYEE, PARENT = DEPARTMENT, BYTES = 79
8 FIELD NAME = NAME, BYTES = 31, START = 1
9 FIELD  NAME = (SSN, SEQ), BYTES = 9, START = 32
10 FIELD NAME = BDATE, BYTES = 9, START = 41
11 FIELD NAME = ADDRESS, BYTES = 30, START = 50

12 SEGM NAME = DEPENDENT, PARENT = EMPLOYEE, BYTES = 25
13 FIELD NAME = (DEP_NAME, SEQ), BYTES = 15, START = 1
14 FIELD NAME = SEX, BYTES = 1, START = 16
15 FIELD NAME = BIRTHDATE, BYTES = 9, START = 17

16 SEGM NAME =  SUPERVISEE, PARENT = EMPLOYEE, BYTES = 24
17 FIELD NAME = NAME, BYTES = 15, START = 1
18 FIELD NAME = SSN, BYTES = 9, START = 16

19 SEGM NAME =  PROJECT, PARENT = DEPARTMENT, BYTES = 16
20 FIELD NAME = PNAME, BYTES = 10, START = 1
21 FIELD NAME = (PNUMBER, SEQ), BYTES = 6, START = 11

22 SEGM NAME = WORKER, PARENT = PROJECT, BYTES = 26
23 FIELD NAME = NAME, BYTES = 15, START = 1
24 FIELD NAME = (SSN, SEQ), BYTES = 9, START = 16
25 FIELD NAME = HOURS, BYTES = 2, START = 25
26 DBDGEN
27 FINISH
28 END
```

Figure 11.16   Physical database definition corresponding to the hierarchy of Figure 11.5.

- Sequence fields may be unique (which is the default) or nonunique. To designate a nonunique sequence field, one uses M (for multiple) in the FIELD definition, as:

   FIELD NAME = (PARTNAME, SEQ.M), ...

- A unique sequence field is required for the root segment if the database is stored by using HISAM and HIDAM (see Section 11.7.5), because this provides an index key for the primary index.

- Combinations of two or more fields are recognized as new fields. This allows a combination of fields to be treated as a composite key. For example, STATENAME, CITYNAME may together be given a new field name, say SCNAME, which can be defined as a sequence field.

An occurrence tree in our terminology is called a **physical database record** in IMS. The linearized form of an occurrence tree within a physical database record is produced by a *preorder traversal* of the segment occurrences (see Section 11.1.4). The sequence of segments from any segment up to the root—obtained by going through a series of successive parent segments—is called the segment's **hierarchical path**. A concatenation of keys (including segment type codes) along this path is called the **hierarchical sequence key** of that segment. The hierarchical sequence key of a DEPENDENT occurrence in a physical database record for the database of Figure 11.5 may be as follows:

1 | '000005' | 2 | '369278157' | 4 | 'JOHN. . .'.

Here, 1, 2, and 4 are, respectively, the segment type codes of DEPARTMENT, EMPLOYEE, and DEPENDENT, assigned automatically by IMS, and '000005', '369278157', and 'JOHN. . .' are sequence keys along the hierarchical path up to that segment occurrence for JOHN.

The physical database records in an IMS database occur in sequence by the key of its root segment. Within a physical database record, the segments occur in ascending order of their hierarchical sequence key.

Type 1 Views in IMS — Subsets of Physical Databases. IMS allows two kinds of views, or "logical databases"* (an IMS term), to be constructed from physical databases. For easy reference we call them type 1 and type 2 logical databases, or type 1 and type 2 views, which is our own nomenculture. Incidentally, additional confusion arises in IMS because only type 2 views are actually defined with a logical database definition; type 1 views are defined by using a PCB.

A type 1 logical database schema defines a *subhierarchy* of a physical database schema by observing these rules:

1. The root segment type must be part of the view.

2. Nonroot segment types may be omitted.

3. If a segment type is omitted, all its children segment types must be omitted.

4. From the segments that are included, any field type may be omitted.

For example, a large number of type 1 views can be defined for the database of Figure 11.5. Two valid type 1 views are shown in Figure 11.17(a). They are meaningful for two different applications. One deals with dependents, and the other deals with workers who work on projects.

Two other subhierarchies are shown in Figure 11.17(b). In the first, the EMPLOYEE segment is omitted but its child segment is included. This violates rule 3 of the preceding list. In the second subhierarchy, the root segment DEPARTMENT is omitted, which violates rule 1. Hence both of these subhierarchies are invalid views in IMS. Every type 1 hierarchy is defined by means of a PCB. We will not describe the PCB syntax here.

This view facility accomplishes the usual objectives of permitting selective access to only the relevant portion of a database, and it provides a certain amount of security. When the PROCOPT specification allows updates, the corresponding change allows updates to the "base" physical record. This is governed by a complicated set of rules in IMS and may lead to inconsistencies if not done properly. One PSB for a given application may include several PCBs that correspond to several type 1 views.

---

*IMS uses the term *logical database* loosely, with two meanings corresponding to the two types of views. A logical database or LDB is, however, defined only for the virtual hierarchy or type 2 view.

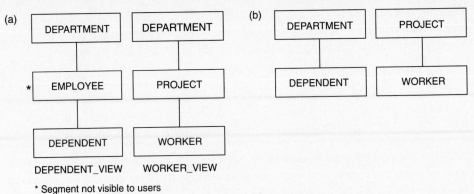

* Segment not visible to users

Figure 11.17   Type 1 views in IMS on the database in Figure 11.5. (a) Two
valid views. (b) Two invalid views.

Type 2 Views in IMS over Multiple Physical Databases. This facility in IMS is a true
view facility in that it allows one to create views that are virtual hierarchies. A **virtual
hierarchy** consists of segments, some of which are connected by *logical parent-child relationships* (an IMS term)—we called them virtual parent-child relationships (VPCRs) in
Section 11.2. By setting up logical relationships among segments from different physical
databases, one can create a complex network. The type 2 view facility allows us to carve
out any hierarchies from such a network. In Figure 11.18 we show virtual hierarchies
based on the hierarchies of Figure 11.10. Type 2 views must be defined explicitly in IMS
as logical databases (LDBs) by using the DBD macro and with ACCESS = LOGICAL.

Various rules govern logical parent-child relationships and the construction of logical databases from physical databases. Among the more important ones are:

1. The root of an LDB must be the root of some PDB.

2. A logical child segment must have one physical and only one logical parent. As
   a consequence, a root segment *cannot* be a logical child segment.

3. A physical child of a logical parent may appear as a dependent of a concatenated
   (logical child/logical parent) segment in the LDB. By virtue of this facility, we
   can create a logical database from Figure 11.10 as shown in Figure 11.18, which
   shows the use of an EMPLOYEE segment type twice (once as a supervisor and once
   as a supervisee) in the same logical database. This makes tracking currencies of
   segments even more difficult than we indicated in Section 11.6.1. This feature
   is a very powerful one in IMS and expands the scope of generating new hierarchies a great deal.

4. A logical parent segment type may have multiple logical child segment types.
   This is already seen for the EMPLOYEE segment in Figure 11.10.

Views in IMS versus Views in Relational Systems. We saw two types of view definitions
or external schema facilities in IMS. Type 1 allowed views over single hierarchies; type

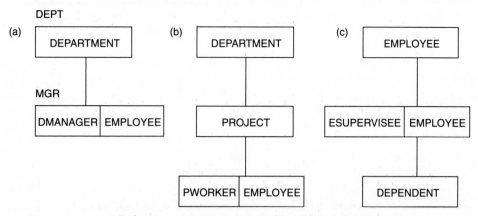

Figure 11.18 Type 2 views in IMS on the database in Figure 11.10. (a) Manager_View. (b) Project_View. (c) Dependent_View.

2 allowed views over multiple hierarchies. Let us compare this view facility to the views in relational systems:

1. A relational view does not have to be contemplated at the time of defining a conceptual schema or a set of base relations. In contrast, the definition of PDBs is determined by what LDBs need to use them. The IMS type 2 views are therefore not purely external schemas; they influence and determine the definition of the conceptual schema. The spirit of the three-schema architecture (see Section 2.2.1) is thus *not* fully maintained.

2. Relational views do not assume any physical access structure to support the views. IMS type 2 views, in contrast, require explicit definitions of pointers to link segments from multiple PDBs. The feasible LDBs are restricted by the types of pointers declared in the physical database(s).

3. The definition of a type 1 view is compulsory for an application to access a physical (or a logical) database. Even if the entire physical database is accessed by one application, a PCB (type 1 view) must be defined for it. In fact, a PCB is still required on top of an LDB to access it. There is no corresponding requirement in relational systems.

The type 2 view facility is a useful feature that extends the capabilities of IMS as follows:

- It allows a **limited network facility** by allowing two segments to have an M:N relationship via a common child pointer segment. N-ary relationships with N > 2 are *not* possible, unlike the situation in the network model.

- It reduces redundant storage of data. Correspondingly, updates may also be saved.

- Most important, it allows users to view the data in a variety of hierarchical ways besides the rigidly defined physical database hierarchies. This is done by combining segments from multiple existing hierarchies.

Unfortunately, the physical and logical database definitions, the different types of pairing of segments—physical and virtual—in "bidirectional relationships," and the complicated loading procedures for logical databases make type 2 views a very complex feature of IMS. We have left out a number of details in this discussion. It appears that some IMS installations do without the use of logical databases and are satisfied to rely entirely on physical databases.

11.7.4 *Data Manipulation in* IMS

Data manipulation operations in IMS closely parallel the HDML operations of Section 11.6. DL/1 includes the data manipulation language (DML) of IMS as well as the data definition language (DDL). We will not describe the detailed language syntax here. Instead we will show how DL/1 applications interface with IMS and will point out a few special features of DL/1. Calls to DL/1 are embedded in an IMS application program written in COBOL, PL/1, System 360/370 basic assembly language, or FORTRAN. This call has the following syntax:

CALL <procedure name> (<parameter list>).

The procedure name to be called varies depending on the language in which the application program is written. A PL/1 program must use the name PL1TDL1 (for PL/1 to DL/1), which is fixed. Consider the following query: "Obtain a list of dependents born after JAN-01-1980 for the employees in the departments with DNUMBER = 4". A call to DL/1 would be coded as

CALL PL1TDL1 (SIX, GU, PCB_1, DEPND_IO_AREA, DEPT,D_SSA, EMPL_SSA, DEPND_SSA)

This call appears in the application program that is assumed to be in PL/1. The parameter list is interpreted as follows:

- SIX refers to a variable containing the string 'SIX'. It indicates the number of remaining parameters in the list. Different queries can have different numbers of parameters.

- GU represents a variable containing the string 'GU', which stands for the operation to be performed—in this case, "get unique."

- PCB_1 is the name of the structure defined in the PL/1 program that acts as a mask to address an area called the program communication block (PCB). It is the common area through which information is passed back and forth between IMS and the application program. Among other things, it includes a hierarchy level indicator, the processing options in effect, the current segment name, the current hierarchical sequence key; and the number of sensitive segments for the corresponding PCB definition.

- DEPND_IO_AREA is a 25-byte input-output area reserved in the program to receive the entire DEPENDENT segment.

- D_SSA, EMPL_SSA, and DEPND_SSA are segment search arguments, one per query. They stand for variable-containing strings that specify the search conditions for that statement. In our example the three strings would contain 'DEPARTMENT

(DNUMBER = '000004')', 'EMPLOYEE', and 'DEPENDENT(BDATE > 'JAN-01-1980')', . respectively.

In the HDML language of Section 11.6, the effect of the above CALL would be to do the following query:

GET FIRST PATH DEPARTMENT, EMPLOYEE, DEPENDENT
WHERE DNUMBER = '000004' AND DEPENDENT.BDATE > 'JAN-01-1980'

The only difference is that in HDML we assumed that this would retrieve data for each of the segments; in IMS, with the Get Unique command, *only* the DEPENDENT segment (the terminal node of the path) is fetched into memory.

CALL Interface versus Embedded Query Language Interface. The above scenario demonstrates the use of a parameterized 'CALL interface' between a high-level programming language such as PL/1 and the DBMS. This should be contrasted with the embedded query language interface exemplified by the use of SQL in relational systems. The advantages of a CALL interface are:

1. The compiler for the host language remains unchanged; hence no precompilation is necessary.

2. The application program looks homogeneous; there is no intervention of any foreign syntax.

The main disadvantages are:

1. The positional parameters in a CALL can easily be interchanged or omitted.

2. By looking at a CALL statement, it is impossible to judge the embedded data retrieval update operations. Hence application programs become difficult to read.

3. There are no semantic checks on the parameters in a CALL. Hence errors may surface later at execution time without being detected at compile time.

In our opinion the CALL interface may be convenient for the implementer but it is not desirable for application development.

Table 11.3 summarizes the correspondence between the operations proposed in HDML and those that exist in DL/1. The DL/1 operations are invoked using the CALL facility described above. In Section 11.6 we used a different notation, where the HDML commands were embedded in PASCAL programs and the search conditions were written with a WHERE clause. This distinction must be kept in mind while reading this table. We offer next a few additional explanations corresponding to the notes in Table 11.3.

- *Note 1:* Each time a hierarchy is processed, in general, IMS requires that the first command be a Get Unique (GU), which must address a hierarchical path in the hierarchy, starting with the root. Accessing segments within the hierarchy directly is not possible. (Exceptions exist but are beyond the scope of this discussion.)

- *Note 2:* Get Unique in DL/1 is used to account for GET FIRST as well as GET FIRST PATH of HDML. For Examples 1, 2, and 3 of Section 11.6.2, GU of DL/1 would work exactly like GET FIRST of HDML. Example 4 of Section 11.6.3 is shown in DL/1 plus a host language below (in a pseudosyntax *without* coding as an exact CALL).

Table 11.3   Operations Proposed in HDML (Section 11.6) and Those Existing in IMS DL/1

HDML Operation	DL/1 Operation	Meaning
Get First (GF)	Get Unique (GU)	Get the first occurrence of a specified record (*see Note 1*)
Get Next (GN)	Get Next (GN)	Get the next occurrence of a specified record
Get First Path	Get Unique (GU) plus command code *D	Get the first occurrence of all records along a hierarchical path (*see Note 2*)
Get Next Path	Get Next within Parent (GNP) or Get Next (GN)	Get the next occurrence of a specified hierarchical path (*see Note 3*)
Get Next within Parent	Get Next within Parent (GNP)	Get the next child occurrence for the current parent occurrence
Get Next within Virtual Parent	No special operation	Get the next child occurrence for the current virtual parent occurrence (*see Note 3*)
INSERT DELETE REPLACE	INSERT (ISRT) DELETE (DLET) REPLACE (REPL)	Insert new record occurrence Delete old record occurrence Replace current record occurrence with a new occurrence
Get with Hold	Get Unique with Hold (GHU) Get Next with Hold (GHN) Get Next within Parent with Hold (GHNP)	Perform a corresponding GET operation with a hold on the record so that it can be subsequently replaced or deleted

This query retrieves employee-dependent pairs where both have the first name John. The segment search arguments (e.g., "EMPLOYEE*D (FNAME = 'JOHN')") are shown next to the operation for notational convenience.

```
GU EMPLOYEE *D (FNAME = 'JOHN')
   DEPENDENT (DEPNAME = 'JOHN')
while DB_STATUS = 'segment found' do
      begin
            WRITE EMPLOYEE NAME, EMPLOYEE BIRTHDATE, DEPENDENT
                  BIRTHDATE
            GN EMPLOYEE *D (FNAME = 'JOHN')
               DEPENDENT (DEPNAME = 'JOHN')
      end;
```

The *D for data in the preceding example is called a **command code**. Notice that Get Next with a *D produces the same effect as Get Next Path in HDML. It would be possible in DL/1 to code this example without using *D. In that case, instead of the entire path, only the terminal segment (DEPENDENT, in the above example) would be retrieved.

- *Note 3:* There are no special commands in IMS for processing virtual ("logical" in IMS) parent-child relationships, because virtual relationships *cannot be processed directly without defining a logical database.*

A few additional observations comparing DL/1 with HDML are in order. The hold option was demonstrated for HDML in Example 10 of Section 11.6.5. It applies to all forms of the GET operation in IMS. The while . . . do . . . end loops shown in the PASCAL plus HDML examples in Section 11.6 were controlled by a DB_STATUS code. Loops must be explicitly coded in the same way in the host language for IMS. Status code is available as part of the PCB area.

IMS provides a command code *F that allows an application to search in the hierarchy to determine whether a condition is satisfied and then move back to a previous named segment within the same physical database record and retrieve data. The *V command code is used to position the retrieval processing in the current of a particular segment type (see Section 11.6.2). With these command codes, it is possible to change the normal forward direction of processing through the linearized hierarchical sequences.

An IMS application program can open several PCBs or type 1 views and process them concurrently. Currency of segment types within each PCB is maintained by the system. Each CALL includes one parameter referring to a specific PCB.

11.7.5 *Storage of Databases in IMS*

We shall review the different types of file organizations available to store physical databases in IMS without going into details. In IMS these are referred to as access methods. Compared to most DBMSs, IMS provides a far wider array of access methods. We mention all of them here:

- Each physical database in IMS is a stored database. The logical databases are virtual hierarchical databases that may be viewed as such, but in storage they do not represent separate data. Logical databases consist of the physical databases plus linkages provided by pointer structures.

- Each stored segment contains stored data fields plus a prefix (not visible to user programs) containing a segment type code, pointers, a delete flag, and other control information.

- Regardless of the access method, a stored database is always stored as a sequence of occurrence trees, called **physical database records**, where each occurrence tree contains a preorder sequence of segments (see Sections 11.1.3 and 11.1.4). It is owned by a specific root segment. For brevity, we shall sometimes refer to an occurrence tree as a **tree**.

- Various IMS access methods differ as to how the sequence of segments is "tied together" within a physical database record and what type of access structure is provided to locate the physical database record or individual segment occurrences within it.

- Based on the type of access provided to the physical database records, two types of structures are provided in IMS: **hierarchical sequential** (HS) and **hierarchical direct** (HD). They are further divided into HSAM, HISAM, HDAM, and HIDAM, as shown in Figure 11.19.

The IMS access methods may be regarded as high-level ones. IMS provides routines for HISAM, HDAM, and so on, that in turn use the lower-level access methods called SAM (sequential access method), OSAM (overflow sequential access method), and ISAM (indexed sequential access method). A combination of files at the lower-level access method is used by the higher-level access method (see Figure 11.19).

HSAM. HSAM ties together the segments within a tree by *physical contiguity*. The trees themselves are placed in physical sequence in storage. Each physical database record represents one occurrence tree. HSAM "strings out" the physical records sequentially, in order of the sequence key of the root segment, with a fixed block size. This organization is

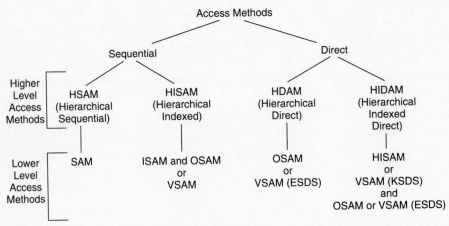

Figure 11.19   An overview of IMS access methods.

"tapelike" and is of academic importance only, since it supports no updating. However, it can be used for dumping and transporting databases. Once a database is loaded (by using ISRT commands), only the GET operations (excluding GET HOLD) are allowed. To do modification/deletion/insertion of data, the old database is read in and an entire new copy is written out. This organization is used to process data that remains fixed over an extended period of time.

HISAM. In the HISAM organization, the database consists of two files or storage areas or data sets: one file (prime area) contains root segments (plus some additional segments that fit within the record in that file); another file (overflow area) contains the remaining tail portion of each linearized tree. Figure 11.20 shows how the physical database record corresponding to Figure 11.7 would be stored in IMS using HISAM. It shows how a record is split into two files and how fixed-length blocks are linked together within the overflow.

Both files have fixed-length records. Hence, because of the uneven lengths of segments, some space is wasted at the end of records. The first file is either an ISAM or a prime VSAM area that is accessible via an index on the sequence field of the root segment. This is a popular access method with IMS.

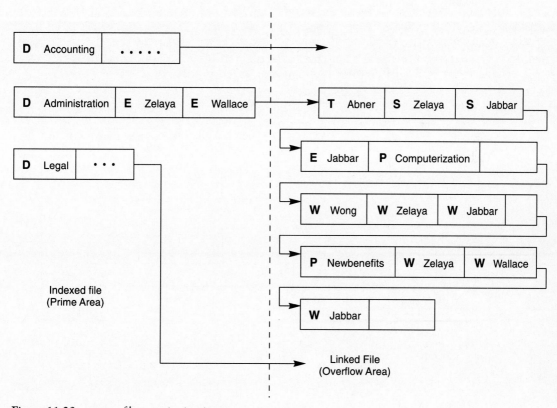

Figure 11.20 HISAM file organization in IMS.

HDAM. An HDAM database consists of a single OSAM or VSAM file. In both HD structures, the root segment is accessed by a hash on the sequence field; segments are stored independently and linked by means of two types of pointers:

- *Hierarchical pointers:* With hierarchical pointers, each segment points to the next in hierarchical sequence, except for the last dependent segment in the hierarchy, which does not bear a pointer. This is essentially the preorder threading of the tree.
- *Child/twin pointers:* Figure 11.21 shows the use of child/twin pointers. Each segment type has a *designated number* of child pointers equal to the number of children segment types defined in the database definition and has *one* twin pointer. For a given tree, the child pointer in a segment can be (a) a null value if it has no child segment of the corresponding type (for example, no DEPENDENT for Zelaya or Jabbar in Figure 11.21) or (b) the location of the first child segment of the corresponding type. Children of the same parent are linked by using a twin pointer. The twin pointer of the last child is a null.

Note that the HDAM organization provides *no sequential access on the root* segment. It can be provided by means of a secondary index. Backward pointers can be created in addition to forward pointers. Declaration of pointers is done as part of the database definition.

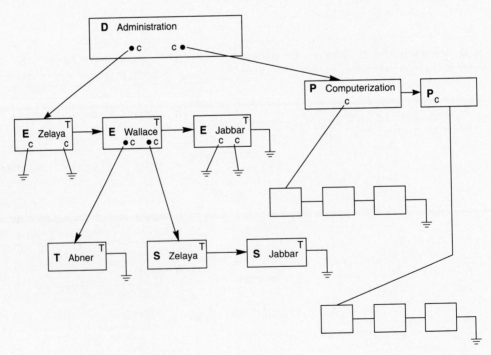

Figure 11.21   HDAM with child/twin pointers in IMS.

From a performance standpoint, hierarchical pointers are favored when requirements dictate direct access to the root coupled with sequential access on dependent segments, as in producing reports, where a variety of different segments must be listed. Child/twin pointers are favored when quick access to lower levels in the hierarchy or to the right bottom part of the tree is desired. HDAM differs from the other three access methods in that the initial loading of the database can be done in any (random) sequence, a tree at a time.

HIDAM. A HIDAM database consists of two parts: an index database and a "data" database. The data database is a single OSAM or VSAM (entry-sequenced data set) file consisting of fixed-length records that are initially loaded in hierarchical sequence. It is treated as an HDAM database by itself. Either hierarchical or child/twin pointer schemes are used to link segments.

The INDEX database is a HISAM database in which the hierarchy consists of only one type of segment, an index segment. Each index segment contains a root sequence field value as its key and the pointer to that root segment in the data database as its data field. The index database is much smaller than the data database. If VSAM is used, a single key-sequenced data set suffices as the index database. Space utilization of the index database is more efficient with VSAM than with ISAM/OSAM. HIDAM databases are popular because they combine the advantages of HISAM and HDAM. Direct access to the root segments in the database is provided by using the root sequence key as a hash key; indexed access is available by going through the index database.

Other IMS Storage Structures. Besides the access methods described previously, IMS provides the following additional storage structures:

1. **Simple HSAM** (SHSAM), **and simple HISAM** (SHISAM) are variants of HSAM and HISAM, respectively, where a database contains only one segment type (the root segment).

2. **The fast path feature** in IMS is designed for on-line transaction systems with high transaction rates and relatively simple processing. It provides data communication facilities and two special database structures:

   a. **Main storage databases** (MSDBs): An MSDB is a root-only database. It is kept in primary memory throughout system operation. Small reference tables such as conversion tables and timetables are good candidates for MSDBs.

   b. **Data entry databases** (DEDBs): A DEDB is a special form of HDAM database designed for better availability and performance. It is a restricted form of hierarchy with only two levels, and it may be partitioned into up to 240 areas. The leftmost segment at the second level, called the *sequential dependent segment type*, is given special treatment. Each area is a separate VSAM data set, and each database record (root plus all dependents) is wholly contained in the area. The partitioning is not visible to the application.

3. **Secondary data set groups** (DSGs): A HISAM, HDAM, or HIDAM database can be partitioned into groups of segment types. One primary data set group and nine secondary data set groups can be created. The primary DSG contains the root

segment. Each secondary DSG is a separate database containing all segment occurrences for the type of segments that belong to it.

Secondary Indexing in IMS. In Chapter 5 we saw the importance of secondary indexes for improving access times in various types of files. IMS provides only the following two types of secondary indexes:

1. An index that provides access to a root or a dependent segment based on the value of any field in it.

2. An index that indexes a given segment on the basis of a field in some *segment at a lower level*. For our database of Figure 11.5, some of the possible secondary indexes are:

   A. An index to DEPARTMENT by department name (DNAME).

   B. An index on DEPENDENT by birthdate (BIRTHDATE).

   C. An index on DEPARTMENT by location of project in that department (PLO-CATION in PROJECT).

There are two shortcomings with secondary index processing in IMS:

1. The DL/1 code must refer explicitly to an index if it is to be used; otherwise processing is done *without* the index.

2. When a field in a lower-level segment in the hierarchy is used for indexing, the hierarchy is visualized as if it were restructured with that segment as the root.

Both of these characteristics directly violate the objective of data independence (see Section 2.2) whereby a user's external view is insulated from the internal organization of the database.

11.8 Summary

In this chapter we discussed the hierarchical model, which represents data by emphasizing hierarchical relationships. The presentation was general, although some aspects were patterned after the major hierarchical system—IBM's IMS. Departures from IMS were mostly pointed out (without detailed discussion) in the text and in footnotes. The main structures used by the hierarchical model are record types and parent-child relationship (PCR) types. Each PCR type defines a hierarchical 1:N relationship between a parent record type and a child record type. Relationships are strictly hierarchical in that a record type can participate as child in at most one PCR type. This restriction makes it difficult to represent a database where numerous relationships exist.

We then saw how hierarchical database schemas can be defined as a number of hierarchical schemas of record types. A hierarchical schema is basically a tree data structure. Corresponding to a hierarchical schema, a number of occurrence trees will exist in the database. The hierarchical sequence of storing database records from an occurrence tree is a preorder traversal of the records in an occurrence tree. The type of each record is stored with the record so that the DBMS can identify the records while searching through records of a hierarchical sequence.

We then discussed the limitations of hierarchical representation when we try to represent M:N relationships, or relationships in which more than two record types participate. It is possible to represent some of these cases by allowing redundant records to exist in the database. The concept of virtual parent-child relationship (VPCR) types is used to permit a record type to have two parents—a real parent and a virtual parent. This VPCR type can also be used to represent M:N relationships without redundancy of database records. We also discussed the types of implicit integrity constraints in hierarchies.

In Section 11.5, we discussed hierarchical database design from an ER conceptual schema. In general, the hierarchical model works well for database applications that are naturally hierarchical. However, when there are many nonhierarchical relationships, trying to fit those relationships into a hierarchical form is difficult, and the resulting representations are often unsatisfactory. We then presented the commands of a hypothetical hierarchical data definition language (HDDL) and of a record-at-a-time hierarchical data manipulation language (HDML). The HDML is based on the hierarchical sequence. We saw how to write programs with embedded HDML commands to retrieve information from a hierarchical database and to update the database.

Finally, we gave the basic architecture, language features, and storage organization of the popular hierarchical database system, IMS.

Although the relational model and relational DBMSs have recently become quite popular, the hierarchical model will be with us for several years to come because a big investment has been made in hierarchical DBMSs in the commercial world. In addition, the hierarchical model is quite suitable for situations where the majority of relationships are hierarchical and where database access mainly uses these hierarchical relationships.

Review Questions

11.1. Define the following terms: *parent-child relationship (PCR) type, root of a hierarchy, leaf of a hierarchy*.

11.2. Discuss the main properties of a hierarchy.

11.3. Discuss the problems with using a PCR type to represent an M:N relationship.

11.4. What is an occurrence tree of a hierarchy?

11.5. What is the hierarchical sequence? Why is it necessary to assign a record type field to each record when the hierarchical sequence is used to represent an occurrence tree?

11.6. Define the following terms: *hierarchical path, broom, forest of trees, hierarchical database*.

11.7. What are virtual parent-child relationship (VPCR) types? How do they enhance the modeling power of the hierarchical model?

11.8. Discuss different techniques that may be used for implementing VPCR types in a hierarchical database.

11.9. Discuss the inherent integrity constraints of the hierarchical model.

11.10. Show how each of the following types of relationships is represented in the hierarchical model: (a) M:N relationships; (b) n-ary relationships, with n > 2; (c) 1:1 relationships. Discuss how an ER schema can be mapped to a hierarchical schema.

11.11. Why is it necessary to embed the HDML commands in a host programming language such as PASCAL?

11.12. Discuss the following concepts, and identify what each is used for when writing an HDML database program: (a) the user work area (UWA); (b) currency indicators; (c) database status indicator.

11.13. Discuss the different types of GET commands of the HDML, and tell how each affects the currency indicators.

11.14. Discuss how parent records are established as a result of a retrieval command. Why does the GET NEXT WITHIN PARENT command *not* establish a new parent?

11.15. Discuss the update commands of the HDML.

Exercises

11.16. Specify the queries of Exercise 6.19 in HDML embedded in PASCAL on the hierarchical database schema of Figure 11.10. Use the PASCAL program variables declared in Figure 11.11, and declare any additional variables you may need.

11.17. Consider the hierarchical database schema shown in Figure 11.22, which corresponds to the relational schema of Figure 2.1. Write appropriate HDDL statements to define the record types and set types of the schema.

11.18. There is some redundancy in the schema of Figure 11.22; what data items are repeated redundantly? Can you specify a hierarchical database schema for this database without redundancy by using VPCRs?

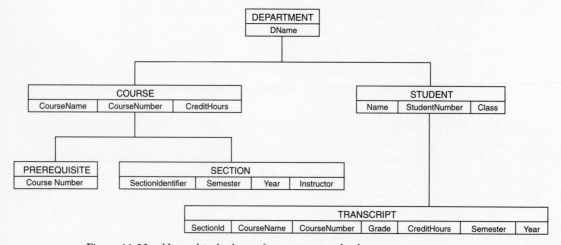

Figure 11.22 Hierarchical schema for a university database.

11.19. Write PASCAL program segments with embedded HDML commands to specify the queries of Exercise 7.16 on the schema of Figure 11.22. Repeat the same queries for your schema of Exercise 11.18.

11.20. Write PASCAL program segments with embedded HDML commands to do the updates and tasks of Exercises 7.17 and 7.18 on the hierarchical database schema of Figure 11.22. Specify any program variables that you need. Repeat the same queries for your schema of Exercise 11.18.

11.21. Choose some database application that you are familiar with or interested in.

  a. Design a hierarchical database schema for your database application.

  b. Declare your record types, PCR types, and VPCR types, using the HDDL.

  c. Specify a number of queries and updates that are needed by your database application, and write a PASCAL program segment with embedded HDML commands for each of your queries.

  d. Implement your database if you have a hierarchical DBMS system available.

11.22. Map the following ER schemas into hierarchical schemas. Specify for each ER schema one or more hierarchical schemas, and state which have redundancies and which do not.

  a. The AIRLINES ER schema of Figure 3.19.

  b. The BANK ER schema of Figure 3.20.

  c. The SHIP_TRACKING ER schema of Figure 6.21.

Selected Bibliography

The first hierarchical DBMS—IMS and its DL/1 language—was developed by IBM and North American Aviation (Rockwell International) in the late 1960s. Few early documents exist that describe IMS. McGee (1977) gives an overview of IMS in an issue of *IBM Systems Journal* devoted to IMS. Bjoerner and Lovengren (1982) formalize some aspects of the IMS data model.

The Time-shared Data Management System (TDMS) of System Development Corporation (now Burroughs) (Vorhaus and Mills 1967; Bleier and Vorhaus 1968) and the Remote File Management System (RFMS) developed at the University of Texas at Austin (Everett et al. 1971) are precursors of another major commercial hierarchical system called System 2000, which is now marketed by SAS Inc. Hardgrave (1974, 1980) describes a language, BOLT, for the hierarchical model.

Tsichritzis and Lochovsky (1976) surveys hierarchical database management, and general descriptions of the hierarchical model appear in several textbooks, including Korth and Silberschatz (1991). Kroenke and Dolan (1988) discusses DL/1 processing, and Date (1990) presents IMS as an example of a hierarchical system. Kapp and Leben (1978) discusses the DL/1 language in detail from the programmer's viewpoint. Recent work has attempted to incorporate hierarchical structures in the relational model (Gyssens et al. 1989; Jagadish 1989). This includes nested relational models (see Section 21.6.2).

CHAPTER 12

Functional Dependencies and Normalization for Relational Databases

In Chapters 6 to 8, we presented various aspects of the relational model, including examples of relational databases. Each *relation schema* consists of a number of attributes, and the *relational database schema* consists of a number of relation schemas. So far, we have assumed that attributes are grouped to form a relation schema by using the common sense of the database designer or by mapping a schema specified in the Entity-Relationship model into a relational schema. However, we did not have any formal measure of why one grouping of attributes into a relation schema may be better than another. There was no measure of the appropriateness or quality of the design, other than the intuition of the designer.

In this chapter we discuss some of the theory that has been developed to attempt to choose "good" relation schemas—that is, to measure formally why one set of groupings of attributes into relation schemas is better than another. There are two levels at which we can discuss the "goodness" of relation schemas. The first is the **logical level**, which refers to how the users interpret the relation schemas and the meaning of their attributes. Having good relation schemas at this level helps the users to understand clearly the meaning of the data tuples in the relations, and hence to formulate their queries correctly. The second is the **manipulation** (or **storage**) **level**, which refers to how the tuples in a base relation are stored and updated. This level applies only to schemas of base relations—which will be physically stored as files—whereas at the logical level we are interested in schemas of both base relations and views (virtual relations). The relational database design theory developed in this chapter applies mainly to base relations, although some criteria of appropriateness also apply to views, as we shall discuss in Section 12.1.

We start in Section 12.1 by informally discussing some criteria for good and bad relation schemas. Then, in Section 12.2 we define the concept of functional dependency, which is the main tool for formally measuring the appropriateness of attribute groupings into relation schemas. Properties of functional dependencies are also studied and analyzed. In Section 12.3 we show how functional dependencies can be used to group attributes into relation schemas that are in a normal form. A relation schema is in a normal form when it satisfies a number of desirable features. Normal forms for relation schemas can be defined, leading to progressively better groupings. In Section 12.4 we discuss more general definitions of some normal forms.

Chapter 13 continues the development of the theory related to the design of good relational schemas. Whereas in Chapter 12 we concentrate on the normal forms for single relation schemas, in Chapter 13 we discuss measures of appropriateness for a whole set of relation schemas that together form a relational database schema. We specify two such properties—the nonadditive (lossless) join property and the dependency preservation property—and discuss algorithms for relational database design that are based on functional dependencies, normal forms, and the aforementioned properties. In Chapter 13 we also define additional types of dependencies and advanced normal forms that further enhance the properties of relation schemas.

For the reader interested in only an informal introduction to normalization, Sections 12.1.4, 12.2.3, 12.2.4, and 12.5 may be skipped.

12.1 Informal Design Guidelines for Relation Schemas

We discuss four *informal measures* of quality for relation schema design in this section:

- Semantics of the attributes.
- Reducing the redundant values in tuples.
- Reducing the null values in tuples.
- Disallowing spurious tuples.

These measures are not always independent of one another, as we shall see.

12.1.1 *Semantics of the Relation Attributes*

Whenever we group attributes to form a relation schema, we assume that a certain meaning is associated with the attributes. In Chapter 6 we discussed how each relation can be interpreted as a set of facts or statements. This meaning, or **semantics,** specifies how to interpret the attribute values stored in a tuple of the relation—in other words, how the attribute values in a tuple relate to one another. The easier it is to explain the semantics of the relation, the better will be the relation schema design.

To illustrate this, consider a simplified version of the COMPANY relational database schema of Figure 6.5, shown in Figure 12.1. Example populated relations of this schema are shown in Figure 12.2. The meaning of the EMPLOYEE relation schema is quite simple: each tuple represents an employee, with values for the employee's name (ENAME), social security number (SSN), birthdate (BDATE), and address (ADDRESS), and the number of

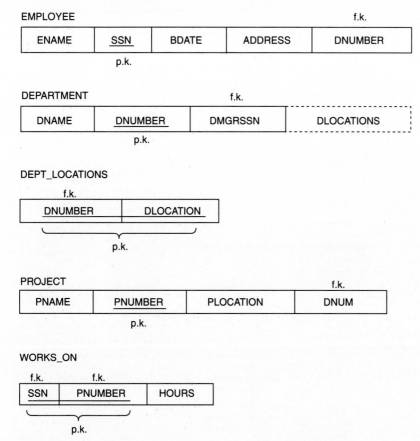

Figure 12.1 Simplified version of the COMPANY relational database schema.

the department that the employee works for (DNUMBER). The DNUMBER attribute is a foreign key that represents an *implicit relationship* between EMPLOYEE and DEPARTMENT. The semantics of the DEPARTMENT and PROJECT schemas are also straightforward; each DEPARTMENT tuple represents a department entity, and each PROJECT tuple represents a project entity. The attribute DMGRSSN of DEPARTMENT relates a department to the employee who is its manager, while DNUM of PROJECT relates a project to its controlling department; both are foreign key attributes. The reader should ignore the attribute DLOCATIONS of DEPARTMENT for the time being, as it is used to illustrate normalization concepts in Section 12.3.

The semantics of the other two relation schemas in Figure 12.1 are slightly more complex. Each tuple in DEPT_LOCATIONS gives a department number (DNUMBER) and *one of* the locations of the department (DLOCATION). Each tuple in WORKS_ON gives an employee social security number (SSN), the project number of *one of* the projects that the employee works on (PNUMBER), and the number of hours per week that the employee works on that project (HOURS). However, both schemas have a well-defined and unam-

EMPLOYEE

ENAME	SSN	BDATE	ADDRESS	DNUMBER
Smith,John B.	123456789	09-JAN-55	731 Fondren,Houston,TX	5
Wong,Franklin T.	333445555	08-DEC-45	638 Voss,Houston,TX	5
Zelaya,Alicia J.	999887777	19-JUL-58	3321 Castle,Spring,TX	4
Wallace,Jennifer S.	987654321	20-JUN-31	291 Berry,Bellaire,TX	4
Narayan,Remesh K.	666884444	15-SEP-52	975 Fire Oak,Humble,TX	5
English,Joyce A.	453453453	31-JUL-62	5631 Rice,Houston,TX	5
Jabbar,Ahmad V.	987987987	29-MAR-59	980 Dallas,Houston,TX	4
Borg,James E.	888665555	10-NOV-27	450 Stone,Houston,TX	1

DEPT_LOCATIONS

DNUMBER	DLOCATION
1	Houston
4	Stafford
5	Bellaire
5	Sugarland
5	Houston

DEPARTMENT

DNAME	DNUMBER	DMGRSSN
Research	5	333445555
Administration	4	987654321
Headquarters	1	888665555

WORKS_ON

SSN	PNUMBER	HOURS
123456789	1	32.5
123456789	2	7.5
666884444	3	40.0
453453453	1	20.0
453453453	2	20.0
333445555	2	10.0
333445555	3	10.0
333445555	10	10.0
333445555	20	10.0
999887777	30	30.0
999887777	10	10.0
987987987	10	35.0
987987987	30	5.0
987654321	30	20.0
987654321	20	15.0
888665555	20	null

PROJECT

PNAME	PNUMBER	PLOCATION	DNUM
ProductX	1	Bellaire	5
ProductY	2	Sugarland	5
ProductZ	3	Houston	5
Computerization	10	Stafford	4
Reorganization	20	Houston	1
Newbenefits	30	Stafford	4

Figure 12.2   Example relations for the schema of Figure 12.1.

biguous meaning. The schema DEPT_LOCATIONS represents a multivalued attribute of DEPARTMENT, whereas WORKS_ON represents an M:N relationship between EMPLOYEE and PROJECT. Hence, all the relation schemas in Figure 12.1 may be considered good from the standpoint of having clear semantics. We can state the following guideline for a relation schema design:

GUIDELINE 1: Design a relation schema so that it is easy to explain its meaning. Do not combine attributes from multiple entity types and relationship types into a single relation. Intuitively, if a relation schema corresponds to one entity type or one relationship type, the meaning tends to be clear. Otherwise, it tends to be a mixture of multiple entities and relationships and hence semantically unclear. ■

The relation schemas in Figures 12.3(a) and (b) also have clear semantics. (The reader should ignore the lines under the relations for now, as they are used to illustrate functional dependency notation in Section 12.2.) A tuple in the EMP_DEPT relation schema of Figure 12.3(a) represents a single employee but includes additional information—namely, the name (DNAME) of the department for which the employee works and the social security number (DMGRSSN) of the department manager. For the EMP_PROJ relation of Figure 12.3(b), each tuple relates an employee to a project but also includes the employee name (ENAME), project name (PNAME), and project location (PLOCATION). Although there is nothing wrong logically with these two relations, they are considered poor designs because they violate Guideline 1 by *mixing attributes from distinct real-world entities;* EMP_DEPT mixes attributes of employees and departments, and EMP_PROJ mixes attributes of employees and projects. They may be used as views, but they cause problems when used as base relations, as we shall discuss in the following section.

12.1.2 *Redundant Information in Tuples and Update Anomalies*

One goal of schema design is to minimize the storage space that the base relations (files) occupy. Grouping attributes into relation schemas has a significant effect on storage space. For example, compare the space used by the two base relations EMPLOYEE and DEPARTMENT in Figure 12.2 with the space for an EMP_DEPT base relation in Figure 12.4, which is the result of applying the NATURAL-JOIN operation to EMPLOYEE and DEPARTMENT. In EMP_DEPT, the attribute values pertaining to a particular department (DNUMBER, DNAME, DMGRSSN) are repeated for every employee who works for that department. By contrast, each department's information appears only in the DEPARTMENT relation in Figure 12.2. Only the department number (DNUMBER) is repeated in the EMPLOYEE rela-

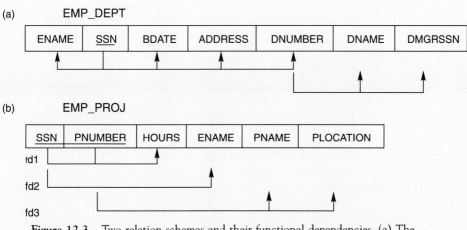

Figure 12.3 Two relation schemas and their functional dependencies. (a) The EMP_DEPT relation schema. (b) The EMP_PROJ relation schema.

tion for each employee who works in that department. Similar comments apply to the EMP_PROJ relation (Figure 12.4), which augments the WORKS_ON relation with additional attributes from EMPLOYEE and PROJECT.

Another serious problem with using the relations in Figure 12.4 as base relations is the problem of **update anomalies**. These can be classified into insertion anomalies, deletion anomalies, and modification anomalies.*

Insertion Anomalies. These can be differentiated into two types, illustrated by the following examples based on EMP_DEPT relation:

- To insert a new employee tuple into EMP_DEPT, we must include either the attribute values for the department that the employee works for, or nulls (if the employee does not work for a department as yet). For example, to insert a new tuple for an employee who works in department number 5, we must enter the attribute values of department 5 correctly so that they are *consistent* with values

EMP_DEPT

ENAME	SSN	BDATE	ADDRESS	DNUMBER	DNAME	DMGRSSN
Smith,John B.	123456789	09-JAN-55	731 Fondren,Houston,TX	5	Research	333445555
Wong,Franklin T.	333445555	08-DEC-45	638 Voss,Houston,TX	5	Research	333445555
Zelaya, Alicia J.	999887777	19-JUL-58	3321 Castle,Spring,TX	4	Administration	987654321
Wallace,Jennifer S.	987654321	19-JUN-31	291 Berry,Bellaire,TX	4	Administration	987654321
Narayan,Ramesh K.	666884444	15-SEP-52	975 FireOak,Humble,TX	5	Research	333445555
English,Joyce A.	453453453	31-JUL-62	5631 Rice,Houston,TX	5	Research	333445555
Jabbar,Ahmad V.	987987987	29-MAR-59	980 Dallas,Houston,TX	4	Administration	987654321
Borg,James E.	888665555	10-NOV-27	450 Stone,Houston,TX	1	Headquarters	888665555

EMP_PROJ

SSN	PNUMBER	HOURS	ENAME	PNAME	PLOCATION
123456789	1	32.5	Smith,John B.	ProductX	Bellaire
123456789	2	7.5	Smith,John B.	ProductY	Sugarland
666884444	3	40.0	Narayan,Ramesh K.	ProductZ	Houston
453453453	1	20.0	English,Joyce A.	ProductX	Bellaire
453453453	2	20.0	English,Joyce A.	ProductY	Sugarland
333445555	2	10.0	Wong,Franklin T.	ProductY	Sugarland
333445555	3	10.0	Wong,Franklin T.	ProductZ	Houston
333445555	10	10.0	Wong,Franklin T.	Computerization	Stafford
333445555	20	10.0	Wong,Franklin T.	Reorganization	Houston
999887777	30	30.0	Zelaya,Alicia J.	Newbenefits	Stafford
999887777	10	10.0	Zelaya,Alicia J.	Computerization	Stafford
987987987	10	35.0	Jabbar,Ahmad V.	Computerization	Stafford
987987987	30	5.0	Jabbar,Ahmad V.	Newbenefits	Stafford
987654321	30	20.0	Wallace,Jennifer S.	Newbenefits	Stafford
987654321	20	15.0	Wallace,Jennifer S.	Reorganization	Houston
888665555	20	null	Borg,James E.	Reorganization	Houston

Figure 12.4   Example relations for the schemas in Figure 12.3 that result from applying NATURAL-JOIN to the relations in Figure 12.2.

*These anomalies were identified by Codd (1972a) to justify the need for normalization of relations, as we shall discuss in Section 12.3.

for department 5 in other tuples in EMP_DEPT. In the design of Figure 12.2 we do not have to worry about this consistency problem because we enter only the department number in the employee tuple; all other attribute values of department 5 are recorded only once in the database, as a single tuple in the DEPARTMENT relation.

- It is difficult to insert a new department that has no employees as yet in the EMP_DEPT relation. The only way to do this is to place null values in the attributes for employee. This causes a problem because SSN is the primary key of EMP_DEPT, and each tuple is supposed to represent an employee entity—not a department entity. Moreover, when the first employee is assigned to that department, we do not need the tuple with null values any more. This problem does not occur in the design of Figure 12.2, because a department is entered in the DEPARTMENT relation whether or not any employees work for it, and whenever an employee is assigned to that department, a corresponding tuple is inserted in EMPLOYEE.

Deletion Anomalies. This problem is related to the second insertion anomaly situation discussed above. If we delete from EMP_DEPT an employee tuple that happens to represent the last employee working for a particular department, the information concerning that department is lost from the database. This problem does not occur in the database of Figure 12.2 because DEPARTMENT tuples are stored separately.

Modification Anomalies. In EMP_DEPT, if we change the value of one of the attributes of a particular department—say, the manager of department 5—we must update the tuples of all employees who work in that department; otherwise, the database will become inconsistent. If we fail to update some tuples, the same department will be shown to have two different values for manager in different employee tuples, which should not be the case.

Based on the preceding three anomalies, we can state the following guideline:

GUIDELINE 2: Design the base relation schemas so that no insertion, deletion, or modification anomalies occur in the relations. If any anomalies are present, note them clearly so that the programs that update the database will operate correctly. ∎

The second guideline is consistent with and, in a way, a restatement of the first guideline. We can also see the need for a more formal approach to evaluating whether a design meets these guidelines. Sections 12.2 to 12.4 provide these needed formal concepts. It is important to note that these guidelines may sometimes *have to be violated* in order to *improve the performance* of certain queries. For example, if an important query retrieves information concerning the department of an employee, along with employee attributes, the EMP_DEPT schema may be used as a base relation. However, the anomalies in EMP_DEPT must be noted and well understood so that, whenever the base relation is updated, we do not end up with inconsistencies. In general, it is advisable to use anomaly-free base relations and to specify views that include the JOINs for placing together the attributes frequently referenced in important queries. This reduces the number of

JOIN terms specified in the query, making it simpler to write the query correctly, and in many cases* it improves the performance.

12.1.3 *Null Values in Tuples*

In some schema designs we may group many attributes together into a "fat" relation. If many of the attributes do not apply to all tuples in the relation, we end up with many nulls in those tuples. This can waste space at the storage level and may also lead to problems with understanding the meaning of the attributes and with specifying JOIN operations at the logical level. Another problem with nulls is how to account for them when aggregate operations such as COUNT or SUM are applied. Moreover, nulls can have multiple interpretations, such as:

- The attribute *does not apply* to this tuple.
- The attribute value for this tuple is *unknown*.
- The value is *known but absent;* that is, it has not been recorded yet.

Having the same representation for all nulls compromises the different meanings they may have. Therefore, we may state another guideline as follows:

GUIDELINE 3:   As far as possible, avoid placing attributes in a base relation whose values may be null. If nulls are unavoidable, make sure that they apply in exceptional cases only and do not apply to a majority of tuples in the relation. ▪

For example, if only 10% of employees have individual offices, there is little justification for including an attribute OFFICE_NUMBER in the EMPLOYEE relation; rather, a relation EMP_OFFICES(ESSN, OFFICE_NUMBER) can be created to include tuples for only the employees with individual offices.

12.1.4 *Spurious Tuples*★

Consider the two relation schemas EMP_LOCS and EMP_PROJ1 in Figure 12.5(a), which can be used instead of the EMP_PROJ relation of Figure 12.3(b). A tuple in EMP_LOCS means that the employee whose name is ENAME works on *some project* whose location is PLOCATION. A tuple in EMP_PROJ1 means that the employee whose social security number is SSN works HOURS per week on the project whose name, number, and location are PNAME, PNUMBER, and PLOCATION. Figure 12.5(b) shows relation extensions of EMP_LOCS and EMP_PROJ1 corresponding to the EMP_PROJ relation of Figure 12.4, which are obtained by applying the appropriate PROJECT (π) operations to EMP_PROJ (ignore the dotted lines in Figure 12.5(b) for now).

Suppose that we used EMP_PROJ1 and EMP_LOCS as the base relations instead of EMP_PROJ. This produces a particularly bad schema design, because we cannot recover

---

*The performance of a query specified on a view that is the JOIN of several base relations depends on how the DBMS implements the view. Many relational DBMSs materialize a frequently used view so that they do not have to perform the JOINs often. The DBMS remains responsible for automatically updating the materialized view when the base relations are updated.

(a)

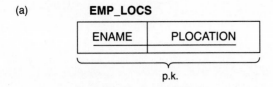

EMP_LOCS

ENAME	PLOCATION

p.k.

EMP_PROJ1

SSN	PNUMBER	HOURS	PNAME	PLOCATION

p.k.

(b)

EMP_LOCS

ENAME	PLOCATION
Smith, John B.	Bellaire
Smith, John B.	Sugarland
Narayan, Ramesh K.	Houston
English, Joyce A.	Bellaire
English, Joyce A.	Sugarland
Wong, Franklin T.	Sugarland
Wong, Franklin T.	Houston
Wong, Franklin T.	Stafford
Zelaya, Alicia J.	Stafford
Jabbar, Ahmad V.	Stafford
Wallace, Jennifer S.	Stafford
Wallace, Jennifer S.	Houston
Borg,James E.	Houston

EMP_PROJ1

SSN	PNUMBER	HOURS	PNAME	PLOCATION
123456789	1	32.5	Product X	Bellaire
123456789	2	7.5	Product Y	Sugarland
666884444	3	40.0	Product Z	Houston
453453453	1	20.0	Product X	Bellaire
453453453	2	20.0	Product Y	Sugarland
333445555	2	10.0	Product Y	Sugarland
333445555	3	10.0	Product Z	Houston
333445555	10	10.0	Computerization	Stafford
333445555	20	10.0	Reorganization	Houston
999887777	30	30.0	Newbenefits	Stafford
999887777	10	10.0	Computerization	Stafford
987987987	10	35.0	Computerization	Stafford
987987987	30	5.0	Newbenefits	Stafford
987654321	30	20.0	Newbenefits	Stafford
987654321	20	15.0	Reorganization	Houston
888665555	20	null	Reorganization	Houston

Figure 12.5 Alternative representation of EMP_PROJ. (a) Representing EMP_PROJ of Figure 12.3(b) by two relation schemas: EMP_LOCS and EMP_PROJ1. (b) Result of projecting the EMP_PROJ relation of Figure 12.4 on the attributes of EMP_PROJ1 and EMP_LOCS.

the information that was originally in EMP_PROJ from EMP_PROJ1 and EMP_LOCS. If we attempt a NATURAL-JOIN operation on EMP_PROJ1 and EMP_LOCS, we get many more tuples than EMP_PROJ had. In Figure 12.6 the result of applying the join to only the tuples *above* the dotted lines in Figure 12.5(b) is shown to reduce the size of the resulting relation. Additional tuples that were not in EMP_PROJ are called **spurious tuples** because they represent spurious or *wrong* information that is not valid. The spurious tuples are marked by asterisks (*) in Figure 12.6.

Decomposing EMP_PROJ into EMP_LOCS and EMP_PROJ1 is bad because, when we JOIN them back using NATURAL-JOIN, we do not get the correct original information. This is because PLOCATION is the attribute that relates EMP_LOCS and EMP_PROJ1, and PLOCATION is neither a primary key nor a foreign key in either EMP_LOCS or EMP_PROJ1. We can now informally state another design guideline:

GUIDELINE 4:   Design relation schemas so that they can be JOINed with equality conditions on attributes that are either primary keys or foreign keys in a way that guarantees that no spurious tuples are generated. ■

This informal guideline obviously needs to be stated more formally. In Chapter 13 we discuss a formal condition, called the nonadditive (or lossless) join property, that guarantees that certain joins do not produce spurious tuples.

SSN	PNUMBER	HOURS	PNAME	PLOCATION	ENAME
123456789	1	32.5	ProductX	Bellaire	Smith,John B.
* 123456789	1	32.5	ProductX	Bellaire	English,Joyce A.
123456789	2	7.5	ProductY	Sugarland	Smith,John B.
* 123456789	2	7.5	ProductY	Sugarland	English,Joyce A.
* 123456789	2	7.5	ProductY	Sugarland	Wong,Franklin T.
666884444	3	40.0	ProductZ	Houston	Narayan,Ramesh K.
* 666884444	3	40.0	ProductZ	Houston	Wong,Franklin T.
* 453453453	1	20.0	ProductX	Bellaire	Smith,John B.
453453453	1	20.0	ProductX	Bellaire	English,Joyce A.
* 453453453	2	20.0	ProductY	Sugarland	Smith,John B.
453453453	2	20.0	ProductY	Sugarland	English,Joyce A.
* 453453453	2	20.0	ProductY	Sugarland	Wong,Franklin T.
* 333445555	2	10.0	ProductY	Sugarland	Smith,John B.
* 333445555	2	10.0	ProductY	Sugarland	English,Joyce A.
333445555	2	10.0	ProductY	Sugarland	Wong,Franklin T.
* 333445555	3	10.0	ProductZ	Houston	Narayan,Ramesh K.
333445555	3	10.0	ProductZ	Houston	Wong,Franklin T.
333445555	10	10.0	Computerization	Stafford	Wong,Franklin T.
* 333445555	20	10.0	Reorganization	Houston	Narayan,Ramesh K.
333445555	20	10.0	Reorganization	Houston	Wong,Franklin T.

Figure 12.6   Result of applying the NATURAL JOIN operation to EMP_PROJ1 and EMP_LOCS, with spurious tuples marked by *.

12.1.5 *Discussion*

In Sections 12.1.1 to 12.1.4, we informally discussed situations that lead to problematic relation schemas, and we proposed informal guidelines for a good relational design. In the rest of this chapter we present formal concepts and theory that may be used to define concepts of the "goodness" and the "badness" of *individual* relation schemas more precisely. We specify several normal forms for relation schemas. In Chapter 13 we give additional criteria for specifying that a *set of relation schemas* together forms a good relational database schema. We also present algorithms that use this theory to design relational database schemas and define additional normal forms beyond BCNF. The normal forms defined in this chapter are based on the concept of a functional dependency, which we describe next, whereas the normal forms discussed in Chapter 13 use additional types of data dependencies called multivalued dependencies and join dependencies.

12.2 Functional Dependencies

The single most important concept in relational schema design is that of a functional dependency. In this section we formally define the concept, and in Section 12.3 we see how it leads to relation schemas in normal forms.

12.2.1 *Definition of Functional Dependency*

A functional dependency is a constraint between two sets of attributes from the database. Suppose that our relational database schema has n attributes $A_1, A_2, \ldots A_n$; let us think of the whole database as being described by a single **universal** relation schema R = $\{ A_1, A_2, \ldots A_n \}$.* We do not imply that we will actually store the database as a single universal table; we use this concept only in developing the formal theory of data dependencies.**

A **functional dependency,** denoted by $X \rightarrow Y$, between two sets of attributes X and Y that are subsets of R specifies a constraint on the possible tuples that can form a relation instance r of R. The constraint states that, for any two tuples t_1 and t_2 in r such that $t_1[X] = t_2[X]$, we must also have $t_1[Y] = t_2[Y]$. This means that the values of the Y component of a tuple in r depend on, or are determined by, the values of the X component; or alternatively, the values of the X component of a tuple uniquely (or **functionally**) **determine** the values of the Y component. We also say that there is a functional dependency from X to Y or that Y is **functionally dependent** on X. We abbreviate functional dependency by **FD.** The set of attributes X is called the **left-hand side** of the FD, and Y is called the **right-hand side**.

---

*This concept of a universal relation is important when we discuss the algorithms for relational database design in Chapter 13.

**This assumption means that every attribute in the database should have a *distinct name*. In Chapter 6 we prefixed attribute names by relation names to achieve uniqueness whenever attributes in distinct relations had the same name.

Thus, X functionally determines Y in a relation schema R if and only if, whenever two tuples of r(R) agree on their X-value, they must necessarily agree on their Y-value. Notice that:

- If a constraint on R states that there cannot be more than one tuple with a given X-value in any relation instance r(R)—that is, X is a **candidate key** of R—this implies that X → Y for any subset of attributes Y of R.
- If X → Y in R, this does not say whether or not Y → X in R.

A functional dependency is a property of the meaning or **semantics** of the attributes. We use our understanding of the semantics of the attributes of R—that is, how they relate to one another—to specify the functional dependencies that should hold on *all* relation states (extensions) r of R. Whenever the semantics of two sets of attributes in R indicate that a functional dependency should hold, we specify the dependency as a constraint. Relation extensions r(R) that satisfy the functional dependency constraints are called **legal extensions** (or **legal relation states**) of R, because they obey the functional dependency constraints. Hence, the main use of functional dependencies is to describe further a relation schema R by specifying constraints on its attributes that must hold *at all times*.

Consider the relation schema EMP_PROJ in Figure 12.3(b); from the semantics of the attributes, we know that the following functional dependencies should hold:

(a) SSN → ENAME
(b) PNUMBER → {PNAME, PLOCATION}
(c) {SSN, PNUMBER} → HOURS

These functional dependencies specify that (a) the value of an employee's social security number (SSN) uniquely determines the employee name (ENAME), (b) the value of a project's number (PNUMBER) uniquely determines the project name (PNAME) and location (PLOCATION), and (c) a combination of SSN and PNUMBER values uniquely determines the number of hours the employee works on the project per week (HOURS). Alternatively, we say that ENAME is functionally determined by (or functionally dependent on) SSN, or "given a value of SSN, we know the value of ENAME," and so on.

Figure 12.3 also introduces a diagrammatic notation for displaying functional dependencies: Each FD is displayed as a horizontal line. The attributes on the left-hand side of the FD are connected by vertical lines to the horizontal line that represents the FD. The right-hand-side attributes of the FD are connected to the horizontal line by arrows pointing toward the attributes, as shown in Figures 12.3(a) and (b).

A functional dependency is a *property of the relation schema* (intension) R, and not of a particular legal relation state (extension) r of R. Hence, an FD *cannot* be inferred automatically from a given relation extension r but must be defined explicitly by someone who knows the semantics of the attributes of R. For example, Figure 12.7 shows a particular relation instance of the TEACH relation schema. Although at first glance we may be tempted to say that TEXT → COURSE, we cannot confirm this unless we know that it is true for all possible relation states of TEACH. It is, however, sufficient to demonstrate a single counterexample to disprove a functional dependency. For example, because 'Smith' teaches both 'Data Structures' and 'Data Management', we can conclude that TEACHER does not functionally determine COURSE. We denote this by TEACHER ↛ COURSE. From Figure 12.7 we can also say that COURSE ↛ TEXT.

TEACH

TEACHER	COURSE	TEXT
Smith	Data Structures	Bartram
Smith	Data Management	Al-Nour
Hall	Compilers	Hoffman
Brown	Data Structures	Augenthaler

Figure 12.7 The TEACH relation.

12.2.2 *Inference Rules for Functional Dependencies*

We denote by F the set of functional dependencies that are specified on relation schema R. Typically, the schema designer specifies the functional dependencies that are *semantically obvious*; usually, however, numerous other functional dependencies hold in *all* legal relation instances that satisfy the dependencies in F. The set of all such functional dependencies is called the **closure** of F and is denoted by F^+. For example, suppose that we specify the following set F of obvious functional dependencies on the relation schema of Figure 12.3(a):

F = { SSN → {ENAME, BDATE, ADDRESS, DNUMBER} ,
 DNUMBER → {DNAME, DMGRSSN} }

We can **infer** the following additional functional dependencies from F:

SSN → {DNAME, DMGRSSN},
SSN → SSN,
DNUMBER → DNAME

An FD X → Y is **inferred from** a set of dependencies F specified on R if X → Y holds in *every* relation state r that is a legal extension of R; that is, whenever r satisfies all the dependencies in F, X → Y also holds in r. The closure F^+ of F is the set of all functional dependencies that can be inferred from F. To determine a systematic way to infer dependencies, we must discover a set of **inference rules** that can be used to infer new dependencies from a given set of dependencies. We consider some of these inference rules next. We use the notation F ⊨ X→Y to denote that the functional dependency X→Y is inferred from the set of functional dependencies F.

In the following discussion, we use an abbreviated notation when discussing functional dependencies. We concatenate attribute variables and drop the commas for convenience. Hence, the FD {X,Y} → Z is abbreviated to XY → Z, and the FD {X,Y,Z} → {U,V} is abbreviated to XYZ → UV. The following six rules (IR1 through IR6) are well-known inference rules for functional dependencies:

(IR1) (Reflexive rule) If X ⊇ Y, then X →Y.

(IR2) (Augmentation rule*) { X →Y } ⊨ XZ →YZ.

(IR3) (Transitive rule) { X →Y, Y→Z } ⊨ X →Z.

(IR4) (Decomposition (or projective) rule) { X →YZ } ⊨ X →Y.

---

*The augmentation rule can also be stated as { X→Y } ⊨ XZ→Y; that is, augmenting the left-hand-side attributes of an FD produces another valid FD.

(IR5) (Union (or additive) rule) $\{ X \rightarrow Y, X \rightarrow Z \} \vDash X \rightarrow YZ$.

(IR6) (Pseudotransitive rule) $\{ X \rightarrow Y, WY \rightarrow Z \} \vDash WX \rightarrow Z$.

The reflexive rule (IR1) says that a set of attributes always determines itself, which is obvious. The augmentation rule (IR2) says that adding the same set of attributes to both the left- and right-hand sides of a dependency results in another valid dependency. According to IR3, functional dependencies are transitive. The decomposition rule (IR4) says that we can remove attributes from the right-hand side of a dependency; applying this rule repeatedly can decompose the FD $X \rightarrow \{A_1, A_2, \ldots, A_n\}$ into the set of dependencies $\{X \rightarrow A_1, X \rightarrow A_2, \ldots, X \rightarrow A_n\}$. The union rule (IR5) allows us to do the opposite; we can combine a set of dependencies $\{X \rightarrow A_1, X \rightarrow A_2, \ldots, X \rightarrow A_n\}$ into the single FD $X \rightarrow \{A_1, A_2, \ldots, A_n\}$.

Each of the preceding inference rules can be proved from the definition of functional dependency, either by direct proof or **by contradiction**. A proof by contradiction assumes that the rule does not hold and shows that this is not possible. We now prove that the first three rules (IR1 to IR3) are valid. The second proof is by contradiction.

PROOF OF IR1
Suppose that $X \supseteq Y$ and that two tuples t_1 and t_2 exist in some relation instance r of R such that $t_1[X] = t_2[X]$. Then $t_1[Y] = t_2[Y]$ because $X \supseteq Y$; hence, $X \rightarrow Y$ must hold in r.

PROOF OF IR2 (BY CONTRADICTION)
Assume that $X \rightarrow Y$ holds in a relation instance r of R but that $XZ \rightarrow YZ$ does not hold. Then there must exist two tuples t_1 and t_2 in r such that (1) $t_1[X] = t_2[X]$, (2) $t_1[Y] = t_2[Y]$, (3) $t_1[XZ] = t_2[XZ]$, and (4) $t_1[YZ] \neq t_2[YZ]$. This is not possible because from (1) and (3) we deduce (5) $t_1[Z] = t_2[Z]$, and from (2) and (5) we deduce (6) $t_1[YZ] = t_2[YZ]$, contradicting (4).

PROOF OF IR3
Assume that (1) $X \rightarrow Y$ and (2) $Y \rightarrow Z$ both hold in a relation r. Then for any two tuples t_1 and t_2 in r such that $t_1[X] = t_2[X]$, we must have (3) $t_1[Y] = t_2[Y]$ (from assumption (1)), and hence we must also have (4) $t_1[Z] = t_2[Z]$, (from (3) and assumption (2)); hence, $X \rightarrow Z$ must hold in r.

Using similar proof arguments, we can prove the inference rules IR4 to IR6 and any additional valid inference rules. However, a simpler way to prove that an inference rule for functional dependencies is valid is to prove it by using inference rules that have already been shown to be valid. For example, we can prove IR4 through IR6 by using IR1 through IR3 as follows:

PROOF OF IR4
1. $X \rightarrow YZ$ (given).
2. $YZ \rightarrow Y$ (using IR1 and knowing that $YZ \supseteq Y$).
3. $X \rightarrow Y$ (using IR3 on 1 and 2).

PROOF OF IR5

1. X→Y (given).
2. X→Z (given).
3. X→XY (using IR2 on 1 by augmenting with X; notice that XX = X).
4. XY→YZ (using IR2 on 2 by augmenting with Y).
5. X→YZ (using IR3 on 3 and 4).

PROOF OF IR6

1. X→Y (given).
2. WY→Z (given).
3. WX→WY (using IR2 on 1 by augmenting with W).
4. WX→Z (using IR3 on 3 and 2).

It has been shown by Armstrong (1974) that inference rules IR1 through IR3 are **sound** and **complete**. By sound, we mean that, given a set of functional dependencies F specified on a relation schema R, any dependency that we can infer from F by using IR1 through IR3 holds in every relation state r of R that *satisfies the dependencies* in F. By complete, we mean that using IR1 through IR3 repeatedly to infer dependencies until no more dependencies can be inferred results in the complete set of *all possible dependencies* that can be inferred from F. In other words, the set of dependencies F^+, which we called the closure of F, can be determined from F by using only inference rules IR1 through IR3. Inference rules IR1 through IR3 are known as **Armstrong's inference rules.***

Typically, database designers first specify the set of functional dependencies F that can easily be determined from the semantics of the attributes of R. Then we can use Armstrong's inference rules to infer additional functional dependencies that will also hold on R. A systematic way to determine these additional functional dependencies is first to determine each set of attributes X that appears as a left-hand side of some functional dependency in F and then to use Armstrong's inference rules to determine the set of all attributes that are dependent on X. Thus, for each set of attributes X, we determine the set X^+ of attributes that are functionally determined by X; X^+ is called the **closure of X under F**. Algorithm 12.1 can be used to calculate X^+.

ALGORITHM 12.1 Determining X^+, the closure of X under F

$X^+ := X;$
repeat
       $oldX^+ := X^+;$
       for each functional dependency Y→ Z in F do
              if $Y \subseteq X^+$ then $X^+ := X^+ \cup Z;$
until $(oldX^+ = X^+);$

Algorithm 12.1 starts by setting X^+ to all the attributes in X. By IR1, we know that all these attributes are functionally dependent on X. Using inference rules IR3 and IR4, we add attributes to X^+, using each functional dependency in F. We keep going through

---

*They are actually known as **Armstrong's axioms,** although they are not axioms in the mathematical sense. Strictly speaking, the axioms are the functional dependencies in F, since we assume that they are correct, while IR1 through IR3 are the inference rules for deducing new functional dependencies.

all the dependencies in F (the repeat loop) until no more attributes are added to X^+ during a complete cycle through the dependencies in F. For example, consider the relation schema EMP_PROJ in Figure 12.3(b); from the semantics of the attributes, we specify the following set F of functional dependencies that should hold on EMP_PROJ:

$$F = \{ \text{SSN} \rightarrow \text{ENAME},$$
$$\text{PNUMBER} \rightarrow \{\text{PNAME, PLOCATION}\},$$
$$\{\text{SSN, PNUMBER}\} \rightarrow \text{HOURS} \}$$

Using Algorithm 12.1, we calculate the following closure sets with respect to F:

$$\{ \text{SSN} \}^+ = \{ \text{SSN, ENAME} \}$$
$$\{ \text{PNUMBER} \}^+ = \{ \text{PNUMBER, PNAME, PLOCATION} \}$$
$$\{ \text{SSN, PNUMBER} \}^+ = \{ \text{SSN, PNUMBER, ENAME, PNAME, PLOCATION},$$
$$\text{HOURS} \}$$

12.2.3 Equivalence of Sets of Functional Dependencies★

In this section we discuss the equivalence of two sets of functional dependencies. First, we give some preliminary definitions. A set of functional dependencies E is **covered by** a set of functional dependencies F—or alternatively, F is said to **cover** E—if every FD in E is also in F^+; that is, E is covered if every dependency in E can be inferred from F. Two sets of functional dependencies E and F are **equivalent** if $E^+ = F^+$. Hence, equivalence means that every FD in E can be inferred from F, and every FD in F can be inferred from E; that is, E is equivalent to F if both the conditions E covers F *and* F covers E hold.

We can determine whether F covers E by calculating X^+ with respect to F for each FD X→Y in E, and then checking whether this X^+ includes the attributes in Y. If this is the case for *every* FD in E, then F covers E. We determine whether E and F are equivalent by checking that E covers F and F covers E.

12.2.4 Minimal Sets of Functional Dependencies★

A set of functional dependencies F is **minimal** if it satisfies the following conditions:

1. Every dependency in F has a single attribute for its right-hand side.
2. We cannot remove any dependency from F and still have a set of dependencies that is equivalent to F.
3. We cannot replace any dependency X→A in F with a dependency Y→A, where Y is a proper subset of X, and still have a set of dependencies that is equivalent to F.

We can think of a minimal set of dependencies as being a set of dependencies in a standard or canonical form with no redundancies. Conditions 2 and 3 make sure that there are no redundancies in the dependencies, and condition 1 ensures that every dependency is in a canonical form with a single attribute on the right-hand side. A **minimal cover** of a set of functional dependencies F is a minimal set of dependencies F_{min} that is equivalent to F. Unfortunately, there can be several minimal covers for a set of functional dependencies. We can always find *at least one* minimal cover F_{min} for any set of dependencies F (see Section 13.1.2).

12.3 Normal Forms Based on Primary Keys

In this section we discuss the normalization process and define the first three normal forms for relation schemas. The definitions of second and third normal form presented here are based on the functional dependencies and primary keys of a relation schema. We will discuss how these normal forms were developed historically and the intuition behind them. More general definitions of these normal forms, which take into account *all candidate keys* of a relation rather than *just the primary key*, are presented in Section 12.4. In Section 12.5 we define Boyce-Codd normal form (BCNF), and in Chapter 13 we define further normal forms that are based on other types of data dependencies.

We first informally discuss what normal forms are and what the motivation behind their development was in Section 12.3.1, as well as recalling some of the definitions from Chapter 6 that are needed here. We then present first normal form (1NF) in Section 12.3.2. In Sections 12.3.3 and 12.3.4, we present definitions of second normal form (2NF) and third normal form (3NF), respectively, that are based on primary keys.

12.3.1 *Introduction to Normalization*

The normalization process, as first proposed by Codd (1972a), takes a relation schema through a series of tests to "certify" whether or not it belongs to a certain **normal form**. Initially, Codd proposed three normal forms, which he called first, second, and third normal form. A stronger definition of 3NF was proposed later by Boyce and Codd and is known as Boyce-Codd normal form. All these normal forms are based on the functional dependencies among the attributes of a relation. Later, a fourth normal form (4NF) and a fifth normal form (5NF) were proposed, based on the concepts of multivalued dependencies and join dependencies, respectively; these are discussed in Chapter 13.

Normalization of data can be looked on as a process during which unsatisfactory relation schemas are decomposed by breaking up their attributes into smaller relation schemas that possess desirable properties. One objective of the original normalization process is to ensure that the update anomalies discussed in Section 12.1.2 do not occur. Normal forms provide database designers with:

- A formal framework for analyzing relation schemas based on their keys and on the functional dependencies among their attributes.
- A series of tests that can be carried out on individual relation schemas so that the relational database can be **normalized** to any degree. When a test fails, the relation violating that test must be decomposed into relations that individually meet the normalization tests.

Normal forms, when considered *in isolation* from other factors, do not guarantee a good database design. It is generally not sufficient to check separately that each relation schema in the database is, say, in BCNF or 3NF. Rather, the process of normalization through decomposition must also confirm the existence of additional properties that the relational schemas, taken together, should possess. Two of these properties are:

- The lossless join or nonadditive join property, which guarantees that the spurious tuple problem discussed in Section 12.1.4 does not occur.

- The dependency preservation property, which ensures that all functional dependencies are represented in some of the individual resulting relations.

We will defer the presentation of the formal concepts and techniques that guarantee the above two properties to Chapter 13. In this section we concentrate on an *intuitive discussion* of the normalization process. Notice that the normal forms mentioned in this section are not the only possible ones. Additional normal forms may be defined to meet other desirable criteria, based on additional types of constraints. The normal forms up to BCNF are defined by considering only the functional dependency and key constraints, whereas 4NF considers an additional constraint called a multivalued dependency and 5NF considers an additional constraint called a join dependency. The practical utility of normal forms becomes questionable when the constraints on which they are based are hard to understand or to detect by the database designers and users who must discover these constraints.

Another point worth noting is that the database designers *need not* normalize to the highest possible normal form. Relations may be left in lower normal forms for performance reasons, such as those discussed at the end of Section 12.1.2.

Before proceeding further, we recall from Chapter 6 the definitions of keys of a relation schema. A **superkey** of a relation schema $R = \{A_1, A_2, \ldots, A_n\}$ is a set of attributes $S \subseteq R$ with the property that no two tuples t_1 and t_2 in any legal relation state r of R will have $t_1[S] = t_2[S]$. A **key** K is a superkey with the additional property that removal of any attribute from K will cause K not to be a superkey any more. The difference between a key and a superkey is that a key has to be "minimal"; that is, if we have a key $K = \{A_1, A_2, \ldots, A_k\}$, then $K - A_i$ is not a key for $1 \leq i \leq k$. In Figure 12.1 {SSN} is a key for EMPLOYEE, whereas {SSN}, {SSN, ENAME}, {SSN, ENAME, BDATE}, etc. are all superkeys.

If a relation schema has more than one "minimal" key, each is called a **candidate key**. One of the candidate keys is *arbitrarily* designated to be the **primary key,** and the others are called secondary keys. Each relation schema must have a primary key. In Figure 12.1 {SSN} is the only candidate key for EMPLOYEE, so it is also the primary key.

An attribute of relation schema R is called a **prime attribute** of R if it is a member of *any key* of R. An attribute is called **nonprime** if it is not a prime attribute—that is, if it is not a member of any candidate key. In Figure 12.1 both SSN and PNUMBER are prime attributes of WORKS_ON, whereas other attributes of WORKS_ON are nonprime.

We now present the first three normal forms: 1NF, 2NF, and 3NF. These were proposed by Codd (1972a) as a sequence to ultimately achieve the desirable state of 3NF relations by progressing through the intermediate states of 1NF and 2NF if needed.

12.3.2 *First Normal Form (1NF)*

First normal form is now considered to be part of the formal definition of a relation; historically, it was defined to disallow multivalued attributes, composite attributes, and their combinations. It states that the domains of attributes must include only *atomic* (simple, indivisible) *values* and that the value of any attribute in a tuple must be a *single value* from the domain of that attribute. Hence, 1NF disallows having a set of values, a tuple of values, or a combination of both as an attribute value for a *single tuple*. In other words, 1NF disallows "relations within relations" or "relations as attributes of tuples." The only attribute values permitted by 1NF are single **atomic** (or **indivisible**) **values**.

Consider the DEPARTMENT relation schema shown in Figure 12.1, whose primary key is DNUMBER, and suppose that we extend it by including the DLOCATIONS attribute shown within dotted lines. We assume that each department can have *a number of* locations. The DEPARTMENT schema and an example extension are shown in Figure 12.8. As we can see, this is not in 1NF because DLOCATIONS is not an atomic attribute, as illustrated by the first tuple in Figure 12.8(b). There are two ways we can look at the DLOCATIONS attribute:

- The domain of DLOCATIONS contains atomic values, but some tuples can have a set of these values. In this case, DNUMBER $\not\to$ DLOCATIONS.

- The domain of DLOCATIONS contains sets of values and hence is nonatomic. In this case, DNUMBER $\to$ DLOCATIONS, because each set is considered a single member of the attribute domain.*

(a) DEPARTMENT

DNAME	DNUMBER	DMGRSSN	DLOCATIONS

(b) DEPARTMENT

DNAME	DNUMBER	DMGRSSN	DLOCATIONS
Research	5	333445555	{Bellaire, Sugarland, Houston}
Administration	4	987654321	{Stafford}
Headquarters	1	888665555	{Houston}

(c) DEPARTMENT

DNAME	DNUMBER	DMGRSSN	DLOCATION
Research	5	333445555	Bellaire
Research	5	333445555	Sugarland
Research	5	333445555	Houston
Administration	4	987654321	Stafford
Headquarters	1	888665555	Houston

Figure 12.8 Normalization into 1NF. (a) A relation schema that is not in 1NF. (b) Example relation instance. (c) 1NF relation with redundancy.

---

*In this case we can consider the domain of DLOCATIONS to be the **power set** of the set of single locations; that is, the domain is made up of *all possible subsets* of the set of single locations.

In either case, the DEPARTMENT relation of Figure 12.8 is not in 1NF; in fact, it does not even qualify as a relation, according to our definition of relation in Section 6.1. To normalize it into 1NF relations, we break up its attributes into the two relations DEPARTMENT and DEPT_LOCATIONS shown in Figure 12.2. The idea is to remove the attribute DLOCATIONS that violates 1NF and place it in a separate relation DEPT_LOCATIONS along with the primary key DNUMBER of DEPARTMENT. The primary key of this relation is the combination {DNUMBER, DLOCATION}, as shown in Figure 12.2. A distinct tuple in DEPT_LOCATIONS exists for *each location* of a department. The DLO-CATIONS attribute is removed from the DEPARTMENT relation of Figure 12.8, de-composing the non-1NF relation into the two 1NF relations DEPARTMENT and DEPT_DLOCATIONS of Figure 12.2.

Notice that a second way to normalize into 1NF is to have a tuple in the original DEPARTMENT relation for each location of a DEPARTMENT, as shown in Figure 12.8(c). In this case, the primary key becomes the combination {DNUMBER, DLOCATION}, and redundancy exists in the tuples. The first solution is superior because it does not suffer from this redundancy problem. In fact, if we choose the second solution, it will be decomposed further during subsequent normalization steps into the first solution.

The first normal form also disallows composite attributes that are themselves mul-tivalued. These are called **nested relations** because each tuple can have a relation *within it*. Figure 12.9 shows how an EMP_PROJ relation can be shown if nesting is allowed. Each tuple represents an employee entity, and a relation PROJS(PNUMBER, HOURS) *within each tuple* represents the employee's projects and the hours per week that the employee works on each project. The schema of the EMP_PROJ relation can be represented as follows:

EMP_PROJ(SSN, ENAME, {PROJS(PNUMBER, HOURS)})

The set braces { } identify the attribute PROJS as multivalued, and we list the com-ponent attributes that form PROJS between parentheses ( ). Interestingly, recent research into the relational model is attempting to allow and formalize nested relations, which were disallowed early on by 1NF (see Section 21.6.2).

Notice that SSN is the primary key of the EMP_PROJ relation in Figures 12.9(a) and (b), while PNUMBER is the **partial** primary key of each nested relation; that is, within each tuple, the nested relation must have unique values of PNUMBER. To normalize this into 1NF, we remove the nested relation attributes into a new relation and **propagate the primary key** into it; the primary key of the new relation will combine the partial key with the primary key of the original relation. Decomposition and primary key prop-agation yield the schemas shown in Figure 12.9(c).

This procedure can be applied recursively to a relation with multiple-level nesting to **unnest** the relation into a set of 1NF relations. This is useful in converting hierarchical schemas into 1NF relations. As we shall see in Chapter 13, restricting relations to 1NF leads to the problems associated with multivalued dependencies and 4NF.

12.3.3 *Second Normal Form (2NF)*

Second normal form is based on the concept of full functional dependency. A functional dependency X→Y is a **full functional dependency** if removal of any attribute A from X means that the dependency does not hold any more; that is, for any attribute A ∈ X,

(a)   **EMP_PROJ**

SSN	ENAME	PROJS	
		PNUMBER	HOURS

(b)   **EMP_PROJ**

SSN	ENAME	PNUMBER	HOURS
123456789	Smith,John B.	1	32.5
		2	7.5
666884444	Narayan,Ramesh K.	3	40.0
453453453	English,Joyce A.	1	20.0
		2	20.0
333445555	Wong,Franklin T.	2	10.0
		3	10.0
		10	10.0
		20	10.0
999887777	Zelaya,Alicia J.	30	30.0
		10	10.0
987987987	Jabbar,Ahmad V.	10	35.0
		30	5.0
987654321	Wallace,Jennifer S.	30	20.0
		20	15.0
888665555	Borg,James E.	20	null

(c)   **EMP_PROJ1**

SSN	ENAME

EMP_PROJ2

SSN	PNUMBER	HOURS

Figure 12.9 Normalizing nested relations into 1NF.
(a) Schema of the EMP_PROJ relation with a "nested relation" PROJS within EMP_PROJ. (b) Example extension of the EMP_PROJ relation with nested relations within each tuple. (c) Decomposing EMP_PROJ into 1NF relations by migrating the primary key.

$(X - \{A\}) \not\twoheadrightarrow Y$. A functional dependency $X \rightarrow Y$ is a **partial dependency** if some attribute $A \in X$ can be removed from X and the dependency still holds; that is, for some $A \in X$, $(X - \{A\}) \rightarrow Y$. In Figure 12.3(b), {SSN, PNUMBER}$\rightarrow$HOURS is a full dependency (neither SSN$\rightarrow$HOURS nor PNUMBER$\rightarrow$HOURS holds). However, the dependency {SSN, PNUMBER}$\rightarrow$ENAME is partial because SSN$\rightarrow$ENAME holds.

A relation schema R is in **2NF** if every nonprime attribute A in R is *fully functionally dependent* on the primary key of R. The EMP_PROJ relation in Figure 12.3(b) is in 1NF but is not in 2NF. The nonprime attribute ENAME violates 2NF because of fd2, as do the nonprime attributes PNAME and PLOCATION because of fd3. The functional dependencies fd2 and fd3 make ENAME, PNAME, and PLOCATION partially dependent on the primary key {SSN, PNUMBER} of EMP_PROJ, thus violating 2NF.

If a relation schema is not in 2NF, it can be further normalized into a number of 2NF relations in which nonprime attributes are associated only with the part of the primary key on which they are fully functionally dependent. The functional dependencies fd1, fd2, and fd3 in Figure 12.3(b) hence lead to the decomposition of EMP_PROJ into the three relation schemas EP1, EP2, and EP3 shown in Figure 12.10(a), each of which is in 2NF. We can see that the relations EP1, EP2, and EP3 are devoid of the update anomalies from which EMP_PROJ of Figure 12.3(b) suffers.

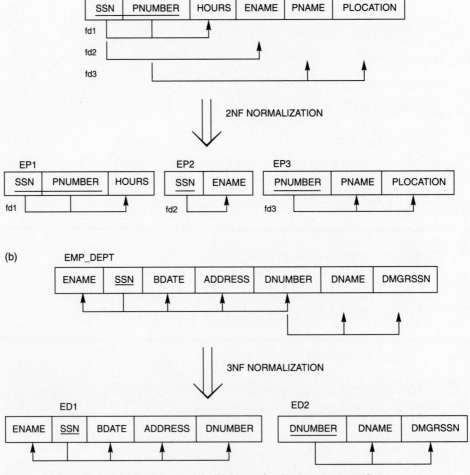

Figure 12.10   The normalization process. (a) Normalizing EMP_PROJ into 2NF relations. (b) Normalizing EMP_DEPT into 3NF relations.

12.3.4 *Third Normal Form (3NF)*

Third normal form is based on the concept of transitive dependency. A functional dependency X→Y in a relation schema R is a **transitive dependency** if there is a set of attributes Z that is *not a subset* of any key* of R, and both X→Z and Z→Y hold. The dependency SSN→DMGRSSN is transitive through DNUMBER in EMP_DEPT of Figure 12.3(a) because both the dependencies SSN→DNUMBER and DNUMBER→DMGRSSN hold *and* DNUMBER is not a subset of the key of EMP_DEPT. Intuitively, we can see that the dependency of DMGRSSN on DNUMBER is undesirable in EMP_DEPT since DNUMBER is not a key of EMP_DEPT.

According to Codd's original definition, a relation schema R is in **3NF** if it is in 2NF and no nonprime attribute of R is transitively dependent on the primary key. The relation schema EMP_DEPT in Figure 12.3(a) is in 2NF, since no partial dependencies on a key exist. However, EMP_DEPT is not in 3NF because of the transitive dependency of DMGRSSN (and also DNAME) on SSN via DNUMBER. We can normalize EMP_DEPT by decomposing it into the two 3NF relation schemas ED1 and ED2 shown in Figure 12.10(b). Intuitively, we see that ED1 and ED2 represent independent entity facts about employees and departments. A NATURAL JOIN operation on ED1 and ED2 will recover the original relation EMP_DEPT without generating spurious tuples.

12.4 General Definitions of Second and Third Normal Forms

In general, we want to design our relation schemas so that they have neither partial nor transitive dependencies, because these types of dependencies cause the update anomalies discussed in Section 12.1.2. According to the definitions of second and third normal forms presented in Section 12.3, the steps for normalization into 3NF relations disallow partial and transitive dependencies on the *primary key*. These definitions, however, do not take other candidate keys of a relation, if any, into account.

In this section we give the more general definitions of 2NF and 3NF that take *all* candidate keys of a relation into account. Notice that this does not affect the definition of 1NF, since it is independent of keys and functional dependencies. We will use the *general definitions* of prime attributes, partial and full functional dependencies, and transitive dependencies given earlier that consider all candidate keys of a relation.

12.4.1 *General Definition of Second Normal Form (2NF)*

A relation schema R is in **second normal form (2NF)** if every nonprime attribute A in R is not partially dependent on *any key* of R.** Consider the relation schema LOTS shown in Figure 12.11(a), which describes parcels of land for sale in various counties of

---

*This is the general definition of transitive dependency. Because we are only concerned with primary keys in this section, we allow transitive dependencies where X is the primary key but Z may be (a subset of) a candidate key.

**This definition can be restated as follows: A relation schema R is in 2NF if every nonprime attribute A in R is fully functionally dependent on *every key* of R.

(a)

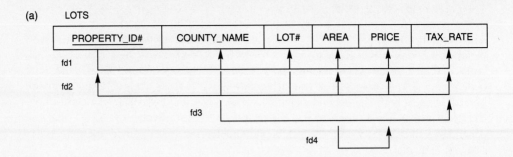

(b)

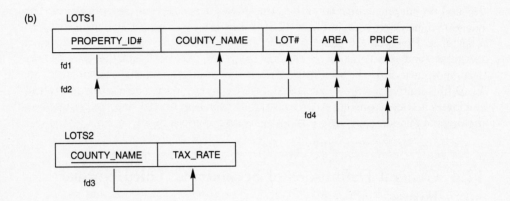

(c)

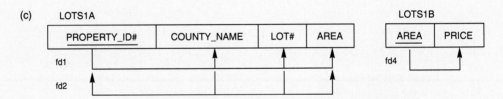

(d)

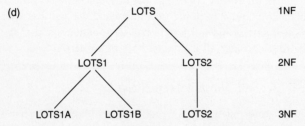

Figure 12.11   Normalization to 2NF and 3NF. (a) The LOTS relation schema and its functional dependencies fd1 through fd4. (b) Decomposing LOTS into the 2NF relations LOTS1 and LOTS2. (c) Decomposing LOTS1 into the 3NF relations LOTS1A and LOTS1B. (d) Summary of normalization of LOTS.

a state. Suppose that there are two candidate keys: PROPERTY_ID# and {COUNTY_NAME, LOT#}; that is, LOT#'s are unique only within each county but PROPERTY_ID#'s are unique across counties for the entire state.

Based on the two candidate keys PROPERTY_ID# and {COUNTY_NAME, LOT#}, we know that the functional dependencies fd1 and fd2 of Figure 12.11(a) hold. We choose PROPERTY_ID# as the primary key, so it is underlined in Figure 12.11(a). Suppose that the following two additional functional dependencies hold in LOTS:

fd3: COUNTY_NAME → TAX_RATE
fd4: AREA → PRICE

In words, the dependency fd3 says that the tax rate is fixed for a given county (does not vary lot by lot within the same county), while fd4 says that the price of a lot is determined by its area regardless of which county it is in (assume that this is the price of the lot for tax purposes).

The LOTS relation schema violates the general definition of 2NF because TAX_RATE is partially dependent on the candidate key {COUNTY_NAME, LOT#}, due to fd3. To normalize LOTS into 2NF, we decompose it into the two relations LOTS1 and LOTS2, shown in Figure 12.11(b). We construct LOTS1 by removing the attribute TAX_RATE that violates 2NF from LOTS and placing it with COUNTY_NAME (the left-hand side of fd3 that causes the partial dependency) into another relation LOTS2. Both LOTS1 and LOTS2 are in 2NF. Notice that fd4 does not violate 2NF and is carried over to LOTS1.

12.4.2 *General Definition of Third Normal Form (3NF)*

A relation schema R is in **3NF** if, whenever a functional dependency X→A holds in R, either (a) X is a superkey of R, or (b) A is a prime attribute of R. According to this definition, LOTS2 (Figure 12.11(b)) is in 3NF. However, fd4 in LOTS1 violates 3NF because AREA is not a superkey of LOTS1 and PRICE is not a prime attribute. To normalize it into 3NF, we decompose LOTS1 into the relation schemas LOTS1A and LOTS1B shown in Figure 12.11(c). We construct LOTS1A by removing the attribute PRICE that violates 3NF from LOTS1 and placing it with AREA (the left-hand side of fd4 that causes the transitive dependency) into another relation LOTS1B. Both LOTS1A and LOTS1B are in 3NF. Two points are worth noting about the general definition of 3NF:

- This definition can be applied *directly* to test whether a relation schema is in 3NF; it does *not* have to go through 2NF first. If we apply the 3NF definition to LOTS with the dependencies fd1 through fd4, we find that *both* fd3 and fd4 violate 3NF. We could hence decompose LOTS into LOTS1A, LOTS1B, and LOTS2 directly.

- LOTS1 violates 3NF because PRICE is transitively dependent on each of the candidate keys of LOTS1 via the nonprime attribute AREA.

12.4.3 *Interpreting the General Definition of 3NF*

A relation schema R violates the general definition of 3NF if a functional dependency X→A holds in R that violates *both* conditions (a) and (b) of 3NF. Violating (b) implies that A is a nonprime attribute. Violating (a) implies that X is not a superset of any key of R; hence, X could be nonprime or it could be a proper subset of a key of R. If X is nonprime we typically have a transitive dependency that violates 3NF, whereas if X is a proper subset of a key of R we have a partial dependency that violates 3NF (and also 2NF). Hence, we can state a **general alternative definition of 3NF** as follows: A relation schema R is in 3NF if every nonprime attribute of R is:

- Fully functionally dependent on every key of R, and
- Nontransitively dependent on every key of R.

12.5 Boyce-Codd Normal Form (BCNF)★

Boyce-Codd normal form is stricter than 3NF, meaning that every relation in BCNF is also in 3NF; however, a relation in 3NF is *not necessarily* in BCNF. Intuitively, we can see the need for a stronger normal form than 3NF by going back to the LOTS relation schema of Figure 12.11(a) with its four functional dependencies fd1 through fd4. Suppose that we have thousands of lots in the relation but the lots are from only two counties: Marion County and Liberty County. Suppose also that lot sizes in Marion County are only 0.5, 0.6, 0.7, 0.8, 0.9, and 1.0 acres, whereas lot sizes in Liberty County are restricted to 1.1, 1.2, . . . , 1.9, and 2.0 acres. In such a situation we would have the additional functional dependency fd5: AREA → COUNTY_NAME. If we add this to the other dependencies, the relation schema LOTS1A still is in 3NF because COUNTY_NAME is a prime attribute.

The area versus county relationship represented by fd5 can be represented by 16 tuples in a separate relation R(AREA, COUNTY_NAME), since there are only 16 possible AREA values. This representation reduces the redundancy of repeating the same information in the thousands of LOTS1A tuples. BCNF is a *stronger normal form* that would disallow LOTS1A and suggest the need for decomposing it.

This definition of Boyce-Codd differs slightly from the definition of 3NF. A relation schema R is in **BCNF** if whenever a functional dependency X→A holds in R, then X is a superkey of R. The only difference between BCNF and 3NF is that condition (b) of 3NF, which allows A to be prime if X is not a superkey, is absent from BCNF.

In our example, fd5 violates BCNF in LOTS1A because AREA is not a superkey of LOTS1A. Note that fd5 satisfies 3NF in LOTS1A because COUNTY_NAME is a prime attribute (condition (b)), but this condition does not exist in the definition of BCNF. We can decompose LOTS1A into two BCNF relations LOTS1AX and LOTS1AY, shown in Figure 12.12(a).

In practice, most relation schemas that are in 3NF are also in BCNF. Only if a dependency X→A exists in a relation schema R with X not a superkey *and* A a prime attribute will R be in 3NF but not in BCNF. The relation schema R shown in Figure 12.12(b) illustrates the general case of such a relation. It is best to have relation schemas in BCNF. If that is not possible, 3NF will do. However, 2NF and 1NF are not considered good relation schema designs. These normal forms were developed historically as stepping stones to 3NF and BCNF.

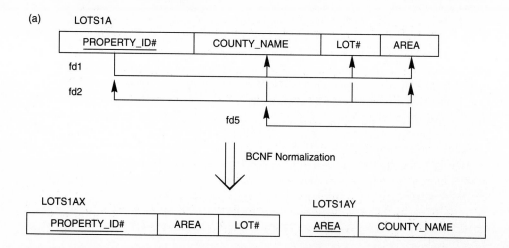

(b)

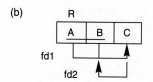

Figure 12.12 BCNF. (a) BCNF normalization with the dependency of fd2 being "lost" in the decomposition. (b) A relation R in 3NF but not in BCNF.

12.6 Summary

In this chapter we discussed on an intuitive basis several pitfalls in relational database design, and then we presented some basic formal concepts that are important in designing a relational database. The topics discussed in this chapter are continued in Chapter 13, where we discuss more advanced concepts in relational design theory.

In Section 12.1 we discussed informally some of the measures for indicating whether a relation schema is "good" or "bad," and we provided informal guidelines for a good design. We discussed the problems of update anomalies that occur when redundancies are present in relations. Additional informal measures of good relation schemas include simple and clear attribute semantics and few nulls in the relations corresponding to schemas.

In Section 12.1.4 we discussed the problem of spurious tuples. This problem is formalized and dealt with in Chapter 13, where we present decomposition algorithms for relational database design based on functional dependencies. There, we discuss the concepts of "lossless join" and "dependency preservation," which are enforced by some of these algorithms. The lossless join property ensures that no spurious tuples will occur. Other topics we discuss in Chapter 13 include multivalued dependencies, join dependencies, and additional normal forms that take these dependencies into account.

In Section 12.2 we presented the concept of functional dependency and discussed some of its properties. Functional dependencies are fundamental constraints that are specified among the attributes of a relation schema. We showed how functional dependencies can be inferred from a set of dependencies and how we can check whether two sets of functional dependencies are equivalent.

In Section 12.3 we used the concept of functional dependency to define normal forms based on primary keys. We provided more general definitions of second normal form (2NF) and third normal form (3NF)—taking all candidate keys of a relation into account—in Section 12.4. Finally, we presented Boyce-Codd normal form (BCNF) in Section 12.5 and discussed how it differs from 3NF. We illustrated by examples how these normal forms can be used to decompose an unnormalized relation into a set of relations in 3NF or BCNF.

Review Questions

12.1. Discuss the attribute semantics as an informal measure of goodness for a relation schema.

12.2. Discuss insertion, deletion, and modification anomalies. Why are they considered bad?

12.3. Why are many **null**s in a relation considered bad?

12.4. Discuss the problem of spurious tuples and how we may prevent it.

12.5. Discuss the informal guidelines for relation schema design.

12.6. What is a functional dependency? Who specifies the functional dependencies that hold among the attributes of a relation schema?

12.7. Why can we not deduce a functional dependency from a particular relation instance?

12.8. What is meant by the completeness and soundness of Armstrong's inference rules?

12.9. What is meant by the closure of a set of functional dependencies?

12.10. When are two sets of functional dependencies equivalent? How can we determine their equivalence?

12.11. What is a minimal set of functional dependencies? Does every set of dependencies have a minimal equivalent set?

12.12. Define first, second, and third normal forms when only primary keys are considered. How do the general definitions of 2NF and 3NF, which consider all keys of a relation, differ from those that consider only primary keys?

12.13. Why is a relation that is in 3NF generally considered good?

12.14. Define Boyce-Codd normal form. How does BCNF differ from 3NF?

12.15. How did the normal forms develop historically?

Exercises

12.16. Suppose that we have the following requirements for a university database that is used to keep track of students' transcripts:

a. The university keeps track of each student's name (SNAME), student number (SNUM), social security number (SSSN), current address (SCADDR) and phone (SCPHONE), permanent address (SPADDR) and phone (SPPHONE), birthdate (BDATE), sex (SEX), class (CLASS) (freshman, sophomore, . . . , graduate), major department (MAJORDEPTCODE), minor department (MINORDEPTCODE) (if any), and degree program (PROG) (B.A., B.S., . . . , Ph.D.). Both SSN and student number have unique values for each student.

b. Each department is described by a name (DEPTNAME), department code (DEPTCODE), office number (DEPTOFFICE), office phone (DEPTPHONE), and college (DEPTCOLLEGE). Both name and code have unique values for each department.

c. Each course has a course name (CNAME), description (CDESC), code number (CNUM), number of semester hours (CREDIT), level (LEVEL), and offering department (CDEPT). The code number value is unique for each course.

d. Each section has an instructor (INSTRUCTORNAME), semester (SEMESTER), year (YEAR), course (SECCOURSE), and section number (SECNUM). The section number distinguishes different sections of the same course that are taught during the same semester/year; its values are 1, 2, 3, . . .; up to the total number of sections taught during each semester.

e. A transcript refers to a student (SSSN), a particular section, and a grade (GRADE).

Design a relational database schema for this database application. First show all the functional dependencies that should hold among the attributes. Then design relation schemas for the database that are each in 3NF or BCNF. Specify the key attributes of each relation. Note any unspecified requirements, and make appropriate assumptions to render the specification complete.

12.17. Prove or disprove the following inference rules for functional dependencies. A proof can be made either by a proof argument or by using inference rules IR1 through IR3. A disproof should be performed by demonstrating a relation instance that satisfies the conditions and functional dependencies in the left-hand side of the inference rule but does not satisfy the dependencies in the right-hand side.

a. $\{W \rightarrow Y, X \rightarrow Z\} \vDash \{WX \rightarrow Y\}$.

b. $\{X \rightarrow Y\}$ and $Z \subseteq Y \vDash \{X \rightarrow Z\}$.

c. $\{X \rightarrow Y, X \rightarrow W, WY \rightarrow Z\} \vDash \{X \rightarrow Z\}$.

d. $\{XY \rightarrow Z, Y \rightarrow W\} \vDash \{XW \rightarrow Z\}$.

e. $\{X \rightarrow Z, Y \rightarrow Z\} \vDash \{X \rightarrow Y\}$.

f. $\{X \rightarrow Y, XY \rightarrow Z\} \vDash \{X \rightarrow Z\}$.

g. $\{X \rightarrow Y, Z \rightarrow W\} \vDash \{XZ \rightarrow YW\}$.

h. $\{XY \rightarrow Z, Z \rightarrow X\} \models \{Z \rightarrow Y\}$.

i. $\{X \rightarrow Y, Y \rightarrow Z\} \models \{X \rightarrow YZ\}$.

j. $\{XY \rightarrow Z, Z \rightarrow W\} \models \{X \rightarrow W\}$.

12.18. Why are the three inference rules IR1 through IR3 (Armstrong's inference rules) important?

12.19. Consider the following two sets of functional dependencies: F = $\{A \rightarrow C, AC \rightarrow D, E \rightarrow AD, E \rightarrow H\}$ and G = $\{A \rightarrow CD, E \rightarrow AH\}$. Check whether they are equivalent.

12.20. Consider the relation schema EMP_DEPT in Figure 12.3(a) and the following set G of functional dependencies on EMP_DEPT: G = $\{SSN \rightarrow \{ENAME, BDATE, ADDRESS, DNUMBER\}$, DNUMBER $\rightarrow \{DNAME, DMGRSSN\}\}$. Calculate the closures $\{SSN\}^+$ and $\{DNUMBER\}^+$ with respect to G.

12.21. Is the set of functional dependencies G in Exercise 12.20 minimal? If not, try to find a minimal set of functional dependencies that is equivalent to G. Prove that your set is equivalent to G.

12.22. Why are transitive dependencies and partial dependencies considered bad in a relational schema?

12.23. What update anomalies occur in the EMP_PROJ and EMP_DEPT relations of Figures 12.3 and 12.4?

12.24. In what normal form is the LOTS relation schema in Figure 12.11(a) with respect to the restrictive interpretations of normal form that take *only the primary key* into account? Would it be in the same normal form if the general definitions of normal form were used?

12.25. Why is BCNF considered better than 3NF?

12.26. Prove that any relation schema with two attributes is in BCNF.

12.27. Why do spurious tuples occur in the result of joining the EMP_PROJ1 and EMP_LOCS relations of Figure 12.5 (result shown in Figure 12.6)?

12.28. Consider the universal relation R = $\{A, B, C, D, E, F, G, H, I, J\}$ and the set of functional dependencies F = $\{ \{A, B\} \rightarrow \{C\}, \{A\} \rightarrow \{D, E\}, \{B\} \rightarrow \{F\}, \{F\} \rightarrow \{G, H\}, \{D\} \rightarrow \{I, J\} \}$. What is the key for R? Decompose R into 2NF, then 3NF relations.

12.29. Repeat exercise 12.28 for the following different set of functional dependencies G = $\{ \{A, B\} \rightarrow \{C\}, \{B, D\} \rightarrow \{E, F\}, \{A, D\} \rightarrow \{G, H\}, \{A\} \rightarrow \{I\}, \{H\} \rightarrow \{J\} \}$.

12.30. Consider the relation R, which has attributes that hold schedules of courses and sections at a university; R = {CourseNo, SecNo, OfferingDept, CreditHours, CourseLevel, InstructorSSN, Semester, Year, Days_Hours, RoomNo, NoOfStudents}. Suppose that the following functional dependencies hold on R:

{CourseNo} $\rightarrow$ {OfferingDept, CreditHours, CourseLevel}
{CourseNo, SecNo, Semester, Year} $\rightarrow$
    {Days_Hours, RoomNo, NoOfStudents, InstructorSSN}
{RoomNo, Days_Hours, Semester, Year} $\rightarrow$
    {InstructorSSN, CourseNo, SecNo}

Try to determine which sets of attributes form keys of R. How would you normalize this relation?

Selected Bibliography

Functional dependencies were originally introduced by Codd (1970). The original definitions of first, second, and third normal form were also defined by Codd (1972a), where a discussion on update anomalies can be found. Boyce-Codd normal form was defined in Codd (1974). The alternative definition of third normal form is given in Ullman (1988), as is the definition of BCNF that we give here. The textbooks by Ullman (1988) and Maier (1983) contain many of the theorems and proofs concerning functional dependencies.

Armstrong (1974) shows the soundness and completeness of the inference rules IR1 through IR3. Additional references to relational design theory are given in Chapter 13.

CHAPTER 13

Relational Database Design Algorithms and Further Dependencies

There are two main techniques for relational database schema design. The first technique involves designing a conceptual schema in a high-level data model, such as the ER model, and then mapping the conceptual schema into a set of relations using a mapping procedure such as the one discussed in Section 6.8. This can be called a **top-down** design. In this technique we can informally apply the normalization principles discussed in Chapter 12, such as avoiding transitive or partial dependencies, *both* during the conceptual schema design and afterward to the relations resulting from the mapping procedure. The second, more purist approach involves viewing relational database schema design strictly in terms of functional and other types of dependencies specified on the database attributes. This is sometimes called **relational synthesis,** because relation schemas in 3NF or BCNF are *synthesized* by having the appropriate attributes grouped together. Each individual relation schema should represent a logically coherent grouping of attributes and should possess the measures of goodness associated with normalization.

In Chapter 12 we discussed some measures of goodness for individual relation schemas based on their keys and functional dependencies—namely, that they are in BCNF or, barring that, in 3NF. During the process of normalization, we **decompose** a relation that is not in a certain normal form into multiple relation schemas until a final design with relations in the desired normal form is reached. An extreme case of this design process is termed **strict decomposition**. In this approach we start by synthesizing one giant relation schema, called the **universal relation,** that includes all the database attributes. We then repeatedly perform decomposition until it is no longer feasible or no longer desirable.

In this chapter we first present several algorithms based on functional dependencies that can be used for relational database design. In Section 13.1 we discuss the concepts of dependency preservation and lossless (or nonadditive) joins, which are used by the design algorithms to achieve desirable decompositions. We show that normal forms are *insufficient on their own* as criteria for a good relational database schema design.

We then discuss other types of data dependencies and some of the normal forms they lead to. These data dependencies specify constraints that *cannot be* expressed by functional dependencies. We discuss multivalued dependencies, join dependencies, inclusion dependencies, and template dependencies. We also define fourth normal form (4NF), fifth normal form (5NF), and, briefly, domain-key normal form (DKNF).

It is possible to skip some or all of the following sections: 13.3, 13.4, 13.5.

13.1 Algorithms for Relational Database Schema Design

In Section 13.1.1 we give examples to show that looking at an *individual* relation to test whether it is in a higher normal form does not, on its own, guarantee a good design; rather, a *set of relations* that together form the relational database schema must possess certain additional properties to ensure a good design. In Section 13.1.2 we discuss one of these properties—the dependency preservation property. In Section 13.1.3 we discuss another of these properties—the lossless or nonadditive join property. We present decomposition algorithms that guarantee these properties (which are formal concepts), as well as guaranteeing that the individual relations are normalized appropriately. Section 13.1.4 discusses problems associated with null values, and Section 13.1.5 summarizes the design algorithms and their properties.

13.1.1 *Relation Decomposition and Insufficiency of Normal Forms*

The relational database design algorithms that we present here start from a single **universal relation schema** $R = \{A_1, A_2, \ldots, A_n\}$ that includes *all* the attributes of the database. We implicitly make the universal relation assumption, which states that every attribute name is unique. The set F of functional dependencies that should hold on the attributes of R is specified by the database designers and is made available to the design algorithms. Using the functional dependencies, the algorithms **decompose** the universal relation schema R into a set of relation schemas $D = \{R_1, R_2, \ldots, R_m\}$ that will become the relational database schema; D is called a **decomposition** of R.

We must make sure that each attribute in R will appear in at least one relation schema R_i in the decomposition so that no attributes are "lost"; formally:

$$\bigcup_{i=1}^{m} R_i = R$$

This is called the **attribute preservation** condition of a decomposition.

Another goal is to have each individual relation R_i in the decomposition D be in BCNF (or 3NF). However, this condition is not sufficient to guarantee a good database design on its own. We must consider the decomposition as a whole, in addition to looking at the individual relations. To illustrate this point, consider the EMP_LOCS relation of Figure 12.5, which is in 3NF and also in BCNF. In fact, any relation schema with only two attributes is automatically in BCNF (Exercise 12.26). Although EMP_LOCS is in BCNF, it still gives rise to spurious tuples when joined with EMP_PROJ1 (which is not in BCNF) (Figure 12.6). Hence, EMP_LOCS represents a particularly bad relation schema because of its convoluted semantics by which PLOCATION gives the location of *one of the projects* on which an employee works. Joining EMP_LOCS with PROJECT of Figure 12.2 (which *is* in BCNF) also gives rise to spurious tuples. We need other criteria that, together with the conditions of 3NF or BCNF, prevent such bad designs. In the next three subsections we discuss such additional conditions that should hold on a decomposition D as a whole.

13.1.2 *Decomposition and Dependency Preservation*

It would be useful if each functional dependency X→Y specified in F either appeared directly in one of the relation schemas R_i in the decomposition D or could be inferred from the dependencies that appear in some R_i. Informally, this is the dependency preservation condition. We want to preserve the dependencies because each dependency in F represents a constraint on the database. If one of the dependencies is not represented in some individual relation R_i of the decomposition, we cannot enforce this constraint by looking only at an individual relation; instead, we have to join two or more of the relations in the decomposition and then check that the functional dependency holds in the result of the join operation. This is clearly an inefficient procedure that cannot be adopted in a practical system.

It is not necessary that the exact dependencies specified in F appear themselves in individual relations of the decomposition D. It is sufficient that the union of the dependencies that hold on the individual relations in D be equivalent to F. We now define these concepts more formally. First we need a preliminary definition. Given a set of dependencies F on R, the **projection** of F on R_i, denoted by $\pi_F(R_i)$ where R_i is a subset of R, is the set of dependencies X→Y in F^+ such that the attributes in X ∪ Y are all contained in R_i. Hence, the projection of F on each relation schema R_i in the decomposition D is the set of functional dependencies in F^+, the closure of F, such that all their left- and right-hand-side attributes are in R_i. We say that a decomposition D = {R_1, R_2, ..., R_m} of R is **dependency-preserving** with respect to F if the union of the projections of F on each R_i in D is equivalent to F; that is,

$$((\pi_F(R_1)) \cup \cdots \cup (\pi_F(R_m)))^+ = F^+$$

If a decomposition is not dependency-preserving, some dependency is **lost** in the decomposition. As we mentioned earlier, to check that a lost dependency holds, we must take the JOIN of several relations in the decomposition to get a relation that includes all left- and right-hand-side attributes of the lost dependency, and then check that the dependency holds on the result of the JOIN—an option that is not practical.

An example of a decomposition that does not preserve dependencies is shown in Figure 12.12(a), where the functional dependency fd2 is lost when LOTS1A is decomposed into {LOTS1AX, LOTS1AY}. The decompositions in Figure 12.11, however, are dependency-preserving. It is always possible to find a dependency-preserving decomposition D with respect to F such that each relation R_i in D is in 3NF. Algorithm 13.1 will create such a decomposition. This algorithm guarantees only the dependency-preserving property; it does *not* guarantee the lossless join property that will be discussed in the next section. The first step of Algorithm 13.1 is to find a minimal cover G for F. An algorithm for accomplishing this step is outlined as Algorithm 13.1*a* below. Recall from Section 12.2.4 that a minimal cover G of F is a *minimal set* of functional dependencies that is equivalent to F. Algorithm 13.1*a* is based on the three conditions that a minimal set of dependencies must satisfy (see Section 12.2.4). Step 2 of the algorithm ensures that every functional dependency in G has a single attribute as its right-hand side. Step 3 removes any redundant attributes from the left-hand side of a functional dependency. Step 4 ensures that no redundant functional dependencies remain in G.

ALGORITHM 13.1   Dependency-preserving decomposition into 3NF relation schemas

1. find a minimal cover G for F ;
2. for each left-hand side X of a functional dependency that appears in G
   create a relation schema {X UNION A_1 UNION A_2 . . . UNION A_m} in D,
   where $X \rightarrow A_1$, $X \rightarrow A_2$, . . . , $X \rightarrow A_m$ are the only dependencies in G with
   X as left-hand side ;
3. place any remaining (unplaced) attributes in a single relation schema to ensure
   the attribute preservation property ;

ALGORITHM 13.1*a*   Finding a minimal cover G for F

1. set G := F ;
2. replace each functional dependency $X \rightarrow A_1, A_2, \ldots , A_n$ in G by the n
   functional dependencies $X \rightarrow A_1$, $X \rightarrow A_2$, . . . , $X \rightarrow A_n$;
3. for each functional dependency $X \rightarrow A$ in G
      for each attribute B that is an element of X
         { compute X^+ with respect to the set of functional dependencies
                    $((G - (X \rightarrow A)) \text{ UNION } ((X - B) \rightarrow A))$;
         if X^+ contains A, then replace $X \rightarrow A$ with $(X - B) \rightarrow A$ in G } ;
4. for each remaining functional dependency $X \rightarrow A$ in G
      {compute X^+ with respect to the set of dependencies $(G - (X \rightarrow A))$;
      if X^+ contains A, then remove $X \rightarrow A$ from G } ;

We will not provide a formal proof, but it can be shown that every relation schema created by Algorithm 13.1 is in 3NF. The proof is based on the fact that G is a minimal cover so the dependencies in G satisfy the properties in Section 12.2.4. It is obvious that all the dependencies in G are preserved by the algorithm because each dependency appears in one of the relations R_i in the decomposition D. Since G is a minimal cover of F, it is equivalent to F, and all the dependencies in F are either preserved directly in the decomposition or are derivable from those in the resulting relations. Algorithm 13.1 is called the **relational synthesis** algorithm, because each relation schema R_i in the decomposition is "synthesized" from a set of dependencies in G with the same left-hand side.

13.1.3 *Decomposition and Lossless (Nonadditive) Joins*

Another property a decomposition D should possess is the lossless join or nonadditive join property, which ensures that no spurious tuples are generated when a NATURAL JOIN operation is applied to the relations in the decomposition. We already illustrated this problem in Section 12.1.4 with the example of Figures 12.5 and 12.6. Because this is a property of a decomposition of relation schemas, the condition of no spurious tuples should hold on *every legal relation instance*—that is, every relation instance that satisfies the functional dependencies specified on the schemas. Hence, the lossless join property is always defined with respect to a specific set F of dependencies. Formally, a decomposition $D = \{R_1, R_2, \ldots, R_m\}$ of R has the **lossless (nonadditive) join** property with respect to the set of dependencies F on R if, for *every* relation state r of R that satisfies F, the following holds:

$$* \, (\pi_{<R1>}(r), \ldots, \pi_{<Rm>}(r) \,) = r$$

The word *lossless* refers to loss of information, not to loss of tuples. If a decomposition does not have the lossless join property, we may get additional spurious tuples after the PROJECT(π) and NATURAL JOIN(*) operations are applied; these additional tuples represent erroneous information. We prefer the term **nonadditive join** because it describes the situation more accurately; if the property holds on a decomposition, we are guaranteed that no spurious tuples bearing wrong information are *added* to the result after the PROJECT and NATURAL JOIN operations are applied.

The decomposition of EMP_PROJ into EMP_LOCS and EMP_PROJ1 in Figure 12.5 obviously does not have the lossless join property. In general, we want to be able to check whether a given decomposition D has the lossless join property with respect to a set of functional dependencies F. We can use Algorithm 13.2 to do this checking.

Algorithm 13.2 creates a relation instance r in the matrix S that satisfies all the functional dependencies in F. At the end of the loop of applying functional dependencies, any two rows in S—which represent two tuples in r—that agree in their values for the left-hand-side attributes X of a functional dependency X→Y in F will also agree in their values for the right-hand-side attributes Y. It can be shown that, if any row in S ends up with all "a" symbols at the end of the algorithm, the decomposition has the lossless join property with respect to F. If, on the other hand, no row ends up being all "a" symbols, the relation instance r represented by S at the end of the algorithm is an example of a relation instance r of R that satisfies the dependencies in F but does not have the lossless join property. This relation serves as a counterexample, so the decomposition D does not have the lossless join property in this case. Note that the "a" and "b" symbols have no special meaning at the end of the algorithm.

Figure 13.1(a) shows how we apply Algorithm 13.2 to the decomposition of the EMP_PROJ relation schema from Figure 12.3(b) into the two relation schemas EMP_PROJ1 and EMP_LOCS of Figure 12.5(a). The algorithm cannot change any "b" symbols to "a" symbols; hence, the resulting matrix S does not have a row with all "a" symbols, and so the decomposition does not have the lossless join property.

Figure 13.1(b) shows another decomposition of EMP_PROJ that has the lossless join property, and Figure 13.1(c) shows how we apply the algorithm to that decomposition. Once a row consists only of "a" symbols, we know that the decomposition has the lossless join property, and we can stop applying the functional dependencies to the matrix S.

ALGORITHM 13.2   Testing for the lossless join property

1. create a matrix S with one row i for each relation R_i in the decomposition D, and one column j for each attribute A_j in R;
2. set $S(i,j):= b_{ij}$ for all matrix entries;
   (* each b_{ij} is a distinct symbol associated with indices (i,j) *)
3. for each row i representing relation schema R_i
      for each column j representing attribute A_j
         if R_i includes attribute A_j
            then set $S(i,j):= a_j$;
   (* each a_j is a distinct symbol associated with index (j) *)
4. repeat the following until a loop execution results in no changes to S
      for each functional dependency X→Y in F
         for all rows in S *which have the same symbols* in the columns corresponding to attributes in X
            make the symbols in each column that correspond to an attribute in Y be the same in all these rows as follows: if any of the rows has an "a" symbol for the column, set the other rows to that *same* "a" symbol in the column—if no "a" symbol exists for the attribute in any of the rows choose one of the "b" symbols that appear in one of the rows for the attribute and set the other rows to that "b" symbol in the column;
5. if a row is made up entirely of "a" symbols, then the decomposition has the lossless join property—otherwise, it does not;

We can now test whether a particular decomposition D obeys the lossless join property with respect to a set of functional dependencies F. The next question is whether there is an algorithm to decompose a relation schema R = $\{A_1, A_2, \ldots, A_n\}$ into a decomposition D = $\{R_1, R_2, \ldots, R_m\}$ such that each R_i is in BCNF *and* the decomposition D has the lossless join property with respect to F. The answer is yes; there is such an algorithm. Before we give the algorithm, however, we need to present some properties of lossless join decompositions.

PROPERTY LJ1

A decomposition D = $\{R_1, R_2\}$ of R has the lossless join property with respect to a set of functional dependencies F on R *if and only if* either:

• The FD $((R_1 \cap R_2) \to (R_1 - R_2))$ is in F^+, or
• The FD $((R_1 \cap R_2) \to (R_2 - R_1))$ is in F^+.

Notice that property LJ1 constitutes an easier test for the lossless join property than does Algorithm 13.2. However, LJ1 is applicable to decompositions into *two relation schemas only*. The reader is encouraged to verify that this property holds on our informal successive normalization examples in Sections 12.3 and 12.4.

(a)   R={SSN, ENAME, PNUMBER, PNAME, PLOCATION, HOURS}   D={R1, R2}
       R1=EMP_LOCS={ENAME, PLOCATION}
       R2=EMP_PROJ1={SSN, PNUMBER, HOURS, PNAME, PLOCATION}

       F={SSN→ENAME;PNUMBER→{PNAME, PLOCATION} ;{SSN,PNUMBER}→HOURS}

	SSN	ENAME	PNUMBER	PNAME	PLOCATION	HOURS
R1	b_{11}	a_2	b_{13}	b_{14}	a_5	b_{16}
R2	a_1	b_{22}	a_3	a_4	a_5	a_6

(no changes to matrix after applying functional dependencies)

(b)

EMP		**PROJECT**			**WORKS_ON**		
SSN	ENAME	PNUMBER	PNAME	PLOCATION	SSN	PNUMBER	HOURS

(c)   R={SSN, ENAME, PNUMBER, PNAME, PLOCATION, HOURS}   D={R1, R2, R3}
       R1=EMP={SSN, ENAME}
       R2=PROJ={PNUMBER, PNAME, PLOCATION}
       R3=WORKS_ON={SSN, PNUMBER, HOURS}

       F={SSN→ENAME;PNUMBER→{PNAME, PLOCATION} ;{SSN,PNUMBER}→HOURS}

	SSN	ENAME	PNUMBER	PNAME	PLOCATION	HOURS
R1	a_1	a_2	b_{13}	b_{14}	b_{15}	b_{16}
R2	b_{21}	b_{22}	a_3	a_4	a_5	b_{26}
R3	a_1	b_{32}	a_3	b_{34}	b_{35}	a_6

(original matrix S at start of algorithm)

	SSN	ENAME	PNUMBER	PNAME	PLOCATION	HOURS
R1	a_1	a_2	b_{13}	b_{14}	b_{15}	b_{16}
R2	b_{21}	b_{22}	a_3	a_4	a_5	b_{26}
R3	a_1	$\cancel{b_{32}}\,a_2$	a_3	$\cancel{b_{34}}\,a_4$	$\cancel{b_{35}}\,a_5$	a_6

(matrix S after applying the first two functional dependencies -
last row is all "a" symbols, so we stop)

Figure 13.1   The lossless join testing algorithm. (a) Applying the algorithm to
test for lossless join to the decomposition of EMP_PROJ into
EMP_PROJ1 and EMP_LOCS. (b) Another decomposition of
EMP_PROJ. (c) Applying the algorithm for testing lossless join to
the decomposition of Figure 13.1(b).

PROPERTY LJ2

If a decomposition $D = \{R_1, R_2, \ldots, R_m\}$ of R has the lossless join property with respect to a set of functional dependencies F on R, and if a decomposition $D_1 = \{Q_1, Q_2, \ldots, Q_k\}$ of R_i has the lossless join property with respect to the *projection of F on R_i*, then the decomposition $D_2 = \{R_1, R_2, \ldots, R_{i-1}, Q_1, Q_2, \ldots, Q_k, R_{i+1}, \ldots, R_m\}$ of R has the lossless join property with respect to F.

Property LJ2 says that, *if* a decomposition D already has the lossless join property—with respect to F—*and* we further decompose one of the relation schemas R_i in D into another decomposition D_1 that also has the lossless join property—with respect to $\pi_F(R_i)$—*then* replacing R_i in D by D_1 will result in a decomposition that also has the lossless join property—with respect to F. We implicitly assumed this property in the informal normalization examples of Sections 12.3 and 12.4.

Using the properties LJ1 and LJ2, we can develop Algorithm 13.3 to create a lossless join decomposition D for R with respect to F such that each relation schema R_i in the decomposition D is in BCNF.

ALGORITHM 13.3   Lossless join decomposition into BCNF relations

1. set D := { R } ;
2. while there is a relation schema Q in D that is not in BCNF do
    begin
        choose a relation schema Q in D that is not in BCNF ;
        find a functional dependency X→Y in Q that violates BCNF ;
        replace Q in D by two schemas (Q − Y) and (X ∪ Y)
    end;

Each time through the loop in Algorithm 13.3, we decompose one relation schema Q that is not in BCNF into two relation schemas. By properties LJ1 and LJ2, the decomposition D has the lossless join property. At the end of the algorithm, all relation schemas in D will be in BCNF. The reader can check that the normalization example in Figures 12.11 and 12.12 basically follows this algorithm. The functional dependencies fd3, fd4, and later fd5 violate BCNF, so the LOTS relation is decomposed appropriately into BCNF relations, and the decomposition then satisfies the lossless join property. In step 2 of Algorithm 13.3, it is necessary to determine whether a relation schema Q is in BCNF or not. One method for doing this is to test, for each functional dependency X→Y in Q, whether X^+ fails to include all the attributes in Q. If it does, X→Y violates BCNF, since X cannot then be a (super)key. Another technique is based on an observation that, whenever a relation schema Q violates BCNF, there exists a pair of attributes A and B in Q such that $(Q - \{A, B\})$→A; by computing the closure $(Q - \{A, B\})^+$ for each pair of attributes {A, B} of R, and checking whether the closure includes A (or B), we can determine whether Q is in BCNF.

If we want a decomposition to have the lossless join property *and* to preserve dependencies, we have to be satisfied with relation schemas in 3NF, rather than in BCNF. A simple modification to Algorithm 13.1, shown as Algorithm 13.4, yields a decomposition D of R that:

- Preserves dependencies.
- Has the lossless join property.
- Is such that each resulting relation schema in the decomposition is in 3NF.

ALGORITHM 13.4 Lossless join and dependency-preserving decomposition into 3NF relation schemas

1. find a minimal cover G for F ;
    (* F is the set of functional dependencies specified on R *)
2. for each left-hand side X that appears in G
    create a relation schema {X ∪ A_1 ∪ A_2 . . . ∪ A_m} where
    X→A_1, X→A_2, . . . , X→A_m are all the dependencies in G with X as
    left-hand side ;
3. place all remaining (unplaced) attributes in a single relation schema ;
4. if none of the relation schemas contains a key of R, create one more relation
    schema that contains attributes that form a key for R;

It can be shown that the decomposition formed from the set of relation schemas created by the preceding algorithm is dependency-preserving and has the lossless join property. In addition, each relation schema in the decomposition is in 3NF. Step 4 of Algorithm 13.4 involves identifying a key of R. Algorithm 13.4*a* can be used to identify a key K of R based on the set of given functional dependencies. We start by setting K to all the attributes of R; then we remove one attribute at a time and check whether the remaining attributes still form a superkey. Notice that the set of functional dependencies used to determine a key in Algorithm 13.4 could be either F or G, since they are equivalent. Notice, too, that Algorithm 13.4*a* determines only *one key* for R; the key returned depends on the order in which attributes are removed from R in step 2.

ALGORITHM 13.4*a* Finding a key K for relation schema R

1. set K := R ;
2. for each attribute A in K
    { compute $(K - A)^+$ with respect to the given set of functional
    dependencies;
    if $(K - A)^+$ contains all the attributes in R, then set K := K − {A} } ;

It is not always possible to find a decomposition into relation schemas that preserves dependencies and allows each relation schema in the decomposition to be in BCNF—rather than 3NF, as in Algorithm 13.4. We can check the 3NF relation schemas in the decomposition individually to see whether each satisfies BCNF. If some relation schema R_i is not in BCNF, we can choose to decompose it further or to leave it as it is in 3NF (with some possible update anomalies). The fact that we cannot always find a decomposition into relation schemas in BCNF that preserves dependencies can be illustrated by the examples in Figure 12.12. The relations LOTS1A (Figure 12.12(a)) and R (Figure 12.12(b)) are not in BCNF but are in 3NF. Any attempt to decompose either relation further into BCNF relations results in loss of the dependency fd2 in LOTS1A or loss of fd2 in R.

It is important to note that the theory of lossless join decompositions is based on the assumption that *no **null** values are allowed for the join attributes*. The next section discusses some of the problems that **null**s may cause in relational decompositions.

13.1.4 *Problems with Null Values and Dangling Tuples*

We must carefully consider the problems associated with **null**s when designing a relational database schema. There is no fully satisfactory relational design theory as yet that includes **null** values. One problem occurs when some tuples have **null** values for attributes that will be used to JOIN individual relations in the decomposition. To illustrate this, consider the database shown in Figure 13.2(a), where two relations EMPLOYEE and DEPARTMENT are shown. The last two employee tuples—Berger and Benitez—present newly hired employees who have not yet been assigned to a department (assume that this does not violate any integrity constraints). Now suppose that we want to retrieve a list of (ENAME, DNAME) values for all the employees. If we apply the * operation on EMPLOYEE and DEPARTMENT (Figure 13.2(b)), the two aforementioned tuples will *not* appear in the result. The OUTER JOIN operation, discussed in Chapter 6, can deal with this problem. Recall that, if we take the LEFT OUTER JOIN of EMPLOYEE with DEPARTMENT, tuples in EMPLOYEE that have **null** for the join attribute will still appear in the result, joined with an "imaginary" tuple in DEPARTMENT that has **null**s for all its attribute values. Figure 13.2(c) shows the result.

In general, whenever a relational database schema is designed where two or more relations are interrelated via foreign keys, particular care must be devoted to watching for potential null values in foreign keys. This can cause unexpected loss of information in queries that involve joins. Moreover, if nulls occur in other attributes, such as SALARY, their effect on built-in functions such as SUM and AVERAGE must be carefully evaluated.

A related problem is that of **dangling tuples,** which may occur if we carry a decomposition too far. Suppose that we decompose the EMPLOYEE relation of Figure 13.2(a) further into EMPLOYEE_1 and EMPLOYEE_2, shown in Figure 13.3(a) and 13.3(b).* If we apply the * operation to EMPLOYEE_1 and EMPLOYEE_2, we get the original EMPLOYEE relation. However, we may use an alternative representation for the case when an employee has not yet been assigned a department. This is shown in Figure 13.3(c), where we *do not include a tuple* in EMPLOYEE_3 if the employee has not been assigned a department. This representation contrasts with including a tuple with **null** for DNUM, as in EMPLOYEE_2. Suppose that we use EMPLOYEE_3 instead of EMPLOYEE_2. Now if we apply a NATURAL JOIN on EMPLOYEE_1 and EMPLOYEE_3, the tuples for Berger and Benitez will disappear. These are called **dangling tuples** because they are represented in only one of the two relations that represent employees and hence are lost if we apply an (inner) join operation.

13.1.5 *Discussion*

In the preceding subsections we presented several algorithms for relational database design. These algorithms decompose a universal relation schema into a set of relation

---

*This sometimes happens when we apply vertical fragmentation to a relation in the context of a distributed database (see Chapter 23).

(a)

EMPLOYEE

ENAME	SSN	BDATE	ADDRESS	DNUM
Smith, John B.	123456789	09-JAN-55	731 Fondren, Houston, TX	5
Wong, Franklin T.	333445555	08-DEC-45	638 Voss, Houston, TX	5
Zelaya, Alicia J.	999887777	19-JUL-58	3321 Castle, Spring, TX	4
Wallace, Jennifer S.	987654321	20-JUN-31	291 Berry, Bellaire, TX	4
Narayan, Ramesh K.	666884444	15-SEP-52	975 Fire Oak, Humble, TX	5
English, Joyce A.	453453453	31-JUL-62	5631 Rice, Houston, TX	5
Jabbar, Ahmad V.	987987987	29-MAR-59	980 Dallas, Houston, TX	4
Borg, James E.	888665555	10-NOV-27	450 Stone, Houston, TX	1
Berger, Anders C.	999775555	26-APR-55	6530 Braes, Bellaire, TX	**null**
Benitez, Carlos M.	888664444	09-JAN-53	7654 Beech, Houston, TX	**null**

DEPARTMENT

DNAME	DNUM	DMGRSSN
Research	5	333445555
Administration	4	987654321
Headquarters	1	888665555

(b)

ENAME	SSN	BDATE	ADDRESS	DNUM	DNAME	DMGRSSN
Smith, John B.	123456789	09-JAN-55	731 Fondren, Houston, TX	5	Research	333445555
Wong, Franklin T.	333445555	08-DEC-45	638 Voss, Houston, TX	5	Research	333445555
Zelaya, Alicia J.	999887777	19-JUL-58	3321 Castle, Spring, TX	4	Administration	987654321
Wallace, Jennifer S.	987654321	20-JUN-31	291 Berry, Bellaire, TX	4	Administration	987654321
Narayan, Ramesh K.	666884444	15-SEP-52	975 Fire Oak, Humble, TX	5	Research	333445555
English, Joyce A.	453453453	31-JUL-62	5631 Rice, Houston, TX	5	Research	333445555
Jabbar, Ahmad V.	987987987	29-MAR-59	980 Dallas, Houston, TX	4	Administration	987654321
Borg, James E.	888665555	10-NOV-27	450 Stone, Houston, TX	1	Headquarters	888665555

(c)

ENAME	SSN	BDATE	ADDRESS	DNUM	DNAME	DMGRSSN
Smith, John B.	123456789	09-JAN-55	731 Fondren, Houston, TX	5	Research	333445555
Wong, Franklin T.	333445555	08-DEC-45	638 Voss, Houston, TX	5	Research	333445555
Zelaya, Alicia J.	999887777	19-JUL-58	3321 Castle, Spring, TX	4	Administration	987654321
Wallace, Jennifer S.	987654321	20-JUN-31	291 Berry, Bellaire, TX	4	Administration	987654321
Narayan, Ramesh K.	666884444	15-SEP-52	975 Fire Oak, Humble, TX	5	Research	333445555
English, Joyce A.	453453453	31-JUL-62	5631 Rice, Houston, TX	5	Research	333445555
Jabbar, Ahmad V.	987987987	29-MAR-59	980 Dallas, Houston, TX	4	Administration	987654321
Borg, James E.	888665555	10-NOV-27	450 Stone, Houston, TX	1	Headquarters	888665555
Berger, Anders C.	999775555	26-APR-55	6530 Braes, Bellaire, TX	**null**	**null**	**null**
Benitez, Carlos M.	888664444	09-JAN-53	7654 Beech, Houston, TX	**null**	**null**	**null**

Figure 13.2 The null value join problem. (a) A database with nulls for some join attributes. (b) Result of applying the NATURAL JOIN operation to the EMPLOYEE and DEPARTMENT relations. (c) Result of applying the OUTER JOIN operation to EMPLOYEE with DEPARTMENT.

(a) **EMPLOYEE_1**

ENAME	SSN	BDATE	ADDRESS
Smith, John B.	123456789	09-JAN-55	731 Fondren, Houston, TX
Wong, Franklin T.	333445555	08-DEC-45	638 Voss, Houston, TX
Zelaya, Alicia J.	999887777	19-JUL-58	3321 Castle, Spring, TX
Wallace, Jennifer S.	987654321	20-JUN-31	291 Berry, Bellaire, TX
Narayan, Ramesh K.	666884444	15-SEP-52	975 Fire Oak, Humble, TX
English, Joyce A.	453453453	31-JUL-62	5631 Rice, Houston, TX
Jabbar, Ahmad V.	987987987	29-MAR-59	980 Dallas, Houston, TX
Borg, James E.	888665555	10-NOV-27	450 Stone, Houston, TX
Berger, Anders C.	999775555	26-APR-55	6530 Braes, Bellaire, TX
Benitez, Carlos M.	888664444	09-JAN-53	7654 Beech, Houston, TX

(b) **EMPLOYEE_2**

SSN	DNUM
123456789	5
333445555	5
999887777	4
987654321	4
666884444	5
453453453	5
987987987	4
888665555	1
999775555	null
888664444	null

(c) **EMPLOYEE_3**

SSN	DNUM
123456789	5
333445555	5
999887777	4
987654321	4
666884444	5
453453453	5
987987987	4
888665555	1

Figure 13.3 The "dangling tuple" problem. (a) The relation EMPLOYEE_1, which includes all the attributes of the EMPLOYEE relation except for DNUMBER. (b) The relation EMPLOYEE_2, which includes the DNUMBER attribute of EMPLOYEE with null values. (c) The relation EMPLOYEE_3, which does not include the tuples for which DNUMBER has a null value.

schemas and are based on the concepts of functional dependencies, normal forms, dependency preservation, and lossless join decomposition. We also discussed the problems with null values and dangling tuples in relational design.

One of the problems with the algorithms discussed here is that the database designer must first specify *all* the relevant functional dependencies among the database attributes. This is *not a simple task* for a large database with hundreds of attributes. Failure to specify one or two important dependencies may result in an undesirable design. Another problem is that these algorithms are not deterministic in general. For example, the synthesis algorithms require the specification of a minimal cover for the set of functional dependencies. Because there may be, in general, many minimal covers corresponding to a set of functional dependencies, the algorithm can give different designs for the same set of functional dependencies, each design depending on the particular minimal cover. Some of these designs may not be desirable. Other algorithms produce a decomposition that depends on the order in which the functional dependencies are supplied to the algorithm; again, potentially many different designs may arise corresponding to the same set of functional dependencies.

For the preceding reasons, these algorithms cannot be used blindly. They have not proved to be very popular in practice up to now; top–down database design based on the ER model and other high-level data models is currently used more often. One technique combines the two approaches. For example, we may start with the ER model to produce a conceptual schema and map it to relations. Then we can apply these algorithms to the individual relations obtained from the ER design, specify their functional dependencies, and see whether they need to be decomposed further. Another alternative is to analyze the entity types of the ER design itself and decompose them if needed by applying a similar theory.

So far we have discussed only functional dependency, which is by far the most important type of dependency in relational database design theory. However, in many cases relations have constraints that cannot be specified as functional dependencies. In the following sections we describe additional types of dependencies that may be used to represent other types of constraints on relations. Some of these dependencies lead to further normal forms. In Section 13.2 we discuss the multivalued dependency and define fourth normal form, which is based on this dependency. Next, in Section 13.3, we briefly discuss join dependencies and fifth normal form. Finally, we briefly discuss inclusion dependencies, template dependencies, and domain-key normal form.

13.2 Multivalued Dependencies and Fourth Normal Form

Multivalued dependencies are a consequence of first normal form, which disallowed an attribute in a tuple to have a set of values. If we have two or more multivalued independent attributes in the same relation schema, we get into a problem of having to repeat every value of one of the attributes with every value of the other attribute to keep the relation instances consistent. This constraint is specified by a multivalued dependency.

For example, consider the relation EMP shown in Figure 13.4(a). A tuple in this EMP relation represents the fact that an employee whose name is ENAME *works on the project* whose name is PNAME and *has a dependent* whose name is DNAME. An employee may work on several projects and may have several dependents, and the employees projects and dependents are not directly related to one another.* To keep the tuples in the relation consistent, we must keep a tuple to represent every combination of an employee's dependent and an employee's project. This constraint is specified as a multivalued dependency on the EMP relation. Informally, whenever two *independent* 1:N relationships A:B and A:C are mixed in the same relation, an MVD may arise.

13.2.1 *Formal Definition of Multivalued Dependency*

Formally, a **multivalued dependency** (MVD) X—↠Y specified on relation schema R, where X and Y are both subsets of R, specifies the following constraint on any relation r of R:

---

*In an ER diagram, each would be represented as a multivalued attribute or a weak entity type (see Chapter 3).

(a) **EMP**

ENAME	PNAME	DNAME
Smith	X	John
Smith	Y	Anna
Smith	X	Anna
Smith	Y	John

(b) **EMP_PROJECTS**

ENAME	PNAME
Smith	X
Smith	Y

EMP_DEPENDENTS

ENAME	DNAME
Smith	John
Smith	Anna

(c) **SUPPLY**

SNAME	PARTNAME	PROJNAME
Smith	Bolt	ProjX
Smith	Nut	ProjY
Adamsky	Bolt	ProjY
Walton	Nut	ProjZ
Adamsky	Nail	ProjX
Adamsky	Bolt	ProjX
Smith	Bolt	ProjY

(d) **R1**

SNAME	PARTNAME
Smith	Bolt
Smith	Nut
Adamsky	Bolt
Walton	Nut
Adamsky	Nail

R2

SNAME	PROJNAME
Smith	ProjX
Smith	ProjY
Adamsky	ProjY
Walton	ProjZ
Adamsky	ProjX

R3

PARTNAME	PROJNAME
Bolt	ProjX
Nut	ProjY
Bolt	ProjY
Nut	ProjZ
Nail	ProjX

Figure 13.4   4NF and 5NF. (a) The EMP relation with two MVDs ENAME→→ PNAME and ENAME→→DNAME. (b) Decomposing EMP into two relations in 4NF. (c) The SUPPLY relation with no MVDs that is in 4NF (however, it would not be in 5NF if the JD(R1,R2,R3) holds). (d) Decomposing the SUPPLY relation with the join dependency into three 5NF relations.

If two tuples t_1 and t_2 exist in r such that $t_1[X] = t_2[X]$, then two tuples t_3 and t_4 should also exist* in r with the following properties:

- $t_3[X] = t_4[X] = t_1[X] = t_2[X]$.
- $t_3[Y] = t_1[Y]$ and $t_4[Y] = t_2[Y]$.
- $t_3[R - (XY)] = t_2[R - (XY)]$ and $t_4[R - (XY)] = t_1[R - (XY)]$.

Whenever X→→Y holds, we say that X **multidetermines** Y. Because of the symmetry in the definition, whenever X→→Y holds in R, so does X→→(R − (XY)). Recall that

*The tuples t_1, t_2, t_3, and t_4 are not necessarily distinct.

$(R - XY)$ is the same as $R - (X \cup Y) = Z$. Hence, $X \twoheadrightarrow Y$ implies $X \twoheadrightarrow Z$, and therefore it is sometimes written as $X \twoheadrightarrow Y/ Z$.

The formal definition specifies that, given a particular value of X, the set of values of Y determined by this value of X is completely determined by X alone and *does not depend* on the values of the remaining attributes Z of the relation schema R. Hence, whenever two tuples exist that have distinct values of Y but the same value of X, these values of Y must be repeated with every distinct value of Z that occurs with that same value of X. This informally corresponds to Y being a multivalued attribute of the entities represented by tuples in R.

In Figure 13.4(a) the MVDs ENAME$\twoheadrightarrow$PNAME and ENAME$\twoheadrightarrow$DNAME, or ENAME$\twoheadrightarrow$ PNAME/DNAME hold in the EMP relation. The employee with ENAME 'Smith' works on projects with PNAME 'X' and 'Y' and has two dependents with DNAME 'John' and 'Anna'. If we stored only the first two tuples in EMP (<'Smith', 'X', 'John'> and <'Smith', 'Y', 'Anna'>), we would incorrectly show associations between project 'X' and 'John' and between project 'Y' and 'Anna'; these should not be conveyed, because no such meaning is intended in this relation. Hence, we must store the other two tuples (<'Smith', 'X', 'Anna'> and <'Smith', 'Y', 'John'>) to show that {'X', 'Y'} and {'John', 'Anna'} are associated only with 'Smith'; that is, there is no association between PNAME and DNAME.

An MVD $X \twoheadrightarrow Y$ in R is called a **trivial MVD** if (a) Y is a subset of X or (b) $X \cup Y$ = R. For example, the relation EMP_PROJECTS in Figure 13.4(b) has the trivial MVD ENAME$\twoheadrightarrow$PNAME. An MVD that satisfies neither (a) nor (b) is called a **nontrivial MVD**. A trivial MVD will hold in *any* relation instance r of R; it is called trivial because it does not specify any constraint on R.

If we have a nontrivial MVD in a relation, we may have to repeat values redundantly in the tuples. In the EMP relation of Figure 13.4(a), the values 'X' and 'Y' of PNAME are repeated with each value of DNAME (or by symmetry, the values 'John' and 'Anna' of DNAME are repeated with each value of PNAME). This redundancy is clearly undesirable. However, the EMP schema is in BCNF because *no* functional dependencies hold in EMP. Therefore, we need to define a fourth normal form that is stronger than BCNF and disallows relation schemas such as EMP. We first discuss some of the properties of MVDs and consider how they are related to functional dependencies.

13.2.2 *Inference Rules for Functional and Multivalued Dependencies*

As with functional dependencies (FDs), we can develop inference rules for MVDs. It is better, though, to develop a unified framework that includes both FDs and MVDs so that both types of constraints can be considered together. The following inference rules IR1 through IR8 form a sound and complete set for inferring functional and multivalued dependencies from a given set of dependencies. Assume that all attributes are included in a "universal" relation schema $R = \{A_1, A_2, \ldots, A_n\}$ and that X, Y, Z, and W are subsets of R.

(IR1) (Reflexive rule for FDs): If $X \supseteq Y$, then $X \rightarrow Y$.

(IR2) (Augmentation rule for FDs): $\{X \rightarrow Y\} \vDash XZ \rightarrow YZ$.

(IR3) (Transitive rule for FDs): $\{X \rightarrow Y, Y \rightarrow Z\} \vDash X \rightarrow Z$.

(IR4) (Complementation rule for MVDs): $\{X \twoheadrightarrow Y\} \vDash \{X \twoheadrightarrow (R - (X \cup Y))\}$.

(IR5) (Augmentation rule for MVDs): If $X \twoheadrightarrow Y$ and $W \supseteq Z$ then $WX \twoheadrightarrow YZ$.

(IR6) (Transitive rule for MVDs): $\{X \twoheadrightarrow Y, Y \twoheadrightarrow Z\} \models X \twoheadrightarrow (Z - Y)$.

(IR7) (Replication rule (FD to MVD)): $\{X \rightarrow Y\} \models X \twoheadrightarrow Y$.

(IR8) (Coalescence rule for FDs and MVDs): If $X \twoheadrightarrow Y$ and there exists W with the properties that (a) $W \cap Y$ is empty, (b) $W \rightarrow Z$, and (c) $Y \supseteq Z$, then $X \rightarrow Z$.

IR1 through IR3 are Armstrong's inference rules for FDs alone. IR4 through IR6 are inference rules pertaining to MVDs only. IR7 and IR8 relate FDs and MVDs. In particular, IR7 says that a functional dependency is a *special case* of a multivalued dependency; that is, every FD is also an MVD. An FD $X \rightarrow Y$ is an MVD $X \twoheadrightarrow Y$ with the additional restriction that at most one value of Y is associated with each value of X. Given a set F of functional and multivalued dependencies specified on $R = \{A_1, A_2, \ldots, A_n\}$, we can use IR1 through IR8 to infer the (complete) set of all dependencies (functional or multivalued) F^+ that will hold in every relation instance r of R that satisfies F. We again call F^+ the **closure** of F.

13.2.3 *Fourth Normal Form (4NF)*

We now present the definition of 4NF, which is violated when a relation has undesirable multivalued dependencies, and hence can be used to identify and decompose such relations. A relation schema R is in **4NF** with respect to a set of dependencies F if, for every *nontrivial* multivalued dependency $X \twoheadrightarrow Y$ in F^+, X is a superkey for R.

The EMP relation of Figure 13.4(a) is not in 4NF because in the nontrivial MVDs ENAME $\twoheadrightarrow$ PNAME and ENAME $\twoheadrightarrow$ DNAME, ENAME is not a superkey of EMP. We decompose EMP into EMP_PROJECTS and EMP_DEPENDENTS, shown in Figure 13.4(b). Both EMP_PROJECTS and EMP_DEPENDENTS are in 4NF, because ENAME $\twoheadrightarrow$ PNAME is a trivial MVD in EMP_PROJECTS and ENAME $\twoheadrightarrow$ DNAME is a trivial MVD in EMP_DEPENDENTS. In fact, no nontrivial MVDs hold in either EMP_PROJECTS or EMP_DEPENDENTS. No FDs hold in these relation schemas either.

To illustrate why it is important to keep relations in 4NF, Figure 13.5(a) shows the EMP relation with an additional employee, 'Brown', who has three dependents ('Jim', 'Joan', and 'Bob') and works on four different projects ('W', 'X', 'Y', and 'Z'). There are 16 tuples in EMP in Figure 13.5(a). If we decompose EMP into EMP_PROJECTS and EMP_DEPENDENTS, as shown in Figure 13.5(b), we need only store a total of 11 tuples in both relations. Moreover, these tuples are much smaller than the tuples in EMP. In addition, the update anomalies associated with multivalued dependencies are avoided. For example, if Brown starts working on another project, we must insert three tuples in EMP—one for each dependent. If we forget to insert any one of those, the relation becomes inconsistent in that it incorrectly implies a relationship between project and dependent. However, only a single tuple need be inserted in the 4NF relation EMP_PROJECTS. Similar problems occur with deletion and modification anomalies if a relation is not in 4NF.

The EMP relation in Figure 13.4(a) is not in 4NF, because it represents two *independent* 1:N relationships—one between employees and the projects they work on, and the other between employees and their dependents. We sometimes have a relationship between three entities that depends on all three participating entities, such as the SUPPLY relation shown in Figure 13.4(c) (consider only the tuples in Figure 13.4(c) *above* the

(a) **EMP**

ENAME	PNAME	DNAME
Smith	X	John
Smith	Y	Anna
Smith	X	Anna
Smith	Y	John
Brown	W	Jim
Brown	X	Jim
Brown	Y	Jim
Brown	Z	Jim
Brown	W	Joan
Brown	X	Joan
Brown	Y	Joan
Brown	Z	Joan
Brown	W	Bob
Brown	X	Bob
Brown	Y	Bob
Brown	Z	Bob

(b) **EMP_PROJECTS**

ENAME	PNAME
Smith	X
Smith	Y
Brown	W
Brown	X
Brown	Y
Brown	Z

EMP_DEPENDENTS

ENAME	DNAME
Smith	Anna
Smith	John
Brown	Jim
Brown	Joan
Brown	Bob

Figure 13.5 Benefits of 4NF. (a) The EMP relation with some additional tuples. (b) Projecting EMP on EMP_PROJECTS and EMP_DEPENDENTS.

dotted line for now). In this case a tuple represents a supplier supplying a specific part *to a particular project,* so there are *no* nontrivial MVDs. The SUPPLY relation is already *in 4NF* and should not be decomposed. Notice that relations containing nontrivial MVDs tend to be "all key" relations; that is, their key is all their attributes taken together.

13.2.4 *Lossless Join Decomposition into 4NF Relations*

Whenever we decompose a relation schema R into $R_1 = (X \cup Y)$ and $R_2 = (R - Y)$ based on an MVD $X \twoheadrightarrow Y$ that holds in R, the decomposition has the lossless join property. It can be shown that this is a necessary and sufficient condition for decomposing a schema into two schemas that have the lossless join property, as given by property LJ1'.

PROPERTY LJ1'
The relation schemas R_1 and R_2 form a lossless join decomposition of R if and only if $(R_1 \cap R_2) \twoheadrightarrow (R_1 - R_2)$ (or by symmetry, if and only if $(R_1 \cap R_2) \twoheadrightarrow (R_2 - R_1)$).

This is similar to property LJ1 of Section 13.1.3, except that LJ1 dealt with FDs only, whereas LJ1' deals with both FDs and MVDs (recall that an FD is also an MVD). We can use a slight modification of Algorithm 13.3 to develop Algorithm 13.5, which creates a lossless join decomposition into relation schemas that are in 4NF (rather than in BCNF). Algorithm 13.5 does *not* necessarily produce a decomposition that preserves FDs.

ALGORITHM 13.5 Lossless join decomposition into 4NF relations

```
set D := { R } ;
while there is a relation schema Q in D that is not in 4NF do
    begin
```

choose a relation schema Q in D that is not in 4NF ;
find a nontrivial MVD X→→Y in Q that violates 4NF ;
replace Q in D by two schemas (Q - Y) and (X ∪ Y)
end;

13.3 Join Dependencies and Fifth Normal Form*

We saw that LJ1 and LJ1' give the condition for a relation schema R to be decomposed into two schemas R_1 and R_2, where the decomposition has the lossless join property. However, in some cases there may be no lossless join decomposition into two relation schemas but there may be a lossless join decomposition into more than two relation schemas. These cases are handled by join dependency and fifth normal form. It is important to note that these cases occur very rarely and are difficult to detect in practice.

A **join dependency** (JD), denoted by $JD(R_1, R_2, \ldots, R_n)$, specified on relation schema R, specifies a constraint on instances r of R. The constraint states that *every legal instance* r of R should have a lossless join decomposition into $R_1, R_2, \ldots, R_n$; that is,

$$* \ (\pi_{<R1>}(r), \pi_{<R2>}(r), \ldots, \pi_{<Rn>}(r) \ ) = r$$

Notice that an MVD is a special case of a JD where n = 2. A join dependency $JD(R_1, R_2, \ldots, R_n)$, specified on relation schema R, is a **trivial JD** if one of the relation schemas R_i in $JD(R_1, R_2, \ldots, R_n)$ is equal to R. Such a dependency is called trivial because it has the lossless join property for *any* relation instance r of R and hence does not specify any constraint on R. We can now specify fifth normal form, which is also called project-join normal form. A relation schema R is in **fifth normal form (5NF)** (or **project-join normal form (PJNF)**) with respect to a set F of functional, multivalued, and join dependencies if, for every nontrivial join dependency $JD(R_1, R_2, \ldots, R_n)$ in F^+ (that is, implied by F), every R_i is a superkey of R.

For an example of a JD, consider once again the SUPPLY relation of Figure 13.4(c). Suppose that the following additional constraint always holds: Whenever a supplier s supplies part p, *and* a project j uses part p, *and* the supplier s supplies *at least one* part to project j, *then* supplier s will also be supplying part p to project j. This constraint can be restated in other ways and specifies a join dependency JD(R1, R2, R3) among the three projections R1(SNAME, PARTNAME), R2(SNAME, PROJNAME), and R3(PARTNAME, PROJNAME) of SUPPLY. If this constraint holds, the tuples below the dotted line in Figure 13.4(c) must exist in any legal instance of the SUPPLY relation that also contains the tuples above the dotted line. Figure 13.4(d) shows how the SUPPLY relation *with the join dependency* is decomposed into three relations R1, R2, and R3 that are each in 5NF. Notice that applying NATURAL JOIN to *any two* of these relations produces spurious tuples, but applying NATURAL JOIN to *all three together* does not. The reader should verify this on the example relation of Figure 13.4(c) and its projections in Figure 13.4(d). This is because only the JD exists, but no MVDs are specified. Notice, too, that the JD(R1, R2, R3) is specified on all legal relation instances, not just on the one shown in Figure 13.4(c).

Discovering JDs in practical databases with hundreds of attributes is difficult; hence, current practice of database design pays scant attention to them.

13.4 Inclusion Dependencies*

Inclusion dependencies were defined in order to formalize interrelational constraints. For example, the foreign key (or referential integrity) constraint cannot be specified as a functional or multivalued dependency because it relates attributes across relations; but it can be specified as an inclusion dependency.* Formally, an **inclusion dependency** R.X < S.Y between two sets of attributes—X of relation schema R, and Y of relation schema S—specifies the constraint that, at any time when r is a relation state of R and s a relation state of S, we must have:

$$\pi_{<X>}(r) \subseteq \pi_{<Y>}(s)$$

The $\subseteq$ relationship does not necessarily have to be a proper subset. Obviously, the sets of attributes on which the inclusion dependency is specified—X of R and Y of S—must have the same number of attributes. In addition, the domains of corresponding attributes should be compatible. For example, if $X = \{A_1, A_2, \ldots, A_n\}$ and $Y = \{B_1, B_2, \ldots, B_n\}$, one possible correspondence is to have DOM(A_i) COMPATIBLE-WITH DOM(B_i) for $1 \leq i \leq n$. In this case we say that A_i **corresponds-to** B_i.

For example, we can specify the following inclusion dependencies on the relational schema in Figure 12.1:

DEPARTMENT.DMGRSSN < EMPLOYEE.SSN
WORKS_ON.SSN < EMPLOYEE.SSN
EMPLOYEE.DNUMBER < DEPARTMENT.DNUMBER
WORKS_ON.PNUMBER < PROJECT.PNUMBER

All the preceding inclusion dependencies represent **referential integrity constraints**. We can also use the inclusion dependencies to represent **class/subclass relationships**. For example, in the relational schema of Figure 21.12 (see Chapter 21), we can specify the following inclusion dependencies:

EMPLOYEE.SSN < PERSON.SSN
ALUMNUS_DEGREES.SSN < PERSON.SSN
STUDENT.SSN < PERSON.SSN

There are inference rules for inclusion dependencies. Three examples of these are:

(IDIR1) R.X < R.X.
(IDIR2) If R.X < S.Y where $X = \{A_1, A_2, \ldots, A_n\}$ and $Y = \{B_1, B_2, \ldots, B_n\}$ and A_i corresponds-to B_i, then $R.A_i < S.B_i$ for $1 \leq i \leq n$.
(IDIR3) If R.X < S.Y and S.Y < T.Z, then R.X < T.Z.

The preceding inference rules were shown to be sound and complete for inclusion dependencies. So far, no normal forms have been developed based on inclusion dependencies.

---

*Inclusion dependencies can also be used to represent the constraint between two relations that represent a higher-level class/subclass relationship, which we will discuss in Chapter 21.

13.5 Other Dependencies and Normal Forms⋆

13.5.1 *Template Dependencies*

No matter how many types of dependencies we develop, some peculiar constraint may come up that cannot be represented by any of them. The idea behind template dependencies is to specify a template—or example—that defines each constraint or dependency. There are two types of templates: tuple-generating templates and constraint-generating templates. A template consists of a number of **hypothesis tuples** that are meant to show an example of the tuples that may appear in one or more relations. The other part of the template is the **template conclusion**. For tuple-generating templates, the conclusion is a *set of tuples* that must also exist in the relations if the hypothesis tuples are there. For constraint-generating templates, the template conclusion is a *condition* that must hold on the hypothesis tuples.

Figure 13.6 shows how we may define functional, multivalued, and inclusion dependencies by templates. Figure 13.7 shows how we may specify the constraint that "an employee's salary cannot be higher than the salary of his or her direct supervisor" on the relation schema EMPLOYEE in Figure 6.5.

(a)
$$R = \{ A, B, C, D \}$$

hypothesis
$$a_1 \; b_1 \; c_1 \; d_1$$
$$a_1 \; b_1 \; c_2 \; d_2$$

$$X = \{ A, B \}$$
$$Y = \{ C, D \}$$

conclusion
$$c_1 = c_2 \text{ and } d_1 = d_2$$

(b)
$$R = \{ A, B, C, D \}$$

hypothesis
$$a_1 \; b_1 \; c_1 \; d_1$$
$$a_1 \; b_1 \; c_2 \; d_2$$

$$X = \{ A, B \}$$
$$Y = \{ C \}$$

conclusion
$$a_1 \; b_1 \; c_2 \; d_1$$
$$a_1 \; b_1 \; c_1 \; d_2$$

(c)
$$R = \{ A, B, C, D \} \qquad S = \{ E, F, G \}$$

$$X = \{ C, D \}$$
$$Y = \{ E, F \}$$

hypothesis
$$a_1 \; b_1 \; c_1 \; d_1$$

conclusion
$$\qquad\qquad\qquad c_1 \; d_1 \; g$$

Figure 13.6   Templates for common types of dependencies. (a) Template for the functional dependency $X \rightarrow Y$. (b) Template for the multivalued dependency $X \twoheadrightarrow Y$. (c) Template for the inclusion dependency $R.X < S.Y$.

EMPLOYEE = { NAME , SSN , ... , SALARY , SUPERVISORSSN }

	a	b	c	d
hypothesis	e	d	f	g
conclusion		c < f		

Figure 13.7 Template for the constraint that an employee's salary should be less than the supervisor's salary.

13.5.2 *Domain-Key Normal Form (DKNF)*

We can also always define stricter normal forms that take into account additional types of dependencies and constraints. The idea behind domain-key normal form is to specify, (theoretically, at least) the "ultimate normal form" that takes into account all possible types of dependencies and constraints. A relation is said to be in **DKNF** if all constraints and dependencies that should hold on the relation can be enforced simply by enforcing the domain constraints and the key constraints specified on the relation. For a relation in DKNF, it becomes very straightforward to enforce the constraints by simply checking that each attribute value in a tuple is of the appropriate domain and that every key constraint on the relation is enforced. However, it seems unlikely that complex constraints can be included in a DKNF relation; hence, its practical utility is limited.

13.6 Summary

In Section 13.1 we presented the concept of relation decomposition. We then gave algorithms for decomposing a universal relation schema into a set of relation schemas that are in normal forms and that satisfy the lossless join property, the dependency-preserving property, or both properties. Both properties are based on the functional dependencies specified on the attributes of the universal relation.

We then defined additional types of dependencies and some additional normal forms. Multivalued dependencies led to fourth normal form, and join dependencies led to fifth normal form. We also discussed inclusion dependencies, which are used to specify referential integrity and class/subclass constraints, and template dependencies, which can be used to specify arbitrary types of constraints. Finally, we discussed very briefly the domain-key normal form.

Review Questions

13.1. What is meant by the attribute preservation condition on a decomposition?

13.2. Why are normal forms alone insufficient as a condition for a good schema design?

13.3. What is the dependency preservation property for a decomposition? Why is it important?

13.4. Why can we not guarantee that the relation schemas in a dependency-preserving decomposition will be in BCNF?

13.5. What is the lossless join property of a decomposition? Why is it important?

13.6. Discuss the null value and dangling tuple problems.

13.7. What is a multivalued dependency? What type of constraint does it specify? When does it arise?

13.8. Define fourth normal form. Why is it useful?

13.9. Define join dependencies and fifth normal form.

13.10. What types of constraints are inclusion dependencies meant to represent?

13.11. How do template dependencies differ from the other types of dependencies we discussed?

Exercises

13.12. Show that the relation schemas produced by Algorithm 13.1 are in 3NF.

13.13. Show that, if the matrix S resulting from Algorithm 13.2 does not have a row that is all "a" symbols, projecting S on the decomposition and joining it back will always produce at least one spurious tuple.

13.14. Show that the relation schemas produced by Algorithm 13.3 are in BCNF.

13.15. Show that the relation schemas produced by Algorithm 13.4 are in 3NF.

13.16. Specify a template dependency for join dependencies.

13.17. Specify all the inclusion dependencies for the relational schema of Figure 6.5.

13.18. Prove that a functional dependency is also a multivalued dependency.

13.19. Consider the example of normalizing the LOTS relation in Section 12.4. Determine whether the decomposition of LOTS into {LOTS1AX, LOTS1AY, LOTS1B, LOTS2} has the lossless join property, by applying Algorithm 13.2.

13.20. Show how the MVDs ENAME→→PNAME and ENAME→→DNAME in Figure 13.4(a) may arise during normalization into 1NF of a relation, where the attributes PNAME and DNAME are multivalued (nonsimple).

13.21. Apply Algorithm 13.4a to the relation in Exercise 12.28 to determine a key for R. Create a minimal set of dependencies F that is equivalent to F, and apply the synthesis algorithm (Algorithm 13.4) to decompose R into 3NF relations.

13.22. Repeat Exercise 13.21 for the functional dependencies in Exercise 12.29.

13.23. Apply the decomposition algorithm (Algorithm 13.3) to the relation R and the set of dependencies F in Exercise 12.28. Repeat for the dependencies G in Exercise 12.29.

13.24. Apply Algorithm 13.4a to the relation in Exercise 12.30 to determine a key for R. Apply the synthesis algorithm (Algorithm 13.4) to decompose R into 3NF relations and the decomposition algorithm (Algorithm 13.3) to decompose R into BCNF relations.

13.25. Write programs that implement Algorithms 13.3 and 13.4.

13.26. Consider the following decompositions for the relation schema R of Exercise 12.28. Determine whether each decomposition has (i) the dependency preservation property, and (ii) the lossless join property, with respect to F. Also determine which normal form each relation in the decomposition is in.

    a. $D_1 = \{R_1, R_2, R_3, R_4, R_5\}; = \{A, B, C\}, R_2 = \{A, D, E\}, R_3 = \{B, F\}, R_4 = \{F, G, H\}, R_5 = \{D, I, J\}$.

    b. $D_2 = \{R_1, R_2, R_3\}; R_1 = \{A, B, C, D, E\}, R_2 = \{B, F, G, H\}, R_3 = \{D, I, J\}$.

    c. $D_3 = \{R_1, R_2, R_3, R_4, R_5\}; R_1 = \{A, B, C, D\}, R_2 = \{D, E\}, R_3 = \{B, F\}, R_4 = \{F, G, H\}, R_5 = \{D, I, J\}$.

Selected Bibliography

The theory of dependency preservation and lossless joins is given in the textbook by Ullman (1988), where proofs of some of the algorithms discussed here appear. The lossless join property is analyzed in Aho et al. (1979). The books by Maier (1983) and Atzeni (1992) include a comprehensive discussion of relational dependency theory.

The decomposition algorithm is due to Bernstein (1976), and other normalization algorithms are presented in Biskup et al. (1979) and Tsou and Fischer (1982). Algorithms to determine the keys of a relation from functional dependencies are given in Osborn (1976); testing for BCNF is discussed in Osborn (1979). Testing for 3NF is discussed in Jou and Fischer (1983). Algorithms for designing BCNF relations are given in Wang (1990) and Hernandez and Chan (1991).

Multivalued dependencies and fourth normal form are defined in Zaniolo (1976) and Fagin (1977). The set of sound and complete rules for functional and multivalued dependencies was given by Beeri et al. (1977). Join dependencies are discussed by Rissanen (1977) and Aho et al. (1979). Inference rules for join dependencies are given by Sciore (1982). Fifth normal form (called project-join normal form) is introduced in Fagin (1979). Inclusion dependencies are discussed by Casanova et al. (1981), and their use in optimizing relational schemas is discussed in Casanova et al. (1989). Template dependencies are discussed by Sadri and Ullman (1982). Other dependencies are discussed in Nicolas (1978), Furtado (1978), and Mendelzon and Maier (1979). Domain-key normal form is defined by Fagin (1981).

C H A P T E R   1 4

Overview of the Database Design Process

In this chapter we discuss different phases of the database design process. For small databases that will be used by a small number of users, database design need not be very complicated. However, when medium-size or large databases are designed for use as part of a large organization's information system, database design becomes quite complex. This is because the system must satisfy the requirements of many diverse users. Careful design and testing phases are imperative to ensure that all these requirements are satisfactorily met. Medium to large databases are used by from about 25 to hundreds of users, contain millions of bytes of information, and involve hundreds of queries and application programs. Such databases are widely used in government, industry, and commercial organizations. Service industries such as banking, utility, insurance, travel, hotel, and communications companies are totally dependent on successful around-the-clock operation of their databases. The systems for these types of applications are often called **transaction processing systems** because of the large number of transactions that are applied to the database every day. We will concentrate on the database design process for such medium-size and large databases here. For the remainder of this chapter, *database design* refers to the design process for such an environment. We also discuss how a database fits within the information system of a large organization and review the life cycle of a typical information system and its component database system.

In Section 14.1 we discuss why databases have become an important part of information resource management in many organizations and we examine life-cycle issues. In Section 14.2 we discuss the typical phases of database design for medium-size or large databases. Section 14.3 offers an overview of physical database design. Finally, in Section 14.4 we briefly discuss automated design tools. The latter two sections may be skipped for a less detailed overview.

14.1 Role of Information Systems in Organizations

14.1.1 *Organizational Context for Using Database Systems*

We now discuss briefly how database systems have become a part of the information systems of many organizations. Information systems in the 1960s were dominated by file systems. Organizations have been gradually moving from these to database systems since the early 1970s. Many organizations have set up departments under a database administrator (DBA) to oversee and control database life-cycle activities. Similarly, information resource management (IRM) is recognized by large organizations to be a key to successful management of the business. There are several reasons for this:

- More functions in organizations are computerized, increasing the need to keep large volumes of data available in an up-to-the-minute current state.
- As the complexity of the data and applications grows, complex relationships among the data need to be modeled and maintained.
- There is a tendency toward consolidation of information resources in many organizations.

Database systems satisfy the preceding three requirements in large measure. Two additional characteristics of database systems are also very valuable in the design and management of large databases:

- *Data independence* protects application programs from changes in the underlying logical organization and in physical access paths and storage structures.
- *External schemas* (views) allow the same data to be used for multiple applications, each application having its own view of the data.

An additional justification for moving to database systems is the low cost of developing new applications in comparison to the cost for older file systems. This often justifies the high initial cost of database design and system conversion. The availability of high-level data access languages simplifies the task of writing database applications, while high-level query languages make ad hoc querying of information by higher-level managers feasible.

From the early 1970s to the mid-1980s, the move was toward creating large centralized repositories of data managed by a single centralized DBMS. Recently, this trend has been *reversed*, because of the following developments:

1. Personal computers and databaselike software products, such as VISICALC, LOTUS 1-2-3, SYMPHONY, PARADOX, and DBASE IV and V, are being heavily utilized by users who previously belonged to the category of casual and occasional database users. Many administrators, engineers, scientists, architects, and the like belong to this category. As a result, the practice of creating **personal databases** is gaining popularity. It is now possible to check out a copy of part of a large database from a mainframe computer or a database server, work on it from a personal workstation, and then re-store it on the mainframe. Similarly, users can design and create their own databases and then merge them into a larger one.

2. The advent of distributed database management systems (DDBMSs; see Chapter 23) is opening up the option of distributing the database over multiple computer systems for better local control and faster local processing. At the same time, local users can access remote data by using the facilities provided by the DDBMS.

3. Many organizations now use **data dictionary systems,** which are mini DBMSs that manage **meta-data** for a database system—that is, data that describes the database structure, constraints, applications, authorizations, and so on. These are often used as an *integral tool* for information resource management. A useful data dictionary system should store and manage the following types of information:

   a. Descriptions of the schemas of the database system.

   b. Detailed information on physical database design, such as storage structures, access paths, and file and record sizes.

   c. Descriptions of the database users, their responsibilities, and their access rights.

   d. High-level descriptions of the database transactions and applications and of the relationships of users to transactions.

   e. The relationship between database transactions and the data items referenced by them. This is useful in determining which transactions are affected when certain data definitions are changed.

   f. Usage statistics such as frequencies of queries and transactions and access counts to different portions of the database.

This information is available to database administrators, designers, and authorized users as on-line system documentation. This improves the database administrators' control over the information system, and the users' understanding and use of the system. In many large organizations, a data dictionary system is considered to be as important as a DBMS.

Recently, great emphasis has been placed on high-performance **transaction processing systems,** which require around-the-clock nonstop operation and are used in the service industry. These databases are often accessed by hundreds of transactions per minute from remote and local terminals. Transaction performance, in terms of the average number of transactions per minute and the average and maximum transaction response time, is critical in these applications. A careful physical database design that meets the organization's transaction-processing needs is a must in such types of systems.

Some organizations have committed their information resource management to certain DBMS and data dictionary products. Their investment in the design and implementation of very large and complex systems makes it very difficult for them to change to newer DBMS products, so the organizations become locked in to their current DBMS system. With regard to such large and complex databases, one cannot overemphasize the importance of a careful design that takes into account the need for possible system modifications in the future due to changing requirements. The cost can be very high if a large and complex system cannot evolve and it becomes necessary to move to other DBMS products.

14.1.2 *Information System Life Cycle*

In a large organization, the database system is typically part of a much larger information system that is used to manage the information resources of the organization. An **information system** includes all resources within the organization that are involved in the collection, management, use, and dissemination of information. In a computerized environment, these resources include the data itself, the DBMS software, the computer system hardware and storage media, the personnel who use and manage the data (DBA, end users, parametric users, and so on), the applications software that accesses and updates the data, and the application programmers who develop these applications. Hence, the database system is only part of a much larger organizational information system.

In this section we examine a typical life cycle of an information system and how the database system fits into this life cycle. The information system life cycle is often called the **macro life cycle,** whereas the database system life cycle is referred to as the **micro life cycle**. The macro life cycle typically includes the following phases:

1. Feasibility analysis: This is concerned with analyzing potential application areas, performing preliminary cost-benefit studies, and setting up priorities among applications.

2. Requirements collection and analysis: Detailed requirements are collected by interacting with potential users to identify their particular problems and needs.

3. Design: This phase has two aspects: the design of the database system, and the design of the application systems (programs) that use and process the database.

4. Implementation: The information system is implemented, the database is loaded, and the database transactions are implemented and tested.

5. Validation and acceptance testing: The acceptability of the system in meeting users' requirements and performance criteria is validated. The system is tested against performance criteria and behavior specifications.

6. Operation: This may be preceded by conversion of users from an older system, as well as by user training. The operational phase starts when all system functions are operational and have been validated. As new requirements or applications crop up, they pass through all the previous phases until they are validated and incorporated into the system. Monitoring of system performance and system maintenance are important activities during the operational phase.

14.1.3 *Database Application System Life Cycle*

Activities related to the database application system (micro) life cycle include the following phases:

1. System definition: The scope of the database system, its users, and its applications are defined.

2. Design: At the end of this phase, a complete logical and physical design of the database system on the chosen DBMS is ready.

3. Implementation: This comprises the process of writing the conceptual, external, and internal database definitions, creating empty database files, and implementing the software applications.

4. Loading or data conversion: The database is populated either by loading the data directly or by converting existing files into the database system format.

5. Application conversion: Any software applications from a previous system are converted to the new system.

6. Testing and validation: The new system is tested and validated.

7. Operation: The database system and its applications are put into operation.

8. Monitoring and maintenance: During the operational phase, the system is constantly monitored and maintained. Growth and expansion can occur in both data content and software applications. Major modifications and reorganizations may be needed from time to time.

Activities 2, 3, and 4 together are part of the design and implementation phases of the larger information system life cycle. Our emphasis in Section 14.2 is on activity 2, which covers the database design phase. Most databases in organizations undergo all of the preceding life-cycle activities. The conversion steps (4 and 5) are not applicable when both the database and the applications are new. When an organization moves from an old established system to a new one, activities 4 and 5 tend to be the most time-consuming and the effort to accomplish them is often underestimated. In general, there is often feedback among the various steps because new requirements frequently arise at every stage.

14.2 The Database Design Process

We now focus on step 2 of the database application system life cycle, which we call database design. The problem of database design can be stated as follows: *Design the logical and physical structure of one or more databases to accommodate the information needs of the users in an organization for a defined set of applications.*

The *goals* of database design are multiple: to satisfy the information *content* requirements of the specified users and applications; to provide a natural and easy-to-understand *structuring* of the information; and to support *processing requirements* and any performance objectives such as response time, processing time, and storage space. These goals are very hard to accomplish and measure. The problem is aggravated because the database design process often begins with very informal and poorly defined requirements. By contrast, the result of the design activity is a rigidly defined database schema that cannot easily be modified once the database is implemented. We can identify six main phases of the database design process:

1. Requirements collection and analysis.

2. Conceptual database design.

3. Choice of a DBMS.

4. Data model mapping (also called logical database design).

5. Physical database design.

6. Database system implementation.

The design process consists of two parallel activities, as illustrated in Figure 14.1. The first activity involves the design of the **data content and structure** of the database; the second relates to the design of **database processing and software applications**. These two activities are closely intertwined. For example, we can identify data items that will

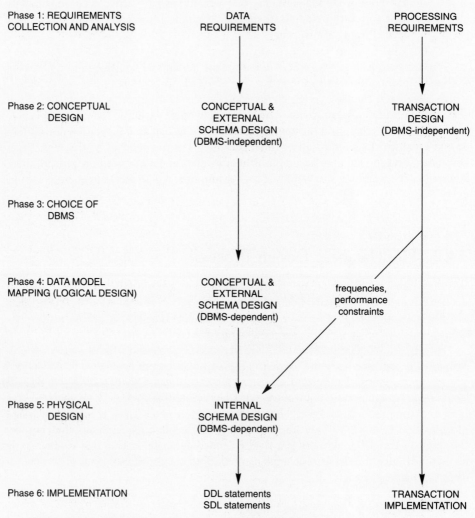

Phase 1: REQUIREMENTS
COLLECTION AND ANALYSIS

DATA
REQUIREMENTS

PROCESSING
REQUIREMENTS

Phase 2: CONCEPTUAL
DESIGN

CONCEPTUAL &
EXTERNAL
SCHEMA DESIGN
(DBMS-independent)

TRANSACTION
DESIGN
(DBMS-independent)

Phase 3: CHOICE OF
DBMS

Phase 4: DATA MODEL
MAPPING (LOGICAL DESIGN)

CONCEPTUAL &
EXTERNAL
SCHEMA DESIGN
(DBMS-dependent)

frequencies,
performance
constraints

Phase 5: PHYSICAL
DESIGN

INTERNAL
SCHEMA DESIGN
(DBMS-dependent)

Phase 6: IMPLEMENTATION

DDL statements
SDL statements

TRANSACTION
IMPLEMENTATION

Figure 14.1 Phases of database design for large databases.

be stored in the database by analyzing database applications. In addition, the physical database design phase, during which we choose the storage structures and access paths of database files, depends on the applications that will use these files. On the other hand, we usually specify the design of database applications by referring to the database schema constructs, which are specified during the first activity. Clearly, these two activities strongly influence one another. Traditionally, database design methodologies have primarily focused on one or the other of these activities; this may be called **data-driven** or **process-driven** database design. It is now recognized that the two activities should proceed hand in hand.

The six phases mentioned above do not have to proceed strictly in sequence. In many cases we may have to modify the design from an earlier phase during a later phase. These **feedback loops** among phases—and also within phases—are common during database design. We do not show feedback loops in Figure 14.1 to avoid complicating the diagram. Phase 1 in Figure 14.1 involves collecting information about the intended use of the database, whereas phase 6 concerns database implementation. Phases 1 and 6 are sometimes considered *not* to be part of database design per se, but part of the more general information system life cycle. The heart of the database design process is phases 2, 4, and 5, which we briefly summarize here:

- *Conceptual database design (phase 2)*: The goal of this phase is to produce a conceptual schema for the database that is independent of a specific DBMS. We often use a high-level data model such as the ER or EER model (see Chapter 21) during this phase. In addition, we specify as many of the known database applications or transactions as possible, using a notation that is independent of any specific DBMS.

- *Data model mapping (phase 4)*: This is also called **logical database design**. During this phase we **map** (or **transform**) the conceptual schema from the high-level data model used in phase 2 into the data model of the DBMS chosen in phase 3. We can start this phase after choosing an implementation data model, rather than waiting for a specific DBMS to be chosen—for example, if we decide to use some relational DBMS but have not yet decided on a particular one. We call the latter *system-independent* (but *data model–dependent*) logical design. In terms of the three-level DBMS architecture discussed in Chapter 2, the result of this phase is a *conceptual schema* in the chosen data model. In addition, the design of *external schemas* (views) for specific applications is often done during this phase.

- *Physical database design (phase 5)*: During this phase we design the specifications for the stored database in terms of physical storage structures, record placement, and access paths. This corresponds to designing the *internal schema* in the terminology of the three-level DBMS architecture.

In the following subsections we discuss each of the six phases of database design.

14.2.1 *Phase 1: Requirements Collection and Analysis*

Before we can effectively design a database, we must know the expectations of the users and the intended uses of the database in as much detail as possible. The process of identifying and analyzing the intended uses is called **requirements collection and analysis**.

To specify the requirements, we must first identify the other parts of the information system that will interact with the database system. These include new and existing users and applications. The requirements of these users and applications are then collected and analyzed. Typically, the following activities are part of this phase:

- The major application areas and user groups that will use the database are identified. Key individuals within each group are chosen as the main participants in the subsequent steps of requirements collection and specification.

- Existing documentation concerning the applications is studied and analyzed. Other documentation—policy manuals, forms, reports, and organization charts—is reviewed to determine whether it has any influence on the requirements collection and specification process.

- The current operating environment and planned use of the information is studied. This includes analysis of the types of transactions and their frequencies, as well as of the flow of information within the system. The input and output data for the transactions are specified.

- Written responses to sets of questions are collected from the potential database users. These questions involve the users' priorities and the importance they place on various applications. Key individuals may be interviewed to help in assessing the worth of information and in setting up of priorities.

The preceding modes of collecting requirements give poorly structured and mostly informal statements of requirements, which are then transformed into a better structured form by using one of the more formal **requirements specification techniques**. These include HIPO (hierarchical input process output), SADT (structured analysis and design technique), DFDs (data flow diagrams), Orr-Warnier diagrams, and Nassi-Schneiderman diagrams. All of these are diagrammatic methods for organizing and presenting information-processing requirements. The diagrams can take the form of hierarchies, flowcharts, sequential and loop structures, or something else, depending on the method. Additional documentation in the form of text, tables, charts, and decision requirements usually accompanies the diagrams. There are whole books that discuss the requirements collection and analysis phase (see the bibliographic notes at the end of this chapter). This phase can be quite time-consuming, but it is crucial to the future success of the information system.

Some computer-aided techniques have been proposed to deal with requirements collection and analysis. These techniques include automated tools for requirements analysis, to check the consistency and completeness of specifications. The requirements are stored in a single repository, usually called the design database, and can be displayed and updated as the design progresses. An early example is the PROBLEM STATEMENT LANGUAGE and PROBLEM STATEMENT ANALYZER (PSL/PSA) developed by the ISDOS project at the University of Michigan (see the bibliographic notes).

14.2.2 *Phase 2: Conceptual Database Design*

The second phase of database design involves two parallel activities. The first activity, **conceptual schema design,** examines the data requirements resulting from phase 1 and produces a conceptual database schema. The second activity, **transaction design,** examines the database applications analyzed in phase 1 and produces high-level specifications for these transactions.

Phase 2a: Conceptual Schema Design. The conceptual schema produced by this phase is usually contained in a DBMS-independent high-level data model and hence cannot be used directly to implement the database. The importance of a DBMS-independent conceptual schema cannot be overestimated, for the following reasons:

1. The goal of conceptual schema design is a complete understanding of the database structure, meaning (semantics), interrelationships, and constraints. This is best achieved independently of a specific DBMS because each DBMS typically has idiosyncrasies and restrictions that should not be allowed to influence the conceptual schema design.

2. The conceptual schema is invaluable as a *stable description* of the database contents. The choice of DBMS and later design decisions may change without changing the DBMS-independent conceptual schema.

3. A good understanding of the conceptual schema is crucial for database users and application designers. Use of a high-level data model that is more expressive and general than the data models of individual DBMSs is hence quite important.

4. The diagrammatic description of the conceptual schema can serve as an excellent vehicle of communication among database users, designers, and analysts. Because high-level data models usually rely on concepts that are easier to understand than lower-level DBMS-specific data models, any communication concerning the schema design becomes more exact and more straightforward.

In this phase of database design, it is important to use a high-level data model—also known as a semantic or conceptual data model—that has the following characteristics:

1. Expressiveness: The data model should be expressive enough to distinguish different types of data, relationships, and constraints.

2. Simplicity: The model should be simple enough for typical nonspecialist users to understand and use its concepts.

3. Minimality: The model should have a small number of basic concepts that are distinct and nonoverlapping in meaning.

4. Diagrammatic representation: The model should have a diagrammatic notation for displaying a conceptual schema that is easy to interpret.

5. Formality: A conceptual schema expressed in the data model must represent a formal nonambiguous specification of the data. Hence, the model concepts must be defined accurately and unambiguously.

These requirements are sometimes conflicting. In particular, requirement 1 conflicts with the other requirements. Many high-level conceptual models have been proposed for database design (see the selected bibliography for Chapter 21). In the following discussion, we will use the terminology of the Enhanced Entity-Relationship (EER) model presented in Chapters 3 and 21, and we will assume that it is being used in this phase.

APPROACHES TO CONCEPTUAL SCHEMA DESIGN: For conceptual schema design, we must identify the basic components of the schema: the entity types, the relationship types, and their attributes. We should also specify key attributes, cardinality and participation constraints on relationships, weak entity types, and specialization/generalization hierarchies and lattices (if needed). This design is derived from the requirements collected during phase 1.

There are two approaches to designing the conceptual schema. In the first, which we call the **centralized (or one-shot) schema design approach,** the requirements of the different applications and user groups from phase 1 are merged into a single set of requirements *before schema design begins*. A single schema corresponding to the merged set of requirements is then designed. When many users and applications exist, merging all the requirements can be an arduous and time-consuming task. The assumption behind this approach is that a centralized authority, the DBA, is responsible for deciding how to merge the requirements of different users and applications, and for designing the conceptual schema for the whole database. Once the conceptual schema is designed and finalized, external schemas for the various user groups and applications can be specified by the DBA.

In the second approach, which we call the **view integration approach,** we do not merge the requirements; rather, a schema (or view) is designed for each user group or application based only on its requirements. As a result, we develop one high-level schema (view) for each such user group or application. During a subsequent **view integration** phase, these schemas are merged or integrated into a **global conceptual schema** for the entire database. The individual views can be reconstructed as external schemas after view integration.

The main difference between the two approaches lies in the manner and stage in which multiple views or requirements of the many users and applications are reconciled and merged. In the centralized approach, the reconciliation is done manually by the DBA's staff prior to designing any schemas and is applied directly to the requirements collected in phase 1. This approach has traditionally been used in spite of the burden it places on the DBA's staff to reconcile the differences and conflicts among user groups in order to come up with a clear definition of the global requirements *before* the conceptual schema design is attempted. Because of the difficulties in accomplishing this task, the view integration approach is now gaining more acceptance.

In the view integration approach, each user group or application actually designs its own conceptual (EER) schema from its requirements. Then an integration process is applied to these schemas (views) by the DBA to form the global integrated schema. Although view integration can be done manually, its application to a large database involving tens of user groups requires a methodology and the use of automated tools to help in carrying out the integration. The correspondences among the attributes, entity types, and relationship types in various views must be specified before the integration can be applied. In addition, problems such as integrating conflicting views and verifying the consistency of the specified interschema correspondences must be resolved.

STRATEGIES FOR SCHEMA DESIGN: Given a set of requirements, whether for a single user or for a large user community, we must create a conceptual schema that satisfies these requirements. There are various strategies for designing such a schema. Most of these strategies follow an incremental approach; that is, they start with some schema constructs derived from the requirements, and then they incrementally modify, refine, or build on them. We now discuss some of these strategies:

1. Top–down strategy: Start with a schema containing high-level abstractions, and then apply successive top–down refinements. For example, we may start by specifying only a few high-level entity types. Then, as we specify their attributes, we split them into lower-level entity types and relationships. The process of specialization to refine an entity type into subclasses (see Section 21.1) is another example of a top–down design strategy.

2. Bottom–up strategy: Start with a schema containing basic abstractions, and then combine or add to these abstractions. For example, we may start with the attributes and group these into entity types and relationships. We may add new relationships among entity types as the design progresses. The process of generalizing subclasses into higher-level generalized classes (see Section 21.1) is another example of a bottom–up design strategy.

3. Inside–out strategy: This is a special case of a bottom–up strategy, where attention is focused on a central set of concepts that are most evident. Modeling then *spreads outward* by considering new concepts in the vicinity of existing ones. For example, we could specify a few clearly evident entity types in the schema and continue by adding other entity types and relationships that are related to each.

4. Mixed strategy: Instead of following any particular strategy throughout the design, the requirements are partitioned according to a top–down strategy, and part of the schema is designed for each partition according to a bottom–up strategy. The various schema parts are then combined.

Figures 14.2 and 14.3 illustrate top–down and bottom–up refinement, respectively. An example of a top–down refinement primitive is decomposition of an entity type into several entity types. Figure 14.2(a) shows a COURSE being refined into COURSE and SEMINAR, and the TEACHES relationship is correspondingly split into TEACHES and OFFERS. Figure 14.2(b) shows a COURSE_OFFERING entity type being refined into two entity types and a relationship between them. Figure 14.3(a) shows the bottom–up refinement primitive of generating new relationships among entity types. The bottom–up refinement using generalization is illustrated in Figure 14.3(b), where the new concept of VEHICLE_OWNER is "discovered" from the existing entity types FACULTY, STUDENT, and STAFF; this generalization process and the related diagrammatic notation are discussed in Chapter 21.

SCHEMA (VIEW) INTEGRATION: For large databases with many expected users and applications, the view integration approach of designing individual schemas and then merging them can be used. Because the individual views can be kept relatively small, design of the schemas is simplified. However, a methodology for integrating the views into a global database schema is needed. Schema integration can be divided into the following subtasks:

1. Identifying correspondences and conflicts among the schemas: Because the schemas are designed individually, it is necessary to specify constructs in the schemas

that represent the same real-world concept. These correspondences must be identified before integration can proceed. During this process, several types of conflicts among the schemas may be discovered:

a. Naming conflicts: These are of two types: synonyms and homonyms. A **synonym** occurs when two schemas use different names to describe the same concept; for example, an entity type CUSTOMER in one schema may describe the same concept as an entity type CLIENT in another schema. A **homonym** occurs when two schemas use the same name to describe different concepts; for example, an entity type PART may represent computer parts in one schema and furniture parts in another schema.

b. Type conflicts: The same concept may be represented in two schemas by different modeling constructs. For example, the concept of a DEPARTMENT may be an entity type in one schema and an attribute in another.

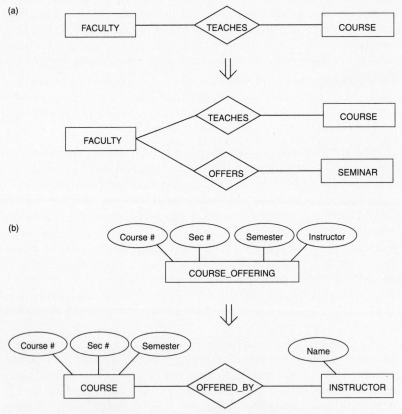

Figure 14.2 Examples of top–down refinement. (a) Generating a new entity type. (b) Decomposing an entity type into two entity types and a relationship.

c. **Domain (value set) conflicts:** An attribute may have different domains in two schemas. For example, SSN may be declared as an integer in one schema and as a character string in the other. A conflict of the unit of measure could occur if one schema represented WEIGHT in pounds and the other used kilograms.

d. **Conflicts among constraints:** Two schemas may impose different constraints; for example, the key of an entity type may be different in each schema. Another example involves different structural constraints on a relationship such as TEACHES; one schema may represent it as 1:N (a course has one instructor), while the other schema represents it as M:N (a course may have more than one instructor).

2. **Modifying views to conform to one another:** Some schemas are modified so that they conform to other schemas more closely. Some of the conflicts identified in step 1 are resolved during this step.

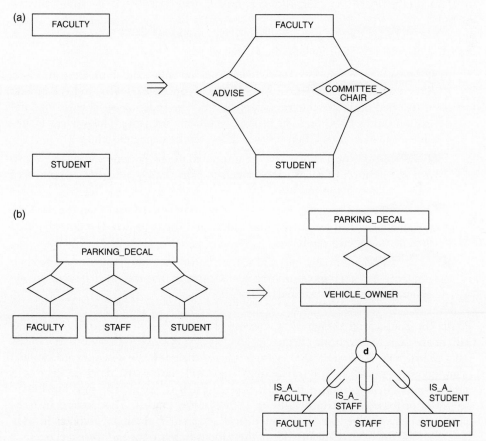

Figure 14.3 Examples of bottom–up refinement. (a) Discovering and adding new relationships. (b) Discovering a new generalized entity type and relating it.

3. Merging of views: The global schema is created by merging the individual schemas. Corresponding concepts are represented only once in the global schema, and mappings between the views and the global schema are specified.

4. Restructuring: As a final optional step, the global schema may be analyzed and restructured to remove any redundancies or unnecessary complexity.

Some of these ideas are illustrated by the rather simple example presented in Figures 14.4 and 14.5. In Figure 14.4, two views are merged to create a bibliographic database. During identification of correspondences between the two views, we discover that RESEARCHER and AUTHOR are synonyms (as far as this database is concerned), as are CONTRIBUTED_BY and WRITTEN_BY. Further, we decide to modify VIEW 1 to include a SUBJECT for ARTICLE, as shown in Figure 14.4, *to conform to* VIEW 2. Figure 14.5 shows the result of merging MODIFIED VIEW 1 with VIEW 2. The relationships BELONGS_TO and WRITTEN_BY are merged, as are the entity types AUTHOR and SUBJECT. We also generalize the entity types ARTICLE and BOOK into the entity type PUBLICATION, with their common attribute Title. The attribute Publisher applies only to the entity type BOOK, whereas the attribute Size and the relationship type PUBLISHED_IN apply only to ARTICLE.

Several strategies have been proposed for the process of view integration. As illustrated in Figure 14.6, these include the following:

1. Binary ladder integration: Two schemas that are quite similar are integrated first. The resulting schema is then integrated with another schema, and the process is repeated until all schemas are integrated. The ordering of schemas for integration can be based on some measure of schema similarity. This strategy is suitable for manual integration because of its step-by-step approach.

2. N-ary integration: All the views are integrated in one procedure after an analysis and specification of their correspondences. This strategy requires computerized tools for large design problems.

3. Binary balanced strategy: Pairs of schemas are integrated first; then the resulting schemas are paired for further integration; and the procedure is repeated until a final global schema results.

4. Mixed strategy: Initially, the schemas are partitioned into groups based on their similarity, and each group is integrated separately. The intermediate schemas are grouped again and integrated, and so on.

Phase 2b: Transaction Design. The purpose of phase 2b, which proceeds in parallel with phase 2a, is to design the characteristics of known database transactions in a DBMS-independent way. When a database system is being designed, the designers are aware of many known applications (or **transactions**) that will run on the database once it is implemented. An important part of database design is to specify the functional characteristics of these transactions early on in the design process. This ensures that the database schema will include all the information required by these transactions. In addition, knowing the relative importance of the various transactions and the expected rates of their invocation plays a crucial part in physical database design (phase 5). Usually, only some of the database transactions are known at design time; after the database system is implemented, new transactions are continuously identified and implemented. However, the most important transactions are often known in advance of system implementation and should be specified at an early stage.

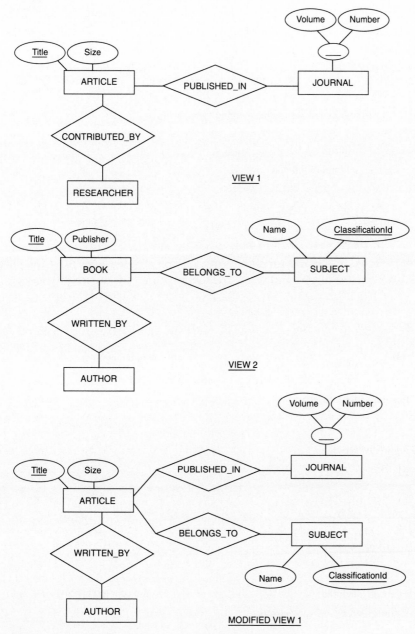

Figure 14.4   Modifying views to conform before integration.

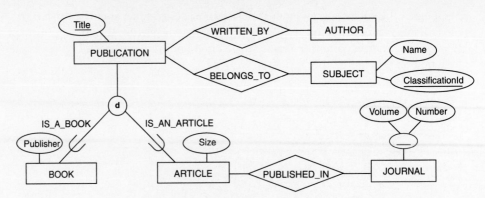

Figure 14.5   Integrated schema after merging views 1 and 2.

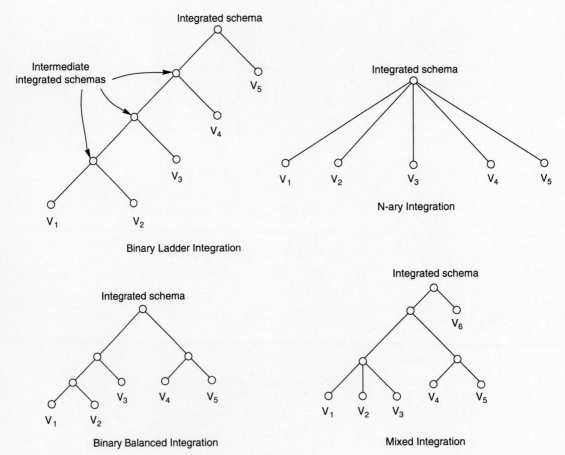

Figure 14.6   Different strategies for view integration.

One common technique for specifying transactions at a conceptual level is to identify their **input/output** and **functional** behavior. By specifying the input data, output data, and internal functional flow of control, designers can specify a transaction in a conceptual and system-independent way. Transactions usually can be grouped into three categories: retrieval transactions, update transactions, and mixed transactions. **Retrieval transactions** are used to retrieve data for display on a screen or for production of a report. **Update transactions** are used to enter new data or to modify existing data in the database. **Mixed transactions** are used for more complex applications that do some retrieval and some update. For example, suppose that we are designing an airline reservations database. An example of a retrieval transaction is to list all morning flights on a given date between two cities. An example of an update transaction is to book a seat on a particular flight. A mixed transaction may first display some data, such as showing a customer reservation on some flight, and then update the database, such as canceling the reservation by deleting it.

Several techniques for requirements specification include notation for specifying **processes,** which in this context are more complex operations that can consist of several transactions. Other proposals for specifying transactions include TAXIS, GALILEO (see the bibliography), and GORDAS (see Section 21.5). Transaction design is just as important as schema design. Unfortunately, many current design methodologies emphasize one over the other. One should go through phases 2a and 2b in parallel, using feedback loops for refinement, until a stable design of schema and transactions is reached.

14.2.3 *Phase 3: Choice of a DBMS*

The choice of a DBMS is governed by a number of factors. Some factors are technical, others are economic, and still others are concerned with the politics of the organization. The technical factors are concerned with the suitability of the DBMS for the task at hand. Issues to consider here are the type of DBMS (relational, network, hierarchical, object-oriented, other), the storage structures and access paths that the DBMS supports, the user and programmer interfaces available, the types of high-level query languages, and so on. We discuss these technical factors in Appendix C, when we compare data models. In this section we concentrate on discussing the economic and organizational factors that affect the choice of DBMS. The following costs must be considered when selecting a DBMS:

1. Software acquisition cost: This is the "up-front" cost of buying the software, including language options, different interfaces such as forms and screens, recovery/backup options, special access methods, and documentation. The correct DBMS version for a specific operating system must be selected.

2. Maintenance cost: This is the recurring cost of receiving standard maintenance service from the vendor and for keeping the DBMS version up to date.

3. Hardware acquisition cost: New hardware may be needed, such as additional memory, terminals, disk units, or specialized DBMS storage.

4. Database creation and conversion cost: This is the cost of either creating the database system from scratch or converting an existing system to the new DBMS

software. In the latter case it is customary to operate the existing system in parallel with the new system until all the new applications are fully implemented and tested. This cost is hard to project and is often underestimated.

5. Personnel cost: Acquisition of DBMS software for the first time by an organization is often accompanied by a reorganization of the data-processing department. New positions of database administrator (DBA) and staff are created in most companies that adopt DBMSs.

6. Training cost: Because DBMSs are often complex systems, personnel must often be trained to use and program the DBMS.

7. Operating cost: The cost of continued operation of the database system is typically not worked into an evaluation of alternatives because it is incurred regardless of the DBMS selected.

The benefits of acquiring a DBMS are not so easy to measure and quantify. A DBMS has several intangible advantages over traditional file systems, such as ease of use, wider availability of data, and faster access to information. More tangible benefits include reduced application development cost, reduced redundancy of data, and better control and security. Based on a cost–benefit analysis, an organization has to decide when to switch to a DBMS. This move is generally driven by the following factors:

- Data complexity: As data relationships become more complex, the need for a DBMS is felt more strongly.

- Sharing among applications: The greater the sharing among applications, the more the redundancy among files, and hence the greater the need for a DBMS.

- Dynamically evolving or growing data: If the data changes constantly, it is easier to cope with these changes using a DBMS than using a file system.

- Frequency of ad hoc requests for data: File systems are not at all suitable for ad hoc retrieval of data.

- Data volume and need for control: The sheer volume of data and the need to control it sometimes demands a DBMS.

Finally, several economic and organizational factors affect the choice of one DBMS over another:

1. Structure of the data: If the data to be stored in the database follows a hierarchical structure, a hierarchical-type DBMS should be considered. For data with many interrelationships, a network or relational system may be more appropriate. Relational technology is gaining in popularity. For complex data structures and data types, object-oriented systems may be suitable.

2. Familiarity of personnel with the system: If the programming staff within the organization is familiar with a particular DBMS, it may be favored to reduce training cost and learning time.

3. Availability of vendor services: The existence of a vendor service facility nearby is desirable to assist in solving any problems with the system. Moving from a non-DBMS to a DBMS environment is generally a major undertaking and requires much vendor assistance at the start.

Before purchasing a DBMS, an organization must take into account the hardware/software configuration required to run the DBMS and the DBMS portability among different types of hardware. Many commercial DBMSs now have versions that run on many hardware/software configurations (or **platforms**). The need of applications for backup, recovery, performance, integrity, and security must also be considered. Many DBMSs are currently being designed as *total solutions* to the information-processing and information resource management needs within organizations. Most DBMS vendors are combining their products with the following options or built-in features, which are often categorized as 4GL (fourth generation languages) by commercial vendors:

- Text editors and browsers.
- Report generators and listing utilities.
- Communication software (often called teleprocessing monitors).
- Data entry and display features such as forms, screens, and menus with automatic editing features.
- Graphical design tools.

In some cases it may not be appropriate to use a DBMS; instead, it may be preferable to develop in-house software for the applications. This may be the case if the applications are very well defined and are *all* known beforehand. In such a case, an in-house custom-designed system may be appropriate to implement the known applications in the most efficient way. In most cases, however, new applications that were not foreseen at design time come up *after* system implementation. This is precisely why DBMSs have become very popular: they facilitate the incorporation of new applications without major changes to the existing system.

14.2.4 *Phase 4: Data Model Mapping (Logical Database Design)*

The next phase of database design is to create a conceptual schema and external schemas in the data model of the selected DBMS. This is done by mapping the conceptual and external schemas produced in phase 2a from the high-level data model to the data model of the DBMS. The mapping can proceed in two stages:

1. System-independent mapping: In this step the mapping into the data model of the DBMS does not consider any specific characteristics or special cases that apply to the DBMS implementation of the data model. We discuss DBMS-independent mapping of an ER schema to a relational, object-oriented, hierarchical, or network schema in Sections 6.8, 22.8, 10.4, and 11.5, respectively.

2. Tailoring the schemas to a specific DBMS: Different DBMSs implement a data model by using specific modeling features and constraints. We may have to adjust the schemas obtained in step 1 to conform to the specific implementation features of a data model as used in the selected DBMS.

The result of this phase should be DDL statements in the language of the chosen DBMS that specify the conceptual and external level schemas of the database system. But if the DDL statements include some physical design parameters, a complete DDL specification must wait until after the physical database design phase is completed. Many automated CASE (computer assisted software engineering) design tools (see Section 14.4) can generate DDL for commercial systems from a conceptual schema design.

14.2.5 *Phase 5: Physical Database Design*

Physical database design is the process of choosing specific storage structures and access paths for the database files to achieve good performance for the various database applications. Each DBMS offers a variety of options for file organization and access paths. These usually include various types of indexing, clustering of related records on disk blocks, linking related records via pointers, and various types of hashing. Once a specific DBMS is chosen, the physical database design process is restricted to choosing the most appropriate structures for the database files from among the options offered by that DBMS. In this section we give guidelines for physical design decisions in various types of DBMSs. The following criteria are often used to guide the choice of physical database design options:

1. Response time: This is the elapsed time between submitting a database transaction for execution and receiving a response. A major influence on response time that is under the control of the DBMS is the database access time for data items referenced by the transaction. Response time is also influenced by factors not under DBMS control, such as system load, operating system scheduling, or communication delays.

2. Space utilization: This is the amount of storage space used by the database files and their access path structures.

3. Transaction throughput: This is the average number of transactions that can be processed per minute by the database system; it is a critical parameter of transaction systems such as those used for airline reservations or banking. Transaction throughput must be measured under peak conditions on the system.

Typically, average and worst-case limits on the preceding parameters are specified as part of the system performance requirements. Analytical or experimental techniques, which can include prototyping and simulation, are used to estimate the average and worst-case values under different physical design decisions, to determine whether they meet the specified performance requirements.

Performance depends on record size and number of records in the file. Hence, we must estimate these parameters for each file. In addition, we should estimate the update and retrieval patterns for the file cumulatively from all the transactions. Attributes used for selecting records should have primary access paths and secondary indexes constructed for them. Estimates of file growth, either in the record size because of new attributes or in the number of records, should also be taken into account during physical database design.

The result of the physical database design phase is an *initial* determination of storage structures and access paths for the database files. It is almost always necessary to **tune** the design on the basis of its observed performance after the database system is implemented. Most systems include a monitoring utility to collect performance statistics, which are kept in the system catalog or data dictionary for later analysis. These include statistics on the number of invocations of predefined transactions or queries, input/output activity against files, counts of file pages or index records, and frequency of index usage. As the database system requirements change, it often becomes necessary to reorganize some files by constructing new indexes or by changing primary access methods. In Section 14.3 we discuss physical design issues related to different types of DBMSs.

14.2.6 *Phase 6: Database System Implementation*

After the logical and physical designs are completed, we can implement the database system. Language statements in the DDL (data definition language) and SDL (storage definition language) of the selected DBMS are compiled and used to create the database schemas and (empty) database files. The database can then be **loaded** (populated) with the data. If data is to be converted from an earlier computerized system, **conversion routines** may be needed to reformat the data for loading into the new database.

Database transactions must be implemented by the application programmers at this stage. Conceptual specifications of transactions are examined, and corresponding program code with embedded DML (data manipulation language) commands is written and tested. Once the transactions are ready and the data is loaded into the database, the design and implementation phase is over and the operational phase of the database system begins.

14.3 Physical Database Design Guidelines★

In this section we first discuss the physical design factors that affect the performance of applications and transactions; then we comment on the specific guidelines for relational, network, and hierarchical DBMSs.

14.3.1 *Factors That Influence Physical Database Design*

Physical design is an activity where the goal is not only to come up with the appropriate structuring of data in storage but to do so in a way that guarantees good performance. For a given conceptual schema, there are many physical design alternatives in a given DBMS. It is not possible to make meaningful physical design decisions and performance analyses until we know the queries, transactions, and applications that are expected to run on the database. We must analyze these applications, their expected frequencies of invocation, any time constraints on their execution, and the expected frequency of update operations. We discuss each of these factors next.

Analyzing the Database Queries and Transactions. Before undertaking physical database design, we must have a good idea of the intended use of the database by defining the queries and transactions that we expect to run on the database in a high-level form. For each *query*, we should specify the following:

1. The files that will be accessed by the query.
2. The fields on which any selection conditions for the query are specified.
3. The fields on which any join conditions or conditions to link multiple record types for the query are specified.
4. The fields whose values will be retrieved by the query.

The fields listed in items 2 and 3 above are candidates for definition of access structures. For each update transaction or operation, we should specify the following:

1. The files that will be updated.
2. The type of update operation on each file (insert, modify, or delete).
3. The fields on which any selection conditions for a delete or modify operation are specified.
4. The fields whose values will be changed by a modify operation.

Again, the fields listed in part 3 above are candidates for access structures. On the other hand, the fields listed in part 4 are candidates for avoiding an access structure, since modifying them will require updating the access structures.

Analyzing the Expected Frequency of Invocation of Queries and Transactions. Besides identifying the characteristics of expected queries and transactions, we must consider their expected rates of invocation. This frequency information, along with the field information collected on each query and transaction, is used to compile a cumulative list of expected frequency of use for all queries and transactions. This is expressed as the expected frequency of using each field in each file as a selection field or a join field, over all the queries and transactions. Generally, for large volumes of processing, the informal "80–20 rule" applies. This rule states that approximately 80% of the processing is accounted for by only 20% of the queries and transactions. Therefore, in practical situations it is rarely necessary to collect exhaustive statistics and invocation rates on all the queries and transactions; it is sufficient to determine the 20% or so most important ones.

Analyzing the Time Constraints of Queries and Transactions. Some queries and transactions may have stringent performance constraints. For example, a certain transaction may have the constraint that it should terminate within 5 seconds on 95% of the occasions when it is invoked and that it should never take more than 20 seconds. Such additional performance considerations can be used to place further priorities on the fields that are candidates for access paths. The selection fields used by queries and transactions with time constraints become higher-priority candidates for access structures.

Analyzing the Expected Frequencies of Update Operations. A minimum number of access paths should be specified for a file that is updated frequently, because updating the access paths themselves slows down the update operations.

Once we have compiled the preceding information, we can address the physical database design decisions, which consist mainly of deciding on the storage structures and access paths for the database files. Rarely are all queries and transactions on the database known at the time of physical database design. New applications often come up after the database system has been implemented, requiring that new queries and transactions be specified. In such cases it is often necessary to modify some of the physical database design decisions in order to incorporate the new applications into the system. This is called **tuning** the physical design. If some of the transactions or queries with response time constraints fail to meet their specified response times, modifications to the original physical design are needed to improve the efficiency of the transactions.

14.3.2 *Physical Database Design Guidelines for Relational Systems*

Most relational systems represent each base relation as a physical database file. The access path options include specifying the type of file for each relation and the attributes on which indexes should be defined. One of the indexes of each file may be a primary or clustering index. In addition, there are several techniques for speeding up frequently used EQUIJOIN or NATURAL JOIN operations. We first discuss these techniques and then discuss choosing file organizations and selecting indexes.

Techniques for Speeding Up EQUIJOIN or NATURAL JOIN Operations. Some relational systems offer an option to store two relations with a 1:N relationship between them, represented by a *foreign key*, as a two-level hierarchical file, where each record of the 1 side (primary key) is stored, followed by the records of the N side (with matching foreign keys). This type of storage structure makes the JOIN between the two files on this 1:N relationship very efficient. For example, consider the relational database schema in Figure 6.5, and suppose that each relation is implemented as a file. If the EQUIJOIN with condition EMPLOYEE.SSN = WORKS_ON.ESSN must be done as efficiently as possible, we can use a mixed file of the EMPLOYEE and WORKS_ON records. Each EMPLOYEE record will be stored followed by the WORKS_ON records that have the same SSN value. It is also possible to *cluster* the WORKS_ON records on ESSN while maintaining separate files.

Another option is to **denormalize** the logical database schema when we design the physical files. This is done to situate the attributes that are frequently required in a query in the same file records with other attributes involved in the query. We do this by **replicating** (or **duplicating**) the attributes in the file where they are needed. We must compensate for this denormalization by requiring that update transactions maintain the values of replicated attributes consistent with one another. For example, suppose that the same query that requires the preceding JOIN operation also requires retrieval of the PNAME attribute of the PROJECT record with PROJECT.PNUMBER = WORKS_ON.PNO. We can then replicate the PNAME attribute in the WORKS_ON records so that the latter join does not need to be executed. This technique can be carried one step further by physically storing a file that is the result of the JOIN of two files, although this extreme denormalization should be used only with the utmost care. All types of update anomalies discussed in Chapter 12 may now occur and must be dealt with explicitly whenever updates are applied to the file.

Choice of File Organization and Index Selection Guidelines. A popular option for organizing a separate file in a relational system is to keep the file records unordered and create as many secondary indexes as needed. Attributes that are used often for selection and join conditions are candidates for secondary indexes.

Another option is to specify an ordering attribute for the file by specifying a primary or clustering index. The attribute that is used most often for join operations should be chosen for ordering or clustering the records, since this makes the join operation more efficient (see Chapter 16). If the records are often accessed in order of an attribute, this is another indication that it should be chosen for ordering the file records. Only one of the attributes of each file can be chosen for physically ordering the file records, with a corresponding primary index (if the attribute is a key) or a clustering index (if the attribute is not a key). Many relational systems use the keywords UNIQUE to specify a key and CLUSTER to specify an ordering index.

Choice of Hashing. Some relational systems also offer the option of specifying a hash key attribute rather than an ordering attribute for a relation. If a key attribute is to be used mainly for equality selection and for join operations, but not for accessing the records in order, we can choose a hash file instead of an ordered file. Another criterion for choosing a hash file is that the size of the file is known and the file is not expected to grow or shrink. If the file changes in size and the relational DBMS offers some dynamic hashing scheme (see Chapter 4), we can choose dynamic hashing for that file.

We can summarize the guidelines for choosing a physical organization for a separate relational file as follows:

1. Choose an attribute that is either used frequently for retrieving the records in order or used most frequently for join operations on the file as an ordering attribute for the file. Create a primary index (if the attribute is a key) or a clustering index (if it is a nonkey) on that attribute. This is the *primary access path* to the file records. If no attribute qualifies, use an unordered file.

2. For each attribute (other than the ordering attribute) that is used frequently in selection or join conditions, specify a secondary index which serves as a *secondary access path* to the file records.

3. If the file is to be updated very frequently with record insertions and deletions, try to minimize the number of indexes for the file.

4. If an attribute is used frequently for equality selection and join operations but not for retrieving the records in order, a hash file can be used. Static hashing can be used for files whose size does not change much; dynamic hashing is needed for files that are likely to grow rapidly or fluctuate in size. Secondary indexes can be built on other attributes of the hash file.

Of course, the choice among these options is limited by the storage structures and access paths available on the chosen relational DBMS.

14.3.3 *Physical Database Design Guidelines for Network Systems*

There are several important physical design options for a network database. The first involves deciding on the implementation of each set type. Another choice, similar to the denormalization issue for relational databases, involves deciding whether any fields from an owner record type should be replicated in a member record type for efficiency purposes. In addition, some network DBMSs allow the definition of hash keys or indexes on a record type. These, together with SYSTEM-owned set types, provide entry points into the database, which are often followed by *navigating from the entry point* by tracing the pointers of sets (**set processing**). Finally, decisions must be made on any ordering fields of record types or of member records within a set type.

Guidelines for Choosing Among Set Implementation Options. There are many options for implementing a set type. We review these options, which were discussed in Chapter 10, and present guidelines for deciding which option to use, as follows:

1. Implementing a set type by physical contiguity: In some network DBMSs, the member records can be physically stored following the owner record; this option is called set implementation by **physical contiguity**. If a record type is a member of several set types, *only one* of those can be chosen for implementation by physical contiguity. Accessing the member records of a set instance is most efficient in this option, so the set types that are used most often to access *all member records* of an owner are candidates for this implementation option.

2. Implementing a set type by pointer arrays: Another implementation option is to store an array of pointers to the member records with the owner record. If a *single member record* is selected by its order in the set (such as the FIRST, LAST, or ith) and often from the owner, this is a good option.

3. Using different options for pointer implementation: Most sets are implemented by pointers and linked lists. We can have a single **next** pointer or both **next** and **prior** pointers in member records of a set. With either of these two options, we can also have an **owner** pointer in each member record. If the set members are mainly accessed by using FIND NEXT, the next pointer is sufficient. If FIND PRIOR is often used, a prior pointer should be included. Finally, if the owner is often accessed from a member record by using FIND OWNER, an owner pointer should be included. This last option is useful for record types that participate as members in multiple set types—for example, linking record types for M:N relationships, such as the WORKS_ON record type in Figure 10.9. With this option, a program can retrieve member records by using one set type—say, E_WORKSON—and then directly find the owner record by using the owner pointer of the other set type (P_WORKSON).

In a network database, the equivalents of most relational EQUIJOIN operations are *prespecified* as set types, as can be seen by comparing the COMPANY database schema in the relational model (Figure 6.5) and in the network model (Figure 10.9). For example, the join condition EMPLOYEE.SSN = WORKS_ON.ESSN on the relational schema is represented by the E_WORKSON set type. In the same way, the join condition PROJECT.NUMBER = WORKS_ON.PNUMBER is represented by the P_WORKSON set type. Hence, joins that are executed frequently in the relational model correspond to sets that are traversed frequently in the network model. Such set types are candidates for efficient implementation by physical contiguity.

Denormalization for Efficiency or for Structural Constraints. We may wish to replicate some of the fields from an *owner* record type in the *member* record type of a set type, for the following reasons:

- If a NO DUPLICATES ALLOWED (key) field from the owner is replicated, it can be used to specify a structural constraint for a MANUAL set type, or AUTOMATIC SET SELECTION for an AUTOMATIC set type. These replicated fields can have their values accessed from the member record directly, *without the DBMS having to locate and access the owner record,* reducing the access time, especially if there is no owner pointer in the member record.

- Other, nonkey fields may also be replicated in the member for efficiency. However, this replication means that updates to a field in the owner that is replicated in the members must be propagated to all member records by the update program to preserve consistency, thus slowing down some update operations.

Record-accessing Options. The network model requires **entry points** into the database to commence navigational searches for records. These are provided either by means of SYSTEM-owned set types or by specifying an access structure for a record type. The default is to do a linear search in an **AREA**—a DBTG concept that stands for a logical partition of the database that is assigned to a physically contiguous area on disk. Other **LOCATION MODE**s for record types in the original DBTG report, which are still followed in many commercial network DBMSs, include the following:

- *CALC*—The records of the record type are hashed on a specified field of the record type called a CALC KEY. A record is retrieved directly by the value of its CALC KEY.

- *VIA SET*—This causes the member records to be stored near the owner; no direct access to the records is available.

- *DIRECT*—The application program suggests an actual physical page on or near which the record should be stored. The actual storage location address (in the form of a record pointer) is returned in a **DBKEY** (database key). The database key concept was suggested in the original DBTG report as an efficiency mechanism, but it was dropped from later reports.

The direct option is used when a program saves a pointer to the record and later uses this pointer to fetch the record directly. The AREA concept allows the database designer to specify that the records of certain record types be placed *physically near each other* on disk, perhaps on the same cylinder. This makes accessing several of these records, especially when related via sets, much faster. Specification of AREAs is an important physical design decision in systems that support this concept.

Selection of SYSTEM-owned Sets and Record Ordering. SYSTEM-owned sets are defined for processing all the records of a record type in some desired order, typically for use in report generation applications. The records in a SYSTEM-owned set can be ordered by values of a field specified in the ORDER clause. SYSTEM-owned sets should be specified if we intend to use records of a record type as "entry points" and then locate records related to them by other sets. For example, if we frequently make reports that print information on departments and display employee and project information for those departments, we can use a SYSTEM-owned set to access the DEPARTMENT records in Figure 10.9. We can then retrieve the related EMPLOYEE and PROJECT records via the WORKS_FOR, MANAGES, and CONTROLS sets. If we often want the departments accessed in order of department number, we can order the SYSTEM-owned set by the DNO field.

14.3.4 *Physical Database Design Guidelines for Hierarchical Systems*

The main decisions for physical database design for hierarchical systems are closely interrelated with the logical design because of the many options we have for specifying hierarchies for the same conceptual database schema. However, there are many additional options, such as choice of hashing or indexing fields for the root record type or choice of "secondary" indexing for nonroot record types and implementation of virtual parent–child relationships. Access to data in a hierarchical database is constrained by the hierarchical structure and typically proceeds by first locating the root record. Within an occurrence tree, the search is conducted either sequentially on the records in the tree or by following certain pointer schemes. The root records may have indexed or hashed access on certain fields to locate the required occurrence tree efficiently. We are faced with the following decisions that affect database performance:

1. Choice of root record types of hierarchies: Root record types are entry points to the database, because all the descendent records can be accessed from the root. In addition, access paths such as hashing and indexes can easily be specified on the root. Record types that are often used to start a retrieval are good candidates to be chosen as roots of hierarchies.

2. Implementation options for parent–child relationships (PCRs): The most common implementation of a PCR is as a hierarchical file, which uses physical contiguity and stores the records as a hierarchical sequence (preorder traversal), as discussed in Chapter 11. However, pointers to facilitate the location of descendent records of a certain record type (called *secondary indexes* in IMS) may be added. Similarly, pointers to facilitate location of an ancestor record (called *physical parent pointers* in IMS) may be also added.

3. Choice of pointer records: The pointer record type option minimizes redundancy at the cost of having to define a virtual parent–child relationship (VPCR). Choosing between this option and the option of replicating records in a hierarchy is an important design decision. The former minimizes redundancy, while the latter provides more efficient retrieval at the cost of complicating the update process tremendously.

4. Different options for virtual parent–child relationship implementation: Most VPCRs are implemented by pointers in the child records, which facilitates locating the parent record from the child record. This is similar to the owner pointer of the network model. To provide access from a virtual parent to its first virtual child, a pointer (called a *logical child pointer* in IMS) can be used. The child then points to the next virtual child record having the same virtual parent (using a *logical twin pointer*). This is similar to the next pointers of a set type in network databases.

5. Dummy virtual parent records: Because VPCRs do not have names, it is desirable to have a record be a virtual parent in *at most one* VPCR. If the logical design chosen has a record type that is a virtual parent in several VPCRs, we can create a dummy record type that is a real child of that record type for each additional VPCR. Each dummy record is now a virtual parent in a *single* VPCR.

Hierarchical databases also allow partitioning of a hierarchy into groups of record types for efficiency reasons. This is similar to the AREA concept of DBTG network DBMSs. A group, called a **data set group** in IMS, contains a subtree from the hierarchical schema and is mapped to a contiguous physical storage area. This improves access to records within the subtree by storing them in close proximity. A root of such a group may be given direct access via a secondary index.

14.4 Automated Design Tools⋆

Most database design is still carried out manually by expert designers, who use their experience and knowledge in the design process. However, many aspects of database design are difficult to carry out by hand and are amenable to automation. For example, it is relatively straightforward to automate much of the data model mapping phase. Detecting conflicts among schemas before integrating them may be quite difficult to do manually. Similarly, evaluating different alternatives quantitatively for physical database design can be very time-consuming. A number of design tools exist that help with special aspects of database design, such as conceptual, mapping, and physical aspects, as well as with requirements collection and analysis. We will not survey database design tools here, but only mention the following characteristics that a good design tool should possess:

- An easy-to-use interface: This is critical because it enables the designers to focus on the task at hand and not on understanding the tool. Graphical and natural language interfaces are commonly used. Different interfaces may be tailored to end users or to expert database designers.

- Analytical components: Most tools provide analytical components for tasks that are difficult to perform manually, such as evaluating physical design alternatives or detecting conflicting constraints among views.

- Heuristic components: Aspects of the design that cannot be precisely quantified can be automated by entering heuristic rules in the design tool. These rules are used to evaluate design alternatives heuristically.

- Trade-off analysis: A tool should present the designer with adequate comparative analysis whenever it presents multiple alternatives to choose from.

- Display of design results: Design results, such as schemas, are often displayed in diagrammatic form. Other types of results can be shown as tables, lists, or reports that can easily be interpreted.

- Design verification: This is a highly desirable feature. Its purpose is to verify that the resulting design satisfies the initial requirements.

Currently there is increasing awareness of the value of design tools, and they are becoming a must for dealing with large database design problems. The database design process is becoming unthinkable without adequate tool support for large, organization-wide databases. There is also an increasing awareness that schema design and application design should go hand in hand. The emerging CASE (computer-assisted software engineering) tools address both these areas. Some tools use expert system technology to guide the design process by including design expertise in the form of rules. Expert system technology is also useful in the requirements collection and analysis phase, which is typically a laborious and frustrating process. The trend is to use both data dictionaries and design tools to achieve better designs for complex databases.

14.5 Summary

In this chapter we discussed the different phases of the database design process. We also discussed how databases fit within an information system for information resource management in an organization. The database design process includes six phases, but the three commonly included as a part of database design are conceptual design, logical design (data model mapping), and physical design. We also discussed the initial phase of requirements collection and analysis, which is often considered to be a *predesign phase*. In addition, at some point during the design, a specific DBMS package must be chosen. We discussed some of the organizational criteria that come into play in selecting a DBMS.

The importance of designing both the schema and the applications (or transactions) was highlighted. We discussed different approaches to conceptual schema design and the difference between centralized schema design and the view integration approach. In Section 14.3 we discussed the factors that affect physical database design decisions and gave guidelines for choosing among physical design alternatives for relational, network, and hierarchical DBMSs. Finally, we briefly discussed the use of automated design tools.

Review Questions

14.1. What are the six phases of database design? Discuss each phase.

14.2. Which of the six phases are considered the main activities of the database design process itself? Why?

14.3. Why is it important to design the schemas and applications in parallel?

14.4. Why is it important to use an implementation-independent data model during conceptual schema design?

14.5. Discuss the characteristics that a data model for conceptual schema design should possess.

14.6. Compare and contrast the two main approaches to conceptual schema design.

14.7. Discuss the strategies for designing a single conceptual schema from its requirements.

14.8. What are the steps of the view integration approach to conceptual schema design? How would a view integration tool work? Design a sample modular architecture for such a tool.

14.9. What are the different strategies for view integration?

14.10. Discuss the factors that influence the choice of a DBMS package for the information system of an organization.

14.11. What is system-independent data model mapping?

14.12. What are the important factors that influence physical database design?

14.13. Discuss the decisions made during physical database design.

14.14. Discuss the macro and micro life cycles of an information system.

14.15. Discuss the guidelines for physical database design in relational DBMSs.

14.16. Discuss the guidelines for physical database design in network DBMSs.

14.17. Discuss the guidelines for physical database design in hierarchical DBMSs.

Selected Bibliography

There is a vast amount of literature on database design. We first list some of the books that address database design. Wiederhold (1986) is a comprehensive textbook covering all phases of database design, with an emphasis on physical design. Two books (Ceri 1983; Albano et al. 1985) have been published by the DATAID project in Italy, a comprehensive project addressing many aspects of database design. Batini et al. (1992), Teorey (1990), and McFadden and Hoffer (1988) emphasize conceptual and logical database design. Brodie et al. (1984) gives a collection of chapters on conceptual modeling, constraint specification and analysis, and transaction design. Teorey and Fry (1982) presents a methodology for access path design at the logical level. Yao (1985) is a collection of works ranging from requirements specification techniques to schema restructuring. The book by Atre (1980) discusses database administration and data dictionaries.

We now give references to selected papers that discuss the topics covered in this chapter. Navathe and Kerschberg (1986) discusses all phases of database design and point out the role of data dictionaries. Goldfine and Konig (1988) and ANSI (1989) discuss the role of data dictionaries in database design. Eick and Lockemann (1985) proposes a model for requirements collection. Rozen and Shasha (1991), Schkolnick (1978), and Carlis and March (1984) present models for the problem of physical database design. March and Severance (1977) discusses record segmentation. Approaches to structured application design are discussed in Gane and Sarson (1979) and De Marco (1979). Whang et al. (1982) presents a methodology for physical design of network DBMS.

Navathe and Gudgil (1982) defined approaches to view integration. Schema integration methodologies are compared in Batini et al. (1986). Detailed work on n-ary view integration can be found in Navathe et al. (1986), Elmasri et al. (1986), and Larson et al. (1989). An integration tool based on Elmasri et al. (1986) is described in Sheth et al. (1988). Another view-integration system is discussed in Hayne and Ram (1990). Casanova et al. (1991) describes a tool for modular database design. Motro (1987) discusses integration with respect to preexisting databases. The binary balanced strategy to view integration is discussed in Teorey and Fry (1982). A formal approach to view integration, which uses inclusion dependencies, is given in Casanova and Vidal (1982). Other aspects of integration are discussed in Elmasri and Wiederhold (1979), Elmasri and Navathe (1984), Mannino and Effelsberg (1984), and Navathe et al. (1984a).

All aspects of database administration are reviewed in Weldon (1981). Surveys of data dictionaries are given in Curtice (1981) and Allen et al. (1982). Some well-known commercial database design tools are ERMA, developed by Arthur D. Little Inc. in Cambridge, Massachusetts; the ADW family of CASE tools, developed at Knowledgeware in Atlanta, Georgia; MAST_ER of Infodyne, Inc.; and DDEW of CCA (Computer Corporation of America). Automated design tools are discussed in Bubenko et al. (1971), Albano et al. (1985), Navathe (1985), and Chapter 15 of Batini et al. (1992).

Transaction design is a relatively less thoroughly researched topic. Mylopoulos et al. (1980) proposed the TAXIS language, and Albano et al. (1987) developed the GALILEO system, both of which are comprehensive systems for specifying transactions. The GOR-DAS language for the ECR model (Elmasri et al. 1985) contains a transaction specification capability. Navathe and Balaraman (1991) and Ngu (1991) discuss transaction modeling in general for semantic data models.

CHAPTER 15

The System Catalog

The system **catalog** is at the heart of any general-purpose DBMS. It is a "minidatabase" itself, and its function is to store the **schemas,** or *descriptions*, of the databases that the DBMS maintains. The catalog stores data that describes each database; such data is often called **meta-data**. It includes a description of the conceptual database schema, the internal schema, any external schemas, and the mappings between the schemas at different levels. In addition, information needed by specific DBMS modules—for example, the query optimization module or the security and authorization module—is stored in the catalog.

The term **data dictionary** is often used to indicate a more general software utility than a catalog. A **catalog** is closely coupled with the DBMS software; it provides the information stored in it to users and the DBA, but it is *mainly* accessed by the various software modules of the DBMS itself, such as DDL and DML compilers, the query optimizer, the transaction processor, report generators, and the constraint enforcer. On the other hand, a *stand-alone* **data dictionary** software package may interact with the software modules of the DBMS but is *mainly* used by the designers, users, and administrators of a computer system for information resource management. Data dictionary systems are also used to maintain information on system hardware and software, documentation, and users, as well as other information relevant to system administration. If a data dictionary is used *only* by designers, users, and administrators and not by the DBMS software, it is called a **passive data dictionary;** otherwise, it is called an **active data dictionary** or **data directory**. Figure 15.1 illustrates the types of active data dictionary interfaces.

Data dictionaries are also used to document the database design process itself, by storing information on the results of every design phase and the design decisions. This helps in automating the design process by making the design decisions and changes available to all the database designers. Modifications to the database description are made by

479

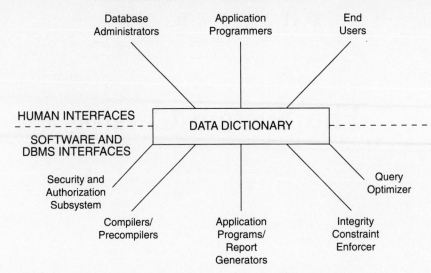

Figure 15.1   Human and software interfaces to a data dictionary.

changing the data dictionary contents. Using the data dictionary during database design means that, at the conclusion of the design phase, the meta-data is already in the data dictionary.

In this chapter we concentrate on discussing the system catalog rather than general data dictionary systems. In Section 15.1 we discuss catalogs for relational DBMSs; then we discuss network catalogs in Section 15.2. In Section 15.3 we discuss how a catalog is used by various modules of a DBMS, and we describe other types of information that may be stored in a catalog. Because a catalog is itself a minidatabase, we can describe the catalog structure by reference to a schema in some data model. We give a description of a conceptual schema for each catalog in the EER model (see Chapter 21) to help clarify the conceptual structure of a catalog.

15.1 Catalogs for Relational DBMSs

The information stored in a catalog of a relational DBMS includes descriptions of the relation names, attribute names, attribute domains (data types), primary keys, secondary key attributes, foreign keys, and other types of constraints, as well as external-level descriptions of views and internal-level descriptions of storage structures and indexes. Security and authorization information, which specifies the users' authority to access the database relations and views and the creators or owners of each relation (see Chapter 20), is also included.

In relational DBMSs it is common practice to store the catalog itself as relations and to use the DBMS software for querying, updating, and maintaining the catalog. This allows DBMS routines (as well as users) to access the information stored in the catalog whenever they are authorized to do so, using the query language of the DBMS.

REL_AND_ATTR_CATALOG

REL_NAME	ATTR_NAME	ATTR_TYPE	MEMBER_OF_PK	MEMBER_OF_FK	FK_RELATION
EMPLOYEE	FNAME	VSTR15	no	no	
EMPLOYEE	MINIT	CHAR	no	no	
EMPLOYEE	LNAME	VSTR15	no	no	
EMPLOYEE	SSN	STR9	yes	no	
EMPLOYEE	BDATE	STR9	no	no	
EMPLOYEE	ADDRESS	VSTR30	no	no	
EMPLOYEE	SEX	CHAR	no	no	
EMPLOYEE	SALARY	INTEGER	no	no	
EMPLOYEE	SUPERSSN	STR9	no	yes	
EMPLOYEE	DNO	INTEGER	no	yes	EMPLOYEE
DEPARTMENT	DNAME	VSTR10	no	no	DEPARTMENT
DEPARTMENT	DNUMBER	INTEGER	yes	no	
DEPARTMENT	MGRSSN	STR9	no	yes	
DEPARTMENT	MGRSTARTDATE	STR10	no	no	EMPLOYEE
DEPT_LOCATIONS	DNUMBER	INTEGER	yes	yes	
DEPT_LOCATIONS	DLOCATION	VSTR15	yes	no	DEPARTMENT
PROJECT	PNAME	VSTR10	no	no	
PROJECT	PNUMBER	INTEGER	yes	no	
PROJECT	PLOCATION	VSTR15	no	no	
PROJECT	DNO	INTEGER	no	yes	
WORKS_ON	ESSN	STR9	yes	yes	DEPARTMENT
WORKS_ON	PNO	INTEGER	yes	yes	EMPLOYEE
WORKS_ON	HOURS	REAL	no	no	PROJECT
DEPENDENT	ESSN	STR9	yes	yes	
DEPENDENT	DEPENDENT_NAME	VSTR15	yes	no	EMPLOYEE
DEPENDENT	SEX	CHAR	no	no	
DEPENDENT	BDATE	STR9	no	no	

Figure 15.2   Basic catalog for the relational schema of Figure 6.5.

A possible catalog structure for base relation information is shown in Figure 15.2, which stores relation names, attribute names, attribute types, and primary key information. Figure 15.2 also shows how foreign key constraints may be included. The *description* of the relational database schema in Figure 6.5 is shown as the tuples (contents) of the catalog file in Figure 15.2, which we call REL_AND_ATTR_CATALOG. The primary key of REL_AND_ATTR_CATALOG is the combination of attributes {REL_NAME, ATTR_NAME}, because all relation names should be unique and all attribute names within a particular relation schema should also be unique. Another catalog file can store information for each relation, such as tuple size, number of tuples, number of indexes, and creator name.

To include information on secondary key attributes of a relation, we can simply extend the preceding catalog if we assume that an attribute can be a *member of one key only*. In this case we can replace the MEMBER_OF_PK attribute of REL_AND_ATTR_CATALOG with an attribute KEY_NUMBER; the value of KEY_NUMBER is 0 if the attribute is not a member of any key, 1 if it is a member of the primary key, and $i > 1$ for the ith secondary key, where the secondary keys of a relation are numbered 2, 3, . . . , n. However, if an attribute can be a member of *more than one key*, which is the general case, the above representation is not sufficient. One possibility is to store information on key attributes separately in a second catalog relation RELATION_KEYS, with attributes {REL_NAME, KEY_NUMBER, MEMBER_ATTR} that together are the key of RELA-TION_KEYS. This is shown in Figure 15.3(a). The DDL compiler assigns the value 1 to KEY_NUMBER for the primary key and values 2, 3, . . . , n for the secondary keys. Each

(a)   **RELATION_KEYS**

REL_NAME	KEY_NUMBER	MEMBER_ATTR

(b)   **RELATION_INDEXES**

REL_NAME	INDEX_NAME	MEMBER_ATTR	INDEX_TYPE	ATTR_NO	ASC_DESC

(c)   **VIEW_QUERIES**

VIEW_NAME	QUERY

VIEW_ATTRIBUTES

VIEW_NAME	ATTR_NAME	ATTR_NUM

Figure 15.3   Other possible catalog relations for a relational system. (a) Catalog relation for storing general key information. (b) Catalog relation for storing index information. (c) Catalog relations for storing view information.

key will have a tuple in RELATION_KEYS for each attribute that is part of that key, and the value of MEMBER_ATTRIBUTE gives the name of that attribute. A similar structure can be used to store information involving foreign keys.

Next, consider information regarding indexes. In the general case where an attribute can be a member of more than one index, the RELATION_INDEXES catalog relation shown in Figure 15.3(b) can be used. The key of RELATION_INDEXES is the combination {INDEX_NAME, MEMBER_ATTR} (assuming that index names are unique). MEMBER_ATTR is the name of an attribute included in the index. For example, if we specify three indexes on the WORKS_ON relation of Figure 6.5—a clustering index on ESSN, a secondary index on PNO, and another secondary index on the combination {ESSN, PNO}—the attributes ESSN and PNO are members of two indexes each. The ATTR_NO and ASC_DESC fields in INDEXES specify the order of each attribute in the index and specify whether the attribute is ordered in ascending or descending order in the index.

The definitions of views must also be stored in the catalog. A view is specified by a query, with a possible renaming of the values appearing in the query result (see Chapter 7). We can use the two catalog relations shown in Figure 15.3(c) to store view definitions. The first, VIEW_QUERIES, has two attributes {VIEW_NAME, QUERY} and stores the query (the entire text string) corresponding to the view. The second, VIEW_ATTRIBUTES, has attributes {VIEW_NAME, ATTR_NAME, ATTR_NUM} to store the names of the attributes of the view, where ATTR_NUM is an integer number greater than zero specifying the correspondence of each view attribute to the attributes in the query result. The key of VIEW_QUERIES is VIEW_NAME, and that of VIEW_ATTRIBUTES is the combination {VIEW_NAME, ATTR_NAME}.

The preceding examples illustrate the types of information stored in a catalog, which typically includes many more files and information. Most relational systems store their catalog files as DBMS relations. However, because the catalog is accessed very frequently by the DBMS modules, it is important to implement catalog access as efficiently as possible. It may be more efficient to implement the catalog using a specialized set of data structures and access routines, thus trading generality for efficiency.

Finally, we take a conceptual look at the basic information stored in a relational catalog. Figure 15.4 shows a high-level EER schema diagram (see Chapters 3 and 21) describing part of a relational catalog. In Figure 15.4 the RELATION entity type stores the names of relations that appear in a relational schema. Two disjoint subclasses, BASE_RELATION and VIEW_RELATION are created for RELATION. The entity type ATTRIBUTE is a weak entity type of RELATION, and its partial key is AttrName. BASE_RELATIONs also have general key and foreign key constraints, as well as indexes, whereas VIEW_RELATIONs have their defining query (as well as the AttrNum) to specify correspondence of view attributes to query attributes. Notice that an additional unspecified constraint in Figure 15.4 is that all attributes related to a KEY or INDEX entity—via the relationships KEY_ATTRS or INDEX_ATTRS—must be related to the same BASE_RELATION entity to which the KEY or INDEX entity is related. KeyType specifies whether the key is foreign, primary, or secondary. FKEY is a subclass for foreign keys and is related to the referenced relation via REFREL.

We discuss additional information that must be stored in a catalog in Section 15.3, and we discuss security and authorization in Chapter 20.

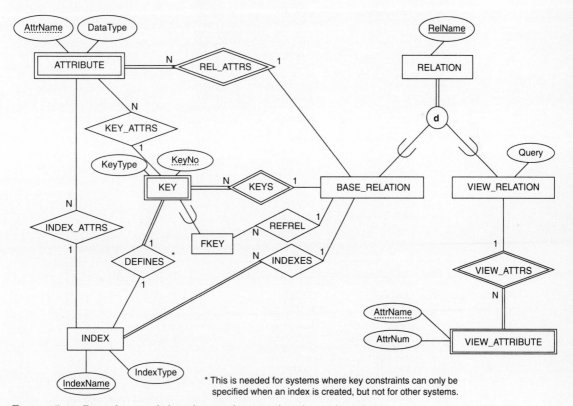

Figure 15.4 Example extended ER diagram for part of a relational catalog.

15.2 Catalogs for Network DBMSs

The basic information that must be stored in a catalog of a network DBMS is a description of the record types and set types. Information on how each set type is implemented and other physical storage choices must also be included in the catalog, as well as security and authorization information and information concerning external subschemas. Figure 15.5 shows a possible network catalog for describing the record types and set types. The catalog consists of two files—one for describing record types, and the other for listing set types—and includes the minimal information necessary for describing a network database schema. The contents of these two files correspond to the network schema of Figure 10.9.

We can easily extend the SET_TYPES_CATALOG by adding information on how each set type is implemented. For example, we could add the flag fields NEXT_POINTER,

RECORD_TYPES_CATALOG

RECORD_TYPE_NAME	FIELD_NAME	FIELD_TYPE
EMPLOYEE	FNAME	VSTR15
EMPLOYEE	MINIT	CHAR
EMPLOYEE	LNAME	VSTR15
EMPLOYEE	SSN	STR9
EMPLOYEE	BDATE	STR9
EMPLOYEE	ADDRESS	VSTR30
EMPLOYEE	SEX	CHAR
EMPLOYEE	SALARY	INTEGER
EMPLOYEE	DEPTNAME	VSTR10
DEPARTMENT	NAME	VSTR10
DEPARTMENT	NUMBER	INTEGER
DEPARTMENT	LOCATION	VSTR15
DEPARTMENT	MGRSTART	STR10
PROJECT	NAME	VSTR10
PROJECT	NUMBER	INTEGER
PROJECT	LOCATION	VSTR15
WORKS_ON	ESSN	STR9
WORKS_ON	PNUMBER	INTEGER
WORKS_ON	HOURS	REAL
DEPENDENT	EMPSSN	STR9
DEPENDENT	DEP_NAME	VSTR15
DEPENDENT	SEX	CHAR
DEPENDENT	BDATE	STR9
SUPERVISOR		

SET_TYPES_CATALOG

SET_TYPE_NAME	OWNER_RECORD_TYPE	MEMBER_RECORD_TYPE
ALL_DEPTS	SYSTEM	DEPARTMENT
WORKS_FOR	DEPARTMENT	EMPLOYEE
MANAGES	EMPLOYEE	DEPARTMENT
CONTROLS	DEPARTMENT	PROJECT
IS_A_SUPERVISOR	EMPLOYEE	SUPERVISOR
SUPERVISEES	SUPERVISOR	EMPLOYEE
E_WORKSON	EMPLOYEE	WORKS_ON
P_WORKSON	PROJECT	WORKS_ON
DEPENDENTS_OF	EMPLOYEE	DEPENDENT

Figure 15.5 Basic catalog files for storing information on record types and set types.

(a) SET_TYPES_CATALOG

SET_TYPE_NAME	· · ·	NEXT_POINTER	OWNER_POINTER	PRIOR_POINTER	CONTIGUOUS_MEMBERS

(b) SET_TYPES_CATALOG

SET_TYPE_NAME	· · ·	RETENTION_OPTION	INSERTION_OPTION

(c) RECORD_TYPES_CATALOG

RECORD_TYPE_NAME	FIELD_NAME	FIELD_TYPE	VECTOR	REPEATING_GROUP

COMPOSITE_FIELD_COMPONENTS

RECORD_TYPE_NAME	FIELD_NAME	COMPONENT_FIELD_NAME

UNIQUE-(NO-DUPLICATE)-CONSTRAINTS

RECORD_TYPE_NAME	KEY_NUMBER	FIELD_NAME

Figure 15.6 Some extensions to the basic network catalog. (a) Extending the SET_TYPES_CATALOG to include set implementation information. (b) Including the set type options in the SET_TYPES_CATALOG file. (c) Representing repeating and vector fields and the NO DUPLICATES ALLOWED constraint.

OWNER_POINTER, PRIOR_POINTER, CONTIGUOUS_MEMBERS, and so on, where each flag field has a value of either TRUE or FALSE. This is shown in Figure 15.6(a). The set options for each set type must also be stored in the catalog, by adding the fields RETEN-TION_OPTION and INSERTION_OPTION (see Figure 15.6(b)), where the possible values for RETENTION_OPTION are {MANDATORY, OPTIONAL, FIXED} and for INSERTION_OPTION are {AUTOMATIC, MANUAL}. Any structural constraints on set types and the AUTOMATIC SET SELECTION method for AUTOMATIC set types must be specified in the catalog, too.

We must also be able to represent composite **group** fields such as vector fields and repeating groups. In addition, constraints on fields, such as the NO DUPLICATES ALLOWED option specified for key fields, must be recorded in the catalog. Figure 15.6(c) shows how we may represent the NO DUPLICATES ALLOWED constraint by using the same technique as for representing general keys in a relational catalog. Figure 15.6(c) also shows how to represent group fields in the catalog. The VECTOR and REPEATING_GROUP fields in RECORD_TYPES_CATALOG are flag fields that have values of either TRUE or FALSE. The component fields of a group (composite) field are stored in the COMPOSITE_FIELD_COMPONENTS file.

As we did with the relational model, we show a conceptual description of part of a network system catalog as an EER schema (see Chapters 3 and 21) in Figure 15.7. The relationship set MEMBER relates a SET_TYPE entity to its member RECORD_TYPE entity. MULTI_MEMBER set types have additional member record types. SYSTEM_OWNED set types do not have an owner record type; but other set types, which we call REGULAR in Figure 15.7, are related via the OWNER relationship set to their owner RECORD_TYPE entity.

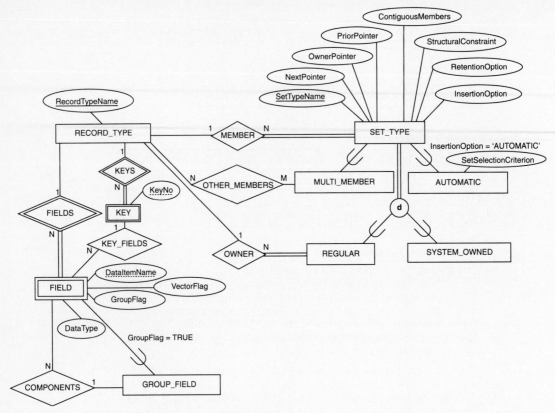

Figure 15.7   ERR diagram for part of a network catalog.

AUTOMATIC set types are a subclass of SET_TYPE with the membership condition InsertionOption = 'AUTOMATIC', and they have the additional specific attribute SetSelectionCriterion. GROUP_FIELDS are a subclass of fields that are formed of COMPONENTS.

15.3 Other Catalog Information Accessed by DBMS Software Modules

The DBMS modules use and access a catalog very frequently; that is why it is important to implement access to the catalog as efficiently as possible. In this section we discuss the different ways in which some of the DBMS software modules use and access the catalog. These include the following:

    1. DDL (and SDL) compilers: These DBMS modules process and check the specification of a database schema in the data definition language and store that description in the catalog. Schema constructs and constraints at all levels—con-

ceptual, internal, and external—are extracted from the DDL (data definition language) and SDL (storage definition language) specifications and entered into the catalog, as is any mapping information among levels, if necessary. Hence, these software modules actually *populate* the catalog's minidatabase (or **meta–database**) with data, the data being descriptions of database schemas.

2. Query and DML parser and verifier: These modules parse queries, DML retrieval statements, and database update statements; and they check the catalog to verify whether all the schema names referenced in these statements are valid. For example, in a relational system, a query parser would check that all the relation names specified in the query exist in the catalog and that the attributes specified belong to the appropriate relations. Similarly, in a network system, any record types or set types referenced in DML commands are extracted from the catalog, and the DML commands are verified.

3. Query and DML compiler: These compilers convert high-level queries and DML commands into low-level file access commands. The mapping between the conceptual schema and the internal schema file structures is accessed from the catalog during this process. For example, the catalog must include a description of each file and its fields and the correspondences between fields and conceptual-level attributes.

4. Query and DML optimizer: The query optimizer accesses the catalog for access path and implementation information, to determine the best way to execute a query or DML command (see Chapter 16). For example, the optimizer accesses the catalog to check which fields of a relation have hash access or indexes, before deciding how to execute a selection or join condition on the relation. Similarly, a set-processing DML command in a network database such as FIND OWNER checks the catalog to determine whether an OWNER pointer exists for the member record type or whether it must trace through NEXT pointers until the owner record is reached.

5. Authorization and security checking: The DBA has privileged commands to update the authorization and security portion of the catalog (see Chapter 20). All access by a user to a relation or record type is checked by the DBMS for proper authorization by accessing the catalog.

6. External-to-conceptual mapping of queries and DML commands: Queries and DML commands specified with reference to an external view or schema must be transformed to refer to the conceptual schema before they can be processed by the DBMS. This is accomplished by accessing the catalog description of the view in order to perform the transformation.

Information stored in the catalog is accessed very frequently by practically all the DBMS software modules. The catalog information that we discussed in Sections 15.1 and 15.2 is only the basic information. More sophisticated DBMSs need to store additional information in the catalog, such as the number of records in each base relation or record type, the average selectivity of different fields in a base relation, the number of levels in an index, and the average number of members in a set instance of a set type. This information must be updated automatically by the DBMS. In addition, an expanded catalog/

data dictionary system may include information that is useful for database system users, such as design decisions and justifications. Clearly, the catalog is a very important component of any generalized DBMS.

15.4 Summary

In this chapter we discussed the type of information that is included in a DBMS catalog. In Section 15.1 we discussed catalog structure for a relational DBMS and showed how it can store the constructs of the relational model, including information concerning key constraints, indexes, and views. We also gave a conceptual description—in the form of an EER schema diagram—of the relational model constructs and how they are related to one another. In Section 15.2 we covered the constructs for network system catalogs and presented a conceptual EER diagram to describe the concepts of the network model. The hierarchical model is discussed in the exercises. In Section 15.3 we discussed how different DBMS modules access the information stored in a DBMS catalog. We also discussed other types of information stored in a catalog.

Review Questions

15.1. What is meant by the term *meta-data?*

15.2. How are relational DBMS catalogs usually implemented?

15.3. Discuss the types of information included in a relational catalog at the conceptual, internal, and external levels.

15.4. Discuss the types of information included in a network catalog at the conceptual, internal, and external levels.

15.5. Discuss how some of the different DBMS modules access a catalog and the type of information each accesses.

15.6. Why is it important to have efficient access to a DBMS catalog?

Exercises

15.7 Expand the relational catalog of Figure 15.3 to include a more complete description of a relational schema, plus internal descriptions of storage files and any needed mapping information.

15.8. For each of the EER diagrams shown in Figures 15.4 and 15.7, use the mapping algorithms discussed in Chapters 6 and 10 to create an equivalent relational schema. What can each of the relational schemas be used for?

15.9. Write (in English) sample queries against the EER schemas of Figures 15.4 and 15.7 that would retrieve meaningful information about the database schemas from the catalog.

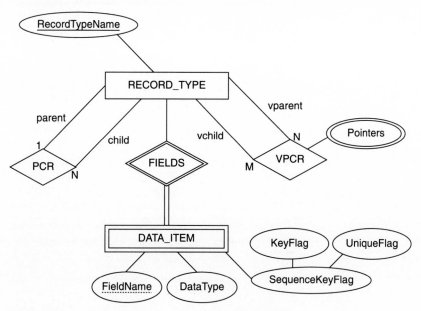

Figure 15.8   ER schema for a basic hierarchical catalog.

15.10. Using the relational schemas from Exercise 15.8, write the queries you specified in 15.9 in some relational query language (SQL, QUEL, relational algebra).

15.11. Figure 15.8 shows an ER schema diagram representing the basic information in a catalog for a hierarchical database system. Map this schema to a set of relations, and repeat Exercises 15.9 and 15.10 for this schema.

15.12 Suppose that we have a "generalized" DBMS that uses the EER model at the conceptual schema level and relationlike files at the internal level. Draw an EER diagram to represent the basic information for a catalog that represents such an EER database system. First describe the EER concepts as an EER schema (!), and then add mapping information from the conceptual schema to the internal schema into the catalog.

CHAPTER 16

Query Processing and Optimization

In this chapter we discuss the techniques used by a DBMS to process, optimize, and execute high-level queries. A query expressed in a high-level query language such as SQL must first be scanned, parsed, and validated.* The **scanner** identifies the language components (tokens) in the text of the query, while the **parser** checks the query syntax to determine whether it is formulated according to the syntax rules (rules of grammar) of the query language. The query must also be **validated,** by checking that all attribute and relation names are valid and semantically meaningful. An internal representation of a query is then created, usually as a tree or graph data structure; this is called a **query tree** or **query graph**. The DBMS must then devise an **execution strategy** for retrieving the result of the query from the internal database files. A query typically has many possible execution strategies, and the process of choosing a suitable one for processing a query is known as **query optimization**.

Figure 16.1 shows the different steps of processing a high-level query. The **query optimizer** module has the task of producing an execution plan, and the **code generator** generates the code to execute that plan. The **runtime database processor** has the task of running the query code, whether compiled or interpreted, to produce the query result. If a runtime error results, an error message is generated by the runtime database processor.

The term *optimization* is actually a misnomer because, in some cases, the chosen execution plan is not the optimal (best) strategy; it is just a **reasonably efficient strategy**

---

*We will not discuss the parsing and syntax-checking phase of query processing here; this material is discussed in most compiler textbooks.

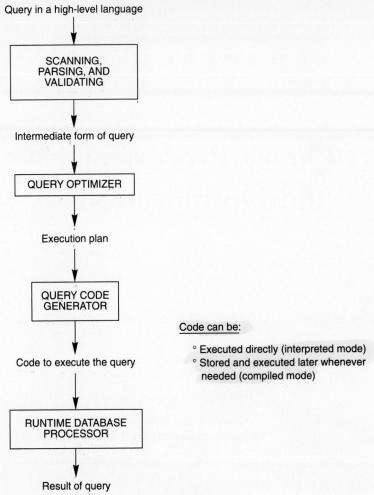

Figure 16.1 Steps of processing a high-level query.

for executing the query. Finding the optimal strategy is usually too time-consuming except for the simplest of queries, and it may require information on how the files are implemented and even on the contents of the files—information that may not be available in the DBMS catalog. Hence, the term "planning of an execution strategy" may be more accurate than "query optimization" for the material discussed in this chapter.

For lower-level navigational database languages, such as the network DML or the hierarchical HDML (see Chapters 10 and 11) the programmer must choose the query execution strategy while writing a database program. If a DBMS provides only a navigational language, there is *limited need or opportunity* for extensive query optimization by the DBMS; instead, the programmer is given the capability to choose the "optimal" execution strategy. On the other hand, a high-level relational query is more declarative in nature: it specifies what the intended result of the query is, rather than identifying the details of how the result should be obtained. Hence, query optimization is necessary for high-level relational queries. A relational DBMS must systematically evaluate alternative query execution strategies and choose an optimal strategy.

Each DBMS typically has a number of general database access algorithms that implement relational operations such as SELECT or JOIN or combinations of these operations. Only execution strategies that can be implemented by the DBMS access algorithms and that apply to the particular database design can be considered by the query optimization module. We discuss algorithms for implementing relational operations in Section 16.1.

There are two main techniques for query optimization. The first approach is based on **heuristic rules** for ordering the operations in a query execution strategy. The rules typically reorder the operations in a query tree (defined in Section 16.2.1) or determine an order for executing the operations specified by a query graph (defined in Section 16.2.2). The second approach involves **systematically estimating** the cost of different execution strategies and choosing the execution plan with the lowest cost estimate. The two strategies are usually combined in a query optimizer. We discuss heuristic optimization in Section 16.2 and cost estimation in Section 16.3.

16.1 Basic Algorithms for Executing Query Operations

A relational DBMS, or a nonrelational DBMS with a high-level relational query language interface, must include **algorithms** for implementing the types of relational operations that can appear in a query execution strategy. These include the basic relational algebra operations discussed in Chapter 6 and, in many cases, combinations of these operations. The DBMS must also have algorithms for processing special operations such as aggregation functions and grouping. For each such operation or combination of operations, one or more algorithms are available to execute the operation. An algorithm may apply to particular storage structures and access paths; if so, it can be used only if the files involved in the operation include these access paths (see Chapters 4 and 5). In this section we discuss typical algorithms used to implement SELECT, JOIN, and other relational operations.

16.1.1 *Implementing the SELECT Operation*

There are many options for executing a SELECT operation; some options depend on the file's having specific access paths and may apply only to certain types of selection conditions. We discuss some of the algorithms for implementing SELECT in this section. We will use the following operations, specified on the relational database of Figure 6.5, to illustrate our discussion:

(OP1): $\sigma_{SSN=123456789}(EMPLOYEE)$

(OP2): $\sigma_{DNUMBER>5}(DEPARTMENT)$

(OP3): $\sigma_{DNO=5}(EMPLOYEE)$

(OP4): $\sigma_{DNO=5 \text{ AND } SALARY>30000 \text{ AND } SEX=F}(EMPLOYEE)$

(OP5): $\sigma_{ESSN=123456789 \text{ AND } PNO=10}(WORKS\_ON)$

Search Methods for Selection

A number of search algorithms are possible for selecting records from a file. These are also known as **file scans,** because they scan the records of a file to search for and retrieve records that satisfy a selection condition. If the search algorithm involves the use of an index, the index search is called an **index scan**. The following search methods (S1 through S6) are examples of some of the search algorithms that can be used to implement a select operation:

S1. Linear search (brute force): Retrieve *every record* in the file, and test whether its attribute values satisfy the selection condition.

S2. Binary search: If the selection condition involves an equality comparison on a key attribute on which the file is ordered, binary search (which is more efficient than linear search) can be used. An example is OP1 if SSN is the ordering attribute for the EMPLOYEE file.

S3. Using a primary index or hash key to retrieve a single record: If the selection condition involves an equality comparison on a key attribute with a primary index (or a hash key)—for example, SSN = 123456789 in OP1—use the primary index (or the hash key) to retrieve the record.

S4. Using a primary index to retrieve multiple records: If the comparison condition is >, ≥, <, or ≤ on a key field with a primary index—for example, DNUMBER > 5 in OP2—use the index to find the record satisfying the corresponding equality condition (DNUMBER = 5); then retrieve all subsequent records in the (ordered) file. For the condition DNUMBER < 5, retrieve all the preceding records.

S5. Using a clustering index to retrieve multiple records: If the selection condition involves an equality comparison on a nonkey attribute with a clustering index—for example, DNO = 5 in OP3—use the clustering index to retrieve all the records satisfying the selection condition.

S6. Using a secondary (B$^+$-tree) index: On an equality comparison, this search method can be used to retrieve a single record if the indexing field has unique values (is a key) or to retrieve multiple records if the indexing field is not a key. In addition, it can be used to retrieve records on conditions involving >, ≥, <, or ≤.

In Section 16.3.3, we discuss how to develop formulas that estimate the access cost of these search methods in terms of the number of block accesses and the access time involved. Method S1 applies to any file, but all the other methods depend on having the appropriate access path on the attributes involved in the selection condition. Methods S4 and S6 can also be used to retrieve records in a certain *range*—for example, 30000≤SALARY≤35000. Queries involving such conditions are called **range queries**.

If a condition of a SELECT operation is a **conjunctive condition**—that is, if it is made up of several simple conditions connected with the AND logical connective, such as OP4 above—the DBMS can use the following additional methods to implement the operation:

S7. Conjunctive selection: If an attribute involved in any single *simple condition* in the conjunctive condition has an access path that permits the use of one of the methods S2 to S6, use that condition to retrieve the records and then check whether each retrieved record satisfies the remaining simple conditions in the conjunctive condition.

S8. Conjunctive selection using a composite index: If two or more attributes are involved in equality conditions in the conjunctive condition and a composite index (or hash structure) exists on the combined fields—for example, if an index has been created on the composite key (ESSN, PNO) of the WORKS_ON file for OP5—we can use the index directly.

S9. Conjunctive selection by intersection of record pointers:* This method is possible if secondary indexes are available on all (or some of) the fields involved in equality comparison conditions in the conjunctive condition and if the indexes include record pointers (rather than block pointers). Each index can be used to retrieve the *record pointers* that satisfy the individual condition. The *intersection* of these sets of record pointers gives the record pointers that satisfy the conjunctive condition, which are then used to retrieve those records directly. If only some of the conditions have secondary indexes, each retrieved record is further tested to determine whether it satisfies the remaining conditions.

Whenever a single condition specifies the selection—such as OP1, OP2, or OP3—we can only check whether an access path exists on the attribute involved in that condition. If an access path exists, the method corresponding to that access path is used; otherwise, the "brute force" linear search approach of method S1 is used. Query optimization for a SELECT operation is needed mostly for conjunctive select conditions whenever *more than one* of the attributes involved in the conditions have an access path. The optimizer should choose the access path that *retrieves the fewest records* in the most efficient way.

In choosing between multiple simple conditions in a conjunctive select condition, it is important to consider the **selectivity** of each condition; this is defined as the ratio of the number of records (tuples) that satisfy the condition to the total number of records (tuples) in the file (relation). The smaller the selectivity, the fewer tuples the condition selects and the higher the desirability of using that condition first to retrieve records. Although exact selectivities of all conditions may not be available, *estimates of selectivities* are often kept in the DBMS catalog and used by the optimizer. For example, the selectivity of an equality condition on a key attribute of relation $r(R)$ is $1/|r(R)|$, where $|r(R)|$ is the number of tuples in relation $r(R)$. The selectivity of an equality condition on an attribute with i *distinct values* is estimated by $(|r(R)|/i)/|r(R)|$ or $1/i$, assuming that the records are evenly distributed among the distinct values. Under this assumption, $|r(R)|/i$ records will satisfy an equality condition on this attribute.

Compared to a conjunctive selection condition, a **disjunctive condition** (where simple conditions are connected by the OR logical connective rather than by AND) is much

---

*A record pointer uniquely identifies a record and provides the address of the record on disk; hence, it is also called the **record identifier** or **record id**.

harder to process and optimize. For example, consider OP4':

(OP4'): $\sigma_{DNO=5 \text{ OR } SALARY>30000 \text{ OR } SEX=F}$(EMPLOYEE)

With such a condition, little optimization can be done, because the records satisfying the disjunctive condition are the *union* of the records satisfying the individual conditions. Hence, if any *one* of the conditions does not have an access path, we are compelled to use the brute force linear search approach. Only if an access path exists on *every* condition can we optimize the selection by retrieving the records satisfying each condition and then applying the union operation to eliminate duplicate records. We can apply the union to record pointers rather than to records if the appropriate access paths that provide record pointers exist for every condition.

A DBMS will have available many of the methods discussed above. The query optimizer must choose the appropriate one for executing each SELECT operation in a query. This optimization uses formulas that estimate the costs for each available access method, as we discuss in Section 16.3. The optimizer chooses the access method with the lowest estimated cost.

16.1.2 *Implementing the JOIN Operation*

The JOIN operation is one of the most time-consuming operations in query processing. Most join operations encountered in queries are of the EQUIJOIN and NATURAL JOIN varieties, so we consider only these two here. For the remainder of this chapter, the term **join** refers to an EQUIJOIN (or NATURAL JOIN). There are many possible ways to implement a **two-way join,** which is a join on two files. Joins involving more than two files are called **multiway joins**. The number of possible ways to execute multiway joins grows very rapidly. In this section we discuss some of the techniques for implementing two-way joins. To illustrate our discussion, we refer to the relational schema of Figure 6.5 once more—specifically, to the EMPLOYEE, DEPARTMENT, and PROJECT relations. The algorithms we consider are for join operations of the form

$R \bowtie_{A=B} S$

where A and B are domain-compatible attributes of R and S, respectively. The methods we discuss can be extended to more general forms of join. We illustrate four of the most common techniques for performing such a join, using the following example operations:

(OP6): EMPLOYEE $\bowtie_{DNO=DNUMBER}$ DEPARTMENT
(OP7): DEPARTMENT $\bowtie_{MGRSSN=SSN}$ EMPLOYEE

Methods for Implementing Joins

J1. **Nested (inner-outer) loop** approach (brute force): For each record t in R(outer loop), retrieve every record s from S (inner loop) and test whether the two records satisfy the join condition t[A] = s[B].

J2. Using an **access structure to retrieve the matching record(s):** If an index (or hash key) exists for one of the two join attributes—say, B of S—retrieve each record t in R, one at a time, and then use the access structure to retrieve directly all matching records s from S that satisfy s[B] = t[A].

J3. **Sort–merge join:** If the records of R and S are *physically sorted* (ordered) by value of the join attributes A and B, respectively, we can implement the join in the most efficient way possible. Both files are scanned in order of the join attributes, matching the records that have the same values for A and B. In this method, the records of each file are scanned only once each for matching with the other file—unless both A and B are nonkey attributes, in which case the method needs to be modified slightly. A sketch of the sort–merge join algorithm is given in Figure 16.2(a). We use R(i) to refer to the ith record in R. A variation of the sort–merge join can be used when secondary indexes exist on both join attributes. The indexes provide the ability to access (scan) the records in order of the join attributes, but the records themselves are physically scattered all over the file blocks, so this method may be quite inefficient, as every record access may involve accessing a disk block.

J4. **Hash-join:** The records of files R and S are both hashed to the *same hash file,* using the *same hashing function* on the join attributes A of R and B of S as hash keys. A single pass through the file with fewer records (say, R) hashes its records to the hash file buckets. A single pass through the other file (S) then hashes each of its records to the appropriate bucket, where the record is combined with all matching records from R.

In practice, techniques J1 to J4 are implemented by accessing *whole disk blocks* of a file, rather than individual records. Depending on the available buffer space in memory, the number of blocks read in from the file can be adjusted. In the nested-loop approach (J1), it makes a difference which file is chosen for the outer loop and which for the inner loop. To illustrate this, consider OP6 and assume that the DEPARTMENT file consists of $r_D = 50$ records stored in $b_D = 10$ disk blocks and that the EMPLOYEE file consists of $r_E = 5000$ records stored in $b_E = 2000$ disk blocks. In addition, assume that $n_B = 6$ blocks (buffers) in main memory are available for implementing the join. It is advantageous to read as many blocks as possible at a time into memory from the file whose records are used for the outer loop ($n_B - 1$ blocks) and one block at a time for the inner-loop file. This reduces the total number of block accesses.

If EMPLOYEE is used for the outer loop, each block of EMPLOYEE is read once, and the entire DEPARTMENT file (each of its blocks) is read once for *each time* we read in $n_B - 1$ blocks of the EMPLOYEE file. We get

Total number of blocks accessed for outer file = b_E
Number of times ($n_B - 1$) blocks of outer file are loaded = $\lceil b_E/(n_B - 1) \rceil$
Total number of blocks accessed for inner file = $b_D * \lceil (b_E/(n_B - 1)) \rceil$

Hence, we get the following total number of block accesses:

$b_E + (\lceil (b_E/(n_B - 1)) \rceil * b_D) = 2000 + (\lceil (2000/5) \rceil * 10) = 6000$ block accesses

On the other hand, if we use the DEPARTMENT records in the outer loop, by symmetry we get the following total number of block accesses:

$b_D + (\lceil (b_D/(n_B - 1)) \rceil * b_E) = 10 + (\lceil (10/5) \rceil * 2000) = 4010$ block accesses

(a)   sort the tuples in R on attribute A; (* assume R has n tuples (records) *)
       sort the tuples in S on attribute B; (* assume S has m tuples (records) *)
       set i←1, j←1 ;
       while (i ≤ n) and (j ≤ m)
       do{   if R(i)[A] > S(j)[B]
                       then   set j←j+1
                       elseif R(i)[A] < S(j)[B]
                       then   set i←i+1
                       else   {   (* R(i)[A]=S(j)[B] , so we output a matched tuple *)
                                    output the combined tuple <R(i) , S(j)> to T;
                                                (* output other tuples that match R(i) , if any *)
                                                set l←j+1 ;
                                                while (l ≤ m) and (R(i)[A]=S(l)[B])
                                                do   {   output the combined tuple <R(i) , S(l)> to T ;
                                                                       set l←l+1
                                                                       }
                                                (* output other tuples that match S(j) , if any *)
                                                set k←i+1 ;
                                                while (k ≤ n) and (R(k)[A]=S(j)[B])
                                                do   {   output the combined tuple <R(k) , S(j)> to T ;
                                                                       set k←k+1
                                                                       }
                                                set i←k, j←l
                              }
             }

(b)   create a tuple t[<attribute list>] in T' for each tuple t in R;
             (* T' contains the projection result <u>before</u> duplicate elimination *)
       if <attribute list> includes a key of R
             then T ← T'
             else   {   sort the tuples in T';
                          set i←1, j←2;
                          while i ≤ n
                              do {   output the tuple T'[i] to T;
                                       while T'[i] = T'[j] do j←j+1; (* eliminate duplicates *)
                                       i←j ; j←i+1
                                  }
                     }
       (* T contains the projection result after duplicate elimination *)

Figure 16.2   Implementing the JOIN, PROJECT, UNION, INTERSECTION, and SET
                   DIFFERENCE operations by sorting where R has n tuples and S has
                   m tuples.
                   (a) Implementing the operation T←R ⋈ $_{A=B}$S.
                   (b) Implementing the operation T←$\pi_{<\text{attribute list}>}$(R).   *(con-
                   tinued on next page)*

(c) sort the tuples in R and S using the same unique sort attributes;
     set i←1, j←1;
     while (i ≤ n) and (j ≤ m)
     do {   if R(i) > S(j)
                 then   {   output S(j) to T;
                             set j←j+1
                         }
                 elseif R(i) < S(j)
                 then   {   output R(i) to T;
                             set i←i+1
                         }
                 else set j←j+1 (* R(i)=S(j) , so we skip one of the duplicate tuples *)
         }
     if (i ≤ n) then add tuples R(i) to R(n) to T;
     if (j ≤ m) then add tuples S(j) to S(m) to T;

(d) sort the tuples in R and S using the same unique sort attributes;
     set i←1, j←1;
     while (i ≤ n) and (j ≤ m)
     do {   if R(i) > S(j)
                 then   set j←j+1
                 elseif R(i) < S(j)
                 then   set i←i+1
                 else   {   output R(i) to T ; (* R(i)=S(j) , so we output the tuple *)
                             set i←i+1, j←j+1
                         }
         }

(e) sort the tuples in R and S using the same unique sort attributes;
     set i←1, j←1;
     while (i ≤ n) and (j ≤ m)
     do {   if R(i) > S(j)
                 then   set j←j+1
                 elseif R(i) < S(j)
                 then   {   output R(i) to T; (* R(i) has no matching S(j), so output R(i) *)
                             set i←i+1
                         }
                 else   set i←i+1, j←j+1
         }
     if (i ≤ n) then add tuples R(i) to R(n) to T ;

Figure 16.2   *(continued)* (c) Implementing the operation T←R ∪ S.
                   (d) Implementing the operation T←R ∩ S.
                   (e) Implementing the operation T←R − S.

In addition to the preceding costs, the join algorithm needs a buffer to hold the joined records of the *result file*. Once the buffer is filled, it is written to disk. Double buffering can be used to speed the algorithm (see Section 4.3). If the result file of the join operation has b_R disk blocks, each block is written once, so additional b_R block accesses should be added to the preceding formulas in order to estimate the cost of the join operation. The same holds for the formulas developed later for other join algorithms. As this example shows, it is advantageous to use the file *with fewer blocks* as the outer-loop file in method J1, if more than two buffers exist in memory for implementing the join. Hence, the *size* of the files being joined directly affects the performance of the different join techniques. Another factor that affects the performance of a join, particularly method J2, is the percentage of records in a file that will be joined with records in the other file. We call this the **join selection factor** of a file with respect to an equijoin condition with another file. This factor depends on the particular equijoin condition between the two files.

To illustrate this, consider the operation OP7, which joins each DEPARTMENT record with the EMPLOYEE record for the manager of that department. Here, each DEPARTMENT record (50 records in our example) is expected to be joined to a single EMPLOYEE record, but many EMPLOYEE records (4950 of them) will not be joined. Suppose that secondary indexes exist on both the attributes SSN of EMPLOYEE and MGRSSN of DEPARTMENT, with the number of index levels $x_{SSN} = 4$ and $x_{MGRSSN} = 2$, respectively. We have two options for implementing method J2. The first retrieves each EMPLOYEE record and then uses the index on MGRSSN of DEPARTMENT to find a matching DEPARTMENT record. In this case, no matching record will be found for employees who do not manage a department. The number of block accesses for this case is approximately

$$b_E + (r_E*(x_{MGRSSN} + 1)) = 2000 + (5000*3) = 17,000 \text{ block accesses}$$

The second option retrieves each DEPARTMENT record and then uses the index on SSN of EMPLOYEE to find a matching EMPLOYEE record. In this case, every DEPARTMENT record will have one matching EMPLOYEE record. The number of block accesses for this case is approximately

$$b_D + (r_D*(x_{SSN} + 1)) = 10 + (50*5) = 260 \text{ block accesses}$$

The second option is more efficient because the join selection factor of DEPARTMENT with respect to the join condition SSN = MGRSSN is 1, whereas the selection factor of EMPLOYEE with respect to the same join condition is (50/5000). For method J2, either the smaller file or the file that has a match for every record (high join selection factor) should be used in the outer loop. In some cases an index may be created specifically for performing the join operation if one does not already exist.

Merge-join method J3 is quite efficient. Only a single pass is made through both files. Hence, the number of blocks accessed is equal to the sum of the numbers of blocks in both files. For this method, both OP6 and OP7 would need $b_E + b_D = 2000 + 10 = 2010$ block accesses. However, both files are required to be ordered by the join attributes; if one or both are not, they may be sorted specifically for performing the join operation. If we estimate the cost of sorting an external file by ($b \log_2 b$) block accesses, and if both files need to be sorted, the total cost of a sort-merge join can be estimated by ($b_E + b_D + b_E \log_2 b_E + b_D \log_2 b_D$).

Hash-join method J4 is also quite efficient. In this case only a single pass is made through both files, whether or not they are ordered, to produce the hash file entries. If the hash file can be kept in main memory, the implementation is straightforward. If parts of the hash file must be stored on disk, the method becomes less efficient; a number of variations to improve the efficiency have been proposed. Here we discuss the technique known as *hybrid hash join*, which has been shown to be quite efficient.

In the **hybrid hash join** algorithm, a number of *in-memory buffers* are available for holding hashed records; records that do not fit in memory are held in disk blocks. Let us assume that the size of a memory buffer is one disk block, that N such buffers are available, and that the hash function used is $h(K) = K \bmod M$ so that M hash buckets are needed. The idea behind the hybrid hash join is first to hash the *smaller* of the two files being joined into the hash buckets. If the memory buffer space is large enough to hold *all the buckets*, then the records of the smaller file are all in memory after being hashed in the first phase of the algorithm. In this case, the second phase hashes the records in each block of the second file—one record at a time—and combines those records with the matching records from the first file. The resulting joined records are written into the result file. In our example, the smaller file is the DEPARTMENT file; hence, if the number of available memory buffers $N > b_D$, the whole DEPARTMENT file is held in main memory. Each EMPLOYEE block is then read into a buffer, and each record in the buffer is hashed to a bucket and joined with the corresponding DEPARTMENT record(s). The joined records are written to a buffer and eventually to the result file on disk. The cost in terms of block accesses is hence $(b_D + b_E)$, plus b_R—the cost of writing the result file.

If the memory buffer space is *not* large enough to hold all the buckets for the smaller of the files being joined, part of each hash bucket must be stored on disk. The hybrid hash join algorithm divides the buffer space among the hash buckets such that all the blocks of the *first bucket* completely reside in main memory. For each of the other hash buckets, only a single in-memory buffer—whose size is one disk block—is allocated; the remainder of the bucket's blocks are stored on disk. Whenever the in-memory buffer for a bucket gets filled, its contents are written to a disk block such that all disk blocks for a bucket are contiguous (or linked together). At the end of the first phase, the smaller of the two files being joined is hashed to the buckets; the first bucket resides wholly in main memory, whereas each of the other buckets resides on disk except for the first block of each bucket.

For the second phase, the records of the second file being joined—the larger file— are hashed using the same hash function on the join attribute(s). If a record hashes to the first bucket, it is joined with the matching record(s) and the joined records are written to the result buffer (and eventually to disk). If a record hashes to a bucket *other than the first*, it is written to disk into buckets for the second file's records. At the end of the second phase, all records that hash to the first bucket have been joined; now there are $M - 1$ buckets on disk containing the remaining records of the first file, and another $M - 1$ buckets containing the remaining records of the second file. We therefore have additional $M - 1$ phases—one for each pair of buckets. For buckets i, first the records that hashed from the first file are copied into the memory buffers; then each of the records from the second file that hashed to the same bucket are read, matched, joined, and written into the result file.

We can approximate the cost of this join as $3 * (b_D + b_E)$ for our example, since each record—except for records that hash to the first bucket—is read once, written back to disk in one of the hash buckets, and then read a second time to perform the join. The actual cost is less, because records that hash to the first bucket from either file are read only once. Exercise 16.16 addresses how the formulas for hybrid hash join may be developed.

16.1.3 Implementing the PROJECT Operation

A PROJECT operation $\pi_{<\text{attribute list}>}(R)$ is straightforward to implement if <attribute list> includes a key of relation R, because in this case the result of the operation will have the same number of tuples as R, but with only the values for the attributes in <attribute list> in each tuple. If <attribute list> does not include a key of R, duplicate tuples must be eliminated. This is usually done by sorting the result of the operation and then eliminating duplicate tuples, which appear consecutively after sorting, as in Figure 16.2(b). Hashing can also be used to eliminate duplicates: as each record is hashed and inserted into a bucket of the hash file, it is checked against those already in the bucket; if it is a duplicate, it is not inserted.

16.1.4 Implementing Set Operations

Set operations—UNION, INTERSECTION, SET DIFFERENCE, and CARTESIAN PRODUCT—are sometimes expensive to implement. In particular, the Cartesian product operation R X S is quite expensive, because its result includes a record for each combination of records from R and S. In addition, the attributes of the result include all attributes of R and S. If R has n records and j attributes and S has m records and k attributes, the resulting relation will have n * m records and j + k attributes. Hence, it is important to avoid the CARTESIAN PRODUCT operation and to substitute other equivalent operations during query optimization (see Section 16.2).

The other three set operations—UNION, INTERSECTION, and SET DIFFERENCE—apply only to union-compatible relations, which have the same attributes. The customary way to implement these operations is to sort the two relations on the same attributes. After sorting, a single scan through each relation is sufficient to produce the result. For example, we can implement R ∪ S by scanning both sorted files concurrently; and whenever the same tuple exists in both relations, only one is kept. For R ∩ S, we keep in the result only the tuples that appear in both relations. Figure 16.2(c) to (e) sketches the implementation of these operations by sorting and scanning. If sorting is done on unique key attributes, the operations are further simplified.

Hashing can also be used to implement UNION, INTERSECTION, and SET DIFFERENCE by hashing both files to the same hash file buckets. For example, to implement R ∪ S, first hash the records of R to the hash file; then, while hashing the records of S, do not insert duplicate records. To implement R ∩ S, first hash the records of R to the hash file. Then, while hashing each record of S, if an identical record is found in the bucket, add the record to the result file. To implement R − S, first hash the records of R to the hash file. While hashing each record of S, if an identical record is found in the bucket, remove that tuple.

16.1.5 *Combining Operations for Query Execution*

It is not advisable to have a separate access routine for each relational algebra operation. Creating a **temporary** file to hold the tuples in the result of the operation is generally not efficient. Typically, a query specified in the relational algebra consists of a sequence of operations. If we execute a single operation at a time, we must generate as many temporary files as there are operations. Many of these temporary files will then be used as input files to subsequent operations. Generating and storing a large temporary file on disk is time-consuming. To reduce the number of temporary files, it is common to generate algorithms for *combinations of operations*.

For example, rather than being implemented separately, a JOIN can be combined with two SELECT operations on the input files and a final PROJECT operation on the resulting file; all this is implemented by one algorithm with two input files and a single output file. Rather than creating four temporary files, we apply the algorithm directly and get just one result file. In Section 16.2.1 we discuss how heuristic relational algebra optimization can group operations together for execution.

It is now common to create the code dynamically to implement multiple operations. The generated code for producing the query combines several algorithms that correspond to individual operations. As the result tuples from one operation are produced, they are provided as input for a subsequent operation. For example, if a join operation follows two select operations on base relations, the tuples resulting from each select are provided as input for the join algorithm as they are produced.

16.2 Using Heuristics in Query Optimization

In this section we discuss optimization techniques that apply heuristic rules to modify the internal representation of a query—which is usually in the form of a tree or a graph data structure—to improve its expected performance on execution. The parser of a high-level query generates the internal representation, which is then optimized according to heuristic rules. Following that, access routines to execute groups of operations based on the access paths available on the files are chosen by the query optimizer.

The main **heuristic rule** is to apply SELECT and PROJECT operations *before* applying the JOIN or other binary operations. This is because the size of the file resulting from a binary operation is a function of the sizes of the input files—in some cases, a multiplicative function. The SELECT and PROJECT operations typically reduce the size of a single file and never increase its size; hence, they should be applied *before* a join or other binary operation.

In Section 16.2.1 we introduce the query tree notation, which is used to represent a relational algebra expression. We then show how heuristic optimization rules are applied to convert the tree into an **equivalent** query tree, which represents a relational algebra expression that is more efficient to execute but gives the same result as the original one. Then, in Section 16.2.2, we introduce the query graph notation, which is used to represent a relational calculus expression. We then show how heuristic rules can be applied to the query graph to produce an efficient execution strategy.

16.2.1   *Heuristic Optimization of Query Trees (Relational Algebra)*

A **query tree** is a tree structure that corresponds to a relational algebra expression by representing the input relations as *leaf nodes* of the tree and the relational algebra operations as *internal nodes*. An **execution of the query tree** consists of executing an internal node operation whenever its operands are available and then replacing that internal node by the relation that results from executing the operation. The execution terminates when the root node is executed and produces the result relation.

Figure 16.3(a) shows a query tree for query Q2 of Chapters 6 to 8: For every project located in 'Stafford', retrieve the project number, the controlling department number, and the department manager's last name, address, and birthdate. This query is specified on the relational schema of Figure 6.5 and corresponds to the following relational algebra expression (recall that ⋈ stands for JOIN):

$$\pi_{\text{PNUMBER,DNUM,LNAME,ADDRESS,BDATE}} (((\sigma_{\text{PLOCATION='Stafford'}}(\text{PROJECT}))$$
$$\bowtie_{\text{DNUM=DNUMBER}} (\text{DEPARTMENT})) \bowtie_{\text{MGRSSN=SSN}} (\text{EMPLOYEE}))$$

This corresponds to the following SQL query:

```
Q2:   SELECT   PNUMBER, DNUM, LNAME, ADDRESS, BDATE
      FROM     PROJECT, DEPARTMENT, EMPLOYEE
      WHERE    DNUM=DNUMBER AND MGRSSN=SSN AND
               PLOCATION='Stafford'
```

In Figure 16.3(a) the three relations PROJECT, DEPARTMENT, and EMPLOYEE are represented by leaf nodes, while the relational algebra operations of the expression are represented by internal tree nodes. When this query tree is executed, the node marked (1) in Figure 16.3(a) is executed before node (2) because the result of operation (1) must be available before we can execute operation (2). Similarly, node (2) must be executed before node (3), and so on.

In general, many different relational algebra expressions—and hence many different query trees—can be equivalent; that is, they can correspond to the same query. A query may also be stated in various ways in a high-level query language such as SQL (see Chapter 7). The query parser will typically generate a standard **canonical** query tree to correspond to an SQL query, without doing any optimization. For example, for a select–project–join query, such as Q2, the canonical tree is shown in Figure 16.3(b). The Cartesian product of the relations specified in the FROM clause is first applied; then the selection and join conditions of the WHERE clause are applied, followed by the projection on the SELECT clause attributes.

Such a canonical query tree represents a relational algebra expression that is very inefficient if executed directly, because of the Cartesian product (X) operations. For example, if the PROJECT, DEPARTMENT, and EMPLOYEE relations had record sizes of 100, 50, and 150 bytes and contained 100, 20, and 5000 tuples, respectively, the result of the Cartesian product would contain 10 million tuples of record size 300 bytes each. However, the query tree is in a simple standard form. It is now the job of the heuristic query optimizer to transform this **initial query tree** into a **final query tree** that is efficient to execute. The optimizer must include rules for equivalence among relational algebra expressions that can be applied to the initial tree, guided by the heuristic query opti-

(a)

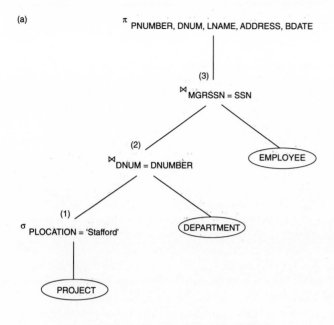

(b)

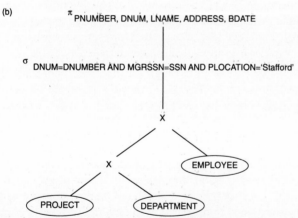

Figure 16.3   Two query trees for the query Q2. (a) Query tree corresponding
to the relational algebra expression for Q2. (b) Initial (canonical) query tree for SQL query Q2.

mization rules, to produce the final, optimized query tree. We first discuss informally how
a query tree is transformed by using heuristics. Then we discuss general transformation
rules (guidelines) and show how they may be used in an algebraic heuristic optimizer.

Example of Transforming a Query.   In relation to the database of Figure 6.5, consider
a query Q: Find the last names of employees born after 1957 who work on a project
named "Aquarius." This query can be specified in SQL as follows:

Q: **SELECT** LNAME
  FROM EMPLOYEE, WORKS_ON, PROJECT
  WHERE PNAME='Aquarius' **AND** PNUMBER=PNO **AND** ESSN=SSN
  AND BDATE>'DEC-31-1957'

The initial query tree for Q is shown in Figure 16.4(a). Executing this tree directly first creates a very large file containing the Cartesian product of the entire EMPLOYEE, WORKS_ON, and PROJECT files. However, we need only one PROJECT record—for the 'Aquarius' project—and only the EMPLOYEE records for those whose birthdate is after 'DEC-31-1957'. Figure 16.4(b) shows an improved query tree that first applies the SELECT operations to reduce the number of tuples that appear in the Cartesian product.

A further improvement is achieved by switching the positions of the EMPLOYEE and PROJECT relations in the tree, as shown in Figure 16.4(c). This uses the information that PNUMBER is a key attribute of the PROJECT relation, and hence the SELECT operation on the PROJECT relation will retrieve a single record only. We can further improve the query tree by replacing any CARTESIAN PRODUCT operation that is followed by a join condition with a JOIN operation, as shown in Figure 16.4(d). Another improvement is to keep only the attributes needed by subsequent operations in the temporary intermediate relations, by including PROJECT (π) operations as early as possible in the query tree, as shown in Figure 16.4(e). This reduces the attributes (columns) of the intermediate temporary relations, whereas the SELECT operations reduce the number of tuples (records) only.

As the preceding example demonstrates, we can convert a query tree step by step into another query tree that is more efficient to execute. However, we must make sure that the conversion steps always lead to an equivalent query tree. To do this, we must know which transformation rules *preserve this equivalence*. We discuss some of these transformation rules next.

General Transformation Rules for Relational Algebra Operations. There are many rules for transforming relational algebra operations into equivalent ones. Here we are interested in the meaning of the operations and the resulting relations. Hence, if two relations have the same set of attributes in a *different order* but the two relations represent the same information, we consider the relations equivalent. In Section 6.1.2 we gave an alternative definition of *relation* that makes order of attributes unimportant; we will use this definition here. We now state some transformation rules, without proving them:

1. Cascade of σ: A conjunctive selection condition can be broken up into a cascade (sequence) of individual σ operations:

    $$\sigma_{c1 \text{ AND } c2 \text{ AND } \ldots \text{ AND } cn}(R) \equiv \sigma_{c1}(\sigma_{c2}(\ldots(\sigma_{cn}(R))\ldots))$$

2. Commutativity of σ: The σ operation is commutative:

    $$\sigma_{c1}(\sigma_{c2}(R)) \equiv \sigma_{c2}(\sigma_{c1}(R))$$

3. Cascade of π: In a cascade (sequence) of π operations, all but the last one can be ignored:

    $$\pi_{List1}(\pi_{List2}(\ldots(\pi_{Listn}(R))\ldots)) = \pi_{List1}(R)$$

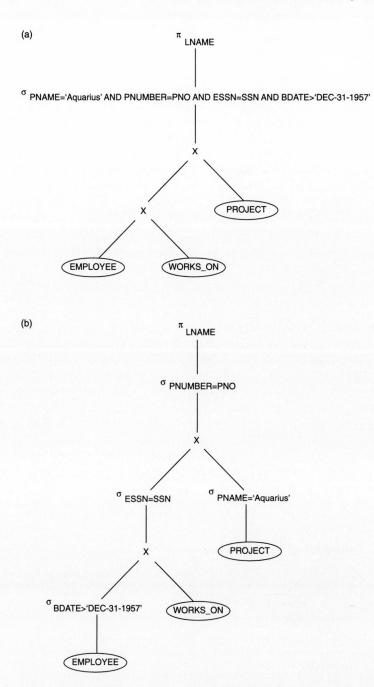

Figure 16.4   Steps in converting a query tree during heuristic optimization.
(a) Initial (canonical) query tree for SQL query Q. (b) Moving
SELECT operations down the query tree.   *(continued on next page)*

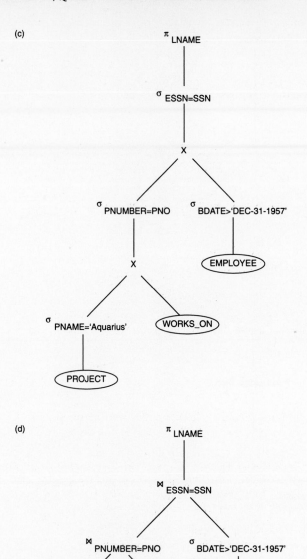

Figure 16.4   *(continued)* (c) Applying the more restrictive SELECT operation first. (d) Replacing CARTESIAN PRODUCT and SELECT with JOIN operations.   *(continued on next page)*

(e)

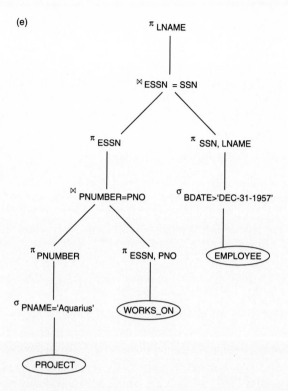

Figure 16.4 *(continued)* (e) Moving PROJECT operations down the query tree.

4. Commuting σ with π: If the selection condition c involves only the attributes A1, ..., An in the projection list, the two operations can be commuted:

$$\pi_{A1, A2, ..., An} (\sigma_c (R)) \equiv \sigma_c (\pi_{A1, A2, ..., An} (R))$$

5. Commutativity of ⋈ (or X): The ⋈ operation is commutative:

$$R \bowtie_c S \equiv S \bowtie_c R$$

Notice that, although the order of attributes may not be the same in the relations resulting from the two joins, the "meaning" is the same because order of attributes is not important in the alternative definition of *relation* that we use here. The X operation is commutative in the same sense as the ⋈ operation.

6. Commuting σ with ⋈ (or X): If all the attributes in the selection condition c involve only the attributes of one of the relations being joined—say, R—the two operations can be commuted as follows:

$$\sigma_c (R \bowtie S) \equiv (\sigma_c (R)) \bowtie S$$

Alternatively, if the selection condition c can be written as (c1 and c2), where condition c1 involves only the attributes of R and condition c2 involves only the attributes of S, the operations commute as follows:

$$\sigma_c (R \bowtie S) \equiv (\sigma_{c1} (R)) \bowtie (\sigma_{c2} (S))$$

The same rules apply if the $\bowtie$ is replaced by a $\times$ operation. These transformations are very useful during heuristic optimization.

7. Commuting π with $\bowtie$ (or $\times$): Suppose that the projection list is L = {A1, ..., An, B1, ..., Bm}, where A1, ..., An are attributes of R and B1, ..., Bm are attributes of S. If the join condition c involves only attributes in L, the two operations can be commuted as follows:

$$\pi_L (R \bowtie_c S) \equiv (\pi_{A1, \ldots, An} (R)) \bowtie_c (\pi_{B1, \ldots, Bm} (S))$$

If the join condition c contains additional attributes not in L, these must be added to the projection list, and a final π operation is needed. For example, if attributes An + 1, ..., An + k of R and Bm + 1, ..., Bm + p of S are involved in the join condition c but are not in the projection list L, the operations commute as follows:

$$\pi_L (R \bowtie_c S) \equiv$$
$$\pi_L ((\pi_{A1, \ldots, An, An+1, \ldots, An+k} (R)) \bowtie_c (\pi_{B1, \ldots, Bm, Bm+1, \ldots, Bm+p} (S)))$$

For $\times$, there is no condition c, so the first transformation rule always applies by replacing $\bowtie_c$ with $\times$.

8. Commutativity of set operations: The set operations $\cup$ and $\cap$ are commutative but $-$ is not.

9. Associativity of $\bowtie$, $\times$, $\cup$, and $\cap$: These four operations are individually associative; that is, if θ stands for any *one* of these four operations (throughout the expression), we have

$$(R \theta S) \theta T \equiv R \theta (S \theta T)$$

10. Commuting σ with set operations: The σ operation commutes with $\cup$, $\cap$, and $-$. If θ stands for any *one* of these three operations, we have

$$\sigma_c (R \theta S) \equiv (\sigma_c (R)) \theta (\sigma_c (S))$$

11. The π operation commutes with $\cup$. If θ stands for $\cup$, we have

$$\pi_L (R \theta S) \equiv (\pi_L (R)) \theta (\pi_L (S))$$

12. Other transformations: There are other possible transformations. For example, a selection or join condition c can be converted into an equivalent condition by using the following rules (known as DeMorgan's laws):

$$c \equiv \textbf{NOT} (c1 \textbf{ AND } c2) \equiv (\textbf{NOT } c1) \textbf{ OR } (\textbf{NOT } c2)$$
$$c \equiv \textbf{NOT} (c1 \textbf{ OR } c2) \equiv (\textbf{NOT } c1) \textbf{ AND } (\textbf{NOT } c2)$$

Additional transformations discussed in Chapter 6 are not repeated here.

We discuss next how these rules are used in heuristic optimization.

Outline of a Heuristic Algebraic Optimization Algorithm. We can now outline the steps of an algorithm that utilizes some of the above rules to transform an initial query tree into an optimized tree that is more efficient to execute (in most cases). The steps of the algorithm will lead to transformations similar to those discussed in our example of Figure 16.4. The steps of the algorithm are as follows:

1. Using rule 1, break up any SELECT operations with conjunctive conditions into a cascade of SELECT operations. This permits a greater degree of freedom in moving select operations down different branches of the tree.

2. Using rules 2, 4, 6, and 10 concerning the commutativity of SELECT with other operations, move each SELECT operation as far down the query tree as is permitted by the attributes involved in the select condition.

3. Using rule 9 concerning associativity of binary operations, rearrange the leaf nodes of the tree so that the leaf node relations with the most restrictive SELECT operations are executed first in the query tree representation. By "most restrictive SELECT operations," we mean the ones that produce a relation with the fewest tuples or with the smallest absolute size. Either definition can be used, since these rules are heuristic. Another possibility is to define the most restrictive SELECT as the one with the smallest selectivity; this is more practical because estimated selectivities are often available in the catalog.

4. Combine a CARTESIAN PRODUCT operation with a subsequent SELECT operation whose condition represents a join condition into a JOIN operation.

5. Using rules 3, 4, 7, and 11 concerning the cascading of PROJECT and the commuting of PROJECT with other operations, break down and move lists of projection attributes down the tree as far as possible by creating new PROJECT operations as needed.

6. Identify subtrees that represent groups of operations that can be executed by a single algorithm.

In our example, Figure 16.4(b) shows the tree of Figure 16.4(a) after applying steps 1 and 2 of the algorithm; Figure 16.4(c) shows the tree after applying step 3; Figure 16.4(d) after applying step 4; and Figure 16.4(e) after applying step 5. In step 6 we may group together the operations in the subtree whose root is the operation $\bowtie_{\text{PNUMBER=PNO}}$ into a single algorithm. We may also group the remaining operations into another subtree, where the tuples resulting from the first algorithm replace the subtree whose root is the operation $\bowtie_{\text{PNUMBER=PNO}}$, because the first grouping means that this subtree is executed first.

Summary of Heuristics for Algebraic Optimization. We now summarize the basic heuristics for algebraic optimization. The main heuristic is to apply first the operations that reduce the size of intermediate results. This includes performing SELECT operations as early as possible to reduce the number of tuples and performing PROJECT operations as early as possible to reduce the number of attributes. This is done by moving SELECT and PROJECT operations as far down the tree as possible. In addition, the SELECT and JOIN operations that are most restrictive—that is, result in relations with the fewest tuples or with the smallest absolute size—should be executed before other similar operations. This is done by reordering the leaf nodes of the tree among themselves and adjusting the rest of the tree appropriately.

16.2.2 *Heuristic Optimization of Query Graphs (Relational Calculus)*★

The approach we describe now is often called **query decomposition** and was first proposed as a heuristic optimization technique for implementing the QUEL language (Chapter 8) in the INGRES DBMS. QUEL queries are very similar to tuple relational calculus (Chapter 8) and are represented as query graphs. We discuss only select–project–join queries here, although the technique may be extended to more general queries. Recall that a QUEL query may include a number of **tuple variables**—one variable for each relation involved in a certain role in the query.

A **query graph** is a representation of a select–project–join tuple relational calculus expression or QUEL query. Each tuple variable is represented by a **node** in the graph, and **edges** among these nodes represent **join conditions** involving these variables. Constant values appearing in the query are represented by special nodes called **constant nodes**. Constant nodes are connected by edges representing selection conditions to the nodes that represent the tuple variables involved in these conditions.

Figure 16.5 shows a query graph for the following QUEL query, which is specified on the relational schema shown in Figure 6.5 and corresponds to query Q2 of Chapters 6 to 8: For every project located in 'Stafford', retrieve the project number, the controlling department number, and the department manager's last name, address, and birthdate:

Q2:	**RANGE OF**	P **IS** PROJECT, D **IS** DEPARTMENT, E **IS** EMPLOYEE
	RETRIEVE	(P.PNUMBER, D.DNUMBER, E.LNAME, E.BDATE, E.ADDRESS)
	WHERE	P.DNUM=D.DNUMBER **AND** D.MGRSSN=E.SSN **AND** P.PLOCATION='Stafford'

In Figure 16.5 the tuple variables P, D, and E and the constant value 'Stafford' are represented by nodes in the graph. Constant nodes are displayed in double ovals. The

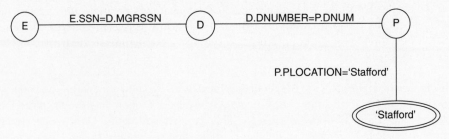

Figure 16.5   Query graph for the query Q2.

edges are labeled by the corresponding selection or join conditions. Notice that the query graph does *not* specify any *order of execution* on the operations, unlike the query tree, which has implicit order. This makes the query graph a completely neutral representation, specifying *what* the query will retrieve but not *how* to execute the query. The query graph is a **canonical representation** of a select–project–join relational calculus query; each query corresponds to one and only one graph. This is unlike query trees, where many different trees can represent the same query.

Optimizing and Executing a Query Graph by Query Decomposition. We now describe the query decomposition method that heuristically optimizes (derives a "good" execution strategy for) and executes a query graph. We illustrate our discussion by using the query Q': Find the last names of employees born after 1957 who work on a project located in 'Stafford' and controlled by department number 4. This query refers to the database of Figure 6.5 and is specified in QUEL as follows:

Q':	**RANGE OF**	P **IS** PROJECT, W **IS** WORKS_ON, E **IS** EMPLOYEE
	RETRIEVE	(E.LNAME)
	WHERE	P.PLOCATION='Stafford' **AND** P.DNUM=4 **AND**
		P.PNUMBER=W.PNO **AND**
		W.ESSN=E.SSN **AND** E.BDATE>'DEC-31-1957'

Figure 16.6(a) shows the query graph for Q'. The query decomposition approach uses the heuristic of executing SELECT operations before JOIN or CARTESIAN PRODUCT by identifying **single-variable subqueries** of a query, which involve a single tuple variable and a SELECT condition. These subqueries are executed first, and the projection list of each subquery includes any attributes that are needed in subsequent processing. A multivariable query is broken into a sequence of single-variable subqueries by detachment and tuple substitution. **Detachment** is the process of identifying and separating a subquery that has a single variable in common with the rest of the query. **Tuple substitution** is the process of substituting a single tuple at a time for one of the variables in the query; that is, the variable is instantiated with *actual corresponding tuples* from the database. This generates for an n-variable query a number of simpler (n − 1)-variable queries—one for each tuple substituted.

Detachment is applied before tuple substitution, because it generates two queries from one. Tuple substitution is applied only when detachment is not possible. By using these two operations repeatedly, we can eventually reduce the query into a number of irreducible (constant) components, and combining those gives the query result. For query Q', the following single-variable subqueries are detached and executed first:

Qa:	**RETRIEVE**	**INTO** P' (P.PNUMBER)
	WHERE	P.PLOCATION='Stafford' **AND** P.DNUM=4
Qb:	**RETRIEVE**	**INTO** E' (E.LNAME, E.SSN)
	WHERE	E.BDATE>'DEC-31-1957'

The graph of Figure 16.6(a) is now reduced to the graph of Figure 16.6(b) by removing the constant nodes and including nodes to represent the intermediate relations P' and E' corresponding to the results of the subqueries Qa and Qb. Intermediate relations are represented by **small nodes,** shown as double circles in Figure 16.6(b), to indicate that the number of tuples in these relations has been reduced by applying a select-project query to a relation. When *no more single-variable subqueries can be detached and executed,* and if more than one node remains, the graph represents one or more multivariable queries. Each connected subgraph represents a subquery, and each arc represents a join condition. The Cartesian product operation must be applied to the subqueries corresponding to graph partitions. In our example, the graph in Figure 16.6(b) has only one partition and represents a modified original query Q", which is a three-variable query that refers to the WORKS_ON (W) relation and the intermediate relations P' and E':

> Q":   **RETRIEVE**   (E'.LNAME)
>   **WHERE**   P'.PNUMBER=W.PNO **AND** W.ESSN=E'.SSN

The next step is to apply tuple substitution, which specifies an order on the join and Cartesian product operations based on the nested loop method of executing joins (method J1 of Section 16.1.2, but extended for multiway joins). However, in the actual implementation, method J2 may be used if appropriate access structures exist on the join attributes. The main optimization decision involves choosing which of the relations to put in the outer loop and which in the inner loop. During tuple substitution of this n-variable query, the tuple variable for the outer relation is substituted with one of its tuples at a time during the query evaluation process. For *each tuple* in the outer relation, an $(n - 1)$-variable query, with the outer relation variable substituted for by that constant tuple, is generated, and we may apply detachment followed by tuple substitution recursively on each of these queries.

The main heuristic for picking a relation for tuple substitution is the number of tuples in the relation. A small relation should be picked first. If the reduced graph has more than one small relation, choose the one estimated to have the smallest number of tuples, if this can be determined.*

We illustrate tuple substitution for our example of Figure 16.6(b). Based on the database extension in Figure 6.6, the relation P' will have two PROJECT tuples with PNUMBER values of 10 and 30, while E' will have three EMPLOYEE tuples with SSN values of 999887777, 453453453, and 987987987. If we choose relation P' for tuple substitution, we can replace the graph of Figure 16.6(b) by the two graphs shown in Figure 16.6(c)—one graph for each tuple t in P'. After retrieving the result of each of these graphs, we take their UNION to form the result of the original graph of Figure 16.6(b). For each of the graphs shown in Figure 16.6(c), the node on which tuple substitution was applied can be broken down into one (or more) constant nodes, and we reapply the decomposition algorithm recursively to each graph. At the end of the algorithm, the

---

*In practice, the process of choosing the variable for tuple substitution, called **variable selection,** is more involved. Other factors such as the availability of access paths on relations can be used to estimate the costs of choosing different variables.

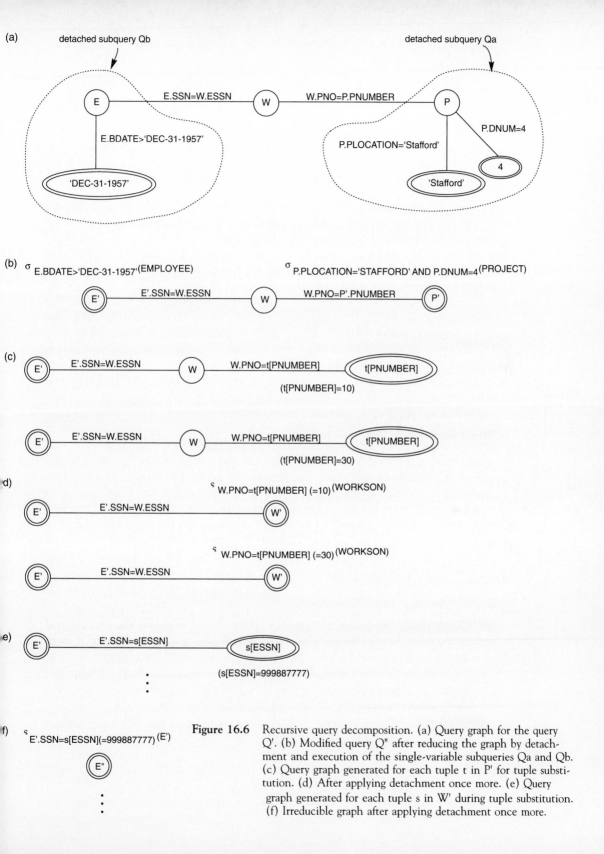

Figure 16.6 Recursive query decomposition. (a) Query graph for the query Q′. (b) Modified query Q″ after reducing the graph by detachment and execution of the single-variable subqueries Qa and Qb. (c) Query graph generated for each tuple t in P′ for tuple substitution. (d) After applying detachment once more. (e) Query graph generated for each tuple s in W′ during tuple substitution. (f) Irreducible graph after applying detachment once more.

result of the original query is produced. Figure 16.6(d) to (f) illustrates the remainder of the process for our query. The results of each graph produced by tuple substitution are "UNIONed" together.

16.3   Using Cost Estimates in Query Optimization*

A query optimizer should not depend solely on heuristic rules; it should also estimate and compare the costs of executing a query using different execution strategies and should choose the strategy with the *lowest cost estimate*. For this approach to work, accurate cost estimates for each execution strategy are required so that different strategies are compared fairly and realistically. In addition, we must limit the number of execution strategies to be considered; otherwise, too much time will be spent making cost estimates for the many possible execution strategies. Hence, this approach is more suitable for **compiled queries** where the optimization is done at compile time and the resulting execution strategy code is stored and executed directly at runtime. For **interpreted queries,** where the entire process shown in Figure 16.1 occurs at runtime, a full-scale optimization may slow down the response time. A more elaborate optimization is indicated for compiled queries; and a partial, less time-consuming optimization works best for interpreted queries.

We call this approach **systematic query optimization,*** and it is similar to traditional optimization techniques according to which a solution to a problem is sought in the solution space while a minimized objective (cost) function is maintained. The cost functions used in query optimization are estimates and not exact cost functions, so the optimization may select a query execution strategy that is not the optimal one. In Section 16.3.1 we discuss the components of query execution cost. In Section 16.3.2 we discuss the type of information needed in cost functions. This information is kept in the DBMS catalog. In Section 16.3.3 we give examples of cost functions for a SELECT operation, and in Section 16.3.4 we discuss cost functions for two-way JOIN operations.

16.3.1   *Cost Components for Query Execution*

The cost of executing a query includes the following components:

1. Access cost to secondary storage: This is the cost of searching for, reading, and writing data blocks that reside on secondary storage, mainly on disk. The cost of searching for records in a file depends on the type of access structures on that file, such as ordering, hashing, and primary or secondary indexes. In addition, factors such as whether the file blocks are allocated contiguously on the same disk cylinder or scattered on the disk affect the access cost.

2. Storage cost: This is the cost of storing any intermediate files that are generated by an execution strategy for the query.

---

*This approach was first used in the optimizer for the SYSTEM R experimental DBMS developed at IBM.

3. Computation cost: This is the cost of performing in-memory operations on the data buffers during query execution. Such operations include searching for records, sorting records, merging records for a join, and performing computations on field values.

4. Communication cost: This is the cost of shipping the query and its results from the database site to the site or terminal where the query originated.

For large databases, the main emphasis is on minimizing the access cost to secondary storage. In fact, many cost functions ignore other factors and compare different query execution strategies in terms of the number of block transfers between disk and main memory. For smaller databases, where most of the data in the files involved in the query can be completely stored in memory, the emphasis should be on minimizing computation cost. In distributed databases, where many sites are involved (see Chapter 23), communication cost must be minimized also. It is difficult to include all the cost components in a (weighted) cost function because of the difficulty of assigning suitable weights to the cost components. That is why many cost functions consider a single factor only—disk access. In the next section we discuss some of the information that is needed for formulating cost functions.

16.3.2 *Catalog Information Used in Cost Functions*

To estimate the costs of various execution strategies, we must keep track of any information that is needed for cost functions. This information may be stored in the DBMS catalog, where it is accessed by the query optimizer. First, we must know the size of each file. For a file whose records are all of the same type, the **number of records (tuples)** r and the **number of blocks** b (or close estimates of them) are needed. The **blocking factor** bfr for the file may also be needed. We must also keep track of the primary access method and the primary access attributes. The file records may be unordered, ordered by an attribute with or without a primary or clustering index, or hashed on a key attribute. Information is kept on all secondary indexes and indexing attributes. The **number of levels** x of each multilevel index (primary, secondary, or clustering) is needed for cost functions that estimate the number of block accesses that occur during query execution. In some cost functions the **number of first-level index blocks** b_{I1} is needed.

Another important parameter is the **number of distinct values** d of an indexing attribute. This allows estimation of the **selection cardinality** s of an attribute, which is the *average* number of records that will satisfy an equality selection condition on that attribute. For a key attribute, s = 1. For a nonkey attribute, by making an assumption that the d distinct values are uniformly distributed among the records, we get

$$s = (r/d)$$

Information such as the number of index levels is easy to maintain because it does not change very often. However, other information may change frequently; for example, the number of records r in a file changes every time a record is inserted or deleted. The query optimizer will need reasonably close but not necessarily completely up-to-the-minute values of these parameters for use in estimating the cost of various execution strategies. In the next two sections we examine how some of these parameters are used in cost functions for a systematic query optimizer.

16.3.3 Examples of Cost Functions for SELECT

We now give cost functions for the selection algorithms S1 to S8 discussed in Section 16.1.1 in terms of *number of block transfers* between memory and disk. These cost functions are estimates that ignore computation time, storage cost, and other factors, as discussed in Section 16.3.1. The cost for method Si is referred to as C_{Si} block accesses.

S1. Linear search (brute force) approach: Search all the file blocks to retrieve all records satisfying the selection condition; hence, C_{S1a} = b. For an equality condition on a key, only half the file blocks are searched on the average before finding the record, so C_{S1b} = (b/2).

S2. Binary search: This search accesses approximately C_{S2} = $\log_2 b$ + $\lceil (s/bfr) \rceil$ − 1 file blocks. This reduces to $\log_2 b$ if the equality condition is on a unique (key) attribute, because s = 1 in this case.

S3. Using a primary index (S3a) or hash key (S3b) to retrieve a single record: For a primary index, retrieve one more block than the number of index levels; hence, C_{S3a} = x + 1. For hashing, the cost function is approximately C_{S3b} = 1.

S4. Using an ordering index to retrieve multiple records: If the comparison condition is >, ≥, <, or ≤ on a key field with an ordering index, roughly half the file records will satisfy the condition. This gives a cost function of C_{S4} = x + (b/2). This is a very rough estimate, and although it may be correct on the average, it may be quite inaccurate in individual cases.

S5. Using a clustering index to retrieve multiple records: Given an equality condition, s records will satisfy the condition, where s is the selection cardinality of the indexing attribute. This means that $\lceil (s/bfr) \rceil$ file blocks will be accessed, giving C_{S5} = x + $\lceil (s/bfr) \rceil$.

S6. Using a secondary (B⁺-tree) index: On an *equality* comparison, s records will satisfy the condition, where s is the selection cardinality of the indexing attribute. However, because the index is nonclustering, each of the records may reside on a different block, so the cost estimate is C_{S6a} = x + s. This reduces to x + 1 for a key indexing attribute. If the comparison condition is >, ≥, <, or ≤ and half the file records are assumed to satisfy the condition, then (very roughly) half the first-level index blocks are accessed, plus half the file records via the index. The cost estimate for this case, very approximately, is C_{S6b} = x + (b_{I1}/2) + (r/2).

S7. Conjunctive selection: Either use S1 or one of the methods S2 to S6 discussed above. In the latter case, use one condition to retrieve the records and then check in the memory buffer whether each retrieved record satisfies the remaining conditions in the conjunction.

S8. Conjunctive selection using a composite index: Same as S3a, S5, or S6a, depending on the type of index.

Example of Using the Cost Functions. In a query optimizer, it is common to enumerate the various possible strategies for executing a query and to estimate the costs for different strategies. An optimization technique, such as dynamic programming, may be used to find the optimal (least) cost estimate efficiently, without having to consider all possible execution strategies. We do not discuss optimization algorithms here; rather, we use a simple example to illustrate how cost estimates may be used. Suppose that the EMPLOYEE file of Figure 6.5 has $r_E = 10,000$ records stored in $b_E = 2000$ disk blocks with blocking factor $bfr_E = 5$ records/block and the following access paths:

1. A clustering index on SALARY, with levels $x_{SALARY} = 3$ and selection cardinality $s_{SALARY} = 20$.

2. A secondary index on the key attribute SSN, with $x_{SSN} = 4$ ($s_{SSN} = 1$).

3. A secondary index on the nonkey attribute DNO, with $x_{DNO} = 2$ and first-level index blocks $b_{I1DNO} = 4$. There are $d_{DNO} = 125$ distinct values for DNO, so the selection cardinality of DNO is $s_{DNO} = (r_E / d_{DNO}) = 80$.

4. A secondary index on SEX, with $x_{SEX} = 1$. There are $d_{SEX} = 2$ values for the sex attribute, so the selection cardinality is $s_{SEX} = (r_E / d_{SEX}) = 5000$.

We illustrate the use of cost functions with the following examples:

(OP1): $\sigma_{SSN=123456789}$(EMPLOYEE)
(OP2): $\sigma_{DNO>5}$(EMPLOYEE)
(OP3): $\sigma_{DNO=5}$(EMPLOYEE)
(OP4): $\sigma_{DNO=5 \text{ AND } SALARY>30000 \text{ AND } SEX=F}$(EMPLOYEE)

The cost of the brute force (linear search) option S1 will be estimated as $C_{S1a} = b_E = 2000$ (for a selection on a nonkey attribute) or $C_{S1b} = (b_E / 2) = 1000$ (average cost for a selection on a key attribute). For OP1 we can use either method S1 or method S6a; the cost estimate for S6a is $C_{S6a} = x_{SSN} + 1 = 4 + 1 = 5$, and it is chosen over method S1, whose average cost is $C_{S1b} = 1000$. For OP2 we can use either method S1 (with estimated cost $C_{S1a} = 2000$) or method S6b (with estimated cost $C_{S6b} = x_{DNO} + (b_{I1DNO} / 2) + (r_E / 2) = 2 + (4/2) + (10,000/2) = 5004$), so we choose the brute force approach for OP2. For OP3 we can use either method S1 (with estimated cost $C_{S1a} = 2000$) or method S6a (with estimated cost $C_{S6a} = x_{DNO} + s_{DNO} = 2 + 80 = 82$), so we choose method S6a.

Finally, consider OP4, which has a conjunctive selection condition. We need to estimate the cost of using any one of the three components of the selection condition to retrieve the records, plus the brute force approach. The latter gives cost estimate $C_{S1a} = 2000$. Using the condition (DNO = 5) first gives the cost estimate $C_{S6a} = 82$. Using the condition (SALARY > 30,000) first gives a cost estimate $C_{S4} = x_{SALARY} + (b_E / 2) = 3 + (2000/2) = 1003$. Using the condition (SEX = F) first gives a cost estimate $C_{S6a} = x_{SEX} + s_{SEX} = 1 + 5000 = 5001$. The optimizer would then choose method S6a on the secondary index on DNO because it has the lowest cost estimate. The condition (DNO = 5) is used to retrieve the records, and the remaining part of the conjunctive condition (SALARY > 30,000 AND SEX = F) is checked for each selected record in memory.

16.3.4 Examples of Cost Functions for JOIN

To develop reasonably accurate cost functions for join operations, we need to have an estimate for the size (number of tuples) of the file that results *after* the join operation.

This is usually kept as a ratio of the size (number of tuples) of the join file to the size of the Cartesian product file, if both are applied to the same input files, and is called the **join selectivity** js. If we denote the number of tuples of a relation R by $|R|$, we have

$$js = |(R \bowtie_c S)| \,/\, |(R \times S)| = |(R \bowtie_c S)| \,/\, (\,|R| * |S|\,)$$

If there is no join condition c, then js = 1 and the join is the same as the Cartesian product. If no tuples from the relations satisfy the join condition, then js = 0. In general, $0 \le js \le 1$. For a join where the condition c is an equality comparison R.A = S.B, we get the following two special cases:

1. If A is a key of R, then $|(R \bowtie_c S)| \le |S|$, so js $\le (1/|R|)$.
2. If B is a key of S, then $|(R \bowtie_c S)| \le |R|$, so js $\le (1/|S|)$.

Having an estimate of the join selectivity for commonly occurring join conditions enables the query optimizer to estimate the size of the resulting file after the join operation, given the sizes of the two input files, by using the formula $|(R \bowtie_c S)| = js * |R| * |S|$. We can now give some sample *approximate* cost functions for estimating the cost of some of the join algorithms given in Section 16.1.2. The join operations are of the form

$$R \bowtie_{A=B} S$$

where A and B are domain-compatible attributes of R and S, respectively. Assume that R has b_R blocks and that S has b_S blocks:

J1. Nested loop approach: Suppose that we use R for the outer loop; then we get the following cost function to estimate the number of block accesses for this method, assuming *two memory buffers*. We assume that the blocking factor for the resulting file is bfr_{RS} and that the join selectivity is known:

$$C_{J1} = b_R + (b_R * b_S) + ((js * |R| * |S|)/bfr_{RS})$$

The last part of the formula is the cost of writing the resulting file to disk. This cost formula can be modified to take into account different numbers of memory buffers, as discussed in Section 16.1.2.

J2. Using an access structure to retrieve the matching record(s): If an index exists for the join attribute B of S with index levels x_B, we can retrieve each record in R and then use the index to retrieve all the matching records t from S that satisfy t[B] = s[A]. The cost depends on the type of index. For a secondary index where s_B is the selection cardinality* for the join attribute B of S, we get

$$C_{J2a} = b_R + (|R| * (x_B + s_B)) + ((js * |R| * |S|)/bfr_{RS})$$

For a clustering index where s_B is the selection cardinality of B, we get

$$C_{J2b} = b_R + (|R| * (x_B + (s_B/bfr_B))) + ((js * |R| * |S|)/bfr_{RS})$$

---

*Selection cardinality was defined as the average number of records that satisfy an equality condition on an attribute, which is the average number of records that have the same value for the attribute and hence will be joined to a single record in the other file.

For a primary index, we get

$$C_{J2c} = b_R + (|R| * (x_B + 1)) + ((js * |R| * |S|)/bfr_{RS})$$

If a hash key exists for one of the two join attributes—say, B of S—we get

$$C_{J2d} = b_R + (|R| * h) + ((js * |R| * |S|)/bfr_{RS})$$

where $h \geq 1$ is the average number of block accesses to retrieve a record, given its hash key value.

J3. Sort–merge join: If the files are already sorted on the join attributes, the cost function for this method is

$$C_{J3a} = b_R + b_S + ((js * |R| * |S|)/bfr_{RS})$$

If we must sort the files, the cost of sorting must be added. We can approximate the sorting cost by $k * b * \log_2 b$ for a file of b blocks, where k is a constant factor. Hence, we get the following cost function:

$$C_{J3b} = k * ((b_R * \log_2 b_R) + (b_S * \log_2 b_S)) + b_R + b_S$$
$$+ ((js * |R| * |S|)/bfr_{RS})$$

Example of Using the Cost Functions. Suppose that we have the EMPLOYEE file described in the example of the previous section, and assume that the DEPARTMENT file of Figure 6.5 consists of $r_D = 125$ records stored in $b_D = 13$ disk blocks. Consider the join operations:

(OP6): EMPLOYEE $\bowtie_{DNO=DNUMBER}$ DEPARTMENT
(OP7): DEPARTMENT $\bowtie_{MGRSSN=SSN}$ EMPLOYEE

Suppose that we have a primary index on DNUMBER of DEPARTMENT with $x_{DNUMBER} = 1$ level and a secondary index on MGRSSN of DEPARTMENT with selection cardinality $s_{MGRSSN} = 1$ and levels $x_{MGRSSN} = 2$. Assume that the join selectivity for OP6 is $js_{OP6} = (1/|DEPARTMENT|) = 1/125$ because DNUMBER is a key of DEPARTMENT. Also assume that the blocking factor for the resulting join file $bfr_{ED} = 4$ records per block. We can estimate the costs for the JOIN operation OP6 using the applicable methods J1 and J2 as follows:

1. Using method J1 with EMPLOYEE as outer loop:

$$C_{J1} = b_E + (b_E * b_D) + ((js_{OP6} * r_E * r_D)/bfr_{ED})$$
$$= 2000 + (2000 * 13) + (((1/125) * 10,000 * 125)/4) = 30,500$$

2. Using method J1 with DEPARTMENT as outer loop:

$$C_{J1} = b_D + (b_E * b_D) + ((js_{OP6} * r_E * r_D)/bfr_{ED})$$
$$= 13 + (13 * 2000) + (((1/125) * 10,000 * 125)/4) = 28,513$$

3. Using method J2 with EMPLOYEE as outer loop:

$$C_{J2c} = b_E + (r_E * (x_{DNUMBER} + 1)) + ((js_{OP6} * r_E * r_D)/bfr_{ED})$$
$$= 2000 + (10,000 * 2) + (((1/125) * 10,000 * 125)/4) = 24,500$$

4. Using method J2 with DEPARTMENT as outer loop:

$$C_{J2a} = b_D + (r_D * (x_{DNO} + s_{DNO})) + ((js_{OP6} * r_E * r_D)/bfr_{ED})$$
$$= 13 + (125 * (2 + 80)) + (((1/125) * 10,000 * 125)/4) = 12,763$$

Case 4 has the lowest cost estimate and will be chosen. Notice that if 14 memory buffers (or more) were available for executing the join instead of just 2, 13 of them could be used to hold the entire DEPARTMENT relation in memory, and the cost for case 2 could be drastically reduced to just $b_E + b_D + ((js_{OP6} * r_E * r_D)/bfr_{ED})$ or 4513, as discussed in Section 16.1.2. As an exercise, the reader should perform a similar analysis for OP7.

16.4 Semantic Query Optimization*

A different approach to query optimization, called **semantic query optimization**, has been suggested. This technique, which may be used in combination with the techniques discussed previously, uses constraints specified on the database schema in order to modify one query into another query that is more efficient to execute. We will not discuss this approach in detail but only illustrate it with an example. Consider the SQL query:

```
SELECT    E.LNAME, M.LNAME
FROM      EMPLOYEE E M
WHERE     E.SUPERSSN=M.SSN AND E.SALARY>M.SALARY
```

This query retrieves the names of employees who earn more than their supervisors. Suppose that we had a constraint on the database schema that stated that no employee can earn more than his or her direct supervisor. If the semantic query optimizer checks for the existence of this constraint, it need not execute the query at all because it knows that the result of the query will be empty. Techniques known as **theorem proving** can be used for this purpose. This may save considerable time if the constraints checking can be done efficiently. However, searching through many constraints to find ones that are applicable to a given query and that may semantically optimize it can also be quite time-consuming. With the advent of knowledge-based and expert systems, semantic query optimization techniques may eventually be incorporated into the DBMSs of the future.

16.5 Summary

In this chapter we gave an overview of the techniques used by DBMSs in processing and optimizing high-level queries. In Section 16.1 we discussed how various relational algebra operations may be executed by a DBMS. We saw that some operations, particularly SELECT and JOIN, may have many execution options. We also discussed how access routines to the database can implement combinations of operations.

In Section 16.2 we discussed heuristic approaches to query optimization, which use heuristic rules to improve the efficiency of query execution. In Section 16.2.1 we showed how a query tree that represents a relational algebra expression can be heuristically optimized by reorganizing the tree nodes. We also gave equivalence-preserving transformation rules that may be applied to a query tree. In Section 16.2.2 we discussed the query graph notation, which represents a relational calculus expression, and showed how it may be optimized and executed by a technique called *query decomposition*. This technique breaks up a query into simpler ones and includes heuristics to order the execution of query operations.

In Section 16.3 we discussed the systematic or cost estimation approach to query optimization. We showed how cost functions are developed for some access routines and how these cost functions are used to estimate the cost of different execution strategies. Finally, we mentioned the technique of semantic query optimization in Section 16.4.

Review Questions

16.1. What is meant by the term *access routine*? Why is it important to implement several relational operations in a single access routine?

16.2. Discuss the different algorithms for implementing each of the following relational operators and the circumstances under which each algorithm can be used: SELECT, JOIN, PROJECT, UNION, INTERSECT, MINUS, XPROD.

16.3. What is meant by the term *heuristic optimization*? Discuss the main heuristics that are applied during query optimization.

16.4. How does a query tree represent a relational algebra expression? What is meant by an *execution* of a query tree? Discuss the rules for transformation of query trees, and identify when each rule should be applied during optimization.

16.5. How do query graphs represent relational calculus expressions? Discuss the query decomposition approach to optimizing and executing a query graph.

16.6. What is meant by *systematic query optimization*?

16.7. Discuss the cost components for a cost function that is used to estimate query execution cost. Which cost components are used most often as the basis for cost functions?

16.8. Discuss the different types of parameters that are used in cost functions. Where is this information kept?

16.9. List the cost functions for the SELECT and JOIN methods discussed in Section 16.1.

16.10. What is meant by semantic query optimization? How does it differ from other query optimization techniques?

Exercises

16.11. Consider SQL queries Q1, Q8, Q1B, Q4, and Q27 from Chapter 7.

a. Draw at least two query trees that can represent *each* of these queries. Under what circumstances would you use each of your query trees?

   b. Draw the initial query tree for each of these queries; then show how the query tree is optimized by the algorithm outlined in Section 16.2.1.

   c. For each query, compare your own query trees of part a and the initial and final query trees of part b.

16.12. Draw the query graph for each of the QUEL queries Q0, Q1, Q3', Q8, Q1D, and Q27 from Chapter 9; then show how the query graph is optimized and executed by the query decomposition algorithm of Section 16.2.2.

16.13. Develop cost functions for the PROJECT, UNION, INTERSECTION, SET DIFFERENCE, and CARTESIAN PRODUCT algorithms discussed in Sections 16.1.3 and 16.1.4.

16.14. Develop cost functions for an algorithm that consists of two SELECTs, a JOIN, and a final PROJECT, in terms of the cost functions for the individual operations.

16.15. Calculate the cost functions for different options of executing the JOIN operation OP7 discussed in Section 16.3.4.

16.16. Develop formulas for the hybrid hash join algorithm for calculating the size of the buffer for the first bucket. Develop more accurate cost estimation formulas for the algorithm.

16.17. Estimate the cost of operations OP6 and OP7, using the formulas developed in Exercise 16.16.

Selected Bibliography

A recent survey (Graefe 1993) discusses query processing in database systems and includes an extensive bibliography. A survey paper by Jarke and Koch (1984) gives a taxonomy of query optimization and includes a bibliography of work in this area. An early reference to query optimization is Rothnie (1975), which describes optimization of two-variable queries in the DAMAS experimental DBMS. Palermo (1974) shows how relational calculus expressions can be converted into relational algebra and then optimized. A detailed algorithm for relational algebra optimization is given by Smith and Chang (1975). Hall (1976) discusses relational algebra transformations in the PRTV experimental DBMS.

The decomposition algorithm for QUEL, used in the experimental INGRES DBMS, was presented by Wong and Youssefi (1976); and Youssefi and Wong (1979) discusses its performance. Whang (1985) discusses query optimization in OBE (Office-By-Example), which is a system based on QBE.

Systematic optimization using cost functions was used in the SYSTEM R experimental DBMS and is discussed in Astrahan et al. (1976). Selinger et al. (1979) discusses the optimization of multiway joins in SYSTEM R. Join algorithms are discussed in Gotlieb (1975), Blasgen and Eswaran (1976), and Whang et al. (1982). Hashing algorithms for implementing joins are described and analyzed in DeWitt et al. (1984), Bratbergsengen (1984), Shapiro (1986), Kitsuregawa et al. (1989), and Blakeley and Martin (1990), among others. Kim (1982) discusses transformations of nested SQL queries into canonical representations. Optimization of aggregate functions is discussed in Klug (1982) and Muralikrishna (1992).

Salzberg et al. (1990) describes a fast external sorting algorithm, and Lipton et al. (1990) discusses selectivity estimation. Yao (1979) gives a comparative analysis of many known query processing algorithms. Kim et al. (1985) discusses advanced topics in query optimization. Semantic query optimization is discussed in King (1981) and Malley and Zdonick (1986). More recent work on semantic query optimization is reported in Chakravarthy et al. (1990), Shenoy and Ozsoyoglu

(1989), and Siegel et al. (1992). Aho et al. (1979*a*) discusses a technique of optimization for relational calculus queries with only equality comparisons, ANDs, and existential quantifiers based on tableaus, which are tables where columns represent attributes and rows represent conditions. Ullman (1982) discusses tableaus. Sagiv and Yannakakis (1980) extend tableaus to handle UNION and SET DIFFERENCE.

Beck et al. (1989) discusses a technique called classification, which can be used to optimize queries on a semantic data model. Recently, there has been increasing interest in parallel algorithms for executing queries, such as the work by Mikkilineni and Su (1988).

CHAPTER 17

Transaction Processing Concepts

In this chapter we present the concept of an atomic transaction; this is used to represent a logical unit of database processing. We discuss the concurrency control problem, which occurs when multiple transactions submitted by various users interfere with one another in a way that produces incorrect results. We also discuss recovery from transaction failures. Section 17.1 informally discusses why concurrency control and recovery are necessary in a database system. Section 17.2 introduces the concept of an **atomic transaction** and discusses additional concepts related to transaction processing in database systems. Section 17.3 presents the concepts of atomicity, consistency, isolation, and durability—the so-called **ACID properties** that are considered desirable in transactions. Section 17.4 introduces the concept of **schedules** (or **histories**) of executing transactions and characterizes the recoverability of schedules. Section 17.5 discusses the concept of serializability of concurrent transaction executions, which can be used to define correct execution sequences of concurrent transactions. In Chapter 18 we discuss concurrency control techniques. Chapter 19 presents an overview of recovery techniques.

17.1 Introduction to Transaction Processing

In this section we informally introduce the concepts of concurrent execution of transactions and recovery from transaction failures. In Section 17.1.1 we compare single-user and multiuser database systems and show how concurrent execution of transactions can take place in multiuser systems. Section 17.1.2 presents a simple model of transaction execution, based on read and write database operations, that is used to formalize concurrency control and recovery concepts. Section 17.1.3 shows by informal examples why concurrency control techniques are needed in multiuser systems. Finally, Section 17.1.4 discusses why techniques are needed to permit recovery from failure by presenting the different ways in which transactions can fail while executing.

17.1.1 *Single-User Versus Multiuser Systems*

One criterion for classifying a database system is by the number of users who can use the system *concurrently*—that is, at the same time. A DBMS is **single-user** if at most one user at a time can use the system, and it is **multiuser** if many users can use the system concurrently. Single-user DBMSs are mostly restricted to some microcomputer systems; most other DBMSs are multiuser. For example, an airline reservations system is used by hundreds of travel agents and reservation clerks concurrently. Systems in banks, insurance agencies, stock exchanges, and the like are also operated by many users who submit transactions concurrently to the system.

Multiple users can use computer systems simultaneously because of the concept of **multiprogramming,** which allows the computer to process multiple programs (or transactions) at the same time. If only a single central processing unit (CPU) exists, it can actually process at most one program at a time. However, **multiprogramming operating systems** execute some commands from one program, then suspend that program and execute some commands from the next program, and so on. A program is resumed at the point where it was suspended when it gets its turn to use the CPU again. Hence, concurrent execution of the programs is actually **interleaved,** as illustrated in Figure 17.1 (same as Figure 4.3), which shows two programs A and B executing concurrently in an interleaved fashion. Interleaving keeps the CPU busy when an executing program requires an input or output (I/O) operation, such as reading a block from disk. The CPU is switched to execute another program rather than remaining idle during I/O time.

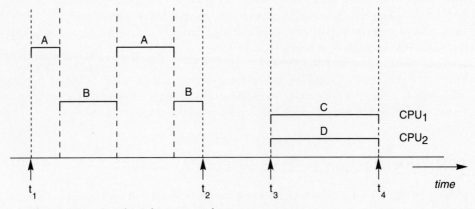

Figure 17.1   Interleaved versus simultaneous concurrency.

If the computer system has multiple hardware processors (CPUs), **simultaneous** processing of multiple programs is possible, leading to simultaneous rather than interleaved concurrency, as illustrated by programs C and D in Figure 17.1. Most of the theory concerning concurrency control in databases is developed in terms of interleaved concurrency, although it may be adapted to simultaneous concurrency. For the remainder of this chapter, we assume the *interleaved model of concurrent execution*.

In a multiuser DBMS, the stored data items are the primary resources that may be accessed concurrently by user programs, which are constantly retrieving information from and modifying the database. The *execution of a program* that accesses or changes the contents of the database is called a **transaction**.

17.1.2   *Read and Write Operations of a Transaction*

We deal with transactions at the level of data items and disk blocks for the purpose of discussing concurrency control and recovery techniques. At this level, the database access operations that a transaction can include are:

- **read_item(X)**: Reads a database item named X into a program variable. To simplify our notation, we assume that *the program variable is also named* X.

- **write_item(X)**: Writes the value of program variable X into the database item named X.

As we discussed in Chapter 4, the basic unit of data transfer from the disk to the computer main memory is one block. In general, a data item will be the field of some record in the database, although it may be a larger unit such as a record or even a whole block. Executing a read_item(X) command includes the following steps:

1. Find the address of the disk block that contains item X.
2. Copy that disk block into a buffer in main memory (if that disk block is not already in some main memory buffer).
3. Copy item X from the buffer to the program variable named X.

Executing a write_item(X) command includes the following steps:

1. Find the address of the disk block that contains item X.
2. Copy that disk block into a buffer in main memory (if that disk block is not already in some main memory buffer).
3. Copy item X from the program variable named X into its correct location in the buffer.
4. Store the updated block from the buffer back to disk (either immediately or at some later point in time).

Step 4 is the one that actually updates the database on disk. In some cases the buffer is not immediately stored to disk, in case additional changes are to be made to the buffer. Usually, the decision about when to store back a modified disk block that is in a main memory buffer is handled by the recovery manager or the operating system.

(a) read_item (X);   (b) read_item (X);
     X:=X-N;   X:=X+M;
     write_item (X);   write_item (X);
     read_item (Y);
     Y:=Y+N;
     write_item (Y);

Figure 17.2   Two sample transactions. (a) Transaction T_1.
(b) Transaction T_2.

A transaction will include read_item and write_item operations to access the database. Figure 17.2 shows examples of two very simple transactions. Concurrency control and recovery mechanisms are mainly concerned with the database access commands in a transaction.

Transactions submitted by the various users may execute concurrently and may access and update the same database items. If this concurrent execution is uncontrolled, it may lead to problems such as an *inconsistent database*. In the next section we *informally* introduce three of the problems that may occur when concurrent transactions execute in an uncontrolled manner.

17.1.3 Why Concurrency Control Is Needed

Several problems can occur when concurrent transactions execute in an uncontrolled manner. We illustrate some of these problems by referring to a simple airline reservation database in which a record is stored for each airline flight. Each record includes the number of reserved seats on that flight as a *named data item*, among other information. Figure 17.2(a) shows a transaction T_1 that *cancels* N reservations from one flight whose number of reserved seats is stored in the database item named X and *reserves* the same number of seats on another flight whose number of reserved seats is stored in the database item named Y. Figure 17.2(b) shows a simpler transaction T_2 that just *reserves* M seats on the first flight referenced in transaction T_1. To simplify our example, we do not show additional portions of the transactions, such as checking whether a flight has enough seats available before reserving additional seats.

When a database program is written, it has the flight numbers, their dates, and the number of seats to be booked as parameters; hence, the same program can be used to execute many transactions, each with different flights and numbers of seats to be booked. For concurrency control purposes, a transaction is a *particular execution* of a program on a specific date, flight, and number of seats. In Figure 17.2(a) and (b), the transactions T_1 and T_2 are *specific executions* of the programs that refer to the specific flights whose numbers of seats are stored in data items X and Y in the database. We now discuss the types of problems we may encounter with these two transactions.

The Lost Update Problem. This occurs when two transactions that access the same database items have their operations interleaved in a way that makes the value of some database item incorrect. Suppose that transactions T_1 and T_2 are submitted at approximately the same time, and suppose that their operations are interleaved by the operating system, as shown in Figure 17.3(a); then the final value of item X is incorrect, because T_2 reads the value of X *before* T_1 changes it in the database, and hence *the updated value resulting from T_1 is lost.* For example, if X = 80 at the start (originally there were 80 reservations on the flight), N = 5 (T_1 cancels 5 seats on the flight corresponding to X and reserves them on the flight corresponding to Y), and M = 4 (T_2 reserves 4 seats on X), the final result should be X = 79; but in the schedule of Figure 17.3(a), it is X = 84 because the update that canceled 5 seats was *lost.*

The Temporary Update (or Dirty Read) Problem. This occurs when one transaction updates a database item and then the transaction fails for some reason (see Section 17.1.4). The updated item is accessed by another transaction before it is changed back to its original value. Figure 17.3(b) shows an example where T_1 updates item X and then

(a)

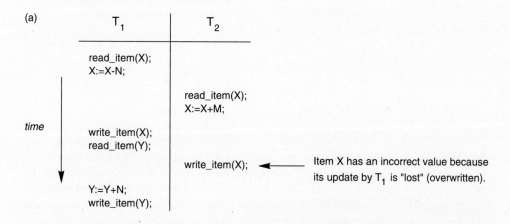

(b)

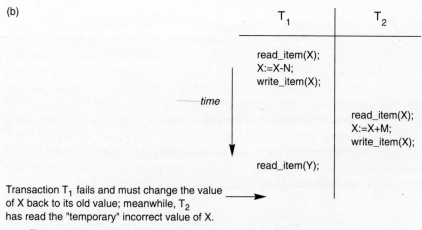

Figure 17.3 Some problems that occur when concurrent execution is uncontrolled. (a) The lost update problem. (b) The temporary update problem. *(continued on next page)*

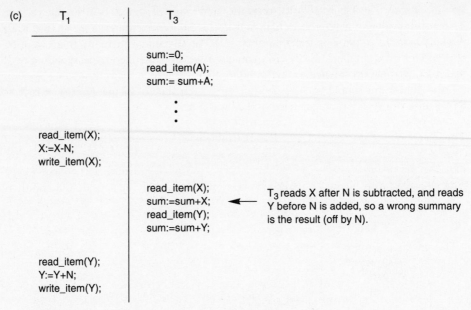

Figure 17.3 *(continued)* (c) The incorrect summary problem.

fails before completion, so the system must change X back to its original value. Before it can do so, however, transaction T_2 reads the "temporary" value of X, which will not be recorded permanently in the database because of the failure of T_1. The value of item X that is read by T_2 is called *dirty data*, because it has been created by a transaction that has not completed and committed yet; hence, this problem is also known as the *dirty read* problem.

The Incorrect Summary Problem. If one transaction is calculating an aggregate summary function on a number of records while other transactions are updating some of these records, the aggregate function may calculate some values before they are updated and others after they are updated. For example, suppose that a transaction T_3 is calculating the total number of reservations on all the flights; meanwhile, transaction T_1 is executing. If the interleaving of operations shown in Figure 17.3(c) occurs, the result of T_3 will be off by an amount N because T_3 reads the value of X *after* N seats have been subtracted from it but reads the value of Y *before* those N seats have been added to it.

Another problem that may occur is the **unrepeatable read,** where a transaction T reads an item twice, and the item is changed by another transaction T′ between the two reads. Hence, T receives *different values* for its two reads of the same item.

17.1.4 *Why Recovery Is Needed*

Whenever a transaction is submitted to a DBMS for execution, the system is responsible for making sure that either (a) all the operations in the transaction are completed successfully and their effect is recorded permanently in the database, or (b) the transaction has no effect whatsoever on the database or on any other transactions. The DBMS must not permit some operations of a transaction T to be applied to the database while other operations of T are not. This may happen if a transaction **fails** after executing some of its operations but before executing all of them.

Types of Failures. There are several possible reasons for a transaction to fail in the middle of execution:

1. A computer failure (system crash): A hardware or software error occurs in the computer system during transaction execution. If the hardware crashes, the contents of the computer's internal memory may be lost.

2. A transaction or system error: Some operation in the transaction may cause it to fail, such as integer overflow or division by zero. Transaction failure may also occur because of erroneous parameter values or because of a logical programming error. In addition, the user may interrupt the transaction during its execution on purpose—for example, by issuing a control-C in a VAX/VMS or UNIX environment.

3. Local errors or exception conditions detected by the transaction: During transaction execution, certain conditions may occur that necessitate cancellation of the transaction. For example, data for the transaction may not be found. A condition, such as insufficient account balance in a banking database, may cause a transaction, such as a fund withdrawal from that account, to be canceled. This may be done by a programmed ABORT in the transaction itself.

4. Concurrency control enforcement: The concurrency control method may decide to abort the transaction, to be restarted later, because it violates serializability or because several transactions are in a state of deadlock (see Chapter 18).

5. Disk failure: Some disk blocks may lose their data because of a read or write malfunction or because of a disk read/write head crash. This may happen during a read or a write operation of the transaction.

6. Physical problems and catastrophes: This refers to an endless list of problems that includes power or air-conditioning failure, fire, theft, sabotage, overwriting disks or tapes by mistake, and mounting of a wrong tape by the operator.

Failures of types 1, 2, 3, and 4 are more common than those of types 5 or 6. Whenever a failure of type 1 through 4 occurs, the system must keep sufficient information to recover from the failure. Disk failure or other catastrophic failures of type 5 or 6 do not happen frequently; if they do occur, it is a major task to recover from these types of failure. We discuss concepts and techniques for recovery from failure in Chapter 19.

The concept of an atomic transaction is fundamental to many techniques for concurrency control and recovery from failures. In the next section we present the transaction concept and discuss why it is important.

17.2 Transaction and System Concepts

As mentioned earlier, the *execution of a program* that includes database access operations is called a **database transaction** or simply a **transaction**. If the database operations in a transaction do not update any data in the database but only retrieve data, the transaction is called a **read-only transaction**. In this chapter we are mainly interested in transactions that do some updates to the database, so the word *transaction* refers to a program execution that *updates the database* unless we explicitly state otherwise.

17.2.1 *Transaction States and Additional Operations*

A transaction is an atomic unit of work that is either completed in its entirety or not done at all. For recovery purposes, the system needs to keep track of when the transaction starts, terminates, and commits or aborts (see below). Hence, the recovery manager keeps track of the following operations:

- BEGIN_TRANSACTION: This marks the beginning of transaction execution.
- READ or WRITE: These specify read or write operations on the database items that are executed as part of a transaction.
- END_TRANSACTION: This specifies that READ and WRITE transaction operations have ended and marks the end limit of transaction execution. However, at this point it may be necessary to check whether the changes introduced by the transaction can be permanently applied to the database (committed) or whether the transaction has to be aborted because it violates concurrency control or for some other reason.
- COMMIT_TRANSACTION: This signals a *successful end* of the transaction so that any changes (updates) executed by the transaction can be safely **committed** to the database and will not be undone.
- ROLLBACK (or ABORT): This signals that the transaction has *ended unsuccessfully*, so that any changes or effects that the transaction may have applied to the database must be *undone*.

In addition to the preceding operations, some recovery techniques require additional operations that include the following:

- UNDO: Similar to rollback except that it applies to a single operation rather than to a whole transaction.
- REDO: This specifies that certain *transaction operations* must be *redone* to ensure that all the operations of a committed transaction have been applied successfully to the database.

Figure 17.4 shows a state transition diagram that describes how a transaction moves through its execution states. A transaction goes into an **active** state immediately after it starts execution, where it can issue READ and WRITE operations. When the transaction ends, it moves to the **partially committed** state. At this point, some concurrency control techniques require that certain *checks* be made to ensure that the transaction did not

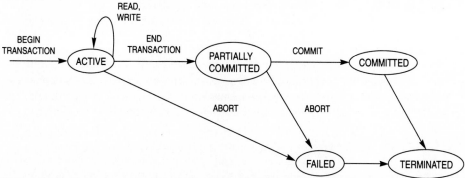

Figure 17.4 State transition diagram for transaction execution.

interfere with other executing transactions. In addition, some recovery protocols need to ensure that a system failure will not result in an inability to record the changes of the transaction permanently (usually by recording changes in a system log, discussed in the next subsection). Once both checks are successful, the transaction is said to have reached its commit point and enters the **committed state**. Commit points are discussed in more detail in Section 17.2.3. Once a transaction enters the committed state, it has concluded its execution successfully.

However, a transaction can go to the **failed** state if one of the checks fails or if it is aborted during its active state. The transaction may then have to be rolled back to undo the effect of its WRITE operations on the database. The **terminated** state corresponds to the transaction leaving the system. Failed or aborted transactions may be *restarted* later, either automatically or after being resubmitted, as *brand new* transactions.

17.2.2 *The System Log*

To be able to recover from transaction failures, the system maintains a **log** (sometimes called a **journal**). The log keeps track of all transaction operations that affect the values of database items. This information may be needed to permit recovery from transaction failures. The log is kept on disk, so it is not affected by any type of failure except for disk or catastrophic failure. In addition, the log is periodically backed up to archival storage (tape) to guard against such catastrophic failures. We now list the types of entries that are written to the log and the action each performs. In these entries, T refers to a unique **transaction-id** that is generated automatically by the system and is used to identify each transaction:

1. [start_transaction,T]: Records that transaction T has started execution.
2. [write_item,T,X,old_value,new_value]: Records that transaction T has changed the value of database item X from old_value to new_value.
3. [read_item,T,X]: Records that transaction T has read the value of database item X.

4. [commit,T]: Records that transaction T has completed successfully, and affirms that its effect can be committed (recorded permanently) to the database.

5. [abort,T]: Records that transaction T has been aborted.

As we shall see in Chapter 19, protocols for recovery that avoid cascading rollbacks do not require that READ operations be written to the system log, whereas other protocols require these entries for recovery. In the former case, the overhead of recording operations in the log is reduced, since fewer operations—only WRITEs—are recorded in the log. In addition, strict protocols require simpler WRITE entries that do not include new_value (see Section 17.4).

Notice that we assume here that transactions cannot be nested. We also assume that *all* permanent changes to the database occur within transactions, so the notion of recovery from a transaction failure amounts to either undoing or redoing the *recoverable* transaction operations individually from the log. If the system crashes, we can recover to a consistent database state by examining the log and using one of the techniques described in Chapter 19. Because the log contains a record of every WRITE operation that changes the value of some database item, it is possible to **undo** the effect of these WRITE operations of a transaction T by tracing backward through the log and resetting all items changed by a WRITE operation of T to their old_values. We can also **redo** the effect of the WRITE operations of a transaction T by tracing forward through the log and setting all items changed by a WRITE operation of T to their new_values. Redoing the operations of a transaction may be required if all its updates are recorded in the log but a failure occurs before we can be sure that all the new_values have been written permanently in the actual database.

17.2.3 *Commit Point of a Transaction*

A transaction T reaches its **commit point** when all its operations that access the database have been executed successfully *and* the effect of all the transaction operations on the database has been recorded in the log. Beyond the commit point, the transaction is said to be **committed,** and its effect is assumed to be *permanently recorded* in the database. The transaction then writes an entry [commit,T] into the log. If a system failure occurs, we search back in the log for all transactions T that have written a [start_transaction,T] entry into the log but have not written their [commit,T] entry yet; these transactions may have to be *rolled back* to undo their effect on the database during the recovery process. Transactions that have written their commit entry in the log must also have recorded all their WRITE operations in the log; otherwise they would not be committed, so their effect on the database can be *redone* from the log entries.

Notice that the log file must be kept on disk. As discussed in Chapter 4, updating a disk file involves copying the appropriate block of the file from disk to a buffer in main memory, updating the buffer in main memory, and copying the buffer back from main memory to disk. It is common to keep one block of the log file in main memory until it is filled with log entries and then to write it back to disk only once, rather than writing it to disk every time a log entry is added. This saves the overhead of multiple disk writes of the same file block. At the time of a system crash, only the log entries that have been *written back to disk* are considered in the recovery process because the contents of main memory may be lost. Hence, *before* a transaction reaches its commit point, any portion of the log that has not been written to the disk yet must now be written to the disk. This process is called **force-writing** the log file before committing a transaction.

17.2.4 *Checkpoints in the System Log*

Another type of entry in the log is called a **checkpoint**.* A [checkpoint] record is written into the log periodically at that point when the system writes out to the database on disk the effect of all WRITE operations of committed transactions. Hence, all transactions that have their [commit,T] entries in the log before a [checkpoint] entry do not need to have their WRITE operations *redone* in case of a system crash.

The recovery manager of a DBMS must decide at what intervals to take a checkpoint. The interval may be measured in time—say, every m minutes—or the number t of committed transactions since the last checkpoint, where the values of m or t are system parameters. Taking a checkpoint consists of the following actions:

1. Suspend execution of transactions temporarily.
2. Force-write all update operations of committed transactions from main memory buffers to disk.
3. Write a [checkpoint] record to the log, and force-write the log to disk.
4. Resume executing transactions.

A checkpoint record in the log may also include additional information, such as a list of active transaction ids, and the locations (addresses) of the first and most recent (last) records in the log for each active transaction. This can facilitate undoing transaction operations in the event that a transaction must be rolled back.

17.3 Desirable Properties of Transactions

Atomic transactions should possess several properties. These are often called the ACID **properties,** and they should be enforced by the concurrency control and recovery methods of the DBMS. The following are the ACID properties:

1. **Atomicity**: A transaction is an atomic unit of processing; it is either performed in its entirety or not performed at all.
2. **Consistency preservation**: A correct execution of the transaction must take the database from one consistent state to another.
3. **Isolation**: A transaction should not make its updates visible to other transactions until it is committed; this property, when enforced strictly, solves the temporary update problem and makes cascading rollbacks of transactions unnecessary (see Chapter 19).

---

*The term *checkpoint* has been used to describe more restrictive situations in some systems, such as DB2. It has also been used in the literature to describe altogether different concepts.

4. **Durability or permanency**: Once a transaction changes the database and the changes are committed, these changes must never be lost because of subsequent failure.

The atomicity property requires that we execute a transaction to completion. It is the responsibility of the recovery method to ensure atomicity. If a transaction fails to complete for some reason, such as a system crash in the midst of transaction execution, the recovery method must undo any effects of the transaction on the database.

The consistency preservation property is generally considered to be the responsibility of the programmers who write the database programs or of the DBMS module that enforces integrity constraints. Recall that a **database state** is a collection of all the stored data items (values) in the database at a given point in time. A **consistent state** of the database satisfies the constraints specified in the schema as well as any other constraints that should hold on the database. A database program should be written in a way that guarantees that, if the database is in a consistent state before executing the transaction, it will be in a consistent state after the *complete* execution of the transaction, assuming that *no interference with other transactions* occurs.

Isolation is enforced by the currency control method. There have been attempts to define the *level* or *degree of isolation* of a transaction. A transaction is said to have degree 0 (zero) isolation if it does not overwrite the dirty reads of higher-degree transactions. A degree 1 (one) isolation transaction has no lost updates; and degree 2 isolation has no lost updates and no dirty reads. Finally, degree 3 isolation (also called *true isolation*) has, in addition to degree 2 properties, repeatable reads. The durability property is the responsibility of the recovery method.

17.4 Schedules and Recoverability

When transactions are executing concurrently in an interleaved fashion, the order of execution of operations from the various transactions forms what is known as a transaction **schedule** (or **history**). In this section, we first define the concept of schedule, and then we characterize the types of schedules that facilitate recovery when failures occur. In Section 17.5, we characterize schedules in terms of the interference of participating transactions, leading to the concepts of serializability and serializable schedules.

17.4.1 *Schedules (Histories) of Transactions*

A **schedule** (or **history**) S of n transactions $T_1, T_2, \ldots, T_n$ is an ordering of the operations of the transactions subject to the constraint that, for each transaction T_i that participates in S, the operations of T_i in S must appear in the same order in which they occur in T_i. Note, however, that operations from other transactions T_j can be interleaved with the operations of T_i in S. For now, consider the order of operations in S to be a *total ordering*, although it is possible to deal with schedules whose operations form *partial orders* (as we discuss later).

Figure 17.3(a) and (b) shows two possible schedules for the transactions T_1 and T_2. For the purpose of recovery and concurrency control, we are mainly interested in the read_item and write_item operations of the transactions, as well as the commit and abort operations. A shorthand notation for describing a schedule uses the symbols r, w, c, and a for the operations read_item, write_item, commit, and abort, respectively, and appends as subscript the transaction id (transaction number) to each operation in the schedule. In this notation, the database item X that is read or written follows the r and w operations in parentheses. For example, the schedule of Figure 17.3(a), which we shall call S_a, can be written as follows when augmented with the commit operations:

S_a: $r_1(X)$; $r_2(X)$; $w_1(X)$; $r_1(Y)$; $w_2(X)$; c_2; $w_1(Y)$; c_1;

Similarly, the schedule for Figure 17.3(b), which we call S_b, can be written as follows, if we assume that transaction T_1 aborted after its read_item(Y) operation:

S_b: $r_1(X)$; $w_1(X)$; $r_2(X)$; $w_2(X)$; c_2; $r_1(Y)$; a_1;

Two operations in a schedule are said to **conflict** if they belong to different transactions, if they access the same item X, and if one of the two operations is a write_item(X). For example, in schedule S_a, the operations $r_1(X)$ and $w_2(X)$ conflict, as do the operations $r_2(X)$ and $w_1(X)$, and the operations $w_1(X)$ and $w_2(X)$. However, the operations $r_1(X)$ and $r_2(X)$ do not conflict, since they are both read operations; and the operations $w_2(X)$ and $w_1(Y)$ do not conflict, because they operate on distinct data items X and Y.

A schedule S of n transactions T_1, T_2, ..., T_n, is said to be a **complete schedule** if the following conditions hold:

1. The operations in S are exactly those operations in T_1, T_2, ..., T_n, including a commit or abort operation as the last operation for each transaction in the schedule.

2. For any pair of operations from the same transaction T_i, their order of appearance in S is the same as their order of appearance in T_i.

3. For any two conflicting operations, one of the two must occur before the other in the schedule.

The preceding conditions allow for two *nonconflicting operations* to occur in the schedule without defining which occurs first, thus leading to the definition of a schedule as a **partial order** of the operations in the n transactions. However, a total order must be specified in the schedule for any pair of conflicting operations (condition 3) and for any pair of operations from the same transaction (condition 2). Condition 1 simply states that all operations in the transactions must appear in the complete schedule. Since every transaction has either committed or aborted, a complete schedule will not contain any active transactions.

In general, it is difficult to encounter complete schedules in a transaction-processing system, because new transactions are continually being submitted to the system. Hence, it is useful to define the concept of the **committed projection** C(S) of a schedule S, which includes only the operations in S that belong to committed transactions—that is, transactions T_i whose commit operation c_i is in S.

17.4.2 *Characterizing Schedules Based on Recoverability*

For some schedules it is easy to recover from transaction failures, whereas for other schedules the recovery process can be quite involved. Hence, it is important to characterize the types of schedules for which recovery is possible, as well as those for which recovery is relatively simple. First, we would like to ensure that, once a transaction T is committed, it should *never be necessary* to roll back T. The schedules that meet this criterion are called *recoverable schedules*.

A schedule S is said to be **recoverable** if no transaction T in S commits until all transactions T' that have written an item that T reads have committed. A transaction T is said to **read from** transaction T' in a schedule S if some item X is first written by T' and later read by T. In the schedule S, T' should not have aborted before T reads item X, and there should be no transactions that write X after T' writes it and before T reads it (unless those transactions, if any, have aborted before T reads X).

The schedule S_a given in the preceding section is recoverable. However, consider the two (partial) schedules S_c and S_d that follow:

S_c: $r_1(X)$; $w_1(X)$; $r_2(X)$; $r_1(Y)$; $w_2(X)$; c_2; a_1;
S_d: $r_1(X)$; $w_1(X)$; $r_2(X)$; $r_1(Y)$; $w_2(X)$; $w_1(Y)$; c_1; c_2;

S_c is not recoverable, because T_2 reads item X from T_1, and then T_2 commits before T_1 commits. If T_1 aborts after the c_2 operation in S_c, then the value of X that T_2 read is no longer valid and T_2 must be aborted *after it had already committed*, leading to a schedule that is not recoverable. For the schedule to be recoverable, the c_2 operation in S_c must be postponed until after T_1 commits, as shown in S_d.

In a recoverable schedule, no committed transaction ever needs to be rolled back. However, it is still possible for a phenomenon known as *cascading rollback* (or *cascading abort*) to occur, where an uncommitted transaction has to be rolled back because it read an item from a transaction that failed. This is illustrated in schedule S_e, where transaction T_2 has to be rolled back because it read item X from T_1, and T_1 then aborted:

S_e: $r_1(X)$; $w_1(X)$; $r_2(X)$; $r_1(Y)$; $w_2(X)$; $w_1(Y)$; a_1;

Because cascading rollback can be quite time-consuming—since numerous transactions can be rolled back (see Chapter 19)—it is important to characterize the schedules where this phenomenon is guaranteed not to occur. A schedule is said to **avoid cascading rollback** if every transaction in the schedule only reads items that were written by *committed* transactions. In this case, all items read will be committed, so no cascading rollback will occur. To satisfy this criterion, the $r_2(X)$ command in schedule S_e must be postponed until after T_1 has committed (or aborted), thus delaying T_2 but ensuring no cascading rollback if T_1 aborts.

Finally, there is a third, more restrictive type of schedule, called a **strict schedule,** in which transactions can neither read *nor write* an item X until the last transaction that wrote X has committed (or aborted). Strict schedules simplify the process of recovering write operations to a matter of restoring the **before image** of a data item X, which is the value that X had prior to the aborted write operation. This simple procedure may not always work correctly unless a schedule is strict. For example, consider schedule S_f:

S_f: $w_1(X, 5)$; $w_2(X, 8)$; a_1;

Suppose that the value of X was originally 9, which is the before image stored in the system log along with the $w_1(X, 5)$ operation. If T_1 aborts, as in S_f, the recovery procedure that restores the before image of an aborted write operation will restore the value of X to 9, even though it has already been changed to 8 by transaction T_2, thus leading to potentially incorrect results. Although S_f avoids cascading aborts, it is not a strict schedule, since it permits T_2 to write item X even though the transaction T_1 that last wrote X had not yet committed (or aborted). A strict schedule does not have this problem; it is also recoverable and avoids cascading rollback.

We have now characterized schedules in terms of their recoverability. In the next section we characterize the type of schedules that are considered correct when concurrent transactions are executing; these are called *serializable schedules*.

17.5 Serializability of Schedules

Suppose that two users—airline reservation clerks—submit to the DBMS transactions T_1 and T_2 of Figure 17.2 at approximately the same time. If no interleaving is permitted, there are only two possible ways of ordering the operations of the two transactions for execution:

1. Execute all the operations of transaction T_1 (in sequence) followed by all the operations of transaction T_2 (in sequence).
2. Execute all the operations of transaction T_2 (in sequence) followed by all the operations of transaction T_1 (in sequence).

These alternatives are shown in Figure 17.5(a) and (b), respectively. If interleaving of operations is allowed, there will be many possible orders in which the system can execute the individual operations of the transactions. Two possible schedules are shown in Figure 17.5(c).

An important aspect of concurrency control, called **serializability theory,** attempts to determine which schedules are "correct" and which are not and to develop techniques that allow only correct schedules. This section defines serializability of schedules, presents some of this theory, and discusses how it may be used in practice.

17.5.1 *Serial, Nonserial, and Conflict-Serializable Schedules*

Figure 17.5 shows several possible schedules for transactions T_1 and T_2 of Figure 17.2. Schedules A and B in Figure 17.5(a) and (b) are called *serial schedules* because the operations of each transaction are executed consecutively, without any interleaved operations from the other transaction. In a serial schedule, entire transactions are performed in serial order: T_1 and then T_2 in Figure 17.5(a), and T_2 and then T_1 in Figure 17.5(b). Schedules C and D in Figure 17.5(c) are called *nonserial* because each sequence interleaves operations from the two transactions.

Formally, a schedule S is **serial** if, for every transaction T participating in the schedule, all the operations of T are executed consecutively in the schedule; otherwise, the schedule is called **nonserial**. One reasonable assumption we can make, if we consider

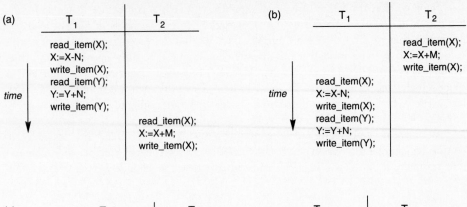

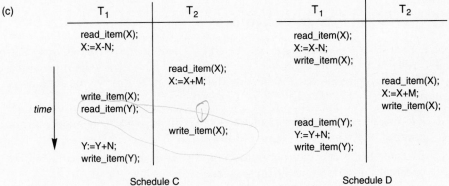

Schedule C   Schedule D

Figure 17.5   Some schedules involving transactions T_1 and T_2. (a) Schedule
A: T_1 followed by T_2. (b) Schedule B: T_2 followed by T_1.
(c) Two schedules with interleaving of operations.

the transactions to be *independent*, is that *every serial schedule is considered correct*. This
is so because we assume that every transaction is correct if executed on its own (by the
consistency preservation property of Section 17.3) and that transactions do not depend
on one another. Hence, it does not matter which transaction is executed first. As long
as every transaction is executed from beginning to end without any interference from
the operations of other transactions, we get a correct end result on the database. The
problem with serial schedules is that they limit concurrency or interleaving of operations.
In a serial schedule, if a transaction waits for an I/O operation to complete, we cannot
switch the CPU processor to another transaction, thus wasting valuable CPU processing
time and making serial schedules generally unacceptable.

To illustrate our discussion, consider the schedules in Figure 17.5, and assume that
the initial values of database items are X = 90, Y = 90 and that N = 3 and M = 2.
After executing transactions T_1 and T_2, we would expect the database values to be
X = 89 and Y = 93, according to the meaning of the transactions. Sure enough, executing
either of the serial schedules A or B gives the correct results. Now consider the nonserial
schedules C and D. Schedule C (same as Figure 17.3(a)) gives the results X = 92 and
Y = 93, in which the X value is erroneous, whereas schedule D gives the correct results.

n. possible

Schedule C gives an erroneous result because of the lost update problem discussed in Section 17.1.3; transaction T_2 reads the value of X *before* it is changed by transaction T_1, so only the effect of T_2 on X is reflected in the database. The effect of T_1 on X is *lost*, overwritten by T_2, leading to the incorrect result for item X. However, some non-serial schedules give the correct expected result, such as schedule D. We would like to determine which of the nonserial schedules *always* give a correct result and which may give erroneous results. The concept used to characterize schedules in this manner is that of serializability of a schedule.

A schedule S of n transactions is **serializable** if it is *equivalent to some serial schedule* of the same n transactions. We will define the concept of equivalence of schedules shortly. Notice that there are (n)! possible serial schedules of n transactions and many more possible nonserial schedules. We can form two disjoint groups of the nonserial schedules: those that are equivalent to one (or more) of the serial schedules, and hence are serializable; and those that are not equivalent to *any* serial schedule, and hence are not serializable.

Saying that a nonserial schedule S is serializable is equivalent to saying that it is correct, because it is equivalent to a serial schedule, which is considered correct. The remaining question is: When are two schedules considered "equivalent"? There are several ways to define equivalence of schedules. The simplest, but least satisfactory, definition of schedule equivalence involves comparing the effects of the schedules on the database. Two schedules are called **result equivalent** if they produce the same final state of the database. However, two different schedules may accidentally produce the same final state. For example, in Figure 17.6, schedules S_1 and S_2 will produce the same final database state if they execute on a database with an initial value of X = 100; but for other initial values of X, the schedules are *not* result equivalent. In addition, these two schedules execute different transactions, so they definitely should not be considered equivalent. Hence, result equivalence is *not* used to define equivalence of schedules.

The safest and most general approach to defining schedule equivalence is not to make any assumption about the types of operations included in the transactions. For two schedules to be equivalent, the operations applied to each data item affected by the schedules should be applied to that item in both schedules *in the same order*. Two definitions of equivalence of schedules are generally accepted: *conflict equivalence* and *view equivalence*. We discuss each of these next.

Two schedules are said to be **conflict equivalent** if the order of any two *conflicting* operations is the same in both schedules. Recall from Section 17.4.1 that two operations in a schedule are said to *conflict* if they belong to different transactions, if they access the same database item, and if one of the two operations is a write_item operation. If

S_1	S_2
read_item(X);	read_item(X);
X:=X+10;	X:=X*1.1;
write_item(X);	write_item(X);

Figure 17.6 Two schedules that are equivalent for the initial value of X = 100 but are not equivalent in general.

two conflicting operations are applied in *different orders* in two schedules, the effect of the schedules can be different on either the transactions or the database, and hence the schedules are not conflict equivalent. For example, if a read and write operation occur in the order $r_1(X)$, $w_2(X)$ in a schedule S_a, and in the reverse order $w_2(X)$, $r_1(X)$ in a schedule S_b, the value read by the $r_1(X)$ operation can be different in the two schedules. Similarly, if two write operations occur in the order $w_1(X)$, $w_2(X)$ in a schedule S_a, and in the reverse order $w_2(X)$, $w_1(X)$ in another schedule S_b, the next $r(X)$ operation in the two schedules will read potentially different values; or if these are the last operations accessing item X in the schedules, the final value of item X will be different for the two schedules.

Using the notion of conflict equivalence, we define a schedule S to be **conflict serializable** if it is (conflict) equivalent to some serial schedule S'. In such a case, we can reorder the *nonconflicting* operations in S until we form the equivalent serial schedule S'. According to this definition, schedule D of Figure 17.5(c) is equivalent to the serial schedule A of Figure 17.5(a). In both these schedules, the read_item(X) of T_2 reads the value of X written by T_1, while the other read_item operations read the database values from the initial database state. In addition, T_1 is the last transaction to write item Y, and T_2 is the last transaction to write X in both schedules. Because A is a serial schedule and schedule D is equivalent to A, D is a *serializable schedule*. Notice that the operations $r_1(Y)$ and $w_1(Y)$ of schedule D do not conflict with the operations $r_2(X)$ and $w_2(X)$, since they access different data items. Hence, we can move $r_1(Y)$, $w_1(Y)$ before $r_2(X)$, $w_2(X)$, leading to the equivalent serial schedule T_1, T_2.

Schedule C of Figure 17.5(c) is not equivalent to either of the two possible serial schedules A and B. It is not equivalent to A, because the read_item(X) operation in T_2 reads the value written by T_1 in schedule A but reads the original value of X in schedule C, thus violating rule 1 for equivalence. At the same time, schedule C is not equivalent to B. Hence, schedule C is *not serializable*. If we try to reorder the operations of schedule C to find an equivalent serial schedule, we fail because $r_2(X)$ and $w_1(X)$ conflict, so we cannot move $r_2(X)$ down to get the equivalent serial schedule T_1, T_2. Similarly, because $w_1(X)$ and $w_2(X)$ conflict, we cannot move $w_1(X)$ down to get the equivalent serial schedule T_2, T_1.

Another, more complex definition of equivalence—called *view equivalence*, which leads to the concept of *view serializability*—is discussed in Section 17.5.4.

17.5.2 *Testing for Conflict Serializability of a Schedule*

There is a simple algorithm for determining the conflict serializability of a schedule. Most concurrency control methods *do not* actually test for serializability. Rather, protocols, or rules, are developed that guarantee that a schedule will be serializable. We discuss the algorithm for testing conflict serializability of schedules here to gain a better understanding of these protocols, which are discussed in Chapter 18.

Algorithm 17.1 can be used to test a schedule for conflict serializability. The algorithm looks at only the read_item and write_item operations in the schedule to construct a **precedence graph** (or **serialization graph**). A precedence graph is a **directed graph** $G = (N,E)$ that consists of a set of nodes $N = \{T_1, T_2, \ldots, T_n\}$ and a set of directed edges $E = \{e_1, e_2, \ldots, e_m\}$. There is one node in the graph for each transaction T_i in the schedule. Each edge e_i in the graph is of the form $(T_j \rightarrow T_k)$, $1 \leq j \leq n$, $1 \leq k \leq n$, where T_j is called the **starting node** of e_i and T_k is called the **ending node** of e_i such that one of the operations in T_j appears in the schedule before some *conflicting operation* in T_k.

ALGORITHM 17.1 Testing conflict serializability of a schedule S

(1) for each transaction T_i participating in schedule S
      create a node labeled T_i in the precedence graph;
(2) for each case in S where T_j executes a read_item (X) after a write_item (X) command executed by T_i
      create an edge $(T_i \rightarrow T_j)$ in the precedence graph;
(3) for each case in S where T_j executes write_item(X) after T_i executes a read_item(X)
      create an edge $(T_i \rightarrow T_j)$ in the precedence graph;
(4) for each case in S where T_j executes a write_item(X) command after T_i executes a write_item(X) command
      create an edge $(T_i \rightarrow T_j)$ in the precedence graph;
(5) the schedule S is serializable if and only if the precedence graph has no cycles;

The precedence graph is constructed as shown in Algorithm 17.1. If there is a cycle in the precedence graph, schedule S is not (conflict) serializable; if there is no cycle, S is serializable. A **cycle** in a directed graph is a *sequence* of edges $C = ((T_j \rightarrow T_k),$ $(T_k \rightarrow T_p), \ldots, (T_i \rightarrow T_j))$ with the property that the starting node of each edge— except the first edge—is the same as the ending node of the previous edge, and the starting node of the first edge is the same as the ending node of the last edge. Hence, the sequence starts and ends at the same node.

In the precedence graph, an edge from T_i to T_j means that transaction T_i must come before transaction T_j in any serial schedule that is equivalent to S, because two conflicting operations appear in the schedule in that order. If there is no cycle in the precedence graph, we can create an **equivalent serial schedule** S' that is equivalent to S, by ordering the transactions that participate in S as follows: Whenever an edge exists in the precedence graph from T_i to T_j, T_i must appear before T_j in the equivalent serial schedule S'. The latter process is known as topological sorting. Notice that the edges $(T_i \rightarrow T_j)$ in a precedence graph can optionally be labeled by the name(s) of the data item(s) that led to creating the edge.

In general, several serial schedules can be equivalent to S if the precedence graph has no cycle. On the other hand, if the precedence graph has a cycle, it is easy to show that we cannot create any equivalent serial schedule, so schedule S is not serializable. The precedence graphs created for schedules A to D, respectively, of Figure 17.5 appear in Figure 17.7(a) to (d). The precedence graph for schedule C has a cycle, so it is not serializable. The graph for schedule D has no cycle, so it is serializable; and the equivalent serial schedule is T_1 followed by T_2. The graphs for schedules A and B have no cycles, as expected, because the schedules are *serial* and hence serializable.

Another example, in which three transactions participate, is shown in Figure 17.8. Figure 17.8(a) shows the read_item and write_item operations in each transaction. Two

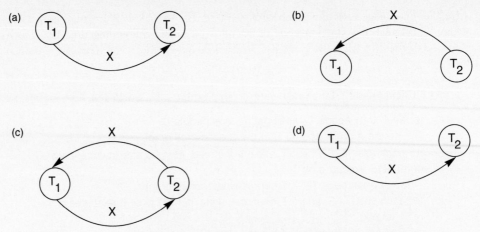

Figure 17.7 Constructing the precedence graphs for schedules A to D to test for conflict serializability. (a) Precedence graph for schedule A of Figure 17.5. (b) Precedence graph for schedule B of Figure 17.5. (c) Precedence graph for schedule C of Figure 17.5 (not serializable). (d) Precedence graph for schedule D of Figure 17.5 (serializable, equivalent to schedule A).

schedules E and F for these transactions are shown in Figure 17.8(b) and (c), respectively. We show the precedence graphs for schedules E and F in Figure 17.8(d) and (e). Schedule E is not serializable, because the corresponding precedence graph has cycles. Schedule F is serializable, and the serial schedule equivalent to F is shown in Figure 17.8(e). Although only one equivalent serial schedule exists for schedule F, in general there may be more than one equivalent serial schedule for a serializable schedule. Figure 17.8(f) shows a precedence graph representing a schedule that has two equivalent serial schedules.

17.5.3 *Uses of Serializability*

As we discussed earlier, saying that a schedule S is (conflict) serializable—that is, that S is (conflict) equivalent to a serial schedule—is tantamount to saying that S is correct. Being *serializable* is distinct from being *serial*, however. A serial schedule represents inefficient processing because no interleaving of operations from different transactions is permitted. This can lead to low CPU utilization while a transaction waits for disk I/O, thus slowing down processing considerably. A serializable schedule gives us the benefits of concurrent execution without giving up any correctness.

In practice, it is quite difficult to test for the serializability of a schedule. The interleaving of operations from concurrent transactions is typically determined by the operating system scheduler. Factors such as system load, time of transaction submission, and priorities of transactions contribute to the ordering of operations in a schedule by the operating system. Hence, it is practically impossible to determine how the operations of a schedule will be interleaved beforehand to ensure serializability.

(a)

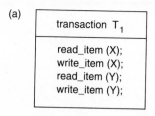

transaction T_1	transaction T_2	transaction T_3
read_item (X); write_item (X); read_item (Y); write_item (Y);	read_item (Z); read_item (Y); write_item (Y); read_item (X); write_item (X);	read_item (Y); read_item (Z); write_item (Y); write_item (Z);

(b)

	transaction T_1	transaction T_2	transaction T_3
		read_item (Z); read_item (Y); write_item (Y);	
			read_item (Y); read_item (Z);
time	read_item (X); write_item (X);		
			write_item (Y); write_item (Z);
		read_item (X);	
	read_item (Y); write_item (Y);	write_item (X);	

(c)

	transaction T_1	transaction T_2	transaction T_3
			read_item (Y); read_item (Z);
time	read_item (X); write_item (X);		
			write_item (Y); write_item (Z);
		read_item (Z);	
	read_item (Y); write_item (Y);		
		read_item (Y); write_item (Y); read_item (X); write_item (X);	

Figure 17.8 Another example of serializability testing. (a) The READ and WRITE operations of three transactions. (b) Schedule E of the transactions T_1, T_2, and T_3. (c) Schedule F of the transactions T_1, T_2, and T_3. *(continued on next page)*

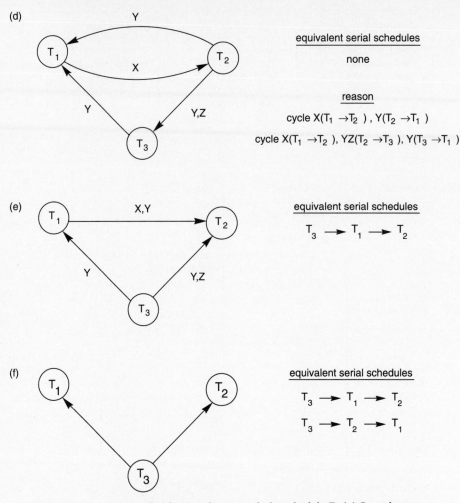

Figure 17.8 *(continued)* (d) Precedence graph for schedule E. (e) Precedence graph for schedule F. (f) A precedence graph with two equivalent serial schedules.

If transactions are executed at will and then the resulting schedule is tested for serializability, we must cancel the effect of the schedule if it turns out not to be serializable. This is a serious problem that makes this approach impractical. Hence, the approach taken in most practical systems is to determine methods that ensure serializability without having to test the schedules themselves for serializability after they are executed. One such method uses the theory of serializability to determine **protocols** or sets of rules that, if followed by *every* individual transaction or if enforced by a DBMS concurrency control subsystem, will ensure serializability of *all schedules in which the transactions participate*. Hence, in this approach we never have to concern ourselves with the schedules themselves.

Another problem is that, when transactions are submitted continuously to the system, it is difficult to determine when a schedule begins and when it ends. Serializability theory can be adapted to deal with this problem by considering only the committed projection of a schedule S. Recall from Section 17.4.1 that the *committed projection* C(S) of a schedule S includes only the operations in S that belong to committed transactions. We can define a schedule S to be serializable if its committed projection C(S) is equivalent to some serial schedule, since only committed transactions are guaranteed by the DBMS.

In Chapter 18, we discuss a number of different concurrency control protocols that guarantee serializability. The most common technique, called *two-phase locking,* is based on locking data items to prevent concurrent transactions from interfering with one another. Another technique is based on *timestamp ordering,* where each transaction is assigned a unique timestamp and the protocol ensures that any conflicting operations are executed in the order of the transaction timestamps. Other techniques are based on maintaining *multiple versions* of data items and on *certification* or *validation.*

Another factor that affects concurrency control is the **granularity** of the items— that is, what portion of the database an item represents. An item can be as small as a single value or as large as the database itself. Of course, in the latter case, very little concurrency is allowed. We discuss granularity of items in Section 18.5.

17.5.4 *View Equivalence and View Serializability*★

In Section 17.5.1, we defined the concepts of conflict equivalence of schedules, and of conflict serializability. Another, less restrictive definition of equivalence of schedules is called *view equivalence.* This leads to another definition of serializability called *view serializability.* Two schedules are said to be **view equivalent** if the following three conditions hold:

1. The same set of transactions participates in S and S', and S and S' include the same operations of those transactions.

2. For any operation $r_i(X)$ of T_i in S, if the value of X read by the operation has been written by an operation $w_j(X)$ of T_j (or if it is the original value of X before the schedule started), the same condition must hold for the value of X read by operation $r_i(X)$ of T_i in S'.

3. If the operation $w_k(Y)$ of T_k is the last operation to write item Y in S, then $w_k(Y)$ of T_k must also be the last operation to write item Y in S'.

The idea behind view equivalence is that, as long as each read operation of a transaction reads the result of *the same write operation* in both schedules, the write operations of each transaction must produce the same results. The read operations are hence said to *see the same view* in both schedules. Condition 3 ensures that the final write operation on each data item is the same in both schedules, so the database state should be the same at the end of both schedules. A schedule S is said to be **view serializable** if it is view equivalent to a serial schedule.

The definitions of conflict serializability and view serializability are similar if a condition known as the **constrained write** assumption holds on all transactions in the schedule. This condition states that any write operation $w_i(X)$ in T_i is preceded by a $r_i(X)$ in T_i *and* that the value written by $w_i(X)$ in T_i depends only on the value of X read by $r_i(X)$. This assumes that computation of the new value of X is a function $f(X)$ based on the old value of X read from the database. However, the definition of view serializability is less restrictive than that of conflict serializability under the **unconstrained write** assumption, where the value written by an operation $w_i(X)$ in T_i can be independent of any old value from the database. This is called a **blind write,** and is illustrated by the following schedule of three transactions T_1: $r_1(X)$, $w_1(X)$; T_2: $w_2(X)$; and T_3: $w_3(X)$:

S_a: $r_1(X)$; $w_2(X)$; $w_1(X)$; $w_3(X)$; c_1; c_2; c_3;

In S_a, the operations $w_2(X)$ and $w_3(X)$ are blind writes, since T_1 and T_3 do not read the value of X. The schedule S_a is view serializable, since it is view equivalent to the serial schedule T_1, T_2, T_3. However, S_a is not conflict serializable, since it is not conflict equivalent to any serial schedule.

It has been shown that any conflict-serializable schedule is also view serializable, but not vice versa, as illustrated by the preceding example. There is an algorithm to test whether a schedule S is view serializable or not. However, the problem of testing for view serializability has been shown to be NP-complete, meaning that finding an efficient algorithm for this problem is highly unlikely.

17.5.5 *Other Types of Equivalence of Schedules*★

Serializability of schedules is sometimes considered to be too restrictive as a condition for ensuring the correctness of concurrent executions. Some applications can produce schedules that are correct by satisfying conditions less stringent than either conflict serializability or view serializability. An example is the type of transactions known as debit-credit transactions—for example, those that apply deposits and withdrawals to a data item whose value is the current balance of a bank account. The semantics of debit-credit operations is that they update the value of a data item X by either subtracting from or adding to the value of the data item. Because addition and subtraction operations are commutative—that is, they can be applied in any order—it is possible to produce correct schedules that are not serializable. For example, consider the following two transactions, each of which may be used to transfer an amount of money between two bank accounts:

T_1: $r_1(X)$; X := X − 10; $w_1(X)$; $r_1(Y)$; Y := Y + 10; $w_1(Y)$;
T_2: $r_2(Y)$; Y := Y − 20; $w_2(Y)$; $r_2(X)$; X := X + 20; $w_2(X)$;

Consider the following schedule S for the two transactions:

S: $r_1(X)$; $w_1(X)$; $r_2(Y)$; $w_2(Y)$; $r_1(Y)$; $w_1(Y)$; $r_2(X)$; $w_2(X)$;

With the additional knowledge, or *semantics*, that the operations between each $r_i(X)$ and $w_i(X)$ are commutative, we know that the order of executing the sequences consisting of (read, update, write) is not important as long as each (read, update, write) sequence is not interrupted. Hence, the schedule S is considered to be correct even though it is not serializable. Recently, researchers have been working on extending concurrency control theory to deal with cases where serializability is considered to be too restrictive as a condition for correctness of schedules.

17.6 Summary

In this chapter we discussed DBMS concepts for transaction processing. In Section 17.1 we introduced the concept of a database transaction and the operations relevant to transaction processing. We compared single-user systems to multiuser systems and then presented examples of how uncontrolled execution of concurrent transactions in a multiuser system can lead to incorrect results and database values. We also discussed the various types of failures that may occur during transaction execution.

In Section 17.2, we first introduced the typical states that a transaction passes through during execution; then we discussed several concepts that are used in recovery and concurrency control methods. The system log keeps track of database accesses and uses this information to recover from failures. A transaction either succeeds and reaches its commit point or fails and has to be rolled back. A committed transaction has its changes permanently recorded in the database. Checkpoints are used to indicate that all committed transactions up to the checkpoint have recorded their updates permanently in the database. In Section 17.3, we presented an overview of the desirable properties of transactions—namely, atomicity, consistency preservation, isolation, and durability—which are often referred to as the ACID properties.

In Section 17.4, we first defined a schedule (or history) as an execution sequence of the operations of several transactions with possible interleaving. We then characterized schedules in terms of their recoverability. Recoverable schedules ensure that, once a transaction commits, it never needs to be undone. Cascadeless schedules ensure that no aborted transaction requires the cascading abort of other transactions. Strict schedules allow a simple recovery scheme consisting of rewriting the old values of items that have been changed by an aborted transaction.

In Section 17.5 we defined equivalence of schedules and saw that a serializable schedule is equivalent to some serial schedule. We defined the concepts of conflict equivalence and view equivalence, leading to definitions for conflict serializability and view serializability. A serializable schedule is considered correct. We then presented algorithms for testing the (conflict) serializability of a schedule. Finally, we discussed why testing for serializability is impractical in a real system, although it can be used to define and verify concurrency control protocols, and we briefly mentioned less restrictive definitions of schedule equivalence.

We will discuss a number of concurrency control techniques in Chapter 18, and we will discuss the techniques for recovery from transaction failures in Chapter 19.

Review Questions

17.1. What is meant by *concurrent execution of database transactions* in a multiuser system? Discuss why concurrency control is needed, and give informal examples.

17.2. Discuss the different types of transaction failures. What is meant by *catastrophic failure*?

17.3. Discuss the actions taken by the read_item and write_item operations on a database.

17.4. Draw a state diagram, and discuss the typical states that a transaction goes through during execution.

17.5. What is the system log used for? What are the typical kinds of entries in a system log? What are checkpoints, and why are they important? What are transaction commit points, and why are they important?

17.6. Discuss the atomicity, durability, isolation, and consistency preservation properties of a database transaction.

17.7. What is a schedule (history)? Define the concepts of recoverable, cascadeless, and strict schedules, and compare them in terms of their recoverability.

17.8. Discuss the different measures of transaction equivalence. What is the difference between conflict equivalence and view equivalence?

17.9. What is a serial schedule? What is a serializable schedule? Why is a serial schedule considered correct? Why is a serializable schedule considered correct?

17.10. What is the difference between the constrained write and the unconstrained write assumptions? Which is more realistic?

17.11. Discuss how serializability is used to enforce concurrency control in a database system. Why is serializability sometimes considered too restrictive as a measure of correctness for schedules?

Exercises

17.12. Change transaction T_2 in Figure 17.2b to read:

```
read_item(x);
X:= X+M;
if X > 90 then exit
            else write_item(X);
```

Discuss the final result of the different schedules in Figure 17.3, where M = 2 and N = 2, with respect to the following questions. Does adding the above condition change the final outcome? Does the outcome obey the implied consistency rule (that the capacity of X is 90)?

17.13. Repeat Exercise 17.12, adding a check in T_1 so that Y does not exceed 90.

17.14. Add the operation commit at the end of each of the transactions T_1 and T_2 from Figure 17.2; then list all possible schedules for the modified transactions. Determine which of the schedules are recoverable, which are cascadeless, and which are strict.

17.15. List all possible schedules for transactions T_1 and T_2 from Figure 17.2, and determine which are conflict serializable (correct) and which are not.

17.16. How many *serial* schedules exist for the three transactions in Figure 17.8(a)?

17.17. Write a program to create all possible schedules for the three transactions in Figure 17.8(a), and to determine which of those schedules are conflict serializable and which are not. For each conflict serializable schedule, your program should print the schedule and list all equivalent serial schedules.

Selected Bibliography

The concept of atomic transaction is discussed in Gray (1981). The book by Bernstein, Hadzilacos, and Goodman (1987) is devoted to concurrency control and recovery techniques in both centralized and distributed database systems; it is an excellent reference. The book by Papadimitriou (1986) offers a more theoretical perspective. A large reference book of over 1000 pages by Gray and Reuter (1993) offers a more practical perspective of transaction processing concepts and techniques. Two edited volumes—Elmagarmid (1992) and Bhargava (1989)—offer collections of research papers on transaction processing.

The concepts of serializability are introduced in Gray et al. (1975). View serializability is defined in Yannakakis (1984). Recoverability of schedules is discussed in Hadzilacos (1983, 1986).

CHAPTER 18

Concurrency Control Techniques

In this chapter, we discuss a number of concurrency control techniques that are used to ensure noninterference or isolation of concurrently executing transactions. Most of these techniques ensure serializability of schedules (see Section 17.5), using **protocols** or sets of rules that guarantee serializability. One important set of protocols employs the technique of **locking** data items to prevent multiple transactions from accessing the items concurrently; a number of locking protocols are described in Section 18.1. Another set of concurrency control protocols use transaction **timestamps**. A timestamp is a unique identifier for each transaction generated by the system. Concurrency control protocols that use timestamp ordering to ensure serializability are described in Section 18.2. In Section 18.3, we discuss **multiversion** concurrency control protocols that use multiple versions of a data item. In Section 18.4, we present a protocol based on the concept of *validation* or *certification* of a transaction after it executes its operations; these are sometimes called **optimistic** protocols.

Another factor that affects concurrency control is the **granularity** of the items—that is, what portion of the database an item represents. An item can be as small as a single value or as large as a disk block, a file, or even the entire database. We discuss granularity of items in Section 18.5. Finally, in Section 18.6, we discuss some additional concurrency control issues.

18.1 Locking Techniques for Concurrency Control

One of the main techniques used to control concurrent execution of transactions is based on the concept of locking data items. A **lock** is a variable associated with a data item in the database and describes the status of that item with respect to possible operations that can be applied to the item. Generally, there is one lock for each data item in the database. We use locks as a means of synchronizing the access by concurrent transactions to the database items. In Section 18.1.1 we discuss the nature and types of locks. Then, in Section 18.1.2, we present protocols that use locking to guarantee serializability of transaction schedules. Finally, in Section 18.1.3 we discuss two problems associated with the use of locks—namely, deadlock and livelock—and show how these problems are handled.

18.1.1 Types of Locks

Several types of locks can be used in concurrency control. We first present binary locks, which are simple but somewhat restrictive in their use. Then we discuss shared and exclusive locks, which provide more general locking capabilities.

Binary Locks. A **binary lock** can have two **states** or **values**: locked and unlocked (or 1 and 0, for simplicity). A distinct lock is associated with *each* database item X. If the value of the lock on X is 1, item X *cannot be accessed* by a database operation that requests the item. If the value of the lock on X is 0, the item can be accessed when requested. We refer to the *value* of the lock associated with item X as LOCK(X).

Two operations, lock_item and unlock_item, must be included in the transactions when binary locking is used. A transaction requests access to an item X by issuing a **lock_item(X)** operation. If LOCK(X) = 1, the transaction is forced to wait; otherwise, the transaction sets LOCK(X) := 1 (locks the item) and is allowed access. When the transaction is through using the item, it issues an **unlock_item(X)** operation, which sets LOCK(X) := 0 (unlocks the item) so that X may be accessed by other transactions. Hence, a binary lock enforces *mutual exclusion* on the data item. A description of the lock_item(X) and unlock_item(X) operations is shown in Figure 18.1.

Notice that the lock_item and unlock_item operations must be implemented as indivisible units (known as *critical sections* in operating systems); that is, no interleaving should be allowed once a lock or unlock operation is started until the operation terminates or the transaction waits. In Figure 18.1, the wait command within the lock_item(X) operation is usually implemented by putting the transaction on a waiting queue for the item X until X is unlocked and the transaction is granted access to it. Other transactions that also want to access X are placed on the same queue. Hence, the wait command is considered to be outside the lock_item operation. The DBMS has a **lock manager** subsystem to keep track of and control access to locks.

When the binary locking scheme is used, every transaction must obey the following rules:

1. A transaction T must issue the operation lock_item(X) before any read_item(X) or write_item(X) operations are performed in T.

2. A transaction T must issue the operation unlock_item(X) after all read_item(X) and write_item(X) operations are completed in T.

3. A transaction T will not issue a lock_item(X) operation if it already holds the lock on item X.

4. A transaction T will not issue an unlock_item(X) operation unless it already holds the lock on item X.

These rules can be enforced by a module of the DBMS. Between the lock_item(X) and unlock_item(X) operations in transaction T, T is said to **hold the lock** on item X. At most one transaction can hold the lock on a particular item. No two transactions can access the same item concurrently. Notice that it is quite simple to implement a binary lock; all that is needed is a binary-valued variable, LOCK, associated with each data item X in the database. In its simplest form, each lock can be a record with two fields: <data item name, LOCK> plus a queue for waiting transactions. The system only needs to maintain these records for locked items in a **lock table**.

Shared and Exclusive Locks. The preceding binary locking scheme is too restrictive in general, because at most one transaction can hold a lock on a given item. We should allow several transactions to access the same item X if they all access X for *reading purposes only*. However, if a transaction is to write an item X, it must have exclusive access to X. For this purpose, we can use a different type of lock called a **multiple-mode lock**. In this scheme there are three locking operations: read_lock(X), write_lock(X), and unlock(X). A lock associated with an item X, LOCK(X), now has three possible states: "read-locked," "write-locked," or "unlocked." A read-locked item is also called **share-locked,** because other transactions are allowed to read the item, whereas a write-locked item is called **exclusive-locked,** because a single transaction exclusively holds the lock on the item.

One simple, though not completely general, method for implementing the preceding three operations on a multiple-mode lock is to keep track of the number of transactions that hold a shared lock on an item. Each lock can be a record with three fields:

```
lock_item (X):
   B: if LOCK (X)=0  (* item is unlocked *)
      then LOCK (X)← 1  (* lock the item *)
      else begin
         wait  (until lock (X)=0  and
            the lock manager wakes up the transaction);
         go to B
         end;


unlock_item (X):
   LOCK (X)←0  (* unlock the item *)
   if any transactions are waiting
      then wakeup one of the waiting transactions;
```

Figure 18.1 Lock and unlock operations for binary locks.

<data item name, LOCK, no_of_reads>. The value of LOCK is one of read-locked, write-locked, or unlocked, suitably coded. Again, to save space, the system need only maintain lock records for locked items in the lock table. The three operations read_lock(X), write_lock(X), and unlock(X) are described in Figure 18.2. As before, each of the three operations should be considered indivisible; no interleaving should be allowed once one of the operations is started until either the operation terminates or the transaction is placed on a waiting queue for the item.

```
read_lock (X):
    B: if LOCK (X)="unlocked"
        then begin LOCK (X)← "read-locked";
                        no_of_reads(X)← 1
            end
        else if LOCK(X)="read-locked"
                then no_of_reads(X)← no_of _reads(X) + 1
                else begin wait (until LOCK (X)="unlocked" and
                            the lock manager wakes up the transaction);
                        go to B
                    end;


write_lock (X):
    B: if LOCK (X)="unlocked"
        then LOCK (X)← "write-locked"
        else begin
                wait (until LOCK(X)="unlocked" and
                  the lock manager wakes up the transaction);
                go to B
            end;


unlock_item (X):
    if LOCK (X)="write-locked"
        then begin LOCK (X)← "unlocked;"
            wakeup one of the waiting transactions, if any
            end
        else if LOCK(X)="read-locked"
                then begin
                        no_of_reads(X)← no_of_reads(X) - 1;
                        if no_of_reads(X)=0
                            then begin LOCK (X)="unlocked";
                                    wakeup one of the waiting transactions, if any
                                end
                    end;
```

Figure 18.2   Locking and unlocking operations for two-mode (read-write or shared-exclusive) locks.

When we use the multiple-mode locking scheme, the system must enforce the following rules:

1. A transaction T must issue the operation read_lock(X) or write_lock(X) before any read_item(X) operation is performed in T.

2. A transaction T must issue the operation write_lock(X) before any write_item(X) operation is performed in T.

3. A transaction T must issue the operation unlock(X) after all read_item(X) and write_item(X) operations are completed in T.

4. A transaction T will not issue a read_lock(X) operation if it already holds a read (shared) lock or a write (exclusive) lock on item X. This rule may be relaxed, as we discuss shortly.

5. A transaction T will not issue a write_lock(X) operation if it already holds a read (shared) lock or write (exclusive) lock on item X. This rule may be relaxed, as we discuss shortly.

6. A transaction T will not issue an unlock(X) operation unless it already holds a read (shared) lock or a write (exclusive) lock on item X.

Sometimes it is desirable to relax conditions 4 and 5 in the preceding list. For example, it is possible for a transaction T to issue a read_lock(X) and then later on to **upgrade** the lock by issuing a write_lock(X) operation. If T is the only transaction with a read lock on X at the time it issues the write_lock operation, we can upgrade the lock. It is also possible for a transaction T to issue a write_lock(X) and then later on to **downgrade** the lock by issuing a read_lock(X) operation. If we allow upgrading and downgrading of locks, we must include transaction identifiers in the record structure for each lock to store the information on which transactions hold locks on the item, and we must change the descriptions of the read_lock(X) and write_lock(X) operations in Figure 18.2 appropriately. We leave this as an exercise for the reader.

Using binary locks or multiple-mode locks in transactions, as described earlier, *does not guarantee serializability* of schedules in which the transactions participate. Figure 18.3 shows an example where the preceding locking rules are followed but a nonserializable schedule may still result. This is because in Figure 18.3(a) the items Y in T_1 and X in T_2 were *unlocked too early*. This allows a schedule such as the one shown in Figure 18.3(c) to occur; this is not a serializable schedule and hence gives incorrect results. To guarantee serializability, we must follow *an additional protocol* concerning the positioning of locking and unlocking operations in every transaction. The best known protocol, two-phase locking, is described in the next section.

18.1.2 *Guaranteeing Serializability by Two-phase Locking*

A transaction is said to follow the **two-phase locking protocol*** if *all* locking operations (read_lock, write_lock) precede the *first* unlock operation in the transaction. Such a transaction can be divided into two phases: an **expanding** (or **growing**) **phase,** during which new locks on items can be acquired but none can be released; and a **shrinking**

---

*This is unrelated to the two-phase commit protocol for recovery in distributed databases (see Chapter 19).

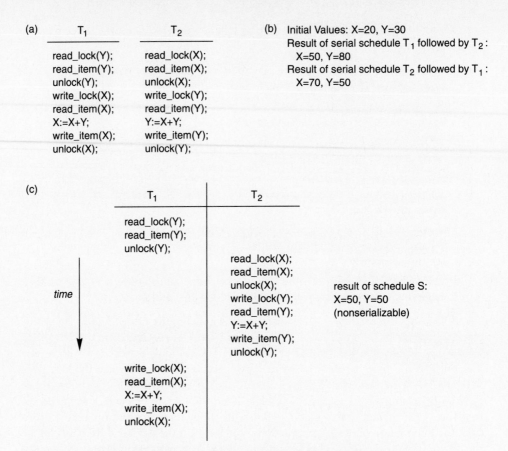

Figure 18.3 Transactions that do not obey two-phase locking. (a) Two transactions T_1 and T_2. (b) Results of possible serial schedules of T_1
and T_2. (c) A nonserializable schedule S that uses locks.
nonserializable schedule S that uses locks.

phase, during which existing locks can be released but no new locks can be acquired. If
upgrading of locks is allowed, this definition is unchanged. However, if downgrading of
locks is also allowed, the definition must be changed slightly, because *all downgrading
must be done in the shrinking phase.* Hence, a read_lock(X) operation that downgrades an
already held write lock on X can appear only in the shrinking phase of the transaction.

Transactions T_1 and T_2 of Figure 18.3(a) do not follow the two-phase locking protocol. This is because the write_lock(X) operation follows the unlock(Y) operation in
T_1, and similarly the write_lock(Y) operation follows the unlock(X) operation in T_2. If
we enforce two-phase locking, the transaction can be rewritten as T_1' and T_2', as shown
in Figure 18.4. Now, the schedule shown in Figure 18.3(c) is not permitted for T_1' and
T_2' under the rules of locking described in Section 18.1.1. This is because T_1' will issue
its write_lock(X) *before* it unlocks item Y; consequently, when T_2' issues its read_lock(X),
it is forced to wait until T_1' issues its unlock (X) in the schedule.

T_1'	T_2'
read_lock (Y);	read_lock (X);
read_item (Y);	read_item (X);
write_lock (X);	write_lock (Y);
unlock (Y);	unlock (X);
read_item (X);	read_item (Y);
X:=X+Y;	Y:=X+Y;
write_item (X);	write_item (Y);
unlock (X);	unlock (Y);

Figure 18.4 Transactions T_1' and T_2', which are the same as T_1 and T_2 of Figure 18.3 but which follow the two-phase locking protocol.

It can be proved that, if *every* transaction in a schedule follows the two-phase locking protocol, the schedule is guaranteed to be serializable, obviating the need to test for serializability of schedules any more. The locking mechanism, by enforcing two-phase locking rules, also enforces serializability.

Two-phase locking may limit the amount of concurrency that can occur in a schedule. This is because a transaction T may not be able to release an item X after it is through using it if T must lock an additional item Y later on; or conversely, T must lock the additional item Y before it needs it so that it can release X. Hence, X must remain locked by T until all items that the transaction needs have been locked; only then can X be released by T. Meanwhile, another transaction seeking to access X may be forced to wait, even though T is through using X; conversely, if Y is locked earlier than it is needed, another transaction seeking to access Y is forced to wait even though T is not using Y yet. This is the price for guaranteeing serializability of all schedules without having to check the schedules themselves.

Basic, Conservative, and Strict Two-phase Locking. There are a number of variations of two-phase locking (2PL). The technique just described is known as **basic 2PL**. A variation known as **conservative 2PL** (or **static 2PL**) requires a transaction to lock all the items it accesses *before the transaction begins execution*, by **predeclaring** its read set and write set. Recall that the read set of a transaction is the set of all items that the transaction reads, and the write set is the set of all items that the transaction writes. If any of the predeclared items needed cannot be locked, the transaction does not lock any item; instead, it waits until all the items are available for locking. Conservative 2PL is a deadlock-free protocol, as we shall see in Section 18.1.3 when we discuss the deadlock problem.

In practice, the most popular variation of 2PL is **strict 2PL,** which guarantees strict schedules (see Section 17.4.2). In this variation, a transaction T does not release any of its locks until after it commits or aborts. Hence, no other transaction can read or write an item that is written by T unless T has committed, leading to a strict schedule for recoverability. Notice the difference between conservative and strict 2PL; the former must lock all its items *before it starts*, whereas the latter does not unlock any of its items until *after it terminates* (by committing or aborting). Strict 2PL is not deadlock-free unless it is combined with conservative 2PL.

Although two-phase locking guarantees serializability, the use of locks can cause two additional problems: deadlock and livelock. We discuss these problems and their solutions in the next section.

18.1.3 *Dealing with Deadlock and Livelock*

Deadlock occurs when each of two transactions is waiting for the other to release the lock on an item. A simple example is shown in Figure 18.5(a), where the two transactions T_1' and T_2' are deadlocked in a partial schedule; T_1' is waiting for T_2' to release item X, while T_2' is waiting for T_1' to release item Y. Meanwhile, neither can proceed to unlock the item that the other is waiting for, and other transactions can access neither item X nor item Y. Deadlock is also possible when more than two transactions are involved, as we shall see.

One way to prevent deadlock is to use a **deadlock prevention protocol**. One deadlock prevention protocol, which is used in conservative two-phase locking, requires that every transaction lock all the items it needs in advance; if any of the items cannot be obtained, none of the items are locked. Rather, the transaction waits and then tries again to lock all the items it needs. This solution obviously further limits concurrency. A second protocol, which also limits concurrency, involves ordering all the items in the database and making sure that a transaction that needs several items will lock them according to that order. This requires that the programmer be aware of the chosen order of the items, which is not very practical in the database context.

A number of other deadlock prevention schemes have been proposed that make a decision on whether a transaction involved in a possible deadlock situation should be blocked and made to wait, should be aborted, or should preempt and abort another transaction. These techniques use the concept of **transaction timestamp** TS(T), which is a unique identifier assigned to each transaction. The timestamps are ordered based on the order in which transactions are started; hence, if transaction T_1 starts before transaction T_2, then $TS(T_1) < TS(T_2)$. Notice that the *older* transaction has the *smaller* timestamp value. Two schemes that prevent deadlock are called wait-die and wound-wait. Suppose that transaction T_i tries to lock an item X, but is not able to because X is locked by some other transaction T_j with a conflicting lock. The rules followed by these schemes are as follows:

- **wait-die**: if $TS(T_i) < TS (T_j)$ (T_i is older than T_j)
  then T_i is allowed to wait
  otherwise abort T_i (T_i *dies*) and restart it later *with the same timestamp*

- **wound-wait**: if $TS(T_i) < TS(T_j)$ (T_i is older than T_j)
  then abort T_j (T_i *wounds* T_j) and restart it later *with the same timestamp*
  otherwise T_i is allowed to wait

In wait-die, an older transaction is allowed to wait on a younger transaction, whereas a younger transaction requesting an item held by an older transaction is aborted and restarted. The wound-wait approach does the opposite: a younger transaction is allowed to wait on an older one, whereas an older transaction requesting an item held by a younger transaction *preempts* the younger transaction by aborting it. Both schemes

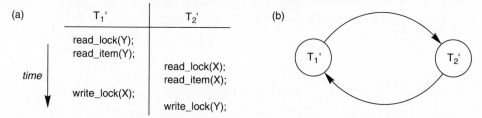

Figure 18.5   The deadlock problem. (a) A partial schedule of T_1' and T_2' that
is in a state of deadlock. (b) Wait-for graph for the partial schedule in Figure 18.5(a).

end up aborting the *younger* of the two transactions that *may be involved* in a deadlock, and it can be shown that these two techniques are deadlock-free. However, both techniques cause some transactions to be aborted and restarted even though those transactions may *never actually cause a deadlock*. Another problem can occur with the wait-die, where the transaction T_i may be aborted and restarted several times in a row because an older transaction T_j continues to hold the data item that T_i needs.

Another group of protocols that prevent deadlock do not require timestamps. These include the no waiting (NW) and cautious waiting (CW) algorithms. In the **no waiting** algorithm, if a transaction is unable to obtain a lock, it is immediately aborted and then restarted after a certain time delay without checking whether a deadlock will actually occur or not. Because this scheme can cause transactions to abort and restart needlessly, the **cautious waiting** approach was proposed to try to reduce the number of needless aborts/restarts. Suppose that transaction T_i tries to lock an item X but is not able to do so because X is locked by some other transaction T_j with a conflicting lock. The cautious waiting rules are as follows:

- **cautious waiting**: if T_j is not blocked (not waiting for some other locked item)
    then T_i is blocked and allowed to wait
    otherwise abort T_i

It can be shown that cautious waiting is deadlock-free, by considering the times at which a transaction T gets blocked, b(T). If the two transactions T_i and T_j above both become blocked, and T_i is waiting on T_j, then $b(T_i) < b(T_j)$, since a transaction can only wait on a transaction when it is not blocked. Hence, the blocking times form a total ordering on all blocked transactions, so no cycle that causes deadlock can occur.

Another deadlock prevention scheme involves using **timeouts**. If a transaction waits longer than a system-defined timeout, the system assumes that the transaction is deadlocked and aborts it, regardless of whether a deadlock situation actually exists.

A second approach to dealing with deadlock is **deadlock detection,** where we periodically check to see if the system is in a state of deadlock. This solution is attractive if we know there will be little interference among the transactions—that is, if different transactions will rarely access the same items at the same time. This can happen if the transactions are short and each transaction locks only a few items, or if the transaction load is light. On the other hand, if transactions are long and each transaction uses many items, or if the transaction load is quite heavy, it is advantageous to use a deadlock prevention scheme.

A simple way to detect a state of deadlock is to construct a **wait-for graph**. One node is created in the wait-for graph for each transaction that is currently executing in the schedule. Whenever a transaction T_i is waiting to lock an item X that is currently locked by a transaction T_j, create a directed edge $(T_i \rightarrow T_j)$. When T_j releases the lock(s) on the items that T_i was waiting for, the directed edge is dropped from the wait-for graph. We have a state of deadlock if and only if the wait-for graph has a cycle. One problem with this approach is the matter of determining *when* the system should check for deadlock. Criteria such as the number of currently executing transactions or the period of time several transactions have been waiting to lock items may be used to determine that the system should check for deadlock. Figure 18.5(b) shows the wait-for graph for the partial schedule shown in Figure 18.5(a). If we discover that the system is in a state of deadlock, some of the transactions causing the deadlock must be aborted. Choosing which transaction to abort is known as *victim selection*. The algorithm for victim selection should generally avoid selecting transactions that have been running for a long time and that have performed many updates, and should try instead to select transactions that have not made many changes or that are involved in more than one deadlock cycle in the wait-for graph. A problem known as *cyclic restart* may occur, where a transaction is aborted and restarted only to be involved in another deadlock. The victim selection algorithm can use higher priorities for transactions that have been aborted multiple times so that they are not selected as victims repeatedly.

Another problem that may occur when we use locking is **livelock**. A transaction is in a state of livelock if it cannot proceed for an indefinite period of time while other transactions in the system continue normally. This may occur if the waiting scheme for locked items is unfair, giving priority to some transactions over others. The standard solution for livelock is to have a fair waiting scheme. One such scheme uses a **first-come-first-serve** queue; transactions are enabled to lock an item in the order in which they originally requested to lock the item. Another scheme allows some transactions to have priority over others but increases the priority of a transaction the longer it waits, until it eventually gets the highest priority and proceeds. A similar problem to livelock, called **starvation,** can occur in the algorithms for dealing with deadlock. It occurs if the algorithms select the same transaction as victim repeatedly, thus causing it to abort and never finish execution. The wait-die and wound-wait schemes discussed above avoid starvation.

18.2 Concurrency Control Based on Timestamp Ordering*

The use of locks, combined with the two-phase locking protocol, allows us to guarantee serializability of schedules. The order of transactions in the equivalent serial schedule is based on the order in which executing transactions lock the items they require. If a transaction needs an item that is already locked, it may be forced to wait until the item is released. A different approach that guarantees serializability involves using transaction timestamps to order transaction execution for an equivalent serial schedule. In Section

18.2.1 we define timestamps. Then we discuss how serializability is enforced by ordering transactions based on their timestamps, in Section 18.2.2.

18.2.1 *Timestamps*

A **timestamp** is a unique identifier created by the DBMS to identify a transaction. Typically, timestamp values are assigned in the order in which the transactions are submitted to the system, so a timestamp can be thought of as the *transaction start time*. We will refer to the timestamp of transaction T as **TS(T)**. Concurrency control techniques based on timestamps do not use locks; hence, deadlocks *cannot* occur.

Timestamps can be generated in several ways. One possibility is to use a counter that is incremented each time its value is assigned to a transaction. The transaction timestamps are numbered 1, 2, 3, . . . in this scheme. A computer counter has a finite maximum value, so the system must periodically reset the counter to zero when no transactions are executing for some short period of time. Another way to implement timestamps is to use the current value of the system clock and ensure that no two timestamp values are generated during the same tick of the clock.

18.2.2 *The Timestamp Ordering Algorithm*

The idea for this scheme is to order the transactions based on their timestamps. A schedule in which the transactions participate is then serializable, and the equivalent serial schedule has the transactions in order of their timestamp values. This is called **timestamp ordering** (TO). Notice how this differs from two-phase locking. In two-phase locking, a schedule is serializable by being equivalent to *some* serial schedule allowed by the locking protocols; in timestamp ordering, however, the schedule is equivalent to the *particular* serial order that corresponds to the order of the transaction timestamps. The algorithm must ensure that, for each item accessed by more than one transaction in the schedule, the order in which the item is accessed does not violate the serializability of the schedule. To do this, the **basic TO** algorithm associates with each database item X two timestamp (**TS**) values:

1. **read_TS(X)**: The **read timestamp** of item X; this is the largest timestamp among all the timestamps of transactions that have successfully read item X.

2. **write_TS(X)**: The **write timestamp** of item X; this is the largest of all the timestamps of transactions that have successfully written item X.

Whenever some transaction T tries to issue a read_item(X) or a write_item(X) operation, the basic TO algorithm compares the timestamp of T with the read timestamp and the write timestamp of X to ensure that the timestamp order of execution of the transactions is not violated. If the timestamp order is violated by the operation, then transaction T will violate the equivalent serial schedule, so T is aborted. Then T is resubmitted to the system as a new transaction with a *new* timestamp. If T is aborted and rolled back, any transaction T_1 that may have used a value written by T must also be rolled back. Similarly, any transaction T_2 that may have used a value written by T_1 must also be rolled back, and so on. This effect is known as **cascading rollback** and is one of the problems associated with basic TO, since the schedules produced are not recoverable. The concurrency control algorithm must check whether the timestamp ordering of transactions is violated in the following two cases:

1. Transaction T issues a write_item(X) operation:

    a. If read_TS(X) > TS(T) or if write_TS(X) > TS(T), then abort and roll back T and reject the operation. This should be done because some transaction with a timestamp greater than TS(T)—and hence *after* T in the timestamp ordering—has already read or written the value of item X before T had a chance to write X, thus violating the timestamp ordering.

    b. If the condition in part a does not occur, then execute the write_item(X) operation of T and set write_TS(X) to TS(T).

2. Transaction T issues a read_item(X) operation:

    a. If write_TS(X) > TS(T), then abort and roll back T and reject the operation. This should be done because some transaction with timestamp greater than TS(T)—and hence *after* T in the timestamp ordering—has already written the value of item X before T had a chance to read X.

    b. If write_TS(X) ≤ TS(T), then execute the read_item(X) operation of T and set read_TS(X) to the larger of TS(T) and the current read_TS(X).

Hence, the basic TO algorithm checks whenever two *conflicting operations* occur in the incorrect order, and rejects the later of the two operations by aborting the transaction that issued it. The schedules produced by basic TO are hence guaranteed to be conflict serializable. A modification of the algorithm, known as **Thomas's write rule,** does not enforce conflict serializability; but it rejects fewer write operations, by modifying the checks for the write_item(X) operation as follows:

    a. If read_TS(X) > TS(T), then abort and roll back T and reject the operation.

    b. If write_TS(X) > TS(T), then do not execute the write operation but continue processing. This is because some transaction with timestamp greater than TS(T)—and hence after T in the timestamp ordering—has already written the value of X. Hence, we must ignore the write_item(X) operation of T because it is already outdated and obsolete. Notice that any conflict arising from this situation would be detected by case a.

    c. If neither the condition in part a nor the condition in part b occurs, then execute the write_item(X) operation of T and set write_TS(X) to TS(T).

The timestamp ordering protocol, like the two-phase locking protocol, guarantees serializability of schedules. However, some schedules are possible under each protocol that are not allowed under the other. Hence, neither protocol allows *all possible* serializable schedules. As mentioned earlier, deadlock does not occur with timestamp ordering. However, cyclic restart (and hence starvation) may occur if a transaction is continually aborted and restarted.

As was mentioned earlier, the basic TO algorithm enforces conflict serializability, but it does not ensure recoverable schedules; and hence it does not ensure cascadeless or strict schedules either (see Section 17.4.2). A variation of basic TO called **strict TO** ensures that the schedules are both strict and (conflict) serializable. In this variation, a transaction T that issues a read_item(X) or write_item(X) such that TS(T) > write_TS(X) has its read or write operation *delayed* until the transaction T' that *wrote* the value of X (hence TS(T') = write_TS(X)) has committed or aborted. To implement this algorithm, it is necessary to simulate the locking of an item X that has been written by transaction T' until T' is either committed or aborted. This algorithm does not cause deadlock, since T waits for T' only if TS(T) > TS(T').

18.3 Multiversion Concurrency Control Techniques⋆

Other protocols for concurrency control keep the old values of a data item when the item is updated. These are known as **multiversion concurrency control** techniques, because several versions (values) of an item are maintained. When a transaction requires access to an item, an appropriate version is chosen to maintain the serializability of the currently executing schedule, if possible. The idea is that some read operations that would be rejected in other techniques can still be accepted by reading an *older version* of the item to maintain serializability. When a transaction writes an item, it writes a *new version* and the old version of the item is retained. In general, multiversion concurrency control algorithms use the concept of view serializability rather than conflict serializability.

An obvious drawback of multiversion techniques is that more storage is needed to maintain multiple versions of the database items. However, older versions may have to be maintained anyway—for example, for recovery purposes. In addition, some database applications require older versions to be kept to maintain a history of the evolution of data item values. The extreme case is a *temporal database*, which keeps track of all changes and the times at which they occurred. In such cases, there is no additional penalty for multiversion techniques, since older versions are already maintained.

Several multiversion concurrency control schemes have been proposed. We discuss two schemes here, one based on timestamp ordering and the other based on two-phase locking.

18.3.1 *Multiversion Technique Based on Timestamp Ordering*

In this multiversion technique, several versions X_1, X_2, . . ., X_k of each data item X are kept by the system. For each version, the value of version X_i and the following two timestamps are kept:

1. read_TS(X_i): The **read timestamp** of X_i; this is the largest of all the timestamps of transactions that have successfully read *version* X_i.

2. write_TS(X_i): The **write timestamp** of X_i; this is the timestamp of the transaction that wrote the value of version X_i.

Whenever a transaction T is allowed to execute a write_item(X) operation, a new version X_{k+1} of item X is created, with both the write_TS(X_{k+1}) and the read_TS(X_{k+1}) set to TS(T). Correspondingly, when a transaction T is allowed to read the value of version X_i, the value of read_TS(X_i) is set to the larger of read_TS(X_i) and TS(T).

To ensure serializability, we use the following two rules to control the reading and writing of data items:

1. If transaction T issues a write_item(X) operation, and version i of X has the highest write_TS(X$_i$) of all versions of X that is also *less than or equal to* TS(T), and TS(T) < read_TS(X$_i$), then abort and roll back transaction T; otherwise, create a new version X$_j$ of X with read_TS(X$_j$) = write_TS(X$_j$) = TS(T).

2. If transaction T issues a read_item(X) operation, find the version i of X that has the highest write_TS(X$_i$) of all versions of X that is also *less than or equal to* TS(T); then return the value of X$_i$ to transaction T, and set the value of read_TS(X$_i$) to the larger of TS(T) and the current read_TS(X$_i$).

In case 1, transaction T may be aborted and rolled back. This happens if T is attempting to write a version of X that should have been read by another transaction T' whose timestamp is read_TS(X$_i$); however, T' has already read version X$_i$, which was written by the transaction with timestamp equal to write_TS(X$_i$). If this conflict occurs, T is rolled back; otherwise, a new version of X, written by transaction T, is created. Notice that, if T is rolled back, cascading rollback may occur. Hence, to ensure recoverability, a transaction T is not allowed to commit until after all the transactions that have written versions that T has read have committed.

18.3.2 *Multiversion Two-phase Locking*

In this scheme, there are three locking modes for an item: read, write, and certify. Hence, the state of an item X can be one of "read locked," "write locked," "certify locked," and "unlocked." In the standard locking scheme with only read and write locks (see Section 18.1.1), a write lock is an exclusive lock. We can describe the relationship between read and write locks in the standard scheme by means of the **lock compatibility table** shown in Figure 18.6(a). An entry of *yes* means that, if a transaction T holds the type of lock specified in the column header on item X and if transaction T' requests the type of lock specified in the row header on the same item X, then T' can *obtain the lock* because the locking modes are compatible. On the other hand, an entry of *no* in the table indicates that the locks are not compatible, so T' must wait until T releases the lock.

In the standard locking scheme, once a transaction obtains a write lock on an item, no other transactions can access that item. The idea behind multiversion two-phase locking is to allow other transactions T' to read an item X while a single transaction T holds a write lock on X. This is accomplished by allowing **two versions** for each item X; one version must always have been written by some committed transaction. The second version X' is created when a transaction T acquires a write lock on the item. Other transactions can continue to read the committed version X while T holds the write lock. Now transaction T can change the value of X' as needed, without affecting the value of the committed version X. However, once T is ready to commit, it must obtain a **certify lock** on all items that it currently holds write locks on before it can commit. The certify lock is not compatible with read locks, so the transaction may have to delay its commit until all its write-locked items are released by any reading transactions. At this point, the committed version X of the data item is set to the value of version X', version X' is

(a)

	Read	Write
Read	yes	no
Write	no	no

(b)

	Read	Write	Certify
Read	yes	yes	no
Write	yes	no	no
Certify	no	no	no

Figure 18.6 Lock compatibility. (a) Compatibility table for standard locking scheme. (b) Compatibility table for multiversion two-phase locking.

discarded, and the certify locks are then released. The lock compatibility table for this scheme is shown in Figure 18.6(b).

In this multiversion two-phase locking scheme, reads can proceed concurrently with a write operation—an arrangement not permitted under the standard two-phase locking schemes. The cost is that a transaction may have to delay its commit until it obtains exclusive certify locks on all the items it has updated. It can be shown that this scheme avoids cascading aborts, since transactions are only allowed to read the version X that was written by a committed transaction. However, deadlocks may occur if conversion of a read lock to a write lock is allowed, and these must be handled by variations of the techniques discussed in Section 18.1.3.

18.4 Validation (Optimistic) Concurrency Control Techniques*

In all the concurrency control techniques we have discussed so far, a certain degree of checking is done *before* a database operation can be executed. For example, in locking, a check is done to determine whether the item being accessed is locked. In timestamp ordering, the transaction timestamp is checked against the read and write timestamps of the item. Such checking represents overhead during transaction execution, with the effect of slowing down the transactions.

In **optimistic concurrency control** techniques, also known as **validation** or **certification** techniques, *no checking* is done while the transaction is executing. Several proposed concurrency control methods use the validation technique. We will describe only one scheme here. In this scheme, updates in the transaction are *not* applied directly to the database items until the transaction reaches its end. During transaction execution, all updates are applied to *local copies* of the data items that are kept for the transaction. At the end of transaction execution, a **validation phase** checks whether any of the transaction updates violate serializability. Certain information needed by the validation phase must be kept by the system. If serializability is not violated, the transaction is committed and the database is updated from the local copies; otherwise, the transaction is aborted and then restarted later.

There are three phases for this concurrency control protocol:

1. The **read phase:** A transaction can read values of data items from the database. However, updates are applied only to local copies of the data items kept in the transaction workspace.

2. The **validation phase:** Checking is performed to ensure that serializability will not be violated if the transaction updates are applied to the database.

3. The **write phase:** If the validation phase is successful, the transaction updates are applied to the database; otherwise, the updates are discarded and the transaction is restarted.

The idea behind optimistic concurrency control is to do all the checks at once; hence, transaction execution proceeds with a minimum of overhead until the validation phase is reached. If there is little interference among the transactions, most transactions will be validated successfully. However, if there is much interference, many transactions that execute to completion will have their results discarded and must be restarted later. Under these circumstances, optimistic techniques do not work well. The techniques are called "optimistic" because they assume that little interference will occur and hence that there is no need to do checking during transaction execution.

The optimistic protocol we describe uses transaction timestamps and also requires that the write_sets and read_sets of the transactions be kept by the system. In addition, start and end times for some of the three phases need to be kept for each transaction. The **write_set** of a transaction is the set of items written by the transaction, whereas the **read_set** is the set of items read by the transaction. In its validation phase for transaction T_i, the protocol checks that T_i does not interfere with any committed transactions or with any other transactions currently in their validation phase. The validation phase for T_i checks that, for each such transaction T_j that is committed or is in its validation phase, *one* of the following conditions holds:

1. Transaction T_j completes its write phase before T_i starts its read phase.

2. T_i starts its write phase after T_j completes its write phase, and the read_set of T_i has no items in common with the write_set of T_j.

3. Both the read_set and the write_set of T_i have no items in common with the write_set of T_j, and T_j completes its read phase before T_i completes its read phase.

If any one of these three conditions holds, there is no interference and T_i is validated successfully. If none of these three conditions holds, the validation of transaction T_i fails and it is aborted and restarted later because interference may have occurred.

18.5 Granularity of Data Items

All concurrency control techniques assumed that the database was formed of a number of items. A database item could be chosen to be one of the following:

- A database record.
- A field value of a database record.
- A disk block.
- A whole file.
- The whole database.

Several trade-offs must be considered in choosing the data item size. We shall discuss data item size in the context of locking, although similar arguments can be made for other concurrency control techniques.

First, notice that the larger the data item size is, the lower is the degree of concurrency permitted. For example, if the data item size is a disk block, a transaction T that needs to lock a record A must lock the whole disk block X that contains A. This is because a lock is associated with the whole data item X. Now if another transaction S wants to lock a different record B that happens to reside in the same block X in a conflicting lock mode, it is forced to wait until the first transaction releases the lock on block X. If the data item size was a single record, transaction S could proceed as it would by locking a different data item (record B) than that locked by T (record A).

On the other hand, the smaller the data item size is, the more items will exist in the database. Because every item is associated with a lock, the system will have a larger number of active locks to be handled by the lock manager. More lock and unlock operations will be performed, causing a higher overhead. In addition, more storage space will be required for the lock table. For timestamps, storage is required for the read_TS and write_TS for each data item, and the overhead of handling a large number of items is similar to that in the case of locking.

The size of data items is often called the **data item granularity**. *Fine granularity* refers to small item sizes, whereas *coarse granularity* refers to large item sizes. Given the above trade-offs, the obvious question to ask is: What is the best item size? The answer is that *it depends on the types of transactions involved.* If a typical transaction accesses a small number of records, it is advantageous to have the data item granularity be one record. On the other hand, if a transaction typically accesses many records of the same file, it may be better to have block or file granularity so that the transaction will consider all those records as one (or a few) data items.

Most concurrency control techniques have a uniform data item size. However, some techniques have been proposed that permit variable item sizes. In these techniques, the data item size may be changed to the granularity that best suits the transactions that are currently executing on the system.

18.6 Some Other Concurrency Control Issues

In this section, we discuss some other issues relevant to concurrency control. In Section 18.6.1, we discuss problems associated with insertion and deletion of records and the so-called "phantom problem," which may occur when records are inserted. Then, in Section 18.6.2, we discuss problems that may occur when a transaction outputs some data to a terminal before it commits, and then the transaction is later aborted.

18.6.1 Insertion, Deletion, and Phantom Records

When a new data item is **inserted** in the database, it obviously cannot be accessed until after the item is created and the insert operation is completed. In a locking environment, a lock for the item can be created and set to exclusive (write) mode; the lock can be released at the same time as other write locks would be released, based on the concurrency control protocol being used. For a timestamp-based protocol, the read and write timestamps of the new item are set to the timestamp of the creating transaction.

A **deletion** operation is applied on an existing data item. For locking protocols, again an exclusive (write) lock must be obtained before the transaction can delete the item. For timestamp ordering, the protocol must ensure that no later transaction has read or written the item before allowing a transaction to delete the item.

A problem known as the **phantom problem** can occur when a new record that is being inserted by some transaction T satisfies a condition that a set of records accessed by another transaction T' must satisfy. For example, suppose that transaction T is inserting a new EMPLOYEE record belonging to department number 5 (that is, whose DNO attribute is 5), whereas transaction T' is accessing all EMPLOYEE records whose DNO = 5 in order to add up all their SALARY values (to calculate the personnel budget for department 5). If the equivalent serial order is T followed by T', then T' must read the new EMPLOYEE record and include its SALARY in the sum calculation. For the equivalent serial order T' followed by T, the new salary should not be included. Notice that, although the transactions logically conflict, in the latter case there is really no record (data item) in common between the two transactions, since T' may have locked all the records with DNO = 5 *before* T inserted the new record. This is because the record that causes the conflict is a **phantom record** that has suddenly appeared in the database on being inserted. If other operations in the two transactions conflict, the conflict due to the phantom record may not be recognized by the concurrency control protocol.

One solution to the phantom record problem is known as **index locking**, and can be used in conjunction with a two-phase locking protocol. Recall from Chapter 5 that an index includes entries that have an attribute value, plus a set of pointers to all records in the file with that value. For example, an index on the DNO attribute of the EMPLOYEE file would include an entry for each distinct DNO value, plus a set of pointers to all EMPLOYEE records with that value. If the index entry is locked *before* the record itself can be accessed, then the conflict on the phantom record can be detected. This is because transaction T' would request a read lock on the *index entry* for DNO = 5, and T would request a write lock on the same entry *before* they could place the locks on the actual records. Since the index locks conflict, the phantom conflict would be detected. A more general technique, called **predicate locking,** would lock access to all records that satisfy an *arbitrary predicate* (condition) in a similar manner; however predicate locks have proved to be difficult to implement efficiently.

18.6.2 *Interactive Transactions*

Another problem occurs when interactive transactions read input and write output to an interactive device, such as a terminal screen, before they are committed. The problem is that a user can input a value of a data item to a transaction T that is based on some value written to the screen by transaction T', which may not have committed. This dependency between T and T' cannot be modeled by the system concurrency control method, since it is only based on the user interacting with the two transactions.

An approach to dealing with this problem is to postpone output of transactions to the screen until they have committed.

18.7 Summary

In this chapter we discussed DBMS techniques for concurrency control. In Section 18.1 we discussed the two-phase locking protocol and a number of its variations. We introduced the concepts of shared (read) and exclusive (write) locks, and showed how locking can guarantee serializability when used in conjunction with the two-phase locking rule. We discussed the basic two-phase locking protocol, as well as conservative and strict two-phase locking. We also presented various techniques for dealing with the deadlock problem, which can occur with locking.

In Section 18.2, we presented the timestamp ordering protocol, which ensures serializability based on the order of transaction timestamps. Timestamps are unique, system-generated transaction identifiers. We discussed Thomas's write rule, which improves performance but does not guarantee conflict serializability. The strict timestamp ordering protocol was also presented.

In Section 18.3 we discussed two multiversion protocols, which assume that older versions of data items can be kept in the database. One technique, called multiversion two-phase locking, assumes that two versions can exist for an item and attempts to increase concurrency by making write and read locks compatible (at the cost of introducing an additional certify lock mode). We also presented a multiversion protocol based on timestamp ordering. Section 18.4 presented an example of an optimistic protocol, which is also known as a certification or validation protocol. Section 18.5 briefly discussed the issue of data item granularity, and Section 18.6 introduced the phantom problem and problems with interactive transactions.

In the next chapter, we give an overview of recovery techniques.

Review Questions

18.1. What is the two-phase locking protocol? How does it guarantee serializability?

18.2. What are some variations of the two-phase locking protocol? Why is strict two-phase locking often preferred?

18.3. Discuss the problems of deadlock, livelock, and starvation, and the different approaches to dealing with these problems.

18.4. Compare binary locks to exclusive/shared locks. Why is the latter type of locks preferable?

18.5. Describe the wait-die and wound-wait protocols for deadlock prevention.

18.6. Describe the cautious waiting, no waiting, and timeout protocols for deadlock prevention.

18.7. What is a timestamp? How does the system generate timestamps?

18.8. Discuss the timestamp ordering protocol for concurrency control. How does strict timestamp ordering differ from basic timestamp ordering?

18.9. Discuss two multiversion techniques for concurrency control.

18.10. What is a certify lock? What are the advantages and disadvantages of using certify locks?

18.11. How do optimistic concurrency control techniques differ from other concurrency control techniques? Why are they also called validation or certification techniques? Discuss the typical phases of an optimistic concurrency control method.

18.12. How does the granularity of data items affect the performance of concurrency control? What factors affect selection of granularity size for data items?

18.13. What type of locks are needed for insert and delete operations?

18.14. What is a phantom record? Discuss the problem that a phantom record can cause for concurrency control.

18.15. How does index locking resolve the phantom problem?

18.16. What is a predicate lock?

Exercises

18.17. Prove that the basic two-phase locking protocol guarantees conflict serializability of schedules. (*Hint:* Show that, if a serializability graph for a schedule has a cycle, then at least one of the transactions participating in the schedule does not obey the two-phase locking protocol.)

18.18. Modify the data structures for multiple-mode locks and the algorithms for read_lock(X), write_lock(X), and unlock(X) so that upgrading and downgrading of locks are possible. (*Hint:* The lock needs to keep track of the transaction id(s) that hold the lock, if any.)

18.19. Prove that strict two-phase locking guarantees strict schedules.

18.20. Prove that the wait-die and wound-wait protocols avoid deadlock and livelock.

18.21. Prove that cautious waiting avoids deadlock.

18.22. Apply the timestamp ordering algorithm to the schedules of Figure 17.8(b) and (c), and determine whether the algorithm will allow the execution of the schedules.

18.23. Repeat Exercise 18.22, but use the multiversion timestamp ordering method.

Selected Bibliography

The two-phase locking protocol, and the concept of predicate locks is presented in Eswaran et al. (1976). The books by Bernstein et al. (1988), Gray and Reuter (1993), and Papadimitriou (1986) are devoted to concurrency control and recovery. Locking is discussed in Gray et al. (1975), Lien and Weinberger (1978), Kedem and Silbershatz (1980), and Korth (1983). Deadlocks and wait-for graphs were formalized by Holt (1972), and the wait-wound and wound-die schemes are presented in Rosenkrantz et al. (1978). Cautious waiting is discussed in Hsu et al. (1992). Helal et al. (1993) compares various locking approaches. Timestamp-based concurrency control techniques are discussed in Bernstein and Goodman (1980) and Reed (1983). Optimistic concurrency control is discussed in Kung and Robinson (1981) and Bassiouni (1988). Papadimitriou and Kanellakis (1979) and Bernstein et al. (1983) discuss multiversion techniques. Multiversion timestamp ordering was proposed in Reed (1978, 1983), and multiversion two-phase locking is discussed in Lai and Wilkinson (1984). A method for multiple locking granularities was proposed in Gray et al. (1975), and the effects of locking granularities are analyzed in Ries and Stonebraker (1977). Bhargava and Reidl (1988) presents an approach for dynamically choosing among various concurrency control and recovery methods.

Other recent work on concurrency control includes semantic-based concurrency control (Badrinath and Ramamritham 1992), transaction models for long running activities (Dayal et al. 1991), and multilevel transaction management (Hasse and Weikum 1991).

CHAPTER 19

Recovery Techniques

In this chapter we discuss some of the techniques that can be used to recover from transaction failures. We have already discussed the different causes of failure (such as system crashes and transaction errors), in Section 17.1.4. We have also covered many of the concepts that are used by recovery processes (such as the system log, checkpoints, and commit points), in Section 17.2.

We first introduce recovery concepts in Section 19.1, including an outline of recovery procedures and categorization of recovery algorithms. We also discuss write-ahead logging, in-place versus shadow updates, and the process of rolling back (undoing) the effect of a transaction. In Section 19.2, we present recovery techniques based on deferred update, also known as the NO-UNDO/REDO technique. In Section 19.3, we discuss recovery techniques based on immediate update; these include the UNDO/REDO and UNDO/NO-REDO algorithms. We discuss the technique known as shadowing or shadow paging, which can be categorized as a NO-UNDO/NO-REDO algorithm in Section 19.4. Recovery in multidatabase transactions is briefly discussed in Section 19.5. Finally, techniques for recovery from catastrophic failure are discussed in Section 19.6.

The techniques we discuss here are *not* descriptions of recovery as implemented in a specific system. Our emphasis is on conceptually describing several different approaches to recovery. For descriptions of recovery features in specific systems, the reader should consult the bibliographic notes and the user manuals for those systems.

Recovery techniques are often intertwined with the concurrency control mechanisms. Certain recovery techniques are best used with specific concurrency control methods. We will attempt to discuss recovery concepts independently of concurrency control mechanisms, but we will discuss the circumstances under which a particular recovery mechanism is best used with a certain concurrency control protocol.

19.1 Recovery Concepts

19.1.1 Recovery Outline

Recovery from transaction failures usually means that the database is *restored* to some state from the past so that a correct state—close to the time of failure—can be *reconstructed* from that past state. To do this, the system must keep information about changes to data items during transaction execution outside the database. This information is typically kept in the **system log,** as discussed in Section 17.2.2. A typical strategy for recovery may be summarized informally as follows:

1. If there is extensive damage to a wide portion of the database due to catastrophic failure, such as a disk crash, the recovery method restores a past copy of the database that was *dumped* to archival storage (typically tape) and reconstructs a more current state by reapplying or *redoing* committed transaction operations from the log up to the time of failure.

2. When the database is not physically damaged but has become inconsistent due to noncatastrophic failures of types 1 through 4 of Section 17.1.4, the strategy is to reverse the changes that caused the inconsistency by *undoing* some operations. It may also be necessary to *redo* some operations in order to restore a consistent state of the database, as we shall see. In this case we do not need a complete archival copy of the database. Rather, the entries kept in the system log are consulted during recovery.

We can distinguish two main techniques for recovery from noncatastrophic transaction failures. The **deferred update** techniques do not actually update the database until *after* a transaction reaches its commit point; then the updates are recorded in the database. Before commit, all transaction updates are recorded in the local transaction workspace. During commit, the updates are first recorded persistently in the log and then written to the database. If a transaction fails before reaching its commit point, it will not have changed the database in any way, so UNDO is not needed. It may be necessary to REDO the effect of the operations of a committed transaction from the log, because their effect may not yet have been recorded in the database. Hence, deferred update is also known as the **NO-UNDO/REDO algorithm**. We discuss this technique in Section 19.2.

In the **immediate update** techniques, the database may be updated by some operations of a transaction *before* the transaction reaches its commit point. However, these operations are typically recorded in the log *on disk* by force-writing before they are applied to the database, making recovery still possible. If a transaction fails after recording some changes in the database but before reaching its commit point, the effect of its operations on the database must be undone; that is, the transaction must be rolled back. In the general case of immediate update, both *undo* and *redo* are required during recovery, so it is known as the **UNDO/REDO algorithm**. A variation of the algorithm where all updates are recorded in the database before a transaction commits requires *undo* only, so it is known as the **UNDO/NO-REDO algorithm**. We discuss these techniques in Section 19.3.

19.1.2 System Concepts for Recovery

The recovery process is often closely intertwined with operating system functions—in particular, the buffering and caching of disk pages in main memory. Typically, one or more disk pages that include the data item to be updated are **cached** into a main memory buffer and then updated in memory before being written back to disk. The caching of disk pages is traditionally an operating system function, but because of its importance to the efficiency of recovery procedures, it is sometimes handled by the DBMS by calling low-level operating systems routines. In general, it is convenient to consider that each data item corresponds to one disk page for recovery purposes.

Typically a collection of in-memory buffers, called the **DBMS cache,** is kept under the control of the DBMS for the purpose of holding database items. A **directory** for the cache is used to keep track of which database items are in the buffers. This can be a table of <item name, buffer location> entries. When the DBMS requests action on some item, it first checks the directory to determine whether the item is in the cache. If it is not in the cache, the item must be located on disk, and the appropriate disk pages are copied into the cache. It may be necessary to **flush** some of the cache buffers to make space available for the new item. Some page-replacement strategy from operating systems, such as least recently used (LRU) or first-in-first-out (FIFO), can be used to select the buffers for flushing.

Associated with each item in the cache is a **dirty bit,** which can be included in the directory entry, to indicate whether or not the item has been modified. When the item is first read from disk into a cache buffer, the buffer directory is updated with the new item name, and the dirty bit is set to 0 (zero). As soon as the item is modified, the dirty bit for the corresponding directory entry is set to 1 (one). When an item is flushed, it is written back to disk only if its dirty bit is 1.

Two main strategies are employed when flushing a modified data item back to disk. The first strategy, known as **in-place updating,** writes the data item in the *same disk location*, thus overwriting the old value of the data item on disk. Hence, a single copy of each data item is maintained on disk. The second strategy, known as **shadowing,** writes a new item at a different disk location, so multiple copies of a data item can be maintained. In general, the old value of the data item before updating is called the **before image (BFIM)**, and the new value after updating is called the **after image (AFIM)**. In shadowing, both the BFIM and the AFIM are kept on disk; hence, it is not strictly necessary to maintain a log for recovering. We discuss recovery based on shadowing in Section 19.4.

When in-place updating is used, it is necessary to use a log for recovery (see Section 17.2.2). In this case, the recovery mechanism must ensure that the BFIM of the data item is recorded in the appropriate log entry and that log entry is flushed to disk before the BFIM is overwritten with the AFIM. This process is generally known as a **write-ahead logging**. Before we can describe a protocol for write-ahead logging, we need to distinguish between two types of log entries: those needed for UNDO, and those needed for REDO. A **REDO-type log entry** is a log entry corresponding to a write_item operation of some transaction that includes the new value (AFIM) of the item; such an entry is needed if the recovery technique must *redo* the effect of the operation from the log by setting the item value in the database to its AFIM. The **UNDO-type log entries** include write_item entries that include the old value (BFIM) of the item; such an entry is needed if the recovery technique must *undo* the effect of the operation from the log by setting the item value in the database back to its BFIM. In addition, when cascading rollback is possible, read_item entries in the log are considered to be UNDO-type entries (see Section 19.1.3).

To permit recovery when in-place updating is used, the appropriate entries required for recovery must be permanently recorded in the log on disk before changes are applied to the database. For example, consider the following **write-ahead logging (WAL)** protocol for a recovery algorithm that requires both UNDO and REDO:

1. The before image of an item cannot be overwritten by its after image on disk until all UNDO-type log records for the updating transaction—up to this point in time—have been force-written to disk.

2. The commit operation of a transaction cannot be completed until all the REDO-type and UNDO-type log records for that transaction have been force-written to disk.

To facilitate the recovery process, the DBMS recovery subsystem maintains a number of lists related to the transactions being processed in the system. These include a list for **active transactions** that have started but not committed as yet, a list of all **committed transactions** since the last checkpoint, and a list of **aborted transactions** since the last checkpoint. Maintaining these lists makes the recovery process more efficient.

19.1.3 *Transaction Rollback*

If a transaction fails for whatever reason after updating the database, it may be necessary to **roll back** or UNDO the transaction. Any data item values that have been changed by the transaction must be returned to their previous values (BFIMs). The log entries are used to recover the old values of data items that must be rolled back.

If a transaction T is rolled back, any transaction S that has, in the interim, read the value of some data item X written by T must also be rolled back. Similarly, once S is rolled back, any transaction R that has read the value of some data item Y written by S must also be rolled back; and so on. This phenomenon is called **cascading rollback,** and can occur when the recovery protocol ensures *recoverable* schedules but does not ensure *strict* or *cascadeless* schedules (see Section 17.4.2). Cascading rollback, understandably, can be quite time-consuming. That is why most recovery mechanisms are designed such that cascading rollback *is never required.*

Figure 19.1 shows an example where cascading rollback is required. The read and write operations of three individual transactions are shown in Figure 19.1(a). Figure 19.1(b) shows the system log at the point of a system crash for a particular execution schedule of these transactions. The values of data items A, B, C, and D, which are used

	T_1	T_2	T_3
(a)	read_item(A)	read_item(B)	read_item(C)
	read_item(D)	write_item(B)	write_item(B)
	write_item(D)	read_item(D)	read_item(A)
		write_item(D)	write_item(A)

		A	B	C	D
		30	15	40	20
(b)	[start-transaction,T_3]				
	[read_item,T_3,C]				
*	[write_item,T_3,B,15,12]		12		
	[start-transaction,T_2]				
	[read_item,T_2,B]				
**	[write_item,T_2,B,12,18]		18		
	[start-transaction,T_1]				
	[read_item,T_1,A]				
	[read_item,T_1,D]				
	[write_item,T_1,D,20,25]				25
	[read_item,T_2,D]				
**	[write_item,T_2,D,25,26]				26
	[read_item,T_3,A]				

←System crash

* T_3 is rolled back because it did not reach its commit point.
** T_2 is rolled back because it reads the value of item B written by T_3.
The rest of the [write,...] entries in the log are redone.

(c)

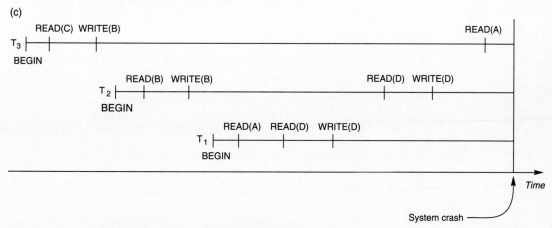

Figure 19.1 Cascading rollback. (a) The read and write operations of three transactions. (b) System log at point of crash. (c) Operations before the crash.

by the transactions, are shown to the right of the system log entries. We assume that the original item values, shown in the first line, are A = 30, B = 15, C = 40, and D = 20. At the point of system failure, transaction T_3 has not reached its conclusion and must be rolled back. The WRITE operations of T_3, marked by a single * in Figure 19.1(b), are the T_3 operations that are undone during transaction rollback. Figure 19.1(c) graphically shows the operations of the different transactions along the time axis.

We must now check for cascading rollback. From Figure 19.1(c) we see that transaction T_2 reads the value of item B that was written by transaction T_3; this can also be determined by examining the log. Because T_3 is rolled back, T_2 must now be rolled back, too. The WRITE operations of T_2, marked by ** in the log, are the ones that are undone. Note that only write_item operations need to be undone during transaction rollback; read_item operations are recorded in the log only to determine whether cascading rollback of additional transactions is necessary.

If rollback of transactions is *never* required by the recovery method (because the method guarantees cascadeless or strict schedules), we can keep *more limited information* in the system log. There is also no need to record any read_item operations in the log, because these are needed only for determining cascading rollback.

19.2 Recovery Techniques Based on Deferred Update

The idea behind deferred update techniques is to defer or postpone any actual updates to the database itself until the transaction completes its execution successfully and reaches its commit point. During transaction execution, the updates are recorded only in the log and in the transaction workspace. After the transaction reaches its commit point and the log is force-written to disk, the updates are recorded in the database itself. If a transaction fails before reaching its commit point, there is no need to undo any operations, because the transaction has not affected the database in any way.

We can state a typical deferred update protocol as follows:

1. A transaction cannot change the database until it reaches its commit point.
2. A transaction does not reach its commit point until all its update operations are recorded in the log *and* the log is force-written to disk.

Notice that step 2 of this protocol is a variation on the write-ahead logging (WAL) protocol. Because the database is never updated until after the transaction commits, there is never a need to UNDO any operations. Hence, this technique is known as the NO-UNDO/REDO algorithm. The REDO is needed in case the system fails after the transaction commits but before all its changes are recorded in the database. In this case, the transaction operations are redone from the log entries.

Usually, the method of recovery from failure is closely related to the concurrency control method in multiuser systems. First we discuss recovery in single-user systems, where no concurrency control is needed, so that we can understand the recovery process independently of any concurrency control method. Then we discuss how concurrency control may affect the recovery process.

19.2.1 *Recovery Using Deferred Update in a Single-user Environment*

In such an environment, the recovery algorithm can be rather simple. The algorithm RDU_S (recovery using deferred update in a single-user environment) uses a REDO procedure, given subsequently, for redoing certain write_item operations; it works as follows:

PROCEDURE RDU_S   Use two lists of transactions: the committed transactions since the last checkpoint, and the active transactions (at most one transaction will fall in this category, because the system is single-user). Apply the REDO operation to all the write_item operations of the committed transactions from the log *in the order in which they were written to the log*. Restart the active transactions.

The REDO procedure is defined as follows:

REDO(WRITE_OP)   Redoing a write_item operation WRITE_OP consists of examining its log entry [write_item,T,X,new_value] and setting the value of item X in the database to new_value, which is the after image (AFIM).

The REDO operation is required to be **idempotent;** that is, executing it over and over is equivalent to executing it just once. In fact, the whole recovery process should be idempotent. This is so because, if the system were to fail during the recovery process, the next recovery attempt might REDO certain write_item operations that had already been redone during the first recovery process. The result of recovery from a crash *during recovery* should be the same as the result of recovering *when there is no crash during recovery!*

Notice that the transaction in the active list will have had no effect on the database because of the deferred update protocol and is ignored completely by the recovery process. It is *implicitly rolled back*, because none of its operations were reflected in the database. However, the transaction must now be restarted, either automatically by the recovery process or manually by the user.

Figure 19.2 shows an example of recovery in a single-user environment, where the first failure occurs during execution of transaction T_2, as shown in Figure 19.2(b). The recovery process will redo the [write_item,T_1,D,20] entry in the log by resetting the value of item D to 20 (its new value). The [write,T_2, . . .] entries in the log are ignored by the recovery process because T_2 is not committed. If a second failure occurs during recovery from the first failure, the same recovery process is repeated from start to finish, with identical results.

(a) T_1 T_2

read_item(A)   read_item(B)
read_item(D)   write_item(B)
write_item(D)   read_item(D)
                          write_item(D)

(b)   [start-transaction,T_1]
        [write_item,T_1,D,20]
        [commit,T_1]
        [start-transaction,T_2]
        [write_item,T_2,B,10]
        [write_item,T_2,D,25] ← System crash

The [write-item, ...] operations of T_1 are redone.

T_2 log entries are ignored by the recovery process.

Figure 19.2   Recovery using deferred update in a single-user environment. (a)
                    The read and write operations of two transactions. (b) System
                    log at the point of crash.

19.2.2 Deferred Update with Concurrent Execution in a Multiuser Environment

For multiuser systems with concurrency control, the recovery process may be more complex, depending on the protocols used for concurrency control. In many cases, the concurrency control and recovery processes are interrelated. In general, the greater the degree of concurrency we wish to achieve, the more difficult the task of recovery becomes.

Consider a system in which concurrency control uses two-phase locking and prevents deadlock by preassigning all locks to items needed by a transaction before the transaction starts execution. To combine the deferred update method for recovery with this concurrency control technique, we can keep all the locks on items in effect *until the transaction reaches its commit point*. After that, the locks can be released. This ensures strict and serializable schedules. Assuming that [checkpoint] entries are included in the log, a possible recovery algorithm for this case, which we call RDU_M (recovery using deferred update in a multiuser environment), is given next. This procedure uses the REDO procedure defined earlier.

PROCEDURE RDU_M (WITH CHECKPOINTS)   Use two lists of transactions maintained by the system: the committed transactions T since the last checkpoint, and the active transactions T'. REDO all the WRITE operations of the committed transactions from the log, *in the order in which they were written into the log*. The transactions that are active and did not commit are effectively canceled and must be resubmitted.

Figure 19.3 shows a possible schedule of executing transactions. When the checkpoint was taken at time t_1, transaction T_1 had committed, whereas transactions T_3 and T_4 had not. Before the system crash at time t_2, T_3 and T_2 were committed but not T_4 and T_5. According to the RDU_M method, there is no need to redo the write_item operations of transaction T_1—or any transactions committed before the last checkpoint time t_1. Write_item operations of T_2 and T_3 must be redone, however, because both transactions reached their commit points after the last checkpoint. Recall that the log is force-written before committing a transaction. Transactions T_4 and T_5 are ignored: they are effectively canceled or rolled back because none of their write_item operations were recorded in the database under the deferred update protocol. We will refer to Figure 19.3 later to illustrate other recovery protocols.

We can make the NO-UNDO/REDO recovery algorithm *more efficient* by noting that, if a data item X has been updated more than once by committed transactions, it is only necessary to REDO *the last update of X* from the log during recovery, since the other updates would be overwritten by this last REDO in any case. In this case, we start from *the end of the log*; then, whenever an item is redone, it is added to a list of redone items. Before REDO is applied to an item, the list is checked; if the item appears on the list, it is not redone, since its last value has already been recovered.

A drawback of the method described here is that it limits the concurrent execution of transactions because *all items remain locked until the transaction reaches its commit point.* The method's main benefit is that transaction operations never need to be undone, for two reasons:

1. A transaction does not record its changes in the database until it reaches its commit point—that is, until it completes its execution successfully. Hence, a transaction is never rolled back because of failure during transaction execution.

2. A transaction will never read the value of an item that is written by an uncommitted transaction, because items remain locked until a transaction reaches its commit point. Hence, no cascading rollback will occur.

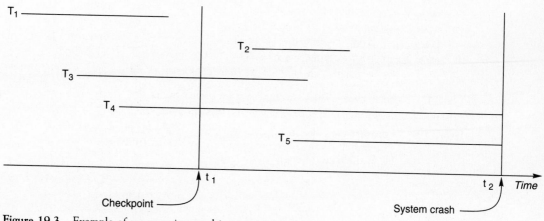

Figure 19.3 Example of recovery in a multiuser environment.

Figure 19.4 shows an example of recovery for a multiuser system that utilizes the recovery and concurrency control method just described.

19.2.3 Transaction Actions That Do Not Affect the Database

In general, a transaction will have actions that do not affect the database, such as generating and printing messages or reports from information retrieved from the database. If a transaction fails before completion, we may not want the user to get these reports, since the transaction has failed to complete. Hence, such reports should be generated only *after the transaction reaches its commit point*. A common method of dealing with such actions is to issue the commands that generate the reports but keep them as batch jobs. The batch jobs are executed only after the transaction reaches its commit point. If the transaction does not reach its commit point because of a failure, the batch jobs are canceled.

	T_1	T_2	T_3	T_4
(a)	read_item(A)	read_item(B)	read_item(A)	read_item(B)
	read_item(D)	write_item(B)	write_item(A)	write_item(B)
	write_item(D)	read_item(D)	read_item(C)	read_item(A)
		write_item(D)	write_item(C)	write_item(A)

(b)   [start_transaction,T_1]
[write_item,T_1,D,20]
[commit,T_1]
[checkpoint]
[start_transaction,T_4]
[write_item,T_4,B,15]
[write_item,T_4,A,20]
[commit,T_4]
[start_transaction,T_2]
[write_item,T_2,B,12]
[start_transaction,T_3]
[write_item,T_3,A,30]
[write_item,T_2,D,25] ←System crash

T_2 and T_3 are ignored because they did not reach their commit points.
T_4 is redone because its commit point is after the last system checkpoint.

Figure 19.4   Recovery using deferred update with concurrent transactions. (a) The read and write operations of four transactions. (b) System log at the point of crash.

19.3 Recovery Techniques Based on Immediate Update★

In these techniques, when a transaction issues an update command, the database can be updated "immediately," without any need to wait for the transaction to reach its commit point. In many of these techniques, however, an update operation must still be recorded in the log (on disk) *before* it is applied to the database so that we can recover, in case of failure, by using the write-ahead logging protocol (see Section 19.1.2).

When immediate update is allowed, provisions must be made for *undoing* the effect of update operations on the database, because a transaction can fail after it has applied some updates to the database itself. Hence, recovery schemes based on immediate update must include the capability to roll back a transaction by undoing the effect of its write_item operations.

In general, we can distinguish two main categories of immediate update algorithms. If the recovery technique ensures that all updates of a transaction are recorded in the database on disk *before the transaction commits*, there is never a need to REDO any operations of committed transactions. Such an algorithm is called **UNDO/NO-REDO**. On the other hand, if the transaction is allowed to commit before all its changes are written to the database, we have the most general recovery algorithm, known as **UNDO/REDO**. This is also the most complex technique. Next, we discuss two examples of UNDO/REDO algorithms and leave it as an exercise for the reader to develop the UNDO/NO-REDO variation.

19.3.1 *UNDO/REDO Recovery Based on Immediate Update in a Single-user Environment*

We first consider a single-user system so that we can examine the recovery process separately from concurrency control. If a failure occurs in a single-user system, the executing transaction at the time of failure may have recorded some changes in the database. The effect of all such operations must be undone as part of the recovery process. Hence, the recovery algorithm needs an UNDO procedure, described subsequently, to undo the effect of certain write_item operations that have been applied to the database following examination of their system log entry. The recovery algorithm RIU_S (recovery using immediate update in a single-user environment) also uses the REDO procedure defined earlier.

PROCEDURE RIU_S

1. Use two lists of transactions maintained by the system: the committed transactions since the last checkpoint, and the active transactions (at most one transaction will fall in this category, because the system is single-user).
2. Undo all the write_item operations of the *active* transaction from the log, using the UNDO procedure described hereafter.
3. Redo all the write_item operations of the *committed* transactions from the log, in the order in which they were written in the log, using the REDO procedure.

The UNDO procedure is defined as follows:

UNDO(WRITE_OP)   Undoing a write_item operation WRITE_OP consists of examining its log entry [write_item,T,X,old_value,new_value] and setting the value of item X in the database to old_value which is the before image (BFIM). Undoing a number of write_item operations from one or more transactions from the log must proceed in the *reverse order* from the order in which the operations were written in the log.

19.3.2   *UNDO/REDO Immediate Update with Concurrent Execution*

When concurrent execution is permitted, the recovery process again depends on the protocols used for concurrency control. The procedure RIU_M (recovery using immediate updates for a multiuser environment) outlines a recovery technique for concurrent trans-actions with immediate update. Assume that the log includes checkpoints and that the concurrency control protocol produces *strict schedules*—as, for example, the strict two-phase locking protocol does. Recall that a strict schedule does not allow a transaction to read or write an item unless the transaction that last wrote the item has committed. However, deadlocks can occur in strict two-phase locking, thus requiring UNDO of trans-actions. For a strict schedule, UNDO of an operation requires changing the item back to its old value (BFIM).

PROCEDURE RIU_M

1. Use two lists of transactions maintained by the system: the committed transactions since the last checkpoint, and the active transactions.
2. Undo all the write_item operations of the *active* (uncommitted) transactions, using the UNDO procedure. The operations should be undone in the reverse of the order in which they were written into the log.
3. Redo all the write_item operations of the *committed* transactions from the log, in the order in which they were written into the log.

19.4   Shadow Paging*

This recovery scheme does not require the use of a log in a single-user environment. In a multiuser environment, it may require a log if a log is needed for the concurrency control method.* Shadow paging considers the database to be made up of a number of fixed-size disk pages (or disk blocks)—say, n—for recovery purposes. A **page table** (or **directory**) with n entries is constructed, where the ith page table entry points to the ith database page on disk. The page table is kept in main memory if it is not too large, and all references—reads or writes—to database pages on disk go through the page table. When a transaction begins executing, the **current page table**—whose entries point to the most recent or current database pages on disk—is copied into a **shadow page table**. The shadow page table is then saved on disk while the current page table is used by the transaction.

---

*For example, the experimental DBMS SYSTEM R uses shadow paging along with checkpointing and logging.

During transaction execution, the shadow page table is *never* modified. When a write_item operation is performed, a new copy of the modified database page is created, but the old copy of that page is *not overwritten*. Instead, the new page is written else-where—on some previously unused disk block. The current page table entry is modified to point to the new disk block, whereas the shadow page table is not modified and continues to point to the old unmodified disk block. Figure 19.5 illustrates the concepts of a shadow page table and a current page table. For pages updated by the transaction, two versions are kept. The old version is referenced by the shadow page table, and the new version by the current page table.

To recover from a failure during transaction execution, it is sufficient to free the modified database pages and to discard the current page table. The state of the database before transaction execution is available through the shadow page table, and that state is recovered by reinstating the shadow page table so that it becomes the current page table once more. The database thus is returned to its state prior to the transaction that was executing when the crash occurred, and any modified pages are discarded. Committing a transaction corresponds to discarding the previous shadow page table and freeing the old page tables that it references. Since recovery involves neither undoing nor redoing data items, this technique can be categorized as a NO-UNDO/NO-REDO technique for recovery.

The advantage of shadow paging is that it makes undoing the effect of the executing transaction very simple. There is no need to undo or redo any transaction operations. In a multiuser environment with concurrent transactions, logs and checkpoints must be incorporated into the shadow paging technique. One disadvantage of shadow paging is

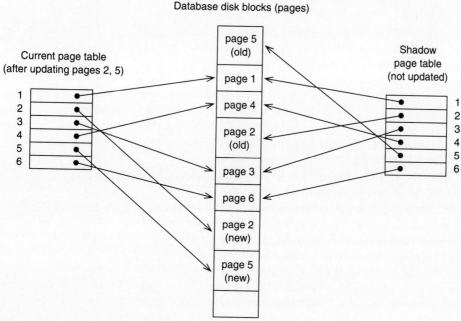

Figure 19.5 Shadow paging.

that the updated database pages change location on disk. This makes it difficult to keep related database pages close together on disk without complex storage management strategies. Furthermore, if the page table (directory) is large, the overhead of writing shadow page tables to disk as transactions commit is significant. A further complication is how to handle **garbage collection** when a transaction commits. The old pages referenced by the shadow page that have been updated must be released and added to a list of free pages for future use. These pages are no longer needed after the transaction commits, and the current page table replaces the shadow page table to become the valid page table.

19.5 Recovery in Multidatabase Transactions★

So far, we have implicitly assumed that a transaction accesses a single database. In some cases a single transaction, called a **multidatabase transaction,** may require access to multiple databases. These databases may even be stored on different types of DBMSs; for example, some DBMSs may be relational, whereas others are hierarchical or network DBMSs. In such a case, each DBMS involved in the multidatabase transaction will have its own recovery technique and transaction manager separate from those of the other DBMSs. This situation is somewhat similar to the case of a distributed database management system (see Chapter 23), where parts of the database reside at different sites that are connected by a communication network.

To maintain the atomicity of a multidatabase transaction, it is necessary to have a two-level recovery mechanism. A **global recovery manager,** or **coordinator,** is needed in addition to the local recovery managers. The coordinator usually follows a protocol called the **two-phase commit protocol,** whose two phases can be stated as follows:

PHASE 1:   When all participating databases signal the coordinator that the part of the multidatabase transaction involving each has concluded, the coordinator sends a message "prepare for commit" to each participant to get ready for committing the transaction. Each participating database receiving that message will force-write all log records to disk and then send a "ready to commit" or "OK" signal to the coordinator. If the force-writing to disk fails or the local transaction cannot commit for some reason, the participating database sends a "cannot commit" or "not OK" signal to the coordinator. If the coordinator does not receive a reply from a database within a certain time interval, it assumes a "not OK" response.

PHASE 2:   If *all* participating databases reply "OK," the transaction is successful, and the coordinator sends a "commit" signal for the transaction to the participating databases. Because all the local effects of the transaction have been recorded in the logs of the participating databases, recovery from failure is now possible. Each participating database completes transaction commit by writing a [commit] entry for the transaction in the log and permanently updating the database if needed. On the other hand, if one or more of the participating databases have a "not OK" response to the coordinator, the transaction has failed, and the coordinator sends a message to "roll back" or UNDO the local effect of the transaction to each participating database. This is done by undoing the transaction operations, using the log. ∎

The net effect of the two-phase commit protocol is that either all participating databases commit the effect of the transaction or none of them do. In case any of the participants—or the coordinator—fails, it is always possible to recover to a state where either the transaction is committed or it is rolled back. A failure during or before phase 1 usually requires the transaction to be rolled back, whereas a failure during phase 2 means that a successful transaction can recover and commit.

19.6 Database Backup and Recovery from Catastrophic Failures

So far, all the techniques we have discussed apply to noncatastrophic failures. A key assumption has been that the system log is maintained on the disk and is not lost as a result of the failure. Similarly, the shadow page table must be stored on disk to allow recovery when shadow paging is used. The recovery techniques we have discussed use the entries in the system log or the shadow page table to recover from the failure by bringing the database back to a consistent state.

The recovery manager of a DBMS must also be equipped to handle more catastrophic failures such as disk crashes. The main technique used to handle such crashes is that of **database backup**. The whole database and the log are periodically copied onto a cheap storage medium such as magnetic tapes. In case of a catastrophic system failure, the latest backup copy can be reloaded from the tape to the disk, and the system can be restarted.

To avoid losing all the effects of transactions that have been executed since the last backup, it is customary to back up the system log by periodically copying it to magnetic tape. The system log is usually substantially smaller than the database itself and hence can be backed up more frequently. When the system log is backed up, users do not lose all transactions they have performed since the last database backup. All committed transactions recorded in the portion of the system log that has been backed up can have their effect on the database reconstructed. A new system log is started after each database backup operation. Hence, to recover from disk failure, the database is first re-created on disk from its latest backup copy on tape. Following that, the effects of all the committed transactions whose operations have been entered in the backed-up copy of the system log are reconstructed.

19.7 Summary

In this chapter we discussed the techniques for recovery from transaction failures. The main goal of recovery is to ensure the atomicity property of a transaction. If a transaction fails before completing its execution, the recovery mechanism has to make sure that the transaction has no lasting effects on the database. We first gave an informal outline for a recovery process and then discussed system concepts for recovery. These included a discussion of caching, in-place updating versus shadowing, before and after images of a data item, UNDO versus REDO recovery operations, and the write-ahead logging protocol.

Next we discussed two different approaches to recovery: deferred update and immediate update. Deferred update techniques postpone any actual updating of the database until a transaction reaches its commit point. The transaction force-writes the log to disk before recording the updates in the database. This approach, when used with certain concurrency control methods, is designed never to require transaction rollback, and recovery simply consists of redoing the operations of transactions committed after the last checkpoint from the log. Deferred update can lead to a recovery algorithm known as NO-UNDO/REDO. Immediate update techniques may apply changes to the database before the transaction reaches a successful conclusion. In some protocols, any changes applied to the database must first be recorded in the log and force-written to disk so that these operations can be undone if necessary. We also gave an overview of a recovery algorithm for immediate update known as UNDO/REDO. Another algorithm, known as UNDO/NO-REDO, can also be developed for immediate update if all transaction actions are recorded in the database before commit.

We discussed the shadow paging technique for recovery, which keeps track of old database pages by using a shadow page table. This technique, which is classified as NO-UNDO/NO-REDO, does not require a log in single-user systems but still needs the log for multiuser systems. We then discussed the two-phase commit protocol, which is used for recovery from failures involving multidatabase transactions. Finally, we discussed recovery from catastrophic failures, which is typically done by backing up the database and the log to tape. The log can be backed up more frequently than the database, and the backup log can be used to redo operations starting from the last database backup.

Review Questions

19.1. Discuss the different types of transaction failures. What is meant by catastrophic failure?

19.2. Discuss the actions taken by the read_item and write_item operations on a database.

19.3. (Review from Chapter 17) What is the system log used for? What are the typical kinds of entries in a system log? What are checkpoints, and why are they important? What are transaction commit points, and why are they important?

19.4. How are buffering and caching techniques used by the recovery subsystem?

19.5. What are the before image (BFIM) and the after image (AFIM) of a data item? What is the difference between in-place updating and shadowing, with respect to their handling of BFIM and AFIM?

19.6. What are UNDO-type log entries and REDO-type log entries?

19.7. Describe the write-ahead logging protocol.

19.8. Identify three typical lists of transactions that are maintained by the recovery subsystem.

19.9. What is meant by transaction rollback? Why is it necessary to check for cascading rollback? Which recovery techniques do not require rollback?

19.10. Discuss the UNDO and REDO operations and the recovery techniques that use each.

19.11. Discuss the deferred update technique of recovery. What is the main advantage of this technique? Why is it called the NO-UNDO/REDO method?

19.12. How can recovery handle transaction operations that do not affect the database, such as the printing of reports by the transaction?

19.13. Discuss the immediate update recovery technique in both single-user and multiuser environments. What are the advantages and disadvantages of immediate update?

19.14. What is the difference between the UNDO/REDO and the UNDO/NO-REDO algorithms for recovery with immediate update? Develop the outline for an UNDO/NO-REDO algorithm.

19.15. Describe the shadow paging recovery technique. Under what circumstances does it not require a log?

19.16. Describe the two-phase commit protocol for multidatabase transactions.

19.17. Discuss how recovery from catastrophic failures is handled.

Exercises

19.18. Suppose that the system crashes before the [read_item,T_3,A] entry is written to the log in Figure 19.1(b); will that make any difference in the recovery process?

19.19. Suppose that the system crashes before the [write_item,T_2,D,25,26] entry is written to the log in Figure 19.1(b); will that make any difference in the recovery process?

19.20. Figure 19.6 shows the log corresponding to a particular schedule at the point of a system crash for the four transactions T_1, T_2, T_3, and T_4 of Figure 19.4. Suppose

[start_transaction,T_1]
[read_item,T_1,A]
[read_item,T_1,D]
[write_item,T_1,D,20]
[commit,T_1]
[checkpoint]
[start_transaction,T_2]
[read_item,T_2,B]
[write_item,T_2,B,12]
[start_transaction,T_4]
[read_item,T_4,B]
[write_item,T_4,B,15]
[start_transaction,T_3]
[write_item,T_3,A,30]
[read_item,T_4,A]
[write_item,T_4,A,20]
[commit,T_4]
[read_item,T_2,D]
[write_item,T_2,D,25] ← System crash

Figure 19.6 Example schedule and corresponding log.

that we use the *immediate update protocol* with checkpointing. Describe the recovery process from the system crash. Specify which transactions are rolled back, which operations in the log are redone and which (if any) are undone, and whether any cascading rollback takes place.

19.21. Suppose that we use the deferred update protocol for the example in Figure 19.6. Show how the log would be different in the case of deferred update by removing the unnecessary log entries; then describe the recovery process, using your modified log. Assume that only redo operations are applied, and specify which operations in the log are redone and which are ignored.

Selected Bibliography

The books by Bernstein et al. (1987) and Papadimitriou (1986) are devoted to the theory and principles of concurrency control and recovery. The book by Gray and Reuter (1993) is an encyclopedic work on concurrency control, recovery, and other transaction-processing issues.

Verhofstad (1978) presents a tutorial and survey of recovery techniques in database systems. Categorizing algorithms based on their UNDO/REDO characteristics is discussed in Haerder and Reuter (1983) and in Bernstein et al. (1983). Gray (1978) discusses recovery, along with other system aspects of implementing operating systems for databases. The shadow paging technique is discussed in Lorie (1977), Verhofstad (1978), and Reuter (1980). Gray et al. (1981) discusses the recovery mechanism in SYSTEM R. Lockeman and Knutsen (1968), Davies (1972), and Bjork (1973) are early papers that discuss recovery. Chandy et al. (1975) discusses transaction rollback. Lilien and Bhargava (1985) discusses the concept of integrity block and its use to improve the efficiency of recovery.

Recovery using write-ahead logging is analyzed in Jhingran and Khedkar (1992) and is used in the ARIES system (Mohan et al. 1992a). More recent work on recovery includes compensating transactions (Korth et al. 1990) and main memory database recovery (Kumar 1991). The ARIES recovery algorithms (Mohan et al. 1992) have been quite successful in practice. Franklin et al. (1992) discusses recovery in the EXODUS system.

Database Security
and Authorization

In this chapter we discuss the techniques used for protecting the database against persons who are not authorized to access a part of the database or the whole database. Section 20.1 provides an introduction to security issues and an overview of the topics covered in the rest of this chapter. Section 20.2 discusses the mechanisms used to grant and revoke privileges in relational database systems and in SQL; these mechanisms are often referred to as *discretionary access control*. Section 20.3 offers an overview of the mechanisms for enforcing multiple levels of security—a more recent concern in database system security that is known as *mandatory access control*. Section 20.4 briefly discusses the security problem in statistical databases.

Readers who are only interested in the basic database security mechanisms will find it sufficient to cover the material in Sections 20.1 and 20.2.

20.1 Introduction to Database Security Issues

20.1.1 *Types of Security*

Database security is a very broad area that addresses many issues, including the following:

- Legal and ethical issues regarding the right to access certain information. Some information may be deemed to be private and cannot be accessed legally by unauthorized persons. In the United States, several states and the federal government have privacy-of-information laws.

- Policy issues at the governmental, institutional, or corporate level as to what kinds of information should not be made publicly available—for example, credit ratings and personal medical records.

- System-related issues such as the *system levels* at which various security functions should be handled—for example, physical hardware level, operating system level, or DBMS level.

- The need in some organizations to identify multiple *security levels* and to categorize the data and users based on these classifications—for example, top secret, secret, confidential, and unclassified. The security policy of the organization with respect to permitting access to various classifications of data must be enforced.

In a multiuser database system, the DBMS must provide techniques to enable certain users or user groups to access selected portions of a database without gaining access to the rest of the database. This is particularly important when a large integrated database is to be used by many different users within the same organization. Sensitive information such as employee salaries should be kept confidential from most of the database system's users. A DBMS typically includes a **database security and authorization subsystem** that is responsible for ensuring the security of portions of a database against unauthorized access.

It is now customary to refer to two types of database security mechanisms:

- **Discretionary security mechanisms** are used to grant privileges to users, including the capability to access specific data files, records, or fields in a specified mode (such as read, write, or update mode).

- **Mandatory security mechanisms** are used to enforce multilevel security by classifying the data and users into various security classes (or levels) and then implementing the appropriate security policy of the organization. For example, a typical security policy is to permit users at a certain classification level to see only the data items classified at the user's own (or lower) classification level.

We discuss discretionary security in Section 20.2 and mandatory security in Section 20.3.

Another security problem common to all computer systems is that of preventing unauthorized persons from accessing the system itself—either to obtain information or to make malicious changes in a portion of the database. The security mechanism of a DBMS must include provisions for restricting access to the database system as a whole. This function is called **access control** and is handled by creating user accounts and passwords to control the log-in process by the DBMS. We discuss access control techniques in Section 20.1.3.

A third security problem associated with databases is that of controlling the access to a **statistical database**, which is used to provide statistical information or summaries of values based on various criteria. For example, a database for population statistics may provide statistics based on age groups, income levels, size of household, education levels, and other criteria. Statistical database users such as government statisticians or market research firms are allowed to access the database to retrieve statistical information about a population but not to access the detailed confidential information on specific individuals. Security for statistical databases must ensure that information on individuals cannot be accessed. It is sometimes possible to deduce certain facts concerning individuals from queries that involve only summary statistics on groups; consequently this must not be permitted either. This problem, called **statistical database security**, is discussed briefly in Section 20.4.

Another security technique is **data encryption**, which is used to protect sensitive data that is being transmitted via satellite or some other type of communications network. Encryption can be used to provide additional protection for sensitive portions of a database, as well. The data is **encoded** by using some coding algorithm. An unauthorized user who accesses encoded data will have difficulty deciphering it, but authorized users are given decoding or decrypting algorithms (or keys) to decipher the data. Encrypting techniques that are very difficult to decode without a key have been developed for military applications. We will not discuss encryption algorithms here.

A complete discussion of security in computer systems and databases is outside the scope of this textbook. We give only a brief overview of database security techniques here. The interested reader can refer to one of the textbooks in the bibliography at the end of this chapter for a more comprehensive discussion.

20.1.2 *Database Security and the* DBA

As we discussed in Chapter 1, the DBA is the central authority for managing a database system. The DBA's responsibilities include granting privileges to users who need to use the system and classifying users and data in accordance with the policy of the organization. The DBA has a **privileged account** in the DBMS, sometimes called a **system account**, which provides powerful capabilities that are not made available to regular database accounts and users. This account is similar to the *root* or *superuser* accounts that are given to computer system administrators, allowing access to restricted operating systems commands. DBA privileged commands include commands for granting and revoking privileges to individual accounts, users, or user groups and for performing the following types of actions:

1. *Account creation:* This action creates a new account and password for a user or a group of users to enable them to access the DBMS.

2. *Privilege granting:* This action permits the DBA to grant certain privileges to certain accounts.

3. *Privilege revocation:* This action permits the DBA to revoke (cancel) certain privileges that were previously given to certain accounts.

4. *Security level assignment:* This action consists of assigning user accounts to the appropriate security classification level.

The DBA is responsible for the overall security of the database system. Action 1 in the preceding list is used to control access to the DBMS as a whole, whereas actions 2 and 3 are used to control discretionary database authorizations, and action 4 is used to control mandatory authorization.

20.1.3 *Access Protection, User Accounts, and Database Audits*

Whenever a person or a group of persons needs to access a database system, the individual or group must first apply for a user account. The DBA will then create a new **account number** and **password** for the user if there is a legitimate need to access the database. The user must **log in** to the DBMS by entering the account number and password whenever database access is needed. The DBMS checks that the account number and password are valid; if they are, the user is permitted to use the DBMS and to access the database. Application programs can also be considered as users and can be required to supply passwords.

It is straightforward to keep track of database users and their accounts and passwords by creating an encrypted table or file with the two fields Account_Number and Password. This table can easily be maintained by the DBMS. Whenever a new account is created, a new record is inserted into the table. When an account is canceled, the corresponding record must be deleted from the table.

The database system must also keep track of all operations on the database that are applied by a certain user throughout each **log-in session**, which consists of the sequence of database interactions that a user performs from the time of logging in to the time of logging off. When a user logs in, the DBMS can record the user's account number and associate it with the terminal from which the user logged in. All operations applied from that terminal are attributed to the user's account until the user logs off. It is particularly important to keep track of update operations that are applied to the database so that, if the database is tampered with, the DBA can find out which user did the tampering.

To keep a record of all updates applied to the database and of the particular user who applied each update, we can modify the system log. Recall that the **system log** includes an entry for each operation applied to the database that may be required for recovery from a transaction failure or system crash. We can expand the log entries so that they also include the account number of the user and the on-line terminal id that applied each operation recorded in the log. If any tampering with the database is suspected, a **database audit** is performed, which consists of reviewing the log to examine all accesses and operations applied to the database during a certain time period. When an illegal or unauthorized operation is found, the DBA can determine the account number used to perform this operation. Database audits are particularly important for sensitive databases that are updated by many transactions and users, such as a banking database that is updated by many bank tellers. A database log that is used mainly for security purposes is sometimes called an **audit trail**.

20.2 Discretionary Access Control Based on Privileges

The typical method of enforcing **discretionary access control** in a database system is based on granting and revoking privileges. Let us consider privileges in the context of a relational DBMS. In particular, we will discuss a system of privileges somewhat similar to the one originally developed for the SQL language (see Chapter 7). Many current relational DBMSs use some variation of this technique. The main idea is to include additional statements in the query language that allow the DBA and selected users to grant and revoke privileges.

20.2.1 *Types of Discretionary Privileges*

In SQL2, the concept of *authorization identifier* is used to refer, roughly speaking, to a user account. We will use the word *user* or *account* informally in place of authorization identifier; hence, we use the terms *user* and *account* interchangeably. The DBMS must provide selective access to each relation in the database based on specific accounts. Operations may also be controlled; thus, having an account does not necessarily entitle the account holder to all the functionality provided by the DBMS. Informally, there are two levels for assigning privileges to use the database system:

1. *The account level*: At this level, the DBA specifies the particular privileges that each account holds independently of the relations in the database.

2. *The relation level*: At this level, we can control the privilege to access each individual relation or view in the database.

The privileges at the **account level** apply to the capabilities provided to the account itself and can include the CREATE SCHEMA or CREATE TABLE privilege, to create a schema or base relation; the CREATE VIEW privilege; the ALTER privilege, to add or remove attributes from relations; the DROP privilege, to delete relations or views; the MODIFY privilege, to insert, delete, or update tuples; and the SELECT privilege, to retrieve information from the database by using a SELECT query. Notice that these account privileges apply to the account in general. If a certain account does not have the CREATE TABLE privilege, no relations can be created from that account. Account-level privileges *are not* defined as part of SQL2; they are left to the DBMS implementers to define. In earlier versions of SQL, a CREATETAB privilege existed to give an account the privilege to create tables (relations).

The second level of privileges applies to the individual relations, whether they are base relations or virtual (view) relations. These privileges *are* defined for SQL2. In the following discussion, the term *relation* may refer either to a base relation or to a view, unless we explicitly specify one or the other. Privileges at the relation level specify for each user the individual relations on which each type of command can be applied. Some privileges also refer to individual columns (attributes) of relations. SQL2 commands provide privileges at the *relation and attribute level only*. Although this is quite general, it makes it difficult to create accounts with limited privileges. The granting and revoking of privileges generally follows an authorization model for discretionary privileges known as the **access matrix model**, where the rows of a matrix M represent *subjects* (users, accounts, programs) and the columns represent *objects* (relations, records, columns, views, operations). Each position $M(i, j)$ in the matrix represents the types of privileges (read, write, update) that subject i holds on object j.

To control the granting and revoking of relation privileges, each relation R in a database is assigned an **owner account**, which is typically the account that was used when the relation was created in the first place. The owner of a relation is given *all* privileges on that relation. In SQL2, the DBA can assign an owner to a whole schema by creating the schema and associating the appropriate authorization identifier with that schema, using the CREATE SCHEMA command (see Section 7.1.1). The owner account holder can pass privileges on any of the owned relations to other users by **granting** privileges to their accounts. In SQL the following types of privileges can be granted on each individual relation R:

- SELECT (retrieval) privilege on R: Gives the account retrieval privilege. In SQL the account can use the SELECT statement to retrieve tuples from R.

- MODIFY privileges on R: This gives the account the capability to modify tuples of R. In SQL this privilege is further divided into UPDATE, DELETE, and INSERT privileges to apply the corresponding SQL command to R. In addition, both the INSERT and UPDATE privileges can specify that only certain attributes of R can be updated by the account.

- REFERENCES privilege on R: This gives the account the capability to reference the relation R when specifying integrity constraints. This privilege can also be restricted to specific attributes of R.

Notice that to create a view, the account must have SELECT privilege on *all relations* involved in the view definition.

20.2.2 *Specifying Authorization by Using Views*

The mechanism of **views** is an important discretionary authorization mechanism in its own right. For example, if the owner A of a relation R wants another account B to be able to retrieve only some fields of R, then A can create a view V of R that includes only those attributes and then grant SELECT on V to B. The same applies to limiting B to retrieving only certain tuples of R; a view V' can be created by defining the view by means of a query that selects only those tuples from R that A wants to allow B to access. We illustrate this discussion with the example given in Section 20.2.5.

20.2.3 *Revoking Privileges*

In some cases it is desirable to grant some privilege to a user temporarily. For example, the owner of a relation may want to grant the SELECT privilege to a user for a specific task and then revoke that privilege once the task is accomplished. Hence, a mechanism for **revoking** privileges is needed. In SQL a REVOKE command is included for the purpose of canceling privileges. We will see how the REVOKE command is used in our subsequent example (Section 20.2.5).

20.2.4 *Propagation of Privileges and the GRANT OPTION*

Whenever the owner A of a relation R grants a privilege on R to another account B, the privilege can be given to B with or without the **GRANT OPTION**. If the GRANT OPTION is given, this means that B can also grant that privilege on R to other accounts. Suppose that B is given the GRANT OPTION by A and that B then grants the privilege on R to a third account C, also with GRANT OPTION. In this way, privileges on R can **propagate** to other accounts without the knowledge of the owner of R. If the owner account A now revokes the privilege granted to B, all the privileges that B propagated based on that privilege should automatically be revoked by the system. Hence, a DBMS that allows propagation of privileges must keep track of how all the privileges were granted so that revoking of privileges can be done correctly and completely.

Techniques to limit the propagation of privileges have been developed, although they have not yet been implemented in most DBMSs. Limiting **horizontal propagation** to an integer number i means that an account B given the GRANT OPTION can grant the privilege to at most i other accounts. **Vertical propagation** is more complicated; it limits the depth of the granting of privileges. Granting a privilege with vertical propagation of zero is equivalent to granting the privilege with *no GRANT OPTION*. If account A grants a privilege to account B with vertical propagation set to an integer number j > 0, this means that the account B has the GRANT OPTION on that privilege, but B can grant the privilege to other accounts only with a vertical propagation *less than j*. In effect, vertical propagation limits the sequence of grant options that can be given from one account to the next based on a single original grant of the privilege. We will illustrate this in the following example.

20.2.5 *An Example*

Suppose that the DBA creates four accounts—A1, A2, A3, and A4—and wants only A1 to be able to create base relations; then the DBA must issue the following GRANT command in SQL:

GRANT CREATETAB **TO** A1;

The CREATETAB (create table) privilege gives account A1 the capability to create new database tables (base relations) and is hence an *account privilege*. This privilege was part of earlier versions of SQL, but now is left to each individual system implementation to define. In SQL2, the same effect can be accomplished by having the DBA issue a CREATE SCHEMA command, as follows:

CREATE SCHEMA EXAMPLE **AUTHORIZATION** A1;

Now user account A1 can create tables under the schema called EXAMPLE. It is also possible to introduce a system-defined CREATE_SCHEMA *account privilege* to replace CREATETAB. CREATE_SCHEMA would give the user the privilege to create a database schema, and would thus imply the CREATETAB privilege.

Now, to continue our example, suppose that A1 creates the two base relations EMPLOYEE and DEPARTMENT shown in Figure 20.1; then A1 is the owner of these two relations and hence has all the *relation privileges* on each of them. Next, suppose that account A1 wants to grant to account A2 the privilege to insert and delete tuples in

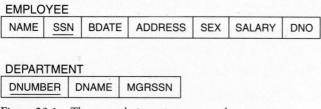

EMPLOYEE

NAME	SSN	BDATE	ADDRESS	SEX	SALARY	DNO

DEPARTMENT

DNUMBER	DNAME	MGRSSN

Figure 20.1 The two relations EMPLOYEE and DEPARTMENT.

both of these relations. However, A1 does not want A2 to be able to propagate these privileges to additional accounts. Then A1 can issue the following command:

GRANT INSERT, DELETE **ON** EMPLOYEE, DEPARTMENT **TO** A2;

Notice that the owner account A1 of a relation automatically has the GRANT OPTION, allowing it to grant privileges on the relation to other accounts. However, account A2 cannot grant INSERT and DELETE privileges on the EMPLOYEE and DEPARTMENT tables, because A2 was not given the GRANT OPTION in the preceding command. Next, suppose that A1 wants to allow account A3 to retrieve information from either of the two tables and also to be able to propagate the SELECT privilege to other accounts. Then A1 can issue the following command:

GRANT SELECT **ON** EMPLOYEE, DEPARTMENT **TO** A3
WITH GRANT OPTION;

The clause "WITH GRANT OPTION" means that A3 can now propagate the privilege to other accounts by using GRANT. For example, A3 can grant the SELECT privilege on the EMPLOYEE relation to A4 by issuing the following command:

GRANT SELECT **ON** EMPLOYEE **TO** A4;

Notice that A4 cannot propagate the SELECT privilege to other accounts, because the GRANT OPTION was not given to A4. Now suppose that A1 decides to revoke the SELECT privilege on the EMPLOYEE relation from A3; then A1 can issue this command:

REVOKE SELECT **ON** EMPLOYEE **FROM** A3;

The DBMS must now automatically revoke the SELECT privilege on EMPLOYEE from A4, too, because A3 granted that privilege to A4 and A3 does not have the privilege any more. Next, suppose that A1 wants to give back to A3 a limited capability to SELECT from the EMPLOYEE relation and wants to allow A3 to propagate the privilege. The limitation is to retrieve only the NAME, BDATE, and ADDRESS attributes and only the tuples with DNO = 5. Then A1 can create the following view:

CREATE VIEW A3EMPLOYEE **AS**
SELECT NAME, BDATE, ADDRESS
FROM EMPLOYEE
WHERE DNO=5;

After the view is created, A1 can grant SELECT on the view A3EMPLOYEE to A3 as follows:

GRANT SELECT **ON** A3EMPLOYEE **TO** A3 **WITH GRANT OPTION;**

Finally, suppose that A1 wants to allow A4 to update only the SALARY attribute of EMPLOYEE; then A1 can issue the following command:

GRANT UPDATE **ON** EMPLOYEE (SALARY) **TO** A4;

The UPDATE or INSERT privilege can specify particular attributes that may be updated or inserted in a relation. Other privileges (SELECT, DELETE) are not attribute-specific, as this specificity can easily be controlled by creating the appropriate views that include only the desired attributes. However, because updating views is not always possible, the UPDATE and INSERT privileges are given the option to specify particular attributes of a base relation that may be updated.

It is possible for a user to receive a certain privilege from two or more sources. For example, A4 may receive a certain UPDATE R privilege from *both* A2 and A3. In such a case, even though A2 may revoke this privilege from A4, A4 continues to have the privilege by virtue of having been granted it from A3. If A3 later revokes the privilege from A4, A4 totally loses the privilege.

We now briefly illustrate horizontal and vertical propagation limits, which are not currently available in SQL or other relational systems. Suppose that A1 grants SELECT to A2 on the EMPLOYEE relation with horizontal propagation = 1 and vertical propagation = 2. Then A2 can grant SELECT to at most one account, because the horizontal propagation limitation is set to 1. In addition, A2 cannot grant the privilege to another account except with vertical propagation = 0 (no GRANT OPTION) or 1, because the vertical propagation limitation is set to 2. This means that A2 must reduce the vertical propagation by at least 1 when passing the privilege to others. As this example shows, horizontal and vertical propagation techniques are designed to limit the propagation of privileges.

20.3 Mandatory Access Control for Multilevel Security*

The discretionary access control technique of granting and revoking privileges on relations has traditionally been the main security mechanism for database systems. This is an all-or-nothing method: a user either has or does not have a certain privilege. In many applications, an additional security policy is needed that classifies data and users based on security classes. This approach, known as **mandatory access control**, is *combined* with the discretionary access control mechanisms described in Section 20.2. It is important to note that most commercial DBMSs currently provide mechanisms only for discretionary access control. However, the need for multilevel security exists in government, military, and intelligence applications, as well as in many industrial and corporate applications.

The typical **security classes** used are top secret (TS), secret (S), confidential (C), and unclassified (U), where TS is the highest level and U the lowest. Other more complex security classification schemes exist, in which the security classes are organized in a lattice. For simplicity, we will use the system with four security classification levels, where TS > S > C > U, to illustrate our discussion. The commonly used model for multilevel security, known as the Bell-LaPadula model, classifies each *subject* (user, account, program) and *object* (relation, tuple, column, view, operation) into one of the security classifications TS, S, C, or U. We will refer to the classification of a subject S as **class(S)** and to the classification of an object O as **class(O)**. Two restrictions are enforced on data access based on the subject/object classifications:

1. A subject S is not allowed read access to an object O unless class(S) ≥ class(O). This is known as the *simple security property*.

2. A subject S is not allowed write access to an object O unless class(S) ≤ class(O). This is known as the *-property (or *star property*).

The first restriction enforces the obvious rule that no subject can read an object whose security classification is higher than the subject's security clearance. The second restriction prohibits a subject from writing an object that has lower security classification than the subject's security clearance. Violation of this rule would allow information to flow from higher to lower classifications, which violates a basic tenet of multilevel security.

To incorporate multilevel security notions into the relational database model, it is common to consider attribute values and tuples as data objects. Hence, each attribute A is associated with a **classification attribute** C in the schema, and each attribute value in a tuple is associated with a corresponding security classification. In addition, in some models, a **tuple classification** attribute TC is added to the relation attributes to provide a classification for each tuple as a whole. Hence, a **multilevel** relation schema R with n attributes would be represented as:

$$R(A_1, C_1, A_2, C_2, \ldots, A_n, C_n, TC)$$

where each C_i represents the classification attribute associated with attribute A_i.

The value of the TC attribute in each tuple provides a general classification for the tuple itself, whereas each C_i provides a finer security classification for each attribute value within the tuple. The value of TC within a tuple t should be the *highest* of all attribute value classifications within t. The **apparent key** of a multilevel relation is the set of attributes that would have formed the primary key in a regular (single-level) relation. A multilevel relation will appear to contain different data to subjects (users) with different classification levels. In some cases, it is possible to store a single tuple in the relation at a higher classification level and produce the corresponding tuples at a lower level classification through a process known as **filtering**. In other cases, it is necessary to store two or more tuples at different classification levels with the same value for the *apparent key*. This leads to the concept of **polyinstantiation**, where several tuples can have the same apparent key value but have different attribute values for users at different classification levels.

We illustrate these concepts with the simple example of a multilevel relation shown in Figure 20.2(a), where we display the classification attribute values next to each attribute's value. Assume that the Name attribute is the apparent key, and consider the query SELECT * FROM EMPLOYEE. A user with security clearance S would see the same relation shown in Figure 20.2(a), since all tuple classifications are less than or equal to S. However, a user with security clearance C would not be allowed to see values for Salary of Brown and JobPerformance of Smith, since they have higher classification. The tuples would be filtered to appear as shown in Figure 20.2(b). For a user with security clearance U, the filtering allows only the name attribute of Smith to appear (Figure 20.2(c)). Notice how filtering introduces null values for attribute values whose security classification is higher than the user's security clearance.

In general, the **entity integrity** rule for multilevel relations states that all attributes that are members of the apparent key must not be null and must have the *same* security classification within each individual tuple. In addition, all other attribute values in the

(a)

EMPLOYEE

Name		Salary		JobPerformance		TC
Smith	U	40000	C	Fair	S	S
Brown	C	80000	S	Good	C	S

(b)

EMPLOYEE

Name		Salary		JobPerformance		TC
Smith	U	40000	C	null	C	C
Brown	C	null	C	Good	C	C

(c)

EMPLOYEE

Name		Salary		JobPerformance		TC
Smith	U	null	U	null	U	U

(d)

EMPLOYEE

Name		Salary		JobPerformance		TC
Smith	U	40000	C	Fair	S	S
Smith	U	40000	C	Excellent	C	C
Brown	C	80000	S	Good	C	S

Figure 20.2 A multilevel relation. (a) The original EMPLOYEE tuples. (b) Appearance of EMPLOYEE after filtering for classification C users. (c) Appearance of EMPLOYEE after filtering for classification U users. (d) Polyinstantiation of the Smith tuple.

tuple must have a security classification greater than or equal to that of the key. This constraint ensures that a user can see the key if the user can see any part of the tuple at all. Other integrity rules, called **null integrity** and **inter-instance integrity**, informally ensure that, if a tuple value at some security level can be filtered (derived) from a higher-classified tuple, then it is sufficient to store the higher-classified tuple in the multilevel relation.

To illustrate polyinstantiation, suppose that a user with *security clearance* C tries to update the value of JobPerformance of Smith to "Excellent"; this corresponds to the following SQL query:

UPDATE EMPLOYEE
SET JobPerformance = "Excellent"
WHERE Name = "Smith" ;

Since the view provided to users with security clearance C (see Figure 20.2(b)) permits such an update, the system should not reject it; otherwise, the user could infer that some nonnull value exists for the JobPerformance attribute of Smith rather than the null value that appears. This is an example of inferring information through what is known as a **covert channel**, which should not be permitted in highly secure systems. However, the user should not be allowed to overwrite the existing value of JobPerformance at the higher classification level. The solution is to create a *polyinstantiation* for the Smith tuple at the lower classification level C, as shown in Figure 20.2(d). This is necessary since the new tuple cannot be filtered from the existing tuple at classification S.

The basic update operations of the relational model (insert, delete, update) must be modified to handle this and similar situations, but this aspect of the problem is outside the scope of our presentation. We refer the interested reader to the end-of-chapter bibliography for further details.

In order to achieve a truly secure system, the Department of Defense (DoD) of the United States has developed metrics for **security levels** achieved by various systems. These levels are named A1, B3, B2, B1, C2, C1, and D, with A1 being the most secure and D the least secure. Systems at C1 and C2 levels must provide discretionary access control, while those at level B1 must also provide mandatory access control. Systems at higher levels provide security against covert channels, and A1 systems must provide verifiable security. An implementation architecture with a **security kernel** (or **reference monitor**)—which handles all basic security actions but is small enough to verify the security levels achieved—has been proposed to ensure the concept; it is called a **trusted computing base** (TCB).

20.4 Statistical Database Security★

Statistical databases are used mainly to produce statistics on various populations. The database may contain confidential data on many individuals, which should be protected from user access. However, users are allowed to retrieve statistical information on the populations, such as averages, counts, sums, and standard deviations. The techniques developed to protect the privacy of individual information in statistical databases are outside the scope of this book. We will only illustrate the problem very briefly here with a simple example. The interested reader can refer to the bibliography for texts that provide a complete discussion of statistical databases and their security. We illustrate the problem with the relation shown in Figure 20.3, which shows a PERSON relation with the attributes NAME, SSN, INCOME, ADDRESS, CITY, STATE, ZIP, SEX, and LAST_DEGREE.

A **population** is a set of tuples of a file that satisfy some selection condition. Hence, each selection condition on the PERSON relation will specify a particular population of PERSON tuples. For example, the condition SEX = 'M' specifies the male population, the condition (SEX = 'F' AND (LAST_DEGREE = 'M.S.' OR LAST_DEGREE = 'PH.D.')) specifies the female population that has an M.S. or PH.D. degree as the highest degree, and the condition CITY = 'Houston' specifies the population that lives in Houston.

Statistical queries involve applying statistical functions to a population of tuples. For example, we may want to retrieve the number of individuals in a population or the

PERSON

NAME	SSN	INCOME	ADDRESS	CITY	STATE	ZIP	SEX	LAST_DEGREE

Figure 20.3 The PERSON relation.

average income in the population. However, statistical users are not allowed to retrieve individual data, such as the income of a specific person. **Statistical database security** techniques must prohibit the retrieval of individual data. This can be controlled by prohibiting queries that retrieve attribute values and by allowing only queries that involve statistical aggregate functions such as COUNT, SUM, MIN, MAX, AVERAGE, and STANDARD DEVIATION. Such queries are sometimes called **statistical queries**.

In some cases it is possible to **deduce** the values of individual tuples from a sequence of statistical queries. This is particularly true when the conditions result in a population consisting of a small number of tuples. As an illustration, suppose that we use the following two statistical queries:

Q1:   **SELECT** COUNT(*) **FROM** PERSON
      WHERE <condition>

Q2:   **SELECT** AVERAGE(INCOME) **FROM** PERSON
      WHERE <condition>

Now suppose that we are interested in finding the SALARY of 'Jane Smith', and we know that she has a PH.D. degree and that she lives in the city of Bellaire, Texas. We issue the statistical query Q1 with the following condition:

(LAST_DEGREE='PH.D.' AND SEX='F' AND CITY='Bellaire' AND STATE='Texas')

If we get a result of 1 for this query, we can issue Q2 with the same condition and find the INCOME of 'Jane Smith'. Even if the result of Q1 on the preceding condition is not 1 but is a small number—say, 2 or 3—we can issue statistical queries using the functions MAX, MIN, and AVERAGE to identify the possible range of values for the INCOME of 'Jane Smith'.

The possibility of deducing individual information from statistical queries is reduced if no statistical queries are permitted whenever the number of tuples in the population specified by the selection condition falls below some threshold. Another technique for prohibiting retrieval of individual information is to prohibit sequences of queries that refer repeatedly to the same population of tuples. It is also possible to introduce slight inaccuracies or "noise" into the results of statistical queries deliberately, to make it difficult to deduce individual information from the results. The interested reader is referred to the bibliography for a discussion of these techniques.

20.5 Summary

In this chapter we discussed several techniques for enforcing security in database systems. Security enforcement deals with controlling access to the database system as a whole and controlling authorization to access specific portions of a database. The former is usually done by assigning accounts with passwords to users. The latter can be accomplished by using a system of granting and revoking privileges to individual accounts for accessing specific parts of the database. This approach, which is generally referred to as *discretionary security*, was discussed in Section 20.2. We presented some SQL commands for granting and revoking privileges, and we illustrated their use with examples. Then in Section

20.3, we gave an overview of mandatory security mechanisms that enforce multilevel security. These require the classifications of users and data values into security classes and enforce the rules that prohibit flow of information from higher to lower security levels. Some of the key concepts underlying the multilevel relational model, including filtering and polyinstantiation, were presented. Finally, in Section 20.4, we briefly discussed the problem of controlling access to statistical databases to protect the privacy of individual information while concurrently providing statistical access to populations of records.

Review Questions

20.1. Discuss what is meant by each of the following terms: *database authorization, access control, data encryption, privileged (system) account, database audit, audit trail*.

20.2. Discuss the types of privileges at the account level and those at the relation level.

20.3. Which account is designated as the owner of a relation? What privileges does the owner of a relation have?

20.4. How is the view mechanism used as an authorization mechanism?

20.5. What is meant by granting a privilege?

20.6. What is meant by revoking a privilege?

20.7. Discuss the system of propagation of privileges and the restraints imposed by horizontal and vertical propagation limits.

20.8. List the types of privileges available in SQL.

20.9. What is the difference between discretionary access control and mandatory access control?

20.10. What are the typical security classifications? Discuss the simple security property and the *-property, and explain the justification behind these rules for enforcing multilevel security.

20.11. Describe the multilevel relational data model. Define the following terms: *apparent key, polyinstantiation, filtering*.

20.12. What is a statistical database? Discuss the problem of statistical database security.

Exercises

20.13. Consider the relational database schema of Figure 6.5. Suppose that all the relations were created by (and hence are owned by) user X, who wants to grant the following privileges to user accounts A, B, C, D, and E:

a. Account A can retrieve or modify any relation except DEPENDENT and can grant any of these privileges to other users.

b. Account B can retrieve all the attributes of EMPLOYEE and DEPARTMENT except for SALARY, MGRSSN, and MGRSTARTDATE.

c. Account C can retrieve or modify WORKS_ON but can only retrieve the FNAME, MINIT, LNAME, SSN attributes of EMPLOYEE and the PNAME, PNUMBER attributes of PROJECT.

d. Account D can retrieve any attribute of EMPLOYEE or DEPENDENT and can modify DEPENDENT.

e. Account E can retrieve any attribute of EMPLOYEE but only for EMPLOYEE tuples that have DNO = 3.

Write SQL statements to grant these privileges. Use views where appropriate.

20.14. Suppose that privilege a of Exercise 20.13 is to be given with GRANT OPTION but only so that account A can grant it to at most five accounts, and each of these accounts can propagate the privilege to other accounts but *without* the GRANT OPTION privilege. What would the horizontal and vertical propagation limits be in this case?

20.15. Consider the relation shown in Figure 20.2(d). How would it appear to a user with classification U? Suppose a classification U user tries to update the salary of "Smith" to $50,000; what would be the result of this action?

Selected Bibliography

Authorization based on granting and revoking privileges was proposed for the SYSTEM R experimental DBMS and is presented in Griffiths and Wade (1976). Several books discuss security in databases and computer systems in general, including the books by Leiss (1982a) and Fernandez et al. (1981). Denning and Denning (1979) is a tutorial paper on data security.

Many papers discuss different techniques for the design and protection of statistical databases. These include McLeish (1989), Chin and Ozsoyoglu (1981), Leiss (1982), Wong (1984), and Denning (1980). Ghosh (1984) discusses the use of statistical databases for quality control. There are also many papers discussing cryptography and data encryption, including Diffie and Hellman (1979), Rivest et al. (1978), and Akl (1983).

Multilevel security is discussed in Jajodia and Sandhu (1991), Denning et al. (1987), Smith and Winslett (1992), Stachour and Thuraisingham (1990), and Lunt et al. (1990). Overviews of research issues in database security are given by Lunt and Fernandez (1990) and Jajodia and Sandhu (1990). The effects of multilevel security on concurrency control are discussed in Kogan and Jajodia (1990).

Recently, a number of works have been published that discuss security in next-generation, semantic, and object-oriented databases (see Chapter 22), such as Bertino (1992), Rabbiti et al. (1991), and Smith (1990).

CHAPTER 21

Advanced Data Modeling Concepts

The ER modeling concepts discussed in Chapter 3 are sufficient for representing many database schemas for traditional database applications, which mainly include data-processing applications in business and industry. Since the late 1970s, however, newer applications of database technology have become commonplace; these include engineering design (CAD/CAM*) databases, image and graphics databases, cartographic and geological databases, multimedia databases,** and knowledge bases for artificial intelligence applications. These types of databases have more complex requirements than do the more traditional applications. To represent these requirements as accurately and explicitly as possible, designers must use additional "semantic" modeling concepts. Various semantic data models have been proposed in the literature. In this chapter, we describe many of the features that have been incorporated into these models. We start in Section 21.1 by enhancing the ER model (see Chapter 3) with additional concepts of specialization, generalization, inheritance, and categories, leading to the **enhanced-ER** or **EER** model. After presenting the EER model concepts in Section 21.1, we show how these concepts can be mapped to the relational model in Section 21.2; this augments the discussion of mapping the regular ER model concepts that was given in Section 6.8. In Section 21.3 we discuss fundamental abstractions that are used as the basis of many semantic data models. In Section 21.4 we classify the different types of integrity constraints used in data modeling. Section 21.5 describes the operations of the EER model and shows how they can be used in conceptually designing the transactions of a database application. Finally, Section 21.6

---

*CAD/CAM is an abbreviation for computer-aided design/computer-aided manufacturing.
**Multimedia databases store data that represent traditional entities, as well as unstructured data such as text, pictures, and voice recordings.

gives a brief overview of several other conceptual data models: the functional data model, the nested relational data model, the structural data model, and the semantic data model.

The reader may choose to skip some or all of the later sections of this chapter (Sections 21.2 through 21.6). In addition, the material in Section 21.1 may be covered immediately after the completion of Chapter 3, if desired.

21.1 Enhanced-ER (EER) Model Concepts

The EER model includes all the modeling concepts of the ER model that were presented in Chapter 3. In addition, it includes the concepts of **subclass** and **superclass** and the related concepts of **specialization** and **generalization**. Another concept included in the EER model is that of a **category**. Associated with these concepts is the important mechanism of **attribute inheritance**. Unfortunately, no standard terminology exists for these concepts, so we use the terminology that is used most commonly. Alternative terminology is given in footnotes. We also describe a diagrammatic technique for displaying these concepts when they arise in an EER schema. We call the resulting schema diagrams **enhanced-ER** or **EER diagrams**.

21.1.1 *Subclasses, Superclasses, and Specialization*

Subclasses and Superclasses. The first EER model concept we take up is that of a subclass of an entity type. As we discussed in Chapter 3, an entity type is used to represent a set of entities of the same type, such as the set of EMPLOYEE entities in a company database. In many cases an entity type has numerous additional subgroupings of its entities that are meaningful and need to be represented explicitly because of their significance to the database application. For example, the entities that are members of the EMPLOYEE entity type may be further grouped into SECRETARY, ENGINEER, MANAGER, TECHNICIAN, SALARIED_EMPLOYEE, HOURLY_EMPLOYEE, and so on. The set of entities in each of the latter groupings is a subset of the entities that belong to the EMPLOYEE entity type, meaning that every entity that is a member of one of these subgroupings is also an employee. We call each of these subgroupings a **subclass** of the EMPLOYEE entity type, and EMPLOYEE is called the **superclass** for each of these subclasses.

We call the relationship between a superclass and any one of its subclasses a **superclass/subclass** or simply **class/subclass relationship.*** In our previous example, EMPLOYEE/ SECRETARY and EMPLOYEE/TECHNICIAN are two class/subclass relationships. Notice that a member entity instance of the subclass represents the *same real-world entity* as some member of the superclass; for example, a SECRETARY entity 'Joan Logano' is also the EMPLOYEE 'Joan Logano'. Hence, the subclass member is the same as the entity in the superclass, but in a distinct *specific role*. When we implement a superclass/subclass relationship in the database system, however, we may represent a member of the subclass as a distinct database object—say, a distinct record that is related via the key attribute to

---

*A class/subclass relationship is often called an IS-A (or IS-AN) relationship because of the way one refers to the concept. We say "a SECRETARY IS-AN EMPLOYEE," "a TECHNICIAN IS-AN EMPLOYEE," etc.

its superclass entity. In Section 21.2 we discuss various options for representing super-class/subclass relationships in relational databases.

An entity cannot exist in the database merely by being a member of a subclass; it must also be a member of the superclass. Such an entity can optionally be included as a member of any number of subclasses. For example, a salaried employee who is also an engineer belongs to the two subclasses ENGINEER and SALARIED_EMPLOYEE of the EMPLOYEE entity type. However, it is not necessary that every entity in a superclass be a member of some subclass.

Attribute Inheritance in Superclass/Subclass Relationships. An important concept associated with subclasses is that of **attribute inheritance**. Because an entity in the sub-class represents the same real-world entity from the superclass, it should possess values for its specific attributes *as well as* values of its attributes as a member of the superclass. We say that an entity that is a member of a subclass **inherits** all the attributes of the entity as a member of the superclass. The entity also inherits all relationship instances for relationship types in which the superclass participates. Notice that a subclass, together with all the attributes it inherits from the superclass, is an *entity type* in its own right.

Specialization. **Specialization** is the process of defining a *set of subclasses* of an entity type; this entity type is called the **superclass** of the specialization. The set of subclasses forming a specialization is defined on the basis of some distinguishing characteristic of the entities in the superclass. For example, the set of subclasses {SECRETARY, ENGINEER, TECHNICIAN} is a specialization of the superclass EMPLOYEE that distinguishes among EMPLOYEE entities based on the *job type* of each entity. We may have several speciali-zations of the same entity type based on different distinguishing characteristics. For example, *another specialization* of the EMPLOYEE entity type may yield the set of subclasses {SALARIED_EMPLOYEE, HOURLY_EMPLOYEE}; this specialization distinguishes among employees based on the *method of compensation.*

Enhanced-ER (EER) Diagrams. Figure 21.1 shows how we represent a specialization dia-grammatically in an **EER diagram**. The subclasses that define a specialization are attached by lines to a circle, which is connected to the superclass. The subset symbol on each line connecting a subclass to the circle indicates the direction of the superclass/subclass relationship. Any attributes that apply only to entities of a particular subclass—such as TypingSpeed of SECRETARY—are attached to the rectangle representing that subclass. These are called **specific attributes** of the subclass. Similarly, a subclass can participate in **specific relationship types**, such as HOURLY_EMPLOYEE participating in BELONGS_TO in Figure 21.1. We will explain the **d** symbol in the circles of Figure 21.1 and additional EER diagram notation shortly.

Figure 21.2 shows a few entity instances that belong to subclasses of the {SECRE-TARY, ENGINEER, TECHNICIAN} specialization. Again, notice that an entity that belongs to a subclass represents *the same real-world entity* as the entity connected to it in the EMPLOYEE superclass, even though the same entity is shown twice; for example, e_1 is shown in both EMPLOYEE and SECRETARY in Figure 21.2. As this figure suggests, a super-

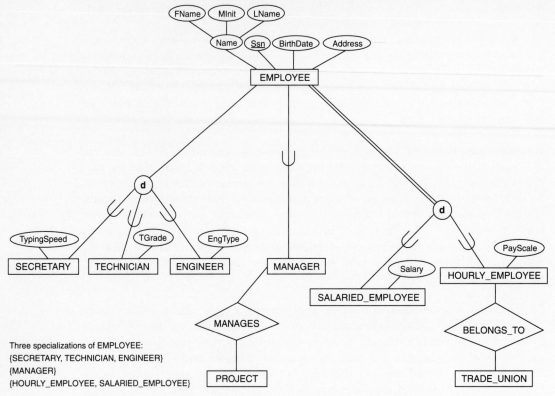

Three specializations of EMPLOYEE:
{SECRETARY, TECHNICIAN, ENGINEER}
{MANAGER}
{HOURLY_EMPLOYEE, SALARIED_EMPLOYEE}

Figure 21.1   EER diagram for representing specialization and subclasses.

class/subclass relationship such as EMPLOYEE/SECRETARY somewhat resembles a 1:1 relationship *at the instance level* (see Figure 3.12). The main difference is that, in a 1:1 relationship, two *distinct entities* are related. We can consider an entity in the subclass as being the same as the entity in the superclass but playing a *specialized role*—for example, an EMPLOYEE specialized in the role of SECRETARY, or an EMPLOYEE specialized in the role of TECHNICIAN.

Use of Subclasses in Data Modeling.   There are two main reasons for including class/ subclass relationships in a data model. The first is that certain attributes may apply to some but not to all entities of the (superclass) entity type. A subclass is defined in order to group the entities to which these attributes apply. The members of the subclass may still share the majority of their attributes with the other members of the superclass. For example, the SECRETARY subclass may have an attribute TypingSpeed, whereas the ENGI-NEER subclass may have an attribute EngineerType, but SECRETARY and ENGINEER share their other attributes as members of the EMPLOYEE entity type.

The second reason for using subclasses is that some relationship types may be participated in only by entities that are members of the subclass. For example, if only HOURLY_ EMPLOYEEs can belong to a trade union, we can represent that fact by creating

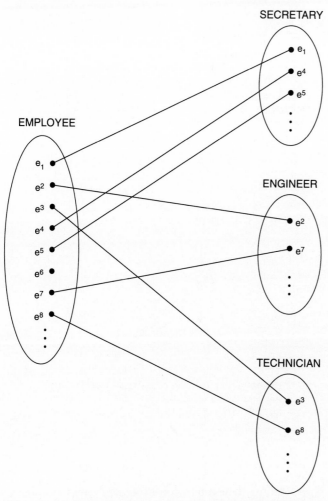

Figure 21.2   Some instances of the specialization of EMPLOYEE into the {SECRETARY, ENGINEER, TECHNICIAN} set of subclasses.

the subclass HOURLY_EMPLOYEE of EMPLOYEE and relating the subclass to an entity type TRADE_UNION via the BELONGS_TO relationship type, as illustrated in Figure 21.1.

21.1.2 *Generalization*

The specialization process discussed in the preceding subsection allows us to:

- Define a set of subclasses of an entity type.
- Associate additional specific attributes with each subclass.
- Establish additional specific relationship types between each subclass and other entity types, or other subclasses.

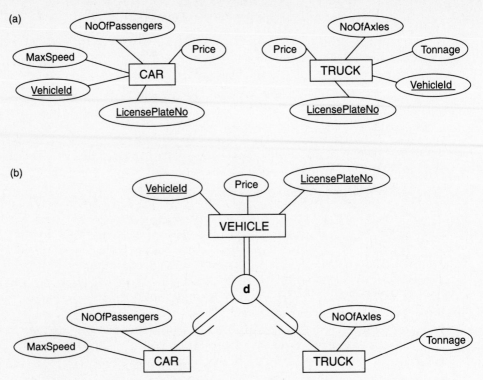

Figure 21.3   Examples of generalization. (a) Two entity types CAR and TRUCK.
(b) Generalizing CAR and TRUCK into VEHICLE.

We can think of a *reverse process* of abstraction in which we suppress the differences among several entity types, identify their common features, and **generalize** them into a single **superclass** of which the original entity types are special **subclasses**. For example, consider the entity types CAR and TRUCK shown in Figure 21.3(a); they can be generalized into the entity type VEHICLE, as shown in Figure 21.3(b). Both CAR and TRUCK are now subclasses of the **generalized superclass** VEHICLE. We use the term **generalization** to refer to the process of defining a generalized entity type from the given entity types.

Notice that the generalization process can be viewed as being functionally the inverse of the specialization process. Hence, in Figure 21.3 we can view {CAR, TRUCK} as a specialization of VEHICLE, rather than viewing VEHICLE as a generalization of CAR and TRUCK. Similarly, in Figure 21.1 we can view EMPLOYEE as a generalization of SEC-RETARY, TECHNICIAN, and ENGINEER. A diagrammatic notation to distinguish between generalization and specialization is sometimes used in practice. An arrow pointing to the generalized superclass represents a generalization, whereas arrows pointing to the specialized subclasses represent a specialization. We will *not* use this notation, because the decision as to which process is more appropriate in a particular situation is often subjective. Appendix A gives some of the suggested alternative diagrammatic notations.

21.1.3   *Data Modeling with Specialization and Generalization*

So far we have introduced the concepts of subclasses and superclass/subclass relationships, as well as the specialization and generalization processes. In general, a superclass or subclass represents a set of entities and hence is also an *entity type*; that is why (like entity types) superclasses and subclasses are shown in rectangles in EER diagrams. We now discuss in more detail the properties of specializations and generalizations.

Constraints on Specialization and Generalization. In the paragraphs following, we discuss constraints that apply to a single specialization or a single generalization; however, for brevity, our discussion refers to specialization only even though it applies to *both specialization and generalization*.

In general, we may have several specializations defined on the same (superclass) entity type, as shown in Figure 21.1. In such a case, entities may belong to subclasses in each of the specializations. However, a specialization may consist of a single subclass only, such as the {MANAGER} specialization in Figure 21.1; in such a case, we do not use the circle notation.

In some specializations we can determine exactly the entities that will become members of each subclass, by placing a condition on the value of some attribute of the superclass. Such subclasses are called **predicate-defined** (or **condition-defined**) **subclasses**. For example, if the EMPLOYEE entity type has an attribute JobType, as shown in Figure 21.4, we can specify the condition of membership in the SECRETARY subclass by the predicate (JobType = 'Secretary'), which we call the **defining predicate** of the sub-

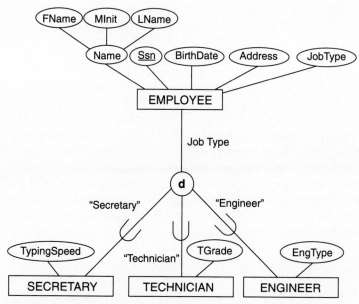

Figure 21.4   Attribute-defined specialization on the JobType attribute of EMPLOYEE.

class. This condition is a *constraint* specifying that members of the SECRETARY subclass must satisfy the predicate and that all entities in the EMPLOYEE entity type whose attribute value for JobType is 'Secretary' must belong to the subclass. We display a predicate-defined subclass by writing the predicate condition next to the line that connects the subclass to its superclass.

If *all subclasses* in a specialization have the membership condition on the *same attribute* of the superclass, the specialization itself is called an **attribute-defined specialization**, and the attribute is called the **defining attribute** of the specialization. We display an attribute-defined specialization, as shown in Figure 21.4, by placing the defining attribute name next to the arc from the circle to the superclass.

When we do not have such a condition for determining membership, the subclass is called **user-defined**. Membership in such a subclass is determined by the database users when they apply the operation to add an entity to the subclass; hence, membership is *specified individually for each entity by the user*, not by any condition that may be evaluated automatically.

Two other constraints may apply to a specialization. The first is the **disjointness constraint**, which specifies that the subclasses of the specialization must be disjoint. This means that an entity can be a member of *at most one* of the subclasses of the specialization. A specialization that is attribute-defined implies the disjointness constraint if the attribute used to define the membership predicate is single-valued. Figure 21.4 illustrates this case, where the **d** in the circle stands for disjoint. We also use the **d** notation to specify the constraint that user-defined subclasses of a specialization must be disjoint, as illustrated by the specialization {HOURLY_EMPLOYEE, SALARIED_EMPLOYEE} in Figure 21.1. If the subclasses are not disjoint, their sets of entities may **overlap**; that is, the same entity may be a member of more than one subclass of the specialization. This case, which is the default, is displayed by placing an **o** in the circle, as shown in the example of Figure 21.5.

The second constraint on specialization is called the **completeness constraint**, which may be either total or partial. A **total specialization** constraint specifies that every entity in the superclass must be a member of some subclass in the specialization. For example, if every EMPLOYEE must be either an HOURLY_EMPLOYEE or a SALARIED_EMPLOYEE, then the specialization {HOURLY_EMPLOYEE, SALARIED_EMPLOYEE} of Figure 21.1 is a total specialization of EMPLOYEE; this is shown in EER diagrams by using a double line to connect the superclass to the circle. A single line is used to display a **partial specialization**, which allows an entity not to belong to any of the subclasses. For example, if some EMPLOYEE entities do not belong to any of the subclasses {SECRETARY, ENGINEER, TECHNICIAN} of Figures 21.1 and 21.4, then that specialization is partial. This notation is similar to the notation for total participation of an entity type in a relationship type of the ER model presented in Chapter 3. Notice that the disjointness and completeness constraints are *independent*. Hence, we have the following four types of specialization:

- disjoint, total
- disjoint, partial
- overlapping, total
- overlapping, partial

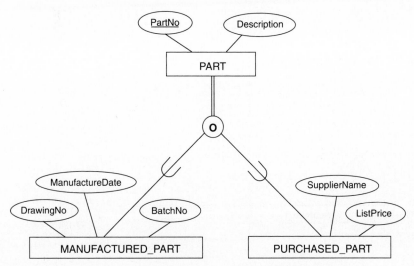

Figure 21.5 Specialization with nondisjoint (overlapping) subclasses.

Of course, the correct constraint is determined from the real-world meaning that applies to each specialization. But a generalization superclass usually is **total**, because the superclass is *derived from* the subclasses and hence contains only the entities that are in the subclasses.

Insertion and Deletion Rules for Specialization and Generalization. Certain insertion and deletion rules apply to specialization (and generalization) as a consequence of the constraints specified earlier. Some of these rules are:

- Deleting an entity from a superclass implies that it is automatically deleted from all the subclasses it belongs to.

- Inserting an entity in a superclass implies that the entity is mandatorily inserted in all *predicate-defined* subclasses for which the entity satisfies the defining predicate.

- Inserting an entity in a superclass of a *total specialization* implies that the entity is mandatorily inserted in at least one of the subclasses of the specialization.

The reader is encouraged to make a complete list of rules for insertions and deletions for the various types of specializations.

Specialization Hierarchies, Specialization Lattices, and Multiple Inheritance. A subclass may itself have further subclasses specified on it, forming a hierarchy or a lattice of specializations. For example, in Figure 21.6 ENGINEER is a subclass of EMPLOYEE and is also a superclass of ENGINEERING_MANAGER; this represents the real-world constraint that every engineering manager is required to be an engineer. A **specialization hierarchy** has the constraint that every subclass participates (as subclass) in *one* class/subclass rela-

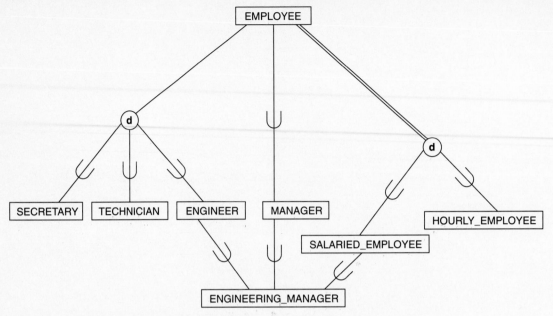

Figure 21.6   Specialization lattice with the shared subclass ENGINEERING_
MANAGER.

tionship; in contrast, for a **specialization lattice** a subclass can be subclass in *more than one* class/subclass relationship. Hence, Figure 21.6 is a lattice.

Figure 21.7 shows another specialization lattice of more than one level. This may be part of a conceptual schema for a UNIVERSITY database. Notice that this arrangement would have been a hierarchy except for the STUDENT_ASSISTANT subclass, which is a subclass in two distinct class/subclass relationships. All person entities represented in the database are members of the PERSON entity type, which is specialized into the subclasses {EMPLOYEE, ALUMNUS, STUDENT}. This specialization is overlapping; for example, an alumnus may also be an employee. An alumnus may also be a student going for an advanced degree after receiving an undergraduate degree. The subclass STUDENT is super-class for the specialization {GRADUATE_STUDENT, UNDERGRADUATE_STUDENT}, while EMPLOYEE is superclass for the specialization {STUDENT_ASSISTANT, FACULTY, STAFF}. Notice that STUDENT_ASSISTANT is also a subclass of STUDENT. Finally, STU-DENT_ASSISTANT is superclass for the specialization into {RESEARCH_ASSISTANT, TEACHING_ASSISTANT}.

In such a specialization lattice or hierarchy, a subclass inherits the attributes not only of its direct superclass but also of all its predecessor superclasses *all the way to the root.* For example, an entity in GRADUATE_STUDENT inherits all the attribute values of that entity as a STUDENT *and* as a PERSON. Note that an entity may exist in several leaf nodes of the hierarchy; for example, a member of GRADUATE_STUDENT may also be a member of RESEARCH_ASSISTANT.

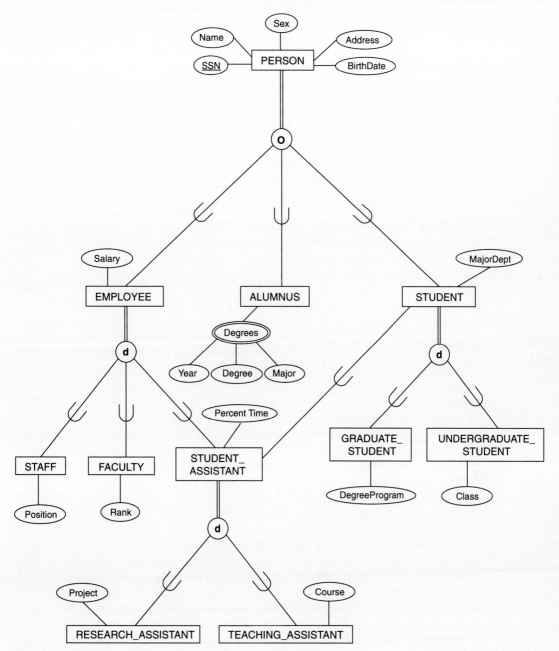

Figure 21.7 Specialization lattice for a UNIVERSITY database.

A subclass with *more than one* superclass is called a **shared subclass**. For example, if every ENGINEERING_MANAGER must be an ENGINEER but must also be a SALARIED_EMPLOYEE and a MANAGER, then ENGINEERING_MANAGER should be a shared subclass of all three superclasses (Figure 21.6). This leads to the concept known as **multiple inheritance**, since the shared subclass ENGINEERING_MANAGER directly inherits attributes and relationships from multiple subclasses. Notice that shared subclasses lead to a lattice; if no shared subclasses existed, we would have a hierarchy rather than a lattice.

Although we have used specialization to illustrate our discussion, similar concepts *apply equally* to generalization, as we mentioned at the beginning of this subsection. Hence, we can also speak of **generalization hierarchies** and **generalization lattices**. The next subsection elaborates on the differences between the specialization and generalization processes.

Top–Down versus Bottom–Up Conceptual Design.   In the specialization process, we typically start with an entity type and then define subclasses of the entity type by successive specialization; that is, we repeatedly define more specific groupings of the entity type. For example, when designing the specialization lattice in Figure 21.7, we may first specify an entity type PERSON for a university database. Then we discover that three types of persons will be represented in the database: university employees, alumni, and students. We create the specialization {EMPLOYEE, ALUMNUS, STUDENT} for this purpose and choose the overlapping constraint because a person may belong to more than one of the subclasses. We then specialize EMPLOYEE further into {STAFF, FACULTY, STUDENT_ASSISTANT}, and specialize STUDENT into {GRADUATE_STUDENT, UNDERGRADUATE_STUDENT}. Finally, we specialized STUDENT_ASSISTANT into {RESEARCH_ASSISTANT, TEACHING_ASSISTANT}. This successive specialization corresponds to a **top–down conceptual refinement** process during conceptual schema design. So far, we have a hierarchy; we then discover that STUDENT_ASSISTANT is a shared subclass, since it is also a subclass of STUDENT, leading to the lattice.

It is possible to arrive at the same hierarchy or lattice from the other direction. In such a case, the process involves generalization rather than specialization and corresponds to a **bottom–up conceptual synthesis**. In structural terms, hierarchies or lattices resulting from either process may be identical; the only difference relates to the manner or order in which the schema superclasses and subclasses were specified.

In practice, it is likely that neither the generalization process nor the specialization process is followed strictly, but a combination of the two processes is employed. In this case, new classes are continually incorporated into a hierarchy or lattice as they become apparent to users and designers. Notice that the notion of representing data and knowledge by using superclass/subclass hierarchies and lattices is quite common in knowledge-based systems and expert systems, which combine database technology with artificial intelligence techniques. For example, frame-based knowledge representation schemes closely resemble class hierarchies.

21.1.4 *Categories and Categorization**

All of the superclass/subclass relationships we have seen thus far have a *single superclass*. Even a shared subclass such as ENGINEERING_MANAGER in the lattice of Figure 21.6 is the subclass in three *distinct* superclass/subclass relationships, where each of the three relationships has a *single* superclass. In some cases, however, the need arises for modeling a single superclass/subclass relationship with *more than one* superclass, where the superclasses represent different entity types. In this case we call the *subclass* a **category**.*

For example, suppose that we have three entity types: PERSON, BANK, and COMPANY. In a database for vehicle registration, an owner of a vehicle can be a person, a bank (holding a lien on a vehicle), or a company. We need to create a class that includes entities of all three types to play the role of vehicle owner. A category OWNER that is a *subclass of the **union*** of the three classes COMPANY, BANK, and PERSON is created for this purpose. We display categories in an EER diagram as shown in Figure 21.8. The superclasses COMPANY, BANK, and PERSON are connected to the circle with the **U** symbol, which stands for the *set union operation*. An arc with the subset symbol connects the circle to the (subclass) OWNER category. If a defining predicate is needed, it is displayed next to the line from the superclass to which the predicate applies. In Figure 21.8, we have two categories: OWNER, which is a subclass of the union of PERSON, BANK, and COMPANY; and REGISTERED_VEHICLE, which is a subclass of the union of CAR and TRUCK.

A category has two or more superclasses that may represent *distinct entity types*, whereas other superclass/subclass relationships always have a single superclass. We can compare a category, such as OWNER in Figure 21.8, with the ENGINEERING_MANAGER shared subclass of Figure 21.6. The latter is a subclass of *each of* the three superclasses ENGINEER, MANAGER, and SALARIED_EMPLOYEE, so an entity that is a member of ENGINEERING_MANAGER must exist in *all three*. This represents the constraint that an engineering manager must be an ENGINEER, a MANAGER, *and* a SALARIED_EMPLOYEE; that is, ENGINEERING_MANAGER is a subset of the *intersection* of the three subclasses. On the other hand, a category is a subset of the *union* of its superclasses. Hence, an entity that is a member of OWNER must exist in *at least one* of the superclasses but does not have to be a member of *all* of them. This represents the constraint that an OWNER may be a COMPANY, a BANK, *or* a PERSON in Figure 21.8. In this example, as in most cases where categories are used, an entity in the category is a member of *exactly one* of the superclasses.

Attribute inheritance works more selectively in the case of categories. For example, in Figure 21.8 each OWNER entity inherits the attributes of a COMPANY, a PERSON, or a BANK, depending on the superclass to which the entity belongs. This is known as **selective inheritance**. On the other hand, a shared subclass such as ENGINEERING_MANAGER (Figure 21.6) inherits *all* the attributes of its superclasses SALARIED_EMPLOYEE, ENGINEER, and MANAGER.

It is interesting to note the difference between the category REGISTERED_VEHICLE (Figure 21.8) and the generalized superclass VEHICLE (Figure 21.3(b)). In Figure 21.3(b),

---

*Our use of the term *category* is based on the ECR model (Elmasri et al. 1985).

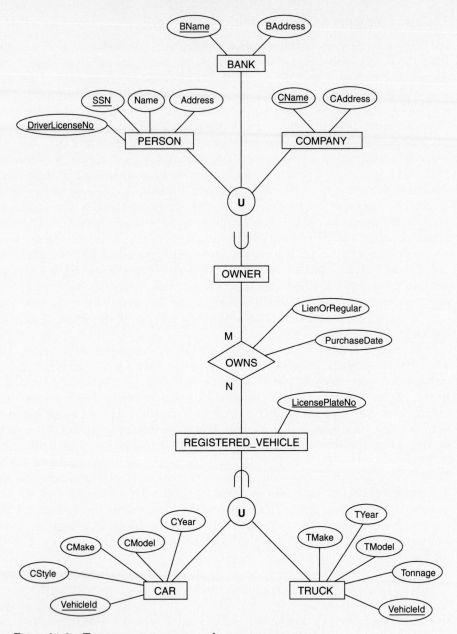

Figure 21.8   Two categories: OWNER and REGISTERED_VEHICLE.

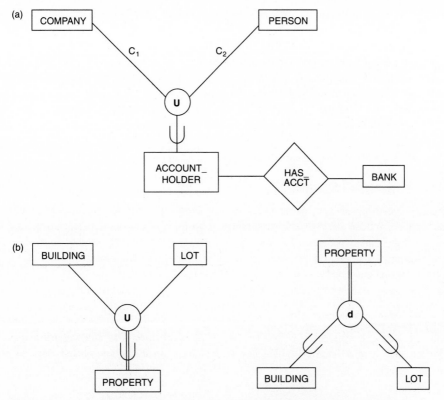

Figure 21.9 Categories. (a) Partial category ACCOUNT_HOLDER that is a subset of the union of two entity types COMPANY and PERSON. (b) Total category PROPERTY and a similar generalization.

every car and every truck is a VEHICLE; but in Figure 21.8, the REGISTERED_VEHICLE category includes some cars and some trucks but not necessarily all of them (for example, some cars or trucks may not be registered). In general, a specialization or generalization such as that in Figure 21.3(b), if it were *partial*, would not preclude VEHICLE from containing other types of entities, such as motorcycles. However, a category such as REGISTERED_VEHICLE in Figure 21.8 implies that only cars and trucks, but not other types of entities, can be members of REGISTERED_VEHICLE.

A category can be **total** or **partial**. For example, ACCOUNT_HOLDER is a predicate-defined partial category in Figure 21.9(a), where c_1 and c_2 are predicate conditions that specify which COMPANY and PERSON entities, respectively, are members of ACCOUNT_HOLDER. However, the category PROPERTY in Figure 21.9(b) is total because every building and lot must be a member of PROPERTY; this is shown by a double line connecting the category to the circle. Partial categories are indicated by a single line connecting the category to the circle, as in Figures 21.8 and 21.9(a).

The superclasses of a category may have different key attributes, as demonstrated by the OWNER category of Figure 21.8; or they may have the same key attribute, as demonstrated by the REGISTERED_VEHICLE category. Notice that, in the case where the category is *total* (not partial), it may alternatively be represented as a specialization (or a generalization), as illustrated in Figure 21.9(b). In this case the choice of which representation to use is subjective. If the two classes represent the same type of entities and share numerous attributes, including the same key attributes, specialization/generalization is preferred; otherwise, categorization is more appropriate.

21.1.5 *Formal Definitions**

In the preceding subsections we extended the basic Entity-Relationship model with the concepts of subclasses, class/subclass relationships, specialization, generalization, and categories. We called the resulting model the enhanced-ER or EER model. In this section we summarize these concepts and define them formally in the manner in which we formally defined the concepts of the basic ER model in Chapter 3.

A **class*** is a set of entities; this includes any of the EER schema constructs that group together entities such as entity types, subclasses, superclasses, and categories. A **subclass** S is a class whose entities must always be a subset of the entities in another class, called the **superclass** C of the **superclass/subclass** (or **IS-A**) **relationship**. We denote such a relationship by C/S. For such a superclass/subclass relationship, we must always have

$$S \subseteq C$$

A **specialization** $Z = \{S_1, S_2, \ldots, S_n\}$ is a set of subclasses that have the same superclass G; that is, G/S_i is a superclass/subclass relationship for $i = 1, 2, \ldots, n$. G is called a **generalized entity type** (or the **superclass** of the specialization, or a **generalization** of the subclasses $\{S_1, S_2, \ldots, S_n\}$). Z is said to be **total** if we always have

$$(\bigcup_{i=1}^{n} S_i) = G$$

otherwise, Z is said to be **partial**. Z is said to be **disjoint** if we always have

$$S_i \cap S_j = \phi \qquad \text{for } i \neq j$$

Otherwise, Z is said to be **overlapping**.

A subclass S of C is said to be **predicate-defined** if a predicate p on the attributes of C is used to specify which entities in C are members of S; that is, $S = C[p]$, where $C[p]$ is the set of entities in C that satisfy p. A subclass that is not defined by a predicate is called **user-defined**.

A specialization Z (or generalization G) is said to be **attribute-defined** if a predicate $(A = c_i)$, where A is an attribute of G and c_i is a constant value from the domain of

---

*The use of the word *class* in conceptual modeling differs from its use in object-oriented programming languages such as C^{++}. In C^{++}, a class is a structured type definition along with its applicable functions (operations).

A, is used to specify membership in each subclass S_i in Z. Notice that, if $c_i \neq c_j$ for i $\neq$ j, and A is a single-valued attribute, then the specialization will be disjoint.

A **category** T is a class that is a subset of the union of n defining superclasses D_1, $D_2, \ldots, D_n$, n > 1, and is formally specified as follows:

$$T \subseteq (D_1 \cup D_2 \ldots \cup D_n)$$

A predicate p_i on the attributes of D_i can be used to specify the members of each D_i that are members of T. If a predicate is specified on every D_i, we get

$$T = (D_1[p_1] \cup D_2[p_2] \cdots \cup D_n[p_n])$$

We should now extend the definition of **relationship type** given in Chapter 3 by allowing any class—not only any entity type—to participate in a relationship. Hence, we should replace the words *entity type* with *class* in that definition. The graphical notation of EER is consistent with ER because all classes are represented by rectangles.

21.1.6 *Example Database Schema in the EER Model*

In this section we give an example of a database schema in the EER model to illustrate the use of the various concepts discussed here and in Chapter 3. Consider a UNIVERSITY database that keeps track of students, their majors, their transcripts, and their registration, as well as of the university's course offerings. The database also keeps track of the sponsored research projects of faculty and graduate students. This schema is shown in Figure 21.10. Following is a discussion of the requirements that led to this schema.

For each person in the database, the database maintains information on the person's Name [Name], social security number [Ssn], address [Address], sex [Sex], and birthdate [BDate]. Two subclasses of the PERSON entity type were identified: FACULTY and STUDENT. Specific attributes of FACULTY are rank [Rank] (assistant, associate, adiunct, research, visiting, etc.), office [FOffice], office phone [FPhone], and salary [Salary], and we also relate each faculty member to the academic department(s) with which the faculty member is affiliated [BELONGS] (a faculty member can be associated with several departments, so the relationship is M:N). A specific attribute of STUDENT is [Class] (freshman = 1, sophomore = 2, ..., graduate student = 5). Each student is also related to his or her major and minor departments, if known ([MAJOR] and [MINOR]), to the course sections he or she is currently attending [REGISTERED], and to the courses completed [TRANSCRIPT]. Each transcript instance includes the grade the student received [Grade] in the course section.

GRAD_STUDENT is a subclass of STUDENT, with the defining predicate Class = 5. For each graduate student, we keep a list of previous degrees in a composite, multivalued attribute [Degrees]. We also relate the student to a faculty advisor [ADVISOR] and to a thesis committee [COMMITTEE] if one exists.

An academic department has the attributes name [DName], telephone [DPhone], and office number [Office] and is related to the faculty member who is its chairperson [CHAIRS] and to the college to which it belongs [CD]. Each college has attributes college name [CName], office number [COffice], and the name of its dean [Dean].

A course has attributes course number [C#], course name [Cname], and course description [CDesc]. Several sections of each course are offered, with each section having

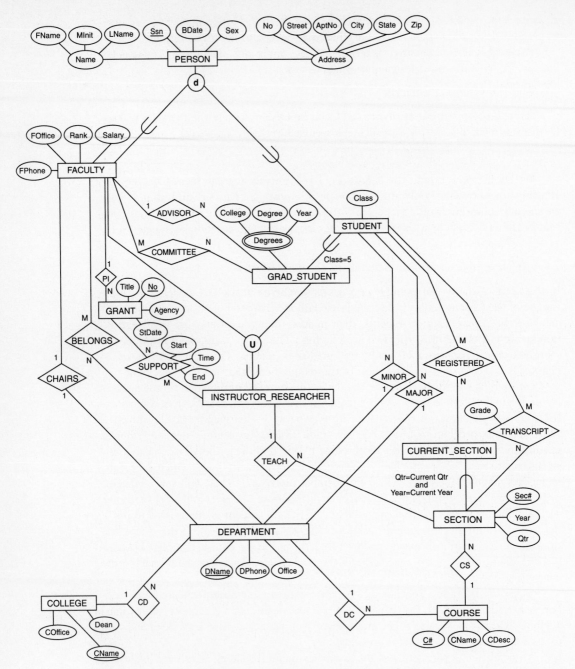

Figure 21.10   ERR conceptual schema for a UNIVERSITY database.

the attributes section number [Sec#] and the year and quarter in which the section was offered ([Year] and [Qtr]). Section numbers uniquely identify each section. The sections being offered during the current semester are in a subclass CURRENT_SECTION of SECTION, with the defining predicate Qtr = CurrentQtr and Year = CurrentYear. Each section is related to the instructor who taught it or is teaching it (if that instructor is in the database).

The category INSTRUCTOR_RESEARCHER is a subset of the union of FACULTY and GRAD_STUDENT and includes all faculty, as well as graduate students who are supported by teaching or research. Finally, the entity type GRANT keeps track of research grants and contracts awarded to the university. Each grant has attributes grant title [Title], grant number [No], the awarding agency [Agency], and the starting date [StDate]. A grant is related to one principal investigator [PI] and to all researchers it supports [SUPPORT]. Each instance of support has as attributes the starting date of support [Start], the ending date of the support (if known) [End], and the percent of time currently being spent on the project [Time] by the person supported.

21.2 EER-to-Relational Mapping

We now discuss the mapping of EER model concepts to relations by extending the ER-to-relational mapping algorithm that was presented in Section 6.8.

21.2.1 *Superclass/Subclass Relationships and Specialization (or Generalization)*

There are several options for mapping a number of subclasses that together form a specialization (or alternatively, that are generalized into a superclass), such as the {SECRETARY, TECHNICIAN, ENGINEER} subclasses of EMPLOYEE in Figure 21.4. We can add a further step to our ER-to-relational mapping algorithm from Section 6.8, which has seven steps, to handle the mapping of specialization. Step 8, which follows, gives the most common options; other mappings are also possible. We then discuss the conditions under which each option should be used. We use Attrs(R) to denote the attributes of relation R and PK(R) to denote the primary key of R.

STEP 8: Convert each specialization with m subclasses $\{S_1, S_2, \ldots, S_m\}$ and (generalized) superclass C, where the attributes of C are $\{k, a_1, \ldots, a_n\}$ and k is the (primary) key, into relation schemas using one of the four following options:

Option 8A: Create a relation L for C with attributes Attrs(L) = $\{k, a_1, \ldots, a_n\}$ and PK(L) = k. Create a relation L_i for each subclass S_i, $1 \leq i \leq m$, with the attributes Attrs(L_i) = $\{k\} \cup \{$attributes of $S_i\}$ and PK(L_i) = k.

Option 8B: Create a relation L_i for each subclass S_i, $1 \leq i \leq m$, with the attributes Attrs(L_i) = $\{$attributes of $S_i\} \cup \{k, a_1, \ldots, a_n\}$ and PK(L_i) = k.

Option 8C: Create a single relation L with attributes Attrs(L) = {k, a_1, ..., a_n} ∪ {attributes of S_1} ∪ ··· ∪ {attributes of S_m} ∪ {t} and PK(L) = k. This option is for a specialization whose subclasses are *disjoint*, and t is a **type** attribute that indicates the subclass to which each tuple belongs, if any. This option has the potential for generating a large number of null values.

Option 8D: Create a single relation schema L with attributes Attrs(L) = {k, a_1, ..., a_n} ∪ {attributes of S_1} ∪ ··· ∪ {attributes of S_m} ∪ {t_1, t_2, ..., t_m} and PK(L) = k. This option is for a specialization whose subclasses are *overlapping* (not disjoint), and each t_i, $1 \leq i \leq m$, is a Boolean attribute indicating whether a tuple belongs to subclass S_i. ∎

Option 8A creates a relation L for the superclass C and its attributes, plus a relation L_i for each subclass S_i; each L_i includes the specific attributes of S_i, plus the primary key of the superclass C, which is propagated to L_i and becomes its primary key. An EQUIJOIN operation on the primary key between any L_i and L produces all the specific and inherited attributes of the entities in S_i. This option is illustrated in Figure 21.11(a) for the EER schema in Figure 21.4. Option 8A works for any constraints on the specialization: disjoint or overlapping, total or partial. Notice that the constraint

$$\pi_{<k>}(L_i) \subseteq \pi_{<k>}(L)$$

must hold for each L_i. This specifies an *inclusion dependency* L_i.k < L.k (see Section 13.4).

In option 8B, the EQUIJOIN operation is *built into* the schema and the relation L is done away with, as illustrated in Figure 21.11(b) for the EER specialization in Figure 21.3(b). This option works well only with both the disjoint and total constraints. If the specialization is not total, an entity that does not belong to any of the subclasses S_i is lost. If the specialization is not disjoint, an entity belonging to more than one subclass will have its inherited attributes from the superclass C stored redundantly in more than one L_i. With option 8B, no relation holds all the entities in the superclass C; consequently, we must apply an OUTER UNION operation to the L_i relations to retrieve all the entities in C. The result of the outer union will be similar to the relations under options 8C and 8D except that the type fields will be missing. Whenever we search for an arbitrary entity in C, we must search all the m relations L_i.

Options 8C and 8D create a single relation to represent the superclass C and all its subclasses. An entity that does not belong to some of the subclasses will have null values for the specific attributes of these subclasses. These options are hence not recommended if many specific attributes are defined for the subclasses. If few specific subclass attributes exist, however, these mappings are preferable to options 8A and 8B because they do away with the need to specify EQUIJOIN and OUTER UNION operations and hence can yield a more efficient implementation. Option 8C is used to handle disjoint subclasses by including a single **type** (or **image**) **attribute** t to indicate the subclass to which each tuple belongs; hence, the domain of t could be {1, 2, ..., m}. If the specialization is partial, t can have null values in tuples that do not belong to any subclass. If the specialization is attribute-defined, that attribute serves the purpose of t and t is not needed; this option is illustrated in Figure 21.11(c) for the EER specialization in Figure 21.4. Option 8D is used to handle overlapping subclasses by including m *Boolean*

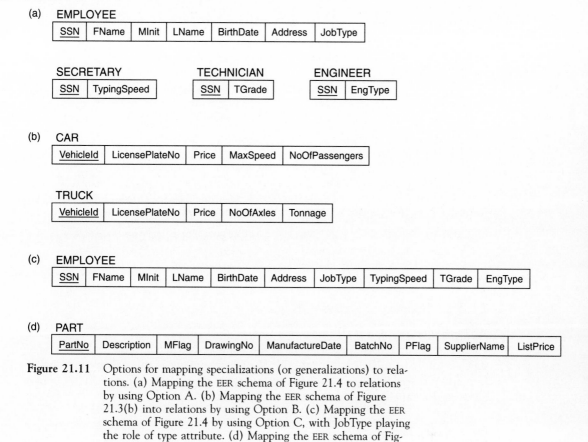

Figure 21.11   Options for mapping specializations (or generalizations) to relations. (a) Mapping the EER schema of Figure 21.4 to relations by using Option A. (b) Mapping the EER schema of Figure 21.3(b) into relations by using Option B. (c) Mapping the EER schema of Figure 21.4 by using Option C, with JobType playing the role of type attribute. (d) Mapping the EER schema of Figure 21.5 by using Option D, with two Boolean type fields MFlag and PFlag.

type fields, one for *each* subclass. Each type field t_i can have a domain {yes, no}, where a value of yes indicates that the tuple is a member of subclass S_i. This option is illustrated in Figure 21.11(d) for the EER specialization in Figure 21.5, where MFlag and PFlag are the type fields. Notice that it is also possible to create a single type field of m bits instead of the m type fields.

When we have a multilevel specialization (or generalization) hierarchy or lattice, we do not have to follow the same mapping option for all the specializations. Instead, we can use one mapping option for part of the hierarchy or lattice and other options for other parts. Figure 21.12 shows one possible mapping into relations for the lattice of Figure 21.7. Here we used option 8A for PERSON/ {EMPLOYEE, ALUMNUS, STUDENT}, option 8C for both EMPLOYEE/ {STAFF, FACULTY, STUDENT_ASSISTANT} and STUDENT/STUDENT_ASSISTANT, and option 8D for both STUDENT_ASSISTANT/ {RESEARCH_ASSISTANT, TEACHING_ ASSISTANT} and STUDENT/ {GRADUATE_STUDENT, UNDERGRADUATE_STUDENT}. In Figure 21.12, all attributes whose names end with 'Type' or 'Flag' are type fields.

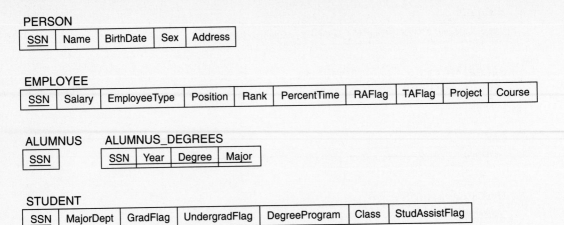

PERSON

SSN	Name	BirthDate	Sex	Address

EMPLOYEE

SSN	Salary	EmployeeType	Position	Rank	PercentTime	RAFlag	TAFlag	Project	Course

ALUMNUS   **ALUMNUS_DEGREES**

SSN

SSN	Year	Degree	Major

STUDENT

SSN	MajorDept	GradFlag	UndergradFlag	DegreeProgram	Class	StudAssistFlag

Figure 21.12   Mapping the EER specialization lattice shown in Figure 21.7 using multiple options.

21.2.2 Mapping of Shared Subclasses

A shared subclass, such as ENGINEERING_MANAGER of Figure 21.6, is a subclass of several superclasses. These classes must all have the same key attribute; otherwise, the shared subclass would be modeled as a category. We can apply any of the options discussed in step 8 to a shared subclass, although usually option 8A is used. In Figure 21.12, option 8D is used for the shared subclass STUDENT_ASSISTANT.

21.2.3 Mapping of Categories

A category is a subclass of the *union* of two or more superclasses that can have different keys because they can be of different entity types. An example is the OWNER category shown in Figure 21.8, which is a subset of the union of three entity types PERSON, BANK, and COMPANY. The other category in Figure 21.8, REGISTERED_VEHICLE, has two superclasses that have the same key attribute.

For mapping a category whose defining superclasses have different keys, it is customary to specify a new key attribute, called a **surrogate key**, when creating a relation to correspond to the category. This is because the keys of the defining classes are different, so we cannot use any one of them exclusively to identify all entities in the category. We can now create a relation schema OWNER to correspond to the OWNER category, as illustrated in Figure 21.13, and include any attributes of the category in this relation. The primary key of OWNER is the surrogate key OwnerId. We also add the surrogate key attribute OwnerId as foreign key to each relation corresponding to a superclass of the category, to specify the correspondences in values between the surrogate key and the key of each superclass.

For a category whose superclasses have the same key, such as VEHICLE in Figure 21.8, there is no need for a surrogate key. The mapping of the REGISTERED_VEHICLE category, which illustrates this case, is also shown in Figure 21.13.

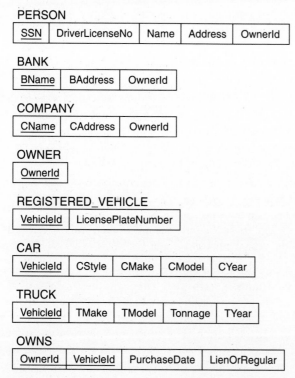

Figure 21.13   Mapping the categories of Figure 21.8 to relations.

21.3 Data Abstraction and Knowledge Representation Concepts★

In this section we discuss in abstract terms some of the modeling concepts that were described quite specifically in our presentation of the ER and EER models in Chapter 3 and Section 21.1. The terminology is used both in conceptual data modeling and in artificial intelligence literature when discussing **knowledge representation** (abbreviated as **KR**), whose goal is to develop concepts for accurately modeling some "domain of discourse" in order to store and manipulate knowledge for drawing inferences, making decisions, or just answering questions. The goals of KR are similar to those of *semantic data models*, but there are also some important differences between the two disciplines. We summarize the similarities and differences here:

- Both disciplines use an abstraction process to identify common properties and important aspects of objects in the miniworld while suppressing insignificant differences and unimportant details.

- Both disciplines provide concepts, constraints, operations, and languages for defining data and representing knowledge.

- KR is generally broader in scope than semantic data models. Different forms of knowledge, such as rules (used in inference, deduction, and search), incomplete and default knowledge, and temporal and spatial knowledge, are represented in KR schemes. Semantic data models are being expanded to include some of these concepts.

- KR schemes include **reasoning mechanisms** that deduce additional facts from the facts stored in a database. Hence, whereas most current database systems are limited to answering direct queries, knowledge-based systems using KR schemes can answer queries that involve **inferences** over the stored data. Database technology is being extended with inference mechanisms (see Chapter 24).

- Whereas most data models concentrate on the representation of database schemas, or meta-knowledge, KR schemes often mix up the schemas with the instances themselves in order to provide flexibility in representing exceptions. This often results in inefficiencies when these KR schemes are implemented, compared to databases, especially when a large amount of data (or facts) needs to be stored.

In this section we discuss five **abstraction concepts** that are used in both semantic data models, such as the EER model, and KR schemes. These are the concepts of classification/instantiation, identification, generalization/specialization, aggregation, and association. The paired concepts of classification and instantiation are inverses of one another, as are generalization and specialization. The concepts of aggregation and association are also related. We discuss these abstract concepts and their relation to the concrete representations used in the EER model to clarify the data abstraction process and to improve our understanding of the related process of conceptual schema design.

21.3.1 *Classification and Instantiation*

The process of **classification** involves systematically assigning similar objects to object classes. We can now describe (in DB) or reason about (in KR) the classes rather than the individual objects themselves. Groups of objects share the same types of attributes and constraints, and by classifying objects we simplify the process of discovering their properties. **Instantiation** is the inverse of classification and refers to the generation and specific examination of distinct objects of a class. Hence, an object instance is related to its object class by the **IS-AN-INSTANCE-OF** relationship.

In general, the objects of a class should have a similar type structure. However, some objects may display properties that differ in some respects from the other objects of the class; these **exception objects** also need to be modeled, and KR schemes allow more varied exceptions than do semantic data models. In addition, certain properties apply to the class as a whole and not to the individual objects themselves; KR schemes allow such **class properties**.

In the EER model, entities are classified into entity types according to their basic properties and structure. Entities are further classified into subclasses and categories based on additional similarities and differences (exceptions) among them. Relationship instances are classified into relationship types. Hence, entity types, subclasses, categories, and relationship types are the different types of classes in the EER model. The EER model does not provide explicitly for class properties, but it may be extended to do so.

Knowledge representation models allow multiple classification schemes in which one class is an *instance* of another class (called a **meta-class**). Notice that this *cannot be* directly represented in the EER model, because we have only two levels—classes and instances. The only relationship among classes in the EER model is a superclass/subclass relationship, whereas in some KR schemes an additional class/instance relationship can be represented directly in a class hierarchy. An instance may itself be another class, allowing multiple-level classification schemes.

21.3.2 *Identification*

Identification is the abstraction process whereby classes and objects are made uniquely identifiable by means of some **identifier**. For example, a class name uniquely identifies a whole class. An additional mechanism is necessary for telling distinct object instances apart by means of object identifiers. Moreover, it is necessary to identify multiple manifestations in the database of the same real-world object. For example, we may have a tuple <*Matthew Clarke*, 610618, 376-9821> in a PERSON relation and another tuple <301-54-0836, CS, 3.8> in a STUDENT relation that happens to represent the same real-world entity. There is no way to identify the fact that these two database objects (tuples) represent the same real-world entity unless we make a provision *at design time* for appropriate cross-referencing to supply this identification. Hence, identification is needed at two levels:

- To distinguish among database objects and classes.
- To identify database objects and to relate them to their real-world counterparts.

In the EER model, identification of schema constructs is based on a system of unique names for the constructs. For example, every class in an EER schema—whether it is an entity type, a subclass, a category, or a relationship type—must have a distinct name. The names of attributes of a given class must also be distinct. Rules for unambiguously identifying attribute name references in a specialization or generalization lattice or hierarchy are needed, as well.

At the object level, the values of key attributes are used to distinguish among entities of a particular entity type. For weak entity types, entities are identified by a combination of their own partial key values and the entities they are related to in the owner entity type(s). Relationship instances are identified by the combination of entities that they relate; this includes one entity from each participating class.

21.3.3 *Specialization and Generalization*

Specialization is the process of further classifying a class of objects into more specialized subclasses. Generalization is the inverse process of generalizing several classes into a higher-level abstract class that includes the objects in all these classes. Specialization is conceptual refinement, whereas generalization is conceptual synthesis. Subclasses are used in the EER model to represent specialization and generalization. We call the relationship between a subclass and its superclass an **IS-A-SUBCLASS-OF** relationship.

21.3.4 *Aggregation and Association*

Aggregation is an abstraction concept for building composite objects from their component objects. There are two cases where this concept can be related to the EER model. The first case is the situation where we aggregate attribute values of an object to form the whole object. The second case, which the EER model does not provide for explicitly, involves the possibility of combining objects that are related by a particular relationship instance into a *higher-level aggregate object*. This is sometimes useful when the higher-level aggregate object is itself to be related to another object. We call the relationship between the primitive objects and their aggregate object IS-A-PART-OF; and the inverse is called IS-A-COMPONENT-OF.

The abstraction of **association** is used to associate objects from several *independent classes*. Hence, it is somewhat similar to the second use of aggregation. It is represented in the EER model by relationship types. This relationship is called IS-ASSOCIATED-WITH.

To understand aggregation better, consider the ER schema shown in Figure 21.14(a), which stores information about interviews by job applicants to various companies. The class COMPANY is an aggregation of the attributes (or component objects) CName (company name) and CAddress (company address), whereas JOB_APPLICANT is an aggregate of Ssn, Name, Phone, and Address. The relationship attributes ContactName and ContactPhone represent the name and phone number of the contact person in the company responsible for the interview. Suppose that some interviews result in job offers, while others do not. We would like to treat INTERVIEW as a class to associate it with JOB_OFFER. The schema shown in Figure 21.14(b) is *incorrect* because it requires each interview relationship instance to have a job offer. The schema shown in Figure 21.14(c) is not allowed, because the ER model does not allow relationships among relationships.

One way to represent this situation is to create a higher-level aggregate class composed of COMPANY, JOB_APPLICANT, and INTERVIEW and to relate this class to JOB_OFFER as shown in Figure 21.14(d). Although the EER model as described here does not have this facility, some semantic data models do allow it and call the resulting object a **composite** or **molecular object**. Other models treat entity types and relationship types uniformly and hence permit relationships among relationships.

To represent this situation correctly in the EER model, we need to create a new weak entity type INTERVIEW, as shown in Figure 21.14(e), and relate it to JOB_OFFER. Hence, we can always represent these situations correctly in the EER model by creating additional entity types, although it may be conceptually more desirable to allow direct representation of aggregation as in Figure 21.14(d) or to allow relationships among relationships as in Figure 21.14(c).

The main distinction between aggregation and association is that, when an association instance is deleted, the participating objects continue to exist. However, if we support the notion of an aggregate object—for example, a CAR that is made up of objects ENGINE, CHASSIS, and TIRES—then deleting the aggregate CAR object amounts to deleting its component objects.

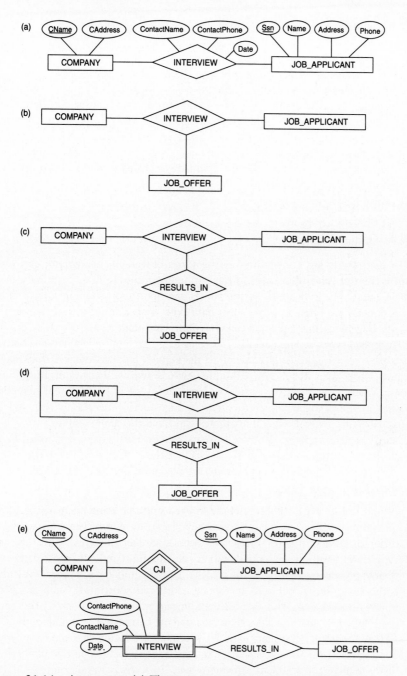

Figure 21.14   Aggregation. (a) The INTERVIEW relationship type. (b) Including JOB_OFFER in a ternary relationship type (incorrect). (c) Including JOB_OFFER by having a relationship in which another relationship participates (not allowed). (d) Using aggregation and a composite (molecular) object. (e) Correct representation.

21.4 Integrity Constraints in Data Modeling*

A database stores information about some *part of the real world,* which we called the **miniworld** or **universe of discourse.** Certain rules, called **integrity constraints,** govern the miniworld. These are sometimes called the *business rules.* When we design a schema for a particular database application, one important activity consists of identifying the integrity constraints that must hold on the database. We want to specify as many of these integrity constraints as possible to the DBMS and have the DBMS be responsible for enforcing them. In this section, we summarize the main types of integrity constraints that occur frequently in database modeling. We have already discussed integrity constraints in each of the individual data models we presented. This section describes types of integrity constraints independently of a specific data model.

21.4.1 *Domain Constraints*

Domain constraints are constraints on the types of values an attribute can have. A **domain** is a *set of values* representing some inherent meaning. It is customary to assign a **domain name** that indicates how the values can be interpreted. The values that constitute a domain are often specified via a **data type,** such as integer, real number, string, and so on. In general, many domains can have the same data type, since there is a limited set of basic data types in most database systems or programming languages. The domain name is used as a higher-level concept to distinguish among domains that may have the same basic data type. For example, two domains *Weights_in_Kilograms* and *Heights_in_Meters* may both have the low-level data type of positive real numbers, but the values in the domains represent different high-level concepts, as reflected in the domain names. In general, several attributes can have the same domain.

Data type definitions in database systems are constantly being expanded to reflect more of the meaning associated with the data values. It is now common in object-oriented systems to define the appropriate set of **operations** associated with each data type. The following are some of the data types commonly included in database systems:

- **Numeric data types:** These include integers and real numbers in various formats. To reflect the low-level data types available on most computers, integers may be differentiated into short-integer (2-bytes), integer (4-bytes), and long-integer types; and similarly real numbers can be differentiated into floating-point and double-precision floating-point types. To accommodate higher-level domain constraints, it is possible to introduce additional constraints, such as restricting a domain to nonnegative or positive numeric values only, or explicitly specifying a subrange of numeric values that the attribute can take. For example, the domain *Person_Weights_in_Kilograms* can be specified as having the data type positive floating-point numbers less than 300. The operations for numeric data types typically include the standard arithmetic $(+, -, *, /, \ldots)$ and comparison $(=, <, >, \ldots)$ operators.

- **Character and String data types:** Single-character data types can include any character in the standard computer ASCII character set. Data types for strings of characters are often characterized by the length of allowed strings. Fixed-length string data types include values that all have the same length, whereas variable-length strings do not have this restriction. It is common to specify a maximum length on variable-length strings for implementation purposes. A string data type can also be restricted to include only certain characters, the most common restriction being to limit the characters to alphabetic, decimal, or binary bits. The operators for character and string data types typically include equality and inequality comparison, and string concatenation.

- **Boolean data types**: The values are of Boolean data types restricted to True and False (or 0 and 1), with the associated logical operations AND, OR, and NOT.
- **Enumerated data types**: These are identified by an explicit set of values. For example, the domain *Student_Letter_Grades* can be specified as the set of characters {A, B, C, D, F, I, P}. It is also possible, though not very common, to define a *dynamic* enumerated data type; for example, the domain of *Department_Names* in a university can include the set of all current department names. If a new department is created, it must be added to the enumerated set.
- **Date and Time data types**: Because calendar dates and time play an increasingly important role in database systems, it is becoming increasingly important to define basic data types to accommodate these concepts.* There are composite data types that typically include multiple fields for **date** (year, month, day) and **time** (hour, minute, second). A **timestamp** includes both date and time fields. Both absolute values (a specific time at a specific date) and relative values (called **intervals**) should be included, as well as operations for comparing and manipulating the values of these data types. A difference operation between two absolute timestamps yields an interval, whereas an operation that increments or decrements an absolute timestamp by a fixed interval yields another absolute timestamp.
- **User-defined data types**: The capability of allowing a user to define domains with a new composite data type and its operations adds flexibility to a database system; it is becoming available in some object-oriented database systems.

21.4.2 *Key and Relationship Constraints*

The **key constraint** is one of the standard constraints that occur frequently in database applications. Key constraints are treated slightly differently in various data models. In the ER model, a key is an attribute of an entity type that must have a unique value for every entity belonging to the entity type *at any specific point in time*. The value of the key attribute can hence serve to identify each entity uniquely. A key attribute must be single-valued, but it may be simple or composite. A **regular** entity type may have one or more keys. A **weak** entity type has no key, but it usually has a *partial key* whose values uniquely identify the weak entities *that are related to the same owner entity* via an identifying relationship (see Section 3.3.4). Subclasses inherit the key from their superclass.

The concept of key in the network model is similar, except that the keyword **UNIQUE** is used to identify keys. In addition, it is possible for some record types not to have any keys. In the relational model, each base relation has a **primary key** and may

---

*For example, such data types are included in the new SQL2 standard (see Section 7.1).

have additional secondary keys (identified by the keyword UNIQUE in SQL). SQL also permits relations that do not have keys. A class of entities without a key is sometimes called a **bag**; such a class allows multiple identical entities and hence is not a set.

Structural constraints on relationships are used to specify restrictions on the way in which entities of an entity type can participate in relationship instances of a particular relationship type. There are two main types of relationship constraints in the ER model. The **cardinality ratio** specifies whether an entity can participate in only one relationship instance or in multiple relationship instances. The common cardinality ratios for binary relationships are 1:1, 1:N, N:1, and M:N. The **participation constraint** specifies whether an entity *must* participate in a relationship instance, or whether it can exist on its own independently of being related to another entity. The former is called *total participation* or *existence dependency*, and the latter is called *partial participation*. An alternative, more general technique for specifying structural constraints on relationships specifies a pair of integers (*min, max*) attached to each participation of an entity type E in a relationship type R; this restricts each entity e in E to participate in *at least min* and *at most max* relationship instances in R at any point in time. This technique covers both cardinality ratio and participation constraint, and it is applicable to relationships of any degree.

In the relational model, relationships are represented by means of foreign keys. In SQL, the behavior of each foreign key when the referenced primary key is updated or deleted can be specified by using one of the options REJECT, PROPAGATE, SET TO NULL, or SET TO DEFAULT. In the network model, relationships are specified via set types, and their behavior is defined by using the INSERTION and RETENTION options.

21.4.3 *General Semantic Integrity Constraints*

Many constraints from a miniworld for a database application can be specified as key constraints and relationship constraints. Often, however, there are other, more complex constraints that cannot be specified on the basis of these concepts. These are known as general *semantic integrity constraints*. The mechanisms for specifying such **explicit constraints** are still being refined in commercial database systems. In general, there are two proposed approaches to specifying such constraints: the *procedural* approach and the *declarative* approach.

Specifying Constraints Procedurally in the Transactions. One method of specifying explicit constraints involves writing statements to check for constraints in the update programs (or transactions) that will be applied to the database. This is called the **procedural specification of constraints** (or the **coded constraints** technique). The constraints are coded into appropriate transactions by the programmer. For example, consider the general constraint that "the salary of an employee must not be greater than the salary of the manager of the department that the employee works for," specified on the ER schema of Figure 3.14. To ensure proper enforcement, this constraint must be checked in *every update transaction* that may violate the constraint. This includes any transaction that modifies the salary of an employee, any transaction that inserts a new employee or relates an employee to a department, any transaction that assigns a new manager to a department, and so on. In every such transaction, part of the code of the transaction must explicitly check that the constraint is not being violated. If the constraint is being violated, the transaction must be aborted without its introducing any changes to the database. This ensures that the transaction behaves as an atomic unit for semantic integrity control.

The preceding technique for handling explicit constraints is used by many existing DBMSs. It is also used in object-oriented databases, where explicit constraints can be encoded as part of the methods or operations that are **encapsulated** with the objects. This approach is completely general, since the checks are programmed in a general-purpose programming language, and it allows the programmer to code the checks efficiently. It is not very flexible, however, and places an extra burden on the programmer, who must know all the constraints that a transaction may violate and must include checks to ensure that none of these constraints are violated. An omission, misunderstanding, or error by the programmer may leave the database in an inconsistent state.

Another drawback of specifying constraints procedurally is that constraints can change with time, as the business rules in a miniworld situation change. If a constraint changes, the DBA must instruct appropriate programmers to recode all the transactions and operations affected by the change. This again leaves open the possibility of overlooking some transactions and hence of producing errors in constraint representation and enforcement.

Specifying Constraints Declaratively as Assertions. A more formal technique for representing explicit constraints is to use a **constraint specification language**, usually based on some variation of the relational calculus. This **declarative approach** establishes a clean separation between the **constraint base** (in which the constraints are stored in a suitably encoded form) and the **integrity control subsystem** of the DBMS (which accesses the constraint base to apply the constraints appropriately to the affected transactions).

When this technique is used, constraints are often called **assertions**. This approach has been suggested for use with relational DBMSs.* The integrity control subsystem compiles the assertions, which are then stored in the DBMS catalog, where the integrity control subsystem can refer to them and *automatically* enforce them. Consequently, update transactions can be written *without any constraint-checking statements*. This approach is very appealing from the standpoint of the users and programmers because of its flexibility. Update transactions are written without any concomitant check for constraint violations. A constraint can be changed independently of the transactions without the designer's having to recode any transactions; the designer need only cancel the old assertion and specify its replacement in the assertion specification language. The new assertion is compiled and thereupon replaces the canceled assertion in the DBMS catalog. Unfortunately, this technique has proved very difficult to implement efficiently, because the integrity control subsystems have proved to be quite complex. Research on making this approach more efficient is continuing; it includes the use of rule systems, deductive databases (see Chapter 24), and active databases (see Chapter 25).

21.4.4 Inherent, Implicit, and Explicit Constraints

In this section, we summarize the three main techniques by which constraints can be specified in a database system. Every data model has a set of built-in constraints asso-

---

*The SQL language includes the ASSERT statement for assertion specification (see Chapter 7), although this statement is *not* implemented in many current relational DBMSs.

ciated with the constructs of the data model. We call these the **inherent constraints** of the data model. Inherent constraints *need not be specified* in the DDL when a database schema is being defined; they are inherent properties of the data model constructs themselves. An example of an inherent constraint in the ER model is that every relationship instance of an n-ary relationship type R relates *exactly one entity from each entity type participating in R in a specific role*, and that each relationship instance relates a unique association of entities at any point in time. The inherent constraints are hence the *rules* that define the data model constructs.

Implicit constraints, on the other hand, are specified to the DBMS through the data definition language during the process of creating the database schema. They are *implied* by the various specifications that describe each entity type, attribute, and relationship in a particular schema DDL. For example, specifying that a certain attribute is a key of an entity type implies the constraint that the attribute must have a unique value for each entity. Similarly, specifying a structural constraint on a relationship type R implicitly defines the corresponding constraints on R. The DDL compiler interprets and stores these constraints in the DBMS catalog so that the DBMS software can automatically enforce the constraints each time an update occurs. Implicit constraints that are supported by a DBMS are *specified in the DDL* during schema definition.

Each data model includes a different set of inherent and implicit constraints. A given implementation of a data model in a *particular DBMS* will usually provide automatic support for only some of the inherent and implicit constraints of the data model. In general, high-level data models represent more inherent and implicit constraints than do lower-level data models. However, no data model is capable of representing all types of constraints that may occur in a miniworld. Hence, it is necessary to specify additional **explicit constraints** on each particular database schema. Examples of explicitly specified constraints are the general semantic integrity constraints discussed in Section 21.4.3. These constraints are specified by the programmers either procedurally when they implement database transactions or declaratively via an assertion specification language.

21.4.5 *State Versus Transition Constraints*

Finally, we can classify constraints based on whether they refer to a single database state or to multiple states. A **state constraint** is a constraint on every **nontransient state** of the database—that is, every state where the database is not in the process of being updated. Recall that a *database state* refers to all the data in the database at a particular point in time. A nontransient database state is **consistent** if it satisfies all state constraints. Examples of state constraints are domain constraints, key constraints, structural constraints on relationship, and most of the other constraints we have discussed so far.

State constraints should be checked whenever the database state is changed by an update transaction. A transaction should include sufficient checks to guarantee that, if the database is in a consistent state before transaction execution, it will also be in a consistent state after transaction execution. A transaction is considered an atomic update unit, not only for integrity constraints, but also for concurrency control and recovery, as we discussed in Chapters 17 through 19.

Another type of constraint applies to multiple database states and is called a database **transition constraint**. A transition constraint is a constraint on the transition from one state to another, not on an individual state. An example is that the Salary attribute of an employee can only be increased; this means that any update to the Salary attribute is accepted only if the new value of Salary is greater than the old value. Notice that the constraint is neither on the state of the database before the update nor on the state of it after the update; it is specified on the transition between states and involves values of attributes both *before* and *after* the transaction. In general, transition constraints occur less frequently than state constraints, and they are mainly specified as *explicit constraints*.

21.5 EER Update Operations and Transaction Specification★

There are two complementary parts in the database design process, as illustrated in Figure 3.1. So far, we have concentrated on the conceptual design of the data requirements of a database application. The specification of the functional and processing requirements should proceed in parallel. This is typically done by using a high-level process specification technique, such as data flow diagrams, followed by a more detailed design. In general, programming language constructs such as if statements, looping constructs, and input-output must be used to specify complex database transactions. In addition, a set of database operations must be included to specify database accesses. In this section, we introduce the basic update operations of the EER model. We then show how simple database transactions can be specified during database design by combining these operations.

Eight basic operations can be used to specify updates on an EER schema. The operations **insert_entity** and **delete_entity** specify the creation and removal of an entity in an entity type. The operations **add_relationship** and **remove_relationship** serve similar functions for relationship types. We shall abbreviate these four operations as **insert_E**, **delete_E**, **add_R**, and **remove_R**, respectively. Two other operations, **modify_E** and **modify_R**, are needed to specify modification of entity and relationship attribute values, respectively. Finally, the two operations **add_to_class** and **remove_from_class**, abbreviated as **add_C** and **remove_C**, respectively, are used to add and to remove an entity in a subclass or category. We now informally specify the form and arguments for each of these operations:

- **insert_E** *entity_type_name* **attributes** *attribute_name ← value*, . . .
- **delete_E** *entity_type_name* **where** *condition*
- **add_R** *relationship_type_name* **where** *entity_type_name : condition*, . . .
  attributes *attribute_name ← value*, . . .
- **remove_R** *relationship_type_name* **where** *entity_type_name : condition*, . . .
- **modify_E** *entity_type_name* **where** *condition*
  attributes *attribute_name ← value*, . . .
- **modify_R** *relationship_type_name* **where** *entity_type_name : condition*, . . .
  attributes *attribute_name ← value*, . . .
- **add_C** *subclass_or_category_name* **from** *superclass_name* **where** *condition*
  attributes *attribute_name ← value*, . . .
- **remove_C** *subclass_or_category_name* **where** *condition*

In the preceding list, *entity_type_name* is the name of one of the entity types in the database schema; and similarly, *relationship_type_name*, *subclass_or_category_name*, and *attribute_name* are the names of appropriate relationship types, subclasses or categories, and attributes from the same schema. A *value* can be a constant value from the attribute domain, or a parameter (variable) that holds such a value. Finally, *condition* specifies a predicate that selects one or more entities from an entity type or class. Here are six examples showing some of these operations on the COMPANY ER schema shown in Figure 3.14:

insert_E PROJECT
attributes Name ← "ProductA", Number ← 9, Location ← "Dallas" ;
delete_E PROJECT **where** (Name = "ProductA") ;
add_R WORKS_ON
where PROJECT:(Name = "ProductA"), EMPLOYEE:(SSN="123456789")
attributes Hours ← 20 ;
remove_R WORKS_ON
where PROJECT:(Name = "ProductA"), EMPLOYEE:(SSN="123456789") ;
modify_E PROJECT **where** (Name = "ProductA")
attributes Location ← "Arlington" ;
modify_R WORKS_ON
where PROJECT:(Name = "ProductA"), EMPLOYEE:(SSN="123456789")
attributes Hours ← 30 ;

The first two commands specify the addition and the removal of a PROJECT entity; the next two specify the addition and the removal of a relationship instance in WORKS_ON; and the final two specify modifications of attributes. Notice that a relationship instance is identified by specifying a condition on each of the entities that participates in the relationship. If any of these conditions specifies multiple entities, multiple relationship instances are affected by the command. For example, the operation

remove_R WORKS_ON
where PROJECT:(Location = "Houston"), EMPLOYEE:(Salary > 50000) ;

would specify the removal of all relationship instances that relate *any* PROJECT located in "Houston" with *any* EMPLOYEE whose Salary is greater than $50,000. If one of the participating entity types is not specified, all its entities are selected. For example, the operation

remove_R WORKS_ON **where** PROJECT:(Name = "ProductA") ;

would specify the removal of all relationship instances that relate *any* EMPLOYEE to the specified PROJECT entity. We can also append role names to the participating entity types, if needed, as shown in the examples that follow.

These basic update operations can be combined to specify logical update transactions on a particular schema during database design. In this case, a transaction is given a name, a number of parameters, and a body of code specification that includes the appropriate database operations. For example, consider the transaction

HIRE_EMP_IN_DEPARTMENT, which hires a new employee to work for a particular department. The parameters include all relevant attributes of the new employee entity, plus a means of identifying the department that the employee is joining, and possibly the name of the direct supervisor of the employee. This can be specified as follows:

```
DEFINE TRANSACTION HIRE_EMP_IN_DEPARTMENT
    PARAMETERS FN, MI, LN, SSN, BD, SEX, SAL, ADDR, DNAME, SUPERSSN
    BEGIN_TRANS
        insert_E EMPLOYEE attributes
            Name.Fname ← FN, Name.Minit ← MI, Name.Lname ← LN, Ssn ← SSN,
            Bdate ← BD, Sex ← SEX, Salary ← SAL, Address ← ADDR ;
        add_R WORKS_FOR where
            EMPLOYEE : (Ssn = SSN), DEPARTMENT : (Name = DNAME) ;
        add_R SUPERVISION where
            EMPLOYEE.supervisor : (Ssn = SUPERSSN),
            EMPLOYEE.supervisee : (Ssn = SSN) ;
    END_TRANS ;
```

Here, the transaction parameters are specified as variables, which must be instantiated by providing appropriate values whenever a new employee is actually inserted in the database. We used *dot notation* when specifying component attributes of a composite attribute (Name.Fname), or when specifying roles (EMPLOYEE.supervisor); similar notation can be used to specify entities related via a relationship. This high-level transaction specification is precise enough to specify the transaction actions clearly, and to form a basis for implementing the transaction later. Notice that we did not specify any checking for integrity constraints in this transaction, since the goal of the specification process here is to define unambiguously the meaning of the transaction. All the integrity constraints specified in the COMPANY schema, as well as any additional explicit constraints, must be enforced when the database system is implemented.

We now specify four other transactions—CHANGE_EMP_SUPERVISOR, END_PROJECT, ASSIGN_EMP, and DEASSIGN_EMP—on the COMPANY ER schema:

```
DEFINE TRANSACTION CHANGE_EMP_SUPERVISOR
    PARAMETERS EMPSSN, NEWSUPERSSN
    BEGIN_TRANS
        remove_R SUPERVISION where
            EMPLOYEE.supervisee : (Ssn = EMPSSN) ;
        add_R SUPERVISION where
            EMPLOYEE.supervisor : (Ssn = NEWSUPERSSN),
            EMPLOYEE.supervisee : (Ssn = EMPSSN) ;
    END_TRANS ;
```

DEFINE TRANSACTION END_PROJECT
   PARAMETERS PNAME
   BEGIN_TRANS
     delete_E PROJECT **where** Name = PNAME ;
     remove_R WORKS_ON **where**
       PROJECT : (Name = PNAME) ;
     remove_R CONTROLS **where**
       PROJECT : (Name = PNAME) ;
   END_TRANS ;

DEFINE TRANSACTION ASSIGN_EMP
   PARAMETERS EMPSSN, PNAME, HOURSPERWEEK
   BEGIN_TRANS
     add_R WORKS_ON **where**
       EMPLOYEE : (Ssn = EMPSSN), PROJECT : (Name = PNAME)
       attributes Hours ← HOURSPERWEEK ;
   END_TRANS ;

DEFINE TRANSACTION DEASSIGN_EMP
   PARAMETERS EMPSSN, PNAME
   BEGIN_TRANS
     remove_R WORKS_ON **where**
       EMPLOYEE : (Ssn = EMPSSN),
       PROJECT : (Name = PNAME) ;
   END_TRANS ;

Finally, we illustrate subclass operations by a transaction on the UNIVERSITY EER schema of Figure 21.10. The following transaction specifies the hiring of a new FACULTY entity, by inserting the new entry in the PERSON entity type, then adding it to the FACULTY subclass and INSTRUCTOR_RESEARCHER category, and finally relating the FACULTY to a DEPARTMENT via the BELONGS relationship.

DEFINE TRANSACTION HIRE_NEW_FACULTY
   PARAMETERS FN, MI, LN, SSN, BD, SEX, ADDR, SAL, RANK, OFF, PHONE, DNAME
   BEGIN_TRANS
     insert_E PERSON **attributes**
       Name.Fname ← FN, Name.Minit ← MI, Name.Lname ← LN, Ssn ← SSN,
       Bdate ← BD, Sex ← SEX, Address ← ADDR ;
     add_C FACULTY **from** PERSON **where** Ssn = SSN **attributes**
       Rank ← RANK, Salary ← SAL, FOffice ← OFF, FPhone ← PHONE ;
     add_C INSTRUCTOR_RESEARCHER **from** FACULTY **where** Ssn = SSN ;
     add_R BELONGS **where**
       FACULTY : (Ssn = SSN), DEPARTMENT : (DName = DNAME) ;
   END_TRANS ;

Notice that inherited attributes, such as Ssn of FACULTY, can be used in specifying conditions on a subclass. The process of specifying simple transactions is evidently quite straightforward. For more complex transactions, it is necessary to use regular programming language constructs, such as if and case statements, looping, input and output, and (in many cases) displays of the results of database queries. For example, a complex transaction for specifying the process of reserving seats on an airline may require first retrieving the appropriate flights from the database and displaying these on the screen for the travel agent, followed by updating the database to specify the reservation of seats on a particular flight. Because there is no standard notation for specifying this, we leave it to our readers to use their favored programming language or pseudo-code constructs when specifying complex transactions during database design.

21.6 Overview of Other Data Models★

As we mentioned at the beginning of this chapter, many conceptual data models have been proposed. In Section 21.1 we presented the most important semantic modeling concepts as part of the EER model. In this section we give overviews of four other data models: the functional, nested relational, structural, and semantic data models.

21.6.1 *Functional Data Models*

Functional data models (**FDMs**) use the concept of a mathematical function as their fundamental modeling construct. Any request for information can be visualized as a function call with certain arguments, and the function returns the required information. There are several proposals for functional data models and query languages (see the bibliography at the end of this chapter). The DAPLEX model and language are perhaps the best-known example.

The main modeling primitives of an FDM are **entities** and **functional relationships**. Several standard types of entities exist at the most basic level; these include STRING, INTEGER, CHARACTER, and REAL (among others) and are called **printable entity types**. Abstract entity types that correspond to real-world objects are given the type **ENTITY**. For example, consider the EER diagram in Figure 21.10; we will show how some of the entity types and relationship types in that schema can be specified in a functional DAPLEX-like notation. The PERSON, STUDENT, COURSE, SECTION, and DEPARTMENT entity types are declared as follows:

```
PERSON( ) → ENTITY
STUDENT( ) → ENTITY
COURSE( ) → ENTITY
SECTION( ) → ENTITY
DEPARTMENT( ) → ENTITY
```

These statements specify that the functions PERSON, STUDENT, COURSE, SECTION, and DEPARTMENT return abstract entities; and hence, these statements serve to define the corresponding entity types. An attribute of an entity type is also specified as a function whose argument (domain) is the entity type and whose result (range) is a printable entity. The following function declarations specify the attributes of PERSON:

SSN(PERSON) → STRING
BDATE(PERSON) → STRING
SEX(PERSON) → CHAR

Applying the SSN function to an entity of type PERSON returns that PERSON's social security number, which is a printable value of type STRING. To declare composite attributes, such as NAME in Figure 21.10, we must declare them to be entities and then declare their component attributes as functions, as shown here for the NAME attribute:

NAME( ) → ENTITY
NAME(PERSON) → NAME
FNAME(NAME) → STRING
MINIT(NAME) → CHAR
LNAME(NAME) → STRING

To declare a relationship type, we give it a **role name** in one direction and define it also as a function. For example, the MAJOR and MINOR relationship types of Figure 21.10 may be declared as follows:

MAJOR(STUDENT) → DEPARTMENT
MINOR(STUDENT) → DEPARTMENT

These declarations specify that applying a function MAJOR or MINOR to a STUDENT entity should return as its result an entity of type DEPARTMENT. To declare an inverse role name for the same relationship types, we write:

MAJORING_IN(DEPARTMENT) →» STUDENT INVERSE OF MAJOR
MINORING_IN(DEPARTMENT) →» STUDENT INVERSE OF MINOR

The INVERSE OF clause declares that these functions are the inverses of the two previously declared functions and hence that they specify *the same* relationship types as the other two, but in the *reverse direction*. Notice also the double arrows (→»), which specify that applying the MAJORING-IN or MINORING-IN function on a single DEPARTMENT entity can return a *set of entities* of type STUDENT. This specifies that the relationship types are 1:N. This notation can also be used to specify multivalued attributes. To specify an M:N relationship type, we use double arrows in *both directions*, as in the following example:

COURSES_COMPLETED(STUDENT) →» SECTION
STUDENTS_ATTENDED(SECTION) →» STUDENT INVERSE OF
                                        COURSES_COMPLETED

This declares the TRANSCRIPT relationship of Figure 21.10 in both directions. Some functions may have more than one argument; for example, to declare the GRADE attribute of the preceding relationship, we write:

GRADE(STUDENT, SECTION) → CHAR

Notice that we need not declare an inverse for each relationship. For example, the DC and CS relationship types of Figure 21.10, which relate a course to its offering department and a course to its sections, may be declared in only one direction, as follows:

```
OFFERING_DEPARTMENT(COURSE) → DEPARTMENT
SECTIONS_OF(COURSE) ↠ SECTION
```

Figure 21.15(a) shows a declaration of part of the EER schema of Figure 21.10 in FDM notation, and Figure 21.15(b) shows a diagrammatic notation for that schema. There is also notation available for specifying IS-A relationships, derived values, and other advanced modeling concepts in DAPLEX. In Figure 21.15(a), the function IS_A_PERSON specifies an IS-A relationship (a subclass/superclass relationship, in EER terminology) between STUDENT and PERSON.

A fundamental concept in FDM is **function composition**. By writing DNAME(OFFERING_DEPARTMENT(COURSE)), we compose the two functions DNAME and OFFERING_DEPARTMENT. This is called a **path expression** and can be written in an alternative *dot notation* as COURSE.OFFERING_DEPARTMENT.DNAME. Function composition can be used to declare **derived functions**; for example, the functions of FNAME(PERSON) or FNAME(STUDENT) in Figure 21.15(a) are declared to be compositions of previously declared functions. This approach can also be used to specify the inherited attributes explicitly, as shown in Figure 21.15(a). Notice that we did not show any derived functions or inverse relationships in the schema diagram of Figure 21.15(b), although we could have done so.

Function composition is also the main concept used in **functional query languages**. We illustrate this by a simple example. Suppose that we want to retrieve the last names of all students majoring in 'Math'; we could do so by writing the following query:

```
RETRIEVE LNAME(NAME(IS_A_PERSON(MAJORING_IN(DEPARTMENT))))
WHERE DNAME(DEPARTMENT) = 'Math'
```

Here we use the MAJORING_IN function, which is the inverse of MAJOR. Alternatively, we can use the derived function LNAME(STUDENT) to shorten the preceding query to:

```
RETRIEVE LNAME(MAJORING_IN(DEPARTMENT))
WHERE DNAME(DEPARTMENT) = 'Math'
```

The inverse function MAJORING_IN(DEPARTMENT) returns STUDENT entities, so we can apply the derived function LNAME(STUDENT) to those entities.

21.6.2 *The Nested Relational Data Model*

The **nested relational model** removes the restriction of *first normal form* (1NF; see Sections 6.1 and 12.3.2) from the basic relational model. The resulting model is also known as the **Non-1NF** or **N1NF** relational model. In the standard relational model—also called the *flat* model—attributes are required to be single-valued and to have atomic domains. The nested relational model allows composite and multivalued attributes, thus leading to complex tuples with a hierarchical structure. This is useful for representing objects

(a) ENTITY TYPE DECLARATIONS (INCLUDING THE COMPOSITE ATTRIBUTE NAME):

PERSON( ) → ENTITY   STUDENT( ) → ENTITY
COURSE( ) → ENTITY   SECTION( ) → ENTITY
DEPARTMENT( ) → ENTITY   NAME( ) → ENTITY

ATTRIBUTE DECLARATIONS (INCLUDING THREE DERIVED ATTRIBUTES):

SSN(PERSON) → STRING   BDATE(PERSON) → STRING
SEX(PERSON) → CHAR   NAME(PERSON) → NAME
FNAME(NAME) → STRING   FNAME(PERSON) → FNAME(NAME(PERSON))
MINIT(NAME) → CHAR   MINIT(PERSON) → MINIT(NAME(PERSON))
LNAME(NAME) → STRING   LNAME(PERSON) → LNAME(NAME(PERSON))
CLASS(STUDENT) → STRING   SEC# (SECTION) → INTEGER
YEAR(SECTION) → STRING   QTR(SECTION) → STRING
DNAME(DEPARTMENT) → STRING   DPHONE(DEPARTMENT) → STRING
OFFICE(DEPARTMENT) → STRING   C# (COURSE) → STRING
CNAME(COURSE) → STRING   CDESC(COURSE) → STRING

RELATIONSHIP TYPE DECLARATIONS (INCLUDING INVERSES AND RELATIONSHIP
ATTRIBUTES):

MAJOR(STUDENT) → DEPARTMENT
MINOR(STUDENT) → DEPARTMENT
MAJORING_IN(DEPARTMENT)→→ STUDENT INVERSE OF MAJOR
MINORING_IN(DEPARTMENT) →→ STUDENT INVERSE OF MINOR
COURSES_COMPLETED(STUDENT)→→ SECTION
STUDENTS_ATTENDED(SECTION)→→ STUDENT INVERSE OF COURSES_COMPLETED
GRADE(STUDENT, SECTION) → CHAR
OFFERING_DEPARTMENT(COURSE) → DEPARTMENT
SECTIONS_OF(COURSE) →→ SECTION

IS_A RELATIONSHIP AND INHERITED ATTRIBUTE DECLARATIONS:

IS_A_PERSON(STUDENT) → PERSON
SSN(STUDENT) → SSN(IS_A_PERSON(STUDENT))
BDATE(STUDENT) → BDATE(IS_A_PERSON(STUDENT))
SEX(STUDENT) → SEX(IS_A_PERSON(STUDENT))
NAME(STUDENT) → NAME(IS_A_PERSON(STUDENT))
FNAME(STUDENT) → FNAME(IS_A_PERSON(STUDENT))
MINIT(STUDENT) → MINIT(IS_A_PERSON(STUDENT))
LNAME(STUDENT) → LNAME(IS_A_PERSON(STUDENT))

Figure 21.15 The functional data model. (a) Declaring part of the EER
schema of Figure 21.10 as functions. *(continued on next page)*

that are naturally hierarchically structured. Figure 21.16(a) shows a nested (N1NF) relation schema DEPT based on part of the COMPANY database, and Figure 21.16(b) gives
an example of a N1NF tuple in DEPT. To define the DEPT schema as a nested structure,
we can write the following:

DEPT = (DNO, DNAME, MANAGER, EMPLOYEES, PROJECTS, LOCATIONS)
EMPLOYEES = (ENAME, DEPENDENTS)
PROJECTS = (PNAME, PLOC)
LOCATIONS = (DLOC)
DEPENDENTS = (DNAME, AGE)

(b)

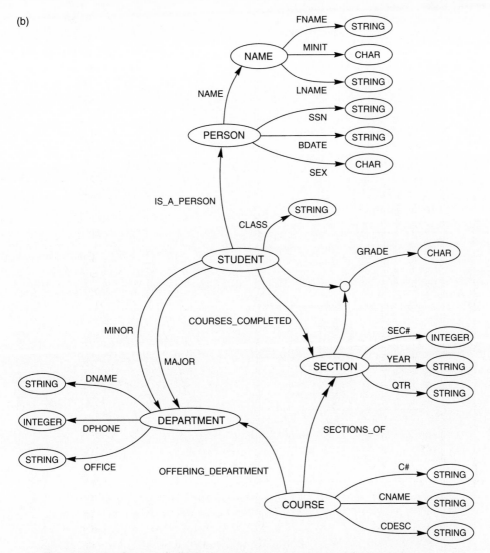

Figure 21.15   *(continued)* (b) Diagrammatic representation of the FDM schema declared in Figure 21.15(a).

First, all attributes of the DEPT relation are defined. Next, any nested attributes of DEPT—namely, EMPLOYEES, PROJECTS, and LOCATIONS—are themselves defined. Next, any second-level nested attributes, such as DEPENDENTS of EMPLOYEES, are defined; and so on. All attribute names must be distinct in the nested relation definition. Notice that a nested attribute is typically a *multivalued composite* attribute, thus leading to a "nested relation" within each tuple. For example, the value of the PROJECTS attribute *within* each DEPT tuple is a relation with two attributes (PNAME, PLOC). In the DEPT tuple of Figure 21.16(b), the PROJECTS attribute contains three tuples as its value. Other nested attributes may be *multivalued simple* attributes, such as LOCATIONS of DEPT. It is also possible

(a) DEPT (schema)

DNO	DNAME	MANAGER	EMPLOYEES		PROJECTS		LOCATIONS
			ENAME	DEPENDENTS	PNAME	PLOC	DLOC
				DNAME	AGE			

(b) DEPT (example of a nested tuple)

4	Administration	Wallace	Zelaya	Thomas	8	New benefits	Stafford	Stafford
				Jennifer	6	Computerization	Stafford	Greenway
			Wallace	Jack	18	Phone System	Greenway	
				Robert	15			
				Mary	10			
			Jabbar					

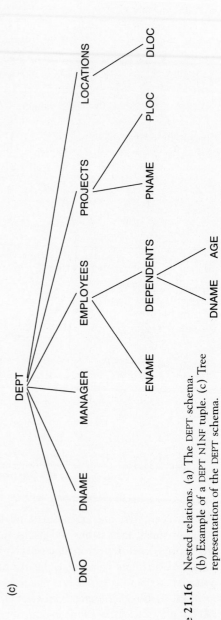

(c)

Figure 21.16 Nested relations. (a) The DEPT schema.
(b) Example of a DEPT N1NF tuple. (c) Tree
representation of the DEPT schema.

to have a nested attribute that is *single-valued* and *composite*, although most nested relational models treat such an attribute as though it were multivalued.

When a nested relational database schema is defined, it consists of a number of **external** relation schemas; these define the top level of the individual nested relations. In addition, nested attributes are called **internal** relation schemas, since they define relational structures that are *nested inside* another relation. In our example, DEPT is the only external relation; all the others—EMPLOYEES, PROJECTS, LOCATIONS, and DEPENDENTS—are internal relations. Finally, **attributes** appear at the leaf level and are not nested. We can represent each relation schema by means of a tree structure, as shown in Figure 21.16(c), where the root is an external relation schema, the leaves are attributes, and the internal nodes are internal relation schemas. Notice the similarity between this representation and a hierarchical schema (see Chapter 11).

It is important to be aware that the three first-level nested relations in DEPT represent *independent* information. Hence, EMPLOYEES represents the employees *working for* the department, PROJECTS represents the projects *controlled by* the department, and LOCATIONS represents the various department locations. The relationship between EMPLOYEES and PROJECTS is not represented in the schema; this is an M:N relationship, which is difficult to represent in a hierarchical structure.

Extensions to the relational algebra and to the relational calculus, as well as to SQL, have been proposed for nested relations. The interested reader is referred to the bibliography at the end of this chapter for details. Here, we illustrate two operations, **NEST** and **UNNEST**, that can be used to augment standard relational algebra operations for converting between nested and flat relations. Consider the flat EMP_PROJ relation of Figure 12.4, and suppose that we project it over the attributes SSN, PNUMBER, HOURS, ENAME as follows:

EMP_PROJ_FLAT ← π SSN, ENAME, PNUMBER, HOURS (EMP_PROJ)

To create a nested version of this relation, where one tuple exists for each employee and the (PNUMBER, HOURS) are nested, we use the NEST operation as follows:

EMP_PROJ_NESTED ← NEST PROJS = (PNUMBER, HOURS) (EMP_PROJ_FLAT)

The effect of this operation is to create an internal nested relation PROJS = (PNUMBER, HOURS) within the external relation EMP_PROJ_NESTED. Hence, NEST groups together the tuples *with the same value* for the attributes that are *not specified* in the NEST operation; these are the SSN and ENAME attributes in our example. For each such group, which represents one employee in our example, a single nested tuple is created with an internal nested relation PROJS = (PNUMBER, HOURS). Hence, the EMP_PROJ_NESTED relation looks like the EMP_PROJ relation shown in Figure 12.9(a) and (b). Notice the similarity between nesting and grouping for aggregate functions (see Section 6.6.1). In the former, each group of tuples becomes a single nested tuple; whereas, in the latter, each group becomes a single summary tuple after an aggregate function is applied to the group.

The UNNEST operation is the inverse of NEST. We can reconvert EMP_PROJ_NESTED to EMP_PROJ_FLAT as follows

EMP_PROJ_FLAT ← UNNEST PROJS = (PNUMBER, HOURS) (EMP_PROJ_NESTED)

Here, the PROJS nested attribute is flattened into its components PNUMBER, HOURS.

21.6.3   *The Structural Data Model*

Various data models proposed extending the early relational model with additional constraints and semantics. Eventually, some of the proposed extensions became incorporated into the relational model and SQL2. We give an overview of the **structural data model** as a representative example of these extensions to the early relational model. The structural model used two types of structures: relations and connections. The concept of a **relation** is similar to that of the standard (flat) relational model. However, relations were categorized into several types to indicate their update behavior and their connections to other relations.

Each relation in the structural model has a **ruling part**; this corresponds to the concept of a primary key in the relational model described in Chapter 6. The original structural model categorized six types of relations: primary, referenced, nest, association, lexicon, and subrelation. Connections were categorized into three types: ownership, reference, and identity connection. We illustrate these concepts with the schema shown in Figure 21.17, which is the structural model representation of a simplified COMPANY database schema.

Primary relations do not have any references to them; hence, a tuple can be deleted from a primary relation without the user's having to check referencing tuples in other relations. In Figure 21.17, PROJECT is the only primary relation. **Referenced** relations have an attribute in some other relation that refers to their ruling part; hence, they correspond to relations that are referenced by a foreign key. However, for referenced relations, the *behavior* of the foreign key is defined to be *reject* on delete. This means that, if an attempt is made to delete a referenced tuple, the deletion is rejected unless no tuples from the referencing relation actually refer to the tuple being deleted. In Figure 21.17, DEPT and EMPLOYEE are referenced relations. Referenced relations are connected to their referencing relations via a **reference connection**; this is displayed as a directed arc (arrow) to the referenced relation, as shown in Figure 21.17. Notice that this is the same graphical notation we used *for all foreign keys* in Figure 6.7; in the structural model, only foreign keys with *reject on delete* semantics are defined by a reference connection.

Nest relations typically correspond to multivalued attributes or weak entity types in the ER model, and they are typically represented by a *nested internal relation* in the nested relational model. In the structural model, a nest relation is owned by another relation. In Figure 21.17, DEPENDENT is a nest relation that is owned by EMPLOYEE. A nest relation includes a foreign key attribute *within its ruling part* that refers to the owner relation; the *behavior* for the foreign key is defined to be *cascade* on delete, which means that, if the owner (referenced) tuple is deleted, the nest (referencing) tuples are automatically deleted. **Association** relations typically represent binary M:N or n-ary relationships. Their ruling part is entirely formed of *two or more* foreign keys, each referencing an owner relation. The foreign keys are again defined with the *cascade on delete* behavior. In Figure 21.17, WORKS_ON is an association relation.

An **ownership connection** is used to connect an owner relation to an owned nest or association relation, and hence it represents a foreign key from the owned relation to the owner, with *cascade on delete* semantics. It is displayed as a line with an asterisk at the owned (nest or association) relation end, as shown in Figure 21.17. The main difference between nest and association relations is that the nest relation has only one

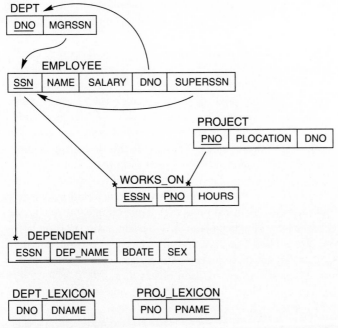

Figure 21.17   Simplified COMPANY schema in the structural model.

owner (and hence represents a strictly hierarchical relationship), whereas an association has two or more owners.

Lexicon relations are used to store one-to-one correspondences between pairs of attributes. Hence, secondary keys may be removed into a lexicon if desired. This is illustrated by the DEPT_LEXICON and PROJ_LEXICON relations in Figure 21.17. Finally, sub-relations and identity connections are used to represent class/subclass relationships, specialization, and generalization. An **identity connection** represents a foreign key—which is also a primary key—from a **subrelation** to another relation, with *cascade on delete* semantics.

The structural model was proposed before foreign keys were incorporated into the relational model. The concepts of connections defined foreign keys with different types of behaviors. Several of the structural model concepts—and similar concepts proposed by other researchers—eventually made their way into the standard relational model and SQL2.

21.6.4 *The Semantic Data Model*

The **semantic data model** (or SDM) introduced the concepts of classes and subclasses into data modeling; hence, it was the initial source for many of the concepts that have since been incorporated into conceptual data models, including object-oriented models (see Chapter 22). It also categorized classes whose objects represented information with various types of semantics. In this section, we give a very brief introduction to some of the concepts of SDM.

The main modeling concept of SDM is the **class**, which is a collection of objects of the same type. The **properties** (attributes) of a class specify the type of objects in the class. Properties are classified as *optional* (null allowed) versus *mandatory* (null not allowed); *simple* (atomic) versus *compound* (composite); *single-valued* versus *multivalued*; *derivable* versus *stored*; and *unique* versus *nonunique*. An object exists independently of any of its attribute values. Each property is associated with a domain (value set) from which its values for individual objects can be chosen. If the domain of a property is another class, the values of the property *refer to* objects from the other class.

Object classes are also classified into several types. A *concrete object class* represents objects with a concrete existence in the miniworld. An *abstraction class* represents groups of objects from other classes with identical properties. For example, an AIRPLANES class that contains an object for each individual plane owned by an airline is a concrete object class, whereas a PLANE_TYPES class that contains an object for each plane type (B737, B747, MD-11, DC-9, . . .) is an abstraction class. An *aggregate class* contains objects that are aggregates of other objects; for example, each object in a SHIP_CONVOYS aggregate class consists of an aggregate of objects from the concrete object class SHIPS. An *event class* includes temporal objects, such as VOYAGES or ARRIVALS.

A *subclass* is a subset of objects from a *base class*. For example, OIL_TANKERS and CRUISE_SHIPS are subclasses of a SHIPS base class. A *restriction subclass* is predicate-defined, whereas a *nonrestriction subclass* is not. In addition to subclasses that are defined by the users, abstraction and aggregation classes typically define certain subclasses. For example, each object in the abstraction class PLANE_TYPES defines a subclass of objects from AIRPLANES that are of a particular plane type.

This concludes our brief overview of some SDM concepts. Historically, SDM introduced many concepts that have been adapted into advanced data models. Some of the EER model concepts (see Section 21.1) have their origins in SDM concepts.

21.7 Summary

In this chapter we first discussed extensions to the ER model that improve its representational capabilities. We called the resulting model the enhanced-ER or EER model. The concept of a subclass and its superclass and the related mechanism of attribute inheritance were presented. We saw how it is sometimes necessary to create additional classes of entities, either because of additional specific attributes or because of specific relationship types. We discussed two main processes for defining superclass/subclass hierarchies and lattices—namely, specialization and generalization.

We then showed how to display these new constructs in an EER diagram. We also discussed the various types of constraints that may apply to specialization or generalization. The two main constraints are total/partial and disjoint/overlapping. In addition, a defining predicate for a subclass or a defining attribute for a specialization may be specified. We discussed the differences between user-defined and predicate-defined subclasses and between user-defined and attribute-defined specializations. Finally, we discussed the concept of a category, which is a subset of the union of two or more classes, and we gave formal definitions of all the concepts presented.

We then showed in Section 21.2 how EER model constructs can be mapped to relational structures. These mappings can be used during the logical phase of database design.

In Section 21.3 we discussed types of abstract data representation concepts. The concepts discussed were classification and instantiation, generalization and specialization, identification, aggregation and association. We saw how the EER model concepts are related to each of these. We also discussed briefly the discipline of knowledge representation and how it is related to semantic data modeling.

Section 21.4 provided a general categorization of the types of integrity constraints used frequently in data modeling. Section 21.5 presented the update operations associated with the EER model and illustrated their use in defining transactions at the conceptual level during database design. Finally, Section 21.6 gave a brief overview of four additional data models: functional, nested relational, structural, and semantic.

Review Questions

21.1. What is a subclass? When is a subclass needed in data modeling?

21.2. Define the following terms: *superclass of a subclass, superclass/subclass relationship, IS-A relationship, specialization, generalization, category, specific attributes.*

21.3. Discuss the mechanism of attribute inheritance. Why is it useful?

21.4. Discuss user-defined and predicate-defined subclasses, and identify the differences between the two.

21.5. Discuss user-defined and attribute-defined specializations, and identify the differences between the two.

21.6. Discuss the two main types of constraints on specializations and generalizations.

21.7. What is the difference between a subclass hierarchy and a subclass lattice?

21.8. What is the difference between specialization and generalization? Why do we not display this difference in schema diagrams?

21.9. How does a category differ from a regular shared subclass? What is a category used for? Illustrate your answer with examples.

21.10. List the various data abstraction concepts and the corresponding modeling concepts in the EER model.

21.11. What aggregation feature is missing from the EER model? How can the EER model be further enhanced to support it?

21.12. Discuss the following types of constraints: *domain constraints, key constraints, relationship (structural) constraints, semantic integrity constraints.* What are the differences between and the advantages/disadvantages of each of the following?

    a. Procedural versus declarative specification of constraints.

b. Inherent constraints, implicitly declared constraints, and explicitly declared constraints.

c. State constraints versus transition constraints.

21.13. List the update operations of the EER model, and discuss their use in designing database transactions at the conceptual level.

21.14. How is the nested relational data model different from the standard (flat) relational model? Describe the operations that can be used to map from one to the other.

Exercises

21.15. Design an EER schema for a database application that you are interested in. Specify all constraints that should hold on the database. Make sure that the schema has at least five entity types, four relationship types, a weak entity type, a superclass/subclass relationship, a category, and an n-ary (n > 2) relationship type.

21.16. Figure 21.18 shows an example of an EER diagram for a small airport database. The database is used to keep track of airplanes, their owners, airport employees, and pilots for a small private airport. From the requirements for this database, the following information was collected. Each airplane has a registration number [Reg#], is of a particular plane type [OF-TYPE], and is stored in a particular hangar [STORED-IN]. Each plane type has a model number [Model], a capacity [Capacity], and a weight [Weight]. Each hangar has a number [Number], a capacity [Capacity], and a location [Location]. The database also keeps track of the owners of each plane [OWNS] and the employees who have maintained the plane [MAINTAIN]. Each relationship instance in OWNS relates an airplane to an owner and includes the purchase date [Pdate]. Each relationship instance in [MAINTAIN] relates an employee to a service record [SERVICE]. Each plane undergoes service many times; hence, it is related by [PLANE-SERVICE] to a number of service records. A service record includes as attributes the date of maintenance [Date], the number of hours spent on the work [Hours], and the type of work done [Workcode]. We use a weak entity type [SERVICE] to represent airplane service, because the airplane registration number is used in identifying a service record. An owner is either a person or a corporation. Hence, we use a generalization category [OWNER] that is a subset of the union of corporation [CORPORATION] and person [PERSON] entity types. Both pilots [PILOT] and employees [EMPLOYEE] are subclasses of PERSON. Each pilot has specific attributes license number [LicNum] and restrictions [Restr]; each employee has specific attributes salary [Salary] and shift worked [Shift]. All person entities in the database have data kept on their social security number [Ssn], name [Name], address [Address], and telephone number [Phone]. For corporation entities, the data kept includes name [Name], address [Address], and telephone number [Phone]. The database also keeps track of the types of planes each pilot is authorized to fly [FLIES] and the types of planes each employee can do maintenance work on [WORKS-ON].

a. Map the EER schema of Figure 21.18 into a relational schema.

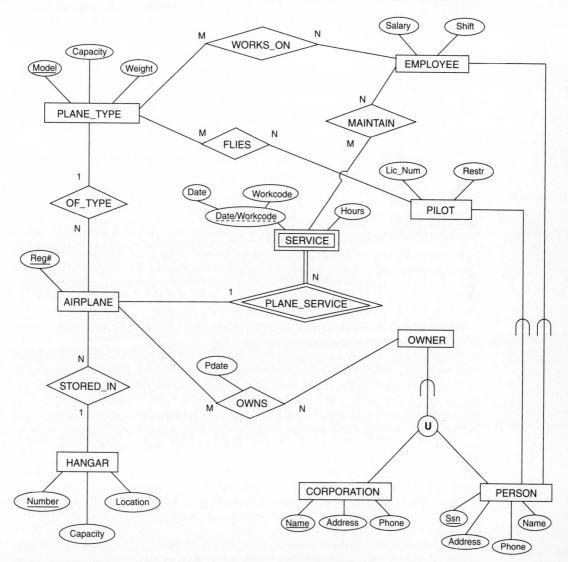

Figure 21.18 Extended-ER schema diagram for the small airport database.

b. Create a functional data model schema to correspond to the EER schema in Figure 21.18. Use the FDM notation of Figure 21.15(b).

21.17. Map the UNIVERSITY EER schema of Figure 21.10 into a relational schema.

21.18. Create a functional data model schema to correspond to the UNIVERSITY EER schema of Figure 21.10. Use the FDM notation of Figure 21.15(b).

21.19. Consider the BANK ER schema of Figure 3.23, and suppose that it is necessary to keep track of different types of ACCOUNTS (SAVINGS_ACCTS, CHECKING_ACCTS, . . .) and LOANS (CAR_LOANS, HOME_LOANS, . . .). Suppose that it is also desirable to keep track of each account's TRANSACTIONs (deposits, withdrawals, checks, . . .) and each loan's PAYMENTs; both of these include the amount, date, time, ... Modify the BANK schema, using ER and EER concepts of specialization and generalization. State any assumptions you make about the additional requirements.

21.20. How do nested relations compare to hierarchies of the hierarchical data model (see Chapter 11)? Would you want to change the LIBRARY relational schema of Figure 6.22 if you had the nested relational model constructs? Explain.

21.21. Draw a functional data model schema and a structural data model schema for the LIBRARY schema of Figure 6.22.

Selected Bibliography

Many papers have proposed conceptual or semantic data models. We give a representative list here. One group of papers, including Abrial (1974), Senko's DIAM model (1975), the NIAM method (Verheijen and VanBekkum 1982), and Bracchi et al. (1976), presents semantic models that are based on the concept of binary relationships. Another group of early papers discusses methods for extending the relational model to enhance its modeling capabilities. This includes the papers by Schmid and Swenson (1975), Navathe and Schkolnick (1978), Codd's RM/T model (1979), Furtado (1978), and the structural model of Wiederhold and Elmasri (1979).

The ER model was originally proposed by Chen (1976) and is formalized in Ng (1981). Since then, numerous extensions of its modeling capabilities have been proposed, as in Scheuermann et al. (1979), Dos Santos et al. (1979), Teorey et al. (1986), Gogolla and Hohenstein (1991), and the Entity-Category-Relationship (ECR) model of Elmasri et al. (1985). Smith and Smith (1977) presents the concepts of generalization and aggregation. The semantic data model of Hammer and McLeod (1981) introduced the concepts of class/subclass lattices, as well as other advanced modeling concepts. Weddell (1992) discusses functional dependencies in the context of semantic data models.

Another class of data models, called functional data models, was originally proposed by Sibley and Kerschberg (1977) and extended by Shipman (1981), which included many advanced modeling concepts as well as the functional query language DAPLEX. Another functional query language is FQL (Buneman and Frankel 1979). The book by Tsichritzis and Lochovsky (1982) discusses and compares data models.

The nested relational model is discussed in Schek and Scholl (1985), Jaeshke and Schek (1982), Chen and Kambayashi (1991), and Makinouchi (1977), among others. Algebras and query languages for nested relations are presented in Paredaens and VanGucht (1992), Pistor and Andersen (1986), Roth et al. (1988), and Ozsoyoghu et al. (1987), among others. Implementation of prototype nested relational systems is described in Dadam et al. (1986), Deshpande and VanGucht (1988), and Schek and Scholl (1989).

Although we did not discuss languages for the entity-relationship model and its extensions, there have been several proposals for such languages. Elmasri and Wiederhold (1981) proposes the GORDAS query language for the ER model, and it is extended to the ECR model in Elmasri et al. (1985). Another ER query language is proposed by Markowitz and Raz (1983). Senko (1980) presents a query language for Senko's DIAM model. A formal set of operations called the ER algebra was presented by Parent and Spaccapietra (1985). Campbell et al. (1985) presents a set of ER operations and shows that they are relationally complete. The TAXIS language for specifying trans-actions conceptually was proposed in Mylopoulos et al. (1981). User-friendly interfaces based on the ER model and other semantic models are presented in Elmasri and Larson (1985) and Czejdo et al. (1987), among many others. Kent (1978, 1979) discusses the shortcomings of traditional data models. Bradley (1978) extends the network model with a high-level language.

A survey of semantic data modeling appears in Hull and King (1987). Another survey of conceptual modeling is Pillalamarri et al. (1988). Eick (1991) discusses design and transformations of conceptual schemas.

CHAPTER 22

Object-Oriented
Databases

In this chapter we discuss object-oriented data models and database systems. As we have seen throughout this book, data models of many different types have been proposed. In Chapter 3, we presented the ER model. In Part 2, we presented the concepts and languages for the relational model. The network and hierarchical models were discussed in Part 3. In Chapter 21, we incorporated many advanced modeling concepts into the ER model, leading to the EER model, and we gave brief overviews of several additional data models: functional, nested relational, structural, and semantic. Many of the data models and systems discussed earlier have proved quite successful in developing the database technology required for traditional business database applications. However, they have certain shortcomings in relation to more complex applications, such as engineering design and manufacturing (CAD/CAM and CIM*), image and graphics databases, scientific databases, geographic information systems, multimedia databases, and efforts to provide uniform access to multiple database systems. These newer applications have requirements and characteristics that differ from those of traditional business applications, including more complex structures for objects, longer-duration transactions, new data types for storing images or large textual items, and the need to define nonstandard application-specific operations. Object-oriented databases were proposed to meet the needs of these more complex applications. The object-oriented approach offers the flexibility to handle some of these requirements without being limited by the data types and query languages available in traditional database systems. A key feature of object-oriented databases is the power they give the designer to specify both the structure of complex objects and the operations that can be applied to these objects.

---

*Computer-aided design/computer-aided manufacturing and computer-integrated manufacturing.

In the past few years, many experimental prototypes and commercial object-oriented database systems have become available. The experimental prototypes include the ORION system developed at MCC,* OpenOODB at Texas Instruments, the IRIS system developed at Hewlett-Packard laboratories, the ODE system at ATT Bell Labs, and the ENCORE/ObServer project at Brown University. Commercially available systems include GEM-STONE/OPAL of ServioLogic, ONTOS of Ontologic, Objectivity of Objectivity Inc., Versant of Versant Technologies, ObjectStore of Object Design, and O2 of O2 Technology. These represent only a partial list of the experimental prototypes and the commercially available object-oriented database systems. Unfortunately, it is still too early to tell which systems will emerge as leaders in this field. We have selected two systems—O2 and ObjectStore—to illustrate object-oriented database systems in Section 22.7.

Object-oriented databases have adopted many of the concepts that were developed for object-oriented programming languages. In Section 22.1, we examine the origins of the object-oriented approach and discuss how it applies to database systems. We then describe the key concepts utilized in many object-oriented database systems. In Section 22.2, we discuss object identity, object structure, and type constructors. Section 22.3 presents the concept of encapsulation of operations and the definition of methods as part of class declarations. Section 22.4 describes type and class hierarchies and inheritance in object-oriented databases, and Section 22.5 provides an overview of the issues that arise when complex objects need to be represented and stored. Section 22.6 discusses additional concepts, including polymorphism, operator overloading, dynamic binding, multiple and selective inheritance, and versioning of objects.

Section 22.7 presents examples from existing object-oriented database systems to illustrate data definition and data manipulation. Section 22.7.1 offers an overview of the O2 system, and Section 22.7.2 gives examples from the ObjectStore system. Section 22.8 discusses object-oriented database design by mapping an EER conceptual schema into an object-oriented schema.

The reader may skip some or all of Sections 22.5 through 22.8, if a less detailed introduction to the topic is desired.

22.1 Overview of Object-oriented Concepts

The term **object-oriented**—abbreviated by OO or O-O—has its origins in OO programming languages. OO concepts are now applied in the areas of databases, software engineering, knowledge bases, artificial intelligence, and computer systems in general. OO programming languages have their roots in the SIMULA language, which was proposed in the late 1960s. In SIMULA, the concept of a *class* groups together the internal data structure of an object in a class declaration. Subsequently, researchers proposed the concept of *abstract data type*, which hides the internal data structures and specifies all possible external operations that can be applied to an object, leading to the concept of *encapsulation*. The programming language SMALLTALK, developed at Xerox PARC** in the

---

*Microelectronics and Computer Technology Corporation, Austin, Texas.
**Palo Alto Research Center, Palo Alto, California.

1970s, was one of the first languages to explicitly incorporate additional OO concepts, such as message passing and inheritance. It is known as a *pure* OO programming language, meaning that it was explicitly designed to be object-oriented. This contrasts with *hybrid* OO programming languages, which incorporate OO concepts into an already existing language. An example of the latter is C^{++}, which incorporates OO concepts into the popular C programming language.

Objects in an OO programming language exist only during program execution. An OO database provides capabilities so that objects can be created to exist permanently, or *persist*, and be shared by numerous programs. Hence, OO databases store *persistent objects* permanently on secondary storage, and allow the sharing of these objects among multiple programs and applications. This requires the incorporation of other well-known features of database management systems, such as indexing mechanisms, concurrency control, and recovery. An OO database system interfaces with one or more OO programming languages to provide persistent and shared object capabilities.

One goal of OO databases is to maintain a direct correspondence between real-world and database objects so that objects do not lose their integrity and identity and can easily be identified and operated upon. Hence, OO databases provide a unique system-generated *object identifier* (*OID*) for each object. We can compare this to the relational model, for example, where each relation must have a primary key attribute whose value identifies each tuple uniquely. In the relational model, if the value of the primary key is changed, the tuple will have a new identity, even though it may still represent the same real-world object. Alternatively, a real-world object may possess different keys in different relations, making it difficult to ascertain that the keys do indeed stand for the same object (for example, the object identifier may be represented as Emp_id in one relation and as Ssn in another relation).

Another feature of OO databases is that objects may have an *object structure* of *arbitrary complexity* in order to contain all of the significant information that describes the object. In contrast, in traditional database systems, information about a complex object is often *scattered* over many relations or records, leading to loss of direct correspondence between a real-world object and its database representation.

The internal structure of an object includes the specification of *instance variables*, which hold the values that define the internal state of the object. Hence, an instance variable is similar to the concept of an *attribute*, except that instance variables may be encapsulated within the object and thus are not necessarily visible to external users. Instance variables may also be of arbitrarily complex data types. Object-oriented systems allow definition of the operations or functions that can be applied to objects of a particular type. In fact, some OO models insist that all operations a user can apply to an object must be predefined. This forces a complete *encapsulation* of objects. This rigid approach has since been relaxed in most OO data models, since it implies that any simple retrieval requires a predefined operation.

To encourage encapsulation, an operation is defined in two parts. The first part, called the *signature* or *interface* of the operation, specifies the operation name and arguments (or parameters). The second part, called the *method* or *body*, specifies the *implementation* of the operation. Operations can be invoked by passing a *message* to an object, which includes the operation name and the parameters. The object then executes the method for that operation. This encapsulation permits modification of the internal structure of an object and implementation of its operations without the need to disturb the external programs that invoke these operations. Hence, encapsulation provides for a form of data and operation independence (see Chapter 2).

Another key concept in OO systems is that of type and class hierarchies and *inheritance*. This permits specification of new types and classes that inherit much of their structure and operations from previously defined types or classes. Hence, specification of the object types can proceed systematically. This makes it easier to develop the data types of a system incrementally, and to *reuse* existing type definitions when creating new types of objects.

One problem in OO database systems involves representing *relationships* among objects. The insistence on complete encapsulation in early OO data models led to the argument that relationships should not be explicitly represented, but instead should be described by defining appropriate methods that locate related objects. However, this approach does not work very well for complex databases with multiple relationships, because it is useful to identify these relationships and make them visible to users. Many OO data models now allow the representation of relationships via *references*—that is, by placing the OIDs of related objects within an object itself.

Some OO systems provide capabilities for dealing with *multiple versions* of the same object—a feature that is essential in design and engineering applications. For example, an old version of an object that represents a tested and verified design should be retained until the new version is tested and verified. A new version of a complex object may include only a few new versions of its component objects, whereas other components remain unchanged. In addition to permitting versioning, OO databases should ideally allow for *schema evolution*, which occurs when type declarations are changed or when new types or relationships are created.

Another OO concept is *operator polymorphism*, which refers to an operation's ability to be applied to different types of objects; in such a situation, an *operation name* may refer to several distinct *implementations*, depending on the type of objects it is applied to. This feature is also called *operator overloading*. For example, an operation to calculate the area of a geometric object may differ in its method (implementation), depending on whether the object is of type triangle, circle, or rectangle. This may require the use of *late binding* of the operation name to the appropriate method at run-time, when the type of object to which the operation is applied becomes known.

In Sections 22.2 through 22.6, we discuss the main concepts of OO databases in more detail.

22.2 Object Identity, Object Structure, and Type Constructors

In this section we discuss the concept of object identity, and then we present the typical structuring operations for defining the structure of the value of an object. These structuring operations are often called **type constructors**. They define basic data-structuring operations that can be combined to form objects of arbitrary complexity.

22.2.1 *Object Identity*

An OO database system provides a **unique identity** to each independent object stored in the database. This unique identity is typically implemented via a unique, system-generated **object identifier**, or OID. The value of an OID is not visible to the external user, but it is used internally by the system to identify each object uniquely and to create and manage inter-object references.

The main property required of an OID is that it be **immutable**; that is, the value of an OID for a particular object should not change. This preserves the identity of the real-world object being represented. It is also desirable that each OID be used only once; that is, even if an object is removed from the database, its OID should not be assigned to another object. These two properties imply that the OID should not depend on any attribute values of the object, since the value of an attribute may be changed. It is also generally considered inappropriate to base the OID on the physical address of the object in storage, since physical reorganization of the database objects could change the OIDs in such a case. However, some systems do use the physical address as OID to increase the efficiency of object retrieval. If the physical address changes, an *indirect pointer* can be placed at the former address, which gives the new physical location of the object. An OO database system must have some mechanism for generating OIDs with the immutability property.

Some OO data models require that everything be represented as an object, whether it is a simple value or a complex object; hence, every basic value, such as an integer, string, or Boolean value, has an OID. This allows two basic values to have different OIDs, which can be useful in some cases. For example, the integer value 50 can be used sometimes to mean a weight in kilograms, and other times to mean the age of a person. Then, two basic objects with distinct OIDs could be created, and both objects would have the same basic value of 50. Although useful as a theoretical model, this is not very practical, since it may lead to the generation of too many OIDs. Hence, most OO database systems allow for the representation of both objects and **values**. Every object must have an immutable OID, whereas a value has no OID and just stands for itself.

22.2.2 *Object Structure*

In OO databases, the values (or states) of complex objects may be constructed from other objects by using certain **type constructors**. One way of representing such objects is to view each object as a triple (i, c, v), where i is a unique *object identifier* (the OID), c is a *constructor* (that is, an indication of how the object value is constructed), and v is the object *value* (or state). There can be several constructors, depending on the data model or the OO system. The three most basic constructors are the **atom**, **tuple**, and **set** constructors. Other commonly used constructors include the **list** and **array** constructors. There is also a **domain** D that contains all basic atomic values that are directly available in the system. These typically include integers, real numbers, character strings, Booleans, dates, and any other data types that the system supports directly.

An object value v is interpreted on the basis of the value of the constructor c in the triple (i, c, v) that represents the object. If c = atom, the value v is an atomic value from the domain D of basic values supported by the system. If c = set, the value v is a set of object identifiers $\{i_1, i_2, \ldots, i_n\}$, which are the identifiers (OIDs) for a set of objects that are typically of the same type. If c = tuple, the value v is a tuple of the form $<a_1{:}i_1, a_2{:}i_2, \ldots, a_n{:}i_n>$, where each a_j is an attribute name (sometimes called an *instance variable name* in OO terminology) and each i_j is an object identifier (OID). If c = list, the value v is an *ordered list* of object identifiers $[i_1, i_2, \ldots, i_n]$ of the same type. For c = array, the value is an array of object identifiers.

The preceding model allows arbitrary nesting of set, list, tuple, and other constructors. All values in nonatomic objects refer to other objects by their object identifiers. Hence, the only case where an actual value appears is in atomic objects. It is not practical to generate a unique system identifier for every value, so most systems allow both OIDs and *structured values*. Values can be structured by using the same type constructors as objects, except that a value *does not have* an OID.

The type constructors **set, list, array,** and **bag** are called **collection types** or **bulk types**, to distinguish them from basic types and tuple types. A list is similar to a set except that the OIDs in a list are *ordered,* and hence we can refer to the first, second, or i^{th} object in a list. A bag is also similar to a set, except that it allows duplicate values to exist. The main characteristic of a collection type is that a value will be a *collection of objects* that may be unstructured (such as a set or a bag) or structured (such as a list or an array).

Let us assume for the following example that everything is an object, including basic values. Let us also assume that we have the constructors atom, set, and tuple. We now represent some objects from the relational database shown in Figure 6.6, using the preceding model. We use $i_1, i_2, i_3, \ldots$ to stand for unique system-generated object identifiers. An object is defined by a triple (OID, type constructor, value). Consider the following objects:

$o_1 = (i_1,$ atom, Houston$)$

$o_2 = (i_2,$ atom, Bellaire$)$

$o_3 = (i_3,$ atom, Sugarland$)$

$o_4 = (i_4,$ atom, 5$)$

$o_5 = (i_5,$ atom, Research$)$

$o_6 = (i_6,$ atom, 22-MAY-78$)$

$o_7 = (i_7,$ set, $\{i_1, i_2, i_3\})$

$o_8 = (i_8,$ tuple, $<$DNAME$:i_5,$ DNUMBER$:i_4,$ MGR$:i_9,$ LOCATIONS$:i_7,$ EMPLOYEES$:i_{10},$ PROJECTS$:i_{11}>)$

$o_9 = (i_9,$ tuple, $<$MANAGER$:i_{12},$ MANAGERSTARTDATE$:i_6>)$

$o_{10} = (i_{10},$ set, $\{i_{12}, i_{13}, i_{14}\})$

$o_{11} = (i_{11},$ set $\{i_{15}, i_{16}, i_{17}\})$

.

.

.

The first five objects (o_1–o_5) listed here are just atomic values. There are many similar objects, one for each distinct constant atomic value in the database. These atomic objects are the ones that may cause a problem, due to the use of too many object identifiers, if this model is implemented directly. Object o_7 is a set-valued object that represents the set of locations for department 5; the set $\{i_1, i_2, i_3\}$ refers to the atomic objects with values {Houston, Bellaire, Sugarland}. Object o_8 is a tuple-valued object that represents department 5 itself, and has the attributes DNAME, DNUMBER, MGR, LOCATIONS, and so on. The first two attributes DNAME and DNUMBER have atomic objects o_5 and o_4 as their values. The MGR attribute has a tuple object o_9 as its value, which in turn has two attributes. The value of the manager attribute is the object whose OID is i_{12} (not shown), which is the employee object that manages the department, whereas the value of MANAGERSTARTDATE is another atomic object whose value is a date. The value of the EMPLOYEES attribute of o_8 is a set object with OID $= i_{10}$, whose value is the set of object identifiers for the employees who work for the DEPARTMENT (objects i_{12}, i_{13}, i_{14}, which are not shown). Similarly, the value of the PROJECTS attribute of o_8 is a set object with OID $= i_{11}$, whose value is the set of object identifiers for the projects that are controlled by department number 5 (objects i_{15}, i_{16}, and i_{17}, which are not shown).

In this model, an object can be represented as a graph structure, since it can be constructed by repeatedly applying the three basic constructors. The graph representing an object o_i can be constructed by first creating a node for the object o_i itself. The node for o_i is labeled with the OID and the object constructor c. We also create a node in the graph for each basic value in the domain D of all atomic values. If the object has an atomic value, we draw a directed arc from the node representing o_i to the node representing its basic value. If the object value is constructed, we draw directed arcs from the object node to a node that represents the constructed value. In general, the graph for an *individual object* should not have cycles, since that would indicate an object that contains itself as a component. However, the graph that represents a *type of object* may have cycles that represent recursive relationships. For example, in a type graph, an EMPLOYEE object may refer to a SUPERVISOR object, which is also of type EMPLOYEE. However, in the graph for the individual EMPLOYEE objects, the supervisor must be a distinct employee object, and hence there are no cycles. Figure 22.1 shows the graph for the example DEPARTMENT object given earlier.

The preceding model permits two types of definitions in a comparison of the values of two objects for equality. Two objects are said to have **identical values** if the graphs representing their values are identical in every respect, including the OIDs at every level. Another, weaker definition of equality is when two objects have **equal values.** In this case, the graph structures must be the same, and all the corresponding atomic values in the graphs should also be the same. However, some corresponding internal nodes in the two graphs may have objects with different OIDs.

A simple example can illustrate the difference between the two definitions for comparing objects for equality. Consider the following objects o_1, o_2, o_3, o_4, o_5, and o_6:

$$o_1 = (i_1, \text{tuple}, <a_1{:}i_4, a_2{:}i_6>)$$
$$o_2 = (i_2, \text{tuple}, <a_1{:}i_5, a_2{:}i_6>)$$
$$o_3 = (i_3, \text{tuple}, <a_1{:}i_4, a_2{:}i_6>)$$

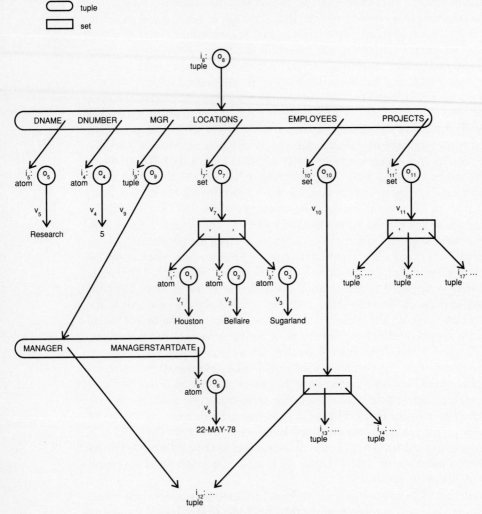

Figure 22.1 Graphical representation of a complex object.

$$o_4 = (i_4, \text{atom}, 10)$$
$$o_5 = (i_5, \text{atom}, 10)$$
$$o_6 = (i_6, \text{atom}, 20)$$

The objects o_1 and o_2 have *equal* values, since their values at the atomic level are the same but the values are reached through distinct objects o_4 and o_5. However, the values of objects o_1 and o_3 are *identical*. Similarly, o_4 and o_5 are equal but not identical, because they have distinct OIDs.

22.2.3 *Type Constructors*

An OO **data definition language** (OODDL) that incorporates the preceding type constructors can be used to define object types for a particular database application. Hence, these type constructors can be used to define the data structures for an OO *database schema*. We will see in Section 22.3 how to incorporate the definition of operations (or methods) into the OO schema. Figure 22.2 shows how we may declare Employee and Department types based on the objects in Figure 22.1 We also define a Date type as a tuple (rather than an atomic value, as in Figure 22.1). We use the keywords tuple, set, and list for the type constructors, and we use the available standard data types (integer, string, real, and so on) for atomic types. We use our own syntax—somewhat similar to O2 syntax—because of the current lack of a standard OODDL syntax.

Attributes that refer to other objects—such as dept of Employee or projects of Department—are basically **references**, and hence serve to represent *relationships* among the object types. A binary relationship can be represented in one direction, or it can have an *inverse reference*. The latter representation makes it easy to traverse the relationship in both directions. For example, the attribute employees of Department has as

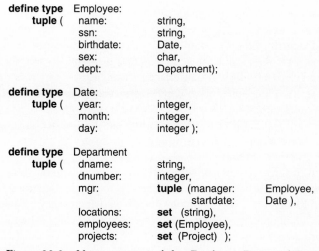

Figure 22.2   Using OODDL to define Employee, Date, and Department types.

its value a *set of references* to objects of type Employee; these are the employees who work for the department. The inverse reference attribute dept of Employee refers to the particular department that an employee works for. We will see later that some OODBMSs allow inverses to be explicitly declared (see Section 22.7.2), to ensure that inverse references are consistent.

22.3 Encapsulation of Operations, Methods, and Persistence

The concept of encapsulation is one of the main characteristics of OO languages and systems. It is also related to the concepts of abstract data types and of information hiding in programming languages. In traditional databases, this concept was not applied, since it is customary to make the structure of database objects visible to users and external programs. Typically, a number of standard database operations are applicable to objects of all types. For example, in the relational model, the operations for selecting, inserting, deleting, and modifying tuples are generic and may be applied to any type of relation in the database. The relation and its attributes are visible to users and to external programs that access the relation tuples and attributes by using these operations.

The concepts of information hiding and encapsulation can be applied to database objects. The main idea is to define the behavior of a type of object based on the operations that can be externally applied to objects of that type. The internal structure of the object is hidden, and the object is only accessible through a number of predefined operations. Some operations may be used to create or destroy objects; other operations may update the object value (or object state); and others may be used to retrieve parts of the object value or to apply some calculations to the object value. Still other operations may perform a combination of retrieval, calculation, and update. In general, the *implementation* of an operation can be specified in a *general-purpose programming language* that provides flexibility and power in defining the operations.

The external users of the object are only made aware of the **interface** of the object, which defines the names and arguments (parameters) of each operation. The **implementation** of the object is hidden from the external users; it includes the definition of the internal data structures of the object and the implementation of the operations that access these structures. In OO terminology, the interface part of each operation is called the **signature**, and the operation implementation is called a **method**. Typically, a method is invoked by sending a **message** to the object to execute the corresponding method. Notice that, as part of executing a method, a subsequent message to another object may be invoked, and this mechanism may be used to return values from the objects to the external environment or to other objects.

For database applications, the requirement that all objects be completely encapsulated is too stringent. One way of relaxing this requirement is to divide the structure of an object into **visible** and **hidden** attributes (variables). Visible attributes may be directly accessed for reading by external operators, or by a high-level query language. The hidden attributes of an object are completely encapsulated, and can only be accessed through predefined operations. Most OODBMSs employ high-level query languages for accessing

```
define class  Employee:
type
     tuple (   name:          string,
               ssn:           string,
               birthdate:     Date,
               sex:           char,
               dept:          Department);

operations
  age (e: Employee):              integer,
  create_new_emp:                 Employee,
  destroy_emp (e: Employee):      boolean ;


define class  Department
type
     tuple (   dname:         string,
               dnumber:       integer,
               mgr:           tuple (manager:     Employee,
                                     startdate:   Date ),
               locations:     set  (string),
               employees:     set (Employee),
               projects:      set  (Project) )

operations
  number_of_emps(d: Department):            integer,
  create_new_dept:                          Department,
  destroy_dept (d: Department):             boolean,
  add_emp (d: Department, e: Employee):     boolean,
        (* adds a new employee to the department *)
  remove_emp (d: Department, e: Employee):  boolean,
        (* removes an employee from the department *) ;
```

Figure 22.3   Using OODDL to define Employee and Department classes.

visible attributes, and several proposals attempt to extend the SQL language for use with OO databases.

In most cases, operations that *update* the state of an object are encapsulated. This is a way of defining the update semantics of the objects, given that in many OO data models, few integrity constraints are predefined in the schema. Each type of object has its integrity constraints *programmed into the methods* that create, delete, and update the objects. In such cases, all update operations are implemented by encapsulated operations. The term **class** is used to refer to an object type definition, along with the definitions of the operations for that type.* Figure 22.3 shows how the OODDL of Figure 22.2 may be extended to define classes. A number of operations are declared for each object class, and the signature (interface) of each operation is included in the class definition. A method (implementation) for each operation must be defined elsewhere, using a programming language. Typical operations include the *object constructor* operation—which is used to create a new object—and the *destructor* operation—which is used to destroy

---

*In the EER model, the term *class* was used to refer to an object type, along with the set of all objects of that type.

an object. A number of *object modifier* operations can also be declared to modify various attributes (variables) of an object.

It is customary for an OODBMS to be closely coupled with an OO programming language. The OO programming language is used to specify the method implementations. An object is typically created by some executing program, by invoking the object constructor operation. Not all objects are meant to be stored permanently in the database. **Transient objects** exist in the executing program and disappear once the program terminates. **Persistent objects** are stored in the database and persist after program termination. The typical mechanism for persistence involves either giving an object a unique persistent **name** through which it can be retrieved by this and other programs or making the object *reachable* from some persistent object. An object B is said to be **reachable** from an object A if a sequence of references in the object graph lead from object A to object B. For example, all the objects in Figure 22.1 are reachable from object o8; hence, if o8 is made persistent, all the other objects in Figure 22.1 also become persistent.

If we first create a named persistent object N, whose value is a *set* or *list* of objects of some class C, we can make objects of C persistent by *adding them* to the set or list, and thus making them reachable from N. Hence, N defines a **persistent collection** of objects of class C. For example, we can define a class DepartmentSet (see Figure 22.4) whose objects are of type **set**(Department). Suppose that an object of type DepartmentSet is created, and suppose that it is named AllDepartments and thus made persistent, as illustrated in Figure 22.4. Any Department object that is added to the set of AllDepartments by using the add_dept operation becomes persistent by virtue of its being reachable from AllDepartments.

Notice the difference between standard database models and OO databases in this respect. In a typical database model, such as the EER or the relational model, *all* objects are assumed to be persistent. Hence, when an entity type or subclass such as EMPLOYEE

```
define class DepartmentSet
type
        set (Department)


operations
  create_dept_set:                                 DepartmentSet,
  destroy_dept_set (ds: DepartmentSet):            boolean,
  add_dept (ds: DepartmentSet, d: Department):     boolean,
  remove_dept (ds: DepartmentSet, d: Department):  boolean ;

persistent name AllDepartments: DepartmentSet ;
          (* AllDepartments is a persistent named object of type set(Department) *)


    ...

d := create_new_department ;
    ...   (* creates a new department object in the variable d *)
b := add_dept(AllDepartments, d) ;
          (* makes d persistent by adding it to the persistent named object AllDepartments *)
```

Figure 22.4   Creating persistent objects by naming and reachability.

is defined in the EER model, it represents both the *type declaration* for EMPLOYEE and a *persistent set* of *all* EMPLOYEE objects. In the typical OO approach, a class declaration of EMPLOYEE only specifies the type and operations for a class of objects. The user must separately define a persistent object of type set(EMPLOYEE) or list(EMPLOYEE) whose value is the *collection of references* to all persistent EMPLOYEE objects, if this is desired, as illustrated in Figure 22.4. In fact, it is possible to define several persistent collections for the same class definition, if desired. The main reason for this difference is that it allows transient and persistent objects to follow the same type and class declarations of the OODDL and the OO programming language. Because we are mainly interested in database applications here, we assume that, for every class declaration, the class name refers to both the *type* and the *operations* definitions, as well as to *the set of all persistent objects* of that class. This makes our use of the word **class** consistent with its use in Chapter 21.

22.4 Type and Class Hierarchies and Inheritance

Another main characteristic of OO systems is that they should allow type or class hierarchies and inheritance. Type hierarchies and class hierarchies are conceptually different; but because in the end result they often lead to structures that behave similarly, they are often taken to mean the same thing. In our presentation, we first discuss type hierarchies (in Section 22.4.1), and then class hierarchies (in Section 22.4.2). We use a *different OO model* in this section—a model in which attributes and operations are treated uniformly—since both attributes and operations can be inherited. In addition, the term **class** in this section refers to the *set of objects* of a particular type.

22.4.1 *Type Hierarchies and Inheritance*

In most database applications, there are numerous objects of the same type. Hence, OO databases must provide a capability for classifying objects based on their type, as do other database systems. But in OO databases, a further requirement is that the system permit the definition of new types based on other predefined types, leading to a **type hierarchy**.

Typically, a type is defined by assigning it a type name and then defining a number of attributes (instance variables) and operations (methods) for the type. In some cases, the attributes and operations are together called *functions*, to simplify the terminology. Subsequently, a function name can be used to refer to the value of an attribute or to refer to the implementation of an operation (method). In this section, we use the term **function** to refer to both attributes *and* operations of an object type.

A type can be defined by giving it a **type name** and then listing the names of its **functions**. In this section, when specifying a type, we use the following simplified format:

TYPE_NAME: function, function, . . ., function

For example, a type that describes characteristics of a PERSON may be defined as follows:

PERSON: Name, Address, Birthdate, Age, SSN

In the PERSON type, the Name, Address, SSN, and Birthdate functions are implemented as stored attributes, whereas the Age function is implemented as a method that calculates the Age from the value of the Birthdate attribute and the current date.

The concept of **subtype** is useful when the designer or user must create a new type that is similar, but not identical to an already defined type. The subtype then **inherits** all the functions of the predefined type, which we shall call the **supertype**. For example, suppose that we want to define two new types EMPLOYEE and STUDENT as follows:

EMPLOYEE: Name, Address, Birthdate, Age, SSN, Salary, HireDate, Seniority
STUDENT: Name, Address, Birthdate, Age, SSN, Major, GPA

Since both STUDENT and EMPLOYEE include all the functions defined for PERSON *plus* some additional functions of their own, we can declare them to be **subtypes** of PERSON. Each will inherit the previously defined functions of PERSON—namely, Name, Address, Birthdate, Age, and SSN. For STUDENT, it is only necessary to define the new functions Major and GPA, which are not inherited. Presumably, Major can be defined as a stored attribute, whereas GPA may be implemented as a method that accesses the Grade values that are internally stored within each STUDENT object. For EMPLOYEE, the Salary and HireDate functions may be stored attributes, whereas Seniority may be a method that calculates Seniority from the value of HireDate.

The idea of defining a type involves defining all of its functions and implementing them either as attributes or as methods. When a subtype is defined, it can then inherit all of these functions and their implementation. Only functions that are specific to the subtype, and hence are not implemented in the supertype, need to be defined and implemented. Therefore, we can declare EMPLOYEE and STUDENT as follows:

EMPLOYEE **subtype-of** PERSON: Salary, HireDate, Seniority
STUDENT **subtype-of** PERSON: Major, GPA

By declaring each of EMPLOYEE and STUDENT to be *subtype-of* PERSON, we are specifying that each inherits all the functions of PERSON. In general, a subtype includes *all* of the functions that are defined for its supertype, *plus* some additional functions that are specific only to the subtype. Hence, it is possible to generate a **type hierarchy** to show the supertype/subtype relationships among all the types declared in the system.

As another example, consider a type that describes objects in plane geometry, which may be defined as follows:

GEOMETRY_OBJECT: Shape, Area, ReferencePoint

For the GEOMETRY_OBJECT type, Shape is implemented as an attribute (its values can be triangle, rectangle, circle, and so on), and Area is a method that is applied to calculate the area. Now suppose that we want to define a number of subtypes for the GEOMETRY_OBJECT type, as follows:

RECTANGLE **subtype-of** GEOMETRY_OBJECT: Width, Height
TRIANGLE **subtype-of** GEOMETRY_OBJECT: Side1, Side2, Angle
CIRCLE **subtype-of** GEOMETRY_OBJECT: Radius

Notice that the Area operation may be implemented by a different method for each subtype, since the procedure for area calculation is different for rectangles, triangles, and circles. Similarly, the attribute ReferencePoint may have a different meaning for each subtype; it might be the center point for RECTANGLE and CIRCLE objects, and the vertex point between the two given sides for a TRIANGLE object. Some OO systems allow the

renaming of inherited functions in different subtypes to reflect the meaning more closely (see Section 22.7.1).

An alternative way of declaring these three subtypes is to specify the value of the Shape attribute as a condition that must be satisfied for objects of each subtype:

RECTANGLE **subtype-of** GEOMETRY_OBJECT (Shape='rectangle'): Width, Height
TRIANGLE **subtype-of** GEOMETRY_OBJECT (Shape='triangle'): Side1, Side2, Angle
CIRCLE **subtype-of** GEOMETRY_OBJECT (Shape='circle'): Radius

Here, only GEOMETRY_OBJECT objects whose Shape='rectangle' are of the subtype RECTANGLE, and similarly for the other two subtypes. In this case, all functions of the GEOMETRY_OBJECT supertype are inherited by each of the three subtypes, but the value of the Shape attribute is restricted to a specific value for each.

Notice that type definitions *do not* generate objects on their own. They are just declarations of certain types; and as part of that declaration, the implementation of the functions of each type is specified. In a database application, there are many objects of each type. When an object is created, it typically belongs to one or more of these types that have been declared. For example, a circle object is of type CIRCLE *and* GEOMETRY_OBJECT (by inheritance). Each object also becomes a member of one or more object classes, which are used to group together collections of objects that are meaningful to the database application. We discuss object classes and class hierarchies in the next section.

22.4.2 *Class Hierarchies*

A **class** is a collection of objects that is meaningful to some application.* In most OO databases, the collection of objects in a class has the same type. However, this is not a necessary condition. For example, SMALLTALK, a so-called *typeless* OO language, allows a class to contain a collection of objects regardless of their type. This can also be the case when other non-object-oriented typeless languages, such as LISP, are extended with OO concepts.

A class is typically defined by its name and by the collection of objects that are included in the class. It is often useful to be able to define a **subclass** of another class of objects, where the latter is called the **superclass**. In this case, the constraint is that every object in the subclass must also be a member of the superclass. Some OO systems have a predefined system class (called the ROOT class or the OBJECT class) that contains all the objects in the system. Classification then proceeds by specializing objects into additional classes that are meaningful to the application, creating a **class hierarchy** for the system. All system- and user-defined classes are subclasses of the class OBJECT, directly or indirectly.

Notice that the type constructors discussed in Section 22.2 permit the value of one object to be a collection of objects, which is essentially a class. Hence, a class of objects whose values are based on the *set constructor* defines a number of collections—one cor-

---

*We used the term *class* in Section 22.3 to indicate a type declaration and the operations applicable. In this section *class* refers to a collection of objects.

responding to each object. The set-valued objects themselves are members of another class. This allows for multilevel classification schemes, where an object in one class defines as its value a class of objects.

In OO databases that are based on types (that is, in the majority of OO databases), a class hierarchy often has a corresponding type hierarchy, since all objects in a class are constrained to being of the same type. Hence, it is possible to create a *default class* for each type (or subtype), to hold all persistent objects of that type.* Such systems would always possess a class hierarchy that corresponds to the type hierarchy. Because of this, there often is no clear distinction between the type hierarchy and the class hierarchy; instead, the two are combined into a single hierarchy. Each class then has a particular type and holds the collection of all persistent objects of that type.

In most OO systems, a distinction is made between persistent and transient objects and classes. A **persistent class** is a class whose collection of objects is stored permanently in the database and hence can be accessed and shared by multiple programs. A **transient class** is a class whose collection of objects exists temporarily during the execution of a program but is not kept when the program terminates. For example, a transient class may be created in a program to hold the result of a query that selects some objects from a persistent class and copies those objects into the transient class. The transient class has the same type as the persistent class. The program can then manipulate the objects in the transient class; and once the program terminates, the transient class ceases to exist. In general, numerous classes—transient or persistent—may contain objects of the same type.

22.5 Complex Objects★

One principal motivation that led to the development of OO systems was the desire to represent complex objects. There are two main types of complex objects: structured and unstructured. A structured complex object is made up of component objects assembled by applying the available type constructors recursively at various levels. An unstructured complex object typically is a data type that requires a large amount of storage, such as a data type that represents an image or a large textual object. In Sections 22.5.1 and 22.5.2, we discuss the various types of complex objects.

22.5.1 *Unstructured Complex Objects and Type Extensibility*

An **unstructured complex object** facility provided by a DBMS permits the storage and retrieval of large objects that are needed by the database application. Typical examples of such objects are *bitmap images* and *long text strings;* they are also known as **binary large objects**, or **BLOBs** for short. These objects are unstructured in the sense that the DBMS does not know what their structure is—only the application that uses them can interpret the objects' meaning. For example, the application may have functions to display an image or to search for certain keywords in a long text string. The objects are considered

---

*Most OO systems do not create such classes automatically.

complex because they require a large area of storage and are not part of the standard data types provided by typical DBMSs. Because the object size is quite large, a DBMS may retrieve a portion of the object and provide it to the application program before the whole object is retrieved. The DBMS may also use buffering and caching techniques to prefetch portions of the object before the application program needs to access them.

The DBMS software does not have the capability to directly process selection conditions and other operations based on values of these objects, unless the application provides the code to do the comparison operations needed for the selection. In an OODBMS, this can be accomplished by defining a new abstract data type for the uninterpreted objects and by providing the methods for selecting, comparing, and displaying such objects. For example, consider objects that are two-dimensional bitmap images. Suppose that the application needs to select from a collection of such objects only those that include a certain pattern. In this case, the user must provide the pattern recognition program as a method on objects of the bitmap type. The OODBMS then retrieves an object from the database and runs the method for pattern recognition on it to determine whether the object includes the required pattern.

Because an OODBMS allows users to create new types, and because a type includes both structure and operations, we can view an OODBMS as having an **extensible type system**. We can create libraries of new types by defining their structure and operations, including complex types. Applications can then use or modify these types, in the latter case by creating subtypes of the types provided in the libraries. However, the DBMS internals must provide the underlying storage and retrieval capabilities for objects that require large amounts of storage so that the operations may be applied efficiently. Many OODBMSs provide for the storage and retrieval of large unstructured objects as character strings or bit strings, which can be passed "as is" to the application program for interpretation.

22.5.2 *Structured Complex Objects*

A **structured complex object** differs from an unstructured complex object in that the object's structure is defined by repeated application of the type constructors provided by the OODBMS. Hence, the object structure is defined and known to the OODBMS. As an example, consider the DEPARTMENT object shown in Figure 22.1. At the first level, the object has a tuple structure with six attributes: DNAME, DNUMBER, MGR, LOCATIONS, EMPLOYEES, and PROJECTS. However, only two of these attributes—namely, DNAME and DNUMBER—have basic values; the other four have complex values and hence build the second level of the complex object structure. One of these four (MGR) has a tuple structure, and the other three (LOCATIONS, EMPLOYEES, PROJECTS) have a set structure. At the third level, for a MGR tuple value, we have one basic attribute (MANAGERSTART-DATE) and one attribute (MANAGER) that refers to an employee object, which has a tuple structure. For a LOCATIONS set, we have a set of basic values, but for both the EMPLOYEES and the PROJECTS sets, we have sets of tuple-structured objects.

Two types of reference semantics exist between a complex object and its components at each level. The first type, which we call **ownership semantics**, applies when the subobjects of a complex object are encapsulated within the complex object and are hence considered part of the complex object. The second type, which we call **reference semantics**, applies when the components of the complex object are themselves independent objects but at times may be considered part of the complex object. For example, we may consider the DNAME, DNUMBER, and LOCATIONS attributes to be owned by a DEPARTMENT, whereas MGR, EMPLOYEES, and PROJECTS should be referenced because they represent independent subobjects. The first type is also referred to as the *is-part-of* or *is-component-of* relationship; and the second type is called the *is-associated-with* relationship, since it describes an equal association between two independent objects. The is-part-of relationship (ownership semantics) for constructing complex objects has the property that the component objects are encapsulated within the complex object and are considered part of the internal object structure. They can only be accessed by methods of that object, and they are deleted if the object itself is deleted. On the other hand, a complex object whose components are referenced is considered to consist of independent objects that can have their own identity and methods. When a complex object needs to access its referenced components, it must do so by invoking the appropriate methods of the components, since they are not encapsulated within the complex object. In addition, a referenced component object may be referenced by more than one complex object and hence is not automatically deleted when the complex object is deleted.

An OODBMS should provide storage options for *clustering* the component objects of a complex object together on secondary storage in order to increase the efficiency of operations that access the complex object. In many cases, the object structure is stored on disk pages in an uninterpreted fashion. When a disk page that includes an object is retrieved into memory, the OODBMS can build up the structured complex object from the information on the disk pages, which may refer to additional disk pages that must be retrieved. This is known as **complex object assembly.**

22.6 Other OO Concepts★

In this section we give an overview of some additional OO concepts, including polymorphism (operator overloading), multiple inheritance, selective inheritance, versioning, and configurations.

22.6.1 *Polymorphism (Operator Overloading)*

Another characteristic of OO systems is that they provide for **polymorphism** of operations, which is also sometimes referred to as **operator overloading**. This concept allows the same *operator name* or *symbol* to be bound to two or more different *implementations* of the operator, depending on the type of objects to which the operator is applied. A simple example from programming languages can illustrate this concept. In some languages, the operator symbol "+" can mean different things when applied to operands (objects) of different types. If the operands of "+" are of type *integer*, the operation invoked is integer addition. If the operands of "+" are of type *set*, the operation invoked is set union. The compiler can determine which operation to execute based on the types of operands supplied in the program.

In OO databases, a similar situation may occur. We can use the GEOMETRIC_OBJECT example discussed in Section 22.4 to illustrate polymorphism* in OO databases. Suppose that we declare GEOMETRY_OBJECT and its subtypes as follows:

GEOMETRY_OBJECT: Shape, Area, CenterPoint
RECTANGLE **subtype-of** GEOMETRY_OBJECT (Shape='rectangle'): Width, Height
TRIANGLE **subtype-of** GEOMETRY_OBJECT (Shape='triangle'): Side1, Side2, Angle
CIRCLE **subtype-of** GEOMETRY_OBJECT (Shape='circle'): Radius

Here, the function Area is declared for all objects of type GEOMETRY_OBJECT. However, the implementation of the method for Area may differ for each subtype of GEOMETRY_OBJECT. One possibility is to have a general implementation for calculating the area of a generalized GEOMETRIC_OBJECT (for example, by writing a general algorithm to calculate the area of a polygon) and then to rewrite more efficient algorithms to calculate the areas of specific types of geometric objects, such as a circle, a rectangle, a triangle, and so on. In this case, the Area function is *overloaded* by different implementations.

The OODBMS must now select the appropriate method for the Area function based on the type of geometric object to which it is applied. In strongly typed systems, this can be done at compile time, since the object types must be known. This is termed **early binding**, since the choice of which method to use can be done at compile time. However, in systems with weak typing or no typing (such as SMALLTALK and LISP), the type of the object to which a function is applied may not be known until run-time. In this case, the function must check the type of object at run-time and then invoke the appropriate method. This is often referred to as **late binding** of the function to the implementation method, since the binding is done at run-time.

22.6.2 *Multiple Inheritance and Selective Inheritance*

Multiple inheritance in a type hierarchy occurs when a certain subtype T is a subtype of two (or more) different types and hence inherits the functions (attributes and methods) of both supertypes. For example, we may create a subtype ENGINEERING_MANAGER that is a subtype of both MANAGER and ENGINEER. This leads to the creation of a **type lattice** rather than a type hierarchy. One problem that may occur with multiple inheritance is that the two supertypes from which the subtype inherits may have distinct functions of the same name, creating an ambiguity. For example, both MANAGER and ENGINEER may have a function called Salary. If the Salary function is implemented by different methods in the MANAGER and ENGINEER supertypes, an ambiguity exists as to which of the two is inherited by the subtype ENGINEERING_MANAGER. It is possible, however, that both ENGINEER and MANAGER inherit Salary from the same supertype (such as EMPLOYEE) higher up in the lattice. In such a case, there is no ambiguity; the problem only arises if the functions are distinct in the two supertypes.

---

*In programming languages, there are several types of polymorphism. The interested reader is referred to the bibliographic notes for works that include a more complete discussion.

There are several techniques for dealing with ambiguity in multiple inheritance. One solution is to have the system check for ambiguity when the subtype is created, and to let the user explicitly choose which function is to be inherited at this time. Another solution is to use some system default. A third solution is to disallow multiple inheritance if ambiguity occurs, instead forcing the user to change the name of one of the functions in one of the supertypes. Indeed, some OO systems do not permit multiple inheritance at all.

Selective inheritance occurs when a subtype inherits only some of the functions of a supertype. Other functions are not inherited. In this case, an EXCEPT clause may be used to list the functions in a supertype that are *not* to be inherited by the subtype. The mechanism of selective inheritance is not typically provided in OO database systems, but it is used more frequently in artificial intelligence applications.

22.6.3 *Versions and Configurations*

Many database applications that use OO systems require the existence of several **versions** of the same object. For example, consider a database application for a software engineering environment that stores various software artifacts, such as design modules, source code modules, configuration information to describe which modules should be linked together to form a complex program, and test cases for testing the system. Commonly, *maintenance activities* are applied to a software system as its requirements evolve. Maintenance usually involves changing some of the design and implementation modules. If the system is already operational, and if one or more of the modules must be changed, the designer should create a **new version** of each of these modules to implement the changes. Similarly, new versions of the test cases may have to be generated to test the new versions of the modules. However, the existing versions should not be discarded until the new versions have been thoroughly tested and approved; only then should the new versions replace the older ones.

Notice that there may be more than two versions of an object. For example, consider two programmers working to update the same software module concurrently. In this case, two versions, in addition to the original module, are needed. The programmers can update their own versions *of the same software module* concurrently. This is often referred to as **concurrent engineering**. However, it eventually becomes necessary to merge these two versions together so that the hybrid version can include the changes made by both programmers. During merging, it is also necessary to make sure that their changes are compatible. This necessitates creating yet another version of the object: one that is the result of merging the two independently updated versions.

As can be seen from the preceding discussion, an OODBMS should be able to store and manage multiple versions of the same object. Several systems do provide this capability, by allowing the application to maintain multiple versions of an object and to refer explicitly to particular versions as needed. However, the problem of merging and reconciling changes made to two different versions is typically left to the application developers, who know the semantics of the application. Some DBMSs have certain facilities that can compare the two versions with the original object and determine whether any changes made are incompatible, in order to assist with the merging process. Other systems maintain a **version graph** that shows the relationships among versions. Whenever a version v_1 originates by copying another version v, a directed arc can be drawn from v to v_1. Similarly, if two versions v_2 and v_3 are merged to create a new version v_4, directed arcs are drawn from v_2 and from v_3 to v_4. The version graph can help users understand the relationships among the various versions, and can be used internally by the system to manage the creation and deletion of versions.

When versioning is applied to complex objects, further issues arise that must be resolved. A complex object, such as a software system, may consist of many modules. When versioning is allowed, each of these modules may have a number of different versions and a version graph. A **configuration** of the complex object is a collection consisting of one version of each module arranged in such a way that the module versions in the configuration are compatible and together form a valid version of the complex object. A new version or configuration of the complex object does not have to include new versions for every module. Hence, certain module versions that have not been changed may belong to more than one configuration of the complex object. Notice that a configuration is a collection of versions of *different objects* that together make up a complex object, whereas the version graph describes the collection of versions of the *same object*. A configuration should follow the type structure of a complex object; multiple configurations of the same complex object are analogous to multiple versions of a component object.

22.7 Examples of OODBMSs⋆

We now illustrate the concepts discussed in this chapter by examining two OODBMSs. Section 22.7.1 presents an overview of the O2 system by O2 Technology, and Section 22.7.2 gives an overview of the ObjectStore system by Object Design Inc. As we mentioned at the beginning of this chapter, there are many other commercial and prototype OODBMSs; we use these two as examples to illustrate specific systems.

22.7.1 *Overview of the O2 System*

In our overview of the O2 system, we first illustrate data definition and then consider examples of data manipulation in O2. Thereafter, we give a brief discussion of the system architecture of O2.

Data Definition in O2. In O2, the schema defines the system's object types and object classes. An object type is defined by using the atomic types provided by O2 and by applying the O2 type constructors. The *atomic types* include Boolean, character, integer, real, string, and bits. The *type constructors* include tuple, list, set, and unique set. The *set* constructor, when specified alone, allows duplicate elements (similar to what we called a *bag* in Section 22.2.2), whereas the *unique set* constructor does not (similar to what we called a *set* in Section 22.2.2). In O2, methods are not included as part of a type definition. Rather, a *class definition* consists of two parts: the *type* of the objects that can be members of the class, and the *methods* that can be applied to these objects.

There is a distinction in O2 between values and objects. A *value* has a type only and represents itself. An *object* belongs to a class and hence has a type and a behavior specified by the methods of the class. In addition, an object has a *unique identity* (an OID) and a current value (or state), whereas a value does not have an OID. Both values and objects can have complex types, and the different levels of the complex type either can be values (representing ownership semantics) or can refer to other objects by using their OIDs (representing reference semantics). The O2 system has a language, O2C, that can be used to define classes, methods, and types, and to create objects and values. Objects are *persistent* (if they are stored permanently in the database) or *transient* (if they only exist during execution of a program). Values are transient unless they become part of a persistent object.

Figure 22.5 shows possible type and class declarations in O2C for a portion of the UNIVERSITY database, whose EER schema was given in Figure 21.10. We have included a few methods to illustrate how methods can be declared. It is possible in O2 to define a new class E' that inherits the type and methods of another class E. In our terminology, E' is a subclass of E, *and* the type of E' must be a subtype of E. For example, in Figure

```
type Phone: tuple (    area_code: integer,
                       number: integer );

type Date: tuple (     year: integer,
                       month: integer,
                       day: integer );

class Person
    type tuple (       ssn: string,
                       name: tuple (      firstname: string,
                                          middlename: string,
                                          lastname: string ),
                       address: tuple (   number: integer,
                                          street: string,
                                          apt_no: string,
                                          city: string,
                                          state: string,
                       birthdate: Date,   zipcode: string ),
                       sex: character )

        method         age: integer
    end

class Student inherit Person
    type tuple (       class: string,
                       majors_in: Department,
                       minors_in: Department,
                       registered_in: set (Section),
                       transcript: set (tuple (    grade: character,
                                                   ngrade: real,
                                                   section: Section ) ) )

        method         grade_point_average: real,
                       change_class: boolean,
                       change_major (new_major: Department): boolean
    end
```

Figure 22.5   O2 class declarations for part of the UNIVERSITY database of Figure 21.10.   *(continued on next page)*

```
class Grad_Student inherit Student
      type tuple (      degrees: set (tuple ( college: string,
                                             degree: string,
                                             year: integer ) ),
                        advisor: Faculty )
end

class Faculty inherit Person
      type tuple (      salary: real,
                        rank: string,
                        foffice: string,
                        fphone: Phone,
                        belongs_to: set (Department),
                        grants: set (Grant),
                        advises: set (Student) )

      method           promote_faculty,
                        give_raise (percent: real)
end

class Department
      type tuple (      dname: string,
                        office: string,
                        dphone: Phone,
                        members: set (Faculty),
                        majors: set (Student),
                        chairperson: Faculty,
                        courses: set (Course) )

      method           add_major (s: Student),
                        remove_major (s: Student): boolean
end

class Section
      type tuple (      sec_num: integer,
                        qtr: Quarter,
                        year: Year,
                        students: set ( tuple ( stud: Student,
                                                grade: character ) ),
                        course: Course,
                        teacher: Instructor )

      method           change_grade (s: Student, g: character)
end

class Course
      type tuple (      cname: string,
                        cnumber: string,
                        cdescription: string,
                        sections: set (Section),
                        offering_dept: Department )

      method           update_description (new_d: string)
end
```

Figure 22.5   *(continued)*

22.5, Student and Faculty are declared to be subclasses of Person by using the **inherit** Person statement in the definitions of Student and Faculty. It is possible to **rename** the inherited attributes or methods and to **redefine** the structure of inherited attributes or the implementation of inherited methods for a subclass. For example, if we want to rename the ssn attribute of Person as student_id in the subclass Student of Person, we can include the following statement in the class definition of Student:

> **rename** ssn **as** student_id

To redefine a method, we first rename it, and then include a definition of the renamed method.

O2 also permits **multiple inheritance**, where a class inherits the type and the methods of two or more classes. If the two classes have an attribute or a method with the same name, it is best to rename these two so that their names can be distinguished in the subclass. In the rename statement, we can qualify the attribute or method name with the class name by attaching _classname to the attribute or method name, thereby obviating the name ambiguity problem that can arise with multiple inheritance.

Class/subclass relationships and inheritance are specified in O2 by using the keyword **inherit** in the subclass declaration. For example, in Figure 22.5, the O2 classes Faculty and Student inherit the type and methods from the Person class, and each includes its own additional attributes and methods. The Faculty class has the following additional attributes: rank, salary, foffice, and fphone. In addition, we include in the Faculty O2 class three set-valued attributes—belongs_to, grants, and advises—to represent the BELONGS, PI, and ADVISOR relationships, respectively.

Data Manipulation in O2. O2 applications can be developed in two ways using programming languages. The first is to use O2's own query language, O2SQL, and programming language, O2C, to write application programs. The second is to use O2 as a persistent object storage system for another stand-alone language, such as C^{++}, and to develop the applications in that language. O2 also has a user interface generator called O2Look, which can be used to speed up application development by facilitating interaction with O2C through a user-friendly interface. Another tool, called O2Tools, is a graphical program-development environment that includes tools such as a browser, a debugger, a shell that allows editing and execution of O2 commands and interaction with Unix files, and a workspace manager that can temporarily store database objects.

We first illustrate the O2C language and its use in writing methods for classes. This language is a subset of the C language that has been extended to handle O2 types, including operations for set and list types. Figure 22.6(a) shows the definition of a few of the methods that are declared in the O2 classes of Figure 22.5. The first method, age, calculates a person's age from the birthdate and today's date, using only C language constructs. Notice that the use of the keyword **self** inside a method refers to the object for which the method is invoked. Thus, the word *self* in the age method refers to an object of type Person and has the type and methods of such an object. The second method, grade_point_average, uses a for loop that iterates over the set of values in the transcript attribute of Student to get the sum of the numeric grades and the number of transcript records; then it calculates and returns the grade-point average. The third method is an example of an update, and it changes the major of a student. This method also invokes two methods of the Department class—remove_major and add_major—which are also shown in Figure 22.6(a). It does so to ensure that the values of the inverse attribute—majors of the Department class—remain consistent with the value of the majors_in attribute of the Student class. This provides an example of how the programmer can implement bidirectional relationships by defining appropriate O2 methods.

There are two ways to create a persistent object in O2. One way is to make the object itself a **root**, by giving it a name via the **name** statement. In this case, the object is called a *persistent root*. The other way is to make the object *reachable* from a persistent root—for example, by making it a member of a set-valued persistent object or by making it a component of a complex object. In general, O2 does not create a persistent object set to correspond to each class declaration; instead, it leaves this task for the user to do explicitly. Hence, if a set of all persistent objects of type Person is needed, the programmer must create a persistent root of type set(Person) and give it a name, as shown in Figure 22.6(b), where the set is called All_Persons. Any object that is added to that set automatically becomes persistent, since it becomes *attached to a persistent root*. The Person object "Franklin Wong" shown in Figure 22.6(b) is not persistent when it is created, but it becomes persistent when it is added to the All_Persons object. One can also create an individual persistent object just by giving it a name—without its having to belong to any persistent set—as illustrated by the Person object named "John Smith" in Figure 22.6(b).

O2 also has a query language, O2SQL, which can be used to retrieve a set of values into a transient class in an O2C program. O2SQL allows the creation of a new type *on the fly* for a query result. The query language has a **SELECT . . . FROM . . . WHERE** structure, similar to that of SQL, but it is possible in O2SQL to use functional reference within the query to refer to components of complex objects and values. Functional reference uses the *dot notation* to refer to components of complex objects; for example, by writing

    s.majors_in.dname

in Q1 of Figure 22.7, we first locate the DEPARTMENT object related to STUDENT s via the majors_in function, and then locate the dname attribute of that department.

In an O2SQL query, the SELECT clause defines the data to be retrieved and the structure (type) of the values in the query result. The FROM clause specifies the collections of objects that are referenced by the query and gives variable names that range over objects in those collections. A **collection** is typically a set of objects. We assumed in Figure 22.7 that Student is the name of a collection of all persistent Student objects. Finally, the WHERE clause specifies the conditions for selecting the individual objects involved in the query result. Figure 22.7 shows examples of two queries. Query Q1 retrieves the names of all students majoring in computer science, and the query result type is a set of tuples with two attributes: fname and lname. Query Q2 retrieves the transcripts of students majoring in computer science, and the result has a complex type whose structure is specified in the SELECT clause of the query. The facility to define a new type structure for the values in a query result is not available in all OODBMSS. Some systems only allow the retrieval of whole objects from a collection as is, without restructuring them for the query result. The programmer may then explicitly restructure these objects as transient objects of new types that are declared in the user program.

(a)
method body age: integer **in class** Person

```
{    int a ;
     Date d ;
     d = today() ;
     a = d->year  -  self->birthdate->year ;
     i f ( d->month  <  self->birthdate->month ) ||
        ( ( d->month  ==  self->birthdate->month )  &&  ( d->day  <  self->birthdate->day ) )
        --a ;    /* decrements a by 1 */
     return a;
}
```

method body grade_point_average: real **in class** Student

```
{    float sum = 0.0 ;
     int count = 0 ;
     struct {
         char gr ;
         float ngrade ;
         o2_Section sec ;
     } t ;
     for ( t in self->transcript ) {
     sum += t->ngrade ;  ++count ;  /* increments sum by ngrade, count by 1 */
        }
        return sum/count ;
}
```

method body change_major (new_major: Department): boolean **in class** Student

```
{    if (self->majors_in-> remove_major (self) ) {
        return 0 ;
        }
     else {
        new_major-> add_major (self) ;
        self->majors_in = new_major ;
        return 1;
        }
}
```

method body remove_major (s: Student): boolean **in class** Department

```
{    if (s in  self->majors) {
        self->majors  -= set(s)  ;  /* -= applies set difference to remove object s from set of majors */
        return 1 ;
        }
     else return 0 ;
}
```

method body add_major (s: Student) **in class** Department

```
{    self->majors += set(s) ;  /* += applies set union to add object s to set of majors */
}
```

Figure 22.6   O2 programming. (a) Method body declarations in O2 for some of the methods included in Figure 22.5. (b) Creating persistent objects in O2.   *(continued on next page)*

(b)
name All_Persons: **set** (Person) /* a persistent root to hold all persistent Person objects */

name John_Smith: Person ; /* a persistent root to hold a single Person object */

run body {
    o2 Person p = **new** Person ; /* creates a new Person object p */

    *p = **tuple** (ssn: "333445555",
                name: **tuple** (firstname: "Franklin", middlename: "T", lastname: "Wong"),
                address: **tuple** (number: 638, street: "Voss Road", city: "Houston",
                              state: "Texas", zipcode: "77079"),
                birthdate: **tuple** (year: 1945, month: 12, day: 8),
                sex: M);
    All_Persons += **set** (p) ; /* p becomes persistent by attaching to persistent root */

      /* now put values in persistent named object John_Smith */
    John_Smith->ssn = "123456789",
    John_Smith->name: **tuple** (firstname: "John", middlename: "B", lastname: "Smith"),
    John_Smith->address: **tuple** (number:731, street: "Fondren Road", city: "Houston",
                        state: "Texas", zipcode: "77036"),
    John_Smith->birthdate: tuple (year: 1955, month: 1, day: 9),
    John_Smith->sex: M ;
}

Figure 22.6   *(continued)*

Q1:select tuple (fname: s.name.firstname,
                lname: s.name.lastname)
    from s **in** Student
    where s.majors_in.dname = "Computer Science"

Q2:select tuple (fname: s.name.firstname,
                lname: s.name.lastname,
                transcript: **select tuple** (
                              cname: sc.section.course.cname,
                              sec_no: sc.section.sec_num,
                              quarter: sc.section.qtr,
                              year: sc.section.year,
                              grade: sc.grade)
                      from sc **in** sec)
    from s **in** Student , sec **in** s.transcript
    where s.majors_in.dname = "Computer Science"

Figure 22.7   Two queries in o2sql.

An alternative to using the o2c language is to use a stand-alone language, such as C^{++}, in conjunction with the O2 system. To facilitate this, O2 provides an **export facility** that creates C^{++} classes corresponding to the O2 class declarations. Figure 22.8 shows a C^{++} class that corresponds to the Person class declared in Figure 22.5. Objects from the O2 persistent Person class can now be directly retrieved into C^{++} program variables that are defined to be of the corresponding C^{++} class type, and these can be manipulated by C^{++} program code.

Overview of the O2 System Architecture. In this section, we give a brief overview of the O2 system architecture. A part of the O2 system, called O2Engine, is responsible for

```
class Person: o2_root {
public:
    char* ssn ;
    struct {
        char* firstname ;
        char* middlename ;
        char* lastname } name ;
    struct {
        int    number
        char* street ;
        char* apt_no ;
        char* city ;
        char* state ;
        char* zipcode } address ;
    struct {
        int  year
        int  month
        int  day } birthdate ;
    char sex ;

    int age () ;
    }
```

Figure 22.8   C^{++} class declaration corresponding to the O2 class Person.

much of the DBMS functionality. This includes providing support for storing, retrieving, and updating persistently stored objects that may be shared by multiple programs. O2Engine implements the concurrency control, recovery, and security mechanisms that are typical in database systems. In addition, O2Engine implements a transaction management model and schema evolution mechanisms.

The implementation of O2Engine at the system level was based on a *client/server architecture*, to accommodate the current trend toward networked and distributed computer systems (see Chapter 23). The *server component*, which can be a file server machine, is a *page server*; it only deals with storage at the page (disk block) level and does not know the object structures. Its responsibility is to retrieve pages efficiently when instructed to do so by a client, and to maintain the appropriate concurrency control and recovery information at the page level. In O2, concurrency control uses locking, and recovery is based on a write-ahead logging technique. The server also does a certain amount of page caching to reduce disk I/O, and it is accessed via a remote procedure call (RPC) interface from the clients. A *client* is typically a workstation; and most of the O2 functionality is provided at the client level.

At the functional level, O2Engine has three main components. The *storage component*, at the lowest level, is an extension of a storage system called WISS (Wisconsin Storage System), which was developed at the University of Wisconsin. The implementation of this layer is split between the client and the server. The server process provides disk management, page storage and retrieval, concurrency control, and recovery. The client process caches pages and locks that have been provided by the server and makes them available to the higher-level functional modules of the O2 client.

The next functional component, called the *object manager*, deals with structuring objects and values, clustering related objects on disk pages, indexing objects, maintaining object identity, performing operations on objects, and so on. Object identifiers were implemented in O2 as the physical disk address of an object, to avoid the overhead of logical-to-physical id mapping, and they are based on the WISS record identifiers. The OID includes a disk volume identifier, a page number within the volume, and a slot number within the page. Structured complex objects are broken down into record components, and indexes are used to access set-structured or list-structured components of an object.

The top functional level of O2Engine is called the *schema manager*. It keeps track of class, type, and method definitions; provides the inheritance mechanisms; checks the consistency of class declarations; and provides for schema evolution, which includes the creation and deletion of class declarations incrementally. For the interested reader, references to material that discusses various aspects of the O2 system are given in the bibliographic notes at the end of this chapter.

22.7.2 *Overview of the ObjectStore System*

In this section, we give an overview of the ObjectStore OODBMS. First we illustrate data definition in ObjectStore, and then we give examples of queries and data manipulation.

Data Definition in ObjectStore. The ObjectStore system is closely integrated with the C^{++} language and provides persistent storage capabilities for C^{++} objects. This choice was made to avoid the *impedance mismatch* problem between a database system and its programming language, where the structures provided by the database system are distinct from those provided by the programming language. Hence, ObjectStore can use the C^{++} class declarations as its data definition language. It uses an extended C^{++} that includes additional constructs specifically useful in database applications. Objects of a class can be transient in the program, or they can be persistently stored by ObjectStore. Persistent objects can be shared by multiple programs. A pointer to an object has the same syntax regardless of whether the object is persistent or transient, so persistence is somewhat transparent to the programmers and users.

Figure 22.9 shows possible ObjectStore C^{++} class declarations for a portion of the UNIVERSITY database, whose EER schema was given in Figure 21.10. ObjectStore's extended C^{++} compiler supports inverse relationship declarations and additional functions.* In C^{++}, an asterisk (*) specifies a reference (pointer), and the type of a field (attribute) is listed before the attribute name. For example, the declaration

    Faculty *advisor

in the Grad_Student class specifies that the attribute *advisor* has the type *pointer to a Faculty object*. The basic types in C^{++} include character (char), integer (int), and real number (float). A character string can be declared to be of type char* (a pointer to an array of characters).

In C^{++}, a *derived* class E' inherits the description of a *base* class E by including the name of E in the definition of E' following a colon (:) and either the keyword **public** or

---

*ObjectStore can also be used with other C^{++} compilers, by including ObjectStore's C^{++} library interface.

```
/* this is the file univ_schema.H that includes the database class declarations */

struct Phone {
    int area_code ;
    int number ;
}

struct Date {
    int year ;
    int month ;
    int day ;
}

class Person {
public:
    char  ssn[9] ;
    struct {
        char* firstname ;
        char* middlename ;
        char* lastname ;
        } name ;
    struct {
        int    number
        char* street ;
        char* apt_no ;
        char* city ;
        char* state ;
        char* zipcode ;
        } address ;
    Date birthdate ;
    char  sex ;

    int age () ;
}

struct Transcript {
    char
    float     grade ;
    Section ngrade ;
}          *section ;

class Student: public Person {
    /* Student inherits  (is derived from) Person */ public:
    char*               class ;
    Department          *majors_in ;
    Department          *minors_in ;
    os_Set<Section*>    registered_in ;
    os_Set<Transcript*> transcript ;

    float grade_point_average () ;
    void change_class () ;
    void change_major (Department *new_major) ;
}
```

Figure 22.9   Some C^{++} class declarations for an ObjectStore UNIVERSITY database.
(continued on next page)

```
    struct Degree {
        char* college ;
        char* degree ;
        int   year ;
    }

    class Grad_student: public Student {
        /* Grad_student inherits (is derived from) Student */public :
        os_Set<Degree*>      degrees ;
        Faculty              *advisor ;
    }

    class Faculty: public Person {   /* Faculty inherits (is derived from) Person */
        float                salary ;
        char*                rank ;
        char*                foffice ;
        char*                fphone ;
        os_Set<Department*>  belongs_to ;
        Department           *chairs ;
        os_Set<Grant*>       grants ;
        os_Set<Student*>     advises ;

        void promote_faculty () ;
        void give_raise (float  percent) ;
    }

    class Department {
        char*                dname ;
        char*                office ;
        Phone                dphone ;
        os_Set<Faculty*>     members ;
        os_Set<Student*>     majors ;
        Faculty              chairperson ;
        os_Set<Course*>      courses ;

        void add_major (Student *s) ;
        void remove_major (Student *s) ;
    }
```

Figure 22.9   (*continued*)

the keyword **private**.* For example, in Figure 22.9, both the Faculty and the Student classes are derived from the Person class, and both inherit the fields (attributes) and the functions (methods) declared in the description of Person. Functions are distinguished from attributes by including parameters between parentheses after the function name. If a function has no parameters, we just include the parentheses (). A function that does not return a value has the type **void**. There is a direct correspondence between the O2 declarations in Figure 22.5 and the C^{++} declarations in Figure 22.9, as can be seen by comparing the two. ObjectStore adds its own **set constructor** to C^{++} by using the keyword **os_Set** (for ObjectStore set). For example, the declaration

```
    os_Set<Transcript*> transcript
```

---

*C^{++} has two types of derivations: public and private. We will only consider public derivations here.

within the Student class, specifies that the value of the attribute transcript in each Student object is a *set of pointers* to objects of type Transcript. The tuple constructor is *implicit* in C^{++} declarations whenever various attributes are declared in a class (or a struct, which is the C^{++} concept corresponding to a type). ObjectStore also has added bag and list constructors to C^{++}, called os_Bag and os_List, respectively.

The class declarations in Figure 22.9 include reference attributes in both directions for the relationships from Figure 21.10. For example, for the MAJORS relationship, we included the attribute majors_in—with type pointer to Department—in the Student class, and the attribute majors—with type set of pointers to Student—in the Department class. ObjectStore includes a **relationship facility** that acts as an extension to the C^{++} declarations, permitting the specification of inverse attributes that represent a binary relationship. Figure 22.10 illustrates the syntax of this facility, which is specified by adding the keyword **inverse_member** to an attribute and then listing its inverse attribute in the other class. For example, in Figure 22.10, the CHAIRS and BELONGS relationships between Faculty and Department (Figure 21.10) are declared in this way. The *belongs_to* attribute of the Faculty class is declared to be the inverse of the *members* attribute of the Department class. ObjectStore then keeps the relationship consistent automatically; if a reference to a Faculty object is added to the *members* set of a particular Department object, the system automatically adds a reference to the Department in the *belongs_to* set of that Faculty object. References in the 1:1 or N:1 direction (whose *max* participation is 1) are declared as single pointers, whereas references in the 1:N or M:N directions (whose *max* participation is greater than 1) are declared by using the os_Set (set of pointers) construct.

Figure 22.10 also illustrates another C^{++} feature: the **constructor** function for a class. A class can have a function with the same name as the class name, which is used to create *new objects* of the class. In Figure 22.10, the constructor for Faculty only supplies the ssn value for a Faculty object (ssn is *inherited* from Person), and the constructor for Department only supplies the dname value. The values of other attributes can be added to the objects later, although in a real system the constructor function would include more parameters to construct a more complete object. We discuss how constructors can be used to create persistent objects next.

Data Manipulation in ObjectStore. ObjectStore uses C^{++} to develop its applications. It also has a graphical user interface tool to facilitate application development. The collection types—os_Set, os_Bag, and os_List—can have additional functions applied to them. These include the functions **insert**(e), **remove**(e), and **create**, which can be used to insert an element e into a collection, to remove an element e from a collection, and to create a new collection, respectively. In addition, a **foreach**(c, collection) programming construct allows the program to loop over each element c in a collection. These functions are illustrated in Figure 22.11(a), which shows how a few of the methods declared in Figure 22.9 may be specified in ObjectStore. The function *add_major* adds a (pointer to a) student to the set attribute *majors* of the Department class, by invoking the insert function via the statement majors−>insert. Similarly, the *remove_major* function removes a student pointer from the same set. Here, we assume that the appropriate *inverse_of* declarations have been made, so any inverse attributes are automatically maintained by the system. In the *grade_point_average* function, the foreach(t, transcript) con-

```
extern database *univ_db ;

class Person ;

class Faculty: public Person {    /* Faculty inherits (is derived from) Person */
    float  salary ;
    char* rank ;
    char* foffice ;
    char* fphone ;
    os_Set<Department*> belongs_to
        inverse_member  Department::members ;
    Department  *chairs
        inverse_member  Department::chairperson ;
    os_Set<Grant*>    grants ;
    os_Set<Student*> advises ;

    Faculty (char  s[9]) { ssn = new (univ_db) char[9] ; strcpy(ssn, s) ; }
        /* the ssn attribute is inherited from Person */
    void promote_faculty () ;
    void give_raise (float  percent) ;
}

class Department {
    char*  dname ;
    char*  office ;
    Phone dphone ;
    os_Set<Faculty*> members
        inverse_member  Faculty::belongs_to ;
    os_Set<Student*> majors ;
    Faculty   *chairperson
        inverse_member  Faculty::chairs ;
    os_Set<Course*> courses ;

    Department (char*  d) { dname = new (univ_db) char[strlen(d)+1] ; strcpy(dname,  d) ; }
    void add_faculty (Faculty  *f) ;
    void add_major (Student  *s) ;
    int   remove_major (Student  *s) ;
}
```

Figure 22.10 Declaring inverse relationships in ObjectStore.

struct is used to range over the set of transcript records within a Student object to calculate the gpa.

In C^{++}, functional reference to components within an object o uses the *arrow notation* when a *pointer* to o is provided, and uses the *dot notation* when a variable whose value is the *object o itself* is provided. These references can be used to refer to both attributes and functions of an object. For example, the references d.year and t–>ngrade in the age and grade_point_average functions refer to component attributes, whereas the reference to majors–>remove in remove_major invokes the remove function of ObjectStore on the majors set.

To create persistent objects and collections in ObjectStore, the programmer or user must assign a **name**, which is also called a *persistent variable*. The persistent variable can be viewed as a shorthand reference to the object, and it is permanently "remembered" by ObjectStore. For example, in Figure 22.11(b), we created two persistent set-valued

```
(a)
int  Person::age () {
        Date d = today() ; int a = d.year - birthdate.year ;
        if ( d.month < birthdate.month ) ||
          ( d.month == birthdate.month ) && ( d.day < birthdate.day ) ) --a ;
        return a;
} ;

float  Student::grade_point_average () {
        float sum = 0.0 ; int count = 0 ; Transcript*  t ;
        foreach (t, transcript) {
            sum += t->ngrade ; ++count ;  /* increments sum by ngrade, count by 1 */
            }
        return sum/count ;
} ;

void Student::change_major (Department  *new_major) {majors_in = new_major ; }
void Department::remove_major (Student  *s) {majors->remove(s) ; }
void Department::add_faculty (Faculty  *f) { members->insert (f) ; }
void Department::add_major (Student*  s) { majors->insert(s) ; }


(b)
main () {
    database  *univ_db = database::open ("/database/univ" ) ;

    transaction::begin () ;
/* create two persistent sets to hold all Faculty and all Department objects *
    os_Set<Faculty*>  &all_faculty = os_Set<Faculty*>::create(univ_db) ;
    os_Set<Department*>  &all_depts = os_Set<Department*>::create(univ_db) ;

/* create a new Faculty object and a new Department object using the constructors */
    Faculty    *f = new (univ_db) Faculty ("123456789") ;
    Department    *d = new (univ_db) Department ("Computer Science") ;
/* relate the objects by invoking the appropriate method */
    d->add_faculty (f) ;
/* add the objects to their persistent sets */
    all_faculty.insert(f) ; all_depts.insert(d) ;

    transaction::commit () ;
}
```

Figure 22.11   ObjectStore programming. (a) Function definitions in C^{++} for some of the methods included in Figure 22.9. (b) Creating persistent objects in ObjectStore.

objects—all_faculty and all_depts—and made them persistent in the database called univ_db. These objects are used by the application to hold pointers to all persistent objects of type faculty and department, respectively. An object that is a member of a defined class may be created by invoking the object constructor function for that class, with the keyword **new**. For example, in Figure 22.11(b), we created a Faculty object and a Department object, and then related them by invoking the method add_faculty. Finally, we added them to the all_faculty and all_dept sets to make them persistent.

ObjectStore also has a query facility, which can be used to select a set of objects from a collection by specifying a selection condition. The result of a query is a collection of pointers to the objects that satisfy the query. Query language statements can be embed-

```
os_Set<Faculty*> &asst_profs =
    all_faculty [: rank == 'Assistant Professor' :]

os_Set<Faculty*> &rich_asst_profs =
    all_faculty [: rank == 'Assistant Professor' && salary > 5000.00 :]

os_Set<Faculty*> &dept_chairs =
    all_faculty [: chairs :]

os_Set<Faculty*> &cs_faculty =
    all_faculty [: belongs_to [: dname == 'Computer Science' :] :]
```

Figure 22.12   Queries in ObjectStore.

ded within a C^{++} program, and can be considered a means of associative high-level access to select objects that avoids the need to create an explicit looping construct. Figure 22.12 illustrates a few queries, each of which returns a subset of objects from the all_faculty collection that satisfy a particular condition. The first query in Figure 22.12 selects all Faculty objects from the all_faculty collection whose rank is Assistant Professor. The second query retrieves assistant professors whose salary is greater than $5,000.00. The third query retrieves department chairs, and the fourth query retrieves computer science faculty.

ObjectStore also allows the user to specify the creation of indexes, which the system can use to optimize the retrieval of objects that satisfy a selection criterion. Another useful feature is the support of multiple versions of an object that can exist concurrently. The preceding discussion has offered a brief overview of some features of ObjectStore; references to documents that describe ObjectStore in more detail are given in the bibliography.

22.8   OO Database Design by EER-to-OO Mapping*

It is straightforward to design the type declarations of object classes for an OODBMS from an EER schema that contains *neither* categories *nor* n-ary relationships with n greater than two. However, the methods are not specified in the EER diagram and must be added to the class declarations after the structural mapping is completed. Every class should include a constructor and a destructor method for creating and destroying objects of the class, plus any additional methods required by the application. If transactions were designed conceptually as discussed in Section 21.5, these could be used as the basis for defining and implementing the methods. The outline of the mapping from EER to OO is as follows:

STEP 1:   Create an OO class for each EER class. The type of the OO class should include all the attributes of the EER class by using a tuple constructor at the top level of the type. *Multivalued attributes* are declared by using the set, bag, or list constructors.* If the

---

*We must decide whether a set constructor or a list constructor is used, because this information is not available from the EER schema.

values of the multivalued attribute for an object should be ordered, the list constructor is chosen; if duplicates are allowed, the bag constructor should be chosen. *Composite attributes* are mapped into a tuple constructor. ■

STEP 2:   Add reference attributes for each binary relationship into the OO classes that participate in the relationship. The attributes may be created in one direction or in both directions. The attributes are single-valued for binary relationships in the 1:1 or N:1 direction; they are set-valued or list-valued for relationships in the 1:N or M:N direction. If a binary relationship is represented by references in both directions, declare the references to be inverses of one another, if such a facility exists. If relationship attributes exist, a tuple constructor can be used to create a structure of the form <reference, relationship attributes>, which is included instead of the reference attribute. ■

STEP 3:   Include appropriate methods for each class. These are not available from the EER schema and must be added to the database design as needed. A constructor method should include code that checks any constraints that must hold when a new object is created. A destructor method should check any constraints that may be violated when an object is deleted. Other methods should include any further constraint checks that are relevant. ■

STEP 4:   An OO class that corresponds to a subclass in the EER schema inherits the type and methods of its superclass(es) in the OO schema. Its specific attributes and references are specified as discussed in steps 1 and 2. ■

STEP 5:   Weak entity types that do not participate in any relationships except their identifying relationship can be mapped as though they were composite multivalued attributes of the owner entity type, by using the set(tuple(. . .)) constructor. ■

STEP 6:   n-ary relationships with n > 2 can be mapped into a separate object type, with appropriate references to each participating object type. These references are based on mapping a 1:N relationship from each participating entity type to the n-ary relationship. M:N binary relationships may also use this option, if desired. ■

These general mapping steps can be applied to both O2 and ObjectStore, as well as to other OO data models and systems. Consider the O2 declarations in Figure 22.5, which show some of the O2 type and class declarations for the UNIVERSITY database of Figure 21.10. We included reference attributes in both directions for most relationships. For example, for the MAJORS relationship we included the attribute majors_in—with type Department—in the STUDENT class, and the attribute majors—with type **set**(Student)—in the DEPARTMENT class. However, for the MINORS relationship, we only included the reference attribute minors_in in the STUDENT class. The choice of whether to represent a binary relationship in one direction only or in both directions is left to the OO database designer, based on the expected use of the objects. For example, if we mainly expect to use the MINORS relationship to refer to the minor department of a student object, but we expect hardly ever to refer to the set of all students minoring in a department, the choice identified here would be adequate.

Notice that O2 can be characterized as a bit weak in its handling of relationships in general, since the class declarations do not note that two attributes in two classes are representing the same relationship. ObjectStore allows two attributes to be declared as inverses of one another, so the system itself can maintain the consistency of the relationship, as illustrated in Figure 22.10. In O2 and similar systems, the programmers must maintain every relationship explicitly by coding the methods that update the objects appropriately. Thus, in a sense, these systems do *not* recognize the concept of a bidirectional relationship as such; instead, they leave it to the programmers to implement such relationships.

22.9 Summary

In this chapter we discussed the object-oriented approach to database systems, which was proposed to meet the needs of complex database applications and to add database functionality to object-oriented programming languages such as C^{++}. We first discussed the main concepts used in OO databases, which include the following:

- *Object identity:* Objects have unique identities that are independent of their attribute values.

- *Type constructors:* Complex object structures can be constructed by recursively applying a set of basic constructors, such as tuple, set, list, and bag.

- *Encapsulation:* Both the object structure and the operations that can be applied to objects are included in the object class definitions.

- *Programming language compatibility:* Both persistent and transient objects are handled uniformly. Objects are made persistent by being attached to a persistent collection.

- *Type hierarchies and inheritance:* Object types can be specified by using a type hierarchy, which allows the inheritance of both attributes and methods of previously defined types.

- *Support for complex objects:* Both structured and unstructured complex objects can be stored and manipulated.

- *Polymorphism and operator overloading:* Operations and method names can be "overloaded" to apply to different object types with different implementations.

- *Versioning:* Some OO systems provide support for maintaining several versions of the same object.

We then provided an overview of two OODBMSs—namely, O2 and ObjectStore—and gave an outline of a mapping procedure that can be used to design an OO database schema from an EER conceptual design. Database researchers have debated the advisability of trying a completely new approach to database management—namely, the object-oriented approach—versus extending the capabilities of commercial relational database management systems to meet the needs of more complex database applications. Work is progressing on an SQL3 standard, which will incorporate OO concepts into the

SQL2 standard relational language. Extended relational prototypes include the POSTGRES and STARBURST projects (see selected bibliography).

Review Questions

22.1. What are the origins of the object-oriented approach?

22.2. What primary characteristics should an OID possess?

22.3. Discuss the various type constructors. How are they used to create complex object structures?

22.4. How does a class differ from a type in OO terminology? Discuss the concept of encapsulation, and tell how it is used to create abstract data types.

22.5. Explain what the following terms mean in object-oriented terminology: *method, signature, message, collection.*

22.6. What is the relationship between a type and its subtype in a type hierarchy? What is the difference between a type hierarchy and a class hierarchy?

22.7. What is the difference between persistent and transient objects? How is persistence handled in typical OO database systems?

22.8. How do regular inheritance, multiple inheritance, and selective inheritance differ?

22.9. Discuss the concept of polymorphism/operator overloading.

22.10. What is the difference between structured and unstructured complex objects?

22.11. What is the difference between ownership semantics and reference semantics in structured complex objects?

22.12. What is versioning? Why is it important? What is the difference between versions and configurations?

22.13. What is the difference between values and objects in O2? How are objects made persistent in O2?

22.14. How are relationships represented in an OO data model? What are inverse references? How are inverse references declared in ObjectStore?

Exercises

22.15. Design an OO schema for a database application that you are interested in. First construct an EER schema for the application; then create the corresponding classes in O2. Specify a number of methods for each class. Repeat by specifying the classes for ObjectStore.

22.16. Consider the AIRPORT database described in Exercise 21.18. Specify a number of operations/methods that you think should be applicable to that application. Specify the O2 classes and methods for the database. Repeat for ObjectStore.

22.17. Map the complete UNIVERSITY EER schema of Figure 21.10 into O2 and ObjectStore classes. Include appropriate methods for each class.

22.18. Map the COMPANY ER schema of Figure 3.2 into O2 and ObjectStore classes. Include appropriate methods for each class.

Selected Bibliography

Object-oriented database concepts are an amalgam of concepts from OO programming languages and from database systems and conceptual data models. A number of textbooks describe OO programming languages—for example, Stroustrup (1986) and Pohl (1991) for C^{++}, and Goldberg (1989) for SMALLTALK. A recent book by Cattell (1991) describes OO database concepts.

There is a vast bibliography on OO databases, so we can only provide a representative sample here. The October 1991 issue of CACM and the December 1990 issue of *IEEE Computer* describe object-oriented database concepts and systems. Dittrich (1986) and Zaniolo et al. (1986) survey the basic concepts of object-oriented data models. An early paper on object-oriented databases is Baroody and DeWitt (1981). Data modeling issues in OO databases are discussed in Banerjee et al. (1987), Borgida et al. (1989), Kappel and Schrefl (1991), and Bouzeghoub and Metais (1991). Su et al. (1988) presents an object-oriented data model that is being used in CAD/CAM applications. Mitschang (1989) extends the relational algebra to cover complex objects. Query languages and graphical user interfaces for OO are described in Gyssens et al. (1990), Kim (1989), Alashqur et al. (1989), Bertino et al. (1992), Agrawal et al. (1990), and Cruz (1992).

Osborn (1989) and Zicari (1991) discuss schema evolution in OO databases. Heiler and Zdonick (1990) and Rudensteiner (1992) discuss object views, and Barsalou et al. (1991) discusses object views that are constructed over a relational database. Bertino and Kim (1989) discusses indexing in OO databases. Storage, architecture, and performance issues in OO databases are discussed in Biliris (1992), Cattell and Skeen (1992), Cheng (1991), DeWitt et al. (1990), Shekita and Carey (1989), Willshire (1991), Chang and Katz (1989), and Tsangaris and Naughton (1992). Lehman and Lindsay (1989) discusses the implementation of large objects. Tsotras and Gopinath (1992) discusses object versioning.

The O2 system is described in Deux et al. (1991) and in a recent book (Bancilhon et al. 1992) that includes a list of references to other publications describing various aspects of O2. The O2 model was formalized in Velez et al. (1989). The ObjectStore system is described in Lamb et al. (1991). Fishman et al. (1987) and Wilkinson et al. (1990) discuss IRIS, an object-oriented DBMS developed at Hewlett-Packard laboratories. Maier et al. (1986) and Butterworth et al. (1991) describe the design of GEMSTONE. An OO system supporting open architecture developed at Texas Instruments is described in Thompson et al. (1993). The ODE system developed at ATT Bell Labs is described in Agrawal and Gehani (1989). The ORION system developed at MCC is described in Kim et al. (1990). Morsi et al. (1992) describes an OO testbed.

Polymorphism in databases and object-oriented programming languages is discussed in Osborn (1989), Atkinson and Buneman (1987), and Danforth and Tomlinson (1988). Object identity is discussed in Abiteboul and Kanellakis (1989). OO programming languages for databases are discussed in Kent (1991). Object constraints are discussed in Delcambre et al. (1991) and Elmasri et al. (1993). Authorization and security in OO databases are examined in Rabitti et al. (1991) and Bertino (1992).

Distributed Databases and Client–Server Architecture

In a **centralized database system**, all system components reside at a single computer or **site**. The components include the data, the DBMS software, and the associated secondary storage devices such as disks for on-line database storage and tapes for backup. A centralized database can be accessed remotely via terminals connected to the site; however, the data and DBMS software principally reside at a single site. In recent years there has been a rapid trend toward the **distribution** of computer systems over multiple sites that are interconnected via a **communication network**. In this chapter we discuss the development of **distributed database systems (DDBSs)** and the techniques used in their implementation. The software used to implement such a system is called a **distributed database management system (DDBMS)**.

In Section 23.1 we discuss the reasons for moving toward distribution, and we introduce DDBS concepts. Section 23.2 gives an overview of the client–server architecture, which is becoming popular for distributed systems in general, and for distributed databases in particular. Section 23.3 presents techniques for fragmenting a database and distributing its portions over multiple sites; this is also known as distributed database design. Section 23.4 categorizes the various types of distributed database systems. Sections 23.5 and 23.6 introduce distributed query processing and concurrency control/recovery techniques, respectively.

For a shorter introduction to the topic of distributed databases, some or all of Sections 23.3.3, 23.5, and 23.6 may be skipped.

23.1 Introduction to Distributed DBMS Concepts

A distributed database is a collection of data that belongs logically to the same system but is physically spread over the sites of a computer network. Several factors have led to the development of DDBSs. Potential advantages of DDBSs include the following:

- *Distributed nature of some database applications:* Many database applications are *naturally distributed* over different locations. For example, a company may have locations at different cities, or a bank may have multiple branches. It is natural for databases used in such applications to be distributed over these locations. Many **local users** access only the data at this location, but other **global users**—such as company headquarters—may require occasional access to data stored at several of these locations. Notice that the data at each local site typically describes a "miniworld" at that site. The sources of data and the majority of users and applications for the local database physically reside at that site.

- *Increased reliability and availability:* These are two of the most common potential advantages cited for distributed databases. **Reliability** is broadly defined as the probability that a system is up at a particular moment, whereas **availability** is the probability that the system is continuously available during a time interval. When the data and DBMS software are distributed over several sites, one site may fail while other sites continue to operate. Only the data and software that exist at the failed site cannot be accessed. This improves both reliability and availability. Further improvement is achieved by judiciously *replicating* data and software at more than one site. In a centralized system, failure at a single site makes the whole system unavailable to all users.

- *Allowing data sharing while maintaining some measure of local control:* In some types of DDBSs (see Section 23.4), it is possible to control the data and software locally at each site. However, certain data can be accessed by users at other remote sites through the DDBMS software. This allows *controlled* sharing of data throughout the distributed system.

- *Improved performance:* When a large database is distributed over multiple sites, smaller databases exist at each site. As a result, local queries and transactions accessing data at a single site have better performance because of the smaller local databases. In addition, each site has a smaller number of transactions executing than if all transactions are submitted to a single centralized database. For transactions that involve access to more than one site, processing at the different sites may proceed in parallel, reducing response time.

Distribution leads to increased complexity in the system design and implementation. To achieve the potential advantages listed previously, the DDBMS software must be able to provide the following *additional functions* to those of a centralized DBMS:

- The ability to access remote sites and transmit queries and data among the various sites via a communication network.
- The ability to keep track of the data distribution and replication in the DDBMS catalog.

- The ability to devise execution strategies for queries and transactions that access data from more than one site.
- The ability to decide on which copy of a replicated data item to access.
- The ability to maintain the consistency of copies of a replicated data item.
- The ability to recover from individual site crashes and from new types of failures such as the failure of a communication link.

These functions themselves increase the complexity of a DDBMS over a centralized DBMS. Before we can realize the full potential advantages of distribution, we must find satisfactory solutions to these issues. Including all this additional functionality is hard to accomplish, and finding optimal solutions is a step beyond that. Additional complexities appear when we consider the design of a distributed database. Specifically, we must decide on how to distribute the data over sites and what data, if any, to replicate.

At the physical **hardware** level, the following main factors distinguish a DDBS from a centralized system:

- There are multiple computers, called **sites** or **nodes**.
- These sites must be connected by some type of **communication network** to transmit data and commands among sites, as shown in Figure 23.1.

The sites may all be located in physical proximity—say, within the same building or group of adjacent buildings—and connected via a **local area network,** or they may be geographically distributed over large distances and connected via a **long-haul net-**

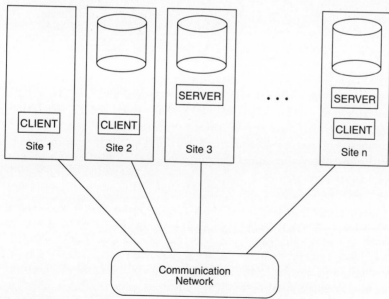

Figure 23.1 Simplified physical client–server architecture for a DDBS.

work. Local area networks typically use cables, whereas long-haul networks use telephone lines or satellites. It is also possible to use a combination of the two types of networks.

Networks may have different **topologies** that define the direct communication paths among sites. For example, direct links may exist between sites 1 and 2 and between sites 2 and 3 but not between sites 1 and 3; in such a case, communication between sites 1 and 3 must pass through site 2. The type and topology of the network used may have a significant effect on performance and hence on the strategies for distributed query processing and distributed database design. For high-level architectural issues, however, it does not matter which type of network is used; it only matters that each site is able to communicate, directly or indirectly, with every other site. For the remainder of this chapter, we assume that some type of communication network exists among sites, regardless of the particular topology.

23.2 Overview of Client–Server Architecture

The **client–server architecture** has been developed to deal with new computing environments in which a large number of personal computers, workstations, file servers, printers, and other equipment are connected together via a network. The idea is to define **specialized servers** with specific functionalities. For example, it is possible to connect a number of diskless workstations or personal computers as clients to a *file server* machine that maintains the files of the client's users. Another machine could be designated as a *printer server* by being connected to various printers; thereafter, all print requests would be forwarded to this machine. In this way, the resources provided by specialized servers can be accessed by many clients. This idea can be carried over to software, with specialized software—such as a DBMS or a CAD (computer-aided design) package—being stored on specific server machines, and this software being made accessible to multiple clients.

The client–server architecture is increasingly being incorporated into commercial DBMS packages as they move toward the support of distribution. The idea is to divide the DBMS software into two levels—client and server—to reduce its complexity. This is illustrated in Figure 23.1; some sites may run the client software only (these could be diskless machines, such as site 1, or machines with disks, such as site 2), while other sites may be dedicated server machines that run the server software only, such as site 3. Still other sites may support both client and server modules, such as site n in Figure 23.1.

Exactly how to divide the DBMS functionality between client and server has not yet been established. Different approaches have been proposed. One possibility is to include the functionality of a centralized DBMS at the server level. A number of relational DBMS products have taken this approach, where an **SQL server** is provided to the clients. Each client must then formulate the appropriate SQL queries and provide the user interface and programming language interface functions. Since SQL is a relational standard, various different SQL servers, possibly provided by different vendors, can accept SQL commands. The client may also refer to a data dictionary that includes information on the distribution of data among the various SQL servers, as well as modules for decomposing a global query into a number of local queries that can be executed at the various sites. We discuss such a module further in Section 23.5. Interaction between client and server might proceed as follows during processing of an SQL query:

1. The client parses a user query and decomposes it into a number of independent site queries. Each site query is sent to the appropriate server site.

2. Each server processes the local query and sends the resulting relation to the client site.

3. The client site combines the results of the subqueries to produce the result of the originally submitted query.

In this approach, the SQL server has also been called a **database processor (DP)** or a **back-end machine**, whereas the client has been called an **application processor (AP)** or a **front-end machine**. The interaction between client and server can be specified by the user at the client level or via a specialized client module. For example, the user may know what data is stored in each server, break down a query request into site subqueries manually, and submit individual subqueries to the various sites. The resulting tables may be combined explicitly by a further user query at the client level. The alternative is to have the client module undertake these actions automatically.

Another approach, taken by some object-oriented DBMSs (see Chapter 22), divides the software modules of the DBMS between client and server in a more integrated way. For example, the *server level* may include the part of the DBMS software responsible for handling data storage on disk pages, local concurrency control and recovery, buffering and caching of disk pages, and other such functions. Meanwhile, the *client level* may handle the user interface, data dictionary functions, DBMS interaction with programming language compilers, global query optimization/concurrency control/recovery, structuring of complex objects from the data in the buffers, and other such functions. In this approach, the client–server interaction is more tightly coupled and is done internally by the DBMS modules, rather than by the users.

In a typical DDBMS, it is customary to divide the software modules into three levels:

- The **server** software is responsible for local data management at a site, much like centralized DBMS software.

- The **client** software is responsible for most of the distribution functions; it accesses data distribution information from the DDBMS catalog and processes all requests that require access to more than one site.

- The **communications software** (sometimes in conjunction with a **distributed operating system**) provides the communication primitives that are used by the client to transmit commands and data among the various sites as needed. This is not strictly part of the DDBMS, but it provides essential communication primitives and services.

The **client** is responsible for generating a distributed execution plan for a multisite query or transaction and for supervising distributed execution by sending commands to servers. These commands include local queries and transactions to be executed, as well as commands to transmit data to other clients or servers. Hence, client software should be included at any site where multisite queries are submitted. We discuss distributed

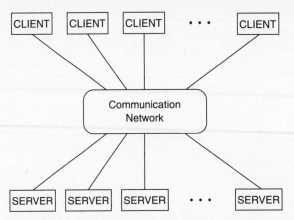

Figure 23.2   Simplified logical client–server architecture for a DDBS.

query processing further in Section 23.5. Another function controlled by the client is that of ensuring consistency of replicated copies of a data item by employing distributed (or global) concurrency control techniques. The client must also ensure the atomicity of global transactions by performing global recovery when certain sites fail. We discuss distributed recovery and concurrency control in Section 23.6. Figure 23.2 shows a logical view of a DDBS; here, clients and servers are shown without specifying the site on which each resides.

One possible function of the client is to *hide* the details of data distribution from the user; that is, it enables the user to write global queries and transactions as though the database were centralized, without having to specify the sites at which the data referenced in the query or transaction resides. This property is called **distribution transparency**. Some DDBMSs do not provide distribution transparency, instead requiring that users be aware of the details of data distribution. In this case, users must specify the sites at which the data referenced in global queries and transactions reside. In the latter situation, a user typically *appends the site name* to any references to a relation, file, or record type. In the former situation, the user is presented with a schema that does not include any distribution information, and the DDBMS itself keeps track of the sites at which data is located in the **DDBMS catalog**. Using this information, the client software can break down a query into a number of subqueries that can be executed at the various sites, and it can plan how to transmit results of subqueries to other sites for further processing and for producing the result. DDBMSs that provide distribution transparency make it simpler for a user to specify queries and transactions, but they require more complex software. DDBMSs that do not provide distribution transparency make it the responsibility of the user to specify the site of each relation or file, leading to simpler software.

23.3 Data Fragmentation, Replication, and Allocation Techniques for Distributed Database Design

In this section we discuss techniques that are used to break up the database into logical units, called **fragments**, that may be assigned for storage at the various sites. We also discuss the use of **data replication**, which permits certain data to be stored in more than one site, and the process of **allocating** fragments—or replicas of fragments—for storage at the various sites. These techniques are used during the process of **distributed database design**. The information concerning data fragmentation, allocation, and replication is stored in a **global system catalog** that is accessed by the client software as needed.

23.3.1 Data Fragmentation

In a DDBS, decisions must be made regarding which site should be used to store which portions of the database. For now, we will assume that there is *no replication*; that is, each file—or portion of a file—is to be stored at only one site. We discuss replication and its effects later in this section. We also use the terminology of *relational databases*; similar concepts apply to other data models. We assume that we are starting with a relational database schema and must decide on how to distribute the relations over the various sites. To illustrate our discussion, we use the relational database schema in Figure 6.5.

Before we decide on how to distribute the data, we must determine the *logical units* of the database that are to be distributed. The simplest logical units are the relations themselves; that is, each *whole* relation is to be stored at a particular site. In our example, we must decide on a site to store each of the relations EMPLOYEE, DEPARTMENT, PROJECT, WORKS_ON, and DEPENDENT of Figure 6.5. In many cases, however, a relation can be divided into smaller logical units for distribution. For example, consider the company database shown in Figure 6.6, and assume there are three computer sites—one for each department in the company. Of course, in an actual situation, there are many more tuples in the relations. We may want to store the database information relating to each department at the computer site for that department. To do so, we need to partition each relation by using a technique called horizontal fragmentation.

Horizontal Fragmentation. A **horizontal fragment** of a relation is a subset of the tuples in that relation. The tuples that belong to the horizontal fragment are specified by a condition on one or more attributes of the relation. Often, only a single attribute is involved. For example, we may define three horizontal fragments on the EMPLOYEE relation of Figure 6.6 with the following conditions: (DNO = 5), (DNO = 4), and (DNO = 1); each fragment contains the EMPLOYEE tuples working for a particular department. Similarly, we may define three horizontal fragments for the PROJECT relation of Figure 6.6 with the conditions (DNUM = 5), (DNUM = 4), and (DNUM = 1); each fragment contains the PROJECT tuples controlled by a particular department. Horizontal fragmentation divides a relation "horizontally" by grouping rows to create subsets of tuples, where each subset has a certain logical meaning. These fragments can then be assigned to different sites in the distributed system.

Vertical Fragmentation. A **vertical fragment** of a relation keeps only certain attributes of the relation. For example, we may want to fragment the EMPLOYEE relation into two vertical fragments. The first fragment includes personal information—NAME, BDATE, ADDRESS, and SEX—and the second includes work-related information—SSN, SALARY, SUPERSSN, DNO. This vertical fragmentation is not quite proper because, if the two fragments are stored separately, we cannot put the original employee tuples back together, since there is *no common attribute* between the two fragments. It is necessary to include the *primary key attribute* in *every* vertical fragment so that the full relation can be reconstructed from the fragments. Hence, we must add the SSN attribute to the personal information fragment. Vertical fragmentation divides a relation "vertically" by columns.

Notice that each horizontal fragment on a relation R can be specified by a $\sigma_{Ci}(R)$ operation in the relational algebra. A set of horizontal fragments whose conditions C1, C2, ..., Cn include all the tuples in R—that is, every tuple in R satisfies (C1 OR C2 OR $\cdots$ OR Cn)—is called a **complete horizontal fragmentation** of R. In many cases a complete horizontal fragmentation is also **disjoint**; that is, no tuple in R satisfies (Ci AND Cj) for any i $\neq$ j. Our two earlier examples of horizontal fragmentation for the EMPLOYEE and PROJECT relations were both complete and disjoint. To reconstruct the relation R from a *complete* horizontal fragmentation, we need to apply the UNION operation to the fragments.

A vertical fragment on a relation R can be specified by a $\pi_{Li}(R)$ operation in the relational algebra. A set of vertical fragments whose projection lists L1, L2, ..., Ln include all the attributes in R but share only the primary key attribute of R is called a **complete vertical fragmentation** of R. In this case the projection lists satisfy the following two conditions:

- $L1 \cup L2 \cup \cdots \cup Ln = $ ATTRS(R).
- $Li \cap Lj = $ PK(R) for any i $\neq$ j, where ATTRS(R) is the set of attributes of R and PK(R) is the primary key of R.

To reconstruct the relation R from a *complete* vertical fragmentation, we apply the OUTER UNION operation to the fragments. Notice that we could also apply the FULL OUTER JOIN operation and get the same result for a complete vertical fragmentation. The two vertical fragments of the EMPLOYEE relation with projection lists L1 = {SSN, NAME, BDATE, ADDRESS, SEX} and L2 = {SSN, SALARY, SUPERSSN, DNO} constitute a complete vertical fragmentation of EMPLOYEE.

Two horizontal fragments that are neither complete nor disjoint are those defined on the EMPLOYEE relation of Figure 6.5 by the conditions (SALARY > 50000) and (DNO = 4); they may not include all EMPLOYEE tuples, and they may include common tuples. Two vertical fragments that are not complete are those defined by the attribute lists L1 = {NAME, ADDRESS} and L2 = {SSN, NAME, SALARY}; these lists violate both conditions of a complete vertical fragmentation.

Mixed Fragmentation. We can intermix the two types of fragmentation, yielding a **mixed fragmentation**. For example, we may combine the horizontal and vertical fragmentations of the EMPLOYEE relation given earlier into a mixed fragmentation that includes six fragments. In this case the original relation can be reconstructed by applying

UNION *and* OUTER UNION (or OUTER JOIN) operations in the appropriate order. In general, a **fragment** of a relation R can be specified by a SELECT-PROJECT combination of operations $\pi_L(\sigma_C(R))$. If C = TRUE and L ≠ ATTRS(R), we get a vertical fragment, and if C ≠ TRUE and L = ATTRS(R), we get a horizontal fragment. Finally, if C ≠ TRUE and L ≠ ATTRS(R), we get a mixed fragment. Notice that a relation can itself be considered a fragment with C = TRUE and L = ATTRS(R). In the following discussion, the term *fragment* is used to refer to a relation or to any of the preceding types of fragments.

A **fragmentation schema** of a database is a definition of a set of fragments that includes *all* attributes and tuples in the database and satisfies the condition that the whole database can be reconstructed from the fragments by applying some sequence of OUTER UNION (or OUTER JOIN) and UNION operations. It is also sometimes useful—although not necessary—to have all the fragments be disjoint except for the repetition of primary keys among vertical (or mixed) fragments. In the latter case, all replication and distribution of fragments is clearly specified at a subsequent stage, separately from fragmentation.

An **allocation schema** describes the allocation of fragments to sites of the DDBS; hence, it is a mapping that specifies for each fragment the site(s) at which it is stored. If a fragment is stored at more than one site, it is said to be **replicated**. We discuss data replication and allocation next.

23.3.2 *Data Replication and Allocation*

Replication is useful in improving the availability of data. The most extreme case is replication of the *whole database* at every site in the distributed system, thus creating a **fully replicated** distributed database. This can improve availability remarkably because the system can continue to operate as long as at least one site is up. It also improves performance of retrieval for global queries, because the result of such a query can be obtained locally from any one site; hence, a retrieval query can be processed at the local site where it is submitted, if that site includes a server module. The disadvantage of full replication is that it can slow down update operations drastically, since a single logical update must be performed on every copy of the database to keep the copies consistent. This is especially true if many copies of the database exist. Full replication makes the concurrency control and recovery techniques more expensive than they would be if there were no replication, as we shall see in Section 23.6.

The other extreme from full replication involves having **no replication**; that is, each fragment is stored at exactly one site. In this case all fragments *must* be disjoint, except for the repetition of primary keys among vertical (or mixed) fragments. This is also called **nonredundant allocation**.

Between these two extremes, we have a wide spectrum of **partial replication** of the data; that is, some fragments of the database may be replicated whereas others are not. The number of copies of each fragment can range from one up to the total number of sites in the distributed system. A description of the replication of fragments is sometimes called a **replication schema**.

Each fragment—or each copy of a fragment—must be assigned to a particular site in the distributed system. This process is called **data distribution** (or **data allocation**).

The choice of sites and the degree of replication depend on the performance and availability goals of the system and on the types and frequencies of transactions submitted at each site. For example, if high availability is required and if transactions can be submitted at any site and if most transactions are retrieval only, a fully replicated database is a good choice. However, if certain transactions that access particular parts of the database are mostly submitted at a particular site, the corresponding set of fragments can be allocated at that site only. Data that is accessed at multiple sites can be replicated at those sites. If many updates are performed, it may be useful to limit replication. Finding an optimal or even a good solution to distributed data allocation is a complex optimization problem.

23.3.3 *Example of Fragmentation, Allocation, and Replication**

We now consider an example of fragmenting and distributing the company database of Figures 6.5 and 6.6. Suppose that the company has three computer sites—one for each current department. Sites 2 and 3 are for departments 5 and 4, respectively. At each of these sites, we expect frequent access to the EMPLOYEE and PROJECT information for the employees *who work in that department* and the projects *controlled by that department*. Further, we assume that these sites mainly access the NAME, SSN, SALARY, and SUPERSSN attributes of EMPLOYEE. Site 1 is used by company headquarters and accesses all employee and project information regularly, in addition to keeping track of DEPENDENT information for insurance purposes.

According to these requirements, the whole database of Figure 6.6 can be stored at site 1. To determine the fragments to be replicated at sites 2 and 3, we can first horizontally fragment the EMPLOYEE, PROJECT, DEPARTMENT, and DEPT_LOCATIONS relations by department number—called DNO, DNUM, and DNUMBER, respectively, in Figure 6.5. We can then vertically fragment the resulting EMPLOYEE fragments to include only the attributes {NAME, SSN, SALARY, SUPERSSN, DNO}. Figure 23.3 shows the mixed fragments EMPD5 and EMPD4, which include the EMPLOYEE tuples satisfying the conditions DNO = 5 and DNO = 4, respectively. The horizontal fragments of PROJECT, DEPARTMENT, and DEPT_LOCATIONS are similarly fragmented by department number. All these fragments—stored at sites 2 and 3—are replicated because they are also stored at the headquarters site 1.

We must now fragment the WORKS_ON relation and decide which fragments of WORKS_ON to store at sites 2 and 3. We are confronted with the problem that no attribute of WORKS_ON directly indicates the department to which each tuple belongs. In fact, each tuple in WORKS_ON relates an employee e to a project p. We could fragment WORKS_ON based on the department d in which e works *or* based on the department d' that controls p. Fragmentation becomes easy if we have a constraint stating that d = d' for all WORKS_ON tuples—that is, if employees can work only on projects controlled by the department they work for. However, there is no such constraint in our database of Figure 6.6. For example, the WORKS_ON tuple <333445555, 10, 10.0> relates an employee who works for department 5 with a project controlled by department 4. In this case we could fragment WORKS_ON based on *both* the department in which the employee works *and* the department that controls the project, as shown in Figure 23.4.

In Figure 23.4, the union of fragments G1, G2, and G3 gives all WORKS_ON tuples for employees who work *for department* 5. Similarly, the union of fragments G4, G5, and

(a)

EMPD5	FNAME	MINIT	LNAME	SSN	SALARY	SUPERSSN	DNO
	John	B	Smith	123456789	30000	333445555	5
	Franklin	T	Wong	333445555	40000	888665555	5
	Ramesh	K	Narayan	666884444	38000	333445555	5
	Joyce	A	English	453453453	25000	333445555	5

DEP5	DNAME	DNUMBER	MGRSSN	MGRSTARTDATE
	Research	5	333445555	22- MAY-78

DEP5_LOCS	DNUMBER	LOCATION
	5	Bellaire
	5	Sugarland
	5	Houston

WORKS_ON5	ESSN	PNO	HOURS
	123456789	1	32.5
	123456789	2	7.5
	666884444	3	40.0
	453453453	1	20.0
	453453453	2	20.0
	333445555	2	10.0
	333445555	3	10.0
	333445555	10	10.0
	333445555	20	10.0

PROJS5	PNAME	PNUMBER	PLOCATION	DNUM
	Product X	1	Bellaire	5
	Product Y	2	Sugarland	5
	Product Z	3	Houston	5

(b)

EMPD4	FNAME	MINIT	LNAME	SSN	SALARY	SUPERSSN	DNO
	Alicia	J	Zelaya	999887777	25000	987654321	4
	Jennifer	S	Wallace	987654321	43000	888665555	4
	Ahmad	V	Jabbar	987987987	25000	987654321	4

DEP4	DNAME	DNUMBER	MGRSSN	MGRSTARTDATE
	Administration	4	987654321	01-JAN-85

DEP4_LOCS	DNUMBER	LOCATION
	4	Stafford

WORKS_ON4	ESSN	PNO	HOURS
	333445555	10	10.0
	999887777	30	30.0
	999887777	10	10.0
	987987987	10	35.0
	987987987	30	5.0
	987654321	30	20.0
	987654321	20	15.0

PROJS4	PNAME	PNUMBER	PLOCATION	DNUM
	Computerization	10	Stafford	4
	Newbenefits	30	Stafford	4

Figure 23.3 Allocation of fragments to sites. (a) Relation fragments at site 2. (b) Relation fragments at site 3.

(a)

G1	ESSN	PNO	HOURS
	123456789	1	32.5
	123456789	2	7.5
	666884444	3	40.0
	453453453	1	20.0
	453453453	2	20.0
	333445555	2	10.0
	333445555	3	10.0

C1=C AND (PNO IN (SELECT PNUMBER
FROM PROJECT
WHERE DNUM=5))

G2	ESSN	PNO	HOURS
	333445555	10	10.0

C2=C AND (PNO IN (SELECT PNUMBER
FROM PROJECT
WHERE DNUM=4))

G3	ESSN	PNO	HOURS
	333445555	20	10.0

C3=C AND (PNO IN (SELECT PNUMBER
FROM PROJECT
WHERE DNUM=1))

(b)

G4	ESSN	PNO	HOURS

C4=C AND (PNO IN (SELECT PNUMBER
FROM PROJECT
WHERE DNUM=5))

G5	ESSN	PNO	HOURS
	999887777	30	30.0
	999887777	10	10.0
	987987987	10	35.0
	987987987	30	5.0
	987654321	30	20.0

C5=C AND (PNO IN (SELECT PNUMBER
FROM PROJECT
WHERE DNUM=4))

G6	ESSN	PNO	HOURS
	987654321	20	15.0

C6=C AND (PNO IN (SELECT PNUMBER
FROM PROJECT
WHERE DNUM=1))

(c)

G7	ESSN	PNO	HOURS

C7=C AND (PNO IN (SELECT PNUMBER
FROM PROJECT
WHERE DNUM=5))

G8	ESSN	PNO	HOURS

C8=C AND (PNO IN (SELECT PNUMBER
FROM PROJECT
WHERE DNUM=4))

G9	ESSN	PNO	HOURS
	888665555	20	null

C9=C AND (PNO IN (SELECT PNUMBER
FROM PROJECT
WHERE DNUM=1))

Figure 23.4 Complete and disjoint fragments of the WORKS_ON relation.
(a) Fragments of WORKS_ON for employees working in department 5 (C=ESSN IN (SELECT SSN FROM EMPLOYEE WHERE DNO=5)). (b) Fragments of WORKS_ON for employees working in department 4 (C=ESSN IN (SELECT SSN FROM EMPLOYEE WHERE DNO=4)). (c) Fragments of WORKS_ON for employees working in department 1 (C=ESSN IN (SELECT SSN FROM EMPLOYEE WHERE DNO=1)).

G6 gives all WORKS_ON tuples for employees who *work for department 4*. On the other hand, the union of fragments G1, G4, and G7 gives all WORKS_ON tuples for projects *controlled by department 5*. The condition for each of the fragments G1 through G9 is shown in Figure 23.4. The relations that represent M:N relationships, such as WORKS_ON, often have several possible logical fragmentations. In our distribution of Figure 23.3, we choose to include all fragments that can be joined to either an EMPLOYEE tuple or a PROJECT tuple at sites 2 and 3. Hence, we place the union of fragments G1, G2, G3, G4, and G7 at site 2 and the union of fragments G4, G5, G6, G2, and G8 at site 3. Notice that fragments G2 and G4 are replicated at both sites. This allocation strategy permits the join between the local EMPLOYEE or PROJECT fragments at site 2 or site 3 and the local WORKS_ON fragment to be performed completely locally. This clearly demonstrates how complex the problem of database fragmentation and allocation is for large databases. The bibliographic notes give references to some of the work done in this area.

23.4 Types of Distributed Database Systems

The term *distributed database management system* can describe various systems that differ from one another in many respects. The main thing that all such systems have in common is the fact that data and software are distributed over multiple sites connected by some form of communication network. In this section we discuss a number of types of DDBMSs and the criteria and factors that make some of these systems different.

The first factor we consider is the **degree of homogeneity** of the DDBMS software. If all servers (or individual local DBMSs) use identical software and all clients use identical software, the DDBMS is called **homogeneous;** otherwise, it is called **heterogeneous.** Another factor related to the degree of homogeneity is the **degree of local autonomy.** If all access to the DDBMS must be gained through a client, then the system has **no local autonomy**. On the other hand, if *direct access* by local transactions to a server is permitted, the system has some degree of local autonomy.

At one extreme of the autonomy spectrum, we have a DDBMS that "looks like" a centralized DBMS to the user. A single conceptual schema exists, and all access to the system is obtained through a client, so no local autonomy exists. At the other extreme we encounter a type of DDBMS called a **federated DDBMS** (or a **multidatabase system**). In such a system, each server is an independent and autonomous centralized DBMS that has its own local users, local transactions, and DBA and hence has a very high degree of *local autonomy*. Each server can authorize access to particular portions of its database by specifying an **export schema**, which specifies the part of the database that may be accessed by a certain class of nonlocal users. A client in such a system is essentially an additional interface to several servers (local DBMSs) that allows a multidatabase (or global) user to access data stored in several of these *autonomous databases*. Notice that a federated system is a hybrid between distributed and centralized systems; it is a centralized system for local autonomous users and a distributed system for global users.

In a heterogeneous multidatabase system, one server may be a relational DBMS, another a network DBMS, and a third a hierarchical DBMS; in such a case it is necessary to have a canonical system language and to include language translators in the client to translate subqueries from the canonical language to the language of each server.

A third aspect that may be used to categorize distributed databases is the **degree of distribution transparency** or, alternatively, the **degree of schema integration**. If the user sees a single integrated schema without any information concerning fragmentation, replication, or distribution, the DDBMS is said to have a *high degree of distribution transparency* (or schema integration). On the other hand, if the user sees all fragmentation, allocation, and replication, the DDBMS has *no distribution transparency* and no schema integration. In the latter case, the user must refer to specific fragment copies at specific sites when formulating a query, by appending the site name before a relation or fragment name.

This is part of the complex problem of **naming** in distributed systems. In the case of a DDBMS that does not provide distribution transparency, it is up to the user to *unambiguously specify* the name of a particular relation or fragment copy. This task is more severe in a multidatabase system, because each server (local DBMS) presumably was developed independently, and as a result conflicting names may have been used at different servers. In the case of a DBMS that provides an integrated schema, however, naming becomes an internal system problem, because the user is provided with a single unambiguous schema. The DDBMS must store *all correspondences* among the integrated schema objects and the objects distributed across the various DPs in the **distribution catalog**.

23.5 Query Processing in Distributed Databases*

We now give an overview of how a DDBMS processes and optimizes a query. We first discuss the communication costs of processing a distributed query; then we discuss a special operation, called a *semijoin*, that is used in optimizing some types of queries in a DDBMS.

23.5.1 *Data Transfer Costs of Distributed Query Processing*

We discussed the issues involved in processing and optimizing a query in a centralized DBMS in Chapter 16. In a distributed system, several additional factors further complicate query processing. The first is the cost of transferring data over the network. This data includes intermediate files that are transferred to other sites for further processing, as well as the final result files that may have to be transferred to the site where the query result is needed. Although these costs may not be very high if the sites are connected via a high-performance local area network, they become quite significant in other types of networks. Hence, DDBMS query optimization algorithms consider the goal of reducing the *amount of data transfer* as an optimization criterion in choosing a distributed query execution strategy.

We illustrate this with two simple example queries. Suppose that the EMPLOYEE and DEPARTMENT relations of Figure 6.5 are distributed as shown in Figure 23.5. We will assume in this example that neither relation is fragmented. According to Figure 23.5, the size of the EMPLOYEE relation is $100 * 10{,}000 = 10^6$ bytes, and the size of the DEPARTMENT relation is $35 * 100 = 3500$ bytes. Consider the query Q: "For each employee, retrieve the employee name and the name of the department for which the employee works." This can be stated as follows in the relational algebra:

Q: $\pi_{\text{FNAME,LNAME,DNAME}}(\text{EMPLOYEE} \bowtie_{\text{DNO=DNUMBER}} \text{DEPARTMENT})$

The result of this query will include 10,000 records, assuming that every employee is related to a department. Suppose that each record in the query result is *40 bytes long*. The query is submitted at a distinct site 3, which is called the **result site** because the

SITE 1:

EMPLOYEE

FNAME	MINIT	LNAME	SSN	BDATE	ADDRESS	SEX	SALARY	SUPERSSN	DNO

10,000 records
each record is 100 bytes long
SSN field is 9 bytes long   FNAME field is 15 bytes long
DNO field is 4 bytes long   LNAME field is 15 bytes long

SITE 2:

DEPARTMENT

DNAME	DNUMBER	MGRSSN	MGRSTARTDATE

100 records
each record is 35 bytes long
DNUMBER field is 4 bytes long   DNAME field is 10 bytes long
MGRSSN field is 9 bytes long

Figure 23.5   Example to illustrate volume of data transferred.

query result is needed there. Neither the EMPLOYEE nor the DEPARTMENT relations reside at site 3. There are three simple strategies for executing this distributed query:

1. Transfer both the EMPLOYEE and the DEPARTMENT relations to the result site, and perform the join at site 3. In this case we need to transfer a total of 1,000,000 + 3500 = 1,003,500 bytes.

2. Transfer the EMPLOYEE relation to site 2, execute the join at site 2, and send the result to site 3. The size of the query result is 40 * 10,000 = 400,000 bytes, so we must transfer 400,000 + 1,000,000 = 1,400,000 bytes.

3. Transfer the DEPARTMENT relation to site 1, execute the join at site 1, and send the result to site 3. In this case we have to transfer 400,000 + 3500 = 403,500 bytes.

If minimizing the amount of data transfer is our optimization criterion, we should choose strategy 3. Now consider another query Q': "For each department, retrieve the department name and the name of the department manager." This can be stated as follows in the relational algebra:

Q: $\pi_{DNAME,FNAME,LNAME}$(DEPARTMENT $\bowtie_{MGRSSN=SSN}$ EMPLOYEE)

Again, suppose that the query is submitted at site 3. The same three strategies for executing query Q apply to Q', except that the result of Q' includes only 100 records, assuming that each department has a manager:

1. Transfer both the EMPLOYEE and the DEPARTMENT relations to the result site, and perform the join at site 3. In this case we need to transfer a total of 1,000,000 + 3500 = 1,003,500 bytes.

2. Transfer the EMPLOYEE relation to site 2, execute the join at site 2, and send the result to site 3. The size of the query result is 40 * 100 = 4000 bytes, so we must transfer 4000 + 1,000,000 = 1,004,000 bytes.

3. Transfer the DEPARTMENT relation to site 1, execute the join at site 1, and send the result to site 3. In this case we have to transfer 4000 + 3500 = 7500 bytes.

Again, we would choose strategy 3—in this case by an overwhelming margin over strategies 1 and 2. The preceding three strategies are the most obvious ones for the case where the result site (site 3) is different from all the sites that contain files involved in the query (sites 1 and 2). However, suppose that the result site is site 2; then we have two simple strategies:

4. Transfer the EMPLOYEE relation to site 2, execute the query, and present the result to the user at site 2. Here, we need to transfer the same number of bytes— 1,000,000—for both Q and Q'.

5. Transfer the DEPARTMENT relation to site 1, execute the query at site 1, and send the result back to site 2. In this case we must transfer 400,000 + 3500 = 403,500 bytes for Q and 4000 + 3500 = 7500 bytes for Q'.

A more complex strategy, which sometimes works better than these simple strategies, uses an operation called **semijoin**. We introduce this operation and discuss distributed execution using semijoins next.

23.5.2 Distributed Query Processing Using Semijoin

The idea behind distributed query processing using the semijoin operation is to reduce the number of tuples in a relation before transferring it to another site. Intuitively, the idea is to send the *joining column* of one relation R to the site where the other relation S is located; this column is then joined with S. Following that, the join attributes, along with the attributes required in the result, are projected out and shipped back to the original site and joined with R. Hence, only the joining column of R is transferred in one direction, and a subset of S with no extraneous tuples is transferred in the other direction. If only a small fraction of the tuples in S participate in the join, this can be quite an efficient solution to minimizing data transfer.

To illustrate this, consider the following strategy for executing Q or Q':

1. Project the join attributes of DEPARTMENT at site 2, and transfer them to site 1. For Q, we transfer $F = \pi_{DNUMBER}(DEPARTMENT)$, whose size is 4 * 100 = 400 bytes, whereas, for Q', we transfer $F' = \pi_{MGRSSN}(DEPARTMENT)$, whose size is 9 * 100 = 900 bytes.

2. Join the transferred file with the EMPLOYEE relation at site 1, and transfer the required attributes from the resulting file to site 2. For Q, we transfer $R = \pi_{<DNO, FNAME, LNAME>}(F \bowtie_{DNUMBER=DNO} EMPLOYEE)$, whose size is 34 * 10,000 = 340,000 bytes, whereas, for Q', we transfer $R' = \pi_{<MGRSSN, FNAME, LNAME>}(F' \bowtie_{MGRSSN=SSN} EMPLOYEE)$, whose size is 39 * 100 = 3900 bytes.

3. Execute the query by joining the transferred file R or R' with DEPARTMENT, and present the result to the user at site 2.

Using this strategy, we transfer 340,400 bytes for Q and 4800 bytes for Q'. We limited the EMPLOYEE attributes and tuples transmitted to site 2 in step 2 to only those that will *actually be joined* with a DEPARTMENT tuple in step 3. For query Q, this turned out to include all EMPLOYEE tuples, so little improvement was achieved. However, for Q' only 100 out of the 10,000 EMPLOYEE tuples were needed.

The semijoin operation was devised to formalize this strategy. A **semijoin** operation $R \ltimes_{A=B} S$, where A and B are domain-compatible attributes of R and S, respectively, produces the same result as the relational algebra expression $\pi_{<R>}(R \bowtie_{A=B} S)$. In a distributed environment where R and S reside at different sites, the semijoin is typically implemented by first transferring $F = \pi_{<B>}(S)$ to the site where R resides and then joining F with R, thus leading to the strategy discussed here.

Notice that the semijoin operation is not commutative; that is,

$$R \ltimes S \neq S \ltimes R$$

23.5.3 Query and Update Decomposition

In a DDBMS with *no distribution transparency*, the user phrases a query directly in terms of specific fragments. For example, consider another query Q: "Retrieve the names and hours per week for each employee who works on some project controlled by department 5," which is specified on the distributed database where the relations at sites 2 and 3 are shown in Figure 23.3, and those at site 1 are shown in Figure 6.6, as in our earlier example. A user who submits such a query must specify whether it references the PROJS5 and WORKS_ON5 relations at site 2 (Figure 23.3) or the PROJECT and WORKS_ON relations at site 1 (Figure 6.6). The user must also maintain consistency of replicated data items when updating a DDBMS with *no replication transparency*.

On the other hand, a DDBMS that supports *full distribution, fragmentation, and replication transparency* allows the user to specify a query or update request on the schema of Figure 6.5 just as though the DBMS were centralized. For updates, the DDBMS is responsible for maintaining *consistency among replicated items* by using one of the distributed concurrency control algorithms discussed in Section 23.6. For queries, a **query decomposition** module must break up or **decompose** a query into **subqueries** that can be executed at the individual sites. In addition, a strategy for combining the results of the subqueries to form the query result must be generated. Whenever the DDBMS determines that an item referenced in the query is replicated, it must choose or **materialize** a particular replica that is referenced during query execution.

To determine which replicas include the data items referenced in a query, the DDBMS refers to the fragmentation, replication, and distribution information stored in the DDBMS catalog. For vertical fragmentation, the attribute list for each fragment is kept in the catalog. For horizontal fragmentation, a condition, sometimes called a **guard**, is kept for each fragment. This is basically a selection condition that specifies which tuples exist in the fragment; it is called a *guard* because *only tuples that satisfy this condition* are permitted to be stored in the fragment. For mixed fragments, both the attribute list and the guard condition are kept in the catalog.

In our earlier example, the guard conditions for fragments at site 1 (Figure 6.6) are TRUE (all tuples), and the attribute lists are * (all attributes). For the fragments shown

(a) EMPD5
        attribute list: FNAME,MINIT,LNAME,SSN,SALARY,SUPERSSN, DNO
      guard condition: DNO=5
      DEP5
        attribute list: $\star$ (all attributes DNAME,DNUMBER,MGRSSN,MGRSTARTDATE)
      guard condition: DNUMBER=5
      DEP5_LOCS
        attribute list: $\star$ (all attributes DNUMBER,LOCATION)
      guard condition: DNUMBER=5
      PROJS5
        attribute list: $\star$ (all attributes PNAME,PNUMBER,PLOCATION,DNUM)
      guard condition: DNUM=5
      WORKS_ON5
        attribute list: $\star$ (all attributes ESSN,PNO,HOURS)
      guard condition: ESSN IN (π_{SSN} (EMPD5))
      OR PNO IN ($\pi_{PNumber}$ (PROJS5))

(b) EMPD4
        attribute list: FNAME,MINIT,LNAME,SSN,SALARY,SUPERSSN, DNO
      guard condition: DNO=4
      DEP4
        attribute list: $\star$ (all attributes DNAME,DNUMBER,MGRSSN,MGRSTARTDATE)
      guard condition: DNUMBER=4
      DEP4_LOCS
        attribute list: $\star$ (all attributes DNUMBER,LOCATION)
      guard condition: DNUMBER=4
      PROJS4
        attribute list: $\star$ (all attributes PNAME,PNUMBER,PLOCATION,DNUM)
      guard condition: DNUM=4
      WORKS_ON4
        attribute list: $\star$ (all attributes ESSN,PNO,HOURS)
      guard condition: ESSN IN (π_{SSN} (EMPD4))
      OR PNO IN ($\pi_{PNumber}$(PROJS4))

Figure 23.6   Guard conditions and attribute lists for fragments. (a) Guards
and attribute lists for relation fragments at site 2. (b) Guards and
attribute lists for relation fragments at site 3.

in Figure 23.3, we have the guard conditions and attribute lists shown in Figure 23.6.
When the DDBMS decomposes an update request, it can determine which fragments must
be updated by examining their guard conditions. For example, a user request to insert a
new EMPLOYEE tuple <'Alex', 'B', 'Coleman', '345671239', '22-APR-64', '3306 Sand-
stone, Houston, TX', M, 33000, '987654321', 4> would be decomposed by the DDBMS
into two update requests: the first inserts the preceding tuple in the EMPLOYEE fragment
at site 1, and the second inserts the projected tuple <'Alex', 'B', 'Coleman', '345671239',
33000, '987654321', 4> in the EMPD4 fragment at site 3.

For query decomposition, the DDBMS can determine which fragments may contain
the required tuples by comparing the query condition with the guard conditions. For
example, consider the query Q: "Retrieve the names and hours per week for each
employee who works on some project controlled by department 5"; this can be specified
in SQL on the schema of Figure 6.5 as follows:

Q: **SELECT**   FNAME, LNAME, HOURS
         FROM   EMPLOYEE, PROJECT, WORKS_ON
         WHERE   DNUM=5 **AND** PNUMBER=PNO **AND** ESSN=SSN

Suppose that the query is submitted at site 2, which is where the query result will be needed. The DDBMS can determine from the guard condition on PROJS5 and WORKS_ON5 that all tuples satisfying the conditions (DNUM = 5 AND PNUMBER = PNO) reside at site 2. Hence, it may decompose the query into the following relational algebra subqueries:

$$T1 \leftarrow \pi_{ESSN} (PROJS5 \bowtie_{PNUMBER=PNO} WORKS\_ON5)$$
$$T2 \leftarrow \pi_{ESSN, FNAME, LNAME} (T1 \bowtie_{ESSN=SSN} EMPLOYEE)$$
$$RESULT \leftarrow \pi_{FNAME, LNAME, HOURS} (T2 * WORKS\_ON5)$$

This decomposition can be used to execute the query by using a semijoin strategy. The DDBMS knows from the guard conditions that PROJS5 contains exactly those tuples satisfying (DNUM = 5) and that WORKS_ON5 contains all tuples to be joined with PROJS5; hence, subquery T1 can be executed at site 2, and the projected column ESSN can be sent to site 1. Subquery T2 can then be executed at site 1, and the result can be sent back to site 2, where the final query result is calculated and displayed to the user. An alternative strategy would be to send the query Q itself to site 1, which includes all the database tuples, where it would be executed locally and from which the result would be sent back to site 2. The query optimizer would estimate the costs of both strategies and would choose the one with the lower cost estimate.

23.6 Overview of Concurrency Control and Recovery in Distributed Databases*

For concurrency control and recovery purposes, numerous problems arise in a distributed DBMS environment that are not encountered in a centralized DBMS environment. These problems include the following:

- *Dealing with* **multiple copies** *of the data items:* The concurrency control method is responsible for maintaining consistency among these copies. The recovery method is responsible for making a copy consistent with other copies if the site on which the copy is stored fails and recovers later.

- *Failure of individual sites:* The DDBMS should continue to operate with its running sites, if possible, when one or more individual sites fail. When a site recovers, its local database must be brought up to date with the rest of the sites before it rejoins the system.

- *Failure of communication links:* The system must be able to deal with failure of one or more of the communication links that connect the sites. An extreme case of this problem is that **network partitioning** may occur. This breaks up the sites into two or more partitions, where the sites within each partition can communicate only with one another and not with sites in other partitions.

- *Distributed commit:* Problems can arise with committing a transaction that is accessing databases stored on multiple sites if some sites fail during the commit process. The **two-phase commit protocol** (see Section 19.5) is often used to deal with this problem.

- *Distributed deadlock:* Deadlock may occur among several sites, so techniques for dealing with deadlocks must be extended to take this into account.

Distributed concurrency control and recovery techniques must deal with these and other problems. In the following subsections, we review some of the techniques that have been suggested to deal with recovery and concurrency control in DDBMSs.

23.6.1 *Distributed Concurrency Control Based on a Distinguished Copy of a Data Item*

To deal with replicated data items in a distributed database, a number of concurrency control methods have been proposed that extend the concurrency control techniques for centralized databases. We discuss these techniques in the context of extending centralized *locking*. Similar extensions apply to other concurrency control techniques. The idea is to designate *a particular copy* of each data item as a **distinguished copy**. The locks for this data item are associated *with the distinguished copy*, and all locking and unlocking requests are sent to the site that contains that copy.

A number of different methods are based on this idea, but they differ in their method of choosing the distinguished copies. In the **primary site** technique, all distinguished copies are kept at the same site. A modification of this approach is the primary site with a **backup site**. Another approach is the **primary copy** method, where the distinguished copies of the various data items can be stored in different sites. A site that includes a distinguished copy of a data item basically acts as the **coordinator site** for concurrency control on that item. We discuss these techniques next.

Primary Site Technique. In this method a single **primary site** is designated to be the **coordinator site** *for all database items*. Hence, all locks are kept at that site, and all requests for locking or unlocking are sent to that site. This method is thus an extension of the centralized locking approach. For example, if all transactions follow the two-phase locking protocol, serializability is guaranteed. The advantage of this approach is that it is a simple extension of the centralized approach and hence is not overly complex. However, it has certain inherent disadvantages. One disadvantage is that all locking requests are sent to a single site, possibly overloading that site and causing a system bottleneck. Another disadvantage is that failure of the primary site paralyzes the system, since all locking information is kept at that site. This can limit system reliability and availability.

Although all locks are accessed at the primary site, the items themselves can be accessed at any site at which they reside. For example, once a transaction obtains a read_lock on a data item from the primary site, it can access any copy of that data item. However, once a transaction obtains a write_lock and updates a data item, the DDBMS is responsible for updating *all copies* of the data item before releasing the lock.

Primary Site with Backup Site. This approach addresses the second disadvantage of the primary site method by designating a second site to be a **backup site**. All locking information is maintained at both the primary and the backup sites. In case of failure of the primary site, the backup site can take over as primary site, and a new backup site can be chosen. This simplifies the process of recovery from failure of the primary site, since the backup site takes over and processing can resume after a new backup site is chosen and the lock status information is copied to that site. It slows down the process of acquiring locks, however, because all lock requests and granting of locks must be recorded at *both the primary and the backup sites* before a response is sent to the requesting transaction. The problem of the primary and backup sites becoming overloaded with requests and slowing down the system remains undiminished.

Primary Copy Technique. This method attempts to distribute the load of lock coordination among various sites by having the distinguished copies of different data items *stored at different sites*. Failure of one site affects any transactions that are accessing locks on items whose primary copies reside at that site, but other transactions are not affected. This method can also use backup sites to enhance reliability and availability.

Choosing a New Coordinator Site in Case of Failure. Whenever a coordinator site fails in any of the preceding techniques, the sites that are still running must choose a new coordinator. In the case of the primary site approach with *no* backup site, all executing transactions must be aborted and restarted, and the recovery process is quite tedious. Part of the recovery process involves choosing a new primary site and creating a lock manager process and a record of all lock information at that site. For methods that use backup sites, transaction processing is suspended while the backup site is designated as the new primary site and a new backup site is chosen and is sent copies of all the locking information from the new primary site.

If a backup site X is about to become the new primary site, X can choose the new backup site from among the system's running sites. However, if no backup site existed, or if both the primary and the backup sites are down, a process called **election** can be used to choose the new coordinator site. In this process, any site Y that attempts to communicate with the coordinator site repeatedly and fails to do so can assume that the coordinator is down and can start the election process by sending a message to all running sites proposing that Y become the new coordinator. As soon as Y receives a majority of yes votes, Y can declare that it is the new coordinator. The election algorithm itself is quite complex, but this is the main idea behind the election method. The algorithm also resolves any attempt by two or more sites to become coordinator at the same time. The references in the bibliography at the end of this chapter discuss the process in detail.

23.6.2 *Distributed Concurrency Control Based on Voting*

The concurrency control methods for replicated items discussed earlier all use the idea of a distinguished copy that maintains the locks for that item. In the **voting method**, there is no distinguished copy; rather, a lock request is sent to all sites that include a copy of the data item. Each copy maintains its own lock and can grant or deny the request for it. If a transaction that requests a lock is granted that lock by *a majority* of the copies, it holds the lock and informs *all copies* that it has been granted the lock. If a transaction does not receive a majority of votes granting it a lock within a certain *time-out period*, it cancels its request and informs all sites of the cancellation.

The voting method is considered a truly distributed concurrency control method, since the responsibility for a decision resides with all the sites involved. Simulation studies have shown that voting has higher message traffic among sites than do the distinguished copy methods. If the algorithm takes into account possible site failures during the voting process, it becomes extremely complex.

23.6.3 *Distributed Recovery*

The recovery process in distributed databases is quite involved. We give only a very brief idea of some of the issues here. In some cases it is quite difficult even to determine whether a site is down without exchanging numerous messages with other sites. For example, suppose that site X sends a message to site Y and expects a response from Y but does not receive it. There are several possible explanations:

- The message was not delivered to Y because of communication failure.
- Site Y is down and could not respond.
- Site Y is running and sent a response, but the response was not delivered.

Without additional information or the sending of additional messages, it is difficult to determine what actually happened.

Another problem with distributed recovery is distributed commit. When a transaction is updating data at several sites, it cannot commit until it is sure that the effect of the transaction on *every* site cannot be lost. This means that every site must first have recorded the local effects of the transactions permanently in the local site log on disk. The two-phase commit protocol, discussed in Section 19.5, is often used to ensure the correctness of distributed commit.

23.7 Summary

In this chapter we provided an introduction to distributed databases. This is a very broad topic, and we discussed only some of the basic techniques used with distributed databases. We first discussed the reasons for distribution and the potential advantages of distributed databases over centralized systems. We then described the client–server architecture of a DDBMS. We defined the concepts of data fragmentation, replication, and distribution, and we distinguished between horizontal and vertical fragments of relations. We discussed the use of data replication to improve system reliability and availability. We also defined the concept of distribution transparency and the related concepts of fragmentation transparency and replication transparency. We categorized DDBMSs by using criteria such as degree of homogeneity of software modules and degree of local autonomy.

In Section 23.5, we illustrated some of the techniques used in distributed query processing. The cost of communication among sites is considered a major factor in distributed query optimization. We compared different techniques for executing joins and presented the semijoin technique for joining relations that reside on different sites.

In Section 23.6, we briefly discussed the concurrency control and recovery techniques used in DDBMSs. We reviewed some of the additional problems that must be dealt with in a distributed environment that do not appear in a centralized environment.

Review Questions

23.1. What are the main reasons for and potential advantages of distributed databases?

23.2. What additional functions does a DDBMS have over a centralized DBMS?

23.3. What are the main software modules of a DDBMS? Discuss the main functions of each of these modules in the context of the client–server architecture.

23.4. What is a fragment of a relation? What are the main types of fragments? Why is fragmentation a useful concept in distributed database design?

23.5. Why is data replication useful in DDBMSs? What typical units of data are replicated?

23.6. What is meant by *data allocation* in distributed database design? What typical units of data are distributed over sites?

23.7. How is a horizontal partitioning of a relation specified? How can a relation be put back together from a complete horizontal partitioning?

23.8. How is a vertical partitioning of a relation specified? How can a relation be put back together from a complete vertical partitioning?

23.9. Discuss what is meant by the following terms: *degree of homogeneity of a DDBMS, degree of local autonomy of a DDBMS, federated DBMS, distribution transparency, fragmentation transparency, replication transparency, multidatabase system.*

23.10. Discuss the naming problem in distributed databases.

23.11. Discuss the different techniques for executing an equijoin of two files located at different sites. What main factors affect the cost of data transfer?

23.12. Discuss the semijoin method for executing an equijoin of two files located at different sites. Under what conditions is an equijoin strategy efficient?

23.13. Discuss the factors that affect query decomposition. How are guard conditions and attribute lists of fragments used during the query decomposition process?

23.14. How is the decomposition of an update request different from the decomposition of a query? How are guard conditions and attribute lists of fragments used during the decomposition of an update request?

23.15. Discuss the factors that do not appear in centralized systems that affect concurrency control and recovery in distributed systems.

23.16. Compare the primary site method with the primary copy method for distributed concurrency control. How does the use of backup sites affect each?

23.17. When are voting and elections used in distributed databases?

Exercises

23.18. Consider the data distribution of the COMPANY database, where the fragments at sites 2 and 3 are as shown in Figure 23.3 and the fragments at site 1 are as shown in Figure 6.6. For each of the following queries, show at least two strategies of decomposing and executing the query. Under what conditions would each of your strategies work well?

  a. For each employee in department 5, retrieve the employee name and the names of the employee's dependents.

  b. Print the names of all employees who work in department 5 but who work on some project *not* controlled by department 5.

Selected Bibliography

The textbooks by Ceri and Pelagatti (1984a) and Ozsu and Valduriez (1990) are devoted to distributed databases. Fragmentation is discussed in Chang and Cheng (1980) and Ceri and Pelagatti (1984a). Federated database systems are discussed in McLeod and Heimbigner (1985). Principles of computer communication networks are discussed in the textbook by Tanenbaum (1981).

Distributed query processing, optimization, and decomposition are discussed in the papers by Hevner and Yao (1979), Apers et al. (1983), Ceri and Pelagatti (1984), Bodorick et al. (1992), and Kerschberg et al. (1982). Bernstein and Goodman (1981) discusses the theory behind semijoin processing. Wong (1983) discusses the use of relationships in relation fragmentation. Concurrency control and recovery schemes are discussed and compared in Garcia-Molina (1978), Ries (1979), and Bernstein and Goodman (1981a). Elections in distributed systems are discussed in Garcia-Molina (1982).

A concurrency control technique for replicated data that is based on voting is presented by Thomas (1979). Gifford (1979) proposes the use of weighted voting, and Paris (1986) describes a method called voting with witnesses. Jajodia and Mutchler (1990) discusses dynamic voting. A technique called *available copy* is proposed by Bernstein and Goodman (1984), and one that uses the idea of a group is presented in ElAbbadi and Toueg (1988). Other recent work that discusses replicated data includes Gladney (1989), Agrawal and ElAbbadi (1990), ElAbbadi and Toueg (1990), Kumar and Segev (1993), Mukkamala (1989), and Wolfson and Milo (1991). Schlageter (1981), Bassiouni (1988), and Ceri and Owicki (1983) discuss optimistic methods for DDB concurrency control. Garcia-Molina (1983) and Kumar and Stonebraker (1987) discuss a technique that uses the semantics of the transactions. Distributed concurrency control techniques based on locking and distinguished copies are presented by Menasce et al. (1980) and Minoura and Wiederhold (1982). Obermark (1982) presents algorithms for distributed deadlock detection. Lamport (1978) discusses problems with generating unique timestamps in a distributed system.

A survey of recovery techniques in distributed systems is given by Kohler (1981). Skeen (1981) discusses nonblocking commit protocols, and Reed (1983) discusses atomic actions on distributed data. A book edited by Bhargava (1987) presents various approaches and techniques for distributed recovery and concurrency control.

Techniques for schema integration in federated databases are presented by Elmasri et al. (1986), Hayne and Ram (1990), and Motro (1987). Onuegbe et al. (1983) discusses the translation and local optimization problem. Elmagarmid and Helal (1988) and Gamal-Eldin et al. (1988) discuss the update problem in heterogeneous DDBSs. Heterogeneous distributed databases are also discussed in Kaul et al. (1990), Hsiao and Kamel (1989), and Perrizo et al. (1991).

Techniques for distributed data allocation are proposed in Blankenship et al. (1991), Morgan and Levin (1977), Ramamoorthy and Wah (1979), Chu and Hurley (1982), and Kamel and King (1985), among others. Distributed database design involving horizontal and vertical fragmentation, allocation, and replication is addressed in Ceri et al. (1983), Navathe et al. (1984), Ceri et al. (1982), Wilson and Navathe (1986), and Elmasri et al. (1987).

Recently, multidatabase systems and interoperability have become important topics. Techniques for dealing with semantic incompatibilities among multiple databases are examined in DeMichiel (1989), Siegel and Madnick (1991), Krishnamurthy et al. (1991), and Wang and Madnick (1989). Transaction processing in multidatabases is discussed in Mehrotra et al. (1992), Georgakopoulos et al. (1991), Elmagarmid et al. (1990), and Brietbart et al. (1990), among others.

A number of experimental distributed DBMSs have been implemented. These include distributed INGRES (Epstein et al. 1978), DDTS (Devor and Weeldreyer 1980), SDD-1 (Rothnie et al. 1980), System R* (Lindsay et al. 1984), SIRIUS-DELTA (Ferrier and Stangret 1982), and MULTIBASE (Smith et al. 1981). The OMNIBASE system (Rusinkiewicz et al. 1988) is a federated DDBMS. Many commercial DBMS vendors have announced distributed versions of their systems. Commercial DDBMSs are now applying the client–server architecture in their newer versions. Some issues concerning client–server systems are discussed in Carey et al. (1991), DeWitt et al. (1990), and Wang and Rowe (1991).

CHAPTER 24

Deductive Databases

A deductive database system is a database system that includes capabilities to define **rules**, which can deduce or infer additional information from the facts that are stored in a database. Because part of the theoretical foundation for some deductive database systems is mathematical logic, they are often referred to as **logic databases**. Other types of systems, referred to as **expert database systems** or **knowledge-based systems**, also incorporate reasoning and inferencing capabilities; such systems use techniques that were developed in the field of artificial intelligence, including semantic networks, frames, or rules for capturing domain-specific knowledge. The main differences between these systems and the ones we discuss here are twofold:

1. Knowledge-based expert systems have traditionally assumed that the data needed resides in main memory; hence, secondary storage management is not an issue. Deductive database systems attempt to change this restriction so that either a DBMS is enhanced to handle an expert system interface or an expert system is enhanced to handle secondary storage resident data.

2. The knowledge in an expert or knowledge-based system is extracted from application experts and refers to an application domain rather than to knowledge inherent in the data.

Whereas a close relationship exists between these and the deductive databases we are about to discuss, a detailed discussion goes beyond our scope. In this chapter, we only discuss logic-based systems and give an overview of the formal foundations of deductive database systems.

For a brief introduction to deductive databases, the reader can cover only Sections 24.1 and 24.2.

The bibliographic references for this chapter are placed at the anonymous ftp site bc.aw.com as bc/elmasri/ch24.biblio

24.1 Introduction to Deductive Databases

In a deductive database system, a declarative language is typically used to specify rules. By a **declarative language**, we mean a language that defines what a program wants to achieve rather than one that specifies the details of how to achieve it. An **inference engine** (or **deduction mechanism**) within the system can deduce new facts from the database by interpreting these rules. The model used for deductive databases is closely related to the relational data model, and particularly to the relational calculus formalism (see Chapter 8). It is also related to the field of **logic programming** and the **Prolog** language. The deductive database work based on logic has used Prolog as a starting point. A subset of Prolog called **Datalog** is used to define rules declaratively in conjunction with an existing set of relations, which are themselves treated as literals in the language. Although the language structure of Datalog resembles that of Prolog, its operational semantics—that is, how a Datalog program is to be executed—is left open.

A deductive database uses two main types of specifications: facts and rules. **Facts** are specified in a manner similar to the way relations are specified, except that it is not necessary to include the attribute names. Recall that a tuple in a relation describes some real-world fact whose meaning is partly determined by the attribute names. In a deductive database, the meaning of an attribute value in a tuple is determined solely by its *position* within the tuple. **Rules** are somewhat similar to relational views. They specify virtual relations that are not actually stored but that can be formed from the facts by applying inference mechanisms based on the rule specifications. The main difference between rules and views is that rules may involve recursion and hence may yield views that cannot be defined in terms of standard relational views.

The evaluation of Prolog programs is based on a technique called *backward chaining*, which involves a top–down evaluation of goals. In the deductive databases that use Datalog, attention has been devoted to handling large volumes of data stored in a relational database. Hence, evaluation techniques have been devised that resemble those for a bottom–up evaluation. Prolog suffers from the limitation that the order of specification of facts and rules is significant in evaluation; moreover, the order of literals within a rule is significant. The execution techniques for Datalog programs attempt to circumvent these problems.

We discussed object-oriented databases (OODBs) in Chapter 22. It is instructive to put deductive databases (DDBs) in a proper context with respect to OODBs. The emphasis in OODBs has been on providing a natural modeling mechanism for real-world objects by encapsulating their structure with behavior. The emphasis in DDBs, in contrast, has been on deriving new knowledge from existing data by supplying the real-world relationships in the form of rules. OODBs have traditionally left optimization of navigational queries up to the programmer, whereas DDBs use internal mechanisms for evaluation and optimization. Signs of a marriage of these two different enhancements to traditional databases have started appearing, in the form of adding deductive capabilities to OODBs and adding programming language interfaces like C^{++} to DDBs.

The rest of this chapter is organized as follows. In Section 24.2, we introduce the Prolog/Datalog notation; Datalog is a deductive query language similar to Prolog but more suitable for database applications. In Section 24.3 we discuss theoretical interpretations of the meaning of rules. The two standard approaches to inference mechanisms in logic programming languages, called *forward chaining* and *backward chaining*, are discussed in Section 24.4. Section 24.5 presents concepts related to Datalog programs, their evaluation, and their execution. Section 24.6 discusses a commercial system called the LDL deductive database system; next, in Section 24.7, we briefly cover two university research systems called CORAL and NAIL!

24.2 Prolog/Datalog Notation

In this section we introduce the basic notation for writing Prolog/Datalog rules. Then we discuss the two main theoretical **interpretations** of the meaning of rules in Section 24.3. The notation used in Prolog/Datalog is based on providing **predicates** with unique names. A predicate has an implicit meaning, which is suggested by the predicate name, and a fixed number of **arguments**. If the arguments are all constant values, the predicate simply states that a certain fact is true. If, on the other hand, the predicate has variables as arguments, it is either considered as a query or as part of a rule or constraint. Throughout this chapter, we adopt the Prolog convention that all **constant values** in a predicate either are *numeric* or are character strings starting with *lowercase letters* only, whereas **variable names** always start with an *uppercase letter*.

24.2.1 An Example

Consider the example shown in Figure 24.1, which is based on the relational database of Figure 6.6, but in a much simplified form. There are three predicate names: *supervise*, *superior*, and *subordinate*. The supervise predicate is defined via a set of facts, each of which has two arguments: a supervisor name, followed by the name of a *direct* supervisee (subordinate) of that supervisor. These facts correspond to the actual data that is stored in the database, and they can be considered as constituting a set of tuples in a relation SUPERVISE with two attributes whose schema is:

SUPERVISE(Supervisor,Supervisee)

Thus, supervise(X,Y) states the fact that "X supervises Y." Notice the omission of the attribute names in the Prolog notation. Attribute names are only represented by virtue of the position of each argument in a predicate: the first argument represents the supervisor, and the second argument represents a direct subordinate.

The other two predicate names are defined by rules. The main contribution of deductive databases is the ability to specify recursive rules, and to provide a framework for inferring new information based on the specified rules. A rule is of the form **head :- body**, and usually has a **single predicate** to the left of the :- symbol (called the **head** or left-hand side (LHS) or conclusion of the rule), and **one or more predicates** to the right of the :- symbol (called the **body** or right-hand side (RHS) or premise(s) of the rule). A predicate with constants as arguments is said to be **ground**; we also refer to it as an **instantiated predicate**. The arguments of the predicates that appear in a rule typically include a number of variable symbols, although predicates can also contain constants as arguments. A rule specifies that, if a particular assignment or **binding** of constant values

(a)

Facts
supervise(franklin,john).
supervise(franklin,ramesh).
supervise(franklin,joyce).
supervise(jennifer,alicia).
supervise(jennifer,ahmad).
supervise(james,franklin).
supervise(james,jennifer).
...
Rules
superior(X,Y) :- supervise(X,Y).
superior(X,Y) :- supervise(X,Z), superior(Z,Y).
subordinate(X,Y) :- superior(Y,X).
Queries
superior(james,Y)?
superior(james,joyce)?

(b)

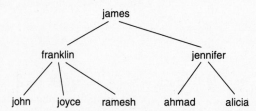

Figure 24.1   (a) Prolog notation for facts, rules, and queries. (b) The supervisory tree based on the given facts.

to the variables in the body (RHS predicates) makes *all* the RHS predicates **true**, it also makes the head (LHS predicate) true by using the same assignment of constant values to variables. Hence, a rule provides us with a way of generating new facts that are instantiations of the head of the rule. These new facts are based on facts that already exist, corresponding to the instantiations (or bindings) of predicates in the body of the rule.

Notice that, by listing multiple predicates in the body of a rule, we implicitly apply the **logical and** operator to these predicates. Hence, the commas between the RHS predicates may be read as meaning "and."

Consider the definition of the predicate superior in Figure 24.1, whose first argument is an employee name and whose second argument is an employee who is either a *direct* or an *indirect* subordinate of the first employee. By *indirect subordinate*, we mean the subordinate of some subordinate down to any number of levels. Thus, superior (X,Y) stands for the fact that "X is a superior of Y" through direct or indirect supervision. We can write two rules that together specify the meaning of the new predicate. The first rule under Rules in the figure states that, for every value of X and Y, if supervise(X,Y)— the rule body—is true, then superior(X,Y)—the rule head—is also true, since Y would be a direct subordinate of X (at one level down). This rule can be used to generate all direct superior/subordinate relationships from the facts that define the supervise predicate. The second recursive rule states that, if supervise(X,Z) *and* superior(Z,Y) are *both* true, then superior(X,Y) is also true. This is an example of a **recursive rule**, where one of the rule body predicates in the RHS is the same as the rule head predicate in the LHS. In general, the rule body defines a number of premises such that, if they are all true, we can deduce that the conclusion in the rule head is also true. Notice that, if we have two (or more) rules with the same head (LHS predicate), it is equivalent to saying that the predicate is true (that is, that it can be instantiated) if *either one* of the bodies is true; and hence, it is equivalent to a **logical or** operation. For example, if we have two rules X :- Y and X :- Z, they are equivalent to a rule X :- Y **or** Z. The latter form is not used in deductive systems, however, because it is not in the standard form of rule, called a Horn clause, as we discuss in Section 24.2.3.

A Prolog system contains a number of **built-in** predicates that the system can interpret directly. These typically include the equality comparison operator =(X,Y), which returns true if X and Y are identical and can also be written as X=Y by using the standard infix notation.* Other comparison operators for numbers, such as $<$, $<=$, $>$, and $>=$, can be treated as binary functions. Arithmetic functions such as $+$, $-$, $*$, and $/$ can be used as arguments in predicates in Prolog. In contrast, Datalog (in its basic form) does *not* allow functions such as arithmetic operations as arguments; indeed, this is one of the main differences between Prolog and Datalog. However, later extensions to Datalog have been proposed to include functions.

A **query** typically involves a predicate symbol with some variable arguments, and its meaning (or "answer") is to deduce the different constant combinations that, when **bound** (assigned) to the variables, can make the predicate true. For example, the first query in Figure 24.1 requests the names of all subordinates of "james" at any level. A different type of query, which has only constant symbols as arguments, returns either a true or a false result, depending on whether the arguments provided can be deduced from the facts and rules. For example, the second query in Figure 24.1 returns true if superior(james,joyce) can be deduced, and returns false otherwise.

24.2.2 *Datalog Notation*

We provide here some basic concepts and notation associated with Datalog. In Datalog, as in other logic-based languages, a program is built from basic objects called **atomic formulas**. It is customary to define the syntax of logic-based languages by describing the syntax of atomic formulas and identifying how they can be combined to form a program. In Datalog, atomic formulas are **literals** of the form $p(a_1, a_2, \ldots, a_n)$, where p is the predicate name and n is the number of arguments for predicate p. Different predicate symbols can have different numbers of arguments, and the number of arguments n of predicate p is sometimes called the **arity** of p. The arguments can be either constant values or variable names. As mentioned earlier, we use the convention that constant values either are numeric or start with a *lowercase* character, whereas variable names always start with an *uppercase* character.

---

*A Prolog system typically has a number of different equality predicates that have different interpretations.

A number of **built-in predicates** are included in Datalog, which can also be used to construct atomic formulas. The built-in predicates are of two main types: the binary comparison predicates $<$ (less), $<=$ (less_or_equal), $>$ (greater), and $>=$ (greater_or_equal) over ordered domains; and the comparison predicates $=$ (equal) and $/=$ (not_equal) over ordered or unordered domains. These can be used as binary predicates with the same syntax as other predicates—for example by writing less(X,3)—or they can be specified by using the customary infix notation X<3. Notice that, because the domains of these predicates are potentially infinite, they should be used with care in rule definitions. For example, the predicate greater(X,3), if used alone, generates an infinite set of values for X that satisfy the predicate (all integer numbers greater than 3). We discuss this problem a bit later.

A **literal** is either an atomic formula as defined earlier—called a **positive literal**—or an atomic formula preceded by **not**. The latter is a negated atomic formula, called a **negative literal**. Datalog programs can be considered to be a *subset* of the **predicate calculus** formulas, which are somewhat similar to the formulas of the domain relational calculus (see Chapter 8). In Datalog, however, these formulas are first converted into what is known as **clausal form** before they are expressed in Datalog; and only formulas given in a restricted clausal form, called **Horn clauses,**[*] can be used in Datalog.

24.2.3 *Clausal Form and Horn Clauses*

Recall from Section 8.1.2 that a formula in the relational calculus is a condition that includes predicates called *atoms* (based on relation names). In addition, a formula can have quantifiers—namely, the *universal quantifier* (for all) and the *existential quantifier* (there exists). In clausal form, a formula must be transformed into another formula with the following characteristics:

- All variables in the formula are universally quantified. Hence, it is not necessary to include the universal quantifiers (for all) explicitly; the quantifiers are removed, and all variables in the formula are *implicitly* quantified by the universal quantifier.

- In clausal form, the formula is made up of a number of **clauses**, where *each clause* is composed of a number of *literals* connected by OR logical connectives only. Hence, each **clause** is a *disjunction* of literals.

- The *clauses themselves* are connected by AND logical connectives only, to form a formula. Hence, the *clausal form of a formula* is a *conjunction* of clauses.

It can be shown that any formula can be converted into clausal form. For our purposes, we are mainly interested in the form of the individual clauses, each of which is a disjunction of literals. Recall that literals can be positive literals or negative literals. Consider a clause of the form:

$$\text{not}(P_1) \text{ OR } \text{not}(P_2) \text{ OR } \cdots \text{ OR } \text{not}(P_n) \text{ OR } Q_1 \text{ OR } Q_2 \text{ OR } \cdots \text{ OR } Q_m \qquad (1)$$

---

[*]Named after the mathematician Alfred Horn.

This clause has n negative literals and m positive literals. Such a clause can be transformed into the following equivalent logical formula:

$$P_1 \text{ AND } P_2 \text{ AND } \cdots \text{ AND } P_n => Q_1 \text{ OR } Q_2 \text{ OR } \cdots \text{ OR } Q_m \qquad (2)$$

where => is the **implies** symbol. The formulas (1) and (2) are equivalent, meaning that their truth values are always the same. This is the case because, if all the P_i literals (i = 1, 2, ..., n) are true, the formula (2) is true only if at least one of the Q_i's is true, which is the meaning of the => (implies) symbol. Similarly, for formula (1), if all the P_i literals (i = 1, 2, ..., n) are true, their negations are all false; so in this case formula (1) is true only if at least one of the Q_i's is true. In Datalog, rules are expressed as a restricted form of clauses called **Horn clauses**, in which a clause can contain *at most one* positive literal. Hence, a Horn clause is either of the form

$$\text{not}(P_1) \text{ OR } \text{not}(P_2) \text{ OR } \cdots \text{ OR } \text{not}(P_n) \text{ OR } Q \qquad (3)$$

or of the form

$$\text{not}(P_1) \text{ OR } \text{not}(P_2) \text{ OR } \cdots \text{ OR } \text{not}(P_n) \qquad (4)$$

The Horn clause in (3) can be transformed into the clause:

$$P_1 \text{ AND } P_2 \text{ AND } \cdots \text{ AND } P_n => Q \qquad (5)$$

which is written in Datalog as the following rule:

$$Q \text{ :- } P_1, P_2, \ldots, P_n. \qquad (6)$$

The Horn clause in (4) can be transformed into:

$$P_1 \text{ AND } P_2 \text{ AND } \cdots \text{ AND } P_n => \qquad (7)$$

which is written in Datalog as follows:

$$P_1, P_2, \ldots, P_n. \qquad (8)$$

A Datalog rule, as in (6), is hence a Horn clause; and its meaning (based on formula (5)) is that, if the predicates P_1 and P_2 and ... and P_n are all true for a particular binding to their variable arguments, then Q is also true and can hence be inferred. The Datalog expression (8) can be considered as an integrity constraint, where all the predicates must be true to satisfy the query.

In general, a query in Datalog consists of two components:

• A Datalog program, which is a finite set of rules.
• A literal $P(X_1, X_2, \ldots, X_n)$, where each X_i is a variable or a constant.

A Prolog or Datalog system has an internal **inference engine** that can be used to process and compute the results of such queries. Prolog inference engines typically return one result to the query (that is, one set of values for the variables in the query) at a time and must be prompted to return additional results.

24.3 Interpretations of Rules*

There are two main alternatives for interpreting the theoretical meaning of rules: proof-theoretic and model-theoretic. In practical systems, the inference mechanism within a system defines the exact interpretation, which may not coincide with either of the two theoretical interpretations. The inference mechanism is a computational procedure and hence provides a computational interpretation of the meaning of rules. In this section, we first discuss the two theoretical interpretations. Inference mechanisms are then discussed briefly as a way of defining the meaning of rules. We discuss specific inference mechanisms in more detail in Section 24.4.

One interpretation is called the **proof-theoretic** interpretation of rules. In this interpretation, we consider the facts and rules to be true statements, or **axioms. Ground axioms** contain no variables. The facts are ground axioms that are given to be true. Rules are called **deductive axioms**, since they can be used to deduce new facts. The deductive axioms can be used to construct proofs that derive new facts from existing facts. For example, Figure 24.2 shows how to prove the fact superior(james, ahmad) from the rules and facts given in Figure 24.1. The proof-theoretic interpretation gives us a procedural or computational approach for computing an answer to the Datalog query. The process of proving whether a certain fact (theorem) holds is otherwise known as *theorem proving*.

The second type of interpretation is called the **model-theoretic** interpretation. Here, given a finite* or an infinite domain of constant values, we assign to a predicate every possible combination of values as arguments. Then we must determine whether the predicate is true or false. In general, it is sufficient to specify the combinations of arguments that make the predicate true, and to state that all other combinations make the predicate false. If this is done for every predicate, it is called an **interpretation** of the set of predicates. For example, consider the interpretation shown in Figure 24.3 for the predicates supervise and superior. This interpretation assigns a truth value (true or false) to every possible combination of argument values (from a finite domain) for the two predicates.

An interpretation is called a **model** for a *specific set of rules* if those rules are *always true* under that interpretation; that is, for any values assigned to the variables in the rules, the head of the rules is true when we substitute the truth values assigned to the predicates in the body of the rule by that interpretation. Hence, whenever a particular substitution (binding) to the variables in the rules is applied, if all the predicates in the body of a rule are true under the interpretation, the predicate in the head of the rule must also be true. The interpretation shown in Figure 24.3 is a model for the two rules shown, since it can never cause the rules to be violated. Notice that a rule is violated if a particular binding of constants to the variables make all the predicates in the rule body true but makes the predicate in the rule head false. For example, if supervise(a,b) and superior(b,c) are both true under some interpretation, but superior(a,c) is not true, the interpretation cannot be a model for the recursive rule:

superior(X,Y) :- supervise(X,Z), superior(Z,Y)

In the model-theoretic approach, the meaning of the rules is established by providing a model for these rules. We can consider the head of a rule to be a query defined

---

*The most commonly chosen domain is finite and is called the "Herbrand Universe."

1. superior(X,Y) :- supervise(X,Y).	(rule 1)
2. superior(X,Y) :- supervise(X,Z), superior(Z,Y).	(rule 2)
3. supervise(jennifer,ahmad).	(ground axiom, given)
4. supervise(james,jennifer).	(ground axiom, given)
5. superior(jennifer,ahmad).	(apply rule 1 on 3)
6. superior(james,ahmad) :- supervise(james,jennifer), superior(jennifer,ahmad).	(apply rule 2 on 4 and 5)

Figure 24.2 Proving a new fact.

by its body (RHS predicates). The result of the query is the set of values (bindings for the arguments of the predicates) that are defined to make the predicate true.

A model is called a **minimal model** for a set of rules if we cannot change any fact from true to false and still get a model for these rules. For example, consider the interpretation in Figure 24.3, and assume that the supervise predicate is defined by a set of known facts, whereas the superior predicate is defined as an interpretation (model) for the rules. Suppose that we add the predicate superior(james, bob) to the true predicates. This remains a model for the rules shown, but it is not a minimal model, since changing

Rules

superior(X,Y) :- supervise(X,Y).
superior(X,Y) :- supervise(X,Z), superior(Z,Y).

Interpretation

Known Facts:

supervise(franklin,john) is **true**.
supervise(franklin,ramesh) is **true**.
supervise(franklin,joyce) is **true**.
supervise(jennifer,alicia) is **true**.
supervise(jennifer,ahmad) is **true**.
supervise(james,franklin) is **true**.
supervise(james,jennifer) is **true**.
supervise(X,Y) is **false** for all other possible (X,Y) combinations.

Derived Facts:

superior(franklin,john) is **true**.
superior(franklin,ramesh) is **true**.
superior(franklin,joyce) is **true**.
superior(jennifer,alicia) is **true**.
superior(jennifer,ahmad) is **true**.
superior(james,franklin) is **true**.
superior(james,jennifer) is **true**.
superior(james,john) is **true**.
superior(james,ramesh) is **true**.
superior(james,joyce) is **true**.
superior(james,alicia) is **true**.
superior(james,ahmad) is **true**.
superior(X,Y) is **false** for all other possible (X,Y) combinations.

Figure 24.3 An interpretation that is a model for the two rules listed.

the truth value of superior(james,bob) from true to false still provides us with a model for the rules. The model shown in Figure 24.3 is the minimal model for the set of facts that are defined by the supervise predicate.

In general, the minimal model that corresponds to a given set of facts in the model-theoretic interpretation should be the same as the facts generated by the proof-theoretic interpretation for the same original set of ground and deductive axioms. However, this is generally true only for rules with a simple structure. Once we allow negation in the specification of rules, the correspondence between interpretations *does not* hold. In fact, with negation, numerous minimal models are possible for a given set of facts.

A third approach to interpreting the meaning of rules involves defining an inference mechanism that is used by the system to deduce facts from the rules. This inference mechanism would define a **computational interpretation** to the meaning of the rules. The Prolog logic programming language uses its inference mechanism to define the meaning of the rules and facts in a Prolog program. Not all Prolog programs correspond to the proof-theoretic or model-theoretic interpretations; it depends on the type of rules in the program. However, for many simple Prolog programs, the Prolog inference mechanism infers the facts that correspond either to the proof-theoretic interpretation or to a minimal model under the model-theoretic interpretation.

24.4 Basic Inference Mechanisms for Logic Programs⋆

In this section we discuss the two main approaches to computational inference mechanisms that are based on the proof-theoretic interpretation of rules. In Section 24.4.1, we discuss bottom–up inference mechanisms, where the inference starts from the given facts and generates additional facts that are matched to the goal of a query. Section 24.4.2 discusses top–down inference mechanisms, where the inference starts from the goal of a query and tries to find constant values that make it true. The latter approach has been used in Prolog.

24.4.1 *Bottom–Up Inference Mechanisms (Forward Chaining)*

In bottom–up inference, which is also called **forward chaining** or **bottom–up resolution**, the inference engine starts with the facts and applies the rules to generate new facts. As facts are generated, they are checked against the query predicate goal for a match. The term *forward chaining* indicates that the inference moves forward from the facts toward the goal. For example, consider the first query shown in Figure 24.1, and assume that the facts and rules shown are the only ones that hold. In bottom–up inference, the inference mechanism first checks whether any of the existing facts directly matches the query—superior(james,Y)?—that is given. Since all the facts are for the supervise predicate, no match is found; so the first rule is now applied to the existing facts to generate new facts. This causes the facts for the superior predicate to be generated by the first (nonrecursive) rule in the order shown in Figure 24.3. As each fact is generated, it is checked for a match against the query predicate. No matches are found until the fact superior(james,franklin) is generated, which results in the first answer to the query—namely, Y=franklin.

In a Prolog-like system, where one answer at a time is generated, additional prompts must be entered to search for the next answer; in this case, the system continues to generate new facts and returns the next answer, Y=jennifer, from the generated fact superior(james,jennifer). At this point, all possible applications of the first (nonrecursive) rule are exhausted, having generated the first seven facts of the superior predicate that are shown in Figure 24.3. If additional results are needed, the inference continues to the next (recursive) rule to generate additional facts. It must now match each supervise fact with each superior fact, searching for a match in the second argument of supervise with the first argument of superior, in order to satisfy both the RHS predicates: supervise(X,Z) *and* superior(Z,Y). This results in the generation of the subsequent facts listed in Figure 24.3, and the additional answers Y=john, Y=ramesh, Y=joyce, Y=alicia, and Y=ahmad. Any new superior facts that are generated recursively must also be matched, using the recursive rule until no more facts can be generated. In this particular example, no additional facts are generated.

In the bottom–up approach, a search strategy to generate only the facts that are relevant to a query should be used; otherwise, all possible facts are generated in some order that is irrelevant to the particular query, which can be very inefficient for large sets of rules and facts.

24.4.2 *Top–Down Inference Mechanisms (Backward Chaining)*

The top–down inference mechanism is the one used in Prolog interpreters. The top–down inference, also called **backward chaining** and **top–down resolution**, starts with the query predicate goal and attempts to find matches to the variables that lead to valid facts in the database. The term *backward chaining* indicates that the inference moves backward from the intended goal to determine facts that would satisfy the goal. In this approach, facts are not explicitly generated, as they are in forward chaining. For example, in processing the query superior(james,Y)?, the system first searches for any facts with the superior predicate whose first argument matches "james". If any such facts exist, the system generates the results in the same order in which the facts were specified. Since there are no such facts in our example, the system then locates the first rule whose head (LHS) has the same predicate name as the query, leading to the (nonrecursive) rule:

superior(X,Y) :- supervise(X,Y)

The inference mechanism then matches X to james, leading to the rule:

superior(james,Y) :- supervise(james,Y)

The variable X is now said to be **bound** to the value "james". The system proceeds to substitute superior(james,Y) with supervise(james,Y), and it searches for facts that match supervise(james,Y) to find an answer for Y. The facts are searched in the order in which they are listed in the program, leading to the first match Y=franklin, followed by the match Y=jennifer. At this point, the search using the first rule is exhausted, so the system searches for the next rule whose head (LHS) has the predicate name superior, which leads to the recursive rule. The inference mechanism then binds X to "james", resulting in the modified rule:

superior(james,Y) :- supervise(james,Z), superior(Z,Y)

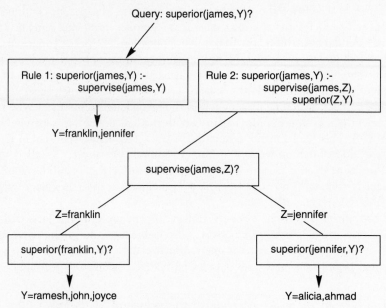

Figure 24.4   Top–down evaluation of a query.

It then substitutes the LHS with the RHS and starts searching for facts that satisfy *both* of the RHS predicates. These are now called **subgoals** of the query. In this case, to find a match for the query, the system must find facts that satisfy more than one predicate—supervise(james,Z) *and* superior(Z,Y)—which is known as a **compound goal**. To satisfy a compound goal, a standard approach is to employ **depth-first** search, meaning that the program first tries to find a binding that makes the first predicate true, and then moves on to search for a corresponding match for the next predicate. If the first predicate binding does not result in any match that makes the second predicate true, the system **backtracks** and searches for the next binding that makes the first predicate true, and then continues the search as before.

In our example, the system finds the match supervise(james,franklin) for the first subgoal, which **binds** Z to "franklin", resulting in Z=franklin. It then searches for a match to superior(franklin,Y) for the second subgoal, which continues the matching process by utilizing the first (nonrecursive) rule again and eventually returns Y=john, Y=ramesh, and Y=joyce. The process is then repeated with Z=jennifer, returning Y=alicia and Y=ahmad. These are shown pictorially in Figure 24.4.

In this example, there are no additional "third-level" superior relationships; but if there were, these would also be generated at their appropriate order in the inference process (see Exercise 24.1).*

---

*Notice that, in our example, the order of search is quite similar for both forward and backward chaining. However, this is not generally the case in more complex cases.

There has been a lot of research in devising more efficient inference mechanisms in the field of logic programming. In particular, one can employ **breadth-first** search techniques instead of depth-first search for compound goals, where the search for matches to multiple subgoals can proceed in parallel. Optimization techniques designed to guide the search by using more promising rules first during inference have also been proposed.

The top–down depth-first inference mechanism leads to certain problems because of its dependence on the order in which rules and facts are written. For example, when rules are written to define a predicate recursively, such as in the definition of the superior predicate, one must write the subgoals in the order shown so that no infinite recursion occurs during the inference process. Another problem occurs when rule definitions involve negation, which we will not be able to address in detail, except for a brief mention in Section 24.5.5. These problems have led to the definition of some different inference mechanisms or query evaluation strategies for the Datalog language in the case of applications that involve databases.

24.5 Datalog Programs and Their Evaluation[*]

There are two main methods of defining the truth values of predicates in actual Datalog programs. **Fact-defined predicates** (or **relations**) are defined by listing all the combinations of values (the tuples) that make the predicate true. These correspond to base relations whose contents are stored in a database system. Figure 24.5 shows the fact-defined predicates employee, male, female, department, supervise, project, and workson, which correspond to part of the relational database shown in Figure 6.6. **Rule-defined predicates** (or **views**) are defined by being the head (LHS) of one or more Datalog rules; they correspond to *virtual relations* whose contents can be inferred by the inference engine. Figure 24.6 shows a number of rule-defined predicates that refer to the database of Figure 24.5.

24.5.1 *Safety of Programs*

A program or a rule is said to be **safe** if it generates a *finite* set of facts. The general theoretical problem of determining whether a set of rules is safe is undecidable. However, one can determine the safety of restricted forms of rules. For example, the rules shown in Figure 24.5 are safe. One situation where we get unsafe rules that can generate an infinite number of facts arises when one of the variables in the rule can range over an infinite domain of values, and that variable is not limited to ranging over a finite relation. For example, consider the rule:

    big_salary(Y) :- Y>60000

Here, we can get an infinite result if Y ranges over all possible integers. But suppose that we change the rule as follows:

    big_salary(Y) :- employee(X),salary(X,Y),Y>60000

employee(john).	male(john).
employee(franklin).	male(franklin).
employee(alicia).	male(ramesh).
employee(jennifer).	male(ahmad).
employee(ramesh).	male(james).
employee(joyce).	female(alicia).
employee(ahmad).	female(jennifer).
employee(james).	female(joyce).
salary(john,30000).	project(productx).
salary(franklin,40000).	project(producty).
salary(alicia,25000).	project(productz).
salary(jennifer,43000).	project(computerization).
salary(ramesh,38000).	project(reorganization).
salary(joyce,25000).	project(newbenefits).
salary(ahmad,25000).	workson(john,productx,32).
salary(james,55000).	workson(john,producty,8).
department(john,research).	workson(ramesh,productz,40).
department(franklin,research).	workson(joyce,productx,20).
department(alicia,administration).	workson(joyce,producty,20).
department(jennifer,administration).	workson(franklin,producty,10).
department(ramesh,research).	workson(franklin,productz,10).
department(joyce,research).	workson(franklin,computerization,10).
department(ahmad,administration).	workson(franklin,reorganization,10).
department(james,headquarters).	workson(alicia,newbenefits,30).
supervise(franklin,john).	workson(alicia,computerization,10).
supervise(franklin,ramesh).	workson(ahmad,computerization,35).
supervise(franklin,joyce).	workson(ahmad,newbenefits,5).
supervise(jennifer,alicia).	workson(jennifer,newbenefits,20).
supervise(jennifer,ahmad).	workson(jennifer,reorganization,15).
supervise(james,franklin).	workson(james,reorganization,10).
supervise(james,jennifer).	

Figure 24.5   Fact predicates that describe part of the database in Figure 6.6.

In the second rule, the result is not infinite, since the values that Y can be bound to are now restricted to values that are the salary of some employee in the database—presumably, a finite set of values. We can also rewrite the rule as follows:

```
big_salary(Y) :- Y>60000,employee(X),salary(X,Y)
```

In this case, the rule is still theoretically safe. Notice, however, that, in Prolog or any other system that uses a top–down, depth-first inference mechanism, the rule creates an infinite loop, since we first search for a value for Y and then check whether it is a salary of an employee. The result is generation of an infinite number of Y values, even though

```
superior(X,Y) :- supervise(X,Y).
superior(X,Y) :- supervise(X,Z), superior(Z,Y).
subordinate(X,Y) :- superior(Y,X).
supervisor(X) :- employee(X), supervise(X,Y).
over_40K_emp(X) :- employee(X), salary(X,Y), Y>=40000.
under_40K_supervisor(X) :- supervisor(X), not(over_40_K_emp(X)).
main_productx_emp(X) :- employee(X), workson(X,productx,Y), Y>=20.
president(X) :- employee(X), not(supervise(Y,X)).
```

Figure 24.6   Rule-defined predicates.

these, after a certain point, cannot lead to a set of true RHS predicates. One definition of Datalog considers both rules to be safe, since it does not depend on a particular inference mechanism. Nonetheless, it is generally advisable to write such a rule in the safest form, with the predicates that restrict possible bindings of variables placed first. As another example of an unsafe rule, consider the following rule:

    has_something(X,Y) :- employee(X)

Here, an infinite number of Y values can again be generated, since the variable Y appears only in the head of the rule and hence is not limited to a finite set of values. To define safe rules more formally, we use the concept of a limited variable. A variable X is **limited** in a rule if: (a) it appears in a regular (not built-in) predicate in the body of the rule; (b) it appears in a predicate of the form X=c or c=X or (c1<=X and X<=c2) in the rule body, where c, c1, and c2 are constant values; or (c) it appears in a predicate of the form X=Y or Y=X in the rule body, where Y is a limited variable. A rule is said to be **safe** if all its variables are limited.

24.5.2 *Use of Relational Operations*

It is straightforward to specify many operations of the relational algebra in the form of Datalog rules that define the result of applying these operations on the database relations (fact predicates). This means that relational queries and views based on queries can easily be specified in Datalog. The additional power that Datalog provides is in the specification of recursive queries, and views based on recursive queries. In this section, we show how some of the standard relational operations can be specified as Datalog rules. Let us assume that the base relations (fact-defined predicates) rel_one, rel_two, and rel_three, whose schemas are shown in Figure 24.7, are available, and that the relational operations are applied to those relations. Notice that, in Datalog, we do not need to specify the attribute names in Figure 24.7; rather, the arity of each predicate is the important aspect. In a practical system, the domain (data type) of each attribute is also important for operations such as UNION, INTERSECTION, and JOIN, and we assume that the attribute types are compatible for the various operations, as discussed in Chapter 6.

Figure 24.7 illustrates a number of basic relational operations. Notice that, if the Datalog model is based on the relational model and hence assumes that predicates (fact relations and query results) specify sets of tuples, duplicate tuples in the same predicate are automatically eliminated. This may or may not be true, depending on the Datalog inference engine. However, it is definitely *not* the case in Prolog, so any of the rules in Figure 24.7 that involve duplicate elimination are not correct for Prolog. For example, if we want to specify Prolog rules for the UNION operation with duplicate elimination, we must rewrite them as follows:

    union_one_two(X,Y,Z) :- rel_one(X,Y,Z).
    union_one_two(X,Y,Z) :- rel_two(X,Y,Z), not(rel_one(X,Y,Z)).

However, the rules shown in Figure 24.6 should work for Datalog, if duplicate records are automatically eliminated. Similarly, the rules for the Project operation shown in Figure 24.7 should work for Datalog in this case, but they are not correct for Prolog, since duplicates would appear in the latter case.

```
rel_one(A,B,C).
rel_two(D,E,F).
rel_three(G,H,I,J).

select_one_A_eq_c(X,Y,Z) :- rel_one(c,Y,Z).
select_one_B_less_5(X,Y,Z) :- rel_one(X,Y,Z), Y<5.
select_one_A_eq_c_and_B_less_5(X,Y,Z) :- rel_one(c,Y,Z), Y<5.

select_one_A_eq_c_or_B_less_5(X,Y,Z) :- rel_one(c,Y,Z).
select_one_A_eq_c_or_B_less_5(X,Y,Z) :- rel_one(X,Y,Z), Y<5.

project_three_on_G_H(W,X) :- rel_three(W,X,Y,Z).

union_one_two(X,Y,Z) :- rel_one(X,Y,Z).
union_one_two(X,Y,Z) :- rel_two(X,Y,Z).

intersect_one_two(X,Y,Z) :- rel_one(X,Y,Z), rel_two(X,Y,Z).

difference_two_one(X,Y,Z) :- rel_two(X,Y,Z), not(rel_one(X,Y,Z)).

cart_prod_one_three(T,U,V,W,X,Y,Z) :-
                    rel_one(T,U,V), rel_three(W,X,Y,Z).

natural_join_one_three_C_eq_G(U,V,W,X,Y,Z) :-
                    rel_one(U,V,W), rel_three(W,X,Y,Z).
```

Figure 24.7 Predicates for illustrating relational operations.

24.5.3 *Evaluation of Nonrecursive Datalog Queries*

Implementations of Prolog have been based on the backward chaining approach where
ordering of predicates is significant. Since Datalog has been defined as a subset of Prolog,
the inference mechanisms for logic programming languages, such as forward chaining or
backward chaining, can be used with Datalog. However, if Datalog is to be used in a
deductive database system, it is appropriate to define an inference mechanism based on
relational database query processing concepts. In relational query processing, the inherent strategy involves a bottom–up evaluation, starting with base relations; the order of
operations is kept flexible and subject to query optimization. In this section, we discuss
an inference mechanism based on relational operations that can be applied to **nonrecursive** Datalog queries. We use the fact and rule base shown in Figures 24.5 and 24.6
to illustrate our discussion.

    If a query involves only fact-defined predicates, the inference becomes one of
searching among the facts for the query result. For example, a query such as

    department(X,research)?

is a selection of all employee names X who work for the "research" department, and it
can be answered by searching through the fact-defined predicate department(X,Y). Such
a query is similar to a relational SELECT operation on a base relation, and it can be
handled by the database query processing and optimization techniques discussed in
Chapter 16.

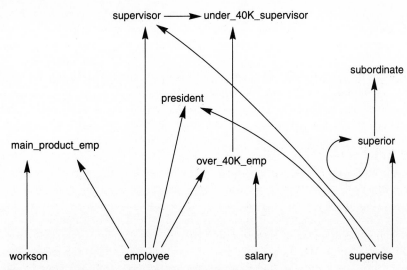

Figure 24.8   Predicate dependency graph for Figure 24.6.

When a query involves rule-defined predicates, the inference mechanism must compute the result based on the rule definitions. If a query is nonrecursive and involves a predicate p that appears as the head of a rule p :- $p_1, p_2, \ldots, p_n$, the strategy is first to compute the relations corresponding to $p_1, p_2, \ldots, p_n$ and then to compute the relation corresponding to p, which can be used to generate the query result. To determine the relationship among predicates, it is useful to keep track of the dependency among the predicates of a deductive database in a **predicate dependency graph**. Figure 24.8 shows the predicate dependency graph for the fact and rule predicates shown in Figures 24.6 and 24.7. The dependency graph contains a **node** for each predicate. Whenever a predicate A is specified in the body (RHS) of a rule, and the head (LHS) of that rule is the predicate B, we say that B **depends on** A, and we draw a directed edge from A to B. This indicates that, in order to compute the facts for the predicate B (the rule head), we must first compute the facts for all the predicates A in the rule body. If the dependency graph has no cycles, we call the rule set **nonrecursive**. If there is at least one cycle, the rule set is called **recursive**. In Figure 24.8, there is one recursively defined predicate—namely, superior—which has a recursive edge pointing back to itself, since its rule is recursively defined. In addition, because the predicate subordinate depends on superior, it also requires recursion in computing its result.

A query that includes only nonrecursive predicates is called a **nonrecursive query**. In this section, we only discuss inference mechanisms for nonrecursive queries. In Figure 24.8, any query that does not involve the predicates subordinate or superior is nonrecursive. In the predicate dependency graph, the nodes corresponding to fact-defined predicates do not have any incoming edges, since all fact-defined predicates have their facts stored in a database relation. The contents of a fact-defined predicate can be computed independently of other predicates by retrieving the tuples in the corresponding database relation.

The main function of an inference mechanism is to compute the facts that correspond to query predicates. This can be accomplished by generating a **relational expression** involving relational database operators as SELECT, PROJECT, JOIN, UNION, and SET DIFFERENCE (with appropriate provision for dealing with safety issues) that, when executed, provides the query result. The query can then be executed by utilizing the internal query processing and optimization operations of a relational database management system. Whenever the inference mechanism needs to compute the fact set corresponding to a nonrecursive rule-defined predicate p, it first locates all the rules that have p as their head. The idea is to compute the fact set for each such rule and then to apply the *union* operation to the results, since union corresponds to a logical OR operation. The dependency graph indicates all predicates q on which each p depends, and since we assume that the predicate is nonrecursive, we can always determine a partial order among such predicates q. Before computing the fact set for p, we first compute the fact sets for all predicates q on which p depends, based on their partial order. For example, if a query involves the predicate under_40K_supervisor, we must first compute both supervisor and over_40K_emp. Since the latter two depend only on the fact-defined predicates employee, salary, and supervise, they can be computed directly from the stored database relations.

We must also deal with built-in predicates, such as the comparison operators $>$, $<$, and $=$, if they appear in a rule body. In specifying an inference algorithm that computes the fact set of any nonrecursive query, it is common to convert the rules into a canonical form called **rectified rules**. A rule is said to be rectified if all the arguments in the predicate of the rule head are *distinct variables*. If a rule head has constants, or if a variable is repeated twice in the rule head, it can easily be rectified: a constant c is replaced by a variable X, and a predicate equal(X,c) is added to the rule body. Similarly, if a variable Y appears twice in a rule head, one of those occurrences is replaced by another variable Z, and a predicate equal(Y,Z) is added to the rule body.

Notice that, in the case of nonrecursive queries, the evaluation of the query can be expressed as a tree whose leaves are the base relations. What is needed is appropriate application of the relational operations of SELECT, PROJECT, and JOIN, together with set operations of UNION and SET DIFFERENCE, until the predicate in the query gets evaluated. An outline of an inference algorithm GET_EXPR(Q) that generates a relational expression for computing the result of a DATALOG query $Q = p(arg_1, arg_2, . . ., arg_n)$ can informally be stated as follows:

1. Locate all rules S whose head involves the predicate p. If there are no such rules, then p is a fact-defined predicate corresponding to some database relation R_p; in this case, one of the following expressions is returned and the algorithm is terminated (we use the notation $i to refer to the name of the ith attribute of relation R_p);

    a. If all arguments are distinct variables, the relational expression returned is R_p.

    b. If some arguments are constants or if the same variable appears in more than one argument position, the expression returned is

        SELECT<condition>(R_p),

where the selection <condition> is a conjunctive condition made up of a number of simple conditions connected by AND, and constructed as follows:

    i. If a constant c appears as argument i, include a simple condition ($i = c) in the conjunction.

    ii. If the same variable appears in both argument locations j and k, include a condition ($j = $k) in the conjunction.

  c. For an argument that is not present in any predicate, a unary relation containing values that satisfy all conditions is constructed. Since the rule is assumed to be safe, this unary relation turns out to be finite.

2. At this point, one or more rules S_i, i = 1, 2, . . ., n, n > 0, exist with predicate p as their head. For each such rule S_i, generate a relational expression as follows:

  a. Apply selection operations on the predicates in the RHS for each such rule, as discussed in step 1.

  b. A natural join is constructed among the relations that correspond to the predicates in the body of the rule S_i over the common variables. For arguments that gave rise to the unary relations in step 1(c), the corresponding relations are brought as members into the natural join. Let the resulting relation from this join be R_s.

  c. If any built-in predicate X theta Y was defined over the arguments X and Y, the result of the join is subjected to an additional selection:

$$\text{SELECT}_{<X \text{ theta } Y>}(R_s),$$

  d. Repeat step 2(b) until no more built-in predicates apply.

3. Take the UNION of the expressions generated in step 2 (if more than one rule exists with predicate p as its head).

24.5.4 *Concepts for Recursive Query Processing in Datalog*

In general, for deductive database queries, the query optimization problem can be separated into two problems:

• The problem of query evaluation, which arises in relation to a program that produces an answer to the query.

• A strategy part that comes up when optimal execution of the rules entails rewriting those rules.

Many approaches have been presented for both recursive and nonrecursive queries. We discussed an approach to nonrecursive query evaluation earlier. Here we first define some terminology for recursive queries, then briefly describe naive and semi-naive approaches to query evaluation that belongs to the first of the preceding problems and then the magic set approach that belongs to the second of these.

We have already seen examples involving recursive rules where the same predicate occurs in the head and in the body of a rule. Another example is

ancestor(X,Y) :- ancestor(X,Z), parent(Z,Y)

which states that Y is an ancestor of X if Z is an ancestor of X and Y is a parent of Z.

A rule is said to be **linearly recursive** if the recursive predicate (ancestor) appears once and only once in the RHS of the rule. For example,

sg(X,Y) :- parent(X,XP), parent(Y,YP), sg(XP,YP)

is a linear rule in which the predicate sg (same-generation cousins) is used only once in RHS. The rule states that X and Y are same-generation cousins if their parents are same-generation cousins. Notice that the rule

ancestor(X,Y) :- ancestor(X,Z), ancestor(Z,Y)

is *not* linearly recursive. It is believed that most "real-life" rules can be described as linear recursive rules; algorithms have been defined to execute linear sets of rules efficiently. The preceding definitions become more involved when a set of rules with predicates that occur on both the LHS and the RHS of rules are considered.

Given a Datalog program with relations corresponding to the predicates, the :- symbol may be replaced by an equality sign to form **Datalog equations**, without any loss of meaning. A **fixed point** of a set of equations with respect to relations $R_1, R_2, \ldots, R_n$ is a solution for these relations that satisfies the given equations. A fixed point then forms a model of the rules from which the equations were defined. It is possible in a given set of equations that there are two solution sets, $S_1 <= S_2$, such that each predicate in solution S_1 is a subset of (or is equal to) the corresponding predicate in the solution S_2. A solution S_o is called the **least fixed point** if $S_o <= S$ for any solution S to those equations.

If we represent a directed graph by the predicate edge(X,Y) such that edge (X,Y) is true if and only if there is an edge from node X to node Y in the graph, the paths in the graph may be expressed by the following rules:

path(X,Y) :- arc(X,Y)
path(X,Y) :- path(X,Z), path (Z,Y)

Notice that there are other ways of defining paths recursively. Let us assume that relations P and A correspond to the predicates path and arc in the preceding rules. The **transitive closure** of relation P contains all possible pairs of nodes that have a path between them, and it corresponds to the least fixed point solution corresponding to the equations that result from the preceding rules.*

For evaluating a set of Datalog rules (equations) that may contain recursive rules, a large number of strategies have been proposed, details of which are beyond our scope. Here we illustrate three important techniques: the naive strategy, the semi-naive strategy, and the use of magic sets.

---

*For a detailed discussion of fixed points, consult Ullman (1988).

Naive Strategy. The input is a set of Datalog rules with a set of base relations corresponding to the fact-defined predicates and another set of relations corresponding to the rule-defined predicates. The output is the least fixed point (LFP) solution to the Datalog equations corresponding to these rules.

The procedure involves first setting up the equations for the rules. Permanent values in the fact-defined relations and current values in the rule-defined relations are used to compute new values for the rule-defined relations. The process is repeated until, at some point, none of the rule-defined predicates has any change of values. At that stage, the LFP solution is supposed to be reached. For details of the procedure, see the references given in bibliographic notes at the end of this chapter.

Semi-naive Strategy. The main problem with naive evaluation is that, at each iteration of evaluating the rule-defined relations, a redundant computation of the same tuples occurs. We should rather concentrate on the "incremental change" to the rule-defined predicate at each round and use these in computing additional tuples on the next round. The semi-naive strategy is an efficient strategy because of its approach to compute the "differential" of the tuples in each of the rule-defined predicates at each iteration. See the bibliographic notes at the end of this chapter for more details.

Other approaches to recursive query processing include the recursive query/subquery strategy of Vielle which is a top–down interpreted strategy, and the Henschen-Naqvi top–down compiled iterative strategy.[*]

The second problem is that of query optimization, which addresses the following shortcomings of the preceding approaches:

- The naive and semi-naive strategies do *not* make good use of the query bindings.
- These strategies still do a lot of duplicate computation.

Many techniques have been proposed that qualify as query-rewriting techniques, with the goal of dealing with these two drawbacks. We describe one such technique next.

The Magic Set Rule Rewriting Technique. The problem addressed by the magic sets rule rewriting technique is that frequently a query asks not for the entire relation corresponding to an intentional predicate, but for a small subset of this relation. Consider the following program:

```
sg(X,Y) :- flat(X,Y).
sg(X,Y) :- up(X,U), sg(U,V), down(V,Y).
```

Here, sg is a predicate ("same-generation cousin"), and the head of each of the two rules is the atomic formula sg(X,Y). The other predicates found in the rules are flat, up, and down. These are presumably stored extensionally as facts, while the relation for sg is intentional—that is, defined only by the rules. For a query like sg(john,Z)—that is, "who are the same generation cousins of John?"—asked of the predicate, our answer to the query must examine only the part of the database that *is relevant*—namely the part that involves individuals somehow connected to John.

---

[*]These are described in Vielle (1986) and Henschen and Naqvi (1984).

A top–down, or backward-chaining search would start from the query as a goal and use the rules from head to body to create more goals; none of these goals would be irrelevant to the query, although some might cause us to explore paths that happen to "dead-end."

On the other hand, a bottom–up or forward-chaining search, working from the bodies of the rules to the heads, would cause us to infer sg facts that would never even be considered in the top–down search. Yet bottom–up evaluation is desirable because it avoids the problems of looping and repeated computation that are inherent in the top–down approach. Moreover, the bottom–up approaches allow us to use set-at-a-time operations, such as relational joins, that are very efficient in the context of disk-resident data, while the pure top–down methods use tuple-at-a-time operations.

Magic sets rule rewriting is a technique that allows us to rewrite the rules, as a function of the query form only, that is, it considers which arguments of the predicate are bound to constants, and which are variable, so that the advantages of top–down and bottom–up methods are combined. The technique focuses on the goal inherent in the top–down evaluation but combines this with the looping freedom, easy termination testing, and efficient evaluation of bottom–up evaluation. Instead of giving the method, of which many variations are known and used in practice, we explain the idea with an example.

Given the previously stated rules and the query sg(john,Z), a typical magic sets transformation of the rules would be:

```
sg(X,Y)        :- magic-sg(X), flat(X,Y).
sg(X,Y)        :- magic-sg(X), up(X,U), sg(U,V), down(V,Y).
magic-sg(U)    :- magic-sg(X), up(X,U).
magic-sg(john).
```

Intuitively, we can see that the magic-sg facts correspond to queries or subgoals. The definition of the magic-sg predicate mimics how goals are generated in a top–down evaluation. The set of magic-sg facts is used as a filter in the rules defining sg, to avoid generating facts that are not answers to some subgoal. Thus, a purely bottom–up, forward-chaining evaluation of the rewritten program achieves a restriction of search similar to that achieved by top–down evaluation of the original program. Further details of this technique are beyond our scope.

While the magic sets technique was originally developed to deal with recursive queries, it is applicable to nonrecursive queries as well. Indeed, it has been adapted to deal with SQL queries (which contain features such as grouping, aggregation, arithmetic conditions, and multiset relations that are not present in pure logic queries), and has been found to be useful for evaluating nonrecursive "nested" SQL queries.

24.5.5 Stratified Negation

A deductive database query language can be enhanced by permitting negated literals in the bodies of rules in programs. Once we permit negated literals in the rules, however, we lose an important property of the rules called the *minimal model*, which we discussed earlier. This model is computed by naive or seminaive evaluation, as discussed in the preceding section. But in the presence of negated literals, a program may not have a least model. For example, the program

p(a):- not p(b).

has two minimal models: {p(a)} and {p(b)}.

A detailed history of the concept of negation is beyond our scope. But for practical purposes, we discuss next the important notion of *stratified negation*, which is used in deductive system implementations.

The meaning of a program with negation is usually given by some "intended" model. The challenge is to develop algorithms for choosing an intended model that:

1. Makes sense to the user of the rules.
2. Allows us to answer queries about the model efficiently.

In particular, it is desirable that the model work well with the magic sets transformation, in the sense that we can modify the rules by some suitable generalization of magic sets, and the resulting rules allow (only) the relevant portion of the selected model to be computed efficiently. (Alternatively, other efficient evaluation techniques must be developed.)

One important class of negation that has been extensively studied is **stratified negation**. A program is **stratified** if there is no recursion through negation. Programs in this class have a very intuitive semantics and can be efficiently evaluated. The example that follows describes a stratified program. Consider the following program P_2:

r_1: ancestor(X,Y) :- parent (X,Y).
r_2: ancestor(X,Y) :- parent(X,Z), ancestor(Z,Y).
r_3: nocyc(X,Y):- ancestor(X,Y), not ancestor(Y,X).

Notice that the third rule has a negative literal in its body. This program is stratified because the definition of the predicate nocyc depends (negatively) on the definition of ancestor, but the definition of ancestor *does not* depend on the definition of nocyc. We are not equipped to give a more formal definition without giving additional notation and definitions. A bottom–up evaluation of P_2 would first compute a fixed point of rules r_1 and r_2 (the rules defining ancestor). Rule r_3 is applied only when all the ancestor facts are known.

A natural extension of stratified programs is the class of locally stratified programs. Intuitively, a program P is *locally stratified* for a given database if, when we substitute constants for variables in all possible ways, the resulting instantiated rules do not have any recursion through negation.

24.6 The LDL System⋆

The Logic Data Language (LDL) project at Microelectronics and Computer Technology Corporation (MCC) was started in 1984 with two primary objectives:

- To develop a system that extends the relational model, yet exploits some of the desirable features of an RDBMS (relational database management system).

- To enhance the functionality of a DBMS so that it works as a deductive DBMS and also supports the development of general-purpose applications.

The resulting system is now a commercial deductive DBMS. In this section, we briefly survey the highlights of the technical approach taken by LDL and consider its important features.

24.6.1 *Background, Motivation, and Overview*

The design of the LDL language may be viewed as a rule-based extension to domain calculus–based languages. We reviewed domain calculus in Section 8.3 and discussed the QBE language in Section 8.4. The LDL system has tried to achieve the expressive and deductive power of Prolog while also matching the ease of use of QBE. Another challenge it faced was to combine the expressive capability of Prolog with the functionality and facility of a general-purpose DBMS. The latter includes the modeling and storage of data, as we discussed in the first two parts of this book, and transaction-processing and query optimization support that we discussed in Part 4 of the book. MCC built an integrated system, rather than coupling Prolog with relational databases.

The main drawback experienced by earlier systems that coupled Prolog with an RDBMS is that Prolog is navigational whereas in RDBMSs the user formulates a correct query and leaves the optimization of query execution to the system. The navigational nature of Prolog is evident in the ordering of rules and goals to achieve an optimal execution and termination. Two options are available:

- Make Prolog more "database-like" by adding navigational database management features (discussed in Chapter 10).

- Modify Prolog into a general-purpose declarative logic language.

The latter option has been chosen in LDL, yielding a language that is different from Prolog in its constructs and style of programming.

LDL differs from the Prolog/Datalog style of programming in the following ways:

- Rules are compiled in LDL.

- There is a notion of a "schema" of the fact base in LDL at compile time. The fact base is freely updated at run-time. Prolog, on the other hand, treats facts and rules identically, and it subjects facts to interpretation when they are changed.

- LDL does not follow the resolution and unification technique used in Prolog systems that are based on backward chaining.

- The LDL execution model is simpler, based on the operation of matching and the computation of "least fixed points." These operators, in turn, use simple extensions to the relation algebra.

The first LDL implementation, completed in 1987, was based on a language called FAD. The current prototype implementation, completed in 1988, is called SALAD and is undergoing further changes as it is tested against the "real-life" applications described in Section 24.6.4. The current prototype is an efficient portable system for UNIX that assumes a single tuple get-next interface between the compiled LDL program and an underlying fact manager.

24.6.2 *The LDL Data Model and Language*

With the design philosophy of LDL being to combine the declarative style of relational languages with the expressive power of Prolog, constructs in Prolog such as negation, set-of, updates, and cut have been dropped. Instead, the declarative semantics of Horn clauses was extended to support complex terms through the use of function symbols, called functors in Prolog.

A particular employee record can therefore be defined as:

```
Employee (Name (John Doe), Job(VP),
        Education ({(High school, 1961),
                (College (Harvard, bs, math), 1965),
                (College (Michigan, phd, ie), 1975)}))
```

In the preceding record, VP is a simple term, whereas education is a complex term that consists of a term for high school and a nested relation containing the term for college and the year of graduation. LDL thus supports complex objects with an arbitrarily complex structure including lists, set terms, trees, and nested relations. We can think of a compound term as a Prolog structure with the function symbol as the functor.

LDL allows updates in the bodies of rules. For instance, a rule

```
happy (Dept, Raise, Name) <-
        emp (Name, Dept, Sal), Newsal = Sal+Raise,
        -emp (Name, Dept,-), +emp(Name,Dept,Newsal).
```

combined with

```
?happy(software, 1000, Name).
```

gives a $1,000 raise to all employees in the software department and returns the names of those happy employees. This query is regarded as an indivisible transaction.

LDL offers an if—then—else construct of clean declarative semantics, for the clear expression and efficient implementation of mutually disjunctive rules. In addition, it offers a nonprocedural "choice" predicate, for situations where any answer will do. The choice predicate can be used to obtain a single-answer response, rather than the all-answer solution that represents the default response for LDL queries. In the declarative semantics of LDL, negation has been treated by using stratification and nondeterminism, which is supported through the same construct called "choice."

24.6.3 *Query Evaluation and Optimization in LDL*

Even though LDL's semantics is defined in a bottom–up fashion (for example, via stratification), the implementor can use any execution that is faithful to this declarative semantics. In particular, the execution can proceed bottom–up or top–down, or it may be a hybrid execution. These choices enable the compiler/optimizer to be selective in customizing the most appropriate modes of execution for the given program.

As a first approximation, it is easy to view the LDL execution as a bottom–up computation using relational algebra. For instance, let $p(\ldots)$ be the query with the following rule, where p_1 and p_2 are either database or derived predicates:

$$p(X,Y) <\!\!-\!\!- p_1(X,Z), p_2(Z,Y).$$

This query can be answered by first computing the relations representing p_1 and p_2 and then computing their join, followed by a projection. In actuality, the LDL optimizer and compiler can select and implement the preceding rule by using any of four different execution modes:

- *Pipelined Execution* computes *only* the tuples in p_2 that join with tuples of p_1 in a pipelined fashion. This avoids the computation of any tuple of p_2 that does not join with p_1 (resulting in *no superfluous work*); in contrast, if a tuple in p_2 joins with many tuples in p_1, it is computed many times.

- *Lazy Pipelined Execution* is a pipelined execution in which, as the tuples are generated for p_2, they are stored in a temporary relation, say rp_2, for subsequent use. Therefore, any tuple in p_2 is computed exactly once, even if it is used many times (resulting in *amortized work* as well as no superfluous work of pipelined execution). Further, since both of these pipelined executions compute p_2-tuples one at a time, it is possible to avoid residual computation in the case of intelligent backtracking; this is called *backtrackable advantage*.

- *Lazy Materialized Execution* proceeds as in the lazy pipelined case except that, for a given Z-value, all tuples in p_2 that join with the tuple in p_1 are computed and stored in a relation before proceeding. The main advantage of this execution is that the execution is *reentrant* (a property that is important in the context of recursion), whereas the previous two forms of pipelined execution are not, since they compute tuples of p_2 one at a time. On the other hand, this execution does not have the backtrackable advantage.

- *Materialized Execution* computes *all* tuples in p_2 and stores them in the relation (say, rp_2). Then the computation proceeds, using the tuples from rp_2. Notice that this has the amortized work and reentrant advantages but lacks the backtrackable and superfluous work advantages.

The pipelined execution is useful if the joining column is a key for p_1, whereas the materialized execution is the best if all the Z-values of p_2 are joined with some p_1 tuple. In both of these cases, the respective lazy evaluation incurs more overhead, due to the checking that is needed for each p_1 tuple. The reentrant property is especially useful if the predicate is in the scope of a recursive query that is being computed top–down. Therefore, in such cases, lazy materialized execution is preferred over lazy pipelined execution. Otherwise, lazy pipelined execution is preferred, to exploit the backtrackable property.

The preceding discussion can be generalized to any predicate occurrence with a (possible empty) set of bound arguments. Even though we have limited our discussion here to a single nonrecursive rule, it can be generalized to include arbitrary rules with recursion.

LDL queries pose a new set of problems, stemming from the following observations. First, the model of data is enhanced to include complex objects (such as hierarchies and heterogeneous data allowed for an attribute). Second, new operators are needed not only to operate on complex data, but also to handle new operations such as recursion and negation. Thus, the complexity of data, as well as the set of operations, emphasizes the need for new database statistics and new estimations of cost.

24.6.4   *LDL Applications*

The LDL system has been applied to the following application domains:

- *Enterprise modeling:* This domain involves modeling the structure, processes, and constraints within an enterprise. Data related to an enterprise may result in an extended ER model containing hundreds of entities and relationships and thousands of attributes. A number of applications useful to designers of new applications (as well as for management) can be developed based on this "meta-database" (see Chapter 15), which contains dictionary-like information about the whole enterprise.

- *Hypothesis testing or data dredging:* This domain involves formulating a hypothesis, translating it into an LDL rule set and a query, and then executing the query against given data to test the hypothesis. The process is repeated by reformulating the rules and the query. This has been applied to genome data analysis (see Section 25.2.3 for more details) in the field of microbiology. Data dredging consists of identifying the DNA sequences from low-level digitized autoradiographs from experiments performed on *E. coli* bacteria.

- *Software reuse:* The bulk of the software for an application is developed in standard procedural code, and a small fraction is rule-based and encoded in LDL. The rules give rise to a knowledge base that contains the following elements:

  – A definition of each C module used in the system.

  – A set of rules that defines ways in which modules can export/import functions, constraints, and so on.

  The "knowledge base" can be used to make decisions that pertain to the reuse of software subsets. Modules can be recombined to satisfy specific tasks, as long as the relevant rules are satisfied. This is being experimented with in banking software.

24.7 Other Deductive Database Systems★

24.7.1 *The CORAL System*

The CORAL system, which was developed at the University of Wisconsin at Madison, builds on experience gained from the LDL project. Like LDL, the system provides a declarative language based on Horn clauses with an open architecture. There are many important differences, however, in both the language and its implementation. The CORAL system can be seen as a database programming language that combines important features of SQL and Prolog.

From a language standpoint, CORAL adapts LDL's set-grouping construct to be closer to SQL's GROUP BY construct. For example, consider:

budget(Dname,sum(<Sal>)) :- dept(Dname,Ename,Sal).

This rule computes one budget tuple for each department, and each salary value is counted as often as there are people with that salary in the given department. This is exactly what the corresponding SQL query would do. In LDL, the grouping and the sum operation cannot be combined in one step; more importantly, the grouping is defined to produce a *set* of salaries for each department. Therefore, computing the budget is harder in LDL. A related point is that SQL supports a *multiset* semantics for queries when the DISTINCT clause is not specified. CORAL supports such a multiset semantics as well. Thus, the following rule can be defined to compute either a set of tuples or a multiset of tuples in CORAL, just as in SQL:

budget2(Dname,Sal) :- dept(Dname,Ename,Sal)

This raises an important point: how can a user specify which semantics (set or multiset) is desired? In SQL, the keyword DISTINCT is used; similarly, an *annotation* is provided in CORAL. In fact, CORAL supports a number of annotations that can be used to choose a desired semantics or to provide optimization hints to the CORAL system. The added complexity of queries in a recursive language makes optimization difficult, and the use of annotations often makes a big difference in the quality of the optimized evaluation plan.

CORAL supports a class of programs with negation and grouping that is strictly larger than the class of stratified programs. The bill-of-materials problem, in which the cost of a composite part is defined as being the sum of the costs of all atomic parts, is an example of a problem that requires this added generality.

CORAL is closer to Prolog than to LDL in supporting nonground tuples; thus, the tuple equal(X,X) can be stored in the database and denotes that every binary tuple in which the first and the second field values are the same is in the relation called equal. From an evaluation standpoint, CORAL's main evaluation techniques are based on bottom−up evaluation, which is very different from Prolog's top−down evaluation. However, CORAL also provides a Prolog-like top−down evaluation mode.

Since many different semantics and evaluation methods are supported, CORAL provides a *module* mechanism for organizing programs. Each module exports a query predicate and can be considered to be simply a definition of this predicate. A module contains one or more rules defining the exported predicate and possibly some local predicates. The semantics and evaluation of a module can be controlled by adding per-module annotations, and each module's controls are completely independent of those for other modules. This makes it possible to mix top–down evaluation in one module with bottom–up evaluation in another module, for example.

From an implementation perspective, CORAL implements several optimizations to deal with nonground tuples efficiently, in addition to techniques such as magic templates for pushing selections into recursive queries, pushing projections, and special optimizations of different kinds of (left- and right-linear) linear programs. It also provides an efficient way to compute nonstratified queries. A "shallow-compilation" approach is used, whereby the run-time system interprets the compiled plan. This results in very fast compilation of even large programs. CORAL uses the EXODUS storage manager to provide support for disk-resident relations. It also has a good interface with C^{++} and is *extensible*, enabling a user to customize the system for special applications by adding new data types or relation implementations, for example. An interesting feature is an *explanation* package that allows a user to examine graphically how a fact is generated; this is useful for debugging as well as for providing explanations. In summary, CORAL supports declarative queries, extending relational query languages and logic programs, but it is also a sophisticated programming language for data-intensive applications. The current focus is on extending the data model with object-oriented features, leading to a deductive and object-oriented system.

24.7.2 *The NAIL! Project*

The NAIL! (Not Another Implementation of Logic!) project was started at Stanford in 1985. The initial goal was to study the optimization of logic by using the database-oriented "all-solutions" model. In collaboration with the MCC group, this project is responsible for the first paper on magic sets and the first work on regular recursions. In addition, many important contributions to coping with negation and aggregation in logical rules were made by the project. Stratified negation, well-founded negation, and modularly stratified negation were also developed in connection with this project.

An initial prototype system was built but later abandoned because the purely declarative paradigm was found to be unworkable for many applications. The revised system uses a core language, called GLUE, which is essentially single logical rules, with the power of SQL statements, wrapped in conventional language constructs such as loops, procedures, and modules. The original NAIL! language becomes a view mechanism for GLUE; it permits fully declarative specifications in situations where declarativeness is appropriate.

24.8 Summary

In this chapter we gave an introduction to a relatively new branch of database management called *deductive database systems*. This field has been influenced by logic programming languages, particularly by Prolog. A subset of Prolog called Datalog, which contains function-free Horn clauses, is primarily used as the basis of current deductive database work. Concepts of Datalog were introduced in this chapter. We discussed the standard backward-chaining inferencing mechanism of Prolog and a forward-chaining bottom–up strategy. The latter has been adapted to evaluate queries dealing with relations (extensional databases), by using standard relational operations together with Datalog. Procedures for evaluating nonrecursive and recursive query processing were discussed informally. Negation is particularly difficult to deal with in such deductive databases; a popular concept called *stratified negation* was introduced in this regard.

We surveyed a commercial deductive database system called LDL from MCC and other experimental systems called CORAL and NAIL!. The deductive database area is still in an experimental stage. Its adoption by industry will give a boost to its development. Toward this end, we mentioned practical applications in which LDL is being used.

Exercises

24.1. Add the following facts to the example database in Figure 24.3:

supervise (ahmad,bob), supervise (franklin,gwen).

First modify the supervisory tree in Figure 24.1(b) to reflect this change. Then modify the diagram in Figure 24.4 showing the top–down evaluation of the query supervisor(james,Y).

24.2. Consider the following set of facts for the relation parent(X,Y), where Y is the parent of X:

parent(a,aa), parent(a,ab), parent(aa,aaa), parent(aa,aab), parent(aaa,aaaa), parent(aaa,aaab).

Consider the rules

r_1: ancestor(X,Y) :- parent(X,Y)
r_2: ancestor(X,Y) :- parent(X,Z), ancestor(Z,Y)

which define ancestor Y of X as above.

(a) Show how to solve the Datalog query

ancestor(aa,X)?

using the naive strategy. Show your work at each step.

(b) Show the same query by computing only the changes in the ancestor relation and using that in rule 2 each time.

[This question is derived from (Bancilhon and Ramakrishnan 1986).]

24.3. Consider a deductive database with the following rules:

ancestor(X,Y) :- father(X,Y)
ancestor(X,Y) :- father(X,Z), ancestor(Z,Y)

Notice that "father(X,Y)" means that Y is the father of X; "ancestor(X,Y)" means that Y is the ancestor of X. Consider the fact base

father(Harry,Issac), father(Issac,John), father(John,Kurt).

(a) Construct a model theoretic interpretation of the above rules using the given facts.

(b) Consider that a database contains the above relations father(X,Y), another relation brother(X,Y), and a third relation birth(X,B), where B is the birthdate of person X. State a rule that computes the first cousins of the following variety: their fathers must be brothers.

(c) Show a complete Datalog program with fact-based and rule-based literals that computes the following relation: list of pairs of cousins, where the first person is born after 1960 and the second after 1970. You may use "greater than" as a built-in predicate. [*Note:* Sample facts for brother, birth, and person must also be shown.]

24.4. Consider the following rules:

```
reachable(X,Y) :- flight(X,Y)
reachable(X,Y) :- flight(X,Y), reachable(Y,Z)
```

Where reachable(X,Y) means that city Y can be reached from city X, and flight(X,Y) means that there is a flight to city Y from city X.

(a) Construct fact predicates that describe the following:

(i) Los Angeles, New York, Chicago, Atlanta, Frankfurt, Paris, Singapore, Sydney are cities.

(ii) The following flights exist: LA to NY, NY to Atlanta, Atlanta to Frankfurt, Frankfurt to Atlanta, Frankfurt to Singapore, and Singapore to Sydney. [*Note:* No flight in reverse direction can be automatically assumed.]

(b) Is the given data cyclic? If so, in what sense?

(c) Construct a model theoretic interpretation (that is, an interpretation similar to the one shown in Figure 24.3) of the above facts and rules.

(d) Consider the query:

```
reachable(Atlanta,Sydney)?
```

How will this query be executed using naive and semi-naive evaluation? List the series of steps it will go through.

(e) Consider the following rule defined predicates:

```
round-trip-reachable(X,Y) :- reachable(X,Y), reachable(Y,X)
duration(X,Y,Z)
```

Draw a predicate dependency graph for the above predicates. [*Note:* duration(X,Y,Z) means that you can take a flight from X to Y in Z hours.]

(f) Consider the query: what cities are reachable in 12 hours from Atlanta? Show how to express it in Datalog. Assume built-in predicates like greater-than(X,Y). Can this be converted into a relational algebra statement in a straightforward way? Why or why not?

(g) Consider the predicate population(X,Y) where Y is the population of city X. Consider the query: list all possible bindings of the predicate pair(X,Y), where Y is a city that can be reached in two flights from city X, which has over 1 million people. Show this query in Datalog. Draw a corresponding query tree in relational algebraic terms.

Selected Bibliography

In relation to the early development of the logic and database approach, a survey by Gallaire et al. (1984), Reiter's (1984) reconstruction of relational database theory, and the discussion of incomplete knowledge in light of logic by Levesque (1984) are worth studying. Gallaire and Minker (1978) is an early book on this topic. A detailed treatment of logic and databases appears in Ullman (1989), vol. II, and there is a related chapter in vol. I (1988). Ceri, Gottlob, and Tanca (1990) presents a comprehensive yet concise treatment of logic and databases.

Excellent survey articles on deductive databases and recursive query processing include Bancilhon and Ramakrishnan (1986), Warren (1992), and Ramakrishnan and Ullman (1993). Aho and Ullman (1979) provides an early algorithm for dealing with recursive queries, using the least fixed point operator. Bancilhon and Ramakrishnan (1986) gives an excellent and detailed description of the approaches to recursive query processing, with detailed examples of the naive and seminaive approaches. A complete description of the seminaive approach based on relational algebra is given in Bancilhon (1985). The original paper on magic sets is by Bancilhon et al. (1986). Beeri and Ramakrishnan (1987) extends it. Mumick et al. (1990) shows the applicability of magic sets to nonrecursive nested SQL queries. Other approaches to optimizing rules without rewriting them appear in Vielle (1986, 1987). Kifer and Lozinskii (1986) proposes a different technique. Bry (1990) discusses how the top–down and bottom–up approaches can be reconciled. Whang and Navathe (1992) describes an Extended Disjunctive Normal Form technique to deal with recursion in relational algebra expressions for providing an expert system interface over a relational DBMS.

Chang (1981) describes an early system for combining deductive rules with relational databases. The LDL System prototype is described in Chimenti et al. (1990); an overview of the system appeared in Chimenti et al. (1987). Krishnamurthy and Naqvi (1988) deals with updates in LDL; Krishnamurthy and Naqvi (1989) introduces the "choice" notion in LDL. Zaniolo (1988) discusses the language issues for the LDL system.

A language overview of CORAL is provided in Ramakrishnan et al. (1992), and the implementation is described in Ramakrishnan et al. (1993). An extension to support object-oriented features, called CORAL^{++}, is described in Srivastava et al. (1993). Ullman (1985) provides the basis for the NAIL! system, which is described in Morris et al. (1987). Phipps et al. (1991) describes the GLUE-NAIL! deductive database system. The early implementation of EDUCE at ECRC is described in Bocca (1986a, 1986b); it was later distributed under the name Megalog.

CHAPTER 25

Emerging Database
Technologies and
Applications

So far in this book we have discussed the various techniques for modeling data, designing databases, and implementing them on computers. The term **database technology** is used to refer collectively to the *proven techniques* used on a *wide scale* in industry and government, as well as by individual personal database users, to perform these functions on a *day-to-day* basis. The bulk of what we have discussed is already a part of current database technology. In every discipline of human endeavor, technology always lags behind ongoing research by several years. Database technology is no exception. Therefore, the research work underway today that has the potential of becoming a viable technology will not be available for general consumption for another 5 to 10 years. In this textbook it is impossible for us to include details of a number of such ongoing promising research efforts. We intend, however, to give the reader a broad perspective on the current state of the art in databases and database systems research in this chapter. We will attempt to bring out the major issues and to point out the difficult problems, rather than to discuss the proposed solutions in detail. References to pertinent literature are given whenever appropriate. A few additional references appear in the bibliography.

This chapter is organized as follows: Section 25.1 is an overview of the progression of database technology, roughly over the last 30 years. Section 25.2 discusses the emerging nonconventional areas of applications that are making use of this technology and will continue to place further demands on it. Section 25.3 describes a number of new technologies that are expected to be incorporated in future DBMSs. We end the chapter with Section 25.4, where we outline some emerging technologies and give pointers to research needed in the near future.

One **disclaimer:** This chapter does *not* provide a complete summary of ongoing research. Omissions of some research areas should not be considered to imply any bias. The vast field of database management research, where every year at least 200 to 300

The bibliographic references for this chapter are placed at the anonymous ftp site bc.aw.com as bc/elmasri/ch25.biblio papers are published through refereed conferences and journals, is difficult to condense in this small chapter.

25.1 Progression of Database Technology

Table 25.1 summarizes the progression of database technology for the last three decades or so. The table's first three columns correspond roughly to the three identifiable periods. The last column lists expected future developments. We discuss this table row by row.

25.1.1 *Data Models*

The network and hierarchical models emerged in the 1960s. Since its introduction in 1970, the relational model has excited rapidly increasing interest because of its desirable properties, including its formal basis, homogeneity, well-defined set of algebraic operations, and calculus-based languages. Shortcomings of the relational model in terms of its semantic expressive power led to interest in semantic models. This has grown since the late 1970s, particularly with the advent of the Entity-Relationship (ER) model (Chen 1976), Semantic Hierarchy Model (Smith and Smith 1977), and Semantic Data Model (Hammer and McLeod 1981). In his RM/T model, Codd (1979) suggested that there is a need to add more expressive power to the relational data model by providing it with certain abstractions from the preceding models. The interest in semantic models continued in the 1980s. And today, with the expanding horizons of database applications (Section 25.2), the need for the abstractions that we discussed in Chapter 21 is being felt even more intensely.

A major trend in the next several years will be object-oriented (OO) data models and object-oriented database management systems (OODBMSs); we discussed both of these in detail in Chapter 22. OO data models bring an expressive power similar to that of semantic data models, but go beyond them by explicitly modeling behavior. They are claimed to be easier to implement and use for application development due to the built-in modularity, encapsulation and reuse of code.

Logic is being proposed as an underlying data model for relational and other representation schemas. The relational calculus (see Chapter 8) is based on a branch of logic called first-order predicate calculus; hence, use of logic already exists to characterize relational queries. The relationship between logic and relational databases is well brought out in Gallaire et al. (1984). Logic provides a formalism that can be used in query languages, integrity modeling, query evaluation, treatment of null values, dealing with incomplete information, and so on. Logic also leads to a formal understanding of deduction in databases, which we discussed in Chapter 24.

The future is likely to see further proliferation of object-oriented DBMSs, further use of logic for deductive databases, and a merging of knowledge representation, programming languages, and data models (Brodie et al. 1984; Bancilhon and Buneman 1990; Atkinson and Buneman 1987).

Another distinct trend in commercial DBMS development involves producing unified systems with "hybrid" data models. One example is the UniSQL system which supports a full object-oriented data model that is completely compatible with the relational

Table 25.1 Database Technology Trends

	1960s to Mid-1970s	1970s to Mid-1980s	1980s to Early 1990s	Future
Data Model	Network Hierarchical	Relational	Semantic Object-oriented Logic	Merging data models with knowledge representation Hybrid models
Database Hardware	Mainframes	Mainframes Minis PCs	Faster PCs Workstations Database machines Back ends	Client-server configuration Parallel processing Optical memories
User Interface	None	Query languages Forms	Graphics Menus Query-by-forms	Multimedia Natural languages Speech input Freehand text
Program Interface	Procedural	Embedded query languages	Standardized SQL 4GL Logic programming	Integrated database and programming languages
Presentation and Display	Reports	Report generators	Business graphics Image output	Generalized presentation managers
Processing	Processing data	Information and transaction processing	Transaction processing Knowledge processing	Distributed, heterogeneous data and knowledge processing with multimedia information Parallel database management

model. The open ODB product of Hewlett-Packard, based on the IRIS DBMS developed earlier, combines an object-oriented data model with a functional data model. Vendors of conventional DBMS products have already begun implementing a relational SQL-based interface to allow concurrent development of relational applications. This has happened with network DBMSs such as UNISYS's DMS1100 and Computer Associates' IDMS, and it will continue as a trend.

25.1.2 *Database Hardware*

Over the last 30 years there has been quite a revolution in growth of storage capacities of computers, microminiaturization of the circuitry, and increased processing speeds. The cost of components has fallen steadily and dramatically. The amount of data that can be processed in a certain amount of time has been growing. Moreover, larger databases are becoming feasible on smaller equipment. Until a few years ago, sizable databases could only be handled by mainframes and minis. With the advent of powerful hardware, it is now possible to implement major DBMS products on workstations and personal computers. Relational DBMSs such as DB2/2, ORACLE, and INFORMIX and object-oriented DBMSs such as ObjectStore and O2 (which we discussed in Chapter 22) are available on these. The functionality of low-end database products such as Lotus 1-2-3, the DBase series, ACCESS, and Paradox is also continuously expanding with more powerful hardware that affords windowing and graphics capabilities as well as higher speeds.

Even though storage costs have declined and main storage capacities of systems have grown considerably, the overall performance of database systems is still a great concern. In addition, the advances in software, which incorporate sophisticated data modeling, have been very gradual (as we shall see in Section 25.2) compared to those in processors and I/O architecture. This is due to the mismatch between access speeds of secondary storage devices and those of central processing units, leading to inevitable delays in processing large volumes of data stored on disk. Compared to the advances in speeds of processors (attributed to new logic technologies as well as to the availability of parallel processing), the rate of increase in speeds of secondary storage devices (mainly disks) has been slow.

To deal with these problems, several alternative suggestions have been made for special hardware geared for the data management functions. These alternatives, generically known as **database machines** or computers, include back-end processors, intelligent (logic per track) devices, multiprocessor systems, associative memory systems, and special-purpose processors. The Intelligent Database Machine (IDM) introduced by Britton-Lee in 1982 is the first commercial database machine. Teradata's DBC/1012 is a recent entry; it is the only multiprocessor database computer available commercially that has a very flexible reconfigurable architecture. Another database machine called the Teradata DBC/1012 has been introduced. A parallel database management system implementation of the ORACLE relational DBMS exists on the KSR (Kendall Square Research) parallel processing hardware, as well as on the Ncube processor. Research on alternative architectures and simulation of their performance are ongoing activities. Su (1988) provides an excellent survey of research efforts in database computers. Typically, however, most of them have remained as designs on paper or small prototype implementations because of lack of resources to build actual full-scale hardware or even prototypes.

Because of the demands of high-volume transaction processing and of ever-increasing processor speeds (especially in supercomputers), much attention will be given in the future to database machines and to parallel processing architectures. From the experience of the last 15 years, however, it is hard to predict what, if anything, will emerge in the way of economically viable and commercially feasible solutions.

From the standpoint of new storage hardware, optical storage devices (which are currently write-once and read-forever types) are being modified into read-write devices and will soon be economically affordable. They have very high capacities (in the range of 10^{12} bytes) and open up the possibility of storing vast amounts of information by recording updated information without erasing old information. Read-write optical disks have already been introduced on the market. Even with the moderate-cost write-once optical disks available today, which have a physical write rate of one page per second, a disk used for a normal workload can last one year (Gait 1988). This opens up a number of exciting new prospects for historical data storage and retrieval (see temporal applications in Section 25.3.4).

25.1.3 *User Interfaces*

In Chapter 1 we pointed out the large spectrum of people who are typical users of DBMSs. When DBMSs were introduced in the late 1960s, end users had *no* direct access to databases. Their interactions were limited to verbally communicating their requirements to programmers. Filling forms was one of the first interactive modes of data entry suitable for a large population of end users such as sales or insurance clerks. Most interaction still occurred with batch programs in procedural languages.

Query languages became popular in the 1970s. We discussed the query languages SQL (Chapter 7) and QBE and QUEL (Chapter 8) for the relational data model. It is quite remarkable that, for all practical purposes, such a major DBMS product as IMS (see Chapter 11 for details) does *not* have a query language. The network data model has also survived without much query language support except for specialized high-level user commands that customers and vendors may have developed on their own. The availability of graphics workstations and windowing has tremendously increased the potential for creating nonsyntactic interfaces to DBMSs, where a user is not burdened with having to use a specific syntax. Interfaces making extensive use of windowing capabilities, pull-down menus, and icons are likely to grow and become more sophisticated.

Most DBMSs are aiming to add facilities called **Query by Forms**. These allow users to invoke "parameterized" queries for which run-time parameters are supplied and a predefined query is recompiled or reinterpreted and executed. Other user facilities include *icon-based* interfaces, where a user touches icons or images on the screen to formulate a query, and mouse-based interfaces, where a *mouse* or *touch-sensitive* screen permits cursor movement while specifying a query. Some interfaces access actual data and provide values existing in the database in a scrollable window so that these values can be used as constants in queries.

Natural language interfaces have been explored for some time. Three basic approaches are used to interpret natural language:

• *Keyword extraction or pattern matching:* In keyword systems, the program relates words in natural language to specific fields in a database, where an application developer defines the relationships. However, pattern matching without a grammatical basis is of limited use.

• *Parsing:* Parsing converts a potentially ambiguous phrase in English to an internal format that should accurately represent the user's intended query. Two variations on this approach are possible: one based on a grammar of the natural language, and another based on the semantics of the language in terms of a lexicon and a series of production rules. The LADDER system (Hendrix 1978) used a semantic grammar for accessing U.S. Navy databases. Harris's (1978) INTELLECT system, now a commercial product, is also based on grammar rules. Codd's (1978) Rendezvous system used a lexicon and converted natural language queries into relational calculus based on a phrase grammar.

• *Query mapping:* A knowledge base or a "world model" is used with canonical representations of sentences from a certain application domain, together with linguistic knowledge and mapping knowledge, to map natural language queries at a conceptual level into database queries in a specific language. The KDA system (Wu and Ichikawa 1992) is an example of this approach.

Today's natural language systems suffer from the fact that they represent a heavy overhead, require a database-specific lexicon to be built, and allow ambiguities in query specification. As a result, the user may not be aware of how the system has actually interpreted a query and the system has no way of predicting exactly what the user may want. Icon- and mouse-based interfaces are equally easy to operate at times and are much more economical.

The technology of *speech recognition and understanding* is still not sophisticated enough to allow speech input to be viable in a major way in the near future. That approach, however, has a phenomenal potential for opening the doors of databases to people of all ages and all levels of sophistication and for making database-based computer-aided instruction available to the masses.

25.1.4 *Program Interfaces*

Even today, the bulk of programming in the commercial world, which may account for 70 to 80% (a rough guess!) of actual database processing, is done in conventional programming languages—mostly in COBOL, PL/1, and (now) C. These languages, plus FORTRAN, Assembler, and ALGOL, have been the mainstay of database applications. The C^{++} language has recently entered the scene and is gaining ground rapidly, especially in object-oriented DBMSs.

The 1970s saw the emergence of query languages that were embedded in programming languages for large-scale application program development. We saw examples of *embedding* SQL in Chapter 7.

A departure from this trend came in two areas. First, the **Fourth-Generation Languages** (4GLs, a term coined commercially without a precise definition) became popular in the 1980s. They allow the user to give a high-level specification of an application in the 4GL language. The system (or a tool) then *automatically generates* the application code. For example, INGRES and most RDBMSs provide an Application by Forms interface, where the application designer develops an application by using forms displayed on the screen rather than by writing a program for it. 4GLs, however, have not been uniformly accepted for general-purpose data management and for most report generation. Their built-in database support is minimal.

Another major development in the 1980s has been the standardization of SQL, first the ANSI SQL and SQL 89 standards, and more recently SQL2 and SQL3. Chapter 7 follows SQL2 syntax. Most RDBMS vendors are trying to comply with these standards, which will facilitate interoperability among these systems. SQL3 is in a draft form at the time of our publication; it combines many object-oriented features (see Chapter 22) in SQL. Many nonrelational DBMS vendors have opted to provide SQL programming interfaces for their DBMS—for example, in the IDMS network model–based system (see Section 10.7) and in the ADABAS system of software AG.

Use of logic programming languages for deductive database management* (see Chapter 24) has not had much impact to date. One reason for this is the lack of full-scale commercial systems. We discussed the only such system, LDL, in Section 24.7. We expect that the trend will be toward *integrated programming systems*, where the inferencing and recursion of the logic programming language are coupled with the efficient manipulation of facts in the DBMS. With the merger of object-oriented and relational data models, or with a relational interface developed on top of a network DBMS, future systems will continue to present multiple programming interface options within a single system for application development.

25.1.5 *Presentation and Display*

The original output devices on computer systems were line printers and card punchers. Most output was presented either as line-by-line reports or as calculated values punched into cards and subjected to further processing. The language RPG (Report Generation Language) was the beginning of a trend toward making report generation a specialized activity that could be specified in terms of high-level report generation commands.

Today, report generators are a standard feature of most DBMSs. Examples are INGRES's report writer, IDMS's CULPRIT package, and UNIFY's lst and rpt processors. Special report definition languages are provided in which users specify formatting, spacing, pagination, levels of totals, headers, justification, and so on.

With interactive access to databases for a variety of users, report generation became possible by invoking the report generator or by specifying reports via forms (for example, INGRES's Report by Forms). With the advent of PCs, users have come to expect to be presented with a great deal of information on the screen. Most DBMS packages supply **business graphics** output in a variety of forms, including xy plots (scatter plots) using linear regression, bar charts, pie charts, and line plots (containing piecewise linear approximations of curves that appear as a set of connected lines). With color graphics, aesthetically pleasing as well as impressive displays are now commonplace. These types of displays require the query output to be postprocessed by a display manager.

---

*We do not intend to define deductive databases formally here. Suffice it to say that a conventional database becomes deductive by the addition of a theory with certain axioms and deductive laws. See Gallaire et al. (1984).

By integrating image technology with database processing and by storing digitized voice as data, some of today's experimental systems are able to produce image and voice output. Digitized image storage is becoming quite common. Specialized hardware for speech synthesis may become commercially available in the next few years.

25.1.6 Nature of Processing

Database technology was originally introduced as a response to the problems of file processing and its associated disadvantages (see Section 1.3). The main applications are in business data processing—inventory management, payroll, general ledger billing, order processing, sales reporting, and so on.

During the late 1970s, the technology began to be applied in a variety of domains from different disciplines. High-level applications that summarized data into information for tactical and strategic planning were generated. Reliable and secure DBMSs became a resource of centralized information with which a large number of geographically separated applications/users could interact. This has been made possible by advances in **data communications technology**, including broadband and satellite communication networks. The major users of DBMS technology today use it for **transaction processing**.

Airlines, major hotel chains, insurance companies, banks, retail chain stores, automobile and appliance dealerships, and the like operate today by using reliable rapid transaction processing and on-line real-time updates. Today it is possible to book a seat in a theatre on Broadway from a remote town in Oregon. These applications will continue to place higher and higher demands on the technology of on-line transaction processing.

25.1.7 Current Trends in Technology

The trend of technology for the next several years will be dominated by the following themes:

- *Distributed, heterogeneous environments:* Large centralized databases will be replaced by distributed databases. These databases may be implemented from conventional network and hierarchical DBMSs, the current relational DBMSs, or the object-oriented DBMSs that are gaining popularity. The "client-server" architecture is becoming extremely popular and will afford users various options with regard to the functionality of the DBMS and the location of data.

- *Open systems:* Several standardization efforts such as SQL Access Group, ANSI/X3H7, Object Management Group's (OMG) Object Data Management Group (ODMG), Microsoft's ODBS, IDAPI, and ODAPI (Borland) are striving to improve the "openness" of future database system and applications. Systems that comply with these standards will be able to communicate among themselves easily. SQL2 and SQL3 standards will play a major role here. The trend will be toward designing global applications that run on clients' systems and draw data from a variety of servers with standardized data access protocols.

- *More functionality:* The sheer functionality of DBMSs will go beyond the conventional define, store, access, query, and report functions. The deductive capability described in Chapter 24, the processing of meta-data, and better specification of behavior through methods (Chapter 22) will be included. Additionally, the "active" capability (which we describe in Section 25.3) to make databases more responsive, multimedia database management, better processing of temporal and spatial data, special DBMSs for scientific users, and so on are likely to dominate the development of database technology in coming years. We address a few of these areas and their special needs in Section 25.3.

• *Parallel Database Management:* A new breed of database management systems is likely to be offered on a commercial scale based on the MIMD (multiple instruction, multiple data paths) architectures such as Intel's iPSC hypercube or the Kendall Square Research machine. Current work involves new algorithms for parallel query strategies for data allocation and effective use of the overall system to minimize the cost per transaction. Hardly any work has thus far been done on how an existing array of database applications should be parallelized to benefit from the parallel DBMSs of the future.

25.2 Emerging Database Applications

The applications of database technology are expanding continually. Since data is at the heart of any information system, as computing becomes more widely available, each discipline will come up with its own unique set of applications. It is not our objective to go through such lists of applications in detail. We wish to identify major categories of applications that are recognized today as presenting good potential as well as a great challenge to database technology. Special modeling characteristics of each application area will be highlighted.

25.2.1 *Engineering Design and Manufacturing*

The difficult goal of computer-integrated design and manufacturing requires the effective management of design and manufacturing information. This topic spans subareas denoted by several acronyms: CAD (computer-aided design), CAM (computer-aided manufacturing), CAE (computer-aided engineering), and CIM (computer-integrated manufacturing). An integrated approach to managing manufacturing information requires compatible representation and manipulation of information in different phases of the product life cycle. This includes business applications such as sales forecasting, order processing, product planning, production control, inventory control, and cost accounting; design and engineering of the product together with planning for materials requirements; manufacturing-related applications, including manufacturing resource planning and control; and applications of group technology for parts classification, robotics, and manufacturing process control (including NC—numerical control programming) (Bray 1988).

The standard advantages of database technology help to integrate these areas (see Sections 1.6 and 1.7). A great deal of research is being directed toward both the design and the manufacturing problems, and a major emphasis today is placed on developing DBMSs particularly suited to computer-aided design applications. Figure 25.1 shows the variety of data that is relevant and how a number of applications may be supported in the design environment once this data is captured.

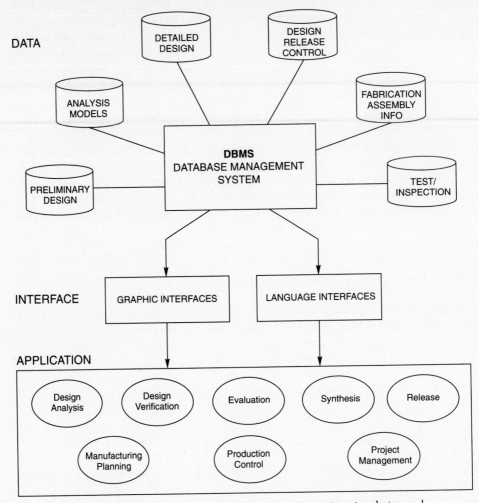

Figure 25.1 Use of a database management system in engineering design and applications.

Engineering design is an exploratory and iterative process. The engineering design activity for complex systems such as airplanes or automobiles is conducted by project teams, and the design of a component or a subsystem continuously evolves under a set of design guidelines, resource limitations, and design constraints. Intermittently, designs are cross-checked against other independently evolving designs, and finally, "permanent" designs or versions are stored.

Role of Database Management in CAD. Two important areas of investigation are the design of VLSI (very large-scale integration) electronic systems and the design of mechanical structures and systems. A basic challenge in mechanical design is **geometric modeling**, which refers to representing the physical shape of mechanical parts. The shape of parts provides a common thread through the design, analysis, and manufacturing cycle for parts. Different CAD systems employ different geometric modeling techniques, including wire frame modeling, surface modeling, and solid modeling. It is a traumatic experience for the user to transport data among different CAD systems or from a CAD system to a CAM system. The National Bureau of Standards defined a common neutral interface or format of data called Initial Graphics Exchange Specification (IGES 1983) to facilitate such interchange of data. IGES defines standard design entities for 2D drawings and 3D objects as well as electrical diagrams. For three-dimensional solids, two types of representations, called boundary representation and constructive solid geometry, are more common.

Structural engineering deals with problems ranging from the design of trusses in buildings to the design of complex launch pad assemblies for spacecraft. Whether buildings, mechanical assemblies, bridges, or spaceships are involved, structures are constrained by geometries and require the selection of an optimal set of members to meet weight constraints and design limits and provide reliability under different loadings. Databases can play an important role in storing information centrally for use with analytical tools (such as finite-element analysis), graphics (typically three-dimensional graphics on CAD systems), simulations, and optimal design algorithms. In chemical engineering, databases are used for plant design and process control. There are two main reasons for using a centralized database system for design data:

- Part of a design can be synthesized, analyzed, coordinated, and documented while individual project teams work on different parts of the design.

- Constraints related to identical standards, designs, and specifications and other physical properties, design style, and topological relationships can be verified and enforced automatically.

Engineering design data is difficult to capture and represent with conventional data models (Chapters 6–11) and DBMSs for the following reasons:

- Engineering design data contains a nonhomogeneous collection of design objects. Classical data models deal with homogeneous collections.

- Classical DBMSs are good for formatted data (scalars), short strings, and fixed-length records. Digitized designs are long strings; they have variable-length records or textual information; they often contain vectors and matrices of values.

- Temporal and spatial (see Section 25.3.4) relationships are important in designs for layout, placement, and assembly operations.

- Design data is characterized by a large number of types, each with a small number of instances. Conventional databases have just the opposite situation.

- Schemas *evolve constantly* in design databases because designs go through a long period of evolution.

- Transactions in design databases are of long duration; a designer may "check out" a design object and work on it for several weeks before restoring it (in its modified form) to the database. Similarly, updates are far-reaching because of topological relationships, functional relationships, tolerances, and so on. One change is likely to affect a large number of design objects.

- It is necessary to keep old versions and to create new versions of the same object. A design log must be maintained for tracing the evolution of a design and possibly for backtracking through it.

- Making a design permanent, releasing it to production, archiving it, and so on are specialized functions in a design database.

- Design data must not be duplicated at lower levels of design; since design elements (such as gates in electrical circuits or nuts and bolts in mechanical design) are used in a highly repetitive way, redundancy control is required to suppress certain common attributes. For example, when identical bolts are used at two places, the positional coordinates are stored but other attributes are not repeated. In such cases, a library of design objects can be maintained.

Because of these demands, new data modeling approaches are being proposed to manage VLSI designs, as well as mechanical designs. Object-oriented models are favored because they possess the following characteristics (for a detailed discussion, see Spooner 1986 and Ketabchi 1986):

- *Common model:* The designer's miniworld can be mapped into the database objects by a one-to-one mapping.

- *Uniform interface:* All objects are treated uniformly by accessing them through methods (or user-defined operations).

- *Support of complex objects:* Object-oriented models for engineering designs must allow creation of arbitrarily complex objects involving hierarchies and lattices (Batory and Buchmann 1984).

- *Information hiding and support of abstractions:* The abstraction mechanism can provide the essential external features of objects for design while hiding internal representation or implementation details. Generalization and aggregation are easily supported (see Ahmed and Navathe 1991).

- *Versioning:* A design object may undergo evolution through a series of versions; it may also have different representations. It is necessary to treat a *generic object* and its versions independently. At the same time, there should not be an overuse of the "create version" operation as opposed to an update. ORION (Chou and Kim 1986) supports transient versions and working versions. Ahmed and Navathe (1991) defines a versioning scheme based on intrinsic and extrinsic properties of design objects. A version is created when intrinsic properties are unchanged, but extrinsic properties change. The proposed versioning scheme prevents unnecessary version proliferation.

- *Modularity, flexibility, extensibility, and tailorability:* Object-oriented databases support schema evolution more easily than do conventional models; new objects or new operations can easily be added, and old ones can be modified or deleted.

Early efforts in this direction included a project at the University of Southern California (Afsarmanesh et al. 1985), the ORION system (Kim et al. 1987) at the Microelectronics and Computer Technology Corporation, and an effort at the University of California, Berkeley (Katz 1985). More recently, the ROSE (Relational Object System for

Engineering) system was developed at Rensselaer Polytechnic by Hardwick and Spooner (1989). It is a structurally object-oriented DBMS supporting aggregation, generalization, and association. It has an open architecture with facilities for providing front-end and back-end tools.

Extensions of the relational and network models to accommodate CAD data have been reported but have not been very successful (Wiederhold et al. 1982; Stonebraker et al. 1983). Long transactions and concurrency control of design transactions remain research issues.

Another important development is the standardization of the product data for exchange purposes across vendors, designers, and manufacturers. The PDES (Product Data Exchange using STEP, where STEP is an ISO STandard for the Exchange of Product Model Data) standard is now drawing a very large following (PDES Inc. 1991). It is applied in diverse industries such as building and construction, electrical components, and architecture. An accompanying language called EXPRESS is also gaining popularity as a descriptive language for specifying parts, identifying various types of constraints on them, and providing a uniform way of representing design objects for further analysis/synthesis. The PDES/STEP and EXPRESS standards promote sharing and integration of data for product design. Both of these developments are likely to lead to a new generation of systems and tools in engineering design and manufacturing.

There is also a need for further work on modeling of the design data due to its peculiarities. One promising direction involves the separation of the structure and function in complex physical systems so that each can be independently represented and analyzed (Navathe and Cornelio 1990). This approach further facilitates modeling of the dynamics of such systems using the active database approach (see Section 25.3.1) and aids in simulation (Cornelio and Navathe 1993).

25.2.2 *Office Systems and Decision Support Systems*

Automation of office work has been one of the fastest-growing areas of application of information systems (Ellis and Nutt 1980). The growing interest and activity in **office information systems (OISs)** is evident from the fact that a journal called *ACM Transactions on Office Information Systems* was launched in 1983 by the Association for Computing Machinery. Subsequently, noting that office information systems are only one specific type of information system, the journal changed its title to *Transactions on Information Systems* in 1990. Database technology is having a major impact on office work because much of it falls in the category of *programmable work*, where the events are predictable and the responses are known. Computers and, in particular, database systems can greatly influence this type of work. The other extreme is *emergent creative work*, according to the taxonomy of Ciborra et al. (1984), where the events are unpredictable and the responses are unknown. The office work of top management, international money traders, and the like falls into this category and requires the assistance of decision support systems. We first briefly point out the differences between information systems and OISs; then we briefly review a data-based model of an OIS; and finally we make a few comments on decision support systems.

Office Information Systems Versus Conventional Database Applications. * Like CAD applications, OIS applications place a higher demand on a DBMS while centralizing the information in a given office environment. This is due to the following characteristics of OIS applications:

- *Semantic richness:* Office data tends to be semantically rich and requires support for unstructured messages, letters, text, annotations, chains of forwarding addresses, oral communications, and so on. There are *stereotypical information groupings* in an office, such as business letters or quarterly progress reports with standardized formats.

- *Time factor:* The time factor and timing constraint must be modeled to capture the following types of information: the total travel time of a document along a path; duration of activities, calendars, and schedules; allowable response time to reply to a message; automatic generation of reminders; and so on.

- *Lack of structure:* Office activities tend to be much less structured than other information systems. Instructions to perform work are incomplete and irregular; constant communication and dialogue are necessary.

- *High interconnectivity:* Compared to a manufacturing workcell that uses machine tools, an office typically represents a much more complex group of elements, each performing a variety of functions and interconnected in multiple directions to elements of different types. It is therefore difficult to model the workflow in an office accurately, and automation and productivity improvements are difficult to achieve via a well-defined office design methodology.

- *Office constraints and evolution:* Because an office is a group of humans, it is subject to constant evolution in which the authorities and job responsibilities of individuals change. It is therefore difficult to model all constraints definitively.

- *Interactive interface:* OISs are highly interactive. It should be possible for even the lowest-level worker in an office to communicate to an OIS. User groups are diverse and span the whole spectrum from naive to sophisticated. This makes interface design challenging.

- *Filtering of information:* Most offices have a built-in hierarchy. It is necessary to filter and summarize information in a pyramid style within the system. Low-level transactions must be summarized before being passed up to the next level of management. Aggregation of data elements should be performed automatically at different prespecified and user-controlled intervals.

- *Priorities, scheduling, reminders:* All of these are important characteristics of different elements of work; a variety of interrupts are generated and must be handled in the office constantly.

It is evident that office automation is not an easy task. A database at the heart of an OIS must be capable of meeting all of the preceding requirements. Because of these factors, we see "islands of mechanization" in offices today rather than a totally automated office. Many conceptual modeling and design methodologies for OISs have been pro-

---

*This section is largely derived from Bracchi and Pernici (1984, 1987).

posed; examples are OFFIS (Konsynski et al. 1982), OAM (Sirbu et al. 1981), and MOBILE-Burotique (Dumas et al. 1982). Recent research in office information systems has concentrated on modeling the office workflow, defining the database requirements, and dealing with query processing specific to the office setting. An example is the TODOS (Pernici 1989) project, which stands for TOols for Designing Office Systems. Multimedia database technology (see Section 25.3.2) is expected to play a major role in office systems (Masunaga 1987, Woelk 1987, Bertino 1988).

Data-based Model of an Office Information System. Data-based models group data into forms that resemble paper forms in an office. The Office-By-Example project at IBM Research (Zloof 1982) developed a language called Office By Example (OBE) that is an extension of the QBE language described in Chapter 9. OBE models a variety of objects using the basic relational table paradigm: forms, reports, documents, address lists, message lists, menus, and so on. The system allows data types such as image, text, and time. The functions specified on these objects include word processing, querying, and automatic triggering of activities (for example, send letter when payment is more than n days overdue, where n is a run-time parameter or is obtained from some table). Authorization, message communication and forwarding, and document manipulation are examples of other functions handled through the same interface. The main point of data-based office models is to represent the office from the viewpoint of objects manipulated by office workers. The object-oriented approach again seems promising here. Products specific to document processing, electronic multimedia mail, audio/video communication, and the like are appearing for PC Windows–type user environments. One example is the NEWWAVE system of Hewlett-Packard.

Decision Support Systems (DSSs). Office systems or business data-processing systems in general offer decision support to upper-level office workers in several ways:

- *Analysis of office data:* Data must be presented to the user at the right level of detail, using the right display after performing the proper filtering.

- *Controlling the state of the system:* An OIS must have features to determine its own state and to evaluate it. Any discrepancies or exceptional conditions requiring review should be brought to the attention of the right individuals.

- *Support of analytical decision-making tools:* Besides making ad hoc decisions, managers are called on to make long-term strategic and business planning decisions. Alternative choices must be considered and analyzed. A DSS must have knowledge of alternatives as well as the models needed to perform optimization or to reach "intelligent" choices.

- *Support for organizational design and office system design changes:* The DSS should have some features that allow organizational restructuring or information flow modification without disrupting normal operations.

DSSs are being designed today with a DBMS as their central component. In general, a DSS allows the user to perform control and monitoring functions; it must also allow the user to enforce policy decisions (constraints) and actions (procedures). To permit partial automation of decision making in offices, one may resort to an "active" database system (see Section 25.3.1), where actions can involve generating messages, notices, letters, and so on, or can be more involved in terms of enforcing policies that span the entire set of functions and databases in the office. Various systems have been proposed, but the literature is too vast to be summarized here.

25.2.3 *The Human Genome Initiative*

Introduction and Goals of the Project. The Human Genome Initiative (HGI) is a good example of a trend in biology that is giving it a new aspect: that of a computational analytical science. The Human Genome Initiative is an international effort aimed at determining the location of the estimated 100,000 human genes that compose the entire human genome. HGI is a monumental scientific adventure that can be compared with efforts in the fourteenth century to draw the most complete and detailed possible map of the earth, given the tools of those days when the earth was believed to be flat. The scientific, medical, and economic implications of the HGI are profound. HGI would ultimately pave the way for a routine decoding of genes that make life possible as well as providing an improved understanding of the diseases afflicting mankind.

The most ambitious goal of the genome project is to complete the most detailed map: a reference sequence of the entire human genome. HGI is a long-term project, with an expected duration of between 25 and 40 years. It involves three key computational challenges: sequence analysis, information storage and retrieval, and protein structure prediction. These elements break down as follows:

- *Sequence analysis problem:* Given a set of DNA sequences, efficient alignment-matching algorithms are needed that can deal elegantly with insertion, deletion, substitution, and even gaps in the series of sequence elements.

- *Storage and retrieval problem:* Effectively storing and retrieving data, and making the information easily accessible to distributed users while effectively dealing with errors, conflicts, and updates is a challenging problem—the more so because the rate at which new sequence information will be generated by the turn of the century will be about 1.6 billion base pairs per year.

- *DNA and protein structure prediction problem:* Within cells, most DNA is associated with proteins that, among other things, influence the torsional stress on the DNA double helix. Under negative torsional stress, the DNA helix may assume alternative structures. Specific sequences favor such structures, and predicting the probabilities of alternative structures for a given sequence is a challenging problem. Another difficulty is the protein-folding problem. After a protein is synthesized by the cell, the protein chain folds according to the laws of physics into a specialized form, based on the particular properties and order of the amino acids. The protein-folding problem is expected to challenge our most powerful supercomputers for the foreseeable future.

In multicellular organisms, DNA is generally found as two linear strands wrapped around each other in the form of a double helix. A DNA strand is a polymeric chain made of nucleotides, each consisting of a nitrogenous base, a deoxyribose sugar, and a phosphate molecule. The arrangement of nucleotides along the DNA backbone is called the DNA sequence. Four nucleotides are used in the DNA sequences: adenosine (A), guanosine (G), cytidine (C), and thymidine (T). In nature, base pairs form only between A's and T's and between G's and C's. The size of the genome is generally given as its total number of base pairs. A **gene** is a region of a chromosome whose DNA sequence can be transcribed to produce a biologically active RNA molecule. With this background, the goals of HGI related to computing are as follows:

- To establish, maintain, and enhance databases containing information about DNA sequences, location of DNA markers and genes, function of identified genes, and other related information.

- To create maps of human chromosomes consisting of DNA markers that would permit scientists to locate genes quickly.

- To create repositories of research materials, including ordered sets of DNA fragments that fully represent DNA in the human chromosome.

- To determine the DNA sequence of a large fraction of the human genome and that of other organisms.

Requirements of a Genome Database. It is crucial for the scientific community to be able to access information on a topic from a variety of databases that may handle different aspects of the problem. Databases must use standardized or easily translatable formats and must be interconnected. The genome database must be heterogeneous and interoperable. The main problems in achieving these objectives are as follows:

- Different (and seemingly conflicting) views of a sequence must be represented adequately.

- A nucleotide sequence as represented in a database is an imperfect and incomplete picture of an idealized molecule: imperfect, because experimental data always contains errors; incomplete, because there is always a scope to learn more about it; and idealized, because it ordinarily ignores variation.

- The concepts are fluid, and their meanings change all the time. Currently, no good database technology supports a fluid environment of this type.

- The "construction process" of the model of the universe produces inconsistency, ambiguity, and outright contradiction. It is important that the genome database support dynamic schema evolution, while the construction process continues on the basis of the new experimental data and new inferences.

Since the concepts and the schema are continually changing, the query language should be powerful enough to satisfy the needs of the users, each of whom has a different degree of expertise and knowledge. The genome database must perform pattern matching to identify relevant sequences, gaps, and so on, requiring a powerful pattern-matching facility.

The choice and the design of the data model that reflects the biology of the problem are themselves major issues. The relational data model is poorly suited for a genome database because it fails to capture the order in a sequence. Existing object-oriented models are useful in that they can capture complex objects and can perform incremental consistency checking. However, they have a weak query capability. As we noted in Section 24.7, the LDL system, with its deductive capability, is currently being applied to this problem for the *E. coli* genome.

Current Efforts. Existing databases and repositories that gather, maintain, analyze, and distribute data and materials are already struggling to keep up with the exponential growth of molecular biology. Some databases specialize in map and sequence information from one specific genome; for example, there are databases exclusively devoted to mouse, to *E. coli* bacteria, to drosophila, and to nematode genomes. Others carry particular kinds of information from all the relevant genomes. Some existing U.S. databases and repositories are given next. More information on these databases is summarized in Table 25.2.

> On-line Mendelian Inheritance in Man (OMIM). This is a computerized atlas of human traits that are known to be inherited—that is, the expressed genes.
>
> Human Gene Mapping Library (HGML). This library consists of five linked databases—one each for map information, relevant literature, RFLP maps, DNA probes, and contacts (researchers with information on data and materials).
>
> GenBank. This is the major U.S. database for nucleic acid sequence information from humans and other organisms.
>
> Protein Identification Resource (PIR). This resource contains sequence data for proteins and amino acids, with annotations that indicate known functional regions.
>
> Protein Data Bank (PDB). This library gathers information on the atomic structure of nucleic acids, messenger RNA, amino acids, proteins, and carbohydrates that has been derived from crystallographic studies.

25.3 Next Generation of Databases and Database Management Systems

In this section we will briefly survey the major types of databases and the associated database technology that is currently under development. This includes the following: active databases (Section 25.3.1), multimedia databases (Section 25.3.2), statistical and scientific databases (Section 25.3.3), and spatial and temporal databases (Section 25.3.4). This is followed by a section on unified and extensible database management (Section 25.3.5), where we survey two extensible systems—EXODUS and GENESIS—and a commercial product called UniSQL, which unifies the object-oriented and relational approaches to database management.

25.3.1 *Active Databases**

Traditionally, DBMSs are passive; they execute queries or transactions only when explicitly requested to do so by a user or an application program. But many applications, such as process control, power generation/distribution networks, automated office workflow

---

*This section is largely based on Chakravarthy 1990.

Table 25.2 Some Existing Genome Databases

Name	Institution	Contents	Format	On-line Access
GenBank	Los Alamos National Laboratory	DNA	MT/CD-ROM	on-line/anonymous FTP
EMBL	European Molecular Biology Laboratory	DNA	MT/CD-ROM	N/A
PIR	National Biomedical Research Foundation	protein	MT/CD-ROM	on-line
SWISS-PROT	Geneva University	protein	MT/CD-ROM	anonymous FTP
PDB	Brookhaven National Laboratory	protein	MT	anonymous FTP
GDB/OMIM	Johns-Hopkins University	generic map	CD-ROM	on-line
MEDLINE	National Library of Medicine	bibliography	CD-ROM	on-line

control, program trading, battle management, and hospital patient monitoring, which require timely response to critical situations, are not well served by these "passive" DBMSs. For these **time-constrained** applications, conditions defined on states of the database must be monitored, and once these conditions occur, specified actions must be invoked, possibly subject to some timing constraints. A possible scenario in automated manufacturing involves monitoring for an event—widgets coming out of an assembly line machine M1 over an interval—evaluation of a condition—10% of widgets being defective over the time interval—and taking one or more actions—bringing the machine M2 on-line and notifying appropriate personnel. All of this may involve access to shared databases that are constantly being updated by several users and have to be maintained in a consistent state.

Approaches. Traditionally, two approaches to meeting the requirements of time-constrained applications have been taken (see Figure 25.2). The first is to write a special application program that polls (periodically queries) the database to determine whether the situation being monitored has occurred. The second is to augment each program that updates the database to check the situation being monitored. The first is difficult to implement because the optimal polling frequency is hard to determine; the second compromises modularity and reuse of code. Active databases support condition monitoring (including triggers and alerters) at a level of abstraction that has three characteristics: its semantics are well-defined; it satisfies the modeling and efficiency requirements of nontraditional database applications; and it seamlessly integrates with a DBMS.

An active DBMS continually monitors the database state (including the system clock) and reacts spontaneously when predefined events occur. Functionally, an active database management system monitors *conditions* triggered by *events* representing data-

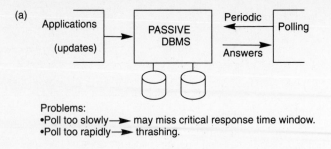

Problems:
- Poll too slowly → may miss critical response time window.
- Poll too rapidly → thrashing.

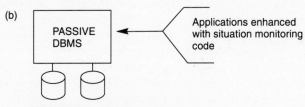

Problems:
- Need to augment application programs.
- Management and maintenance of application is costly.

Figure 25.2   Conventional passive DBMS mimicking active behavior: (a) the polling approach; (b) the enhanced application approach.

base events (for instance, updates) or nondatabase events (for instance, hardware failure detected by a diagnostic program); and if the condition evaluates to true, the *action* is executed. An active DBMS provides both modularity and timely response. The integrated approach to an active DBMS illustrated in Figure 25.3 can be viewed as the next logical step beyond deductive database systems. In an active DBMS, the notion of an event is generalized and made explicit. Rules include events, conditions, and actions. Figure 25.4 shows an active database for automatic reordering of items in an inventory control application.

Issues in Active Databases. Six important issues set active DBMSs apart from passive DBMSs:

- **Efficiency:** The set of all event–condition–action rules is likely to form a large set of predefined queries that need to be efficiently managed and evaluated when specified events occur. Evaluation of complex rules under time constraints is a challenge when sets of rules that represent a highly dynamic environment become very large. This opens new possibilities for optimization by using results from multiple-query optimization (Chakravarthy 1991; Shim et al. 1993).

- **Modes of rule execution:** Rules can be fired and executed under different modes: immediate, deferred, or detached. Under immediate mode of execution, the processing of the remaining steps of the original transaction (that is, the triggering

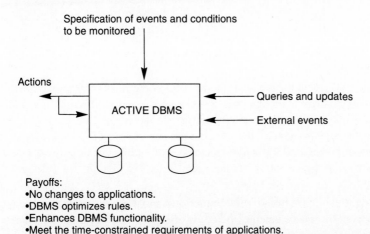

Payoffs:
•No changes to applications.
•DBMS optimizes rules.
•Enhances DBMS functionality.
•Meet the time-constrained requirements of applications.

Figure 25.3 The integrated approach to active databases.

transaction that caused the event to occur) is suspended until the fired rule has been completely processed. Response time and concurrency can be improved if the condition evaluation or action execution is detached from the original trans-action (that is, run in a separate transaction). If a rule is allowed to trigger another rule as a part of its execution, the transaction model becomes nested, leading to further complexity.

- **Data model extensions:** Active DBMSs require enhancements to the data model in at least two ways: for specifying events, and for specifying conditions and actions. In addition to events that correspond to database operations (such as insert, delete, and modify), temporal and/or periodic events (for example, that the balance in all bank accounts should be checked at 5 P.M. every day), and user- or

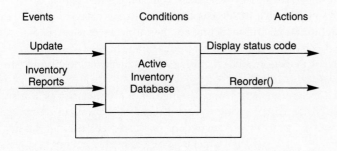

EVENT: Update Quantity on Hand (item).

CONDITION: Quantity_on_Hand (item) +
                    Quantity_on_Order(item) < Threshold (item).

ACTION: Reorder (item).

Figure 25.4 Active DBMS example (from Chakravarthy 1989).

application-generated events (such as a failure signal from a diagnostic routine on a hardware component) need to be supported. The language can be made to support a specification of complex events based on an event algebra (Jagdish and Gehani 1992).

- **Management of rules:** First, the ability to manipulate rules (add/delete/modify) as if they were any other data object in the system is essential. Second, mechanisms for enabling and disabling individual rules or rule sets are often needed. For example, the set of rules activated while an aircraft is taxiing needs to be disabled when it becomes airborne, and a different set of rules for the current context needs to be activated. Finally, selective enabling and selective disabling of rules are also important.

- **Supporting DBMS functions:** DBMS functions can be supported by the active DBMS. Constraint management (including integrity and security enforcement), maintenance of derived data (such as views), and rule-based inferencing are a few examples.

- **Interaction with parts of DBMS:** Unlike in a conventional query optimizer, in an active DBMS, rules cannot be optimized in isolation. Optimization of rules requires interaction with several components of a DBMS (such as the transaction manager, the object manager, and the scheduler).

State of the Art of Active Databases. Following is a brief overview of the research and commercial efforts in the active database area.

HiPAC (Chakravarthy 1989, 1990), which stands for High Performance ACtive database system, was a research effort focussing on active time-constrained data management. The knowledge model of HiPAC included primitives for events, conditions, and actions, and it formulated the notion of "rules as first-class objects." In the execution model, the interaction between rule execution and conventional transaction execution was investigated; coupling modes and algorithms for supporting rules that had various coupling modes were developed. Various other issues were addressed as part of the HiPAC project: an architecture of an active DBMS; combining real-time processing with databases; multiple query optimization; and modeling and performance evaluation of various coupling modes. For the battle management application, PROBE (Dayal 1985) was extended to include event detection and processing of conditions consisting of spatial queries.

An Event/Trigger Mechanism (ETM) was designed at the University of Karlsruhe (Dittrich 1986; Kotz 1988) to enforce complex consistency constraints in design databases. The effort addressed the general problem of constraint enforcement and was implemented on top of the DAMASCUS design database system. Event, action, and trigger tables are maintained for efficient access and determination of triggers when a specific event occurs. The active capability is an add-on to the underlying system, and consequently the modes in which a trigger can be executed with respect to a transaction are limited. In POSTGRES (Stonebraker 1987), commercially designated Miro, database operations and other predefined events (such as date) trigger the rule evaluation. Rules are expressed in QUEL by using keywords (such as *always* and *demand*), and the system uses special types of locks for the database items mentioned in the condition for the implementation of rules. Trigger implementation (also called *tuple-level processing*) is embedded in the executor and uses three types of locks. Query rewrite uses the well-known query modification approach outlined in Chapter 17. Only the equivalent of immediate coupling mode is supported.

The Starburst project at IBM has addressed the problem of set-oriented rules (Widom 1990) triggered by database state transitions in the context of relational databases. Events corresponding to database operations (inserted/deleted/updated) can be associated with a condition and an action by using the SQL syntax. The interaction between transaction execution and rule execution is addressed in detail.

Sybase (1992) supports simple triggers, where the triggering conditions involve only a single relation, and can be viewed as being an active DBMS in principle. Sybase recognizes events that correspond only to database operations—namely, insert, delete, and update. Triggers cannot return data to the user and cannot be specified on views or temporary objects. One trigger cannot fire another trigger, and triggers are always executed in immediate mode.

InterBase (Interbase 90), on the other hand, does not impose most of the restrictions seen in Sybase. In InterBase, a trigger specification consists of an event, a sequence number associated with the trigger, and a trigger action. An event can be one of the database operations (store, erase, or modify). Any number of triggers can be defined on a relation. The user can also specify whether the trigger action is to be executed before or after the operation corresponding to the event is performed. Multiple rule execution is supported by using the priority information (an integer) to resolve conflicts. Access to new and old tuple values is provided through the keywords *old* and *new*.

ORACLE version 7, INGRES, INFORMIX, and so on all provide some degree of rule and trigger support. In terms of commercial DBMS products, rule-based facilities are likely to be offered with increasing frequency in the coming years.

25.3.2 *Multimedia Databases*

Multimedia databases store information that originates from different media, including numeric data, text, bitmap images, yaster graphics images, audio, and video. They also use appropriate display devices in presenting the information. Large-scale applications of multimedia databases can be expected in the following disciplines in the coming years:

- *Documents and records management*: A large number of industries and businesses keep very detailed records and a variety of documents. The data may include engineering design and manufacturing data, medical records of patients, publishing material, and insurance claim records, depending on the organization.

- *Knowledge dissemination*: The multimedia mode is a very effective mode of knowledge dissemination. As such, we hope to see electronic books and repositories of information on many topics for public consumption.

- *Education and training*: Teaching materials for different audiences, from kindergarten children up to professional equipment operators, can be designed from multimedia sources.

- *Marketing, advertising, retailing, and travel:* There are virtually no limits to using multimedia information in these applications for effective presentations.

- *Real-time control and monitoring:* Coupled with active database technology (see Section 25.3.1), multimedia presentation of information can be a very effective means for monitoring and controlling manufacturing operations, nuclear power plants, patients in intensive care units, transportation systems, and so on.

Issues in Multimedia Databases. Multimedia applications dealing with thousands of images, documents, audio and video segments, and free text data depend critically on appropriate modeling of the structure and content of data. Multimedia information systems are very complex and embrace a large set of issues, including the following:

- *Modeling:* This area gets into the controversy of applying database versus information retrieval techniques to the problem. There are problems of dealing with complex objects (see Chapter 22) made up of types of data that range over numeric, text, graphic (computer-generated image), animated graphic image, audio stream, and video sequence. Documents constitute a specialized area and deserve special consideration.

- *Design:* The conceptual, logical, and physical design of multimedia databases has not been researched yet. It can be based on the general methodology described in Chapter 14, but the issues at each level are far more complex.

- *Storage:* Storage of multimedia data on standard disklike devices presents problems of representation, compression, mapping to device hierarchies, archiving, and buffering during the I/O operation. Adhering to standards such as JPEG or MPEG is one way most vendors of multimedia products are likely to deal with this issue. In DBMSs, a "BLOB" (Binary Large OBject) facility allows untyped bitmaps to be stored and retrieved. Standardized software will be required to deal with synchronization, compression/decompression, and so on, which are still in the research domain (Vin 1991).

- *Retrieval:* The "database way" of retrieving information is based on query languages and internally kept index structures. The "information retrieval" way of dealing with it relies strictly on keywords or predefined index terms. For images, video data, and audio data, this opens up many issues. We discuss a few of them later.

- *Performance:* For multimedia applications involving simply documents and text, performance constraints are subjectively determined by the user population. For applications involving video playback or audio-video synchronization, however, physical limitations dominate. For instance, video must be delivered at a steady rate of 60 frames per second. Techniques for query optimization may compute expected response time before evaluating the query. The use of parallel processing of data may alleviate some problems, but currently such efforts are largely experimental.

The preceding issues have given rise to a variety of open research problems. We only address a few of them as representative problems in this section.

Databases Versus Information Retrieval Perspectives. In database models and systems, modeling the data content has not been an issue because the data has a rigid structure and the meaning of a data instance can be inferred from the schema. On the other hand, information retrieval (IR) is mainly concerned with modeling the content of text documents (by keywords, phrasal indexes, semantic networks, and so on) for which structure is generally neglected. By modeling the content, the system can determine whether a document is relevant to an inquirer's query by examining the content-descriptors of the document. Consider, for instance, an insurance company's accident claim report as a multimedia object: it contains images of the accident, structured insurance forms, audio recordings of the parties involved in the accident, the text report of the insurance company's representative, and other information. What data models to employ in representing multimedia information remains an open issue.

Requirements of Multimedia/Hypermedia Data Modeling and Retrieval. To capture the full expressive power of multimedia, the system should have a modeling construct that lets the user specify links between any two arbitrary nodes. **Hypermedia links** can take on a number of different forms, including the following:

- Links can be specified with or without associated information. A link may have large descriptions associated with it.

- A link can start from a specific point inside a node, or it can start from the whole node.

- A link can be directional or nondirectional.

The link capability of the data model should account for all of these variations. When a content-based retrieval of multimedia data is needed, the query mechanism should have access to the links and the link-associated information. The system should provide facilities for defining views over links, as well as private and public links. Valuable contextual information can be obtained from the structural information. An automatically generated hypermedia link does not reveal anything new about the two nodes, because the link was created automatically by some method. On the other hand, manually generated hypermedia links and the link information can be utilized to gain more knowledge about the nodes that are being connected. Facilities for creating and utilizing such links, navigational query languages to utilize the links, and so on are important features of any system permitting effective use of multimedia information.

Indexing of Images. There are two approaches to the problem of indexing images. One uses image-processing techniques to identify the different objects automatically. The other uses manual indexing techniques to assign index terms and phrases. One important problem in using image-processing techniques to index pictures relates to scalability. The current state of the art allows only simple patterns in images. The complexity increases with the number of recognizable features. Another important problem relates to the complexity of the query. Rules and inference mechanisms, as discussed in Chapter 24, can be used to derive higher-level facts from simple features of images. This allows high-level queries like "find the apartment designs that allow maximum sunshine in the living room," in an architectural application.

The information retrieval approach to image indexing is based on one of the following three indexing schemes:

- *Classificatory systems* (Gordon 1988) classify the images hierarchically into certain predetermined categories. In this approach, the indexer and the user should have a good knowledge of the available categories. Finer details of a complex image and relationships among objects in an image cannot be captured.

- *Keyword-based systems* use an uncontrolled (alternately, a controlled) vocabulary as in indexing of textual documents. Simple facts represented in the image (like "ice-capped region") and facts derived as a result of high-level interpretation by humans (like permanent ice, recent snowfall, and polar ice) can be captured.

- In the *entity-attribute-relation scheme* (Leung 1992), all the objects in the picture and the relationships between objects and the attributes of the objects are identified.

In the case of text documents, a human indexer can choose the keywords from the pool of words available in the document to be indexed. This is not possible in the case of image and video data.

Open Problems in Text Retrieval. Although text retrieval has existed in business applications and library systems for a long time, the following open problems still confront the designers of text retrieval systems:

- *Phrase indexing:* Substantial improvements can be realized if phrase descriptors (as opposed to single-word index terms) are assigned to documents and used in queries, provided that these descriptors are good indicators of document content and information need (Fagan 1987).

- *Use of thesaurus:* One reason for the poor recall of current systems is that the vocabulary of the user differs from the vocabulary used to index the documents. One solution is to use a thesaurus to expand the user's query with related terms. The problem then becomes one of finding a thesaurus for the domain of interest.

- *Resolving ambiguity:* One of the reasons for low precision (the ratio of the number of relevant items retrieved to the total number of retrieved items) in text information retrieval systems is that words have multiple meanings. One way to resolve ambiguity is to use an on-line dictionary (Krovetz 1992) while the other is to compare the contexts in which the two words occur (Salton 1991).

Multimedia information systems promise to bring about a marriage of the disciplines of information retrieval and database management, which have heretofore tended to diverge.

25.3.3 *Scientific and Statistical Databases*

The use of computers to manage scientific and statistical information is not new. However, database technology was rather late in reaching statisticians and scientists. In March, 1990, the National Science Foundation sponsored a workshop, hosted by the University of Virginia, at which representatives from the earth, life, and space sciences gathered together with computer scientists to discuss the problems facing the scientific community in the area of database management. These problems are likely to grow exponentially over the next decade. We summarize in this section the important issues raised in this report (French et al. 1990).

Scientific data is unique because of its relatively static nature and indefinite retention. The typical transaction-processing environment of conventional databases is absent for scientific databases; they have a low update frequency, and old data is rarely discarded. We referred earlier to the large volume of scientific data in the human genome initiative: it involves 3 billion nucleotide bases. The Magellan planetary probe will generate about 1 trillion bytes of data over five years.

Scientific database systems comprise three "dimensions": level of interpretation, intended analysis, and sources of information. In the following discussion, *data set* is used to mean data related to a single experiment or mission; *database* is used for any aggregate of data that is summarized or compiled from multiple experiments.

The Interpretation Dimension. This dimension refers to the continuum reflecting the raw (versus processed) nature of the information. It affects what one expects of the data set and how the data set is used. Based on this dimension, data can be divided into the following categories:

- *Raw/sensor data:* This consists of (seldom saved) raw values obtained directly from the measurement device.

- *Calibrated data:* This consists of (normally preserved) raw physical values, corrected with calibration operators.

- *Validated data:* This consists of calibrated data that has been filtered through quality-assurance procedures; it is the most commonly used type of data for scientific purposes.

- *Derived data:* This consists of frequently aggregated data, such as gridded or averaged data, for which the detail of the underlying measurements has been lost.

- *Interpreted data:* This consists of derived data that is related to other data sets or to the literature of the field.

Typically, information about the processing must be retained and propagated together with a data set. The raw data and its summary may need to be interrelated.

Intended Scientific Analysis. Most stored scientific data is subjected to some type of analysis. Earth science data is subjected to statistical, time-series analysis. Genome data is analyzed for patterns over character storage. Space data in large arrays is transformed (for example, by using the Fourier transform) for spectral analysis. The relational data model is unsuitable because of its inability to represent sequences and because of the lack of representation for characteristics of data used during analysis. Sometimes, data is to be "corrected" rather than "updated," but there are no facilities for accomplishing this in relational DBMSs.

Sources of Data. This is a fundamental discriminatory feature of scientific databases. In a single-source database environment, raw data is collected and further processes by filtering or calibration techniques; the resulting validated data is used in light of the scientific mission. The syntactic and semantic complexity of the interpreted data is much higher than that of the original data. Multisource databases add a new dimension of complexity, with multiple methodologies of data collection, instruments for data recording, and different protocols affecting encoding and accuracy. These databases may be independently used and managed by diverse computing systems and DBMSs. However, the goal typically is to create a common data archive such as GENBANK for the human genome initiative (see Section 25.2.3), to be used by the original research teams that are generating and managing the raw data. This inherits the problems of distributed and multi-databases we discussed in Chapter 23.

Traditional DBMSs have proved inadequate to deal with the above set of requirements mainly for the following reasons:

- They lack features to deal with the built-in redundancies and inaccuracies of data during scientific experimentation and its recording. The progression of data along the interpretation dimension cannot be handled gracefully.

- Analysis of data using multivariate statistical functions and aggregations is lacking.

- DBMSs have the overhead of transaction processing, which is unnecessary for most scientific applications.

- The inherent distinction in statistical data between a value and what it stands for (such as a number (value) representing the number of households in Fulton County that have an income in the range of \$75,000–\$100,000 per year and at least one child in a private school) is not supported in traditional DBMSs. Abstractions such as the cross-product proposed in the data model OSAM* (Su et al. (1988) are useful.

Important issues in the areas of data definition, data manipulation, and technology standards need to be addressed to meet the requirements of scientific and statistical databases. In the area of data definition, the following issues arise:

- New data models, including those covered in Chapter 21, need to be explored. They should support special data types such as time series and DNA sequences.

- Meta-data management is crucial, with a provision needed for dealing with citations, different types of documentation, and experimental details.

- Evolution of data must be supported with an appropriate audit trail.

- Standards are needed across scientific disciplines for recording experimental results and even for sharing citations.

In the area of data manipulation, the following points are relevant:

- It is not adequate to perform conventional querying and report generation. Statistical and analytical functions must become an integrated part of the system. A trend is also visible to add a relational querying language interface such as SQL to existing statistical packages such as SAS.

- Various summarization and aggregation operations, together with a facility to describe the summary statistic, must be provided.

- Export and import features must exist for transferring data into and out of the scientific database and into statistical utilities.

- Since a typical statistician or scientist is a novice database user initially, a range of user interfaces and browsing and navigational facilities must be provided. Provision should be made to allow users to "learn" the data management aspect of the system through a graduation of those features and interfaces.

In the area of technology standards, the following issues are prominent:

- Physical encoding of data is important, with compression and indexing techniques needed for efficient storage and retrieval. Encryption of data is essential for privacy where human subjects are involved.

- For long-term experiments (such as a space probe or long-term tracking of patients with a certain disease), schemas may have to undergo changes as experimental techniques evolve.

- Standards including data formats and associated analysis tools are needed within disciplines and across disciplines. An example is the FITS standard used by the astrophysics community.

- Transmission of entire data sets over high-speed networks is becoming feasible. Extensive catalogs are needed with names, aliases, codes, data derivation procedures, data quality-control measures, and usage information. Appropriate archiving of data sets is necessary.

It is evident from the preceding discussion that the community of scientific database users has a very special set of needs. French et al. (1990) contains a series of recommendations that include addressing sociological as well as technical problems; professional societies are called upon to encourage cooperation among scientists through easier exchange of information.

25.3.4 *Spatial and Temporal Database Management*

In this subsection we cover two important types of data that have started receiving attention from database modeling researchers only recently. In Section 25.2.1, while discussing CAD/CAM applications, we alluded to geometric modeling. Whether in the context of CAD/CAM, of architectural and civil engineering design, or of cartography and geological surveys, it is important to model the spatial dimension. Today's data models are lacking in this area. The spatial semantics can be captured by three common representations:

- *Solid representation:* The space is divided into pieces of various sizes. The spatial characteristics of an entity are then represented by the set of these pieces associated with that entity.

- *Boundary representation (or wire frame models):* The spatial characteristics are represented by line segments or boundaries.

- *Abstract representation:* Relationships with spatial semantics, such as ABOVE, NEAR, IS-NEXT-TO, and BEHIND, are used to associate entities.

The PROBE project at Computer Corporation of America (Dayal et al. 1987) provided support for spatial data in the functional data model DAPLEX (Shipman 1981). While it is clear that many applications would benefit from such facilities, different application domains have varying requirements. For example, in VLSI applications, space is two-dimensional and discrete; basic objects to be stored are points, line segments, rectangles, and polygons. In solid modeling for most manufacturing applications, space is three-dimensional and continuous, and the basic objects are parametrically defined curves and surfaces. The operations relevant to each application area also differ.

If we assume that a 2D or 3D space is represented by using line segments and polygons, the following representative queries might be made:

- Queries about line segments:

  - All segments that intersect a given point or set of points.

  - All segments that have a given set of endpoints.

  - All segments that intersect a given line segment.

- Proximity queries:

  - The nearest line segment to a given point.

  - All segments within a given distance from a given point (also known as a range or window query).

- Queries involving attributes of line segments:

  - Given a point, the minimum enclosing polygon whose constituent line segments are all of a specified type.

  - Given a point, all the polygons that are incident on it.

Different ways of storing objects in space have been proposed by decomposing space. Examples include the following:

- *Minimum bounding rectangles:* Objects are grouped into hierarchies, which in turn are organized into structures similar to B-trees. Examples include R-tree (Guttman 1984) and R*tree.

- *Disjoint cells:* Objects are decomposed into subobjects. Each subobject is in a different cell.

- *Uniform grid:* The space is divided by overlaying a uniform grid structure. Objects appear in a specific cell of this structure.

- *Quad trees:* This is a hierarchical variable-resolution data structure; there are many variations of it.

The representation of objects in space and the processing of queries on those objects are specific areas of investigation that are being heavily pursued by the developers of Geographic Information Systems (GISs). For a thorough review of spatial data structures and their applications, the reader should consult Samet (1990a, 1990b).

Temporal Data Management. Temporal information is a special one-dimensional case of spatial information. Temporal aspects built into databases must include three types of support for time: time points, time intervals, and abstract relationships involving time (before, after, during, simultaneously, concurrently, and so on). The **history** aspect of databases is very important for applications such as project management, patient histories in hospitals, maintenance histories of equipment, and administrative and operational control in office systems.

One limitation of current databases is that information becomes effective at the same moment as it is recorded in the database. There are no provisions for making a distinction between the *registration time* (or *transaction time*) when certain data is entered and the *logical time* (or *valid time*) period during which the specific data values are valid. In fact, sometimes a transaction time must be recorded for an event. Many database updates in real applications are either *retroactive* (they became effective at some previous point in time) or *proactive* (they become effective at some time in the future). Another limitation is that current systems maintain no history of changes. Each update destroys old facts. The database thus represents only the current state of some domain rather than a history of that domain. To deal with the preceding requirements, data models are needed that explicitly incorporate time, separating time-varying information from time-invariant information and representing them separately. One proposed model is the Temporal Relational Model (TRM) of Navathe and Ahmed (1989). In this model, attributes are divided into time-varying and non-time-varying ones, and so are relations. In time-varying relations, two timestamp attributes are appended, representing the start time and the end time of the logical time over which the tuple is valid. This approach is called *tuple time stamping*. Figure 25.5 shows a time-varying EMPLOYEE relation in TRM.

For this model, a time normalization procedure is proposed to avoid temporal anomalies; the SQL query language is extended into Temporal SQL (TSQL) with a variety of features, including the WHEN clause, temporal ordering, time-slice, aggregate functions, grouping, and a moving-time window. Another school of thinking proposes *attribute time stamping*, which appends a new attribute value with a timestamp at each update time (Ben-Zvi 1982; Clifford and Tansel 1985; Gadia 1988). This results in unnormalized relations with a much more complicated algebra and query language; furthermore, relationships involving non-time-varying keys *cannot* be represented in this approach.

A recent landmark in temporal database research was the publication of a comprehensive collection of works representing the state of the art in this field, edited by Tansel

EmpNo	Salary	Position	T_S	T_E
33	20K	Typist	12	24
33	25K	Secretary	25	35
45	27K	Jr. Engineer	28	37
45	30K	Sr. Engineer	38	42

Notes: T_S: Time start

T_E: Time end

Figure 25.5   A time-varying relation in the Temporal Relational Model.

et al. (1993). The organization of this collection indicates topics in which interesting work has appeared in temporal database management in the recent past:

- *Extensions to the relational model:* This work has emphasized the different ways of adding timestamp information to a static relational model that contains "snapshot" relations. Different types of time may be added by using the two primary approaches: triple timestamping, which was illustrated earlier; and attribute timestamping, which gives rise to unnormalized (non-1NF) relations. Extensions to SQL and QUEL have been proposed to handle temporal operations. Temporal relational algebras, calculi, and aggregate functions have been proposed. An organized effort is underway to "standardize" temporal enhancements to SQL.

- *Other data models:* This work includes extensions to the ER model and to the functional data model. A spreadsheet history model and a temporal deductive database model have also been proposed.

- *Implementation issues:* Query processing and optimization take a new form, depending on the data model and the language used. Indexing of temporal information in various ways (Elmasri et al. 1990) and updating as well as concurrency control and recovery of *transaction-time* (or *rollback*) databases have been investigated. The temporal join operator may assume many forms; its optimization has been studied. Finally, incremental and decremental computation of transaction-time databases has been investigated.

Open problems include reasoning with temporal information, processing transactions over valid-time and transaction-time databases, mixing temporal processing with active and deductive databases, and integrating temporal information over heterogeneous environments.

With the advent of optical write-once disks that can store 10^{13} bytes of data, appending updates to history data becomes viable. Further work in the implementation aspects and commercial feasibility of these models is necessary, however. Implementation of these data models also places demands on operating systems for time management, recording, and synchronization of multiuser time frames.

25.3.5 *Extensible and Unified Database Management*

As we saw earlier in this chapter, there is a need to build new DBMSs to meet the challenges of the new applications. DBMSs are complex pieces of software with complicated algorithms and relationships among components. Because it takes a long time to develop a DBMS, a new modular approach has been proposed that builds DBMSs out of "DBMS parts" or building blocks.

Such an **extensible database management system** would assemble prewritten modules (algorithms) into new "tailor-made DBMSs." This approach has several obvious advantages:

- New DBMS development is rapid and economical.

- Technological or algorithmic improvements can quickly be incorporated into the reusable modules, and as a result, the system can always remain up to date.

• Proposed new techniques and algorithms can be evaluated without making significant modifications to the system.

This approach has been pursued by the GENESIS project at the University of Texas (Batory et al. 1986) and by EXODUS at the University of Wisconsin (Graefe and Dewitt 1987; Carey et al. 1986, 1986a, 1988). GENESIS takes the approach of defining the components of a DBMS and the interfaces among them in such a way that a new DBMS can be configured within minutes from a menu-driven user interface, just by selecting appropriate options. Plug-compatible modules are designed for access methods, query optimization, concurrency control, recovery, and other functions by preimplementing a set of alternative algorithms. The common interfaces allow them to be pieced together as building blocks.

EXODUS is architected differently. It provides certain kernel facilities, including a versatile storage manager and a type manager. The type manager permits definition of class hierarchies with multiple inheritance. The storage object is an untyped, uninterpreted variable-length byte sequence of arbitrary size. Buffer management, concurrency control, and recovery mechanisms are provided on top of the storage manager and can be modified. Type-independent index structures, including B+ trees, grid files, and linear hashing, can be selected from a library of access methods. The language E is provided for the database implementor (DBI). It extends C by adding the notion of persistent objects to C, and it frees the implementor from worrying about the internal structure of those objects. The "operator methods" layer in the architecture contains a mix of DBI-supplied and EXODUS-supplied code to operate on the typed, stored objects. Query processing is divided into query optimization and query evaluation. The DBI supplies the description of operators (in a target query language), methods to implement the operators, and cost formulas for those methods. The rule-based optimizer generator transforms these descriptions into C source code, which constitutes a tailored optimizer for the target system. The EXODUS storage manager has been used by various vendors (including O2, which we discussed in Chapter 22) to implement their own DBMSs.

The preceding approach to configuring, which involves generating a tailored DBMS, contrasts with another approach proposed to deal with new applications: that of building DBMSs with extensible functionality by providing a wide set of features. This **full-functionality approach** is exemplified by the PROBE (Dayal et al. 1987) and STARBURST (Haas et al. 1988) projects.

We have already referred to PROBE and STARBURST, while discussing active databases; and we mentioned spatial query processing in PROBE. The POSTGRES DBMS, now called Miro (Stonebraker et al. 1993) also combines object-oriented and active database capabilities with the relational model.

A third trend in this category is toward unified database management. An example of a system in this category is UniSQL, which claims to combine "the sophistication, power, and ease of use in the popular application development tools" while "delivering on the promise of object-oriented development and multimedia database integration." The UniSQL product is organized as follows:

• *UniSQL/X:* This component provides the client-server DBMS platform. It allows traditional relational applications to coexist with the new object-oriented database application. The SQL/S is an ANSI SQL–compliant object-oriented query language.

- *UniSQL/M:* This component is a heterogeneous database manager that allows access to databases from other relational and prerelational DBMSs. It supports an object-oriented query language, SQL/M, that allows the definition and processing of a multi-database schema.
- *UniSQL/4GE Tools:* Object Master is a tool for dynamically generating applications for the creation and management of objects within SQL/X and SQL/M environments. Other tools, called Visual Editor and Media Master, allow for viewing and editing of schemas and for sophisticated report generation.

The next generation of DBMSs is likely to be patterned after the UniSQL DBMS. They will combine features of relational and other data models and provide a combination of the active, multimedia, scientific, spatial, and temporal facilities we have discussed so far.

25.4 Interfaces with Other Technologies and Future Research

Database technology is not developing in isolation. It is very closely tied to several other disciplines, some of which have already been pointed out. For example, the distributed and multi-database area (Chapter 23) is closely tied to telecommunications and networking. Multimedia databases are closely tied to information retrieval. In this section, we comment on a few such interfaces and some likely areas for future development.

25.4.1 *Interface with Software Engineering Technology*

The primary goal of software engineering is to develop ways to make the software development process easier, more effective, and more efficient. A prime end product of the software engineering activity is application software. With DBMSs becoming so commonplace, the application software development should be considered in the context of DBMSs. A merging of the concepts from both of these disciplines should occur in the following areas:

- *Design databases:* A large design activity such as developing a large software system is like large design projects in other areas, such as building a skyscraper, a power station, or a manufacturing facility. A large system design can be hierarchically decomposed into designs of smaller and smaller components. Each component evolves, design specifications change, and new design alternatives appear. A proper way to consolidate and track the design information is to create a database for it.
- *Application generation from high-level specification:* This area is of great interest in commercial application development. Several commercial application generators are on the market, as part of CASE (computer-assisted software engineering) tools. The main incentive is that such generators reduce the effort and cost of application development. Since this goal is shared by DBMSs, in the future we are likely to see application generators closely coupled with underlying DBMSs.

- *Software tools:* This is an important area of future development. Software tools have two purposes: to reduce the drudgery of certain tasks for humans, and to improve the performance of certain machines. Various types of tools are needed with DBMSs. Tools of the first type include requirements specification and analysis tools, conceptual design tools, tools for view integration, tools for schema mapping among models, tools for physical design and optimization, and partitioning and allocation tools. Tools of the second type include performance monitoring, tuning, reorganizing, and restructuring tools. The past few years have seen tremendous activity in tool development. However, few current tools provide good interfaces and can interface easily with other tools. Of course, there are a few exceptions. Vigorous activity in tool development is likely to continue in the next few years.

- *Prototyping:* This is a popular topic among software engineering enthusiasts, but it has received little attention in the database area. Prototyping of databases and applications can go a long way toward validating the design of schemas, refining their structures, and evaluating the relative frequencies of queries (transactions). We are likely to see substantial development in this area. Increasing availability of personal computers and workstations makes the role of prototyping even more significant.

25.4.2 *Interface with Artificial Intelligence Technology*

In Chapter 24, we discussed the relationship between logic and databases and saw how it led to the development of the deductive database technology. Today there is growing interest in moving from databases to **knowledge bases** (KBs). Knowledge is information at a higher level of abstraction. For example, "Mr. Jones is 45 years old" may be considered to be a fact in a database. "Mr. Jones is middle aged" is not such a precise fact; it is a broader, higher form of knowledge. Similarly, while "Mr. Jones had an accident on January 17, 1988, in New York at the ramp leading in from I-495 to I-278" is a fact, "Mr. Jones is a reckless driver" is knowledge. "All middle-aged men are reckless" is another higher-level element of knowledge, although it may represent a poor inference because it is not generally correct.

It is very hard to define and quantify knowledge. Knowledge is typically generated by experts in some domain of expertise. Thus knowledge is used to define, control, and interpret the data in a database.

Knowledge comes in various forms (Wiederhold 1984):

- *Structural knowledge:* This is knowledge about dependencies and constraints among the data (for example, "insertion into benefit plan x is subject to preregistration in benefit plan y").

- *General procedural knowledge:* This is knowledge that can be described only by a procedure or a method (for example, a procedure to determine the "creditworthiness" of a customer).

- *Application-specific knowledge:* This is knowledge determined by the rules and regulations applicable in a specific domain (for example, computation of the cheapest airline fare between two cities).

- *Enterprise-directing knowledge:* This is a higher form of knowledge that allows an enterprise to make decisions. For example, on a companywide basis, this knowledge includes the cost of relocating and retraining employees as well as some measure of the benefit in the form of morale and loyalty of keeping employees on the job for more than n years.

Intensional knowledge is defined as knowledge that underlies and precedes the factual content of the database. Such knowledge can be fully specified *before* the database is established. Database systems exist to manage the data and the meta-data, which together constitute **extensional knowledge** or knowledge embedded in facts and instances. Knowledge systems use not only the extensional knowledge but also the intensional knowledge, possibly in the form of rules in a rule base. **Derived knowledge** is a form in which extensional knowledge and intensional knowledge are mixed. A database may store relations called father (Father_name, Child_name), mother (Mother_name, Child_name), and person (Person_name, Sex). From these three basic relations, it would be possible to define a variety of family relationships, from cousins to uncles to grandfathers, which is the job of a rule base.

Most KB systems today store intensional knowledge in the form of rules. Other representations include logical assertions, semantic networks, and frames. We refer to the inferencing and control strategy of a KB as *strategic knowledge*.

A promising new area of research is *knowledge mining*, which involves extracting previously unknown but useful information from a database (Piatesky-Shapiro and Frawley 1991; Anwar et al. 1992). Potential areas of development include case-based reasoning (Kolodner 1993), applied as an aid to reasoning with databases; automated schema design by means of conceptual clustering (Beck et al. 1993); and explanation-based learning, applied to maintain the consistency of a database (as in the XCON system; Schimmler et al. 1991), among others. Many learning strategies may be used as new paradigms for query processing in database systems.

25.4.3 *User Interfaces for Databases*

Despite the current advances in user interfaces, a few areas remain to be explored, particularly for the benefit of database users:

- *Customized languages:* Casual and occasional users need languages that are easy to use and fit well with their problem domains. An account executive in an investment firm deals with a different set of terms and processing requirements than does a production supervisor in a manufacturing company. If both are using the same system, each should be given a customized interface. Currently, these are not impossible to provide, but they involve a heavy programming effort. Future systems should make it easier to generate a customized set of language constructs for each set of users.

- *Alternative paradigms for accessing databases:* The system called Spatial Data Management System (SDMS) of Computer Corporation of America (Herot 1980) is a good example of getting away from the records- and files-oriented approach to data management. SDMS simulates an environment in which data is organized in a three-dimensional space such as an office. It bases the search for data on the principle that people are good at locating information by knowing where it is placed and by knowing some physical appearance attributes of the medium or container in which it is recorded. Such a system allows a natural "spatial exploration" through the database, encourages browsing, and uses icons as dictionary information (meta-data). This system is able to store and display illustrations and pictures from videodisks and other media. Visualization of scientific data and even of document repositories by using clever techniques is receiving a lot of attention (Korfhage 1991; Chalmers 1992). In the future we might see more developments along these lines that would also incorporate other forms of information, including movies, animations, and (going a step farther) even smells and tastes!

- *Natural-language interface in multiple languages:* With faster means of communication, it is already becoming necessary to make the same database under the same DBMS available to Americans, Italians, Japanese, and others at the same time. Today's natural-language interfaces are inefficient and inadequate. Future interfaces will demand multilingual support. There are related problems of displaying information in different scripts, allowing editing of text involving multiple languages (for example, English and Arabic, where the latter is read from right to left), storing aliases in different languages, and so on.

25.4.4 *Database Machines and Architecture*

Research on database machines has focused primarily on the efficient retrieval and storage of large quantities of data. One future direction of research on database machines would be to design a computer that integrates the problem-solving components with the data management functions. Another is to develop hardware for database management functions, such as security and integrity control, concurrency control, and transaction management, that are currently implemented by software and constitute a major source of performance overhead. Research into parallel architectures for knowledge-based systems is also needed.

25.4.5 *Interface with Programming Language Technology*

Research on query languages—query language design and query modification, optimization, and compilation—is ongoing in relation to hard application areas of CAD, office systems, and statistical, scientific, spatial, and temporal database management. Further work is needed on proving the equivalence of models and languages and on formalizing their semantics.

A new field of research called Database Programming Languages (DBPLs) is emerging (Bancilhon and Buneman 1990). These languages will minimize the "impedance mismatch" among traditional programming languages and database query languages. However, none of the proposals made so far have been demonstrated on a practical scale.

Many other fields can benefit from the application of database technology. We cannot attempt to name them all here. One promising area is Computer Supported Cooperative Work or CSCW (Kling 1991). It stands to gain by facilitating problem solving in

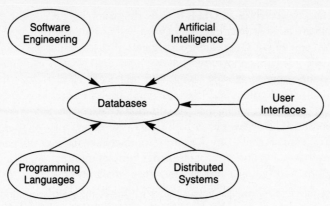

Figure 25.6   Future integration of technologies.

a group context, using principles of active database management (Chakravarthy et al. 1993).

We conclude this chapter with Figure 25.6, which shows that, in future information modeling and processing applications in the diverse areas to which databases will be applied, database technology must work hand in hand with the related technologies of software engineering, artificial intelligence, programming languages, user interfaces, and distributed systems. Users will engage in problem-solving activities with the database as a focus and with these other technologies supporting various facets of the problem-solving process.

Selected Bibliography

Much of the relevant bibliography for this chapter has been already referenced in the various sections. Here we give a few additional references. Several journals and conference proceedings may be consulted to keep track of developments in the database systems field. Among the prominent ones are *ACM Transactions on Database Systems*, *IEEE Transactions on Knowledge and Data Engineering*, *IEEE Transactions on Software Engineering* (particularly prior to 1990), *Information Systems*, and *Data and Knowledge Engineering* (North Holland). In the last couple of years, the following new journals have started: *The VLDB Journal*, *Journal of Distributed and Parallel Databases*, *Journal of Intelligent Information Systems*, and *Journal of Intelligent Cooperative Information Systems*. Several heavily refereed international conferences publish proceedings of the papers. The major conferences are the ACM SIGMOD annual conference (since 1974), the VLDB conference (since 1975), the IEEE Data Engineering Conference (since 1984), the Conference on Extending Database Technology (since 1989), and the Entity-Relationship Conference (since 1980). Because of rapidly growing interest in the emerging technologies, a new workshop called Research Issues in Data Engineering was started in 1991. It has devoted itself to interoperability and multi-databases in 1991 and 1993, to multimedia in 1992, and to active databases in 1994. Proceedings are published by IEEE. A new conference called Parallel and Distributed Information Systems has also been launched since 1991.

A series of international workshops called the Statistical Database Workshops has been held at irregular intervals starting in 1982. The International Federation of Information Processing Societies has a special interest group on databases that has been conducting Database Semantics workshops. The series of conference proceedings on Expert Database Systems (EDS 1984, 1986, 1988) has provided papers related to databases, logic, expert and knowledge-based systems, and techniques related to the integration of database and artificial intelligence technologies.

A special issue (2:1, March 1990) of *IEEE Transactions on Knowledge and Data Engineering* was devoted to the description of prototype database systems, some of which were mentioned in this and earlier chapters.

Reports of certain workshops summarize the results of panels invited by the National Science Foundation. One such report (Silberschatz et al. 1991) relates to the future of database systems research. Highlights from the report on scientific databases (French et al. 1990) were presented in Section 25.3.3.

Among specialized reading books, Stonebraker (1988) is a collection of research papers on database systems. Mylopoulos and Brodie (1989) has contributions on the interface of artificial intelligence and databases. Specialized books have started appearing on application areas such as geographic databases (Laurini 1992).

Another topic of current research, which we have not discussed elsewhere, involves the incorporation of incomplete and imprecise (fuzzy) information in databases. Papers that discuss incomplete information include Lipski (1979), Vassiliou (1980), Imielinski and Lipski (1981), and Liu and Sunderraman (1988). Techniques for dealing with fuzzy information are discussed in Zadeh (1983) and Zvieli (1986).

An early survey paper on back-end database machines is Maryanski (1980). Techniques for implementing main-memory databases are discussed by DeWitt et al. (1984). Applications of multimedia databases are discussed in Christodoulakis and Faloutsos (1986).

Dittrich (1986) is a survey of the object-oriented approach. Maier et al. (1986) describes the GEMSTONE /OPAL object-oriented system. The Darmstadt Database Kernel System is described in Paul et al. (1987). Navathe and Pillalamarri (1988) discusses how to make the ER model (discussed in Chapters 3 and 21) into an object-oriented model.

Many projects address databases for engineering design. Haskin and Lorie (1982) and Lorie and Plouffe (1983) discuss complex design objects in databases. Eastman (1987) discusses the facilities needed for engineering databases. Kemper et al. (1987) describes an object-oriented DBMS for engineering applications. Geometric modeling and spatial data processing are discussed by Kemper and Wallrath (1987) and Orenstein (1986). The R-tree data structure for indexing spatial data is presented in Guttman (1984). Schema evolution is discussed by Banerjee et al. (1987*a*), and CAD databases for VLSI are discussed in Du and Ghanta (1987).

Recently, interest has been growing in real-time databases, such as the work by Abbott and Garcia-Molina (1988). A temporal data model and query language for relational databases is described in Gadia (1988). Tsichritzis (1982) discusses forms management.

APPENDIX A

Alternative Diagrammatic Notations

Figure A.1 shows a number of different diagrammatic notations for representing ER and EER model concepts. Unfortunately, there is no standard notation: different database design practitioners prefer different notations. Similarly, various CASE (computer-aided software engineering) tools and OOA (object-oriented analysis) methodologies use various notations. Some notations are associated with models that have additional concepts and constraints beyond those of the ER and EER models described in Chapters 3 and 21, while other models have fewer concepts and constraints. The notation we used in Chapter 3 is quite close to the original notation for ER diagrams, which is still widely used. We discuss some alternate notations here.

Figure A.1(a) shows different notations for displaying entity types/classes, attributes, and relationships. In Chapters 3 and 21, we used the symbols marked (i) in Figure A.1(a)—namely, rectangle, oval, and diamond. Notice that symbol (ii) for entity types/ classes, symbol (ii) for attributes, and symbol (ii) for relationships are similar, but they are used by different methodologies to represent three different concepts. The straight line symbol (iii) for representing relationships is used by several tools and methodologies.

Figure A.1(b) shows some notations for attaching attributes to entity types. We used notation (i). Notation (ii) uses the third notation (iii) for attributes from Figure A.1(a). The last two notations in Figure A.1(b)—(iii) and (iv)—are popular in OOA methodologies and in some CASE tools. In particular, the last notation displays both the attributes and the methods of a class, separated by a horizontal line.

Figure A.1(c) shows various notations for representing the cardinality ratio of binary relationships. We used notation (i) in Chapters 3 and 21. Notation (ii)—known as the *chicken feet* notation—is quite popular. Notation (iv) uses the arrow as a functional reference (from the N to the 1 side) and resembles our notation for foreign keys in the relational model (see Figure 6.7); notation (v)—used in *Bachman diagrams*—uses the

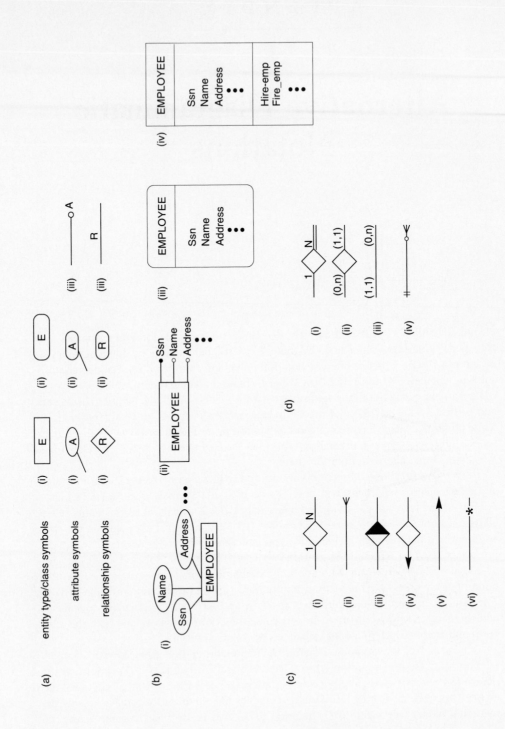

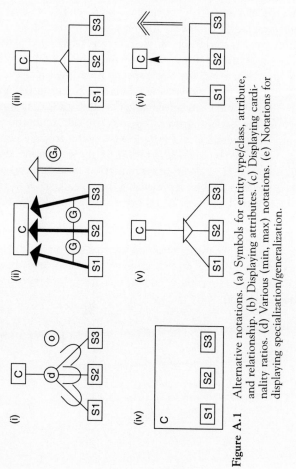

Figure A.1 Alternative notations. (a) Symbols for entity type/class, attribute, and relationship. (b) Displaying attributes. (c) Displaying cardinality ratios. (d) Various (min, max) notations. (e) Notations for displaying specialization/generalization.

arrow *in the reverse direction* (from the 1 to the N side). For a 1:1 relationship, (ii) uses a straight line without any chicken feet; (iii) makes both halves of the diamond white; and (iv) places arrowheads on both sides. For an M:N relationship, (ii) uses chicken feet at both ends of the line; (iii) makes both halves of the diamond black; and (iv) does not display any arrowheads.

Figure A.1(d) shows several variations for displaying (min, max) constraints, which are used to display both cardinality ratio and total/partial participation. Notation (ii) is the alternative notation we used in Figure 3.14 and discussed in Section 3.4. Recall that our notation specifies the constraint that each entity must participate in at least min and at most max relationship instances. Hence, for a 1:1 relationship, both max values are 1; and for M:N, both max values are n. A min value greater than 0 (zero) specifies total participation (existence dependency). In methodologies that use the straight line for displaying relationships, it is common to *reverse the positioning* of the (min, max) constraints, as shown in (iii). Another popular technique—which follows the same positioning as (iii)—is to display the *min* as o ("oh" or circle, which stands for zero) or as | (vertical dash, which stands for 1), and to display the max as | (vertical dash, which stands for 1) or as chicken feet (which stands for n), as shown in (iv).

Figure A.1(e) shows some notations for displaying specialization/generalization. We used notation (i) in Chapter 15, where a d in the circle specifies that the subclasses (S1, S2, and S3) are disjoint and an o specifies overlapping subclasses. Notation (ii) uses G (for generalization) to specify disjoint, and Gs to specify overlapping; some notations use the solid arrow, while others use the double arrow (shown at the side). Notation (iii) uses a triangle pointing toward the superclass, and notation (v) uses a triangle pointing toward the subclasses; it is also possible to use both notations in the same methodology, with (iii) indicating generalization and (v) indicating specialization. Notation (iv) places the boxes representing subclasses within the box representing the superclass. Of the notations based on (vi), some use a single-lined arrow, and others use a double-lined arrow (shown at the side).

The notations shown in Figure A.1 show only some of the diagrammatic symbols that have been used or suggested for displaying database conceptual schemas. Other notations, as well as various combinations of the preceding, have also been used. It would be useful to establish a standard that everyone would adhere to, in order to prevent misunderstandings and reduce confusion.

Parameters of Disks

The most important disk parameter is the time required to locate an arbitrary disk block, given its block address, and then to transfer the block between the disk and a main memory buffer. This is the **random access time** for accessing a disk block. There are three time components to consider:

1. **Seek time (s):** This is the time needed to mechanically position the read/write head on the correct track for movable-head disks. (For fixed-head disks, it is the time needed to electronically switch to the appropriate read/write head.) For movable-head disks this time varies, depending on the distance between the current track under the read/write head and the track specified in the block address. Usually, the disk manufacturer provides an average seek time in milliseconds. The typical range of average seek time is 10 to 60 msec. This is the main "culprit" for the delay involved in transferring blocks between disk and memory.

2. **Rotational delay (rd):** Once the read/write head is at the correct track, the user must wait for the beginning of the required block to rotate into position under the read/write head. On the average, this takes about the time for half a revolution of the disk, but it actually ranges from immediate access (if the start of the required block is in position under the read/write head right after the seek) to a full disk revolution (if the start of the required block just passed the read/write head after the seek). If the speed of disk rotation is p revolutions per minute (rpm), then the average rotational delay rd is given by

   $$rd = (1/2)*(1/p) \text{ min} = (60*1000)/(2*p) \text{ msec}$$

   A typical value for p is 3600 rpm, which gives a rotational delay of rd = 8.33 msec. For fixed-head disks, where the seek time is negligible, this component causes the greatest delay in transferring a disk block.

3. **Block transfer time (btt):** Once the read/write head is at the beginning of the required block, some time is needed to transfer the data in the block. This block transfer time depends on the block size, the track size, and the rotational speed. If the **transfer rate** for the disk is tr bytes/msec and the block size is B bytes, then

$$btt = B/tr \text{ msec}$$

If we have a track size of 50 Kbytes and p is 3600 rpm, the transfer rate in bytes/msec is

$$tr = (50*1000)/(60*1000/3600) = 3000 \text{ bytes/msec}$$

In this case, btt = B/3000 msec, where B is the block size in bytes.

The average time needed to find and transfer a block, given its block address, is estimated by

$$(s + rd + btt) \text{ msec}$$

This holds for either reading or writing a block. The principal method of reducing this time is to transfer several blocks that are stored on one or more tracks of the same cylinder; then the seek time is required only for the first block. To transfer consecutively k *noncontiguous* blocks that are on the *same cylinder*, we need approximately

$$s + (k * (rd + btt)) \text{ msec}$$

In this case, we need two or more buffers in main storage, because we are continuously reading or writing the k blocks, as we discussed in Section 4.3. The transfer time per block is reduced even further when *consecutive blocks* on the same track or cylinder are transferred. This eliminates the rotational delay for all but the first block, so the estimate for transferring k consecutive blocks is

$$s + rd + (k * btt) \text{ msec}$$

A more accurate estimate for transferring consecutive blocks takes into account the interblock gap (see Section 4.2.1), which includes the information that enables the read/write head to determine which block it is about to read. Usually, the disk manufacturer provides a **bulk transfer rate** (btr) that takes the gap size into account when reading consecutively stored blocks. If the gap size is G bytes, then

$$btr = (B/(B + G)) * tr \text{ bytes/msec}$$

The bulk transfer rate is the rate of transferring *useful bytes* in the data blocks. The disk read/write head must go over all bytes on a track as the disk rotates, including the bytes in the interblock gaps, which store control information but not real data. When the bulk transfer rate is used, the time needed to transfer the useful data in one block out of several consecutive blocks is B/btr. Hence, the estimated time to read k blocks consecutively stored on the same cylinder becomes

$$s + rd + (k * (B/btr)) \text{ msec}$$

Another parameter of disks is the **rewrite time.** This is useful in cases when we read a block from the disk into a main memory buffer, update the buffer, and then write the buffer back to the same disk block on which it was stored. In many cases, the time required to update the buffer in main memory is less than the time required for one disk revolution. If we know that the buffer is ready for rewriting, the system can keep the disk heads on the same track, and during the next disk revolution the updated buffer is rewritten back to the disk block. Hence, the rewrite time T_{rw} is usually estimated to be the time needed for one disk revolution:

$T_{rw} = 2 * rd$ msec

To summarize, here is a list of the parameters we have discussed and the symbols we use for them:

seek time: s msec

rotational delay: rd msec

block transfer time: btt msec

rewrite time: T_{rw} msec

transfer rate: tr bytes/msec

bulk transfer rate: btr bytes/msec

block size: B bytes

interblock gap size: G bytes

APPENDIX C

Comparison of Data Models and Systems

In this appendix, we briefly compare the various data models described in this book, and the database systems based on these models. We compare model representation capabilities, languages, typical system storage structures, and integrity constraints.

C.1 Comparison of Data Model Representations

One main difference between representations in data models relates to how relationships are represented. In the *relational model*, connections between two relations are represented by foreign key attributes in one relation that reference the primary key of another relation. Individual tuples that have matching values in the foreign and primary key attributes are logically related, even though they are not physically connected. In the *network model*, 1:N connections between two record types are explicitly represented by the set type construct, and the DBMS physically connects related records together in a set instance.

We can say that the relational model uses *logical* or *symbolic* references, whereas the network model uses *physical references*. We can keep the logical references in a network database—in addition to the physical references—by duplicating the key field of the owner record in the member records, and we use the duplicate values to specify structural constraints or for automatic set selection. If this duplication is done for all set types, the record types in the network schema resemble the corresponding relations of the relational schema. On the other hand, if we do not duplicate the owner key in the member record, the system does not have any means of checking for valid set membership; it is the user's responsibility to link member records physically to set instances, using the

CONNECT, DISCONNECT, RECONNECT, or STORE command. The STORE command accomplishes the linking when AUTOMATIC set membership is specified.

The *hierarchical model* also represents relationships explicitly, but it has serious limitations compared to the network model. Whereas a record type in the network model can be a member in *any number* of set types, it can have only one real parent and one virtual parent in the hierarchical model. This creates problems when modeling M:N and n-ary relationship types. If a schema contains mainly 1:N relationship types in the same direction, it can be modeled naturally as a hierarchy. However, if many relationship types exist, it is difficult to come up with a good hierarchical representation without duplicating some records or using pointers. Consequently, the hierarchical model is generally considered inferior to both the relational and the network models in its modeling capability.

In *object-oriented* (OO) models, relationships are typically represented by references via the object identifier (OID). This is somewhat similar to foreign keys, except that internal system identifiers are used rather than user-defined attributes. The OO models support complex object structures by using tuple, set, list, and other constructors. In addition, they support the specification of methods and the inheritance mechanisms that permit creation of new class definitions from existing ones. The *nested relational model* supports the creation of hierarchically structured relations in addition to flat relations. In some sense, nested relations resemble the use of the tuple and set constructor in a nested fashion, so we can consider the structuring capabilities of nested relations to be a subset of the OO type of constructors.

Table C.1 compares the terminology used in the ER, relational, network, hierarchical, and OO models. Table C.2 summarizes the mapping of ER constructs to these models.

C.2 Comparison of Data Manipulation Languages

We have differentiated between two types of database languages: high-level languages that operate on sets of records, and low-level languages that operate on a single record at a time. Most high-level database languages are associated with the relational model, whereas the network and hierarchical models are associated with record-at-a-time low-level languages. OO systems typically support object-at-a-time programming in an OO programming language, in addition to having some high-level query language to support the selection of a subset of objects from a collection.

The *relational model* has several high-level languages. The formal operations of the relational algebra apply to sets of tuples; a query is specified by a *sequence* of operations on relations. In relational calculus, a single expression (rather than a sequence of operations) specifies a query; we specify *what* we want to retrieve without stating any order of *how* to retrieve it. Hence, relational calculus is considered to be at a higher declarative level than relational algebra. Commercial languages for the relational model—such as SQL, QUEL, and QBE—are based primarily on the relational calculus. They also incorporate facilities for aggregate functions, grouping, sorting, keeping duplicate tuples, and arithmetic, which fall outside the realm of basic relational algebra or calculus. Most relational systems allow users to enter queries directly and interactively or to embed the queries in a programming language.

Table C.1 Comparative Terminology of Data Models

Entity-Relationship Model	Relational Model		Network Model	Hierarchical Model	OO Model
	Formal	Informal			
Entity type schema	Relation schema	Table description	Record type description	Record type description	Class description
Entity set	Relation state	Table	Record type instances	Record type (segment in IMS)	Collection of objects
Entity instance	Tuple	Row	Record occurrence	Record occurrence	Object
1:N relationship type	—[a]	—[a]	Set type	Parent-child relationship (PCR) type	—[c]
1:N relationship instance	—[a]	—[a]	Set occurrence (or set instance)	PCR occurrence (or PCR instance)	—[c]
Attribute	Attribute	Column	Field or data item	Field or data item	Attribute
Value set	Domain	Data type	Data type	Data type	Atomic data type
Key	Candidate key	Candidate key	—[b]	—[b]	—[b]
—[b]	Primary key	Primary key	Key or unique field	Sequence key or sequence field	Object identifier
Multivalued attribute	—[b]	—[b]	Vector or repeating group	—[b]	Set constructor
Composite attribute	—[b]	—[b]	Repeating group	—[b]	Tuple constructor

[a]No corresponding concept; relationship is established by using foreign keys.
[b]No equivalent concept or term.
[c]No corresponding concept; relationship is established by using references.

Table C.2   Summary of Mapping ER Model Concepts to Relational, Network, Hierarchical, and OO

ER Model Concept	Relational Model	Network Model	Hierarchical Model	OO Model
Entity type	As a relation	As a record type	As a record type	As a class
Weak entity type	As a relation, but include the primary key of the identifying relation	As a record type that is a member in a set type with the identifying record type as owner (or as a repeating group)	As a record type that is a child of the identifying record type	As a class, or as a set of tuples within an owner class
1:1 relationship type	Include primary key of one relation as foreign key of the other relation, or merge into a single relation	Use a set type whose instances are restricted to having one member record, or merge into a single record type	Use a PCR type whose instances are restricted to having a single child record, or merge into a single record type	Two reference attributes that are inverses; both are simple
1:N relationship type	Include the primary key of the "1-side" relation as foreign key in the "N-side" relation	Use a set type	Use a parent-child relationship type	Two reference attributes that are inverses; one is set-valued
M:N relationship type	Set up a new relation that includes as foreign keys the primary keys of the participating relations	Set up a linking record type and make it a member in set types owned by the participating record types	(a) Use a single hierarchy and duplicate records (b) Use multiple hierarchies and VPCR types	Both reference attributes are set-valued; or as below
n-ary relationship type	Same as M:N	Same as M:N	(a) Same as M:N (b) Make relationship as parent and participating entity types as children in a single hierarchy.	Create a new class with n references.

The *network* and *hierarchical* DML commands that we discussed are low-level because they search for and retrieve single records. We must use a general-purpose programming language and embed the database commands in the program. In both these languages, the concept of current record is crucial to interpreting the meaning of DML commands, because the effect of a command depends on the current record. The network model DML uses additional currency indicators such as current of set types and current of record types, which also affect the outcome of DML commands. Although these currency concepts facilitate record-at-a-time access, the programmer must be thoroughly familiar with how the different commands affect currency indicators in order to write correct programs. These record-at-a-time commands have their origin in traditional file-processing commands.

From the preceding discussion, it is clear that the relational model has a distinct advantage as far as languages are concerned. Both the formal and commercial languages associated with the relational model are quite powerful and are high-level. The existence of an SQL standard is another big advantage, although the standard itself is continually evolving. Current work on an SQL3 standard extends SQL2 with OO features and structures. Several network and hierarchical DBMSs have implemented high-level query languages that resemble the relational languages for use with their systems along with the traditional DML commands.

In *OO systems,* the DML is typically incorporated into some OO programming language, such as C^{++}. Hence, the structures of both stored *persistent* objects and programming-language *transient* objects is often compatible. This feature is generally considered very desirable for integrating database services into complex software systems. Query languages have been developed for OO databases. Work on a standard OO model and language is progressing, but no complete detailed standard has emerged as yet.

C.3 Comparison of Storage Structures

We discussed some storage structures used by DBMSs to physically store a database in Chapters 4 and 5. By far the most important current technique is that of indexing. As we saw, a wide variety of options can be used to implement indexes, ranging from B^+-trees to dense indexes. Hashing techniques are also being increasingly utilized.

For the *relational model,* the general technique is to implement each base relation as a separate file. If the user does not specify any storage structure, most relational DBMSs will store the tuples as unordered records in the file. Many relational DBMSs allow the user to specify dynamically on each file a single primary or clustering index and any number of secondary indexes. The user has the responsibility to choose the attributes on which the indexes are set up. An increasing number of DBMSs allow the specification of hashing techniques, both as the primary organization to store records, and as indexing structures. In general, it is recommended to create indexes (or hash keys) on all attributes that will be used frequently in either selection or join conditions. Unique indexes and hash keys also provide an efficient technique for enforcing key constraints. Most relational DBMSs also allow users to drop indexes dynamically.

Some relational DBMSs give the user the option of mixing records from several base relations together, which is useful when related records from more than one relation are often accessed together. This clustering of records physically places a record from one relation followed by the related records from another relation so that the related records may be retrieved in the most efficient way possible. This is also used frequently in hierarchical and network systems, which initiated this type of structure.

The *network model* is usually implemented by using pointers and circularly linked lists (ring files). Most network DBMSs also present the option of implementing some sets by clustering; that is, the owner record is followed by the member records in physical contiguity for each set instance. This clustering of member records next to their owner record can be done only for a single set type that a record type participates in as member, because we can physically cluster the member records based on only one logical 1:N relationship type. The set type that is used most frequently in accessing the records should be chosen for physical clustering. In many cases, indexing or hashing on certain attributes of a record type can also be implemented on the ring file for fast access to individual records of a particular type.

The *hierarchical model* is usually implemented by using hierarchical files, which preserve the hierarchical sequence of the database. In addition, various options including hashing, indexing, and pointers are available, so we can have efficient access to individual records and to related records. Most hierarchical systems provide many such options for "tuning" the performance of a database system.

OO systems provide persistent storage for complex-structured objects. They typically employ indexing techniques to locate disk pages that store the object. The objects are often stored as bytes strings, and the object structure is reconstructed after copying the disk pages that contain the object into system buffers. A number of OO—and relational—systems are using some form of client–server architecture.

C.4 Comparison of Integrity Constraints

The *relational model* constraints include keys, entity integrity, and referential integrity. In the SQL2 standard, different *behavior options* for foreign keys are available, such as PROPAGATE and SET NULL. General assertions can also be used to specify additional types of constraints. Hence, the relational model has made great strides from its earlier versions in incorporating useful mechanisms for integrity constraints.

The *hierarchical model* has the built-in hierarchical constraint that a record type can have at most one real parent in a hierarchy. Other constraints exist in each individual DBMS; for example, IMS allows only one virtual parent for a record type. There is *no provision* for enforcing consistency among duplicate records; this must be enforced by the application programs that update the database. Key constraints can be specified. The implicit constraint that a child record must be related to a parent record is enforced; moreover, child records are automatically deleted when their parent or ancestor is deleted.

The *network model* constraints include set retention options, which specify whether every member record must have an owner (MANDATORY or FIXED) or not (OPTIONAL). Automatic set types with SET SELECTION BY STRUCTURAL match the key field of an owner with a field in the member record. The CHECK option can be used to specify a similar constraint for MANUAL nonautomatic set types. Key constraints are specified by the DUPLICATES NOT ALLOWED clause. Hence, many structural constraints on relationship types can be specified to a network DBMS. Unfortunately, not all of these features are implemented on current network DBMSs.

The constraints supported by *OO systems* vary from system to system. The philosophy that constraints should be specified procedurally in the methods, while quite general, makes it difficult to ascertain which constraints have been specified and to check the consistency of the constraints. The inverse relationship mechanism supported by some OO systems makes a good start in providing some declarative constraints. It is possible that more of the typical database constraints will be incorporated into OO database models and systems as they mature, much as happened with the relational model.

Selected Bibliography

Abbreviations Used in the Bibliography

ACM: Association for Computing Machinery.

AFIPS: American Federation of Information Processing Societies.

CACM: Communications of the ACM (journal).

CIKM: Proceedings of the International Conference on Information and Knowledge Management.

EDS: Proceedings of the International Conference on Expert Database Systems.

ER Conference: Proceedings of the International Conference on Entity-Relationship Approach.

ICDE: Proceedings of the IEEE International Conference on Data Engineering.

IEEE: Institute of Electrical and Electronics Engineers.

IEEE Computer: Computer magazine (journal) of the IEEE CS.

IEEE CS: IEEE Computer Society.

IFIP: International Federation for Information Processing.

JACM: Journal of the ACM.

NCC: Proceedings of the National Computer Conference (published by AFIPS).

OOPSLA: Proceedings of the ACM Conference on Object-Oriented Programming Systems, Languages, and Applications.

PODS: Proceedings of the ACM Symposium on Principles of Database Systems.

SIGMOD: Proceedings of the ACM SIGMOD International Conference on Management of Data.

TKDE: IEEE Transactions on Knowledge and Data Engineering (journal).

TOCS: ACM Transactions on Computer Systems (journal).

TODS: ACM Transactions on Database Systems (journal).

TOIS: ACM Transactions on Information Systems.

TOOIS: ACM Transactions on Office Information Systems (journal).

TSE: IEEE Transactions on Software Engineering (journal).

VLDB: Proceedings of the International Conference on Very Large Data Bases (issues after 1981 available from Morgan Kaufmann, Menlo Park, California).

Format for Bibliographic Citations

Book titles are in boldface; for example, **Database Computers**. Conference proceedings names are in italics; for example, *NCC* or *Proceedings of the ACM Pacific Conference*. Journal names are in boldface; for example, **TODS** or **Information Systems**. For journal citations, we give the volume number:issue number (within the volume, if any) and date of issue. For example "**TODS,** 3:4, December 1978" refers to the December 1978 issue of ACM Transactions on Database Systems, which is Volume 3, Number 4. Articles that appear in books or conference proceedings that are themselves cited in the bibliography are referenced as "in" these references; for example, "in VLDB [1978]" or "in Rustin [1974]". For citations with more than four authors, we will give the first author only followed by et al. In our selected bibliography at the end of each chapter, we use et al. if there are more than two authors. All author names are given with *a single initial* (for example, Codd, E. instead of Codd, E.F.).

Bibliographic References

Abbott, R. and Garcia-Molina, H. [1989] "Scheduling Real-Time Transactions with Disk Resident Data", in VLDB [1989].

Abiteboul, S. and Kanellakis, P. [1989] "Object Identity as a Query Language Primitive", in SIGMOD [1989].

Abrial, J. [1974] "Data Semantics", in Klimbie and Koffeman [1974].

Adam, N. and Gongopadhyay, A. [1993] "Integrating Functional and Data Modeling in a Computer Integrated Manufacturing System", in ICDE [1993].

Afsarmanesh, H., McLeod, D., Knapp, D., and Parker, A. [1985] "An Extensible Object-Oriented Approach to Databases for VLSI/CAD", in VLDB [1985].

Agrawal, D. and ElAbbadi, A. [1990] "Storage Efficient Replicated Databases", **TKDE**, 2:3, September 1990.

Agrawal, R. and Gehani, N. [1989] "ODE: The Language and the Data Model", in SIGMOD [1989].

Agrawal, R., Gehani, N., and Srinivasan, J. [1990] "OdeView: The Graphical Interface to Ode", in SIGMOD [1990].

Ahad, R. and Basu, A. [1991] "ESQL: A Query Language for the Relational Model Supporting Image Domains", in ICDE [1991].

Ahmed, R. and Navathe, S. [1991] "Version Management of Composite Objects in CAD Databases", in SIGMOD [1991].

Aho, A., Beeri, C., and Ullman, J. [1979] "The Theory of Joins in Relational Databases", **TODS**, 4:3, September 1979.

Aho, A., Sagiv, Y., and Ullman, J. [1979a] "Efficient Optimization of a Class of Relational Expressions", **TODS**, 4:4, December 1979.

Aho, A. and Ullman, J. [1979] "Universality of Data Retrieval Languages", *Proceedings of the POPL Conference*, San Antonio Tx, ACM, 1979.

Akl, S. [1983] "Digital Signatures: A Tutorial Survey", **IEEE Computer**, 16:2, February 1983.

Alashqur, A., Su, S., and Lam, H. [1989] "OQL: A Query Language for Manipulating Object-Oriented Databases", in VLDB [1989].

Albano, A., Cardelli, L., and Orsini, R. [1985] "GALILEO: A Strongly-Typed Interactive Conceptual Language", TODS, 10:2, June 1985.

Albano, A., de Antonellis, V., and di Leva, A. (editors) [1985] **Computer-Aided Database Design: The DATAID Project,** North-Holland, 1985.

Allen, F., Loomis, M., and Mannino, M. [1982] "The Integrated Dictionary/Directory System", ACM **Computing Surveys,** 14:2, June 1982.

Andrews, T. and Harris, C. [1987] "Combining Language and Database Advances in an Object-Oriented Development Environment", OOPSLA, 1987.

ANSI [1975] American National Standards Institute Study Group on Data Base Management Systems: Interim Report, FDT, 7:2, ACM, 1975.

ANSI [1986] American National Standards Institute: The Database Language SQL, Document ANSI X3.135, 1986.

ANSI [1986a] American National Standards Institute: The Database Language NDL, Document ANSI X3.133, 1986.

ANSI [1989] American National Standards Institute: Information Resource Dictionary Systems, Document ANSI X3.138, 1989.

Anwar, T., Beck, H., and Navathe, S. [1992] "Knowledge Mining by Imprecise Querying: A Classification Based Approach", in ICDE [1992].

Apers, P., Hevner, A., and Yao, S. [1983] "Optimization Algorithms for Distributed Queries", TSE, 9:1, January 1983.

Armstrong, W. [1974] "Dependency Structures of Data Base Relationships", *Proceedings of the IFIP Congress,* 1974.

Astrahan, M. et al. [1976] "System R: A Relational Approach to Data Base Management", TODS, 1:2, June 1976.

Atkinson, M. and Buneman, P. [1987] "Types and Persistence in Database Programming Languages" in ACM **Computing Surveys,** 19:2, June 1987.

Atre, S. [1980] **Structured Techniques for Design, Performance, and Management,** Wiley, 1980.

Atzeni, P. and De Antonellis, V. [1993] **Relational Database Theory,** Benjamin/Cummings, 1993.

Bachman, C. [1969] "Data Structure Diagrams", **Data Base** (Bulletin of ACM SIGFIDET), 1:2, March 1969.

Bachman, C. [1973] "The Programmer as a Navigator", CACM, 16:1, November 1973.

Bachman, C. [1974] "The Data Structure Set Model", in Rustin [1974].

Bachman, C. and Williams, S. [1964] "A General Purpose Programming System for Random Access Memories", *Proceedings of the Fall Joint Computer Conference,* AFIPS, 26, 1964.

Badal, D. and Popek, G. [1979] "Cost and Performance Analysis of Semantic Integrity Validation Methods", in SIGMOD [1979].

Badrinath, B. and Ramamritham, K. [1992] "Semantics-Based Concurrency Control: Beyond Commutativity", TODS, 17:1, March 1992.

Baeza-Yates, R. and Larson, P. [1989] "Performance of B+-trees With Partial Expansions", TKDE, 1:2, June 1989.

Bancilhon, F. and Buneman, P. (editors) [1990] **Advances in Database Programming Languages,** ACM Press, 1990.

Bancilhon, F., Maier, D., Sagiv, Y. and Ullman, J. [1986] "Magic sets and other strange ways to implement logic programs", PODS [1986].

Bancilhon, F., and Ramakrishnan, R. [1986] "An Amateur's Introduction to Recursive Query Processing Strategies, " in SIGMOD [1986].

Banerjee, J. et al. [1987] "Data Model Issues for Object-Oriented Applications", TOOIS, 5:1, January 1987.

Banerjee, J., Kim, W., Kim, H., and Korth, H. [1987a] "Semantics and Implementation of Schema Evolution in Object-Oriented Databases", in SIGMOD [1987].

Baroody, A. and DeWitt, D. [1981] "An Object-Oriented Approach to Database System Implementation", TODS, 6:4, December 1981.

Barsalou, T., Siambela, N., Keller, A., and Wiederhold, G. [1991] "Updating Relational Databases Through Object-Based Views", in SIGMOD [1991].

Bassiouni, M. [1988] "Single-Site and Distributed Optimistic Protocols for Concurrency Control", TSE, 14:8, August 1988.

Batini, C., Ceri, S., and Navathe, S. [1992] **Database Design: An Entity-Relationship Approach,** Benjamin/Cummings, 1992.

Batini, C., Lenzerini, M., and Navathe, S. [1987] "A Comparative Analysis of Methodologies for Database Schema Integration", ACM **Computing Surveys,** 18:4, December 1986.

Batory, D. and Buchmann, A. [1984] "Molecular Objects, Abstract Data Types, and Data Models: A Framework", in VLDB [1984].

Batory, D. et al. [1986] "GENESIS: An Extensible Database Management System", TSE, **14:11,** November 1988.

Bayer, R., Graham, M., and Seegmuller, G. (editors) [1978] **Operating Systems: An Advanced Course,** Springer-Verlag, 1978.

Bayer, R. and McCreight, E. [1972] "Organization and Maintenance of Large Ordered Indexes", **Acta Informatica,** 1:3, February 1972.

Beck, H., Anwar, T., and Navathe, S. [1993] "A Conceptual Clustering Algorithm for Database Schema Design", TKDE, to appear.

Beck, H., Gala, S., and Navathe, S. [1989] "Classification as a Query Processing Technique in the CANDIDE Semantic Data Model", in ICDE [1989].

Beeri, C., Fagin, R., and Howard, J. [1977] "A Complete Axiomatization for Functional and Multivalued Dependencies", in SIGMOD [1977].

Beeri, C. and Ramakrishnan, R. [1987] "On the Power of Magic" in PODS [1987].

Ben-Zvi, J. [1982] "The Time Relational Model", Ph.D. Thesis, University of California, Los Angeles, 1982.

Berg, B. and Roth, J. [1989] **Software for Optical Disk,** Meckler, 1989.

Bernstein, P. [1976] "Synthesizing Third Normal Form Relations from Functional Dependencies", TODS, 1:4, December 1976.

Bernstein, P., Blaustein, B., and Clarke, E. [1980] "Fast Maintenance of Semantic Integrity Assertions Using Redundant Aggregate Data", in VLDB [1980].

Bernstein, P. and Goodman, N. [1980] "Timestamp-Based Algorithms for Concurrency Control in Distributed Database Systems", in VLDB [1980].

Bernstein, P. and Goodman, N. [1981] "The Power of Natural Semijoins", SIAM **Journal of Computing,** 10:4, December 1981.

Bernstein, P. and Goodman, N. [1981a] "Concurrency Control in Distributed Database Systems", ACM **Computing Surveys,** 13:2, June 1981.

Bernstein, P. and Goodman, N. [1984] "An Algorithm for Concurrency Control and Recovery in Replicated Distributed Databases", TODS, 9:4, December 1984.

Bernstein, P., Hadzilacos, V., and Goodman, N. [1988] **Concurrency Control and Recovery in Database Systems**, Addison-Wesley, 1988.

Bertino, E. [1992] "Data Hiding and Security in Object-Oriented Databases", in ICDE [1992].

Bertino, E., Negri, M., Pelagatti, G., and Sbattella, L. [1992] "Object-Oriented Query Languages: The Notion and the Issues", TKDE, 4:3, June 1992.

Bertino, E. and Kim, W. [1989] "Indexing Techniques for Queries on Nested Objects", TKDE, 1:2, June 1989.

Bertino, F., Rabbitti and Gibbs, S. [1988] "Query Processing in a Multimedia Environment", TOIS, 6, 1988.

Bhargava, B. (editor) [1987] **Concurrency and Reliability in Distributed Systems,** Van Nostrand-Reinhold, 1987.

Bhargava, B. and Helal, A. [1993] "Efficient Reliability Mechanisms in Distributed Database Systems", CIKM, November 1993.

Bhargava, B. and Reidl, J. [1988] "A Model for Adaptable Systems for Transaction Processing", in ICDE [1988].

Biliris, A. [1992] "The Performance of Three Database Storage Structures for Managing Large Objects", in SIGMOD [1992].

Biller, H. [1979] "On the Equivalence of Data Base Schemas—A Semantic Approach to Data Translation", **Information Systems,** 4:1, 1979.

Bjork, A. [1973] "Recovery Scenario for a DB/DC System", *Proceedings of the ACM National Conference,* 1973.

Bjorner, D. and Lovengren, H. [1982] "Formalization of Database Systems and a Formal Definition of IMS", in VLDB [1982].

Blakeley, J., Coburn, N., and Larson, P. [1989] "Updated Derived Relations: Detecting Irrelevant and Autonomously Computable Updates", TODS, 14:3, September 1989.

Blakeley, J. and Martin, N. [1990] "Join Index, Materialized View, and Hybrid-Hash Join: A Performance Analysis", in ICDE [1990].

Blankinship, R., Hevner, A., and Yao, S. [1991] "An Iterative Method for Distributed Database Design", in VLDB [1991].

Blasgen, M. and Eswaran, K. [1976] "On the Evaluation of Queries in a Relational Database System", IBM **Systems Journal,** 16:1, January 1976.

Blasgen, M., et al. [1981] "System R: An Architectural Overview", IBM **Systems Journal,** 20:1, January 1981.

Bleier, R. and Vorhaus, A. [1968] "File Organization in the SDC TDMS", *Proceedings of the IFIP Congress,* 1968.

Bocca, J. [1986] "EDUCE—A Marriage of Convenience: Prolog and a Relational DBMS", *Proceedings of the Third International Conference on Logic Programming,* Springer-Verlag, 1986.

Bocca, J. [1986a] "On the Evaluation Strategy of EDUCE", in SIGMOD [1986].

Bodorick, P., Riordon, J., and Pyra, J. [1992] "Deciding on Correct Distributed Query Processing", TKDE, 4:3, June 1992.

Borgida, A., Brachman, R., McGuinness, D., and Resnick, L. [1989] "CLASSIC: A Structural Data Model for Objects", in SIGMOD [1989].

Borkin, S. [1978] "Data Model Equivalence", in VLDB [1978].

Bouzeghoub, M. and Metais, E. [1991] "Semantic Modelling of Object-Oriented Databases", in VLDB [1991].

Boyce, R., Chamberlin, D., King, W., and Hammer, M. [1975] "Specifying Queries as Relational Expressions", CACM, 18:11, November 1975.

Bracchi, G., Paolini, P., and Pelagatti, G. [1976] "Binary Logical Associations in Data Modelling", in Nijssen [1976].

Bracchi, G. and Pernici, B. [1984] "The Design Requirements of Office Systems", TOOIS, 2:2, April 1984.

Bracchi, G. and Pernici, B. [1987] "Decision Support in Office Information Systems", in Holsapple and Whinston [1987].

Brachman, R. and Levesque, H. [1984] "What Makes a Knowledge Base Knowledgeable? A View of Databases from the Knowledge Level", in EDS [1984].

Bradley, J. [1978] "An Extended Owner-Coupled Set Data Model and Predicate Calculus for Database Management", TODS, 3:4, December 1978.

Bray, O. [1988] **Computer Integrated Manufacturing—The Data Management Strategy,** Digital Press, 1988.

Breitbart, Y., Silberschatz, A., and Thompson, G. [1990] "Reliable Transaction Management in a Multidatabase System", in SIGMOD [1990].

Brodie, M. and Mylopoulos, J. (editors) [1985] **On Knowledge Base Management Systems,** Springer-Verlag, 1985.

Brodie, M., Mylopoulos, J., and Schmidt, J. (editors) [1984] **On Conceptual Modeling,** SpringerVerlag, 1984.

Brosey, M. and Shneiderman, B. [1978] "Two Experimental Comparisons of Relational and Hierarchical Database Models", **International Journal of Man-Machine Studies,** 1978.

Bry, F. [1990] "Query Evaluation in Recursive databases: Bottom-up and Top-down Reconciled", TKDE, 2, 1990.

Bubenko, J., Berild, S., Lindercrona-Ohlin, E., and Nachmens, S. [1976] "From Information Requirements to DBTG Data Structures", *Proceedings of the ACM SIGMOD/SIGPLAN Conference on Data Abstraction,* 1976.

Bubenko, J., Langefors, B., and Solvberg, A. (editors) [1971] **Computer-Aided Information Systems Analysis and Design,** Studentlitteratur, Lund, Sweden, 1971.

Bukhres, O. [1992] "Performance Comparison of Distributed Deadlock Detection Algorithms", in ICDE [1992].

Buneman, P. and Frankel, R. [1979] "FQL: A Functional Query Language", in SIGMOD [1979].

Bush, V. [1945] "As We May Think", *The Atlantic Monthly,* 176:1, January 1945 (reprinted in Kochen, M. (editor) **The Growth of Knowledge,** Wiley, 1967).

Cammarata, S., Ramachandra, P., and Shane, D. [1989] "Extending a Relational Database with Deferred Referential Integrity Checking and Intelligent Joins", in SIGMOD [1989].

Campbell, D., Embley, D., and Czejdo, B. [1985] "A Relationally Complete Query Language for the Entity-Relationship Model", in ER Conference [1985].

Cardenas, A. [1985] **Data Base Management Systems,** Second Edition, Allyn and Bacon, 1985.

Carey, M. et al. [1986] "The Architecture of the EXODUS Extensible DBMS", in Dittrich and Dayal [1986].

Carey, M., DeWitt, D., Richardson, J. and Shekita, E. [1986a] "Object and File Management in the EXODUS Extensible Database System", in VLDB [1986].

Carey, M., DeWitt, D., and Vandenberg, S. [1988] "A Data Model and Query Language for Exodus", in SIGMOD [1988].

Carey, M., Franklin, M., Livny, M., and Shekita, E. [1991] "Data Caching Tradeoffs in Client-Server DBMS Architectures", in SIGMOD [1991].

Carlis, J. [1986] "HAS, a Relational Algebra Operator or Divide Is Not Enough to Conquer", in ICDE [1986].

Carlis, J. and March, S. [1984] "A Descriptive Model of Physical Database Design Problems and Solutions", in ICDE [1984].

Casanova, M., Fagin, R., and Papadimitriou, C. [1981] "Inclusion Dependencies and Their Interaction with Functional Dependencies", PODS, 1981.

Casanova, M., Furtado, A., and Tuchermann, L. [1991] "A Software Tool for Modular Database Design", TODS, 16:2, June 1991.

Casanova, M., Tuchermann, L., Furtado, A., and Braga, A. [1989] "Optimization of Relational Schemas Containing Inclusion Dependencies", in VLDB [1989].

Casanova, M. and Vidal, V. [1982] "Toward a Sound View Integration Method", PODS, 1982.

Cattell, R. and Skeen, J. [1992] "Object Operations Benchmark", TODS, 17:1, March 1992.

Ceri, S. (editor) [1983] **Methodology and Tools for Database Design,** North-Holland, 1983.

Ceri, S., Gottlob, G., Tanca, L. [1990], **Logic Programming and Databases**, Springer-Verlag, 1990.

Ceri, S., Navathe, S., and Wiederhold, G. [1983] "Distribution Design of Logical Database Schemas", TSE, 9:4, July 1983.

Ceri, S., Negri, M., and Pelagatti, G. [1982] "Horizontal Data Partitioning in Database Design", in SIGMOD [1982].

Ceri, S. and Owicki, S. [1983] "On the Use of Optimistic Methods for Concurrency Control in Distributed Databases", *Proceedings of the Sixth Berkeley Workshop on Distributed Data Management and Computer Networks*, February 1983.

Ceri, S. and Pelagatti, G. [1984] "Correctness of Query Execution Strategies in Distributed Databases", TODS, 8:4, December 1984.

Ceri, S. and Pelagatti, G. [1984a] **Distributed Databases: Principles and Systems,** McGraw-Hill, 1984.

Ceri, S. and Tanca, L. [1987] "Optimization of Systems of Algebraic Equations for Evaluating Datalog Queries", in VLDB [1987].

Cesarini, F. and Soda, G. [1991] "A Dynamic Hash Method With Signature", TODS, 16:2, June 1991.

Chakravarthy, S. [1990] "Active Database Management Systems: Requirements, State-of-the-Art, and an Evaluation", in ER Conference [1990].

Chakravarthy, S. [1991] "Divide and Conquer: A Basis for Augmenting a Conventional Query Optimizer with Multiple Query Processing Capabilities", in ICDE [1991].

Chakravarthy, S. et al. [1989] "HiPAC: A Research Project in Active, Time Constrained Database Management", Final Technical Report, XAIT-89-02, Xerox Advanced Information Technology, August 1989.

Chakravarthy, S., Karlapalem, K., Navathe, S. and Tanaka, A. [1993] "Database Supported Co-operative Problem Solving", in **International Journal of Intelligent Co-operative Information Systems**, 2:3, September 1993.

Chakravarthy, U., Grant, J., and Minker, J. [1990] "Logic-Based Approach to Semantic Query Optimization", TODS, 15:2, June 1990.

Chalmers, M. and Chitson, P. [1992] "Bead: Explorations in Information Visualization", *Proceedings of the ACM SIGIR International Conference*, June 1992.

Chamberlin, D. and Boyce, R. [1974] "SEQUEL: A Structured English Query Language", in SIGMOD [1984].

Chamberlin, D., et al. [1976] "SEQUEL 2: A Unified Approach to Data Definition, Manipulation, and Control", IBM **Journal of Research and Development,** 20:6, November 1976.

Chamberlin, D., et al. [1981] "A History and Evaluation of System R", CACM, 24:10, October 1981.

Chan, C., Ooi, B., and Lu, H. [1992] "Extensible Buffer Management of Indexes", in VLDB [1992].

Chandy, K., Browne, J., Dissley, C., and Uhrig, W. [1975] "Analytical Models for Rollback and Recovery Strategies in Database Systems", TSE, 1:1, March 1975.

Chang, C. [1981] "On the Evaluation of Queries Containing Derived Relations in a Relational Database" in Gallaire et al. [1981].

Chang, C. and Walker, A. [1984] "PROSQL: A Prolog Programming Interface with SQL/DS", in EDS [1984].

Chang, E. and Katz, R. [1989] "Exploiting Inheritance and Structure Semantics for Effective Clustering and Buffering in Object-Oriented Databases", in SIGMOD [1989].

Chang, N. and Fu, K. [1981] "Picture Query Languages for Pictorial Databases", IEEE **Computer,** 14:11, November 1981.

Chang, P., and Myre, W. [1988] "OS/2 EE Database Manager: Overview and Technical Highlights", IBM **Systems Journal,** 27:2, 1988.

Chang, S., Lin, B., and Walser, R. [1979] "Generalized Zooming Techniques for Pictorial Database Systems", *NCC,* AFIPS, 48, 1979.

Chen, M. and Yu, P. [1991] "Determining Beneficial Semijoins for a Join Sequence in Distributed Query Processing", in ICDE [1991].

Chen, P. [1976] "The Entity Relationship Mode—Toward a Unified View of Data", TODS, 1:1, March 1976.

Chen, Q. and Kambayashi, Y. [1991] "Nested Relation Based Database Knowledge Representation", in SIGMOD [1991].

Cheng, J. [1991] "Effective Clustering of Complex Objects in Object-Oriented Databases", in SIGMOD [1991].

Childs, D. [1968] "Feasibility of a Set Theoretical Data Structure—A General Structure Based on a Reconstituted Definition of Relation", *Proceedings of the IFIP Congress,* 1968.

Chimenti, D. et al. [1987] "An Overview of the LDL System", MCC Technical Report #ACA-ST-370-87, Austin, Tx, November 1987.

Chimenti, D. et al. [1990] "The LDL System Prototype", TKDE, 2:1, March 1990.

Chin, F. [1978] "Security in Statistical Databases for Queries with Small Counts", TODS, 3:1, March 1978.

Chin, F. and Ozsoyoglu, G. [1981] "Statistical Database Design", TODS, 6:1, March 1981.

Chou, H. and Kim, W. [1986] "A Unifying Framework for Version Control in a CAD Environment", in VLDB [1986].

Christodoulakis, S. et al. [1984] "Development of a Multimedia Information System for an Office Environment", in VLDB [1984].

Christodoulakis, S. and Faloutsos, C. [1986] "Design and Performance Considerations for an Optical Disk-Based Multimedia Object Server", IEEE **Computer,** 19:12, December 1986.

Chu, W. and Hurley, P. [1982] "Optimal Query Processing for Distributed Database Systems", IEEE **Transactions on Computers,** 31:9, September 1982.

Ciborra, C., Migliarese, P., and Romano, P. [1984] "A Methodological Inquiry of Organizational Noise in Socio Technical Systems", **Human Relations,** 37:8, 1984.

Claybrook, B. [1983] **File Management Techniques,** Wiley, 1983.

Claybrook, B. [1992] OLTP: **OnLine Transaction Processing Systems,** Wiley, 1992.

Clifford, J. and Tansel, A. [1985] "On an Algebra for Historical Relational Databases: Two Views", in SIGMOD [1985].

CODASYL [1978] Data Description Language Journal of Development, Canadian Government Publishing Centre, 1978.

Codd, E. [1970] "A Relational Model for Large Shared Data Banks", CACM, 13:6, June 1970.

Codd, E. [1971] "A Data Base Sublanguage Founded on the Relational Calculus", *Proceedings of the ACM SIGFIDET Workshop on Data Description, Access, and Control*, November 1971.

Codd, E. [1972] "Relational Completeness of Data Base Sublanguages", in Rustin [1972].

Codd, E. [1972a] "Further Normalization of the Data Base Relational Model", in Rustin [1972].

Codd, E. [1974] "Recent Investigations in Relational Database Systems", *Proceedings of the IFIP Congress*, 1974.

Codd, E. [1978] "How About Recently? (English Dialog with Relational Data Bases Using Rendezvous Version 1)", in Shneiderman [1978].

Codd, E. [1979] "Extending the Database Relational Model to Capture More Meaning", TODS, 4:4, December 1979.

Codd, E. [1982] "Relational Database: A Practical Foundation for Productivity", CACM, 25:2, December 1979.

Codd, E. [1985] "Is Your DBMS Really Relational?" and "Does Your DBMS Run By the Rules?", *COMPUTER WORLD*, October 14 and October 21, 1985.

Codd, E. [1986] "An Evaluation Scheme for Database Management Systems That Are Claimed to be Relational", in ICDE [1986].

Codd, E. [1990] **Relational Model for Data Management-Version 2,** Addison-Wesley, 1990.

Comer, D. [1979] "The Ubiquitous B-tree", ACM **Computing Surveys,** 11:2, June 1979.

Cornelio, A. and Navathe, S. [1993] "Applying Active Database Models for Simulation", in *Proceedings of 1993 Winter Simulation Conference*, Los Angeles, IEEE, December 1993.

Cruz, I. [1992] "Doodle: A Visual Language for Object-Oriented Databases", in SIGMOD [1992].

Curtice, R. [1981] "Data Dictionaries: An Assessment of Current Practice and Problems", in VLDB [1981].

Czejdo, B., Elmasri, R., Rusinkiewicz, M., and Embley, D. [1987] "An Algebraic Language for Graphical Query Formulation Using an Extended Entity-Relationship Model", *Proceedings of the ACM Computer Science Conference*, 1987.

Dahl, R. and Bubenko, J. [1982] "IDBD: An Interactive Design Tool for CODASYL DBTG Type Databases", in VLDB [1982].

Dahl, V. [1984] "Logic Programming for Constructive Database Systems", in EDS [1984].

Date, C. [1983] **An Introduction to Database Systems,** Volume 2, Addison-Wesley, 1983.

Date, C. [1983a] "The Outer Join", *Proceedings of the Second International Conference on Databases (ICOD-2)*, 1983.

Date, C. [1984] "A Critique of the SQL Database Language", ACM SIGMOD **Record,** 14:3, November 1984.

Date, C. [1990] **An Introduction to Database Systems,** Volume 1, Fifth Edition, Addison-Wesley, 1990.

Date, C. and White, C. [1988a] **A Guide to SQL/DS,** Addison-Wesley, 1988.

Date, C. and White, C. [1989] **A Guide to DB2,** Third Edition, Addison-Wesley, 1989.

Davies, C. [1973] "Recovery Semantics for a DB/DC System", *Proceedings of the ACM National Conference*, 1973.

Dayal, U. and Bernstein, P. [1978] "On the Updatability of Relational Views", in VLDB [1978].

Dayal, U., Hsu, M., and Ladin, R. [1991] "A Transaction Model for Long-Running Activities", in VLDB [1991].

Dayal, U. et al. [1987] "PROBE Final Report", Technical Report CCA-87-02, Computer Corporation of America, December 1987.

DBTG [1971] Report of the CODASYL Data Base Task Group, ACM, April 1971.

Delcambre, L., Lim, B., and Urban, S. [1991] "Object-Centered Constraints", in ICDE [1991].

DeMarco, T. [1979] **Structured Analysis and System Specification,** Prentice-Hall Yourdan Inc., 1979.

DeMichiel, L. [1989] "Performing Operations Over Mismatched Domains", in ICDE [1989].

Denning, D. [1980] "Secure Statistical Databases with Random Sample Queries", TODS, 5:3, September 1980.

Denning, D. and Denning, P. [1979] "Data Security", ACM **Computing Surveys,** 11:3, September 1979.

Devor, C. and Weeldreyer, J. [1980] "DDTS: A Testbed for Distributed Database Research", *Proceedings of the ACM Pacific Conference,* 1980.

DeWitt, D. et al. [1984] "Implementation Techniques for Main Memory Databases", in SIGMOD [1984].

DeWitt, D. et al. [1990] "The Gamma Database Machine Project", TKDE, 2:1, March 1990.

DeWitt, D., Futtersack, P., Maier, D., and Velez, F. [1990] "A Study of Three Alternative Workstation Server Architectures for Object-Oriented Database Systems", in VLDB [1990].

Diffie, W. and Hellman, M. [1979] "Privacy and Authentication", **Proceedings of the IEEE,** 67:3, March 1979.

Dittrich, K. [1986] "Object-Oriented Database Systems: The Notion and the Issues", in Dittrich and Dayal [1986].

Dittrich, K. and Dayal, U. (editors) [1986] *Proceedings of the International Workshop on Object-Oriented Database Systems,* IEEE CS, Pacific Grove, California, September 1986.

Dittrich, K., Kotz, A. and Mulle, J. [1986] "An Event/Trigger Mechanism to Enforce Complex Consistency Constraints in Design Databases", in SIGMOD Record, 15:3, 1986.

Dodd, G. [1969] "APL—A Language for Associative Data Handling in PL/I", *Proceedings of the Fall Joint Computer Conference,* AFIPS, 29, 1969.

Dodd, G. [1969] "Elements of Data Management Systems", ACM **Computing Surveys,** 1:2, June 1969.

Dos Santos, C., Neuhold, E., and Furtado, A. [1979] "A Data Type Approach to the Entity-Relationship Model", in ER Conference [1979].

Du, D. and Tong, S. [1991] "Multilevel Extendible Hashing: A File Structure for Very Large Databases", TKDE, 3:3, September 1991.

Du, H. and Ghanta, S. [1987] "A Framework for Efficient IC/VLSI CAD Databases", in ICDE [1987].

Dumas, P. et al. [1982] "MOBILE-Burotique: Prospects for the Future", in Naffah [1982].

Dumpala, S. and Arora, S. [1983] "Schema Translation Using the Entity-Relationship Approach", in ER Conference [1983].

Dwyer, S. et al. [1982] "A Diagnostic Digital Imaging System", *Proceedings of the IEEE CS Conference on Pattern Recognition and Image Processing,* June 1982.

Eastman, C. [1987] "Database Facilities for Engineering Design", **Proceedings of the IEEE**, 69:10, October 1981.

EDS [1984] **Expert Database Systems,** Kerschberg, L. (editor), (*Proceedings of the First International Workshop on Expert Database Systems*, Kiawah Island, South Carolina, October 1984), Benjamin/Cummings, 1986.

EDS [1986] **Expert Database Systems,** Kerschberg, L. (editor), (*Proceedings of the First International Conference on Expert Database Systems*, Charleston, South Carolina, April 1986), Benjamin/Cummings, 1987.

EDS [1988] **Expert Database Systems,** Kerschberg, L. (editor), (*Proceedings of the Second International Conference on Expert Database Systems*, Tysons Corner, Virginia, April 1988), Benjamin/Cummings (forthcoming).

Eick, C. and Lockemann, P. [1985] "Acquisition of Terminological Knowledge Using Database Design Techniques", in SIGMOD [1985].

Eick, C. [1991] "A Methodology for the Design and Transformation of Conceptual Schemas", in VLDB [1991].

ElAbbadi, A. and Toueg, S. [1988] "The Group Paradigm for Concurrency Control", in SIGMOD [1988].

ElAbbadi, A. and Toueg, S. [1989] "Maintaining Availability in Partitioned Replicated Databases", **TODS,** 14:2, June 1989.

Ellis, C. and Nutt, G. [1980] "Office Information Systems and Computer Science", **ACM Computing Surveys,** 12:1, March 1980.

Elmagarmid, A. and Helal, A. [1988] "Supporting Updates in Heterogeneous Distributed Databases Systems", in ICDE [1988].

Elmagarmid, A., Leu, Y., Litwin, W., and Rusinkiewicz, M. [1990] "A Multidatabase Transaction Model for Interbase", in VLDB [1990].

Elmasri, R., James, S., and Kouramajian, V. [1993] "Automatic Class and Method Generation for Object-Oriented Databases", *Proceedings of the Third International Conference on Deductive and Object-Oriented Databases (DOOD-93)*, Phoenix, Arizona, December 1993.

Elmasri, R., Kouramajian, V., and Fernando, S. [1993] "Temporal Database Modeling: An Object-Oriented Approach", *CIKM*, November 1993.

Elmasri, R. and Larson, J. [1985] "A Graphical Query Facility for ER Databases", in ER Conference [1985].

Elmasri, R., Larson, J., and Navathe, S. [1986] "Schema Integration Algorithms for Federated Databases and Logical Database Design", Honeywell CSDD, Technical Report CSC-86-9: 8212, January 1986.

Elmasri, R. and Navathe, S. [1984] "Object Integration in Logical Database Design", in ICDE [1984].

Elmasri, R., Srinivas, P., and Thomas, G. [1987] "Fragmentation and Query Decomposition in the ECR Model", in ICDE [1987].

Elmasri, R., Weeldreyer, J., and Hevner, A. [1985] "The Category Concept: An Extension to the Entity-Relationship Model", **International Journal on Data and Knowledge Engineering,** 1:1, May 1985.

Elmasri, R. and Wiederhold, G. [1979] "Data Model Integration Using the Structural Model", in SIGMOD [1979].

Elmasri, R. and Wiederhold, G. [1980] "Structural Properties of Relationships and Their Representation", *NCC*, AFIPS, 49, 1980.

Elmasri, R. and Wiederhold, G. [1981] "GORDAS: A Formal, High-Level Query Language for the Entity-Relationship Model", in ER Conference [1981].

Elmasri, R. and Wuu, G. [1990] "A Temporal Model and Query Language for ER Databases", in ICDE [1990], in VLDB [1990].

Elmasri, R. and Wuu, G. [1990a] "The Time Index: An Access Structure for Temporal Data", in VLDB [1990].

Engelbart, D. and English, W. [1968] "A Research Center for Augmenting Human Intellect", *Proceedings of the Fall Joint Computer Conference*, AFIPS, December 1968.

Epstein, R., Stonebraker, M., and Wong, E. [1978] "Distributed Query Processing in a Relational Database System", in SIGMOD [1978].

ER Conference [1979] **Entity-Relationship Approach to Systems Analysis and Design,** Chen, P. (editor), (*Proceedings of the First International Conference on Entity-Relationship Approach*, Los Angeles, California, December 1979), North-Holland, 1980.

ER Conference [1981] **Entity-Relationship Approach to Information Modeling and Analysis,** Chen, P. (editor), (*Proceedings of the Second International Conference on Entity-Relationship Approach*, Washington, D.C., October 1981), Elsevier Science, 1981.

ER Conference [1983] **Entity-Relationship Approach to Software Engineering,** Davis, C., Jajodia, S., Ng, P., and Yeh, R. (editors), (*Proceedings of the Third International Conference on Entity-Relationship Approach*, Anaheim, California, October 1983), North-Holland, 1983.

ER Conference [1985] *Proceedings of the Fourth International Conference on Entity-Relationship Approach*, Liu, J. (editor), Chicago, Illinois, October 1985, IEEE CS.

ER Conference [1986] *Proceedings of the Fifth International Conference on Entity-Relationship Approach*, Spaccapietra, S. (editor), Dijon, France, November 1986, Express-Tirages.

ER Conference [1987] *Proceedings of the Sixth International Conference on Entity-Relationship Approach*, March, S. (editor), New York, New York, November 1987.

ER Conference [1988] *Proceedings of the Seventh International Conference on Entity-Relationship Approach*, Batini, C. (editor), Rome, Italy, November 1988.

ER Conference [1989] *Proceedings of the Eighth International Conference on Entity-Relationship Approach*, Lochovsky, F. (editor), Toronto, Canada, October 1989.

ER Conference [1990] *Proceedings of the Ninth International Conference on Entity-Relationship Approach*, Kangassalo, H. (editor), Lausanne, Switzerland, September 1990.

ER Conference [1991] *Proceedings of the Tenth International Conference on Entity-Relationship Approach*, Teorey, T. (editor), San Mateo, California, October 1991.

ER Conference [1992] *Proceedings of the Eleventh International Conference on Entity-Relationship Approach*, Pernul, G. and Tjoa, A. (editors), Karlsruhe, Germany, October 1992.

ER Conference [1993] *Proceedings of the Twelfth International Conference on Entity-Relationship Approach*, Elmasri, R. and Kouramajian, V. (editors), Arlington, Texas, December 1993.

Eswaran, K. and Chamberlin, D. [1975] "Functional Specifications of a Subsystem for Database Integrity", in VLDB [1975].

Eswaran, K., Gray, J., Lorie, R., and Traiger, I. [1976] "The Notions of Consistency and Predicate Locks in a Data Base System", **CACM**, 19:11, November 1976.

Everett, G., Dissly, C., and Hardgrave, W. [1971] RFMS User Manual, TRM-16, Computing Center, University of Texas at Austin, 1981.

Fagan, J. [1987] "Experiments in Automatic Phrase Indexing for Document Retrieval: A Comparison of Syntactic and Non-Syntactic Methods", Ph.D. Dissertation, Department of Computer Science, Cornell University, 1987.

Fagin, R. [1977] "Multivalued Dependencies and a New Normal Form for Relational Databases", **TODS**, 2:3, September 1977.

Fagin, R. [1979] "Normal Forms and Relational Database Operators", in SIGMOD [1979].

Fagin, R. [1981] "A Normal Form for Relational Databases That is Based on Domains and Keys", TODS, 6:3, September 1981.

Fagin, R., Nievergelt, J., Pippenger, N., and Strong, H. [1979] "Extendible Hashing—A Fast Access Method for Dynamic Files", TODS, 4:3, September 1979.

Faloutsos, G., and Jagadish, H. [1992] "On B-Tree Indices for Skewed Distributions", in VLDB [1992].

Farag, W. and Teorey, T. [1993] "FunBase: A Function-based Information Management System", CIKM, November 1993.

Fernandez, E., Summers, R., and Wood, C. [1981] **Database Security and Integrity,** Addison-Wesley, 1981.

Ferrier, A. and Stangret, C. [1982] "Heterogeneity in the Distributed Database Management System SIRIUS-DELTA", in VLDB [1982].

Fishman, D. et al. [1986] "IRIS: An Object-Oriented DBMS", TOOIS, 4:2, April 1986.

Ford, D., Blakeley, J., and Bannon, T. [1993] "Open OODB: A Modular Object-Oriented DBMS", in SIGMOD [1993].

Ford, D. and Christodoulakis, S. [1991] "Optimizing Random Retrievals from CLV Format Optical Disks", in VLDB [1991].

Franaszek, P., Robinson, J., and Thomasian, A. [1992] "Concurrency Control for High Contention Environments", TODS, 17:2, June 1992.

Franklin, F., et al. [1992] "Crash Recovery in Client-Server EXODUS", in SIGMOD [1992].

French, C., Jones, K. and Pfaltz, J.L. (editors) [1990] "Scientific Database Management (Final Report)", Complete Science Report No. TR-90-2-1, Department of Computer Science, University of Virginia, August 1990.

Frenkel, K. [1991] "The Human Genome Project and Informatics", CACM, November 1991.

Fry, J. and Sibley, E. [1976] "Evolution of Data-Base Management Systems", ACM **Computing Surveys,** 8:1, March 1976.

Furtado, A. [1978] "Formal Aspects of the Relational Model", **Information Systems,** 3:2, 1978.

Gadia, S. [1988] "A Homogeneous Relational Model and Query Language for Temporal Databases", TODS, 13:4, December 1988.

Gait, J. [1988] "The Optical File Cabinet: A Random-Access File System for Write-Once Optical Disks", IEEE **Computer,** 21:6, June 1988.

Gallaire, H. and Minker, J. (editors) [1978] **Logic and Databases,** Plenum Press, 1978.

Gallaire, H., Minker, J., and Nicolas, J. [1984] "Logic and Databases: A Deductive Approach", ACM **Computing Surveys,** 16:2, June 1984.

Gallaire, H., Minker, J and Nicolas, J. (editors) [1981], Advances in Database Theory, Volume 1, Plenum press, 1981.

Gamal-Eldin, M., Thomas, G., and Elmasri, R. [1988] "Integrating Relational Databases with Support for Updates", *Proceedings of the International Symposium on Databases in Parallel and Distributed Systems,* IEEE CS, December 1988.

Gane, C. and Sarson, T. [1977] **Structured Systems Analysis: Tools and Techniques,** Improved Systems Technologies Inc., 1977.

Garcia-Molina, H. [1978] "Performance Comparison of Two Update Algorithms for Distributed Databases", *Proceedings of the Berkeley Workshop on Distributed Data Management and Computer Networks,* IEEE CS, February 1978.

Garcia-Molina, H. [1982] "Elections in Distributed Computing Systems", IEEE **Transactions on Computers,** 31:1, January 1982.

Garcia-Molina, H. [1983] "Using Semantic Knowledge for Transaction Processing in a Distributed Database", TODS, 8:2, June 1983.

Gehani, N., Jagdish, H. and Shmueli, O. [1992] "Composite Event Specification in Active Databases: Model and Implementation", in VLDB [1992].

Georgakopoulos, D., Rusinkiewicz, M., and Sheth, A. [1991] "On Serializability of Multidatabase Transactions Through Forced Local Conflicts", in ICDE [1991].

Gerritsen, R. [1975] "A Preliminary System for the Design of DBTG Data Structures", CACM, 18:10, October 1975.

Ghosh, S. [1984] "An Application of Statistical Databases in Manufacturing Testing", in ICDE [1984].

Ghosh, S. [1986] "Statistical Data Reduction for Manufacturing Testing", in ICDE [1986].

Gifford, D. [1979] "Weighted Voting for Replicated Data", *Proceedings of the Seventh ACM Symposium on Operating Systems Principles*, 1979.

Gladney, H. [1989] "Data Replicas in Distributed Information Services", TODS, 14:1, March 1989.

Gogolla, M. and Hohenstein, U. [1991] "Towards a Semantic View of an Extended Entity-Relationship Model", TODS, 16:3, September 1991.

Goldberg, A. and Robson, D. [1983] **Smalltalk-80: The Language and Its Implementation,** Addison-Wesley, 1983.

Goldfine, A. and Konig, P. [1988] A Technical Overview of the Information Resource Dictionary System (IRDS), Second Edition, NBS IR 88-3700, National Bureau of Standards.

Gordon, C. [1988] "Report of Icon class Workshop, November 1987" in **Visual Resources: an International Journal of Documentation,** 5, 1988.

Gotlieb, L. [1975] "Computing Joins of Relations", in SIGMOD [1975].

Graefe, G. and DeWitt, D. [1987] "The EXODUS Optimizer Generator", in SIGMOD [1987].

Gray, J. [1978] "Notes on Data Base Operating Systems", in Bayer, Graham, and Seegmuller [1978].

Gray, J. [1981] "The Transaction Concept: Virtues and Limitations", in VLDB [1981].

Gray, J., Lorie, R., and Putzulo, G. [1975] "Granularity of Locks and Degrees of Consistency in a Shared Data Base", in Nijssen [1976].

Gray, J., McJones, P., and Blasgen, M. [1981] "The Recovery Manager of the System R Database Manager", ACM **Computing Surveys,** 13:2, June 1981.

Gray, J. and Reuter, A. [1993] **Transaction Processing: Concepts and Techniques,** Morgan Kaufmann, 1993.

Griffiths, P. and Wade, B. [1976] "An Authorization Mechanism for a Relational Database System", TODS, 1:3, September 1976.

Guttman, A. [1984] "R-Trees: A Dynamic Index Structure for Spatial Searching", in SIGMOD [1984].

Gyssens, M., Paredaens, J., and Van Gucht, D. [1989] "A Grammar-Based Approach Towards Unifying Hierarchical Data Models", in SIGMOD [1989].

Gyssens, M., Paredaens, J., and Van Gucht, D. [1990] "A Graph-Oriented Object Model for Database End-User Interfaces", in SIGMOD [1990].

Haas, L., Freytag, J., Lohman, G., and Pirahesh, H. [1989] "Extensible Query Processing in STARBURST", in SIGMOD [1989].

Hachem, N. and Berra, P. [1992] "New Order Preserving Access Methods for Very Large Files Derived from Linear Hashing", TKDE, 4:1, February 1992.

Haerder, T. and Rothermel, K. [1987] "Concepts for Transaction Recovery in Nested Transactions", in SIGMOD [1987].

Hall, P. [1976] "Optimization of a Single Relational Expression in a Relational Data Base System", IBM **Journal of Research and Development,** 20:3, May 1976.

Hammer, M. and McLeod, D. [1975] "Semantic Integrity in a Relational Data Base System", in VLDB [1975].

Hammer, M. and McLeod, D. [1981] "Database Description with SDM: A Semantic Data Model", TODS, 6:3, September 1980.

Hammer, M. and Sarin, S. [1978] "Efficient Monitoring of Database Assertions", in SIGMOD [1978].

Hanson, E. [1992] "Rule Condition Testing and Action Execution in Ariel", in SIGMOD [1992].

Hardgrave, W. [1974] "BOLT: A Retrieval Language for Tree-Structured Database Systems", in TOU [1984].

Hardgrave, W. [1980] "Ambiguity in Processing Boolean Queries on TDMS Tree Structures: A Study of Four Different Philosophies", TSE, 6:4, July 1980.

Hardwick, M. and Spooner, D. [1989] "ROSE Data Manager: Using Object Technology to Support Interactive Engineering Applications", TKDE, 1:2, 1989.

Harrington, J. [1987] **Relational Database Management for Microcomputer: Design and Implementation,** Holt Rinehart Winston, 1987.

Harris, L. [1978] "The ROBOT System: Natural Language Processing Applied to Data Base Query", *Proceedings of the ACM National Conference*, December 1978.

Haskin, R. and Lorie, R. [1982] "On Extending the Functions of a Relational Database System", in SIGMOD [1982].

Hasse, C. and Weikum, G. [1991] "A Performance Evaluation of Multi-Level Transaction Management", in VLDB [1991].

Hayes-Roth, F., Waterman, D., and Lenat, D. (editors) [1983] **Building Expert Systems,** Addison-Wesley, 1983.

Hayne, S. and Ram, S. [1990] "Multi-User View Integration System: An Expert System for View Integration", in ICDE [1990].

Heiler, S. and Zdonick, S. [1990] "Object Views: Extending the Vision", in ICDE [1990].

Helal, A., Hu, T., Elmasri, R., and Mukherjee, S. [1993] "Adaptive Transaction Scheduling", *CIKM*, November 1993.

Held, G. and Stonebraker, M. [1978] "B-Trees Reexamined", CACM, 21:2, February 1978.

Hendrix, G., Sacerdoti, D., Sagalowicz D. and Slocum, J. [1978] "Developing a Natural Language Interface to Complex Data", TODS, 3:2, June 1978.

Hernandez, H. and Chan., E. [1991] "Constraint-Time-Maintainable BCNF Database Schemes", TODS, 16:4, December 1991.

Herot, C. [1980] "Spatial Management of Data", TODS, 5:4, December 1980.

Hevner, A. and Yao, S. [1979] "Query Processing in Distributed Database Systems", TSE, 5:3, May 1979.

Hoffer, J. [1982] "An Empirical Investigation with Individual Differences in Database Models", *Proceedings of the Third International Information Systems Conference*, December 1982.

Holsapple, C. and Whinston, A. (editors) [1987] **Decisions Support Systems Theory and Application,** Springer-Verlag, 1987.

Hsiao, D. and Kamel, M. [1989] "Heterogeneous Databases: Proliferation, Issues, and Solutions", TKDE, 1:1, March 1989.

Hsu, A. and Imielinsky, T. [1985] "Integrity Checking for Multiple Updates", in SIGMOD [1985].

Hull, R. and King, R. [1987] "Semantic Database Modeling: Survey, Applications, and Research Issues", ACM **Computing Surveys,** 19:3, September 1987.

IBM [1978] QBE Terminal Users Guide, Form Number SH20-2078-0.

IBM [1978a] QBE Quick Reference Card, Form Number JX20-2030-0.

IBM [1992] Systems Application Architecture Common Programming Interface Database Level 2 Reference, Document Number SC26-4798-01.

ICDE [1984] *Proceedings of the IEEE CS International Conference on Data Engineering*, Berra, P. (editor), Los Angeles, California, April 1984.

ICDE [1986] *Proceedings of the IEEE CS International Conference on Data Engineering*, Wiederhold, G. (editor), Los Angeles, California, February 1986.

ICDE [1987] *Proceedings of the IEEE CS International Conference on Data Engineering*, Wah, B. (editor), Los Angeles, California, February 1987.

ICDE [1988] *Proceedings of the IEEE CS International Conference on Data Engineering*, Carlis, J. (editor), Los Angeles, California, February 1988.

ICDE [1989] *Proceedings of the IEEE CS International Conference on Data Engineering*, Shuey, R. (editor), Los Angeles, California, February 1989.

ICDE [1990] *Proceedings of the IEEE CS International Conference on Data Engineering*, Liu, M. (editor), Los Angeles, California, February 1990.

ICDE [1991] *Proceedings of the IEEE CS International Conference on Data Engineering*, Cercone, N. and Tsuchiya, M. (editors), Kobe, Japan, April 1991.

ICDE [1992] *Proceedings of the IEEE CS International Conference on Data Engineering*, Golshani, F. (editor), Phoenix, Arizona, February 1992.

ICDE [1993] *Proceedings of the IEEE CS International Conference on Data Engineering*, Elmagarmid, A. and Neuhold, E. (editors), Vienna, Austria, April 1993.

IGES [1983] International Graphics Exchange Specification Version 2, National Bureau of Standards, U.S. Department of Commerce, January 1983.

Imielinski, T. and Lipski, W. [1981] "On Representing Incomplete Information in a Relational Database", in VLDB [1981].

Interbase [1990] InterBase DDL Reference Manual : Interbase Version 3.0, Interbase Software Corporation, 1990.

Ioannidis, Y. and Kang, Y. [1990] "Randomized Algorithms for Optimizing Large Join Queries", in SIGMOD [1990].

Ioannidis, Y. and Wong, E. [1988] "Transforming Non-Linear Recursion to Linear Recursion", in EDS [1988].

Iossophidis, J. [1979] "A Translator to Convert the DDL of ERM to the DDL of System 2000", in ER Conference [1979].

Irani, K., Purkayastha, S., and Teorey, T. [1979] "A Designer for DBMS-Processable Logical Database Structures", in VLDB [1979].

Jagadish, H. [1989] "Incorporating Hierarchy in a Relational Model of Data", in SIGMOD [1989].

Jajodia, S. and Mutchler, D. [1990] "Dynamic Voting Algorithms for Maintaining the Consistency of a Replicated Database", TODS, 15:2, June, 1990.

Jajodia, S., Ng, P., and Springsteel, F. [1983] "The Problem of Equivalence for Entity-Relationship Diagrams", TSE, 9:5, September, 1983.

Jajodia, S. and Sandhu, R. [1991] "Toward a Multilevel Secure Relational Data Model", in SIGMOD [1991].

Jardine, D. (editor) [1977] **The ANSI/SPARC DBMS Model,** North-Holland, 1977.

Jarke, M. and Koch, J. [1984] "Query Optimization in Database Systems", **ACM Computing Surveys,** 16:2, June 1984.

Jensen, C. and Snodgrass, R. [1992] "Temporal Specialization", in ICDE [1992].

Johnson, T. and Shasha, D. [1993] "The Performance of Current B-Tree Algorithms", TODS, 18:1, March 1993.

Kaefer, W. and Schoening, H. [1992] "Realizing a Temporal Complex-Object Data Model", in SIGMOD [1992].

Kamel, I. and Faloutsos, C. [1993] "On Packing R-trees", CIKM, November 1993.

Kamel, N. and King, R. [1985] "A Model of Data Distribution Based on Texture Analysis", in SIGMOD [1985].

Kapp, D. and Leben, J. [1978] IMS **Programming Techniques,** Van Nostrand-Reinhold, 1978.

Kappel, G. and Schrefl, M. [1991] "Object/Behavior Diagrams", in ICDE [1991].

Katz, R. [1985] **Information Management for Engineering Design,** Surveys in Computer Science, Springer-Verlag, 1985.

Katz, R. and Wong, E. [1982] "Decompiling CODASYL DML into Relational Queries", TODS, 7:1, March 1982.

Kaul, M., Drosten, K., and Neuhold, E. [1990] "ViewSystem: Integrating Heterogeneous Information Bases by Object-Oriented Views", in ICDE [1990].

Kedem, Z. and Silberschatz, A. [1980] "Non-Two Phase Locking Protocols with Shared and Exclusive Locks", in VLDB [1980].

Keller, A. [1982] "Updates to Relational Database Through Views Involving Joins", in Scheuermann [1982].

Kemper, A., Lockemann, P., and Wallrath, M. [1987] "An Object-Oriented Database System for Engineering Applications", in SIGMOD [1987].

Kemper, A., Moerkotte, G., and Steinbrunn, M. [1992] "Optimizing Boolean Expressions in Object Bases", in VLDB [1992].

Kemper, A. and Wallrath, M. [1987] "An Analysis of Geometric Modeling in Database Systems", **ACM Computing Surveys,** 19:1, March 1987.

Kent, W. [1978] **Data and Reality,** North-Holland, 1978.

Kent, W. [1979] "Limitations of Record-Based Information Models", TODS, 4:1, March 1979.

Kent, W. [1991] "Object-Oriented Database Programming Languages", in VLDB [1991].

Kerschberg, L., Ting, P., and Yao, S. [1982] "Query Optimization in Star Computer Networks", TODS, 7:4, December 1982.

Ketafchi, M. and Berzins, V. [1986] "Component Aggregation: A Mechanism for Organizing Efficient Engineering Databases", in ICDE [1986].

Kifer, M. and Lozinskii, E. [1986] "A Framework for an Efficient Implementation of Deductive Databases", *Proceedings of the Sixth Advanced Database Symposium,* Tokyo, Japan, August 1986.

Kim, W. [1982] "On Optimizing an SQL-like Nested Query", TODS, 3:3, September 1982.

Kim, W. [1989] "A Model of Queries for Object-Oriented Databases", in VLDB [1989].

Kim, W. [1990] "Object-Oriented Databases: Definition and Research Directions", TKDE, 2:3, September 1990.

Kim, W., Garza, J., Ballou, N., and Woelk, D. [1990] "Architecture of the ORION Next Generation Database System", TKDE, 2:1, March 1990.

Kim, W., Reiner, D., and Batory, D. (editors) [1985] **Query Processing in Database Systems,** Springer-Verlag, 1985.

Kim, W. et al. [1987] "Features of the ORION Object-Oriented Database System", Microelectronics and Computer Technology Corporation, Technical Report ACA-ST-308-87, September 1987.

King, J. [1981] "QUIST: A System for Semantic Query Optimization in Relational Databases", in VLDB [1981].

Kitsuregawa, M., Nakayama, M., and Takagi, M. [1989] "The Effect of Bucket Size Tuning in the Dynamic Hybrid GRACE Hash Join Method", in VLDB [1989].

Klimbie, J. and Koffeman, K. (editors) [1974] **Data Base Management,** North-Holland, 1974.

Klug, A. [1982] "Equivalence of Relational Algebra and Relational Calculus Query Languages Having Aggregate Functions", JACM, 29:3, July 1982.

Knuth, D. [1973] **The Art of Computer Programming,** Volume 3: **Sorting and Searching,** Addison-Wesley, 1973.

Kogan, B. and Jajodia, S. [1990] "Concurrency Control in Multilevel Secure Databases Based on Replicated Architecture", in SIGMOD [1990].

Kohler, W. [1981] "A Survey of Techniques for Synchronization and Recovery in Decentralized Computer Systems", ACM **Computing Surveys,** 13:2, June 1981.

Kolodner, J. [1993] **Case Based Reasoning,** Morgan Kaufmann, 1993.

Konsynski, B., Bracker, L., and Bracker, W. [1982] "A Model for Specification of Office Communications", IEEE **Transactions on Communications,** 30:1, January 1982.

Korfhage, R. [1991] "To see, or Not to see: Is that the Query" in *Proceedings of the* ACM SIGIR *International Conference*, June 1991.

Korth, H. [1983] "Locking Primitives in a Database System", JACM, 30:1, January 1983.

Korth, H., Levy, E., and Silberschatz, A. [1990] "A Formal Approach to Recovery by Compensating Transactions", in VLDB [1990].

Korth, H. and Silberschatz, A. [1991] **Database System Concepts,** Second Edition, McGraw-Hill, 1991.

Kotz, A., Dittrich, K., Mulle, J. [1988] "Supporting Semantic Rules by a Generalized Event/Trigger Mechanism", in VLDB [1988].

Krishnamurthy, R., Litwin, W., and Kent, W. [1991] "Language Features for Interoperability of Databases with Semantic Discrepancies", in SIGMOD [1991].

Krishnamurthy, R., and Naqvi, S., [1988] "Database Updates in Logic Programming, Rev. 1", MCC Technical Report #ACA-ST-010-88, Rev. 1, September 1988.

Krishnamurthy, R. and Naqvi, S. [1989] "Non-Deterministic Choice in Datalog," *Proceeedings of the 3rd International Conference on Data and Knowledge Bases*, June 27-30, Jerusalem, Israel.

Kroenke, D. and Dolan, K. [1988] **Database Processing,** Third Edition, Science Research Associates, 1983.

Krovetz, R. and Croft B. [1992] "Lexical Ambiguity and Information Retrieval" in TOIS, 10, April 1992.

Kumar, A. [1991] "Performance Measurement of Some Main Memory Recovery Algorithms", in ICDE [1991].

Kumar, A. and Segev, A. [1993] "Cost and Availability Tradeoffs in Replicated Concurrency Control", TODS, 18:1, March 1993.

Kumar, A. and Stonebraker, M. [1987] "Semantics Based Transaction Management Techniques for Replicated Data", in SIGMOD [1987].

Kung, H. and Robinson, J. [1981] "Optimistic Concurrency Control", TODS, 6:2, June 1981.

Kunii, T. and Harada, M. [1980] "SID: A System for Interactive Design", NCC, AFIPS, 49, June 1980.

Lacroix, M. and Pirotte, A. [1977] "Domain-Oriented Relational Languages", in VLDB [1977].

Lacroix, M. and Pirotte, A. [1977a] "ILL: An English Structured Query Language for Relational Data Bases", in NIJSSEN [1977].

Lafue, G. and Smith, R. [1984] "Implementation of a Semantic Integrity Manager with a Knowledge Representation System", in EDS [1984].

Lamport, L. [1978] "Time, Clocks, and the Ordering of Events in a Distributed System", CACM, 21:7, July 1978.

Langerak, R. [1990] "View Updates in Relational Databases with an Independent Scheme", TODS, 15:1, March 1990.

Lanka, S. and Mays, E. [1991] "Fully Persistent B+-Trees", in SIGMOD [1991].

Larson, J. [1983] "Bridging the Gap Between Network and Relational Database Management Systems", IEEE Computer, 16:9, September 1983.

Larson, J., Navathe, S., and Elmasri, R. [1989] "Attribute Equivalence and its Use in Schema Integration", TSE, 15:2, April 1989.

Larson, P. [1978] "Dynamic Hashing", BIT, 18, 1978.

Larson, P. [1981] "Analysis of Index-Sequential Files with Overflow Chaining", TODS, 6:4, December 1981.

Laurini, R. and Thompson, D. [1992] **Fundamentals of Spatial Information Systems**, Academic Press, 1992.

Lehman, P. and Yao, S. [1981] "Efficient Locking for Concurrent Operations on B-Trees", TODS, 6:4, December 1981.

Lehman, T. and Lindsay, B. [1989] "The Starburst Long Field Manager", in VLDB [1989].

Leiss, E. [1982] "Randomizing, A Practical Method for Protecting Statistical Databases Against Compromise", in VLDB [1982].

Leiss, E. [1982a] **Principles of Data Security,** Plenum Press, 1982.

Lenzerini, M. and Santucci, C. [1983] "Cardinality Constraints in the Entity Relationship Model", in ER Conference [1983].

Leung, C., Hibler, B. and Mwara, N. [1992] "Picture Retrieval by Content Description", in **Journal of Information Science**, 1992, pp. 111-119.

Levesque, H. [1984] " The Logic of Incomplete Knowledge Bases", Chapter 7 in Brodie et al. [1984].

Lien, E. and Weinberger, P. [1978] "Consistency, Concurrency, and Crash Recovery", in SIGMOD [1978].

Lieuwen, L. and DeWitt, D. [1992] "A Transformation-Based Approach to Optimizing Loops in Database Programming Languages", in SIGMOD [1992].

Lilien, L. and Bhargava, B. [1985] "Database Integrity Block Construct: Concepts and Design Issues", TSE, 11:9, September 1985.

Lindsay, B. et al. [1984] "Computation and Communication in R*: A Distributed Database Manager", TOCS, 2:1, January 1984.

Lipton, R., Naughton, J., and Schneider, D. [1990] "Practical Selectivity Estimation through Adaptive Sampling", in SIGMOD [1990].

Lipski, W. [1979] "On Semantic Issues Connected with Incomplete Information", TODS, 4:3, September 1979.

Liskov, B. and Zilles, S. [1975] "Specification Techniques for Data Abstractions", TSE, 1:1, March 1975.

Liskov, B. et al. [1981] CLU Reference Manual, Lecture Notes in Computer Science, Springer-Verlag, 1981.

Litwin, W. [1980] "Linear Hashing: A New Tool for File and Table Addressing", in VLDB [1980].

Liu, K. and Sunderraman, R. [1988] "On Representing Indefinite and Maybe Information in Relational Databases", in ICDE [1988].

Liu, L. and Meersman, R. [1992] "Activity Model: A Declarative Approach for Capturing Communication Behavior in Object-Oriented Databases", in VLDB [1992].

Livadas, P. [1989] **File Structures: Theory and Practice,** Prentice-Hall, 1989.

Lockemann, P. and Knutsen, W. [1968] "Recovery of Disk Contents after System Failure", CACM, 11:8, August 1968.

Lorie, R. [1977] "Physical Integrity in a Large Segmented Database", TODS, 2:1, March 1977.

Lorie, R. and Plouffe, W. [1983] "Complex Objects and Their Use in Design Transactions", in SIGMOD [1983].

Lozinskii, E. [1986] "A Problem-Oriented Inferential Database System", TODS, 11:3, September 1986.

Lu, H., Mikkilineni, K., and Richardson, J. [1987] "Design and Evaluation of Algorithms to Compute the Transitive Closure of a Database Relation", in ICDE [1987].

Lucyk, B. [1993] **Advanced Topics in DB2,** Addison-Wesley, 1993.

Maier, D. [1983] **The Theory of Relational Databases,** Computer Science Press, 1983.

Maier, D., Stein, J., Otis, A., and Purdy, A. [1986] "Development of an Object-Oriented DBMS", OOPSLA, 1986.

Malley, C. and Zdonick, S. [1986] "A Knowledge-Based Approach to Query Optimization", in EDS [1986].

Mannino, M. and Effelsberg, W. [1984] "Matching Techniques in Global Schema Design", in ICDE [1984].

March, S. and Severance, D. [1977] "The Determination of Efficient Record Segmentations and Blocking Factors for Shared Files", TODS, 2:3, September 1977.

Mark, L., Roussopoulos, N., Newsome, T., and Laohapipattana, P. [1992] "Incrementally Maintained Network to Relational Mappings", **Software Practice & Experience,** 22:12, December 1992.

Markowitz, V. and Raz, Y. [1983] "ERROL: An Entity-Relationship, Role Oriented, Query Language", in ER Conference [1983].

Martin, J., Chapman, K., and Leben, J. [1989] **DB2-Concepts, Design, and Programming,** Prentice Hall, 1989.

Maryanski, F. [1980] "Backend Database Machines", ACM **Computing Surveys,** 12:1, March 1980.

Masunaga, Y. [1987] "Multimedia Databases: A Formal Framework", *Proceedings of the IEEE Office Automation Symposium*, , April 1987.

McFadden, F. and Hoffer, J. [1988] **Database Management,** Second Edition, Benjamin/Cummings, 1988.

McGee, W. [1977] "The Information Management System IMS/VS, Part I: General Structure and Operation", IBM **Systems Journal,** 16:2, June 1977.

McLeish, M. [1989] "Further Results on the Security of Partitioned Dynamic Statistical Databases", TODS, 14:1, March 1989.

McLeod, D. and Heimbigner, D. [1985] "A Federated Architecture for Information Systems", TOOIS, 3:3, July 1985.

Mehrotra, S. et al. [1992] "The Concurrency Control Problem in Multidatabases: Characteristics and Solutions", in SIGMOD [1992].

Menasce, D., Popek, G., and Muntz, R. [1980] "A Locking Protocol for Resource Coordination in Distributed Databases", TODS, 5:2, June 1980.

Mendelzon, A. and Maier, D. [1979] "Generalized Mutual Dependencies and the Decomposition of Database Relations", in VLDB [1979].

Mikkilineni, K. and Su, S. [1988] "An Evaluation of Relational Join Algorithms in a Pipelined Query Processing Environment", TSE, 14:6, June 1988.

Miller, N. [1987] **File Structures Using PASCAL,** Benjamin/Cummings, 1987.

Minoura, T. and Wiederhold, G. [1981] "Resilient Extended True-Copy Token Scheme for a Distributed Database", TSE, 8:3, May 1981.

Missikoff, M. and Wiederhold, G. [1984] "Toward a Unified Approach for Expert and Database Systems", in EDS [1984].

Mitschang, B. [1989] "Extending the Relational Algebra to Capture Complex Objects", in VLDB [1989].

Mohan, C. [1993] "IBM's Relational Database Products: Features and Technologies", in SIGMOD [1993].

Mohan, C. and Levine, F. [1992] "ARIEL/IM: An Efficient and High-Concurrency Index Management Method Using Write-Ahead Logging", in SIGMOD [1992].

Mohan, C. and Narang, I. [1992] "Algorithms for Creating Indexes for Very Large Tables without Quiescing Updates", in SIGMOD [1992].

Mohan, C. et al. [1992] "ARIEL: A Transaction Recovery Method Supporting Fine-Granularity Locking and Partial Rollbacks Using Write-Ahead Logging", TODS, 17:1, March 1992.

Morgan, H. and Levin, K. [1977] "Optimal Program and Data Locations in Computer Networks", CACM, 20:5, May 1977.

Morris, K., Ullman, J., and VanGelden, A. [1986] "Design Overview of the NAIL! System", *Proceedings of the Third International Conference on Logic Programming*, Springer-Verlag, 1986.

Morris, K. et al. [1987] "YAWN! (Yet Another Window on NAIL!), in ICDE [1987].

Morris, R. [1968] "Scatter Storage Techniques", CACM, 11:1, January 1968.

Morsi, M., Navathe, S., and Kim, H. [1992] "An Extensible Object-Oriented Database Testbed", in ICDE [1992].

Moss, J. [1982] "Nested Transactions and Reliable Distributed Computing", *Proceedings of the Symposium on Reliability in Distributed Software and Database Systems*, IEEE CS, July 1982.

Motro, A. [1987] "Superviews: Virtual Integration of Multiple Databases", TSE, 13:7, July 1987.

Mukkamala, R. [1989] "Measuring the Effect of Data Distribution and Replication Models on Performance Evaluation of Distributed Systems", in ICDE [1989].

Mumick, I., Finkelstein, S., Pirahesh, H. and Ramakrishnan, R. [1990] "Magic is Relevant", in SIGMOD [1990].

Mumick, I., Pirahesh, H., and Ramakrishnan, R. [1990] "The Magic of Duplicates and Aggregates", in VLDB [1990].

Muralikrishna, M. [1992] "Improved Unnesting Algorithms for Join and Aggregate SQL Queries", in VLDB [1992].

Mylopolous, J., Bernstein, P., and Wong, H. [1980] "A Language Facility for Designing Database-Intensive Applications", TODS, 5:2, June 1980.

Naffah, N. (editor) [1982] **Office Information Systems,** North-Holland, 1982.

Naish, L. and Thom, J. [1982] "The MU-PROLOG Deductive Database", Technical Report 83/10, Department of Computer Science, University of Melbourne, 1983.

Navathe, S. [1980] "An Intuitive View to Normalize Network-Structured Data", in VLDB [1980].

Navathe, S. [1985a] "Important Issues in Database Design Methodologies and Tools", in Albano et al. [1985].

Navathe, S. and Ahmed, R. [1988] "A Temporal Relational Model and Query Language", **Information Sciences** (to appear).

Navathe, S., Ceri, S., Wiederhold, G., and Dou, J. [1984] "Vertical Partitioning Algorithms for Database Design", TODS, 9:4, December 1984.

Navathe, S. and Cornelio, A. [1990] "Modeling Engineering Data by Complex Structural Objects and Complex Functional Objects" *Proceedings of the International Conference on Extending Data Base Technology*, Venice, Italy, March 1990, Springer-Verlag Notes in Computer Science, No. 416, 1990.

Navathe, S., Elmasri, R., and Larson, J. [1986] "Integrating User Views in Database Design", IEEE **Computer**, 19:1, January 1986.

Navathe, S. and Gadgil, S. [1982] "A Methodology for View Integration in Logical Database Design", in VLDB [1982].

Navathe, S. and Kerschberg, L. [1986] "Role of Data Dictionaries in Database Design", **Information and Management,** 10:1, January 1986.

Navathe, S. and Pillalamarri, M. [1988] "Toward Making the ER Approach Object-Oriented", in ER Conference [1988].

Navathe, S., Sashidhar, T., and Elmasri, R. [1984a] "Relationship Merging in Schema Integration", in VLDB [1984].

Navathe, S. and Schkolnick, M. [1978] "View Representation in Logical Database Design", in SIGMOD [1978].

Negri, M., Pelagatti, S., and Sbatella, L. [1991] "Formal Semantics of SQL Queries", TODS, 16:3, September 1991.

Ng, P. [1981] "Further Analysis of the Entity-Relationship Approach to Database Design", TSE, 7:1, January 1981.

Nicolas, J. [1978] "Mutual Dependencies and Some Results on Undecomposable Relations", in VLDB [1978].

Nievergelt, J. [1974] "Binary Search Trees and File Organization", ACM **Computing Surveys,** 6:3, September 1974.

Nijssen, G. (editor) [1976] **Modelling in Data Base Management Systems,** North-Holland, 1976.

Nijssen, G. (editor) [1977] **Architecture and Models in Data Base Management Systems,** North-Holland, 1977.

Obermarck, R. [1982] "Distributed Deadlock Detection Algorithms", TODS, 7:2, June 1982.

Ohsuga, S. [1982] "Knowledge Based Systems as a New Interactive Computer System of the Next Generation", in **Computer Science and Technologies,** North-Holland, 1982.

Olle, T. [1978] **The CODASYL Approach to Data Base Management,** Wiley, 1978.

Olle, T., Sol, H., and Verrijn-Stuart, A. (editors) [1982] **Information System Design Methodology,** North-Holland, 1982.

Omiecinski, E. and Scheuermann, P. [1990] "A Parallel Algorithm for Record Clustering", TODS, 15:4, December 1990.

Onuegbe, E., Rahimi, S., and Hevner, A. [1983] "Local Query Translation and Optimization in a Distributed System", NCC, AFIPS, 52, 1983.

Orenstein, J. [1986] "Spatial Query Processing in an Object Oriented Database System", in SIGMOD [1986].

Osborn, S. [1979] "Towards a Universal Relation Interface", in VLDB [1979].

Osborn, S. [1989] "The Role of Polymorphism in Schema Evolution in an Object-Oriented Database", TKDE, 1:3, September 1989.

Ozsoyoglu, G., Ozsoyoglu, Z., and Matos, V. [1985] "Extending Relational Algebra and Relational Calculus with Set Valued Attributes and Aggregate Functions", TODS, 12:4, December 1987.

Ozsoyoglu, Z. and Yuan, L. [1987] "A New Normal Form for Nested Relations", TODS, 12:1, March 1987.

Ozsu, T. and Valduriez, P. [1991] **Principles of Distributed Database Systems,** Prentice-Hall, 1991.

Palermo, F. [1974] "A Database Search Problem", in Tou [1974].

Papadimitriou, C. [1979] "The Serializability of Concurrent Database Updates", JACM, 26:4, October 1979.

Papadimitriou, C. [1986] **The Theory of Database Concurrency Control,** Computer Science Press, 1986.

Papadimitriou, C. and Kanellakis, P. [1979] "On Concurrency Control by Multiple Versions", TODS, 9:1, March 1974.

Papazoglou, M. and Valder, W. [1989] **Relational Database Management: A Systems Programming Approach,** Prentice-Hall, 1989.

Paredaens, J. and Van Gucht, D. [1992] "Converting Nested Algebra Expressions into Flat Algebra Expressions", TODS, 17:1, March 1992.

Parent, C. and Spaccapietra, S. [1985] "An Algebra for a General Entity-Relationship Model", TSE, 11:7, July 1985.

Paris, J. [1986] "Voting with Witnesses: A Consistency Scheme for Replicated Files", in ICDE [1986].

Paul, H. et al. [1987] "Architecture and Implementation of the Darmstadt Database Kernel System", in SIGMOD [1987].

PDES [1991] "A High-Lead Architecture for Implementing a PDES/STEP Data Sharing Environment." Publication Number PT 1017.03.00, PDES Inc., May 1991.

Pernici, B. et al. [1989] "C-TODOS: an Automatic Tool for Office System Conceptual Design ", TOIS, 7:4, October 1989.

Perrizo, W., Rajkumar, J., and Ram, P. [1991] "HYDRO: A Heterogeneous Distributed Database System", in SIGMOD [1991].

Phipps, G., Derr, M., Ross, K. [1991] "Glue-NAIL!: A Deductive Database System", in SIGMOD [1991].

Piatesky - Shapiro, G. and Frauley, W. (editors) [1991] **Knowledge Discovery in Databases**, AAAI Press/The MIT Press, 1991.

Pillalamarri, M., Navathe, S., and Papachristidis, A. [1988] "Understanding the Power of Semantic Data Models", Working Paper, Database Systems R & D Center, University of Florida.

Prague, C. and Hammit, J. [1985] **Programming with dBase III,** Tab Books, 1985.

Rabitti, F., Bertino, E., Kim, W., and Woelk, D. [1991] "A Model of Authorization for Next-Generation Database Systems", TODS, 16:1, March 1991.

Ramakrishnan, R., Srivastava, D. and Sudarshan, S. [1992] "CORAL: Control, Relations and Logic", in VLDB [1992].

Ramakrishnan, R., Srivastava, D. and Sudarshan, S. [1992] "{CORAL}: {C}ontrol, {R}elations and {L}ogic", in VLDB [1992].

Ramakrishnan, R., Srivastava, D., Sudarshan, S. and Sheshadri, P. [1993] "Implementation of the {CORAL} deductive database system", in SIGMOD [1993].

Ramakrishnan, R., and Ullman, J. [1994] "Survey of Research in Deductive Database Systems", in **Journal Of Logic Programming**, to appear in 1994.

Ramamoorthy, C. and Wah, B. [1979] "The Placement of Relations on a Distributed Relational Database", *Proceedings of the First International Conference on Distributed Computing Systems*, IEEE CS, 1979.

Reed, D. [1983] "Implementing Atomic Actions on Decentralized Data", TOCS, 1:1, February 1983.

Reisner, P. [1977] "Use of Psychological Experimentation as an Aid to Development of a Query Language", TSE, 3:3, May 1977.

Reisner, P. [1981] "Human Factors Studies of Database Query Languages: A Survey and Assessment", ACM **Computing Surveys,** 13:1, March 1981.

Reiter, R. [1984] "Towards a Logical Reconstruction of Relational Database Theory", Chapter 8, in Brodie et al. [1984].

Ries, D. [1979] "The Effect of Concurrency Control on the Performance of a Distributed Database Management System", *Proceedings of the Berkeley Workshop on Distributed Data Management and Computer Networks*, IEEE CS, February 1979.

Ries, D. and Stonebraker, M. [1977] "Effects of Locking Granularity in a Database Management· System", TODS, 2:3, September 1977.

Rissanen, J. [1977] "Independent Components of Relations", TODS, 2:4, December 1977.

Rivest, R., Shamir, A., and Adelman, L. [1978] "On Digital Signatures and Public Key Cryptosystems", CACM, 21:2, February 1978.

Ross, S. [1986] **Understanding and Using dBase III,** West Publishing, 1986.

Roth, M. and Korth, H. [1987] "The Design of Non-1NF Relational Databases into Nested Normal Form", in SIGMOD [1987].

Rothnie, J. [1975] "Evaluating Inter-Entry Retrieval Expressions in a Relational Data Base Management System", NCC, AFIPS, 44, 1975.

Rothnie, J. et al. [1980] "Introduction to a System for Distributed Databases (SDD-1)", TODS, 5:1, March 1980.

RTI [1983] INGRES Reference Manual, Relational Technology Inc., 1983.

Roussopoulos, N. [1991] "An Incremental Access Method for View-Cache: Concept, Algorithms, and Cost Analysis", TODS, 16:3, September 1991.

Rozen, S., and Shasha, D. [1991] "A Framework for Automating Physical Database Design", in VLDB [1991].

Rudensteiner, E. [1992] "Multiview: A Methodology for Supporting Multiple Views in Object-Oriented Databases", in VLDB [1992].

Rusinkiewicz, M. et al. [1988] "OMNIBASE—A Loosely-Coupled: Design and Implementation of a Multidatabase System", IEEE **Distributed Processing Newsletter,** 10:2, November 1988.

Rustin, R. (editor) [1972] **Data Base Systems,** Prentice-Hall, 1972.

Rustin, R. (editor) [1974] *Proceedings of the ACM SIGMOD Debate on Data Models: Data Structure Set Versus Relational,* 1974.

Sacca, D. and Zaniolo, C. [1987] "Implementation of Recursive Queries for a Data Language Based on Pure Horn Clauses", *Proceedings of the Fourth International Conference on Logic Programming*, MIT Press, 1986.

Sadri, F. and Ullman, J. [1982] "Template Dependencies: A Large Class of Dependencies in Relational Databases and Its Complete Axiomatization", JACM, 29:2, April 1982.

Sagiv, Y. and Yannakakis, M. [1981] "Equivalence among Relational Expressions with the Union and Difference Operators", JACM, 27:4, November 1981.

Sakai, H. [1980] "Entity-Relationship Approach to Conceptual Schema Design", in SIGMOD [1980].

Salzberg, B. [1988] **File Structures: An Analytic Approach,** Prentice-Hall, 1988.

Salzberg, B. et al. [1990] "FastSort: A Distributed Single-Input Single-Output External Sort", in SIGMOD [1990].

Salton, G. and Buckley, C. [1991] "Global Text Matching for Information Retrieval" in **Science,** 253, August 1991.

Samet, H. [1990] **The Design and Analysis of Spatial Data Structures,** Addison-Wesley, 1990.

Samet, H. [1990a] **Applications of Spatial Data Structures: Computer Graphics, Image Processing and GIS,** Addison-Wesley, 1990.

Sammut, C. and Sammut, R. [1983] "The Implementation of UNSW-PROLOG", **The Australian Computer Journal,** May 1983.

Schenk, H. [1974] "Implementation Aspects of the DBTG Proposal", *Proceeding of the IFIP Working Conference on Database Management Systems,* 1974.

Scheuermann, P. (editor) [1982] **Improving Database Usability and Responsiveness,** Academic Press, 1982.

Scheuermann, P., Schiffner, G., and Weber, H. [1979] "Abstraction Capabilities and Invariant Properties Modeling within the Entity-Relationship Approach", in ER Conference [1979].

Schkolnick, M. [1978] "A Survey of Physical Database Design Methodology and Techniques", in VLDB [1978].

Schlageter, G. [1981] "Optimistic Methods for Concurrency Control in Distributed Database Systems", in VLDB [1981].

Schlimmer, J., Mitchell, T., McDermott, J. [1991] "Justification Based Refinement of Expert Knowledge" in Piatesky-Shapiro and Frawley [1991].

Schmidt, J. and Swenson, J. [1975] "On the Semantics of the Relational Model", in SIGMOD [1975].

Schwarz, P. et al. [1986] "Extensibility in the Starburst Database System", in Dittrich and Dayal [1986].

Sciore, E. [1982] "A Complete Axiomatization for Full Join Dependencies", **JACM,** 29:2, April 1982.

Selinger, P. et al. [1979] "Access Path Selection in a Relational Database Management System", in SIGMOD [1979].

Senko, M. [1975] "Specification of Stored Data Structures and Desired Output in DIAM II with FORAL", in VLDB [1975].

Senko, M. [1980] "A Query Maintenance Language for the Data Independent Accessing Model II", **Information Systems,** 5:4, 1980.

Shekita, E. and Carey, M. [1989] "Performance Enhancement Through Replication in an Object-Oriented DBMS", in SIGMOD [1989].

Shenoy, S. and Ozsoyoglu, Z. [1989] "Design and Implementation of a Semantic Query Optimizer", **TKDE,** 1:3, September 1989.

Sheth, A., Larson, J., Cornelio, A., and Navathe, S. [1988] "A Tool for Integrating Conceptual Schemas and User Views", in ICDE [1988].

Shim, K., Sellis, T. and Nau, D. [1993] "Improvements on a Heuristic Algorithm for Multiple-Query Optimization" in **Data and Knowledge Engineering,** North Holland, to appear in 1993.

Shipman, D. [1981] "The Functional Data Model and the Data Language DAPLEX", TODS, 6:1, March 1981.

Shneiderman, B. (editor) [1978] **Databases: Improving Usability and Responsiveness,** Academic Press, 1978.

Sibley, E. [1976] "The Development of Database Technology", ACM **Computing Surveys,** 8:1, March 1976.

Sibley, E. and Kerschberg, L. [1977] "Data Architecture and Data Model Considerations", NCC, AFIPS, 46, 1977.

Siegel, M. and Madnick, S. [1991] "A Metadata Approach to Resolving Semantic Conflicts", in VLDB [1991].

Siegel, M., Sciore, E., and Salveter, S. [1992] "A Method for Automatic Rule Derivation to Support Semantic Query Optimization", TODS, 17:4, December 1992.

SIGMOD [1974] *Proceedings of the ACM SIGMOD-SIGFIDET Conference on Data Description, Access, and Control,* Rustin, R. (editor), May 1974.

SIGMOD [1975] *Proceedings of the 1975 ACM SIGMOD International Conference on Management of Data,* King, F. (editor), San Jose, California, May 1975.

SIGMOD [1976] *Proceedings of the 1976 ACM SIGMOD International Conference on Management of Data,* Rothnie, J. (editor), Washington, D.C., June 1976.

SIGMOD [1977] *Proceedings of the 1977 ACM SIGMOD International Conference on Management of Data,* Smith, D. (editor), Toronto, Canada, August 1977.

SIGMOD [1978] *Proceedings of the 1978 ACM SIGMOD International Conference on Management of Data,* Lowenthal, E. and Dale, N. (editors), Austin, Texas, May/ June 1978.

SIGMOD [1979] *Proceedings of the 1979 ACM SIGMOD International Conference on Management of Data,* Bernstein, P. (editor), Boston, Massachusetts, May/ June 1979.

SIGMOD [1980] *Proceedings of the 1980 ACM SIGMOD International Conference on Management of Data,* Chen, P. and Sprowls, R. (editors), Santa Monica, California, May 1980.

SIGMOD [1981] *Proceedings of the 1981 ACM SIGMOD International Conference on Management of Data,* Lien, Y. (editor), Ann Arbor, Michigan, April/ May 1981.

SIGMOD [1982] *Proceedings of the 1982 ACM SIGMOD International Conference on Management of Data,* Schkolnick, M. (editor), Orlando, Florida, June 1982.

SIGMOD [1983] *Proceedings of the 1983 ACM SIGMOD International Conference on Management of Data,* DeWitt, D. and Gardarin, G. (editors), San Jose, California, May 1983.

SIGMOD [1984] *Proceedings of the 1984 ACM SIGMOD International Conference on Management of Data,* Yormark, B. (editor), Boston, Massachusetts, June 1984.

SIGMOD [1985] *Proceedings of the 1985 ACM SIGMOD International Conference on Management of Data,* Navathe, S. (editor), Austin, Texas, May 1985.

SIGMOD [1986] *Proceedings of the 1986 ACM SIGMOD International Conference on Management of Data,* Zaniolo, C. (editor), Washington, D.C., May 1986.

SIGMOD [1987] *Proceedings of the 1987 ACM SIGMOD International Conference on Management of Data,* Dayal, U. and Traiger, I. (editors), San Francisco, California, May 1987.

SIGMOD [1988] *Proceedings of the 1988 ACM SIGMOD International Conference on Management of Data,* Boral, H. and Larson, P. (editors), Chicago, Illinois, June 1988.

SIGMOD [1989] *Proceedings of the 1989 ACM SIGMOD International Conference on Management of Data,* Clifford, J., Lindsay, B., and Maier, D. (editors), Portland, Oregon, June 1989.

SIGMOD [1990] *Proceedings of the 1990 ACM SIGMOD International Conference on Management of Data,* Garcia-Molina, H. and Jagadish, H. (editors), Atlantic City, New Jersey, June 1990.

SIGMOD [1991] *Proceedings of the 1991 ACM SIGMOD International Conference on Management of Data*, Clifford, J. and King, R. (editors), Denver, Colorado, June 1991.

SIGMOD [1992] *Proceedings of the 1992 ACM SIGMOD International Conference on Management of Data*, Stonebraker, M. (editor), San Diego, California, June 1992.

SIGMOD [1993] *Proceedings of the 1993 ACM SIGMOD International Conference on Management of Data*, Buneman, P. and Jajodia, S. (editors), Washington, D.C., June 1993.

Silberschatz, A., Stonebraker, M. and Ullman J., [1990] "Database Systems: Achievements and Opportunities", in **ACM SIGMOD Record**, 19:4, December 1990.

Simpson, A. [1989] **dBase Programmers Reference Guide,** SYBEX Inc., 1989.

Sirbu, M., Schoichet, S., Kunin, J., and Hammer, M. [1981] "OAM: An Office Analysis Methodology", Massachusetts Institute of Technology Office Automation Group, Memo OAM-016, 1981.

Skeen, D. [1981] "Non-Blocking Commit Protocols", in SIGMOD [1981].

Smith, G. [1990] "The Semantic Data Model for Security: Representing the Security Semantics of an Application", in ICDE [1990].

Smith, J. and Chang, P. [1975] "Optimizing the Performance of a Relational Algebra Interface", **CACM,** 18:10, October 1975.

Smith, J. and Smith, D. [1977] "Database Abstractions: Aggregation and Generalization", **TODS,** 2:2, June 1977.

Smith, J. et al. [1981] "MULTIBASE: Integrating Distributed Heterogeneous Database Systems", *NCC*, AFIPS, 50, 1981.

Smith, K. and Winslett, M. [1992] "Entity Modeling in the MLS Relational Model", in VLDB [1992].

Smith, P. and Barnes, G. [1987] **Files & Databases: An Introduction,** Addison-Wesley, 1987.

Snodgrass, R. and Ahn, I. [1985] "A Taxonomy of Time in Databases", in SIGMOD [1985].

Spooner D., Michael, A. and Donald, B. [1986] "Modeling CAD data with Data Abstraction and Object Oriented Technique" in ICDE [1986].

Srinivasan, V. and Carey, M. [1991] "Performance of B-Tree Concurrency Control Algorithms", in SIGMOD [1991].

Srivastava, D., Ramakrishnan, R., Sudarshan, S. and Sheshadri, P. [1993] "Coral++: Adding Object-orientation to a Logic Database Language" in VLDB [1993].

Stachour, P. and Thuraisingham, B. [1990] "The Design and Implementation of INGRES", **TKDE,** 2:2, June 1990.

Stonebraker, M. [1975] "Implementation of Integrity Constraints and Views by Query Modification", in SIGMOD [1975].

Stonebraker, M. [1993] "The Miro DBMS" in SIGMOD [1993].

Stonebraker, M. (editor) [1986] **The INGRES Papers,** Addison-Wesley, 1986.

Stonebraker, M. (editor) [1988] **Readings in Database Systems**, Morgan Kaufmann, 1988.

Stonebraker, M., Hanson, E., and Hong, C. [1987] "The Design of the POSTGRES Rules System", in ICDE [1987].

Stonebraker, M. and Rowe, L. [1986] "The Design of POSTGRES", in SIGMOD [1986].

Stonebraker, M., Rubenstein, B., and Guttman, A. [1983] "Application of Abstract Data Types and Exact Indices to CAD Databases", in SIGMOD [1983].

Stonebraker, M. and Wong, E. [1974] "Access Control in a Relational Database Management System by Query Modification", *Proceedings of the ACM Annual Conference*, 1974.

Stonebraker, M., Wong, E., Kreps, P. and Held, G. [1976] "The Design and Implementation of INGRES", TODS, 1:3, September 1976.

Su, S. [1985] "A Semantic Association Model for Corporate and Scientific-Statistical Databases", **Information Science,** 29, 1983.

Su, S. [1988] **Database Computers,** McGraw-Hill, 1988.

Su, S., Krishnamurthy, V., and Lam, H. [1988] "An Object-Oriented Semantic Association Model (OSAM*)", in **AI in Industrial Engineering and Manufacturing: Theoretical Issues and Applications,** American Institute of Industrial Engineers, 1988.

Sybase [1990] Transact - SQL User's Guide, Sybase Inc., 1990.

Tanenbaum, A. [1981] **Computer Networks,** Prentice-Hall, 1981.

Tansel, A. et al. (editors) [1993] **Temporal Databases: Theory, Design, and Implementation,** Benjamin Cummings, 1993.

Taylor, R. and Frank, R. [1976] "CODASYL Data Base Management Systems", ACM **Computing Surveys,** 8:1, March 1976.

Teorey, T. [1990] **Database Modeling and Design: The Entity-Relationship Approach,** Morgan Kaufmann, 1990.

Teorey, T. and Fry, J. [1982] **Design of Database Structures,** Prentice-Hall, 1982.

Teorey, T., Yang, D., and Fry, J. [1986] "A Logical Design Methodology for Relational Databases Using the Extended Entity-Relationship Model", ACM **Computing Surveys,** 18:2, June 1986.

Thomas, J. and Gould, J. [1975] "A Psychological Study of Query By Example", NCC, AFIPS, 44, 1975.

Thomas, R. [1979] "A Majority Consensus Approach to Concurrency Control for Multiple Copy Data Bases", TODS, 4:2, June 1978.

Thomasian, A. [1991] "Performance Limits of Two-Phase Locking", in ICDE [1991].

Todd, S. [1976] "The Peterlee Relational Test Vehicle—A System Overview", IBM **Systems Journal,** 15:4, December 1976.

Tou, J. (editor) [1984] **Information Systems COINS-IV,** Plenum Press, 1984.

Tsangaris, M. and Naughton, J. [1992] "On the Performance of Object Clustering Techniques", in SIGMOD [1992].

Tsichritzis, D. [1982] "Forms Management", CACM, 25:7, July 1982.

Tsichritzis, D. and Klug, A. (editors) [1978] **The ANSI/X3/SPARC DBMS Framework,** AFIPS Press, 1978.

Tsichritzis, D., and Lochovsky, F. [1976] "Hierarchical Data-base Management: A Survey", ACM **Computing Surveys,** 8:1, March 1976.

Tsichritzis, D. and Lochovsky, F. [1982] **Data Models,** Prentice-Hall, 1982.

Tsotras, V. and Gopinath, B. [1992] "Optimal Versioning of Object Classes", in ICDE [1992].

Ullman, J. [1982] **Principles of Database Systems,** Second Edition, Computer Science Press, 1982.

Ullman, J. [1985] "Implementation of Logical Query Languages for Databases", TODS, 10:3, September 1985.

Ullman, J. [1985] Implementation of Logical Query Languages for Databases, TODS, 10:4.

Ullman, J. [1988] **Principles of Database and Knowledge-Base Systems,** Volume 1, Computer Science Press, 1988.

Ullman, J. [1989] **Principles of Database and Knowledge-Base Systems,** Volume 2, Computer Science Press, 1989.

U.S. Congress [1988] "Office of Technology Report, Appendix D: Databases, Repositories, and Informatics", in **Mapping our Genes: - Genome Projects: How Big, How Fast?** The John Hopkins University Press, 1988.

Valduriez, P. and Gardarin, G. [1989] **Analysis and Comparison of Relational Database Systems,** Addison-Wesley, 1989.

Vassiliou, Y. [1980] "Functional Dependencies and Incomplete Information", in VLDB [1980].

Verheijen, G. and VanBekkum, J. [1982] "NIAM: An Information Analysis Method", in Olle et al. [1982].

Verhofstadt, J. [1978] "Recovery Techniques for Database Systems", ACM **Computing Surveys,** 10:2, June 1978.

Vielle, L. [1986] "Recursive Axioms in Deductive Databases: The Query-Subquery Approach", in EDS [1986].

Vielle, L. [1987] Database Complete Proof production based on SLD-resolution", in *Proceedings of the 4th International Conference on Logic Programming,* 1987.

Vielle, L. [1988] "From QSQ Towards QoSaQ: Global Optimization of Recursive Queries", in EDS [1988].

Vin, H., Zellweger, P., Swinehart, D. and Venkat Rangan, P. [1991] "Multimedia Conferencing in the Etherphone Environment", IEEE **Computer**, Special Issue on Multimedia Information Systems, 24:10, October 1991.

VLDB [1975] *Proceedings of the First International Conference on Very Large Data Bases*, Kerr, D. (editor), Framingham, Massachusetts, September 1975.

VLDB [1976] **Systems For Large Databases,** Lockemann, P. and Neuhold, E. (editors) (*Proceedings of the Second International Conference on Very Large Data Bases*, Brussels, Belgium, July 1976), North-Holland, 1977.

VLDB [1977] *Proceedings of the Third International Conference on Very Large Data Bases*, Merten, A. (editor), Tokyo, Japan, October 1977.

VLDB [1978] *Proceedings of the Fourth International Conference on Very Large Data Bases*, Bubenko, J. and Yao, S. (editors), West Berlin, Germany, September 1978.

VLDB [1979] *Proceedings of the Fifth International Conference on Very Large Data Bases*, Furtado, A. and Morgan, H. (editors), Rio de Janeiro, Brazil, October 1979.

VLDB [1980] *Proceedings of the Sixth International Conference on Very Large Data Bases*, Lochovsky, F. and Taylor, R. (editors), Montreal, Canada, October 1980.

VLDB [1981] *Proceedings of the Seventh International Conference on Very Large Data Bases*, Zaniolo, C. and Delobel, C. (editors), Cannes, France, September 1981.

VLDB [1982] *Proceedings of the Eighth International Conference on Very Large Data Bases*, McLeod, D. and Villasenor, Y. (editors), Mexico City, Mexico, September 1982.

VLDB [1983] *Proceedings of the Ninth International Conference on Very Large Data Bases*, Schkolnick, M. and Thanos, C. (editors), Florence, Italy, October/November 1983.

VLDB [1984] *Proceedings of the Tenth International Conference on Very Large Data Bases*, Dayal, U., Schlageter, G., and Seng, L. (editors), Singapore, August 1984.

VLDB [1985] *Proceedings of the Eleventh International Conference on Very Large Data Bases*, Pirotte, A. and Vassiliou, Y. (editors), Stockholm, Sweden, August 1985.

VLDB [1986] *Proceedings of the Twelfth International Conference on Very Large Data Bases*, Chu, W., Gardarin, G., and Ohsuga, S. (editors), Kyoto, Japan, August 1986.

VLDB [1987] *Proceedings of the Thirteenth International Conference on Very Large Data Bases*, Stocker, P., Kent, W., and Hammersley, P. (editors), Brighton, England, September 1987.

VLDB [1988] *Proceedings of the Fourteenth International Conference on Very Large Data Bases*, Bancilhon, F. and DeWitt, D. (editors), Los Angeles, California, August/September 1988.

VLDB [1989] *Proceedings of the Fifteenth International Conference on Very Large Data Bases*, Apers, P. and Wiederhold, G. (editors), Amsterdam, The Netherlands, August 1989.

VLDB [1990] *Proceedings of the Sixteenth International Conference on Very Large Data Bases*, McLeod, D., Sacks-Davis, R., and Schek, H. (editors), Brisbane, Australia, August 1990.

VLDB [1991] *Proceedings of the Seventeenth International Conference on Very Large Data Bases*, Lohman, G., Sernadas, A., and Camps, R. (editors), Barcelona, Catalonia, Spain, September 1991.

VLDB [1992] *Proceedings of the Eighteenth International Conference on Very Large Data Bases*, Yuan, L. (editor), Vancouver, British Columbia, Canada, August 1992.

VLDB [1993] *Proceedings of the Nineteenth International Conference on Very Large Data Bases*, Dublin, Ireland, August 1993.

Vorhaus, A. and Mills, R. [1967] "The Time-Shared Data Management System: A New Approach to Data Management", System Development Corporation, Report SP-2634, 1967.

Walton, C., Dale, A., and Jenevein, R. [1991] "A Taxonomy and Performance Model of Data Skew Effects in Parallel Joins", in VLDB [1991].

Wang, K. [1990] "Polynomial Time Designs Toward Both BCNF and Efficient Data Manipulation", in SIGMOD [1990].

Wang, Y. and Madnick, S. [1989] "The Inter-Database Instance Identity Problem in Integrating Autonomous Systems", in ICDE [1989].

Wang, Y. and Rowe, L. [1991] "Cache Consistency and Concurrency Control in a Client/Server DBMS Architecture", in SIGMOD [1991].

Warren, D. [1992] "Memoing for Logic Programs", CACM, 35:3, ACM, March 1992.

Weddell, G. [1992] "Reasoning About Functional Dependencies Generalized for Semantic Data Models", TODS, 17:1, March 1992.

Weikum, G. [1991] "Principles and Realization Strategies of Multilevel Transaction Management", TODS, 16:1, March 1991.

Weldon, J. [1981] **Data Base Administration,** Plenum Press, 1981.

Whang, K. [1985] "Query Optimization in Office By Example", IBM Research Report RC 11571, December 1985.

Whang, K., Malhotra, A., Sockut, G. and Burns, L. [1990] "Supporting Universal Quantification in a Two-Dimensional Database Query Language", in ICDE [1990].

Whang, K. and Navathe, S. [1987] "An Extended Disjunctive Normal Form Approach for Processing Recursive Logic Queries in Loosely Coupled Environments", in VLDB [1987].

Whang, K. and Navathe, S. [1992] Integrating Expert Systems with Database Management Systems—an Extended Disjunctive Normal Form Approach, in **Information Sciences,** 64, March 1992.

Whang, K., Wiederhold, G., and Sagalowicz, D. [1982] "Physical Design of Network Model Databases Using the Property of Separability", in VLDB [1982].

Widom, J. and Finkelstein, S. [1990] "Set oriented production rules in relational database systems" in SIGMOD [1990].

Wiederhold, G. [1983] **Database Design,** Second Edition, McGraw-Hill, 1983.

Wiederhold, G. [1984] "Knowledge and Database Management", IEEE **Software,** January 1984.

Wiederhold, G., Beetem, A., and Short, G. [1982] "A Database Approach to Communication in VLSI Design", IEEE **Transactions on Computer-Aided Design of Integrated Circuits and Systems,** 1:2, April 1982.

Wiederhold, G. and Elmasri, R. [1979] "The Structural Model for Database Design", in ER Conference [1979].

Wilkinson, K., Lyngbaek, P., and Hasan, W. [1990] "The IRIS Architecture and Implementation", **TKDE,** 2:1, March 1990.

Willshire, M. [1991] "How Spacey Can They Get? Space Overhead for Storage and Indexing with Object-Oriented Databases", in ICDE [1991].

Wilson, B. and Navathe, S. [1986] "An Analytical Framework for Limited Redesign of Distributed Databases", *Proceedings of the Sixth Advanced Database Symposium*, Tokyo, Japan, August 1986.

Wiorkowski, G., and Kull, D. [1992] **DB2-Design and Development Guide,** Third Edition, Addison-Wesley, 1992.

Wirth, N. [1972] **Algorithms + Data Structures = Programs,** Prentice-Hall, 1972.

Woelk, D., Luther, W. and Kim, W. [1987] "Multimedia Applications and Database Requirements", *Proceedings of IEEE Office Automation Symposium*, April 1987.

Wolfson, O. and Milo, A. [1991] "The Multicast Policy and Its Relationship to Replicated Data Placement", **TODS,** 16:1, March 1991.

Wong, E. [1983] "Dynamic Rematerialization-Processing Distributed Queries Using Redundant Data", **TSE,** 9:3, May 1983.

Wong, E., and Youssefi, K. [1976] "Decomposition—A Strategy for Query Processing", **TODS,** 1:3, September 1976.

Wong, H. [1984] "Micro and Macro Statistical/Scientific Database Management", in ICDE [1984].

Wu, X. and Ichikawa, T. [1992] "KDA: A Knowledge-based Database Assistant with a Query Guiding Facility" in **TKDE** 4:5, October 1992.

Yao, S. [1979] "Optimization of Query Evaluation Algorithms", **TODS,** 4:2, June 1979.

Yao, S. (editor) [1985] **Principles of Database Design,** Volume 1: **Logical Organizations,** Prentice-Hall, 1985.

Youssefi, K. and Wong, E. [1979] "Query Processing in a Relational Database Management System", in VLDB [1979].

Zadeh, L. [1983] "The Role of Fuzzy Logic in the Management of Uncertainty in Expert Systems", **Fuzzy Sets and Systems,** 11, North-Holland, 1983.

Zaniolo, C. [1976] "Analysis and Design of Relational Schemata for Database Systems", Ph.D. Thesis, University of California, Los Angeles, 1976.

Zaniolo, C., [1988] "Design and Implementation of a Logic Based Language for Data Intensive Applications", MCC Technical Report #ACA-ST-199-88, June 1988.

Zaniolo, C. et al. [1986] "Object-Oriented Database Systems and Knowledge Systems", in EDS [1984].

Zicari, R. [1991] "A Framework for Schema Updates in an Object-Oriented Database System", in ICDE [1991].

Zloof, M. [1975] "Query By Example", *NCC*, AFIPS, 44, 1975.

Zloof, M. [1982] "Office By Example: A Business Language That Unifies Data, Word Processing, and Electronic Mail", **IBM Systems Journal,** 21:3, 1982.

Zobel, J., Moffat, A., and Sacks-Davis, R. [1992] "An Efficient Indexing Technique for Full-Text Database Systems", in VLDB [1992].

Zook, W. et al. [1977] **INGRES Reference Manual,** Department of EECS, University of California at Berkeley, 1977.

Zvieli, A. [1986] "A Fuzzy Relational Calculus", in EDS [1986].

Index